Ethernet Protocol Types

Value	Description	If 2 bytes after Source Address
		< 05DC it is 802.3
0000-05DC	IEEE 802.3	> 05DC it is D1X
0600	Xerox XNS IDP	
0800	DOD IP	
0801	X.75 Internet	
0802	NBS Internet	
0803	ECMA Internet	
0004	CHAOSnet	
0805	X.25 Level3	
0806	ARP (for IP and for CHAOS)	
6001	DEC MOP Dump/load Assistance	
6002	DEC MOP Remote Console	
6002	DEC DECnet Phase IV	
6004	DEC LAT	
6005	DEC DECnet Diagnostics	
6010-6014	3Com Corporation	
7000-7002	Ungermann-Bass download	
7030	Proteon	
7034	Cabletron	
8035	Reverse ARP	
8046-8047	AT&T	
8088-808A	Xyplex	
809B	Kenetics Ethertalk - AppleTalk overEthernet	
80C0-80C3	Digital Communication Associates	
80D5	IBM SNA Services over Ethernet	
80F2	Retix	
80F3-80F5	Kenetics	
80F7	Apollo Computer	
80FF-8103	Wellfleet Communications	
8137-8138	Novell	

NIC-Government Systems, Inc., DDN Network Information Center
14200 Park Meadow Drive, Suite 200
Chantilly, VA 22021

1	1	1	6	6	0-18	Variable	4	1	1
Starting Delimiter	Access Control	Frame Control	Destination Address	Source Address	Route Information	Data	FCS	Ending Delimiter	Frame Status

802.5

DSAP AA	SSAP AA	Control 03	Protocol ID 0000000800	IP Packet

IEEE 802.3 Subnetwork Access Protocol (SNAP)

Preamble	SFD	Destination Address	Source Address	Length	DSAP AA	SSAP AA	Control	Data Unit	FCS
7	1	6	6	2	1	1	1 or 2	5	4 Bytes

SFD = Start Frame Delimiter

Novell 802.3 Encapsulation

Preamble	SFD	Destination Address	Source Address	Length	IPX Data	FCS	
7	1	6	6	2	46 - 1500	4	Bytes

Ethernet V2.0 Frame Format/DIX/Standard

Preamble	Destination	Source	Type	Data	FCS	
8	6	6	2	46 - 1500	4	Bytes

CCIE Practical Studies
Volume I

Karl Solie, CCIE #4599

Cisco Press

Cisco Press
201 West 103rd Street
Indianapolis, IN 46290 USA

CCIE Practical Studies

Volume I

Karl Solie

Contributing authors: Daniel Keller (Chapter 7)
Galina Diker Pildush (Chapter 8)
Eric Sandberg (Chapter 6)

Copyright © 2002 Cisco Systems, Inc.

Published by:
Cisco Press
201 West 103rd Street
Indianapolis, IN 46290 USA

Printed in the United States of America 1 2 3 4 5 6 7 8 9 0

First Printing   December 2001

Library of Congress Cataloging-in-Publication Number: 00-105177

ISBN: 1-58720-002-3

Warning and Disclaimer

This book is designed to provide information about selected topics for the CCIE exam for the Routing and Switching track. Every effort has been made to make this book as complete and as accurate as possible, but no warranty or fitness is implied.

The information is provided on an "as is" basis. The authors, Cisco Press, and Cisco Systems, Inc. shall have neither liability nor responsibility to any person or entity with respect to any loss or damages arising from the information contained in this book or from the use of the discs or programs that may accompany it.

The opinions expressed in this book belong to the author and are not necessarily those of Cisco Systems, Inc.

Trademark Acknowledgments

All terms mentioned in this book that are known to be trademarks or service marks have been appropriately capitalized. Cisco Press and Cisco Systems, Inc., cannot attest to the accuracy of this information. Use of a term in this book should not be regarded as affecting the validity of any trademark or service mark.

Feedback Information

At Cisco Press, our goal is to create in-depth technical books of the highest quality and value. Each book is crafted with care and precision, undergoing rigorous development that involves the unique expertise of members from the professional technical community.

Readers' feedback is a natural continuation of this process. If you have any comments regarding how we could improve the quality of this book or otherwise alter it to better suit your needs, you can contact us through e-mail at feedback@ciscopress.com. Please make sure to include the book title and ISBN in your message.

We greatly appreciate your assistance.

Publisher	John Wait
Editor-in-Chief	John Kane
Cisco Systems Management	Michael Hakkert
	Tom Geitner
	William Warren
Production Manager	Patrick Kanouse
Acquisitions Editor	Amy Lewis
Development Editor	Christopher Cleveland
Project Editor	San Dee Phillips
Copy Editor	Krista Hansing
Technical Editors	L.C. Broadnax, Bill Kern, Mike Reid, John Tiso, Sze Jee Wong
Team Coordinator	Tammi Ross
Book Designer	Gina Rexrode
Cover Designer	Louisa Klucznik
Composition	Octal Publishing, Inc.
Indexer	Tim Wright

CISCO SYSTEMS

Corporate Headquarters
Cisco Systems, Inc.
170 West Tasman Drive
San Jose, CA 95134-1706
USA
http://www.cisco.com
Tel: 408 526-4000
    800 553-NETS (6387)
Fax: 408 526-4100

European Headquarters
Cisco Systems Europe
11 Rue Camille Desmoulins
92782 Issy-les-Moulineaux
Cedex 9
France
http://www-europe.cisco.com
Tel: 33 1 58 04 60 00
Fax: 33 1 58 04 61 00

Americas Headquarters
Cisco Systems, Inc.
170 West Tasman Drive
San Jose, CA 95134-1706
USA
http://www.cisco.com
Tel: 408 526-7660
Fax: 408 527-0883

Asia Pacific Headquarters
Cisco Systems Australia,
Pty., Ltd
Level 17, 99 Walker Street
North Sydney
NSW 2059 Australia
http://www.cisco.com
Tel: +61 2 8448 7100
Fax: +61 2 9957 4350

Cisco Systems has more than 200 offices in the following countries.
Addresses, phone numbers, and fax numbers are listed on the
Cisco Web site at www.cisco.com/go/offices

Argentina • Australia • Austria • Belgium • Brazil • Bulgaria • Canada • Chile • China • Colombia • Costa Rica • Croatia • Czech Republic • Denmark • Dubai, UAE • Finland • France • Germany • Greece • Hong Kong • Hungary • India • Indonesia • Ireland • Israel • Italy • Japan • Korea • Luxembourg • Malaysia Mexico • The Netherlands • New Zealand • Norway • Peru • Philippines • Poland • Portugal • Puerto Rico Romania • Russia • Saudi Arabia • Scotland • Singapore • Slovakia • Slovenia • South Africa • Spain Sweden • Switzerland • Taiwan • Thailand • Turkey • Ukraine • United Kingdom • United States • Venezuela Vietnam • Zimbabwe

About the Authors

Karl Solie, CCIE #4599, is a principal network engineer for Comdisco Inc. Karl has more than 13 years of experience in the field designing and implementing LAN/WAN-based networks internally and externally for McDonnell Douglas, Unisys, and Comdisco. Over the past 13 years, Karl has worked on a vast array of internetworks, including some of the largest commercial and government-based IP and SNA networks in the United States. He has performed LAN/WAN design and implementation on networks ranging from his community school district in Hudson, Wisconsin, to large government networks in Atlanta, Georgia, and Los Angeles, California. Karl holds a bachelor of arts degree in law from the University of California, Irvine, and he concentrated in mathematics at the University of Wisconsin-Stout.

Contributing Authors

Dan Keller, CCIE #6489, currently works at Qwest Communications as a senior network architect focusing on WAN design. Dan lives in Huntington Beach, California. Dan contributed Chapter 7, "WAN Protocols and Technologies: Integrated Services Digital Network (ISDN)."

Galina Diker Pildush, CCIE #3176, CCSI, is the president and a senior consultant at Advanced Communications Experts (ACE), Inc. She provides training and course development for Global Knowledge Network, Inc., the largest Cisco Learning Partner in the world. Galina is also the author of the Cisco Press title *Cisco ATM Solutions*. Galina lives in Toronto, Canada. She wrote Chapter 8, "WAN Protocols and Technologies: Asynchronous Transfer Mode (ATM)."

Eric Sandberg, CCIE #4355, is currently a senior network engineer for Enventis, Inc. Eric has 20 years experience in the industry and is currently designing and implementing multiservice converged networks utilizing Cisco's AVVID technology. Eric lives in Minnetonka, Minnesota. Eric wrote Chapter 6, "WAN Protocols and Technologies: Voice over X."

About the Technical Reviewers

Lawrence Broadnax is a consultant systems engineer for Clover Technologies. Lawrence has been a Cisco Certified Internet Expert (CCIE #5258) since 1999 and specializes in ATM, routers, switches, AVVID, security, VPN, IP QoS, and packet voice. Lawrence has over 12 years of experience in Networking and Distributed Systems Implementations with TELCOs, ISPs, and VARs. Lawrence has a B.S. degree in Electronic Engineering and lives in Dallas, Texas with his wife, La Tonia, and three-year-old son, Lawrence II.

Bill Kern, CCIE #5364, CCDP, is a sales engineering specialist with Qwest Communications, where he provides third-level technical support for Qwest's sales force specializing in Internet access and network-based VPN services. Bill has more than 20 years of networking experience, including the design, implementation, and troubleshooting of multiprotocol networks, as well as traditional mainframe environments. He has extensive experience with routing protocols and switching services, as well as the many tools included in Cisco's networking products.

Mike Reid, CCIE #2879, has been with Cisco and the CCIE group for over 4 years. He was the full-time proctor in the Halifax CCIE lab for 3 years and is now responsible for the content and delivery of the Routing and Switching certification. Before joining Cisco, Mike spent 10 years designing, building, and managing networks in eastern Canada.

John Tiso, CCIE #5162, is one of the senior technologists of NIS, a Cisco Systems Silver Partner. He has a bachelor of science degree from Adelphi University. John also holds the CCDP certification, the Cisco Security and Voice Access Specializations, and Sun Microsystems, Microsoft, and Novell certifications. John has been published in several industry publications. He can be reached via e-mail at johnt@jtiso.com.

Sze Jee Wong, CCIE #6791, has been in the data communication industry for more than 10 years. He is currently a Senior Network Engineer with Enventis, Inc., where he helps customers with network design and implementation. In addition to his CCIE, Sze Jee also holds the following network certifications: CCNP/DP with Voice, Access, and Security Specializations, CCNA-WAN, Microsoft MCP, and Novell CNE. Sze Jee also holds a bachelor of science degree in mechanical engineering.

Dedications

This book is dedicated to my family, to my wife, Sandra, for her never-ending support and belief in me—not just throughout the last two years of writing but also for the last 12 years of classes, late nights in the lab, on-call, and traveling across the country. And to my two girls, Amanda and Paige, for their understanding and patience while "dad" was locked in the lab. You three are my light, and you make everything in life worthwhile.

Acknowledgments

This book would not have been possible without the dedication of many friends, CCIEs, and other professionals. First and foremost, I would like to thank the team at Cisco Press for their never-ending encouragement over the past two years. I especially would like to thank John Kane for his belief in me and for bringing the project to fruition. I would also like to thank Amy Lewis for her cheerful support and guidance over the past two years. I would like to acknowledge Chris Cleveland as well, one of the best developmental editors anyone could hope to work with. If you look through your favorite Cisco Press books, these names are a common thread. It was my honor to be on the same team as you three.

I would also like to thank the CCIEs that joined the team as contributory authors, adding valuable field experience in the areas of voice, ISDN, and ATM: Eric Sandberg, Dan Keller, and Galina Diker Pildush for their contributions of the voice, ISDN, and ATM chapters, respectively. I would also like to thank the CCIEs who were technical editors; their input and help was invaluable. Special thanks go to Bill Kern, Sze Jee Wong, John Tiso, and Mike Reid. Without all of your help, this book would not have been possible.

I would especially like to thank my past and present coworkers and management at Comdisco Inc. for all of their support in ways too numerous to mention.

Thanks to my mom and dad for buying me my first computer and all those video games 20 years ago, sending me down the great path of technology, and standing behind me the whole time.

Finally, I would like to thank the good Lord Jesus for giving me strength and always being there.

Contents at a Glance

Table of Contents

Part VII   **Enhanced Network Protocols** **1029**

Chapter 15   Configuring Network Address Translation (NAT) 1031

Foreword

"The will to succeed is useless without the will to prepare"…. Henry David Thoreau

The CCIE program is designed to help individuals, companies, industries, and countries succeed in an era of increasing network reliance by distinguishing the top echelon of internetworking experts. If that sounds like a lofty mission, then our standards for excellence are equally high.

To achieve CCIE certification is to ascend the pinnacle of technical excellence in the IT profession. While CCIEs inevitably gain extensive product knowledge on their way to certification, product training is not the program objective. Rather, the focus is on identifying those experts capable of understanding and navigating the intricacies and potential pitfalls inherent in end-to-end networking, regardless of technology or product brand.

Individuals must first qualify by taking a challenging qualification exam designed to assess their knowledge across the complete range of technologies and topologies relevant today. If their scores indicate expert level knowledge, candidates then become eligible to take part in the CCIE Certification Practical Exam. Administered only by Cisco Systems, this exam truly distinguishes the CCIE program from all others. Candidates must demonstrate true mastery of internetworking through a series of hands-on, performance-based exercises under intense conditions simulating today's mission critical IT world.

Becoming a CCIE requires significant investment in education and preparation by each candidate. Moreover, a rigorous and mandatory biyearly recertification process ensures the commitment is long lasting and helps guarantee program integrity. These rigid requirements ensure that CCIEs are leaders with a proven and enduring commitment to their career, the industry, and the process of ongoing learning.

Cisco does not require candidates to complete specific training in preparation for CCIE certification because the program is intended to identify hands-on experience and acquired expertise rather than the completion of specified course work.

If you have committed yourself to achieving CCIE certification, *CCIE Practical Studies* can help ensure that your preparation time is invested wisely. An ambitious undertaking given the complexity and scope of material covered, *CCIE Practical Studies* is the first volume in a series of books focused on CCIE Practical Exam preparation. The first of its kind, this series is written specifically to help individuals practice for the CCIE Certification Practical Exam. Although it's no substitute for experience and acquired expertise, *CCIE Practical Studies* can help motivated candidates successfully achieve certification by honing and reinforcing the skills and acquired knowledge they already possess.

Lorne Bradock
Sr. Manager, CCIE Program Group
Cisco Systems, Inc.

Introduction

In late 1993, Cisco threw down the certification gauntlet with the introduction of the Cisco Certified Internetworking Expert program. Over the years and preceding this, people were attaining certifications at an unprecedented rate. From this mountain of newly certified people, a new term arose: *paper certifications*. The term "paper" was used because people were passing these tests without ever touching the equipment that they were getting certified on. Essentially, their knowledge existed on paper. The certifications that people worked so hard to achieve were becoming more common and were meaning less each day.

The market had enough paper certifications and demanded a new hands-on approach to certifications. The industry needed a way not only to measure someone's theoretical knowledge, but also to measure a person's hands-on abilities. Cisco developed the CCIE program specifically with this in mind. The CCIE certification starts where most certification programs end, with an intense, two-hour written test. After successful completion of this test—a passing score of 70 is required, the person becomes a CCIE candidate and is eligible to take the CCIE practical or the lab portion of the test. The practical exam is an intensive 8 1/2-hour test. It is during this period that the candidate demonstrates theoretical knowledge by applying it in the lab.

This text is the first book authorized by Cisco Systems addressing the CCIE practical exam. It represents the dedicated work of nine CCIEs, with input from many other CCIEs and authors. Our hope is that this text, along with its successors, will shed some light on the CCIE practical exam as well as help you prepare for it.

Goals

Our goal in this book is not to instruct you on how to pass the CCIE practical exam, but rather to guide the engineer through the process of deploying and modeling different WAN and LAN technologies in laboratory environments—in essence, the same principles that the CCIE exam is measuring. It is our hope that you will use this book not only for your studies but also has a reference in the field.

When we began crafting this book, we originally wanted to include every topic that we could find on the CCIE test. Our first outline had BGP, IPX, AppleTalk, DECnet, and so on, but soon we realized that we simply could not cover all the possible topics on the CCIE practical exam in a single book. Topics such as BGP require more than a hundred pages to cover properly at the CCIE level. We did not want to include these topics just for the sake of having them. Therefore, we have already begun work on *CCIE Practical Studies,* Volume II. This book will cover many of the topics that we simply could not fit into the first volume. These topics include BGP, IPX, multicast, and VPN, among others.

Who Should Read This Book?

This book can be used as a general networking reference guide for configuring Cisco routers. It primarily is designed to help the CCIE candidate prepare for the CCIE practical exam by offering many labs for the candidate to work through. The labs are presented in a way that actually tests the candidate's ability to solve and work on the lab, before seeing the answers. We strongly advise working through the labs because many things have been designed into the labs that can make them very difficult to configure. If you don't actually configure the labs, you might miss some of these "small" things that could make a difference on your actual CCIE exam.

This book is targeted toward network engineers who already have at least a CCNA or CCDA certification. The engineer must have a solid understanding of IP addressing and subnetting before reading this book. A good background on Cisco routers and basic configuration experience on routers also will be helpful during your reading.

How This Book Is Organized

This book's organization follows that of the OSI model and how networks are built in general, from Layer 1 on up. The first chapter deals mostly with the physical layer and basic router setup and access. Part II, "Modeling LANs," and Part III, "Connecting LANs with Wide-Area Networks (WANs)," focus on the data link layer, whereas Part IV, "Routing Protocols," focuses on Layers 3 and 4. Each chapter is followed by one or more complex labs. The labs are designed to be worked through before viewing the walkthrough for the lab.

The major parts of the book cover the following topics:

- **Part I, "Modeling the Internetwork"**—This part addresses basic and advanced router setup, including the 16-bit boot register, password recovery on routers and switches, analog access, and the configuration of an access server. This part also includes modeling the internetwork, which covers Frame Relay switching, and the types of cables and other network equipemnt needed to model complex networks.

- **Part II, "Modeling LANs"**—This part includes detailed information on configuring the Catalyst Ethernet and Token Ring series of switches. It includes information on configuring the Ethernet Catalyst 2900/3500 and 4000/5000/6000 families of switches and the Token Ring 3920 switch. Detailed information on VLANs, VTP and trunking protcols, and Spanning Tree also is covered.

- **Part III, "Connecting LANs with Wide-Area Networks (WANs)"**—This chapters covers the configuration of data link protocols used on the WAN. This includes detailed configuration information on HDLC, PPP, Frame Relay, Voice over X, ISDN, and ATM.

- **Part IV, "Routing Protocols"**—This part focues on the primary interior routing protocols and their configuration. Information is provided on RIP and RIP v2, IGRP, OSPF, and EIGRP.

- **Part V, "Transporting Non-Routable Protocols"**—This part consists of a large single chapter. The chapter addresses configuring transparent bridging, integrated routing and bridging, source-route bridging, remote source-route bridging, and Data Link Switching Plus.

- **Part VI, "Controlling Networks and Network Access"**—This part of the book deals exclusively with the various ways to configure and apply an IP access lists. These include configuring standard and extended access lists, named access lists, and dynamic access lists. Binary math and wildcard masks also are addressed in detail.

- **Part VII, "Enhanced Network Protocols "**—This part is divided into three chapters that cover some of the more common feature sets available on Cisco routers. These features include NAT, HSRP, and NTP/SNTP. This part addressses the details of configuring each feature set.

- **Part VIII, "CCIE Preparation and Self-Assessment"**—This part discusses the current CCIE practical exam. It provides study lists and suggestions to help you prepare for the CCIE Lab Exam. The chapter also includes five CCIE practice exams. The exams are provided to give the candidate a "feel" for what the real exam is like.

Icons Used in This Book

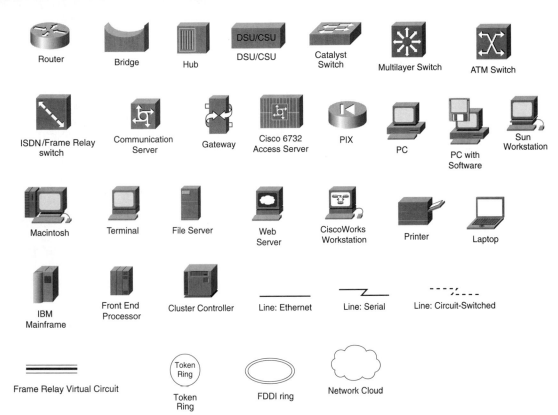

Command Syntax Conventions

The conventions used to present command syntax in this book are the same conventions used in the Cisco IOS Command Reference. The Command Reference describes these conventions as follows:

- Vertical bars (l) separate alternative, mutually exclusive elements.
- Square brackets [ ] indicate optional elements.
- Braces { } indicate a required choice.
- Braces within brackets [{ }] indicate a required choice within an optional element.
- **Boldface** indicates commands and keywords that are entered literally as shown. In actual configuration examples and output (not general command syntax), boldface indicates commands that are manually input by the user (such as a **show** command).
- *Italics* indicate arguments for which you supply actual values.

Modeling the Internetwork

CHAPTER 1

The Key Components for Modeling an Internetwork

Many types of models exist today, from mathematical models and statistical models to the plastic models that you might have built when you were young. Despite their vast differences, they all are models of one type. This book proposes a new kind of model—the internetwork model.

The internetwork model will be defined as a smaller accurate and functional representation of a larger internetwork. Internetwork models, as with all models, are smaller representations of larger networks. The word *accurate* is used because the model will be built to reflect the precise requirements of "real" networks. For example, not only will you design an Open Shortest Path First (OSPF) network, but you also will focus on the details of the design, such as OSPF handling of specific interface types, what areas they are in, and whether they should be transmitting link states or forming adjacencies. Attention to this type of detail will be important in your studies and thereby warrants the use of the word *accurate*. Finally, the model must be functional—that is, it will be tested by running actual data and applications across it.

Just as other models serve a purpose to prove a hypothesis of one sort, the goal of the internetwork model will be to prove the functionality or design theory of the larger internetwork. When you are finished, you will be able to transport many kinds of data across many types of networks. You will see and test the functionality of the network by using test hosts and simulated data.

In summary, an internetwork model is a smaller but accurate representation of the larger internetwork. The goal of this book is to walk the network engineer through assembling and configuring all the necessary hardware and software components required to model complex internetworks.

The term *internetwork* can be defined as a collection of networks, local-area networks (LANs) and wide-area networks (WANs) interconnected by routers, bridges, and switches that function as a singular network. To properly model an internetwork in the lab, you need to simulate different LAN and WAN technologies.

You should go through a logical order when modeling the internetwork. Like mathematics, networking builds on itself. You must first comprehend multiplication and division before you can learn algebra, you must learn algebra before calculus, and so on. Networking follows a similar logical approach:

Step 1 First, build and form all LAN connections.

Step 2 After initial LAN connectivity is established, build and configure all WAN connections.

Step 3 Establish full internetwork connectivity. This is done by laying routing protocols over your LANs and WANs.

Step 4 Finally, apply any filters, features, or any other exterior routing protocols, such as Border Gateway Protocol (BGP), that require a fully functional IP network to operate.

Identifying the Key Components Needed for Modeling Internetworks

You need several key components to fully model complex network designs, including the following:

- Access server
- LANs: switches/hubs and cables
- WANs: routers and cables
- Routers
- Test hosts and applications, preferably Microsoft Windows 95/98/2000 or Windows NT

The preceding list should be viewed more as a list of roles than a list of devices. The specific device type is not relevant; what is relevant is the role that the device plays in the model. There are many ways to simulate a WAN. For example, some network models are more accurate if a Frame Relay switch is deployed in the model, while some models might require only a WAN connection because the protocol needed is irrelevant.

The only component in this list that could be considered optional is the access server. The role of the access server can be a useful one, both in the laboratory environment and in the field. In the field, the access server provides out-of-band management where groups of routers are located. Instead of using multiple modems for dial-in access to routers, an access server can serve as a central point for out-of-band management, requiring only one modem instead of many. The primary role of the access server in the lab will be to provide simple and quick configuration access to a stack of routers. We will go over each one of these components in detail and further discuss their relevance in the lab.

The Access Server

You use the access server as the primary configuration device. From this device, you configure the other routers and switches through a reverse Telnet session. The Cisco routers that accomplish this function the most efficiently are the Cisco routers with the SCSI-II 68-pin async port and the eight-to-one octopus cable. The most common routers that provide this port are the following:

- Cisco 2509/2510
- Cisco 2511/2512
- Cisco 2600/3600 with SCSI-II 68-pin 16/32-port async port

Any Cisco router might be configured for asynchronous communications on its serial ports. A Cisco router with multiple serial ports, such as a Cisco 2522, can also be used as an access server. Regardless of whether you use a router like the 2509 with its SCSI-II 68-pin port or a Cisco 2522 with its 10 serial ports, you need require special cables and a unique configuration.

The most common routers that serve the function of an access server are the Cisco 2509/2510 and the Cisco 2511/2512 routers. The Cisco 2509 has one Ethernet port and eight asynchronous ports, whereas the Cisco 2510 has one Token Ring port and eight asynchronous ports. The eight asynchronous ports utilize a Cisco eight-to-one cable, referred to as the *octal cable*. The part number is CAB-OCTAL-KIT, which also includes modem head-shells for any asynchronous devices, such as modems. The RJ-45 end, of one of the eight cables, plugs into the console port of each router in the lab. You use what Cisco calls reverse Telnet to configure the routers through this cable. This should be called *internal Telnet*—there is nothing reverse about the way Telnet is used to configure the routers. Actually, Telnet is used as the protocol to communicate with a device through a specific internal port or line number.

NOTE   For a complete list of the pinouts of these cables, head-shells, and any other cables mentioned in this book, see Appendix D, "Common Cable Types and Pinouts."

The 2511 access server uses a 68-pin connector and breakout cable, which provides 8 RJ-45 ports on each cable. These ports can also use RJ-45–to–DB-25 adapters to connect to asynchronous devices. The Cisco 2511/2512 is modeled in the same format but supplies an additional eight asynchronous ports.

Figure 1-1 illustrates the back of a Cisco 2511 router and the eight-to one cable.

Figure 1-1 *Cisco 2511 Router and the Eight-to-One Octopus Cable*

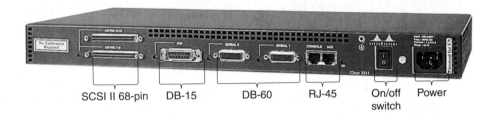

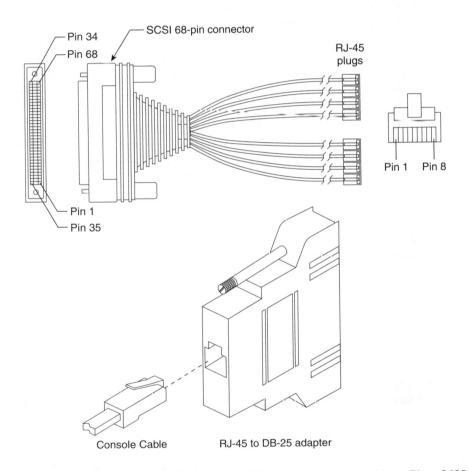

The other form of access server is using serial ports on a router such as a Cisco 3600 series with an eight-port serial module or the Cisco 2522 series with ten serial ports. You can to connect serial cables to various head shells to run asynchronous communications in numerous ways. Essentially, the best combinations require a RS-232 serial cable, either

DTE or DCE, an RJ-45–to–DB-25 adapter, and a rolled or straight-through cable. For the precise pinouts of the RS-232 serial cables and the rolled cable, see Appendix D. The RJ-45–to–DB-25 adapter has three flavors: a DTE M/F, DCE M/F, and MMOD. The female DTE head-shell from Cisco has the label Terminal on one side. The MMOD head-shell (the most common) has the label MODEM on it. This is the same head-shell used on Cisco 4000 and 7000 series routers for the console port, and it is the same head-shell used to connect the terminal server to a modem.

Two common and inexpensive cabling options involve using RS-232 cables as a terminal server cables:

- **Cable method 1**—Use a Cisco female RS-232–to–DB-60 serial cable, the RJ-45–to–DB-25 head-shell labeled MODEM, and a Cisco rolled cable. Connect the cables in the logical fashion; then, from the configuration mode, under the interface mode, enter the **physical-layer async** command. This forces asynchronous communications out the serial port. In the next section, you learn how to completely use this command along with the **transport input** command to configure reverse Telnet sessions to your router's console ports.

- **Cable method 2**—This method is similar to cable method 1, but you use different cables and head-shells. This method requires a Cisco male RS-232–to–DB-60 serial cable, the RJ-45–to–DB-25 head-shell labeled TERMINAL, and a Cisco rolled cable. Again connect the cables in the logical fashion, and add the **physical-layer async** command under the serial interface.

NOTE   The serial port must be a synchronous/asynchronous port to use these cable methods. For example, the ports on a Cisco 2501 are synchronous only, so these cable methods will not work.

Table 1-1 shows all the pinouts for the RJ-45–to–DB-25 adapters, while Table 1-2 shows asynchronous device cabling options.

Table 1-1   *Pinouts for the RJ-45–to–DB-25 Adapters*

Adapter RJ-45 Pins	DTE M/F Pins TERMINAL	DCE M/F Pins	MMOD Pins MODEM
1	4	5	5
2	20	6	8
3	2	3	3
4	7	7	7
5	7	7	7

continues

Table 1-1 *Pinouts for the RJ-45–to–DB-25 Adapters (Continued)*

Adapter RJ-45 Pins	DTE M/F Pins TERMINAL	DCE M/F Pins	MMOD Pins MODEM
6	2	2	2
7	20	20	20
8	4	4	4

Table 1-2 *Asynchronous Device Cabling Options*

Access Server Port	RJ-45 Console Cable Type	Head-Shell Adapter	End Device
Console or aux	Rolled	DTE pinout	Serial cable
Console or aux	Straight	DCE pinout	Serial cable
Console or aux	Rolled	MMOD/MODEM	Modem

The access server can perform multiple roles. Not only can you use this device for easy configuration of the other routers in your stack, but the other serial and LAN ports can be used independently of the terminal server functions. For example, the terminal server could be configured as a route generator or a backbone router. The access server can also be used for remote configuration of the lab through analog dialup. Both of these topics are discussed in detail later in this chapter. The access server is discussed in the section "Simulating LANs by Using Route Generators or Backbone Routers," and the analog dialup is discussed in the section "Configuring Analog Remote Access."

Modeling Local-Area Networks (LANs)

A major part of modeling the internetwork consists of modeling LANs. Each lab in this book has a special section entitled "Equipment Needed." This section lists the minimum hardware requirements needed to complete that particular lab. Some labs might require only a crossover cable or two to connect two routers. Other labs might require a host connection, so you need to use either a hub or a switch when modeling your LANs. Four ways exist in which to model and simulate LANs:

- Modeling LANs by using hubs and media attachment units (MAUs)
- Modeling LANs by using switches
- Simulating LANs by using route generators or backbone routers
- Modeling a LAN with an Ethernet crossover cable

Modeling Versus Simulating

We use the terms *modeling* and *simulating* to describe the character of the network. When the term *model* is used, it means that the network can be used to transport data, and it represents a smaller version of the larger network. When the term *simulated* is used, it implies that the network has only one host and that no data can be sent across the network. The network must be capable of being advertised by a routing protocol to be *simulated*. An example of a simulated network is a loopback interface or an Ethernet interface with the keepalive removed.

Modeling LANs by Using Hubs and MAUs

In a controlled environment, it is necessary to model Layer 1 technologies. The two LAN technologies that we are focusing on are Ethernet and Token Ring. The easiest way to model Layer 1 is by the use of hubs and MAUs. Most of the labs in this book require multiple hubs of multiple types. Physically, the number of network segments are limited by the number of Ethernet or Token Ring interfaces present on the routers in the lab. The type of hubs that you use is not significant; what's important is that the hub is fully operational and has two or more ports. Some hubs are manageable and send IPX SAPs, which can be a useful feature for testing IPX filtering. Other times, it is preferable to have a nice, quiet MAU running in the lab. MAUs generate less heat, no electricity, and no noise. What type you chose to use in your model is up to you.

Modeling LANs by Using Switches

The cleanest way to simulate many LANs is with the use of switches. One switch can be configured to accommodate many virtual LANs (VLANs). A good way to think of a VLAN is as a *standalone hub*. So, instead of having many hubs to accommodate the routers, you need only one switch with a few VLANs. Chapter 2, "LAN Protocols: Configuring Catalyst Ethernet and Token Ring Switches," provides a detailed explanation of VLANs and a switching overview. Using switches to model your LANs also saves on rack space and power requirements, although they are more expensive than hubs.

Simulating LANs by Using Route Generators or Backbone Routers

Two other quick ways to simulate LANs are by using a loopback interfaces and using a **no keepalive** command on the router's Ethernet interface. These two methods can be useful in creating a *route generator* or *backbone router*. A route generator is a device connected to a test network for the purpose of sending and receiving routing updates. A router configured with many loopback addresses with routing protocols will appear as an entire network of routers to a downstream neighbor. We use this functionality in the lab to help simulate networks for route filters and route maps.

Examples 1-1 and 1-2 use a Cisco 2501 as a route generator. Notice that **no keepalive** has been added to the Ethernet to spoof it as up. Also note that the default keepalive value of **10 seconds** is now replaced with **not set**. When you disable the keepalives on the Ethernet segment, you will notice that packets output, output errors, and lost carrier counts all increment together. Do not forget to add a keepalive when you reconnect your Ethernet port back to a real hub or switch. The default value of 10 will automatically be set.

Example 1-1 *Configuring a Two-Route Generator; Simple Loopback Address*

```
Router#conf t
Enter configuration commands, one per line.  End with CNTL/Z.
Router(config)#int loopback 20
Router(config-if)#
%LINEPROTO-5-UPDOWN: Line protocol on Interface Loopback20, changed state to up
Router(config-if)#ip address 172.16.16.1 255.255.255.0
Router(config-if)#exit
Router(config)#int loopback 21
%LINEPROTO-5-UPDOWN: Line protocol on Interface Loopback21, changed state to up
Router(config-if)#ip address 172.16.17.1 255.255.255.0
Router(config-it)#exit
Router(config)#router eigrp 2001
Router(config-router)#network 172.16.0.0
Router(config-router)#^Z
Router#
```

Example 1-2 *Configuring a Route Generator; Spoofing Ethernet*

```
Router#conf t
Enter configuration commands, one per line.  End with CNTL/Z.
Router(config)#int ethernet 0
Router(config-if)#no keepalive
Router(config-if)#^Z
Router#
Router#show int e0
Ethernet0 is up, line protocol is up
  Hardware is Lance, address is 0000.0c8d.54ac (bia 0000.0c8d.54ac)
  MTU 1500 bytes, BW 10000 Kbit, DLY 1000 usec, rely 235/255, load 1/255
  Encapsulation ARPA, loopback not set, keepalive not set
  ARP type: ARPA, ARP Timeout 04:00:00
  Last input never, output 00:00:18, output hang never
  Last clearing of "show interface" counters never
  Queueing strategy: fifo
  Output queue 0/40, 0 drops; input queue 0/75, 0 drops
  5 minute input rate 0 bits/sec, 0 packets/sec
  5 minute output rate 0 bits/sec, 0 packets/sec
     0 packets input, 0 bytes, 0 no buffer
     Received 0 broadcasts, 0 runts, 0 giants, 0 throttles
     0 input errors, 0 CRC, 0 frame, 0 overrun, 0 ignored, 0 abort
     0 input packets with dribble condition detected
     21 packets output, 3030 bytes, 0 underruns
     21 output errors, 0 collisions, 2 interface resets
```

Example 1-2 *Configuring a Route Generator; Spoofing Ethernet (Continued)*

```
        0 babbles, 0 late collision, 0 deferred
        21 lost carrier, 0 no carrier
        0 output buffer failures, 0 output buffers swapped out
Router#
```

Modeling LANs by Using an Ethernet Crossover Cable

A commonly known way to connect two Ethernet hosts is to use an Ethernet crossover cable. An Ethernet crossover cable is simply an RJ-45–to–RJ-45 patch cable, pinned out in a crossover pattern. The obvious limitation is that the crossover cable can be used to connect only two devices. In the lab environment, you can use this cable to connect two routers or to connect a router to one host. Figure 1-2 shows the pinouts for Ethernet crossover cable.

Figure 1-2 *Pinouts for an Ethernet Crossover Cable*

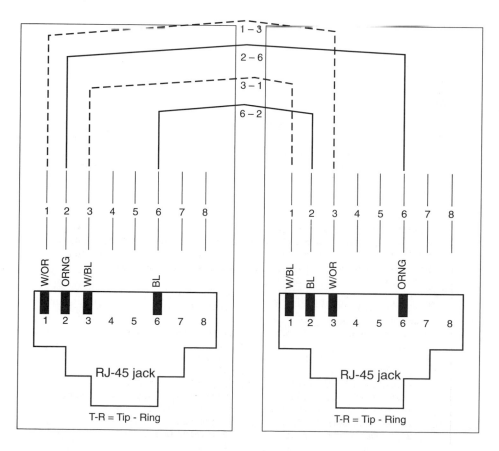

Simulating Wide-Area Network Connections

The other major part of modeling the internetwork consists of WAN connections. At this point in the design, you are concerned only with ISO Layer 1. You will continue to model the internetwork from Layer 1 on up because this is the most logical way to build any network. First, you will build all the physical connections to all your devices, and then you will configure all LAN interfaces, WAN interfaces, and finally your different networks together with routing protocols. Constructing a network in a layered approach allows for future growth and adaptation by upgrading or replacing a single layer at a time, while leaving the remaining layers unchanged. With this in mind, we will focus on physical aspects, such as cable types and pinouts. Part III, "Connecting LANs with Wide Area Networks (WANs)," focuses on ISO Layer 2 protocols.

You can model WAN connections in three primary ways, and you can simulate a WAN in one way in a Cisco environment:

- You can model WANs by using a special crossover cable for routers with WAN Interface Cards (WICs) or external CSU/DSUs.

- You can model WANs by using V.35 DTE cable to a V.35 DCE cable, or any serial cable in a DTE-to-DCE configuration.

- You can simulate WANs by using loopback plugs on CSU/DSUs.

- You can model WANs by using a Cisco router as a Frame Relay or X.25 switch.

NOTE   Of course, no book on networking would be complete without mentioning the OSI model; Appendix B, "The 'Abridged' OSI Reference Model," presents a brief overview of the OSI model.

Modeling WANs by Using Special Crossover Cable Routers with Built-In or External CSU/DSUs

Two routers with built-in or external CSU/DSUs can be connected in a "back-to-back" mode. This functions as the Layer 1 for many WAN protocols, including PPP, HDLC, and others. This is done by utilizing a special crossover cable made from pinning out specific pins of a four-pair Category 5 cable. It is important to note that the crossover cable needed differs slightly from a T1 to a 56-kbps DSU. You must connect a router with a T1 service unit or CSU/DSU to another router with a T1 service unit or CSU/DSU. The same is true for a 56-kbps service unit. Figures 1-3 and 1-4 illustrate what pinouts you need to make a crossover cable, from a Category 5 cable for a T1 CSU/DSU and a 56-kbps CSU/DSU.

Figure 1-3   *Pinouts for a Crossover Cable for T1 Service Module or CSU/DSU*

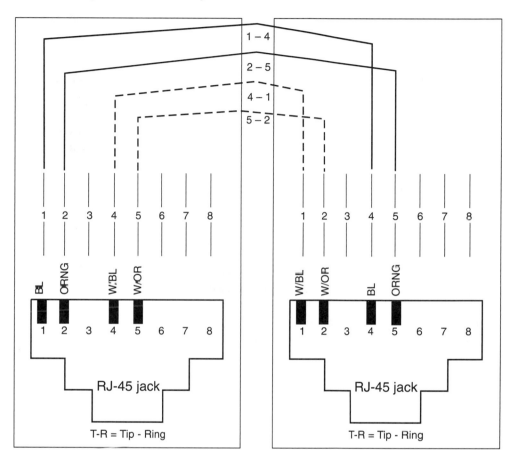

Modeling WANs by Using a V.35 DTE Cable to a V.35 DCE Cable

The most common way to provide Layer 1 connectivity between routers is to connect a female V.35 DCE cable to a male V.35 DTE cable. The key factor in any back-to-back configuration is ensuring that one side of the link sets clocking. This is always the DCE side of the link. To configure the clock rate for an interface, simply add the command **clock rate** [*value*]. Example 1-3 demonstrates how to set the clocking on a serial interface to 64,000 bps.

Example 1-3   *Configuring the Clockrate on a DCE Interface*

```
frame_relay_switch(config)#int serial 5
frame_relay_switch(config-if)#clockrate 64000
frame_relay_switch(config-if)#^Z
frame_relay_switch#
```

Figure 1-4   *Pinouts for a Crossover Cable for 56-kbps Service Module or CSU/DSU*

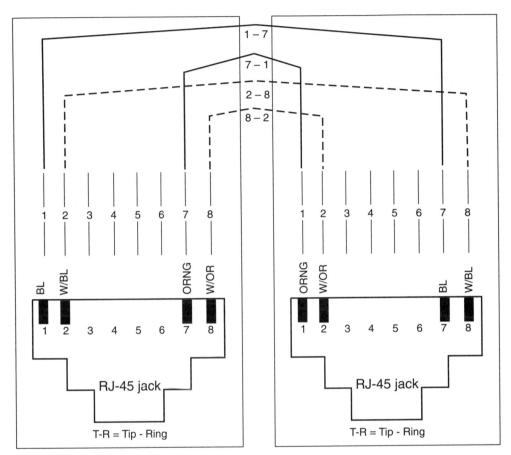

It is important to ensure that the cable is truly a V.35 DTE cable connecting to a V.35 DCE cable. The sex of the DCE or DTE cable is not relevant; however, you must connect a DCE side to a DTE side, and set the clock rate, as demonstrated in Example 1-3. Figure 1-5 illustrates many of the standard Cisco cable connectors, ranging from the common V.35 and RS-232 interfaces to EIA613-HSSI interfaces.

These cables can be ordered from Cisco Systems, part number CAB-V35MT for the V.35 male DTE cable, and CAB-V35FC for the female DCE cable. Several companies also make serial and crossover cables at reasonable prices.

Figure 1-5   *Common Cable Interfaces for Cisco Routers*

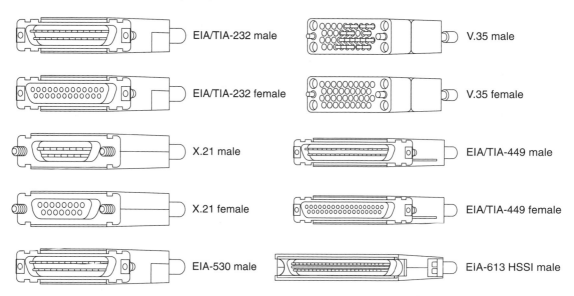

EIA/TIA-232 male

V.35 male

EIA/TIA-232 female

V.35 female

X.21 male

EIA/TIA-449 male

X.21 female

EIA/TIA-449 female

EIA-530 male

EIA-613 HSSI male

At times when the cables are connected in a back-to-back mode, it might be hard to tell which one is the DCE cable. You might be in the field or working remotely, and you might not have physical access to your lab—how, then, can you tell which cable is the DCE cable? The **show controller** command shows the cable type and shows whether the cable is DCE or DTE. Example 1-4 shows two interfaces on a Cisco 2501 router. Using the **show controller** command, you can tell what the interface type is.

Example 1-4   *Example of the* **show controllers** *Command*

```
Router#show controller serial 0
HD unit 0, idb = 0xCED94, driver structure at 0xD3B18
buffer size 1524  HD unit 0, V.35 DTE cable
cpb = 0xE2, eda = 0x4140, cda = 0x4000
RX ring with 16 entries at 0xE24000
00 bd_ptr=0x4000 pak=0x0D66F0 ds=0xE2DDB0 status=80 pak_size=0
***text omitted***

Router#show controller serial 1
HD unit 1, idb = 0xD7788, driver structure at 0xDC508
buffer size 1524  HD unit 1, RS-232 DCE cable
cpb = 0xE3, eda = 0x2140, cda = 0x2000
RX ring with 16 entries at 0xE32000
00 bd_ptr=0x2000 pak=0x0DF0E4 ds=0xE3C468 status=00 pak_size=0
***text omitted***
```

Interface Serial 0 is a V.35 DTE cable, and interface Serial 1 is an RS-232 DCE cable. Other serial cables, such as RS-232, are used for back-to-back connections, as long as a DCE cable is connected to DTE cable. It is important to note that each different cable type has certain speed restrictions. For example, it is not possible to simulate T1 speeds on RS-232 cables. For the most flexibility in lab environments, use V.35 cables whenever possible.

Sometimes, you might want to switch your lab environment rather rapidly. You might want a serial connection attached to one router one day, whereas the next day you might want that same connection to go to another router. In these situations, it is best to use a patch panel of some sort. A V.35 patch panel is a common sight at large labs. The V.35 patch panel is simple to work with. Most V.35 patch panels have a female DTE port located on top, in the rear, and a V.35 male DCE port located in the middle, in the rear. The routers plug into these ports, the DTE cable to the DTE port, and the DCE cable to the DCE port. On the front of the patch panel are small patch ports, with one port in front of each DTE and DCE port. A black patch cable then enables you to patch one DTE port to one DCE port, thereby connecting one router to another router.

To change the configuration, simply move the patch cable to another patch port. Using a patch panel in this manner allows for quick and rapid physical configuration of many serial links. Patch panels should be labeled on the front to designate which is the DCE and DTE port—this can be key when troubleshooting physical layer issues. Figure 1-6 illustrates a V.35 Patch panel.

Most patch panels also have a bottom port, right below the DCE port. This port is used for attaching a line monitor or data scope.

Simulating WANs by Using HDLC and Loopback Plugs on CSU/DSUs

Yet another way to use WAN interfaces in your model is to deploy loopback plugs on your CSU/DSUs combined with running HDLC protocol. In addition, by putting a Layer 3 address, such as an IP or IPX address, on the interface, the interface will respond to **ping**s and will show up in routing tables. The Layer 2 encapsulation must also be set to HDLC when using loopback plugs. Routers with built-in CSU/DSUs or WAN interface cards (WICs), and even on routers with external CSU/DSUs, can have a loopback plug installed into the RJ-45 jack, thus spoofing the WAN interface as up. Example 1-5 illustrates output from the **show interface** command on a Cisco 2524, with a T1 WIC and a loopback plug installed.

Figure 1-6   *V.35 Patch Panels*

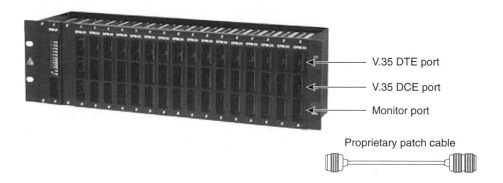

V.35 DTE port

V.35 DCE port

Monitor port

Proprietary patch cable

Example 1-5   *The* **show interface** *Command of a Cisco 2524 with a T1 Loopback Plug Installed in Its WIC*

```
router# show interfaces serial 1
Serial1 is up, line protocol is up (looped)
  Hardware is HD64570 with FT1 CSU/DSU
  MTU 1500 bytes, BW 1544 Kbit, DLY 20000 usec, rely 255/255, load 1/255
  Encapsulation HDLC, loopback not set, keepalive set (10 sec)
  Last input 00:00:02, output 00:00:02, output hang never
  Last clearing of "show interface" counters never
  Input queue: 0/75/0 (size/max/drops); Total output drops: 0
  Queueing strategy: weighted fair
  Output queue: 0/1000/64/0 (size/max total/threshold/drops)
    Conversations  0/1/256 (active/max active/max total)
    Reserved Conversations 0/0 (allocated/max allocated)
  5 minute input rate 0 bits/sec, 0 packets/sec
  5 minute output rate 0 bits/sec, 0 packets/sec
    2537 packets input, 148733 bytes, 0 no buffer
    Received 2537 broadcasts, 0 runts, 0 giants, 0 throttles
    0 input errors, 0 CRC, 0 frame, 0 overrun, 0 ignored, 0 abort
    2537 packets output, 148733 bytes, 0 underruns
    0 output errors, 0 collisions, 1 interface resets
    0 output buffer failures, 0 output buffers swapped out
    1 carrier transitions
    DCD=up  DSR=up  DTR=up  RTS=up  CTS=up
router#
```

NOTE   Loopback plugs can be useful in the field. Whenever a CSU/DSU or WIC is suspected to be malfunctioning, installing a loopback plug can quickly test the physical layer to the CSU/DSU. When the loopback plug is installed, the **show interface** command should show the interface as **line up, protocol up and (looped)**.

A loopback plug can be easy to make. You can use a simple cable kit to construct these plugs, or you can order them from most cable vendors, if they are supplied with the diagrams in Figures 1-7 and 1-8. Figure 1-7 demonstrates the pinouts required for an RJ-45 56-kbps loopback plug, while Figure 1-8 illustrates the pinouts required for an RJ-45 T1 or 1.544-Mbps loopback plug.

Figure 1-7   *Pinouts for an RJ-45 56-kbps Loopback Plug*

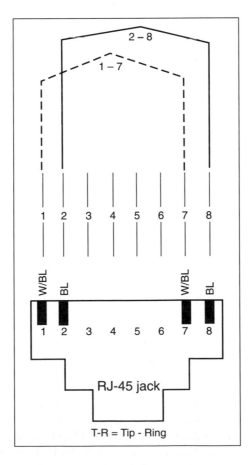

Figure 1-8   *Pinouts for an RJ-45 T1 Loopback Plug*

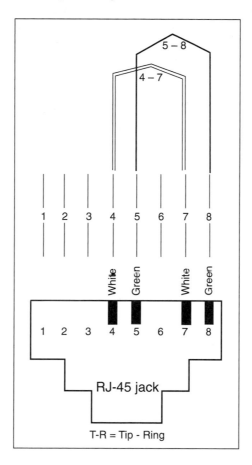

Modeling WANs by Using a Cisco Router as a Frame Relay or X.25 Switch

The third way to model a WAN is to configure a Cisco router as a Frame Relay or an X.25 switch. Any Cisco router with Cisco IOS Software Release 11.0 or later and at least two serial interfaces can be configured as an actual Frame Relay or X.25 switch. When configured as a Frame Relay switch, the router actually sends and receives the Frame Relay Local Management Interface (LMI), and it can even be configured to use Network-to-Network Interface (NNI), the standard interface between Frame Relay switches. Two interfaces are always needed because the switch is primarily a DCE device and requires two routers to serve as the DTE devices. Because the Frame Relay switch is a DCE-only device, it requires DCE serial cables as well.

The Cisco 2522 and the 2523 series routers can perform the function of a Frame Relay switch with ample ports for many end devices. The Cisco 2522 provides two high-speed synchronous serial ports and eight low-speed asynchronous/synchronous serial ports. This router also has one Ethernet port in an RJ-45 or AUI configuration, and one ISDN BRI U interface in an RJ-45 configuration. The Cisco 2523 is exactly the same as the 2522, but instead of the Ethernet port, it has an RJ-45 Token Ring interface. Any Cisco router with multiple serial interfaces is a good choice for a Frame Relay or X.25 switch. The Frame Relay switching functions run independently of normal router functions, such as IP routing. Thus, this router can be used not only as a Frame Relay switch, but also as another routed device or a route generator. The detailed software configuration of a Frame Relay switch is covered later in this chapter, in the section "Configuring a Frame Relay Switch."

TIP

During the course of your studies and career in networking, you will come across many terms and acronyms. Sometimes, it can become difficult to remember all the rules, such as a DCE side requires a clock. One method of memorization that I use is word association. For example, I know that there are DCE and DTE sides to a cable. The *C* is the difference between the two, and *C* stands for "clock." Thus, the DCE side is the side on which you configure the clock signal.

At this point, you might be wondering, "What about ATM? That's a LAN and WAN protocol—where does that fit in?" Asynchronous Transfer Mode (ATM) was originally called the "duck" of networking because it was like a duck in a metaphorical sense. A duck can swim, fly, and walk. It doesn't walk that well and swims okay, but it flies really fast. ATM can do voice, data, and video, although it does some of them better then others. I had the same classification problems in deciding where to talk about ATM. Because ATM is a LAN and WAN technology and is highly specialized, it is covered in Chapter 8, "WAN Protocols and Technologies: Asynchronous Transfer Mode (ATM)."

Routers, Cisco IOS Software, and Memory Requirements for Labs

Throughout this book, every lab has different hardware and software requirements. As mentioned earlier, preceding each lab is a section entitled "Equipment Needed." This section lists the minimum amount of equipment needed to complete that lab. Some labs are rather easy and might require only two or three routers with IP routing software. Other labs, such as those for configuring SNA, are rather complex and require the enterprise feature set and multiple routers. Finding routers, hubs, and such can be difficult.

Unfortunately, it is hard for some companies to realize the benefit of the age-old saying "Practice makes perfect." Companies can have a hard time finding enough room in the budget for labs so that their engineers can finely hone their skills. Sadly, these companies opt to practice and flail on their own networks or those of their customers. There is a reason why companies such as HP, Comdisco Inc., and IBM remain industry leaders: They realize the cost-benefit analysis of having highly skilled engineers to model and deploy complex internetworks.

Personally understanding the difficulty in attaining networking equipment, I have tried to involve the fewest amounts of routers/hubs as possible in these labs. I've also made the studies independent of one another, so if you don't have access to a Token Ring/Ethernet router or a switch, you can still perform a majority of the labs. For example, to perform the translational bridging lab, you need a Token Ring interface and an Ethernet interface on the same physical router. Because many Cisco routers can accommodate multiple LAN segments of different types, I won't go into details on specific router models. A good rule to follow when investing in new routers is, the more modular the router is, the more flexibility you have in creating multiple models. Investing in modular routers also protects your investment because most routers can be upgraded with the installation of new networking modules.

NOTE   The Comdisco lab uses primarily Cisco Catalyst 5500s, Cisco 2500s, 4500s, and 3600 series routers for modeling network scenarios. The Cisco 3600 series router can accommodate almost any networking requirement; this includes ATM, Gigabyte Ethernet, Voice over IP or Frame Relay, along with VPN technology.

When all the hardware is gathered, you are ready to begin discussing the Cisco Internetwork Operating System (IOS) Software releases, DRAM memory, and FLASH memory requirements that the models require. All three are tightly related to each other. The protocols and Cisco feature sets that you use drive the amount of DRAM memory needed to execute that feature. The Cisco IOS feature set is stored in FLASH memory. Therefore, the more features and protocols that are in use, the more DRAM and FLASH memory will be required. The labs listed in this book utilize most of the major routing protocols and most major feature sets. To easily accommodate this, the Enterprise Plus feature set could be installed on all the routers. The Cisco IOS Software release level should be at least 11.2.x or 12.0.x. If you are specifically practicing for the CCIE Lab Exam, use a minimum IOS level of 12.0 on all routers. If the lab requires an IOS feature greater than IP routing, it will be noted as a requirement.

NOTE   To find the exact minimum memory requirements for the specific Cisco IOS Software and feature set in use, consult Cisco's Web page, www.cisco.com.

Test Hosts and Data Simulation

The ultimate goal of all networks is to transport data from one place to another. Without data to transport, there would be no need for networks. To ensure that any model is working properly, test data is always required. Networking has no exception to this rule. Without test data of some sort, it would be difficult to test many networking features. Features such as remote source-route bridging (RSRB) actually need to send and receive data before the RSRB becomes active. A data-link switching (DLSw) peer can be connected, but no circuit becomes active until data is sent. Therefore, to properly test the models, you need to simulate data of many kinds. Your challenge will be testing complex protocols, such as SNA, without installing a mini-mainframe in your labs.

Fortunately, the Microsoft Windows 95/98/2000–based operating systems ship with three major protocols that help in testing your networks. Microsoft Windows 95, 98, and 2000 all ship with TCP/IP, IPX/SPX, and NetBEUI as installable protocols. These three protocols allow numerous testing of many Cisco IOS Software features.

For example, two Windows-based workstations running NetBEUI can be used to test DLSw peers across an internetwork. Browsing Network Neighborhood will force an all-routes explorer frame to be generated. The name that you entered in the Control Panel/Network/Identification Name dialog box will be the name that appears during the **show dlsw reachability** command. As another example, in an RSRB environment, this explorer frame would be enough to bring up the remote source bridge and force a connection to the other remote source bridge.

Installing TCP/IP allows you to use many shareware utilities, such as FTP, TFTP, and DHCP, for testing. By actually setting up end stations, filters will take a more true-to-life form when you can actually see them at work. All these IP-based utilities are shareware that you should be able to find online.

NOTE   I installed my first home network in 1993, on the same day that the computer game DOOM was released. DOOM allowed for 3D multiplayer computer games over a network through IPX. We pooled our money, and hours later, we were stringing coax cable from one end of the apartment to the other. We then proceeded to set up an IPX-based NetWare Lite network. In the days of DOS and the dreaded 640 K limit, we were quite proud of our little network. We ventured forth and immersed ourselves in the 3D world of DOOM well into the wee hours of the morning.

To this day, DOOM and its descendants remain a nemesis to network managers. Bandwidth manager products, such as the one by Packeteer, even have a special data flow for DOOM. (This probably is to secure enough bandwidth for the DOOM players so that they are not slowed down by somebody's print job.) At any rate, computer games continue to be great tests for the speed and for the transport of IP and IPX protocols, as well as for the network manager trying to control them. In the lab or at home, the joys of playing the latest computer game over your new network can be a fun and rewarding experience. Plus, you can amaze your friends with your networking expertise.

Building the Framework for Internetwork Modeling—Configuring Key Components

Every model that you construct in this book starts from a similar framework. Most models involve one or more LANs and WANs—of course, routers and hubs are needed for this. You also need a device for local or remote access to the model, along with a test application to run or test the model. Thus, your framework for most models consist of routers, hubs, a Frame Relay switch, an access server, and a couple of workstations. From this framework, you build and design many models, making only subtle changes to the network topologies. There is a logical process to go through when constructing this initial framework:

Step 1   **Gain privileged level access to devices in the model.** This includes using and modifying the 16-bit boot register to gain privileged level access to a router's configuration.

Step 2   **Upgrade the Cisco IOS Software to the model's requirements.** This includes copying a new IOS image to Flash memory.

Step 3   **Configure local and remote access to the model.** This includes configuring an access server and configuring analog dialup access to the lab.

Step 4   **Configure LAN and WAN devices.** Every model will require slightly different LAN and WAN configurations. This will require only minor cable movement, though, so your primary focus will be on the initial configuration of a Frame Relay switch and its permanent virtual circuits (PVCs).

Step 5   **Configure test applications and test networks.** This includes setting up Microsoft Windows 95/98/2000 networking and configuring network protocols such as TCP/IP, IPX, and Net BEUI. You will also learn about the use of route generators.

Gaining Privileged Access: The 16-Bit Boot Register

I think that one of the best-kept secrets of Cisco routers and switches is the 16-bit boot register. The 16-bit register is located on almost every Cisco platform in one variation or another. For example, this is the same register that was set by jumpers on the AGS series routers in the early 1990s. It is the same register that is found in the Catalyst switches in 2001. And, for the most part, it is the same register on all Cisco routers, sometimes masked in a utility called CONFREG.

Another common example of using the boot register is during password recovery. The boot register, actually bit 6, is the bit that you flip when you change the register from 0x2102 to 0x2142 during password recovery. During password recovery, bit 6 is set to ignore NVRAM on startup. This is perhaps the most common use of the register. Some other uses of the boot register include the following:

- Recovering a lost password
- Enabling or disabling the console Break key
- Allowing manual boot of the OS using the **B** command at the bootstrap program (ROM monitor) prompt
- Changing the router boot configuration to allow a Flash or ROM boot
- Performing maintenance testing from the ROM monitor
- Loading an image into Flash memory
- Permanently disabling a router

Because the boot register represents the "keys" to your router, it is important to explain the entire register rather then covering just bit 6.

To display the boot register, key in the **show version** command. The boot register is displayed at the bottom of the text. Example 1-6 demonstrates the **show version** command.

Example 1-6   *The **show version** Command, with a Boot Register Set to Boot to ROM, 0x2101*

```
router(boot)#show version
Cisco Internetwork Operating System Software
IOS (tm) 3000 Bootstrap Software (IGS-RXBOOT), Version 10.2(8a), RELEASE SOFTWAR
E (fc1)
Copyright (c) 1986-1995 by cisco Systems, Inc.
Compiled Tue 24-Oct-95 15:46 by mkamson
Image text-base: 0x01020000, data-base: 0x00001000

ROM: System Bootstrap, Version 5.2(8a), RELEASE SOFTWARE

router uptime is 34 minutes
System restarted by power-on
Running default software
```

Example 1-6   *The **show version** Command, with a Boot Register Set to Boot to ROM, 0x2101 (Continued)*

```
cisco 2500 (68030) processor (revision L) with 14332K/2048K bytes of memory.
Processor board serial number 03071163 with hardware revision 00000000
X.25 software, Version 2.0, NET2, BFE and GOSIP compliant.
ISDN software, Version 1.0.
1 Ethernet/IEEE 802.3 interface.
2 Serial network interfaces.
1 ISDN Basic Rate interface.
32K bytes of non-volatile configuration memory.
16384K bytes of processor board System flash (Read/Write)

Configuration register is 0x2101

router(boot)#
```

The boot register is formatted with the most-significant bit on the right, as illustrated by Figure 1-9. This figure also shows how the default settings of 0x2102 are derived on Cisco routers.

Figure 1-9   *Default Settings of the 16-Bit Boot Register*

Bit 15	Bit 14	Bit 13	Bit 12	Bit 11	Bit 10	Bit 9	Bit 8	Bit 7	Bit 6	Bit 5	Bit 4	Bit 3	Bit 2	Bit 1	Bit 0
0	0	1	0	0	0	0	1	0	0	0	0	0	0	1	0
	2				1				0				2		

Briefly stepping through the default settings of the register, you can see that bits 1, 8, and 13 are set to 1, or the ON position. Having bit 1 set then sets the boot portion of the register to a hexadecimal value of 2. This tells the router to boot from Flash if a valid IOS is found there. Having bits 4 through 7 set to 0 enables the router to boot normally; from NVRAM, preserve the banner and set "all 1s" as the broadcast. Bit 8 tells the router that the Break key is disabled. The rest of the register sets the network broadcast to 1s, sets the console baud rate to 9600, and determines how the router responds to a netboot failure. As mentioned previously, the most common use of this register is the flipping of bit 6, causing the router to ignore the startup config stored in NVRAM. Again, this is the same procedure used in password recovery.

Table 1-3 illustrates the entire register and its settings in detail. Refer to this table when reading the following detailed descriptions of the boot register.

Table 1-3 *The Entire 16-Bit Boot Register with Default Settings*

Bit	Meaning	Default Setting
0–3	Boot Field: 0x0 = Boot ROM monitor. -------------------------------------- 0x1 = Boot from onboard ROM, or boot to boot mode, if a subset of the IOS exists. -------------------------------------- 0x2 to 0xF Causes the following (listed in order of precedence): Boot from Flash, if a valid IOS file exists. Follow **boot system** commands found in the configuration. Use the register value to form a filename from which to netboot a system image from.	0 0 1 0
4	Fast boot: Force load through the **boot system** commands found in the configuration.	0
5	High-speed console: 1 = console operates at 19.2 or 38.4; works with bits 11 and 12.	0
6	Ignore startup-config file: 1 = ignore NVRAM.	0
7	OEM bit: 1 = disabling the display of the Cisco banner on startup.	0
8	Break key: 1 = disable.	1
9	Not used.	0
10	Netboot broadcast format: Setting bit 10 = 1 causes the processor to use an all-zeros broadcast.	0
11-12	Console baud rate: **Bit 5** = 1 **Bit 11** = 1 **Bit 12** = 0 **Console baud rate** = 38,400 --------------------------------------	0 0

Table 1-3   *The Entire 16-Bit Boot Register with Default Settings (Continued)*

Bit	Meaning	Default Setting
11-12 Cont.	**Bit 5 = 1** **Bit 11 = 0** **Bit 12 = 0** **Console baud rate** = 19,200	0 0

	Bit 5 = 0 **Bit 11 = 0** **Bit 12 = 0** **Console baud rate** = 9600	

	Bit 5 = 0 **Blt 11 = 0** **Bit 12 = 1** **Console baud rate** = 4800	

	Bit 5 = 0 **Bit 11 = 1** **Bit 12 = 1** **Console baud rate** = 2400	

	Bit 5 = 0 **Bit 11 = 1** **Bit 12 = 0** **Console baud rate** = 1200	
13	Response to netboot failure: 1 = boot from ROM after netboot failure, 0 = continue to netboot.	1

continues

Table 1-3   *The Entire 16-Bit Boot Register with Default Settings (Continued)*

Bit	Meaning	Default Setting
14	Netboot subnet broadcast:	0
	Setting bit 14 = 1 forces a subnet broadcast.	
15	Enable diagnostic messages: 1 = ignore NVRAM and display diagnostic messages.	0

Boot Field (Bits 0 Through 3)

The boot field controls the booting of the router. This field starts with the first 4 bits on the right. If this field is set for 0x0, decimal 0, the router will boot to ROM monitor mode. For example, setting the register for 0x2100 causes the router to boot to ROM monitor mode. Setting this value to 0x1 causes the router to boot from its onboard ROM. This ROM may contain a full IOS, such as in the 7000 series, or a subset of the IOS, as in the 2500 series. The prompt, when in boot mode, is represented with (boot) behind the router's host name.

If you set the boot field to a value of 2 through F, and if there is a valid system boot command stored in the configuration file, the router boots the system software as directed by that value. If you set the boot field to any other bit pattern, the router uses the resulting number to form a default boot filename for netbooting. The router creates a default boot filename as part of the automatic configuration processes. To form the boot filename, the router starts with cisco and links the octal equivalent of the boot filename, a dash, and the processor-type name. A Cisco 4000 with the bit pattern of 0x1 set in the first octet will try to load a TFTP file named Cisco2-4000. Table 1-4 lists the default boot filenames or actions for the processor when setting the boot field bits. The xxxx stands for the processor type—for instance, in Cisco 4000, xxxx = 4000.

Table 1-4   *Default Boot Filenames*

Action/Filename	Bit 3	Bit 2	Bit 1	Bit 0
Boot to ROM monitor	0	0	0	0
Boot from ROM	0	0	0	1
cisco2-xxxx	0	0	1	0
cisco3-xxxx	0	0	1	1
cisco4-xxxx	0	1	0	0
cisco5-xxxx	0	1	0	1
cisco6-xxxx	0	1	1	0
cisco7-xxxx	0	1	1	1

Table 1-4   *Default Boot Filenames (Continued)*

Action/Filename	Bit 3	Bit 2	Bit 1	Bit 0
cisco10-xxxx	1	0	0	0
cisco11-xxxx	1	0	0	1
cisco12-xxxx	1	0	1	0
cisco13-xxxx	1	0	1	1
cisco14-xxxx	1	1	0	0
cisco15-xxxx	1	1	0	1
cisco16-xxxx	1	1	1	0
cisco17-xxxx	1	1	1	1

Fast Boot/Force Boot (Bit 4)

Setting this bit forces the router to load the Cisco IOS Software found in the configuration set by the **boot system flash** command. If no Cisco IOS Software matches the filename set by this command, the router will boot to boot mode. For example, adding the line **boot system flash c2500-js56-l.120-3.bin** forces the router to look for the file c2500-js56-1.120-3.bin in Flash memory. If an exact match of this filename isn't found, the router will boot in boot mode.

High-Speed Console (Bit 5)

The setting of bit 5 works in conjunction with bits 11 and 12. Setting this bit is for high-speed console access above 9600 bps. When this bit is set, you can connect to the console port at speeds of 19,200 bps and 38,400 bps. For a complete listing of how the jumper works in conjunction with bits 10, and 11, see Table 1-6.

CAUTION   Bit 5 is an "undocumented" bit for a reason. The console port is critical to router operation and troubleshooting. The higher the data speeds are, the more sensitive the connection is and the higher the probability is that you will not be capable of connecting to the router at these high speeds. If you do not have Telnet access or another "back door" into the router enabled, the consequences can be dire. The gains from operating the console port at 19,200 bps or 38,400 bps instead of 9600 bps are minor. Keep in mind that the uses for this interface are for router key-ins and configuration; it is not necessary to have high-speed console access. Change this bit with extreme caution.

Ignore NVRAM (Bit 6)

Setting this bit forces the router to ignore the configuration file in NVRAM, called the *startup-config*. When you ignore NVRAM, you essentially are ignoring the startup-config. You can still view the startup-config with the **show** command, but the configuration will be absent from the running-config. This is also the bit that is flipped during password recovery.

OEM Bit (Bit 7)

This bit was created for Original Equipment Manufacturers (OEMs) versions of the routers. By setting this bit, the Cisco Systems, Inc. banner will be ignored. If the IOS has encryption software on it, the encryption warning will still be displayed.

Break Key (Bit 8)

Setting this bit disables the Break key. If you set this bit to 0, then at *any time* during the routers uptime—not just during the boot process—you can halt the operating system with the press of a *single key*. This is a powerful setting and should not be changed. Disabling the break—it is disabled by default—does not affect the Break key during the first 60 seconds of initialization. During this time, the Break key will still halt the router.

Reserved (Bit 9)

This bit is currently not in use.

Netboot Broadcast Format (Bits 10 and 14)

Setting bits 10 and 14 controls how the routers and switches handle subnet and host broadcasts. The default broadcast address is all 1s in the host or subnet destination address. Changing these bits allows for backward compatibility for many older UNIX hosts, such as Berkley UNIX 4.2BSD. Most IP implementation today uses a 1s compliment for broadcast messages, so you probably will never modify these settings. Table 1-5 illustrates the use of bit 10 and bit 14.

Table 1-5   *Configuration Settings for Broadcast Address Control, Bit 10 and Bit 14*

Bit 14	Bit 10	Address (<net><host>)
0	0	<1s> <1s>
0	1	<0s> <1s>
1	0	<net> <1s>
1	1	<net> <0s>

System Console Terminal Baud Rate Settings (Bits 5, 11, and 12)

Bits 5, 11, and 12 control the baud rate (bps) of the console port. The routers are shipped with this setting to 9600, which has bits 5, 11, and 12 off, or set at 0. Table 1-6 shows the baud rate settings. For example, to increase the baud settings of the routers console port, use a register of 0x2122 for 19.2 access.

Table 1-6   *Configuration Settings for System Console Baud Rate*

Bit 5	Bit 11	Bit 12	Console Baud Rate
1	1	0	38,400 bps
1	0	0	19,200 bps
0	0	0	9600 bps
0	0	1	4800 bps
0	1	0	1200 bps
0	1	1	2400 bps

Netboot Failure Response (Bit 13)

Setting bit 13 causes the router to load the Cisco IOS Software from the default location after five netboot failures. The default for this bit is on, or 1, which is why most of the routers' jump registers start with 2. Setting this bit to 0 causes the router to continue to netboot and never look at the ROM for booting.

Display Factory Diagnostics (Bit 15)

Setting bit 15 causes the router to display factory diagnostic messages. Setting this bit also forces NVRAM to be ignored. To display these diagnostic messages, configure the register at 0xA102. The A sets bit 15 and bit 13, forcing diagnostics messages to appear during initialization.

Understanding the Boot Process

This next section can be found in a similar format on the Cisco documentation CD that comes with all new Cisco routers. Although everything can be found on the CD, this section is important enough to highlight:

When a router is powered on or rebooted, the following events happen:

- The ROM monitor initializes.
- The ROM monitor checks the configuration register boot field (the lowest 4 bits in the register.)
  - If the boot field is 0x0, the system does not boot an IOS image and waits for user intervention at the ROM monitor prompt.

- If the boot field is 0x1, the ROM monitor boots the boot helper image. (On some platforms the boot helper image is specified by the BOOTLDR environment variable.)
- If the boot field is 0x2 through 0xF, the ROM monitor boots the first valid image specified in the configuration file or specified by the BOOT environment variable.

- When the boot field is 0x2 through 0xF, the router goes through each command in order until it boots a valid image. If bit 13 in the configuration register is set, each command will be tried once. If bit 13 is not set, the **Boot system** command specifying a network server will be tried up to five more times. The timeouts between each consecutive attempt are 2, 4, 16, 256, and finally 300 seconds. If it cannot find a valid image, the following events happen:
  - If all boot commands in the system configuration file specify booting from a network server and all commands fail, the system attempts to boot the first valid file in Flash memory.
  - If the boot-default-ROM-software option in the configuration register is set, the router will start the boot image (the image contained in boot ROM or specified by the BOOTLDR environment variable).
  - If the boot-default-ROM-software option in the configuration register is *not* set, the system waits for user intervention at the ROM monitor prompt. You must boot the router manually.
  - If a fully functional system image is not found, the router will not function and must be reconfigured through a direct console port connection.

- When looking for a bootable file in Flash memory:
  - The system searches for the filename in Flash memory. If a filename is not specified, the software searches through the entire Flash directory for a bootable file instead of picking only the first file.
  - The system attempts to recognize the file in Flash memory. If the file is recognized, the software decides whether it is bootable by performing the following checks:
    - For run-from-Flash images, the software determines whether it is loaded at the correct execution address.
    - For run-from-RAM images, the software determines whether the system has enough RAM to execute the image.

This process changes on platforms with dual processor cards or dual Flash cards, such as those that are found on the 7000 series or in the Catalyst RSM. Figure 1-10 diagrams this rather complicated process as it is found on most platforms (except those noted).

Accessing the Register

The boot register is a 16-bit register represented in hex to the router. The router make and model determine how the register is accessed. As mentioned previously, the AGS used 16 jumpers to set this register. Every router and switch allows access to the register through the configuration, assuming that you have privileged-level access. Switches work much in the same way as routers. First, you will learn about accessing the register on Catalyst switches, and then you will learn about routers.

Figure 1-10 *Router Boot Process*

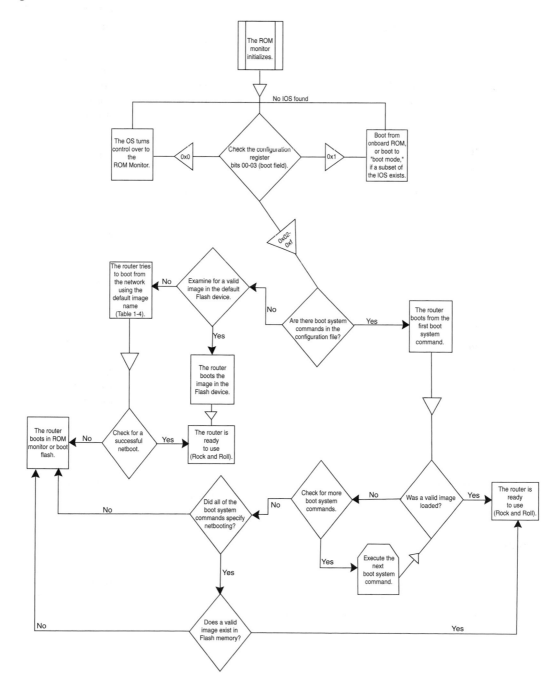

Accessing and Configuring the Register: Catalyst Switches

For the most part, the 16-bit register is identical to its cousin found in the router. The differences are slight. Most of the bits that are used in netbooting are used for broadcast control and are not used on the Catalyst switches. Bit 6 operates differently on the Catalyst than it does on the router. Setting Bit 6 clears the configs from NVRAM, which is the same as entering the **clear config all** command—that is, it clears the entire configuration stored in NVRAM the next time the switch is restarted.

The initialization process on the Catalyst 5000 series Supervisor Engine III and the Catalyst 4000, 2948G, and 2926 series switches involves two software images: the ROM monitor and the supervisor engine system code. When the switch is reset, the ROM monitor code is executed first. Then, depending on the boot register settings in NVRAM, the switch either remains in ROM monitor mode or loads the supervisor system image. If a fatal exception error occurs during powerup, the switch remains in ROM monitor mode. Figure 1-11 illustrates the 16-bit boot register for the Catalyst series of switches. Table 1-7 provides detailed descriptions of the boot register.

Figure 1-11 *The Entire 16-Bit Boot Register for Catalyst Switches with Default Settings*

Bit 15	Bit 14	Bit 13	Bit 12	Bit 11	Bit 10	Bit 9	Bit 8	Bit 7	Bit 6	Bit 5	Bit 4	Bit 3	Bit 2	Bit 1	Bit 0
0	0	0	0	0	0	0	1	0	0	0	0	1	1	1	1
0				1				0				F			

Table 1-7 *Catalyst Switch Boot Register Bit Meanings and Default Settings*

Bit	Meaning	Default Setting
0–3	Boot field: 0x0 = Boot ROM monitor. 0x1 = Boot from onboard ROM, or boot to boot mode if a subset of the IOS exists. 0x2 to 0xF Causes the following (listed in order of precedence): Follow **boot system** commands found in the configuration. If a boot image in the BOOT environment variable list is not found, boot in ROM monitor mode.	1 1 1 1
4	Reserved.	0
5	Reserved.	0

Table 1-7   *Catalyst Switch Boot Register Bit Meanings and Default Settings (Continued)*

Bit	Meaning	Default Setting
6	Clear NVRAM: 1 = Clear NVRAM.	0
7	OEM bit: 1 = disabling the display of the Cisco banner on startup (Not used.)	0
8	Break key: 1 = disable.	1
9	Unsupported baud rate.	0
10	IP will use an all-zeros broadcast. (Not used.)	0
11–12	Console baud rate: 00 = 9600 01 = 4800 10 = 1200 11 = 1200 On the Catalyst 4000 and 2948G, this speed is fixed at 9600.	0 0
13	Boots default Flash if network boot fails. (Not used.)	0
14	Netboot subnet broadcast: Setting bit 14 = 1 forces a subnet broadcast. (Not used.)	0
15	Enable diagnostic messages: 1 = ignore NVRAM and display diagnostic messages. (Not used.)	0

The default register is set for 0x010f. This allows the system to boot from the image specified in the BOOT environment variable; the console will operate at 9600 baud, and any configuration in NVRAM will be loaded. To display the current register settings, use the **show boot** [*module_number*] command. Example 1-7 shows how to display the current configuration register and BOOT environment settings.

Example 1-7   *Demonstration of the **show boot** Command*

```
Console>(enable) show boot
BOOT variable = slot0:cat5000-sup3.4-2-1.bin,1;bootflash:cat5000-sup3.3-2-
1b.bin,1;bootflash:cat5000-sup3.4-1-2.bin,1;

Configuration register is 0x10f
Ignore-config: disabled
Console baud: 9600
Boot: image specified by the boot system commands

Console>(enable)
```

The following is list of register-specific commands for the Catalyst family of switches:

- **set boot config-register 0x**value [mode_num]

  This command directly configures the boot register at the bit level. This commands affects all the bits in the register by modifying the entire boot register at once.

- **set boot config-register baud {1200 | 2400 | 4800 | 9600}**[module_number]

  This configures the ROM monitor console port baud rate. The ROM monitor uses the baud rate specified in the configuration register only if it is different from the baud rate specified by the **set system baud** command.

- **set boot config-register ignore-config enable**

  This command clears the entire configuration stored in NVRAM the next time the switch is restarted. This is essentially the same as using the **clear config all** command, followed by a reload.

- **set boot config-register boot {rommon | bootflash | system}**[module_number]

  This command determines what boot method the switch will use during the next startup:

  — **rommon** = Boot to the ROM monitor

  — **bootflash** = Boot from the first image stored in the onboard Flash

  — **system** = Boot from the image specified in the BOOT environment variable. This is the default setting.

- **set boot system flash** device:[filename] [**prepend**] [module_number]

  This command specifies an image to add to the BOOT environment variable. This also specifies what device that image exists on.

- **clear boot system flash** device:[filename][module_number]

  This command clears a specific image from the BOOT environment variable.

- **clear boot system all**[module_number]

  This command clears the entire BOOT environment variable.

Accessing and Configuring the Register: Cisco Routers

To set the register by the configuration mode, enter **config-register <0x0000-0xFFFF>**. Example 1-8 demonstrates how to change the configuration register from 2102 to 2142. This forces the router to ignore NVRAM during its initialization. To see if the configuration settings have taken effect, perform the **show version** command after changing the register.

TIP	You should always check and document the current configuration register setting before changing it. This might come in handy if you have problems.

Example 1-8   *Changing the Boot Register Through the Configuration*

```
Documenting the current setting
router#
router#show version
Cisco Internetwork Operating System Software
IOS (tm) 2500 Software (C2500-JS56-L), Version 12.0(3), RELEASE SOFTWARE (fc1)
Copyright (c) 1986-1999 by cisco Systems, Inc.
*** text omitted ***
32K bytes of non-volatile configuration memory.
16384K bytes of processor board System flash (Read ONLY)

Configuration register is 0x2102
router#
```

```
Change the setting to 0x2142.

router#conf t
Enter configuration commands, one per line.  End with CNTL/Z.
router(config)#config-register 0x2142
router(config)#^Z
router#
router#show version
Cisco Internetwork Operating System Software
IOS (tm) 2500 Software (C2500-JS56-L), Version 12.0(3), RELEASE SOFTWARE (fc1)
Copyright (c) 1986-1999 by cisco Systems, Inc.
*** text omitted ***
32K bytes of non-volatile configuration memory.
16384K bytes of processor board System flash (Read ONLY)

Configuration register is 0x2102 (will be 0x2142 at next reload)
```

TIP	Whenever you change the boot register from the configuration mode, you are prompted to save your configuration before you reload the router. This prompt is generated from entering the configuration mode and exiting, regardless of any changes made to the configuration. The register setting is not part of the startup-config or running-config, so it is not necessary to save the configuration for the new jump register setting to take place.

Accessing and Configuring the Register: ROM Monitor

If you cannot access the router's configuration, such as in a password-recovery situation, you can force the Cisco IOS Software to halt and go into ROM monitor mode. To enter ROM monitor mode, you must send a break signal to the router. By default, the Break key is disabled by the boot register; consequently, a restart of the router is needed. Almost all Cisco routers and switches can be interrupted by sending the break signal during the first 60 seconds of initialization. There are many ways to send the break signal and to interrupt router and switch operations, the most common of which are documented in Table 1-8.

Table 1-8   *Standard Break Key Combinations*

Terminal-Emulation Software	Platform	Operating System	Key Combination
Hyperterm (version 595160)	IBM-compatible	Windows 9x	Ctrl-F6-Break
Kermit	Sun workstation	Solaris	Ctrl-\L
Kermit	Sun workstation	Solaris	Ctrl-\B
MicroPhone Pro	IBM-compatible	Windows 9.x	Ctrl-Break
Minicom	IBM-compatible	Linux	Ctrl-A-F
ProComm Plus	IBM-compatible	DOS or Windows	Alt-B
Telix	IBM-compatible	DOS	Ctrl-End
Telnet to Cisco	IBM-compatible	—	Ctrl-]
Teraterm	IBM-compatible	Windows 9.x	Alt-B
Hyperterm	IBM-compatible	Windows 9.x	Break
Hyperterm	IBM-compatible	Windows 9.x	Ctrl-Break
Tip	Sun workstation	Solaris	Ctrl-], then Break or Ctrl-C
			~#
VT 100 Emulation	Data general	N/A	F16
Hypterm	IBM-compatible	Windows NT	Shift-6 Shift-4 Shift-B (^$B)
Z-TERMINAL	Mac	Apple	Command-B
—	Break-Out Box	—	Connect pin 2 (X-mit) to +V for half a second
—	Cisco to aux port	—	Control-Shift-6, then B
—	IBM-compatible	—	Ctrl-Break

If your portable or laptop computer is using Windows 95/98/2000 with HyperTerm, the break signal is usually issued by pressing the Function key and the Break key, sometimes located on the Page Down or Pause key.

On a full-size 101 keyboard with Windows 95/98 with HyperTerm, the break signal is issued by pressing the Ctrl-Break/Pause key.

On Windows NT, you must configure NT to send the break signal with a function key. Set the break by entering the characters **^$B** (**Shift 6, Shift 4**, and uppercase **B**). HyperTerm 5.0 private edition sends the break for the windows NT platform without any additional configuration.

To access the register of a Catalyst 5000 or 2926G series switch, you can enter ROM monitor mode by restarting the switch and then pressing the **Break** key during the first 60 seconds of initialization. On the Catalyst 4000 and 2948G series switches, you can enter ROM monitor mode by restarting the switch and then pressing **Control-C** during the first five seconds of initialization.

When using any other terminal-emulation software, consult the manufacturer's instructions on sending a break signal.

When you have successfully sent the break signal, the router prompt will change to a > character or a **rommon** x > prompt. There are two prompts because there are two types of ROM monitors. One is built around the earlier 2000 series boards. It requires more of a manual manipulation of the boot registers. The other type of ROM monitor is built around the newer 3600 and RISC-based platforms. This ROM monitor uses a utility called CONFREG to manipulate the boot register. Table 1-9 lists some common router types and the type of ROM monitor used. The easiest way to tell what type of ROM monitor is used in your router is to simply key in the **?** for help. If the CONFREG utility appears, execute it by typing in **CONFREG**.

Table 1-9 *ROM Monitor Compatibility Matrix*

CONFREG ROM Monitor	Basic ROM Monitor
Cisco 1003 series	Cisco 2000 series
Cisco 1600 series	Cisco 2500 series
Cisco 3600 series	Cisco 3000 series
Cisco 4500 series	Cisco 4000 series with 680x0
Cisco 7200 series	Cisco 7000 series 10.0 ROM
Cisco 7500 series	Cisco IGS series running IOS 9.1 in ROM
IDT Orion-based router	
AS5200 and AS5300 platforms	

First, you will learn about the Basic ROM monitor, and then you will learn about the utility called CONFREG. When you have successfully transmitted a break signal, you should get a screen that resembles Example 1-9; also note the **Abort at** message.

Example 1-9   *Example of a Successful Break into ROM Monitor, Followed by the* **h** *or* **Help** *Command*

```
System Bootstrap, Version 5.2(8a), RELEASE SOFTWARE
Copyright (c) 1986-1995 by cisco Systems
2500 processor with 14336 Kbytes of main memory

Abort at 0x10200C2 (PC)
>
>h$            Toggle cache state
B [filename] [TFTP Server IP address | TFTP Server Name]
             Load and execute system image from ROM or from TFTP server
C [address]  Continue execution [optional address]
D /S M L V   Deposit value V of size S into location L with modifier M
E /S M L     Examine location L with size S with modifier M
G [address]  Begin execution
H            Help for commands
I            Initialize
K            Stack trace
L [filename] [TFTP Server IP address | TFTP Server Name]
             Load system image from ROM or from TFTP server, but do not
             begin execution
O            Show configuration register option settings
P            Set the break point
S            Single step next instruction
T function   Test device (? for help)

Deposit and Examine sizes may be B (byte), L (long) or S (short).
Modifiers may be R (register) or S (byte swap).
Register names are: D0-D7, A0-A6, SS, US, SR, and PC
>
```

The abort message first conveys that the router has aborted and that you successfully halted the router OS. The second indication that you are in the ROM monitor mode is the **>** prompt. Also in Example 1-9, an **h** was entered to display the help listing; this key is the same as the **?** key. Most of the ROM monitor is designed for low-level hardware and software debugging, but a couple of commands are worth mentioning:

- **H**—Displays the help messages, as in Example 1-9.
- **I**—Initializes the router. It is the same as the **reload** command.
- **$**—Toggles the cache; used for debugging by the TAC.
- **P**—Sets the break point; used for TAC diagnostics.
- **S**—Is a single-step instruction used for TAC diagnostics.

- **T** *function*—Use the **?** key behind the **T** command to perform a low-level test of a specific components. This usually performs a detailed hardware memory diagnostic.
- **B**—Allows manual booting from the ROM monitor:
  — **B flash**—Boots the first file in Flash memory.
  — **B** *filename* [**TFTP** *host*]—Boots over the network using TFTP.
  — **B flash** *filename*—Boots the file (filename) from Flash memory.
- **L**—Works the same as the **B** command, but the router will not begin execution of the code.
- **O**—Examines the 16-bit boot register.
- **O/R** *0x0000*—Sets the boot register by using a manual hex setting. For example, O/R 0x2102 will set the register to its default.
- **D** */S M L V*—Deposit value *V* of size *S* into location *L* with modifier *M*.
- **E** */S M L*—Examines location *L* with size *S* with modifier *M*. **E/S 2000002** examines the boot register directly from memory.

At this time, you can verify whether you have a router that supports the CONFREG utility or one that supports only basic ROM monitor commands. By looking at the ROM monitor prompt, you can determine this. By keying in the **?** command, you can determine whether CONFREG is supported. For example, in Example 1-10, notice that the prompt is a **>**, the greater-than sign. This prompt is a good indication that you might have to use basic ROM monitor commands to change the boot register. One last check is to simply key in the **?** command for help, as the example demonstrates.

Example 1-10 *Another Example of a Successful Break into ROM Monitor, Followed by the* **?** *or* **Help** *Command, Showing the Presence of the CONFREG Utility*

```
Abort at 0x10200C2 (PC)
>?
$               Toggle cache state
B [filename] [TFTP Server IP address I TFTP Server Name]
                Load and execute system image from ROM or from TFTP server
C [address]  Continue execution [optional address]
D /S M L V   Deposit value V of size S into location L with modifier M
E /S M L     Examine location L with size S with modifier M
G [address]  Begin execution
H               Help for commands
I               Initialize
K               Stack trace
L [filename] [TFTP Server IP address I TFTP Server Name]
                Load system image from ROM or from TFTP server, but do not
                begin execution
O               Show configuration register option settings
P               Set the break point
S               Single step next instruction
```

continues

Example 1-10 *Another Example of a Successful Break into ROM Monitor, Followed by the* **?** *or* **Help** *Command, Showing the Presence of the CONFREG Utility (Continued)*

```
T function    Test device (? for help)

Deposit and Examine sizes may be B (byte), L (long) or S (short).
Modifiers may be R (register) or S (byte swap).
Register names are: D0-D7, A0-A6, SS, US, SR, and PC
>
```

Example 1-11 shows the output from the **?** command showing the CONFREG utility. Therefore, to configure this router's boot register, you use CONFREG. Notice in Example 1-11 the prompt of **rommon**. This is a good indication that CONFREG is supported.

Example 1-11 *The* **?** *Command Used on a Router That Supports CONFREG*

```
*** System received an abort due to Break Key ***
signal= 0x3, code= 0x0, context= 0x6033f2b8
PC = 0x6005eba4, Cause = 0x20, Status Reg = 0x34408302
rommon 1 >
rommon 1 > ?
alias            set and display aliases command
boot             boot up an external process
break            set/show/clear the breakpoint
confreg          configuration register utility
cont             continue executing a downloaded image
context          display the context of a loaded image
cookie           display contents of cookie PROM in hex
dev              list the device table
dir              list files in file system
dis              disassemble instruction stream
dnld             serial download a program module
frame            print out a selected stack frame
help             monitor builtin command help
history          monitor command history
meminfo          main memory information
repeat           repeat a monitor command
reset            system reset
set              display the monitor variables
stack            produce a stack trace
sync             write monitor environment to NVRAM
sysret           print out info from last system return
unalias          unset an alias
unset            unset a monitor variable
rommon 2 >
```

At times, reading the English wording of CONFREG can actually be harder to understand than just manipulating the bits in the register. To help understand which bits the questions in CONFREG correspond to, consult Table 1-10.

Table 1-10   *CONFREG to BIT Comparison*

CONFREG Text	Bit(s) Set	Default Setting
enable "diagnostic mode"? y/n [n]:	15	Off
enable "use net in IP bcast address"? y/n [n]:	14	Off
disable "load rom after netboot fails"? y/n [n]:	13	On
enable "use all zero broadcast"? y/n [n]:	10	Off
enable "break/abort has effect"? y/n [n]:	8	Off
enable "ignore system config info"? y/n [n]:	6	Off
change console baud rate? y/n [n]:	11&12	Off and Off
change the boot characteristics? y/n [n]:	0-3	0x2

Password Recovery: Routers

When you have a solid understanding of how the boot register works, password recovery becomes straightforward. For all the router platforms, the procedure involves simply changing bit 6, which ignores the startup-config in NVRAM, and then reloading the router. When the router reboots, it will no longer have a running-config. The configuration is still stored in NVRAM and can be viewed by performing the **show startup-config** command from Enable mode. Because there is no running-config, there will be no enable password. Therefore, you can enter Enable mode and copy the startup-config to the running-config, with the **copy startup-config running-config** command. At this time, remember to change the register back, set the enable password, bring up the interfaces (which will be down), and save the new configuration. This entire process is outlined in the step list that follows.

As mentioned previously, the router will always accept a break signal if sent during the first 60 seconds of initialization, regardless of whether bit 8 is set. With this in mind, the following procedure will recover most routers:

Step 1   Attach a PC or PDA with terminal-emulation software to the router's console port through a Cisco rolled cable.

Step 2   Power-cycle the router.

Step 3   Issue a break signal by pressing the **Break** key, or by executing one of the other ways mentioned, within 60 seconds of initialization.

Step 4   Determine what type of ROM monitor you have. Is CONREG supported?

— If Basic ROM monitor:

— Set bit 6: **>O/R 0x2142**. This will set bit 6. Reload the router with the **Initialize** command.

— If CONFREG is supported:

Run the CONFREG utility: >**CONFREG**. Answer every question with the default or Enter, until you come to the question: Enable **ignore system config info**. Answer "yes" to this question. This will also set bit 6. Reload the router with the **RESET** command.

Step 5 When the router reloads, it will try to run setup. Abort the setup utility with a **Ctrl-C**.

Step 6 Enter Enable mode and do a copy startup-config running-config—for example #**copy startup-config running-config**.

Step 7 Enter the configuration mode, and do the following:

— Set the boot register back to its original configuration.

— All interfaces will be shut down; bring up all interfaces to their normal state.

— Set the enable password to a new value.

— Save the new configuration.

CAUTION   Be careful after you have ignored NVRAM and reloaded the router. The router still has a configuration in NVRAM, and it is easy to overwrite this configuration with a slip of a keystroke. This is particularly easy for people of the "old school"—a simple **wr** instead of **wr t** will ruin the config stored in NVRAM.

TIP   Make a backup copy of the current router configuration when modifying the registers or performing any work that could put the router configuration in jeopardy. Taking the small amount of time that it requires to perform this could be priceless if disaster strikes.

Password Recovery: Switches

Password recovery with switches is a little easier than with routers. During the first 30 seconds of initialization, the password and enable password is simply the Enter key. To recover a password on a Catalyst switch, follow this procedure:

Step 1 Power-cycle the switch.

Step 2 As soon as the switch loads, enter Enable mode. This is done by quickly typing in **enable [Enter]**. The switch will prompt you for a password. During the first 30 seconds, the password is the Enter key. Therefore, simply press the **Enter** key. In Enable mode, set a new password with the **set password** command. When you're prompted for the old password, use the **Enter** key again.

Step 3   In Enable mode, set a new enable password with the **set enablepass** command. When setting the enable password, you will be prompted for the old password; again, this is simply the **Enter** key.

Upgrading the Cisco IOS Software

At some time, either for some of the labs in this book or when in the field, you will have to upgrade the router's Cisco IOS Software. Upgrading Cisco IOS Software is a task that can be trivial if you know what you're doing. The Cisco IOS image is stored on Flash memory, either in SIMMs or in credit-card modules. There are four items to account for before upgrading your router's Cisco IOS Software:

- The router Cisco IOS release—must be Release 9.0 or later. (If this rule applies to you, it might also be time to upgrade to IP version 4.)
- The amount of free space available on Flash.
- The size of the new image, including its DRAM requirements.
- A reachable IP address or name of the server to load the image from.

To locate the amount of Flash space available on SIMMs, simply execute the **show flash** command. To view the contents on a credit-card module, enter **dir** [*device*]—for example, **dir slot0:** and/or **dir slot1:**, depending on which slot has the credit-card Flash in. Here are the common Flash commands and their PCMCIA equivalents:

- **show flash**—Displays flash on *SIMMs*, as in Example 1-8.
- **dir** [**/all** | **/deleted** | **/long**][*device*][*filename*].
  - — **/all**—Lists deleted, undeleted, and files with errors
  - — **/deleted**—Lists deleted files only
  - — **/long**—Lists files in a long, detailed format
  - — *device*—Lists files on a specific Flash device: FLASH:, BOOTTFLASH:, SLOT0:, SLOT1:
  - — *filename*—Names a specific Flash file to list
- **cd**—Changes from one Flash device to another.
- **copy** *source-device:filename destination-device:filename*—Copies files from one source to another. If no specific file is listed, you will be prompted later to enter the filename. This is the case when you copy TFTP to Flash.

Here are some examples of Flash manipulation.

- To change from one Flash device to another, key in the command **cd**—for example, **cd SLOT1:**.

- To view the Flash on different devices, use the **dir** [**/all** | **deleted** | **long**] command— for example, **dir flash:**, or simply **dir**.

NOTE   If you are using credit-card Flash, ensure that the write protect is located in the off position before you try to write to Flash. This can be done by moving the tab on the end of the Flash card. Not all Flash cards are the same; either the documentation or the Flash card itself will indicate which position is the write protect mode.

Example 1-12 demonstrates the **show flash** command and a **dir** command on a router.

Example 1-12 *The* **show flash** *and* **dir** *Command*

```
router#show flash

System flash directory:
File  Length   Name/status
  1   10307412  c2500-js56-l.120-3.bin
[10307476 bytes used, 6469740 available, 16777216 total]
16384K bytes of processor board System flash (Read ONLY)

router#
router#dir
Directory of flash:/

  1  -rw-    10307412              <no date>  c2500-js56-l.120-3.bin

16777216 bytes total (6469740 bytes free)
router#
```

In this example, the Cisco IOS Software is *c2500-js56-l.120-3.bin*, and its length is 10307412 bytes. This Flash image leaves only 6.46 kB left. Therefore, when you upgrade the router's Cisco IOS Software, you need to delete the old version.

After you determine what type of Flash device the router has and how much Flash memory is available, you can plan for the Cisco IOS Software upgrade. The first thing in planning for an IOS upgrade is to determine the requirements in terms of Flash main or shared DRAM memory. Every IOS has different Flash and DRAM requirements. The only way to verify the exact requirements of the IOS is to look it up on Cisco's Web page.

If you have the proper access and authority to upgrade your Cisco IOS Software from Cisco, you can find new software releases in the Software Center of Cisco's home page under Service & Support. By clicking on the Software Center, you will be prompted through a series of questions called the Cisco IOS Planner. The planner will guide you through the process by slowly narrowing your choices of a new IOS. In this example, the IP version has been chosen for a Cisco 2600 series router—specifically, 12.0.9. Notice the minimum memory requirements of 4 MB of Flash and 20 MB of DRAM memory, as illustrated in Figure 1-12. You must be logged on and have proper authority to view and download Cisco IOS Software.

Figure 1-12 *Example of a Cisco Web Download of IOS*

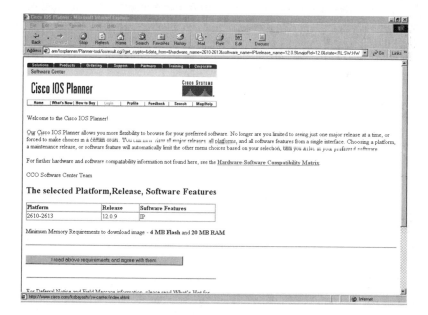

It is important to mention that the Cisco Web page or the Cisco TAC is the first and last authority when it comes to Cisco IOS Software memory requirements. Assuming requirements across multiple platforms and even within a platform is not recommended. Let's use the example in Figure 1-12 to demonstrate this. The same Cisco IOS Software release, 12.0.9, on a Cisco 2500 series platform requires 8 MB of Flash and only 4 MB of DRAM memory. This is exactly why you must verify the requirements of each IOS release to be certain that it will work in the router you're trying to upgrade.

The last phase will be to ensure that there is a valid TFTP server with the new Flash image, in that it is reachable. Finally, the router is ready to upgrade. To copy Cisco IOS Software from a TFTP server to the router, use the **copy tftp flash** command. Before you perform this command, check the following:

* The TFTP server's IP address
* The Cisco IOS Software name as it exists on the server

- That the router can ping the TFTP server (again, this should be a locally connected network)

When performing the **copy tftp flash** command, you will be asked a series of questions, basically matching the preceding list.

NOTE With Cisco IOS Software Release 11.0, Cisco introduced a more "English-like" command structure for handling files. Instead of **configure memory,** it uses **copy startup-config running-config** to write the configuration to NVRAM. Table 1-11 provides a comparative list of the old commands and their new command counterparts. After looking at the list, it becomes clear why Cisco made the change.

Table 1-11 *Changes to Cisco IOS Software File Commands*

Old Command	New Command
configure memory	**copy startup-config running-config**
configure network	**copy {rcp	tftp} running-config**
configure overwrite-network	**copy {rcp	tftp} startup-config**
copy erase flash	**erase flash**
copy verify or copy verify flash	**verify flash**, **verify** (cisco 7000 and Cisco 7500)
copy verify bootflash	**verify boot flash**
show configuration	**show startup-config**
tftp-server system	**tftp-server**
write erase	**erase startup-config**
write memory	**copy running-config startup-config**
write network	**copy running-config {rcp	tftp}**
write terminal	**show running-config**

In the next example, you will be upgrading the IOS of the access server. For this example, the new Cisco IOS file is c2500-js56-l.120-3.bin and is located on a TFTP server at address 206.191.241.45. According to Cisco, the new Cisco IOS Software requires 16 MB of Flash and 8 MB of DRAM Memory.

As mentioned previously, first you must verify that you have IOS 9.0 or later on your router. You also must verify that there is enough Flash and Main memory to run the new Cisco IOS Software. To do this, use the **show version** and **show flash** commands. Example 1-13 is a good exhibition of these commands.

Example 1-13 *Verifying Flash and DRAM Memory with the* **show version** *and* **show flash** *Commands*

```
skynet_access_1#show version
Cisco Internetwork Operating System Software
IOS (tm) 3000 Software (IGS-INR-L), Version 10.3(7), RELEASE SOFTWARE (fc1)
Copyright (c) 1986-1995 by cisco Systems, Inc.
Compiled Wed 01-Nov-95 12:40 by vatran
Image text-base: 0x03022C14, data-base: 0x00001000

ROM: System Bootstrap, Version 5.2(8a), RELEASE SOFTWARE
ROM: 3000 Bootstrap Software (IGS-RXBOOT), Version 10.2(8a), RELEASE SOFTWARE (f
c1)

skynet_access_1 uptime is 1 week, 2 days, 16 hours, 19 minutes
System restarted by reload
System image file is "flash:/junky_old_ios.bin", booted via flash

cisco 2511 (68030) processor (revision L) with 14332K/2048K bytes of memory.
Processor board serial number 05309022
Bridging software.
X.25 software, Version 2.0, NET2, BFE and GOSIP compliant.
1 Ethernet/IEEE 802.3 interface.
2 Serial network interfaces.
16 terminal lines.
32K bytes of non-volatile configuration memory.
16384K bytes of processor board System flash (Read ONLY)

Configuration register is 0x2102

skynet_access_1#
skynet_access_1#show flash

System flash directory:
File  Length   Name/status
  1   4147048  /junky_old_ios.bin
[4147112 bytes used, 12630104 available, 16777216 total]
16384K bytes of processor board System flash (Read ONLY)

skynet_access_1#
```

You can see through the **show version** command that the router does have a version of Cisco IOS Software later than Release 9.0—in this example, it is Release 10.3.7. Next, you check the amount of main memory, which, as indicated on Line 16, is 14332 K/2048 K. Overall, this means that the router has 16 MB of memory, divided into 14 MB of main memory and 2 MB of shared memory. For all practical purposes, you can view this amount as the sum of the two values. Next, you should check the amount of Flash memory available. This example says that the IOS is called *junky_old_ios.bin* and is approximately 4 MB in size. Because you have 16 MB of Flash, the router will prompt you to tell whether you want to erase the current Flash image. If you do not want to erase the Flash image, be sure to add the command **boot system flash** *IOS_filename* to the configuration.

You now know that you can upgrade the Cisco IOS Software. You also know the IP address and the name of the image. Quickly **ping** the TFTP server to ensure that you have IP connectivity. Example 1-14 walks you through the rest of upgrade process.

Example 1-14 *Upgrading the IOS Through the TFTP Server*

```
skynet_access_1#ping 206.191.241.45
Type escape sequence to abort.
Sending 5, 100-byte ICMP Echos to 206.191.241.45, timeout is 2 seconds:
!!!!!
Success rate is 100 percent (5/5), round-trip min/avg/max = 1/3/4 ms
skynet_access_1#copy tftp flash
                      ****  NOTICE  ****
Flash load helper v1.0
This process will accept the copy options and then terminate
the current system image to use the ROM based image for the copy.
Routing functionality will not be available during that time.
If you are logged in via telnet, this connection will terminate.
Users with console access can see the results of the copy operation.
                 ---- ******** ----
[There are active users logged into the system]
Proceed? [confirm]y

System flash directory:
File  Length   Name/status
  1   4147048  /junky_old_ios.bin
[4147112 bytes used, 12630104 available, 16777216 total]
Address or name of remote host [255.255.255.255]? 206.191.241.45
Source file name? c2500-js56-l.120-3.bin
Destination file name [c2500-js56-l.120-3.bin]? c2500-js56-l.120-3.bin
Accessing file 'c2500-js56-l.120-3.bin' on 206.191.241.45...
Loading c2500-js56-l.120-3.bin from 206.191.241.45 (via Ethernet0): ! [OK]

Erase flash device before writing? [confirm]y
Flash contains files. Are you sure you want to erase? [confirm]y

Copy 'c2500-js56-l.120-3.bin' from server
  as 'c2500-js56-l.120-3.bin' into Flash WITH erase? [yes/no]yes

4:23:05: %SYS-5-RELOAD: Reload requested
%FLH: c2500-js56-l.120-3.bin from 206.191.241.45 to flash ...

System flash directory:
File  Length   Name/status
  1   4147048  /junky_old_ios.bin
[4147112 bytes used, 12630104 available, 16777216 total]
Accessing file 'c2500-js56-l.120-3.bin' on 206.191.241.45...
Loading c2500-js56-l.120-3.bin .from 206.191.241.45 (via Ethernet0): ! [OK]

Erasing device... eeeeeeeeeeeeeeeeeeeeeeeeeeeeeeeeeeeeeeeeeeeeeeeeeeeeeeeeeeeeeeee
```

Example 1-14 *Upgrading the IOS Through the TFTP Server (Continued)*

```
ee ...erased
Loading c2500-js56-1.120-3.bin from 206.191.241.45 (via Ethernet0): !!!!!!!!!!!!
<text omitted>
!!
[OK - 10307412/16777216 bytes]

Verifying checksum... OK (0xA519)
Flash copy took 0:06:04 [hh:mm:ss]
%FLH: Re-booting system after download
F3: 10070412+236968+1042784 at 0x3000060
<text omitted>
00:01:46: %SYS-5-RESTART: System restarted --
Cisco Internetwork Operating System Software
IOS (tm) 2500 Software (C2500-JS56-L), Version 12.0(3), RELEASE SOFTWARE (fc1)
Copyright (c) 1986-1999 by cisco Systems, Inc.
Compiled Mon 08-Feb-99 22:55 by phanguye
skynet_access_1>
```

Also notice in Example 1-14 that the router will verify the new IOS one last time before first erasing the existing Flash and reloading the router. By watching the router reload, you can see that the new Cisco IOS Software has been loaded. This can also be confirmed by performing the **show flash** command.

Some common problems that occur during an IOS upgrade are as follows:

- Misspelling the IOS name. A common mistake is mixing up the *J* and *L* letters.

- Having a TFTP server that is not local to the router. Make sure that the TFTP server is adjacent to the router. Remember that the router will reload, and a routing table will not be available during the ROM monitor copy phase.

- Not verifying the proper amount of Flash or main memory needed to support the new IOS.

- If routing is not available, use the global command **IP default-gateway** to direct the router toward a default gateway.

NOTE   When naming an IOS on a router, always use the name as provided by Cisco. The naming convention used by Cisco correlates the filename to the feature set of the software.

Configuring and Using the Access Server

The access server provides out-of-band configuration to several devices at a single time. At a large site where several key routers and switches are located, an access server provides the best method for configuration access. You use the access server to configure the routers and switches in the upcoming lab.

The configuration of the access server requires a logical tie between an IP address and a TTY session. To configure what Cisco refers to as *reverse Telnet*, you need to configure three things:

- A transport statement
- A loopback address
- A host table

Configuring the transport statement requires knowledge of what I refer to as "line entries" and what Cisco calls the absolute line number. To list the lines available for configuration on the router perform, use the **show line** command from the console mode. In Example 1-15, you can observe the absolute line number as the number on the far left under the TTY column.

Example 1-15 *Identifying Line Entries of a Router, the* **show line** *Command*

```
Router>show line
  Tty Typ    Ix/Rx    A Modem  Roty AccO AccI   Uses   Noise  Overruns   Int
*   0 CTY              -   -     -    -    -       0      1     0/0        -
    1 TTY   9600/9600  -   -     -    -    -       0      0     0/0        -
    2 TTY   9600/9600  -   -     -    -    -       0      0     0/0        -
    3 TTY   9600/9600  -   -     -    -    -       0      1     0/0        -
    4 TTY   9600/9600  -   -     -    -    -       0      0     0/0        -
    5 TTY   9600/9600  -   -     -    -    -       0      0     0/0        -
    6 TTY   9600/9600  -   -     -    -    -       0      0     0/0        -
    7 TTY   9600/9600  -   -     -    -    -       0      0     0/0        -
    8 TTY   9600/9600  -   -     -    -    -       0      0     0/0        -
    9 TTY   9600/9600  -   -     -    -    -       0      0     0/0        -
   10 TTY   9600/9600  -   -     -    -    -       0      0     0/0        -
   11 TTY   9600/9600  -   -     -    -    -       0      0     0/0        -
   12 TTY   9600/9600  -   -     -    -    -       0      0     0/0        -
   13 TTY   9600/9600  -   -     -    -    -       0      0     0/0        -
   14 TTY   9600/9600  -   -     -    -    -       0      0     0/0        -
   15 TTY   9600/9600  -   -     -    -    -       0      0     0/0        -
   16 TTY   9600/9600  -   -     -    -    -       0      1     0/0        -
   17 AUX   9600/9600  -   -     -    -    -       0      0     0/0        -
   18 VTY              -   -     -    -    -       0      0     0/0        -
   19 VTY              -   -     -    -    -       0      0     0/0        -
   20 VTY              -   -     -    -    -       0      0     0/0        -
   21 VTY              -   -     -    -    -       0      0     0/0        -
   22 VTY              -   -     -    -    -       0      0     0/0        -

Router>
```

Table 1-12 explains the line numbers and the numbering schemes found in Example 1-15.

Table 1-12 *Line Types and Number Schemes*

Line Type	Port Type	Description	Numbering Scheme
CON or CTY	Console	Used for configuration purposes.	Line 0
AUX	Auxiliary	RS-232 DTE port used as a backup async port (TTY).	Last TTY line number plus 1
TTY	Async	Same as an asynchronous interface. Used typically for remote-node dial-in sessions that use protocols such as SLIP, PPP, and Xremote.	Varies between platforms
VTY	Virtual terminal	Used for incoming Telnet, LAT, X.25 PAD, and protocol translation connections onto synchronous ports.	Last TTY line number plus 2, through the maximum number of VTY lines configured

In Example 1-15, you see that Lines 1 through 16 are TTY lines. You use these lines for the reverse Telnet sessions. To configure a reverse Telnet session, simply add a 20 in front of the absolute line number. The syntax is in one of the following two forms. From the console mode, it is **Telnet** *ip_address* **20xx**, where xx is the absolute line number (in this case, 01 through 16). Be sure to include the leading 0 on single-digit numerals. The next way to configure reverse Telnet is entered from configuration mode, in the form of an IP host table. From the configuration mode, use **IP host** *hostname* **20xx** *ip_address.* The IP address used should be one on a loopback interface. This way, you can still use a reverse Telnet session while other physical interfaces are down. The IP address used needs to be reachable, which is another reason to use a loopback address.

TIP   When configuring loopback interfaces, I like to use a methodology that is logical to the network or model that I am building. For example, on every router, I like to use a Loopback 0, with an address of 201.201.x.x. I use Loopback 0 as the router ID on all the routers, where *x.x* is a unique number in the entire network or model. I chose the 201.201 portion of the address because I wanted a high address on Loopback 0 to force this to be a router ID for OSPF. Looking through an OSPF database can be quite a bit easier with logical identifiable router IDs. I am also careful not to redistribute these addresses into any routing protocols. For protocols such as DLSw and BGP, you will use routable IP addresses on the loopback interfaces. I like to start these loopback interfaces at Loopback 20 and above. The more "self-documenting" the network or model is, the easier it will be to troubleshoot and maintain. Another good IP address range to use is 192.168.00, because it is a private address, as defined in RFC 1918.

In the following example, assume that a loopback interface has been configured with the IP address of 201.201.1.1. The other importance of knowing the proper line entry is to add the **transport input all** command to it. This entry allows the Telnet session to occur through the TTY port. You can modify the line entries one at a time, as in Example 1-16, or you can configure multiple lines at a time by entering the range. To enter a range, key in **line** *x-y*, where *x* is the start of the line entries and *y* is the end of them.

Example 1-16 *Configuration of a Reverse Telnet Session*

```
Router#conf t
Enter configuration commands, one per line.  End with CNTL/Z.
Router(config)#ip host r1 2001 201.201.1.1
Router(config)#line 1
Router(config-line)#transport input all
Router(config-line)#no exec
Router(config-line)#^Z
Router#
```

Example 1-16 also makes use of the **no exec** command entered under the line. This is optional in a reverse Telnet configuration. Adding this command lessens the likelihood of contention over the asynchronous port. An executive process, or exec, exists on all lines. These two process buffer data to each other and, at times, can make it difficult to use a reverse Telnet scssion. The error message **% Connection refused by remote host** is an indication of this type of contention for the line. To clear the line of this contention or any users, enter the command **clear line** *line_entry*. Example 1-17 shows the common error **% Connection refused by remote host** and then shows the effect of clearing the line of this condition to enter r1 successfully.

Example 1-17 *Clearing a Line*

```
Router#r1
Trying r1 (201.201.1.1, 2001)...
% Connection refused by remote host

Router#clear line 1
[confirm]y [OK]
Router#r1
Trying r1 (201.201.1.1, 2001)... Open

R1>
```

Upon successful completion of a reverse Telnet or any Telnet session, you might want to get back to the original starting point or the origination point. Cisco refers to this as *suspending a session*. To accomplish this, use the escape character. To enter the default escape character, press **Ctrl-Shift-6** at the same time, and then let up and press the **X** key by itself. This will take you back to the origination point.

To re-establish the connection, enter a **show session** command to find the connection number that you want to restore, and then key in that connection number. Example 1-18 illustrates the output of the **show sessions** command.

Example 1-18 show sessions *Command*

```
Router#show sessions
Conn Host               Address          Byte  Idle Conn Name
   1 r2                 201.201.1.1         0     3 r2
*  2 r1                 201.201.1.1         0     0 r1
   3 r3                 201.201.1.1         0     3 r3
```

The number that appears on the far left is called the relative line number. For example, to return to the session on host r3, key in **3**; to resume the session on r2, key in **1** and press the **Enter** key. The * character in front of host r1 indicates the last session that was active. To return to this session, simply press **Return** or **Enter**.

The following process makes jumping past the origination point possible:

1 Origination point (the first Cisco router Telnetted to or consoled to)

2 First Telnet or reverse Telnet session from 1

3 First session from 2

4 Second session from 2

5 Third session from 2

At some time, you might Telnet from your origination point to another router, perhaps the access server. Then, from that router or access server, you might want to do a reverse Telnet to all the routers in the model. In this scenario, it would be highly desirable to jump back to the access server while avoiding to have to go all the way back to the origination point. To accomplish this, press **Ctrl-Shift-6** twice fast, followed by the **X** key. This takes you from point 4 to point 2, as listed in the previous process without first going to the origination point. The rule is one (**Ctrl-Shift-6**) to take you back to the origination point; the second one moves you one into the loop, and so on.

Configuring a Frame Relay Switch

Conceivably, the most useful device inside and outside the lab might be the Frame Relay switch. Much like the jump register, the configuration of a Frame Relay switch seems to be one of those untold secrets of router configuration. When I learned how to configure Frame Relay switching, I was able to model many network installations. Because I was the "service provider," I could assign my own DLCIs, matching those exactly as AT&T or MCI might provide. By accurately modeling the network in the lab, you increase your confidence level of the installation, along with lowering the probability of misconfiguration or the chance of sending out bad equipment. This section focuses on configuring the Cisco router as a Frame Relay switch. Further Frame Relay configuration details are covered in Chapter 5, "WAN Protocols and Technologies: Frame Relay."

Essentially, Frame Relay switching is a means of switching frames based upon the data-link connection identifier (DLCI). In the router's Frame Relay ARP table, a DLCI number is associated with an interface. Frame Relay uses its ARP table to examine DLCIs and interface pairings to make its decisions on whether to forward a frame out a specific interface.

The Frame Relay switch is predominately a DCE device, which means two things:

- Any modeling requires a minimum of three routers: one router for the switch and two routers to use the switch to communicate with each other.
- DCE cables are needed on the frame switch's serial interfaces.

At this point, it is important to define some common Frame Relay terms:

- **Permanent virtual circuit (PVC)**—The logical end-to-end circuit used for frame transport. A PVC's endpoints are addressed with DLCIs.

- **Data-link connection identifier (DLCI)**—A logical number between 16 and 1007 used to identify the PVC between the customer premises equipment (CPE) and the Frame Relay switch. In most cases, the DLCI is only locally significant, which implies that only the local devices know what the DLCI numbers are. It is possible to have two PVCs with the same DLCI number on the remote ends referring to the same central site.

- **Local Management Interface (LMI)**—Best defined as the signaling standard used between the router and the Frame Relay switch. LMI is used by the switch to learn which DLCIs are defined and their status. LMI also supports a 10-second keepalive mechanism that verifies that the PVC is active and that data is being exchanged. Three types of LMI are supported on Cisco routers: cisco, ansi, and q933a. The router will try an autonegotiation on all three LMI types.

  — **cisco**—LMI type defined by the "big three," Cisco, Digital, and Northern Telecom. This is the default LMI type, after autonegotiation fails. LMI status information is sent on DLCI 0.

  — **ansi**—LMI type defined by ANSI standard T1.617, commonly called Annex D. This is the most common type of LMI found across all Frame Relay networks. LMI status information is sent on DLCI 1023.

  — **q933a**—LMI type defined as ITU-T Q.933, or simply Annex A. LMI status information is sent on DLCI 0.

- **Network-to-Network Interface (NNI)**— NNI is the standard used for two switches to communicate. NNI is used in both Frame Relay and ATM. In ATM, it is referred to as network node interface.

To configure Frame Relay switching, it is necessary to perform the following tasks:

Step 1   Enable Frame Relay switching.

Step 2   Configure the interface LMI and Frame Relay interface type.

Step 3   Configure PVCs, with the **frame-relay route** command.

In this first example, you configure a Frame Relay switch with two end devices or routers. It is always good to make a PVC diagram of your model before you begin. On your diagram, include the DCE, PVC, and interface denotations. Figure 1-13 exhibits the diagram that you use for this example. The diagram highlights the network from a hardware and service provider perspective. The Frame Relay switch, in the middle, has two V.35 DCE cables to two other routers, R1 and R2. These two routers have V.35 DTE male cables connected to their Serial 0 port. You configure a PVC with DLCI 101 on Serial 0 mapping to DLCI 102 on Serial 5.

Figure 1-13 *Basic Frame Relay Configuration Example*

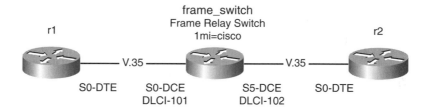

The first step in configuring the Frame Relay switch, excluding drawing your diagram, is to enable Frame Relay switching. This is done with the global configuration command **frame-relay switching**. Next, configure the serial interfaces for frame relay switching. You need to set the encapsulation to Frame Relay with the **encapsulation frame-relay** command, and you must set the LMI type with the **frame-relay lmi-type [ansi | cisco | q993a]** command from the interface prompt. To continue to configure the Frame Relay interface, add the **frame-relay intf-type dce** command. Because the interface is DCE, you need to use the **clock rate** *bps* command. The *bps* values range from 1200 to 8,000,000. Finally, the **frame-relay route** [*16-1007*]*inbound_DLCI* **interface** *outbound_serial_ interface* [*16-1007*]*outbout_DLCI* command creates a PVC on the interface and maps it to another interface. Example 1-19 demonstrates the use of these commands and the basic configuration of a Frame Relay switch.

Example 1-19 *Configuring a Basic Frame Relay Switch*

```
frame_switch#
frame_switch#conf t
Enter configuration commands, one per line.  End with CNTL/Z.
```

continues

Example 1-19 *Configuring a Basic Frame Relay Switch (Continued)*

```
frame_switch(config)#frame-relay switching
frame_switch(config)#interface serial 0
frame_switch(config-if)#encapsulation frame-relay
frame_switch(config-if)#frame-relay intf-type dce
frame_switch(config-if)#frame-relay lmi-type ansi
frame_switch(config-if)#clock rate 56000
frame_switch(config-if)#frame-relay route 101 interface s5 102
frame_switch(config-if)#exit
frame_switch(config)#
frame_switch(config)#interface serial 5
frame_switch(config-if)#encapsulation frame-relay
frame_switch(config-if)#frame-relay intf-type dce
frame_switch(config-if)#clock rate 56000
frame_switch(config-if)#frame-relay route 102 interface s0 101
frame_switch(config-if)#exit
frame_switch(config)#
```

Example 1-20 lists the router's configuration in its entirety.

Example 1-20 *Displaying the Entire Frame Relay Configuration*

```
hostname frame_switch
!
frame-relay switching
!
interface Ethernet0
 ip address 172.16.1.2 255.255.255.0
!
interface Serial0
 no ip address
 encapsulation frame-relay
 clockrate 56000
 frame-relay lmi-type ansi
 frame-relay intf-type dce
 frame-relay route 101 interface Serial5 102
!
<<<text omitted>>>
!
interface Serial5
 no ip address
 encapsulation frame-relay
 clockrate 56000
 frame-relay intf-type dce
 frame-relay route 102 interface Serial0 101
!
<<<text omitted>>>
!
no ip classless
```

Example 1-20 *Displaying the Entire Frame Relay Configuration (Continued)*

```
!
line con 0
line aux 0
line vty 0 4
 login
!
end

frame_switch#
```

At this point, you need to verify that the switch is working. The primary things to look for are an establishment of a PVC and evidence that a PVC is active, with two different DLCI numbers. A PVC becomes active only when the LMI is being exchanged with both DTE devices.

The "Big show" and "Big D" for Frame Relay Switching

I call the following commands the "Big show" and the "Big D," for a couple of reasons. Yes, there are many other useful commands, but when it comes to debugs, fewer is better. I have a friend who was a systems programmer at McDonnell Douglas at the time, and he used to say, "If you're not breaking anything, you're not working." You can easily prove Tom's theory right by "working" with **debug** commands in a production environment. As I am sure you have been told, they can be output-intensive. All **debug** commands should be used in conjunction with the configuration mode key-in **logging buffered 10000**. The second reason that I call these the "big" commands is that there exists a limited set of commands and debugs that can be applied to resolve about 90 percent of most connectivity and routing issues. These "big" commands are the ones that I want to concentrate on.

The key **show** commands, or the "big show," as I like to call them, for Frame Relay switching are as follows:

- **show interface** *xx*—Displays the status of the physical link. The **serial is up/down** stands for Layer 1, or the physical layer. The **line protocol is up/down** stands for the Layer 2 protocol. Both lines should read **up**. **Serial*x* is up, line protocol is down** is a good indication of an LMI mismatch.

- **show frame-relay pvc**—Displays the status of the PVCs. The PVC should be ACTIVE, and input/output packets should be incrementing. The DLCI usage should be SWITCHING not local for Frame Relay switching.

- **show frame-relay lmi**—Displays the status of LMI updates sent and received. The **Num Status Enq. Sent** field should increment with the **Num Status msgs Rcvd** field. The **Num Status Timeouts** field should not be incrementing. The timeout message incrementing is a good indication of a LMI type mismatch.

- **show frame-relay route**—Only valid on Frame Relay switching, shows PVC mapping to interface and DLCI number. Ensure that the PVC is configured correctly with the appropriate DLCIs terminating on the appropriate interfaces. The status should be **active**.

- **debug frame-relay lmi**—Displays LMI keepalive and exchange information. On an inbound LMI frame, a Type 1 means that the frame is normal, whereas a Type 0 is an LMI full status request. The output also notes LMI errors/timeouts and the link status. If there is an invalid LMI type code sent, the code is as follows:

Invalid LMI type 1	Cisco
Invalid LMI type 2	Annex A or Q993a
Invalid LMI type 3	Annex D or ANSI

Still using this example, let's examine each one of these commands in more detail. From the Frame Relay switch, you perform a **show interface** command, as shown in Example 1-21. Notice that Layer 1 is up, but also notice that the line protocol is down and that the line **DCE LMI down** appears. This, in combination with all the **DCD=up DSR=up DTR=up RTS=up CTS=up** verifies that Layer 1 is up and should immediately point us to a frame problem at Layer 2.

Example 1-21 *Example of* **show interface** *Command*

```
frame_switch#show interface serial 0
Serial0 is up, line protocol is down
  Hardware is HD64570
  MTU 1500 bytes, BW 1544 Kbit, DLY 20000 usec, rely 255/255, load 1/255
  Encapsulation FRAME-RELAY, loopback not set, keepalive set (10 sec)
  LMI enq sent  0, LMI stat recvd 0, LMI upd recvd 0
  LMI enq recvd 297, LMI stat sent  297, LMI upd sent  0, DCE LMI down
  LMI DLCI 0  LMI type is ANSI Annex D  frame relay DCE
  FR SVC disabled, LAPF state down
  Broadcast queue 0/64, broadcasts sent/dropped 0/0, interface broadcasts 0
  Last input 00:00:05, output 01:24:05, output hang never
  Last clearing of "show interface" counters never
  Input queue: 0/75/0 (size/max/drops); Total output drops: 0
  Queueing strategy: weighted fair
  Output queue: 0/1000/64/0 (size/max total/threshold/drops)
     Conversations  0/1/256 (active/max active/max total)
     Reserved Conversations 0/0 (allocated/max allocated)
  5 minute input rate 0 bits/sec, 0 packets/sec
  5 minute output rate 0 bits/sec, 0 packets/sec
     2229 packets input, 30711 bytes, 0 no buffer
     Received 82 broadcasts, 0 runts, 0 giants, 0 throttles
     0 input errors, 0 CRC, 0 frame, 0 overrun, 0 ignored, 0 abort
     297 packets output, 4413 bytes, 0 underruns
     0 output errors, 0 collisions, 645 interface resets
```

Example 1-21 *Example of* **show interface** *Command (Continued)*

```
        0 output buffer failures, 0 output buffers swapped out
        1290 carrier transitions
        DCD=up  DSR=up  DTR=up  RTS=up  CTS=up
frame_switch#
```

Focusing more on the frame-related problems, you perform a **show frame-relay pvc** in Example 1-22. Here you are looking for **PVC STATUS = ACTIVE**. The DLCI USAGE will equal SWITCHED on the frame switch and LOCAL on the DTE side of the network. Any DLCI configured on this link will show up. Having a PVC register **INACTIVE** does not necessarily mean that a successful LMI status request was received.

Example 1-22 *The* **show frame-relay pvc** *Command*

```
frame_switch#show frame-relay pvc

PVC Statistics for interface Serial0 (Frame Relay DCE)

DLCI = 101, DLCI USAGE = SWITCHED, PVC STATUS = ACTIVE, INTERFACE = Serial0

  input pkts 0          output pkts 0          in bytes 0
  out bytes 0           dropped pkts 0         in FECN pkts 0
  in BECN pkts 0        out FECN pkts 0        out BECN pkts 0
  in DE pkts 0          out DE pkts 0
  out bcast pkts 0       out bcast bytes 0
  pvc create time 07:01:22, last time pvc status changed 06:59:57
  Num Pkts Switched 0

PVC Statistics for interface Serial5 (Frame Relay DCE)

DLCI = 102, DLCI USAGE = SWITCHED, PVC STATUS = INACTIVE, INTERFACE = Serial5

  input pkts 0          output pkts 0          in bytes 0
  out bytes 0           dropped pkts 0         in FECN pkts 0
  in BECN pkts 0        out FECN pkts 0        out BECN pkts 0
  in DE pkts 0          out DE pkts 0
  out bcast pkts 0       out bcast bytes 0
  pvc create time 07:01:22, last time pvc status changed 02:12:10
  Num Pkts Switched 0
frame_switch#
```

Narrowing the problem even further, you perform the **show frame-relay lmi** command. In Example 1-23, you are focusing on LMI timeouts over a period of time. As mentioned previously, **Num Status Eng Rcvd** should increment with **Num Status msgs Sent**. **Num St Eng. Timeouts** should not increment. LMI type is denoted here. Of course, Invalids also should not increment.

Example 1-23 *The* **show frame-relay lmi** *Command*

```
frame_switch#show frame-relay lmi

LMI Statistics for interface Serial0 (Frame Relay DCE) LMI TYPE = ANSI
  Invalid Unnumbered info 0            Invalid Prot Disc 0
  Invalid dummy Call Ref 0             Invalid Msg Type 0
  Invalid Status Message 0             Invalid Lock Shift 0
  Invalid Information ID 0             Invalid Report IE Len 0
  Invalid Report Request 0             Invalid Keep IE Len 0
  Num Status Enq. Rcvd 297             Num Status msgs Sent 297
  Num Update Status Sent 0             Num St Enq. Timeouts 1677

LMI Statistics for interface Serial5 (Frame Relay DCE) LMI TYPE = CISCO
  Invalid Unnumbered info 0            Invalid Prot Disc 0
  Invalid dummy Call Ref 0             Invalid Msg Type 0
  Invalid Status Message 0             Invalid Lock Shift 0
  Invalid Information ID 0             Invalid Report IE Len 0
  Invalid Report Request 0             Invalid Keep IE Len 0
  Num Status Enq. Rcvd 2806            Num Status msgs Sent 2806
  Num Update Status Sent 0             Num St Enq. Timeouts 4
frame_switch#show frame-relay lmi

LMI Statistics for interface Serial0 (Frame Relay DCE) LMI TYPE = ANSI
  Invalid Unnumbered info 0            Invalid Prot Disc 0
  Invalid dummy Call Ref 0             Invalid Msg Type 0
  Invalid Status Message 0             Invalid Lock Shift 0
  Invalid Information ID 0             Invalid Report IE Len 0
  Invalid Report Request 0             Invalid Keep IE Len 0
  Num Status Enq. Rcvd 297             Num Status msgs Sent 297
  Num Update Status Sent 0             Num St Enq. Timeouts 1678

LMI Statistics for interface Serial5 (Frame Relay DCE) LMI TYPE = CISCO
  Invalid Unnumbered info 0            Invalid Prot Disc 0
  Invalid dummy Call Ref 0             Invalid Msg Type 0
  Invalid Status Message 0             Invalid Lock Shift 0
  Invalid Information ID 0             Invalid Report IE Len 0
  Invalid Report Request 0             Invalid Keep IE Len 0
  Num Status Enq. Rcvd 2807            Num Status msgs Sent 2807
  Num Update Status Sent 0             Num St Enq. Timeouts 4
frame_switch#
```

If you performed this command over a period of time, the timeouts would keep incrementing and no status messages would be received. In this example, it is now becoming clear that you have an LMI problem. You can confirm this with the debug commands. **debug frame-relay lmi** provides useful information. By examining the log, you find the following entry noted in Example 1-24.

Example 1-24 *Output from the* **debug frame-relay lmi** *Command*

```
06:01:52: Serial5(in): StEnq, myseq 122
06:01:52: RT IE 1, length 1, type 1
06:01:52: KA IE 3, length 2, yourseq 123, myseq 122
06:01:52: Serial5(out): Status, myseq 123, yourseen 123, DCE up
06:01:53: Serial0: Invalid LMI type 1
06:01:58: Serial0(down): DCE LMI timeout
```

This log further confirms an LMI problem with Serial 0. An invalid LMI type of 1 indicates that the switch is receiving Cisco LMI from the DTE end, thereby causing the timeout and the "down" condition. If there were an **invalid LMI type 2** or an **invalid LMI type 3**, the LMI would be Q993a or ANSI, respectively. This type field should not be confused with the type field received during normal operation. The type message during normal operation indicates what type of LMI frame is being received. In normal operation, the **myseq** and the **yourseen** fields would be incrementing, along with the **DCE up** indication, as seen with Serial 5. You now can be positive that an LMI problem exists. Changing the LMI type to cisco on the Frame Relay switch, you can observe the results in the log, as seen in Example 1-25.

Example 1-25 *The* **debug** *Output Listed in the Log File During an LMI Correction*

```
09:52:33: Serial0: Invalid LMI type 1
09:52:39: %SYS-5-CONFIG_I: Configured from console by console
09:52:42: Serial5(in): StEnq, myseq 232
09:52:42: RT IE 1, length 1, type 1
09:52:42: KA IE 3, length 2, yourseq 233, myseq 232
09:52:42: Serial5(out): Status, myseq 233, yourseen 233, DCE up
09:52:43: Serial0(down): DCE LMI timeout
09:52:43: Serial0(in): StEnq, myseq 0
09:52:43: RT IE 1, length 1, type 0
09:52:43: KA IE 3, length 2, yourseq 6 , myseq 0
09:52:43: Serial0(out): Status, myseq 1, yourseen 6, DCE down
09:52:52: Serial5(in): StEnq, myseq 233
09:52:52: RT IE 1, length 1, type 1
09:52:52: KA IE 3, length 2, yourseq 234, myseq 233
09:52:52: Serial5(out): Status, myseq 234, yourseen 234, DCE up
09:52:53: Serial0(in): StEnq, myseq 1
09:52:53: RT IE 1, length 1, type 1
09:52:53: KA IE 3, length 2, yourseq 7 , myseq 1
09:52:53: Serial0(out): Status, myseq 2, yourseen 7, DCE up
09:52:53: %LINEPROTO-5-UPDOWN: Line protocol on Interface Serial0, changed state
 to up
09:53:00: %FR-5-DLCICHANGE: Interface Serial5 - DLCI 102 state changed to ACTIVE

09:53:02: Serial5(in): StEnq, myseq 234
09:53:02: RT IE 1, length 1, type 1
```

continues

Example 1-25 *The **debug** Output Listed in the Log File During an LMI Correction (Continued)*

```
09:53:02: KA IE 3, length 2, yourseq 235, myseq 234
09:53:02: Serial5(out): Status, myseq 235, yourseen 235, DCE up
09:53:03: Serial0(in): StEnq, myseq 2
09:53:03: RT IE 1, length 1, type 1
09:53:03: KA IE 3, length 2, yourseq 8 , myseq 2
09:53:03: Serial0(out): Status, myseq 3, yourseen 8, DCE up
```

At this time, you should have a basic understanding of the configuration required to model a Frame Relay switch. The lab exercise addresses subtle changes needed to make this a multipoint Frame Relay connection. We discuss more about Frame Relay LMI frames and their exchange in Chapter 5.

Configuring a Route Generator or Backbone Router

The next component that is helpful in modeling the internetwork is the route generator, or backbone router. A route generator is simply a router configured with virtual networks or loopback interfaces. These virtual networks are given a Layer 3 address and are advertised by a routing protocol. The main use is to make your test network look bigger than it really is, from a physical aspect, by injecting routes into your routing tables. To configure a route generator, perform the following tasks:

Step 1 Add one or more virtual interfaces or loopbacks.

Step 2 Decide what Layer 3 protocols to use, and apply it to the loopback interfaces.

Step 3 Advertise these networks with a routing protocol.

Still using your small frame network, you will configure one router to be a route generator, and then you will examine how the route generator looks to a downstream neighbor. To configure a loopback interface, enter **interface loopback** [*0-2147483647*] from configuration mode. You then must add a Layer 3 address and decide how to advertise the networks. Example 1-26 adds several loopback address with IP addresses. Using EIGRP with an autonomous system ID of 2001, you advertise these networks across the Frame Relay cloud to another router. With Figure 1-14 as your map, you can configure R1 as a route generator.

Figure 1-14 *Route Generator, IP Map*

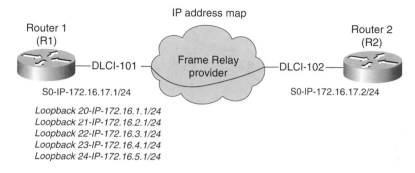

Example 1-26 shows the configuration for R1.

Example 1-26 *Configuring a Route Generator*

```
r1#conf t
Enter configuration commands, one per line.  End with CNTL/Z.
r1(config)#interface loopback 20
r1(config-if)#
02:41:51: %LINK-3-UPDOWN: Interface Loopback20, changed state to up
02:41:52: %LINEPROTO-5-UPDOWN: Line protocol on Interface Loopback20, changed st
ate to up
r1(config-if)#ip address 172.16.1.1 255.255.255.0
r1(config-if)#interface loopback 21
r1(config-if)#ip address 172.16.2.1 255.255.255.0
r1(config-if)#interface loopback 22
r1(config-if)#ip address 172.16.3.1 255.255.255.0
r1(config-if)#interface loopback 23
r1(config-if)#ip address 172.16.4.1 255.255.255.0
r1(config-if)#interface loopback 24
r1(config-if)#ip address 172.16.5.1 255.255.255.0
r1(config-if)#exit
r1(config)#router eigrp 2001
r1(config-router)#network 172.16.0.0
r1(config-router)#exit
r1(config)#interface serial 0
r1(config-if)#ip address 172.16.128.1 255.255.255.252
r1(config-if)#^Z
r1#
```

After configuring R2 for IP and adding EIGRP, you can observe how the virtual networks appear to a downstream router. In later chapters, you use route generators to practice filters and observe how routes are handled by the different routing protocols. Example 1-27 lists the routing table of R2, after the router was configured with the appropriate IP address on the serial interface and a routing protocol.

Example 1-27 *Route Generator Advertising Networks to a Downstream Router*

```
r2#
r2#show ip route
Codes: C - connected, S - static, I - IGRP, R - RIP, M - mobile, B - BGP
       D - EIGRP, EX - EIGRP external, O - OSPF, IA - OSPF inter area
       N1 - OSPF NSSA external type 1, N2 - OSPF NSSA external type 2
       E1 - OSPF external type 1, E2 - OSPF external type 2, E - EGP
       i - IS-IS, L1 - IS-IS level-1, L2 - IS-IS level-2, * - candidate default
       U - per-user static route, o - ODR
       T - traffic engineered route

Gateway of last resort is not set

     172.16.0.0/16 is variably subnetted, 6 subnets, 2 masks
C       172.16.128.0/30 is directly connected, Serial0
D       172.16.4.0/24 [90/2297856] via 172.16.128.1, 00:11:09, Serial0
D       172.16.5.0/24 [90/2297856] via 172.16.128.1, 00:11:09, Serial0
D       172.16.1.0/24 [90/2297856] via 172.16.128.1, 00:11:09, Serial0
D       172.16.2.0/24 [90/2297856] via 172.16.128.1, 00:11:09, Serial0
D       172.16.3.0/24 [90/2297856] via 172.16.128.1, 00:11:09, Serial0
r2#
```

Notice that R2 has EIGRP D routes reported from 172.16.128.1. This router now appears to be part of a much larger EIGRP network.

Configuring Analog Remote Access

Remote access to a network can be considerably useful during your studies and in the field. The Cisco TAC often asks if an analog modem is attached, to help in troubleshooting your problem. Problem solving can be significantly easier when another person can get a firsthand view of the problem. Being able to troubleshoot from a remote location with this type of an out-of-band connection alone can be invaluable. The sections presented here are intended to arm you with enough knowledge to configure a simple analog modem for remote support or for PPP backup. Cisco Systems and Cisco Press have an excellent 1,500–page reference entitled *Cisco IOS Dial Solutions* that covers dialup networks extensively. Most of the information offered in the following section is a derivative of the information presented in that text.

Configuring analog remote access can be abstract at times. A close association exists between the Cisco IOS level, the router port, and the modem, making it difficult to port configurations from one router type to another. Most often, any change in the router platform or switching modem types force you to reconfigure the router. However difficult it might be to configure or reconfigure at times, learning a few commands can get you through a majority of analog dialup issues.

This section focuses on terminal sessions connecting to the routers through their auxiliary or the asynchronous ports on the access server. Chapter 4, "WAN Protocols and Technologies: Point-to-Point Protocol (PPP)," covers PPP and how it is used in conjunction with the AUX, asynchronous (async), and serial ports.

Let's compare the asynchronous interface on the router to the auxiliary port. Both interfaces are capable of all asynchronous functions, which include the following:

- Network protocol support (such as IP, IPX, or AppleTalk)
- Encapsulation support (such as PPP and ARA)
- Authentication support

One of the noticeable differences between the AUX and the async port is the speed at which they can operate. The maximum speed for an asynchronous interface is 115,200 bps, whereas the AUX port operates at a maximum speed of 38,400 bps. Table 1-13 outlines this and other differences between the AUX and async ports.

Table 1-13 *AUX and Asynchronous Comparison*

Enchantments/Features	Asynchronous Interface	Auxiliary Port
Maximum speed	115,200 bps	38,400 bps
Offers DMA buffering for direct memory access without CPU interruption	Yes	No
Supports PPP framing performed on the interface, which removes additional overhead from the CPU	Yes	No
Supports IP fast switching	Yes	No

With these differences aside, the two ports operate and are configured almost identically.

In configuring analog, access is necessary to configure the modem. Modem configuration can vary from modem to modem; however, most of the modems today have standardized the **AT** commands sets that they use. The **AT** command set is a way to set bit registers in the modem with key-ins or strings that you send to the modem. **AT** commands allow you to force compression, answer the phone on one ring, and so on. To configure the router to support modems, you need to perform the following three tasks:

Step 1 Attach the modem to the AUX or asynchronous ports.

Step 2 Configure the modem lines or the line entries.

Step 3 Configure the modem by chat scripts or automatically.

Step 1: Attaching the Modem to the AUX or Asynchronous Ports

The first step in configuring analog communications is to attach the modem to the router. Table 1-14 repeats Table 1-2 from earlier in the chapter so that you can verify what type of cable and what type of head-shell to use on the modem. Most cases involve attaching the Cisco black or blue rolled cable to the AUX port. The MMOD type head-shell is used on the modem.

Table 1-14   *Asynchronous Device Cabling Options from Earlier*

Access Server Port	RJ-45 Console Cable Type	Head-Shell Adapter	End Device
Console or aux	Rolled	DTE pinout	Serial cable
Console or aux	Straight	DCE pinout	Serial cable
Console or aux	Rolled	MMOD/MODEM	Modem

Step 2: Configure the Modem Lines or the Line Entries

The next step is to configure the line commands that correspond to the AUX or the asynchronous line. To find the corresponding line entry, perform the **show line** command. Examine the output, and record the absolute line number that the AUX port is on. Example 1-28 lists the output for the **show line** command. Notice that the absolute line number in this example is 1. To begin to configure the AUX port for asynchronous communications, you need to enter the **Line 1** statement from the configuration mode.

Example 1-28 *Output for the* **show line** *Command*

```
Router#show line
 Tty Typ     Tx/Rx     A Modem  Roty AccO AccI   Uses   Noise  Overruns   Int
*  0 CTY                -    -      -    -    -      0      1     0/0        -
   1 AUX    9600/9600   -    -      -    -    -      0      1     0/0        -
   2 VTY                -    -      -    -    -      0      0     0/0        -
   3 VTY                -    -      -    -    -      0      0     0/0        -
   4 VTY                -    -      -    -    -      0      0     0/0        -
   5 VTY                -    -      -    -    -      0      0     0/0        -
   6 VTY                -    -      -    -    -      0      0     0/0        -


Router#
```

If you perform the same **show line** command on your access server, the output is a little more complicated. In Example 1-29, the absolute line number for the AUX port is 17. Therefore, if you want to add a modem to this AUX port, you need to begin your configuration with the statement **Line 17** from configuration mode.

Example 1-29 *The **show line** Command Performed on the Access Server*

```
skynet_access_1#show line
  Tty Typ     Tx/Rx      A Modem  Roty AccO AccI   Uses   Noise  Overruns   Int
*   0 CTY                -  -        -    -    -      1      0      0/0       -
    1 TTY     9600/9600   -  -        -    -    -      0      0      0/0       -
    2 TTY     9600/9600   -  -        -    -    -      0    103      0/0       -
*   3 TTY     9600/9600   -  -        -    -    -      0      1   1400/4202    -
*   4 TTY     9600/9600   -  -        -    -    -      0      0   1401/4203    -
*   5 TTY     9600/9600   -  -        -    -    -      1      1      2/9       -
*   6 TTY     9600/9600   -  -        -    -    -      0      0    465/1704    -
    7 TTY     9600/9600   -  -        -    -    -      0      0      0/0       -
    8 TTY     9600/9600   -  -        -    -    -      0      0      0/0       -
    9 TTY     9600/9600   -  -        -    -    -      0      0      0/0       -
   10 TTY     9600/9600   -  -        -    -    -      0      0      0/0       -
   11 TTY     9600/9600   -  -        -    -    -      0      0      0/0       -
   12 TTY     9600/9600   -  -        -    -    -      0      0      0/0       -
   13 TTY     9600/9600   -  -        -    -    -      0      0      0/0       -
   14 TTY     9600/9600   -  -        -    -    -      0      0      0/0       -
   15 TTY     9600/9600   -  -        -    -    -      0      0      0/0       -
*  16 TTY   38400/38400   - inout     -    -    .      0      0      0/0       -
   17 AUX     9600/9600   -  -        -    -    -      0      0      0/0       .
   18 VTY                 -  -        -    -    -      0      0      0/0       -
   19 VTY                 -  -        -    -    -      0      0      0/0       -
   20 VTY                 -  -        -    -    -      0      0      0/0       -
   21 VTY                 -  -        -    -    -      0      0      0/0       -
  Tty Typ     Tx/Rx      A Modem  Roty AccO AccI   Uses   Noise  Overruns   Int

   22 VTY                 -  -        -    -    -      0      0      0/0       -

skynet_access_1#
```

When you identify the appropriate line entry to modify, you can configure the line to support a modem. The characteristics that you want to configure at this point apply to Layer 1. That is the speed at which the router communicates with the modem, how the modem handles flow control, and how it handles the carrier.

Addressing speed first, it is important to note that the port speed of the router is not the same as the modem transmission rate. Comparing the two in Table 1-15, you find the following to be true.

Table 1-15 *Modem Transmission Rates Versus Port Speed*

Modem Transmission Rate	Port Speed as Entered Under the *Line x* Interface
9600	38,400
14,400	57,600
28,800	115,200

Table 1-13 noted that the maximum speed for an auxiliary port is 38,400, and the default modem transmission rate is 9600; therefore, you do not need to adjust the speed to get the maximum baud rate. To adjust the speed, in the case of using an asynchronous line, use the **speed [38400 | 57600 | 115200]** command.

If you adjust the speed above 38,400, enable hardware flow control. This is accomplished with the statement **flowcontrol hardware**.

The line must tell the modem also how to handle Carrier. To configure the line to hang up the connection when carrier detect (CD) is lost, use the **modem inout** statement. In some cases, you want the modem only to answer—the **modem dialin** statement would be used in this case.

Step 3: Configure the Modem by Chat Scripts or Automatically

The final step is to configure the modem initialization settings. The easiest and most straightforward method to configure external modems is with the **autoconfigure** command. Cisco IOS Software defines several initialization strings for most major modem brands. To view these predefined stings, enter the **show modemcap** command. Example 1-30 lists the output of the **show modemcap** command and the modems predefined in Cisco IOS Software Release 12.0.3, the current IOS of the router.

Example 1-30 *The Output from the* **show modemcap** *Command*

```
Router#show modemcap
default
codex_3260
usr_courier
usr_sportster
hayes_optima
global_village
viva
telebit_t3000
microcom_hdms
microcom_server
nec_v34
nec_v110
nec_piafs
cisco_v110
mica

Router#
Router#show modemcap default
Modemcap values for default
Factory Defaults (FD):  &F
Autoanswer (AA):  S0=1
Carrier detect (CD):  &C1
Drop with DTR (DTR):  &D2
Hardware Flowcontrol (HFL):  [not set]
```

Example 1-30 *The Output from the* **show modemcap** *Command (Continued)*

```
Lock DTE speed (SPD):  [not set]
DTE locking speed (DTE):  [not set]
Best Error Control (BER):  [not set]
Best Compression (BCP):  [not set]
No Error Control (NER):  [not set]
No Compression (NCP):  [not set]
No Echo (NEC):  E0
No Result Codes (NRS):  Q1
Software Flowcontrol (SFL):  [not set]
Caller ID (CID):  [not set]
On-hook (ONH):  H0
Off-hook (OFH):  H1
Miscellaneous (MSC):  [not set]
Template entry (TPL):  [not set]
Modem entry is built-in.

Router#
```

This listing also shows the predefined AT strings for the modem type called **default**. Over the years, Cisco has made great strides in improving the robustness and ease of configuration for analog support. In the past, and still supported, are what Cisco refers to as chat scripts. The chat script is entered from the configuration mode in the format **chat-script EXPECT SEND EXPECT SEND**. You then call the chat script from the line entry. About 90 percent or more modems function out of the box without complicated **AT** command strings. Try to avoid the use of chat scripts whenever possible, and use the **modem auto-configure discovery** or **modem auto-configure type default**, if your modem is not listed in the **show modemcap** command. Yet one more way to avoid the use of complicated chat scripts is to create your own or modify the existing modemcap entries. This is done using **modemcap edit** *modem-name attribute value* in configuration mode. This command allows for easy manipulation of the **AT** commands through a streamlined interface.

After you identify the modem type to use or have defined your own type, you make the logical connection by adding the **modem auto-configure type** *modem-name*, under the appropriate line entry.

Configuration Walkthrough: Adding a Modem to a Router

Example 1-31 is a complete walkthrough of the configuration needed to add a modem to a router.

Step 1   Verify what line entry you need to modify. This is done with the **show line** command. Record the absolute line number, the number highlighted or to the far right of the display. Refer to this number as *X*.

Step 2 Enter the configuration mode, and enter the appropriate **line** *x* configuration command.

Step 3 Still under the line entry, add the following:

— **transport input all**

— **modem inout**

— **modem autoconfigure discovery**

-or-

— **modem autoconfigure type** [*default | modem-name*]

Step 4 Configure an enable password, to allow privileged mode access.

Example 1-31 *Walkthrough of Configuring Analog Dial Access on an AUX Port*

```
Router#
Router#show line
  Tty Typ     Tx/Rx     A Modem  Roty AccO AccI   Uses   Noise  Overruns   Int
*   0 CTY                -   -     -    -    -      0      9      0/0       -
    1 AUX   9600/9600    -   -     -    -    -      0      1      0/0       -
    2 VTY                -   -     -    -    -      0      0      0/0       -
    3 VTY                -   -     -    -    -      0      0      0/0       -
    4 VTY                -   -     -    -    -      0      0      0/0       -
    5 VTY                -   -     -    -    -      0      0      0/0       -
    6 VTY                -   -     -    -    -      0      0      0/0       -

Router#
Router#conf t
Enter configuration commands, one per line.  End with CNTL/Z.
Router(config)#line 1
Router(config-line)#transport input all
Router(config-line)#modem inout
Router(config-line)#modem autoconfigure discovery
Router(config-line)#^Z
Router#
```

After the **line** commands have been entered, verify modem connectivity by opening a reverse Telnet session to it. In Example 1-32, you add a loopback interface with the IP address of 201.201.201.1, to support the reverse Telnet session. If the session does not open, remember to use the **clear line** command and then try the reverse Telnet again. When you are in session with the modem, you can reset it with the **ATZ** command, as shown. If you can perform a reverse Telnet, this means that the transport is configured properly and that the line was open. If you can perform a reverse Telnet but cannot perform an **ATZ** command, you probably have a cabling issue.

If you still cannot perform the reverse Telnet session or the **ATZ**, ensure that you have added all the previous lines, and then turn on the debugs. To exit from or suspend the reverse

Telnet session, press **Ctrl-Shift-6** and then **X**. To continue troubleshooting the line, use the **disconnect** command to close the reverse Telnet session.

Example 1-32 *A Reverse Telnet Session, Followed by an* **AT** *Command*

```
Router#telnet 201.201.201.1 2001
Trying 201.201.201.1, 2001 ... Open

at7
OK

Router#
Router#disconnect
Closing connection to 201.201.201.1 [confirm]y
Router#
```

The "Big show" and "Big D" for Modems

Two powerful debugs are available to assist in troubleshooting modem connections. The "big D," or debugs, used for modems are **debug modem** and **debug confmodem**. These, used with the **show line** *x* command, can narrow down modem problems quickly. Using the **show line** *x* command, you can observe a few key indicators that this line is working well (refer to Example 1-33). You should see the modem status as **detected**. You should also see the modem state as **idle**, and you finally should see the leads. If the modem state is not idle, try to clear it with the **clear line** *x* command.

Example 1-33 *Example of Working Modem and the* **show line** *Command*

```
Router#show line 1
  Tty Typ     Tx/Rx     A Modem  Roty AccO AccI   Uses   Noise  Overruns   Int
    1 AUX   38400/38400 - inout    -    -    -      0      1      0/0       - Ie

Line 1, Location: "", Type: ""
Length: 24 lines, Width: 80 columns
Baud rate (TX/RX) is 38400/38400, no parity, 2 stopbits, 8 databits
Status: No Exit Banner, Modem Detected
Capabilities: Modem Callout, Modem RI is CD, Modem Discovery
Modem state: Idle
Group codes:    0
Modem hardware state: CTS* noDSR  DTR RTS, Modem Configured
Special Chars: Escape  Hold  Stop  Start  Disconnect  Activation
               ^^x     none   -     -       none
Timeouts:      Idle EXEC    Idle Session   Modem Answer  Session   Dispatch
               00:10:00       never                      none      not set
                             Idle Session Disconnect Warning
                               never
                             Login-sequence User Response
                               00:00:30
```

continues

Example 1-33 *Example of Working Modem and the* **show line** *Command (Continued)*

```
                              Autoselect Initial Wait
                                  not set
Modem type is usr_sportster.
Session limit is not set.
Time since activation: never
Editing is enabled.
History is enabled, history size is 10.
DNS resolution in show commands is enabled
Full user help is disabled
Allowed transports are lat pad v120 mop telnet rlogin nasi.  Preferred is lat.
No output characters are padded
No special data dispatching characters
Router#
```

Example 1-34 shows an invalid line. Notice that the speed changes from listing to listing. This is because the router is constantly trying to communicate with the modem. Also, the status line is missing **modem detected**. Finally, note that the router cannot detect Clear to Send (CTS); this is a good indication of a cabling or head-shell problem.

Example 1-34 *Example of Invalid Line, with the* **show line** *Command*

```
Router#show line 1
  Tty Typ     Tx/Rx    A Modem  Roty AccO AccI   Uses   Noise  Overruns   Int
*  1 AUX    1200/1200  - inout    -    -    -     3       1      0/0        -

Line 1, Location: "", Type: ""
Length: 24 lines, Width: 80 columns
Baud rate (TX/RX) is 1200/1200, no parity, 2 stopbits, 8 databits
Status: Ready, Active, No Exit Banner                    ← notice an absence?
Capabilities: Modem Callout, Modem RI is CD, Modem Discovery ← 'modem detected'
Modem state: Ready
Group codes:    0
Modem hardware state: noCTS noDSR  DTR RTS ←no CTS
Special Chars: Escape  Hold  Stop  Start  Disconnect  Activation
               ^^x     none   -     -      none
Timeouts:      Idle EXEC   Idle Session   Modem Answer  Session   Dispatch
               00:10:00        never                    none      not set
                            Idle Session Disconnect Warning
                               never
                            Login-sequence User Response
                               00:00:30
                            Autoselect Initial Wait
                               not set
Modem type is usr_sportster.
Session limit is not set.
Time since activation: never
Editing is enabled.
History is enabled, history size is 10.
DNS resolution in show commands is enabled
Full user help is disabled
```

Example 1-34 *Example of Invalid Line, with the* **show line** *Command (Continued)*

```
Allowed transports are lat pad v120 mop telnet rlogin nasi.  Preferred is lat.
No output characters are padded
No special data dispatching characters
Router#
```

Turning on the two **debug**s mentioned in the beginning of this section, you can observe the router continually trying to communicate with the modem. The TTY1 session in Example 1-35 stands for the TTY session on Line 1, which is where you have your modem attached.

Example 1-35 *Output from the* **debug confmodem** *and* **debug modem**

```
Router#debug modem
Modem control/process activation debugging is on
Router#debug confmodem
Modem Configuration Database debugging is on
Router#
06:03:15: TTY1: autoconfigure probe started
06:03:18: TTY1: detection speed (38400) response    ••
06:03:21: TTY1: detection speed (19200) response ------
06:03:24: TTY1: detection speed (9600) response ------
06:03:27: TTY1: detection speed (2400) response ------
06:03:30: TTY1: detection speed (1200) response ------
06:03:34: TTY1: detection speed (300) response ------
06:03:34: TTY1: No modem found
06:03:34: TTY1: autoconfigure probe started
06:03:37: TTY1: detection speed (38400) response ------
06:03:40: TTY1: detection speed (19200) response ------
06:03:43: TTY1: detection speed (9600) response ------
06:03:46: TTY1: detection speed (2400) response ------
06:03:49: TTY1: detection speed (1200) response ------
06:03:53: TTY1: detection speed (300) response ------
06:03:53: TTY1: No modem found
06:03:53: TTY1: autoconfigure probe started
```

Fixing the cable, you now can observe a proper operating line, as in Example 1-36. The line **Modem configuration succeeded** and the presence of CTS is a clear indication that a valid modem has been detected.

Example 1-36 *Output from the* **debug confmodem** *and* **debug modem** *Continued*

```
06:38:21: TTY1: autoconfigure probe started
06:38:25: TTY1: detection speed (38400) response ------
06:38:28: TTY1: detection speed (19200) response ------
06:38:31: TTY1: detection speed (9600) response ------
06:38:34: TTY1: detection speed (2400) response ------
06:38:37: TTY1: detection speed (1200) response ------
06:38:40: TTY1: detection speed (300) response ------
```

continues

Example 1-36 *Output from the* **debug confmodem** *and* **debug modem** *Continued (Continued)*

```
06:38:40: TTY1: No modem found
06:38:40: TTY1: CTS came up on IDLE line
06:38:40: TTY1: autoconfigure probe started
06:38:41: TTY1: detection speed (38400) response ---OK---
06:38:44: TTY1: Modem type is usr_sportster
06:38:44: TTY1: Modem command:  --AT&F&C1&D2&M4&K1&B1S0=1H0--
06:38:44: TTY1: Modem configuration succeeded
06:38:46: TTY1: detection speed (38400) response ---OK---
06:38:46: TTY1: Done with modem configuration
```

Finally, you can observe the configuration in its entirety in Example 1-37.

Example 1-37 *A Router Configuration with a Modem Attached to Its AUX Port*

```
hostname router
!
ip subnet-zero
ip host modem 2001 201.201.201.1
!

 interface Loopback0
 ip address 201.201.201.1 255.255.255.0
 no ip directed-broadcast
!
interface Ethernet0
 no ip address
 no ip directed-broadcast
 shutdown
!
interface Serial0
 no ip address
 no ip directed-broadcast
 no ip mroute-cache
 shutdown
!
interface Serial1
 no ip address
 no ip directed-broadcast
 shutdown


!
ip classless
!
line con 0
 transport input none
line aux 0
 modem InOut
 modem autoconfigure discovery
 transport input all
```

Example 1-37 *A Router Configuration with a Modem Attached to Its AUX Port (Continued)*

```
  speed 38400
 line vty 0 4
  login
 !
 end

 Router#
```

Configuring Microsoft Windows 95/98 Networking

The goal of all internetworking is to reliably transfer data from one network to another. Therefore, no model could be called reliable if it were not properly tested with real data and real applications. Therefore, the last components needed to completely model the internetwork are test data and test applications.

As previously mentioned, the entire Microsoft Windows OS line, Windows 95/98/2000 and NT, provides all the network protocols needed to test many network models. The two protocols that we concentrate on are TCP/IP and NetBEUI. You use TCP/IP-related applications such as Telnet, FTP, and TFTP to test filters, verify IP reachability, and upgrade a router with TFTP. You use NetBEUI to test the functionality of bridging and DLSW configurations.

IBrief Overview of Configuring TCP/IP for Windows 95/98

In case you do not have your workstation or laptop configured for TCP/IP, this session briefly walks you through the process:

Step 1 Install your network interface card (NIC), according to the manufacturer's instructions. This might include instructions on how to set up TCP/IP, which supplement this text.

Step 2 Click **Start**, **Settings**, **Control Panel**, **Network**. When the Network dialog box appears, click the **Add** button.

Step 3 A menu pops up listing Client, Adapter, Protocol, and Service. From this selection, click **Protocol**. The manufacturer of the TCP/IP stack that ships with Windows is Microsoft, so click on that manufacturer and then select **TCP/IP**. Windows prompts you through the setup process and then wants to reload your workstation. Avoiding reloads during IP configuration is one of the many improvements in Windows 2000.

Step 4 After the workstation reloads, right-click the **Network Neighborhood** icon located on the desktop, and select **Properties**.

Step 5   The Network dialog box again appears; Step 4 is simply a short cut to this dialog box. Under the Configuration tab, select the entry labeled **TCP/IP**; (*your NIC card*). Then click the **Properties** button. Figure 1-15 illustrates the Network dialog box.

Figure 1-15   *The Network Dialog Box*

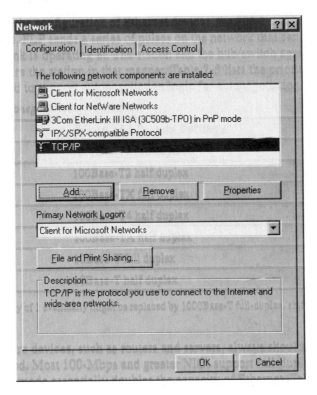

Step 6   In the TCP/IP Properties window, click the **IP Address** tab at the top. Then click **Specify an IP Address**, and enter the address in the field provided.

Step 7   For IP to work properly, you must also add a default gateway. The default gateway should be the IP address of a router on the same LAN segment. This router handles all of the workstation's requests that are not local. To configure a default gateway, click the **Gateway** tab and enter the appropriate IP address.

Step 8   Finally, to use DNS services, click the tab **DNS Configuration**, and enter the DNS server that you want to use. Then click the **Add** button.

After Steps 7 or 8, the workstation reloads. To test your configuration, click the **Start** button and choose **Programs**, **MS-DOS Prompt**. This opens a DOS session. From here, you use the **ping** command to test IP functionality. The **ping** command also can be run with **Start**, **Run**, followed by keying in **ping** *x.x.x.x*. To test DNS functionality, **ping** IP hosts by using the DNS name association instead of the actual IP address.

Brief Overview of Configuring NetBEUI for Windows 95/98

The other host-based protocol that you need to install is NetBEUI. Combined with enabling Windows file and print sharing, the NetBEUI protocol provides a great test application for DLSw and bridging functions. NetBEUI is a nonroutable protocol, which does not have a specific network layer address. To forward these protocols from one network to another, you must use bridging or DLSw. Click the **Start** button and choose **Find**, **Computers**. Key in any name, and click the **Find** button. This sends an all-routes explorer frame. The explorer frame transverses DLSw connections, as well as source-route bridges, transparent bridges, and translational bridges. It is evident that NetBEUI will be of great use in the lab.

To configure NetBEUI, perform the following steps:

Step 1 Right-click the **Network Neighborhood** icon, located on the desktop, and select **Properties**.

Step 2 The Network dialog box appears. Click the **Add** button.

Step 3 A menu pops up listing Client, Adapter, Protocol, and Service. From this selection, left-click **Protocol**. Click **Microsoft** as the manufacturer, and then select **NetBEUI**. Windows prompts you through the setup process, and then it will want to reload your workstation.

Step 4 After the workstation reloads, right-click the **Network Neighborhood** icon, followed by the **Properties** button.

Step 5 The Network dialog box appears again. Click the **Identification** tab at the top. Enter a workstation name that will appear as a DLSw identifier.

Step 6 Finally, to establish end-to-end sessions across the model, you must enable Microsoft file and print sharing. Click the **Add** button. This time, you will be adding a service, so click the **Service** selection.

Step 7 The service that you need to add is Microsoft file and print sharing, so click on this selection. Windows will then install this feature.

Step 8 When file and print sharing is enabled, verify it by clicking the button **Microsoft File** and **Print Sharing**; make sure that both boxes are checked. Then open the Windows Explorer. Click the drive that you would share by right-clicking the drive icon and selecting the **Sharing** selection. If the drive is not shared, click the **Share** box, and be sure to include a password.

CAUTION If you are connected to a cable modem provider in your area, be careful to password-protect your hard drives and any shared resources. The cable modems work on a broadcast mechanism for local access. Therefore, everyone on your local cable modem segment can see your PC and any shared resources.

You need two workstations to properly test the NetBEUI and Windows file and print sharing. To test the configuration, choose **Start**, **Find**. Key in the name that you entered in the Identification tab on Step 5. This locates the workstation. Clicking the workstation name puts you in a session with that workstation. Any shared resources then are displayed. Simply click the resource to use it from your workstation.

Practical Study for Chapter 1: Setting Up

So far, this chapter discussed the key components needed for modeling the internetwork. Now it is time to take what you learned and apply it. Without application, it becomes hard to grasp and retain the concepts put forth so far.

At the heart of practical studies lies the goal of modeling the internetwork. But before you begin with modeling networks and different protocols, you must prepare the lab by configuring the key components discussed in this chapter. As you progress deeper into modeling the internetwork, the labs are increasingly harder. At the end of the study are five complete CCIE practice labs. These labs are for your own personnel challenge when preparing for the CCIE Lab Exam, and answers are not be supplied.

The labs are divided into two major parts, the lab exercise or scenario and then a lab walkthrough. First, try to perform Part I of the lab without looking at Part II, the walk-through. Each lab covers the topics in that chapter, but some labs might also introduce new areas of study.

Lab 1: Password Recovery—Part I

Practical Scenario

You might need to perform password recovery on a router at many times. To model and set up your lab for practical studies, you need at least three routers. Most of the equipment has a high probability of being used. This equipment might require password recovery for privileged-level access. Sometimes, customers forget passwords. In either case, you need to perform password recovery.

Lab Exercise

You received a stack of routers that you can use to model complex networks. Because this equipment is used, it has an existing configuration stored on NVRAM that is password-protected. You are tasked to archive and then erase the current router configuration.

Lab Objectives

- Examine the original configuration of the router.
- Erase the configuration. The router should have no configuration, and, when it boots, it should come up in setup mode.

Equipment Needed

- One Cisco router.
- One Cisco configuration kit (one rolled cable and appropriate head-shell to connect to the PC/laptop's COM port).
- One PC or laptop with terminal-emulation software.
- All labs from this point on require a PC or laptop with the standard configuration kit and terminal-emulation software. This is the only lab in which this basic configuration equipment is mentioned.

Physical Layout and Prestaging

The router used must have some previous configuration and an enable password set.

Lab 1: Password Recovery—Part II

Lab Walkthrough

As discussed previously, password recovery is similar from one router platform to another. Therefore, you can apply the process outlined earlier in this chapter here, with a few modifications to fit the lab exercise.

The procedure outlined in the list that follows is valid for the following routers:

- Cisco 2000 series
- Cisco 2500 series
- Cisco 3000 series
- Cisco 4000 series with the 680x0 Motorola CPU
- Cisco 7000 series running Cisco IOS Software Release 10.0 or later in ROMs installed on the RP card
- IGS series running Cisco IOS Software Release 9.1 or later in ROMs

Step 1   Attach a PC or PDA with terminal-emulation software to the router's console port through Cisco rolled cable.

Step 2   Power-cycle the router.

Step 3   Issue a break signal.

Step 4   Determine what type of ROM monitor you have—is CONREG supported?

— If you have a Basic ROM monitor: Set bit 6: >**O/R 0x2142**. Reload the router with the **initialize** command.

— If CONFREG is supported: Run the CONFREG utility: >**CONFREG.** Answer every question with the default or **Enter** until you come to the question **Enable ignore system config info**. Answer "yes" to this question. This also sets bit 6. Reload the router with the **reset** command.

Step 5   When the router reloads, it will try to run setup, abort the setup utility with **CTRL-C**.

Step 6   Enter enable mode, and examine the configuration found in NVRAM; use the **show startup-config** command to accomplish this.

For this walkthrough, you perform a password recovery operation to gain privileged level access to your access server. In this example, the access server is called *skynet_access_1*.

First, attach a PC or laptop with terminal-emulation software to the console port of the router. Power off the router and turn it back on. Within the first 60 seconds of initialization, issue a break signal from your terminal emulator. Example 1-38 demonstrates a successful break or halt of the OS.

Example 1-38 *A Successful Break*

```
System Bootstrap, Version 5.2(8a), RELEASE SOFTWARE
Copyright (c) 1986-1995 by cisco Systems
2500 processor with 14336 Kbytes of main memory

Abort at 0x10EA888 (PC)
>
```

Getting the terminal-emulation software to send a break signal is a common problem with password recovery. Here are a few tips that might help if you have trouble sending a break signal:

- First, ensure that you are securely plugged into the console port of the router and using the Cisco rolled cable.

- If your portable or laptop computer is using Windows 95/98/2000 with HyperTerminal, the break signal is usually issued by pressing the **Function** key and the **Break** key, sometimes located on the Page Down or Pause key. Table 1-8, earlier in the chapter, documents where you can find standard break key combinations for all terminal-emulation software, platforms, and operating systems.

- On HyperTerminal, the break signal is issued by pressing the **Ctrl-Break/Pause** key sequence.

- On Windows NT, you must configure NT to send the break signal with a function key. Set the Break by entering the characters **^$B** (**Shift 6, Shift 4**, and uppercase **B**). HyperTerm 5.0 private edition sends the Break for the Windows NT platform without any additional configuration.

- When using any other terminal-emulation software, consult the manufacturer's instructions on sending a break signal.

When you see the abort message, you are ready to proceed. If you don't recall what type of routers support CONFREG, this is a good point to key in the **?** for help and look for the CONFREG utility. In Example 1-39, you can see what the output from the **?** looks like on the access server.

Example 1-39 *Output from the **?** Command on Router That Doesn't Support CONFREG*

```
>?
$               Toggle cache state
B [filename] [TFTP Server IP address | TFTP Server Name]
                Load and execute system image from ROM or from TFTP server
```

continues

Example 1-39 *Output from the ? Command on Router That Doesn't Support CONFREG (Continued)*

```
C [address]    Continue execution [optional address]
D /S M L V     Deposit value V of size S into location L with modifier M
E /S M L       Examine location L with size S with modifier M
G [address]    Begin execution
H              Help for commands
I              Initialize
K              Stack trace
L [filename] [TFTP Server IP address | TFTP Server Name]
               Load system image from ROM or from TFTP server, but do not
               begin execution
O              Show configuration register option settings
P              Set the break point
S              Single step next instruction
T function     Test device (? for help)

Deposit and Examine sizes may be B (byte), L (long) or S (short).
Modifiers may be R (register) or S (byte swap).
Register names are: D0-D7, A0-A6, SS, US, SR, and PC
>
```

Example 1-40 illustrates the same break, followed by the **?** command; however, this time, it was performed on a router that supports CONFREG.

Example 1-40 *A Successful Break, Followed by the Output from the ? Command on Router That Supports CONFREG*

```
System Bootstrap, Version 5.3(16) [richardd 16], RELEASE SOFTWARE (fc1)
Copyright (c) 1996 by cisco Systems, Inc.
C4500 processor with 16384 Kbytes of main memory


monitor: command "boot" aborted due to user interrupt
rommon 1 >
rommon 1 > ?
alias           set and display aliases command
boot            boot up an external process
break           set/show/clear the breakpoint
confreg         configuration register utility
cont            continue executing a downloaded image
context         display the context of a loaded image
cookie          display contents of cookie PROM in hex
dev             list the device table
dir             list files in file system
dis             disassemble instruction stream
dnld            serial download a program module
frame           print out a selected stack frame
help            monitor built in command help
history         monitor command history
meminfo         main memory information
repeat          repeat a monitor command
```

Example 1-40 *A Successful Break, Followed by the Output from the **?** Command on Router That Supports CONFREG (Continued)*

```
reset              system reset
set                display the monitor variables
stack              produce a stack trace
sync               write monitor environment to NVRAM
sysret             print out info from last system return
unalias            unset an alias
unset              unset a monitor variable
rommon 2 >
```

Set bit 6 of the register to 1 to ignore NVRAM on startup. This is done by keying in **O/R hex-value** and then pressing **Enter**. Then initialize, or reload, the router by keying in **init**. Example 1-41 demonstrates this procedure.

Example 1-41 *Setting Bit 6 to Ignore NVRAM, Followed by the **initialization** Command*

```
System Bootstrap, Version 5.2(8a), RELEASE SOFTWARE
Copyright (c) 1986-1995 by cisco Systems
2500 processor with 14336 Kbytes of main memory

Abort at 0x10205A6 (PC)
>o/r 0x2142
>init

System Bootstrap, Version 5.2(8a), RELEASE SOFTWARE
Copyright (c) 1986-1995 by cisco Systems
```

On a router that supports CONFREG, this process is just as straightforward. Example 1-42 demonstrates how this procedure is done on such a platform. In this example, a Cisco 4700 series router is used.

Example 1-42 *Setting Bit 6 to Ignore NVRAM, Followed by the **reset** Command*

```
rommon 1 > confreg


    Configuration Summary
enabled are:
load rom after netboot fails
console baud: 9600
boot: image specified by the boot system commands
      or default to: cisco2-C4500

do you wish to change the configuration? y/n  [n]:  y
enable  "diagnostic mode"? y/n  [n]:  n
enable  "use net in IP bcast address"? y/n  [n]:  n
```

continues

Example 1-42 *Setting Bit 6 to Ignore NVRAM, Followed by the* **reset** *Command (Continued)*

```
disable "load rom after netboot fails"? y/n  [n]:  n
enable  "use all zero broadcast"? y/n  [n]:  n
enable  "break/abort has effect"? y/n  [n]:  n
enable  "ignore system config info"? y/n  [n]:  y
change console baud rate? y/n  [n]:  n
change the boot characteristics? y/n  [n]:  n


    Configuration Summary
enabled are:
load rom after netboot fails
ignore system config info
console baud: 9600
boot: image specified by the boot system commands
      or default to: cisco2-C4500

do you wish to change the configuration? y/n  [n]:  n


You must reset or power cycle for new config to take effect
rommon 2 > reset

System Bootstrap, Version 5.3(16) [richardd 16], RELEASE SOFTWARE (fc1)
Copyright (c) 1996 by cisco Systems, Inc.
```

When the router reloads, it will no longer have a running-configuration. The router will still have a startup-configuration, which is stored in NVRAM. To view this configuration, first enter enable mode and then enter the **show startup-configuration** command.

If you want to preserve the existing configuration, perform the following steps, paying strict attention to the order.

Step 1   Enter enable mode with **enable**.

Step 2   Copy the startup-config to running-config with **copy startup-config running-config**.

Step 3   Enter the configuration mode, and change the boot register back to the normal configuration with **configure-register 0x2102**.

Step 4   Bring up all interfaces because they will be in the default down status.

Step 5   Configure a new enable password.

Step 6   Save the configuration with **copy running-config startup-config**.

Lab 2: Password Recovery on a Catalyst 5500—Part I

Practical Scenario

As with routers, sometimes you might need to perform a password-recovery procedure on switches.

Lab Exercise

Along with the routers used for the lab, you have received a used Catalyst 5500 switch. The switch is password-protected. To use the switch in this lab, you must perform password recovery on the switch and secure access with a new password.

Lab Objectives

- Perform password recovery on Catalyst 5500.
- Set a new enable password on the Catalyst 5500.

Equipment Needed

- One Cisco Catalyst switch—the switch can be either a 5000, a 5500, or a 4000 series switch.

Physical Layout and Prestaging

The switch used must have some previous configuration and an enable password set.

Lab 2: Password Recovery on a Catalyst 5500—Part II

Lab Walkthrough

For the first 30 seconds during switch initialization, the password and enable password are both the Enter key. As soon as the **Cisco Systems Console** message appears, you can begin configuration.

First, enter enable mode. The switch will prompt you for a password; simply press the **Enter** key. Second, configure a new password with the **set password** command. Again, the switch will prompt you for an old password, press **Enter** again. Finally, before 30 seconds are up, configure a new enable password. This is done with the command **set enablepass**. For the last time, the switch will prompt you for an old password; press **Enter** one more time. The 30 seconds needed to set the passwords can go by quickly. If you're having trouble getting the passwords set, try setting the new password to just the Enter key. This allows you to type **Enter** twice when prompted for the old and new passwords. Example 1-43 illustrates this process of key-ins.

Example 1-43 *Password Recovery on a Catalyst 5500*

```
Console> en
Enter password:                       <--Enter key pressed
Console> (enable) set pass
Enter old password:                   <--Enter key pressed
Enter new password:                   <--Enter key or new password
Retype new password:                   <--Enter or new password
Password changed.
Console> (enable) set enablepass
Enter old password:                   <--Enter key pressed
Enter new password:                   <--Enter key or new password
Retype new password:                   <--Enter or new password
Password changed.
Console> (enable)
```

Lab 3: Upgrading the IOS and Restoring a Configuration from TFTP Server—Part I

Practical Scenario

Sometimes, in the field, you must perform an Cisco IOS Software upgrade, but you do not have local access to the router. You can still perform the upgrade by making an adjacent Cisco router a TFTP server.

Lab Exercise

In this practical exercise, you upgrade one router's IOS from another router's Flash memory. A second part of this exercise consists of copying configs to and from a TFTP server.

Lab Objectives

- Refer to Figure 1-16, and configure the network as shown—do not configure the loopback address at this time.

- To prevent future "crashes" of the Cisco IOS Software on the router rosewell, copy the new Cisco IOS Software from the router ufo to the router rosewell.

- Using TFTP, TFTP the startup-config from router ufo to the TFTP server 172.16.16.254. Edit the configuration with Wordpad, and change the host name to w-balloon. TFTP the configuration back to the router's startup-config. Reload the router.

Equipment Needed

- Two Cisco routers and one Ethernet hub

- One workstation with terminal-emulation software, TFTP software, and TCP/IP configured per Figure 1-16

Physical Layout and Prestaging

TCP/IP must also be configured on this workstation per Figure 1-16.

Figure 1-16 *Lab 3: Physical Layout and IP Address Map*

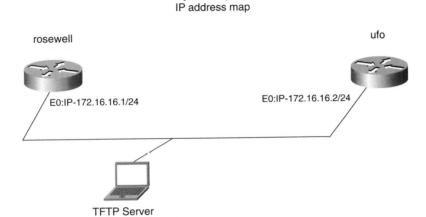

Physical Layout &
IP address map

rosewell

ufo

E0:IP-172.16.16.1/24

E0:IP-172.16.16.2/24

TFTP Server
IP-172.16.16.254/24

Lab 3: Upgrading the IOS and Restoring a Configuration from a TFTP Server—Part II

Lab Walkthrough

The first step in this lab is to configure all the equipment as shown in Figure 1-16. Also attach a workstation to the same physical segment. When all the devices can **ping** each other, you can move on.

This lab introduces another new concept—making the router function as a TFTP server. To make a router perform as a TFTP server, add the command **tftp-server** [**flash** | **rom**] *filename* from configuration mode. In Example 1-44, first you perform a **show flash** command to view the files available on Flash memory (be sure to note the filename). From the configuration mode, enter the command **tftp-server flash** *filename*. To avoid typing mistakes, which is a common problem on Flash upgrades, use cut-and-paste techniques for the filename.

Example 1-44 *Making a Router Serve as a TFTP Server*

```
ufo#
ufo#show flash

System flash directory:
File  Length   Name/status
  1   8102652  c2500-js-l_112-16.bin
[8102716 bytes used, 285892 available, 8388608 total]
8192K bytes of processor board System flash (Read ONLY)

ufo#conf t
Enter configuration commands, one per line.  End with CNTL/Z.
ufo(config)#tftp-server flash c2500-js-l_112-16.bin
ufo(config)#^Z
ufo#
```

Moving over to rosewell, you can now upgrade the IOS through TFTP on router ufo. To perform this task, use the **copy tftp flash** command, and answer the questions accordingly. Use ufo as the TFTP server, and use c2500-js-l_112-16.bin as the filename. Example 1-45 demonstrates the upgrade of rosewell from ufo.

Example 1-45 *Upgrading the IOS by Using TFTP*

```
rosewell#
rosewell#copy tftp flash          ←Copying from the server to the router
                      ****  NOTICE  ****
Flash load helper v1.0
This process will accept the copy options and then terminate
```

continues

Example 1-45 *Upgrading the IOS by Using TFTP (Continued)*

```
the current system image to use the ROM based image for the copy.
Routing functionality will not be available during that time.
If you are logged in via telnet, this connection will terminate.
Users with console access can see the results of the copy operation.
                 ---- ******** ----
Proceed? [confirm]y

System flash directory:
File  Length   Name/status
  1   8034308  c2500-js-l_112-11.bin
[8034372 bytes used, 8742844 available, 16777216 total]
Address or name of remote host [255.255.255.255]? 172.16.16.2
Source file name? c2500-js-l_112-16.bin
Destination file name [c2500-js-l_112-16.bin]? c2500-js-l_112-16.bin
Accessing file 'c2500-js-l_112-16.bin' on 172.16.16.2...
Loading c2500-js-l_112-16.bin .from 172.16.16.2 (via Ethernet0): ! [OK]

Erase flash device before writing? [confirm]y
Flash contains files. Are you sure you want to erase? [confirm]y

Copy 'c2500-js-l_112-16.bin' from server
  as 'c2500-js-l_112-16.bin' into Flash WITH erase? [yes/no]yes

00:01:15: %SYS-5-RELOAD: Reload requested              ←the router reloads
SERVICE_MODULE(1): self test finished: Passed
%SYS-4-CONFIG_NEWER: Configurations from version 11.2 may not be correctly under
stood.
%FLH: c2500-js-l_112-16.bin from 172.16.I6.2 to flash ...

System flash directory:
File  Length   Name/status
  1   8034308  c2500-js-l_112-11.bin
[8034372 bytes used, 8742844 available, 16777216 total]
Accessing file 'c2500-js-l_112-16.bin' on 172.16.16.2...
Loading c2500-js-l_112-16.bin .from 172.16.16.2 (via Ethernet0): ! [OK]

Erasing device... eeeeeeeeeeeeeeeeeeeeeeeeeeeeeeeeeeeeeeeeeeeeeeeeeeeeeeeeeeeeee
ee ...erased                          ←Flash is erased
Loading c2500-js-l_112-16.bin from 172.16.16.2 (via Ethernet0): !!!!!!!!!!!!!!!!!
<<<text omitted>>>
!!!!!!!!!!!!!!!!!!!!!!!!!!!!!!!!!!!!!!!!!!!!!!!!!!!!
[OK - 8102652/16777216 bytes]

Verifying checksum... OK (0x8DCB)
Flash copy took 0:04:40 [hh:mm:ss]
%FLH: Re-booting system after download
F3: 8004052+98568+315656 at 0x3000060
<<<text omitted>>>

00:00:23: %SYS-5-RESTART: System restarted --
Cisco Internetwork Operating System Software
IOS (tm) 2500 Software (C2500-JS-L), Version 11.2(16), RELEASE SOFTWARE (fc1)
```

Example 1-45 *Upgrading the IOS by Using TFTP (Continued)*

```
Copyright (c) 1986-1998 by cisco Systems, Inc.
Compiled Tue 06-Oct-98 11:54 by ashah
rosewell>show flash

System flash directory:
File  Length   Name/status
  1   8102652  c2500-js-l_112-16.bin            ←New IOS
[8102716 bytes used, 8674500 available, 16777216 total]
16384K bytes of processor board System flash (Read ONLY)

rosewell>
```

After the Flash download, the router verifies the checksum of the file before reloading. At the end of the example, you perform a **show flash** command to verify that the new IOS is place.

The second part of the lab requires you to copy the startup-configuration from the router ufo, modify it by changing the hostname to w-balloon, and then copy it back to its original location. To accomplish this, you use the **copy startup-config tftp** command and follow the prompts. Before you do this, it is always a good idea to ensure that the router can **ping** the TFTP server. Example 1-46 demonstrates the use of the **ping** and **copy** commands.

Example 1-46 *Copying the startup-config to a TFTP Server*

```
ufo#ping 172.16.16.254

Type escape sequence to abort.
Sending 5, 100-byte ICMP Echos to 172.16.16.254, timeout is 2 seconds:
!!!!!
Success rate is 100 percent (5/5), round-trip min/avg/max = 1/1/4 ms
ufo#copy startup-config tftp
Remote host []? 172.16.16.254
Name of configuration file to write [ufo-confg]?        ←---- carriage return
Write file ufo-confg on host 172.16.16.254? [confirm]y
Writing ufo-confg !! [OK]
ufo#
```

It is important to note that, as its name implies, TFTP is trivial. That means that TFTP has no way of overwriting files or prompting the user for input after the copy process begins. If you tried this same procedure again, you would get an error because the file already exists from your first copy. You might or might not experience this error; some versions of TFTP have options that automatically overwrite the existing file if it exists. Example 1-47 demonstrates the error when a duplicate file is found and cannot be overwritten.

Example 1-47 *TFTP Copy Error, Duplicate File Found*

```
ufo#copy startup-config tftp
Remote host []? 172.16.16.254
Name of configuration file to write [ufo-confg]?        ←---- carriage return
Write file ufo-confg on host 172.16.16.254? [confirm]y
Writing ufo-confg
TFTP: error code 0 received - File exists
 [Failed]
ufo#
```

When the file is successfully copied to your PC, use Microsoft Wordpad to edit it. Locate the HOSTNAME field and change ufo to w-balloon. Finally, copy the file back to the router by using the **copy tftp startup-config** command. When the file is copied back to the router, you might want to view it; this can be done using the **show startup-config** command. To activate the new configuration, either reload the router or perform the **copy startup-config running-config** command. When this is done, the host name should be changed from ufo to w-balloon. Example 1-48 demonstrates this process.

Example 1-48 *Copy Configurations from a TFTP Server*

```
ufo#copy tftp startup-config
Address of remote host [255.255.255.255]? 172.16.16.254
Name of configuration file [ufo-confg]?
Configure using ufo-confg from 172.16.16.254? [confirm]y
Loading ufo-confg from 172.16.16.254 (via Ethernet0): !
[OK - 564/32723 bytes]
[OK]
ufo#
%SYS-5-CONFIG_NV: Non-volatile store configured from ufo-confg by console tftp f
rom 172.16.16.254

ufo#show startup-config
Using 564 out of 32762 bytes
!
version 11.2
no service password-encryption
no service udp-small-servers
no service tcp-small-servers
!
```

Example 1-48 *Copy Configurations from a TFTP Server (Continued)*

```
hostname W-BALLOON
!
interface Ethernet0
 ip address 172.16.16.2 255.255.255.0
 no ip route-cache
 no ip mroute-cache
!
interface Serial0
 no ip address
 no ip route-cache
 no ip mroute-cache
!
interface Serial1
 no ip address
ufo#
```

Lab 4: Configuring an Access Server—Part I

Practical Scenario

An access server provides out-of-band management to an entire stack of routers. This can provide an easy method of configuring access to a variety of Cisco routers and switches from a single device.

Lab Exercise

In this practical exercise, you configure an access server for reverse Telnet access to all the routers and switches in your rack. This enables you to configure multiple routers and switches without having to manually switch the console cable between them.

Lab Objectives

- Add a loopback interface to the access router. This address should be 201.201.1.1.
- Configure an IP host table so that the following exists:
  - Hostname r1 performs a reverse Telnet to the first router in your stack.
  - Hostname r2 performs a reverse Telnet to the second router in your stack, and so on.
- Minimize contention for the asynchronous lines.
- Prevent router sessions from timing out on all remote routers.

Equipment Needed

- Two Cisco routers and one Cisco 2509-2511, or a 2600 series router with an asynchronous module for the access server. The access server also requires the octal cable.

Physical Layout and Prestaging

- One workstation connected by its COM port to a Cisco 2509-2511, through Cisco black or light-blue rolled cable is required.
- Connect the octal cable labeled 1 to an R1 or the first router's console port. Repeat this process for every router or switch in lab.

Lab 4: Configuring an Access Server—Part II

Lab Walkthrough

After connecting all the console ports to the octal cable of your access server, you can begin to configure the access server to support reverse Telnet sessions. To configure a reverse Telnet session, you need to know what the absolute or line entry numbers are for the TTY lines that you are working on. To display the line entries, perform the **show line** command. In Example 1-49, the line entries are from 1 to 16 for the TTY session. You have two to five routers in this lab, so you use the values 2001 to 2005 for a Telnet port on reverse Telnet sessions.

Example 1-49 *Display of the* **show line** *command*

```
Router#show line
 Tty Typ    Tx/Rx     A Modem  Roty AccO AccI   Uses   Noise   Overruns   Int
*   0 CTY              -   -      -    -    -      0      1      0/0        -
    1 TTY   9600/9600  -   -      -    -    -      0      0      0/0        -
    2 TTY   9600/9600  -   -      -    -    -      0      1      0/0        -
    3 TTY   9600/9600  -   -      -    -    -      0      0      0/0        -
    4 TTY   9600/9600  -   -      -    -    -      0      0      0/0        -
    5 TTY   9600/9600  -   -      -    -    -      0      0      0/0        -
    6 TTY   9600/9600  -   -      -    -    -      0      1      0/0        -
*   7 TTY   9600/9600  -   -      -    -    -      0      2      0/0        -
    8 TTY   9600/9600  -   -      -    -    -      0      0      0/0        -
    9 TTY   9600/9600  -   -      -    -    -      0      0      0/0        -
   10 TTY   9600/9600  -   -      -    -    -      0      0      0/0        -
   11 TTY   9600/9600  -   -      -    -    -      0      0      0/0        -
   12 TTY   9600/9600  -   -      -    -    -      0      0      0/0        -
   13 TTY   9600/9600  -   -      -    -    -      0      0      0/0        -
   14 TTY   9600/9600  -   -      -    -    -      0      0      0/0        -
   15 TTY   9600/9600  -   -      -    -    -      0      0      0/0        -
   16 TTY   9600/9600  -   -      -    -    -      0      0      0/0        -
   17 AUX   9600/9600  -   -      -    -    -      0      0      0/0        -
   18 VTY              -   -      -    -    -      0      0      0/0        -
   19 VTY              -   -      -    -    -      0      0      0/0        -
   20 VTY              -   -      -    -    -      0      0      0/0        -
   21 VTY              -   -      -    -    -      0      0      0/0        -
 Tty Typ    Tx/Rx     A Modem  Roty AccO AccI   Uses   Noise   Overruns   Int

   22 VTY              -   -      -    -    -      0      0      0/0        -

Router#
```

Now that you know the absolute line values, you can configure the access server to support reverse Telnet. From the configuration mode, enter a host name of **access-server**, followed by the lines that you need for the reverse Telnet sessions. Enter **ip host r1 200*x* 201.201.1.1**, where *x* ranges from 1 to 5. You also need to add a Loopback 0 interface with an IP address of 201.201.1.1/24. Example 1-50 illustrates this process.

Example 1-50 *Configuration of IP Host Names for Reverse Telnet Sessions*

```
Router#
Router#conf t
Enter configuration commands, one per line.  End with CNTL/Z.
Router(config)#hostname access-server
access-server(config)#ip host r1 2001 201.201.1.1
access-server(config)#ip host r2 2002 201.201.1.1
access-server(config)#ip host r3 2002 201.201.1.1
access-server(config)#ip host r3 2003 201.201.1.1
access-server(config)#ip host r4 2004 201.201.1.1
access-server(config)#ip host r5 2005 201.201.1.1
access-server(config)#interface loopback 0
access-server(config-if)#ip address 201.201.1.1 255.255.255.0
access-server(config-if)#exit
access-server(config)#
```

The final part of configuring an access server involves configuring the line entries to support reverse Telnet. This can be accomplished by adding **transport input all** on the appropriate lines. In this particular lab, we will go one step further and reduce contention for the line by adding the **no exec** command. This is only for convenience, and it is not a requirement of configuring a reverse Telnet session. Example 1-51 completes the access server's configuration for reverse Telnet.

Example 1-51 *Configuring the Absolute Lines for Support of Reverse Telnet, and Disabling the Exec*

```
access-server(config)#line 1 5
access-server(config-line)#transport input all
access-server(config-line)#no exec
access-server(config-line)#^Z
access-server#
```

To test the configuration, simply key in **r1**, and a session opens to R1. If this session is rejected, be sure to perform a **clear line** *x*, where *x* is the absolute line number of the session that was rejected. Example 1-52 lists the entire configuration of the access server.

Example 1-52 *Complete Listing of a Router Configured as an Access Server*

```
access-server#wr t
Building configuration...

Current configuration:
!
version 12.0
service timestamps debug uptime
service timestamps log uptime
```

Example 1-52 *Complete Listing of a Router Configured as an Access Server (Continued)*

```
no service password-encryption
!
hostname access-server
!
ip subnet-zero
ip host r1 2001 201.201.1.1
ip host r2 2002 201.201.1.1
ip host r3 2003 201.201.1.1
ip host r4 2004 201.201.1.1
ip host r5 2005 201.201.1.1
!
 interface Loopback0
 ip address 201.201.1.1 255.255.255.0
 no ip directed-broadcast
!
interface Ethernet0
 no ip address
 no ip directod-broadcast
 shutdown
!
interface Serial0
 no ip address
 no ip directed-broadcast
 no ip mroute-cache
 shutdown
!
interface Serial1
 no ip address
 no ip directed-broadcast
 shutdown
!
ip classless
!
line con 0
 transport input none
line 1 5
 no exec
 transport input all
line 6 16
line aux 0
line vty 0 4
!
end

access-server#
```

The final part of the lab instructed you to configure the Telnet session so that it would not time out after a period of inactivity. To accomplish this, add the command **no exec-timeout** on Line 0, the console port of the routers connected to the access server. Adding this command forces the routers not to time out the console port and log you off because of inactivity.

Lab 5: Configuring a Frame Relay Switch—Part I

Practical Scenario

A Frame Relay switch can be of great service both in the field and in practice. A Frame Relay switch can be deployed in a lab to help model Frame Relay services that are similar to a production environment.

Lab Exercise

In this practical exercise, you configure a multipoint fully meshed Frame Relay network. This lab focuses only on the switching aspects of Frame Relay, not on the end or DTE devices.

Lab Objectives

- Configure a Cisco router to perform a Frame Relay switching function, as depicted in Figure 1-17.
- Configure all PVCs with ANSI LMI as the diagram depicts. The PVC mapping is as follows:
    - DLCI 112 maps to DLCI 21.
    - DLCI 113 maps to DLCI 31.
    - DLCI 32 maps to DLCI 23.

Equipment Needed

- Three Cisco routers with serial ports and one other Cisco router to perform the role of the Frame Relay switch. The Frame Relay switch must have three usable serial ports.
- A total of six serial cables, or three sets of DTE-to-DCE serial cables.

Physical Layout and Prestaging

Figure 1-17 shows the physical layout for this lab.

Figure 1-17 *Lab 5: Physical Layout for Frame Relay Switching*

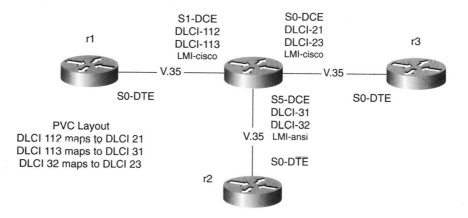

Lab 5: Configuring a Frame Relay Switch—Part II

Lab Walkthrough

The Frame Relay switch in this lab functions as a fully meshed Frame Relay service. A fully meshed Frame Relay service has a PVC not only to a central site, but also to every other site. This can lead to several scaling problems when a large number of sites are involved. Some Layer 3 routing issues, such as split horizons, also can occur on a multipoint network. Chapter 5 discusses this in more depth.

To configure Frame Relay switching, you need to perform the following tasks:

Step 1   Enable Frame Relay switching.

Step 2   Configure interface LMI and Frame Relay interface type.

Step 3   Configure PVCs with the **frame-relay route** command.

First, enable Frame Relay switching using the **frame-relay switching** global command from configuration mode. Second, configure the serial interfaces for Frame Relay switching, as shown in Figure 1-17. To perform this, use the **encapsulation frame-relay** command, along with the commands **frame-relay intf-type dce** command and **frame-relay lmi-type ansi** on serial Interface 5. Example 1-53 highlights the Frame Relay switch configuration.

Example 1-53 *Frame Relay Multipoint Configuration*

```
hostname frame_switch
!

frame-relay switching              ←-Enables Frame Relay switching
!
interface Ethernet0
 no ip address
 shutdown
!
interface Serial0
 no ip address
 encapsulation frame-relay          ←Sets Frame encapsulation
 clockrate 56000    ←Sets the clockrate, needed for DCE interface
 frame-relay intf-type dce          ←Sets Frame Relay to a DCE interface
 frame-relay route 21 interface Serial1 112    ←Creates and maps DLCI 21 to DLCI
112 on Serial 1
 frame-relay route 23 interface Serial5 32    ←Creates and maps DLCI 23 to DLCI 32
on Serial 5
!
interface Serial1
 no ip address
 encapsulation frame-relay
 clockrate 56000
 frame-relay intf-type dce
```

Example 1-53 *Frame Relay Multipoint Configuration (Continued)*

```
 frame-relay route 112 interface Serial0 21        ←Creates and maps DLCI 112 to DLCI
21 on Serial 0
 frame-relay route 113 interface Serial5 31        ←Creates and maps DLCI 113 to DLCI
31 on Serial 5
 !
<<<text omitted>>>
 !
interface Serial5
 no ip address
 encapsulation frame-relay
 clockrate 56000
 frame-relay lmi-type ansi                ←Sets the LMI type to ANSI versus Cisco
 frame-relay intf-type dce
 frame-relay route 31 interface Serial1 113        ←Creates and maps DLCI 31 to DLCI
113 on Serial 1
 frame-relay route 32 interface Serial0 23        ←Creates and maps DLCI 32 to DLCI 23
on Serial 0
 !
<<<text omitted>>>
end
```

To see if your Frame Relay switch is working, you need to configure the DTE, or router side of the network. When this is complete, the PVCs will become "active." Example 1-54 illustrates the Frame Relay configuration of R1, R2, and R3.

Example 1-54 *The Significant Configuration Portions of R1, R2, and R3*

```
hostname r1
!
interface Serial0
 ip address 172.16.17.1 255.255.255.0
 encapsulation frame-relay
 frame-relay map ip 172.16.17.2 112 broadcast
 frame-relay map ip 172.16.17.3 113 broadcast
!

hostname r2
!
interface Serial0
 ip address 172.16.17.2 255.255.255.0
 no ip directed-broadcast
 encapsulation frame-relay
 no ip mroute-cache
 frame-relay map ip 172.16.17.1 21 broadcast
 frame-relay map ip 172.16.17.3 23 broadcast
!

hostname r3
```

continues

Example 1-54 *The Significant Configuration Portions of R1, R2, and R3 (Continued)*

```
!
interface Serial0
 ip address 172.16.17.3 255.255.255.0
 no ip directed-broadcast
 encapsulation frame-relay
 no ip mroute-cache
 frame-relay map ip 172.16.17.1 31 broadcast
 frame-relay map ip 172.16.17.2 32 broadcast
 frame-relay lmi-type ansi
!
```

When this is complete, enter the **show frame-relay route** command to ensure that all connections are up and active. Also verify that LMI is correctly configured with the **show frame-relay lmi** command. These two commands manifest themselves in Example 1-55.

Example 1-55 *The **show frame-relay route** and **show frame-relay lmi** Commands*

```
frame_switch#show frame-relay route
Input Intf      Input Dlci     Output Intf     Output Dlci    Status
Serial0         21             Serial1         112            active
Serial0         23             Serial5         32             active
Serial1         112            Serial0         21             active
Serial1         113            Serial5         31             active
Serial5         31             Serial1         113            active
Serial5         32             Serial0         23             active
frame_switch#
frame_switch#show frame-relay lmi

LMI Statistics for interface Serial0 (Frame Relay DCE) LMI TYPE = CISCO
  Invalid Unnumbered info 0        Invalid Prot Disc 0
  Invalid dummy Call Ref 0         Invalid Msg Type 0
  Invalid Status Message 0         Invalid Lock Shift 0
  Invalid Information ID 0         Invalid Report IE Len 0
  Invalid Report Request 0         Invalid Keep IE Len 0
  Num Status Enq. Rcvd 188         Num Status msgs Sent 188
  Num Update Status Sent 0         Num St Enq. Timeouts 0

LMI Statistics for interface Serial1 (Frame Relay DCE) LMI TYPE = CISCO
  Invalid Unnumbered info 0        Invalid Prot Disc 0
  Invalid dummy Call Ref 0         Invalid Msg Type 0
  Invalid Status Message 0         Invalid Lock Shift 0
  Invalid Information ID 0         Invalid Report IE Len 0
  Invalid Report Request 0         Invalid Keep IE Len 0
  Num Status Enq. Rcvd 188         Num Status msgs Sent 188
  Num Update Status Sent 0         Num St Enq. Timeouts 0
```

Example 1-55 *The* **show frame-relay route** *and* **show frame-relay lmi** *Commands (Continued)*

```
LMI Statistics for interface Serial5 (Frame Relay DCE) LMI TYPE = ANSI
  Invalid Unnumbered info 0        Invalid Prot Disc 0
  Invalid dummy Call Ref 0         Invalid Msg Type 0
  Invalid Status Message 0         Invalid Lock Shift 0
  Invalid Information ID 0         Invalid Report IE Len 0
  Invalid Report Request 0         Invalid Keep IE Len 0
  Num Status Enq. Rcvd 185         Num Status msgs Sent 185
  Num Update Status Sent 0         Num St Enq. Timeouts 1
frame_switch#
```

Lab 6: Configuring Remote Access to the Lab—Part I

Practical Scenario

Attaching a modem to an auxiliary port or an asynchronous line provides a useful out-of-band method of management for routers and switches. You can provide a complete "configuration safety net" for your network with the placement of an access server at a central site. The access server would connect the console ports of all the routers at the central site; when combined with an analog modem, this provides a reliable method of access to your network.

Lab Exercise

This is the final lab of Chapter 1, and it serves as the springboard for all the other labs in this text. From this point on, you use this access server to configure the routers in the lab. To further enhance access to the lab, you add a modem to the last asynchronous port on the access server. This device serves as a key device in modeling some of the most complex internetworks known today. Therefore, the name Skynet is used to give the access server and models some character.

Lab Objectives

- Refer to Figure 1-18, and cable the access server as shown.
- Configure a reverse Telnet session from the access server to all the routers attached to Octal cable. Use an IP host-name table to ease the use of reverse Telnet sessions.
- Configure the modem on the asynchronous line to accept an analog dialup session into the router.

Equipment Needed

- One Cisco 2509-2511, Cisco 2600, or Cisco 3600 for the access server, along with the asynchronous module and octal cable.
- One to five other routers. (Only one is needed to complete this lab.)
- One analog modem, modem head-shell, and Cisco rolled cable.

Physical Layout and Prestaging

Asynchronous connections should be connected as noted in Figure 1-18.

Figure 1-18 *Lab 6: Physical Layout*

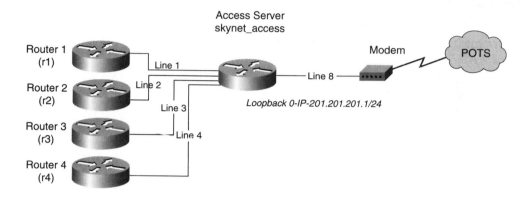

Lab 6: Configuring Remote Access to the Lab—Part II

Lab Walkthrough

The first step in configuring Skynet is to attach the routers and the modem as indicated in Figure 1-18. After attaching all the physical devices, verify what absolute line they exist on through the **show line** command, as demonstrated in Example 1-56. Note the column on the left side—the asynchronous lines are the ones denoted as TTY.

Example 1-56 *The* **show line** *Command Performed on the Access Server*

```
Router#show line
  Tty Typ     Tx/Rx      A Modem  Roty AccO AccI   Uses   Noisc  Overruns   Int
*   0 CTY                 -   -      -    -    -      0      0      0/0        -
    1 TTY     9600/9600   -   -      -    -    -      0      0      0/0        -
*   2 TTY     9600/9600   -   -      -    -    -      0      1     37/110      -
*   3 TTY     9600/9600   -   -      -    -    -      0      1      3/11       -
    4 TTY     9600/9600   -   -      -    -    -      0      1      0/0        -
    5 TTY     9600/9600   -   -      -    -    -      0      1      0/0        -
    6 TTY     9600/9600   -   -      -    -    -      0      1      0/0        -
    7 TTY     9600/9600   -   -      -    -    -      0      0      0/0        -
    8 TTY     9600/9600   -   -      -    -    -      0      0      0/0        -
    9 TTY     9600/9600   -   -      -    -    -      0      0      0/0        -
   10 TTY     9600/9600   -   -      -    -    -      0      0      0/0        -
   11 TTY     9600/9600   -   -      -    -    -      0      0      0/0        -
   12 TTY     9600/9600   -   -      -    -    -      0      0      0/0        -
   13 TTY     9600/9600   -   -      -    -    -      0      0      0/0        -
   14 TTY     9600/9600   -   -      -    -    -      0      0      0/0        -
   15 TTY     9600/9600   -   -      -    -    -      0      0      0/0        -
   16 TTY     9600/9600   -   -      -    -    -      0      0      0/0        -
   17 AUX     9600/9600   -   -      -    -    -      0      0      0/0        -
   18 VTY                 -   -      -    -    -      0      0      0/0        -
   19 VTY                 -   -      -    -    -      0      0      0/0        -
   20 VTY                 -   -      -    -    -      0      0      0/0        -
   21 VTY                 -   -      -    -    -      0      0      0/0        -
  Tty Typ     Tx/Rx      A Modem  Roty AccO AccI   Uses   Noise  Overruns   Int

   22 VTY                 -   -      -    -    -      0      0      0/0        -

Router#
```

Lines 1 through 4 are the TTY lines to which you have attached the routers. Therefore, you need to add the following to these lines:

- **transport input all**
- **no exec**

To make reverse Telnet sessions easier to open, you add a host table for each router, pointing to ports 2001 through 2004. To facilitate the reverse Telnet session, you also need to add a loopback interface. Example 1-57 shows the configuration of skynet_access.

Example 1-57 *Initial Configuration of the Access Server Called skynet_access*

```
Router#conf t
Enter configuration commands, one per line.  End with CNTL/Z.
Router(config)#hostname skynet_access
skynet_access(config)#interface loopback 0                    ← Configuring the
skynet_access(config-if)#ip address 201.201.201.1 255.255.255.0    ← loopback
interface
skynet_access(config-if)#exit
skynet_access(config)#
skynet_access(config)#ip host r1 2001 201.201.201.1          ← Configure the IP
skynet_access(config)#ip host r2 2002 201.201.201.1          ← host table
skynet_access(config)#ip host r3 2003 201.201.201.1
skynet_access(config)#ip host r4 2004 201.201.201.1
skynet_access(config)#ip host modem 2005 201.201.201.1
skynet_access(config)#
skynet_access(config)#line 1 4                               ← Configuring the
skynet_access(config-line)#transport input all                 ← the line entries to
skynet_access(config-line)#no exec                          ← support telnet
skynet_access(config-line)#^Z
skynet_access#
```

To complete the lab, you must configure Line 5 for a modem. To accomplish this task, add the following to Line 5:

- **transport input all**
- **modem inout**
- **modem autoconfigure discovery**

In Example 1-58, you add the preceding commands to Line 5. Be sure to also include an enable password—without this, the remote session will not be capable of entering privilege mode to configure the router.

After adding the new commands, perform the **show line** command, followed by the **show line 5** command. In the resulting output, look for Line 5 to be configured as a modem. Also ensure that the modem is correctly configured and that CTS is detected.

Example 1-58 *The Line Configuration for a Modem and* **show line** *Command in Use*

```
skynet_access(config)#
skynet_access(config)#enable password cisco                 ← Allows privileged access
skynet_access(config)#line 5
skynet_access(config-line)#transport input all              ← Allows terminal sessions
skynet_access(config-line)#modem inout                    ← Configures the modem
skynet_access(config-line)#modem autoconfigure discovery    ← for autodetection
```

continues

Example 1-58 *The Line Configuration for a Modem and* **show line** *Command in Use (Continued)*

```
skynet_access(config)#^Z
skynet_access#


skynet_access#show line
 Tty Typ     Tx/Rx      A Modem  Roty AccO AccI  Uses   Noise  Overruns   Int
*   0 CTY                -   -      -    -    -     0      0      0/0       -
    1 TTY     9600/9600  -   -      -    -    -     0      0      0/0       -
*   2 TTY     9600/9600  -   -      -    -    -     0      1    145/437     -
*   3 TTY     9600/9600  -   -      -    -    -     0      1    109/328     -
    4 TTY     9600/9600  -   -      -    -    -     0      1      0/0       -
    5 TTY 115200/115200- inout     -    -    -     0      1      0/0       -
    6 TTY     9600/9600  -   -      -    -    -     0      1      0/0       -
    7 TTY     9600/9600  -   -      -    -    -     0      0      0/0       -
    8 TTY     9600/9600  -   -      -    -    -     0      0      0/0       -
    9 TTY     9600/9600  -   -      -    -    -     0      0      0/0       -
   10 TTY     9600/9600  -   -      -    -    -     0      0      0/0       -
   11 TTY     9600/9600  -   -      -    -    -     0      0      0/0       -
   12 TTY     9600/9600  -   -      -    -    -     0      0      0/0       -
   13 TTY     9600/9600  -   -      -    -    -     0      0      0/0       -
   14 TTY     9600/9600  -   -      -    -    -     0      0      0/0       -
   15 TTY     9600/9600  -   -      -    -    -     0      0      0/0       -
   16 TTY     9600/9600  -   -      -    -    -     0      0      0/0       -
   17 AUX     9600/9600  -   -      -    -    -     0      0      0/0       -
   18 VTY                -   -      -    -    -     0      0      0/0       -
   19 VTY                -   -      -    -    -     0      0      0/0       -
   20 VTY                -   -      -    -    -     0      0      0/0       -
   21 VTY                -   -      -    -    -     0      0      0/0       -
 Tty Typ     Tx/Rx      A Modem  Roty AccO AccI  Uses   Noise  Overruns   Int

   22 VTY                -   -      -    -    -     0      0      0/0       -

skynet_access#show line 5
 Tty Typ     Tx/Rx      A Modem  Roty AccO AccI  Uses   Noise  Overruns   Int
    5 TTY 115200/115200- inout     -    -    -     0      1      0/0       -

Line 5, Location: "", Type: ""
Length: 24 lines, Width: 80 columns
Baud rate (TX/RX) is 115200/115200, no parity, 2 stopbits, 8 databits
Status: No Exit Banner, Modem Detected
Capabilities: Modem Callout, Modem RI is CD, Modem Discovery
Modem state: Idle
Group codes:    0
Modem hardware state: CTS noDSR  DTR RTS, Modem Configured
Special Chars: Escape  Hold  Stop  Start  Disconnect  Activation
               ^^x      none   -     -       none
Timeouts:      Idle EXEC     Idle Session   Modem Answer  Session   Dispatch
               00:10:00        never                       none     not set
                             Idle Session Disconnect Warning
                               never
                             Login-sequence User Response
                               00:00:30
```

Example 1-58 *The Line Configuration for a Modem and* **show line** *Command in Use (Continued)*

```
                              Autoselect Initial Wait
                                 not set
  Modem type is usr_sportster.
  Session limit is not set.
  Time since activation: never
  Editing is enabled.
  History is enabled, history size is 10.
  DNS resolution in show commands is enabled
  Full user help is disabled
  Allowed transports are lat pad v120 mop telnet rlogin nasi.  Preferred is lat.
  No output characters are padded
  No special data dispatching characters
  skynet_access#
```

When the configuration is complete, you can test it by making an analog connection by using HyperTerminal or another terminal emulator, such as ProComm.

From this point on, the configuration of the access server will remain fairly static. You should have access to all the routers in the stack through reverse Telnet, along with analog access to the lab.

You now should have the groundwork necessary to begin practical studies in internetworking.

Modeling LANs

CHAPTER 2

LAN Protocols: Configuring Catalyst Ethernet and Token Ring Switches

In the realm of networking, no technology is outpacing that of local-area networks (LANs). In less than a decade, LANs have become common in many homes and are a "must" for any small business. Many, if not all, new commercial buildings are wired with some type of copper or fiber cable plant for local-area networking. Even when you travel, many hotels offer the use of a LAN to access the Internet. Many new residential communities are incorporating what you might call *community-area networks*, or CANs, in which homes will be connected through LANs to provide Internet service or another related service.

Not only is the number of LANs multiplying, but bandwidth also is multiplying exponentially. The standards that have been written and adopted for LAN protocols in the last 10 years have been tremendous. For example, in March 2002, 10-Gb Ethernet, 802.3ae, is scheduled for formal ratification, and 100-Gb Ethernet seems inevitable. To put leaps in technology like this in perspective, we use the less than scientific "Twinkie Theory." If a Twinkie represents the bandwidth available on a 10-Mb Ethernet network, a 10-Gb Ethernet network would be a Twinkie roughly 333 feet long and 100 feet tall—now that's a big Twinkie!

NOTE   A *community-area network (CAN)* can be defined as one or more personal homes sharing a common networking architecture.

LAN protocols have changed rapidly, and there have been many winners and losers in the battle for the LAN. Standards such as 100VG AnyLAN never were fully adapted, whereas other LAN protocols, such as FDDI II, have had all development halted. Ethernet currently dominates the vast majority of the market share, with some estimates putting it at more than 90 percent. Although Token Ring networks are not nearly as plentiful as Ethernet Networks, they still are found at most major data centers running IBM mainframes. For these reasons, this text focuses primarily on Ethernet and Token Ring LANs and switching. Specifically, we will discuss Ethernet and Token Ring LANs, and the configuration of Catalyst 4000/5500/6500, Catalyst 2900XL/3500, and Catalyst 2900 families of switches.

Ethernet LANs

Ethernet: A Brief History of an Evolutionary Protocol

Ethernet's history is colorful. Its conception occurred at the Xerox Palo Alto Research Center (PARC), developed by Bob Metcalfe in 1972. In 1979, Digital Equipment Corp., Intel, and Xerox standardized the DIX V1.0 frame; two years later, they refined it with the Version 2.0 frame. In 1981, the Institute of Electrical and Electronic Engineers (IEEE) project 802 decided to form the 802.3 subcommittee, which is almost synonymous with the Ethernet that we know today. Table 2-1 provides a great description of the evolution of the Ethernet standard; this standard can be found in its original form in *Switched, Fast, and Gigabit Ethernet*, 3rd edition, by Robert Breyer and Sean Riley.

Breyer and Riley refer to Ethernet as an evolutionary protocol versus a revolutionary protocol. Evolutionary innovations build on the current installed base and provide some form of migration path. As a revolutionary protocol, it will have some form of radical breakthrough that usually does not build on the current infrastructure. Ethernet is more than 25 years old and still is building a clear future for local-area networks. For further reading on the history of Ethernet, the 100-Mbps wars, and Gigabit Ethernet standards, see *Switched, Fast, and Gigabit Ethernet*, 3rd edition, by Robert Breyer and Sean Riley.

NOTE   The IEEE name convention works in the following manner. In the name 10Base-T, the 10 indicates the transmission speed in megabytes per second. The Base indicates baseband transmission. The *T* stands for unshielded twisted-pair cable, while *F* stands for "fiber." Early versions of Ethernet used a number to indicate cable segment length, such as 10Base-5 and 10Base-2, but this naming convention had to be dropped because of Ethernet's capability to have multiple cable lengths running on the same standard.

Table 2-1   *Evolution of the Ethernet Standard*

Colloquial Ethernet Standard	Official Ethernet Abbreviation	IEEE Spec. Supplement	Speed (Mbps)	LAN Topology	Segment Length in Meters	Medium Support
Thick Ethernet	10Base-5	802.3	10 Mbps	Bus	500 m	50-ohm coaxial (thick)
Thin Ethernet/Thinnet	10Base-2	802.3a	10 Mbps	Bus	185 m	50-ohm coaxial (thin)
Broadband Ethernet	10Broad-36	802.3b	10 Mbps	Bus	1800 m	75-ohm coaxial
10-Mbps Repeaters	Repeaters	802.3c	10 Mbps	Bus	—	50-ohm coaxial (thick/thin)
Fiber-optic Inter-Repeater Link	FOIRL	802.3d	10 Mbps	Star	1000 m	Optical fiber
StarLAN	1Base-5	802.3e	1 Mbps	Star	250 m	100-ohm two-pair Cat 3-UTP
StarLAN Multipoint	1Base-5	802.3f	1 Mbps	Star	250 m	100-ohm two-pair Cat 3-UTP
Layer Management		802.3h	10 Mbps	—	—	—
Twisted-Pair Ethernet	10Base-T	802.3i	10 Mbps	Star	100 m	100-ohm two-pair Cat 3
Fiber Ethernet	10Base-F	802.3j	10 Mbps	Star/bus	< 2000 m	Optical fiber
Layer Management for 10-Mbps Repeaters		802.3k	10 Mbps	Star	—	—

continues

Table 2-1 *Evolution of the Ethernet Standard (Continued)*

Colloquial Ethernet Standard	Official Ethernet Abbreviation	IEEE Spec. Supplement	Speed (Mbps)	LAN Topology	Segment Length in Meters	Medium Support
10Base-T Protocol Implementation Conformance Statement (PICS)	10Base-T PICS	802.3i	10 Mbps	Star	< 2000 m	Multimode or single-mode fiber
Second Maintenance Ballot		802.3m	10 Mbps	—	—	—
Third Maintenance Ballot		802.3n	10 Mbps	—	—	—
Layer Management for MAUs		802.3p	10 Mbps	—	—	—
Guidelines for Development of Managed Objects (GDMO)		802.3q	—	—	—	—
10Base-5 PICS	10Base-5 PICS	802.3r	10 Mbps	—	—	—
Fourth Maintenance Ballot		802.3s	10 Mbps	—	—	—
120-Ohm Cables for 10Base-T		802.3t	10 Mbps	—	100 m	120-ohm two-pair Cat 3 UTP
Fast Ethernet	100Base-TX	802.3u	100 Mbps	Star	100 m	100-ohm two-pair Cat 5 UTP
Fast Ethernet over Cat 3	100Base-T4	802.3u	100 Mbps	Star	100 m	100-ohm four-pair Cat 3 UTP

Table 2-1 *Evolution of the Ethernet Standard (Continued)*

Colloquial Ethernet Standard	Official Ethernet Abbreviation	IEEE Spec. Supplement	Speed (Mbps)	LAN Topology	Segment Length in Meters	Medium Support
Fast Ethernet over Fiber	100Base-FX	802.3u	100 Mbps	Star	< 2000 m	Optical fiber
150-Ohm Cables for 10Base-T		802.3v	10 Mbps	—	100 m	150-ohm two-pair Cat 3 UTP
Enhanced MAC or Binary Logarithmic Arbitration Method	BLAM	802.3w	—	—	—	—
Full-Duplex/Flow Control	FDX	802.3x	10 Mbps	—	—	—
Fast Ethernet over Two-Pair Cat 3	100Base-T2	802.3y	100 Mbps	Star		100-ohm two-pair Cat 3 UTP
Gigabit Ethernet Short Haul	1000Base-SX	802.3z	1000 Mbps	Star	300 m	Multimode fiber
Gigabit Ethernet Long Haul	1000Base-LX	802.3z	1000 Mbps	Star	550 m	Multimode fiber
Gigabit Ethernet	1000Base-CX	802.3z	1000 Mbps	Star	3000 m 25 m	Single-mode fiber Twin-ax 150-ohm copper
Fifth Maintenance Ballot	100Base-T	802.3aa	100 Mbps	—	—	—

continues

Table 2-1 *Evolution of the Ethernet Standard (Continued)*

Colloquial Ethernet Standard	Official Ethernet Abbreviation	IEEE Spec. Supplement	Speed (Mbps)	LAN Topology	Segment Length in Meters	Medium Support
Gigabit Ethernet for Cat 5	1000Base-T	802.3ab	1000 Mbps	Star	100 m	Cat 5 UTP Cat 5e
VLAN Frame Extension	VLAN	802.3ac	—	—	—	—
Trunking	Link aggregation	802.3ad	—	—	—	—
10 Gigabit Ethernet*	10000Base	802.3ae	10,000 Mbps	Star	100 m–300 m 2 km–40 km	Multimode fiber Single-mode fiber
VLAN Tagging	VLAN tagging	802.1Q	—	—	—	—
Secure Data Exchange SDE	Secure VLANs	802.10	—	—	—	—
Traffic Expediting	Priority switching	802.1p	—	—	—	—
MAC Bridges, Spanning Tree	MAC bridges	802.1D	—	—	—	—

* 802.ae is not in its final form, but the drafts indicate these operating specifications.

Ethernet Technical Overview

Ethernet is extremely popular, and many fine books and whitepapers have been written on it. For these reasons, we assume that you have some background in Ethernet technology; therefore, this chapter does not cover Ethernet frames, hubs, and cables in any great length. You should become familiar with the different Ethernet frame types, DIX Version II, and 802.2 frames, as well as the different media types used in Ethernet. This chapter instead focuses more on Spanning Tree, Fast Ethernet, Gigabit Ethernet, and Ethernet and Token Ring switching.

Ethernet Operation

Ethernet operates at the OSI Layer 2, the data link layer. The data link layer actually is divided into two sublayers: the MAC layer and the Logical Link Control (LLC) layer. The LLC layer—802.2, in this case—is a standardized interface between a hardware-specific MAC and a Layer 3 protocol.

The MAC layer has the following responsibilities:

- Generating the physical source and destination address for a frame. These are 48-bit industry-wide unique addresses; the first 3 bytes are assigned by the IEEE, and the last 3 bytes are vendor-unique.

- Ensuring reliable transmissions.

- Synchronizing data transmissions.

- Performing error recognition.

- Performing flow control.

Table 2-2 lists the common physical characteristics of 10-Mbps, 10-Mbps, and 1000-Mbps Ethernet.

Table 2-2   *Common Ethernet Specifications*

Specification	10-Mbps	100-Mbps	1000-Mbps
Minimum frame	512 bits/64 bytes	512 bits/64 bytes	4096 bits/512 bytes
Bit time (μs)	0.1 μs	0.01 μs	0.001 μs
Maximum round-trip delay (μs)	51.2 μs	5.12 μs	4.096 μs
Maximum network diameter, with no repeaters (meters)	Approximately 45710 milleseconds	457 milleseconds	3661 milleseconds
Maximum number of repeaters in a collision domain	Approximately 5	1 Class I repeater or 2 Class II repeaters	1

Ethernet CSMA/CD

Ethernet technology commonly is referred to as carrier-sense multiple access collision detect (CSMA/CD). Ethernet transmits frames in the following manner:

1 **Carrier sense**—This also is known as "listen before talking." An Ethernet station wanting to transmit a frame listens to the medium before it transmits to ensure that the medium is available.

2 **Talk if quiet**—If the channel is quiet for a specific amount of time, the interframe gap (IFG) before the station might begin a transmission. If the channel is busy, it is monitored until it becomes free for the length of IFG timer; after that time, transmission might begin.

3 **Collision**—A collision is measured as an excess of voltage on the "cable" or medium. A collision usually is caused by two stations transmitting data at the same time. If a collision occurs, both frames are destroyed.

4 **Collision detection**—If a station detects a collision during transmission, that transmission immediately stops. A signal jam also is sent on the media to destroy any fragmented frames, preventing corrupted data.

5 **Backoff**—After a collision, a stations waits a period of time called the backoff period. The backoff timer is a random timer generated by a backoff algorithm. This prevents all stations from trying to transmit at the exact same time after a collision. After the backoff timer expires, the station attempts to retransmit the frame. If another collision happens, the station keeps trying to retransmit the frame for 16 times. After 16 unsuccessful attempts, the frame is dropped.

Half- and Full-Duplex Ethernet

Ethernet was developed on older coax type cables capable of transmitting or receiving a signal at any given time. This is precisely why Ethernet needed CSMA/CD technology. With the advent of switches, running Ethernet over UTP and fiber, full-duplex Ethernet became available. Full-duplex Ethernet allows a station to simultaneously transmit and receive data. Ethernet frames are transmitted and received simultaneously on two pairs of UTP or fiber at any given time. Full-duplex Ethernet is essentially Ethernet without CSMA/CD. Full-duplex mode basically doubles the bandwidth of Ethernet! To run full-duplex Ethernet, the station and switch both must be capable and configured for full-duplex operation. A hub with multiple stations cannot operate in full-duplex mode.

NOTE   A station not operating in the correct duplex mode will generate an enormous number of collisions on the port where it is located. These collisions mostly likely will be registered as "late collisions." Be sure that the port on the switch and the end station are operating in the same duplex mode.

Fast Ethernet

In May 1995, the IEEE adopted the Fast Ethernet standard, 802.3u. Years later, after battling FDDI, 100VG AnyLAN, and ATM, this standard became the prominent type of LAN. As costs per port dropped along with the prices of network interface cards (NICs), Fast Ethernet won out over FDDI and 100VG AnyLAN and ATM for many reasons:

- It allows a clean and inexpensive migration path from existing 10-Mbps Ethernet networks. At first, it could run only fiber and Cat 5 UTP, but as Table 2-1 indicates, it now can run over almost every media type.

- Fast Ethernet didn't require costly fiber connections and didn't require complex configurations.

- Fast Ethernet addresses QoS with enormous amounts of bandwidth, while relying on the upper layers or network design to provide QoS.

- Basically, Fast Ethernet became a plug-and-play tenfold upgrade of the LAN. 100-Mb networks evolved out of 10-Mb networks across data centers everywhere.

Some important features and specifications of Fast Ethernet are as follows:

- The 100Base MAC uses the original Ethernet MAC operating at 10 times the speed. This is completely backward compatible with 10-Mbps Ethernet.

- 100Base-T includes a specification for an MII interface. A MII interface is a 100-Mbps version of the AUI adapter.

- Fast Ethernet supports full- and half-duplex functionality.

- Fast Ethernet operates over a wide array of different physical layers: Cat 5, Cat 3, fiber, and so on, as listed in Table 1-2.

Gigabit Ethernet

The ink was hardly dry on the Fast Ethernet standard, and the IEEE started to work on the 802.3z, or Gigabit Ethernet, standard. Three short years later, in June 1998, the 802.3z standard officially was adopted. For the most part, the Gigabit standard is the Fast Ethernet standard multiplied by 10. This is why 10-Gb Ethernet products are right around the corner and 100-Gb Ethernet is an eventuality.

Some important features and specifications of Gigabit Ethernet are as follows:

- Gigabit Ethernet uses the 802.3 frame format, identical to that of 10-Mbps and 100-Mbps Ethernet.

- It includes a specification for a Gigabit MII (GMII). Unlike 10-Mbps Ethernet and 100-Mbps Ethernet, the GMII is an electrical specification and does not include a physical connector. Cisco's physical Gigabit interfaces are called *GBICs*. The type of GBIC determines the physical gigabit connection. There are currently multimode fiber (MMF), single-mode fiber (SMF), and UTP GBICs, as well as a Cisco proprietary GBIC called a *Gigastack*.

One element that makes Gigabit Ethernet one of the most versatile protocols in years is the concept of the GMII. Except for the strictly 1000Base-TX switches, most Gigabit Ethernet switches come with open ports for GBICs. Depending on your network needs, you can put any type of GBIC in this port. With the click of a GBIC, your network can change from a limited 100-m copper-based network to a 10,000-m fiber-based network! The sections that follow cover the more common GBICs, Gigabit standards, and length limitations.

Figure 2-1   *GBIC Installation*

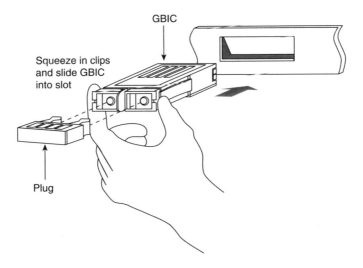

1000Base-SX Gigabit Ethernet

1000Base-SX GBICs use a laser-based wavelength of 850 nms. Depending on the cable type, SX GBIC operates at distances of 220 m to 550 m, as listed in Table 2-3. Wavelengths up to 850 nm are visible to the human eye.

Table 2-3   *1000Base-SX Cable Limitations*

Standard	Cable Size (Microns)	Max. Distance (m)
1000Base-SX	62.5-um multimode fiber	275 m
1000Base-SX	50-um multimode fiber	550 m

1000 Base-LX Gigabit Ethernet

LX GBICs use a laser-based wavelength of 1300 nms. Depending on the cable type, LX GBIC operate at distances of 550 m to 5000 m, as listed in Table 2-4. Cisco also supports an LH and LX GBIC, which extends the IEEE 1000Base-LX maximum distance of 5 km.

Table 2-4   *1000Base-LX Cable Limitations*

Standard	Cable Size (Microns)	Max. Distance (m)
1000Base-LX	62.5-um multimode fiber	550 m
1000Base-LX	50-um multimode fiber	550 m
1000Base-LX	9/10-um single-mode fiber	5 km
1000Base-LH	62.5-um multimode fiber	550 m
1000Base-LH	50-um multimode fiber	550 m
1000Base-LH	9/10-um single-mode fiber	10 km
1000Base-ZX	9/10-um single mode fiber	70 km
1000Base-ZX	9/10 Disposition-shifted fiber	100 km

1000Base-CX Gigabit Ethernet

The CX standard is for operating Gigabit Ethernet over copper for short distances. 1000Base-CX uses a 150-ohm balanced shielded copper cable. The distance of the CX standard is limited to only 25 meters.

1000Base-T Gigabit Ethernet

The IEEE standard for Gigabit Ethernet transmission over Cat 5 UTP is 802.3ab. The standard defines the maximum distance to be 100 meters and the copper to be at least Cat 5 using four pairs of wires, terminated with an RJ-45 jack. Figure 2-1 illustrates a GBIC.

NOTE   The Cisco *Gigastack GBIC* is a Cisco proprietary GBIC used on an uplink port to connect Gigabit Ethernet switches.

Ethernet Autonegotiation

To simplify the configuration of Ethernet devices, the 802.3.u committee defined Fast Link Pulse (FLP). FLP sends a series of pulses on the network that can deduce what duplex and speed the link is operating at. The station and the hub/switch agree on the highest priority and configure the station in that manner. Table 2-5 lists the priority that FLP uses. Both devices need to support autonegotiation logic for autonegotiation to work.

Table 2-5   *Ethernet Autonegotiation Prioritization*

Priority	Speed and Duplex Settings
1*	100Base-T2 full duplex
2	100Base-T2 half duplex
3	100Base-TX full duplex
4	100Base-T4 half duplex
5	100Base-TX half duplex
6	10Base-T full duplex
7	10Base-T half duplex

*   The priority of 1 eventually might be replaced by 1000Base-T full-duplex, shifting the others down by one.

Infrastructure devices, such as routers and servers, always should have speed and duplex settings fixed. Most 100-Mbps and greater NICs support full-duplex operation. Running at full-duplex mode essentially doubles the capacity of Ethernet. Taking advantage of this is the cheapest network upgrade that you will ever do!

NOTE   Duplex modes are a function of the hardware built into the network interface card (NIC). Software upgrades will not allow you to run full-duplex mode. For full-duplex mode to work, the station *and* the switch port must be capable of full-duplex operation.

802.1d Spanning-Tree Protocol (STP)

When Ethernet evolved from a single shared cable to networks with multiple bridges and hubs, a loop-detection and loop-prevention protocol was needed. The 802.1d protocol, developed by Radia Perlman, provided this loop protection. It did such a good job that when most networks went from bridged networks to routed networks, so the importance of Spanning Tree was almost forgotten. Because of this, Spanning Tree is probably the most used but least understood protocol in the modern internetwork. But with the huge success of Ethernet switching, Spanning Tree again becomes an important protocol to control and, more importantly, understand. We will discuss why Spanning Tree has become so important in switched Ethernet networks in upcoming sections.

Spanning Tree Operation

Spanning Tree's purpose in life is to elect a *root bridge* and build loop-free paths leading toward that root bridge for all bridges in the network. When Spanning Tree is converged, every bridge in the network has its bridged interfaces in one of two states: *forwarding* or *blocking*. If the port has the best-cost path to the root bridge, it is forwarding and thus is the shortest path to root. All other interfaces on the bridge are in a blocking state. STP accomplishes this by transmitting special messages called Bridge Protocol Data Units (BPDUs). BPDUs exist in two forms:

- A configuration BPDU, used for initial STP configuration
- A Topology Change Notification (TCN) BPDU used for topology changes

BPDUs are transmitted using a reserved multicast address assigned to all bridges. The BPDU is sent out all bridged LAN ports and is received by all bridges residing on the LAN. The BPDU is not forwarded off the LAN by a router. The BPDU contains the following relevant information:

- **Root ID**—The ID of the bridge assumed to be root. Upon initialization, the bridge assumes that it is root.
- **Transmitting bridge ID and port ID**—The BID of the bridge transmitting the BPDU, and what port the BPDU originated from.
- **Cost to root**—The least-cost path to the root bridge from the bridge transmitting the BPDU. Upon initialization, because the bridge assumes itself to be root, it transmits a 0 for the cost to root.

The *bridge ID (BID)* is an 8-byte field composed from a 6-byte MAC address and a 2-byte bridge priority. The MAC address used for the BID is generated from a number of sources, depending on the hardware in use for the bridge. Routers use a physical address, whereas switches will use an address from the backplane or supervisor module. Figure 2-2 illustrates the BID. The priority value ranges from 0 to 65,535; the default value is 32,768.

Figure 2-2 *The BID*

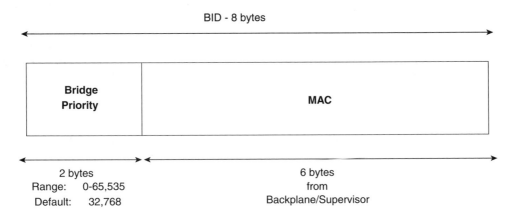

The *path cost* is used by bridges to determine the best possible path to root. Path costs recently have been updated by the IEEE to include Gigabit and greater links. The lower the path cost is, the more preferable the path is. Table 2-6 lists the STP cost values for LAN links.

Table 2-6 *STP Cost Values for LAN Links*

Bandwidth	STP Cost
4 Mbps	250
10 Mbps	100
16 Mbps	62
45 Mbps	39
100 Mbps	19
155 Mbps	14
622 Mbps	6
1 Gbps*	4
10 Gbps	2

* Before the IEEE standard was updated, the lowest value that STP could attain was 1. An STP cost of 1 was used for all links greater than or equal to 1 Gb.

STP has five primary states that it transitions through during its operation. When STP converges, it is in one of two states, forwarding or blocking. Table 2-7 lists the states of STP.

Table 2-7   *Various STP States*

STP State	STP Activity	User Data Being Passed
Disabled	Port is not active; it is not participating in any STP activity.	No
Broken	The 802.1q trunk is misconfigured on one end, or the default/native VLANs do not match on each end.	No
Listening	Port is sending and receiving BPDUs.	No
Learning	A loop-free bridging table is being built.	No
Forwarding	User data is being sent and received.	Yes
Blocking	User traffic is not permitted out the port.	No
PortFast*	Listening/learning states.	Yes

* PortFast is a Cisco-specific states that allow user data traffic to be forwarded during the STP convergence process.

The ports transition from one state to another, as depicted in Figure 2-3.

Let's examine each of these states in more detail.

Disabled

This state appears when a bridge is having problems processing BPDUs, when a trunk is improperly configured, or when the port is administratively down.

Listening

When a bridge port initializes or during the absence of BPDUs for a certain amount of time, STP transitions to the listening state. When STP is in this state, the port is actually blocking and no user data is sent on the link. STP follows a three-step process for convergence:

   1 **Elect one root bridge**—Upon initialization, the bridge begins sending BPDUs on all interfaces. A root bridge is chosen based on the bridge with the lowest BID. Recall that the BID is a combination of a priority and MAC address. In the event of a tie, the bridge with the lowest MAC address is chosen as root. All ports of the root bridge are put in the forwarding state.

Figure 2-3   *The STP Transition*

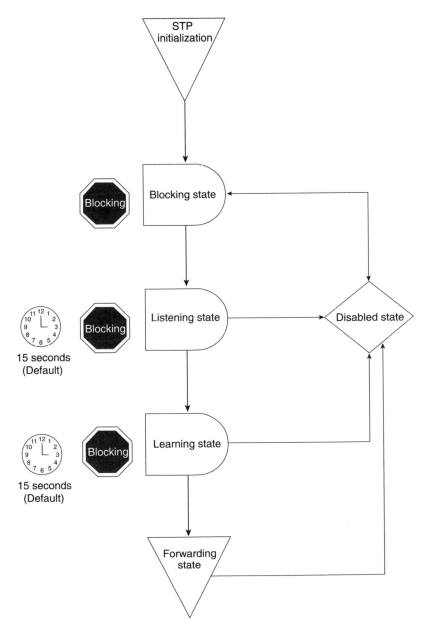

2 Elect one root port for every nonroot bridge—After a single root bridge has been elected, STP elects a *single* root port on each bridge that is not root. The root port is the bridge's best path to the root bridge. When a root port is elected, it is put into the forwarding state. To determine what port should be a root port, STP follows this decision process:

a. Lowest root BID

b. Lowest path cost to root bridge; the cumulative cost of the all paths to root

c. Lowest sender BID

d. Lowest port ID

When a bridge receives a BPDU, it stores it in a bridge table for that port. As new BPDUs are received on that port, they are compared to existing BPDUs. Using the four-step process listed previously, BPDUs that are more attractive or that have lower costs are kept, and the other ones are discarded. The primary variable that influences the root port election is *the cost to the root bridge.* This is the cumulative path cost of all links to the root bridge.

3 Elect one designated port/designated bridge for every segment—For every segment, STP elects one port that will send and receive all information from that segment to the root bridge. A root port can be thought of as the port that forwards information to the root, whereas the designated port can be thought of as the port that sends traffic away from the root. This rule applies mostly to shared-media bridges, or routers. Designated ports on back-to-back switched trunk lines do not follow this rule.

4 All remaining ports become nondesignated ports and are put in blocking mode.

Learning

Ports that remain designated or root ports for a period of 15 seconds, the default forward delay, enter the learning state. The learning state is another 15 seconds that the bridge waits while it builds its bridge table.

Forwarding and Blocking

When the bridge reaches this phase, ports that do not serve a special purpose, such as a root port or a designated port, are called nondesignated ports. All designated ports are put in a forwarding state, while all nondesignated ports are put into a blocking state. In the blocking state, a bridge does not send any configuration BPDUs, but it still listens to them. A blocking port also does not forward any user data.

Figure 2-4 illustrates a basic configuration, with the appropriate ports marked.

Figure 2-4   *STP Ports and Roles*

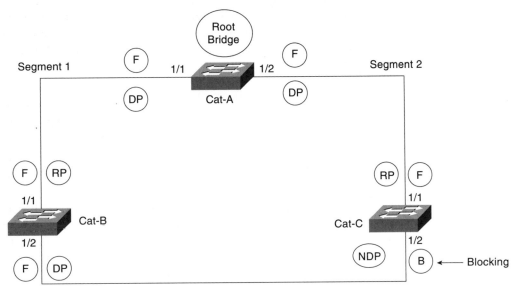

State Port	Symbol
Blocking	B
Forwarding	F
Designated Port	DP
Root Port	RP
Nondesignated Port	NDP

STP Timers

STP has three basic timers that regulate and age BPDUs: a hello timer, a forward delay timer, and a max age time. The timers accomplish the following for STP:

- **Hello timer**—The default hello timer is 2 seconds. This is the amount of time between configuration BPDUs sent by the root bridge.

- **Forward delay timer**—This timer is the default 15 seconds that the routers wait while building its bridging table. The listening and learning stages each use this single 15-second timer.

- **Max age timer**—The max age timer is how long a BPDU is stored before it is flushed. If this timer expires before the interface receives a new BPDU, the interface transitions to the listening state. An expired max ageparameter usually is caused by a link failure. The default value is 20 seconds.

STP uses the hello timer to space BPDUs and has a keepalive mechanism. The hello timer always should prevent the MAX age value from being hit. When the max agetimer expires, it usually indicates a link failure. When this happens, the bridge re-enters the listening state. For STP to recover from a link failure, it takes approximately 50 seconds; it takes 20 seconds for the BPDU to age out, the max age; and it takes 15 seconds for the listening state and 15 seconds for the learning state.

NOTE   Two other forms of STP exist besides IEEE 802.1d. DEC and IBM are two other forms of Spanning Tree in use. The operation of all forms of STP is similar, and Cisco routers support all forms.

By now, you might be asking yourself, how could a protocol like this play a role in the modern network, with a Layer 2 protocol, 2-second hellos, and a 50-second convergence time? Because a switch is a Layer 2 device, all VLANs use Spanning Tree to build loop-free paths between switches. Cisco implements Per VLAN Spanning Tree (PVST). With PVST, there is one instance of Spanning Tree running in every VLAN. Now, take a modern network with 50 VLANs, that's 50 instances of Spanning Tree running on every trunk and every switch! Quickly, the need to understand and control this protocol becomes evident. Because this is so important, controlling Spanning Tree is one of major focuses of the section, "Configuring Catalyst Ethernet Switches."

Ethernet Switching

In the early 1990s, Kalpana, Grand Junction, and Bay Networks started to ship some of the first Ethernet switches. The Bay Networks 28115 was one of the first switches to introduce 10/100 auto-sensing ports and virtual LANs (VLANS). More importantly, all switches put an end to the old Ethernet repeater rules, while increasing bandwidth. Until this point, many people were predicting that ATM would be the only high-speed protocol in use on the LAN—and if it hadn't been for the Ethernet switch, they might have been right.

Ethernet switches provide several key advantages over traditional shared media LANs:

- Significant bandwidth improvement by limiting a collision domain to a single port.
- Scalability. Repeater rules are limited to a single port.
- VLAN capability. Broadcast domains can be located logically and are not limited by geographical boundaries.
- Enhanced security.
- Full-duplex capability.

A switch functions much like a multiport bridge. When VLANs are created, virtual bridges are created to join the ports in the VLAN. Broadcast, unicast, and multicast traffic is forwarded to each member of the VLAN. The Catalyst 5500 series switch builds an address table by recording the source MAC address of frames that it received from its interfaces. When a frame destined for an address not yet in the address table is received, the switch floods the frame out all ports and trunks in the same VLAN as the frame was received. The switch does not forward the frame out the interface that it received it. When a reply for that frame is received, the router records the new address in the address table. The switch forwards subsequent frames to a single port, without flooding it to all ports. Traffic can leave the VLAN only with the aid of a router or a Layer 3 switch providing routing functionality.

Switches forward traffic in three primary modes:

- **Store-and-forward**—The port adapter reads the entire frame into memory and then determines whether the frame should be forwarded. The frame is forwarded only if it does not contain any errors. Store-and-forward mode reduces the amount of errors on the LAN, but there is a delay associated with reading and verifying the frame before forwarding it. In modern ASIC-based switches, the speed of the ASIC has become so great that the latency associated with store-and-forward switches is a nonissue.

- **Cut-through**—In this mode, the port receives the first few bytes of a frame and analyzes the packet header to determine the destination of the frame and immediately begins to forward that frame. The frame is not checked for any errors before forwarding, so this mode does propagate bad frames on the network.

- **Adaptive cut-through**—This mode combines both aspects of cut-through and store-and-forward modes. In this mode, the port operates in cut-through mode until a user-defined threshold of frame errors is detected. When the threshold is exceeded, the port switches to store-and-forward mode.

Broadcast Domains and Collision Domains

Two key concepts in switched networks are *broadcast domains* and *collision domains*. A broadcast domain is the area of the network that forwards broadcasts from one portion of network to the next. A practical example of a broadcast domain is an IP or IPX subnet. A collision domain is a function of the physical properties of a device. Devices in the same collision domain reside on the same "wire" or hub/repeater. Table 2-8 illustrates how various network devices segment collision and broadcast domains.

Figure 2-5 illustrates where collision and broadcast domains reside on various devices.

Table 2-8   *How Various Network Devices Segment Collision and Broadcast Domains*

Hardware Type	Collision Domain	Broadcast Domain
Hub/repeater	All ports are in a single collision domain.	All ports are in a single broadcast domain.
Bridge	Each port is a separate collision domain.	All ports are in a single broadcast domain.
Router	Each port is a separate collision domain.	Each port is in a separate broadcast domain.*
Switch	Each port is a separate collision domain.	Each port is configurable to be in the same or a separate collision domain.

*   Assuming that bridging is disabled

Figure 2-5   *Collision and Broadcast Domains*

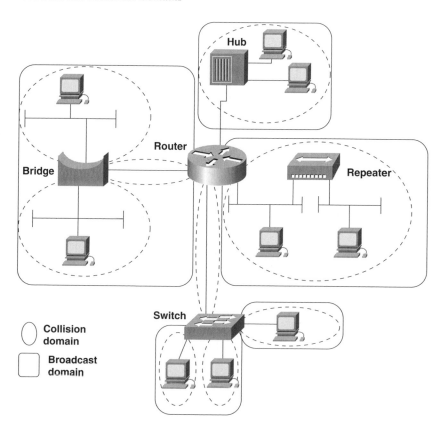

Virtual LANs (VLANS)

Many definitions for a VLAN exist. The definition that we chose to use is simple. Virtual LANS (VLANs) can be easily defined as broadcast domains that can extend geographical distances. When configuring Ethernet switching, every port must be assigned to a VLAN. The default VLAN is always VLAN 1. When switches ship from the factory, they are in some ways plug-and-play. Every port is assigned to VLAN 1, so every port of the switch is in a single broadcast domain. This makes migrating from shared Ethernet hubs to a basic switched network easy. VLANs always should be thought of as simply broadcast domains. Most VLANs eventually become IP/IPX subnets or bridging domains. The basic design rules that apply to broadcast domains also apply to VLANs:

- A single subnet is used per VLAN.
- Do not bridge different VLANs together.
- A router/Layer 3 switch is needed to route between VLANs.
- STP must run in each VLAN to prevent loops. This can be disabled, but it is not recommend.

Let's examine some basic switched networks, focusing on the differences in each one.

Figure 2-6 shows a basic VLAN configuration. The switch has VLANs 1 and 2 configured on it. Each VLAN is configured with a separate IP subnet. If information needs to pass from VLAN 1 to VLAN 2, a router is required. Here, the router has an interface in each VLAN. Traffic going from one VLAN to the other needs to first hit the router. The downfall in this configuration is that a single interface is required for every VLAN that needs to be routed, severely limiting the scalability of networks like this.

Figure 2-7 shows another basic VLAN configuration. The switch has VLANs 1 and 2 configured on it again. Here, the router has a single 100-Mbps interface running a VLAN trunking protocol, such as 802.1q. Traffic going from one VLAN to the other must travel up the trunk to the router and then back down the same trunk. Using a single trunk to route between VLANs is the most economical way to accomplish routing between VLANs. This type of configuration often is referred to as a "router on a stick."

The next evolution was to move the routing function from a standalone router to the switch itself; this is called Layer 3 switching. This move was only logical because traffic is doubled up coming in and exiting the same router interface. At first, this was accomplished through the use of a route switch processor (RSM), installed into a Catalyst 5500 series switch. More switches now are offering this capability. Figure 2-8 illustrates a Layer 3 switch.

Figure 2-6   *Per Interface VLAN Routing*

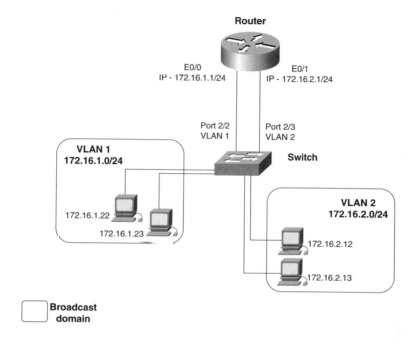

Figure 2-7   *Router on a Stick*

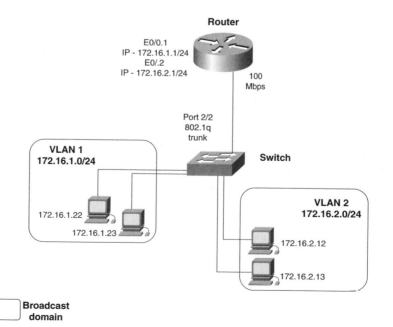

Figure 2-8   *Layer 3 Switching*

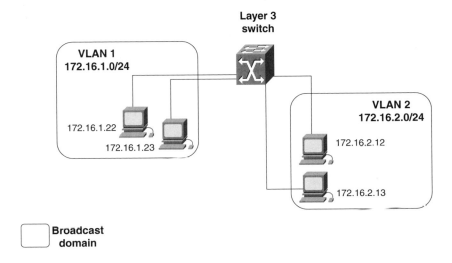

VTP and Trunking Protocols

VTP and Trunking Protocols

A powerful function of VLANs is their capability to span distance. VLANs are communicated from switch to switch by the means of a VLAN Trunking Protocol (VTP). VTP is used to maintain global VLAN information between switches. A VLAN management domain, or VTP domain, consists of one or more switches interconnected and sharing the same administrative responsibility. Anytime that you want the VLANS on one switch to have information about the VLANs on another switch (that is, when you want these two broadcast domains to communicate), you need to configure a VTP domain and a trunk. VTP also tracks all the VLANs in a VTP domain and propagates these in a client/server manner from one switch to another. The intent of VTP is to ease management and provide a common VLAN database across the VTP domain.

VTP advertisements are sent out on all trunk connections in Inter-Switch Link (ISL) frames, 802.1q frames, IEEE 802.10, or ATM LANE. VTP frames are sent to the destination MAC address of 0100.0ccc.ccc with an LLC code of SNAP (AAAA) and a type of 2003 in the SNAP header. For VTP messages to successfully be transmitted, the following must occur:

- VTP will accept only messages with the same domain name. If authentication is configured for that VTP domain, that, too, must match. The VTP name is case-sensitive.

- VTP will accept only messages with the same version, Type I or Type II. This setting is controlled, with the V2 mode being either enabled on both sides of the link or disabled. A switch might be VTP version II–capable and have V2 mode disabled. V2 mode is primarily for Token Ring switches.

- Catalyst switches must be adjacent, and trunking must be configured between them. For Ethernet networks, the trunking protocol is dotq1 (802.1q) or ISL. ATM uses LANE, and FDDI uses IEEE 802.10.

- VTP servers will synchronize with VTP clients only if the VTP client's revision number is less than that of the VTP server. If the VTP client's revision number is equal to or greater than that of the VTP servers the client VLAN database will not synchronize.

After a trunk is established, VTP sends periodic advertisement out each trunk port. The VTP advertisements contain the following:

- VLAN IDs (ISL and 802qQ).
- Emulated LAN names for ATM LANE.
- 802.10 SAID values.
- VTP domain name and configuration revision number. The server with the highest revision number becomes the primary server. The revision number is incremented every time a VLAN configuration change is made.
- VLAN configuration, VLAN ID, VLAN name, and MTU size for each VLAN.
- Ethernet frame format.

VTP has two versions, simply called version I and version II. All the switches in the VTP domain must be on the same version. This rule does not apply to the transparent-mode switches. Version II offers the following, the most important being support for Token Ring:

- **Token Ring support**—VTP VII supports Token Ring LAN switching and VLANs (Token Ring Bridge Relay Function [TrBRF]). We will discuss TrBRF more in upcoming sections.

- **Unrecognized type**—Length value (TLV) support is included. Unrecognized TLV is saved in NVRAM when the switch is in VTP server mode.

- **Version-dependent transparent mode**—VTP will forward VTP messages that do not match the domain name and version to switches operating in VTP transparent mode.

- **Consistency checks**—Consistency checks are performed on VLAN names, and values are performed only upon new entry into the switch.

VTP operates in one of three modes:

- **VTP server mode**—In VTP server mode, VLANs can be created, modified, and deleted. VLAN information automatically is sent to all adjacent VTP servers and clients in the same VTP domain. Caution always should be used when "clearing" a VLAN from the VTP server because that VLAN will be deleted on all VTP servers and clients in that DTP domain. If two devices are configured as servers, the switch/server with the highest VTP configuration revision will be the primary server. VLAN information is stored in the switches NVRAM.

- **VTP client mode**—In VTP client mode, VLANs cannot be created, modified, or deleted. Only the name and the VTP mode and pruning can be changed. The client is at the mercy of the VTP server for all VLAN information. The client still must assign ports to a VLAN, but the VLAN will not be active on the switch unless the VTP server sends information to the client on that VLAN. Furthermore, VLAN information is stored locally in the switch's NVRAM when it is received from the server on the Catalyst 2900XL/2500G series switches. The Catalyst 4000/5500/6500 series of switches do not store the VLAN database if configured has a VTP client.

- **VTP transparent mode**—In VTP transparent mode, VTP information that is local on the switch will not be advertised, but VTP information received form other switches will be forwarded. VLANs can be created, modified, and deleted on transparent switches. VLAN information also is stored in NVRAM. Table 2-9 highlights the various modes and operation.

Table 2-9   *Various VTP Modes of Operation*

VTP Mode	Source VTP Messages	Propagate Local VTP Information	Listen to VTP Messages	Create, Modify, and Delete VLANs	VLAN Database Saved Locally
Server	Yes	Yes	Yes	Yes	Yes
Client	Yes	—	Yes	No	Yes/No*
Transparent	No**	No	Yes**	Yes	Yes

*   The Catalyst 4000/5500/6500 series of switches do not store the VLAN database on VTP client switches. The Catalyst 2900XL/3500G series of switches do save this information and have the VLAN database upon initialization.

**   In transparent mode, the switch does not participate in VTP. That is, it does not synchronize VTP databases. However, VTP information still is received and sent out other trunk ports. Local VLAN information is not propagated by the trunks.

Table 2-10 lists the default VTP mode on Catalyst switches.

Table 2-10   *Default VTP Settings*

VTP Feature	Default Setting
VTP domain name	Null
VTP mode	Server
VTP version 2 updates	Disabled
VTP security/password	Disabled

VLAN Trunking Protocols

VTP requires trunks to transport VTP information. A trunk is considered a point-to-point link between Ethernet switch ports and another networking device such as a router or another switch. Trunks have the capability to carry the traffic of multiple VLANs over a single link and extend VLANs across the internetwork. Without the use of VTP and trunks, an IP subnet could never be partitioned across switches. VTP trunks allow for an effective way to tie two broadcast domains together. Figure 2-9 illustrates how 802.1q trunks are used to tie VLANs 4 and 2 together.

Three primary trunking encapsulations are available for Ethernet:

- **Inter-Switch Link (ISL)**—ISL is a Cisco proprietary trunking encapsulation. ISL is a frame-tagging protocol; the frames on the link contain the standard Ethernet, FDDI, or Token Ring frame and the VLAN information associated with that frame. ISL is supported on links that are 100 Mbps or greater in speed. ISL is an extremely efficient protocol, and it is the protocol that Cisco uses internally for Catalyst to communicate with the route switch modules (RSMs) or other Layer 3 switching fabric. Spanning Tree is run on a per-VLAN basis (PVST) on ISL trunks. This means that every VLAN has a root bridge, and trunks go into a forward/blocking mode for each VLAN on each trunk. PVST is critical to control on large networks, as discussed in upcoming sections.

- **IEEE 802.1q**—802.1q is the industry-standard trunking protocol. 802.1q operates slightly differently than ISL. It runs Mono Spanning Tree (MST) on the default VLAN for all VLANs in the VTP domain. In MST, one root bridge is elected for the entire VTP domain; this is called the Common Spanning Tree (CST). All VLAN information follows one path in this type of configuration. Cisco, understanding the need to control Spanning Tree on large networks while controlling load, implements PVST on all 802.1q VLANs. The following is a list of other restrictions on 802.1q trunks:

  — The default VLAN needs to be the same on both ends of the trunk. MST will run in this VLAN. It is critical that the default VLAN be the same on third-party switches interacting with Cisco switches.

Figure 2-9 *VLAN Trunking*

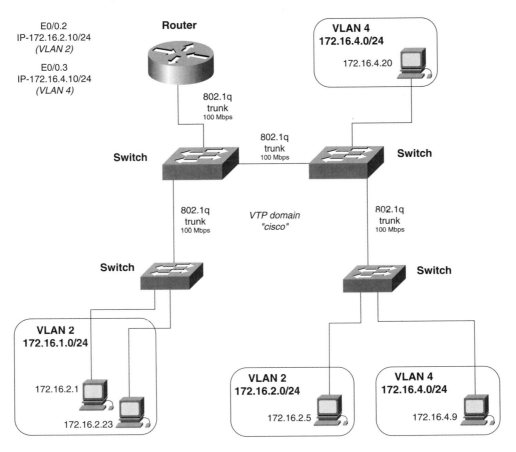

— As mentioned, 802.1q uses MST. Cisco overrides this, by default, with PVST. Because the BPDUs are handled differently between Cisco and third-party switches, care should be taken whenever integrating these domains that Spanning Tree and the default VLANs are consistent in both switches. The entire Cisco VTP domain looks like a single broadcast/spanning tree domain to the third-party switches.

— BPDUs on the native VLAN of the trunk are sent untagged to the reserved IEEE 802.1d Spanning Tree multicast MAC address (0180.c200.0000). The BPDUs on all other VLANs on the trunk are sent and tagged on the reserved Cisco Shared Spanning Tree (SSTP) multicast MAC address (0100.0ccc.cccd).

- **IEEE 802.10**—802.10 was actually the first protocol that the industry tried to use for a VLAN trunking protocol. It originally was developed for extra security on defense networks or large MANs. It primarily is used on FDDI networks today because of its limitations.

Dynamic ISL (DISL) and Dynamic Trunk Protocol (DTP)

Dynamic ISL was Cisco's first trunk-negotiation protocol. It exists on all Catalyst 5500 series software 4.1 and earlier. Originally, it was used to negotiate trunks for the ISL protocol only. Later, in 4.2, DISL was replaced with Dynamic Trunk Protocol (DTP). DTP is essentially DISL that attempts to automate ISL and 802.1q trunk configuration. DTP uses the reserved destination multicast address of 0100.0ccc.cccc for LAN networks to negotiate trunks. In the default auto state, DTP messages are sent out every 30 seconds on all trunk lines. Depending on the mode of the port, the port might become an ISL or 802.1q trunk. DTP operates in the following modes:

- **On**—Puts the port in a permanent trunking state. It also tries to negotiate the link to be a trunk.
- **Off**—Disables the port, and thereby the trunk.
- **Desirable**—Makes the port attempt to convert to a trunk link. The port becomes a trunk if the neighboring port is set to on, desirable, or auto modes.
- **Auto**—The port converts to a trunk if the neighboring port is set to on or desirable modes.
- **Nonegotiate**—Puts the port into trunking mode but prevents the port from sending DTP frames.

In actuality, this is really too many options for a trunk. Network administrators either configure a port as a trunk or they don't. It could be argued that to have a network be so flexible the trunks can or should be added dynamically is a security risk. Table 2-11 illustrates the possible combinations of trunks and the modes. As you will see, the most reliable and simplest way to configure a trunk is to statically configure it on both sides of the link as a trunk and in the "on" mode.

Table 2-11 *Ethernet DTP Configuration Outcomes*

Neighbor Port	Trunk Mode and Trunk Encapsulation	off / ISL or DOT1Q	on / ISL	desirable / ISL	auto / ISL	on / DOT1Q	desirable / DOT1Q	auto / DOT1Q	desirable / negotiate	auto / negotiate
off	ISL or DOT1Q	Local: Nontrunk Neighbor: Nontrunk	Local: ISL trunk Neighbor: Nontrunk	Local: Nontrunk Neighbor: Nontrunk	Local: Nontrunk Neighbor: Nontrunk	Local: 1Q Trunk Neighbor: Nontrunk	Local: Nontrunk Neighbor: Nontrunk	Local: Nontrunk Neighbor: Nontrunk	Local: Nontrunk Neighbor: Nontrunk	Local: Nontrunk Neighbor: Nontrunk
on	ISL	Local: Nontrunk Neighbor: ISL trunk	Local: ISL trunk Neighbor: ISL trunk	Local: ISL trunk Neighbor: ISL trunk	Local: ISL trunk Neighbor: ISL trunk	Local: 1Q trunk Neighbor: ISL trunk	Local: Nontrunk Neighbor: ISL trunk	Local: Nontrunk Neighbor: Nontrunk	Local: ISL Neighbor: ISL	Local: ISL Neighbor: ISL
desirable	ISL	Local: Nontrunk Neighbor: Nontrunk	Local: ISL trunk Neighbor: ISL trunk	Local: ISL trunk Neighbor: ISL trunk	Local: ISL trunk Neighbor: ISL trunk	Local: 1Q trunk Neighbor: ISL trunk	Local: Nontrunk Neighbor: Nontrunk	Local: Nontrunk Neighbor: Nontrunk	Local: ISL Neighbor: ISL	Local: ISL Neighbor: ISL
auto	ISL	Local: Nontrunk Neighbor: Nontrunk	Local: ISL trunk Neighbor: ISL trunk	Local: ISL trunk Neighbor: ISL trunk	Local: Nontrunk Neighbor: Nontrunk	Local: 1Q trunk Neighbor: Nontrunk	Local: Nontrunk Neighbor: Nontrunk	Local: Nontrunk Neighbor: Nontrunk	Local: ISL Neighbor: ISL	Local: Nontrunk Neighbor: Nontrunk
on	DOT1Q	Local: Nontrunk Neighbor: 1Q trunk	Local: ISL trunk Neighbor: 1Q trunk	Local: Nontrunk Neighbor: 1Q trunk	Local: Nontrunk Neighbor: 1Q trunk	Local: 1Q trunk Neighbor: 1Q trunk	Local: 1Q trunk Neighbor: 1Q trunk	Local: 1Q trunk Neighbor: 1Q trunk	Local: 1Q trunk Neighbor: 1Q trunk	Local: 1Q trunk Neighbor: 1Q trunk
desirable	DOT1Q	Local: Nontrunk Neighbor: Nontrunk	Local: ISL trunk Neighbor: Nontrunk	Local: Nontrunk Neighbor: 1Q trunk	Local: Nontrunk Neighbor: 1Q trunk	Local: 1Q trunk Neighbor: 1Q trunk	Local: Nontrunk Neighbor: 1Q trunk	Local: 1Q trunk Neighbor: 1Q trunk	Local: 1Q trunk Neighbor: 1Q trunk	Local: 1Q trunk Neighbor: 1Q trunk

Table 2-11 *Ethernet DTP Configuration Outcomes (Continued)*

Neighbor Port	Trunk Mode and Trunk Encapsulation	off	on	desirable	auto	on	desirable	auto	desirable	auto
		ISL or DOT1Q	ISL	ISL	ISL	DOT1Q	DOT1Q	DOT1Q	negotiate	negotiate
auto	DOT1Q	Local: Nontrunk Neighbor: Nontrunk	Local: ISL trunk Neighbor: Nontrunk	Local: Nontrunk Neighbor: Nontrunk	Local: Nontrunk Neighbor: Nontrunk	Local: 1Q trunk Neighbor: 1Q trunk	Local: 1Q trunk Neighbor: 1Q trunk	Local: Nontrunk Neighbor: Nontrunk	Local: 1Q trunk Neighbor: 1Q trunk	Local: Nontrunk Neighbor: Nontrunk
desirable	negotiate	Local: Nontrunk Neighbor: Nontrunk	Local: ISL trunk Neighbor: ISL trunk	Local: ISL trunk Neighbor: ISL trunk	Local: ISL trunk Neighbor: ISL trunk	Local: 1Q trunk Neighbor: 1Q trunk	Local: 1Q trunk Neighbor: 1Q trunk	Local: ISL trunk Neighbor: ISL trunk	Local: ISL Neighbor: ISL	Local: ISL NEIGHBOR: ISL
auto	negotiate	Local: Nontrunk Neighbor: Nontrunk	Local: ISL Neighbor: ISL trunk	Local: ISL Neighbor: ISL trunk	Local: Nontrunk Neighbor: Nontrunk	Local: 1Q trunk Neighbor: 1Q trunk	Local: 1Q trunk Neighbor: 1Q trunk	Local: Nontrunk Neighbor: Nontrunk	Local: ISL Neighbor: ISL	Local: Nontrunk Neighbor: Nontrunk

Configuring Catalyst Ethernet Switches

The colorful history of Ethernet switching is present in the Catalyst line. Each family of Catalyst switches has a slightly different command-line interface. The Catalyst switches such as the 1900 and 2800 come from Grand Junction and have one type of configuration interface and method. The Catalyst 3000 originated with Kalpana and has another method of configuration. The Catalyst 5500 family started with Cisco's acquisition of Crescendo. The Catalyst 5500 and 6500 families have a unique configuration interface originally called the XDI. Presently, the configuration mode is simply called the command-line interface (CLI); whereas the Catalyst 8500 series uses a hybrid, where the configuration resembles the traditional Cisco router configuration, except that it is a router with hundreds of ports.

The upcoming sections, excluding the section on Token Ring, focus on configuring the Catalyst 2900XL and 3500G family of switches along with the Catalyst 4000/5500/6500 series switches. These two families represent that majority of Cisco Catalyst switches in deployment.

LAN switches were designed to be easy to install and configure. On smaller networks, little to no configuration might be required. On large redundant networks, with multiple VLANs and trunks, switching becomes quite a task. Configuring Ethernet switch configuration can be divided into a four-step process. Most switches, not all, will require a nondefault VTP domain to be created before VLANs can be created.

Step 1 Configure switch management.

Step 2 Configure VTP and VLANs.

Step 3 Configure VLAN trunks, if applicable.

Step 4 (Optional) Control STP and VLAN propagation.

Step 1 involves configuring the management VLAN, IP addresses, and default gateways on the switch so that it can be accessed in-band from the internetwork.

In Step 2, you define the VTP domain and the VLANs on the VTP servers. During this step, you also assign ports to VLANs.

Step 3 involves configuring VLAN trunks, if there are any on the network.

Step 4 is optional but critical to large networks. It involves controlling STP through the setting of root bridges, clearing VLANs from trunks, and using VLAN prune eligibility.

Step 1: Configuring Switch Management

All Catalyst switches have the capability to be managed by an IP address. To accomplish this, an IP address needs to be assigned to the switch, along with a default gateway or default route for IP traffic to get forwarded to. The default management VLAN is VLAN 1. When you assign an IP address to the switch, it will be in VLAN 1 unless you specify another VLAN.

Configuring Switch Management on Catalyst 4000/5500/6500 Switches

The management interface on Catalyst 4000/5500/6500 series is called the SC0 interface. This is a logical in-band interface, which means that it relies on another switch port to forward traffic for it. The 4000 series also has an out-of-band management interface called the ME1 interface. Use the following syntax to set the IP address for the Catalyst switch:

```
set interface sc0 [vlan] [ip_addr [netmask [broadcast]]]
```

A default route also needs to be set for IP to forward traffic to. This is usually a router with an interface on the same VLAN that the switch's IP address is in. A default route can be entered in one of two ways: by entering either a default gateway or the IP default route of 0.0.0.0.

```
set ip route default IP_default_gateway
```

Or

```
set ip route 0.0.0.0 IP_default_gateway
```

For full IP reachability, ensure that a router exists in the same subnet/VLAN as your management IP address. Use the router's Ethernet interface or subinterface as the default gateway IP address for the switch.

Example 2-1 demonstrates the configuration of an IP address and default gateway on the switch sw13. This default gateway is in VLAN 2. You need to proceed to Step 2 and configure VLAN 2 for this configuration to fully work. This is because VLAN 2 will not be in the database yet.

Example 2-1 *Configuring an IP Address and Default Route*

```
sw13 (enable) set int sc0 2 172.16.2.13 255.255.255.0
Interface sc0 vlan set, IP address and netmask set.
sw13 (enable) set ip route default 172.16.2.10
Route added.
```

NOTE   On the Catalyst 4000/5500/6500 series switches, the VTP domain and appropriate VLAN must be configured if the SC0 interface is not on VLAN 1.

Other commands that are useful in configuring general management on the Catalyst 4000/5500/6500 series switches are the following:

- **set prompt**—Sets the prompt of the switch, just like the **hostname** command on routers.
- **set system contact**—Sets a person's name or number to call for support.
- **set system location**—Defines the physical location of the switch.

- **set ip route** *ip_subnet ip_next_hope*—Enables you to enter specific routes into the routing table. The next hop must be a reachable address through the sc0 or me1 interface.

- **show ip route**—Shows the known IP routes, or default routes, and how they are accessed.

Example 2-2 demonstrates the entry of a static route, followed by the **show ip route** command.

Example 2-2 *Configuring Static Routes*

```
sw13 (enable) set ip route 172.18.2.0 172.16.2.10
Route added.
sw13 (enable) show ip route
Fragmentation   Redirect    Unreachable
-------------   --------    -----------
enabled         enabled     enabled

Destination              Gateway                  Flags   Use          Interface
--------------------     --------------------     ------  ----------   ---------
default                  172.16.2.10              UG          165      sc0
172.18.2.0               172.16.2.10              UG            0      sc0
172.16.2.0               172.16.2.13              U           279      sc0
sw13 (enable)
```

Example 2-3 shows how the set system values are displayed with the **show system** command.

Example 2-3 **show system** *Command Output*

```
sw13 (enable) show system
PS1-Status PS2-Status Fan-Status Temp-Alarm Sys-Status Uptime d,h:m:s Logout
---------- ---------- ---------- ---------- ---------- --------------- ---------
ok         ok         ok         off        ok         0,06:59:37      20 min

PS1-Type   PS2-Type   Modem   Baud  Traffic Peak Peak-Time
---------- ---------- ------- ----- ------- ---- ------------------------
WS-C4008   WS-C4008   disable 9600  0%       0% Thu Jun 14 2001, 09:01:43

System Name              System Location          System Contact
---------------------    ---------------------    ---------------------
switch13                 CCIE Lab                 Solie
sw13 (enable)
```

NOTE

VLAN 1: "Just Say No"

VLAN 1 is the default VLAN for all Catalyst switches. MST on 802.1q uses this VLAN for its entire Spanning Tree domain. VLAN 1 has rules that limit how you can control traffic on it. Until recently, you could not even remove VLAN 1 from any trunk line. Any switch added to the network, by default, will be in VLAN 1. This leaves the network vulnerable to potential VLAN and data corruption on VLAN 1. For these reasons, I personally don't run production traffic or management traffic on VLAN 1, which is essentially a "dead" VLAN.

Configuring IP Permit Lists on Catalyst 4000/5500/6500 Switches   When an IP address is configured on the switch, it can be accessed through Telnet and SNMP. There is no need for any additional configuration. Sometimes, you might want to limit Telnet or SNMP access to the switch. To limit this type of traffic, use the **set ip permit** command. Up to 10 line entries can be configured. Networks or single IP addresses can be filtered. For example, to allow only the network 172.16.2.0/24 to pass, the syntax would resemble the following:

```
set ip permit 172.16.2.0 255.255.255.0
```

To limit access to a single address, use a 255.255.255.255 mask or simply omit the mask. After the lines have been entered, enable the "access-list" with the **set ip permit enable** command. The switch will still allow ICMP echo replies and requests; however, it will block SNMP and Telnet traffic. By default, IP permit lists are disabled and need to be enabled to take effect.

The syntax for IP permit is as follows:

```
set ip permit [ip_address] [subnet_mask]
set ip permit [enable | disable]
```

IP permit lists can viewed by entering the **show ip permit** command, such as in Example 2-4.

Example 2-4   **show ip permit** *Command Output*

```
sw13 (enable) show ip permit
IP permit list feature enabled.
Permit List        Mask
----------------   ----------------
172.16.2.0         255.255.255.0

Denied IP Address  Last Accessed Time    Type
----------------   ------------------    ------
172.16.3.1         06/14/01,19:07:43     Telnet
sw13 (enable)
```

Configuring Switch Management on Catalyst 2900XL/3500G Families

The management interface on Catalyst resembles a router with a special *VLAN database* added to it. The commands for assigning ports, trunks, and their management all are performed from the classic configuration mode, or conf t mode. VLAN information is configured from enable mode by using a special key-in, **vlan database**, from the enable mode. From this point on, we will refer to commands in the VLAN database as *VLAN commands*—that is, commands accessed by keying the **vlan database** from the enable mode prompt. Configuration commands entered from the more traditional router-like mode will be called *configuration-mode commands*.

The 2900XL/3500G switch has a default virtual interface called VLAN 1. This is the default VLAN for the switch; if you want to configure the management IP address in VLAN 1, you would simply add it under this interface much like you would a router. To run management on a different VLAN, you will need to shut down the VLAN 1 interface and configure a new virtual interface for the VLAN that you want to run management on. Only one VLAN interface can be active at once; you must shut down VLAN 1 to activate VLAN 2. Example 2-5 demonstrates how to configure the management interface on a VLAN other than VLAN 1.

Example 2-5 *Configuring the Management Interface on Catalyst 2900XL/3500G Switches*

```
sw11#conf t
Enter configuration commands, one per line.  End with CNTL/Z.
sw11(config)#interface vlan 1
sw11(config-if)#shut
sw11(config-if)#exit
sw11(config)#interface vlan 2
sw11(config-subif)#ip address 172.16.2.11 255.255.255.0
sw11(config-subif)#no shut
sw11(config-subif)#^Z
sw11#
```

In this particular example, the management interface will not work until VLAN 2 is defined on the switch. This is Step 2 of the four-part configuration process.

To configure a default route, use the **ip default-gateway** *ip_address* command, the same as it is on a router. Example 2-6 shows how to configure the default gateway. Here, the default gateway points at the router 172.16.2.10.

Example 2-6 *Configuring Default Routing on Catalyst 2900XL/3500G Switches*

```
sw15(config)#ip default-gateway 172.16.2.10
```

Controlling IP Access on Catalyst 2900XL/3500G Families   Controlling IP access on the 2900XL/3500G switches is identical to controlling Telnet access on the router. Recall from Chapter 1, "The Key Components for Modeling an Internetwork," that Telnet access is controlled on the vty lines. These can be viewed on the switch with the same **show line** command. Telnet and SNMP access can be controlled through creating access lists and applying them to the VTY lines on the switch. Because this process is identical to routers, see Chapter 1 for configuring virtual Telnet access.

Step 2: Configuring VTP and VLANs on Catalyst 4000/5500/6500 Switches

This step contains three substeps, all performed with **set** commands. The three substeps are as follows:

Step 1 Configure a VTP domain and mode.

Step 2 Configure physical port properties and assign ports to VLANs.

Step 3 Configure VLANs if the switch is operating as a VTP server or in VTP transparent mode.

Configuring VTP Domain and Mode on Catalyst 4000/5500/6500 Switches

A VTP domain must be configured before any VLANs can be added to the VLAN database. To configure the VTP domain, use this syntax:

```
set vtp [domain name] [mode {client I server I transparent}] [passwd passwd]
    [pruning {enable I disable}] [v2 {enable I disable}]
```

The *name* field sets the VTP domain name and is a case-sensitive field. The default mode of VTP is server mode. If you want to change the mode, use either client, server, or transparent modes. Remember that any VLAN changes on the server are propagated to all client VLANs. For a server to send VTP updates to a client, it *must* have a higher revision number. If the client revision number is higher than the server's, it will not accept updates from the server. If you are having problems with VLANs propagating, be sure to check the revision number of VTP. To reset the VTP revision number, simply change the name of the VTP domain, and then change it back. This will reset the revision counter to 0. This will not work on 2900XL/3500G series switches; these switches must be restarted to clear a corrupt VTP domain.

V2 updates can be enabled or disabled, depending on switch type. You need to use only version 2 updates during Token Ring switching, which is why Ethernet-only switches do not have V2 updates. All switches in the VTP domain must be V2-capable for this mode to work.

VTP also uses and MD5 hash password protection for VTP updates. This can be simply enabled by adding the **password** command to the VTP domain. Example 2-7 demonstrates configuring a VTP domain ciscomd5 with the MD5 password of ccie.

Example 2-7 *Configuring a Password-Protected VTP Domain*

```
sw13 (enable) set vtp domain ciscomd5 password ccie
Generating MD5 secret for the password ....
VTP domain ciscomd5 modified
sw13 (enable)
```

The VTP domain can be viewed with the command **show vtp domain**, as in Example 2-8.

Example 2-8 *Configuring a Password-Protected VTP Domain*

```
sw13 (enable) show vtp domain
Domain Name                          Domain Index VTP Version Local Mode  Password
-------------------------------- ------------ ----------- ----------- ----------
ciscomd5                              1            2           server      configured


Vlan-count Max-vlan-storage Config Revision Notifications
---------- ---------------- --------------- -------------
9          1023             0               disabled


Last Updater   V2 Mode   Pruning   PruneEligible on VLANs
-------------- --------- --------- --------------------------
172.16.2.13    disabled 2-1000
sw13 (enable)
```

The **show vtp domain** command lists the VTP domain name, revision index, and VTP modes and tells whether updates are password-protected. This command also shows the number of VLANs in the domain and tells which ones are prune-eligible. The Last Update row lists the IP address of the switch from which the last VTP update was received. In the previous example, the last update was received from 172.16.2.13.

Configuring Physical Port Properties and Assigning Ports to VLANs on Catalyst 4000/5500/6500 Switches

The next two steps might be combined into one step, depending on whether the switch is configured as a VTP server/transparent or client. Essentially, this step involves configuring VLANs and port characteristics. There is no need to configure VLANs if the switch is a VTP client.

On the Catalyst switch, every port that is not a trunk will be assigned to the default VLAN, VLAN 1. If the port is assigned to any other VLAN, that VLAN must be created in the VLAN database. When trunk lines are configured, the VLANs created on the VTP server will be propagated to other VTP servers and clients.

This step also calls for you to configure physical Ethernet properties, such as full- or half-duplex operation, port speed, and so on. The following commands list some of the most common port configurations:

- **set port disable** [**mod_num/port_num**]—Disables a port, equivalent to the router **shutdown** command.

- **set port enable** [**mod_num/port_num**]—Enables a port, equivalent to the router **no shutdown** command.

- **set port duplex** [**mod_num/port_num**] [**full|half**]—Sets a port transmission type to full or half duplex.

- **set port name** [**mod_num/port_num**] *port_name*—Assigns a logical port name that will appear in the **show port** command.

- **set port speed** [**mod_num/port_num**] [**10|100|auto**]—Sets the port transmission speed to 10, 100, or autonegotiation. Gigabit Ethernet ports currently are fixed at 1000 Mbps; although this might change in the future.

- **set port level** [**mod_num/port_num**] [**normal|high**]—On the Catalyst 4000/5500/6500, if two ports access the switching bus simultaneously, a port with a "high" priority level will be serviced first.

Port status can be viewed with the **show port** command. This version of the command lists all the ports on the switch, along with the VLAN ID of the port, connection status, duplex setting, speed, and interface type. Example 2-9 lists the output of the **show port** command. Notice how the logical port names help identify the port's function. Port 2/19 also is set for a high priority, with the **set port level** command.

Example 2-9 **show port** *Command Output*

```
sw13 (enable) show port
Port  Name               Status     Vlan       Level  Duplex Speed Type
----- ------------------ ---------- ---------- ------ ------ ----- ------------
 2/1  gigabit_trunk_sw11 connected  trunk       normal  full  1000 1000BaseSX
 2/2  gigabit_trunk_sw12 connected  trunk       normal  full  1000 1000BaseSX
 2/3                     notconnect 1           normal  auto  auto 10/100BaseTX
 2/4                     notconnect 1           normal  auto  auto 10/100BaseTX
 2/5                     notconnect 1           normal  auto  auto 10/100BaseTX
 2/6                     notconnect 1           normal  auto  auto 10/100BaseTX
 2/7                     notconnect 1           normal  auto  auto 10/100BaseTX
 2/8                     notconnect 1           normal  auto  auto 10/100BaseTX
 2/9                     notconnect 1           normal  auto  auto 10/100BaseTX
 2/10                    notconnect 1           normal  auto  auto 10/100BaseTX
 2/11                    notconnect 1           normal  auto  auto 10/100BaseTX
 2/12                    notconnect 1           normal  auto  auto 10/100BaseTX
 2/13                    notconnect 1           normal  auto  auto 10/100BaseTX
 2/14                    connected  800         normal a-full a-100 10/100BaseTX
 2/15                    notconnect 200         normal  auto  auto 10/100BaseTX
 2/16                    notconnect 200         normal  auto  auto 10/100BaseTX
```

continues

Example 2-9 **show port** *Command Output (Continued)*

```
2/17                        notconnect 200       normal   auto   auto 10/100BaseTX
2/18                        notconnect 200       normal   auto   auto 10/100BaseTX
2/19 internet_conn          connected  100       high   a-half   a-10 10/100BaseTX
2/20 100_trunk_sw15         connected  trunk     normal a-full  a-100 10/100BaseTX
```

Detailed information about a port can be viewed by appending the port number to the **show port** command. The detailed version of this command provides all the information that the **show port** command provides, plus detailed information on the physical properties of the port. These include security, port errors, and collisions. Example 2-10 lists the detailed version of the **show port** command.

Example 2-10 *Detailed Port Information*

```
sw13 (enable) show port 2/1
Port  Name               Status      Vlan      Level  Duplex Speed Type
----- ------------------ ----------  ----------  ------ ------ ----- ------------
 2/1  gigabit_trunk_sw11 connected   trunk       normal  full  1000 1000BaseSX


Port  Security Secure-Src-Addr   Last-Src-Addr      Shutdown Trap       IfIndex
----- -------- ----------------- -----------------  -------- --------- -------
 2/1  disabled                                      No       disabled 9


Port   Send FlowControl   Receive FlowControl   RxPause TxPause Unsupported
       admin    oper       admin    oper                        opcodes
----- -------- --------   -------- --------     ------- ------- -----------
 2/1  desired  off        off      off             0       0       0


Port  Status     Channel   Channel    Neighbor                  Neighbor
                 mode      status     device                    port
----- ---------- --------  ---------- ------------------------- ----------
 2/1  connected  auto      not channel


Port  Align-Err  FCS-Err   Xmit-Err   Rcv-Err    UnderSize
----- ---------- --------- ---------- ---------- ---------
 2/1     -          0         0          0          0


Port  Single-Col Multi-Coll Late-Coll Excess-Col Carri-Sen Runts    Giants
----- ---------- ---------- ---------- ---------- --------- --------- ---------
 2/1      0          0          0          0         0         0         0


Last-Time-Cleared
-------------------------
Sat Jun 16 2001, 13:29:17
sw13 (enable)
```

Configuring VLANs on Catalyst 4000/5500/6500 Switches

VLANs are created on the Catalyst 4000/5500/6500 series switches with the **set vlan** command. Ports can be added to the VLAN by simply appending the port number to the **set vlan** command:

```
set vlan [1-1001] [mod/ports]
```

The **set vlan** command automatically creates the VLAN, if previously undefined, and adds the port to the VLAN. Multiple ports can be added to a VLAN by adding them with a ",", or denoting a range with a "-". For example, to add ports 1/1 and 1/12 to VLAN 2, you would use the following syntax:

```
set vlan 2 1/1,1/12
```

To add ports 1/10 and ports 2/1, 2/2, and 2/3 to VLAN 3, you would use the following:

```
Set vlan 3 1/10,2/1-2/3
```

Example 2-11 demonstrates the creation of VLAN 33, and adding ports 2/5, 2/10, 2/11, 2/12, and 2/13 to that VLAN in a single statement.

Example 2-11 *VLAN Creation*

```
sw13 (enable) set vlan 33 2/5,2/10-2/13
Vlan 33 configuration successful
VLAN 33 modified.
VLAN 1 modified.
VLAN  Mod/Ports
----  ---------------------
33    2/1-2,2/5,2/10-13,2/20

sw13 (enable)
```

When you create a VLAN, it has certain default values, such as MTU, prune eligibility, and so on. Table 2-12 lists the default values of VLANs. Most of these values can be changed with the **set vlan** command, the syntax for which is as follows:

```
set vlan 1-1001 [name {vlan_name}] [state {active | suspend}] [said {said_value}]
    [mtu mtu] [bridge {bridge_number}] [stp {ieee | ibm | auto}]
```

The parameters for this command are described as follows:

- **name**—Allows you to attach a 32-character name to the VLAN.

- **state**—Allows you to suspend the VLAN. A suspended VLAN is propagated through VTP, but no user traffic will be carried on the VLAN.

- **Security Association ID (SAID)**—Used to change the SAID value of the VLAN. The SAID value is used primarily in 802.10.

- **mtu, bridge, and stp**—Allows you to change the default MTU value, bridge number, and STP type. Extreme caution should be used when changing the MTU, bridge number, and STP type. These values should be changed only when addressing a specific issue that requires it.

Table 2-12 *Default VLAN Settings*

Feature	Default Value
Native or default VLAN	VLAN 1
Port VLAN assignments	All ports assigned to VLAN 1; Token Ring ports assigned to VLAN 1003
VTP mode	Server
VLAN state	Active
Normal VLAN range	VLAN 2 to VLAN 1001
VLAN reserved range*	VLAN 1006 to VLAN 1009
VLAN extended range*	VLAN 1025 to VLAN 2094
MTU size	1500 bytes for Ethernet
	4472 bytes for Token Ring
SAID value	100,000 plus VLAN number
	VLAN2 = SAID 100002
Prune eligibility	VLANS 2 to 1000 are prune-eligible
MAC address reduction	Disabled
Spanning Tree mode	PVST
Default FDDI VLAN	VLAN 1002
Default Token Ring TrCRF VLAN	VLAN 1003
Default FDDI Net VLAN	VLAN 1004
Default Token Ring TrBRF VLAN	VLAN 1005 with bridge number 0F
Spanning Tree version for TrBRF VLANs	IBM
TrCRF bridge mode	SRB

*   The VLAN reserved range is used on the Cat 6500 series to map nonreserved VLANs. The VLAN extended range is available on the Catalyst 6500 series switch. This range is an extension of the normal VLAN range. The extended and reserved VLAN ranges are not be propagated by VTP at this time. Token Ring and FDDI VLANs are listed on Ethernet-only switches because of global VTP information. Likewise, Token Ring switches' VLAN database will list Ethernet VLANs.

VLANs on the switch can be viewed in two ways. The **show vlan** command provides an overview of all the VLANs on the switch, their status, and what ports are assigned to them, along with the default VLAN values. Example 2-12 lists the output of the **show vlan** command. Notice how clear the VLAN name appears on the VLAN's assigned names. Assigning VLAN names will help the network self-document itself.

Example 2-12 show vlan *Command Output*

```
sw13 (enable) show vlan
VLAN Name                                 Status    IfIndex Mod/Ports, Vlans
---- -------------------------------- --------- ------- -----------------------

1    default                          active    4       2/3-4,2/6-9,2/21-34
2    management_VLAN                  active    64
3    Engineering_VLAN                 active    65
4    VLAN0004                         active    70
5    VLAN0005                         active    71
33   VLAN0033                         active    72      2/5,2/10-13
100  Internet_VLAN                    active    66      2/19
200  dummy_VLAN                       active    67      2/15-18
800  VLAN0800                         active    68      2/14
001  VLAN0801                         active    69
1002 fddi-default                     active    5
1003 token-ring-default               active    8
1004 fddinet-default                  active    6
1004 fddinet-default                  active    6


VLAN Type  SAID    MTU   Parent RingNo BrdgNo Stp  BrdgMode Trans1 Trans2
---- ----- ------- ----- ------ ------ ------ ---- -------- ------ ------
1    enet  100001  1500  -      -      -      -    -        0      0
2    enet  100002  1500  -      -      -      -    -        0      0
3    enet  100003  1500  -      -      -      -    -        0      0
4    enet  100004  1500  -      -      -      -    -        0      0
5    enet  100005  1500  -      -      -      -    -        0      0
33   enet  100033  1500  -      -      -      -    -        0      0
100  enet  100100  1500  -      -      -      -    -        0      0
200  enet  100200  1500  -      -      -      -    -        0      0
800  enet  100800  1500  -      -      -      -    -        0      0
801  enet  100801  1500  -      -      -      -    -        0      0
1002 fddi  101002  1500  -      -      -      -    -        0      0
1003 trcrf 101003  1500  -      -      -      -    -        0      0
1004 fdnet 101004  1500  -      -      -      ieee -        0      0
1005 trbrf 101005  1500  -      -      -      ibm  -        0      0

VLAN AREHops STEHops Backup CRF
---- ------- ------- ----------
1003 0       0       off
sw13 (enable)

VLAN AREHops STEHops Backup CRF
---- ------- ------- ----------
1003 0       0       off
sw13 (enable)
```

By adding the VLAN number behind the **show vlan** command, it provides information on just that particular VLAN. Example 2-13 shows the output of the **show vlan 2** command.

Example 2-13 show vlan2 *Command Output*

```
sw13 (enable) show vlan 2
VLAN Name                              Status    IfIndex Mod/Ports, Vlans
---- -------------------------------- --------- ------- ------------------------

2    management_VLAN                   active    64      2/1-2,2/20


VLAN Type  SAID       MTU   Parent RingNo BrdgNo Stp  BrdgMode Trans1 Trans2
---- ----- ---------- ----- ------ ------ ------ ---- -------- ------ ------
2    enet  100002     1500  -      -      -      -    -        0      0


VLAN AREHops STEHops Backup CRF
---- ------- ---- -- ----------
sw13 (enable)
```

VLANs can be deleted from the database with the **clear vlan** *vlan_number* command. VLANs can be deleted only if the switch is in a VTP server or it is in VTP transparent mode. When a VLAN is deleted on a VTP server, it removes the VLAN from the entire VTP domain. All switches in the VTP domain, VTP servers, and clients delete the VLAN from their database. For these reasons, caution should be used when clearing a VLAN. The switch will prompt you before final clearing of the VLAN, as shown in Example 2-14. Only the Cat 4000/5500/6500 will issue this warning when clearing a VLAN. VLANs on the Cat 2900XL and 3500G will be deleted when the changes are applied.

Example 2-14 *Deleting or Clearing a VLAN*

```
sw13 (enable) clear vlan 801
This command will deactivate all ports on vlan 801
in the entire management domain
Do you want to continue(y/n) [n]?y
Vlan 801 deleted
sw13 (enable)
```

Step 2: Configuring VTP and VLANs on Catalyst 2900XL/3500G Switches

Configuring VTP and VLANs on the 2900XL/3500G series switches follows the same three substeps as the Catalyst 5500:

Step 1   Configure a VTP domain and mode.

Step 2 Configure physical port properties and assign ports to VLANs.

Step 3 Configure VLANs if the switch is operating in VTP server mode.

Configuring VTP Domain and Mode on Catalyst 2900XL/3500G Switches

A VTP domain must be configured before any VLANs can be added in the VLAN database. The VLAN database is used to configure the VLAN properties of the switch. This we will refer to as the VLAN configuration mode. This mode is entered by the privileged command **vlan database.** The router-like configuration mode is to configure the physical port properties and assign them to VLANs. To enter this mode, key in **conf t.**

To configure the VTP domain use this syntax:

```
Switch#vlan database
(vlan)#vtp domain domain_name [password]
```

If you add a password behind the domain name, VTP updates will use a MD5 hash. The default VTP mode will be server mode; to change the mode, use the following command from the VLAN configuration mode:

```
(vlan)#vtp [server | client | transparent]
```

For more information on the VTP mode, see the previous section, "VTP and Trunking Protocols."

The VTP domain can be viewed using the **show vtp status** command. This command displays information about the VTP domain, such as configuration revision, domain name, operating mode, and so on. Example 2-15 lists the output of the **show vtp status** command.

Example 2-15 *Viewing the VTP Domain Information*

```
Switch#show vtp status
VTP Version                   : 2
Configuration Revision        : 28
Maximum VLANs supported locally : 254
Number of existing VLANs      : 13
VTP Operating Mode            : Server
VTP Domain Name               : ciscomd5
VTP Pruning Mode              : Disabled
VTP V2 Mode                   : Disabled
VTP Traps Generation          : Disabled
MD5 digest                    : 0xD9 0x50 0xE2 0x4F 0x09 0xDE 0x98 0x07
Configuration last modified by 172.16.2.13 at 6-17-01 18:10:24
sw11#
```

NOTE VLAN information is propagated only if the VTP revision number of the server is *higher* than the client's VTP revision number. If the VTP client's revision number is equal to or higher than the server's, it will not accept any VLAN information. To view the current VTP revision numbers, use the commands **show vtp domain** on Catalyst 4000/5500/6500 series switches and **show vtp status** on Catalyst 2900/3500 series switches.

Configuring Physical Port Properties and Assigning Ports to VLANs on Catalyst 2900XL/3500G Switches

The next step for VTP and VLAN configuration on Catalyst 2900XL/3500G switches is to configure any physical port properties, along with assigning the port to a VLAN. Physical port properties are changed from the configuration mode under the interface, much like you would do on a router. Example 2-16 demonstrates configuring an Ethernet port to 10-Mbps full duplex on a 2800 series switch. This example also assigns the logical name internet_port to the interface.

Example 2-16 *Configuring Physical Port Properties*

```
Switch#conf t
Enter configuration commands, one per line.  End with CNTL/Z.
04:59:58: %SYS-5-CONFIG_I: Configured from console by console
Switch(config)#interface fastEthernet 0/6
Switch(config-if)#speed 10
Switch(config-if)#duplex full
Switch(config-if)#description Internet_port
Switch(config-if)#exit
```

Some of the common physical properties of Ethernet that can be changed are as follows:

- **duplex [full | half | auto]**—Sets the port duplex mode.

- **speed [10 | 100 | auto]**—Sets the port speed.

- **mtu [*1500bytes-2018bytes*]**—Configures the MTU of the interface. Ensure that the MTU of the physical interface matches that of the VLAN, if you change this value.

- **description** *interface_description*—Allows you to set a logical description for the interface.

- **shutdown | no shutdown**—Disables and enables the interface.

The interface command **switchport** is used to assign VLANs to a port in one of three ways. The port can be set up to run as a trunk, or to run multiple or single VLANs. At this time, we will focus on assigning a port to a single VLAN. To accomplish this first, configure the port to be in access mode and then attach a VLAN to the port. The syntax used to accomplish this is as follows:

```
(config-if)#switchport mode [access | multi | trunk]
```

- **access**—Assigns the interface to a single VLAN.

- **multi**—Used to assign the interface to multiple VLANs. The VTP domain must be transparent, and the interface must be attached to a switch or a router.

- **trunk**—Used to configure the port as a trunk. We will discuss this option more in the next section.

To assign the port to a VLAN, use the following command:

```
(config-if)#switchport access vlan [1-1001 | dynamic]
```

The VLAN standard range is 1 to 1001. The **dynamic** keyword is used in VLAN Membership Policy Server (VMPS) configurations. VMPS will not be covered in this text; for more information on VMPS, see the book *Cisco LAN Switching*, by Kennedy Clark and Kevin Hamilton.

Example 2-17 demonstrates the configuration of FastEthernet 0/5 for VLAN 2.

Example 2-17 *Assigning VLAN 2 to Interface fast 0/5*

```
Switch(config)#int fastEthernet 0/5
Switch(config-if)#switchport mode access
Switch(config-if)#switchport access vlan 2
```

When the VTP mode is set to *transparent*, VLANs automatically are created with the **switchport access vlan** command. If the VTP mode is set as a *client*, you cannot configure VLANs on this switch. The VLANs must be configured on the server switch and propagated through VTP over a trunk to the client switch.

Configuring VLANs on Catalyst 2900XL/3500G Switches

The third step for VTP and VLAN configuration on Catalyst 2900XL/3500G switches involves configuring VLANs if the VTP mode is set as a *server*. VLANs are configured in the VLAN database simply by entering **vlan** *[2-1001] options*. Example 2-18 demonstrates the configuration of VLAN 175 with the name backbone. Changes in VLANs must be activated with the **apply** command. All changes will be applied when the VLAN database is exited. If a mistake is made, VLAN changes can be canceled with the **abort** or **reset** commands. The **abort** command exits you from the VLAN database, while the **reset** command cancels the current changes and rereads the current database.

Example 2-18 *Configuration of VLAN 175*

```
Switch#vlan database
Switch(vlan)#vlan 175 name backbone
VLAN 175 added:
    Name: backbone
Switch(vlan)#apply
APPLY completed.
Switch(vlan)#
```

Other options might be configured on the VLAN from this mode. They include the following:

```
Switch(vlan)# vlan vlan_num [name vlan_name] [state {active | suspend}] [said
said_value]
  [mtu mtu] [bridge bridge_number] [stp type {ieee | ibm | auto}]
```

- **name**—Allows you to attach a 32-character name to the VLAN.

- **state**—Allows you to suspend the VLAN. A suspended VLAN is propagated through VTP, but no user traffic will be carried on the VLAN.

- **said**—Used to change the SAID value of the VLAN. The SAID value is used primarily in 802.10.

- **mtu, bridge, and STP**—Allow you to change the default MTU value, bridge number, and STP type.

For the default VLAN values, refer to Table 2-11 in the previous section.

To find the status of VLANs on a 2900XL/3500G switch, use the same command used on the 4000/5500/6500 series switches. The **show vlan** *vlan_number* command displays all the VLANs on the switch, the state, and which ports are assigned to it. To display specific physical and logical information about a single VLAN, use the **show vlan id** [*vlan_number*]. Example 2-19 lists the output of the **show vlan** command, followed by the more specific version of command. Notice again how the VLAN logical names help immediately identify the port purpose.

Example 2-19 **show vlan** *Command Output*

```
sw11#show vlan
VLAN Name                             Status    Ports
---- -------------------------------- --------- -------------------------------
1    default                          active    Fa0/2, Fa0/3, Fa0/4, Fa0/5,
                                                Fa0/6, Fa0/7, Fa0/8, Fa0/9,
                                                Fa0/11, Fa0/12, Fa0/13, Fa0/14,
                                                Fa0/15, Fa0/16, Fa0/17, Fa0/18,
                                                Fa0/19, Fa0/22, Fa0/23, Fa0/24,
                                                Fa0/25, Fa0/26, Fa0/27, Fa0/28,
                                                Fa0/29, Fa0/30, Fa0/31, Fa0/32,
                                                Fa0/33, Fa0/34, Fa0/35, Fa0/36,
                                                Fa0/37, Fa0/38, Fa0/39, Fa0/40,
```

Example 2-19 show vlan *Command Output (Continued)*

```
                                                   Fa0/41, Fa0/42, Fa0/43, Fa0/44,
                                                   Fa0/45, Fa0/46, Fa0/47, Fa0/48,
                                                   Gi0/2
2    management_VLAN                   active
3    Engineering_VLAN                  active    Fa0/1
4    VLAN0004                          active
5    VLAN0005                          active
33   VLAN0033                          active
100  Internet_VLAN                     active
200  dummy_VLAN                        active
800  VLAN0800                          active
1002 fddi-default                      active
1003 token-ring-default                active
1004 fddinet-default                   active
1005 trnet-default                     active

VLAN Type  SAID       MTU   Parent RingNo BridgeNo Stp  BrdgMode Trans1 Trans2
---- ----- ----------   ----  ------ ------ -------- ---- -------- ------ ------
1    enet  100001     1500  -      -      -        -    -        0      0
2    enet  100002     1500  -      -      -        -    -        0      0
3    enet  100003     1500  -      -      -        -    -        0      0
4    enet  100004     1500  -      -      -        -    -        0      0
5    enet  100005     1500  -      -      -        -    -        0      0
33   enet  100033     1500  -      -      -        -    -        0      0
100  enet  100100     1500  -      -      -        -    -        0      0
200  enet  100200     1500  -      -      -        -    -        0      0
800  enet  100800     1500  -      -      -        -    -        0      0
1002 fddi  101002     1500  -      0      -        -    -        0      0
1003 tr    101003     1500  -      0      -        -    srb      0      0
1004 fdnet 101004     1500  -      -      1        ieee -        0      0
1005 trnet 101005     1500  -      -      1        ibm  -        0      0
sw11#

sw11#show vlan id 3
VLAN Name                             Status    Ports
---- -------------------------------- --------- -------------------------------
3    Engineering_VLAN                 active    Fa0/1

VLAN Type  SAID       MTU   Parent RingNo BridgeNo Stp  BrdgMode Trans1 Trans2
---- ----- ---------- ----- ------ ------ -------- ---- -------- ------ ------
3    enet  100003     1500  -      -      -        -    -        0      0
sw11#
```

Step 3: Configuring VLAN trunks on Catalyst 4000/5500/6500 Switches

Configuring trunks on the Catalyst is a two-step process:

Step 1   Configure the port as a trunk.

Step 2   Configure the trunk encapsulation to autonegotiate, or use ISL or 802.1q.

Configuring the autonegotiation, or DTP, is more difficult than simply statically defining the trunk. This is mainly because of some of the differences in the default trunks for the various Catalysts switches. Most Catalysts default to ISL; however, the Catalyst 4000 without the Layer 3 module doesn't support ISL. Another example is that 802.1q auto-negotiation is supported only in Software Release 4.2. It's these little things that can make DTP unreliable in large heterogeneous networks.

However, sometimes this feature is desirable. Table 2-12 lists all the modes and outcomes of DTP. By default, all ports are in a nontrunking status. You will have to configure each port as a trunk and put it into a mode. Recall from earlier that these are the five modes:

- **On**—Sets the port in a permanent trunking state. It also tries to negotiate the link to be a trunk.

- **Off**—Disables the port, and thereby the trunk.

- **Desirable**—Makes the port attempt to convert to a trunk link. The port becomes a trunk if the neighboring port is set to on, desirable, or auto modes.

- **Auto**—Converts the port to a trunk if the neighboring port is set to on or desirable modes.

- **Nonegotiate**—Puts the port into a trunk mode but prevents the port from sending DTP frames.

When the port is configured as a trunk, the encapsulation must be set. There are three types of encapsulation, ISL, 802.1q/DOT1Q, and negotiate. The **negotiate** option will do just that; first it will try to negotiate an ISL trunk, followed by an 802.1q trunk. The syntax to accomplish these two steps is as follows:

```
Switch (enable) set trunk mod_num/port_num [on | off | desirable | auto| nonegotiate]
Switch (enable) set trunk mod_num/port_num [isl | dot1q]
```

As mentioned previously, the most reliable and quickest way to configure a trunk without consulting Table 2-13 is to set the trunk to on and fix the encapsulation type to ISL or 802.1q/dot1q. Example 2-20 exhibits the configuration of an 802.1q trunk on port 2/6.

Example 2-20 *Configuring an 802.1q Trunk*

```
Switch (enable) set trunk 2/6 dot1q
Port(s)  2/6 trunk type set to dot1q.
Switch (enable) set trunk 2/6 on
Port(s)  2/6 trunk mode set to on.
Switch (enable) 2001 Jun 12 09:33:58 %DTP-5-TRUNKPORTON:Port 2/6 has become dot1q
trunk
Switch (enable) 2001 Jun 12 09:34:11 %PAGP-5-PORTTOSTP:Port 2/6 joined bridge port
2/6
```

Table 2-13 *Ethernet DTP Configuration Outcomes*

Neighbor Port	Trunk Mode and Trunk Encapsulation	off / ISL or DOT1Q	on / ISL	desirable / ISL	auto / ISL	on / DOT1Q	desirable / DOT1Q	auto / DOT1Q	desirable / negotiate	auto / negotiate
off	ISL or DOT1Q	Local: Nontrunk Neighbor: Nontrunk	Local: ISL trunk Neighbor: Nontrunk	Local: ISL trunk Neighbor: Nontrunk	Local: ISL trunk Neighbor: Nontrunk	Local: 1Q Trunk Neighbor: Non	Local: Nontrunk Neighbor: Nontrunk	Local: Nontrunk Neighbor: Nontrunk	Local: Nontrunk Neighbor: Nontrunk	Local: Nontrunk Neighbor: Nontrunk
on	ISL	Local: Nontrunk Neighbor: ISL trunk	Local: ISL trunk Neighbor: ISL trunk	Local: ISL trunk Neighbor: ISL trunk	Local: ISL trunk Neighbor: ISL trunk	Local: 1Q trunk Neighbor: ISL trunk	Local: Nontrunk Neighbor: ISL trunk	Local: Nontrunk Neighbor: Nontrunk	Local: ISL Neighbor: ISL	Local: ISL NEIGHBOR: ISL
desirable	ISL	Local: Nontrunk Neighbor: ISL trunk	Local: ISL trunk Neighbor: ISL trunk	Local: ISL trunk Neighbor: ISL trunk	Local: ISL trunk Neighbor: ISL trunk	Local: 1Q trunk Neighbor: Nontrunk	Local: Nontrunk Neighbor: Nontrunk	Local: Nontrunk Neighbor: Nontrunk	Local: ISL Neighbor: ISL	Local: ISL NEIGHBOR: ISL
auto	ISL	Local: Nontrunk Neighbor: Nontrunk	Local: ISL trunk Neighbor: ISL trunk	Local: ISL trunk Neighbor: ISL trunk	Local: Nontrunk Neighbor: Nontrunk	Local: 1Q trunk Neighbor: Nontrunk	Local: Nontrunk Neighbor: Nontrunk	Local: Nontrunk Neighbor: Nontrunk	Local: ISL Neighbor: ISL	Local: Nontrunk Neighbor: Nontrunk
on	DOT1Q	Local: Nontrunk Neighbor: 1Q trunk	Local: ISL trunk Neighbor: 1Q trunk	Local: Nontrunk Neighbor: 1Q trunk	Local: Nontrunk Neighbor: 1Q trunk	Local: 1Q trunk Neighbor: 1Q trunk	Local: 1Q trunk Neighbor: 1Q trunk	Local: 1Q trunk Neighbor: 1Q trunk	Local: 1Q trunk Neighbor: 1Q trunk	Local: 1Q trunk Neighbor: 1Q trunk
desirable	DOT1Q	Local: Nontrunk Neighbor: Nontrunk	Local: ISL trunk Neighbor: Nontrunk	Local: Nontrunk Neighbor: Nontrunk	Local: Nontrunk Neighbor: Nontrunk	Local: 1Q trunk Neighbor: 1Q trunk	Local: Nontrunk Neighbor: 1Q trunk	Local: Nontrunk Neighbor: 1Q trunk	Local: 1Q trunk Neighbor: 1Q trunk	Local: 1Q trunk Neighbor: 1Q trunk

continues

Table 2-13   *Ethernet DTP Configuration Outcomes (Continued)*

Neighbor Port	Trunk Mode and Trunk Encapsulation	off	on	desirable	auto	on	desirable	auto	desirable	auto
		ISL or DOT1Q	ISL	ISL	ISL	DOT1Q	DOT1Q	DOT1Q	negotiate	negotiate
auto	DOT1Q	Local: Nontrunk Neighbor: Nontrunk	Local: ISL trunk Neighbor: Nontrunk	Local: Nontrunk Neighbor: Nontrunk	Local: Nontrunk Neighbor: Nontrunk	Local: 1Q trunk NEIGHBOR: 1Q trunk	Local: 1Q trunk Neighbor: 1Q trunk	Local: Nontrunk Neighbor: Nontrunk	Local: 1Q trunk Neighbor: 1Q trunk	Local: Nontrunk Neighbor: Nontrunk
desirable	Negotiate	Local: Nontrunk Neighbor: Nontrunk	Local: ISL trunk Neighbor: ISL trunk	Local: ISL trunk Neighbor: ISL trunk	Local: ISL trunk Neighbor: ISL trunk	Local: 1Q trunk Neighbor: 1Q trunk	Local: 1Q trunk Neighbor: 1Q trunk	Local: ISL trunk Neighbor: ISL trunk	Local: ISL Neighbor: ISL	Local: ISL Neighbor: ISL
auto	Negotiate	Local: Nontrunk Neighbor: Nontrunk	Local: ISL Neighbor: ISL trunk	Local: ISL trunk Neighbor: ISL trunk	Local: Nontrunk Neighbor: Nontrunk	Local: 1Q trunk Neighbor: 1Q trunk	Local: 1Q trunk Neighbor: 1Q trunk	Local: Nontrunk Neighbor: Nontrunk	Local: ISL Neighbor: ISL	Local: Nontrunk Neighbor: Nontrunk

NOTE   Another autoconfiguration issue might arise with VTP and DISL. When DISL negotiates an ISL trunk, it includes the VTP name in the message. If the VTP domain names differ on the switches, the trunk will not become active. Again to circumvent this, simply configure the trunk to be on, and configure the encapsulation type.

To view the status of a trunk, use the following commands:

```
show trunk [detail]
show trunk [mod_num/port_num] [detail]
show vtp status
```

Example 2-21 lists the output of **show trunk** command. If the trunk is not listed, some key fields to note are the following:

- Status
- Mode
- Encapsulation
- Vlans allowed and active in the management domain
- Peer-Port

The status of the trunk should be trunking, and the mode should be on or should match a valid setting for DTP, as listed in Table 2-12. The encapsulation must match on both sides of the trunk. The "VLANs that are allowed and active in the management domain" states what VLANs the trunk is sending; if no VLANs are listed, the trunk is not configured properly. The native VLAN ID is the VLAN that 802.1q will use this VLAN for its single instance of Spanning Tree (MST). This VLAN must be the same throughout the VTP domain.

Example 2-21 **show trunk** *Command Output*

```
Switch (enable) show trunk detail
Port        Mode           Encapsulation  Status        Native vlan
--------    -----------    -------------  ------------  -----------
  2/1       on             dot1q          trunking      1
  2/2       on             dot1q          trunking      1

Port        Peer-Port  Mode         Encapsulation  Status
--------    ---------  -----------  -------------  ------------
  2/1       GigabitEt  unknown      unknown        unknown
  2/2       GigabitEt  unknown      unknown        unknown

Port        Vlans allowed on trunk
--------    ------------------------------------------------------------------
  2/1       1-1005
  2/2       1-1005
```

continues

Example 2-21 show trunk *Command Output (Continued)*

```
Port      Vlans allowed and active in management domain
--------  ------------------------------------------------------------------
  2/1     1-5,33,100,200,800
  2/2     1-5,33,100,200,800

Port      Vlans in spanning tree forwarding state and not pruned
--------  ------------------------------------------------------------------
  2/1     1-5,33,100,200,800
  2/2     1-3
Switch (enable)
```

Sometimes, it might be hard to determine whether a trunk line is functioning. The trunk can report a status of trunking but not be in a fully exchanging VTP updates. The trunk status should be viewed on each side of the link, to ensure that it is functioning properly. Observing the Peer-Port status is another quick way to tell whether the trunk has recognized the other side of the link. If the Peer-Port status is unknown, it can mean that an encapsulation mismatch has occurred and that the trunk is not operating properly.

As VTP synchronizes within the domain, the VLAN database from server to server and server to client will have the same VLANs listed in them. Only switches in the VTP transparent mode or trunks that have VLANs *cleared* will have different VLAN databases. Comparing the VLAN databases of the two switches connected by a trunk is another way to verify that the trunk is working.

When the trunk becomes active, VTP advertisements will be sent and received. Three types of VTP advertisements occur on the trunk:

- **Subset advertisements**—Subset advertisements are issued when you create, delete, or modify a VLAN.

- **Request advertisements**—Request advertisements are issued from the switch whenever the Catalyst is reset or when a change in the local VTP domain occurs, such as a name change, or when the switch hears a VTP summary advertisement with a higher configuration revision number than its own.

- **Summary advertisements**—Summary advertisements are issued every five minutes by the switch. The main purpose of the summary advertisement is for the switch to verify the VTP revision number, thereby ensuring that the VLAN databases are up-to-date. If it has a lower revision number, it issues a request for new VLAN information.

You can observe VTP advertisements with the **show vtp status** command as demonstrated in Example 2-22. This should be used as another indicator that the trunk line is functioning properly.

Example 2-22 *Observing VTP Advertisements with the* **show vtp status** *Command*

```
Switch (enable) show vtp status
VTP statistics:
summary advts received          66
subset  advts received          4
request advts received          1
summary advts transmitted       16
subset  advts transmitted       13
request advts transmitted       0
No of config revision errors    0
No of config digest errors      0

VTP pruning statistics:

Trunk      Join Transmitted   Join Received   Summary advts received from
                                              non-pruning-capable device
--------   ---------------    -------------   ---------------------------
  2/1      1047               1045            0
  2/2      1041               1046            0
  2/20     631                635            0
Switch (enable)
```

The **show trunk** command also lists the VLANs that are *prune-eligible*. Do not confuse *prune-eligible* VLANs with VLAN propagation. *Prune-eligible* means that unnecessary broadcast and user data, for a specific VLAN, will not be forwarded over trunk lines to switches that do not have an active port in that particular VLAN. By default, all VLAN information and Spanning Tree frames for each VLAN are advertised out all trunking interfaces. VLANs and STP can be removed from a trunk only by using the **clear trunk** command. We will discuss these functions more in the upcoming section "Step 4: Controlling STP and VLAN Propagation."

NOTE   Recall from the previous section that VTP information is communicated only from a VTP server to a VTP client if the VTP server revision number is greater than the client's. Extreme caution should be used whenever changing a VTP server or VTP client in a "synchronized" network. When the network is synchronized, all VTP revision numbers will match. When you make a change to VTP or the VLAN, the revision number will increment, so the switch that you are changing has a chance of becoming the device with the highest VTP revision number. This, in turn, could synchronize the whole network to this switch's VLAN database that you are modifying.

Step 3: Configuring VLAN Trunks on Catalyst 2900XL/3500G Switches

Configuring trunks on this series of Catalyst is a two-step process just like on the Catalyst 5500 family:

Step 1   Configure the port as a trunk.

Step 2   Configure the trunk encapsulation to use ISL or 802.1q.

By default, all ports are set to a nontrunking mode, so the first step is to configure the port as a trunk. The second step calls for you to set the encapsulation of the trunk. These steps are accomplished with the following commands from the interface configuration mode:

```
(config-if)#switchport mode trunk
(config-if)#switchport trunk encapsulation [isl | dot1q]
```

Example 2-23 demonstrates the configuration of an ISL trunk.

Example 2-23 *Configuring an ISL Trunk*

```
Switch#conf t
Enter configuration commands, one per line.  End with CNTL/Z.
Switch(config)#int fastEthernet 0/19
Switch(config-if)#switchport mode trunk
Switch(config-if)#switchport trunk encapsulation isl
Switch(config-if)#^Z
```

To verify that the trunk is working, be sure to check the status of both sides of link, as mentioned previously. The output of the **show interface** *interface_name* **switchport** command presents a general status of the trunk. The information presented here is similar to the information for the **show trunk** command on the Catalyst 4000/5500/6500 switch. This command shows the status of the trunk and the encapsulation. VLAN information such as the default VLAN, the active VLANs on the links, and any prune-eligible VLANs also is listed. Example 2-24 lists the output of the **show interface** *interface_name* **switchport** command.

Example 2-24 *Status of a Trunk Line*

```
sw15#show int fastEthernet 0/19 switchport
Name: Fa0/19
Switchport: Enabled
Administrative mode: trunk
Operational Mode: trunk
Administrative Trunking Encapsulation: isl
Operational Trunking Encapsulation: isl
Negotiation of Trunking: Disabled
Access Mode VLAN: 0 ((Inactive))
Trunking Native Mode VLAN: 1 (default)
Trunking VLANs Enabled: ALL
Trunking VLANs Active: 1-5,33,100,200,800
Pruning VLANs Enabled: 2-1001
```

Example 2-24 *Status of a Trunk Line (Continued)*

```
Priority for untagged frames: 0
Override vlan tag priority: FALSE
Voice VLAN: none
Appliance trust: none
sw15#
```

Along with the trunk lines, the VTP domain counters should be examined using the **show vtp counters** command (see Example 2-25). This will help present a clearer picture on whether the trunk line is operational.

Example 2-25 *Determining the Status of a Trunk by Viewing VTP Counters*

```
sw15#show vtp counters
VTP statistics:
Summary advertisements received      : 10
Subset advertisements received       : 2
Request advertisements received      : 0
Summary advertisements transmitted : 55
Subset advertisements transmitted    : 2
Request advertisements transmitted : 12
Number of config revision errors     : 0
Number of config digest errors       : 0
Number of V1 summary errors          : 0


VTP pruning statistics:

Trunk             Join Transmitted Join Received    Summary advts received from
                                                    non-pruning-capable device
--------------- ---------------- ---------------- ---------------------------
Fa0/19                801              775              0
Fa0/20                1173             1164             0
Fa0/21
```

In 802.1q networks, it is critical to ensure that the default VLAN is the same throughout the entire VTP domain. This is because 802.1q uses MST, and MST makes the entire VTP domain appear as a single-bridged domain to all third-party 802.1q switches. Cisco ensures compatibility with MST domains by implementing PVST+ along with MST. This is an extended version of Per VLAN Spanning Tree (PVST+) that provides seamless transparent integration for 802.1q networks. MST runs on the default VLAN, so it is important to have the same default VLAN throughout the entire internetwork. The default VLAN is 1. To change the default VLAN, use the following interface command on the trunk:

```
(config-if)#switchport trunk native vlan vlan-id
```

To change the native VLAN on a Catalyst 4000/5500/6500 series switches, create a VLAN on the same port that the 802.1 trunk is on.

Step 4: Controlling STP and VLAN Propagation

The final step for configuring Catalyst Ethernet switches is optional but can be extremely important in large networks. Cisco implements a couple of features that allow for switches to be plug-and-play in small networks, but these can have the negative effect of generating significant amounts of traffic in large networks. PVST, coupled with the default setting that every VLAN is communicated on every trunk port, can cause the edge switches to be overrun processing Spanning Tree requests and other broadcasts.

For example, in the network in Figure 2-10, the crane switch has only a single VLAN, VLAN 2. But because this switch is in the same VTP domain as the other switches, it will participate in Spanning Tree for VLAN 3 and VLAN 4. There is no need for this switch to waste resources processing Spanning Tree requests for a VLAN that is not even on the switch. The larger and more redundant the network is, the worse the problem gets. For example, if you had 50 edge switches, there would be 50 separate Spanning Tree topologies on one trunk for one switch! And all of this happens before any user traffic can use the switch.

It is a common misconception that *VLAN pruning* will solve STP issues. But VLAN pruning affects only user traffic—specifically broadcast, multicast, and flooded unicast traffic. Basically, STP constructs the path that data can flow on, and pruning controls the "broadcast" data that flows on that path.

Cisco offers two effective ways for dealing with excessive broadcasts and STP:

- **Clearing VLANs from trunks**—Clearing VLANs off a trunk essentially removes those VLANs from the Spanning Tree topology for that trunk. The downstream switch no longer will receive BPDUs for the VLAN cleared. No user traffic for that VLAN will be capable of passing down this trunk.

- **VLAN pruning**—VLAN pruning states that if VTP pruning is enabled, and if a downstream switch does not have an active port in that VLAN being pruned, the switch prevents the forwarding of flooded traffic to that prune-eligible downstream VLAN. VTP pruning is a method of traffic control that reduces unnecessary broadcast, multicast, and flooded unicast traffic. VTP pruning blocks flooded traffic to VLANs on trunk ports that are included in the pruning-eligible list. If the VLANs are configured as pruning-ineligible, traffic is flooded normally.

In Figure 2-10, VLAN 2 is present on the crane, yin, and yang switches but not on the mantis switch. If VTP pruning is enabled for VLAN 2, the mantis switch will not receive broadcast, multicast, and flooded unicast traffic for VLAN 2. Likewise, the crane switch will not receive the flooded traffic from VLAN 3 and VLAN 4.

The clearing trunks need to be performed on the "core" switches, or the VTP servers. All VLANs should be cleared, except the ones that exist on the downstream switch. Newer versions of Catalyst software allow for the clearing of VLAN 1. However, most switches still will not allow you to clear VLAN 1. To clear VLANs from trunks on the Catalyst 4000/5500/6500 family of switches, use the following command:

```
Switch (enable) clear trunk [mod_num/port_num] vlans_2-1001
```

Figure 2-10 *VLAN Trunking and STP*

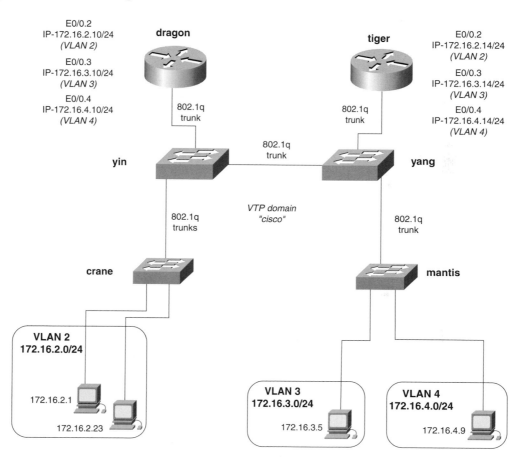

E0/0.2
IP-172.16.2.10/24
(VLAN 2)

E0/0.3
IP-172.16.3.10/24
(VLAN 3)

E0/0.4
IP-172.16.4.10/24
(VLAN 4)

dragon

tiger

E0/0.2
IP-172.16.2.14/24
(VLAN 2)

E0/0.3
IP-172.16.3.14/24
(VLAN 3)

E0/0.4
IP-172.16.4.14/24
(VLAN 4)

802.1q
trunk

802.1q
trunk

802.1q
trunk

yin

yang

802.1q
trunks

*VTP domain
"cisco"*

802.1q
trunk

crane

mantis

**VLAN 2
172.16.2.0/24**

172.16.2.1

172.16.2.23

**VLAN 3
172.16.3.0/24**

172.16.3.5

**VLAN 4
172.16.4.0/24**

172.16.4.9

VLAN

Multiple VLANs can be cleared using a comma as a separator and a hyphen for a range of inclusive VLANs. For example, to clear VLAN 3, VLAN 5, and VLANs 10 to 150, you would use the following command:

```
Switch (enable) clear trunk 2/1 2,5 10-150
```

To clear trunks from VLANs on the Catalyst 2900XL/3500G family of switches, use the following interface command:

```
Switch(config-if)#switchport trunk allowed vlan [add | all | except | remove] vlans_2-1001
```

- **add**—Adds the following VLANs to the trunk
- **all**—Includes all VLANs on the trunk
- **except**—Includes all VLANs except the following
- **remove**—Removes the following VLANs from the trunk

For example, to clear VLAN 3 through VLAN 6, you would use the following command:

```
Switch(config-if)#switchport trunk allowed vlan remove 3-6
```

Figure 2-11 shows the same network as Figure 2-10, with updated interfaces names. In this example, on the yin switch, all VLANs except 1 and 2 on the trunk to the crane switch will be cleared. Before clearing the trunk, examine Spanning Tree for the various VLANs on the yin switch. You will notice that Spanning Tree for all the VLANs is running on all trunks. Example 2-26 lists the output of the **show spanning-tree** command for VLAN 3. This command is key to helping you understand and control Spanning Tree in switched networks. In the next section, we discuss this command in more detail. Notice that in Example 2-26, VLAN 3 is running on the trunk to the dragon router, the yang switch, and the crane switch.

Example 2-26 *Spanning Tree Is Forwarding on All Trunks*

```
yin#show spanning-tree vlan 3

Spanning tree 3 is executing the IEEE compatible Spanning Tree protocol
  Bridge Identifier has priority 32768, address 0004.275e.f5c2
  Configured hello time 2, max age 20, forward delay 15
  Current root has priority 32768, address 0004.275e.f0c2
  Root port is 67, cost of root path is 4
  Topology change flag not set, detected flag not set, changes 1
  Times:  hold 1, topology change 35, notification 2
          hello 2, max age 20, forward delay 15
  Timers: hello 0, topology change 0, notification 0

Interface Fa0/10 (port 23) in Spanning tree 3 is FORWARDING
    Port path cost 19, Port priority 128
    Designated root has priority 32768, address 0004.275e.f0c2
    Designated bridge has priority 32768, address 0004.275e.f5c2
    Designated port is 23, path cost 4
    Timers: message age 0, forward delay 0, hold 0
    BPDU: sent 3766, received 0

Interface Fa0/19 (port 33) in Spanning tree 3 is FORWARDING   ←Trunk to the crane
switch
    Port path cost 19, Port priority 128
    Designated root has priority 32768, address 0004.275e.f0c2
    Designated bridge has priority 32768, address 0004.275e.f5c2
    Designated port is 33, path cost 4
    Timers: message age 0, forward delay 0, hold 0
    BPDU: sent 3768, received 1

Interface Gi0/1 (port 67) in Spanning tree 3 is FORWARDING
    Port path cost 4, Port priority 128
```

Example 2-26 *Spanning Tree Is Forwarding on All Trunks (Continued)*

```
        Designated root has priority 32768, address 0004.275e.f0c2
        Designated bridge has priority 32768, address 0004.275e.f0c2
        Designated port is 67, path cost 0
        Timers: message age 2, forward delay 0, hold 0
        BPDU: sent 5, received 3773
    yin#
```

Figure 2-11 *VLAN Trunking and STP*

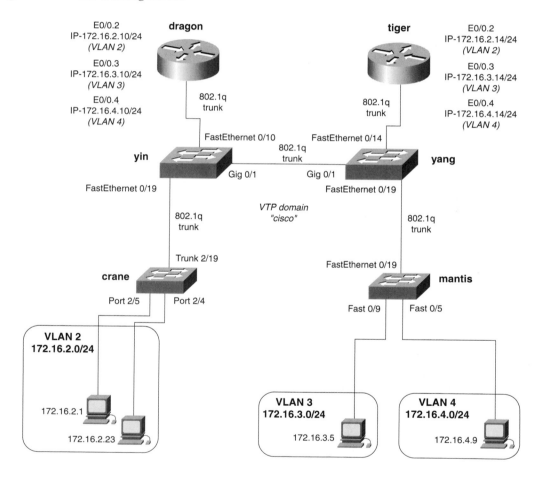

VLAN

In this particular example, the yin switch is a Catalyst 3500G series switch. Therefore, to clear the trunk, you should use the **switchport** command. Example 2-27 demonstrates the clearing of VLANs 3 to 1001 on the trunk between the yin and crane switches. The second portion of the example shows the Spanning Tree for VLAN 3. Notice that VLAN 3 is no longer forwarding out the trunk Fa0/19, the trunk line to the crane switch.

Example 2-27 *Clearing a Trunk of VLANs*

```
yin(config)#int fastEthernet 0/19
yin(config-if)#switchport trunk allowed vlan remove 3-1001
yin(config-if)#^Z


yin#show spanning-tree vlan 3

Spanning tree 3 is executing the IEEE compatible Spanning Tree protocol
  Bridge Identifier has priority 32768, address 0004.275e.f5c2
  Configured hello time 2, max age 20, forward delay 15
  Current root has priority 32768, address 0004.275e.f0c2
  Root port is 67, cost of root path is 4
  Topology change flag set, detected flag not set, changes 4
  Times:  hold 1, topology change 35, notification 2
          hello 2, max age 20, forward delay 15
  Timers: hello 0, topology change 0, notification 0

Interface Fa0/10 (port 23) in Spanning tree 3 is FORWARDING
    Port path cost 19, Port priority 128
    Designated root has priority 32768, address 0004.275e.f0c2
    Designated bridge has priority 32768, address 0004.275e.f5c2
    Designated port is 23, path cost 4
    Timers: message age 0, forward delay 0, hold 0
    BPDU: sent 4589, received 0

Interface Gi0/1 (port 67) in Spanning tree 3 is FORWARDING
    Port path cost 4, Port priority 128
    Designated root has priority 32768, address 0004.275e.f0c2
    Designated bridge has priority 32768, address 0004.275e.f0c2
    Designated port is 67, path cost 0
    Timers: message age 3, forward delay 0, hold 0
    BPDU: sent 14, received 4593
yin#
```

The command **show interface** *interface_name* **switchport allowed-vlan** also shows what VLANs are carried on the trunk. The **show trunk** command is the Catalyst 4000/5500/6500 equivalent of the command. Example 2-28 lists the output of the **switchport** command, showing that VLANs 3 to 1001 no longer appear on the trunk. VLANs 1002 to 1005 are not Ethernet VLANs and cannot be cleared on this trunk.

Example 2-28 *Showing the Allowed VLANs on a Trunk*

```
yin#show int fastEthernet 0/19 switchport allowed-vlan
"1,2,1002-1005"
yin#
```

Clearing trunk lines is one way to control STP, but for the switches that need redundancy, additional methods to control STP must be used.

NOTE

Monitoring Switch Ports with a Network Analyzers

Switches do not forward all frames to every port in a VLAN. Recall that the switch is selective on what ports it forwards frames to, even when they are in the same VLAN. Because of this, you must enter a special command when monitoring a switch port with a network analyzer:

set span {*mod/src_ports*} {*dest_mod/dest_port_of_monitor*} [**rx** | **tx** | **both**]

Without this command, the network analyzer will not properly capture information on the VLAN you're monitoring.

Configuring STP Root Placement

Redundant switched networks do not perform any type of automatic load balancing. Because the STP forwarding/blocking decision is based in part on a static MAC addresses, all traffic tends to follow the same direction and the same path for all VLANs. This leads to some links being overutilized, while others remain idle. Figure 2-12 illustrates a network that has all converged on a single switch. The yang switch is the root of STP for VLANs 2, 3, 4, and 5.

If you want to load-balance between the yin and yang switches, or if you were using HSRP on the dragon and tiger routers, you would want to control STP root placement. For example, if the dragon router was the HSRP primary for VLAN 2, you would want traffic to go through the yin switch instead of the yang switch. To control and distribute traffic in a switched network, the root for STP must be manually configured.

There are multiple ways to configure the root of Spanning Tree for Catalyst switches. The methods that you use to set the root depend mostly on the environment that you trying to control. When setting the root bridge, you essentially are telling STP what ports to put into blocking and what ports to put into forwarding mode. Because STP is run on a per-VLAN basis (PVST), each VLAN can have a different root bridge. This enables you to send traffic over links that normally would not get used. In Figure 2-13, the yin switch is set to be the STP root for VLAN 4 and VLAN 5, while the yang switch is the STP root for VLAN 2 and VLAN 3. This causes the edge switches to balance their load more evenly over the trunks lines. VLANs 4 and 5 will forward to yin, while VLANs 2, 3 will forward to yang.

Figure 2-12 *STP Root*

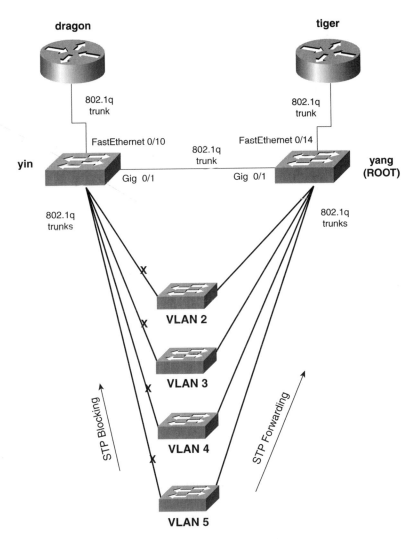

Before we can further discuss how to set STP root, you must learn how to determine where the root bridge is located. The key command for this on the Catalyst 4000/5500/6500 is the **show spantree** *vlan* command. We prefer to use this command because Spanning Tree operates on a per-VLAN basis. Example 2-29 lists the output of the **show spantree** command.

Figure 2-13 *STP Root*

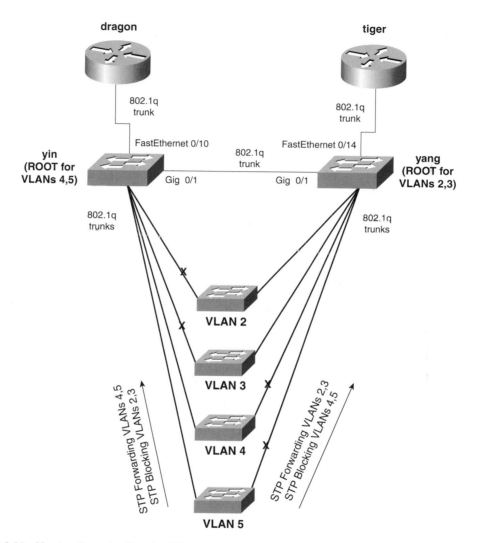

Example 2-29 *Viewing Spanning Tree for VLAN 2*

```
crane (enable) show spantree 2
VLAN 2
Spanning tree enabled
Spanning tree type          ieee

Designated Root             00-30-19-76-4d-01
```

continues

Example 2-29   *Viewing Spanning Tree for VLAN 2 (Continued)*

```
Designated Root Priority     88
Designated Root Cost         0
Designated Root Port         1/0
Root Max Age   20 sec     Hello Time 2  sec    Forward Delay 15 sec

Bridge ID MAC ADDR           00-30-19-76-4d-01
Bridge ID Priority           88
Bridge Max Age 20 sec     Hello Time 2  sec    Forward Delay 15 sec

Port      Vlan  Port-State      Cost   Priority  Fast-Start  Group-Method
--------- ----  --------------  -----  --------  ----------  ------------
  2/4     2     forwarding      100        32    disabled
  2/19    2     forwarding       19        32    disabled
  2/20    2     forwarding       19        32    disabled
crane (enable)
```

Every bit of information provided by this command is useful. The fields are defined as follows (refer to the previous section of STP for more details):

- **Spanning Tree Type**—The type of Spanning Tree Protocol in use—IBM, DEC, or IEEE.

- **Designated Root**—The MAC address of the root bridge.

- **Designated Root Priority**—The bridge priority that was received from the root bridge. The values of the bridge priority range from 0 to 65,535, with 32,768 as the default.

- **Designated Root Cost**—The cumulative cost to the root bridge.

- **Designated Root Port**—The DR root port for that segment.

- **Root Max Age, Hello Time, Forward Delay**—The three STP timers as sent by the root bridge.

- **Bridge ID MAC ADDR**—The MAC address that is being used for this VLAN by this local bridge.

- **Bridge ID Priority**—The priority of the local bridge.

- **Root Max Age, Hello Time, Forward Delay**—The three STP timers on the local bridge.

The final columns show each port that is participating in STP within the VLAN. They also list whether the port is forwarding or blocking, as well as the cost and service priority of the port. Do not confuse this priority with the Spanning Tree bridge priority. The values of the port priority ranges from 0 to 63 (high to low), with 32 as the default.

The command to view Spanning Tree on a Catalyst 2900XL/3500G series switches is as follows:

```
Switch#show spanning-tree vlan vlan
```

The previous example (Example 2-26) demonstrated the output of this command.

Another command that is useful in presenting a general operational picture of Spanning Tree is the **show spantree summary** command. This command provides an overview of the VLANs and tells how many ports and the state of the port. Example 2-30 lists the output for this command.

Example 2-30 *Viewing Spanning Tree for VLAN 2*

```
Switch (enable) show spantree summary
Summary of connected spanning tree ports by vlan

Uplinkfast disabled for bridge.
Backbonefast disabled for bridge.

Vlan  Blocking Listening Learning Forwarding STP Active
----- -------- --------- -------- ---------- ----------
    1        1         0        0          1          2
    ?        0         0        0          3          3
    3        0         0        0          2          2
    4        0         0        0          2          2
  100        0         0        0          2          2
  200        0         0        0          2          2
  300        0         0        0          2          2


      Blocking Listening Learning Forwarding STP Active
----- -------- --------- -------- ---------- ----------
Total        1         0        0         14         15
Switch (enable)
```

To properly set the STP root, it helps to recall the four-step decision process that STP follows when determining root and which ports will forward and which ones will block. The four-step decision process is based on the following:

1 Lowest root BID *<Priority followed by MAC address>*

2 Lowest path cost to root bridge; the cumulative cost of the all paths to root

3 Lowest sender BID

4 Lowest port ID

On the Catalyst 4000/5500/6500 series switches, four primary ways exist to control STP root selection:

- **set spantree root**
- **set spantree priority**
- **set spantree portvlancost**
- **set spantree portvlanpri**

The sections that follow examine the complete syntax and description for what each of these commands do.

set spantree root Command   The syntax for this command is as follows:

```
set spantree root [secondary] [vlan_list] [dia network_diameter] [hello hello_time]
```

This command is a powerful macro that issues Spanning Tree commands to adjust the Spanning Tree timers until the local bridge/switch is elected root. It does this only *once* upon keying in the command. If other switches are added to the network, this command should be performed again. The Catalyst accomplishes this by examining the BDPUs of the existing root bridge. If the value of the priority is greater then 8192, the macro sets the local bridge priority to 8192. If the BPDU contains a priority less then 8192, the macro sets the local bridge priority to 1 less than that value. For example, the root bridge sends a configuration BDPU that is received by the new switch. The new switch, with the macro enabled, examines the priority of the BPDU and finds the value equal to 89. The macro then adjusts the local bridge priority to 88, thereby becoming elected as the new root bridge. The secondary option sets the bridge's local priority to 16,384. Recall that the default bridge priority is 32,768, so the value of 16,384 is a reasonable choice for the backup bridge. The Diameter and Hello timers are used to adjust the hello and max age parameters of STP. Care should be used when adjusting any timers other then the bridge priority. This command exists only on the Catalyst 4000/5500/6500 series switches.

set spantree priority Command   The syntax for this command is as follows:

```
set spantree priority [bridge-priority] [vlans]
```

This command is a direct way to influence the bridge priority. Because the priority is the single most important factor in root selection, this command forces the election of root cleanly. The values of the bridge priority range from 0 to 65535. Valid values are 0, 4096, 8192, 12288, 16384, 20480, 24576, 28672, 32768 (default), 36864, 40960, 45056, 49152, 53248, 57344, and 61440, with 0 indicating high priority and 61440 indicating low priority.

set spantree portvlancost Command   The syntax for this command is as follows:

```
set spantree portvlancost mod_num/port_num [cost 1-65535] [vlans]
```

Use this command to influence the cost that Spanning Tree reports to downstream neighbors. This is the cost that STP uses when adding all the possible paths to root when determining which one is the least-cost path. Remember, a lower-cost path is more preferable. See Table 2-5 for a complete list of the default link cost values.

set spantree portvlanpri Command   The syntax for this command is as follows:

```
set spantree portvlanpri mod_num/port_num [priority 0-63] [vlans]
```

This command sets the port priority that the port will send to its downstream neighbors. Because the command can be performed on per-VLAN per port level, it can be useful. A primary use of this command is when switches want to load-share over multiple trunks among them. The values of the port priority range from 0 to 63, with 32 as the default, where 0 is a high priority and 63 is a low priority.

Table 2-14 lists the commands along with where in the STP decision process the command is exerting influence. The higher up in the chart it is, the more powerful the command is in controlling root selection.

Table 2-14   *Ethernet DTP Configuration Outcomes*

	Catalyst 4k/55k/65k set Command	Catalyst 2900XL/3500G Global Configuration Command
1-Lowest Root BID	set spantree priority set spantree root macro	spanning-tree [vlan *vlan_id*] [priority *0-65535*]
2-Lowest Path Cost to Root	set spantree portvlancost	spanning-tree [vlan *vlan_id*] [cost *1-65535*]
3-Lowest Sender BID	set spantree priority	spanning-tree [vlan *vlan_id*] [priority *0-65535*]
4-Lowest Port ID	set spantree portvlanpri	spanning-tree [vlan *vlan_id*] [port-priority *0-255*]

Practical Example: Configuring a Routed and Switched Network

Let's apply a couple of these concepts to a practical example. Figure 2-14 shows a fairly common network that consists of switches and routers. There are two active VLANs on the network, VLAN2 and VLAN4. VLAN2 is the management VLAN and has some user traffic in it. It has the IP subnet of 172.16.2.0/24. VLAN4 is strictly a user VLAN; it has the IP subnet of 172.16.4.0/24. The dragon router routes between the VLANs and serve as the default gateway for the switches. In this example, you will configure the following:

- Basic IP management, using 172.16.2.10 as the IP default gateway.
- An ISL trunk between the router dragon and the yin switch. The dragon router will route between the VLANs using EIGRP as the routing protocol.
- 802.1q trunks between the yin, crane, and mantis switches.
- The appropriate VLANs, as indicated in Figure 2-14.

This network has two kinds of switches in it, so we can demonstrate the commands used in both families of switches. Beginning with the yin switch, you need to configure an IP address and a default gateway, VLAN trunks, along with VLANs 2 and 4. Recall the four-step process to configure Ethernet switches:

Step 1   Configure switch management.

Step 2   Configure VTP and VLANs.

Step 3   Configure VLAN trunks, if applicable.

Step 4   (Optional) Control STP and VLAN propagation.

Figure 2-14 *Switched and Routed Network*

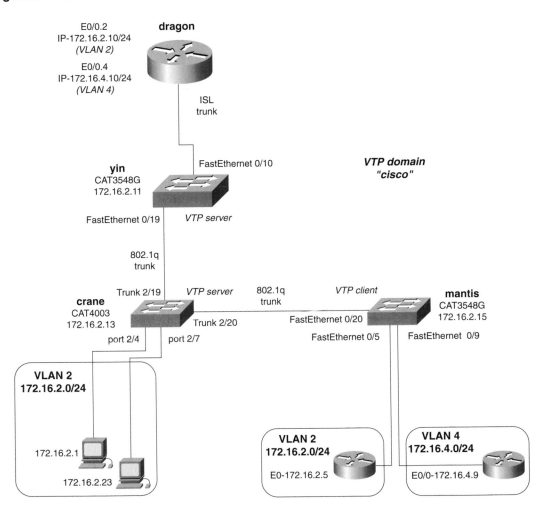

To configure the management VLAN as VLAN 2, you need to define a virtual interface called VLAN 2 on the yin and mantis routers. Assign the management IP address to this interface, and activate it by shutting down the virtual interface vlan 1. Example 2-31 illustrates the first step of the configuration on the yin router.

Example 2-31 *Configuring Basic Management*

```
Switch#conf t
Enter configuration commands, one per line.  End with CNTL/Z.
Switch(config)#hostname yin          ←Sets hostname
yin(config)#int vlan 1               ←Disable interface VLAN 1
yin(config-if)#shut
yin(config-if)#exit

yin(config)#int vlan 2               ←Define interface VLAN 2
yin(config-subif)#ip address 172.16.2.11 255.255.255.0
yin(config-subif)#exit

yin(config)#ip default-gateway 172.16.2.10   ←IP default gateway
yin(config)#
```

The management portion of the configuration on the mantis switch will resemble that of Example 2-31.

Example 2-32 illustrates how to configure basic management on the crane switch, which is a Catalyst 4003. Because this series switch requires VLANs to be defined before the management VLAN can be moved off VLAN 1, you also will proceed to Step 2. Step 2 involves defining VLANs and the VTP domain.

Example 2-32 *Configuring Basic Management and the Default VLAN*

```
Console> (enable) set prompt crane          ←sets host name

crane (enable) set vtp domain cisco         ←Set VTP domain
VTP domain cisco modified
crane (enable) set vlan 2 name management   ←set VLAN 2 and name it
Vlan 2 configuration successful
crane (enable)

crane (enable) set int sc0 2 172.16.2.13 255.255.255.0   ←MNGT interface
Interface sc0 vlan set, IP address and netmask set.
crane (enable) set ip route 0.0.0.0 172.16.2.10          ←Default route to dragon
Route added.
crane (enable)
```

Step 2 requires you to configure the VTP domain—cisco, in this example—and define VLANs on the VTP servers. The mantis switch is the only VTP client, so you can begin with that switch. Example 2-33 demonstrates the configuration of VTP domain and shows how to change the VTP mode to client on the mantis switch.

Example 2-33 *Configuring VTP Domain and VTP Client*

```
mantis#vlan database                    ←enter VLAN database
mantis(vlan)#vtp domain cisco            ←Set VTP domain name to cisco
Changing VTP domain name from Null to cisco
mantis(vlan)#vtp client          ←Set VTP client mode
Setting device to VTP CLIENT mode.
mantis(vlan)#
```

After the VTP domain is created, switch ports can be assigned to VLANs. Example 2-34 illustrates the configuration of the mantis switch, assigning user ports to VLAN 2 and VLAN 4.

Example 2-34 *Assigning Ports to VLAN on the mantis Switch*

```
mantis#conf t
Enter configuration commands, one per line.  End with CNTL/Z.
mantis(config)#interface fastEthernet 0/9
mantis(config-if)#switchport mode access          ←set port to a single VLAN
mantis(config-if)#switchport access vlan 4         ←set VLAN id
mantis(config-if)#exit
mantis(config)#interface fastEthernet 0/5
mantis(config-if)#switchport mode access
mantis(config-if)#switchport access vlan 2
mantis(config-if)#^Z
mantis#
```

Likewise, you must assign the ports 2/4 and 2/7 to VLAN 2 on the crane switch. Example 2-35 demonstrates this type on configuration.

Example 2-35 *Assigning Ports to VLAN on the crane Switch*

```
crane (enable) set vlan 2 2/4,2/7
VLAN 2 modified.
VLAN 1 modified.
VLAN  Mod/Ports
----  ----------------------
2     2/4,2/7,2/19-20

crane (enable) 2001 Jun 26 21:15:08 %PAGP-5-PORTFROMSTP:Port 2/4 left bridge por
t 2/4
```

Example 2-36 shows the configuration of the VTP domain and VLANs on the crane switch, while the second half of the example demonstrates the same configuration on the yin switch.

Example 2-36 *Configuring VTP Domains and VLANs*

```
crane (enable) set vlan 4

yin(vlan)#vtp domain cisco
Changing VTP domain name from Null to cisco
yin(vlan)#vlan 2 name management
VLAN 2 added:
    Name: management
yin(vlan)#
yin(vlan)#vlan 4
VLAN 4 added:
    Name: VLAN0004
yin(vlan)#
```

The third step calls for you to configure VLAN trunks between the switches. As we mentioned previously, configuring static trunks is a lot easier and quicker then trying to memorize the huge autonegotiation table. Example 2-37 demonstrates the configuration of an ISL and 802.1q trunk on the yin switch.

Example 2-37 *Configuring an ISL and 802.1q Trunk*

```
yin(config)#interface fast 0/10
yin(config-if)#switchport mode trunk                  ←Set port to trunk
yin(config-if)#switchport trunk encapsulation isl     ←Set encapsulation to ISL
yin(config-if)#exit
yin(config)#interface fast 0/19
yin(config-if)#switchport mode trunk
yin(config-if)#switchport trunk encapsulation dot1q   ←Set encapsulation to 802.1q
yin(config-if)#^Z
```

Example 2-38 illustrates the configuration of the trunks on the crane switch.

Example 2-38 *Configuring 802.1q Trunks*

```
crane (enable) set trunk 2/19 on          ←Set port 2/19 to trunk
Port(s) 2/19 trunk mode set to on.
crane (enable) set trunk 2/19 dot1q        ←Set trunk type
Port(s) 2/19 trunk type set to dot1q.
2001 Jun 26 17:54:23 %DTP-5-TRUNKPORTON:Port 2/19 has
become dot1q trunk

crane (enable) set trunk 2/20 on
Port(s) 2/20 trunk mode set to on.
crane (enable) set trunk 2/20 dot1q
Port(s) 2/20 trunk type set to dot1q.
crane (enable)
```

After the trunks are configured, you can check the status of the VTP domain on the VTP client switch, mantis. Example 2-39 illustrates that the VTP information is being communicated across the trunks. The **show vlan** command displays the new VLANs that the switch has learned.

Example 2-39 *Status of the VTP Domain on the mantis Switch*

```
mantis#show vtp status
VTP Version                     : 2
Configuration Revision          : 7
Maximum VLANs supported locally : 254
Number of existing VLANs        : 7
VTP Operating Mode              : Client
VTP Domain Name                 : cisco
VTP Pruning Mode                : Disabled
VTP V2 Mode                     : Disabled
VTP Traps Generation            : Disabled
MD5 digest                      : 0x51 0x0C 0x00 0x9A 0x0B 0x13 0xE3 0xBA
Configuration last modified by 172.16.2.13 at 6-26-01 20:39:23    ←VTP is receiving!
mantis#
mantis#show vlan
VLAN Name                             Status    Ports
---- -------------------------------- --------- -------------------------------
1    default                          active    Fa0/1, Fa0/2, Fa0/3, Fa0/4,
                                                Fa0/6, Fa0/7, Fa0/8, Fa0/9,
                                                Fa0/10, Fa0/11, Fa0/12, Fa0/13,
                                                Fa0/14, Fa0/15, Fa0/16, Fa0/17,
                                                Fa0/18, Fa0/19, Fa0/21, Fa0/22,
                                                Fa0/23, Fa0/24

2    management                       active    Fa0/5
4    VLAN0004                         active
1002 fddi-default                     active
1003 token-ring-default               active
1004 fddinet-default                  active
1005 trnet-default                    active

VLAN Type  SAID       MTU   Parent RingNo BridgeNo Stp  BrdgMode Trans1 Trans2
---- ----- ---------- ----- ------ ------ -------- ---- -------- ------ ------
1    enet  100001     1500  -      -      -        -    -        0      0
2    enet  100002     1500  -      -      -        -    -        0      0
4    enet  100004     1500  -      -      -        -    -        0      0
1002 fddi  101002     1500  -      0      -        -    -        0      0
1003 tr    101003     1500  -      0      -        -    srb      0      0
1004 fdnet 101004     1500  -      -      -        ieee -        0      0
1005 trnet 101005     1500  -      -      -        ibm  -        0      0
mantis#
```

Configuring a Trunk on a Router

To route between VLANs, you need to have a router interface in each VLAN. Because solutions like this do not scale well because of the number of physical interfaces needed on large networks, you can configure an ISL or 802.1q trunk on the router. Cisco supports VLAN trunking on Ethernet router interfaces operating at least 100 Mbps.

Configuring a trunk is much like configuring a Frame Relay subinterface. For VLAN trunks, you must create a logical Ethernet subinterface for every VLAN that you want to route between. You also must assign an encapsulation type to that subinterface. Finally, to actually "route," you need to enable a routing protocol. The subinterface will be treated just like a physical interface by the routing protocol. The syntax to accomplish this is as follows:

```
Router(config)interface FastEthernet0.x
Router(config-if)encapsulation [dot1Q [native native_vlan_id | isl] [vlan_id]
```

Continuing from the previous model, Example 2-40 illustrates the configuration of a VLAN trunk on the dragon router.

Example 2-40 *Status of the VTP Domain on the mantis Router*

```
dragon(config)#int fastEthernet 0/0.2
dragon(config-subif)#encapsulation isl 2          ←Set encapsulation and VLAN
dragon(config-subif)#ip address 172.16.2.10 255.255.255.0
dragon(config-subif)#exit
dragon(config)#int fastEthernet 0/0.4
dragon(config-subif)#encapsulation isl 4
dragon(config-subif)#ip address 172.16.4.10 255.255.255.0
dragon(config-subif)#exit

dragon(config)#router eigrp 2001                  ←Configuring EIGRP
dragon(config-router)#network 172.16.0.0
dragon(config-router)#no auto-summary
```

When this stage is complete, full IP connectivity will be established throughout the domain. All switches, routers, and hosts will be capable of **ping**ing each other.

Load Balancing Across Trunks

In the previous model, there were no redundant trunks, so Spanning Tree was really not an issue. But if the model is modified slightly, we can insert some Spanning Tree issues into the network.

Figure 2-15 presents a new network model with some minor changes.

Figure 2-15 *Load Sharing in a Switched Network*

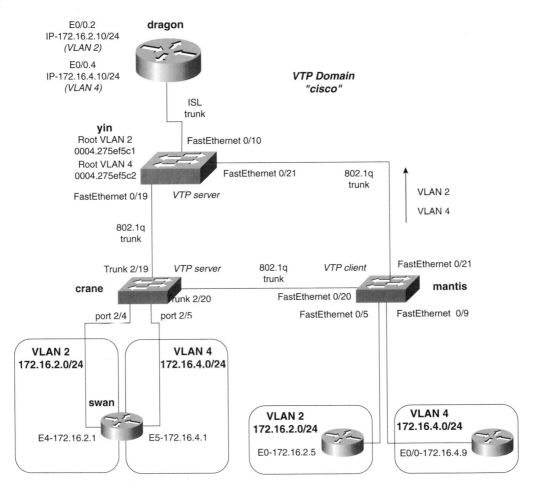

By adding another trunk line between the mantis and yin switches, a loop is created in the network. STP will now put some of the ports into blocking mode, to make the network loop-free. By also adding a two-port router, swan, with an interface in VLAN 2 and VLAN 4, we create a valid reason to want to load-share across this network. In a production environment, the swan router and the dragon router might be running HSRP between them.

The results of how the network converges, or which paths go into forwarding and blocking, can be unpredictable. Most often, but not always, the traffic will tend to follow one path throughout the network. This leaves some links carrying all the traffic, while others are virtually unused.

In Figure 2-15, we have configured another 802.1q between the yin and mantis switches, and added the router as denoted. If STP is observed for VLANs 1, 2, and 4 on the mantis switch, you can see that all the traffic is taking the new trunk, Fast 0/21, to root. The yin switch is root for all the VLANs in the VTP domain. Example 2-41 demonstrates the **show spanning-tree vlan** command on the mantis switch.

Example 2-41 **show spanning-tree** *Command Output on the mantis Switch*

```
mantis#show spanning-tree vlan 2

Spanning tree 2 is executing the IEEE compatible Spanning Tree protocol
  Bridge Identifier has priority 32768, address 00d0.976c.b781
  Configured hello time 2, max age 20, forward delay 15
  Current root has priority 32768, address 0004.275e.f5c1      ← Root MAC for VLAN 2
  Root port is 35, cost of root path is 19
  Topology change flag not set, detected flag not set, changes 7
  Times:  hold 1, topology change 35, notification 2
          hello 2, max age 20, forward delay 15
  Timers: hello 0, topology change 0, notification 0

Interface Fa0/5 (port 17) in Spanning tree 2 is FORWARDING
  Port path cost 100, Port priority 128
  Designated root has priority 32768, address 0004.275e.f5c1
  Designated bridge has priority 32768, address 00d0.976c.b781
  Designated port is 17, path cost 19
  Timers: message age 0, forward delay 0, hold 0
  BPDU: sent 3066, received 0

Interface Fa0/20 (port 34) in Spanning tree 2 is BLOCKING      ←Blocking
  Port path cost 19, Port priority 128
  Designated root has priority 32768, address 0004.275e.f5c1
  Designated bridge has priority 32768, address 0030.1976.4d01
  Designated port is 84, path cost 19
  Timers: message age 3, forward delay 0, hold 0
  BPDU: sent 93, received 2972

Interface Fa0/21 (port 35) in Spanning tree 2 is FORWARDING
  Port path cost 19, Port priority 128
  Designated root has priority 32768, address 0004.275e.f5c1
  Designated bridge has priority 32768, address 0004.275e.f5c1
  Designated port is 35, path cost 0
  Timers: message age 3, forward delay 0, hold 0
  BPDU: sent 5, received 495

mantis#show spanning-tree vlan 4
```

continues

Example 2-41 show spanning-tree *Command Output on the mantis Switch (Continued)*

```
Spanning tree 4 is executing the IEEE compatible Spanning Tree protocol
  Bridge Identifier has priority 32768, address 00d0.976c.b782
  Configured hello time 2, max age 20, forward delay 15
  Current root has priority 32768, address 0004.275e.f5c2   ←Root MAC for VLAN 4
  Root port is 35, cost of root path is 19
  Topology change flag not set, detected flag not set, changes 5
  Times:  hold 1, topology change 35, notification 2
          hello 2, max age 20, forward delay 15
  Timers: hello 0, topology change 0, notification 0

Interface Fa0/9 (port 22) in Spanning tree 4 is FORWARDING
  Port path cost 100, Port priority 128
  Designated root has priority 32768, address 0004.275e.f5c2
  Designated bridge has priority 32768, address 00d0.976c.b782
  Designated port is 22, path cost 19
  Timers: message age 0, forward delay 0, hold 0
  BPDU: sent 1967, received 0

Interface Fa0/20 (port 34) in Spanning tree 4 is BLOCKING
  Port path cost 19, Port priority 128
  Designated root has priority 32768, address 0004.275e.f5c2
  Designated bridge has priority 32768, address 0030.1976.4d03
  Designated port is 84, path cost 19
  Timers: message age 2, forward delay 0, hold 0
  BPDU: sent 1, received 2972

Interface Fa0/21 (port 35) in Spanning tree 4 is FORWARDING
  Port path cost 19, Port priority 128
  Designated root has priority 32768, address 0004.275e.f5c2
  Designated bridge has priority 32768, address 0004.275e.f5c2
  Designated port is 35, path cost 0
  Timers: message age 2, forward delay 0, hold 0
  BPDU: sent 5, received 498
```

In this model, you want to load-balance the VLANs over the trunk lines from the mantis switch. All traffic from VLAN 2 will go to the swan router, while all traffic for VLAN 4 defaults to the dragon router. To accomplish this, you need to set the root for VLAN 2 to be the crane switch, while the root for VLAN 4 should be the yin switch.

By using the **set root** macro command, you can set the root for VLAN 2 on the crane switch. Example 2-42 demonstrates the setting for the root for VLAN 2 on the crane switch. The command is preceded by the **show spant 2** command, displaying the old and new root bridges for VLAN 2.

Example 2-42 *Setting Root for VLAN 2*

```
crane (enable) show spant 2
VLAN 2
Spanning tree enabled
```

Example 2-42 *Setting Root for VLAN 2 (Continued)*

```
Spanning tree type            ieee

Designated Root               00-04-27-5e-f5-c1   ←Current Root, same as in example 2-40
Designated Root Priority      32768
Designated Root Cost          19
Designated Root Port          2/19
Root Max Age  20 sec    Hello Time 2  sec   Forward Delay 15 sec

Bridge ID MAC ADDR            00-30-19-76-4d-01    ←Our MAC for VLAN 2
Bridge ID Priority            32768
Bridge Max Age 20 sec    Hello Time 2  sec   Forward Delay 15 sec

Port      Vlan  Port-State    Cost   Priority  Fast-Start  Group-Method
--------- ----  ------------- -----  --------  ----------  ------------
 2/4       2    forwarding    100        32    disabled
 2/7       2    not-connected 100        32    disabled
 2/19      2    forwarding     19        32    disabled
 2/20      2    forwarding     19        32    disabled
crane (enable)

crane (enable) set spant root 2               ←Set Root macro for VLAN 2
VLAN 2 bridge priority set to 8192.
VLAN 2 bridge max aging time set to 20.
VLAN 2 bridge hello time set to 2.
VLAN 2 bridge forward delay set to 15.
Switch is now the root switch for active VLAN 2.
crane (enable)
crane (enable) show spant 2
VLAN 2
Spanning tree enabled
Spanning tree type            ieee

Designated Root               00-30-19-76-4d-01    ←We are now the Root for VLAN 2
Designated Root Priority      8192
Designated Root Cost          0
Designated Root Port          1/0
Root Max Age  20 sec    Hello Time 2  sec   Forward Delay 15 sec

Bridge ID MAC ADDR            00-30-19-76-4d-01
Bridge ID Priority            8192
Bridge Max Age 20 sec    Hello Time 2  sec   Forward Delay 15 sec

Port      Vlan  Port-State    Cost   Priority  Fast-Start  Group-Method
--------- ----  ------------- -----  --------  ----------  ------------
 2/4       2    forwarding    100        32    disabled
 2/7       2    not-connected 100        32    disabled
 2/19      2    forwarding     19        32    disabled
 2/20      2    forwarding     19        32    disabled
crane (enable)
```

To verify the configuration, also check STP on the mantis switch, as listed in Example 2-43. The mantis switch now shows the root bridge for vlan 2 as 0030.1976.4d01, which is the crane switch. Interface fast 0/20 is now forwarding for VLAN 2, and interface fast 0/21 has been put in blocking mode. VLAN 4 continues to have the yin switch as its root bridge.

Example 2-43 *STP Load Balancing*

```
mantis#show spanning-tree vlan 2

Spanning tree 2 is executing the IEEE compatible Spanning Tree protocol
  Bridge Identifier has priority 32768, address 00d0.976c.b781
  Configured hello time 2, max age 20, forward delay 15
  Current root has priority 8192, address 0030.1976.4d01      ←new Root bridge
  Root port is 34, cost of root path is 19
  Topology change flag not set, detected flag not set, changes 8
  Times:  hold 1, topology change 35, notification 2
          hello 2, max age 20, forward delay 15
  Timers: hello 0, topology change 0, notification 0

Interface Fa0/5 (port 17) in Spanning tree 2 is FORWARDING
    Port path cost 100, Port priority 128
    Designated root has priority 8192, address 0030.1976.4d01
    Designated bridge has priority 32768, address 00d0.976c.b781
    Designated port is 17, path cost 19
    Timers: message age 0, forward delay 0, hold 0
    BPDU: sent 4073, received 0

Interface Fa0/20 (port 34) in Spanning tree 2 is FORWARDING
    Port path cost 19, Port priority 128
    Designated root has priority 8192, address 0030.1976.4d01
    Designated bridge has priority 8192, address 0030.1976.4d01
    Designated port is 84, path cost 0
    Timers: message age 2, forward delay 0, hold 0
    BPDU: sent 95, received 3977

Interface Fa0/21 (port 35) in Spanning tree 2 is BLOCKING
    Port path cost 19, Port priority 128
    Designated root has priority 8192, address 0030.1976.4d01
    Designated bridge has priority 32768, address 0004.275e.f5c1
    Designated port is 35, path cost 19
    Timers: message age 3, forward delay 0, hold 0
    BPDU: sent 6, received 1502
mantis#

mantis#show spanning-tree vlan 4

Spanning tree 4 is executing the IEEE compatible Spanning Tree protocol
  Bridge Identifier has priority 32768, address 00d0.976c.b782
  Configured hello time 2, max age 20, forward delay 15
  Current root has priority 32768, address 0004.275e.f5c2
```

Example 2-43 *STP Load Balancing (Continued)*

```
      Root port is 35, cost of root path is 19
      Topology change flag not set, detected flag not set, changes 5
      Times:  hold 1, topology change 35, notification 2
              hello 2, max age 20, forward delay 15
      Timers: hello 0, topology change 0, notification 0

Interface Fa0/9 (port 22) in Spanning tree 4 is FORWARDING
   Port path cost 100, Port priority 128
   Designated root has priority 32768, address 0004.275e.f5c2
   Designated bridge has priority 32768, address 00d0.976c.b782
   Designated port is 22, path cost 19
   Timers: message age 0, forward delay 0, hold 1
   BPDU: sent 3441, received 0

Interface Fa0/20 (port 34) in Spanning tree 4 is BLOCKING
   Port path cost 19, Port priority 128
   Designated root has priority 32768, address 0004.275e.f5c2
   Designated bridge has priority 32768, address 0030.1976.4d03
   Designated port is 04, path cost 19
   Timers: message age 5, forward delay 0, hold 0
   BPDU: sent 1, received 4445

Interface Fa0/21 (port 35) in Spanning tree 4 is FORWARDING
   Port path cost 19, Port priority 128
   Designated root has priority 32768, address 0004.275e.f5c2
   Designated bridge has priority 32768, address 0004.275e.f5c2
   Designated port is 35, path cost 0
   Timers: message age 3, forward delay 0, hold 0
   BPDU: sent 5, received 1972
mantis#
```

Figure 2-16 now shows how the network is handling and forwarding VLANs.

To enforce consistent Spanning Tree selection throughout the network, you also should set the priority for VLAN 4 on the yin switch. This can be done using the **priority** command, as demonstrated in Example 2-44.

Example 2-44 *Setting Root on a Catalyst 2900XL/3500G Switch*

```
yin(config)#spanning-tree vlan 4 priority 100
```

Figure 2-16 *Load Balancing over Trunks*

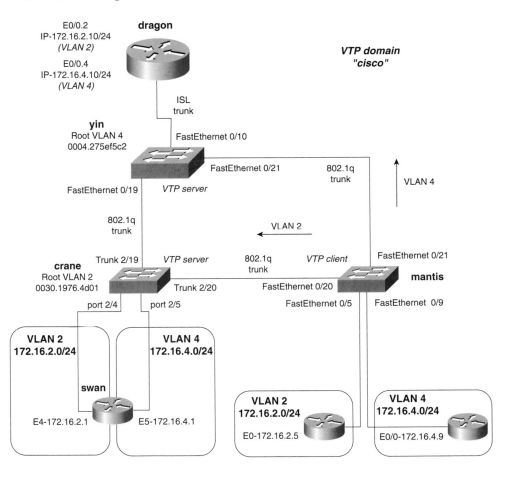

    VLAN

To verify the change, view STP for VLAN 4 on the mantis switch, as in Example 2-45.

Example 2-45 *Verifying the Priority of 100 for VLAN 4*

```
mantis#show spanning-tree vlan 4

Spanning tree 4 is executing the IEEE compatible Spanning Tree protocol
  Bridge Identifier has priority 32768, address 00d0.976c.b782
  Configured hello time 2, max age 20, forward delay 15
```

Example 2-45 *Verifying the Priority of 100 for VLAN 4*

```
Current root has priority 100, address 0004.275e.f5c2
Root port is 35, cost of root path is 19
Topology change flag not set, detected flag not set, changes 5
Times:  hold 1, topology change 35, notification 2
        hello 2, max age 20, forward delay 15
Timers: hello 0, topology change 0, notification 0
```

The world of Ethernet switching is growing at a tremendous pace. There are many more interesting and useful technologies that we simply did not have the time to discuss. We highly recommend reading Kennedy Clark and Kevin Hamilton's book *Cisco LAN Switching*, which is loaded with information on LAN switching for extended reference. Some topics that you might want to pursue on your own that we did not cover in this book are listed here:

- **UplinkFast, PortFast, BackboneFast**—These are ways to help the STP process deal with user traffic during initialization or failure while STP is converging. These technologies are simple to configure and can avoid lost throughput during STP convergence.

- **Fast EtherChannel/Gigabit EtherChannel**—EtherChannel provides a way for the router to aggregate up to four Fast Ethernet ports in a bundle. The technology also applies to Gigabit Ethernet. We like to think of EtherChannel as the PPP multilink of Ethernet. EtherChannel treats the bundle as one large physical link and can distribute traffic in different ways across the bundle. With full-duplex mode, EtherChannel bundles can reach speeds of 800 Mbps to 8,000 Mbps. EtherChannel can help avoid some STP issues because it offers resiliency between switches. When a link goes down, the bundle simply loses bandwidth and does not need to wait for STP to converge before sending user traffic. There are rules to EtherChannel and how ports can be bundled, and they are different for the various families of switches. There is also the drawback that EtherChannel can be used only to connect two switches—for example, bundles cannot be split across switches.

- **Port security**—An advanced security function of all Cisco switches is port security. Port security allows you to limit the access on a port to a single MAC address. When another user plugs into the port with a different MAC address, the port can be shut down, or traps can be sent to a network-management station. This is a helpful feature in the field because it strictly controls physical access to the switch and unwanted moves or changes.

- **Multicast (CGMP/IGMP)**—*CCIE Practical Studies,* Volume I does not address any multicast issues. This does not mean that it is not important, however. Multicast traffic is playing an ever-increasing role in the modern network. *CCIE Practical Studies,* Volume II addresses multicast issues.

IEEE 802.5/Token Ring LANs

Token Ring: 30 Years Old and Still in Service

If you have ever worked on IBM mainframes, AS400s, RS6000s, or any other SNA devices, chances are good that you have worked with Token Ring. And just as the mainframes were supposed to go away with the huge "client/server" push of the 1990s, eventually so would Token Ring networks. But the mainframes never become "extinct" like they were supposed to, and neither did Token Ring networks. The "big iron" mainframes are still present in many large networks, and most of them carry legacy Token Ring networks with them.

Token Ring was conceived by IBM in the early 1970s, and it quickly became IBM's LAN of choice. Soon IBM front-end processors, such as the IBM 3745s, were shipping with Token Ring interfaces. At the time, Token Ring provided a fast LAN medium. Ethernet networks were operating at speeds of 10 Mbps or less on shared-media networks. It was highly debated how much "real" throughput you could get on an Ethernet segment with collisions and a large number of users. As you will see, Token Ring is somewhat deterministic and uses a token-passing technology that allowed it to achieve the speeds that it was advertising, 4 Mbps and 16 Mbps.

Token Ring Technical Overview

The IEEE officially adopted Token Ring as IEEE 802.5. The specifications are almost identical, with a few minor differences. IBM Token Ring calls for the stations to be attached by twisted-pair cable to a multistation access unit (MSAU) in a physical star topology. The IBM 8228 is a common example of a MSAU. The IEEE committee chose not to specify a medium or topology, allowing Token Ring networks to be more flexible.

Token Ring/IEEE 802.5 operates strictly at Layer 2, like most LAN protocols. Like Ethernet, the IEEE committee divides the data link layer into two sublayers: 802.5 as the MAC layer and 802.2 as the LLC layer. Functionally, IEEE 802.5 Token Ring parallels IEEE 802.3. The LLC layer—802.2, in this case—is a standardized interface between a hardware-specific MAC and a Layer 3 protocol.

Token Ring Operation

Tokin Ring networks have a physical topology of a star, but the network is treated as a logical ring. Figure 2-17 shows the logical and physical Token Ring topologies.

Figure 2-17 *Token Ring Topologies*

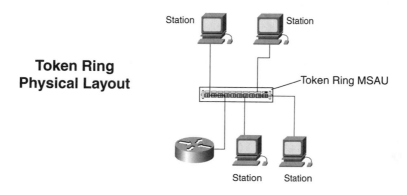

**Token Ring
Physical Layout**

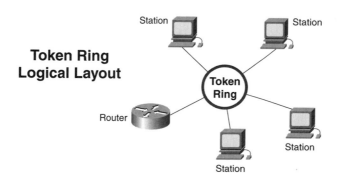

**Token Ring
Logical Layout**

Token Ring networks utilize a token-passing technology on the ring. Token-passing networks move a small frame, called a *token*, around the ring. Token Ring uses two types of frames, a token and an information/data frame. Token frames contain a start delimiter, an access control field, and an end delimiter. The data/command frames contain the same fields, plus a few more for user data, and also contain a source and destination address. When a station wants to transmit information, it must posses the token. Possession of token grants the right of the station to transmit data. If the station has no data to transmit, it simply passes the token along to the next station on the ring.

When a station posses the token and wants to transmit, it changes a single bit in the access control field, the T bit. The station then appends its information to the frame and sends it on to the next station on the ring. The frame circulates the ring until it reaches the destination station, where the frame is then copied by the station and tagged as having been copied. The frame continues around the ring until it reaches the station that originated the frame. At this point, it is removed from the ring by that station. The concept of *early token release* allows a station that seizes a token to transmit a new token onto the ring after first sending its information frame.

The following list describes some other important features that Token Ring employs to help data circulate throughout the ring:

- **Access control field**—The access control field is an 8-bit field found in both types of Token Ring frames, the token and information/data frame. It contains the following information:

P | P | P | T | M | R | R | R

  — **P**—3-bit priority field. Only stations with a priority equal to or higher than the priority of a token can *claim* that token. After the token is claimed and changed to an information frame, only stations with a priority higher than that of the transmitting station can reserve the token for the next pass around the network.

  — **R**—3-bit reservation field used to reserve the token for the next pass around the ring.

  — **T**—Simply called the T bit. If the bit is set to 0, the frame is a token; if it is set to 1, the frame is an information/data frame.

  — **M**—Monitor bit, used by the active monitor to remove endlessly circulating frames from the ring.

- **Active monitor**—One station on the network serves as the active monitor. This station acts as a centralized source of timing information for other stations and performs a variety of ring-maintenance functions. One such function is the removal of endlessly circulating frames from the ring. For example, when an originating station fails, it cannot remove its frame from the ring. This, in turn, will not allow any other stations to transmit on the ring. The active monitor can detect this type of failure through the use of the M bit mentioned previously and can properly remove the frame from the ring.

- **Reliable delivery**—Token Ring uses a 2-bit frame status field to ensure reliable delivery of frames. These bits commonly are referred to as the A and C bits. An originating station generates a frame with the A and C bits set to 0. When the frame transverses the ring and arrives at the originating station, the bits are examined to verify delivery. Receiving stations modify the bits as documented in Table 2-15.

Table 2-15 *A and C Bit Modification by Receiving Station*

A Bit	C Bit	Meaning
0	0	Destination not found. The receiving station did not modify the bits.
0	1	Invalid.
1	0	The frame was accepted, but the station was incapable of copying data from the frame.
1	1	Station found. The frame was accepted and copied.

- **Token Ring frame size**—Token Ring frames have a significantly larger frame size than the 1518-byte Ethernet frame. Token Ring frames have a minimum size of 21 bytes at 4-Mbps and 16-Mbps ring operation. The largest frame size is 4511 bytes on 4-Mbps rings and 17,839 bytes on 16-Mbps rings.

NOTE

Canonical Versus Noncanonical Address Format

Ethernet networks transmit data in what is called a *canonical address format*. This means is that if you have the bit stream 0110 1010, the most significant bit (MSB) is on the left and the least significant bit (LSB) is on the right. Ethernet networks transmit data in a canonical form, with the least significant bits get transmitted first. If an Ethernet network is sending the previous data steam, it would send 0 1 0 1 0 1 1 0. Token Ring and FDDI networks transmit data in a noncanonical format. Noncanonical format transmits the most significant bit first. If a Token Ring network were transmitting the original bit stream mentioned, it would transmit 0 1 1 0 1 0 1 0. Source-route translation bridges and DLSw will perform address translation when needed.

Token Ring Switching

Token Ring switching offers many of the same advantages as Ethernet switching. The major advantage is the speed that Token Ring switching provides. Much as Ethernet bandwidth is affected by the number of stations on a segment causing collisions, Token Ring bandwidth is affected by stations awaiting the token to transmit data. In a switched environment, ports on the same switch can belong to the same ring, but the stations on the switch ports will experience bandwidth as if they were the only stations on the ring.

Token Ring switches also offer dedicated Token Ring (DTR). With traditional 4- or 16-Mbps Token Ring, Token Ring adapters are limited to half-duplex mode. DTR defines a method that allows the switch port to emulate a concentrator port and full-duplex data-passing mode called *transmit immediate (TXI)*, which takes advantage of the fact that there is one end station on a port, and there is no real need to pass a token. Therefore, the adapter can transmit and receive simultaneously, where the ring can now use a theoretical bandwidth of 32 Mbps.

The Token Ring switch ports operate in the following modes:

- **Half-duplex concentrator port**—The port is connected to a single station in half-duplex mode. The port behaves like an active MAU port for classical Token Ring.

- **Half-duplex station emulation**—The port is connected to a port on an MAU. The port behaves like a station connected to a classical Token Ring segment that contains multiple stations.

- **Full-duplex concentrator port**—The port is connected to a single station in full-duplex mode.

- **Full-duplex station emulation**—The port is connected to a switch or a concentrator port in full-duplex mode.

NOTE   Duplex modes are a function of the hardware built into the network interface card. Software upgrades will not allow you to run full-duplex mode. For full-duplex mode to work, the station and switch port must be capable of full-duplex mode.

Token Ring Bridge Relay Function (TrBRF) and the Token Ring Concentrator Function (TrCRF)

The Token Ring bridge relay function (TrBRF) functions like a multiport bridge. Its purpose is to bridge rings. The rings that it bridges are called Token Ring concentrator relay functions (TrCRF). (These probably would have been called virtual rings, but that name was already taken.) Multiple TrCRFs can attach to a single TrBRF, much like multiple rings can attach to a single bridge. TrCRFs can exchange data through source-route bridging (SRB) or source-route transparent bridging (SRT). If you are not familiar with these bridging technologies, you might want to read these sections of Chapter 13, "Configuring Bridging and Data Link Switching Plus."

The TrBRF spans Catalyst switches, much like a Ethernet trunk. This allows TrCRFs on different Catalysts to belong to the same bridge number. Remember that the TrCRF is "the ring." A TrBRF must be created before a TrCRF is defined. Each TrBRF is identified by a bridge number and VLAN ID. When you create a TrCRF, you identify it with a ring number and another *unique* VLAN ID. The TrCRF must be assigned to a parent TrBRF.

Figure 2-18 illustrates the TrBRF TrCRF relationship in the Catalyst 3920. The trbrf-default and the trcrf-default are the actual default TrBRF and TrCRF for all Catalyst switches. Think of them like an abstract VLAN 1 on Ethernet switches. Like Ethernet switches, Token Ring switches were designed to be "plug-and-play" on smaller networks. By default, all ports will be assigned to the trcrf-default, and the trcrf-default has TrBRF as its parent.

Figure 2-18 *Default TrBRF TrCRF Relationship*

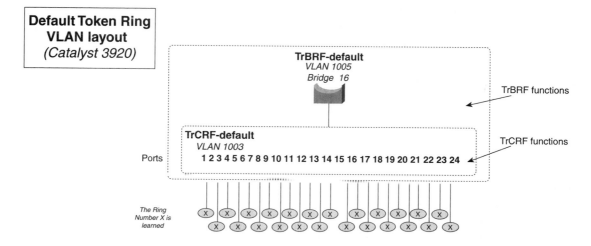

The concept of default TrBRFs and TrCRFs made LAN migrations from shared hub/MSAU environments easy. Out of the box, a Token Ring switch could be deployed without any configuration in place of a hub or MSAU. Like Ethernet switches ports that reside on the same default VLAN, Token Ring ports reside on the same default ring and bridge. Table 2-16 lists the default VLAN settings for Cisco switches.

Table 2-16 *Default VLAN Settings*

Feature	Default Value
Native or Default VLAN	VLAN 1
Port VLAN assignments	All ports assigned to VLAN1; Token Ring ports assigned to VLAN 1003
VTP mode	Transparent
VLAN state	Active
Normal VLAN range	VLAN 2 to VLAN 1001
VLAN reserved range*	VLAN 1006 to VLAN 1009
VLAN extended range*	VLAN 1025 to VLAN 2094
MTU size	1500 bytes for Ethernet
	4472 bytes for Token Ring

continues

Table 2-16 *Default VLAN Settings (Continued)*

Feature	Default Value
SAID value	100,000 plus VLAN number
	VLAN2 = SAID 100002
Prune eligibility	VLANS 2-1000 are prune-eligible
MAC address reduction	Disabled
Spanning Tree mode	PVST
Default FDDI VLAN	VLAN 1002
Default Token Ring TrCRF VLAN	VLAN 1003
Default FDDI Net VLAN	VLAN 1004
Default Token Ring TrBRF VLAN	VLAN 1005 with bridge number 0F
Spanning Tree version for TrBRF VLANs	IBM
TrCRF bridge mode	SRB

*   The VLAN reserved range is used on the Catalyst 6500 series and is used to map nonreserved VLANs. The VLAN extended range is available on the Catalyst 6500 series switch. This range is an extension of the normal VLAN range. The extended and reserved VLAN range is not propagated by VTP. Token Ring and FDDI VLANs are listed on Ethernet-only switches because of global VTP information. Likewise, Token Ring switches' VLAN database lists Ethernet VLANs.

Figure 2-19 diagrams the logical layout of a Token Ring switch. Two TrBRFs were created on the switch. TrBRF brf100 will be bridge 10. This BRF is the parent to the TrCRF crf-ring10, which will be ring 10. All ports on the switch assigned to this CRF will be in ring 10. In this figure, ports 16 to 20 will all be on ring 10. The second TrBRF is used to link bridge 11 to ring 11; ports 21-24 will be on ring 11.

When this switch is configured, you will have two bridging domains. Figure 2-20 shows another conceptual view of the same configuration, represented in a more traditional fashion.

For the bridging domains to communicate, they need to be connected with another source-route bridge, usually in the form of a router. Figure 2-21 illustrates how the two domains can be linked with a router. If the network were transporting a bridged protocol such as SNA, the router could be configured for source-route bridging, and the two domains could be source-route bridged. If the network were transporting a routed protocol such as IP, the router would be configured to "route" traffic between the two domains.

Figure 2-19 *Logical TrBRF TrCRF Relationship*

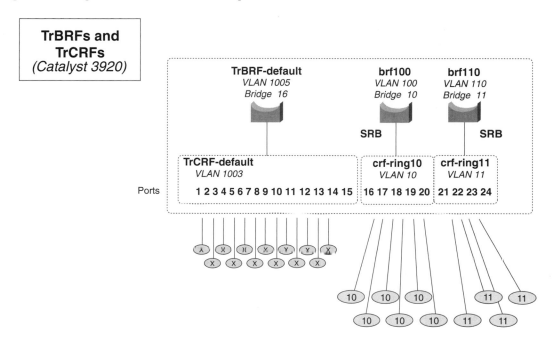

Figure 2-20 *Conceptual View of TrBRFs and TrCRFs*

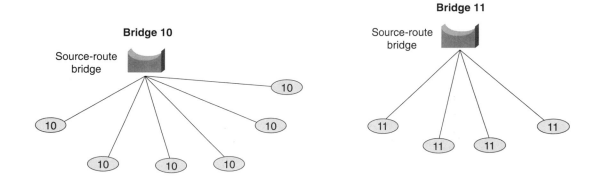

Figure 2-21 *Linking Two Token Ring Bridging Domains*

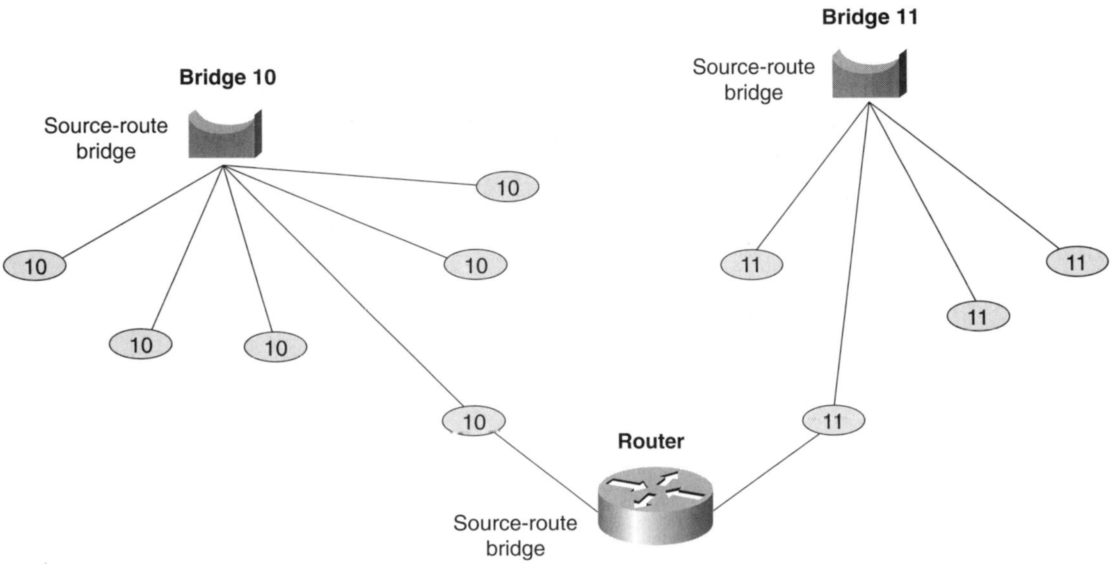

Configuring Token Ring Switching on the Catalyst 3920

Many of the same concepts that are found in Ethernet switching apply directly to Token Ring switches. For example, VLANs, VTP domains, and management VLANs are all found on Token Ring switches. For that reason, we will not spend a lot of time redefining these terms and their application. Instead, we will focus primarily on switch configuration.

The Catalyst 3920 does not have a standard command-line interface for configuration. Instead, the configuration is totally menu or panel-driven. The cursor keys allow you to select different panel options. To a large extent, this makes the configuration of the switches easy because there is no syntax to remember.

Figure 2-22 shows the main panel of the Catalyst 3920 Token Ring switch.

The configuration panel is where the TrBRFs, TrCRFs, VLANs, management, and other software features of the switch are configured. The statistics panel is where the **show** commands for the switch reside. Port status, VTP status, and other important information about the operation of the switch can be viewed. The download/upload panel is where you can upgrade the Catalyst software. Finally, the reset panel is where you can clear NVRAM and reload the switch. Specifically, here is a quick guide to the important setting in each panel.

Figure 2-22 *Initial Configuration Panel*

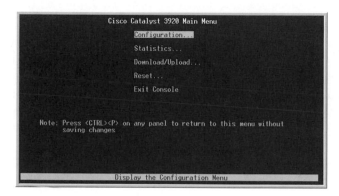

The Switch Configuration Panel

Figure 2-23 shows the switch configuration panel.

Figure 2-23 *Switch Configuration Panel*

The panels available in the switch configuration panel are as follows:

- **Switch configuration**—This panel allows you to display system information and switch hardware information, such as memory and software type. This panel also allows you to set basic switch management, such as system name, date, location, and contact information. You also can assign a MAC address to the switch here, and specify whether the switch will use canonical or noncanonical address formats. The default in Token Ring is noncanonical. Switch uplink information also can be accessed here.

- **Module information**—This panel allows you to display information about the switch modules, their status, uptime, and hardware and firmware revision levels.

- **VLAN and VTP Configuration**—This panel is where you will spend a majority of your time configuring the switch. At this panel, you can access and change the VTP domain, VLAN information, TrBRFs, and TrCRFs. Individual ports also are assigned to TrCRFs here.

- **IP configuration**—This panel allows you to configure basic IP management of the switch. This includes the IP address and subnet mask, the default gateway. The IP address must be assigned to the management TrBRF to become active; that can be performed from the SNMP configuration panel. IP **ping**s also can be sent from this panel when the management TrBRF and IP address are configured.

- **SNMP configuration**—This panel allows you to set basic SNMP read/write, traps, and community strings. RMON is supported on the Catalyst 3920 and also can be activated here. The management VLAN or the management TrBRF must be defined here for SNMP and IP aspects of the switch work. By default, SNMP and IP are configured to use the TrBRF-default entity.

- **Spanning Tree**—This panel allows you to configure STP in the bridged environment. All the same STP parameters and timers discussed earlier can be configured here for Token Ring networks.

- **Token Ring port configuration**—This panel displays and allows you to change physical and some logical port information. From this panel, you can set the duplex mode, early token release, MTU, and ring speed. You also can change the switching mode for the port from auto-cutthrough to one of the other three modes mentioned previously. This panel is where you also can tune explorer broadcasts.

- **CDP configuration**—This panel allows you to configure Cisco CDP information for the switch, as well as display its status. By default, CDP information is turned on for all switch ports.

- **Switched port analyzer**—This panel allows you to attach a network analyzer or similar device to the switch. This is always necessary when you are trying to monitor a switch port. This is because frames are not automatically forwarded to every port in the VLAN.

- **Token Channel**—This panel allows you to create a Token Channel. The first eight ports can be combined to form a Token Channel Interface. This technology is much like EtherChannel.

- **Filters and port security**—This panel allows you to enable MAC address and protocol filters. Port security is enabled from this panel as well.

- **Password**—This panel allows you configure a password for the switch.

- **Console configuration**—This panel allows you to configure and display current Telnet sessions. You also can configure the physical console port form this panel. The default session timeout is set to only 5 seconds; this can be changed to a maximum of 1440 seconds from this panel.

The Statistics Panel

This panel allows you to display various status information of the ports, VLANs, VTP, and other important information. The information panels that you can view include the following:

- Port status
- Port statistics
- Address tables
- Current Spanning Tree information
- VLAN statistics
- CDP neighbor display
- VTP statistics
- Diagnostic test results
- Message log information
- Display summary

The Download/Upload Panel

From this panel, you can upgrade the switch's IOS. You can upgrade the switch through TFTP or the RS-232 interface.

The Reset Panel

From this panel, you can clear the NVRAM on the switch as well as reset it. The download/upload panel allows you to perform the following:

- Reset switch with diagnostics
- Reset switch without diagnostics
- Reset port address table
- Clear nonvolatile RAM

Configuring VLANs on the Catalyst 3920

The logical steps for configuring VLANs for Token Ring resemble the same steps that you use for configuring Ethernet VLANs. With Token Ring, however, you must define rings and bridges, which require a few extra steps. The steps for configuring VLANs on the Catalyst 3920 switch are as follows:

Step 1   Plan TrBRFs, TrCRFs, ring numbers, bridge numbers, and VLANs.

Step 2   Configure VTP.

Step 3   Configure TrBRF VLAN(s) and assign a bridge number to each TrBRF.

Step 4   Configure TrCRFs VLANs and assign a parent TrBRF and an optional
ring number.

Step 5   Assign ports to TrCRFs.

Step 6   Configure switch management.

Configuring Token Ring switching involves configuring a TrBRF VLAN and TrCRF VLAN. This relationship can get rather confusing because there are two VLANs, rings, bridges, and so on. For this reason, you should really take the extra time and lay out a small diagram showing the logical relationships among all these entities.

Figure 2-24 shows two perspectives of the same Token Ring network. The dragon_switch is Cisco Catalyst 3920; it connects two routers and a user workstation. Let's walk through the six-step process to configure this switched Token Ring network.

Step 1: Planning TrBRFs, TrCRFs, Ring Numbers, Bridge Numbers, and VLANs

In Step 1, you plan for VLANs, TrBRFs, and TrCRFs. Figure 2-25 diagrams the network from the dragon_switch perspective. You will define two TrBRFs and the associated VLAN and bridge number for them. You also need to define two TrCRFs, the VLAN for them, and an appropriate ring number. The TrCRF is linked to the TrBRF by declaring it a parent. The TrCRF is not linked to the TrBRF by a common VLAN. The VLANs and bridge numbers do not need to match.

To help self-document the network, try to form some logical naming convention. In this example, TrBRF is called brf5; it is on VLAN 50 and bridge 5. It is the parent of crf-ring5, which is VLAN 5, which contains ring 5. The other TrBRF will be called brf6 and has VLAN 60 and bridge 6. This TrBRF will be the parent of TrCRF crf-ring6, and crf-ring6 contains VLAN 6 and, you guessed it, ring 6.

Figure 2-24 *Token Ring Switched Network Model*

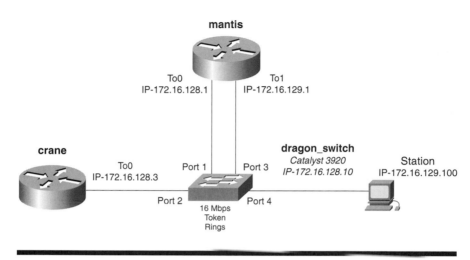

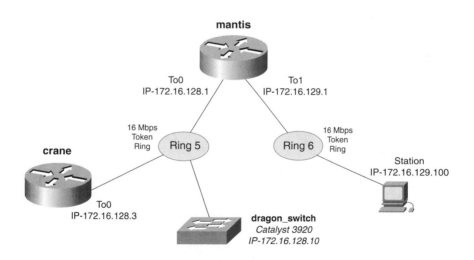

Step 2: Configuring VTP

In Step 2, you can begin to configure the switch. From the initial configuration panel, select the VLAN and VTP configuration panel. From this panel, you can enter the VTP administrative configuration panel, shown in Figure 2-26. In the VTP administrative configuration panel, you can set the VTP domain name, VTP mode, and a password, if you are configuring one.

Figure 2-25 *Defining TrBRFs and TrCRFs*

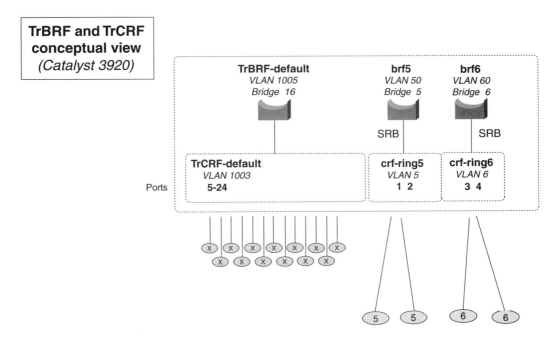

Figure 2-26 *VLAN and VTP Configuration Panel*

Figure 2-27 displays the VTP administrative configuration panel with the configuration of cisco as the VTP domain name.

Figure 2-27 *VTP Administrative Configuration Panel*

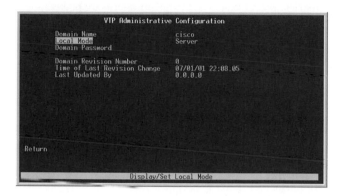

Step 3: Configuring TrBRF VLAN(s) and Assigning a Bridge Number to Each TrBRF

Step 3 tells you to configure TrBRFs and their associated VLANs and assign a bridge number to the TrBRF. As mentioned previously, you will need to configure two TrBRFs. TrBRFs are configured from selecting the VTP VLAN configuration panel under the same VLAN and VTP configuration panel. From this panel, select **Add** to create a new TrBRF. Notice that it says to enter a VLAN; this is the VLAN within the TrBRF. Figures 2-28 and 2-29 display the creation of the TrBRF brf5 VLAN 50.

Figure 2-28 *VTP VLAN Configuration Panel*

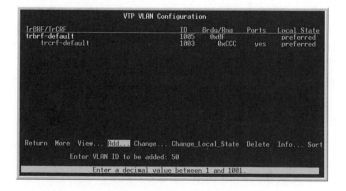

When you create a new VLAN, the switch prompts you to make it either a TrBRF or a TrCRF VLAN. By selecting the TrBRF option when you create the VLAN, you are taken to the VLAN Configuration Parameters menu. From this menu, you can enter the TrBRF name and change the VLAN ID, state, and MTU. This menu also allows you to select the bridge number for the VLAN. The bridge number is displayed and entered in hexadecimal format. When performing source-route bridging in the future, be careful not to get bridge IDs mixed up by entering some in hex and some in decimal. Figure 2-29 displays the VLAN parameters configuration panel.

Figure 2-29   *VLAN Parameters Configuration Panel*

Step 4: Configuring TrCRFs VLANs and Assigning a Parent TrBRF and an Optional Ring Number

After both TrBRF VLANs have been defined, Step 4 calls for you to define the TrCRFs and link them to a parent TrBRFs. To create a TrCRF, create another *unique* VLAN in the same manner as mentioned previously. This VLAN is *not* used to link the TrCRF to the TrBRF, and it needs to have a unique VLAN ID. When prompted for the VLAN type, select TrCRF. Example 2-30 displays the creation of TrCRF VLAN 5.

The VTP VLAN Configuration menu for TrCRFs can be found in Figure 2-31. From this panel, you can assign the VLAN a name and parent VLAN. We have named this VLAN crf-ring5 for some extra documentation. Most important is the parent VLAN; here, you want to assign a parent VLAN of brf5. The ring number is set at a default of auto, which means that the switch will be capable of determining from the RIF what the actual ring number is. In this example, you want to statically configure the ring to be ring 5. The ring number is displayed and entered in hexadecimal.

Figure 2-30 *VTP VLAN Configuration Panel*

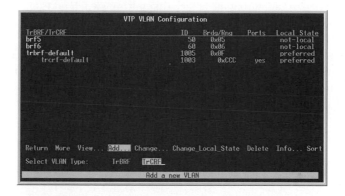

Figure 2-31 *VLAN Parameter Configuration Panel*

Figure 2-32 displays the VTP VLAN configuration panel listing the new VLANs created.

Figure 2-32 *VTP VLAN Configuration Panel*

Step 5: Assigning Ports to TrCRFs

Step 5 involves configuring the actual Token Ring switch ports and assigning them to a TrCRF VLAN. From the VLAN and VTP configuration panel, the third option, Local VLAN Port Configuration, allows you to change the default TrCRF that all the ports are assigned to. As mentioned previously, all ports are assigned to the TrCRF called TrCRF-default. When you select the Change option, the switch prompts you for the port that you want to change. After the port has been entered, the switch presents you with the current TrCRFs that it is aware of and allows you to change these. Figure 2-33 shows the Local VLAN port configuration panel after ports 1 to 3 have been modified.

Figure 2-33 *Local VLAN Port Configuration*

At this point in the configuration, the switch is fully operational. To configure the routers in this network, you simply need to configure the Token Ring interface and basic routing. Example 2-46 illustrates a simple Token Ring configuration, such as the one on the crane router.

Example 2-46 *Basic Token Ring Configuration on the crane Router*

```
crane(config)#int tokenRing 0
crane(config-if)#ring-speed 16
crane(config-if)#ip address 172.16.128.3 255.255.255.0
crane(config-if)#no shut
```

Step 6: Configuring Switch Management

The final step in the configuration is to set up IP access and management. Switch management, such as contact name and information, and canonical address formats can changed from the switch configuration panel. Figure 2-34 displays this panel.

Figure 2-34 *Switch Configuration*

IP configuration, such as an IP address for the switch, and a default gateway are entered from the IP configuration panel. When this panel is selected, the switch prompts you for a TrBRF VLAN to put the address on. It lists all the TrBRFs that it knows about. After a TrBRF is selected, the IP configuration panel displays. In this panel, you can enter an IP address, subnet mask, and default gateway. You also can configure the switch to use BootP from this panel. Figure 2-35 shows the IP configuration panel.

Figure 2-35 *IP Configuration Panel*

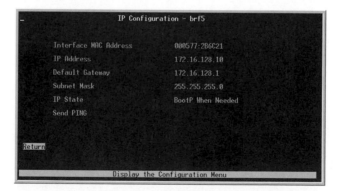

ICMP **ping**s also can be issued from this panel; however, the switch can have only one management address active at a time. Until the management VLAN is changed, the switch uses the VLAN trbrf-default. Much like the Catalyst 2900 and 3500 can have multiple virtual interfaces with IP addresses defined, only one can be active at any given time. To change the active VLAN for management from trbrf-default to another TrBRF VLAN, select the SNMP panel from the configuration panel. The SNMP panel also allows you change the default VLAN, as well as enable RMON and SNMP traps and define community strings. Figure 2-36 displays the SNMP configuration panel, showing the new TrBRF-default to be brf5.

Figure 2-36 *SNMP Configuration Panel*

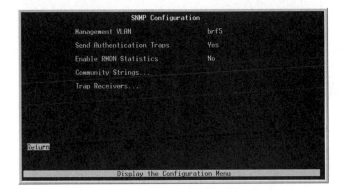

Switch operation can be verified from the main configuration menu. Under the main configuration menu, the Statistics option offers a vast array of statistics to view. The most useful statistics are port statistics and VLAN statistics. The best way to become familiar with the commands that are put into menus such as this is not to spend time reading about them in a book, but to simply spend time selecting and viewing the different options on the switch. Figure 2-37 shows the statistics panel, listing the tip of the iceberg of available options. Figure 2-38 shows the Port Configuration menu, which is another useful way to view the port status.

Figure 2-37 *Statistics Panel*

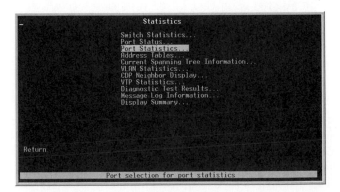

Figure 2-38 *Port Configuration*

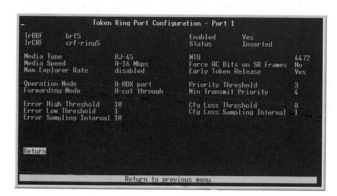

More Practice: Ethernet/Token Ring Labs

Throughout the rest of this book, you will get ample opportunities to configure Ethernet and Token Ring VLANs. All the labs in the chapters on routing protocols and subsequent chapters involve configuring LANs in one form or another. Make the most of these sections if you have the equipment available. For example, instead of using hubs to practice modeling your networks, create VLANs and VLAN trunks.

The following labs involve most of the concepts we've discussed. Instead of having many small labs, one in which you configure a VLAN, one in which you configure a VLAN trunk, and so on, we decided to make the labs in this book rather complex so that they not only challenge you but also present you with "practical" scenarios that you might face in the field.

Lab 7: Ethernet Switching, VLAN Trunking, and Spanning Tree Root Placement—Part I

Practical Scenario

Small Ethernet networks, for the most part, are plug-and-play. Even when Ethernet switches are deployed in small networks, they are user-friendly and not much configuration is needed. It is when redundancy is added to the network that things get more complicated. This lab gives you practice in configuring a redundant Ethernet switched networks and the challenges associated with them.

Lab Exercise

Game LANs, Inc. is a company that provides high-speed backbones for entertainment centers around the country. Game LAN uses Cisco 100-Mbps and Gigabit Ethernet switches to provide the switch fabric for the LANs that the company installs. A part of all Game LAN networks is the redundancy that is built into each design.

Your task is to configure a Game LAN network by using the following parameters as design guidelines:

- Configure an Ethernet switched network as depicted in Figure 2-39.

- Use the VTP domain name, funtime, for all the switches in the network.

- Create three VLANs on this network, and do not use VLAN1. Create one VLAN for management, which is IP subnet 172.16.128.0/24. Mark this VLAN so that it stands out as the management VLAN when being viewed by other switches. Two other VLANs are needed, one for the glaccess_2 router, 172.16.16.0/24, and one for the glaccess_1 router on subnet 172.16.17.0/24.

- Configure the gameserver_1 and the gameserver_2 routers to route among all the VLANs on the network. All VLANs and IP address should be capable of reaching each other. Use EIGRP as the routing protocol, and use 2001 as the Autonomous System ID.

- Tune STP so that the root for all VLANs corresponds to the HSRP configuration. The root for VLANs 128 and 17 should be gl_switch1, and the root for VLAN 16 should be gl_switch2.

- Configure the gl_switch so that only devices on the subnet 172.16.17.0/24 can Telnet to the switch.

- (Optional) Port 2/24 contains a secure workstation. It has a MAC address of 0000.863c.3b41. Configure this port so that only this workstation will work on it, and shut it down if another workstation is plugged into it.

Lab Objectives

- Configure an Ethernet switched network as depicted in Figure 2-39.

- Use a single VTP domain throughout the network. Configure gl_switch1 and gl_switch2 as VTP servers, and configure gl_switch3 as a VTP client. Configure the VLAN trunks and trunk type as denoted in the Figure 2-39. Be sure to configure both types of trunks, 802.1q and ISL.

- Ensure full IP connectivity to all IP interfaces—that is, be sure that you can **ping** all LAN interfaces.

- Create three VLANs on this network, and do not use VLAN1. Create one VLAN for management, which is IP subnet 172.16.128.0/24; one for the glaccess_2 router, 172.16.16.0/24; and one for the glaccess_1 router on subnet 172.16.17.0.

- Configure the gameserver_1 and the gameserver_2 routers to route among all the VLANs on the network. For this lab, you will user EIGRP as the routing protocol. Configure HSRP between these routers. Use the first IP addresses on each subnet as the HSRP shared address. For example, subnet 172.16.128.0/24, the management subnet, should use 172.16.128.1 as the HSRP shared address. Configure HSRP so that the gameserver_2 is the primary for the subnet 172.16.16.0/24 and the gameserver_1 router is the HSRP primary for subnets 172.16.128.0/24 and 172.16.17.0/24. All VLANs and IP address should be capable of reaching each other.

- Configure STP so that the root for VLANs 128 and VLAN 17 is gl_switch1 and the root for VLAN 16 is gl_switch2.

- Configure the gl_switch so that only devices on the 172.16.16.0/24 can Telnet to the switch. This can be the only device that can Telnet and manage the switch.

- (Optional) Port 2/24 contains a secure workstation. It has a MAC address of 0000.863c.3b41. Configure this port so that only this workstation will work on it, and shut it down if another workstation is plugged into it.

Equipment Needed

- Four Cisco routers with Ethernet interfaces. Two routers must have 100-Mbps interfaces. Recall that you need a minimum of a 100 Mbps to run any VLAN trunking protocol. If you do not have routers with 100-Mbps interfaces, routing also can be accomplished by configuring three Ethernet interfaces to the switch from a single router; one interface would be in each VLAN.

- Three Cisco Catalyst Ethernet switches. This lab was designed specifically for two Catalyst 2900/3500 series switches and one Catalyst 4000/5500/6500 series switch.

- To gain practical experience on each type of Cisco Catalyst platform, both types of switches are used in this lab. The gl_switch1 is in the Catalyst 4000/5500/6500 family, while the gl_switch2 and gl_switch3 are in the Catalyst 2900/3500 series family. The specific type of switch is not that important to the functionality of this lab.

Physical Layout and Prestaging

- The networks 172.16.20.0/24 and 172.16.21.0/24 are simulated by loopback interfaces on the glaccess_2 and glaccess_1 routers, respectively.

- This chapter does not focus on the EIGRP and HSRP configurations of this lab. We will show how they are performed during the walkthrough, but for more information on the specifics of how to configure EIGRP and HSRP, see the chapters covering that material.

Figure 2-39 *Game LAN Ethernet Network*

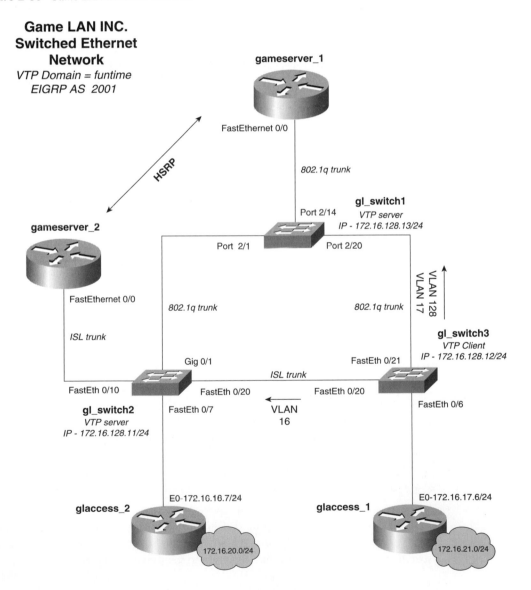

Lab 7: Ethernet Switching, VLAN Trunking, and Spanning Tree Root Placement—Part II

Lab Walkthrough

Attach the switches by using Cat 5 Ethernet crossover cables. A switch in a back-to-back mode requires a crossover cable. Attach the routers with Cat 5 patch cables to the switches, as illustrated in Figure 2-39.

In building this model, you will begin with the configuration of the Ethernet switches and end with the configuration of the routers. Let's begin by defining VLANs and IP subnets to them. Figure 2-40 more accurately reflects the network VLANs, HSRP, and IP address at this point.

You also need to define and create the following VLANs:

- **VLAN 1**—You will not use this VLAN.
- **VLAN 16**—IP subnet 172.16.16.0/24.
- **VLAN 17**—IP subnet 172.16.17.0/24.
- **VLAN 128**—IP subnet 172.16.128.0/24 (new management VLAN).

The VLAN IDs do not need to match the subnet; we purposely match the VLAN ID to the subnet to make the network more self-documenting.

You will begin by configuring the gl_switch1 device. In this model, this device is a Catalyst is in the 4000/5500/6500 family. Recall the four-step configuration process from earlier in this chapter:

Step 1   Configure switch management.

Step 2   Configure VTP and VLANs.

Step 3   Configure VLAN trunks, if applicable.

Step 4   Optional: Control STP and VLAN propagation.

Step 1 calls you to configure basic switch management. Because you are not using VLAN 1 as the default VLAN, you will need to create a new default VLAN before configuring the management interface. To allow IP access to the switch, you also need to configure a password. Example 2-47 demonstrates the creation of the VTP domain, VLANs, and the new management interface on gl_switch1.

Figure 2-40 *Game LAN Ethernet Network*

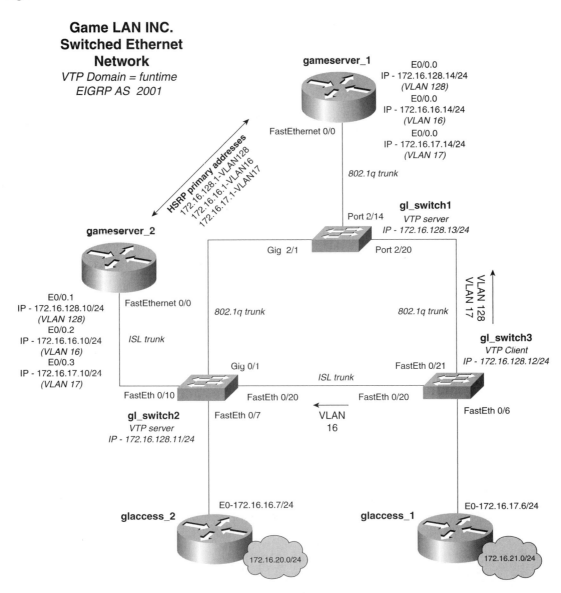

Example 2-47 *Initial Configuration gl_switch1*

```
Console> (enable) set prompt gl_switch1
gl_switch1 (enable) set vtp domain funtime
VTP domain funtime modified
gl_switch1 (enable) set vlan 16
Vlan 16 configuration successful
gl_switch1 (enable) set vlan 17
Vlan 17 configuration successful
gl_switch1 (enable) set vlan 128 name management
Vlan 128 configuration successful
gl_switch1 (enable)
gl_switch1 (enable) set int sc0 128 172.16.128.13 255.255.255.0
Interface sc0 vlan set, IP address and netmask set.
gl_switch1 (enable) set ip route 0.0.0.0 172.16.128.1
Route added.
gl_switch1 (enable)
```

Example 2-47 also shows the addition of a default route. The **set ip route 0.0.0.0 172.16.128.1** command causes the switch to forward all IP traffic to this address. This address needs to be on the same subnet as the management interface—in this case, subnet 172.16.128.0/24.

To ensure that the VTP domain is active, use the **show vtp domain** command to check for configuration errors.

You already have begun to configure the first phase of Step 2, and normally you still would need to assign ports to VLANs. This switch, however, doesn't have any ports in VLANs to configure. This switch has only trunks to the other switches. Therefore, you can skip to Step 3 and define the trunks. To configure the trunks, set them to a static 802.1q trunking mode. Example 2-48 demonstrates the configuration of the trunk lines on gl_switch1.

Example 2-48 *Trunk Configuration on gl_switch1*

```
gl_switch1 (enable) set trunk 2/1 dot1q
Port(s) 2/1 trunk type set to dot1q.
gl_switch1 (enable) set trunk 2/1 on
Port(s) 2/1 trunk mode set to on.
gl_switch1 (enable) set trunk 2/14 dot1q
Port(s) 2/14 trunk type set to dot1q.
gl_switch1 (enable) set trunk 2/14 on
Port(s) 2/14 trunk mode set to on.
gl_switch1 (enable) set trunk 2/20 dot1q
Port(s) 2/20 trunk type set to dot1q.
gl_switch1 (enable) set trunk 2/20 on
Port(s) 2/20 trunk mode set to on.
gl_switch1 (enable)
```

The final step calls for you to fine-tune Spanning Tree. This step cannot be completed until all the trunks are up and operational. When the entire network is converged, routers included, you can come back and tune STP on all the switches. For now, configure the rest of the switches in the domain. The initial configurations of the gl_switch2 and the gl_switch3 are similar. Beginning with other VTP server, gl_switch2, configure basic management. Example 2-49 demonstrates the configuration of the management interface on gl_switch2. Remember, the gl_switch2 and gl_switch3 devices are in the Catalyst 2900/3500 family, so their configuration is different from that of the gl_switch1 device.

Example 2-49 *Management Configuration on gl_switch2*

```
Switch(config)#hostname gl_switch2
gl_switch2(config)#int vlan1
gl_switch2(config-if)#shut
gl_switch2(config-if)#exit
01:35:54: %LINK-5-CHANGED: Interface VLAN1, changed state to administratively do
wn
01:35:55: %LINEPROTO-5-UPDOWN: Line protocol on Interface VLAN1, changed state t
gl_switch2(config)#int vlan128
gl_switch2(config-subif)#ip address 172.16.128.11 255.255.255.0
gl_switch2(config-subif)#no shut
gl_switch2(config-if)#exit
gl_switch2(config)#ip default-gateway 172.16.128.1
```

To allow IP connectivity to the switch, a default-gateway had to be configured, as in Example 2-48. The default gateway must be in the same subnet as the current active management interface, VLAN 128. The IP address of the gateway is the HSRP address of 172.16.128.1.

In Step 2, you define the VTP domain and VLANs. Because you already have VLANs defined on the gl_switch1, there is no need to configure VLANs on any more switches; instead, you can rely on VTP to transport the VLAN information after the trunks are up. Example 2-50 demonstrates the configuration of the VTP domain on gl_switch1.

Example 2-50 *VTP Domain Creation on gl_switch2*

```
gl_switch2#vlan database
gl_switch2(vlan)#vtp domain funtime
Changing VTP domain name from cisco to funtime
```

The gl_switch2 device has a user VLAN on interface fastEthernet 0/7. To assign interface fastEthernet 0/7 to VLAN 16, use the **switchport** command, as in Example 2-51.

Example 2-51 *Assign an Interface to a VLAN on gl_switch2*

```
gl_switch2#conf t
Enter configuration commands, one per line.  End with CNTL/Z.
gl_switch2(config)#interface fastEthernet 0/7
gl_switch2(config-if)#switchport mode access
gl_switch2(config-if)#switchport access vlan 16
```

Proceeding on to Step 3, you can configure the trunks from this switch to the other two. The trunk to gl_switch is an 802.1q trunk, while the trunks to gameserver_2 and gl_switch3 are ISL. Example 2-52 demonstrates the configuration of these trunks on the gl_switch2.

Example 2-52 *Assign an Interface to a VLAN on gl_switch2*

```
Enter configuration commands, one per line.  End with CNTL/Z.
gl_switch2(config)#int gig 0/1
gl_switch2(config if)#switchport mode trunk
gl_switch2(config-if)#switchport trunk encapsulation dot1q
gl_switch2(config-if)#exit
gl_switch2(config)#int fast 0/10
gl_switch2(config-if)#switchport mode trunk
gl_switch2(config-if)#switchport trunk encapsulation isl
gl_switch2(config-if)#exit
gl_switch2(config)#int fast 0/20
gl_switch2(config-if)#switchport mode trunk
gl_switch2(config-if)#switchport trunk encapsulation isl
```

When the trunks are configured on gl_switch2, the trunk to gl_switch1 becomes active. To determine the status of the trunk, use the **show vlan** command along with **show interface gigabitEthernet 0/1 switchport** on gl_switch2. The trunk should be up and trunking. You also should see the VLANs that you created on gl_switch1, and you should be able to **ping** the IP address of 172.16.128.13. Example 2-53 shows the status of an active trunk on gl_switch2.

Example 2-53 *Verifying VLAN and Trunk Operation on gl_switch2*

```
gl_switch2#show vlan
VLAN Name                             Status    Ports
---- -------------------------------- --------- -------------------------------
1    default                          active    Fa0/1, Fa0/2, Fa0/3, Fa0/4,
                                                Fa0/5, Fa0/6, Fa0/8, Fa0/9,
                                                Fa0/11, Fa0/12, Fa0/13, Fa0/14,
                                                Fa0/15, Fa0/16, Fa0/17, Fa0/18,
                                                Fa0/19, Fa0/21, Fa0/22, Fa0/23,
                                                Fa0/24, Fa0/25, Fa0/26, Fa0/27,
                                                Fa0/28, Fa0/29, Fa0/30, Fa0/31,
                                                Fa0/32, Fa0/33, Fa0/34, Fa0/35,
```

continues

Example 2-53 *Verifying VLAN and Trunk Operation on gl_switch2 (Continued)*

```
                                                Fa0/36, Fa0/37, Fa0/38, Fa0/39,
                                                Fa0/40, Fa0/41, Fa0/42, Fa0/43,
                                                Fa0/44, Fa0/45, Fa0/46, Fa0/47,
                                                Fa0/48, Gi0/2
16    VLAN0016                     active       Fa0/7
17    VLAN0017                     active
128   management                   active
1002  fddi-default                 active
1003  token-ring-default           active
1004  fddinet-default              active
1005  trnet-default                active

<<<text omitted>>>
gl_switch2#
gl_switch2#show interface gigabitEthernet 0/1 switchport
Name: Gi0/1
Switchport: Enabled
Administrative mode: trunk
Operational Mode: trunk
Administrative Trunking Encapsulation: dot1q
Operational Trunking Encapsulation: dot1q
Negotiation of Trunking: Disabled
Access Mode VLAN: 0 ((Inactive))
Trunking Native Mode VLAN: 1 (default)
Trunking VLANs Enabled: ALL
Trunking VLANs Active: 1,16,17,128
Pruning VLANs Enabled: 2-1001

Priority for untagged frames: 0
Override vlan tag priority: FALSE
Voice VLAN: none
Appliance trust: none
gl_switch2#
```

You will come back and complete Step 4, tuning STP, after you configure the gl_switch3 switch.

Basic management configuration of the gl_switch3 switch is identical to the configuration in Example 2-49. In that example, you configured a host name, a management interface, and a default gateway. The VTP mode will be transparent, so there is not need to configure VLANs on this switch. The VLANs will be sent when the trunks are configured to the other two switches. Example 2-54 demonstrates the configuration of the VTP and trunks on gl_switch3.

Example 2-54 *VTP Client and VLAN Trunk Configuration on gl_switch3*

```
gl_switch3#vlan database
gl_switch3(vlan)#vtp domain funtime
Changing VTP domain name from Null to funtime
```

Example 2-54 *VTP Client and VLAN Trunk Configuration on gl_switch3 (Continued)*

```
gl_switch3(vlan)#vtp client              ←Setting VTP client
Setting device to VTP CLIENT mode.
gl_switch3(vlan)#exit

gl_switch3#conf t
Enter configuration commands, one per line.  End with CNTL/Z.
gl_switch3(config)#interface fastEthernet 0/21    ←Trunk configuration
gl_switch3(config-if)#switchport mode trunk
gl_switch3(config-if)#switchport trunk encapsulation dot1q
gl_switch3(config-if)#exit
gl_switch3(config)#interface fastEthernet 0/20
gl_switch3(config-if)#switchport mode trunk
gl_switch3(config-if)#switchport trunk encapsulation isl
gl_switch3(config-if)#exit

gl_switch3(config)#interface fastEthernet 0/6         ←User port configuration
gl_switch3(config-if)#switchport mode access
gl_switch3(config-if)#switchport access vlan 17
```

To verify the configuration, view the VTP status with the **show vtp status** command. You also can view the VLANs to be sure that they are being propagated. Example 2-55 lists the output of these status commands on the gl_switch3. At this time, you also should be able to **ping** the IP addresses of the neighboring switches.

Example 2-55 *Verifying VTP Status on gl_switch3*

```
gl_switch3#show vtp status
VTP Version                      : 2
Configuration Revision           : 4
Maximum VLANs supported locally : 254
Number of existing VLANs         : 8
VTP Operating Mode               : Client
VTP Domain Name                  : funtime
VTP Pruning Mode                 : Disabled
VTP V2 Mode                      : Disabled
VTP Traps Generation             : Disabled
MD5 digest                       : 0xC9 0xC8 0x2D 0xEE 0x8D 0xE1 0x46 0x97
Configuration last modified by 172.16.128.13 at 7-2-01 14:43:56

gl_switch3# show vlan
VLAN Name                           Status    Ports
---- -------------------------------- --------- -------------------------------
1    default                         active    Fa0/1, Fa0/2, Fa0/3, Fa0/4,
                                               Fa0/5, Fa0/7, Fa0/8, Fa0/9,
                                               Fa0/10, Fa0/11, Fa0/12, Fa0/13,
                                               Fa0/14, Fa0/15, Fa0/16, Fa0/17,
                                               Fa0/18, Fa0/19, Fa0/22, Fa0/23,
                                               Fa0/24, Fa0/25, Fa0/26, Fa0/27,
```

continues

Example 2-55 *Verifying VTP Status on gl_switch3 (Continued)*

```
                                            Fa0/28, Fa0/29, Fa0/30, Fa0/31,
                                            Fa0/32, Fa0/33, Fa0/34, Fa0/35,
                                            Fa0/36, Fa0/37, Fa0/38, Fa0/39,
                                            Fa0/40, Fa0/41, Fa0/42, Fa0/43,
                                            Fa0/44, Fa0/45, Fa0/46, Fa0/47,
                                            Fa0/48, Gi0/1, Gi0/2
16    VLAN0016                     active
17    VLAN0017                     active   Fa0/6
128   management                   active
1002  fddi-default                 active
1003  token-ring-default           active
1004  fddinet-default              active
1005  trnet-default                active

VLAN Type  SAID       MTU   Parent RingNo BridgeNo Stp  BrdgMode Trans1 Trans2
---- ----- ---------- ----- ------ ------ -------- ---- -------- ------ ------
1    enet  100001     1500  -      -      -        -    -        0      0
16   enet  100016     1500  -      -      -        -    -        0      0
17   enet  100017     1500  -      -      -        -    -        0      0
128  enet  100128     1500  -      -      -        -    -        0      0
1002 fddi  101002     1500  -      0      -        -    -        0      0
1003 tr    101003     1500  -      0      -        -    srb      0      0
1004 fdnet 101004     1500  -      -      -        ieee -        0      0
1005 trnet 101005     1500  -      -      -        ibm  -        0      0
gl_switch3#
gl_switch3#ping 172.16.128.13

Type escape sequence to abort.
Sending 5, 100-byte ICMP Echos to 172.16.128.13, timeout is 2 seconds:
!!!!!
Success rate is 100 percent (5/5), round-trip min/avg/max = 7/7/8 ms
gl_switch3#ping 172.16.128.11

Type escape sequence to abort.
Sending 5, 100-byte ICMP Echos to 172.16.128.11, timeout is 2 seconds:
!!!!!
Success rate is 100 percent (5/5), round-trip min/avg/max = 1/2/3 ms
gl_switch3#
```

The entire switching domain is operational at this point. All the switches will be capable of **ping**ing each other's management interface.

The two routers glaccess_1 and glaccess_2 should be configured for IP now. This involves simply configuring an IP addresses under the Ethernet interface and the loopback interface. In this model, you are using EIGRP as the routing protocol with an Autonomous System ID of 2001. EIGRP must be configured on all the routers. Example 2-56 illustrates the configuration of glaccess_1. The configurations of glaccess_1 and glaccess_2 will be similar except for the IP addresses.

Example 2-56 *Router Configuration of glaccess_1*

```
hostname glaccess_1
!
interface Loopback20
 ip address 172.16.21.6 255.255.255.0
 no ip directed-broadcast
!
interface Ethernet0
 ip address 172.16.17.6 255.255.255.0
 no ip directed-broadcast
!
<<<text omitted>>>
!
router eigrp 2001
 network 172.16.0.0
 no auto-summary
!
```

For the VLANs to communicate with one another, you must configure a router with an interface in each VLAN, or a router with a VLAN trunk. In this model, you will use the routers gameserver_1 and gameserver_2 to not only route between our VLANs, but also to provide resiliency through HSRP. When configuring a VLAN trunk, you need to create subinterfaces on the Ethernet interface and assign a VLAN and VLAN encapsulation to it. You will need one subinterface for each VLAN that you want to route between. Example 2-57 highlights the VLAN trunk configuration for both routers. The trunk of gameserver_1 is an 802.1 trunk, and the trunk of gameserver_2 is an ISL trunk.

Example 2-57 *Router Configuration of gameserver_1 and gameserver_2*

```
hostname gameserver1
!
interface FastEthernet0/0
 no ip address
 duplex auto
 speed auto
!
interface FastEthernet0/0.1
 encapsulation dot1Q 128
 ip address 172.16.128.14 255.255.255.0
!
interface FastEthernet0/0.2
 encapsulation dot1Q 16
 ip address 172.16.16.14 255.255.255.0
!
interface FastEthernet0/0.3
 encapsulation dot1Q 17
 ip address 172.16.17.14 255.255.255.0
```

continues

Example 2-57 *Router Configuration of gameserver_1 and gameserver_2 (Continued)*

```
hostname gameserver_2
!
interface FastEthernet0/0
 no ip address
 duplex auto
 speed auto
!
interface FastEthernet0/0.1
 encapsulation isl 128
 ip address 172.16.128.10 255.255.255.0
 no ip redirects
!
interface FastEthernet0/0.2
 encapsulation isl 16
 ip address 172.16.16.10 255.255.255.0
 no ip redirects
!
interface FastEthernet0/0.3
 encapsulation isl 17
 ip address 172.16.17.10 255.255.255.0
 no ip redirects
!
```

The HSRP configuration requires that the primary router for VLAN 128 and VLAN 17, subnets 172.16.128.0/24 and 172.16.17.0/24, reside on gameserver_1. The HSRP primary address for VLAN 16, subnet 172.16.16.0/24, resides on gameserver_2. To accomplish this, you will need to create an HSRP group for every VLAN, for a total of three groups. You will use a priority of 101 for the interfaces that you want to be active. For more detailed information on configuring HSRP, see Chapter 16, "Configuring Hot Standby Routing Protocol (HSRP)." Example 2-58 lists the HSRP configuration of the gameserver1 and gameserver2 routers.

Example 2-58 *HSRP Configuration of gameserver1 and gameserver2*

```
hostname gameserver1
!
interface FastEthernet0/0
 no ip address
 duplex auto
 speed auto
!
interface FastEthernet0/0.1
 encapsulation dot1Q 128
 ip address 172.16.128.14 255.255.255.0
 standby 1 priority 101 preempt
 standby 1 ip 172.16.128.1
!
```

continues

Example 2-58 *HSRP Configuration of gameserver1 and gameserver2 (Continued)*

```
interface FastEthernet0/0.2
 encapsulation dot1Q 16
 ip address 172.16.16.14 255.255.255.0
 standby 2 priority 95 preempt
 standby 2 ip 172.16.16.1
!
interface FastEthernet0/0.3
 encapsulation dot1Q 17
 ip address 172.16.17.14 255.255.255.0
 standby 3 priority 101 preempt
 standby 3 ip 172.16.17.1
!

!
hostname gameserver_2
!
interface FastEthernet0/0
 no ip address
 duplex auto
 speed auto
!
interface FastEthernet0/0.1
 encapsulation isl 128
 ip address 172.16.128.10 255.255.255.0
 no ip redirects
 standby 1 priority 95 preempt
 standby 1 ip 172.16.128.1
!
interface FastEthernet0/0.2
 encapsulation isl 16
 ip address 172.16.16.10 255.255.255.0
 no ip redirects
 standby 2 priority 101 preempt
 standby 2 ip 172.16.16.1
!
interface FastEthernet0/0.3
 encapsulation isl 17
 ip address 172.16.17.10 255.255.255.0
 no ip redirects
 standby 3 priority 95 preempt
 standby 3 ip 172.16.17.1
!
```

The network is fully redundant and operational now. All IP addresses should be reachable. You can test the network with **ping**s and by unplugging the gameserver_1 or gameserver_2 routers. The network should experience no outages. Example 2-59 lists the route table of glaccess_1, showing the redundant routes.

Example 2-59 *The IP Route Table of glaccess_1*

```
glaccess_1#show ip route
Codes: C - connected, S - static, I - IGRP, R - RIP, M - mobile, B - BGP
       D - EIGRP, EX - EIGRP external, O - OSPF, IA - OSPF inter area
       N1 - OSPF NSSA external type 1, N2 - OSPF NSSA external type 2
       E1 - OSPF external type 1, E2 - OSPF external type 2, E - EGP
       i - IS-IS, L1 - IS-IS level-1, L2 - IS-IS level-2, ia - IS-IS inter area
       * - candidate default, U - per-user static route, o - ODR
       P - periodic downloaded static route

Gateway of last resort is not set

     172.16.0.0/24 is subnetted, 5 subnets
D       172.16.128.0 [90/284160] via 172.16.17.10, 01:04:35, Ethernet0
                     [90/284160] via 172.16.17.14, 01:04:35, Ethernet0
D       172.16.20.0 [90/412160] via 172.16.17.10, 01:04:35, Ethernet0
                    [90/412160] via 172.16.17.14, 01:04:35, Ethernet0
C       172.16.21.0 is directly connected, Loopback20
D       172.16.16.0 [90/284160] via 172.16.17.10, 01:04:35, Ethernet0
                    [90/284160] via 172.16.17.14, 01:04:35, Ethernet0
C       172.16.17.0 is directly connected, Ethernet0
glaccess_1#
```

The final steps in this lab involve setting Spanning Tree root and controlling IP access. To set STP root on the gl_switch1, you will use the **set spantree root** command. By viewing the current STP topology on the gl_switch3, you can see that it is currently root. Example 2-60 shows the STP topology on gl_switch3.

Example 2-60 *STP Topology on gl_switch3*

```
gl_switch3#show spanning-tree vlan 128

Spanning tree 128 is executing the IEEE compatible Spanning Tree protocol
  Bridge Identifier has priority 32768, address 0004.275e.f0c1
  Configured hello time 2, max age 20, forward delay 15
  We are the root of the spanning tree
  Topology change flag not set, detected flag not set, changes 2
  Times:  hold 1, topology change 35, notification 2
          hello 2, max age 20, forward delay 15
  Timers: hello 1, topology change 0, notification 0

Interface Fa0/20 (port 34) in Spanning tree 128 is FORWARDING
    Port path cost 19, Port priority 128
    Designated root has priority 32768, address 0004.275e.f0c1
    Designated bridge has priority 32768, address 0004.275e.f0c1
    Designated port is 34, path cost 0
    Timers: message age 0, forward delay 0, hold 0
    BPDU: sent 1376, received 0
```

Example 2-60 *STP Topology on gl_switch3 (Continued)*

```
Interface Fa0/21 (port 35) in Spanning tree 128 is FORWARDING
   Port path cost 19, Port priority 128
   Designated root has priority 32768, address 0004.275e.f0c1
   Designated bridge has priority 32768, address 0004.275e.f0c1
   Designated port is 35, path cost 0
   Timers: message age 0, forward delay 0, hold 0
   BPDU: sent 1392, received 2
gl_switch3#
```

You will want to set the gl_switch1 switch to be root for VLANs 17 and 128 only. Example 2-61 demonstrates the configuration of gl_switch1.

Example 2-61 *Setting Root for VLAN 17 and VLAN 128 no gl_switch1*

```
gl_switch1 (enable) set spantree root 17,128
VLANs 17,128 bridge priority set to 8192.
VLANs 17,128 bridge max aging time set to 20.
VLANs 17,128 bridge hello time set to 2.
VLANs 17,128 bridge forward delay set to 15.
Switch is now the root switch for active VLANs 17,128.
gl_switch1 (enable)
```

If you view STP on the gl_switch3 in Example 2-62, you will see that this switch is no longer root for VLAN 128. Notice that the priority has changed and that it now points to gl_switch1 as the root.

Example 2-62 *STP for VLAN 128*

```
gl_switch3#show spanning-tree vlan 128

Spanning tree 128 is executing the IEEE compatible Spanning Tree protocol
   Bridge Identifier has priority 32768, address 0004.275e.f0c1
   Configured hello time 2, max age 20, forward delay 15
   Current root has priority 8192, address 0030.1976.4d7f
   Root port is 35, cost of root path is 19
   Topology change flag not set, detected flag not set, changes 5
   Times:  hold 1, topology change 35, notification 2
           hello 2, max age 20, forward delay 15
   Timers: hello 0, topology change 0, notification 0

Interface Fa0/20 (port 34) in Spanning tree 128 is BLOCKING
   Port path cost 19, Port priority 128
   Designated root has priority 8192, address 0030.1976.4d7f
   Designated bridge has priority 32768, address 0004.275e.f5c3
   Designated port is 34, path cost 4
   Timers: message age 3, forward delay 0, hold 0
   BPDU: sent 4762, received 97
```

continues

Example 2-62 *STP for VLAN 128 (Continued)*

```
Interface Fa0/21 (port 35) in Spanning tree 128 is FORWARDING
   Port path cost 19, Port priority 128
   Designated root has priority 8192, address 0030.1976.4d7f
   Designated bridge has priority 8192, address 0030.1976.4d7f
   Designated port is 84, path cost 0
   Timers: message age 3, forward delay 0, hold 0
   BPDU: sent 4777, received 98
gl_switch3#
```

To set the STP root for VLAN 16 on gl_switch2, use the following global command:

```
gl_switch2(config)#spanning-tree vlan 16 priority 100
```

If you exclude the VLAN, all VLANs will have a priority of 100.

The final portion of the lab requires you to limit Telnet access to gl_switch1 to only devices on the subnet 172.16.17.0/24. This can be done by enabling IP permit lists. After an IP permit list is entered, it still must be enabled before it will take effect. Example 2-63 demonstrates the configuration of the IP permit list on gl_switch1.

Example 2-63 *Enabling IP Permit Lists*

```
gl_switch1 (enable) set ip permit 172.16.17.0 255.255.255.0
172.16.17.0 with mask 255.255.255.0 added to IP permit list.
gl_switch1 (enable) set ip permit enable
IP permit list enabled.
gl_switch1 (enable)
```

The optional portion of the lab is about security. By enabling port security, you can force a port to become inactive if it detects a MAC address that isn't specifically allowed on that port. If port security is enabled when a workstation is plugged into the port, it automatically records the MAC address and secures the port for that address. To configure a specific address. add the MAC address to the **set port security** command. Example 2-64 demonstrates enabling port security.

Example 2-64 *Enabling Port Security*

```
gl_switch1 (enable) set port security 2/24 enable 00-00-86-3c-3b-41
Port 2/24 port security enabled with 00-00-86-3c-3b-41 as the secure mac address

Trunking disabled for Port 2/24 due to Security Mode
gl_switch1 (enable)
```

If any other workstation or device is plugged into port 2/24, the port automatically shuts down. Example 2-65 highlights the port status after an unauthorized device is plugged into port 2/24.

Example 2-65 *Port Security*

```
gl_switch1 (enable) show port 2/24
Port  Name                 Status      Vlan       Level   Duplex Speed Type
----- ------------------- ---------- ---------- ------- ------ ----- ------------
 2/24                      shutdown   1          normal  auto   auto  10/100BaseTX

Port  Security Secure-Src-Addr   Last-Src-Addr     Shutdown Trap     IfIndex
----- -------- ----------------- ----------------- -------- -------- -------
 2/24 enabled  00-00-86-3c-3b-41 00-60-5c-f3-5e-65 Yes      disabled 34

Port  Status     Channel   Channel     Neighbor                  Neighbor
                 mode      status      device                    port
----- ---------- --------- ----------- ------------------------- ----------
 2/24 shutdown   auto      not channel

<<<text omitted>>>
```

Lab 8: Configuring Token Ring Switching Using the Catalyst 3920—Part I

Practical Scenario

Token Ring LANs are the second most popular type of network found in modern data centers. Most data centers that have SNA mainframes still have Token Ring networks in place. The following lab gives you practice in configuring Token Ring switching. Throughout the rest of this text, you are encouraged to use Token Ring switches, if you have them available, to enhance the labs on routing protocols and feature sets.

Lab Exercise

Game LANs, Inc., the same company that provides high-speed Ethernet LANs for entertainment centers around the country, also provides Token Ring LANs. One of Game LANs' customers is a small group of people still devoted to playing DOOM on their Token Ring PS/2 PCs. They currently have two Token Ring networks with two IP subnets that they want moved to a switched environment.

Your task is to configure a Game LAN network by using the following parameters as design guidelines:

- Configure a Token Ring switched network as depicted in Figure 2-41.
- Use the VTP domain "rings" and set the switch to be a VTP server.
- Create two VLANs, one for subnet 128.100.1.0/24 and one for 128.100.2.0/24.
- Configure ports 3-24 to be in the VLAN that contains the subnet 128.100.2.0/24.
- Configure IP routing for the network so that there is full IP connectivity to all workstations, routers, and switches. Use RIP as the routing protocol for the internetwork.

Lab Objectives

- Configure a Token Ring switched network as depicted in Figure 2-41.

- Use the VTP domain "rings," and set the switch to be a VTP server. Create two VLANs, one for subnet 128.100.1.0/24 and one for 128.100.2.0/24. The actual configuration might require more VLANs than this.

- Configure ports 3 to 24 to be in the VLAN that contains the subnet 128.100.2.0/24.

- Configure the switch with the IP address as shown in the diagram.

- Use RIP as the routing protocol for the internetwork. Ensure full IP connectivity between all workstations, routers, and switches.

Equipment Needed

- Two Cisco routers with Token Ring interfaces. One router must have two Token Ring interfaces.

- One Catalyst 3920 Token Ring Switch.

- The workstation(s) in the diagram are for extra testing and are not a necessary part of this lab.

Physical Layout and Prestaging

- Connect the switches and the routers, as shown in Figure 2-41.

- The workstation is optional but is recommended to enhance testing and the functionality of network.

Figure 2-41 *Game LAN Token Ring Network*

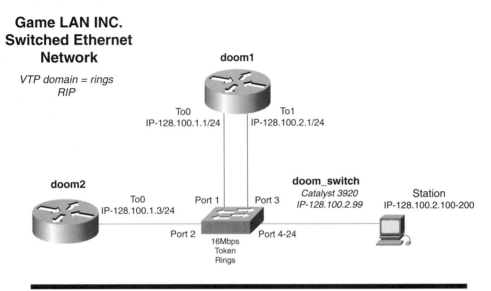

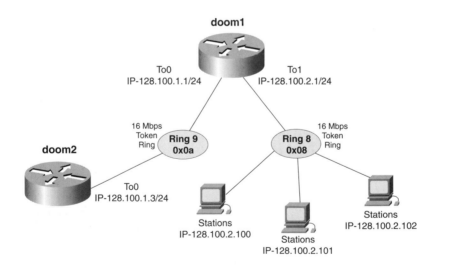

Lab 8: Configuring Token Ring Switching Using the Catalyst 3920—Part II

Lab Walkthrough

Attach the routers to the switch with Cat 5 patch cables, as illustrated in Figure 2-41. When the physical hardware is properly attached, you can begin to follow the six steps for configuring Token Ring switching:

Step 1   Plan TrBRFs, TrCRFs, ring numbers, bridge numbers, and VLANs.

Step 2   Configure VTP.

Step 3   Configure TrBRF VLAN(s) and assign a bridge number to each TrBRF.

Step 4   Configure TrCRFs VLANs and assign a parent TrBRF and an optional ring number.

Step 5   Assign ports to TrCRFs.

Step 6   Configure switch management.

Figure 2-42 diagrams the VLANs that you will need to create. You will need to create two TrBRF VLANs and two TrCRF VLANs. Ports 3-24 will belong to TrCRF crf-ring8, with a parent TrBRF called brf8. Ports 1 and 2 will be in the TrCRF crf-ring9, with a parent TrBRF called brf9.

The switch configuration will be performed entirely from the configuration panel, of the main menu. Step 1 is to configure the VTP domain. Select the VLAN and VTP configuration panel. This is where you will configure VTP and the VLANs needed. Figure 2-43 displays the configuration panel.

From the VLAN and VTP configuration panel, select the VTP administrative configuration panel. Configure the VTP domain to be a server, and assign a name of rings to it. Figure 2-44 displays this panel.

Step 3 involves configuring the TrBRFs. From the VLAN and VTP configuration panel, select the VTP VLAN configuration panel. From the VTP VLAN configuration panel select **Add** to add a new VLAN. The switch prompts you for a VLAN name. The first VLAN that you will create is brf8, VLAN 80. The switch then prompts you for whether the VLAN is a TrBRF or a TrCRF. When you select TrCRF, it takes you to the VLAN configuration menu. From this menu, name the VLAN brf8, and enter a ring number of 8. Remember to enter the ring number in hexadecimal format. Ring 9 will be entered as 0x0a when you configure that ring. Figures 2-45 and 2-46 display the VLAN configuration for TrBRFs.

Figure 2-42 *TrBRF and TrCRF VLAN Conceptual Layout*

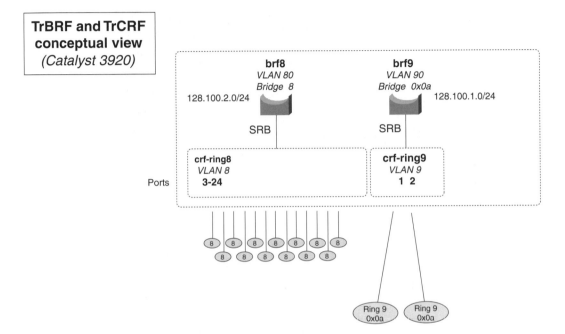

Figure 2-43 *Configuration Panel*

Figure 2-44   *VTP Administrative Panel*

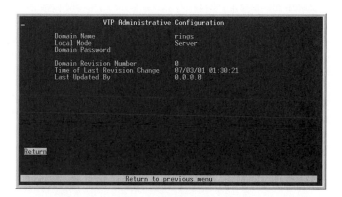

Figure 2-45   *Detailed TrBRF VLAN Configuration*

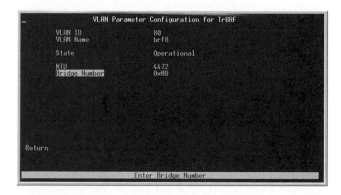

Figure 2-46   *Detailed TrBRF VLAN Configuration*

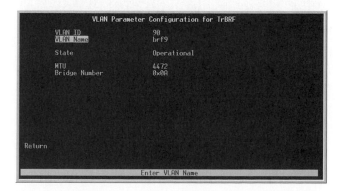

The next step in the configuration is to configure the TrCRF VLANs. These are created from the same menu as the TrBRF VLANs. When you are prompted for the VLAN type, you obviously should select TrCRF instead of TrBRF. When creating the TrCRF VLANs, do not get the VLAN IDs confused. The VLAN IDs for the TrCRF and TrBRFs are unique. The TrCRF is linked to a TrBRF by making it a parent to TrCRF, not by the VLAN ID. Figures 2-47 and 2-48 display the configuration of the TrCRFs VLANs.

Figure 2-47 *Detailed TrCRF VLAN Configuration*

Figure 2-48 *Detailed TrCRF VLAN Configuration*

Figure 2-49 displays the VTP VLAN configuration panel with the newly created VLANs.

Figure 2-49 *VLAN Listing*

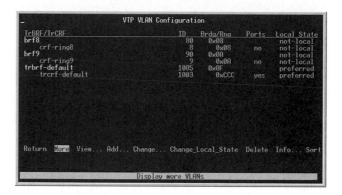

Step 5 involves assigning the ports to the TrCRFs just created. Ports 3 to 24 will be assigned to TrCRF crf-ring8, and ports 1 and 2 will be assigned to TrCRF crf-ring9. From the VLAN VTP configuration panel, select the Local VLAN port configuration option. From this panel, select the port that you want to modify. When the port is selected, the switch prompts you for what TrCRFs are available to attach the port to. Figure 2-50 displays this option.

Figure 2-50 *Port Configuration*

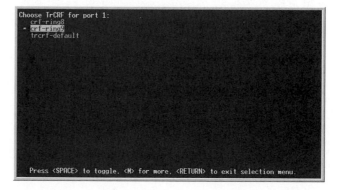

The final step in the configuration is to configure IP access. From the main configuration panel, select IP Configuration to configure an IP address. When this panel is selected, the switch prompts you for a TrBRF to attach the IP address to. In this model, the IP address is 128.100.2.99, so it will attach to TrBRF brf8. When in this menu, enter the IP information; use 128.100.2.1 for the default gateway. Figure 2-51 displays the IP configuration panel.

Figure 2-51 *IP Configuration*

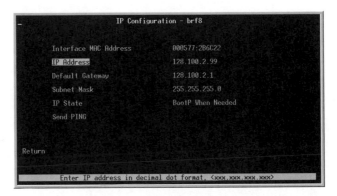

The IP interface will not become active until the same TrBRF becomes the default management interface. This is enabled through the SNMP configuration panel. From the SNMP configuration panel, change the management VLAN from the default to TrBRF brf8.

The switches are fully operational now, and the routers can be configured. The router portion of the lab is rather straightforward. The doom1 router will have two Token Ring interfaces and will run RIP for a routing protocol. The doom2 router will need only one interface configured for IP. Example 2-66 illustrates the relevant configuration of the doom1 and doom2 routers.

Example 2-66 *Configurations of the doom1 and doom2 Routers*

```
hostname doom1
!
<<<text omitted>>>
!
interface TokenRing0
 ip address 128.100.1.1 255.255.255.0
 no ip directed-broadcast
 ring-speed 16
!
interface TokenRing1
 ip address 128.100.2.1 255.255.255.0
 no ip directed-broadcast
 ring-speed 16
!
router rip
 network 128.100.0.0
!
```

Example 2-66 *Configurations of the doom1 and doom2 Routers (Continued)*

```
!
! hostname doom2
!
<<<text omitted>>>
!
interface TokenRing0
 ip address 128.100.1.3 255.255.255.0
 ring-speed 16
!
interface BRI0
 no ip address
 shutdown
!
router rip
 network 128.100.0.0
!
```

When the routers are configured, test the network by **ping**ing all router and switch interfaces. The route table of the doom2 router also shows the subnet 128.100.2.0/24 being reported by RIP.

Connecting LANs with Wide-Area Networks (WANs)

CHAPTER 3

WAN Protocols and Technologies: High-Level Data Link Control (HDLC)

Wide-area networks evolved from the need to share data across vast geographical distances. The definition of WAN is a network spanning a wide geographic area. The purpose of the WAN is to connect local-area networks (LANs) and to transport data from one LAN to another. In our studies, the WAN is used much in the same way.

WAN protocols have changed over time. At first, WAN protocols focused on error correction and were designed to operate on old, unreliable copper lines. WAN protocols today offer high-speed reliable transport on copper and fiber optic lines. Despite the vast evolution of the WAN, it still proves to be the slowest and most expensive part of any modern internetwork.

WAN protocols function at the lower three layers of the OSI model. X.25 PLP is one of the protocols that operates at Layer 3, but most WAN protocols operate at Layer 2. Table 3-1 displays some common WAN protocols and their corresponding layers in the OSI reference model.

Table 3-1 *WAN Protocols and Their Corresponding OSI Layers*

OSI Layers	WAN Protocols					
Network layer	X.25 PLP					
Data link layer	Frame Relay	PPP	HDLC LAPB	X.25	SDLC	ATM-AAL
Physical layer	ISDN-B ISDN-D ISDN-H H11, H12	EIA/TIA-232 EIA/TIA-449 V.24, V.35, HSSI G703, EIA-530				DS-1, DS-3, SONET

In the lab, using Cisco 2500 and 2600 series routers, you can readily model HDLC, PPP, Frame Relay, and X.25. Our studies start with these protocols and end with ISDN and ATM. Modeling ISDN and ATM requires the use of specialized routers and switches.

The Compatibility and Simplicity of HDLC

High-Level Data Link Control (HDLC) is an efficient WAN protocol based primarily on IBM's Synchronous Data Link Control (SDLC) protocol. Cisco's version of HDLC is derived from the ISO 3309 frame. Many forms of the HDLC frame exist, but Cisco's version is not compatible with any other vendors, such as Unisys's implementation of HDLC or the ISO 3309 frame. Even though these frames are similar, they are not compatible.

Cisco's version of HDLC has the following characteristics:

- Incompatibility with other vendors
- Fast and efficient performance
- Support for a keepalive mechanism
- Support for the Serial Link Address Resolution Protocol (SLARP)
- Support for STAC compression

HDLC is the default serial encapsulation, so it does not appear in the configuration listing; however, the HDLC encapsulation appears on the **show interface** display.

The overhead associated with an HDLC frame is small—it has a beginning and ending Flag field, a varied Address field, a Control field, and a variable Information field. Even though these fields vary in size, they vary only from 1 to 4 bytes in length. The overhead of the whole frame ranges from 7 bytes to 12 bytes, which is small. This is where HDLC gains its efficiency.

The HDLC frame uses a keepalive mechanism to verify link integrity. The DCE side of the link sends a sequence number to the DTE side. The DTE side, in turn, sends this number back. The router knows that if it received its last sequence number echoed back from the DTE side of the link, the link is operational. If this sequence number is missed three times in a row, the router deactivates the link. In Example 3-1, you can observe a link going down by not having its keepalives echoed back. This data was displayed with the aid of the **debug serial interface** command.

Example 3-1   *Keepalives on an HDLC Frame Not Being Echoed Back*

```
06:35:59: %LINK-3-UPDOWN: Interface Serial1, changed state to up
06:36:00: Serial1: HDLC myseq 0, mineseen 0, yourseen 0, line up    ←Keepalive(KA)
06:36:00: %LINEPROTO-5-UPDOWN: Line protocol on Interface Serial1, changed state
 to up
06:36:10: HD(1): Deasserting DSR, CTS and DCD
06:36:10: HD(1): Reset from 0x3057C8C
06:36:10: HD(1): Asserting DSR
06:36:10: HD(1): Asserting DCD and CTS
06:36:10: HD(1): Deasserting LTST
06:36:10: HD(1): Asserting DTR and RTS
06:36:10: Serial1: HDLC myseq 1, mineseen 0, yourseen 0, line up    ←KA not received
06:36:18: HD(0): New serial state = 0x0115
```

Example 3-1 *Keepalives on an HDLC Frame Not Being Echoed Back (Continued)*

```
06:36:18: HD(1): got an interrupt state = 0x8055
06:36:18: HD(1): New serial state = 0x005F

06:36:18: HD(1): DTR is up.
06:36:20: HD(1): Deasserting DSR, CTS and DCD
06:36:20: HD(1): Reset from 0x3057C8C
06:36:20: HD(1): Asserting DSR
06:36:20: HD(1): Asserting DCD and CTS
06:36:20: HD(1): Deasserting LTST
06:36:20: HD(1): Asserting DTR and RTS
06:36:20: Serial1: HDLC myseq 2, mineseen 0, yourseen 0, line down    ←Still no KAs
06:36:21: %LINEPROTO-5-UPDOWN: Line protocol on Interface Serial1, changed state
 to down
06:36:28: HD(0): New serial state = 0x0115

06:36:28: HD(1): got an interrupt state = 0x8055
06:36:28: HD(1): New serial state = 0x005F

06:36:28: HD(1): DTR is up.
06:36:30: Serial1: HDLC myseq 3, mineseen 0, yourseen 0, line down
06:36:40: Serial1: HDLC myseq 4, mineseen 0, yourseen 0, line down
06:36:50: Serial1: HDLC myseq 5, mineseen 0, yourseen 0, line down
06:36:51: Serial1: attempting to restart
06:36:51: HD(1): Deasserting DSR, CTS and DCD
06:36:51: HD(1): Reset from 0x3057C8C
```

Notice in Example 3-1 that the sequence number or the myseq field isn't incrementing and matching with the mineseen field. In a correctly operating link, the keepalives will be incrementing and sent to the downstream router. The router will receive these and send them back. The keepalives then show up in the mineseen field of the original router sending it. If the myseq field and mineseen field differ by 3, meaning that three keepalives were dropped, the router reinitializes the link. The yourseen field is the other router's keepalive mechanism and performs the same function. Example 3-2 corrects the problem; observe the debug output.

Example 3-2 *Debug Log of a Correctly Functioning HDLC Link*

```
06:49:30: Serial1: HDLC myseq 81, mineseen 0, yourseen 0, line down
06:49:31: %SYS-5-CONFIG_I: Configured from console by console
06:49:40: Serial1: HDLC myseq 82, mineseen 82*, yourseen 82,
 line up ←First KA seen
06:49:41: %LINEPROTO-5-UPDOWN: Line protocol on Interface Serial1, changed state
 to up
06:49:50: Serial1: HDLC myseq 83, mineseen 83*, yourseen 83, line up
06:50:00: Serial1: HDLC myseq 84, mineseen 84*, yourseen 84, line up
06:50:10: Serial1: HDLC myseq 85, mineseen 85*, yourseen 85, line up
06:50:20: Serial1: HDLC myseq 86, mineseen 86*, yourseen 86, line up
```

continues

Example 3-2 *Debug Log of a Correctly Functioning HDLC Link (Continued)*

```
06:50:31: Serial1: HDLC myseq 87, mineseen 87*, yourseen 87, line up
06:50:41: Serial1: HDLC myseq 88, mineseen 88*, yourseen 88, line up
r3#
06:50:51: Serial1: HDLC myseq 89, mineseen 89*, yourseen 89, line up
```

The exchange of keepalives happens only when Layer 1 of the link is up. If DCD=up, DSR=up, DTR=up, RTS=up, and CTS=up are not present, there will be no keepalive exchanges present.

HDLC also supports SLARP, which is used in the autoinstall process for a serial line to gain and dynamically map its IP address. The Cisco autoinstall process takes advantage of SLARP.

Cisco's implementation of HDLC also supports *payload compression* by the use of the STAC compression algorithm. The STAC compression technique, developed by STAC Electronics, uses the Lempel-Ziv compression algorithm. This algorithm provides good compression but can use many CPU cycles to compress the payload of the frame. STAC compression also can be used with LAPB, X.25, and Frame Relay.

TIP   As a design rule, use HDLC encapsulation for simple configuration with fast, reliable performance between Cisco routers.

Configuring HDLC

HDLC is the default frame encapsulation on all serial interfaces. Therefore, its configuration can be a simple three-step process:

Step 1   Configure the encapsulation from the interface mode by using the **encapsulation hdlc** command.

Step 2   Configure the DCE side of the link by using the **clock rate** *clock_speed* command. This is used only in routers that are attached with back-to-back cables. When using CSU/DSUs, the CSU is the DCE device.

Step 3   (Optional) Configure compression on both ends of the link by using the **compression stac** command.

If you were switching from Frame Relay or another encapsulation to HDLC, you would need to use the **encapsulation hdlc** statement from the interface configuration mode. You can also use the **no** form of the **encapsulation** statement, as in **no encapsulation PPP**. This returns the encapsulation type to the default, which is HDLC. If you are using back-to-back serial cables, or if the interface is cabled as a DCE, you will need to also add the **clock rate** *xxxx* statement in the interface configuration mode on the router with the DCE cable attached. If you want to use STAC compression, enter **compression stac** from the interface configuration mode. Compression must be added to both routers on the link. Make sure that you are aware of the caveats—that is, CPU usage—before implementing any compression technique.

Figure 3-1 illustrates a basic HDLC network. The espn router has two serial connections, one to the atlanta router and one to the bristol_u router. Following the aforementioned multistep process for configuring HDLC, configure this basic HDLC network. To set the encapsulation to HDLC, use the interface command **encapsulation hdlc** on each side of the serial link. For the DCE sides on the link, on the espn router, you need to set the **clock rate** command under the serial interface.

Figure 3-1   *Basic HDLC Network*

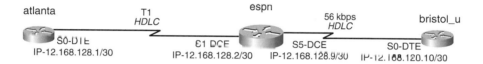

Example 3-3 demonstrates the HDLC configuration of the espn router. Assume that EIGRP as been configured as the routing protocol for the network.

Example 3-3   *HDLC Configuration of the espn Router*

```
espn(config)#interface s1
espn(config-if)#encapsulation hdlc
espn(config-if)#clock rate 2000000
espn(config-if)#ip address 12.168.128.2 255.255.255.252
espn(config-if)#exit
espn(config)#
espn(config)#interface s5
espn(config-if)#encapsulation hdlc
espn(config-if)#clock rate 56000
espn(config-if)#ip address 12.168.128.9 255.255.255.252
```

Example 3-4 demonstrates the HDLC configuration of the bristol_u router.

Example 3-4   *HDLC Configuration of the bristol_u Router*

```
bristol_u(config)#interface s0
bristol_u(config-if)#encapsulation hdlc
bristol_u(config-if)#ip address 12.168.128.10 255.255.255.252
bristol_u(config-if)#exit
```

As you can see, the configuration of HDLC is straightforward. Most of the time, you will not even need to configure an encapsulation, but you will configure simply an IP address.

The "Big show" and "Big D" for HDLC

The **show** and **debug** commands used for HDLC can also be used on most serial interfaces. HDLC is a simple protocol. Therefore, the **show** and **debug** commands are limited but get the job done.

The "big show" and the "big D" commands for HDLC are **show interface** *serial_interface* and **show controllers** *serial_interface*. They're discussed next.

show interface *serial_interface* Command

The **show interface** *serial_interface* command displays the operational status of an interface. The key fields are the interface line [up|down] and the line protocol [up|down]. These fields represent ISO Layer 1 and Layer 2, respectively. The encapsulation type also will be listed along with the keepalive value. DCD, DSR, DTR, RTS, and CTS should all read "up." The interface reset field tells how many times the link has reset itself. Other fields to note indicate the drops, frame, aborts, and CRC errors. Example 3-5 demonstrates output from this command.

Example 3-5   *Output of the **show interface** Command*

```
router#show interface serial 5
Serial5 is up, line protocol is up
  Hardware is CD2430 in sync mode
  Internet address is 12.168.128.9/30
  MTU 1500 bytes, BW 115 Kbit, DLY 20000 usec, rely 255/255, load 1/255
  Encapsulation HDLC, loopback not set, keepalive set (10 sec)
  Last input 00:00:02, output 00:00:00, output hang never
  Last clearing of "show interface" counters never
  Input queue: 0/75/0 (size/max/drops); Total output drops: 0
  Queuing strategy: weighted fair
Output queue: 0/1000/64/0 (size/max total/threshold/drops)
    Conversations  0/1/256 (active/max active/max total)
    Reserved Conversations 0/0 (allocated/max allocated)
  5 minute input rate 0 bits/sec, 0 packets/sec
  5 minute output rate 0 bits/sec, 0 packets/sec
    3870 packets input, 206261 bytes, 0 no buffer
    Received 1524 broadcasts, 0 runts, 0 giants, 0 throttles
    0 input errors, 0 CRC, 0 frame, 0 overrun, 0 ignored, 0 abort
    3907 packets output, 228500 bytes, 0 underruns
    0 output errors, 0 collisions, 44 interface resets
    0 output buffer failures, 0 output buffers swapped out
    24 carrier transitions
    DCD=up  DSR=up  DTR=up  RTS=up  CTS=up
router#
```

show controllers *serial_interface* **Command**

Use the **show controllers** *serial_interface* command to gain physical layer information about a serial controller. This information also helps verify the cable type and whether it is DCE or DTE. Example 3-6 demonstrates output from this command.

Example 3-6 *Output of the* **show interface** *Command*

```
espn#show controllers serial 1
HD unit 1, idb = 0xD7A28, driver structure at 0xDC7A8
buffer size 1524  HD unit 1, V.35 DCE cable, clockrate 2000000
cpb = 0x43, eda = 0x2140, cda = 0x2000
RX ring with 16 entries at 0x432000
00 bd_ptr=0x2000 pak=0x0DF384 ds=0x43C468 status=80 pak_size=0
01 bd_ptr=0x2014 pak=0x0DF1B4 ds=0x43BDB0 status=80 pak_size=0
02 bd_ptr=0x2028 pak=0x0DEFE4 ds=0x43B6F8 status=80 pak_size=0
03 bd_ptr=0x203C pak=0x0DEE14 ds=0x43B040 status=80 pak_size=0
04 bd_ptr=0x2050 pak=0x0DEC44 ds=0x43A988 status=80 pak_size=0
05 bd_ptr=0x2064 pak=0x0DEA74 ds=0x43A2D0 status=80 pak_size=0
06 bd_ptr=0x2078 pak=0x0DE8A4 ds=0x439C18 status=80 pak_size=0
07 bd_ptr=0x208C pak=0x0DE6D4 ds=0x4395D0 status=00 pak_size=0
08 bd_ptr=0x20A0 pak=0x0DE504 ds=0x438EA8 status=80 pak_size=0
09 bd_ptr=0x20B4 pak=0x0DE334 ds=0x4387F0 status=80 pak_size=0
10 bd_ptr=0x20C8 pak=0x0DE164 ds=0x438138 status=80 pak_size=0
11 bd_ptr=0x20DC pak=0x0DDF94 ds=0x437A80 status=80 pak_size=0
12 bd_ptr=0x20F0 pak=0x0DDDC4 ds=0x4373C8 status=80 pak_size=0
13 bd_ptr=0x2104 pak=0x0DDBF4 ds=0x436D10 status=80 pak_size=0
14 bd_ptr=0x2118 pak=0x0DDA24 ds=0x436658 status=80 pak_size=0
15 bd_ptr=0x212C pak=0x0DD854 ds=0x435FA0 status=80 pak_size=0
16 bd_ptr=0x2140 pak=0x0DD684 ds=0x4358E8 status=80 pak_size=0
cpb = 0x43, eda = 0x2800, cda = 0x2800
TX ring with 2 entries at 0x432800
00 bd_ptr=0x2800 pak=0x000000 ds=0x000000 status=80 pak_size=0
01 bd_ptr=0x2814 pak=0x000000 ds=0x000000 status=80 pak_size=0
02 bd_ptr=0x2828 pak=0x000000 ds=0x000000 status=80 pak_size=0
0 missed datagrams, 0 overruns
0 bad datagram encapsulations, 0 memory errors
0 transmitter underruns
0 residual bit errors

espn#
```

debug serial interface **Command**

Remember that, before you turn on debugs on you should always have the **logging buffered 10000** statement present in your configuration. This prevents a flood of console messages form tying up the console.

To demonstrate the usefulness of these commands, we inserted faults into the previously mentioned lab.

We will focus on troubleshooting one side of the problem at a time. Starting with the espn router, perform the **show interface serial 5** command. Example 3-7 lists the output of the **show interface** command.

Example 3-7 *Output of the* **show interface** *Command*

```
espn#show interface serial 5
Serial5 is up, line protocol is up
  Hardware is CD2430 in sync mode
  Internet address is 12.168.128.9/30
  MTU 1500 bytes, BW 115 Kbit, DLY 20000 usec, rely 255/255, load 1/255
  Encapsulation HDLC, loopback not set, keepalive set (10 sec)
  Last input 00:00:02, output 00:00:00, output hang never
  Last clearing of "show interface" counters never
  Input queue: 0/75/0 (size/max/drops); Total output drops: 0
  Queuing strategy: weighted fair
Output queue: 0/1000/64/0 (size/max total/threshold/drops)
     Conversations  0/1/256 (active/max active/max total)
     Reserved Conversations 0/0 (allocated/max allocated)
  5 minute input rate 0 bits/sec, 0 packets/sec
  5 minute output rate 0 bits/sec, 0 packets/sec
     3870 packets input, 206261 bytes, 0 no buffer
     Received 1524 broadcasts, 0 runts, 0 giants, 0 throttles
     0 input errors, 0 CRC, 0 frame, 0 overrun, 0 ignored, 0 abort
     3907 packets output, 228500 bytes, 0 underruns
     0 output errors, 0 collisions, 174 interface resets
     0 output buffer failures, 0 output buffers swapped out
     24 carrier transitions
     DCD=up  DSR=up  DTR=up  RTS=up  CTS=up
espn#
```

Notice that the line is up and the protocol is up. This is good indication that Layer 1 is working, and Layer 2 appears to be working. All the carrier signals show up as well, which is another indication that Layer 1 is working. The number of interface resets and carrier transitions looks suspicious, though. To see whether the counters are incrementing, clear the counters with the **clear counters** command. Then repeat the **show interface** command, and watch to see if they are incrementing. After performing this command, over a period of time, you will see that they do increment, indicating a potential link encapsulation problem.

At this time, the physical aspects of the link to the bristol_u router seem to be working. If you performed the **show controllers** command, this would reaffirm that Layer 1 is operating normally. The problem seems to be a little bit deeper. Therefore, it is necessary to turn on debugs, as demonstrated in Example 3-8 with the **debug serial interface** command. In the preceding example, CIRRUS(5) represents serial interface 5, and HD(1) represents serial interface 1. HD and CIRRUS are controller cards for those ports.

Example 3-8 *Output of the* **debug serial interface** *Command*

```
CIRRUS(5): Asserting DCD                    ←Link asserts DTR
Serial5: HDLC myseq 11, mineseen 0*, yourseen 11, line up    ←NO KA echoed back
CIRRUS(5): DTR is down                  ←DTR drops and the link
Serial5, cd2430_sync_mode_init                    reinitializes
-Traceback= 3078996 3078BE0 30C91DA 315F5B0 315F6E6
CIRRUS(5): Deasserting DSR
CIRRUS(5): Deasserting DCD
CIRRUS(5): Deasserting CTS
CIRRUS(5): Reset from 0x3078BD8
CIRRUS(5): Asserting DSR
CIRRUS(5): Asserting CTS
CIRRUS(5): Asserting DCD
Serial5: HDLC myseq 12, mineseen 0*, yourseen 12, line down
%LINEPROTO-5-UPDOWN: Line protocol on Interface Serial5, changed state to down
Serial1: attempting to restart              ←It attempts to restart
                            And repeats the process
HD(1): Deasserting DSR, CTS and DCD            ← HD(1) is Serial 1 N/A
HD(1): Reset from 0x304562A
HD(1): Asserting DSR
HD(1): Asserting DCD and CTS
HD(1): Deasserting LTST
HD(1): Asserting DTR and RTS
Serial5: HDLC myseq 13, mineseen 0*, yourseen 13, line up
%LINEPROTO-5-UPDOWN: Line protocol on Interface Serial5, changed state to up
Serial5, cd2430_sync_mode_init
-Traceback= 3078996 3078BE0 30C9200 315F5B0 315F6E6
CIRRUS(5): Deasserting DSR
CIRRUS(5): Deasserting DCD
CIRRUS(5): Deasserting CTS
CIRRUS(5): Reset from 0x3078BD8
CIRRUS(5): Asserting DSR
CIRRUS(5): Asserting CTS
CIRRUS(5): Asserting DCD
Serial5: HDLC myseq 14, mineseen 0*, yourseen 14, line up
```

The debugs confirm that an HDLC problem exists on the link, but on what side? Remember that the myseq field should equal the mineseen field. This means that a properly formatted HDLC frame was received and that the keepalive number removed and echoed back.

Starting with the **show interface** command, observe the following about the bristol_u router in Example 3-9:

Example 3-9 *Output of the **show interface** command on bristol_u*

```
bristol_u#show interface serial 0
Serial0 is up, line protocol is down
  Hardware is HD64570
  Internet address is 12.168.128.10/30
  MTU 1500 bytes, BW 1544 Kbit, DLY 20000 usec, rely 255/255, load 1/255
  Encapsulation HDLC, loopback not set, keepalive set (10 sec)
  Last input 00:00:04, output 00:00:10, output hang never
  Last clearing of "show interface" counters never
  Queuing strategy: fifo
Output queue 0/40, 44 drops; input queue 0/75, 0 drops
  5 minute input rate 0 bits/sec, 0 packets/sec
  5 minute output rate 0 bits/sec, 0 packets/sec
     4440 packets input, 258010 bytes, 0 no buffer
     Received 1954 broadcasts, 0 runts, 0 giants, 0 throttles
     0 input errors, 0 CRC, 0 frame, 0 overrun, 0 ignored, 0 abort
     4271 packets output, 227876 bytes, 0 underruns
     0 output errors, 0 collisions, 63 interface resets
     0 output buffer failures, 0 output buffers swapped out
     497 carrier transitions
     DCD=up  DSR=up  DTR=up  RTS=up  CTS=up

bristol_u#show interface serial 0
Serial0 is up, line protocol is down
  Hardware is HD64570
  Internet address is 12.168.128.10/30
  MTU 1500 bytes, BW 1544 Kbit, DLY 20000 usec, rely 255/255, load 1/255
  Encapsulation HDLC, loopback not set, keepalive set (10 sec)
  Last input 00:00:00, output 00:00:01, output hang never
  Last clearing of "show interface" counters never
  Queuing strategy: fifo
Output queue 0/40, 44 drops; input queue 0/75, 0 drops
  5 minute input rate 0 bits/sec, 0 packets/sec
  5 minute output rate 0 bits/sec, 0 packets/sec
     4450 packets input, 258590 bytes, 0 no buffer
     Received 1960 broadcasts, 0 runts, 0 giants, 0 throttles
     0 input errors, 0 CRC, 0 frame, 0 overrun, 0 ignored, 0 abort
     4274 packets output, 227942 bytes, 0 underruns
     0 output errors, 0 collisions, 64 interface resets    ←Note that this field is
     0 output buffer failures, 0 output buffers swapped out      incrementing with
     503 carrier transitions                              ←this field
     DCD=up  DSR=up  DTR=up  RTS=up  CTS=up
bristol_u#
```

This time the line is up, but the line protocol is down. After waiting several seconds, and performing the same command, you see that the Interface Resets field and the Carrier transitions field are also incrementing. At this point, armed with the evidence of keepalives that are not being properly transmitted on one side and the line is up but the protocol is down, you have a clear indication of a Layer 2 HDLC problem. By listing the configuration on the bristol_u router, you find that HDLC compression was not enabled. Adding the **compress stac** statement to the Serial 0 interface of the bristol_u router, you can observe the line becoming active on the espn router. Example 3-10 illustrates Serial 5 recovering on the espn router.

Example 3-10 *Output of the* **debug serial interface** *Command on espn*

```
Serial5: HDLC myseq 165, mineseen 0*, yourseen 67, line down
%LINEPROTO-5-UPDOWN: Line protocol on Interface Serial5, changed state to down
Serial1: attempting to restart
HD(1): Deasserting DSR, CTS and DCD
HD(1): Reset from 0x304562A
HD(1): Asserting DSR
HD(1): Asserting DCD and CTS
HD(1): Deasserting LTST
HD(1): Asserting DTR and RTS
Serial5: HDLC myseq 166, mineseen 166*, yourseen 68, line up
%LINEPROTO-5-UPDOWN: Line protocol on Interface Serial5, changed state to up
Serial5: HDLC myseq 167, mineseen 167*, yourseen 69, line up
Serial5: HDLC myseq 168, mineseen 168*, yourseen 70, line up
Serial1: attempting to restart
HD(1): Deasserting DSR, CTS and DCD
HD(1): Reset from 0x304562A
HD(1): Asserting DSR
HD(1): Asserting DCD and CTS
HD(1): Deasserting LTST
HD(1): Asserting DTR and RTS
Serial5: HDLC myseq 169, mineseen 169*, yourseen 71, line up
Serial5: HDLC myseq 170, mineseen 170*, yourseen 72, line up
Serial5: HDLC myseq 172, mineseen 172*, yourseen 74, line up
Serial5: HDLC myseq 173, mineseen 173*, yourseen 75, line up
Serial5: HDLC myseq 174, mineseen 174*, yourseen 76, line up
```

From the espn router, you can **ping** the bristol_u router and find that the link is up and fully functional.

You can now focus on the problem in the atlanta router. In Example 3-11, start with the **show interface serial 1** command: You see that the line is down and the line protocol is down. You should also see that the DTR and RTS signals are down. This immediately points to a Layer 1 problem. But which side is it on? When you perform the **show controller serial 1** command on the espn router, all is normal—the controller reports no errors and also reports a V.35 DCE cable attached to the port. If you perform this same command on the atlanta router, you see that a serial cable is not detected. Example 3-11 demonstrates the **show controller serial** *x* command on both the espn and the atlanta routers.

Example 3-11 *Output from the* **show controllers** *Command Performed on the atlanta Router and the espn Router*

```
espn#show controllers serial 1
HD unit 1, idb = 0xD7A28, driver structure at 0xDC7A8
buffer size 1524  HD unit 1, V.35 DCE cable, clockrate 1000000 ←DCE Cable attached
cpb = 0x43, eda = 0x2140, cda = 0x2000
RX ring with 16 entries at 0x432000
00 bd_ptr=0x2000 pak=0x0DE8A4 ds=0x439C18 status=80 pak_size=0
01 bd_ptr=0x2014 pak=0x0DDDC4 ds=0x4373C8 status=80 pak_size=0
<<<text omitted>>>
16 bd_ptr=0x2140 pak=0x0DD4B4 ds=0x435230 status=80 pak_size=0
cpb = 0x43, eda = 0x2800, cda = 0x2800
TX ring with 2 entries at 0x432800
00 bd_ptr=0x2800 pak=0x000000 ds=0x000000 status=80 pak_size=0
01 bd_ptr=0x2814 pak=0x000000 ds=0x000000 status=80 pak_size=0
02 bd_ptr=0x2828 pak=0x000000 ds=0x000000 status=80 pak_size=0
165 missed datagrams, 0 overruns
0 bad datagram encapsulations, 0 memory errors
0 transmitter underruns
0 residual bit errors

espn#
```

```
atlanta#
atlanta#show controller serial 0
MK5 unit 0, NIM slot 0, NIM type code 7, NIM version 1
idb = 0x60CF5DF8, driver structure at 0x60CFB100, regaddr = 0x3C000300
IB at 0x40006E64: mode=0x0108, local_addr=0, remote_addr=0
N1=1524, N2=1, scaler=100, T1=1000, T3=2000, TP=1
buffer size 1524
No serial cable attached          ←No serial cable!
RX ring with 32 entries at 0x06EC8 : RLEN=5, Rxhead 0
00 pak=0x60D0322C  ds=0xA8214B44 status=80 max_size=1524 pak_size=0
01 pak=0x60D02E44  ds=0xA8214488 status=80 max_size=1524 pak_size=0
<<<text omitted>>>
30 pak=0x60D03038  ds=0xA801449C status=80 max_size=1524 pak_size=0
31 pak=0x60D02A5C  ds=0xA8213DCC status=80 max_size=1524 pak_size=0
TX ring with 32 entries at 0x07108 : TLEN=5, TWD=7
tx_count = 0, tx_head = 0, tx_tail = 0
00 pak=0x000000 ds=0xA8000000 status=0x38 max_size=1524 pak_size=0
01 pak=0x000000 ds=0xA8000000 status=0x38 max_size=1524 pak_size=0
<<<text omitted>>>
30 pak=0x000000 ds=0xA8000000 status=0x38 max_size=1524 pak_size=0
31 pak=0x000000 ds=0xA8000000 status=0x38 max_size=1524 pak_size=0
XID/Test TX desc at 0xFFFFFF, status=0x30, max_buffer_size=0, packet_size=0
XID/Test RX desc at 0xFFFFFF, status=0x0, max_buffer_size=0, packet_size=0
```

Example 3-11 *Output from the* **show controllers** *Command Performed on the atlanta Router and the espn Router (Continued)*

```
Status Buffer at 0x40007340: rcv=0, tcv=0, local_state=0, remote_state=0
phase=0, tac=0, currd=0x00000, curxd=0x00000
bad_frames=0, frmrs=0, T1_timeouts=0, rej_rxs=0, runts=0
0 missed datagrams, 0 overruns
0 bad datagram encapsulations, 0 memory errors
0 transmitter underruns
0 user primitive errors, 0 spurious primitive interrupts
0 provider primitives lost, 0 unexpected provider primitives
mk5025 registers: csr0 = 0x0E00, csr1 = 0x0302, csr2 = 0x0500
                  csr3 = 0x6E64, csr4 = 0x0214, csr5 = 0x0009

atlanta#
```

After replacing the serial cable, the link becomes active and all is well again in the sports world.

Lab 9: Configuring HDLC—Part I

Practical Scenario

HDLC can have many uses in the field. One instance, as mentioned previously, is to always switch the encapsulation to HDLC when testing a CSU/DSU or an internal CSU/DSU with a loopback plug. HDLC is often used when connecting to a Cisco router administered by a third party. A third-party router is a router that is not part of your autonomous system or one that is not under your direct control. HDLC provides for a quick and easy configuration, minimizing the number of problems that can go wrong because of configuration errors.

Lab Exercise

In this exercise, you are a network engineer for ACME Finance. ACME Finance is about to have a new credit card authorization center and a Wisconsin branch join the network. The credit card center, cc_center, is running HDLC protocol on a 56-kbps link to your distribution router, acme_dist. The credit card center would like to improve performance on this link as soon as possible, by using payload compression. The Wisconsin branch router, wi_branch, has a T1 leased line into acme_dist router, but it is not configured. The WAN is the first circuit in each building, and there are no users; therefore, you won't be concerned with any LAN configurations.

Lab Objectives

- Configure the network as depicted in Figure 3-2.
- Use only the HDLC protocol on the serial links.
- Use payload compression on the 56-kbps link between the cc_center and acme_dist routers.

Equipment Needed

- Three Cisco routers. One must have two serial ports.

- Four serial cables, preferably two V.35 DTE male and two V.35 DCE female cables. Otherwise, you can use the correct speed of DSU/CSUs with a crossover cable between them. When using actual DSU/CSUs, the **clock rate interface** command is not needed. For more information on the various ways to connect routers in a back-to-back manner, review Chapter 1, "The Key Components for Modeling an Internetwork."

Physical Layout and Prestaging

- Connect the serial cables to the routers as shown in Figure 3-2.

Figure 3-2   *ACME Finance Network*

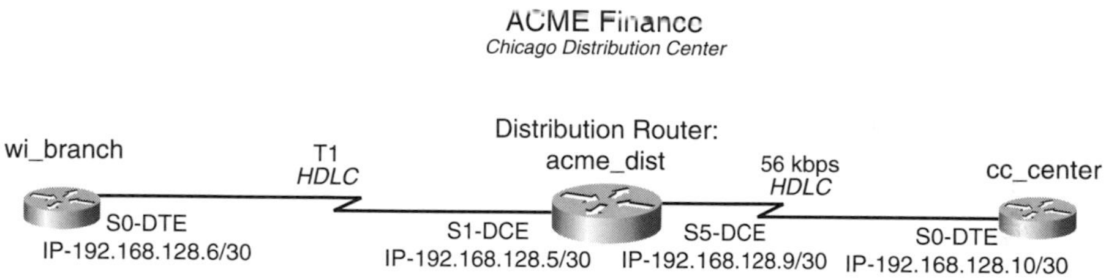

ACME Finance
Chicago Distribution Center

wi_branch
T1
HDLC

Distribution Router:
acme_dist
56 kbps
HDLC
cc_center

S0-DTE
IP-192.168.128.6/30

S1-DCE
IP-192.168.128.5/30

S5-DCE
IP-192.168.128.9/30

S0-DTE
IP-192.168.128.10/30

Lab 9: Configuring HDLC—Part II

Lab Walkthrough

Attach the serial cables as shown in Figure 3-2, ensuring that a DTE side is connected to a DCE side. If you forgot which side is which, perform the **show controller** command to show the cable type (DCE-DTE) attached to this interface. If the routers are connected in a back-to-back manner using serial cables, the **clockrate** command will be needed on the DCE side of the link. If the routers are connected using CSU/DSUs, the CSU/DSU is the DCE device, and the serial interface and cable to the CSU/DSU are DTE devices. Because configurations with CSU/DSUs are actually a DTE configuration to the router, you do not need to use the **clock rate** command.

The distribution router, acme_dist, will be the DCE side of the link for both connections. To configure this router, perform the following:

Step 1   (Optional) Configure a hostname of acme_dist.

Step 2   Configure Serial 5 and Serial 1 for HDLC by using the **Encapsulation hdlc** statement.

Step 3   Configure a clock rate on Serial 1 and Serial 5.

Step 4   Configure STAC compression on Serial 1.

Step 5   Configure an IP address for both serial interfaces.

Step 6   (Optional) Configure a routing protocol.

Example 3-12 demonstrates these steps.

Example 3-12 *Configure HDLC DCE Interfaces*

```
Router#
Router#conf t
Enter configuration commands, one per line.  End with CNTL/Z.
Router(config)#hostname acme_dist
acme_dist(config)#interface serial 5
acme_dist(config-if)#encapsulation hdlc        ←This is optional, HDLC is default
acme_dist(config-if)#clock rate 56000            ←Tells the router to send a clock
acme_dist(config-if)#compress stac      ←Enables STAC compression
acme_dist(config-if)#ip address 192.168.128.9 255.255.255.252
acme_dist(config-if)#no shut
acme_dist(config-if)#exit
acme_dist(config)#
acme_dist(config)#interface serial 1
acme_dist(config-if)#clock rate 1000000
acme_dist(config-if)#ip address 192.168.128.5 255.255.255.252
acme_dist(config-if)#no shut
acme_dist(config-if)#exit
```

Example 3-12 *Configure HDLC DCE Interfaces (Continued)*

```
acme_dist(config)#
acme_dist(config)#router eigrp 2001              →This is optional, configures
acme_dist(config-router)#network 192.168.128.0   →EIGRP as the routing protocol
for this network
acme_dist(config-router)#^Z
acme_dist#
```

Moving on to the credit card center, you must also configure this router for HDLC. The router needs compression configured so that it can understand payload compression. To make this lab practical, you also need to add an IP address, a routing protocol, and a host name. Example 3-13 illustrates the configuration of the credit card center, the cc_center router.

Example 3-13 *HDLC Configuration on the DTE Side of the Network*

```
Router#conf t
Enter configuration commands, one per line.  End with CNTL/Z.
Router(config)#hostname cc center
cc_center(config)#interface serial 0
cc_center(config-if)#encapsulation hdlc
cc_center(config-if)#compress stac
cc_center(config-if)#ip address 192.168.128.10 255.255.255.252
cc_center(config-if)#no shut
cc_center(config-if)#exit
cc_center(config)#
cc_center(config)#router eigrp 2001
cc_center(config-router)#network 192.168.128.0
cc_center(config-router)#^Z
cc_center#
```

Finally, Example 3-14 shows the configuration for the Wisconsin branch. This example takes advantage of the Cisco defaults and the Cisco convention that allows for minimal unique parsing of the command. For example, **co** can be either **configure** or **copy**, but '**cop**' is unique, so **cop** is sufficient. Example 3-14 demonstrates these time-saving steps.

Example 3-14 *HDLC Configuration of wi_branch, Using Defaults and Shortened Keystrokes*

```
Router#conf t
Enter configuration commands, one per line.  End with CNTL/Z.
Router(config)#hostname wi_branch
wi_branch(config)#int s0
wi_branch(config-if)#ip add 192.168.128.6 255.255.255.252
wi_branch(config-if)#no shut
wi_branch(config-if)#
wi_branch(config-if)#
wi_branch(config-if)#router eigrp 2001
wi_branch(config-router)#network 192.168.128.0
wi_branch(config-router)#^Z
wi_branch#
```

Reviewing the configurations in their entirety, you have the following listings in Example 3-15.

Example 3-15 *Configuration Listings for Lab 9, ACME Finance*

```
Distribution Router (acme_dist)

hostname acme_dist
!
<<<text omitted>>>
!
interface Serial1
 ip address 192.168.128.5 255.255.255.252
 clockrate 1000000
!
<<<text omitted>>>
!
interface Serial5
 ip address 192.168.128.9 255.255.255.252
 clockrate 56000
 compress stac
!
<<<text omitted>>>
!
router eigrp 2001
 network 192.169.128.0
```

```
        Credit Card Center (cc_center)

hostname cc_center
!
 interface Serial0
 ip address 192.168.128.10 255.255.255.252
 no ip directed-broadcast
 no ip mroute-cache
 no fair-queue
 compress stac
!
<<<text omitted>>>
!
router eigrp 2001
 network 192.168.128.0
```

```
        Wisconsin Branch (wi_branch)

hostname wi_branch
!
<<<text omitted>>>
```

Example 3-15 *Configuration Listings for Lab 9, ACME Finance (Continued)*

```
!
interface Serial0
 ip address 192.168.128.6 255.255.255.252
 no ip mroute-cache
 no fair-queue
!
<<<text omitted>>>
!
router eigrp 2001
 network 192.168.128.0
```

To verify this particular configuration, a couple of commands are useful: **show interface serial** *x*, **show ip eigrp neighbors**, and, of course, **ping**. When the lab is fully functional you see two EIGRP neighbors on the acme_dist router, one to each of the other routers. The **show interface** commands show the line up, the protocol up, and DCD, DSR, DTR, RTS, and CTS all in an up state.

CHAPTER 4

WAN Protocols and Technologies: Point-to-Point Protocol (PPP)

Along with the explosion of the Internet came the explosion of the Internet's access protocol, the Point-to-Point Protocol (PPP). Most analog dialup connections today run PPP as their data-link protocol. This is primarily because of the Internet-friendly capabilities of PPP:

- Error detection
- Network layer address negotiation
- Authentication using CHAP or PAP
- Data compression
- ISO standard

Before PPP became the dominant Internet access protocol, it was often used—and confused—with the Serial Line Internet Protocol (SLIP). Many people commonly referred to point-to-point connections using SLIP/PPP. Unfortunately, SLIP supported only IP as its only network layer protocol and thereby fell short of the requirements needed for many network administrators running IP, IPX, and AppleTalk protocols.

Cisco's implementation of PPP is modeled after RFC 1661. This RFC explains how PPP is used for encapsulating network layer protocol information over point-to-point links. PPP breaks down the data link layer into three sublayers. Each sublayer has a specific function:

- **Network Control Protocol (NCP)**—Establishes and negotiates network layer protocols and addresses.
- **Link Control Protocol (LCP)**—Establishes, authenticates, and optionally tests the link for quality.
- **High-Level Data Link Control (HDLC)**—Encapsulates datagrams over the link. RFC 1662 describes this procedure.

Table 4-1 outlines PPP and its sublayers.

Table 4-1   *PPP Sublayers of the OSI Mode*

OSI Layer	Common Protocols
Layer 3	Network layer protocols, such as IP, IPX, and AppleTalk
Layer 2	Network Control Protocol (NCP)
	Link Control Protocol (LCP)
	High-Level Data Link Control (HDLC)
Layer 1	Physical layer
	EIA/TIA-232, V.24, V.35, ISDN, and so on

Other RFCs significant to PPP are listed here:

- **RFC 1144**—TCP/IP header compression.
- **RFC 1220**—Point-to-Point Protocol extensions for bridging. This RFC replaces RFC 1220.
- **RFC 1334**—PPP authentication protocols.
- **RFC 1378**—PPP AppleTalk Control Protocol (ATCP).
- **RFC 1552**—PPP Internetworking Packet Exchange Control Protocol (IPXCP).
- **RFC 1570**—PPP LCP extensions.
- **RFC 1661**—Point-to-Point Protocol (PPP).
- **RFC 1662**—PPP in HDLC-like framing.
- **RFC 1990**—PPP Multilink Protocol (MP).

NOTE   You can find all the RFCs online at www.isi.edu/in-notes/rfc*xxxx*.txt, where *xxxx* is the number of the RFC.

As referenced, PPP uses the HDLC protocol as a means by encapsulating datagrams over links. The frame structure and principles of PPP are outlined in the International Organization for Standardization (ISO) HDLC procedures 3309, amended by 1984/PDAD1 to allow use in asynchronous environments and the start/stop transmission.

Many of PPP's extended capabilities, such as error correction and multiple network layer protocols, are controlled by its *Link Control Protocol (LCP)* and the *Network Control*

Protocols (NCP). The LCP frame is sent to configure and optionally test the data link. LCP operates in the following manner:

Step 1 **Link establishment phase**—LCP first opens the connection and then negotiates communications parameters. These include the maximum receive unit, compression type, and link authentication protocol type. After link configuration is complete, a configuration-acknowledgment frame must be sent and received. This step is followed by an optional link-quality determination phase. Here, LCP determines whether the link quality is sufficient to bring up network layer protocols.

Step 2 **"Not so optional" authentication phase**—After the link is established and the authentication protocol is decided on, the peer goes through the authentication specified. Cisco offers the Challenge Handshake Authentication Protocol (CHAP) and the Password Authentication Protocol (PAP) for PPP authentication. The PPP standard does not require any authentication to take place; this is true for nondial connections and ISDN connections. For analog dial configurations running over asynchronous links, however, before a Cisco router can bind a route after Step 3, it requires a lower-level caller ID authentication or CHAP and PAP to take place. This might account for why PPP configs can work in one location and not in another. To protect yourself against this, the Cisco TAC recommends to always use CHAP authentication. RFC 1994 defines PPP CHAP, which obsoletes RFC 1334.

Step 3 **Network layer protocol phase**—At this point, LCP directs NCP to bring up the configured network layer protocols. After this phase is complete, packets from each network layer protocol can be sent over the link.

Step 4 **Link termination phase**—LCP can terminate the link upon user intervention or a physical event. LCP directs the NCP to close the Layer 3 protocols and take appropriate action.

LCP accomplishes these phases with three types of LCP frames:

- **Link establishment frames**—Establishes the link
- **Link termination frames**—Closes the link
- **Link maintenance frames**—Used to manage and debug the link

The Many Uses of PPP

PPP is a versatile protocol, and you can configure it on a number of different interface types:

- Synchronous
- Asynchronous
- ISDN
- High-Speed Serial Interface (HSSI)
- Digital subscriber line (DSL)

As you can already see, PPP can be deployed in a variety of situations. And, as mentioned previously, most people use PPP as their data link layer protocol to access the Internet. PPP is also commonly used as the data-link layer for Integrated Services Digital Network (ISDN) and when configuring a point-to-point link to a non-Cisco device. Another use of PPP can be on a serial backup link, or to "bundle" multiple Basic Rate Interfaces (BRIs) together to maximize bandwidth and load share, such as in a PPP multilink scenario.

When modeling PPP in the internetwork, you will deploy PPP in a number a ways. First, you look at configuring PPP on serial links. Then, the chapter expands and applies the same theory to asynchronous ports using modems. Finally, the chapter discusses how to implement some of the more advanced features of PPP, including PPP compression, PPP multilink, and other PPP features. PPP over ISDN is covered in Chapter 7, "WAN Protocols and Technologies: Integrated Services Digital Network (ISDN)."

Configuring PPP on Synchronous Serial Links

To configure PPP on a serial interface, you must first enable PPP encapsulation on the interface with the **encapsulation ppp** command. If you are configuring both ends of the PPP link, you need to configure PPP encapsulation on each side. If you are configuring a PPP link with two routers, using DTE-to-DCE cable connections, you also need to use the **clock rate** *bps* command on the DCE side of the connection. Essentially, setting the encapsulation coupled with a network layer address is all that is needed for a basic PPP configuration. As you will see, this is just the basic configuration, and you will be using the more advanced features of PPP in the upcoming sections.

The first example involves configuring PPP on a serial interface between two Cisco routers. Use Figure 4-1 as the network diagram and address map, and begin by defining PPP encapsulation on Serial 1 (S1) of r1 and Serial 0 (S0) of r2. Because this is a V.35 back-to-back connection, one side needs to be configured as DCE. Use the **clock rate** statement on the Serial 1 interface of r1 to accomplish this.

Figure 4-1   *PPP Network Diagram and IP Scheme*

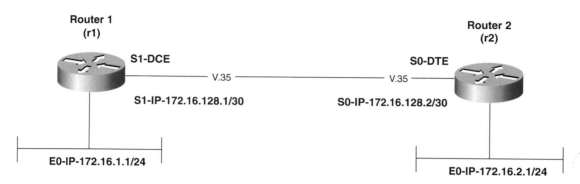

Example 4-1 demonstrates the configuration commands used for a simple PPP back-to-back configuration.

Example 4-1   *PPP on a Serial Interface*

```
r1(config)#interface s1
r1(config-if)#encapsulation ppp              ←Set PPP encapsulation
r1(config-if)#clock rate 56000               ←Needed for DCE connection
r1(config-if)#ip address 172.16.128.1 255.255.255.252
r1(config-if)#no shut
r1(config-if)#^Z
r1#
```

Example 4-2 lists the relevant portions of the configurations for routers r1 and r2.

Example 4-2   *Configuration Listings for PPP Back-to-Back Network on r1 and r2*

```
hostname r1
!
 interface Ethernet0
 ip address 172.16.1.1 255.255.255.0
 no ip directed-broadcast
!
interface Serial1
 ip address 172.16.128.1 255.255.255.252
 no ip directed-broadcast
 encapsulation ppp
 clockrate 56000
!
router ospf 2001
 network 172.16.1.1 0.0.0.0 area 0
 network 172.16.128.1 0.0.0.0 area 1
```

continues

Example 4-2 *Configuration Listings for PPP Back-to-Back Network on r1 and r2 (Continued)*

```
hostname r2
!
interface Ethernet0
 ip address 172.16.2.1 255.255.255.0
!
interface Serial0
 ip address 172.16.128.2 255.255.255.252
 encapsulation ppp
!
router ospf 2001
 redistribute connected subnets
 network 172.16.128.2 0.0.0.0 area 1
 default-metric 100
```

Configuring PPP on Asynchronous Ports for Analog Dial Links

Configuring PPP on asynchronous interfaces for analog dial connections can be more involved than configuring PPP on serial links. This section briefly lists the steps needed to configure PPP and then goes into greater detail on the more complex steps. The steps to configure PPP for use on an asynchronous dialup connection are as follows:

Step 1   Configure the modem and asynchronous port. Step 1 involves attaching and configuring the modem, and configuring the asynchronous port of the router. This step also includes identifying the absolute line number that corresponds to that asynchronous interface. See Chapter 1, "The Key Components for Modeling an Internetwork," for more information on connecting and configuring modems.

Step 2   Define and configure PPP on the asynchronous interface. Configure the asynchronous interface that corresponds to the absolute line number found in Step 1. Configure PPP encapsulation and PPP authentication for the asynchronous interface.

Step 3   Configure network layer addresses or addressing schemas and routing as they corresponds to the asynchronous interface.

Step 4   Configure the asynchronous interface for dial-on-demand routing (DDR).

Step 1: Modem and Asynchronous Port Configuration

Carefully follow the outlined instructions in Chapter 1 to properly connect a modem to either the AUX port or an asynchronous port on a router. This includes using the **modem inout** command and the **modem autoconfigure** command or deploying the use of chat scripts. A chat script is always needed for the remote router to dial into the host. To call the chat script on dial-out use only, use the **script dialer** *script_name* command under the absolute line entry. The chat script should be kept simple and clean. For example, the following chat script will reset the modem, load the factory defaults, and then dial the number 5496561 and wait for a connect message.

```
chat-script dialhost "" "ATZ&F" OK "ATDT5496561" TIMEOUT 60 CONNECT
```

The chat script is where you actually place the number to be called with analog dial communications. The dialer map string also has a telephone number on it, but this is used for authentication and caller identification, not for actually placing the call. When the dialer map is deployed in an ISDN configuration, the dialer map string is used to place the call.

Be sure to perform the **show line** command and make note of the absolute line number that corresponds to the port to which the modem was attached. Example 4-3 attaches a modem to the AUX port of a Cisco 2500 router.

Example 4-3   **show line** *Command Listing the Absolute Line Number of the AUX Port*

```
Router#show line
  Tty Typ     Tx/Rx      A Modem  Roty AccO AccI   Uses   Noise  Overruns  Int
*   0 CTY                 -    -     -    -    -      0      0     0/0       -
    1 AUX   9600/9600  -    -     -    -    -      0      1     0/0       -    ← Aux port
    2 VTY                 -    -     -    -    -      0      0     0/0       -
    3 VTY                 -    -     -    -    -      0      0     0/0       -
    4 VTY                 -    -     -    -    -      0      0     0/0       -
    5 VTY                 -    -     -    -    -      0      0     0/0       -
    6 VTY                 -    -     -    -    -      0      0     0/0       -

Router#
```

You later use the absolute line number (1, in this case) to configure an asynchronous link. The absolute line number can and will change with different router types, so it is important to perform the **show line** command to verify the absolute line number. For example, Example 4-4 attaches a modem to port 16 of the terminal server, and the AUX port is on line 17, not line 1. This example also shows the line as being inactive and shows that a transmit and receive clock is also set. This indicates that a modem is already configured and attached to the line.

Example 4-4   **show line** *Command Listing the Absolute Line Number of the AUX Port*

```
access_server#show line
  Tty Typ     Tx/Rx      A Modem  Roty AccO AccI   Uses   Noise  Overruns  Int
*   0 CTY                 -    -     -    -    -      7      0     0/0       -
*   1 TTY   9600/9600  -    -     -    -    -      1      0     0/0       -
*   2 TTY   9600/9600  -    -     -    -    -      1   1776     0/0       -
*   3 TTY   9600/9600  -    -     -    -    -      1      1     0/0       -
*   4 TTY   9600/9600  -    -     -    -    -      1      0     0/0       -
*   5 TTY   9600/9600  -    -     -    -    -      1      1     0/0       -
```

continues

Example 4-4 **show line** *Command Listing the Absolute Line Number of the AUX Port (Continued)*

```
*   6 TTY   9600/9600   -   -       -   -   -       1       0       0/0         -
*   7 TTY   9600/9600   -   -       -   -   -       1       0       0/0         -
    8 TTY   9600/9600   -   -       -   -   -       0       0       0/0         -
    9 TTY   9600/9600   -   -       -   -   -       0       0       0/0         -
   10 TTY   9600/9600   -   -       -   -   -       0       0       0/0         -
   11 TTY   9600/9600   -   -       -   -   -       0       0       0/0         -
   12 TTY   9600/9600   -   -       -   -   -       0       0       0/0         -
   13 TTY   9600/9600   -   -       -   -   -       0       0       0/0         -
   14 TTY   9600/9600   -   -       -   -   -       0       0       0/0         -
   15 TTY   9600/9600   -   -       -   -   -       0       0       0/0         -
 I 16 TTY 115200/115200- inout     -   -   -       0       0       0/0         -
   17 AUX   9600/9600   -   -       -   -   -       0       0       0/0         -
   18 VTY               -   -       -   -   -       1       0       0/0         -
   19 VTY               -   -       -   -   -       0       0       0/0         -
   20 VTY               -   -       -   -   -       0       0       0/0         -
   21 VTY               -   -       -   -   -       0       0       0/0         -
  Tty Typ     Tx/Rx     A Modem   Roty AccO AccI  Uses   Noise   Overruns   Int

   22 VTY               -   -       -   -   -       0       0       0/0         -

access_server#
```

Step 2: Defining and Configuring PPP on the Asynchronous Interface

Next, configure the asynchronous interface of the router and enable it for PPP. To define the asynchronous interface, simply enter the command **interface async** *interface-number*. To enable PPP on the interface, you must first decide how you want to use PPP and DDR. This is mainly because when PPP originated, it was designed to use PPP strings on call establishment. An example of this is the **/routing** command that can be sent upon PPP establishment, to enable routing protocols to transverse the link. To accommodate this type of flexible session establishment, Cisco offers a variety of commands:

- **async mode {dedicated | interactive}**—This command is off by default—that is, no asynchronous mode is configured. The line will not be capable of accepting inbound networking because PPP and SLIP connections are not enabled. To use any PPP or SLIP protocols, you must use one of the two async modes:

  — **async mode dedicated** means that the router does not wait for any end-user prompts. No end-user commands are required to initiate remote connections, and the interface is automatically configured for SLIP or PPP. The remote end will not be capable of selecting any encapsulation methods, addresses, and other modes.

  — **async mode interactive** means that the router will accept an EXEC command from the end user before a connection is initiated. The **async mode interactive** command should be used if the remote end desires any session-establishment parameters and if you want to route over the link.

- **async {dynamic | default} routing**—When using the **async mode interactive** command, you must use the **async dynamic routing** command as well. The **async dynamic routing** command enables the router to accept the **/routing** keyword when sent by the remote user. If the host interface is set in interactive mode, the **async default routing** command causes the **ppp** and **slip** EXEC commands to be interpreted as if the **/route** keyword was included in the command. The **async default routing** command enables routing protocols on dedicated asynchronous interfaces.

- **autoselect {ppp | slip | during-login | arap}**—This command is used on the absolute line number, where the modem commands are applied. The **autoselect** command enables the router to start a protocol when the appropriate starting character is received. For example, if the router receives a return character, it starts an EXEC session. Table 4-2 lists the frame flags in hex for SLIP, PPP, and ARAP.

Table 4-2   *PPP Frame Flags*

Protocol	Hexadecimal Frame Flag
Return character	0D
SLIP	C0
PPP	7E
ARAP	10

- The **during-login** argument is used when end users or clients of different protocol types might be dialing into the same port on the router. For example, this option might be used when the client runs a TTY session with a terminal emulator, such as Hyperterm, while at the same time another client might want to connect to the same port using PPP.

- **transport input {all | lat | map | nasi | none | pad | rlogin | telnet | v120}**—By default, Cisco routers do not accept incoming network connections to asynchronous ports. You must specify an incoming transport protocol or use the **transport input all** command before the line accepts an incoming connection.

To enable PPP on an asynchronous port, use the following commands:

- **encapsulation ppp**—As stated previously, this command configures the interface for PPP encapsulation.

- **ppp authentication {chap | pap}**—PPP authentication is required on analog dial lines to provide secure and reliable dial connections.

Challenge Handshake Authentication Protocol and Password Authentication Protocol

CHAP and PAP authentication are available on all interfaces running PPP. Both protocols were originally outlined in RFC 1334, and later CHAP was updated in RFC 1994. CHAP and PAP use the concept of each device or router identifying itself with a unique name. The identification process also prevents one router from placing a call to another if the other router port is already connected to the site for which it is configured. PPP operates in the following manner:

Step 1   When a PPP session is established, the router determines the type of authentication required from LCP.

Step 2   The router determines the authentication, either CHAP or PAP, and performs one of the following:

   — Checks the local database for the proper username and password pairing. This is the default setting, and no **login local** is needed.

   — Forwards an authentication request on to a TACACS+ or RADIUS server.

Step 3   The router runs its authentication process based on the response that it received from the local database or the security server. If the response is positive, the router starts the PPP process; if it is negative, the router rejects the user immediately.

The CHAP and PAP process starts when LCP negotiates the parameters of the link. The PAP process sends a clear-text password across the link, which is interpreted by the routers at the remote ends of the link. A data scope or line monitor can capture the response and then can spoof the same process later; therefore, it is a less secure method of authentication.

The CHAP process never sends a clear-text password across the link, making it inherently more secure then PAP. The CHAP process uses a Message Digest 5 (MD5) hash generator to form a 128-bit hash during its challenge process. Only the hash and its modifiers are sent out on the link.

When an initiating router first issues a challenge to a remote router, the initiating router responds with four important parts of information:

- A CHAP challenge packet type identifier
- A supplied version of the ID, a sequential number that identifies the challenge
- A random number
- The host name of the router issuing the challenge

When the remote router receives the response, it performs a reverse lookup on the username and retrieves the password associated with it. The ID, a random number, and the password are fed into the MD5 hash generator. The output from this process is called a *hash*. The

MD5-hashed CHAP challenge is the number that is sent back across the link. When the hash is sent, it is sent along with the CHAP response packet type identifier, the ID, and the host name of the router. The initiating router performs the same process with the values received from the remote router. That is, the initiating router looks up the password associated with the host name sent by the remote router. The initiating router then feeds this information, along with the ID and random number, into the MD5 hash generator. The result of the process is a hash that is equal to the hash value sent by the remote router. If any other result is produced, the remote fails authentication and the link is torn down.

To configure PPP CHAP authentication, perform the following tasks:

Step 1   Ensure that PPP encapsulation is configured on the appropriate interface.

Step 2   On the host router, add a username equal to that of the remote router's host name that is dialing into your network. On the remote router, add a username equal to that of the host router's host name. The passwords that you assign to the two usernames must match exactly. Don't forget that all passwords are case-sensitive.

Step 3   Under the PPP interface, add the following command for CHAP:

```
ppp authentication chap
```

Figure 4-2 and Example 4-5 demonstrate two routers configured for PPP CHAP authentication over an asynchronous interface. Normally, you would enable **service password-encryption**, and the passwords would be encrypted in the router's listing. For readability and educational purposes, however, the passwords have been left unencrypted.

Figure 4-2   *PPP CHAP over Asynchronous Dial Configurations*

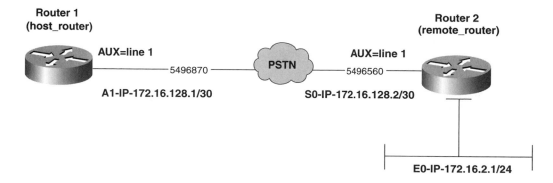

Example 4-5   *CHAP Authentication Configuration for the host_router over an Analog Dial Connection*

```
hostname host_router
!
!
username remote_router password 0 cisco
ip subnet-zero
!
interface Async1
 ip address 172.16.128.1 255.255.255.252
 no ip directed-broadcast
 encapsulation ppp
 dialer in-band
 dialer map ip 172.16.128.2 name remote_router broadcast 5496560
 async mode interactive
 ppp authentication chap
!
ip classless
!
!
!
line con 0
 exec-timeout 0 0
 transport input none
line aux 0
 autoselect ppp
 login local
 modem InOut
 modem autoconfigure discovery
 transport input all
 speed 38400
line vty 0 4
 login
!
end
```

To configure PPP PAP authentication, perform the following tasks:

Step 1   Ensure that PPP encapsulation is configured on the appropriate interface.

Step 2   On the host router, add a username equal to that of the remote router's host name that is dialing into your network. On the remote router add a username equal to that of the host router's host name. The passwords that you assign to the two usernames must match exactly. Don't forget that all passwords are case-sensitive.

Step 3   Under the PPP interface, add the following commands for PAP:

```
ppp authentication pap
ppp pap sent-username local_device_name password password
```

NOTE	Whenever you are running a PPP dial-in client, and during your session establishment, you are prompted for a password, which is a clear indication that the host is issuing you a PAP challenge. Many times, this is the case with Internet service providers (ISPs).

Figure 4-3 illustrates the configuration of PPP PAP in the same network as Figure 4-2.

Figure 4-3 *PPP PAP over Asynchronous Dial Configurations*

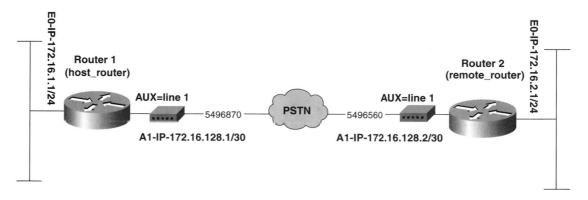

Example 4-6 shows the configurations for the host_router and remote_router for the network in Figure 4-3.

Example 4-6 *PAP Authentication Configuration for the host_router and remote_router over an Analog Dial Connection*

```
hostname host_router
!
username remote_router password 0 cisco1
ip subnet-zero
chat-script dialremote "" "ATZ&F" OK "ATDT5496561" TIMEOUT 60 CONNECT
!
 interface Ethernet0
 ip address 172.16.1.1 255.255.255.0
 no ip directed-broadcast
!
interface Async1
 ip address 172.16.128.1 255.255.255.252
 no ip directed-broadcast
 encapsulation ppp
 dialer in-band
 dialer idle-timeout 305
 dialer map ip 172.16.128.2 name remote_router broadcast 5496560
 dialer-group 1
```

continues

Example 4-6 *PAP Authentication Configuration for the host_router and remote_router over an Analog Dial Connection (Continued)*

```
 async mode interactive
 ppp authentication pap
 ppp pap sent-username host_router password cisco1
!
ip classless
ip route 172.16.2.0 255.255.255.0 172.16.128.2
!
dialer-list 1 protocol ip permit
!
!
line con 0
 exec-timeout 0 0
 transport input none
line aux 0
 autoselect ppp
 script dialer dialremote
 modem InOut
 modem autoconfigure type usr_sportster
 transport input all
 speed 38400
line vty 0 4
 login
!
end

host_router#
```

```
hostname remote_router
!
username host_router password 0 cisco1
chat-script dialhost "" "ATZ&F" OK "ATDT5496870" TIMEOUT 60 CONNECT
!
interface Ethernet0
 ip address 172.16.2.1 255.255.255.0
!
interface Async1
 ip address 172.16.128.2 255.255.255.252
 encapsulation ppp
 async mode interactive
 dialer in-band
 dialer idle-timeout 305
 dialer map ip 172.16.128.1 name host_router broadcast 5496870
 dialer-group 1
 ppp authentication pap
 ppp pap sent-username remote_router password cisco1
!
no ip classless
ip route 172.16.1.0 255.255.255.0 172.16.128.1
!
dialer-list 1 protocol ip permit
!
```

Example 4-6 *PAP Authentication Configuration for the host_router and remote_router over an*
Analog Dial Connection (Continued)

```
line con 0
line aux 0
 autoselect ppp
 script dialer dialhost
 modem InOut
 modem autoconfigure discovery
 transport input all
 rxspeed 38400
 txspeed 38400
line vty 0 4
 login
!
end

remote_router#
```

NOTE   When assigning host names to routers, it's best to use all lowercase names. If you need
more text in the name, you can always use the underscore (_) character. Try to stay
consistent in naming conventions throughout the internetwork or model, to avoid possible
typos and case-sensitive mismatches. Most often, these occur on **map** statements or an
authentication process of one sort. For example, "Host_router" doesn't equal "host_router"
or "host-router," even though they are all called "host router." This might seem confusing
at times because some of the router names used are proper nouns and are lowercase
throughout the book.

Figure 4-4 is a network diagram and IP address map of an asynchronous PPP dial connection
between two routers. To configure this model, begin by attaching and configuring a modem
to the AUX port of each router. You might want to reference Chapter 1 for more detailed
information on modem configuration.

Figure 4-4   *PPP Network Diagram and IP Scheme for an Asynchronous Analog Dial Connection*

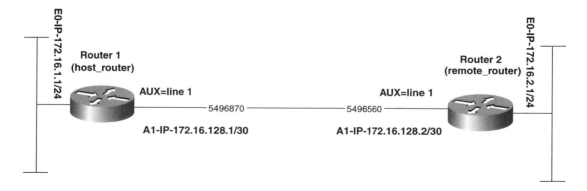

Example 4-7 shows the configuration for the host_router and remote_router in Figure 4-4.

Example 4-7 *PAP Authentication Configuration for host_router and remote_router over an Analog Dial Connection*

```
hostname host_router
!
username remote_router password 0 cisco1
ip subnet-zero
chat-script dialremote "" "ATZ&F" OK "ATDT5496561" TIMEOUT 60 CONNECT
!
 interface Ethernet0
 ip address 172.16.1.1 255.255.255.0
 no ip directed-broadcast
!
interface Async1
 ip address 172.16.128.1 255.255.255.252
 no ip directed-broadcast
 encapsulation ppp
 dialer in-band
 dialer idle-timeout 305
 dialer map ip 172.16.128.2 name remote_router broadcast 5496560
 dialer-group 1
 async mode interactive
 ppp authentication pap
 ppp pap sent-username host_router password cisco
!
ip classless
ip route 172.16.2.0 255.255.255.0 172.16.128.2
!
dialer-list 1 protocol ip permit
!
!
line con 0
 exec-timeout 0 0
 transport input none
line aux 0
 autoselect ppp
 script dialer dialremote
 modem InOut
 modem autoconfigure type usr_sportster
 transport input all
 speed 38400
line vty 0 4
 login
!
end

host_router#
```
```
hostname remote_router
!
username host_router password 0 cisco1
```

Example 4-7   *PAP Authentication Configuration for host_router and remote_router over an*
Analog Dial Connection (Continued)

```
chat-script dialhost "" "ATZ&F" OK "ATDT5496870" TIMEOUT 60 CONNECT
!
interface Ethernet0
 ip address 172.16.2.1 255.255.255.0
!
interface Async1
 ip address 172.16.128.2 255.255.255.252
 encapsulation ppp
 async mode interactive
 dialer in-band
 dialer idle-timeout 305
 dialer map ip 172.16.128.1 name host_router broadcast 5496870
 dialer-group 1
 ppp authentication pap
 ppp pap sent-username remote_router password cisco
!
no ip classless
ip route 172.16.1.0 255.255.255.0 172.16.128.1
!
dialer-list 1 protocol ip permit
!
line con 0
line aux 0
 autoselect ppp
 script dialer dialhost
 modem InOut
 modem autoconfigure discovery
 transport input all
 rxspeed 38400
 txspeed 38400
line vty 0 4
 login
!
end

remote_router#
```

Example 4-8 demonstrates the configuration of an asynchronous port and the corresponding
AUX port of a router for dial-in and dial-out PPP connections. This example also includes
the configuration of the modem. To configure the AUX port for a modem, first perform the
show line command and find the absolute line number to which the modem will be physically
attached. Then, configure that port for modem use. Second, configure the asynchronous
interface for PPP.

Example 4-8   *Configuration of an Asynchronous Port for a Modem and PPP (Steps 1 and 2 Only)*

```
remote_router#show line
  Tty Typ    Tx/Rx     A Modem  Roty AccO AccI   Uses   Noise  Overruns   Int
*  0 CTY                -    -    -    -    -      0      1     0/0        -

   1 AUX   9600/9600 -    -    -    -    -    0      1     0/0       -  ←Modem port
   2 VTY                -    -    -    -    -      0      0     0/0        -
   3 VTY                -    -    -    -    -      0      0     0/0        -
   4 VTY                -    -    -    -    -      0      0     0/0        -
   5 VTY                -    -    -    -    -      0      0     0/0        -
   6 VTY                -    -    -    -    -      0      0     0/0        -

remote_router#
remote_router#conf t
Enter configuration commands, one per line.  End with CNTL/Z.
remote_router(config)#interface async 1
remote_router(config-if)#async mode interactive
remote_router(config-if)#encapsulation ppp
remote_router(config-if)#exit
remote_router(config)#
remote_router(config)#line 1
remote_router(config-line)#modem inout
remote_router(config-line)#modem autoconfigure discovery
remote_router(config-line)#autoselect ppp
remote_router(config-line)#transport input all
remote_router(config-line)#^Z
remote_router#
```

Recall from Chapter 1 that you can add a loopback interface to assist in performing a
reverse Telnet session to test the modem. Another way to try a quick test is to simply Telnet
to the Ethernet interface address with a port of 2001. Example 4-9 exhibits a successful
reverse Telnet to the modem on port 1. When in session with the modem, performing a
quick **ATZ** or a more detailed **AT** command such as **AT&V** displays the current modem
configuration. Be sure that you do not forget to disconnect your modem session after testing
it using the **disconnect** command. To do this, complete the **Ctrl-Shift-6** keyboard function,
which brings you back to the router. Then, enter the **disconnect** command.

Example 4-9   *Performing a Reverse Telnet Session to the Modem*

```
remote_router#telnet 172.16.2.1 2001
Trying 172.16.2.1, 2001 ... Open
atz
OK
at&v
ACTIVE PROFILE:
B1 E1 L1 M1 N1 Q0 T V1 W0 X0 Y0 &C1 &D2 &G0 &J0 &K3 &Q5 &R1 &S0 &T5 &X0 &Y0
S00:001 S01:000 S02:043 S03:013 S04:010 S05:008 S06:002 S07:055 S08:002 S09:006
S10:014 S11:095 S12:050 S18:000 S25:005 S26:001 S36:007 S37:000 S38:020 S46:138
```

Example 4-9   *Performing a Reverse Telnet Session to the Modem (Continued)*

```
S48:007 S95:000

OK
CTRL/SHIFT/6

remote_router#disconnect
Closing connection to 172.16.2.1 [confirm]y
```

The last two configuration phases involve configuring network layer addresses and configuring DDR. These steps are tightly related to one another because DDR naturally requires some form of a network layer addressing to be in place.

Step 3: Configuring Network Layer Addresses or Addressing Schemas, and Routing as It Corresponds to the Asynchronous Interface

The next step involved in configuring PPP over asynchronous interfaces is to configure all network layer addresses for the interfaces. Along with configuring standard addressing, protocol-specific issues, such as OSPF, demand circuits should also be configured at this time.

You can configure IP addressing on the dialer interface in multiple ways. You can configure the router to assign an IP address to the client, or the router could assign multiple addresses from a pool or could simply ignore the addressing requirements of the client and reference only how to get to the address with a **dialer map** statement. The **async dynamic address** and **peer default ip address pool** commands are used to assign an IP address to the client from a pool or from the host router. Table 4-3 lists the combinations that should be used when configuring and assigning IP addresses to a dialer interface.

Table 4-3   *Recommend Router Address and Addressing for PPP*

Host Router Interface Commands	Remote Router or Client PPP Settings
Router static IP:	Router static IP:
ip address *local_ip_address* **dialer map ip** *remote_ip_address*	**ip address** *remote_ip_address* **dialer map ip** *local_ip_address*
Router static IP:	Router dynamic IP:
IP address *local_ip_address* **Dialer map ip** *remote_ip_address*	**ip address** *negotiated* **dialer map ip** *a.b.c.d*
Router static IP	Windows 95/98/2000 static IP:
IP address *local_ip_address* **dialer map ip** *remote_ip_address*	Specify IP address: *remote_ip_address*

continues

Table 4-3 *Recommend Router Address and Addressing for PPP (Continued)*

Host Router Interface Commands	Remote Router or Client PPP Settings
Router static IP dynamic client: **ip address** *local_ip_address* **peer default ip address** *remote_ip_address*	Windows 95/98/2000 dynamic IP: IP address obtained automatically: *remote_ip_address*
Router static IP dynamic client from a pool: **async dynamic address** **ip address** *local_ip_address* **peer default ip address pool** *pool_name* From the global interface, enter the pool: **ip local pool** {**default** | *pool_name low_ip_ address* [*high_ip_address*]}	Windows 95/98/2000 dynamic IP: IP address obtained automatically

Use the **ip address negotiated** statement when you don't have control of the assignment of the IP address on the dialer interface. This might be the case with ISPs. Usually, the ISP will assign you an address when you make a PPP connection. Using the **ip address negotiated** statement enables LCP to properly receive an IP address from the host router. You will use this command for "Easy IP configuration," which is essentially NAT using a dynamic address as its outside address, with TCP overload.

NOTE

The command **peer default ip address** *local_ip_address* must be entered before the **dialer in-band** command is entered. If the **dialer in-band** is entered first, the router will not accept a specific remote peer IP address.

Figure 4-5 illustrates a Windows 95/98 client dialing into an access server. The Windows workstation has its PPP stack configured to receive the IP address automatically. Windows 95/98 dialup networking uses PPP PAP for authentication.

If the workstation wants access to the Internet, a DNS server needs to be configured on the client if DHCP is not used. In Example 4-10, the access_server assigns the address of 172.16.20.2 to the PPP client dialing in. Notice that the access server also has a dialer list on it. This defines interesting traffic so that the link does not terminate while the client is sending data. The dialer idle-timeout terminates the line after 5 minutes and 5 seconds (305 seconds) of inactivity.

Figure 4-5 *Windows 95 PPP Dial-In*

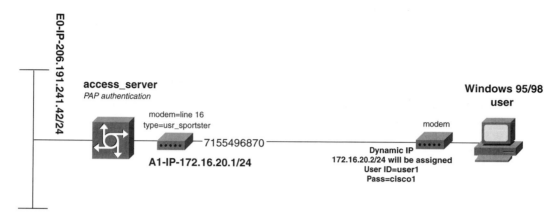

Example 4-10 *WIN 95 PPP Configuration for an Analog Dial Connection*

```
hostname access_server
!
username user1 password 0 cisco1
ip subnet-zero
!
 interface Ethernet0
 ip address 206.191.241.42 255.255.255.248
 no ip directed-broadcast
!
interface Async16
 ip address 172.16.20.1 255.255.255.0
 no ip directed-broadcast
 encapsulation ppp
 dialer in-band
 dialer idle-timeout 305
 dialer-group 1
 async mode interactive
 peer default ip address 172.16.20.2
 no cdp enable
 ppp authentication pap
!
ip classless
!
dialer-list 1 protocol ip permit
!
line con 0
 exec-timeout 0 0
 transport input none
line 1 8
 transport input all
```

continues

Example 4-10 *WIN 95 PPP Configuration for an Analog Dial Connection (Continued)*

```
line 9 15
line 16
 autoselect ppp
 login local
 modem InOut
 modem autoconfigure type usr_sportster
 transport input all
 speed 115200
line aux 0
line vty 0 4
 login
!
end

access_server#
```

NOTE   By default, the Cisco Discovery Protocol (CDP) is enabled on all interfaces. To disable CDP on an interface, use the **no cdp enable** command. CDP is used in ODR routing and to help identify other adjacent Cisco devices. CDP messages can keep dialer lines up if it is not disabled on these type of interfaces. CDP can be considered a security risk if it is enabled and you are not using ODR.

Controlling Routing Updates

The second half of Step 3 involves configuring routing for the DDR link. Proper control of routing updates can be one of the most difficult parts of DDR configuration. To prevent routing updates from constantly bringing up the link and dialing, you must have thorough knowledge of the routing protocol in use. You must also understand how the routing protocol sends and receives updates from one network to another, so as not to filter pertinent information. The dilemma for network engineers is how to propagate routing information without needing to constantly keep the link active.

There are several ways to address how to route on a DDR link without keeping the link active all the time. To accommodate spoofing and routing updates for distance vector protocols for IP, as well as IPX RIP and AppleTalk RTMP, Cisco invented *snapshot routing*. Snapshot routing involves taking a "snapshot" of the routing table and then spoofing the interface that participates in snapshot routing of its routing updates for a certain period. This time, called the *snapshot quiet time*, eventually expires, forcing the router to make a call to the snapshot server to receive a routing update. Snapshot helped solve some problems of routing over a dynamic link, but it does have a limitation: It doesn't support protocols that support variable-length subnet masking (VLSM). To address dynamic links for OSPF networks, OSPF uses a concept called *demand circuits*.

Demand circuits are complex and are covered in more detail in Chapter 12, "Link-State Protocols: Open Shortest Path First (OSPF)." Basically, demand circuits suppress OSPF hellos to the interface, which allows the link or circuit to time out and drop normally. For IP EIGRP and IGRP, Cisco recently introduced the **dialer watch** commands. This feature allows the router to watch for specific routes and make connection decisions based on whether they are in the routing table. Chapter 7 covers snapshot routing and the **dialer watch** commands in greater detail.

As you can see, when modeling or designing any network with dynamic links, it is important to look at the routing schema of the entire network. You must consider whether you need to advertise networks with different bit boundaries over your backup link. As you will learn in upcoming chapters, protocols such as RIP and IGRP accept and advertise only those networks on the same major bit boundary whose subnet masks match those of the interface sending or receiving the routing update.

Table 4-4 lists some suggested methods of routing over dynamic links based on routing schemas that Cisco supports.

Table 4-4   *Dynamic and Static Routing Methods over Dial Links Based on Routing Protocol Type*

Routing Protocol	Dynamic Routing Updates Method	Static Method
EIGRP	dialer watch	Floating static routes AD distance > 170
IGRP	Snapshot routing	Floating static routes AD distance > 100
OSPF	OSPF demand circuit	Floating static routes AD distance > 110
RIP version 1	Snapshot routing	Floating static routes AD distance > 120
RIP version 2	dialer watch	Floating static routes AD distance > 120
IPX RIP/SAP	Snapshot routing	Floating static routes
IPX EIGRP	Snapshot routing	Floating static routes
AppleTalk	Snapshot routing	Floating static routes

A common approach to the routing dilemma, and the approach that this section addresses, is the application of floating static routes or weighted routes. A *floating static route* is a static route defined as a route that is not permanently entered into the routing table. The route appears only under a special set of circumstances. A floating static route is configured as a static route to a destination network with an administrative distance greater than the routing protocols in use. This allows the route to be advertised through the routing protocol first. If the route learned by the routing protocol is lost, the floating static route will be entered into the routing table. The syntax for configuring a weighted or floating static route is as follows:

```
ip route remote_ip_subnet subnet_mask {[ip_next_hop administrative_distance
(1-255)] interface}
```

An administrative distance of 150 to 180 is usually sufficient for weight. Table 4-5 lists the administrative distances for routing protocols and static routes. If no administrative distance is added to the **ip route** command, the default distance is 1. If you point the static route to an interface instead of the next-hop address, the administrative distance will be 0, as in a connected route. A static route that can reach the next-hop IP address will be placed in the forwarding table. A connected route will always be in the forwarding table, unless the interface is in a down state.

Table 4-5   *Default Administrative Distances on Cisco Routers*

Route Source/Type	Default Administrative Distance
Connected interface	0
Static route pointing to an interface	0
Static route to a next-hop interface	1
EIGRP summary route	5
External BGP	20
EIGRP	90
IGRP	100
OSPF	110
IS-IS	115
RIP-1 and RIP-2	120
EGP	140
External EIGRP	170
Internal BGP	200
Unknown route Unreachable	255

Figure 4-6 illustrates the relevant commands needed for using floating static routes to back up a serial connection. In this example, you also need to be sure to use the **IP subnet-zero** command because the address 192.168.1.1/30 is being used on the asynchronous link. The natural network for the asynchronous link as assigned is 192.168.1.0/30, which is the zero subnet on a Class C network. Keeping the DDR link on a separate subnet eliminates the worry of the routing protocol (EIGRP, in this case) bleeding routing updates onto the link. This is yet another way to control routing updates on a link.

Figure 4-6   *Floating Static Route Configuration for Analog Dial Connection*

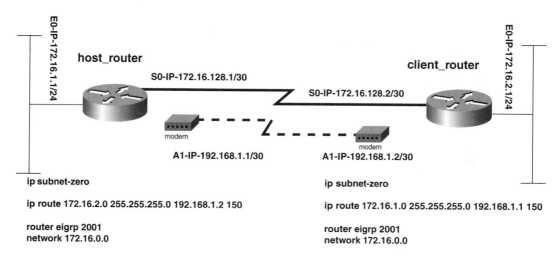

ip subnet-zero

ip route 172.16.2.0 255.255.255.0 192.168.1.2 150

router eigrp 2001
network 172.16.0.0

ip subnet-zero

ip route 172.16.1.0 255.255.255.0 192.168.1.1 150

router eigrp 2001
network 172.16.0.0

Step 4: Configuring the Asynchronous Interface for Dial-on-Demand Routing

Dial-on-demand routing (DDR) can be divided into two subgroups:

- **Legacy DDR**—Enables a temporary connection only when there is *interesting* traffic to send to that destination. Legacy DDR is configured when a static relationship exists between the physical dialing interface and the destination.

- **Advanced DDR with dialer profiles**—Used when multiple logical connections want to share the same physical interface. This form of DDR exists when one or more logical interfaces share the same physical interface on a per-call basis. An example of this is when one router wants to dial two different remote locations and run separate Layer 3 protocols. At times, the router might want to dial the Internet and run only IP, while at other times, the router might want to dial into a headquarters site while running IP and IPX.

This section covers legacy DDR; advanced DDR topics are covered in Chapter 7.

All DDR, whether legacy or advanced, operates in a similar way:

Step 1   When a router receives traffic, it performs a lookup in the routing table to see whether a route exists to the traffic's destination. If a destination exists, an outbound interface is associated with it. If this interface is configured for DDR, the router performs another lookup to determine whether the traffic is *interesting*.

Step 2 The router then locates the next-hop address and uses either the dialing instructions in the **dialer string** command or the **dialer map** command for ISDN TAs. For modems that support V.25*bis* dialing, the dial number is taken off the **chat-script** command. V.25*bis* is an ITU-T standard for in-band signaling to bit synchronous DCE devices.

Step 3 The router checks to see whether the associated interface is in an *up state* and is connected to the remote destination. If the interface is connected, the traffic is sent and the dialer idle timer is reset if the traffic is *interesting*. If the interface is not connected, the router sends call setup information to the DCE device on the interface based on the **dialer string**, **dialer map**, or **chat-script** arguments.

Step 4 While the link is connected, the router sends *interesting* and uninteresting traffic to the destination. When the router finishes sending *interesting* traffic, it sets an idle timer. When the idle timer expires, as defined by the **dialer idle-timeout** command, the router disconnects the call.

Configuring DDR is a four-step process:

Step 1 **Define interesting traffic**—Defining interesting traffic can be done in one of two ways. The whole protocol suite might be defined as interesting, or an access list can be called to further narrow down significant traffic by type or destination. The syntax needed to define DDR is as follows:

```
dialer-list dialer-group_number protocol protocol_name [permit |
    deny | list access-list_number]
```

Step 2 **Enable DDR and assign a dialer list to an interface**—To enable DDR on an interface, use the **dialer in-band** command for V.*25bis* devices, and use the **dialer-group** command on the interface. The **dialer in-band** command specifies for the interface that will be used to perform call setup and teardown between the router and an external dialing device. ISDN devices use the D channel for call setup and teardown, so the **dialer in-band** command is not needed for ISDN BRIs and PRIs. The **dialer-group** command assigns the interface to the dialer list, which, in turn, defines which traffic is interesting. The **dialer-group** must match the dialer list number. The commands to accomplish this are as follows:

— **dialer in-band**

— **dialer-group** *1-10*

Step 3 **Define destination parameters**—This step involves configuring a next-hop address and determining how the router will reach that address. It also involves what name the router will use for authentication and how the router will treat the DDR connection. This is also a good time to define a **dialer idle-timeout**. To configure a next-hop addresses and determine how the router will reach the next hop, use either the **dialer map** or the **dialer string** commands. The **dialer string** command can be used with the **dialer remote-name** command for CHAP authentication.

The **dialer map** statement is the first cousin of the **frame-relay map** statement. The **dialer map** statement tells the router how to reach the next-hop address by protocol type. The current protocols supported are AppleTalk, bridging, ISO CLNS, DECnet, HPR, IP, IPX, LLC2, NetBIOS, snapshot routing protocol, Banyan VINES, and XNS.

```
dialer map protocol_name next_hop_address [name remote_device_name]
    [class class_name] [speed 56 | 64] [broadcast] [dialer_string]
```

The **name** parameter should always equal the host name of the remote router connected to the interface. This parameter is used for authentication purposes.

A class can be added, as you will see in PPP callback. The **speed** and *dialer_string* arguments are used for ISDN interfaces only. The **speed** is set at a default of 64 kbps. The *dialer_string* is for ISDN, where the string is the telephone number that the router will dial when interesting packets to the next-hop address are received. For asynchronous devices, such as modems, you must use a chat script for the router to pass the dial string onto e device. Finally, DDR is nonbroadcast by default; however, if broadcast traffic is to cross the link, the **broadcast** keyword must also be added.

The **dialer map** command enables you to express a lot of DDR commands on one line. Some of these commands can be entered individually:

— **dialer string** *dialer_string*

— **dialer remote-name** *remote_device_name*

— **dialer idle-timeout** *seconds*

The **dialer idle-timeout** is the idle timer that is set to mark when the last interesting traffic was sent. If no further interesting traffic is sent before the idle timer expires, the link is disconnected. The default idle dialer is 120 seconds.

Step 4   **Configure optional call parameters**—Additional call parameters can be added to the interface at this time. Some of the more useful ones are as follows:

— **dialer fast-idle** *seconds*—This command is primarily used with multiple dialer profiles, such as in a DDR with dialer profiles configuration. When two logical dial interfaces are competing for the same physical line, the timer specifies how long the line can remain idle before the current call is disconnected and another dialer interface can place a call. This command should be used when contention for a link is particularly high. You will see this command used in the Chapter 7.

— **dialer load-threshold** *1-255* [**outbound** | **inbound** | **either**]—This command specifies the interface load at which the dialer initiates another call to the destination. The value is set at a load between 1 and 255, as in the **show interface** command; 1 is the lowest load, which makes the dialer call almost immediately. This can be tweaked further by specifying the direction of the traffic. This command is used in conjunction with the **ppp multilink** command, as discussed in an upcoming section.

Using an earlier example of PPP PAP authentication, you can now focus on the DDR portion of the configuration. Figure 4-7 illustrates two routers connected through modems attached to their AUX ports. When each router detects traffic destined toward the subnet defined in the static routes, it dials the other router. This call stays connected until no IP traffic has crossed the subnet for 305 seconds. This time limit is assigned in the **dialer idle-timeout** statements.

Figure 4-7 *Network Topology for the PPP Analog Dial Configuration*

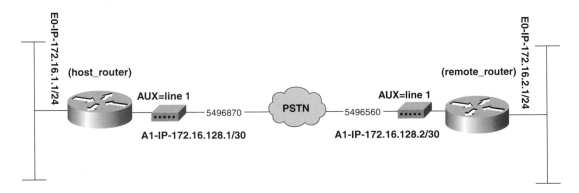

Example 4-11 shows the configurations for the host_router and remote_router in Figure 4-7.

Example 4-11 *PPP Analog Dial Configuration*

```
hostname host_router
!
username remote_router password 0 cisco1
ip subnet-zero
chat-script dialremote "" "ATZ&F" OK "ATDT5496561" TIMEOUT 60 CONNECT
```

Example 4-11 *PPP Analog Dial Configuration (Continued)*

```
 !
  interface Ethernet0
  ip address 172.16.1.1 255.255.255.0
  no ip directed-broadcast
 !
 interface Async1
  ip address 172.16.128.1 255.255.255.252
  no ip directed-broadcast
  encapsulation ppp
  dialer in-band
  dialer idle-timeout 305
  dialer map ip 172.16.128.2 name remote_router broadcast 5496560
  dialer-group 1
  async mode interactive
  ppp authentication chap
 !
 ip classless
 ip route 172.16.2.0 255.255.255.0 172.16.128.2
 !
 dialer-list 1 protocol ip permit
 !
 !
 line con 0
  exec-timeout 0 0
  transport input none
 line aux 0
  autoselect ppp
  script dialer dialremote
  modem InOut
  modem autoconfigure type usr_sportster
  transport input all
  speed 38400
 line vty 0 4
  login
 !
 end

host_router#
```

```
hostname remote_router
!
username host_router password 0 cisco1
chat-script dialhost "" "ATZ&F" OK "ATDT5496870" TIMEOUT 60 CONNECT
!
interface Ethernet0
 ip address 172.16.2.1 255.255.255.0
!
interface Async1
 ip address 172.16.128.2 255.255.255.252
 encapsulation ppp
```

continues

Example 4-11 *PPP Analog Dial Configuration (Continued)*

```
 async mode interactive
 dialer in-band
 dialer idle-timeout 305
 dialer map ip 172.16.128.1 name host_router broadcast 5496870
 dialer-group 1
 ppp authentication chap
!
no ip classless
ip route 172.16.1.0 255.255.255.0 172.16.128.1
!
dialer-list 1 protocol ip permit
!
line con 0
line aux 0
 autoselect ppp
 script dialer dialhost
 modem InOut
 modem autoconfigure discovery
 transport input all
 rxspeed 38400
 txspeed 38400
line vty 0 4
 login
!
end

remote_router#
```

To reiterate, recall the step-by-step list for configuring PPP over asynchronous interfaces. This step-by-step list is a useful tool in configuring PPP over asynchronous interfaces:

Step 1 Modem and asynchronous port configuration: Step 1 involves attaching and configuring the modem, and configuring the asynchronous port of the router. This step also includes identifying the absolute line number that corresponds to that asynchronous interface. See Chapter 1 for more information on connecting and configuring modems.

Step 2 Define and configure PPP on the asynchronous interface. Configure the asynchronous interface that corresponds to the absolute line number found in Step 1. Configure PPP encapsulation and PPP authentication for the asynchronous interface.

Step 3 Configure network layer addresses or addressing schemas, and routing as it corresponds to the asynchronous interface.

Step 4 Configure the asynchronous interface for dial-on-demand routing (DDR).

Configuring PPP Compression

PPP also offers the use of data payload compression to maximize performance across low-bandwidth links. Compression is negotiated by LCP during link initialization. Because LCP negotiates this parameter, it is necessary to have compression configured on both sides of the link. Cisco offers three types of payload compression on PPP links, along with standard *TCP header compression*:

- **Predictor**—Predictor compression is accomplished through a "lossless" predictor algorithm that learns data patterns and can predict the next character in the data stream. The algorithm is called "lossless" because the scheme reproduces the original bit stream exactly, with no degradation or loss. Predictor is more memory-intensive and less CPU-intensive.

- **Stacker**—Stacker, as mentioned in Chapter 3, "WAN Protocols and Technologies: High-Level Data Link Control (HDLC)," is a Lempel-Ziv (LZ)–based compression algorithm. This algorithm tries to predict the next sequence of characters in the data stream by using an index to look up a sequence in compression dictionary. The route sends each data type once with information about where the type occurs within the data stream. Stacker is more CPU-intensive and less memory-intensive than Predictor.

- **MPPC**—Outlined in RFC 2118, Microsoft Point-to-Point Compression (MPPC) allows Cisco routers to exchange data with Microsoft clients. MPPC uses LZ-based compression. Like Stacker, MPPC is more CPU-intensive and less memory-intensive than Predictor.

The preceding compression techniques are configured with the **compress** command at the interface level. To enable payload compression, use the following interface command:

```
compress [predictor | stac | mppc]
```

When enabling compression, the link should always be restarted or cleared with the **clear interface** *interface_name* command. This forces the routers or LCP to renegotiate the link with compression enabled. You cannot use any form of payload compression with TCP header compression.

TCP header compression, as defined in RFC 1144, uses the Van Jacobson algorithm for compressing TCP headers. TCP header compression is most useful when deployed in an environment where there are many small data packets. TCP header compression can significantly cut down on the TCP overhead associated with these packets. To enable TCP header compression, use the following interface command:

```
ip tcp header-compression [passive]
```

The **passive** argument compresses outbound TCP packets only if incoming TCP packets on the same interface are compressed. If the **passive** argument is not specified, all traffic is compressed.

Compression is most effective if the data that you are transferring is highly compressible, such as a text file or ASCII-based data. Files such as JPEG or MPEG files are already compressed to a great extent, and compression merely slows down the router and the transfer of this type of data. Compression will also increase the number of CPU cycles and the amount of memory used by the router. Therefore, you should apply careful consideration to current memory and processor usage before enabling compression.

Two useful commands for analyzing whether compression is in use, are the **show processes** and **show processes buffers** commands. Example 4-12 lists the output of the **show processes** command. Here we see the average utilization of this router is approximately 30 percent. In this case, the router has enough resources to enable compression. Be careful when implementing compression on routers operating at 65 percent of capacity.

Example 4-12 *Output from the* **show processes** *Command*

```
skynet_2#show processes
CPU utilization for five seconds: 29%/2%; one minute: 30%; five minutes: 32%
 PID QTy       PC Runtime (ms)   Invoked   uSecs    Stacks TTY Process
   1 Csp    2E68C       1132      67278       16 3760/4096    0 Load Meter
   2 ME    122648    8882756    6695839 132610432/12288       0 Exec
   3 Lst    17E918     494620      45735    10814 7960/8192    0 Check heaps
   4 Cwe    183AE8          0          1        0 7840/8192    0 Pool Manager
   5 Mst    11A2E8          4          2     2000 7808/8192    0 Timers
   6 Lwe    1D0124     219292     342622      640 7528/8192    0 ARP Input
   7 Mwe    23D924        892       1668      534 7144/8192    0 DDR Timers
   8 Mwe    24DA90          0          2       011920/12288    0 Dialer event
   9 Lwe    260FC0          0          1        0 7856/8192    0 Entity MIB API
  10 Mwe    429FE4          0          2        0 7816/8192    0 Serial Background
  11 Mwe    42DF08          4          1     4000 7856/8192    0 SERIAL A'detect
  12 Cwe    188D94          0          1        0 7848/8192    0 Critical Bkgnd
  13 Mwe    1A0690      16212      49282    32810888/12288     0 Net Background
  14 Lwe    11090C       6900      19588    35211752/12288     0 Logger
  15 Msp    12C25C     274660     335655      818 7472/8192    0 TTY Background
  16 Msp    19FD38       6244     335694       18 7800/8192    0 Per-Second Jobs
  17 Mwe     F0DB0       8092    1186590        6 7648/8192    0 LED Timers
  18 Mwe    4BB398          0         23        0 7976/8192    0 CSM timer process
  19 Mwe    4BE740        212        574      369 7736/8192    0 POTS
  20 Mwe    2004B8      16908      44367      381 7544/8192    0 CDP Protocol
  21 Mrd    2B434C     272492     211068   129110672/12288     0 IP Input
```

NOTE   Cisco offers hardware accelerator cards, or compression service adapters (CSAs), to offset the overhead compression that uses valuable router resources. Cisco compression is performed on the CSA boards if present in the router.

Configuring PPP Multilink

PPP multilink is a mechanism for combining, or bundling, multiple physical links into one large logical link. The logical end-to-end connection is called a *bundle*. This bundle provides increased bandwidth to the destination, along with reduced latency by allowing packets to be disassembled and sent down different links simultaneously to the same destination.

The most common use of PPP multilink is with ISDN, which can use PPP multilink to bind two 64-kbps B channels together to form a single 128-kbps link. ISDN is the most common use of PPP multilink; however, it is also supported on the following interfaces:

- Asynchronous interfaces
- Synchronous interfaces
- ISDN interfaces
  - ISDN BRI
  - ISDN PRI

Figure 4-8 illustrates how a PPP multilink is formed.

Figure 4-8   *PPP Multilink Bundles*

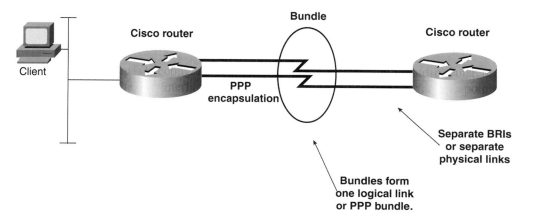

When a bundle is formed, it can be formed with different physical interface types. For example, an asynchronous interface can be joined with a synchronous interface to form a bundle.

NOTE   PPP multilink is outlined in RFC 1990, which replaces RFC 1717. RFC 1990 specifies multivendor interoperability and resolves some earlier ISDN sequencing issues.

PPP multilink is an option negotiated by LCP during its initial negotiation period. After negotiation, PPP multilink operates by first splitting packets into fragments. The fragments then are sent at the same time over multiple point-to-point links to the same remote address. When the fragments arrive at the other side of the connection, LCP reassembles them into a packet.

To configure PPP multilink, use the following commands on the interface or dialer on which you want to configure PPP multilink:

```
ppp multilink
dialer load-threshold load [inbound | outbound | either]
```

The **dialer load-threshold** command specifies the interface load at which the dialer initiates another call to the destination. The value is set at a load between 1 and 255, as in the **show interface** command; 1 is the lowest load, which makes the dialer call almost immediately. This can be tweaked further by specifying the direction of the traffic.

NOTE   Cisco IOS Software Release 11.1 is the first release to support PPP multilink. Cisco IOS Software Release 11.3 includes a feature called the Bandwidth Allocation Control Protocol (BACP). BACP enables two routers to negotiate which peer will add or remove links during a session.

To verify the functionality of PPP multilink, use the **debug ppp negotiation** script along with a source **ping**. By turning on the debug for PPP, you can tell when LCP brings up another channel or link. By performing a extended **ping**, you can easily force a large amount of data quickly across the link to exceed the load threshold and bring up another PPP bundle. The **show ppp multilink** command can also be useful to show the state of a multilink session. Example 4-13 demonstrates the use of the **show ppp multilink** command, followed by an extended **ping**, which brings up the second multilink bundle.

Example 4-13 **show ppp multilink** *Command Output*

```
skynet_2#show ppp multilink

Virtual-Access1, bundle name is cns_isdn_callback
  Dialer interface is Dialer1
  0 lost fragments, 0 reordered, 0 unassigned, sequence 0x0/0x0 rcvd/sent
  0 discarded, 0 lost received, 1/255 load
  Member links: 1 (max not set, min not set)
    BRI0:1                             ←Only one active bundle

skynet_2#ping
Protocol [ip]: ip
Target IP address: 172.16.16.2
Repeat count [5]: 1000
Datagram size [100]: 2000
```

Example 4-13 show ppp multilink *Command Output (Continued)*

```
Timeout in seconds [2]: 5
Extended commands [n]:
Sweep range of sizes [n]:
Type escape sequence to abort.
Sending 1000, 2000-byte ICMP Echos to 172.16.16.2, timeout is 5 seconds:
!!!!!!!!!!!!!!!!!!!!!!!!!!!!!!!!!!!!!!!!!!!!!!!!!!!!!!!!!!!!!!!!!!!!!!!!
<<<text omitted>>>
!!!!!
Success rate is 100 percent (370/370), round-trip min/avg/max = 152/161/284 ms

skynet_2#show ppp multilink

Virtual-Access1, bundle name is cns_isdn_callback
  Dialer interface is Dialer1
  0 lost fragments, 0 reordered, 0 unassigned, sequence 0x496/0x2F1 rcvd/sent
  0 discarded, 0 lost received, 25/255 load
  Member links: 2 (max not set, min not set)
    BRI0:1                          ←Both BRIs are in the bundle
    BRI0:2
skynet_2#
```

Configuring PPP LAPB and LQM

PPP link quality can be enforced or enabled on Cisco routers in two ways. One method is done by enabling LAPB numbered mode negotiation. This is done with the **ppp reliable-link** command. Another method is by enforcing Link Quality Monitoring (LQM) on the link with the **ppp quality** command.

LQM monitors the link quality; if the quality drops below a configured percentage, the router shuts down the link. The percentages are calculated for both incoming and outgoing traffic. The LQM out is calculated by comparing the total number of packets and bytes sent with the total number of packets and bytes received by the destination node. The incoming LQM is measured by comparing the total number of packets and bytes received with the total number of packets and bytes sent by the destination peer.

When LQM is enabled, Link Quality Reports (LQRs) are sent in place of keepalives. LQR is further defined in RFC 1989, "PPP Link Quality Monitoring."

NOTE   LAPB numbered mode inserts essentially another error-correction layer with retransmits, if necessary, while LQM monitors link quality.

To enable LQM, use the following command:

```
ppp quality percentage_of_successful_traffic
```

The other form of increasing link reliability is to use the **ppp reliable-link** command. This command causes the router to provide LAPB numbered mode negotiation. LAPB performed on the data-link layer can provide error detection for many upper-layer protocols, such as PPP, in this case.

You must enable PPP reliable link on both ends of the link. Unlike **ppp quality**, you can use the **ppp reliable-link** command with compression; however, you cannot use PPP reliable link with **PPP multilink**. To verify that these commands are functioning, use **debug ppp negotiation** because LQM will be listed there.

The "Big show" and "Big D" for PPP and DDR

Cisco offers some strong commands for debugging PPP and DDR sessions. Again, this section focuses on the best and most useful **show** and **debug** commands. The "big **show**" and "Big D" for PPP and DDR are as follows:

- **show interface** *interface_name*—The **show interface** command provides useful information about the physical state of the interface. The interface will always show UP and spoofing mode when configured for DDR.

- **show line** *x*—The **show line** command provides useful information on the physical state and, to some degree, the logical state of the interface. For more information on the **show line** command, see Chapter 1.

- **show ip route**—Use the **show ip route** command to verify that the PPP subnet is up and active. The subnet shows "connected" only when the link is actually up and connected on both ends.

- **debug ppp negotiation**—This command is probably the most useful command for debugging PPP sessions. Every aspect of LCP negotiation is listed in the output. Example 4-14 demonstrates a PPP session being negotiated between two routers. Look for IPCP to finish in an open state for IP protocols. You will see a CP negotiate for every PPP option and protocol specified.

- **debug ppp authentication**—This command instantly points out any PPP authentication errors, such as CHAP and PAP errors. See Example 4-15 for a demonstration of PPP authentication failure.

- **debug dialer**—**debug dialer** commands are used primarily to debug when dialing occurs. As the **debug dialer** command shows, successful dialing occurs only when DDR and ACLs have been configured correctly.

The following examples show some of the "big **Show**" and the "big D" commands in action. The debugs should all be used together because they present a clearer picture of what is happening. In Example 4-14, all the debugs from the preceding list, along with debug async state, have been turned on.

Example 4-14 *Output of a Successful **debug ppp negotiation***

```
01:01:57: Async1: Dialing cause ip (s=172.16.128.2, d=172.16.1.1)    ←Dial is
started, Dialer-list is OK
01:01:57: Async1: Attempting to dial 5496561
01:01:57: CHAT1: Attempting async line dialer script
01:01:57: CHAT1: Dialing using Modem script: dialhost & System script: none
01:01:57: TTY1: cleanup pending. Delaying DTR
01:01:57: CHAT1: process started
01:01:57: CHAT1: Asserting DTR
01:01:57: TTY1: Set DTR to 1
01:01:57: CHAT1: Chat script dialhost started.....
01:02:14: CHAT1: Chat script dialhost finished, status = Success    ←Modem connected
01:02:14: TTY1: destroy timer type 1
01:02:14: TTY1: destroy timer type 0
01:02:14: As1 PPP: Async Protocol Mode started for 172.16.128.1    ←PPP started
01:02:14: As1 AAA/ACCT: Using PPP accounting list ""
01:02:14: As1 IPCP: Install route to 172.16.128.1
01:02:16: %LINK-3-UPDOWN: Interface Async1, changed state to up
01:02:16: As1 PPP: Treating connection as a callout
01:02:16: As1 PPP: Phase is ESTABLISHING, Active Open    ←PPP negotiation begins
01:02:16: As1 LCP: O CONFREQ [Closed] id 21 len 20
01:02:16: As1 LCP:    ACCM 0x000A0000 (0x0206000A0000)
01:02:16: As1 LCP:    MagicNumber 0x0069B38A (0x05060069B38A)
01:02:16: As1 LCP:    PFC (0x0702)
01:02:16: As1 LCP:    ACFC (0x0802)
01:02:18: As1 LCP: TIMEout: State REQsent
01:02:18: As1 LCP: O CONFREQ [REQsent] id 22 len 20
01:02:18: As1 LCP:    ACCM 0x000A0000 (0x0206000A0000)
01:02:18: As1 LCP:    MagicNumber 0x0069B38A (0x05060069B38A)
01:02:18: As1 LCP:    PFC (0x0702)
01:02:18: As1 LCP:    ACFC (0x0802)
01:02:20: As1 LCP: TIMEout: State REQsent
01:02:20: As1 LCP: O CONFREQ [REQsent] id 23 len 20
01:02:20: As1 LCP:    ACCM 0x000A0000 (0x0206000A0000)
01:02:20: As1 LCP:    MagicNumber 0x0069B38A (0x05060069B38A)
01:02:20: As1 LCP:    PFC (0x0702)
01:02:20: As1 LCP:    ACFC (0x0802)
01:02:20: As1 LCP: I CONFACK [REQsent] id 23 len 20
01:02:20: As1 LCP:    ACCM 0x000A0000 (0x0206000A0000)
01:02:20: As1 LCP:    MagicNumber 0x0069B38A (0x05060069B38A)
01:02:20: As1 LCP:    PFC (0x0702)
01:02:20: As1 LCP:    ACFC (0x0802)
01:02:20: As1 LCP: I CONFREQ [ACKrcvd] id 180 len 25
01:02:20: As1 LCP:    ACCM 0x000A0000 (0x0206000A0000)
01:02:20: As1 LCP:    AuthProto CHAP (0x0305C22305)
01:02:20: As1 LCP:    MagicNumber 0x0A548C93 (0x05060A548C93)
01:02:20: As1 LCP:    PFC (0x0702)
01:02:20: As1 LCP:    ACFC (0x0802)
01:02:20: As1 LCP: O CONFACK [ACKrcvd] id 180 len 25
01:02:20: As1 LCP:    ACCM 0x000A0000 (0x0206000A0000)
01:02:20: As1 LCP:    AuthProto CHAP (0x0305C22305)
```

continues

Example 4-14 *Output of a Successful **debug ppp negotiation** (Continued)*

```
01:02:20: As1 LCP:      MagicNumber 0x0A548C93 (0x05060A548C93)
01:02:20: As1 LCP:      PFC (0x0702)
01:02:20: As1 LCP:      ACFC (0x0802)
01:02:20: As1 LCP: State is Open
01:02:20: As1 PPP: Phase is AUTHENTICATING, by the peer        ←CHAP begins
01:02:20: As1 CHAP: I CHALLENGE id 39 len 32 from "host_router"   ←CHAP challenge
01:02:20: As1 CHAP: O RESPONSE id 39 len 34 from "remote_router"
01:02:20: As1 CHAP: I SUCCESS id 39 len 4                ←CHAP OK
01:02:20: As1 PPP: Phase is UP
01:02:20: As1 IPCP: O CONFREQ [Closed] id 9 len 10          ←IP Parameters
01:02:20: As1 IPCP:     Address 172.16.128.2 (0x0306AC108002)
01:02:20: As1 CDPCP: O CONFREQ [Closed] id 9 len 4
01:02:20: As1 IPCP: I CONFREQ [REQsent] id 22 len 10
01:02:20: As1 IPCP:     Address 172.16.128.1 (0x0306AC108001)
01:02:20: As1 IPCP: O CONFACK [REQsent] id 22 len 10
01:02:20: As1 IPCP:     Address 172.16.128.1 (0x0306AC108001)
01:02:20: As1 CDPCP: I CONFREQ [REQsent] id 22 len 4
01:02:20: As1 CDPCP: O CONFACK [REQsent] id 22 len 4
01:02:20: As1 IPCP: I CONFACK [ACKsent] id 9 len 10
01:02:20: As1 IPCP:     Address 172.16.128.2 (0x0306AC108002)
01:02:20: As1 IPCP: State is Open                 ←IP OK
01:02:20: dialer Protocol up for As1
01:02:20: As1 CDPCP: I CONFACK [ACKsent] id 9 len 4
01:02:20: As1 CDPCP: State is Open
01:02:21: %LINEPROTO-5-UPDOWN: Line protocol on Interface Async1, changed state to
up
remote_router#
```

Example 4-15 illustrates a PPP CHAP failure on a link with the **debug ppp authentication** command.

Example 4-15 *PPP CHAP Failure*

```
skynet_lab#debug ppp authentication
Se0 PPP: Phase is AUTHENTICATING, by the peer
Se0 CHAP: I CHALLENGE id 51 len 31 from "skynet_lab"
Se0 CHAP: O RESPONSE id 51 len 31 from "isp_router"
Se0 CHAP: I FAILURE id 51 len 25 msg is "MD/DES compare failed"
Se0 PPP: Phase is AUTHENTICATING, by the peer
Se0 CHAP: I CHALLENGE id 52 len 31 from "skynet_lab"
Se0 CHAP: O RESPONSE id 52 len 31 from "isp_router"
```

The **debug ppp negotiation** command can be one of the most powerful debugs available for PPP. It's not too data-intensive, and it provides enough information to solve or narrow down a majority of PPP-related problems.

NOTE   Technique, Technique, Technique

It might seem that some of these examples and labs are overcomplicated with routing protocols and by using VLSM, but there is a reason for this. Too often, many texts and examples use standard 24-bit address space and pay little attention to addressing and other techniques. This just puts the engineer into bad habits of IP address design. In most of this text, IP addresses are assigned just like they would be in the field. Constant reinforcement in examples like this improves your technique. Much in the same way that a martial artist pays strict attention to the smallest detail of every move, you must pay strict attention to every command that you make. If you don't know the purpose of a command in a configuration, ask yourself, "Is it a necessary command?"

Configuring PPP Callback

PPP callback is a way for a remote or calling router to place a call to a *callback server*, terminate the link, and then receive a call from the callback server. This method can be used to enhance security and to control which side of the link gets connection time. Configuring PPP callback is covered in detail in Chapter 7.

Lab 10: Configuring PPP, PAP, and Compression over Asynchronous Dialup—Part I

Practical Scenario

This chapter began describing PPP as the dominant Internet access protocol. PPP is not only used to access the Internet, but it also is widely used by many telecommuters and for remote access to private corporate networks. Many corporate applications such as Citrix or WIN frame, as well as most e-mail servers, require IP as the network layer protocol. To reach these applications, it is necessary to run IP on the remote client workstation and use PPP as the data-link protocol.

Lab Exercise

The Skynet testing facility is a secret networking test site. New Cisco IOS Software features are tested there, and many types of internetwork infrastructures are modeled. At times, engineers require secure remote access to Skynet. Currently, only one engineer, code name JP, has access to the lab. You have been tasked with configuring a secure remote access connection. Use the following guidelines in your design:

- Windows 95/98/2000 will be the client. The IP address should be set to dynamic.
- The user ID is JP, and the password is trashman.
- JP will need to run several Visual Basic programs requiring IP services. This will require IP access to the host 172.16.1.10, which is local to the Ethernet segment.

Lab Objectives

- Configure the access server and network as depicted in Figure 4-9.
- Use PPP on the asynchronous link.
- Configure the proper authentication protocol for Windows 95/98/2000 client, with the username and password specified.
- Allow the link to drop after 10 minutes of inactivity.
- Also allow a TTY session to the access server so it can be used with a standard terminal emulator, such as HyperTerm.
- *Optional:* Increase performance of the link.

Equipment Needed

- One Cisco router, preferably an access server, a Cisco rolled cable, a head-shell labeled MODEM, and a modem.

- One Windows 95/98/2000 workstation with modem.

- *Optional:* To model the actual lab as depicted in Figure 4-9, you will also need an Ethernet hub, and an additional workstation. However, this is not an integral part of the lab.

Physical Layout and Prestaging

- Connect the modem, hub, and workstation to the router, as shown in Figure 4-9.

- Configure a Windows 95/98/2000 dialup networking session. Set the workstation to obtain its IP address automatically. For authentication, use the user ID of JP and the password of trashman. Remember, this is case-sensitive.

Figure 4-9   *PPP Access to Skynet Testing Facility*

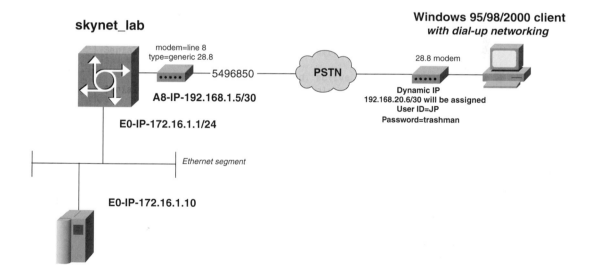

Lab 10: Configuring PPP, PAP, and Compression over Asynchronous Dialup—Part II

Lab Walkthrough

Attach the modem to the access server or auxiliary port with the Cisco rolled cable. Use the Cisco head-shell labeled Modem to attach the modem to the cable. In the lab, use line or port 8 of the access server.

To configure skynet_lab, the access server, you need to perform your four-step process for configuring PPP over asynchronous links. Applying a slight modification to the steps so that they fit this specific lab, you have the following sequence:

Step 1   Perform initial setup of the access server. This includes using a host name of skynet_lab, setting an **enable password**, and configuring the Ethernet interface as shown. To facilitate additional testing from the remote client, you might want to configure the router for Telnet access and reverse Telnet.

Step 2   Configure line 8 for modem use and to autoselect the encapsulation type during login.

Step 3   Configure the asynchronous interface for IP and PPP with PAP authentication and client address negotiation. This includes configuring a username of JP with a password of trashman.

Step 4   Configure the asynchronous interface for DDR.

Step 5   *Optional:* Configure MPPC compression.

First, you need to perform some initial setup on the access server. You set a host name and set an enable password:

```
Router(config)#hostname skynet_lab
skynet_lab(config)#enable password cisco
```

Next, perform the **show line** command to verify the absolute line number to which the modem will be attached. If Telnet access is to be enabled, also note where the vty line numbers start. Example 4-16 demonstrates the **show line** command. Notice that line number for port 8—it is TTY port 8. The lines for Telnet sessions start on 18 and run through 22.

Example 4-16 *The **show line** Command*

```
skynet_lab#show line
  Tty Typ      Tx/Rx     A Modem  Roty AccO AccI   Uses   Noise  Overruns   Int
*   0 CTY                 -    -     -    -    -      0       0     0/0       -
    1 TTY   9600/9600     -    -     -    -    -      0       0     0/0       -
*   2 TTY   9600/9600     -    -     -    -    -      0       1     9/27      -
```

Example 4-16 *The* **show line** *Command (Continued)*

```
   3 TTY   9600/9600  -    -    -    -    -      0      1     0/0      -
   4 TTY   9600/9600  -    -    -    -    -      0      0     0/0      -
   5 TTY   9600/9600  -    -    -    -    -      0      1     0/0      -
   6 TTY   9600/9600  -    -    -    -    -      0      0     0/0      -
   7 TTY   9600/9600  -    -    -    -    -      0      0     0/0      -
   8 TTY   9600/9600  -    -    -    -    -   0      0    0/0        -← Modem port
   9 TTY   9600/9600  -    -    -    -    -      0      0     0/0      -
  10 TTY   9600/9600  -    -    -    -    -      0      0     0/0      -
  11 TTY   9600/9600  -    -    -    -    -      0      0     0/0      -
  12 TTY   9600/9600  -    -    -    -    -      0      0     0/0      -
  13 TTY   9600/9600  -    -    -    -    -      0      0     0/0      -
  14 TTY   9600/9600  -    -    -    -    -      0      0     0/0      -
  15 TTY   9600/9600  -    -    -    -    -      0      0     0/0      -
  16 TTY   9600/9600  -    -    -    -    -      0      0     0/0      -
  17 AUX   9600/9600  -    -    -    -    -      0      0     0/0      -
  18 VTY              -    -    -    -    -   0      0    0/0        -←Telnet lines
  19 VTY              -    -    -    -    -      0      0     0/0      -
  20 VTY              -    -    -    -    -      0      0     0/0      -
  21 VTY              -    -    -    -    -      0      0     0/0      -
  22 VTY              -    -    -    -    -      0      0     0/0      -

skynet_lab#
```

Next, you need to configure line 8 for modem and PPP use. You need to use the **autoselect during-login** command to select what type of session starts on the line. If the client dials in with a terminal emulator, a TTY session starts. If the client starts a PPP session, a PPP session is negotiated. The **autoselect ppp** command must also be used to start the PPP session. You also must configure the modem on line 8. Because you do not know the modem type, the **autoconfigure type default** command is used. Example 4-17 demonstrates the configuration of line 8 for modem and PPP use.

Example 4-17 *Configuration of a Line for Modem and PPP Use*

```
skynet_lab#conf t
Enter configuration commands, one per line.  End with CNTL/Z.
skynet_lab(config)#line 8
skynet_lab(config-line)#modem inout
skynet_lab(config-line)#modem autoconfigure type default
skynet_lab(config-line)#login local
skynet_lab(config-line)#autoselect during-login
skynet_lab(config-line)#autoselect ppp
skynet_lab(config-line)#transport input all
skynet_lab(config-line)#^Z
skynet_lab#
```

To verify that the modem has been properly configured, use the **show line** *x* command—in this case, **show line 8**. Here, you are checking that the modem is configured. You also might want to use the **debug confmodem** command to ensure that the **AT** string was properly received by the mode. Refer back to Chapter 1 for more information on debugging modems, such as using reverse Telnet.

The asynchronous interface should be configured next. The asynchronous interface must match the line number that the modem is on—in this case, 8. At this time, you also want to configure the asynchronous interface for PPP and PAP authentication. Windows 95/98 clients use PAP authentication to authenticate PPP. Example 4-18 shows how to configure PPP encapsulation and PAP authentication.

Example 4-18 *Configuring PPP Encapsulation and PAP Authentication*

```
skynet_lab#conf t
Enter configuration commands, one per line.  End with CNTL/Z.
skynet_lab(config)#int a8
skynet_lab(config-if)#encapsulation ppp
skynet_lab(config-if)#ppp authentication pap
skynet_lab(config-if)#exit
skynet_lab(config)#username JP password trashman
skynet_lab#
```

The next step, demonstrated in Example 4-19, involves setting the IP address of the asynchronous interface and using the **peer default ip address** *remote_ip_address* command to assign an IP address to the PPP client dialing into the router.

Example 4-19 *Configuring Local and Remote IP Addresses*

```
skynet_lab(config)#int a8
skynet_lab(config-if)#ip address 192.168.1.5 255.255.255.252
skynet_lab(config-if)#peer default ip address 192.168.1.6
```

You now can configure the router for DDR. For DDR, you need to add the following the configurations under the asynchronous interface:

- **dialer in-band**
- **dialer idle-timeout** *x*
- **dialer-group** *x*
- **async mode interactive**

The **dialer in-band** allows for V.24*bis* dialing. The **dialer idle-timeout** and **dialer-group** commands define interesting traffic and determine how long the line can be idle of that traffic before disconnecting. Finally, the **async mode interactive** command allows for incoming connections.

Under the global configuration level, you need to enter a **dialer-list 8 protocol ip permit** command. The dialer list can be simple in this config because the router is not initiating a call or routing over the link. Example 4-20 shows the DDR configuration process.

Example 4-20 *Configuring DDR*

```
skynet_lab(config)#int a8
skynet_lab(config-if)#dialer in-band
skynet_lab(config-if)#dialer idle-timeout 600
skynet_lab(config-if)#dialer-group 8
skynet_lab(config-if)#async mode interactive
skynet_lab(config-if)#exit
skynet_lab(config)#dialer-list 8 protocol ip permit
skynet_lab(config)#
```

When this is complete, you can begin to test the configuration. To test the modem, use the **debug confmodem** and **debug modem** commands, as mentioned in Chapter 1. Example 4-21 lists the output of these commands. Here, you can see that the router is properly sending an **AT** command to the modem.

Example 4-21 *Output from* **debug modem** *and* **debug confmodem** *Commands*

```
skynet_lab#debug modem
skynet_lab#debug confmodem
d06h: TTY8: Line reset by "Exec"
1d06h: TTY8: Modem: IDLE->HANGUP
1d06h: TTY8: destroy timer type 0
1d06h: TTY8: destroy timer type 1
1d06h: TTY8: destroy timer type 3
1d06h: TTY8: destroy timer type 4
1d06h: TTY8: destroy timer type 2
1d06h: TTY8: dropping DTR, hanging up
1d06h: tty8: Modem: HANGUP->IDLE
1d06h: TTY8: restoring DTR
1d06h: TTY8: autoconfigure probe started
1d06h: TTY8: Modem command:  --AT&F&C1&D2S0=1H0--
1d06h: TTY8: Modem configuration succeeded
1d06h: TTY8: Detected modem speed 115200
1d06h: TTY8: Done with modem configuration
```

Verifying that the physical layer is working, you can test the network layer. Begin by turning on the "Big D" for PPP: **debug ppp Negotiation**, **debug ppp authentication**, and **debug ppp error**. Initiate a PPP session to the router by a Windows 95/98/2000 workstation. In this particular lab, you are looking for four tasks to complete successfully:

- PPP initializes—that is, the modem picks up and the fist PPP string is received.
- LCP finishes PPP negotiation.

- PAP finishes successfully.

- IPCP installs the proper IP address to the remote end.

Example 4-22 lists the **debug** output, showing all four phases completing successfully and assigning the proper IP address to the Windows 95/98 client.

Example 4-22 debug *Output from a Successful Dial Connection*

```
skynet_lab#debug ppp negotiation
skynet_lab#debug ppp authentication
skynet_lab#debug ppp error
1d06h: As8 IPCP: Install route to 192.168.1.6
1d06h: %LINK-3-UPDOWN: Interface Async8, changed state to up
1d06h: As8 PPP: Treating connection as a callin
1d06h: As8 PPP: Phase is ESTABLISHING, Passive Open        <PPP Initializes
1d06h: As8 LCP: State is Listen                            ←LCP Initializes
1d06h: As8 LCP: I CONFREQ [Listen] id 3 len 23
1d06h: As8 LCP:    ACCM 0x000A0000 (0x0206000A0000)
1d06h: As0 LCP:    MagicNumber 0x00F1EF7A (0x050600F1EF7A)
1d06h: As8 LCP:    PFC (0x0702)
1d06h: As8 LCP:    ACFC (0x0802)
1d06h: As8 LCP:    Callback 6  (0x0D0306)
1d06h: As8 LCP: O CONFREQ [Listen] id 15 len 24
1d06h: As8 LCP:    ACCM 0x000A0000 (0x0206000A0000)
1d06h: As8 LCP:    AuthProto PAP (0x0304C023)
1d06h: As8 LCP:    MagicNumber 0xE7427D86 (0x0506E7427D86)
1d06h: As8 LCP:    PFC (0x0702)
1d06h: As8 LCP:    ACFC (0x0802)
1d06h: As8 LCP: O CONFREJ [Listen] id 3 len 7
1d06h: As8 LCP:    Callback 6  (0x0D0306)
1d06h: As8 LCP: I CONFREQ [REQsent] id 4 len 20
1d06h: As8 LCP:    ACCM 0x000A0000 (0x0206000A0000)
1d06h: As8 LCP:    MagicNumber 0x00F1EF7A (0x050600F1EF7A)
1d06h: As8 LCP:    PFC (0x0702)
1d06h: As8 LCP:    ACFC (0x0802)
1d06h: As8 LCP: O CONFACK [REQsent] id 4 len 20
1d06h: As8 LCP:    ACCM 0x000A0000 (0x0206000A0000)
1d06h: As8 LCP:    MagicNumber 0x00F1EF7A (0x050600F1EF7A)
1d06h: As8 LCP:    PFC (0x0702)
1d06h: As8 LCP:    ACFC (0x0802)
1d06h: As8 LCP: TIMEout: State ACKsent
1d06h: As8 LCP: O CONFREQ [ACKsent] id 16 len 24
1d06h: As8 LCP:    ACCM 0x000A0000 (0x0206000A0000)
1d06h: As8 LCP:    AuthProto PAP (0x0304C023)
1d06h: As8 LCP:    MagicNumber 0xE7427D86 (0x0506E7427D86)
1d06h: As8 LCP:    PFC (0x0702)
1d06h: As8 LCP:    ACFC (0x0802)
1d06h: As8 LCP: I CONFACK [ACKsent] id 16 len 24
1d06h: As8 LCP:    ACCM 0x000A0000 (0x0206000A0000)
1d06h: As8 LCP:    AuthProto PAP (0x0304C023)
1d06h: As8 LCP:    MagicNumber 0xE7427D86 (0x0506E7427D86)
1d06h: As8 LCP:    PFC (0x0702)
1d06h: As8 LCP:    ACFC (0x0802)
```

Example 4-22 debug *Output from a Successful Dial Connection (Continued)*

```
1d06h: As8 LCP: State is Open                        ←LCP completes with
                              OPEN state
1d06h: As8 PPP: Phase is AUTHENTICATING, by this end        ←PAP begins
1d06h: As8 PAP: I AUTH-REQ id 1 len 16 from "JP"
1d06h: As8 PAP: Authenticating peer JP
1d06h: As8 PAP: O AUTH-ACK id 1 len 5
1d06h: As8 PPP: Phase is UP                          ←PAP completes
1d06h: As8 IPCP: O CONFREQ [Closed] id 9 len 10        ←IPCP begins IP setup
1d06h: As8 IPCP:     Address 192.168.1.5 (0x0306C0A80105)
1d06h: As8 CDPCP: O CONFREQ [Closed] id 4 len 4
1d06h: As8 IPCP: I CONFREQ [REQsent] id 1 len 40
1d06h: As8 IPCP:     CompressType VJ 15 slots CompressSlotID (0x0206002D0F01)
1d06h: As8 IPCP:     Address 0.0.0.0 (0x030600000000)
1d06h: As8 IPCP:     PrimaryDNS 0.0.0.0 (0x810600000000)
1d06h: As8 IPCP:     PrimaryWINS 0.0.0.0 (0x820600000000)
1d06h: As8 IPCP:     SecondaryDNS 0.0.0.0 (0x830600000000)
1d06h: As8 IPCP:     SecondaryWINS 0.0.0.0 (0x840600000000)
1d06h: As8 IPCP: O CONFREJ [REQsent] id 1 len 34
1d06h: As8 IPCP:     CompressType VJ 15 slots CompressSlotID (0x0206002D0F01)
1d06h: As8 IPCP:     PrimaryDNS 0.0.0.0 (0x810600000000)
1d06h: As8 IPCP:     PrimaryWINS 0.0.0.0 (0x820600000000)
1d06h: As8 IPCP:     SecondaryDNS 0.0.0.0 (0x830600000000)
1d06h: As8 IPCP:     SecondaryWINS 0.0.0.0 (0x840600000000)
1d06h: As8 CCP: I CONFREQ [Not negotiated] id 1 len 15
1d06h: As8 CCP:     MS-PPC supported bits 0x00000001 (0x120600000001)
1d06h: As8 CCP:     Stacker history 1 check mode EXTENDED (0x1105000104)
1d06h: As8 LCP: O PROTREJ [Open] id 17 len 21 protocol CCP
1d06h: As8 LCP:     (0x80FD0101000F1206000000000111050001)
1d06h: As8 LCP:     (0x04)
1d06h: As8 IPCP: I CONFACK [REQsent] id 9 len 10
1d06h: As8 IPCP:     Address 192.168.1.5 (0x0306C0A80105)
1d06h: As8 LCP: I PROTREJ [Open] id 5 len 10 protocol CDPCP (0x820701040004)
1d06h: As8 CDPCP: State is Closed
1d06h: As8 IPCP: TIMEout: State ACKrcvd
1d06h: As8 IPCP:     Address 192.168.1.5 (0x0306C0A80105)
1d06h: As8 IPCP: I CONFACK [REQsent] id 10 len 10
1d06h: As8 IPCP:     Address 192.168.1.5 (0x0306C0A80105)
1d06h: As8 IPCP: I CONFREQ [ACKrcvd] id 2 len 34
1d06h: As8 IPCP:     Address 0.0.0.0 (0x030600000000)
1d06h: As8 IPCP:     PrimaryDNS 0.0.0.0 (0x810600000000)
1d06h: As8 IPCP:     PrimaryWINS 0.0.0.0 (0x820600000000)
1d06h: As8 IPCP:     SecondaryDNS 0.0.0.0 (0x830600000000)
1d06h: As8 IPCP:     SecondaryWINS 0.0.0.0 (0x840600000000)
1d06h: As8 IPCP: O CONFREJ [ACKrcvd] id 2 len 28
1d06h: As8 IPCP:     PrimaryDNS 0.0.0.0 (0x810600000000)
1d06h: As8 IPCP:     PrimaryWINS 0.0.0.0 (0x820600000000)
1d06h: As8 IPCP:     SecondaryDNS 0.0.0.0 (0x830600000000)
1d06h: As8 IPCP:     SecondaryWINS 0.0.0.0 (0x840600000000)
1d06h: As8 IPCP: I CONFREQ [ACKrcvd] id 3 len 10
1d06h: As8 IPCP:     Address 0.0.0.0 (0x030600000000)
```

continues

Example 4-22 debug *Output from a Successful Dial Connection (Continued)*

```
1d06h: As8 IPCP: O CONFNAK [ACKrcvd] id 3 len 10
1d06h: As8 IPCP:    Address 192.168.1.6 (0x0306C0A80106)
1d06h: As8 IPCP: I CONFREQ [ACKrcvd] id 4 len 10
1d06h: As8 IPCP:    Address 192.168.1.6 (0x0306C0A80106)
1d06h: As8 IPCP: O CONFACK [ACKrcvd] id 4 len 10
1d06h: As8 IPCP:    Address 192.168.1.6 (0x0306C0A80106)
1d06h: As8 IPCP: State is Open                  ←IPCP completes and is Open
skynet_lab#ping 192.168.1.6

skynet_lab#ping                            ← Source PING
Protocol [ip]: ip
Target IP address: 192.168.1.6
Repeat count [5]:
Datagram size [100]:
Timeout in seconds [2]:
Extended commands [n]: y
Source address or interface: 172.16.1.1
Type of service [0]:
Set DF bit in IP header? [no]:
Validate reply data? [no]:
Data pattern [0xABCD]:
Loose, Strict, Record, Timestamp, Verbose[none]:
Sweep range of sizes [n]:
Type escape sequence to abort.
Sending 5, 100-byte ICMP Echos to 192.168.1.6, timeout is 2 seconds:
!!!!!
Success rate is 100 percent (5/5), round-trip min/avg/max = 136/166/196 ms
skynet_lab#
```

Most PPP problems become evident with the "Big D" enabled. Without the **debug**s, it becomes difficult to spot analog dialup errors. Make sure that all four phases are completed, followed by some source **ping**s from 172.16.1.1 to 192.168.1.6 to verify IP connectivity. Some of the most common problems to look for are as follows:

- **PPP not even starting (no ppp debug messages)**—This points to a modem or physical problem. Ensure that autoselect PPP is enabled.

- **PPP authentication fails**—This message is listed clearly in the **debug**; to correct it, ensure that your passwords match.

- **Route not installed to destination networks**—Part of DDR is ensuring that a route exists to the proper networks. This also involves checking for the correct IP address to get negotiated or sent to the PPP client.

To increase performance on this link, you can enable MPPC on interface A8 and disable CDP. To enable MPPC compression, simply add the **compress mppc** command on the interface. After adding this command to the interface, you can see MPPC get successfully negotiated in Example 4-23. To disable CDP on the interface, use the **no cdp enable** command on the interface.

Example 4-23 debug *Output for MPPC Compression*

```
1d07h: As8 CCP: O CONFREQ [Closed] id 2 len 10
1d07h: As8 CCP:    MS-PPC supported bits 0x00000001 (0x120600000001)
<<<text omitted>>>
1d07h: As8 IPCP:    SecondaryWINS 0.0.0.0 (0x840600000000)
1d07h: As8 CCP: I CONFREQ [REQsent] id 1 len 15
1d07h: As8 CCP:    MS-PPC supported bits 0x00000001 (0x120600000001)
1d07h: As8 CCP:    Stacker history 1 check mode EXTENDED (0x1105000104)
1d07h: As8 CCP: O CONFREJ [REQsent] id 1 len 9
1d07h: As8 CCP:    Stacker history 1 check mode EXTENDED (0x1105000104)
1d07h: As8 IPCP: I CONFACK [REQsent] id 13 len 10
1d07h: As8 IPCP:    Address 192.168.1.5 (0x0306C0A80105)
1d07h: As8 CCP: I CONFACK [REQsent] id 2 len 10
1d07h: As8 CCP:    MS-PPC supported bits 0x00000001 (0x120600000001)
1d07h: As8 CCP: I CONFREQ [ACKrcvd] id 2 len 10
1d07h: As8 CCP:    MS-PPC supported bits 0x00000001 (0x120600000001)
1d07h: As8 CCP: O CONFACK [ACKrcvd] id 2 len 10
1d07h: As8 CCP:    MS-PPC supported bits 0x00000001 (0x120600000001)
1d07h: As8 CCP: State is Open
```

NOTE   If you use two routers to test the PAP connection instead of a router and workstation, you need to use the command **ppp pap sent-username** under the async interface for a successful PAP challenge to occur.

Finally, Example 4-24 shows the complete configuration for skynet_lab.

Example 4-24 *Complete Listing of skynet_lab*

```
hostname skynet_lab
!
enable password cisco
!
username JP password 0 trashman
ip subnet-zero
!
interface Ethernet0
 ip address 172.16.1.1 255.255.255.0
 no ip directed-broadcast
!
<<<text omitted>>>
```

continues

Example 4-24 *Complete Listing of skynet_lab (Continued)*

```
!
interface Async8
 ip address 192.168.1.5 255.255.255.252
 no ip directed-broadcast
 encapsulation ppp
 no ip mroute-cache
 dialer in-band
 dialer idle-timeout 600
 dialer-group 8
 async mode interactive
 peer default ip address 192.168.1.6
 compress mppc
 no cdp enable
 ppp authentication pap
!
ip classless
!
dialer-list 8 protocol ip permit
!
line con 0
 exec-timeout 0 0
 transport input none
line 1 7
 transport input all
line 8
 autoselect during-login
 autoselect ppp
 login local
 modem InOut
 modem autoconfigure type default
 transport input all
 speed 115200
line 9 16
line aux 0
line vty 0 4
 login local
!
end

skynet_lab#
```

Lab 11: Configuring PPP, CHAP, and LQM over Synchronous Links—Part I

Practical Scenario

PPP CHAP provides secure authentication for peer-to-peer networking sessions over many types of media. As mentioned earlier, PPP is used over serial, asynchronous, ISDN, and DSL, as well as other media types. Today, PPP is even becoming the encapsulation for some LAN-based networks. Again, this is mainly because of the peer-to-peer authentication that PPP provides.

Lab Exercise

The Skynet testing facility just upgraded its Internet connection to T1. The date of the install coincides with the release of a couple of big Internet games. Skynet views this as the perfect time to stress test the new link. You have the task to provide a quick and secure connection to the Internet. Use the following parameters as your design guidelines:

- Use PPP as your data-link protocol. The host name of the ISP router is isp_router. The CHAP password is 2diablo2. Use CHAP authentication.

- At this time, this is Skynet's only link to the Internet and is the only route out of the Skynet network.

- Configure the link so that it will not tolerate a 40 percent packet loss.

Lab Objectives

- Configure the access server and network, as depicted in Figure 4-10.

- Use PPP with CHAP as the data-link protocol on the synchronous link to the ISP.

- Enforce Link Quality Management on the link.

- *Optional:* There is a DNS server for the ISP; its address is 128.200.1.2. Configure the skynet_lab router to use this DNS server. That is, you should be able to **ping** www.cisco.com when logged on to the skynet_lab router. This might or might not be difficult to test, depending on your lab. What is most important is the correct configuration in the router to forward DNS requests.

Equipment Needed

- Two Cisco routers, connected through V.35 back-to-back cables or in a similar manner
- Two LAN segments, provided through hubs or switches
- One optional workstation functioning as a DNS server

Physical Layout and Prestaging

- Connect the hubs and serial cables to the routers, as shown in Figure 4-10.
- Connect two Ethernet hubs to form two LAN segments, as shown in Figure 4-10.
- Optionally connect and configure a DNS server on the ISP LAN segment.

Figure 4-10 *Skynet Testing Facility PPP Serial Connection Access to an ISP*

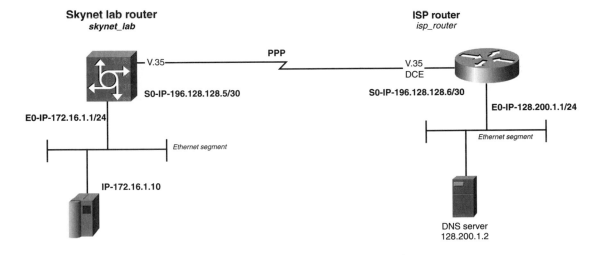

Lab 11: Configuring PPP, CHAP, and LQM over Synchronous Links—Part II

Lab Walkthrough

Attach two routers in a back-to-back fashion, using either a V.35 cable or CSU/DSUs with a crossover cable, as depicted in Figure 4-10.

To configure skynet_lab, you can preserve most of your configuration from the previous lab. Here, you essentially configure PPP over the interface, enable CHAP, and enforce LQM.

First, configure the serial interfaces for PPP by changing the encapsulation type to PPP. At this time, also set a username for the remote router, isp_router, and set the password to 2diablo2:

```
skynet_lab(config)#username isp_router password 2diablo2
skynet_lab(config)#int s0
skynet_lab(config-if)#encapsulation ppp
skynet_lab(config-if)#ppp authentication chap
```

Normally, this would be all that is required for a PPP connection over a serial link; however, you still want to enable and enforce LQM and DNS. To enable LQM on the interface to tolerate a loss of no more then 40 percent, use the **ppp quality** *percentage_of_successful_traffic* command. The PPP quality is measured in a percentage of successful traffic, so you should set this value to 60.

Moving over to the ISP router, you configure that router in much the same way that you configured the Skynet router. Example 4-25 demonstrates the commands needed on the ISP router.

Example 4-25 *Configuration of the ISP PPP Connection*

```
isp_router(config)#username skynet_lab password 2diablo2
isp_router(config)#int s0
isp_router(config-if)#ip address 196.128.128.6 255.255.255.0
isp_router(config-if)#encapsulation ppp
isp_router(config-if)#ppp authentication chap
isp_router(config-if)#clock-rate 2000000
isp_router(config-if)#ppp quality 60
isp_router(config-if)#^Z
```

You can verify the functionality of the serial links by performing a **ping** of the remote serial interface from both routers. If you enable **debug ppp negotiation** and **debug ppp authentication**, you see LQM messages being exchanged on the link, as well as PPP CHAP authentication being performed.

The last step is to configure the router for both the ISP and Skynet. Skynet will have only one route out of the network at this time, so you should use a default route pointing all outbound traffic to the ISP's serial interface. Three commands work together to accomplish this:

- **ip classless**
- **ip default-network 0.0.0.0**
- **ip route 0.0.0.0 0.0.0.0** *196.128.128.6*

The **ip classless** command tells the router to forward any traffic destined toward a subnet not found in its routing table. Without this command, the router will not forward any traffic if the router does not have a route to the destination. The **ip default-network** commands set the default route to 0.0.0.0, and the **ip route** command is a static route pointing to the 0.0.0.0 catchall network. All traffic will be forwarded to the next-hop address entered here.

For the ISP, you should be more specific about the routing. Here, you should simply make one static route pointing toward the remote network:

```
ip route 172.16.1.0 255.255.255.0 196.128.128.5
```

After this is complete, ensure that you have two-way connectivity by issuing extended **ping**s, sourced from each router's Ethernet port. If you perform **show ip route** on Skynet, you should see the default route set, as demonstrated in Example 4-26.

Example 4-26 show ip route *of Skynet and the IP Router—Note the Default Route Set*

```
skynet_lab#show ip route
Codes: C - connected, S - static, I - IGRP, R - RIP, M - mobile, B - BGP
       D - EIGRP, EX - EIGRP external, O - OSPF, IA - OSPF inter area
       N1 - OSPF NSSA external type 1, N2 - OSPF NSSA external type 2
       E1 - OSPF external type 1, E2 - OSPF external type 2, E - EGP
       i - IS-IS, L1 - IS-IS level-1, L2 - IS-IS level-2, * - candidate default
       U - per-user static route, o - ODR
       T - traffic engineered route

Gateway of last resort is 196.128.128.6 to network 0.0.0.0     ←Default route set

C    201.201.201.0/24 is directly connected, Loopback0
     196.128.128.0/24 is variably subnetted, 2 subnets, 2 masks
C       196.128.128.4/30 is directly connected, Serial0
C       196.128.128.6/32 is directly connected, Serial0
     172.16.0.0/24 is subnetted, 1 subnets
C       172.16.1.0 is directly connected, Ethernet0
     192.168.1.0/30 is subnetted, 1 subnets
C       192.168.1.4 is directly connected, Async8
S*   0.0.0.0/0 [1/0] via 196.128.128.6          ←IP next hop of default route
skynet_lab#

isp_router#show ip route
Codes: C - connected, S - static, I - IGRP, R - RIP, M - mobile, B - BGP
       D - EIGRP, EX - EIGRP external, O - OSPF, IA - OSPF inter area
       N1 - OSPF NSSA external type 1, N2 - OSPF NSSA external type 2
```

Example 4-26 show ip route *of Skynet and the IP Router—Note the Default Route Set (Continued)*

```
          E1 - OSPF external type 1, E2 - OSPF external type 2, E - EGP
          i - IS-IS, L1 - IS-IS level-1, L2 - IS-IS level-2, * - candidate default
          U - per-user static route, o - ODR

Gateway of last resort is not set

     128.200.0.0/24 is subnetted, 1 subnets
C       128.200.1.0 is directly connected, Ethernet0
     172.16.0.0/24 is subnetted, 1 subnets
S       172.16.1.0 [1/0] via 196.128.128.5           ←route to Skynet
     196.128.128.0/24 is variably subnetted, 2 subnets, 2 masks
C       196.128.128.5/32 is directly connected, Serial0
C       196.128.128.0/24 is directly connected, Serial0
isp_router#
```

The stage is optional, and it allows the forwarding of DNS requests to a DNS server. To forward DNS requests, two commands are needed:

- **ip name-server** *DNS_server_IP_address*
- **ip domain-lookup**

The **ip name-server** command tells the router the IP address of the DNS server, whereas the **ip domain-lookup** command forwards the UDP DNS packets. Example 4-27 demonstrates the configuration and use of the DNS server at the ISP. This example was taken from a real ISP router; note that the lab has no "real" connection to the Internet, so these statements are shown only for reference and will not be present in Example 4-28.

Example 4-27 *Configuration and Use of DNS Services on a Route*

```
skynet_lab(config)#ip name-server 204.221.151.248
skynet_lab(config)#ip domain-lookup
skynet_lab(config)#^Z
skynet_lab#ping www.cisco.com
Translating "www.cisco.com"...domain server (204.221.151.248) [OK]

Type escape sequence to abort.
Sending 5, 100-byte ICMP Echos to 198.133.219.25, timeout is 2 seconds:
!!!!!
Success rate is 100 percent (5/5), round-trip min/avg/max = 112/114/116 ms
skynet_lab#
```

If you have problems with DNS, ensure that you have IP connectivity to the DNS server, and also make sure that the router's UDP packets are being forwarded.

Example 4-28 shows the router configurations in their entirety.

Example 4-28 *Router Configurations for Skynet and the ISP Route*

```
skynet_lab#show running-config
Building configuration...

Current configuration:
!
version 12.0
service timestamps debug uptime
service timestamps log uptime
no service password-encryption
!
hostname skynet_lab
!
enable password cisco
!
username JP password 0 trashman
username isp_router 0 2diablo2
ip subnet-zero
!
interface Ethernet0
 ip address 172.16.1.1 255.255.255.0
 no ip directed-broadcast
!
interface Serial0
 ip address 196.128.128.5 255.255.255.252
 no ip directed-broadcast
 encapsulation ppp
 no ip mroute-cache
 no fair-queue
 ppp quality 60
!
interface Serial1
 no ip address
 no ip directed-broadcast
 shutdown
!
interface Async8
 ip address 192.168.1.5 255.255.255.252
 no ip directed-broadcast
 encapsulation ppp
 no ip mroute-cache
 dialer in-band
 dialer idle-timeout 600
 dialer-group 8
 async mode interactive
 peer default ip address 192.168.1.6
 compress mppc
 no cdp enable
 ppp authentication pap
!
ip classless
```

Example 4-28 *Router Configurations for Skynet and the ISP Route (Continued)*

```
ip default-network 0.0.0.0
ip route 0.0.0.0 0.0.0.0 196.128.128.6
!
dialer-list 8 protocol ip permit
!
line con 0
 exec-timeout 0 0
 transport input none
line 1 7
 transport input all
line 8
 autoselect during-login
 autoselect ppp
 login local
 modem InOut
 modem autoconfigure type default
 transport input all
 speed 115200
line 9 16
line aux 0
line vty 0 4
 login local
!
end

skynet_lab#
```

```
isp_router#show running-config
Building configuration...

Current configuration:
!
version 11.2
no service password-encryption
no service udp-small-servers
no service tcp-small-servers
!
hostname isp_router
!
!username skynet_lab password 2diablo2
!
interface Ethernet0
 ip address 128.200.1.1 255.255.255.0
```

continues

Example 4-28 *Router Configurations for Skynet and the ISP Route (Continued)*

```
!
interface Serial0
 ip address 196.128.128.6 255.255.255.0
 encapsulation ppp
 clockrate 2000000
 ppp quality 60
!
interface Serial1
 no ip address
 shutdown
!
interface BRI0
 no ip address
 shutdown
!
no ip classless
ip route 172.16.1.0 255.255.255.0 196.128.128.5
!
line con 0
 exec-timeout 0 0
line aux 0
line vty 0 4
 login
!
end

isp_router#
```

Lab 12: Configuring PPP Analog Backup for Synchronous Links—Part I

Practical Scenario

Most sites that have ISDN or analog backup for their serial links use PPP as the data-link protocol. A common struggle with DDR is ensuring that it dials only at the appropriate times. An ISDN or asynchronous line that is dialing because of an improperly configured ACL can be costly. Other limitations put upon the design of your network also might force you to configure dial backup in another fashion. For example, if you had to configure a dial interface in OSPF Area 0 or another regular area, it would dial continuously because of link-state flooding.

Lab Exercise

The SuperGreat Food Corp. runs an IP-based automated inventory system on an IBM 3090x-based platform at its corporate headquarters. Each branch is connected to SuperGreat Foods through a 64-kbps PPP connection. Located at each branch is an RS6000. The RS6000 requires IP connectivity to the mainframe, as well as the SuperGreat IP network. The SuperGreat IP network is in autonomous system 2001; for full IP reachability, you must run EIGRP on all links. Design your network in accordance to the following guidelines set forth form SuperGreat Corp:

* Use PPP as your data-link protocol on all serial links. Authenticate with CHAP on all PPP links. The CHAP password is cub9biggs.

* Using EIGRP as the routing protocol, you must exchange routes on all links. Use 2001 as the autonomous System ID.

* Configure the serial link so that, upon loss of the circuit, the AUX port will provide dial backup. You must send and receive routing updates on the backup port as well.

Lab Objectives

* Configure the SuperGreat network, as depicted in Figure 4-11.

* Use PPP on the serial link between the branch and the corporate router.

* Configure analog dial backup between the two sites so that only a loss of the PPP circuit will trigger a call.

* Use EIGRP as the routing protocol. *Do not use any static routes.*

Equipment Needed

- Two Cisco routers, connected through V.35 back-to-back cables or in a similar manner. The LAN type is not significant.
- Two analog modems, Cisco rolled cables, and MODEM head-shells.
- Two LAN segments, provided through hubs or switches; the LAN type is not important to the configuration of the lab.
- Two Windows 95/98/2000 workstations with IP configured to simulate the IBM mainframe and RS6000, as in Figure 4-11.

Physical Layout and Prestaging

- Connect the hubs, serial cables, and modems to the routers, as shown in Figure 4-11.
- Connect one Token Ring hub to the sub_branch router, and connect the Ethernet hub to the sub_corp router.
- Connect and configure two IP-based workstations for testing purposes.

Figure 4-11 *SuperGreat Foods PPP Network with Dial Backup*

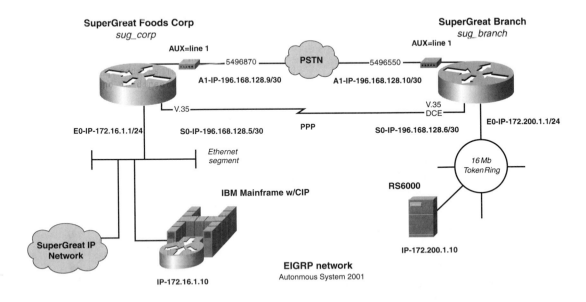

Lab 12: Configuring PPP Analog Backup for Synchronous Links—Part II

Lab Walkthrough

Attach two routers in a back-to-back manner using either V.35 cables or CSU/DSUs with a crossover cable, as depicted in Figure 4-11. Connect the modems with "real" analog lines or a modem eliminator. Connect the modems to the routers' AUX ports, and be sure to use a Cisco rolled cable with the modem head-shell labeled MODEM. See Chapter 1 for additional help in configuring and attaching modems to a router's AUX port.

The design requirements call for you to use EIGRP as the routing protocol. The requirements also call for you to dial only when the PPP circuit is lost. To force an interface to be in a standby mode and to pick up and dial only under a unique circumstance, Cisco offers the **backup interface** command.

The **backup interface** command specifies that an interface stays idle until certain circumstances occur:

- The primary link goes down, resulting in loss of the data link layer.
- The load on the primary link reaches a certain threshold.
- The load on the primary link exceeds a specified threshold.

The **backup interface** command is used on the serial interface that is your primary interface. If you have a 2503 router, two serials, and one ISDN port, and if you were backing up the serial interface with the ISDN interface, the serial interface is referred to as the *primary interface*, and the ISDN is called the *secondary*. The **backup interface** command would go on the serial interface, called the *primary interface*, not the ISDN interface. The syntax for the **backup** command is as follows, entered in interface mode:

```
backup interface interface_name_or_type
```

You also can configure a time period specifying how much time should elapse before a secondary link status changes after primary link status has changed. There are two way to accomplish this:

- A delay that applies after the primary link goes down but before the secondary link is activated.
- A delay that applies after the primary link comes up but before the secondary link is deactivated. The syntax used to insert a delay is as follows:

```
backup delay {enable-delay | never}{disable-delay | never}
```

- A backup load also can be specified. This tells the secondary link to activate based on the amount of traffic on the primary link. This is done with the following command:

```
backup load {enable-threshold | never}{disable-load | never}
```

As soon as the **backup** command is entered on an interface, it immediately forces it into a standby state. Example 4-29 shows a link in backup mode. When the interface is in this state, it does not respond to **ping**s.

Example 4-29 *Status of Link with the* **backup** *Command*

```
Async1 is standby mode, line protocol is down
  Hardware is Async Serial
  Internet address is 192.168.128.10/30
  MTU 1500 bytes, BW 38 Kbit, DLY 100000 usec, rely 255/255, load 1/255
  Encapsulation PPP, loopback not set, keepalive not set
  DTR is pulsed for 5 seconds on reset
  LCP Closed
  Closed: IPCP, CDPCP
```

In this circumstance, the **backup** command will come in handy. When deploying a backup strategy with the **backup** command, you should limit dialing to one side of the network. You might encounter scenarios in which multiple sites dial into the same BRI port or analog ports. If the backup command is places on both ends of the link, you run the risk of having the host stay in a down standby mode on one side of the link. A good example of this could be with Frame Relay, where each side of the link is dependent only on the local Frame Relay switch. In a Frame Relay network, it is possible of have one end of the link "Line UP, Protocol UP"; the **backup** command would not activate the secondary link, while, at the same time, the end of the Frame Relay network might be down. Therefore, it is recommended that you use the **backup** command only on the remote end of the link.

With a backup strategy in mind, focus on configuring the branch router first. To configure the branch router, you need to perform the following:

- Perform initial setup of the router. This includes a host name and a username for sug_corp, along with a password.
- Configure the Token Ring interface for IP, and **ping** RS6000. Use the IP address of 172.200.1.1/24 for the To0 port of the router.
- Configure the Serial 0 interface for PPP and IP. Use the IP address of 196.168.128.6/30.
- Configure EIGRP on the router, use AS 2001, and use the networks 196.168.128.0 and 172.200.0.0.

After this is complete, your config should have parts that resemble the ones in Example 4-30.

Example 4-30 *Initial Setup of the sug_branch*

```
hostname sug_branch
!
enable password cisco
!
username sug_corp password 0 cub9biggs          ←Used for CHAP
ip subnet-zero
 !
 interface Serial0
 ip address 192.168.128.6 255.255.255.252
 no ip directed-broadcast
 encapsulation ppp
 no ip mroute-cache
 no fair-queue
 ppp authentication chap
 !
interface Serial1
 no ip address
 no ip directed-broadcast
 shutdown
 !
interface TokenRing0
 ip address 172.200.1.1 255.255.255.0
 no ip directed-broadcast
 ring-speed 16
 !
router eigrp 2001
 network 192.168.128.0
 network 172.200.0.0
 no auto-summary
 !
no ip classless
 !
line con 0
line aux 0
line vty 0 4
 login
 !
end
```

Before concerning yourself with the modem and the dial backup configuration, you should
configure the host site. Configuring the sug_corp router is similar to configuring the
sug_branch router. To configure the sug_corp router, perform the following actions:

- Perform initial setup of the router. This includes the host name and a username for
  sug_branch, along with a password.

- Configure the Ethernet interface for IP, and **ping** the mainframe. Use the IP address
  of 172.16.1.1/24 for the E0 port of the router.

- Configure the Serial 0 interface for PPP and IP. Use the IP address of 196.168.128.5/30.

- Configure EIGRP on the router, use AS 2001, and use the networks 196.168.128.0 and 172.16.0.0.

After completing this, your configuration should resemble Example 4-31.

Example 4-31 *sug_corp Listing*

```
hostname sug_corp
!
enable password cisco
!
username sug_branch password 0 cub9biggs          ←Used for CHAP
!
interface Ethernet0
 ip address 172.16.1.1 255.255.255.0
!
interface Serial0
 ip address 192.168.128.5 255.255.255.252
 encapsulation ppp
 no fair-queue
 clockrate 64000
ppp authentication chap
!
interface Serial1
 no ip address
 shutdown
!
router eigrp 2001
 network 192.168.128.0
 network 172.16.0.0
 no auto-summary
!
no ip classless
!
line con 0
line aux 0
line vty 0 4
 login
!
end
```

At this time, you should have full IP connectivity from the RS6000 to the mainframe. Test for full connectivity by issuing **ping**s from RS6000 to the mainframe. Also check the route table on each side of the network to ensure that the 172.16.1.0 and 172.200.1.0 networks are being advertised to each other. An EIGRP neighbor also should be built over the serial interface. Example 4-32 lists the route table on sug_branch followed by the **show eigrp neighbors** command.

Example 4-32 *Routing Table on sub_branch and* **show eigrp neighbor** *Command*

```
sug_branch#show ip route
Codes: C - connected, S - static, I - IGRP, R - RIP, M - mobile, B - BGP
       D - EIGRP, EX - EIGRP external, O - OSPF, IA - OSPF inter area
       N1 - OSPF NSSA external type 1, N2 - OSPF NSSA external type 2
       E1 - OSPF external type 1, E2 - OSPF external type 2, E - EGP
       i - IS-IS, L1 - IS-IS level-1, L2 - IS-IS level-2, * - candidate default
       U - per-user static route, o - ODR
       T - traffic engineered route

Gateway of last resort is not set

     192.168.128.0/24 is variably subnetted, 3 subnets, 2 masks
D       192.168.128.8/30 [90/70440192] via 192.168.128.5, 00:09:19, Serial0
C       192.168.128.4/30 is directly connected, Serial0
C       192.168.128.5/32 is directly connected, Serial0
     172.200.0.0/24 is subnetted, 1 subnets
C       172.200.1.0 is directly connected, TokenRing0
     172.16.0.0/24 is subnetted, 1 subnets
D       172.16.1.0 [90/2195456] via 192.168.128.5, 00:09:19, Serial0    ←Corp Subnet
sug_branch#
sug_branch#show ip eigrp neighbors
IP-EIGRP neighbors for process 2001
H    Address                 Interface      Hold Uptime    SRTT   RTO  Q  Seq
                                            (sec)          (ms)        Cnt Num
0    192.168.128.5           Se0             12 00:09:38    32    200  0  5
sug_branch#
```

After you verify that routes are being exchanged and that an EIGRP neighbor is established, you can configure the dial backup portion of the lab.

Starting with the sub_branch router, follow the four-step process for configuring PPP over asynchronous interfaces. The steps to do this are as follows:

Step 1 Configure the modem and asynchronous port of the router. Use the **show line** command to identify the absolute line number.

Step 2 Define and configure PPP on the asynchronous interfaces.

Step 3 Configure IP on the asynchronous interface.

Step 4 Configure DDR on the asynchronous interface.

The configuration for the async ports on both routers will be similar to those in past labs, with the main difference being that of a routing protocol. Under the async port, you will need to have the **async default routing** command for EIGRP. Because you will be using the **backup interface** command, the dialer list can permit all IP traffic on the sug_branch router. Until the **backup interface** command is added, you will see the link immediately dial if EIGRP is configured. If you perform a **debug dialer**, you will see that an EIGRP multicast is bringing up the dialer, as demonstrated in Example 4-33.

Example 4-33 *Example of* **debug dialer**

```
11:25:13: Async1: Dialing cause ip (s=192.168.128.10, d=224.0.0.10)    ←EIGRP
  multicast
11:25:13: Async1: Attempting to dial 5496870
11:25:13: CHAT1: Attempting async line dialer script
11:25:13: CHAT1: Dialing using Modem script: dialsug & System script: none
11:25:13: CHAT1: process started
11:25:13: CHAT1: Asserting DTR
11:25:13: CHAT1: Chat script dialsug started
```

On the sug_corp router, there will be no need for a dialer list because this side of the network will not be responsible for establishing or maintaining the link.

Example 4-34 shows the configurations for the SuperGreat network in their entirety.

Example 4-34 *Complete Configurations for SuperGreat Network with Backup*

```
hostname sug_corp
!
enable password cisco
!
username sug_branch password 0 cub9biggs
!
interface Ethernet0
 ip address 172.16.1.1 255.255.255.0
!
interface Serial0
 ip address 192.168.128.5 255.255.255.252
 encapsulation ppp
 no fair-queue
 clockrate 64000
 ppp authentication chap
!
interface Async1
 ip address 192.168.128.9 255.255.255.252
 encapsulation ppp
 async default routing
 async mode interactive
 dialer in-band
 dialer idle-timeout 300
 dialer map ip 192.168.128.10 name sug_branch broadcast 5496550
 ppp authentication chap
!
router eigrp 2001
 network 192.168.128.0
 network 172.16.0.0
 no auto-summary
```

Example 4-34 *Complete Configurations for SuperGreat Network with Backup (Continued)*

```
!
ip classless
!
line con 0
line aux 0
 autoselect ppp
 modem InOut
 modem autoconfigure discovery
 transport input all
 rxspeed 38400
 txspeed 38400
line vty 0 4
 login
!
end
```

```
hostname sug_branch
!
enable password cisco
!
username sug_corp password 0 cub9biggs
ip subnet-zero
chat-script dialsug "" "ATZ&F" OK "ATDT5496870" TIMEOUT 60 CONNECT
!
 interface Serial0
 ip address 192.168.128.6 255.255.255.252
 no ip directed-broadcast
 encapsulation ppp
 no ip mroute-cache
 backup interface Async1
 no fair-queue
 ppp authentication chap
!
interface TokenRing0
 ip address 172.200.1.1 255.255.255.0
 no ip directed-broadcast
 ring-speed 16
!
interface Async1
 ip address 192.168.128.10 255.255.255.252
 no ip directed-broadcast
 encapsulation ppp
 dialer in-band
 dialer map ip 192.168.128.9 name sug_corp broadcast 5496870
 dialer-group 1
 async default routing
 async mode interactive
 ppp authentication chap
!
```

continues

Example 4-34 *Complete Configurations for SuperGreat Network with Backup (Continued)*

```
router eigrp 2001
 network 172.200.0.0
 network 192.168.128.0
 no auto-summary
!
ip classless
!
dialer-list 1 protocol ip permit
!
line con 0
 transport input none
line aux 0
 autoselect ppp
 script dialer dialsug
 modem InOut
 modem autoconfigure discovery
 transport input all
 speed 38400
line vty 0 4
 login
!
end
```

The SuperGreat network can be tested for backup by unplugging or shutting down the serial interface on the corporate end. Immediately upon link loss, you should see the branch router call the remote. The routing table will then converge over the async interface. Example 4-35 highlights this process in effect.

Example 4-35 *Output from* **debug dialer** *and Route Table Convergence on the sug_branch Router*

```
sug_branch#show ip route
Codes: C - connected, S - static, I - IGRP, R - RIP, M - mobile, B - BGP
       D - EIGRP, EX - EIGRP external, O - OSPF, IA - OSPF inter area
       N1 - OSPF NSSA external type 1, N2 - OSPF NSSA external type 2
       E1 - OSPF external type 1, E2 - OSPF external type 2, E - EGP
       i - IS-IS, L1 - IS-IS level-1, L2 - IS-IS level-2, * - candidate default
       U - per-user static route, o - ODR
       T - traffic engineered route

Gateway of last resort is not set

     192.168.128.0/24 is variably subnetted, 3 subnets, 2 masks
D       192.168.128.8/30 [90/70440192] via 192.168.128.5, 00:04:19, Serial0
C       192.168.128.4/30 is directly connected, Serial0
C       192.168.128.5/32 is directly connected, Serial0
     172.200.0.0/24 is subnetted, 1 subnets
C       172.200.1.0 is directly connected, TokenRing0
     172.16.0.0/24 is subnetted, 1 subnets
D       172.16.1.0 [90/2195456] via 192.168.128.5, 00:04:43, Serial0     ←Corp
   Ethernet
```

Example 4-35 *Output from* **debug dialer** *and Route Table Convergence on the sug_branch Router (Continued)*

```
sug_branch#
sug_branch#
11:34:49: %LINK-3-UPDOWN: Interface Serial0, changed state to down        ←Serial
  Drops
11:34:50: %LINEPROTO-5-UPDOWN: Line protocol on Interface Serial0, changed state
  to down
11:35:06: Async1: re-enable timeout
11:35:06: Async1: Dialing cause ip (s=192.168.128.10, d=224.0.0.10)    ←EIGRP forces
  dial
11:35:06: Async1: Attempting to dial 5496870
11:35:06: CHAT1: Attempting async line dialer script
11:35:06: CHAT1: Dialing using Modem script: dialsug & System script: none
11:35:06: CHAT1: process started
11:35:06: CHAT1: Asserting DTR
11:35:06: CHAT1: Chat script dialsug started
11:35:25: CHAT1: Chat script dialsug finished, status = Success
11:35:25: CHAT1: Chat script dialsug finished, status = Success
11:35:32: dialer Protocol up for As1
11:35:32: %LINEPROTO-5-UPDOWN: Line protocol on Interface Async1, changed state
  to up                                    ←Async UP
sug_branch#
sug_branch#
sug_branch#show ip route
Codes: C - connected, S - static, I - IGRP, R - RIP, M - mobile, B - BGP
       D - EIGRP, EX - EIGRP external, O - OSPF, IA - OSPF inter area
       N1 - OSPF NSSA external type 1, N2 - OSPF NSSA external type 2
       E1 - OSPF external type 1, E2 - OSPF external type 2, E - EGP
       i - IS-IS, L1 - IS-IS level-1, L2 - IS-IS level-2, * - candidate default
       U - per-user static route, o - ODR
       T - traffic engineered route

Gateway of last resort is not set

     192.168.128.0/24 is variably subnetted, 2 subnets, 2 masks
C       192.168.128.8/30 is directly connected, Async1
C       192.168.128.9/32 is directly connected, Async1
     172.200.0.0/24 is subnetted, 1 subnets
C       172.200.1.0 is directly connected, TokenRing0
     172.16.0.0/24 is subnetted, 1 subnets
D       172.16.1.0 [90/69953792] via 192.168.128.9, 00:00:21, Async1←Corp Ethernet
   Reported over the async int.
sug_branch#
sug_branch#ping 172.16.1.1

Type escape sequence to abort.
Sending 5, 100-byte ICMP Echos to 172.16.1.1, timeout is 2 seconds:
!!!!!                                  ←The BANGS are our friends
Success rate is 100 percent (5/5), round-trip min/avg/max = 200/238/324 ms
sug_branch#
```

CHAPTER 5

WAN Protocols and Technologies: Frame Relay

Frame Relay has become "king of the WAN" over the past five to seven years. Many private networks have gone through lengthy migration processes, moving from point-to-point serial links to Frame Relay–based networks. As popular as Frame Relay is, its popularity is starting to wane. Frame Relay circuits eventually might be replaced by lower-cost, higher-speed circuits, such as DSL or cable modems. If a home user can get T3 speed access to Internet service providers (ISP), it is only a matter of time before DSL or some other technology using existing copper replaces the lower-bandwidth Frame Relay service. But it will be years for a new protocol to take the title away from the "king."

This chapter covers Frame Relay terminology and provides a technical overview of Frame Relay and LMI operation. In addition, this chapter examines basic and advanced Frame Relay configuration, including Frame Relay traffic shaping.

Frame Relay Terminology

Some common terms are necessary to know when discussing and configuring Frame Relay. Some of the terms on the following list are recalled from Chapter 1, "The Key Components for Modeling an Internetwork":

- **Permanent virtual circuit (PVC)**—The logical end-to-end circuit, used for frame transport. A PVC's endpoints are addressed with DLCIs.

- **Data-Link Connection Identifier (DLCI)**—A logical number in the range of 16 to 1007 used to identify the PVC between the customer premises equipment (CPE) and the Frame Relay switch. The DLCI is only locally significant, which implies that only the local devices and the Frame Switch that they attach to care what their DLCI numbers are.

- **Local Management Interface (LMI)**—Best defined as the signaling standard used between the router and the Frame Relay switch. LMI is used by the switch to learn which DLCIs are defined and what their status is. LMI also supports a 10-second keepalive mechanism that verifies that the PVC is active and data is being exchanged. Three types of LMI are supported on Cisco routers: CISCO, ANSI, and Q933A. If LMI is not configured, the router tries to autonegotiate on all three LMI types:

    — **CISCO**—LMI type defined by the "big three," Cisco, Digital, and Northern Telecom. This is the default LMI type, if autonegotiation fails. LMI status information is sent on DLCI 0.

    — **ANSI**—LMI type defined by ANSI standard T1.617, commonly called Annex D. This is the most common type of LMI found across all Frame Relay networks. LMI status information is sent on DLCI 1023.

    — **Q933a**—LMI type defined as ITU-T Q.933, or simply Annex A. LMI status information is sent on DLCI 0.

- **Network-to-Network Interface (NNI)**—The standard used for two switches to communicate. NNI is used in both Frame Relay and ATM. In ATM, it is referred to as the Network Node Interface.

- **Local access rate**—The clock speed or "port speed" of the connection to the Frame Relay service provider. Usually, this circuit is 56 kbps, 64 kbps, or T1 speeds, but can operate T3 speeds or on *High Speed Serial Interface (HSSI)*.

Figure 5-1 illustrates a common Frame Relay network, highlighting the preceding terms.

Figure 5-1 *Partially Meshed Frame Relay Network*

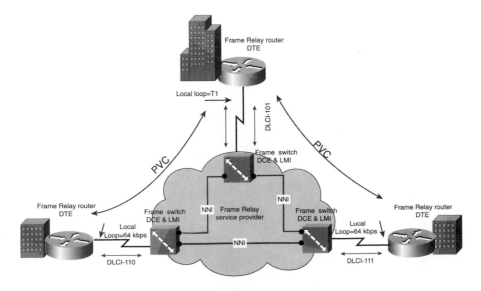

The following terms are called *data rate metrics*. Frame Relay service providers use data rate metrics to define service-level agreements. The following terms also are used when we configure Frame Relay traffic shaping:

- **Committed burst (Bc)**—The number of bits committed to accept and transmit at the CIR.

- **Committed Information Rate (CIR)**The maximum permitted traffic level per PVC. When this is exceeded, the Discard Eligible (DE) bit is set. The DE bit can be used as an indication to the frame carrier that it can drop that frame if capacity between Frame Relay switches is reached. This value is expressed in bits per second.

- **Excess burst (Be)**—The number of bits to transmit after the committed burst value is reached.

- **Maximum data rate (MaxR)**—This value is measured in bits per second and is calculated by the following:

$$MaxR = CIR \times \left(\frac{Bc + Be}{Bc} \right)$$

Figure 5-2 illustrates how these metrics relate to each other.

Figure 5-2   *Frame Relay Data Metrics*

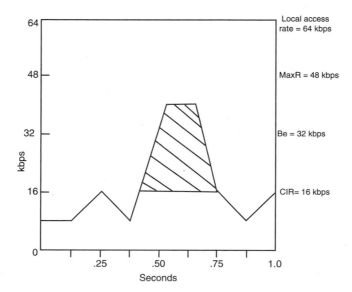

Frame Relay Technical Overview

Necessity is the mother of invention, and this old rule applies to protocols as well. There were many shortcomings in X.25, SDLC, and other WAN protocols when Frame Relay surfaced. Frame Relay brought many useful options that aided in better network design, such as the following:

- Frame Relay provides a means for statistically multiplexing many logical circuits over a single physical circuit.

- Frame Relay helps lower line cost by not requiring dedicated end-to-end circuits for each link.

- Statistical multiplexing provides for increased network scalability by eliminating the need for a router serial port and CSU/DSU for each side of the connection.

- Frame Relay has a scalable network design:

  — It adheres to the three-layer model—core, distribution, and access layers.

  — It allows full, partial, and hybrid meshing strategies.

  — It adds protocol broadcast and performance controls.

Frame Relay is a CCITT and American National Standards Institute (ANSI) standard. It was founded as the next-generation protocol to X.25, which sometimes is referred to as an *overengineered protocol* because it performs extensive error checking and correction at the data link and network layers. X.25 had this type of error correction because it had to deal with many low-quality lines. Frame Relay implements a connection-oriented data stream that relies on the upper-layer protocols to provide error checking and correction. For reference, Frame Relay is outlined in the following standards:

- ANSI T1.606: "Architectural Framework and Service Description for Frame-Relaying Bearer Service" (1991)

- ANSI T1.617: "Signaling Specification for Frame Relay Bearer Service" (1991)

- ANSI T1.618: "Core Aspects of Frame Protocol for Use with Frame Relay Bearer Service" (1991)

- ITU Q.933 and Q.922: User plane control

- RFC 1490: Defines Frame Relay encapsulation

A number of Frame Relay Forum (FRF) implementation agreements can be found at www.frforum.com.

Frame Relay LMI Operation

The LMI is essential for Frame Relay operation. When a Frame Relay link becomes active on a Cisco DTE device, it sends three LMI messages in rapid succession. The order is ANSI, ITU, and then Cisco. The router listens on DLCI 1023 for Cisco LMI and DLCI 0 for ANSI and ITU. The Frame switch responds with the LMI with which it is configured, and the router then sets the LMI type of that interface to match the LMI type that it received. If multiple types of LMI are received, the last one received is used. Cisco refers to this as *LMI autosense*. The router then sends LMI status messages back and forth every 10 seconds. These status messages are referred to as *LMI keepalives*. The router then begins to operate in the manner illustrated by Figure 5-3 and explained in the list that follows.

Figure 5-3   *Frame Relay LMI Operation*

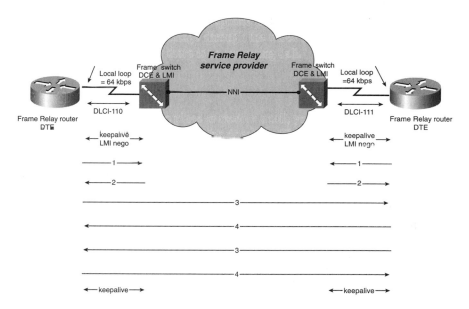

1   On every sixth LMI status request, the DTE device sends a full status request. This request serves as another keepalive and requests the frame switch to respond with a list of all DLCIs that have been defined for that link. Example 5-1 shows this initial exchange happening.

Example 5-1   *Initial LMI Setup and Exchange Output from* **debug frame lmi** *and* **debug frame packet**

```
00:19:19: Serial0(out): StEnq, myseq 1, yourseen 0, DTE up
00:19:19: datagramstart = 0x400002DC, datagramsize = 14
00:19:19: FR encap = 0x00010308
00:19:19: 00 75 95 01 01 00 03 02 01 00
00:19:19:
00:19:19: Serial0(out): StEnq, myseq 1, yourseen 0, DTE up
00:19:19: datagramstart = 0x4000053C, datagramsize = 13
00:19:19: FR encap = 0x00010308
00:19:19: 00 75 51 01 00 53 02 01 00
```

continues

Example 5-1 *Initial LMI Setup and Exchange Output from* **debug frame lmi** *and* **debug frame packet** *(Continued)*

```
00:19:19:
00:19:19: Serial0(out): StEnq, myseq 1, yourseen 0, DTE up
00:19:19: datagramstart = 0x400002DC, datagramsize = 13
00:19:19: FR encap = 0xFCF10309
00:19:19: 00 75 01 01 00 03 02 01 00
00:19:19:
00:19:19: Serial0(in): Status, myseq 1
00:19:19: RT IE 1, length 1, type 0
00:19:19: KA IE 3, length 2, yourseq 1 , myseq 1
00:19:19: PVC IE 0x7 , length 0x6 , dlci 110, status 0x0 , bw 0
00:19:29: Serial0(out): StEnq, myseq 2, yourseen 1, DTE up
00:19:29: datagramstart = 0x400002DC, datagramsize = 13
00:19:29: FR encap = 0xFCF10309
00:19:29: 00 75 01 01 01 03 02 02 01
00:19:29:
00:19:29: Serial0(in): Status, myseq 2
00:19:29: RT IE 1, length 1, type 0
00:19:29: KA IE 3, length 2, yourseq 2 , myseq 2
00:19:29: PVC IE 0x7 , length 0x6 , dlci 110, status 0x0 , bw 0
```

2 When the frame switch receives a status inquiry message, it sends a full status response. This message sends a list of all active DLCIs on that port.

3 For each active DLCI, the router sends an Inverse ARP request per Layer 3 protocol configured on that interface. If IP and IPX are configured, for example, the router sends two Inverse ARP requests. The request also asks the other router to reply with its network layer address. If Inverse ARP is not supported, this transaction and the transaction that follows are accomplished with the **frame-relay map** commands (covered in the "Configuring Frame Relay" section).

4 For each DLCI that each router receives an Inverse ARP message about, the router creates a map entry in its Frame Relay map table. The map table includes the local DLCI and the remote router's network layer address for that request. The table also contains the status of the PVC, which is one of the following (as displayed with the **show frame-relay pvc** command):

— **ACTIVE**—Indicates that the PVC is active and that information can be exchanged

— **INACTIVE**—Indicates that the local connection to the Frame switch is working, but the remote router's connection to the frame switch is not working

— **DELETED**—Indicates that no LMI is being received from the frame switch or that the physical layer is still not established

5   The router continues to exchange keepalive messages every 10 seconds. Again, every 60 seconds, or sixth exchange, a full status LMI request is sent and the process repeats itself. If three consecutive LMI messages are missed, the link is brought down.

Configuring Frame Relay

You need to follow only two physical steps when configuring Frame Relay on Cisco routers. In this text, we list a four-step process; some of these steps do not require configuration. Regardless, you should always be aware of all the components or steps needed to configure the complete frame service. A couple of these commands are set by default, and no additional key-ins are necessary. Further additional steps can be added to the basic steps, but they are not required to get frame service running on your router.

Step 1   **Enable Frame Relay encapsulation on an interface or subinterface**. This is done with the following interface command:

```
router(config-if)#encapsulation frame-relay [cisco | ietf]
```

cisco is the default encapsulation type and should be used when connecting to another Cisco device or an RFC 1490–compliant device.

ietf should be used when connecting to non-Cisco devices.

Step 2   **Set the LMI type**. All Cisco routers running Cisco IOS Software Release 11.2 and later support LMI autosense and require no additional configuration. You can statically configure the LMI with the following interface command:

```
Router(config-if)#frame-relay lmi-type [ansi | cisco | q933i]
```

Refer back to the descriptions on different LMI types in the "Frame Relay Terminology" section if you need to refresh your memory. Cisco is the default LMI type.

Step 3   **Configure static or dynamic protocol and address mapping.** Next, determine what type of address mapping is needed for the specific Frame Relay interface. Your choice to use **frame-relay map** command versus **frame-relay interface-dlci** or no command at all depends on how you have the Frame Relay interface configured and whether the remote device supports Frame Relay Inverse ARP. Subinterfaces are logical divisions of the physical interface. Dynamic address mapping uses Frame Relay Inverse ARP, as previously mentioned. Because you are now splitting the physical interface into multiple subinterfaces, you must provide additional configuration information that ties a specific subinterface to a specific

DLCI. Two types of subinterfaces exist in Frame Relay networks, point-to-point and multipoint. If you are creating a point-to-point subinterface, use the following command:

```
Router(config-if)#frame-relay interface-dlci dlci_number
```

When you are creating a multipoint interface, you need to use static addressing. This is not as much for Frame Relay purposes as it is for general routing issues. Inverse ARP will still be resolved; however, routed protocols will not be capable of forwarding packets to the appropriate next-hop address without the aid of static addressing. Use the following command on multipoint interfaces:

```
Router(config-if)#frame-relay map protocol [ip | dec | appletalk | xns | ipx |
    vines | clns | bridge | llc2 | dlsw] next_hop_address dlci [broadcast]
    [ietf | cisco]
```

The **frame-relay map** statement creates a static map between the local DLCI and the next-hop network address. The **broadcast** keyword is required to forward specific broadcasts, such as the ones needed for OSPF. This keyword should be used at all times. The **ietf** and **cisco** keywords allow for different frame encapsulation types on a PVC basis. The **frame-relay map** statement also can be used to load-share traffic over a frame network. For example, IPX traffic can be mapped to one DLCI, while IP can be mapped to the other. This command also is used to transport protocols in accordance with RFC 1490, such as Spanning-Tree frames and Data Link Switching frames. This command has many uses; refer to the *Cisco IOS Software Configuration Guide* for all **frame-relay map** command options.

Table 5-1 illustrates the recommended use of Inverse ARP address mapping type for each interface.

Table 5-1   *Recommend Address Mapping and Inverse ARP Pairings*

Natural or Standard Interface	Multipoint Subinterface	Point-to-Point Interface	Connecting to a Device Without Inverse ARP
Add a network layer address for each protocol.	Add a network layer address for each protocol. Use **frame-relay map** statements.	Add a network layer address for each protocol. Use the **frame-relay interface-dlci** command.	Add a network layer address for each protocol. Use **frame-relay map** statements.
Static or dynamic addressing	Static addressing	Dynamic addressing	Static addressing

Step 4   **Address protocol-specific issues.** You need to be aware of certain issues when configuring routing protocols over Frame Relay. For example, OSPF works properly only with the network type changed or with **neighbor** statements. All multipoint networks running distance vector protocols, or EIGRP, are subject to split horizons. We discuss these issues in more detail in upcoming chapters. Table 5-2 lists common issues to address with Frame Networks.

Table 5-2   *Common Issues with Frame Networks*

Protocol	Multipoint Subinterface	Point-to-Point Interface
OSPF	Must use **neighbor** statements, or use the **ip ospf network type** command on the interface. Use a priority of 1 to set the DR router. This should be the router with a PVC to all of its neighbors.	Must use **neighbor** statements, or use the **ip ospf network type broadcast** command on the interface.
EIGRP	Disable IP or IPX split horizons. Add **bandwidth** command.	Add **bandwidth** command.
RIP	Disable IP or IPX split horizons.	None.
IGRP	Disable IP or IPX split horizons. Add **bandwidth** command.	Add **bandwidth** command.
BGP	None.	None.
Bridging	Set the root bridge to the router that has PVCs to all *leaves* of the bridge.	Set the root bridge to the router that has PVCs to all *leaves* of the bridge.

NOTE   *Split horizon* refers to the rule that information about a route will not be sent out the same interface or subinterface from which it was received. Split horizon rears its ugly head most predominantly in multipoint configurations. Here, routing updates flow into one subinterface but also must be sent out that same subinterface to reach the other routers on the multipoint network. Split horizon is on by default and prevents routing updates for EIGRP, IGRP, and RIP from being propagated properly in a multipoint configuration. Disable this with the following interface key-in: **no ip split-horizon** for RIP or IGRP networks, and **no ip split-horizon eigrp** *autonomous_system* for EIGRP networks. These commands have similar forms for IPX and AppleTalk. If you have two point-to-point subinterfaces configured, routing updates flow in one subinterface and are forwarded out the other subinterface because each subinterface is on a different network. Therefore, there is no need to disable split horizon when using point-to-point subinterfaces.

Practical Example: Configuring Hybrid Frame Relay Networks

The example that follows walks you through the complete configuration of a Frame Relay network by using the different types of interfaces. Figure 5-4 illustrates a hybrid Frame Relay network.

Figure 5-4   *Frame Relay Hybrid Network*

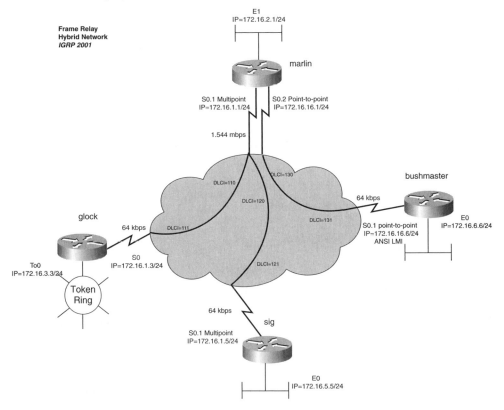

In this example, you configure a Frame Relay multipoint network between the marlin, glock, and sig routers. You also configure a Frame Relay point-to-point network between the marlin and the bushmaster routers. The routing protocol is IGRP.

Let's begin with the marlin router. Following the four-step Frame Relay configuration process, start by setting the encapsulation to Frame Relay on the serial interface. You define two types of subinterfaces. A multipoint is needed for the subnet 172.16.1.0/24, which connects the glock and sig routers. You can use a point-to-point or a multipoint for subnet 172.16.16.0/24 to connect to the bushmaster router.

In this example, you use a point-to-point network. Example 5-2 demonstrates this configuration.

Example 5-2 *Setting Encapsulation and Defining Subinterfaces*

```
marlin#conf t
Enter configuration commands, one per line.  End with CNTL/Z.
marlin(config)#int s0
marlin(config-if)#encapsulation frame-relay
marlin(config-if)#int s0.1 multipoint
marlin(config-subif)#ip address 172.16.1.1 255.255.255.0
marlin(config-subif)#exit
marlin(config)#int s0.2 point-to-point
marlin(config-subif)#ip address 172.16.16.1 255.255.255.0
marlin(config-subif)#^Z
```

You can follow the same steps defining a multipoint subinterface on the glock router and a point-to-point subinterface on the bushmaster router. You will not use any subinterfaces on the glock router, and you should treat it as a multipoint router. At this time, you need only to define the Frame Relay encapsulation on the glock router's s0 interface.

The next step is to configure LMI. As previously mentioned, Frame Relay autosense detects and configure the LMI automatically. No additional configuration is needed. For practice, you will statically configure the LMI on the bushmaster router to ANSI. This is accomplished with the **frame-relay lmi-type ansi** command under the s0 interface.

The third step is to configure static or dynamic addressing. On the marlin router, use a static address on the s0.1 interface, the multipoint interface. The s0.2 interface is a point-to-point interface, so you can use dynamic addressing. You need one **frame-relay map** statement pointing to each remote router on the 172.16.1.0/24 subnet. Example 5-3 demonstrates the configuration for static mapping.

Example 5-3 *Configuring Static Mapping*

```
marlin(config)#int s0.1 multipoint
marlin(config-subif)# frame-relay map ip 172.16.1.3 110 broadcast
marlin(config-subif)# frame-relay map ip 172.16.1.5 120 broadcast
marlin(config-subif)#exit
```

Example 5-4 demonstrates the configuration of dynamic addressing needed for the marlin router.

Example 5-4 *Configuring Dynamic Mapping*

```
marlin(config)#int s0.2 point-to-point
marlin(config-subif)#frame-relay interface-dlci 130
marlin(config-fr-dlci)#^Z
marlin#
```

The glock router's serial interface is a natural interface on a multipoint network; therefore, you use static addressing. Here, you need two **frame-relay map** statements. You configure one **frame-relay map** statement pointing at DLCI 111 for IP address 172.16.1.1, and one pointing at the same DLCI, 111, for IP address 172.16.1.5. Example 5-5 shows the configuration on the glock router serial interface.

Example 5-5 *Configuring the glock Router's Serial Interface*

```
Interface serial0
 ip address 172.16.1.3 255.255.255.0
 no ip directed-broadcast
 encapsulation frame-relay
 no ip mroute-cache
 no fair-queue
 frame-relay map ip 172.16.1.5 111 broadcast
 frame-relay map ip 172.16.1.1 111 broadcast
```

The sig router has a multipoint subinterface on s0; therefore, this router also needs two static **frame-relay map** statements. One **frame-relay map** statement is for the glock router, and one is for the marlin router. Example 5-6 shows the configuration for the serial interface for the sig router.

Example 5-6 *sig Router's Serial Interface*

```
interface serial0.1 multipoint
 ip address 172.16.1.5 255.255.255.0
 no ip directed-broadcast
 no ip mroute-cache
 frame-relay map ip 172.16.1.3 121 broadcast
 frame-relay map ip 172.16.1.1 121 broadcast
 !
```

Returning to the marlin router, you can complete Step 3 for the point-to-point side of the link. The subinterface s0.2 is a point-to-point interface to the bushmaster router. Therefore, you can use dynamic addressing on this interface. To accomplish this, use the **frame-relay interface-dlci** *dlci_number* command under the s0.2 interface, such as in Example 5-7.

Example 5-7 *Configuring marlin Router's serial 0.2 Subinterface*

```
interface serial0.2 point-to-point
 ip address 172.16.16.1 255.255.255.0
 frame-relay interface-dlci 130
 !
```

Repeat this same process for the point-to-point subinterface on the bushmaster router; this time, however, it points toward DLCI 131.

Now, you can move on to Step 4 in the configuration process: address any protocol-specific issues. As previously mentioned, a split-horizon issue occurs on a multipoint network running IGRP, such as this one. With the default of split horizon set to on, the marlin router will not forward sig's Ethernet network of 172.16.5.0/24 back out the s0.1 port toward the glock router. It also will not forward the glock router's Token Ring network 172.16.3.0/24 back out its s0.1 port toward the sig router. To resolve this, use the **no ip split-horizon** command on the marlin router's s0.1 port. You now have full IP connectivity across the Frame Relay network. IGRP uses bandwidth to influence routing decisions. To further tune the network, assign **bandwidth** statements to all serial interfaces to make routing decisions more accurate. Example 5-8 lists the relevant portions of all the router configurations.

Example 5-8 *Relevant Configuration Listing for the Routers in Figure 5-4*

```
hostname marlin
!
interface Ethernet1
 ip address 172.16.2.1 255.255.255.0
 media-type 10BaseT
!
interface Serial0
 no ip address
 encapsulation frame-relay
 no ip mroute-cache
 bandwidth 1544
 no fair-queue
!
interface Serial0.1 multipoint
 ip address 172.16.1.1 255.255.255.0
 no ip split-horizon
 frame-relay map ip 172.16.1.3 110 broadcast
 frame-relay map ip 172.16.1.5 120 broadcast
!
interface Serial0.2 point-to-point
 ip address 172.16.16.1 255.255.255.0
 frame-relay interface-dlci 130
!
router igrp 2001
 network 172.16.0.0
!
```
```
hostname glock
!
<<<text omitted>>>
 !
 interface Serial0
 bandwidth 64
 ip address 172.16.1.3 255.255.255.0
 no ip directed-broadcast
 encapsulation frame-relay
```

continues

Example 5-8 *Relevant Configuration Listing for the Routers in Figure 5-4 (Continued)*

```
 no ip mroute-cache
 no fair-queue
 frame-relay map ip 172.16.1.5 111 broadcast
 frame-relay map ip 172.16.1.1 111 broadcast
!
interface TokenRing0
 ip address 172.16.3.3 255.255.255.0
 no ip directed-broadcast
 ring-speed 16
!
router igrp 2001
 network 172.16.0.0
!
```

```
hostname sig
!
<<<text omitted>>>
!
 interface Ethernet0
 ip address 172.16.5.5 255.255.255.0
 no ip directed-broadcast
!
interface Serial0
 no ip address
 no ip directed-broadcast
 encapsulation frame-relay
 no ip mroute-cache
 no fair-queue
!
interface Serial0.1 multipoint
 bandwidth 64
 ip address 172.16.1.5 255.255.255.0
 no ip directed-broadcast
 no ip mroute-cache
 frame-relay map ip 172.16.1.3 121 broadcast
 frame-relay map ip 172.16.1.1 121 broadcast
!
router igrp 2001
 network 172.16.0.0
!
```

```
hostname bushmaster
!

interface Ethernet0
 ip address 172.16.6.6 255.255.255.0
!
interface Serial0
 no ip address
 encapsulation frame-relay
 frame-relay lmi-type ansi
!
```

Example 5-8 *Relevant Configuration Listing for the Routers in Figure 5-4 (Continued)*

```
interface Serial0.1 point-to-point
 ip address 172.16.16.6 255.255.255.0
 bandwidth 64
 frame-relay interface-dlci 131
!
router igrp 2001
 network 172.16.0.0
```

To verify that your Frame Relay network is operational, you can use standard **ping**s and traces tests; however, sometimes you might want to require more information about the operational status of the Frame network. The "Big **show**" and "Big D" commands for Frame Relay can provide a lot of useful information, as described in the next section.

The "Big show" and "Big D" for Frame Relay

The **show** and **debug** commands for Frame Relay are some of the most useful Cisco commands. They allow you to quickly isolate most problems, and they don't seem to provide excess data that doesn't help you troubleshoot or verify whether the service is running. The "Big **show**" and "Big D" commands for Frame Relay are as follows:

```
show frame-relay pvc [dlci | interface]
show frame-relay lmi
show frame-relay map
debug frame-relay lmi
```

NOTE   For a complete list of the **show** and **debug** commands for Frame Relay, see the *IOS WAN Configuration Guide.*

show frame-relay pvc Command

The **show frame-relay pvc** command displays the statistics about all PVCs on the router, or an optional keyword can be used to display information on a specific DLCI or interface. Most of this command's information is self-explanatory—it shows traffic rates in the form of packets and bytes. It also displays any forward-explicit congestion notification/backward-explicit congestion notification (FECN/BECN) information along with DE packets. The section "Configuring Frame Relay Traffic Shaping (FRTS)" discusses FECN/BECN in more details and gives some additional information that the **show frame pvc** command displays.

One of the key fields to look for is the PVC status. As mentioned previously, the PVC status can be one of the following:

- **ACTIVE**—Indicates that the PVC is active and that information can be exchanged

- **INACTIVE**—Indicates that the local connection to the frame switch is working but that the remote router's connection to the frame switch is not working

- **DELETED**—Indicates that no LMI is being received from the frame switch or that the physical layer is not established

Example 5-9 lists the output from the **show frame pvc** command from the marlin router in the previous example. Notice that traffic is passing on the link, and the PVC status is ACTIVE.

Example 5-9   **show frame pvc** *Output from the marlin Router*

```
marlin#show frame-relay pvc

PVC Statistics for interface Serial0 (Frame Relay DTE)

DLCI = 110, DLCI USAGE = LOCAL, PVC STATUS = ACTIVE, INTERFACE = Serial0.1

    input pkts 500          output pkts 250         in bytes 62900
    out bytes 29762         dropped pkts 2          in FECN pkts 0
    in BECN pkts 0          out FECN pkts 0         out BECN pkts 0
    in DE pkts 0            out DE pkts 0
    out bcast pkts 250       out bcast bytes 29762
    pvc create time 05:31:58, last time pvc status changed 05:29:46

DLCI = 120, DLCI USAGE = LOCAL, PVC STATUS = ACTIVE, INTERFACE = Serial0.1

    input pkts 498          output pkts 249         in bytes 27132
    out bytes 29670         dropped pkts 0          in FECN pkts 0
    in BECN pkts 0          out FECN pkts 0         out BECN pkts 0
    in DE pkts 0            out DE pkts 0
    out bcast pkts 249       out bcast bytes 29670
    pvc create time 05:31:59, last time pvc status changed 05:29:47

DLCI = 130, DLCI USAGE = LOCAL, PVC STATUS = ACTIVE, INTERFACE = Serial0.2

    input pkts 585          output pkts 590         in bytes 107506
    out bytes 118208        dropped pkts 0          in FECN pkts 0
    in BECN pkts 0          out FECN pkts 0         out BECN pkts 0
    in DE pkts 0            out DE pkts 0
    out bcast pkts 590       out bcast bytes 118208
    pvc create time 05:32:00, last time pvc status changed 05:31:07
marlin#
```

The PVC Create Time and the Last Time PVC Status Changed fields are also important. These times should be relatively close if your PVC has not dropped since the interface was brought up. Example 5-10 lists the output of the marlin router with a problem on the PVC. Can you guess where the problem might be just by this one command?

Example 5-10 *Output of* **show frame pvc** *Command on the marlin Router with a PVC Down*

```
marlin#show frame pvc

PVC Statistics for interface Serial0 (Frame Relay DTE)

DLCI = 110, DLCI USAGE = LOCAL, PVC STATUS = INACTIVE, INTERFACE = Serial0.1

  input pkts 508          output pkts 255          in bytes 63860
  out bytes 30362         dropped pkts 2           in FECN pkts 0
  in BECN pkts 0          out FECN pkts 0          out BECN pkts 0
  in DE pkts 0            out DE pkts 0
  out bcast pkts 255       out bcast bytes 30362
  pvc create time 05:38:00, last time pvc status changed 00:00:19

DLCI = 120, DLCI USAGE = LOCAL, PVC STATUS = ACTIVE, INTERFACE = Serial0.1

  input pkts 508          output pkts 254          in bytes 27632
  out bytes 30270         dropped pkts 0           in FECN pkts 0
  in BECN pkts 0          out FECN pkts 0          out BECN pkts 0
  in DE pkts 0            out DE pkts 0
  out bcast pkts 254       out bcast bytes 30270
  pvc create time 05:38:01, last time pvc status changed 05:35:49

DLCI = 130, DLCI USAGE = LOCAL, PVC STATUS = ACTIVE, INTERFACE = Serial0.2

  input pkts 595          output pkts 601          in bytes 109422
  out bytes 120372        dropped pkts 0           in FECN pkts 0
  in BECN pkts 0          out FECN pkts 0          out BECN pkts 0
  in DE pkts 0            out DE pkts 0
  out bcast pkts 601       out bcast bytes 120372
  pvc create time 05:38:01, last time pvc status changed 05:37:09
marlin#
```

Notice that the PVC 110 status has changed. The PVC status is now INACTIVE. Because the other PVC, DLCI 120 on interface Serial0.1, is up and the status of 110 is inactive, it indicates a problem at the remote end. In this example, the glock router's serial interface was shut down, again proving that even in a lab setting, "carrier gremlins" do exist.

show frame-relay lmi Command

Everything that rides over Frame Relay rides over the LMI. If the LMI is not working properly, your frame service will not work. When using the **show frame-relay lmi** command, look for the Num Status Enq. Sent *xx* to increment with the **Num** Status msgs Rcvd *xx* field. If you are sending LMI but are not receiving it, the problem is likely to be with the frame switch or an LMI mismatch. Ensure that the LMI for the interface is the same as what the carrier has the switch set for. Example 5-11 lists the output from the glock router demonstrating an LMI mismatch. Observe how the LMI is being sent, and notice that timeouts are increasing.

Example 5-11 *LMI Mismatch Demonstrated with the* **show frame lmi** *Command*

```
glock#show frame lmi

LMI Statistics for interface Serial0 (Frame Relay DTE) LMI TYPE = ANSI
   Invalid Unnumbered info 0           Invalid Prot Disc 0
   Invalid dummy Call Ref 0            Invalid Msg Type 0
   Invalid Status Message 0            Invalid Lock Shift 0
   Invalid Information ID 0            Invalid Report IE Len 0
   Invalid Report Request 0           Invalid Keep IE Len 0
   Num Status Enq. Sent 82            Num Status msgs Rcvd 18
   Num Update Status Rcvd 0           Num Status Timeouts 63

glock#show frame lmi

LMI Statistics for interface Serial0 (Frame Relay DTE) LMI TYPE = ANSI
   Invalid Unnumbered info 0           Invalid Prot Disc 0
   Invalid dummy Call Ref 0            Invalid Msg Type 0
   Invalid Status Message 0            Invalid Lock Shift 0
   Invalid Information ID 0            Invalid Report IE Len 0
   Invalid Report Request 0           Invalid Keep IE Len 0
   Num Status Enq. Sent 117           Num Status msgs Rcvd 18
   Num Update Status Rcvd 0           Num Status Timeouts 98
glock#
```

After changing the LMI to Cisco and performing a **clear counters** command, you can see what a proper running line looks like. Notice this time in Example 5-12 that the Num Status Enq. Sent messages are incrementing with the Num Status Msgs Rcvd field.

Example 5-12 **show frame lmi** *Command Output*

```
glock#show frame lmi

LMI Statistics for interface Serial0 (Frame Relay DTE) LMI TYPE = CISCO
   Invalid Unnumbered info 0           Invalid Prot Disc 0
   Invalid dummy Call Ref 0            Invalid Msg Type 0
   Invalid Status Message 0            Invalid Lock Shift 0
   Invalid Information ID 0            Invalid Report IE Len 0
   Invalid Report Request 0           Invalid Keep IE Len 0
   Num Status Enq. Sent 1             Num Status msgs Rcvd 1
   Num Update Status Rcvd 0           Num Status Timeouts 0
glock#
glock#show frame lmi

LMI Statistics for interface Serial0 (Frame Relay DTE) LMI TYPE = CISCO
   Invalid Unnumbered info 0               Invalid Prot Disc 0
```

Example 5-12 **show frame lmi** *Command Output (Continued)*

```
Invalid dummy Call Ref 0          Invalid Msg Type 0
Invalid Status Message 0          Invalid Lock Shift 0
Invalid Information ID 0          Invalid Report IE Len 0
Invalid Report Request 0         Invalid Keep IE Len 0
Num Status Enq. Sent 8           Num Status msgs Rcvd 8
Num Update Status Rcvd 0         Num Status Timeouts 0
glock#
```

show frame-relay map Command

The **show frame-relay map** command displays the network layer address and associated DLCI for each remote destination that the local router is connected to. It also displays whether the association is dynamic or static. Use this command to verify your **frame-relay map** statements and to check the operation of Inverse ARP. Example 5-13 demonstrates sample output from this command.

Example 5-13 **show frame-relay map** *Command Output*

```
marlin#show frame-relay map
Serial0.1 (up): ip 172.16.1.3 dlci 110(0x6E,0x18E0), static,
            broadcast,
            CISCO, status defined, active
Serial0.1 (up): ip 172.16.1.5 dlci 120(0x78,0x1C80), static,
            broadcast,
            CISCO, status defined, active
Serial0.2 (up): point-to-point dlci, dlci 130(0x82,0x2020), broadcast
          status defined, active
marlin#
```

debug frame-relay lmi Command

Although many **debug** commands are available for Frame Relay, most of them are for specific configuration types and don't apply to a majority of general frame configurations. Debugging LMI, however, can be helpful for many, if not all, Frame Relay configurations.

The **debug frame-relay lmi** command is useful in displaying LMI exchanges. It allows you to quickly determine whether the router is properly exchanging LMIs. When using this command, look for the yourseq and the myseq numbers to increment. When the router receives a sequence number, it adds 1 to it and sends it back out on the next update as its current sequence number. If three of these LMI messages, or keepalives, are missed consecutively, the link will be reset.

If the output from this command shows only one number changing, it is a strong indication of an LMI mismatch. If no messages appear, there is poor connection between the router and the frame switch. Example 5-14 demonstrates a properly working frame circuit.

Example 5-15 exhibits what happens to a link after carrier gremlins cause an LMI mismatch.

Example 5-14 **debug frame-relay lmi** *Command Output on an Operational Frame Circuit*

```
sig#debug frame-relay lmi
Frame Relay LMI debugging is on
Displaying all Frame Relay LMI data
sig#
18:48:30: Serial0(out): StEnq, myseq 38, yourseen 37, DTE up
18:48:30: datagramstart = 0xE23E94, datagramsize = 13
18:48:30: FR encap = 0xFCF10309
18:48:30: 00 75 01 01 01 03 02 26 25
18:48:30:
18:48:30: Serial0(in): Status, myseq 38
18:48:30: RT IE 1, length 1, type 1
18:48:30: KA IE 3, length 2, yourseq 38, myseq 38
18:48:40: Serial0(out): StEnq, myseq 39, yourseen 38, DTE up
18:48:40: datagramstart = 0xE23E94, datagramsize = 13
18:48:40: FR encap = 0xFCF10309
18:48:40: 00 75 01 01 01 03 02 27 26
18:48:40:
18:48:40: Serial0(in): Status, myseq 39
18:48:40: RT IE 1, length 1, type 1
18:48:40: KA IE 3, length 2, yourseq 39, myseq 39
```

Example 5-15 **debug frame-relay lmi** *Command Output Demonstrating an LMI Mismatch*

```
sig#debug frame-relay lmi
Frame Relay LMI debugging is on
Displaying all Frame Relay LMI data
sig#
18:59:26: Serial0(out): StEnq, myseq 7, yourseen 5, DTE up      ←missed one LMI
18:59:26: datagramstart = 0xE23E94, datagramsize = 13
18:59:26: FR encap = 0xFCF10309
18:59:26: 00 75 01 01 01 03 02 07 05
18:59:26:
18:59:36: Serial0(out): StEnq, myseq 8, yourseen 5, DTE up      ←missed two LMIs
18:59:36: datagramstart = 0xE23E94, datagramsize = 13
18:59:36: FR encap = 0xFCF10309
18:59:36: 00 75 01 01 01 03 02 08 05
18:59:36:
18:59:46: Serial0(out): StEnq, myseq 9, yourseen 5, DTE up      ←Strike three, link
                                                                  down
18:59:46: datagramstart = 0xE23E94, datagramsize = 13
18:59:46: FR encap = 0xFCF10309
18:59:46: 00 75 01 01 01 03 02 09 05
18:59:46:
18:59:56: %FR-5-DLCICHANGE: Interface Serial0 - DLCI 121 state changed to INACTIVE
18:59:56: %LINEPROTO-5-UPDOWN: Line protocol on Interface Serial0.1, changed state
           to down
```

Example 5-15 debug frame-relay lmi *Command Output Demonstrating an LMI Mismatch (Continued)*

```
18:59:56: %FR-5-DLCICHANGE: Interface Serial0 - DLCI 121 state changed to DELETED
18:59:56: Serial0(out): StEnq, myseq 1, yourseen 5, DTE down
18:59:56: datagramstart = 0xE23E94, datagramsize = 13
18:59:56: FR encap = 0xFCF10309
18:59:56: 00 75 01 01 01 03 02 01 05
18:59:56:
18:59:57: %LINEPROTO-5-UPDOWN: Line protocol on Interface Serial0, changed state
          to down
```

Additional Commands for Configuring Frame Relay

Some additional commands are available to control or modify your Frame Relay network. The following list includes some of the more commonly tuned features of Frame Relay. For a complete list, see the *IOS WAN Configuration Guide*.

- **Router(config-if)no frame-relay inverse-arp**—Disables the sending of Inverse ARP requests. Use this command in conjunction with **no arp frame-relay** to prevent the dynamic mapping of PVCs.

- **Router(config-if)no arp frame-relay**—Disables ARP responses. Use this in conjunction with the **no frame-relay inverse-arp** command.

- **Router(config-if)keepalive** *keepalive_interval_in_seconds*—Sets the default 10-second keepalive interval to another value. Be sure to use this command on both sides of the link.

- **clear frame-relay-inarp**—Use this command to clear any dynamically created Frame Relay maps.

- **frame-relay priority-dlci-group** *group-number high-dlci medium-dlci normal-dlci low-dlci*—Use this command to use multiple parallel DLCIs for different Frame Relay traffic types.

Configuring Frame Relay Traffic Shaping

Traffic shaping works on the principle that a router controls outbound traffic to match its data flow to the speed of the remote device. Traffic that fits a particular profile can be "shaped" to meet downstream requirements, eliminating downstream bottlenecks. For example, in Figure 5-5, you can see a partially meshed Frame Relay network.

Figure 5-5 *Partially Meshed Frame Relay Network*

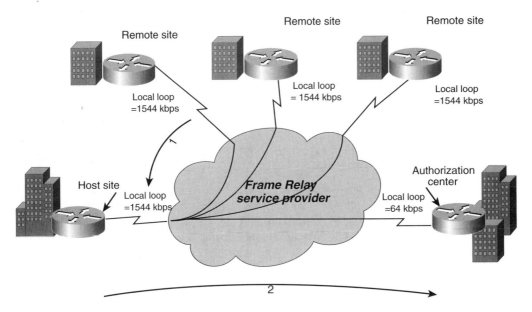

In this model, the remote sites need IP access to the authorization center. At any given time, there are 300 end-to-end TCP connections from the remote sites to the authorization center. If the link between the authorization center fails and then quickly recovers, a flood of TCP connection requests, followed by application data, quickly saturating the 64-kbps link from the host site to the authorization center. Because the remote sites have a full T1, they send at this speed. They have no information letting them know that the authorization center can take in only 64 kbps. FRTS enables you to control bursts of traffic that can occur during these situations.

Let's recall the terms discussed earlier and define them in terms of relevance toward FRTS:

- **Committed burst (Bc)**—The amount of data to send in each Tc interval, measured in bits. Usually set to 1/8 of CIR.

- **Excess burst (Be)**—The number of excess bits to transmit during the first interval over and above Bc, only if *credit* is built up. The Be bit gets set to whatever the burst eligible is set for in the Frame Relay switch. The Be bit is optional. In the field, these parameters are supplied from the WAN provider.

- **Committed Information Rate (CIR)**—The average rate that you want to send traffic out. In this case, this is not that same as the CIR provided by the carrier, but it should be set the same as the physical port speed.

- **Time Interval (Tc)**—Time interval, which cannot exceed 125ms. Tc = Bc/CIR.

- **MinCIR**—The minimum amount of data to be sent during periods of congestion. This value should be set to your actual CIR that the carrier provides you.

- **Byte increment**—This value equals Bc/8. It is the amount of data to send during each time interval.

- **FECN/BECN**—There are two bits in the address field of each frame for explicit signaling, FECN and BECN. The bits might be set by the frame provider when it detects congestion. The frame provider must not clear the bits if it receives a frame with one or both bits set, thereby providing true signaling to the end user.

  — **Backward-explicit congestion notification (BECN)**—This tells the end user that congestion-avoidance procedures should be initiated for traffic destined toward the opposite direction from which the frame was received. Further frames that the user transmits on this VC in this direction might encounter congestion.

  — **Forward-explicit congestion notification (FECN)**—This tells the end user that congestion-avoidance procedures should be initiated for traffic destined toward the same direction from which the frame was received. It also means that this frame on this VC has encountered congestion.

When traffic shaping is enabled, the router checks to see whether there is a *token* or credit available before sending the packet. The token bucket has tokens put in at a certain rate. The bucket itself also has a predefined capacity. If the bucket is already full of tokens, new tokens cannot be held and made available for future packets. Therefore, at any given time, the burst from the router is about the same size as the token bucket. If there are not enough tokens for the router to send a packet, the packet waits until the bucket has enough tokens, or it is discarded. Before the packet is sent out an interface, it is sent through the queue that has been set up for that VC. The default queue is FIFO, but custom queuing or priority queuing also can be used. For more information on queuing, see *Cisco IOS 12.0 Quality of Service*, from Cisco Press.

BECN response mode is one form of traffic shaping. With BECN response mode, traffic shaping is enabled. If a router receives any BECNs during the current time interval, it decreases its transmit rate by 25 percent. This rate continues to drop by 25 percent once per Tc interval until the traffic rate gets to MinCIR, where it levels out. When the traffic rate has decremented, it takes 16 time intervals with no BECNs before it starts to increase the traffic rate. Traffic increases by a rate of (Be+Bc)/16 when it starts to increase.

With this background information in mind, you can move on to the specifics of configuring FRTS. Use the following process to configure Frame Relay traffic shaping:

Step 1   Enable Frame Relay traffic shaping on the interface. Apply the **frame-relay traffic-shaping** command to the serial interface.

Step 2   Create a Frame Relay map class for each VC that you want to apply shaping to. Multiple VCs can use the same map class. Use the **frame-relay class** *class_name_1* [**in** | **out**] command under each VC. Use the global command **map-class frame-relay** *class_name_1* to define the map class. When configuring the map class, the in/out options are optional. If it is omitted, the value applies to inbound and outbound traffic.

Step 3 After you are in the map class configuration mode, configure the following options:

— **frame-relay adaptive-shaping [becn | foresight]**—You will be using BECN shaping; foresight is available if you are connecting to a Cisco IGX or BPX switch.

— **frame-relay cir [in | out]** *bps*—Set this speed to be the physical port speed of the circuit.

— **frame-relay bc [in | out]** *bps*—This is the amount of data sent per interval. A good number to use is 1/8 CIR of the remote circuit.

— **frame-relay be out** *bps*—This is the number of extra bits remaining from previous bursts that will be sent on the first interval. This should not exceed the port speed of the remote router.

— **frame-relay mincir [in | out]** *bps*—This is what the VC will throttle down to when it receives BECNs. Set this value to the actual CIR that the carrier provides to you.

— *(Optional)* **frame-relay traffic-rate** *cir peak*_speed—You can use this command as a shortcut for Steps 2 through 5. For CIR, use the value that the carrier has subscribed on the link. The peak speed should not exceed the physical link speed of the remote router.

Step 4 (Optional) Apply any custom queuing or priority queuing to the map class, not to the interface. FIFO is the default queuing mechanism; apply custom queuing or priority queuing only if you have to. Use the following commands:

```
frame-relay custom-queue-list list_number
frame-relay priority-group list_number
```

Practical Example: Configuring Frame Relay Traffic Shaping

Figure 5-6 shows a Frame Relay point-to-point network.

In this model, you want to prevent the marlin router from flooding the glock router's 64-kbps PVC. At the same time, you want to shape traffic to the sig router. The port speed on the marlin and sig router is 1.544 Mbps, and it is 64 Kbps on the glock router. The PVC between the marlin and glock routers has a 32-kbps CIR set by the carrier. The PVC between the marlin router and the sig router is 512 kbps.

Figure 5-6   *Frame Relay Traffic Shaping*

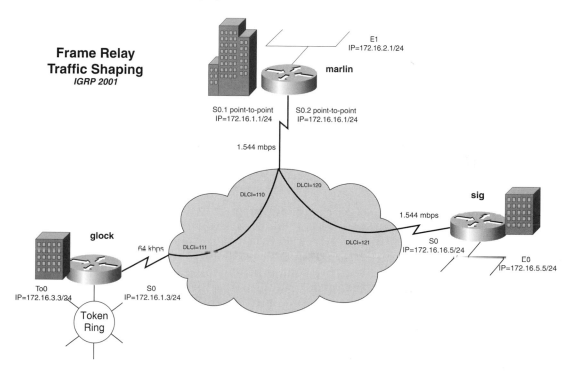

Example 5-16 shows the first portion of the configuration for the marlin router.

Example 5-16 *FRTS: marlin Router Configuration*

```
marlin(config)#int serial 0
marlin(config-if)#frame-relay traffic-shaping        ←Enable FRTS
marlin(config-if)#int s0.1
marlin(config-subif)#frame-relay class 64kb          ←Set map class
marlin(config-subif)#exit
marlin(config)#int s0.2
marlin(config-subif)#frame-relay class t1            ←Set other map class
marlin(config-subif)#^Z
```

Now, you can define two map classes, one called 64kb and the other called t1. Example 5-17 demonstrates the setting of a map classes.

Example 5-17 *Setting the Map Clas*

```
marlin(config)#map-class frame-relay 64kb
marlin(config-map-class)#frame-relay adaptive-shaping becn    ←Enable BENC response
                          mode
marlin(config-map-class)#frame-relay cir 1544000    ←Set to physical port speed
marlin(config-map-class)#frame-relay bc 8000        ←set to remote port speed/8
marlin(config-map-class)#frame-relay be 64000      ←Initial burst
marlin(config-map-class)#frame-relay mincir 32000   ←Carrier enforced CIR
marlin(config-map-class)#exit
marlin(config)#map-class frame-relay t1
marlin(config-map-class)#frame-relay adaptive-shaping becn    ←Enable BENC response
                          mode
marlin(config-map-class)#frame-relay cir 1544000    ←Set to physical port speed
marlin(config-map-class)#frame-relay bc 8000        ←set to remote port speed/8
marlin(config-map-class)#frame-relay be 64000      ← Initial burst
marlin(config-map-class)#frame-relay mincir 512000    ←Carrier enforced CIR
marlin(config-map-class)#
```

To verify your configuration, use the **show traffic-shape** command and add the DLCI number to enhance the **show frame-relay pvc** *dlci_number* command. Example 5-18 lists the output of these commands, respectively.

Example 5-18 **show traffic-shape** *and* **show frame-relay pvc** *Command Output*

```
marlin#show traffic-shape
          Access Target   Byte    Sustain   Excess    Interval  Increment Adap
t
I/F       List   Rate     Limit   bits/int  bits/int  (ms)      (bytes)   Acti
ve
Se0              56000    7875    56000     56000     125       875       BECN
Se0.1            1544000  10412   8000      64000     12        2412      BECN
Se0.2            1544000  10412   8000      64000     12        2412      BECN
marlin#
marlin#
marlin#show frame pvc 120

PVC Statistics for interface Serial0 (Frame Relay DTE)

DLCI = 120, DLCI USAGE = LOCAL, PVC STATUS = ACTIVE, INTERFACE = Serial0.2

    input pkts 904          output pkts 3229       in bytes 94596
    out bytes 477394        dropped pkts 0         in FECN pkts 0
    in BECN pkts 0          out FECN pkts 0        out BECN pkts 0
    in DE pkts 0            out DE pkts 0
    out bcast pkts 3204      out bcast bytes 474980
```

Example 5-18 **show traffic-shape** *and* **show frame-relay pvc** *Command Output (Continued)*

```
 Shaping adapts to BECN
 pvc create time 19:25:28, last time pvc status changed 19:16:38
 cir 1544000    bc 19300     be 64000      limit 10412   interval 12
 mincir 512000    byte increment 2412   BECN response yes
 pkts 3160        bytes 468932     pkts delayed 0         bytes delayed 0
 shaping inactive
 Serial0.2 dlci 120 is first come first serve default queueing

 Output queue 0/40, 0 drop, 0 dequeued
marlin#
```

With the aid of these commands, you can verify that you entered the configuration properly. In this example, shaping is listed as *inactive* because no BECNs have been received from the frame switch.

Lab 13: Configuring Frame Relay Networks and Controlling Frame Relay ARP—Part I

Practical Scenario

We began this chapter stating how prevalent Frame Relay had become in recent years. If you haven't worked on Frame Relay in the field, chances are good that you will. As common as Frame Relay networks are, one thing that isn't common is each network's individual design. Some networks strictly deploy subinterfaces in a point-to-point manner, whereas others might have more of a partially meshed network. This practice lab enables you to configure multiple types of Frame Relay networks.

Lab Exercise

Dr. Evil is in the process of implementing what he refers to as the "Evil Information Freeway" (EIF). The EIF is a Frame Relay network used to connect various factions of the evil empire. Because you are a henchman for the cruel Dr. Evil, you will have additional guidelines to abide by. Use the following parameters as your design guidelines:

- Use the IP subnet 10.10.1.8/29 for the Frame Relay network between the Secret Volcano Lair (sv_lair), Scott's house (scotts_house), and mini-me (mini_me).

- Use the IP subnet of 192.168.1.4/30 for the Frame Relay link between sv_lair and starbucks_90210.

- Use EIGRP as the routing protocol for IP. Use 666 as the autonomous system.

- The frame switch will have a PVC from scotts_house to mini_me. Do not allow any traffic to pass on the PVC directly from scotts_house to mini_me. All traffic must go through the sv_lair first.

- Per Dr. Evil, you can use subinterfaces only on the sv_lair router—or face the consequences.

Lab Objectives

- Configure the EIF network as depicted in Figure 5-7. Configure IP as denoted in the diagram. The LAN topology type is not important in this lab.

- Use Frame Relay as the data link layer protocol on the WAN.

- Prevent dynamic mapping of the PVC between scotts_house and mini_me. Any traceroutes preformed from mini_me to scotts_house, and vice versa, should go through the sv_lair router.

Equipment Needed

- Five Cisco routers, connected through V.35 back-to-back cables or in a similar manner. One router will serve as a frame switch and require four serial ports.

- Four LAN segments, provided through hubs or switches. The LAN segments for mini_me and starbucks_90210 can be substituted with loopbacks.

Physical Layout and Prestaging

- Configure a frame switch to provide the PVCs, as listed in the diagram. See Chapter 1 if you need assistance in configuring a Frame Relay switch. Example 5-19 provides a sample frame switch configuration.

- Connect the hubs and serial cables to the routers as shown in Figure 5-7.

- Connect three Ethernet hubs to form three LAN segments, as shown in Figure 5-7. scotts_house can use either Token Ring or Ethernet for the purposes of this exercise.

Figure 5-7 *EIF Frame Relay Network*

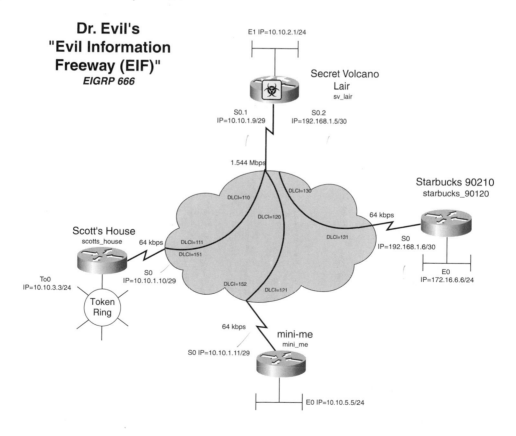

Example 5-19 *Frame Relay Switch Configuration*

```
hostname frame_switch
!
frame-relay switching
!
interface Ethernet0
 no ip address
 shutdown
!
interface Serial0
 no ip address
 encapsulation frame-relay
 no fair-queue
 clockrate 148000
 frame-relay intf-type dce
 frame-relay route 121 interface Serial1 120
 frame-relay route 152 interface Serial5 151
!
interface Serial1
 no ip address
 encapsulation frame-relay
 clockrate 148000
 frame-relay intf-type dce
 frame-relay route 110 interface Serial5 111
 frame-relay route 120 interface Serial0 121
 frame-relay route 130 interface Serial3 131
!
interface Serial2
 no ip address
 shutdown
!
interface Serial3
 no ip address
 encapsulation frame-relay
 clockrate 64000
 frame-relay intf-type dce
 frame-relay route 131 interface Serial1 130
!
interface Serial4
 no ip address
 shutdown
!
interface Serial5
 no ip address
 encapsulation frame-relay
 clockrate 64000
 frame-relay intf-type dce
 frame-relay route 111 interface Serial1 110
 frame-relay route 151 interface Serial0 152
!
```

Lab 13: Configuring Frame Relay Networks and Controlling Frame Relay ARP—Part II

Lab Walkthrough

Attach the four routers in a back-to-back manner to the Frame Relay network cloud. Use V.35 cables or CSU/DSUs with crossover cables to connect the routers to the Frame Relay switch. Create the four LANs by the use of switches or hubs/MAUs.

When the physical connections are complete, assign IP addresses to all LAN interfaces, as depicted in Figure 5-7. Be sure that you can **ping** the router's local LAN interface before moving on.

Begin with the sv_lair router, where you can use subinterfaces. Because the scotts_house, mini_me, and sv_lair routers all have an interface on the same IP subnet, you must create a multipoint interface on sv_lair to accommodate them. There is an additional IP subnet between the sv_lair router and the starbucks_90210 router. For this subnet, you will create an additional point-to-point interface on the Serial 0 interface. With this in mind, you can begin the four-step process for configuring Frame Relay.

First, you define Frame Relay encapsulation on the Serial 0 interface through the **encapsulation frame-relay** interface command. When the encapsulation is entered, you can define the subinterfaces. You need to configure one as a multipoint and one as a point-to-point subinterface, as previously mentioned. Example 5-20 demonstrates the configuration of Step 1 on the sv_lair router.

Example 5-20 *Configuring Frame Encapsulation and Subinterfaces*

```
sv_lair(config)#int s0
sv_lair(config-if)#encapsulation frame-relay
sv_lair(config-if)#exit
sv_lair(config)#int s0.1 multipoint
sv_lair(config-subif)#exit
sv_lair(config)#int s0.2 point-to-point
sv_lair(config-subif)#^Z
sv_lair#
```

The next step in configuring Frame Relay is to set the LMI type. In this case, the LMI type is Cisco, and you are using LMI autosense, so there is no need to do any additional configuration for Step 2. This applies to all the routers in the network.

Step 3 requires the specification of dynamic or static address mapping. The EIF will deploy both kinds of addressing. The sv_lair router uses a multipoint network on interface s0.1, which requires static mapping. You will need one **frame-relay map** statement per protocol per destination site. One **frame-relay map** statement will point to IP address 10.10.1.10 on DLCI 110, while the other will point to IP address 10.10.1.11 on DLCI 120. Example 5-21 shows the configuration necessary to accomplish this.

Example 5-21 *Configuring the Multipoint Interface*

```
sv_lair(config)#int s0.1
sv_lair(config-subif)#ip address 10.10.1.9 255.255.255.248
sv_lair(config-subif)#frame-relay map ip 10.10.1.10 110 broadcast
sv_lair(config-subif)#frame-relay map ip 10.10.1.11 120 broadcast
sv_lair(config-subif)#exit
sv_lair(config)#int s0.2
sv_lair(config-subif)#ip address 192.168.1.5 255.255.255.252
sv_lair(config-subif)#frame-relay interface-dlci 130
sv_lair(config-fr-dlci)#^Z
```

To configure the point-to-point interface, s0.2, use Inverse ARP to resolve the network address. Therefore, the only configuration that you need to make is to add the **interface-dlci** command. The starbucks_90210 router requires only an **encapsulation frame-relay** statement and an **interface-dlci 131** statement.

Before you can address any protocol-specific issues, you must finish bringing up the Frame Relay network on all sides. Before trying to configure a routing protocol, you want to get the network to the point at which the router can **ping** all of its local WAN interfaces, as well as its local LAN interfaces.

scotts_house is not allowed to use subinterfaces or the PVC to mini_me. As soon as both sides of the link between scotts_house and mini_me become active, a dynamic PVC is built by Inverse ARP. To prevent this from happening, you need to shut down the link and disable Inverse ARP. You also need to add two **frame-relay map** statements for IP. They will use the same DLCI but will point to two different IP addresses; basically, they will tell the router to forward all IP traffic out DLCI 111. Example 5-22 lists the configuration for the scotts_house router.

Example 5-22 *Configuration of scotts_house*

```
scotts_house(config)#interface s0
scotts_house(config-if)#encapsulation frame-relay
scotts_house(config-if)#no frame-relay inverse-arp        ←Disables Inverse-ARP
scotts_house(config-if)#no arp frame-relay                ←Disables ARP
scotts_house(config-if)#ip address 10.10.1.10 255.255.255.248
scotts_house(config-if)#frame-relay map ip 10.10.1.9 111 broadcast
scotts_house(config-if)#frame-relay map ip 10.10.1.11 111 broadcast
```

The configuration of mini_me is similar. It requires two **frame-relay map** statements pointing at IP addresses 10.10.1.9 and 10.10.1.10 out DLCI 121. Example 5-23 demonstrates the configuration of mini_me.

Example 5-23 *Configuration of mini_me*

```
mini_me(config)#int s0
mini_me(config-if)#encapsulation frame-relay
mini_me(config-if)#no frame-relay inverse-arp
mini_me(config-if)#no arp frame-relay
mini_me(config-if)#ip address 10.10.1.11 255.255.255.248
mini_me(config-if)#frame-relay map ip 10.10.1.10 121 broadcast
mini_me(config-if)#frame-relay map ip 10.10.1.9 121 broadcast
```

Perform a **show frame-relay map** command on scotts_house and mini_me. Verify that there is not a dynamic PVC on DLCI 151 or 150, as shown in Example 5-24.

Example 5-24 *Correct* **show frame-relay map** *Command Output with No ARP*

```
scotts_house#show frame-relay map
Serial0 (up): ip 10.10.1.9 dlci 111(0x6F,0x18F0), static,
              broadcast,
              CISCO, status defined, active
Serial0 (up): ip 10.10.1.11 dlci 111(0x6F,0x18F0), static,
              broadcast,
              CISCO, status defined, active
scotts_house#
```

If your **frame-relay map** statement looks like Example 5-25, you are using Inverse ARP.

Example 5-25 *Incorrect* **show frame-relay map**, *Using Inverse ARP*

```
scotts_house#show frame-relay map
Serial0 (up): ip 10.10.1.9 dlci 111(0x6F,0x18F0), dynamic,
              broadcast,, status defined, active
Serial0 (up): ip 10.10.1.11 dlci 151(0x97,0x2470), dynamic,
              broadcast,, status defined, active
```

To test your **frame-relay map** statements, **ping** the local routers 10.10.1.9, 10.10.1.10, and 10.10.1.11.

Step 4 of the Frame Relay configuration process (the final step), involves addressing any routing protocol-specific issues. Start by configuring EIGRP on all routers, and use 666 as the Autonomous System ID. On the sv_lair and starbucks_90210 routers, you need to add two **network** statements under EIGRP. The other routers in the network need only the **network 10.0.0.0** and the **no auto-summary** statements. The configuration for sv_lair looks like Example 5-26. For further information on the EIGRP configuration, see Chapter 11, "Hybrid: Enhanced Interior Gateway Routing Protocol (EIGRP)," later in this book.

Example 5-26 *EIGRP Configuration for sv_lair and starbucks_90210*

```
router eigrp 666
 network 10.0.0.0
 network 192.168.1.0
 no auto-summary
!
```

The configuration might appear to be complete at this time—EIGRP neighbors are formed and routes are being exchanged. However, upon close examination of the routing tables of scotts_house and mini_me in Example 5-27, you'll find that sv_lair is not propagating its routes properly. The sv_lair is not forwarding scotts_house routes to mini_me, and it is not forwarding mini_me routes to scotts_house. But sv_lair is forwarding starbucks_90120 routes and its local routes to scotts_house and mini_me.

Example 5-27 *Examining the Routing Tables*

```
scotts_house#show ip route
Codes: C - connected, S - static, I - IGRP, R - RIP, M - mobile, B - BGP
       D - EIGRP, EX - EIGRP external, O - OSPF, IA - OSPF inter area
       N1 - OSPF NSSA external type 1, N2 - OSPF NSSA external type 2
       E1 - OSPF external type 1, E2 - OSPF external type 2, E - EGP
       i - IS-IS, L1 - IS-IS level-1, L2 - IS-IS level-2, * - candidate default
       U - per-user static route, o - ODR
       T - traffic engineered route

Gateway of last resort is not set

     10.0.0.0/8 is variably subnetted, 4 subnets, 2 masks
D       10.10.2.0/24 [90/2195456] via 10.10.1.9, 00:53:29, Serial0
C       10.10.3.0/24 is directly connected, TokenRing0
D       10.10.6.0/24 [90/2707456] via 10.10.1.9, 00:52:27, Serial0
C       10.10.1.8/29 is directly connected, Serial0
     192.168.1.0/30 is subnetted, 1 subnets
D       192.168.1.4 [90/2681856] via 10.10.1.9, 00:53:29, Serial0
scotts_house#

<<<<<no 10.10.5.0 subnet>>>>>

mini_me#show ip route
Codes: C - connected, S - static, I - IGRP, R - RIP, M - mobile, B - BGP
       D - EIGRP, EX - EIGRP external, O - OSPF, IA - OSPF inter area
       N1 - OSPF NSSA external type 1, N2 - OSPF NSSA external type 2
       E1 - OSPF external type 1, E2 - OSPF external type 2, E - EGP
       i - IS-IS, L1 - IS-IS level-1, L2 - IS-IS level-2, * - candidate default
```

Example 5-27 *Examining the Routing Tables (Continued)*

```
            U - per-user static route, o - ODR
            T - traffic engineered route

Gateway of last resort is not set

     10.0.0.0/8 is variably subnetted, 4 subnets, 2 masks
D       10.10.2.0/24 [90/2195456] via 10.10.1.9, 00:53:38, Serial0
C       10.10.5.0/24 is directly connected, Ethernet0
D       10.10.6.0/24 [90/2707456] via 10.10.1.9, 00:52:37, Serial0
C       10.10.1.8/29 is directly connected, Serial0
     192.168.1.0/30 is subnetted, 1 subnets
D       192.168.1.4 [90/2681856] via 10.10.1.9, 00:53:38, Serial0
mini_me#

<<<<<no 10.10.3.0 route>>>>>

─────────────────────────────────────────────────────────────────────
sv_lair#show ip route
Codes: C - connected, S - static, I - IGRP, R - RIP, M - mobile, B - BGP
       D - EIGRP, EX - EIGRP external, O - OSPF, IA - OSPF inter area
       N1 - OSPF NSSA external type 1, N2 - OSPF NSSA external type 2
       E1 - OSPF external type 1, E2 - OSPF external type 2, E - EGP
       i - IS-IS, L1 - IS-IS level-1, L2 - IS-IS level-2, * - candidate default
       U - per-user static route, o - ODR

Gateway of last resort is not set

     10.0.0.0/8 is variably subnetted, 5 subnets, 2 masks
C       10.10.2.0/24 is directly connected, Ethernet0
D       10.10.3.0/24 [90/2185984] via 10.10.1.10, 00:53:10, Serial0.1
D       10.10.5.0/24 [90/2195456] via 10.10.1.11, 00:53:10, Serial0.1
D       10.10.6.0/24 [90/2195456] via 192.168.1.6, 00:52:08, Serial0.2
C       10.10.1.8/29 is directly connected, Serial0.1
     192.168.1.0/30 is subnetted, 1 subnets
C       192.168.1.4 is directly connected, Serial0.2
sv_lair#

<<<<<all routes present>>>>>
```

If you haven't guessed it, the reason for this is because of split horizon. Remember, the rule: A route will not be forwarded back out the same interface or subinterface on which it was received. To resolve this issue, disable split horizon for EIGRP on the sv_lair router. This is accomplished by adding the following command under the s0.1 interface on sv_lair:

```
sv_lair(config-subif)#no ip split-horizon eigrp 666
```

Example 5-28 lists the routing table of scotts_house after the change. Notice now that the 10.10.5.0 route appears.

Example 5-28 **show ip route** *Command Output on the scotts_house Router After Disabling Split Horizon*

```
scotts_house#show ip route
<<<text omitted>>>
Gateway of last resort is not set

     10.0.0.0/8 is variably subnetted, 5 subnets, 2 masks
D       10.10.2.0/24 [90/2195456] via 10.10.1.9, 00:00:09, Serial0
C       10.10.3.0/24 is directly connected, TokenRing0
D       10.10.5.0/24 [90/2707456] via 10.10.1.9, 00:00:09, Serial0
D       10.10.6.0/24 [90/2707456] via 10.10.1.9, 00:00:09, Serial0
C       10.10.1.8/29 is directly connected, Serial0
     192.168.1.0/30 is subnetted, 1 subnets
D       192.168.1.4 [90/2681856] via 10.10.1.9, 00:00:09, Serial0
scotts_house#
```

Another command that will help verify whether EIGRP is working properly is the **show ip eigrp neighbor** command. Performing this command on the sv_lair router, you can see three EIGRP neighbors, one for each remote site. Example 5-29 illustrates the output of this command. Chapter 11 discusses this command and EIGRP neighbors in greater detail.

Example 5-29 **show ip eigrp neighbor** *Command Output*

```
sv_lair#show ip eigrp neighbors
IP-EIGRP neighbors for process 666
H   Address                Interface     Hold Uptime    SRTT   RTO  Q  Seq
                                         (sec)          (ms)       Cnt Num
0   192.168.1.6            Se0.2         128 00:04:34    32    200  0  8
2   10.10.1.10             Se0.1         179 00:08:19    33    200  0  7
1   10.10.1.11             Se0.1         161 00:08:54    24    200  0  7
sv_lair#
```

Example 5-30 lists the relevant portions of all router configurations for this lab.

Example 5-30 *Complete Configuration Listings*

```
hostname sv_lair
!
interface Ethernet0
 ip address 10.10.2.1 255.255.255.0
 media-type 10BaseT
!
<<<text omitted>>>
!
interface Serial0
 no ip address
```

Example 5-30 *Complete Configuration Listings (Continued)*

```
 encapsulation frame-relay
 no ip mroute-cache
!
interface Serial0.1 multipoint
 ip address 10.10.1.9 255.255.255.248
 no ip split-horizon eigrp 666
 frame-relay map ip 10.10.1.10 110 broadcast
 frame-relay map ip 10.10.1.11 120 broadcast
!
interface Serial0.2 point-to-point
 ip address 192.168.1.5 255.255.255.252
 frame-relay interface-dlci 130
!
<<<text omitted>>>
!
router eigrp 666
 network 10.0.0.0
 network 192.168.1.0
 no auto-summary
!
```

```
hostname scotts_house
!
ip subnet-zero
!
 interface Serial0
 ip address 10.10.1.10 255.255.255.248
 no ip directed-broadcast
 encapsulation frame-relay
 no ip mroute-cache
 no arp frame-relay
 frame-relay map ip 10.10.1.9 111 broadcast
 frame-relay map ip 10.10.1.11 111 broadcast
 no frame-relay inverse-arp
!
interface TokenRing0
 ip address 10.10.3.3 255.255.255.0
 no ip directed-broadcast
 ring-speed 16
!
router eigrp 666
 network 10.0.0.0
```

```
hostname mini_me
!
ip subnet-zero
!
 interface Ethernet0
 ip address 10.10.5.5 255.255.255.0
 no ip directed-broadcast
!
```

continues

Example 5-30 *Complete Configuration Listings (Continued)*

```
interface Serial0
 ip address 10.10.1.11 255.255.255.248
 no ip directed-broadcast
 encapsulation frame-relay
 no ip mroute-cache
 no arp frame-relay
 frame-relay map ip 10.10.1.9 121 broadcast
 frame-relay map ip 10.10.1.10 121 broadcast
 no frame-relay inverse-arp
!
interface Serial1
 no ip address
 no ip directed-broadcast
 shutdown
!
interface BRI0
 no ip address
 no ip directed-broadcast
 shutdown
!
router eigrp 666
 network 10.0.0.0
```

```
hostname mini_me
!
ip subnet-zero
!
 interface Ethernet0
 ip address 10.10.5.5 255.255.255.0
 no ip directed-broadcast
!
interface Serial0
 ip address 10.10.1.11 255.255.255.248
 no ip directed-broadcast
 encapsulation frame-relay
 no ip mroute-cache
 no arp frame-relay
 frame-relay map ip 10.10.1.9 121 broadcast
 frame-relay map ip 10.10.1.10 121 broadcast
 no frame-relay inverse-arp
!
router eigrp 666
 network 10.0.0.0
```

```
hostname starbucks_90210
!
interface Ethernet0
 ip address 10.10.6.6 255.255.255.0
!
interface Serial0
```

Example 5-30 *Complete Configuration Listings (Continued)*

```
 ip address 192.168.1.6 255.255.255.252
 encapsulation frame-relay
 frame-relay interface-dlci 131
!
<<text omitted>>>
!
router eigrp 666
 network 10.0.0.0
 network 192.168.1.0
 no auto-summary
```

Lab 14: Configuring Frame Relay Networks, Traffic Shaping, OSPF, & DLSw/LLC2—Part I

Practical Scenario

Most networks don't grow at an even, incremental basis. Some portions of the network might have faster newer links, while other parts of it could be older and slower. Oversubscription of links can be a common problem in Frame Relay networks. Traffic shaping helps address this problem. Enabling traffic shaping allows greater control over bursty traffic and the amount of data sent out an interface at any given time. This greatly helps the problem of high-speed links pushing too much data toward lower-speed links. This practice lab challenges you to configure traffic shaping in a multipoint Frame Relay network.

Lab Exercise

The Jet Propulsion Laboratory (JPL) receives large graphic images from several telescopes. When the JPL receives these images, it immediately downloads them to Cape Canaveral in Florida and Houston, Texas. These images can be large at times and quickly saturate the links of the two NASA sites. To control these sudden bursts of large data, the JPL wants to deploy Frame Relay traffic shaping (FRTS). Use the following guidelines for your design and FRTS configuration:

- Use the IP network of 128.10.0.0 for all your addressing.

- Allow for only 14 host addresses on the JPL LAN.

- Use a 29-bit subnet mask on the WAN.

- Use 24-bit addressing on the remaining LANs.

- Use OSPF as the routing protocol for IP. Assign the areas as depicted in Figure 5-8.

- Configure Frame Relay traffic shaping using the following guidelines: The local port speed of JPL router is 1.544 Mbps. The CIR on the PVC to nasa_houston is 32 kbps. The local port speed of nasa_houston is 64 kbps. Configure FRTS to optimize for the slowest link or the nasa_houston pvc.

- (Optional): Configure DLSw lite between the two NASA routers' Ethernet segments, and use LLC2 as the encapsulation type.

Lab Objectives

- Configure the network as depicted in Figure 5-8. Configure IP by using the previously stated guidelines.

- Use Frame Relay as data link layer protocol on the WAN.

- Configure Frame Relay traffic shaping on the JPL router by using the previously stated guidelines.

- Optional: Configure DLSw between the two NASA routers; use Frame Relay as the peer type.

Equipment Needed

- Four Cisco routers, connected through V.35 back-to-back cable or in a similar manner. One router will serve as a frame switch and require three serial ports.

- Three LAN segments, provided through hubs or switches.

Physical Layout and Prestaging

- Configure a frame switch to provide the PVCs as listed in Figure 5-8. See Chapter 1 if you need assistance in configuring a Frame Relay switch. Example 5-31 provides a sample frame switch configuration.

- Connect the hubs and serial cables to the routers, as shown in Figure 5-8.

- Connect three Ethernet hubs form three LAN segments, as shown in Figure 5-8.

Example 5-31 *Frame Relay Switch Configuration*

```
hostname frame_switch
!
frame-relay switching
!
<<<text omitted>>>
!
interface Serial0
 no ip address
 encapsulation frame-relay
 no fair-queue
 clockrate 148000
 frame-relay lmi-type cisco
 frame-relay intf-type dce
 frame-relay route 121 interface Serial1 120
 frame-relay route 165 interface Serial3 166
!
interface Serial1
```

continues

Example 5-31 *Frame Relay Switch Configuration (Continued)*

```
 no ip address
 encapsulation frame-relay
 clockrate 148000
 frame-relay lmi-type ansi
 frame-relay intf-type dce
 frame-relay route 120 interface Serial0 121
 frame-relay route 130 interface Serial3 131
!
<<<text omitted>>>
!
interface Serial3
 no ip address
 encapsulation frame-relay
 clockrate 64000
 frame-relay lmi-type ansi
 frame-relay intf-type dce
 frame-relay route 131 interface Serial1 130
 frame-relay route 166 interface Serial0 165
```

Figure 5-8 *NASA Frame Relay Network*

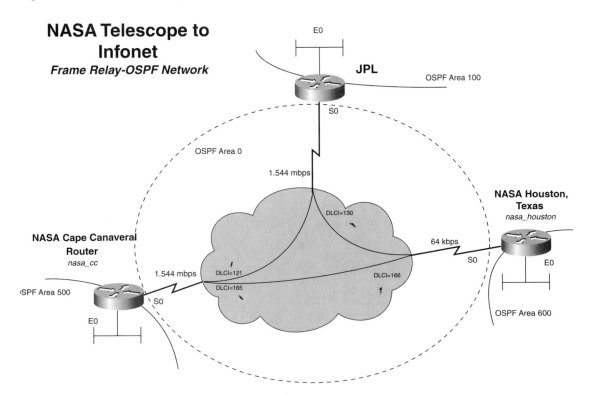

Lab 14: Configuring Frame Relay Networks, Traffic Shaping, OSPF, & DLSw/LLC2—Part II

Lab Walkthrough

Attach the three routers in a back-to-back manner to the frame switch. Use V.35 cables or CSU/DSUs with crossover cables to connect the routers to the frame switch. Create the three LANs by the use of switches or hubs/MAUs.

This lab requires you to configure IP and OSPF. The order in which you will configure the network will be first the LANs for IP, second the WAN for IP, and finally OSPF.

When the physical connections are complete, assign IP addresses to all LAN interfaces, as depicted in Figure 5-9. Be sure that you can **ping** the router's local LAN interface before moving on.

Figure 5-9   *IP Addressing Map*

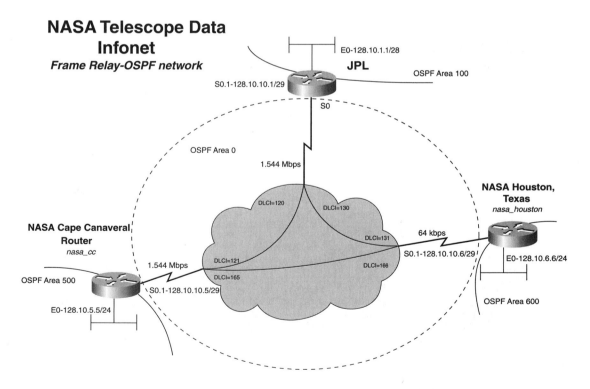

Beginning with the JPL router, follow the four-step process for configuring Frame Relay. First, set the encapsulation type on the s0 interface to **frame-relay**. The second step is to set the LMI type. In this case, it is ANSI. Therefore, you need to statically set it to ANSI with the **frame-relay lmi-type ansi** command. The third step involves statically mapping IP addresses to DLCIs. The JPL router requires two **frame-relay map** statements, one pointing out DLCI 120 for IP address 128.10.10.5, and one pointing out DLCI 130 for IP address 128.10.10.6. Example 5-32 shows the configuration for the JPL router up to this point.

Example 5-32 *JPL Frame Relay Configuration*

```
interface Serial0
 no ip address
 encapsulation frame-relay
 no ip mroute-cache
 frame-relay lmi-type ansi
!
interface Serial0.1 multipoint
 ip address 128.10.10.1 255.255.255.248
 frame-relay map ip 128.10.10.5 120 broadcast
 frame-relay map ip 128.10.10.6 130 broadcast
```

Before you address any routing issues, as Step 4 of the Frame Relay configuration process indicates, you should configure the other two legs of the Frame Relay network.

The nasa_cc and nasa_Houston configurations are similar. Each site will have one **frame-relay map** statement pointing at the jpl router and one pointing at the other nasa site. Example 5-33 lists the nasa_cc and nasa_houston Frame Relay configurations, respectively.

Example 5-33 *Frame Relay Configurations for the NASA Routers*

```
hostname nasa_cc
 interface Serial0
 no ip address
 no ip directed-broadcast
 encapsulation frame-relay
 no ip mroute-cache
 frame-relay lmi-type cisco
!
interface Serial0.1 multipoint
 ip address 128.10.10.5 255.255.255.248
 no ip directed-broadcast
 frame-relay map ip 128.10.10.1 121 broadcast
 frame-relay map ip 128.10.10.6 165 broadcast

hostname nasa_houston
!
interface Serial0
 no ip address
 encapsulation frame-relay
```

Example 5-33 *Frame Relay Configurations for the NASA Routers*

```
!
interface Serial0.1 multipoint
 ip address 128.10.10.6 255.255.255.248
 frame-relay map ip 128.10.10.1 131 broadcast
 frame-relay map ip 128.10.10.5 166 broadcast
!
```

To test the configuration of the **frame-relay map** statements, **ping** the remote serial interface of the NASA routers from the jpl router. When you have connectivity to all your local devices, LAN and WAN, you can begin to configure a routing protocol.

To learn more about configuring OSPF over Frame Relay, skip forward to Chapter 12, "Link-State Protocols: Open Shortest Path First (OSPF)." This lab covers only minor configuration details.

Starting with the jpl router, configure OSPF by adding two **network** statements, one for LAN in Area 100 and one for the WAN in Area 0. Be careful to use a precise wildcard mask of 0.0.0.7 for the LAN and 0.0.0.15 for the WAN. To ensure that adjacencies are built, add a **neighbor** statement for each NASA site. Example 5-34 shows the OSPF configuration for the routers.

Example 5-34 *OSPF Configurations*

```
hostname jpl
!
router ospf 2001
 network 128.10.1.0 0.0.0.15 area 100
 network 128.10.10.0 0.0.0.7 area 0
 neighbor 128.10.10.5 priority 1
 neighbor 128.10.10.6 priority 1
!
─────────────────────────────────────────────
hostname nasa_cc
!
router ospf 2001
 network 128.10.5.0 0.0.0.255 area 500
 network 128.10.10.0 0.0.0.15 area 0
 neighbor 128.10.10.6 priority 1
 neighbor 128.10.10.1 priority 1
!
─────────────────────────────────────────────
hostname nasa_houston
!
router ospf 2001
 network 128.10.6.0 0.0.0.255 area 600
 network 128.10.10.0 0.0.0.7 area 0
 neighbor 128.10.10.5 priority 1
 neighbor 128.10.10.1 priority 1
```

At this point, you should have full IP connectivity. Test this by **ping**ing and viewing the OSPF neighbors with the **show ip ospf neighbors** command. Ensure that every router has two neighbors. If no adjacencies are formed, be sure to check the **network** statements and the IP addresses on the serial interface, along with the **frame-relay map** statements for configuration errors.

The final portion of the lab requires applying FRTS to the serial interface of the JPL router. To accomplish this, you must first enable FRTS and then configure and apply a Frame Relay map class to **frame-relay map** statements. To enable FRTS, use the command **frame-relay traffic-shaping** under the Serial 0 interface.

Next, you need to configure a map class for each PVC, depending on the values given. The key values that you need to set in each map class are as follows:

```
adaptive shaping becn
frame-relay cir
frame-relay bc
frame-relay be
frame-relay mincir
```

You need a map class called 64k, and you need to primarily define the pvc to nasa_houston. The map class has adaptive shaping BECN response mode enabled. The cir is 1544000. bc is 1/8 of the remote port speed, or 8000. The be field should be set not to exceed the other port speed of 64000. The be bit in this model is set to 64000; in the field, this value matches the QoS parameters that the WAN provider supplies. The mincir on this port is set to the actual CIR on the link. In this network, that is set at 32 kbps. Example 5-35 demonstrates the configuration needed for the 64k map class.

Example 5-35 *64k Frame Relay Map Class*

```
!
map-class frame-relay 64k
 frame-relay cir 1544000
 frame-relay bc 8000
 frame-relay be 64000
 frame-relay mincir 32000
 frame-relay adaptive-shaping becn
!
```

When the map class is defined, apply it to the PVC with the **frame-relay class** *class_name* command, specifically **frame-relay class 64k**. To verify that the map class is applied, perform a **show frame-relay pvc** command or the **show frame-relay pvc 130** command for more details, as in Example 5-36. Ensure that the values highlighted are equal to the ones that you entered.

Example 5-36 show frame-relay pvc 130 *Command Output*

```
jpl#show frame-relay pvc 130

PVC Statistics for interface Serial0 (Frame Relay DTE)

DLCI = 130, DLCI USAGE = LOCAL, PVC STATUS = ACTIVE, INTERFACE = Serial0.1

  input pkts 396          output pkts 391          in bytes 30732
  out bytes 30800         dropped pkts 0           in FECN pkts 0
  in BECN pkts 0          out FECN pkts 0          out BECN pkts 0
  in DE pkts 0            out DE pkts 0
  out bcast pkts 0        out bcast bytes 0
  Shaping adapts to BECN
  pvc create time 03:55:53, last time pvc status changed 02:07:28
  cir 1544000    bc 8000       be 64000     limit 9000    interval 5
  mincir 32000      byte increment 1000   BECN response yes
  pkts 225       bytes 17320      pkts delayed 0        bytes delayed 0
  shaping inactive
  Serial0.1 dlci 130 is first come first serve default queueing

  Output queue 0/40, 0 drop, 0 dequeued
jpl#
```

The optional portion of this lab calls for creating a DLSw with LLC2 encapsulation between the two NASA routers, using Frame Relay encapsulation. For the local peer, you can simply use the LAN address. You also need to create a remote peer, with Frame Relay encapsulation type. You will define a bridge group on Ethernet 0 and tie to this to the DLSw bridge group. Using the Frame Relay encapsulation type creates an LLC2 peer. To transport this type of traffic directly encapsulated in Frame Relay, you need to use the **frame-relay map llc** *dlci_number* **broadcast** command.

Example 5-37 lists the configuration for the nasa_cc and nasa_houston routers, respectively, highlighting the DLSw portions of the config.

Example 5-37 *DLSw over Frame Relay, NASA Configurations*

```
hostname nasa_cc
!
ip subnet-zero
 !
 dlsw local-peer peer-id 128.10.5.5
 dlsw remote-peer 0 frame-relay interface Serial0.1 165
 dlsw bridge-group 1
 !
 interface Ethernet0
 ip address 128.10.5.5 255.255.255.0
 no ip directed-broadcast
 bridge-group 1
 !
```

continues

Example 5-37 *DLSw over Frame Relay, NASA Configurations*

```
interface Serial0
 no ip address
 no ip directed-broadcast
 encapsulation frame-relay
 no ip mroute-cache
 frame-relay lmi-type cisco
!
interface Serial0.1 multipoint
 ip address 128.10.10.5 255.255.255.248
 no ip directed-broadcast
 frame-relay map llc2  165 broadcast
 frame-relay map ip 128.10.10.1 121 broadcast
 frame-relay map ip 128.10.10.6 165 broadcast
!
router ospf 2001
 network 128.10.5.0 0.0.0.255 area 500
 network 128.10.10.0 0.0.0.15 area 0
 neighbor 128.10.10.6 priority 1
 neighbor 128.10.10.1 priority 1
!
ip classless
!
bridge 1 protocol ieee
!
```

```
hostname nasa_houston
!
!
dlsw local-peer peer-id 128.10.6.6
dlsw remote-peer 0 frame-relay interface Serial0.1 166
dlsw bridge-group 1
!
interface Ethernet0
 ip address 128.10.6.6 255.255.255.0
 bridge-group 1
!
interface Serial0
 no ip address
 encapsulation frame-relay
!
interface Serial0.1 multipoint
 ip address 128.10.10.6 255.255.255.248
 frame-relay map llc2  166 broadcast
 frame-relay map ip 128.10.10.1 131 broadcast
 frame-relay map ip 128.10.10.5 166 broadcast
!
router ospf 2001
 network 128.10.6.0 0.0.0.255 area 600
 network 128.10.10.0 0.0.0.7 area 0
 neighbor 128.10.10.5 priority 1
```

Example 5-37 *DLSw over Frame Relay, NASA Configurations*

```
 neighbor 128.10.10.1 priority 1
!
no ip classless
!
bridge 1 protocol ieee
```

Use the **show dlsw peer** command to verify the peer is in a "connect" state. For more information on DLSw and verifying and testing the DLSw portion, see Chapter 13, "Configuring Bridging and Data Link Switching Plus."

For reference, Example 5-38 lists the configuration of the jpl router.

Example 5-38 *jpl Router Configuration*

```
hostname jpl
!
interface Ethernet0
 ip address 128.10.1.1 255.255.255.240
 media-type 10BaseT
!
interface Serial0
 no ip address
 encapsulation frame-relay
 no ip mroute-cache
 frame-relay traffic-shaping
 frame-relay lmi-type ansi
!
interface Serial0.1 multipoint
 ip address 128.10.10.1 255.255.255.248
 frame-relay class 64k
 frame-relay map ip 128.10.10.5 120 broadcast
 frame-relay map ip 128.10.10.6 130 broadcast
!
router ospf 2001
 network 128.10.1.0 0.0.0.15 area 100
 network 128.10.10.0 0.0.0.7 area 0
 neighbor 128.10.10.5 priority 1
 neighbor 128.10.10.6 priority 1
!
ip classless
!
map-class frame-relay 64k
 frame-relay cir 1544000
 frame-relay bc 8000
 frame-relay be 64000
 frame-relay mincir 32000
 frame-relay adaptive-shaping becn
!
```

CHAPTER 6

WAN Protocols and Technologies: Voice over X

Authoring contribution by Eric Sandberg

It's possible that the CCIE practical lab might include tasks involving the configuration of Cisco voice-capable routers for voice-over solutions (that is, voice over Frame Relay, Voice over IP and Voice over ATM). The purpose of this chapter is to give you enough information to successfully complete these configuration tasks. This chapter is not intended to be the "be all, end all" for information regarding telephony and voice-over solutions. Many good publications and Cisco classes are available to the general public that can fill that information void. I highly recommend *Cisco Voice over Frame Relay, ATM, and IP* and *Voice over IP Fundamentals* from Cisco Press, and any telephony or voice-related classes from a Cisco certified training partner.

This chapter covers Cisco voice-over technology solutions and tells where they fit into the network, highlights voice-capable Cisco products, discusses configuration and implementation, and enumerates the benefits of a voice-over solution, including reduced long distance costs, more calls with less bandwidth, more and better enhanced services, and more efficient use of the Internet Protocol (IP).

This chapter begins with a quick introduction to the basic elements of analog telephony. The overall objective is to teach engineers how to design, integrate, and configure voice over Frame Relay, ATM, and IP in the enterprise or managed network services using various Cisco 1750, 2600, 3600, and 3810 multiservice access devices.

Introduction to Analog Telephony

This section describes the telephone network with a focus on analog technology and includes the following topics:

- Telephone call components
- Telephone set components
- Telephone signaling

- Local loops
- Voice switches
- Trunks
- Trunk/line seizure signaling types
- Telephone call procedure

Telephone Call Components

Basic telephone call components consist of a telephone, a local loop, a voice switch (CO/PBX), and trunks, as shown in Figure 6-1. Everyone is familiar with the telephone, but there are components within the telephone set that you might not be familiar with. The handset is the part of the phone that you hold in your hand to speak (transmit) and listen (receive) to a voice conversation. The switch hook is the lever that is pushed down while the handset is resting on the cradle (on-hook). When you lift the handset to place a call, the switch hook pops up and is in a state (off-hook) that allows current to flow through the phone.

Figure 6-1 *Basic Telephone Components*

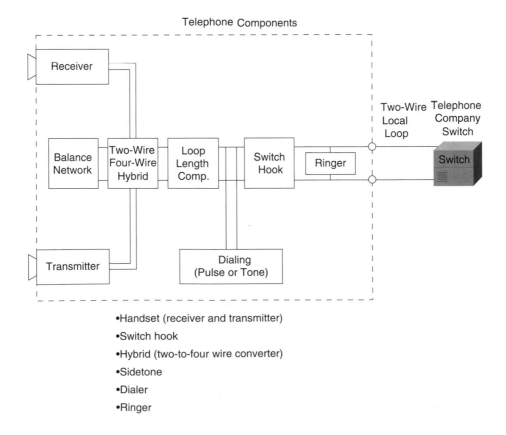

- Handset (receiver and transmitter)
- Switch hook
- Hybrid (two-to-four wire converter)
- Sidetone
- Dialer
- Ringer

In the handset are four wires split into two pairs, one for transmitting and one for receiving. In each phone there is a hybrid two-to-four-wire converter that acts as a communications bridge and provides the conversion between the four-wire handset and the two-wire local loop. Sidetone is another element that emanates from the hybrid, allowing a portion of speech to bleed over into the earpiece so that you can determine how loud you are talking. The dialer, either touch-tone or rotary, signals the telephone company that you are making a call. Pushing buttons on a touch-tone phone or spinning the dialer on a rotary phone sends a signal to the telephone company specifying the location from which you are calling.

Finally, the last component of the telephone is the ringer. When someone is calling you, the telephone company sends voltage through the wires to your telephone, which triggers the ringer alerting you that there is an incoming call.

Telephone Signaling

When you use your phone to place or receive a call, you must communicate your intentions to your telephone company. Signaling does this. The two types of signaling discussed in this chapter are supervisory and address. Supervisory signaling is the means by which you and your telephone company notify each other of call status. The three different types of supervisory signaling are on-hook, off-hook, and ringing.

As discussed previously, allowing the handset to rest in the cradle (on-hook) opens the switch hook and prevents the current from flowing through your phone. Only the ringer is active when the handset is on-hook. On-hook signaling is illustrated in Figure 6-2. Lifting the handset off the cradle allows current to flow through the phone, alerting the phone company that you are requesting to make a call. The phone company, in turn, returns a dial tone to the phone to indicate that it is ready. Figure 6-3 illustrates off-hook signaling. When someone is calling you, the telephone sends voltage to the ringer. The phone company also sends a ringback tone to the caller, alerting the caller that it is sending ringing voltage to the recipient's phone. Ringing is illustrated in Figure 6-4.

Figure 6-2   *Supervisory Signaling—On-Hook*

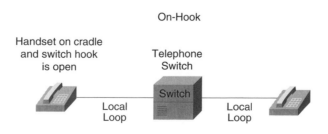

Figure 6-3   *Supervisory Signaling—Off-Hook*

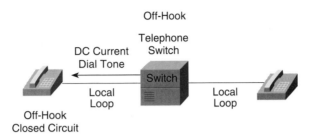

Figure 6-4   *Supervisory Signaling—Ringing*

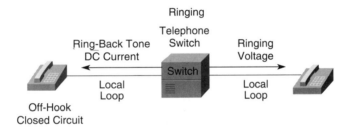

Address signaling can be one of two types, *pulse* or *dual-tone multifrequency (DTMF)*. Rotary-dial phones, while somewhat outdated, are still in use today and use pulse address signaling. Each pulse consists of a make and a break. The make is the period during which the circuit is closed. The break segment is the time that the circuit is open. The cycle should correspond to the following ratio: 60 percent break, 40 percent make. A governor inside the dial controls the rate at which the digits are pulsed. Figure 6-5 illustrates the process for pulse address signaling.

Touch-tone phones use DTMF signaling. When you look at the keypad, each row of keys is identified by a low-frequency tone, and each column is associated with a high-frequency tone. The combination of both tones notifies the phone company of the number you are calling (hence the term DTMF).

Figure 6-6 illustrates the combination of tones that you can generate for each button on the keypad.

Figure 6-5   *Address Signaling—Pulse*

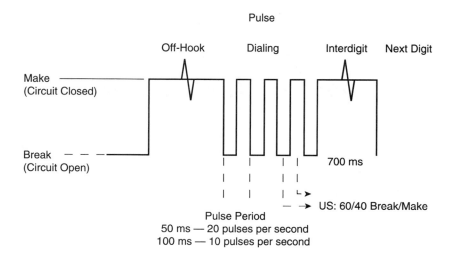

Figure 6-6   *Address Signaling—Dual-Tone Multifrequency (DTMF)*

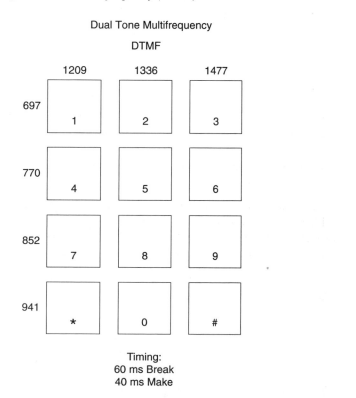

Local Loops

Your telephone is connected to the phone company by a local loop, sometimes referred to as "the last mile." The local loop contains an electrical communication path of two wires, one for transmitting and one for receiving voice signals (see Figure 6-7). The two-wire circuit is referred to as tip and ring. The ring is tied to the negative side of the battery at the phone company, and the tip is tied to the ground. Again, when you lift the handset off the cradle and go off-hook, the current flows down the wires and your phone company provides service to you.

Figure 6-7   *Local Loop*

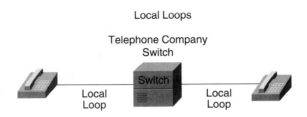

Local Loops

Telephone Company
Switch

Local
Loop

Local
Loop

A loop is the physical pair of wires from the
subscriber to the telephone company switch.

Voice Switches

The next piece of the telephony puzzle is the voice switch. The three types of switches discussed in this section are central office (CO) switches, intermediate switches, and private branch exchange (PBX) switches. A voice switch is a mechanical or electrical device that directs your voice calls to the proper destination. Voice switches typically are located on your premises or at the phone company. The voice switch selectively establishes and releases connections between transmission facilities to provide dedicated paths for the exchange of messages between two calling parties. Paths are established before the information exchanges begin, and, until the callers terminate the sessions, these paths are maintained for the switch's exclusive use.

Private phones are connected directly to a central office switch. When you place a telephone call to a central office switch, it forwards the call to one of the following:

- Another central office switch
- An end user's phone (if it is connected to the same CO)
- An intermediate switch

The CO switch provides all the components to make your phone work—for example, battery, current detector, dial-tone generator, dial register, and ring generator. The battery is the source of power to both the circuit and the phone. The current detector monitors the status of the circuit by detecting whether the circuit is open or closed. The dial-tone generator generates a dial tone to acknowledge the request for service. When the PBX detects current flow on the interface, the dial register receives the dialed digit. The ring generator alerts the called party by sending a ring signal to the called party.

Intermediate switches primarily act as a go between for the switch that forwards a call to other switches in the network, and they also connect trunks.

PBX switches are used in the private sector. It would be inefficient at your place of business to run individual phone lines to the CO for each telephone in your office, for example. Instead, you would install a PBX at your office to provide connectivity between your phones and the CO through trunk lines.

Figure 6-8 shows each of the different types of voice switches.

Figure 6-8   *Voice Switches—Central Office (CO), Intermediate, and Private Branch Exchange (PBX) Switches*

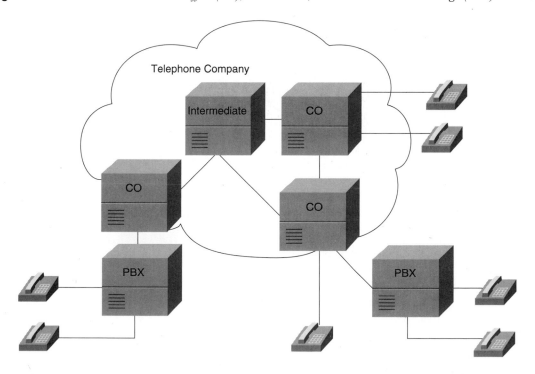

Trunks

The trunk's primary function is to provide the path between switches. Many different subscribers share a trunk, although only one uses it at any given time. There might be many trunks between two switches. A few of the more common trunk types are private trunk lines, central office trunks, foreign exchange trunks, and direct inward/direct outward dialing trunks, as shown in Figure 6-9.

Figure 6-9   *Figure 6-9Trunks—Private, Central Office (CO), and Foreign Exchange*

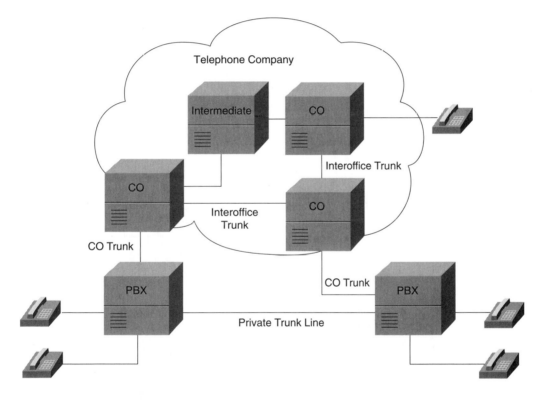

Generally, private-line trunks connect PBXs together, whereas CO trunks are direct connections between the local CO and a PBX. Foreign exchange trunks enable you to fool a switch into thinking that a remote telephone is directly attached to the switch. A *foreign exchange office (FXO)* and *foreign exchange station (FXS)* are needed to fool the switch into thinking that your telephone is directly connected to the switch.

The FXO sits on the switch end of the connection. It plugs directly into the line side of the switch, so the switch thinks that the FXO interface is a telephone. The switch notifies the FXO of an incoming call by sending ringing voltage to the FXO. Likewise, the FXO answers a call by closing the loop to let current flow. When current is flowing, the FXO interface uses any current technology to transport the signal to the FXS.

The FXS sits at the remote site and looks to the telephone like a switch. It provides the dial tone and battery to the telephone. The telephone thinks that it is the switch.

Direct inward dial (DID) trunks are one-way trunks that allow you to dial into a PBX without operator intervention. The CO knows which calls to pass through a DID trunk because it associates a block of numbers with each DID trunk.

Direct outward dial (DOD) trunks are also one-way trunks that allow you to connect directly to the CO. For example, if you want to place a call outside your company's network, you simply dial an access code such as 9, and the PBX forwards your call out to the CO. At that time, the CO provides a second dial tone and uses the remaining dialed digits to forward the call to the final destination.

Figure 6-10 illustrates DID and DOD trunks.

Figure 6-10   *Trunks—Direct Inward/Direct Outward Dialing Trunks*

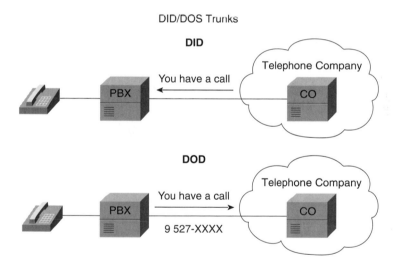

Trunk Line Seizure Signaling Types

This section covers trunk/line seizure signaling types, which are signaling standards that exist between lines and trunks in the telephone network. We focus on loop start signaling, ground start signaling, and E&M signaling. This information is critical to the successful configuration and implementation of your Cisco voice-over solution.

E&M signaling commonly is referred to as *ear and mouth* or *recEive and transMit*, but its origin comes from the terms *earth* and *magnet*. *Earth* represents electrical ground, and *magnet* represents the electromagnet used to generate tones.

Loop start signaling allows you or the telephone company to seize a line or trunk when a call is being initiated, as shown in Figure 6-11. It primarily is used on local loops rather than on trunks. Remember that when the line is in the idle state, it is said to be on-hook. If you lift the handset off the cradle, you cause the switch hook to go off-hook and close the loop. Current can now flow through the circuit, and the CO will detect the current and return a dial tone. Finally, if your telephone is ringing to alert you of an incoming call, the CO is applying AC ring voltage superimposed over the –48 VDC battery, causing the ring generator to notify you of a telephone call. When the PBX or telephone answers the call, the CO removes the ring voltage.

Figure 6-11 *Loop Start Signaling*

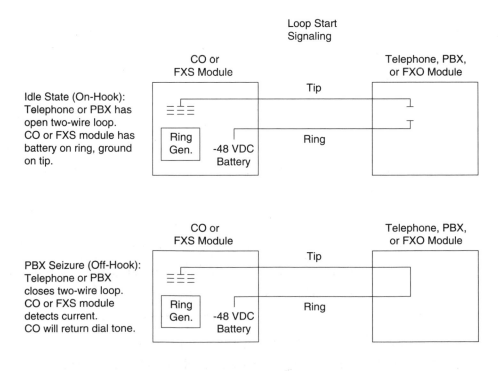

Loop start signaling is a poor signaling solution for high-volume trunks because it is possible to seize the trunk simultaneously from both ends. This problem is known as *glare*. Have you ever picked up the telephone to place an outbound call only to find the person you were calling already on the other end of the connection? Both parties seized the loop simultaneously, and you experienced glare. This might not be a significant problem in your home, but imagine the implications at your place of business, with several times the phone usage. Signaling methods that detect loop or trunk seizure at both ends solve the problem.

Ground start signaling is a modified version of loop start signaling that corrects the probability of glare by providing current detection at both ends of the connection (see Figure 6-12). Ground start signaling is preferable when high-volume trunks are involved.

Figure 6-12 *Ground Start Signaling*

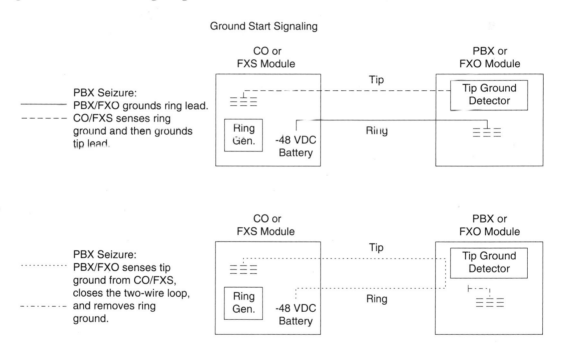

The following summarizes the ground start signaling process:

1 When the line is idle or on-hook, the PBX monitors for ground on the tip lead.

2 The battery from the CO appears on the ring lead.

3 When you go-off hook, the PBX grounds the ring lead.

4 The CO senses the ring ground and grounds the tip lead.

5 The PBX detects the tip ground and closes the circuit to complete the call.

E&M signaling supports tie-line–type facilities or signals between voice switches. Instead of superimposing both voice and signaling over the same wire, E&M uses separate leads

404 Chapter 6: WAN Protocols and Technologies: Voice over X

for each. As you probably guessed, the M lead sends the signal and the E lead receives the signal. For example, if you want to place a call to someone at a remote office, your PBX routes this request over its signal leads for use of the trunk between the two sites. Your PBX makes this request by raising its M lead. The remote PBX detects the request when it detects current on its E lead. The remote PBX attaches a dial register to the trunk and your PBX. Your PBX sends the dialed digits, and the remote PBX raises its M lead to notify you that the call is complete. Five types of E&M signaling exist, as detailed in Table 6-1.

Table 6-1 *E&M Signaling*

PBX to Intermediate Device			
Type	**Lead**	**On-hook**	**Off-hook**
I	M	Ground	Battery (−48 VDC)
II	M	Open	Battery (−48 VDC)
III	M	Ground	Battery (−48 VDC)
IV	M	Open	
V	M	Open	
Intermediate Device to PIX			
Type	**Lead**	**On-hook**	**Off-hook**
I	E	Open	Ground
II	E	Open	Ground
III	E	Open	Ground
IV	E	Open	Ground
V	E	Open	Ground

E&M Type I signaling (see Figure 6-13) is a two-wire signaling type common in North America. One wire is the E lead, and the other is the M lead. Approximately 75 percent of the PBXs in North America are E&M Type I. With the Type I interface, the tie line equipment generates the E signal to the PBX by grounding the E lead. The PBX detects the E signal by sensing the increase in current through a resistive load. Similarly, the PBX generates the M signal by sourcing a current to the tie line equipment, which detects it with a resistive load. The Type I interface requires that the PBX and tie line equipment share a common signaling ground reference.

E&M Type V (see Figure 6-14) is also a two-wire E&M signaling type most common outside North America. As with Type I signaling, Type V uses one wire for the E lead and one wire for the M lead. Type V requires a common ground between the PBX and the tie line equipment. This is provided by the signal ground leads.

Figure 6-13 *E&M Type I*

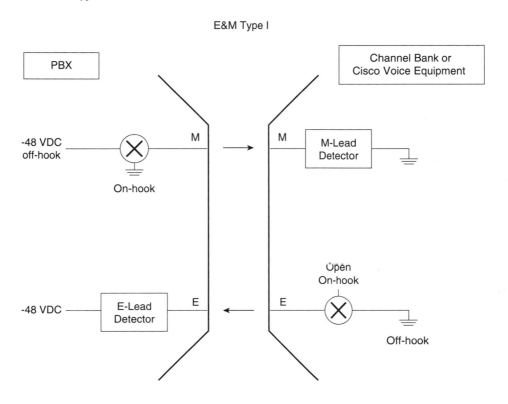

E&M Type II is a four-wire interface (see Figure 6-15). Like Type I and V, Type II uses two wires for the E and M leads. Type II, however, uses the remaining two wires for signal ground and signal battery. These two wires also are used for the return path for the E and M leads. A Type II interface does not require a common ground; instead, each of the two signals has its own return path.

E&M Type III is similar to Type II, but it uses the signal ground lead as the common ground (see Figure 6-16). The E lead operates similar to Type I. In this configuration, the PBX drops the M lead by grounding it rather than by opening a current loop. This is not a common signaling type.

E&M Type IV is symmetric and requires no common ground (see Figure 6-17). Each side closes a current loop to signal; the flow of current is detected by a resistive load to indicate the presence of a signal. E&M Type IV is not supported by Cisco.

Figure 6-14 *E&M Type V*

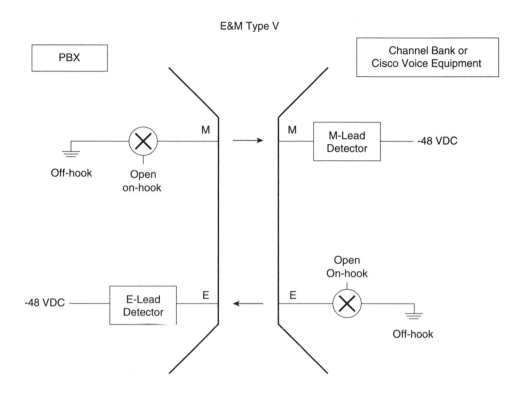

Trunk Supervision

This section covers start protocols for trunk supervision. We will discuss wink start, delay start, and immediate start. Tie trunks have bidirectional supervisory signaling that allows either end to seize the trunk. One PBX seizes the trunk and expects an acknowledgment reply from the other end. The local end needs to differentiate between a return acknowledgment and a remote end request for service.

The most common E&M trunk seizure signal type is *wink start* signaling. With this particular type of signaling, the office initiating the call seizes the line by going off-hook. The remote office does not immediately return an off-hook acknowledgment when it detects the line seizure of the calling office. Instead, the on-hook state is maintained until the receive digit register is attached. The called office toggles the off-hook lead for a specific amount of time (hence the term *wink*). When the calling office receives the wink, it forwards the digits to the remote office. The called office answers the telephone, and the PBX raises the M lead. Figure 6-18 illustrates wink start signaling.

Figure 6-15 *E&M Type II*

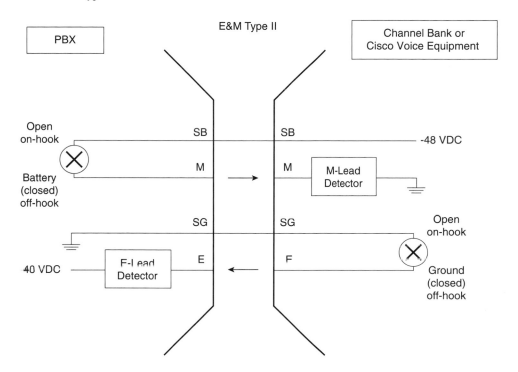

Four-wire, fully looped, nonsymmetrical

With *delay start* signaling, the originating side goes off-hook and waits for about 200 ms; then it checks to see if the far end is on-hook. If the far end is on-hook, it then outputs dial digits. If the far end is off-hook, it waits until it goes on-hook and then outputs dial digits. The delay signal says, in effect, "Wait—I'm not ready to receive digits." Figure 6-19 shows the delay start signaling process.

Now, let's run through the process that takes place with immediate start signaling. With *immediate start* signaling, the calling office PBX seizes the line by going off-hook (see Figure 6-20). Rather than waiting for the double acknowledgment from the remote office, the local PBX waits a predetermined amount of time (say, 150 ms) and then blindly forwards digits. The remote PBX acknowledges the call only after the called party answers the telephone.

Figure 6-16 *E&M Type III*

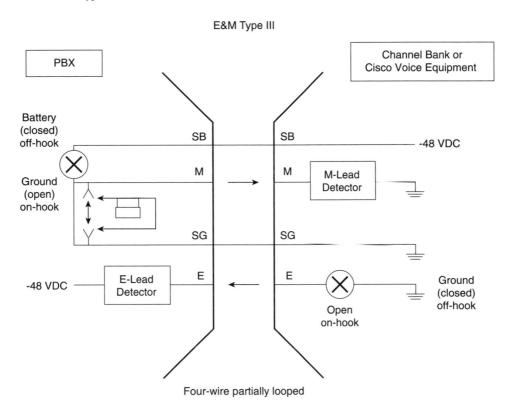

Two-to-Four-Wire Conversion and Echo

Recall that the local loop is made up of two wires. When the local loop reaches the central office switch, it is changed to four wires with a *two-to-four-wire hybrid converter*. This is necessary for your signal to be transported across the trunks in the network. If there is a good impedance match between the lines, the hybrid is said to be balanced with little or no reflected energy. However, if there is an impedance mismatch or inadequate balance between the lines, a portion of the transmitted voice is reflected back toward the receiver side, resulting in *echo*. Some degree of echo is always present. When the magnitude or loudness of the echo becomes too high, it becomes a problem.

Two common types of echo are *talker echo*, in which your voice reflects back to you (above and beyond side tone, which we discussed earlier) and you hear yourself twice. The other is *listener echo*, which gives the effect of hearing the speaker's voice twice. Echo is caused by delay.

Figure 6-17 *E&M Type IV*

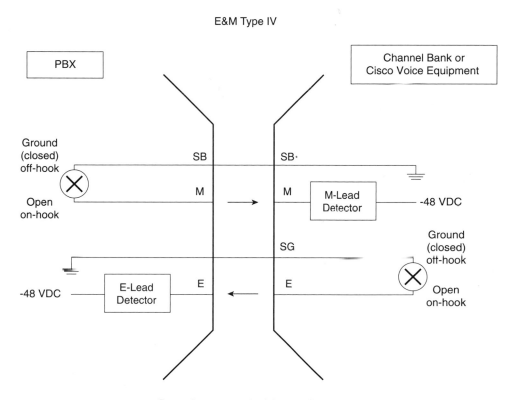

Four-wire, symmetrical, least noise

Figure 6-18 *Trunk Supervision Signaling: Wink Start*

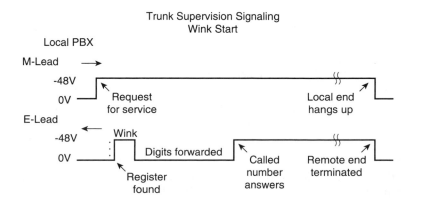

Figure 6-19 *Trunk Supervision Signaling: Delay Start*

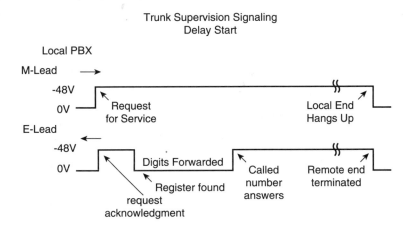

Figure 6-20 *Trunk Supervision Signaling: Immediate Start*

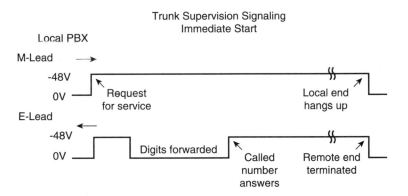

Two ways that you can attempt to solve this problem are echo suppression and echo
cancellation. *Echo suppression* basically suppresses your voice on the return path. The
echo suppressor determines which signals match you and which signals match the person
you are talking to. If the echo suppressor determines that the echo is on the return path, it
either attenuates or breaks the transmission path. However, if it is determined that both
speech and echo are present at the same time from a combination of both parties, the echo
cannot be attenuated without affecting the voice level. A more sophisticated method of
dealing with echo is *echo cancellation*. Rather than breaking or attenuating the transmit
path, as is the case with echo suppression, echo cancellation uses an echo canceller to build
a mathematical model of the speech pattern and subtracts it from the transmit path.

NOTE	An echo canceller removes echo only from one end of the circuit. If echo exists on both ends of the circuit, another echo canceller would need to be applied at the other end.

To summarize, here are the basic elements involved in placing a telephone call. When your telephone is resting on the cradle (on-hook), the line is in an idle state and the telephone or PBX opens the two-wire loop. Lifting the handset off the cradle causes the switch hook to go off-hook, closing the loop and allowing current to flow through the circuit. The switch detects current and returns a dial tone. When a dial tone is received, you request a particular connection by dialing specific numbers. The switch signals the called party by sending ringing voltage. At the same time, the switch also sends an audible ring signal back to the caller notifying the caller that the call is in progress. The analog connection is complete when the called party lifts the handset, closing the loop and allowing current to flow through the circuit.

Digital Voice Technology

Digital loop carrier technology was developed in the early 1970s with the idea of increasing transmission performance through digital technology. In addition to performance enhancements, digital technology is more reliable and easier to maintain than analog signaling. One of the key reasons for converting analog to digital is that digital signals are regenerated and do not accumulate noise in the same manner that analog signals do. Whereas analog signaling is represented as a continuous variable signal quantity such as voltage, digital signaling is represented as a sequence of binary digits indicating the presence of an electrical pulse (1) or lack thereof (0).

Digitizing Analog Signals

Analog-to-digital conversion is accomplished by a codec (coder, decoder). Codecs are used to convert voice frequency channels to 64-kbps digital signal level 0 (DS0) channels. The codec achieves the conversion by sampling, quantizing, and encoding the signal.

Before delving further into the three steps that need to be performed for analog-to-digital conversion, let's take a minute to talk about Nyquist's Theorem (see Figure 6-21). As stated in the Nyquist Theorem:

> A signal is sampled instantaneously at the transmitter at regular intervals and at a rate at least twice the highest frequency in the channel; then samples will contain sufficient information to allow an accurate reconstruction of the signal at the receiver.

The highest frequency for a voice is 4000 Hz—thus, 8000 samples per second, or 1 every 125 microseconds. Use the following formula to calculate the bit rate of digital voice:

2×4 kHz $\times 8$ bits per sample = 64,000 bps (64 kbps), or one DS-0

Figure 6-21 *Digitizing Voice: Nyquist Theorem*

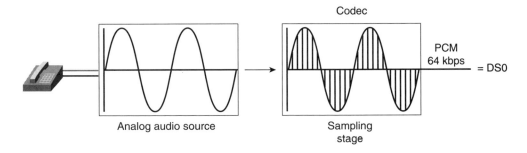

Analog Signal to Digital Signal Conversion Process

Now that you have an understanding of Nyquist's Theorem, we will describe briefly the three steps of the conversion process (sampling, quantizing, and encoding), along with an optional fourth step, compression:

1 **Sampling**—The analog signal is sampled at periodic intervals. The output of the sampling step is a *pulse amplitude modulation (PAM)* signal.

2 **Quantizing**—The PAM signal is matched to a segmented scale. The purpose of this step is to measure the amplitude of the PAM signal and to assign an integer number that defines that amplitude.

3 **Encoding**—The integer base-10 number is converted to an 8-bit binary number. The output is an 8-bit word in which each bit might be either a 1 (pulse) or a 0 (no pulse).

4 **Compression (optional)**—Used to save bandwidth. Compression allows you to carry more voice calls over a single channel.

The sections that follow examine these four steps in greater detail.

Sampling and Quantization

Quantization (see Figure 6-22) divides the range of amplitude values of an analog signal sample into a set of steps that are closest in value to the original analog signal. The voltage range is divided into 16 segments (0 to 7 positive and 0 to 7 negative). Beginning with segment 0, each segment has fewer steps than the previous, which reduces the noise-to-signal ratio. If there is a signal-to-noise ratio problem, it can be solved by converting PAM to PCM using a logarithmic scale. Linear sampling of an analog signal causes small amplitude signals to have a higher signal-to-noise ratio. μ-law and A-law are two quantization methods that help solve this problem by allowing smaller step functions at lower amplitudes. Both compress the signal for transmission and then expand the signal back to its original form at the other end. The result is a more accurate value for smaller amplitude and uniform signal-to-noise quantization ratio across the input range.

Figure 6-22 *Quantization*

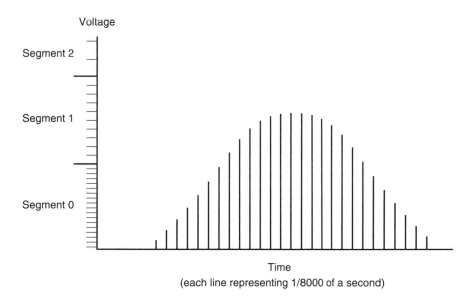

Speech-Encoding Scheme

The three types of speech-encoding schemes discussed here are waveform coders, vocoders, and hybrid coders. Waveform coders start with the analog waveform, taking 8000 samples per second, and then determine the most efficient way to code the analog signal for transmission. Pulse code modulation (PCM), adaptive differential pulse code modulation (ADPCM), μ-law, and A-law are examples of waveform coders. Vocoding schemes use low bit rates but sound synthetic and are typically used in military applications. LPC, channel, and phase are examples of vocoders. Hybrid coders are part of what is called analysis by synthesis (AbS) coding. Because AbS continuously analyzes what a speech waveform should look like in the 5-ms future, hybrid coders are of a much higher quality than simple analysis and synthesis. Examples of hybrid coders are APC, SELP, and CELP.

PCM (repeated 8000 times per second for a telephone voice channel service) is the most common method for converting analog to digital. When the PCM signal is transmitted to the receiver, it must be converted back to an analog signal. This is a two-step process requiring decoding and filtering. In the decoding process, the received 8-bit word is decoded to recover the number that defines the amplitude of that sample. This information is used to rebuild a PAM signal of the original amplitude. The PAM signal then is passed through a properly designed filter that reconstructs the original analog waveform from its digitally coded counterpart.

Voice-Compression Techniques

One of the benefits of compression, of course, is to reduce bandwidth, which, in turn, reduces the time and cost of transmission. Although not necessarily pertinent on high-bandwidth LANs, you can see where this could be beneficial in a voice-over solution across a WAN. However, compression can result in distortion and delay otherwise known as echo.

The two types of voice-compression techniques discussed here are *waveform algorithms* and *source algorithms*. *Adaptive differential pulse code modulation (ADPCM)* is an example of waveform compression. ADPCM is a way of encoding analog voice signals into digital signals by adaptively predicting future encodings by looking at the immediate past. The adaptive part reduces the number of bits required to encode voice signals. The ITU standards for waveform compression are as follows:

G.721 rate—32 kbps = $(2 \times 4$ kHz$) \times 4$ bits/sample

G.723 rate—24 kbps = $(2 \times 4$ kHz$) \times 3$ bits/sample

G.726 rate—16 kbps = $(2 \times 4$ kHz$) \times 2$ bits/sample

---

NOTE   Remember that the standard pulse code modulation (PCM/G.711) requires 64 kbps.

Two examples of source compression are *Low Delay Code Excited Linear Predictive (LD CELP)* and *Conjugate Structure Algebraic Code Excited Linear Predictive (CS-ACELP)*.

CELP is a hybrid coding scheme that delivers high-quality voice at low bit rates, is processor-intensive, and uses DSPs.

CELP transforms analog voice signals as follows:

1 Input to the coder is converted from 8-bit PCM to 16-bit linear PCM sample.

2 A codebook uses feedback to continuously learn and predict the voice waveform.

3 The coder is excited by a white noise generator.

4 The mathematical result is sent to the far-end decoder for synthesis and generation of the voice waveform.

The ITU standards for CELP are listed here:

- G.728 rate = 16 kbps
- G.729 rate = 8 kbps

G.729a is a variant that uses 8 kbps, is less processor-intensive, and allows two voice channels encoded per DSP.

- G.729 is the CS-ACELP that Cisco uses for high-quality 8 kbps in all voice-capable routers. However, it does have a limitation of one voice channel on a single DSP. G.729a, although not quite as high quality, is less processor-intensive and can support two voice channels on a single DSP.

In summary, here is a quick recap of the compression techniques discussed:

- **PCM**—The amplitude of voice signal is sampled and quantized 8000 times per second. Each sample then is represented by one octet (8 bits) and is transmitted. Either A-law or μ-law is used for sampling to reduce the signal-to-noise ratio. PCM is technically a codec, not a compression technique.

- **ADPCM**—In this method, the difference between the current sample and its predicted value based on the past sample is used. This method reduces the bandwidth requirement at the cost of quality of the signal. The sample might be represented by 2, 3, 4, or 5 bits.

- **CELP**—In all these algorithms, an excitation value and a set of linear predictive filters are transmitted. The filter settings transmission are less frequent than excitation values and are sent on an as-needed basis.

Figure 6-23 illustrates the various compression technologies, the amount of bandwidth required to set up and maintain a call with the compression, and the different categories of voice quality.

Digital Speech Interpolation

Similar to statistical multiplexing, *digital speech interpolation (DSI)* multiplexes bandwidth among a larger number of users than there are circuits. DSI uses voice activity detection and silence suppression to allocate the silent periods in human speech and put them to active use. Remember that 50 percent of a voice conversation is silence.

Mean Opinion Scoring (MOS) is a subjective method of grading telephone voice quality. The MOS is a statistical measurement of voice quality derived from a large number of subscribers judging the quality of the connection. The grading scale is 1 to 5, with 5 being excellent and 1 being unsatisfactory.

Figure 6-23 *Cisco's Voice-Compression Technologies*

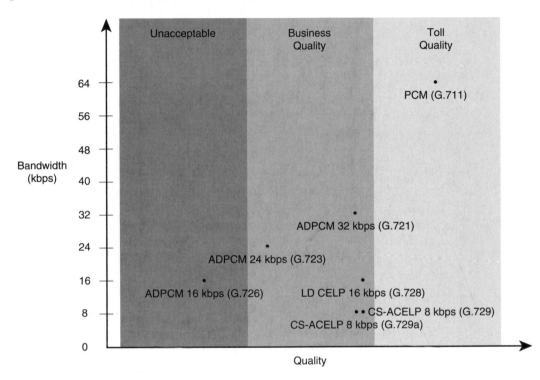

Channel Signaling Types and Frame Formats

Digital service level 0 (DS-0) is the smallest unit of transmission in the hierarchy. It is a 64-kbps circuit. A DS-0 channel can carry one digital PCM voice call. A total of 24 DS-0s can be multiplexed together to form the next level, called a DS1. A digital service level 1 (DS-1) is a 1.544-Mbps circuit. A DS1 carries 24 8-bit byte DS-0s at 1.544 Mbps. A DS-1 frame is 193 bits long, containing 8 bits from each of the 24 DS-0s, plus 1 framing bit. The two major framing formats for T1 are *D4* and *Extended Superframe Format (ESF)*. D4 specifies 12 frames in sequence as a superframe. A superframe uses A- and B-bit signaling or robbed-bit signaling in frames 6 and 12 for control signaling. These robbed bits are the least significant bit from an 8-bit word.

More prevalent in private and public networks is the ESF format. ESF specifies 24 frames in sequence with framing and a *cyclical redundancy check (CRC)*. ESF also uses robbed-bit signaling in frames 6, 12, 18, and 24, also known as *A B C D signaling*. Like D4, these are the least significant bits in the frames. Both formats retain the basic frame structure of 192 data bits followed by 1 framing bit. The 193rd bit of each DS1 frame is used for synchronization. The European equivalent to T1/DS-1 is the E1. The E1 is composed of 32 64-kbps channels that make up a transmission rate of 2.048 Mbps. Thirty of these channels are used for voice and data.

NOTE   The terms DS-1 and T1 are often confused. The T1 actually identifies the physical attributes of a 1.544-Mbps transmission medium.

Channel 0 is used for framing, and channel 16 is used for channel signaling. In E1 frame format, 32 time slots make up a frame. Sixteen E1 frames make up a multiframe.

Two different digital channel signaling types are *Channel Associated Signaling (CAS)* and *Common Channel Signaling (CCS)*. CAS (see Figure 6-24) is signaling in which the signals necessary to switch a given circuit are transmitted through the circuit itself or through a signaling channel permanently associated with it.

Figure 6-24 *Digital Channel Signaling Types—CAS*

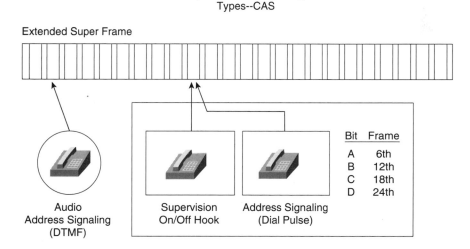

CCS (see Figure 6-25) is signaling in which one channel in each link is used for signaling to control, account for, and manage traffic on all channels of the link. The channel used for CCS does not carry user data.

Figure 6-25 *Common Channel Signaling Types—CCS*

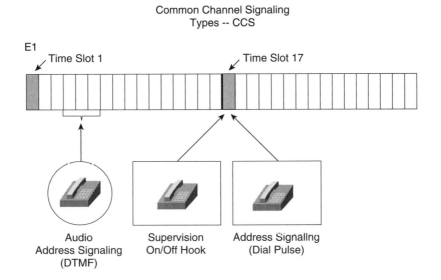

Cisco Voice Products

This section lists each Cisco voice-capable router and gives a brief description of its multiscrvice voice/data integration. We will cover the Cisco 1750, Cisco MC3810, Cisco 2600, Cisco 3600, and Cisco 7200 series routers.

The Voice Network Modules for the Cisco 2600 and 3600 series support up to two voice interface cards that come in three different types. Each of these provides a slightly different interface for connecting to different types of equipment:

- **Foreign exchange office (FXO)**—The FXO interface is a connector that allows an analog connection to be directed at the central office of the PSTN. This interface is of value for an off-premises extension application. This is the only voice interface card that will be approved to connect to off-premises lines. This interface might be used to provide backup over the PSTN or for Centrex-type operations.

- **Foreign exchange station (FXS)**—The FXS interface is a connector that allows connection for normal basic telephone service phones, fax machines, key sets and PBXs; it provides ring voltage, dial tone, and so forth. It is used where phones are connecting directly to the router.

- **Ear and mouth (E&M)**—Thc E&M interface is a connector that allows connection for PBX trunk line (tie lines). It is a signaling technique for two- and four-wire telephone and trunk interfaces. This has been a popular interface for PBX extension-type applications.

Cisco 1750

The Cisco 1750 is a multiservice access router that uses Cisco IOS with QOS to provide voice/fax and data integration. The Cisco 1750 supports the same WAN interface modules as the Cisco 1600, 1720, 2600, and 3600 routers. The Cisco 1750 also supports the same analog voice interface cards and voice over IP technology as the Cisco 2600 and 3600 routers. The voice interface cards include support for FXO, FXS, and E&M.

Cisco 2600

The Voice over IP feature enables the Cisco 2600 and 3600 to carry voice traffic simultaneously with data traffic over an IP network. Voice over IP is primarily a software feature supporting both voice and fax calls. Support for the ISDN BRI signaling type allows a 2600 or 3600 to provide voice access connectivity to either an ISDN telephone network or a digital interface on a PBX/key system. The voice or data also crosses an IP network to which the router connects.

Cisco 3600

The Cisco 3600 supports Voice over IP, Voice over Frame Relay, and Voice over ATM (3640 and 3660), which allows voice traffic to be transported over existing WAN infrastructures, including ISDN, leased lines, ATM, and Frame Relay. Additional features include support for fax relay and interoperability with other H.323 applications.

Cisco MC3810

The key benefits of the MC3810 are voice and data integration. The MC3810 integrates LAN, synchronous data, legacy, voice, video, and fax traffic for transport over a public or private Frame Relay, ATM, TDM, and VoIP networks. The MC3810 optimizes network bandwidth by multiplexing voice and data on the same physical interface. The analog model of the MC3810 has 6 voice ports, and the digital model houses a single digital voice access port (T1/E1) of up to 24 compressed voice channels.

Cisco 7200

The Cisco 7200 series provides both enterprise and service provider customers with a choice of either a four- or a six-slot chassis. The 7200 provides service providers with the foundation for managed router and managed network services with multiservice for data, voice, and video integration. The 7200 extends the multiservice capabilities to support VoIP services, as well as voice-processing extensions such as voice compression and PBX signaling. The 7200 supports multiservice aggregation of lower-end or branch CPE applications for a cost-effective end-to-end solution.

Comparison of Cisco Voice-Capable Routers

In summary, the Cisco voice-capable routers that offer a high level of multiservice voice/data integration include the following:

- The Cisco 1750 offers voice/fax/data integration.
- The Cisco MC3810 provides an end-to-end multiservice solution for VoFR, VoATM, and VoIP.
- The Cisco 2600, 3600, and 7200 support VoFR, VoIP, and VoATM.

Lab 15: Configuring Voice over Frame, Voice over IP, and Voice over ATM

Practical Scenario

Voice over X is a growing technology. We strongly suggest modeling any voice networks in a lab scenario before deploying them in production. This will allow you to have a strong understanding of the configuration required before it is in a production environment. Essentially, we are configuring *toll bypass*. Toll bypass involves placing a voice call over the IP network so that toll charges are not incurred. All the lab modules that follow are configuring toll bypass in one form or another. They represent the first step in moving toward a multiservice *converged* internetwork.

Lab Exercise

This lab is treated in modules that allow you to model the following:

- Voice over Frame
- Voice over IP
- Voice over ATM

Lab Objectives

- In the lab exercises, you configure toll bypass using the following methods:
- Using Voice over Frame Relay. Configure the Frame Relay network in Figure 6-26 so that voice calls can be placed from one router to the next.
- Using Voice over IP across a Frame Relay network. Configure the network in Figure 6-27 so that voice calls can be placed from one router to the next.
- Using a point-to-point voice over ATM application and, as an optional exercise, a private line automatic ring down (PLAR) application. Configure the network in Figure 6-28 so that voice calls can be placed from one router to the next.

The lab is divided into three portions, Voice over Frame, Voice over IP, and Voice over ATM. The Voice over Frame and Voice over IP configurations build upon each other. The walk-through for each lab is presented.

Equipment Needed

- Two Cisco voice-capable routers, each with a foreign exchange station (FXS) interface where you will connect your analog phone sets. We used Cisco 3600s in our labs, but the Cisco 2600s will work nicely as well.

- A Cisco router such as a Cisco 2600 series (something with two serial interfaces) that you will use as your frame relay switch.

- Two analog phone sets.

- For the ATM portion of the lab, two Cisco voice-capable routers, each with an FXS interface where you will connect your analog phone sets. Each should have at least one ATM interface for the point-to-point connection.

Lab 15a: Configuring Voice over Frame Relay—Part I

Physical Layout and Prestaging

- Connect one of the Cisco voice-capable routers to the Serial 1/2 interface on the Cisco 2600 series router (Frame Relay switch), as shown in Figure 6-26.

- Connect the other Cisco voice-capable router to the Serial 1/3 interface on the Cisco 2600 series router (Frame Relay switch), as shown in Figure 6-26.

- Connect an analog phone set to each of the FXS interfaces on the Cisco voice-capable routers, as shown in Figure 6-26.

Figure 6-26 *Voice over Frame Relay Lab*

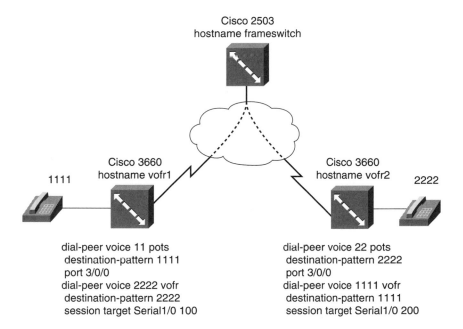

Configuring and Verifying Voice Ports

Configuring the ports on the router for the telephone headsets can be configured in the lab or as part of the prestaging. Example 6-1 shows the configuration for voice ports and for the Frame Relay switch that will be used in both the VoIP and VoFR labs.

Example 6-1 *Configuring the Voice Ports and Frame Relay Switc*

```
hostname frame-switch
!
frame-relay switching
!
<<<text omitted>>>
!
interface Serial1/0
 no ip address
 encapsulation frame-relay
 no fair-queue
 clockrate 64000
 frame-relay intf-type dce
!
interface Serial1/1
 no ip address
 encapsulation frame-relay
 clockrate 64000
 frame-relay intf-type dce
!
interface Serial1/2
 no ip address
 encapsulation frame-relay
 clockrate 64000
 frame-relay intf-type dce
 frame-relay route 200 interface Serial1/3 100
!
interface Serial1/3
 no ip address
 encapsulation frame-relay
 clockrate 64000
 frame-relay intf-type dce
 frame-relay route 100 interface Serial1/2 200
!
<<<text omitted>>>
end

frame-switch#
```

```
hostname vofr1
!
<<<text omitted>>>
!
voice-port 3/0/0
 timeouts call-disconnect 0
!
voice-port 3/0/1
 timeouts call-disconnect 0
!
voice-port 3/1/0
 timeouts call-disconnect 0
!
```

Example 6-1   *Configuring the Voice Ports and Frame Relay Switc (Continued)*

```
voice-port 3/1/1
 timeouts call-disconnect 0
!
dial-peer voice 11 pots
 destination-pattern 1111
 port 3/0/0
!
dial-peer voice 2222 vofr
 destination-pattern 2222
 session target Serial1/0 100
!
<<<text omitted>>>
!
interface Serial1/0
 no ip address
 no ip directed-broadcast
 encapsulation frame-relay
 no ip mroute-cache
 frame-relay traffic-shaping
!
interface Serial1/0.1 point-to-point
 ip address 150.150.10.1 255.255.255.0
 no ip directed-broadcast
 frame-relay interface-dlci 100
  class voice
  vofr cisco
!
<<<text omitted>>>
!
!
map-class frame-relay vofr
 frame-relay voice bandwidth 64000
!
map-class frame-relay voice
 frame-relay cir 768000
 frame-relay bc 1000
 frame-relay mincir 120000
 no frame-relay adaptive-shaping
 frame-relay fair-queue
 frame-relay voice bandwidth 78000
 frame-relay fragment 1500
!
<<<text omitted>>>
!
end

vofr1#
```

Lab 15a: Configuring Voice over Frame Relay—Part II

Lab Walkthrough

POTS peers enable incoming calls to be received by a particular telephony device. To configure a POTS peer, you need to uniquely identify the peer (by assigning it a unique tag number), define its telephone number(s), and associate it with a voice port through which calls will be established. In this example, you are using a four-digit dialing plan.

To configure a POTS dial peer, use the commands in Table 6-2 beginning in global configuration mode.

Table 6-2 *Steps for Configuring POTS Dial Peers*

Step	Command	Purpose
Step 1	Router# **configure terminal**	Enters global configuration mode.
Step 2	Router(config)# **dial-peer voice** *number* **pots**	Enters dial peer configuration mode and defines a local dial peer that will connect to the POTS network.
		The *number* argument is one or more digits identifying the dial peer. Valid entries are from 1 to 2147483647.
		The **pots** keyword indicates a peer using basic telephone service.
Step 3	Router(config-dialpeer)# *destination-pattern* **string**[T]	Configures the destination pattern of the dial peer so that the system can reconcile dialed digits with a telephone number.
		The *string* argument is a series of digits that specify the E.164 or private dialing plan phone number. Valid entries are the numerals 0 through 9 and the letters A through D. The plus symbol (+) is not valid. You can enter the following special characters:
		• The star character (*) that appears on standard touchtone dial pads can be in any dial string but not as a leading character (for example, *650).
		• The period (.) acts as a wildcard character.
		• The comma (,) can be used only in prefixes and inserts a 1-second pause.
		When the timer (T) character is included at the end of the destination pattern, the system collects dialed digits as they are entered until the interdigit timer expires (10 seconds, by default) or the user dials the termination of the end-of-dialing key (default is #).

To configure a VoFR dial peer, you need to uniquely identify the peer (by assigning it a unique tag number) and define the outgoing serial port number and the virtual circuit number.

Depending on your dial plan configuration, you might need to consider how to configure voice networks with variable-length dial plans, number expansion, excess digit playout, forward digits, and default voice routes, or use hunt groups with dial peer preferences.

If you will be sending switched calls over the Frame Relay network, you must configure the VoFR dial peers to specifically support switched calls.

To configure a VoFR dial peer to support switched calls, use the commands shown in Table 6-3 beginning in global configuration mode.

Table 6-3   *Steps for Configuring VoFR Dial Peers to Support Switched Calls*

Step	Command	Purpose
Step 1	Router(config)# **dial-peer voice** *number* **vofr**	Defines a VoFR dial peer and enters dial peer configuration mode. All subsequent commands that you enter in dial peer voice mode before you exit will apply to this dial peer.
		The *number* value tag identifies the dial peer and must be unique on the router. Do not duplicate a specific tag number.
Step 2	Router(config-dial-peer)# **destination-pattern** *string*	Configures the dial peer destination pattern. The same restrictions for the string listed in the POTS dial-peer configuration apply to the VoFR destination pattern.
Step 3	Router(config-dial-peer)# **session target** *interface dlci* [*cid*]	Configures the Frame Relay session target for the dial peer.

The physical serial interface, Serial 1/0, is configured to support Frame Relay encapsulation. You also will notice that Frame Relay traffic shaping is configured. Enabling FRTS on an interface enables both traffic shaping and per-VC queuing on all the PVCs and SVCs on the interface. Traffic shaping enables the router to control the output rate of the circuit and react to congestion notification information, if also configured.

The logical interface Serial 1/0.1 is configured as a basic point-to-point subinterface. Again, notice the two additional configuration parameters on this interface: *class voice* and *vofr cisco*. To associate a map class with a specified data-link connection identifier (DLCI), use the **class** virtual circuit configuration command. To remove the association between the DLCI and the map class, use the **no** form of this command. On the Cisco 2600, 3600, and 7200 series routers, entering the **vofr cisco** command is the only method for configuring Cisco proprietary voice encapsulation. You must then configure a map class to enable voice traffic on the PVCs.

The **map-class frame-relay vofr** is just defining a map class named vofr. To specify how much bandwidth should be reserved for voice traffic on a specific DLCI, use the **frame-relay voice bandwidth** command. To release the bandwidth previously reserved for voice traffic, use the **no** form of this command.

Example 6-2 defines a Frame Relay map class named voice.

Example 6-2   *Defining a Frame Relay Map Class*

```
map-class frame-relay voice
 frame-relay cir 768000
 frame-relay bc 1000
 frame-relay mincir 120000
 no frame-relay adaptive-shaping
 frame-relay fair-queue
 frame-relay voice bandwidth 78000
 frame-relay fragment 1500
```

To specify the incoming or outgoing committed information rate (CIR) for a Frame Relay virtual circuit, use the **frame-relay cir** map class configuration command. To reset the CIR to the default, use the **no** form of this command.

To specify the incoming or outgoing committed burst size (Bc) in bits for a Frame Relay virtual circuit, use the **frame-relay bc** map class configuration command. In this example, 1000 bits is used. To reset the committed burst size to the default, use the **no** form of this command.

To specify the minimum acceptable incoming or outgoing CIR in bits per second for a Frame Relay virtual circuit, use the **frame-relay mincir** map class configuration command. In this example, 120000 bits is used. To reset the minimum acceptable CIR to the default, use the **no** form of this command.

To select the type of backward notification that you want to use, use the **frame-relay adaptive-shaping** map class configuration command. To disable backward notification, use the **no** form of the command.

To enable weighted fair queuing for one or more Frame Relay PVCs, use the **frame-relay fair-queue** map class configuration command in conjunction with the **map-class frame-relay** command. To disable weighted fair queuing for a Frame Relay map class, use the **no** form of this command.

To specify how much bandwidth should be reserved for voice traffic on a specific DLCI, use the **frame-relay voice bandwidth** command. To release the bandwidth previously reserved for voice traffic, use the **no** form of this command.

To enable fragmentation of Frame Relay frames for a Frame Relay map class, use the **frame-relay fragment** map class configuration command. To disable Frame Relay fragmentation, use the **no** form of this command. Fragment size specifies the number of payload bytes from the original Frame Relay frame that will go into each fragment. This number excludes the Frame Relay header of the original frame. All the fragments of a Frame Relay frame except the last will have a payload size equal to *fragment_size*; the last fragment will have a payload less than or equal to *fragment_size*. Valid values are from 16 to 1600 bytes; the default is 53.

In Example 6-3, the configuration parameters on vofr2 are much the same as those in vofr1, with the exception of the dial peers. The destination patterns are reversed and the dlci information in the session target has been changed to point to the correct dlci.

Example 6-3 *Configuring the Voice Ports on vofr2*

```
Current configuration:
!
version 12.0
service timestamps debug uptime
service timestamps log uptime
no service password-encryption
!
hostname vofr2
!
enable password cisco
!
ip subnet-zero
no ip domain-lookup
!
!
!
!
voice-port 3/0/0
 timeouts call-disconnect 0
!
voice-port 3/0/1
 timeouts call-disconnect 0
!
voice-port 3/1/0
 timeouts call-disconnect 0
!
voice-port 3/1/1
 timeouts call-disconnect 0
!
dial-peer voice 22 pots
 destination-pattern 2222
 port 3/0/0
!
dial-peer voice 1111 vofr
 destination-pattern 1111
 session target Serial1/0 200
!
```

continues

Example 6-3 *Configuring the Voice Ports on vofr2 (Continued)*

```
!
interface Ethernet0/0
 no ip address
 no ip directed-broadcast
 shutdown
!
interface TokenRing0/0
 no ip address
 no ip directed-broadcast
 shutdown
 ring-speed 16
!
interface Serial1/0
 no ip address
 no ip directed-broadcast
 encapsulation frame-relay
 frame-relay traffic-shaping
!
interface Serial1/0.1 point-to-point
 ip address 150.150.10.2 255.255.255.0
 no ip directed-broadcast
 frame-relay interface-dlci 200
  class voice
  vofr cisco
!
interface Serial1/1
 no ip address
 no ip directed-broadcast
 shutdown
!
interface Serial1/2
 no ip address
 no ip directed-broadcast
 shutdown
!
interface Serial1/3
 no ip address
 no ip directed-broadcast
 shutdown
!
interface FastEthernet2/0
 no ip address
 no ip directed-broadcast
 shutdown
!
router igrp 1
 network 150.150.0.0
!
ip classless
no ip http server
!
```

Example 6-3 *Configuring the Voice Ports on vofr2 (Continued)*

```
!
map-class frame-relay vofr
 frame-relay voice bandwidth 64000
!
map-class frame-relay voice
 frame-relay cir 768000
 frame-relay bc 1000
 frame-relay mincir 12000
 no frame-relay adaptive-shaping
 frame-relay fair-queue
 frame-relay voice bandwidth 78000
 frame-relay fragment 1500
!
!
line con 0
 password cisco
 transport input none
line aux 0
 password cisco
line vty 0 4
 password cisco
 login
!
end

vofr2#
```

Now that both router configurations are complete, pick up the phone set on vofr1 and dial the digits 2222. If your configurations are correct and your routers are physically connected as described earlier, you should be able to complete a successful call. Hang up the phone set on vofr1 and try placing a call from vofr2 by dialing 1111.

Lab 15b: Configuring Voice over IP—Part I

Equipment Needed

For the voice over IP lab, you need the following equipment:

- Two Cisco voice-capable routers, each with an FXS interface where you will connect your analog phone sets. We used Cisco 3600s in our labs, but the Cisco 2600s will work nicely as well.

- A low-end Cisco router, such as a Cisco 2500 series (something with two serial interfaces), that you will use as your Frame Relay switch.

- Two analog phone sets.

Physical Layout and Prestaging

- Connect one of the Cisco voice-capable routers to the Serial 1/2 interface on the Cisco 2600 series router (Frame switch), as shown in Figure 6-27.

- Connect the other Cisco voice-capable router to the Serial 1/3 interface on the Cisco 2600 series router (Frame switch), as shown in Figure 6-27.

- Connect an analog phone set to each of the FXS interfaces on the Cisco voice-capable routers, as shown in Figure 6-27.

Figure 6-27 *Voice over Frame Relay Lab*

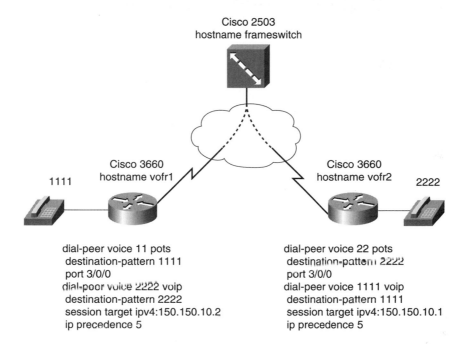

Cisco 2503
hostname frameswitch

Cisco 3660
hostname vofr1

Cisco 3660
hostname vofr2

1111

2222

dial-peer voice 11 pots
 destination-pattern 1111
 port 3/0/0
dial-poor voice 2222 voip
 destination-pattern 2222
 session target ipv4:150.150.10.2
 ip precedence 5

dial-peer voice 22 pots
 destination-pattern 2222
 port 3/0/0
dial-peer voice 1111 voip
 destination-pattern 1111
 session target ipv4:150.150.10.1
 ip precedence 5

Lab 15b: Configuring Voice over IP—Part II

Lab Walkthrough

Example 6-4 shows the configurations that you will use on each of these routers to accomplish your Voice over IP lab. The configuration of the voice ports, dial peers, and QOS mechanisms are discussed. For the purpose of this lab, the Cisco voice-capable routers have host names of voip1 and voip2.

Example 6-4 *Configuring Voice over IP on voip1*

```
Current configuration:
!
version 12.1
service timestamps debug uptime
service timestamps log uptime
no service password-encryption
!
hostname voip1
!
enable password cisco
!
!
!
!
!
!
ces 1/0
!
ip subnet-zero
no ip domain-lookup
!
lane client flush
!
!
!
!
!
controller T1 1/0
!
!
!
interface FastEthernet0/0
 no ip address
 shutdown
 duplex auto
 speed auto
!
interface FastEthernet0/1
 no ip address
```

Example 6-4   *Configuring Voice over IP on voip1 (Continued)*

```
 shutdown
 duplex auto
 speed auto
!
interface ATM1/0
 no ip address
 shutdown
 no atm scrambling cell-payload
 no atm ilmi-keepalive
!
interface Serial2/0
 no ip address
 encapsulation frame-relay
 no ip mroute-cache
 no fair-queue
!
interface Serial2/0.1 point-to-point
 ip address 150.150.10.1 255.255.255.0
 no ip mroute-cache
 frame-relay class voice
 frame-relay interface-dlci 100
 frame-relay ip rtp header-compression
!
interface Serial2/1
 no ip address
 shutdown
!
interface Serial2/2
 no ip address
 shutdown
!
interface Serial2/3
 no ip address
 shutdown
!
router rip
 network 150.150.0.0
!
ip classless
no ip http server
!
!
map-class frame-relay voice
 frame-relay voice bandwidth 78000
 frame-relay fragment 1500
 frame-relay ip rtp priority 16384 16383 312
 no frame-relay adaptive-shaping
 frame-relay cir 768000
 frame-relay bc 1000
 frame-relay mincir 120000
```

continues

Example 6-4 *Configuring Voice over IP on voip1 (Continued)*

```
 frame-relay fair-queue
!
voice-port 3/0/0
!
voice-port 3/0/1
!
voice-port 3/1/0
!
voice-port 3/1/1
!
dial-peer voice 11 pots
 destination-pattern 1111
 port 3/0/0
!
dial-peer voice 2222 voip
 destination-pattern 2222
 session target ipv4:150.150.10.2
 ip precedence 5
!
!
line con 0
 password cisco
 transport input none
line aux 0
 password cisco
line vty 0 4
 password cisco
 login
!
end
```

The configurations for the VoIP lab and VoFR lab are similar, with a few exceptions. These exceptions include the VoIP dial peer, the IP precedence associated with the VoIP dial peer, the Frame Relay IP RTP header compression on the Serial subinterface, and the Frame Relay IP RTP priority defined in the map class.

Let's start with the dial peers. The POTS dial peer is the same as the one defined in the VoFR lab. However, you can see that the session target defined on the VoIP dial peer now points to an IP address rather than an interface and DLCI number. The IP address of the session target can be any interface on the router that you are directing your call to. Best practice would dictate that this address should be the IP address of a loopback interface because it is the most stable. That is, it should always be logically up as long as the router is powered up. In the example, we pointed the session target at the far end IP address of the Serial subinterface.

IP RTP header compression reduces the 40-byte IP+UDP+RTP header to 2 to 4 bytes, thereby reducing the bandwidth required per voice call on point-to-point links. The header is compressed at one end of the link and decompressed at the other end. Another standard name for this technique is CRTP, which stands for compressed RTP. To configure IP RTP header compression, you need to configure the **ip rtp header-compression** command under the serial interface, or the **frame-relay ip rtp header-compression** command under the Frame Relay subinterface.

Frame Relay IP RTP priority is used to reserve a strict priority queue on a Frame Relay PVC for a set of RTP packet flows belonging to a range of User Datagram Protocol (UDP) destination ports. The theory behind IP RTP priority is that VoIP traffic is identified by the fact that it uses a well-known UDP port range (16384-32767). Although the actual ports used are dynamically negotiated between end devices or gateways, all Cisco VoIP products utilize the same port range. When the router recognizes the VoIP traffic, it places this traffic into a strict priority queue. The amount of traffic that is placed into the priority queue is controlled at a user-configurable rate by the system. This priority queue always is serviced before any other traffic, which means that jitter and delay of VoIP traffic is minimized.

IP precedence gives voice packets a higher priority than other IP data traffic. The **ip precedence** command is used by the Cisco 3600 router to differentiate voice traffic from data traffic. So, you need to ensure that the data IP packets do not have the same IP precedence as that of the voice packets. In IP precedence, the numbers 1 through 5 identify classes for IP flows; the numbers 6 through 7 are used for network and backbone routing and updates. It is recommended that IP precedence 5 be used for voice packets.

Example 6-5 shows the configuration for the voip2 router.

Example 6-5 *Configuring Voice over IP on voip2*

```
Current configuration:
!
version 12.1
service timestamps debug uptime
service timestamps log uptime
no service password-encryption
!
hostname voip2
!
enable password cisco
!
!
!
!
!
!
ces 1/0
!
ip subnet-zero
no ip domain-lookup
!
lane client flush
!
```

continues

Example 6-5 *Configuring Voice over IP on voip2 (Continued)*

```
!
!
!
!
controller T1 1/0
!
!
!
interface FastEthernet0/0
 no ip address
 shutdown
 duplex auto
 speed auto
!
interface FastEthernet0/1
 no ip address
 shutdown
 duplex auto
 speed auto
!
interface ATM1/0
 no ip address
 shutdown
 no atm scrambling cell-payload
 no atm ilmi-keepalive
!
interface Serial2/0
 no ip address
 encapsulation frame-relay
 no ip mroute-cache
 no fair-queue
!
interface Serial2/0.1 point-to-point
 ip address 150.150.10.2 255.255.255.0
 no ip mroute-cache
 frame-relay class voice
 frame-relay interface-dlci 200
 frame-relay ip rtp header-compression
!
interface Serial2/1
 no ip address
 shutdown
!
interface Serial2/2
 no ip address
 shutdown
!
interface Serial2/3
 no ip address
 shutdown
!
router rip
```

Example 6-5 *Configuring Voice over IP on voip2 (Continued)*

```
 network 150.150.0.0
 !
 ip classless
 no ip http server
 !
 !
 map-class frame-relay voice
  frame-relay voice bandwidth 78000
  frame-relay fragment 1500
  frame-relay ip rtp priority 16384 16383 312
  no frame-relay adaptive-shaping
  frame-relay cir 768000
  frame-relay bc 1000
  frame-relay mincir 120000
  frame-relay fair-queue
 !
 voice-port 3/0/0
 !
 voice-port 3/0/1
 !
 voice-port 3/1/0
 !
 voice-port 3/1/1
 !
 dial-peer voice 22 pots
  destination-pattern 2222
  port 3/1/0
 !
 dial-peer voice 1111 voip
  destination-pattern 1111
  session target ipv4:150.150.10.1
  ip precedence 5
 !
 !
 line con 0
  password cisco
  transport input none
 line aux 0
  password cisco
 line vty 0 4
  password cisco
  login
 !
 end
```

Now that both router configurations are complete, pick up the phone set on voip1 and dial the digits 2222. If your configurations are correct and your routers are physically connected as described earlier, you should be able to complete a successful call. Hang up the phone set on voip1 and try placing a call from voip2 by dialing 1111.

Lab 15c: Configuring Voice over ATM—Part I

Equipment Needed

For the Voice over ATM lab, you need the following equipment:

- Two Cisco voice-capable routers, each with an FXS interface where you will connect your analog phone sets. Each should have at least one ATM interface for our point-to-point connection.

- Two analog phone sets.

Physical Layout and Prestaging

- Connect the two Cisco voice-capable routers in a point-to-point configuration through the ATM interfaces. Remember to cross over the fiber (refer to Figure 6-28).

- Connect an analog phone set to each of the FXS interfaces on the Cisco voice-capable routers, as shown in Figure 6-28.

Figure 6-28 *Voice over Frame Relay Lab*

```
dial-peer voice 1 pots                    dial-peer voice 1 pots
destination pattern 4444                  destination pattern 1000
port 3/0/0                                port 3/1/0
dial-peer voice 2 voatm                   dial-peer voice 2 voatm
destination pattern 1000                  destination pattern 4444
session target atm 1/0 pvc 1/150          session target atm 1/0 pvc 1/150
```

```
int atm 1/0                               int atm 1/0
pvc 1/150                                 pvc 1/150
encapsulation aal5mux voice               encapsulation aal5mux voice
vbr-rt 128 64 32                          vbr-rt 128 64 32
```

Lab 15c: Configuring Voice over ATM—Part II

Lab Walkthrough

Now, take a look at the configurations that you will use on each of these routers to accomplish your Voice over ATM lab. The configuration of the voice ports, dial peers, and QOS mechanisms is discussed. For the purpose of this lab, the Cisco voice-capable routers have host names of voatm1 and voatm2. Example 6-6 shows the configuration for voatm1.

Example 6-6   *Configuring Voice over ATM on voatm1*

```
Current configuration:
!
version 12.1
service timestamps debug uptime
service timestamps log uptime
no service password-encryption
!
hostname voatm1
!
enable password cisco
!
!
!
!
!
!
ces 1/0
!
ip subnet-zero
!
lane client flush
!
!
!
!
!
controller T1 1/0
!
!
!
interface FastEthernet0/0
 no ip address
 shutdown
 duplex auto
 speed auto
!
```

continues

Example 6-6 *Configuring Voice over ATM on voatm1 (Continued)*

```
interface FastEthernet0/1
 no ip address
 shutdown
 duplex auto
 speed auto
!
interface ATM1/0
 no ip address
 no atm scrambling cell-payload
 no atm ilmi-keepalive
 pvc 1/150
  vbr-rt 128 64 32
  encapsulation aal5mux voice
 !
!
interface Serial2/0
 no ip address
 shutdown
!
interface Serial2/1
 no ip address
 shutdown
!
interface Serial2/2
 no ip address
 shutdown
!
interface Serial2/3
 no ip address
 shutdown
!
ip classless
no ip http server
!
!
voice-port 3/0/0
!
voice-port 3/0/1
!
voice-port 3/1/0
!
voice-port 3/1/1
!
dial-peer voice 1 pots
 destination-pattern 4444
 port 3/0/0
!
dial-peer voice 2 voatm
 destination-pattern 1000
 session target ATM1/0 pvc 1/150
 !
```

Example 6-6   *Configuring Voice over ATM on voatm1 (Continued)*

```
!
line con 0
 transport input none
line aux 0
line vty 0 4
!
end
```

The following is a description of the configuration parameters on the ATM interface.

The **no atm scrambling cell-payload** randomizes the ATM cell payload frames to avoid continuous nonvariable bit patterns and improve the efficiency of ATM's cell delineation algorithms. Normally, the default setting for this command is sufficient, with no specific command required. By default, scrambling is off for T1 or E1 links.

To enable or disable ILMI connectivity procedures and to change the ILMI keepalive poll interval, use the **atm ilmi-keepalive** interface configuration command. To disable ILMI connectivity procedures, use the **no** form of this command. This is disabled by default.

To configure the real-time variable bit rate (VBR) for Voice over ATM connections, use the **vbr-rt** ATM virtual circuit configuration command. **vbr-rt** peak-rate average-rate burst. The parameters for the **vbr-rt** command are described as follows:

- *peak-rate*—The peak information rate (PIR) of the voice connection in kbps. The range is 56 to 10000. Peak value: (2 × the maximum number of calls) × 16 kb.

- *average-rate*—The average information rate (AIR) of the voice connection in kbps. The range is 1 to 56. Average value: (1 × the maximum number of calls) × 16 kb.

- *burst*—Burst size in number of cells. The range is 0 to 65536. Burst value: 4 × the maximum number of calls.

encapsulation aal5mux voice sets the encapsulation of the PVC to support voice traffic.

pvc 1/150 (pvc vpi/vci) creates an ATM PVC for voice traffic and enters virtual circuit configuration mode.

The POTS dial peer is configured the same way as in the VoFR and VoIP labs and is associated with voice port 3/0/0.

The VoATM dial peer is not pointing at an IP address, as it was in the VoIP lab, but now points to an ATM interface and a voice PVC.

Example 6-7 shows the configuration for the second router in your VoATM lab. The configurations are nearly identical with the exception of the **atm clock internal**

configuration parameter on the ATM interface. This means that the transmit clock is
generated internally.

Example 6-7 *Configuring Voice over ATM on voatm2*

```
Current configuration:
!
version 12.1
service timestamps debug uptime
service timestamps log uptime
no service password-encryption
!
hostname voatm2
!
enable password cisco
!
!
!
!
!
!
ces 1/0
!
ip subnet-zero
!
lane client flush
!
!
!
!
!
controller T1 1/0
!
!
!
interface FastEthernet0/0
 no ip address
 shutdown
 duplex auto
 speed auto
!
interface FastEthernet0/1
 no ip address
 shutdown
 duplex auto
 speed auto
!
interface ATM1/0
 no ip address
 atm clock INTERNAL
 no atm scrambling cell-payload
 no atm ilmi-keepalive
 pvc 1/150
```

Example 6-7 *Configuring Voice over ATM on voatm2 (Continued)*

```
  vbr-rt 128 64 32
  encapsulation aal5mux voice
 !
 !
interface Serial2/0
 no ip address
 encapsulation frame-relay
 shutdown
 frame-relay lmi-type cisco
 !
interface Serial2/1
 no ip address
 shutdown
 !
interface Serial2/2
 no ip address
 shutdown
 !
interface Serial2/3
 no ip address
 shutdown
 !
ip classless
no ip http server
 !
 !
voice-port 3/0/0
 !
voice-port 3/0/1
 !
voice-port 3/1/0
 !
voice-port 3/1/1
 !
dial-peer voice 1 pots
 destination-pattern 1000
 port 3/1/0
 !
dial-peer voice 2 voatm
 destination-pattern 4444
 session target ATM1/0 pvc 1/150
 !
 !
line con 0
 transport input none
line aux 0
line vty 0 4
 !
end
```

Now that both router configurations are complete, pick up the phone set on voatm1 and dial the digits 1000. If your configurations are correct and your routers are physically connected as described earlier, you should be able to complete a successful call. Hang up the phone set on voatm1 and try placing a call from voatm2 by dialing 1000.

Lab 15d: Optional Private Line Automatic Ring Down (PLAR) Connection

As on optional lab, we have set up a private line automatic ring down (PLAR) lab. This is sometimes referred to as the *Bat Phone*. You can complete this lab by referring back to the VoFR lab that you did previously. All you need to do to create the PLAR connection is add one configuration statement under your voice port. Example 6-8 shows the configuration for router vofr2 to accomplish this.

Example 6-8 *Configuring a PLAR Connection*

```
hostname vofr2
!
enable password cisco
!
ip subnet-zero
no ip domain-lookup
!
!
!
!
voice-port 3/0/0
 timeouts call-disconnect 0
 connection plar 1111
!
voice-port 3/0/1
 timeouts call-disconnect 0
!
voice-port 3/1/0
 timeouts call-disconnect 0
!
voice-port 3/1/1
 timeouts call-disconnect 0
!
dial-peer voice 22 pots
 destination-pattern 2222
 port 3/0/0
!
dial-peer voice 1111 vofr
 destination-pattern 1111
 session target Serial1/0 200
!
!
interface Ethernet0/0
 no ip address
 no ip directed-broadcast
 shutdown
!
```

continues

Example 6-8 *Configuring a PLAR Connection (Continued)*

```
interface TokenRing0/0
 no ip address
 no ip directed-broadcast
 shutdown
 ring-speed 16
!
interface Serial1/0
 no ip address
 no ip directed-broadcast
 encapsulation frame-relay
 frame-relay traffic-shaping
!
interface Serial1/0.1 point-to-point
 ip address 150.150.10.2 255.255.255.0
 no ip directed-broadcast
 frame-relay interface-dlci 200
  class voice
  vofr cisco
!
interface Serial1/1
 no ip address
 no ip directed-broadcast
 shutdown
!
interface Serial1/2
 no ip address
 no ip directed-broadcast
 shutdown
!
interface Serial1/3
 no ip address
 no ip directed-broadcast
 shutdown
!
interface FastEthernet2/0
 no ip address
 no ip directed-broadcast
 shutdown
!
router igrp 1
 network 150.150.0.0
!
ip classless
no ip http server
!
!
map-class frame-relay voice
 frame-relay cir 768000
 frame-relay bc 1000
 frame-relay mincir 120000
 no frame-relay adaptive-shaping
```

Example 6-8   *Configuring a PLAR Connection (Continued)*

```
 frame-relay fair-queue
 frame-relay voice bandwidth 78000
 frame-relay fragment 1500
!
!
line con 0
 password cisco
 transport input none
line aux 0
 password cisco
line vty 0 4
 password cisco
 login
!
end
```

With this configuration in place, all you have to do is pick up the telephone set on router vofr2 and it will automatically dial 1111 and connect you to the telephone set connected to router vofr1.

CHAPTER 7

WAN Protocols and Technologies: Integrated Services Digital Network (ISDN)

Authoring contribution by Daniel Keller

Integrated Services Digital Network (ISDN) is basically the digital version of the Public Switched Telephone Network (PSTN). It offers a common platform for integrating voice, video, and data services globally. When discussing ISDN, we actually are talking about Narrowband ISDN (N-ISDN). The other type of ISDN is referred to as *Broadband ISDN (B-ISDN)*, which provides high-speed transmissions and is the foundation behind ATM, which is addressed in more depth in Chapter 8, "WAN Protocols and Technologies: Asynchronous Transfer Mode (ATM)."

ISDN Development, Components, and Mechanics

Once upon a time, in the early days of the public telephone network, telephone users were connected through a series of analog circuits. Starting in the early 1960s, telephone companies began replacing the analog circuits in the core of their networks with packet-based digital signals. Analog circuits still were delivered to the telephone users at the local loop level. ISDN delivers the digital circuits directly to the customers, enabling them to carry a wide variety of traffic over the network. Therefore, ISDN enables users to carry voice, video, data, and other traffic over the existing telephone wiring. When ISDN became an emerging technology, it was envisioned to become the leading worldwide digital network technology, providing access to everyone. Now, with the emergence of xDSL and cable modems, ISDN is losing favor with the home access market. However, ISDN is still a major player in the business market, where it is used to back up primary links and where PRI/E1s are used to carry data and V.90 remote dial-in access. It is also more readily available than DSL and cable, allowing the majority of home users who fail to qualify for cable or DSL to purchase ISDN service.

A standards committee was developed in 1984 to coordinate the ISDN movement, called the International Telephone and Telegraph Consultative Committee (CCITT), now known as the *International Telecommunications Union (ITU)*. The ITU organizes the ISDN protocols according to three general topic areas:

- Protocols that begin with the letter *E* deal with telephone network standards for ISDN. For example, the E.164 protocol describes international addressing.

- Protocols that begin with the letter *I* deal with concepts, terminology, and general methods. The I.100 series of protocols deal with general ISDN concepts and the structure of other I-series recommendations. I.200 deals with the service aspects of ISDN, whereas I.300 describes network aspects, and I.400 describes how the *User Network Interface (UNI)* is provided.

- Protocols beginning with the letter *Q* cover how switching and signaling should operate. Q.921 describes the ISDN data-link processes of *Link Access Protocol (LAPD)*, which functions like Layer 2 processes in the OSI model and is an encapsulation option on the ISDN D channel. Q.931 specifies Layer 3 functions.

Debugging Q.921 and Q.931 sometimes can be useful for troubleshooting ISDN connectivity problems, and this is discussed in more detail later in the chapter.

The major advantage of ISDN is that it allows multiple digital channels to operate simultaneously over one circuit. Currently, there are three types of ISDN channels:

- **B (Bearer) channel**—64 kbps used for user traffic. Some ISDN switches limit B channels to a capacity of 56 kbps.

- **D (Data) channel**—16 kbps or 64 kbps, depending on the type of ISDN circuit. This channel is used for ISDN signaling, as well as call setup and teardown.

- **H channel**—Provides a way to bond multiple B channels. They typically are not used in North America. H channels are implemented as follows:

    — **H0**—384 kbps (six B channels) used for high-quality audio/high speed digital information

    — **H10**—1.472 Mbps (23 B channels) used for teleconferencing/digital information

    — **H11**—1.536 Mbps (24 B channels) used for teleconferencing/digital information

    — **H12**—1.92 Mbps (30 B channels) used for teleconferencing/digital information

    — **H4**—150 Mbps (approximate) used for high-definition TV

Cisco supports the following two ISDN interface types, which combine the channel types in the preceding list:

- **Basic Rate Interface (BRI)**—One 16-kbps D channel + two B channels

- **Primary Rate Interface (PRI)**—1 64-kbps D channel + 23 B channels in North America and Japan, for a total capacity of 1536 kbps. 1 64-kbps D channel + 30 B channels in Europe and other parts of the world, for a total capacity of `1984 kbps`.

ISDN Components and Reference Points

To access the ISDN network, *customer premises equipment (CPE)*, which is the local terminating equipment, is used. This equipment performs the functions needed for properly connecting to the ISDN network. The following describes the types of ISDN CPE options:

- **TE1 (Terminal Equipment Type 1)**—Designates a device with a native ISDN interface.

- **TE2 (Terminal Equipment Type 2)**—Designates a device that does not include a native ISDN interface and requires a terminal adapter (TA) for its ISDN signals.

- **NT1 (Network Termination 1)**—Designates a device that converts the BRI signals into a form used by the ISDN digital line, and is the boundary between the carrier's ISDN network and the CPE.

- **NT2 (Network Termination 2)**—Designates a device that aggregates and switches all ISDN lines at a customer location. This typically is incorporated into a corporate private branch exchange (PBX).

- **TA (Terminal Adapter)**—Used by a TE2 device to convert EIA/TIA-232, V.35, and other signals into BRI signals.

Because CPE can include one or more of these functions, the way in which they connect to the other ISDN devices can vary. Because of this, the ISDN standards refer to these various interfaces as *reference points*. The reference points simply define the logical points between the previous CPE groups. Figure 7-1 shows the reference points, which are described as follows:

- **R**—The connection between a non–ISDN-compatible device (TE2) and a TA
- **S**—The connection between the end-user CPE and the NT2
- **T**—The connection between the NT2 and the NT1
- **U**—The connection between the NT1 and the carrier's ISDN network

In most implementations for BRI users, an NT2 is not used and usually is found only in PBXs. In this case, the CPE-to-carrier interface is referred to as the S/T interface.

Generally, routers come with an integrated S/T ISDN interface, so the reference points would look like they do in Figure 7-2.

Figure 7-1 *ISDN Reference Points*

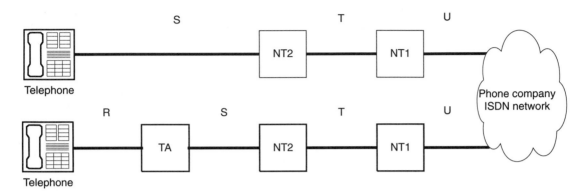

Figure 7-2 *ISDN Reference Points for a Router with an Integrated S/T ISDN Interface*

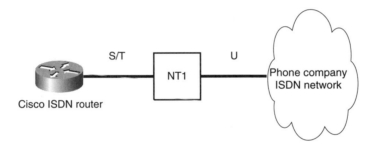

Additionally, Cisco routers can be purchased with an S/T interface and integrated NT1, so reference points S, T, and U would all be incorporated into the BRI/PRI interface of the Cisco router.

In North America, all ISDN lines are connected to the ISDN switch at the local central office (CO) through a U interface. This U interface requires network termination to convert it into an S/T interface that actually connects to your end equipment. An NT-1 is a separate unit that serves this function and also provides power to your ISDN line. In Europe, the NT-1 is included in telco-provisioned ISDN lines, so all you need is the S/T interface.

When working with Cisco routers, it is important to determine whether the unit has an S/T interface, which will require an external NT-1, or a U interface with a built-in NT-1. Check your hardware manual to determine whether you have the proper equipment.

ISDN Layers

ISDN deals with Layers 1, 2, and 3 of the OSI reference model. ISDN connectivity works only if all three of these layers are operational. Layer 1 is the physical layer, dealing with the physical connections between the router and the ISDN circuit. Layer 2, the data link layer, deals with the Q.921 protocol on the D channel and the encapsulation options for each B channel (HDLC and PPP). Q.921 handles the signaling between the router ISDN interface and the ISDN switch. Layer 3, the network layer, includes the Q.931 protocol over the D channel and network layer protocols (IP, IPX, AppleTalk, and so on) over the B channels. Q.931 handles call setup messages between the calling and called parties. It is important to fully understand the various protocols that operate over the D and B channels when configuring and troubleshooting ISDN.

ISDN Encapsulation Options

ISDN routers can support both PPP and HDLC encapsulations. HDLC is the default encapsulation, but the vast majority of ISDN routers use PPP. The main reason that PPP is chosen over HDLC is because HDLC cannot use both B channels simultaneously. With HDLC, both B channels can be up, but one channel is used to send and the other is used to receive traffic. Each B channel has the capability to provide full duplex (send and receive at the same time), so by using HDLC, you are essentially cutting the possible data rate over the link in half.

PPP was covered in Chapter 4, "WAN Protocols and Technologies: Point-to-Point Protocol (PPP)," and the majority of what was discussed in this chapter applies to ISDN. The benefits of using PPP encapsulation include the capability to use both BRI B channels simultaneously, using the PPP **multilink** command, as well as being able to perform the authentication options (PAP and CHAP) discussed in Chapter 4.

ISDN Configuration Basics

Now that the boring specifics of ISDN are behind us, it is time to dive into the more interesting topic of how to actually configure Cisco routers to use ISDN.

Unfortunately, there is currently no method of configuring ISDN in a lab environment without the use of actual ISDN circuits or a costly ISDN simulator. Nonetheless, ISDN is a core topic in the CCIE routing and switching lab exam, and the only way to learn the topic is through a great deal of hands-on practice.

To configure basic ISDN, only two things must be configured:

- ISDN switch type settings
- Service profile identifiers (SPIDs)

The SPID is a number assigned to a fully initializing ISDN terminal that enables the Stored Program Control Switching System (SPCS) to uniquely identify the ISDN terminal at Layer 3 of the D-channel signaling protocol.

A SPID is assigned to each B channel and usually resembles a phone number followed by some extra digits. For example, if your router is connecting to a Siemens ISDN switch, the SPIDs would typically be of the type aaabbbbbbbccdd, where

> aaa is the three-digit area code
> bbbbbbb is the seven-digit phone number

For national ISDN switches, the most frequently used SPID value is NPANXXXXXX0101, based on the configurations being installed today. The NPA/NXX is simply the carrier's term for the local area code/access number.

Not all ISDN switches actually require that the SPIDS be configured, but the majority of them do. The ISDN provider can provide you with the information that you need. Currently, Cisco routers support a number of different switch type options, as documented in Table 7-1.

Table 7-1 *Supported ISDN Switch Types*

Identifier	Description
basic-1tr6	German 1TR6 ISDN switches
basic-5ess	AT&T basic rate switches
basic-dms100	NT DMS-100 basic rate switches
basic-net3	NET3 ISDN and Euro-ISDN switches (UK and others), also called E-DSS1 or DSS1
basic-ni1	National ISDN-1 switches
basic-nwnet3	Norway Net3 switches
basic-nznet3	New Zealand Net3 switches
basic-ts013	Australian TS013 switches
None	No switch defined
Ntt	Japanese NTT ISDN switches (ISDN BRI only)
primary-4ess	AT&T 4ESS switch type for the United States (ISDN PRI only)
primary-5ess	AT&T 5ESS switch type for the United States (ISDN PRI only)
primary-dms100	NT DMS-100 switch type for the United States (ISDN PRI only)
primary-net5	NET5 ISDN PRI switches (Europe)
primary-ntt	INS-Net 1500 for Japan (ISDN PRI only)
primary-ts014	Australian TS014 switches (ISDN PRI only)

Table 7-1   *Supported ISDN Switch Types (Continued)*

Identifier	Description
vn2	French VN2 ISDN switches (ISDN BRI only)
vn3	French VN3 ISDN switches (ISDN BRI only)
vn4	French VN4 ISDN switches (ISDN BRI only)

You need to contact your ISDN service provider to determine which switch type is being used. The switch type can be configured in both *global* and *interface* configuration modes. If it is specified in global mode, the switch type applies to all ISDN interfaces in the router. If it is placed in interface mode, it is applied to the interface only. If both are specified, the switch type that is configured in interface mode overrides the switch type set globally for that interface. For example, if you have a router with six ISDN interfaces and five of them connect to a DMS-100 switch, with the other connecting to an NI switch, you can use the **isdn switch-type basic-dms100** command globally and then use the command **isdn switch-type basic-ni** in interface mode for the specific NI connected BRI interface.

Configuring Dial-on-Demand Routing (DDR)

For ISDN to work properly, *dial-on-demand routing (DDR)* options must be created on the interface. Often, ISDN links are used to back up point-to-point or Frame Relay circuits. If not configured correctly, the ISDN link can stay up constantly or can continuously connect, hang up, and then connect again. Because ISDN carrier's normally charge usage by the minute, a small configuration error can result in a customer getting ISDN bills of more than $1000 per month. Unless you enjoy long "discussions" with your manager, you probably want to avoid this. DDR works using the concept of user-defined "interesting" traffic. The ISDN link will come up only under the circumstances permitted, or when certain interesting traffic is passed to the ISDN interface. The ISDN call will stay up until no interesting traffic has passed through the ISDN interface for a user-specified period of time, using the **dialer idle-timeout** command in interface configuration mode. The default idle timeout length is 120 seconds. The length of time that can be configured is as follows:

```
ISDN_Router(config-if)#dialer idle-timeout ?
  <1-2147483>  Idle timeout before disconnecting a call
```

This time is specified in seconds. An important thing to note here is that *all* types of traffic will pass over the ISDN link as long as the connection is active, not just the traffic specified as "interesting."

However, only traffic specified as interesting will keep the call up. Think of the dialer idle timeout value as a countdown timer. When traffic specified as interesting initiates an ISDN connection, the timer starts, counting down to 0. When the timer reaches 0, the connection is dropped. This timer is reset only when the traffic specified as interesting (which was defined in the dialer lists) passes through the ISDN link. As you will see, there are a number of ways to accomplish DDR; the trick is to configure the routers so that an ISDN connection is established when needed, while suppressing the connection when it is not needed.

The two options that are discussed with DDR in this chapter are legacy DDR and dialer profiles. Legacy DDR deals with the capability to enable a connection only when there is traffic to send. Here, the dialer parameters are specified on the physical ISDN interface. Dialer profiles include the use of logical dialer interfaces, which are separate from the physical ISDN interface, to issue a DDR call. In this setup, the bulk of the configuration commands are placed on the logical dialer interfaces, and only a few necessary commands actually are placed on the physical ISDN interface. Examples of both legacy and dialer profile configurations are covered in this chapter.

To configure DDR, you must keep in mind that there are two ends to an ISDN call: the *calling router* and the *called router*. The calling router is the router that will initiate the ISDN call, and the called router is the destination router where the ISDN link terminates. Note that each router can serve as both a calling and a called router; however, when setting up DDR, you work from one side at a time. One router might have different requirements for placing a call than the other router. Figure 7-3 shows a typical simple ISDN setup.

Figure 7-3   *ISDN Backing up a Primary Link*

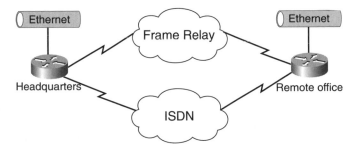

Normally, the remote office will initiate the ISDN connection, therefore becoming the calling router. The headquarters router becomes the called router. Larger networks might have numerous remote offices that use routers with BRI interfaces, with the headquarters router having a PRI interface to handle multiple ISDN calls at once.

In this setup, the Frame Relay link is used as the primary, with the ISDN link backing up the Frame Relay, and is used only when there is a Frame Relay outage. Typically, the remote office is the calling router, and the headquarters location is the called router. As you will see, there are numerous ways in which to accomplish this.

To configure DDR, perform the following steps:

Step 1   Configure the ISDN switch type and SPID information, if necessary.

Step 2   Specify the interesting traffic that will bring up the ISDN call.

Step 3   Configure the dialer information. This includes the number to call to reach the called router, as well as any other parameters associated with the call.

Step 4   Configure any other optional parameters associated with the ISDN interface. These advanced topics include interface encapsulation, dialer idle-timeout, authentication options, callback for billing purposes, and so on. Most of these options are covered later in the chapter.

Step 5   Route traffic over the ISDN line. You can use a number of options here, such as specifying floating static routes, using the backup interface command, or using dynamic routing protocols together with their respective options. These options include the following:

> — For OSPF: OSPF demand circuit
>
> — For EIGRP, IGRP, OSPF: Dialer watch
>
> — IGRP, RIP: Snapshot routing
>
> — All: Backup interface

These routing topics are covered later in the chapter, and these options are demonstrated through different labs. You will find many parallels in these examples to those found in Chapter 4, but because ISDN is such an important topic, some more examples are provided that can be found in Chapter 4 for the sake of completeness.

Within the scope of the CCIE lab, you will be provided the switch type and the SPID numbers, so there won't be a lot of guessing. In the real world, ISDN is a huge pain because of service provider issues; however, most typical noncarrier problems are the result of incorrectly entering information (that is, SPIDS or switch type). The other setup for bringing up an ISDN line is to save the router configuration and power-reset the router. Within the scope of the lab exam, if you are *highly confident* that you have your router configured correctly and that you have the correct *working cable* plugged into the *correct* jack, don't hesitate too long to notify the instructor that you are having problems with the line and you are wondering whether there have been problems with the line in the past. As with all other questions to the instructor, ask questions as if the instructor is a customer!

Step 1: Configure the ISDN Switch Type and SPID Information

Referring back to Figure 7-1, you can specify the ISDN switch type in either global or interface configuration mode. Because the routers in this diagram have only one BRI interface, it does not matter where it is applied. For purposes here, specify it in interface mode along with the SPID information, as demonstrated in Example 7-1.

Example 7-1 *Setting the SPID Information on a BRI Interface*

```
ISDN_Router#config terminal
Enter configuration commands, one per line.  End with CNTL/Z.
ISDN_Router(config)#interface BRI0
ISDN_Router(config-if)#isdn switch-type basic-dms100
ISDN_Router(config-if)#isdn spid1 61293198331111 ldn
ISDN_Router(config-if)#isdn spid2 61293198461111 ldn
```

The LDN is the local directory number, which is the seven-digit number assigned by the service provider and used for call routing. The LDN is not necessary for establishing ISDN-based connections, but it must be specified if you want to receive incoming calls on the second B channel. The LDN is required only when two SPIDs are configured (for example, when connecting to a DMS or NI1 switch). Each SPID is associated with an LDN, and configuring the LDN causes incoming calls to B channel 2 to be answered properly. If the LDN is not configured, incoming calls to B channel 2 might fail.

CAUTION   Take caution when entering the SPID information because it can be easy to "fat finger" the numbers. We have done this often and then have wasted time trying to troubleshoot what I thought was an ISDN circuit problem, only to realize that we typed in the wrong SPID.

Step 2: Specify Interesting Traffic

Interesting traffic is defined as the kind of traffic that is allowed to initiate an ISDN connection. When this connection has been established, the link will stay up as long as the type of traffic that is defined as interesting traverses the ISDN link.

This step is performed using the **dialer-group** interface command, along with a special access list that defines the interesting traffic, called a dialer list, in global configuration mode. The syntax for the **dialer-list** is as follows:

> **dialer-list** *dialer-group* **protocol** *protocol-name* [**permit** | **deny** | **list**] *access-list number.*

Here, the *dialer-group* argument is used to define the interesting traffic for the interface. This is the same number that was entered into the **dialer-group** command. Be sure that the number specified in the *dialer-group* number matches the *dialer-list* number. For example, if you want to specify all IP traffic as interesting, use the command **dialer list 1 protocol ip permit**.

You also can use extended dialer lists to define a more granular set of conditions that will define the interesting traffic, by combining a dialer list with an extended access list. For example, if you want to specify that only traffic originating from 10.1.1.0/24 destined for 10.1.2.0/24 can initiate an ISDN call, you would accomplish this through the following commands:

```
ISDN_Router(config)#dialer-list 1 protocol ip list 101
ISDN_Router(config)#access-list 101 permit ip 10.1.1.0 0.0.0.255 10.1.2.0 0.0.0.255
```

The first command ties the dialer list to an extended access list; this example uses access list 101. By using extended access lists, you can be more specific in what types of traffic you define as interesting.

Step 3: Configure Dialer Information

A few options should be considered when configuring the dialer information. The most basic way to do this is through the **dialer-string** interface command. Configuring the dialer information in this manner has some limitations—namely, the dialer string will be used for all outgoing calls, regardless of the actual destination. This works well if the calling router has only one other router to connect to, but not if the ISDN router has the capability to dial into more than one other ISDN router. A more feature-rich way of accomplishing this step is using the **dialer-map** command. Here, a router can more accurately determine which ISDN router to dial into based on the Layer 3 address. These two options commonly are referred to as legacy DDR. Finally, the last option is to use a set of logical dialer interfaces. A major advantage to using logical dialer interfaces is that an ISDN router has the capability to dial into multiple other ISDN routers simultaneously. We will now demonstrate these three options using the simplified network in Figure 7-4 as a reference.

Figure 7-4   *Simplified ISDN Network*

Configuring Dialer Information, Method 1: Using Dialer Strings

This is the simplest (and least robust) way to configure ISDN. In Example 7-2, all traffic specified as interesting initiates the call, which will be placed to the number specified in the dialer string. This works well for situations in which there is only one possible destination, but not in networks where there are multiple ISDN sites that need access to each other directly. Note that the BRI interface encapsulation in this example has been set to PPP. In this situation, it is not necessary and could have just as easily been left with the default encapsulation, HDLC.

Example 7-2 *Cheech and Chong Router Configurations Using Dialer Strings*

```
Cheech#show running-config

version 11.2
no service password-encryption
no service udp-small-servers
no service tcp-small-servers
!
hostname Cheech
!
enable password cisco
!
isdn switch-type basic-dms100
!
interface Ethernet0
 no ip address
shutdown
!
interface Serial0
no ip address
shutdown
!
interface Serial1
 no ip address
 shutdown
!
interface BRI0
 ip address 175.10.23.1 255.255.255.252
 encapsulation ppp
 isdn spid1 61293199371111   <SPID associated with the first B channel
 isdn spid2 61293199381111   <SPID associated with the second B channel
 dialer string 6129319833    <number to dial for all outgoing connections
 dialer-group 1
!
ip classless
!
dialer-list 1 protocol ip permit  <all ip traffic is interesting
!
line con 0
 exec-timeout 0 0
 privilege level 15
 logging synchronous
line aux 0
line vty 0 4
 password cisco
 login
!
end
```

```
Chong#show running-config
!
version 11.2
```

Example 7-2   *Cheech and Chong Router Configurations Using Dialer Strings (Continued)*

```
no service password-encryption
no service udp-small-servers
no service tcp-small-servers
!
hostname Chong
!
enable password cisco
!
isdn switch-type basic-dms100
!
interface Ethernet0
no ip address
shutdown
!
interface Serial0
no ip address
shutdown

!
interface Serial1
 no ip address
 shutdown
!
interface BRI0
 ip address 175.10.23.2 255.255.255.252
encapsulation ppp
isdn spid1 61293198331111    <SPID for the first B channel
isdn spid2 61293198461111    <SPID for the second B channel
dialer string 6129319937     <number to call for all connections
dialer-group 1
!
no ip classless
!
dialer-list 1 protocol ip permit  <all ip traffic is interesting
!
line con 0
 exec-timeout 0 0
 privilege level 15
 logging synchronous
line aux 0
line vty 0 4
no login
privilege level 15
!
end
```

In this example, both routers can initiate ISDN calls. If you want only Cheech to be capable of calling into Chong, and not vice versa, you could omit the **dialer string** command in Chong's configuration.

NOTE   Although the configurations in Example 7-2 are fairly straightforward, you might not be familiar with some commands. Both routers have some serious security holes that purposely were done. Under the **line con 0**, we added the **privilege level 15** command. This enables anyone connected to the router to go straight to enable mode without typing in the enable password. We also added the **exec-timeout 0 0** command, which means that all console connections will never time out. This was done only to save the time and effort that it takes to go into enable mode and type in a password to get into enable mode. We did something similar under the vty so that when you Telnet to a router, you go automatically into enable mode without a password prompt. Although this is useful in a lab environment, these commands never should be implemented in a live production router. One final command to point out is the **logging synchronous** parameter under the console heading. This prevents the router from interrupting you while you are in the middle of typing a command. By default, the router logs all events to the console, which can make it easy to lose your place while typing in commands. An alternative to this is the **no logging console** command, but we prefer the **logging synchronous** command because it allows you to see the console log entries, which is usually useful, without the bothersome interruptions that occur by default.

Configuring Dialer Information, Method 2: Using Dialer Maps

The problem with using dialer strings occurs when multiple ISDN connections are involved. In the network illustrated in Figure 7-5, the Headquarters router would require two sets of dialer strings to connect to the remote offices, Cheech and Chong. However, because the Headquarters router has no way of associating IP addresses with dialer strings, it might dial the Cheech router when it needs to connect to the Chong router.

Figure 7-5   *Dialer Map Configuration*

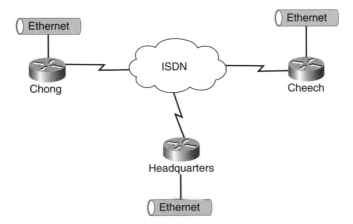

A way to map IP addresses to dialed numbers is to use dialer maps. Using dialer maps tells the router which dial string to call when it wants to connect to a specific IP address. Example 7-3 demonstrates the router configuration using dialer maps.

Example 7-3 *Example Dial String Configuration for the Headquarters Router*

```
interface BRI0
 ip address 175.10.23.3 255.255.255.248
 encapsulation ppp
 isdn spid1 61293193601111
 isdn spid2 61293197761111
 dialer map ip 175.10.23.1 name Cheech 6129319937
 dialer map ip 175.10.23.2 name Chong 6129319833
 dialer-group 1
```

The IP address space is set up so that when the Headquarters router calls either Cheech or Chong, they are in the same subnet.

You should be aware of a couple of other options when using dialer maps. One is that the connection speed for each B channel can be manually set to either 56 kbps or 64 kbps, using the **speed** keyword. Another useful command is the **name** keyword, which can be placed at the end of the dialer map statement. With CHAP and the **name** keyword included in the **dialer map** command, both the telephone number and the name for a given next-hop address are compared to the names of the routers already connected. In this way, calls to destinations to which connections already are established can be avoided.

More important is the **broadcast** keyword option. If you want to pass routing updates across the ISDN connection, (routing protocols use broadcast packets to advertise their routes), you must use the **broadcast** keyword in the dialer map statement, as demonstrated in Example 7-4. This is much like Frame Relay, in that the **broadcast** statement must be configured in all **frame-relay map** statements if you want to pass routing updates.

Example 7-4 *Using the **broadcast** Statement: Headquarters Router Configuration*

```
interface BRI0
 ip address 175.10.23.3 255.255.255.248
 encapsulation ppp
 isdn spid1 61293193601111
 isdn spid2 61293197761111
 dialer map ip 175.10.23.1 name Cheech broadcast 6129319937
 dialer map ip 175.10.23.2 name Chong broadcast 6129319833
 dialer-group 1
```

The configuration in Example 7-4 enables the passing of routing updates and other broadcast traffic. However, if you don't want this traffic to actually trigger calls, you need to specify restrictive dialer lists or make the ISDN interface passive under the routing process.

Configuring Dialer Information, Method 3: Using Logical Dialer Interfaces

Dialer profiles were introduced in Cisco IOS Software Release 11.2, and they offer the capability to separate the configuration parameters used in legacy DDR from the physical interfaces. It is perhaps the most complex method of configuring DDR, but it offers the greatest amount of flexibility and design options. It works through the creation of logical dialer interfaces, where the configuration options are placed. These dialer interfaces are bound to a physical interface only when a connection is made, through the use of dialer pools.

To configure dialer profiles, first you must remove all legacy DDR commands under the BRI 0 interface. Then you create a logical interface, dialer 1, and place all configuration options and Layer 3 information on that interface. The steps for configuring dialer profiles are as follows:

Step 1   Remove all legacy DDR commands from the BRI 0 interface. IOS will not allow you to map a dialer interface to a physical interface until this is done.

Step 2   Configure a logical interface using the **interface dialer** *X* command, where *X* can be any value between 0 and 255.

Step 3   Configure a **dialer remote-name** on the dialer interface. Only one remote name can be specified, and this should be the name of the router with which you want to make an ISDN connection.

Step 4   Map the logical interface to the physical interface. This is done by associating a dialer pool on the logical interface to the **dialer pool-member** on the physical interface. This is done with the **dialer pool-member** *x* command on the physical interface and the **dialer pool** *x* command on the logical dialer interface, where *x* can be any integer from 1 to 255. The number specified must be the same for both interfaces, and there can be only one dialer pool per dialer interface.

Step 5   Define the interesting traffic. This is needed only for routers that initiate calls (calling routers), and it is done the same way as legacy DDR, except that the commands are now placed on the logical interface.

Step 6   Provide a dialer string to call on the logical interface. This is the number to call to connect to another ISDN router. Note here that dialer maps cannot be configured on dialer interfaces. When a connection is made to another router, dialer maps are generated dynamically.

Step 7   Configure the optional parameters on the dialer interface. This is where things like dialer idle timeouts and network addressing are placed.

Example 7-5 illustrates an example configuration that incorporates these seven steps. The important thing to notice in this example is the introduction of the logical dialer interface.

Example 7-5   *Example Dialer Profile Configuration*

```
Remote_Site#show running-config
Building configuration...

Current configuration:
!
version 12.0
service timestamps debug uptime
service timestamps log uptime
no service password-encryption
!
hostname Remote_Site
!
!
username Headquarters password 0 cisco
ip subnet-zero
isdn switch-type basic-dms100
!
interface Loopback0
 ip address 175.10.101.1 255.255.255.255
 no ip directed-broadcast
!
interface Ethernet0
 ip address 175.10.2.1 255.255.255.0
 no ip directed-broadcast
 no keepalive
!
interface Serial0
 no ip address
 no ip directed-broadcast
 shutdown
 no fair-queue
 clockrate 125000
!
interface Serial1
 description PRIMARY LINK TO HQ
 bandwidth 64
 ip address 175.10.200.1 255.255.255.252
 no ip directed-broadcast
!
```

continues

Example 7-5 *Example Dialer Profile Configuration (Continued)*

```
interface BRI0
 no ip address
 no ip directed-broadcast
 encapsulation ppp
 dialer pool-member 1
 isdn switch-type basic-dms100
 isdn spid1 61293199371111
 isdn spid2 61293199381111
!
interface Dialer1
 ip address 175.10.23.1 255.255.255.252
 no ip directed-broadcast
 encapsulation ppp
 dialer remote-name Headquarters
 dialer string 6129319833
 dialer pool 1
 dialer-group 1
!
no ip classless
!
dialer-list 1 protocol ip permit
!
!
line con 0
 privilege level 15
 logging synchronous
 transport input none
line aux 0
line vty 0 4
 login
!
end

! We can verify our configuration by using the show dialer command.  Notice here
that the BRI 0 interface is now bound to the logical dialer interface, dialer 1.
Remote_Site#show dialer

BRI0 - dialer type = ISDN

Dial String      Successes   Failures    Last called   Last status
0 incoming call(s) have been screened.
0 incoming call(s) rejected for callback.

BRI0:1 - dialer type = ISDN
Idle timer (120 secs), Fast idle timer (20 secs)
Wait for carrier (30 secs), Re-enable (15 secs)
Dialer state is data link layer up
Dial reason: ip (s=175.10.23.1, d=175.10.23.2)
Interface bound to profile Di1
Time until disconnect 111 secs
Current call connected 00:00:10
```

Example 7-5   *Example Dialer Profile Configuration (Continued)*

```
Connected to 6129319833 (6129319833)

BRI0:2 - dialer type = ISDN
Idle timer (120 secs), Fast idle timer (20 secs)
Wait for carrier (30 secs), Re-enable (15 secs)
Dialer state is idle

Di1 - dialer type = DIALER PROFILE
Idle timer (120 secs), Fast idle timer (20 secs)
Wait for carrier (30 secs), Re-enable (15 secs)
Dialer state is data link layer up

Dial String      Successes   Failures    Last called    Last status
6129319833               2          0     00:00:11       successful    Default
```

Step 4: Configuring Advanced Optional Parameters

A number of advanced features can be specified using ISDN, including ISDN callback, call screening, and PPP authentication. Most of these options apply only to a PPP encapsulated interface. To demonstrate this, simply look at the number of PPP options available to us on the BRI interface in Example 7-6.

Example 7-6   *Calling Up the Available PPP Options*

```
R2(config-if)#ppp ?
  authentication         Set PPP link authentication method
  bap                    Set BAP bandwidth allocation parameters
  bridge               Enable PPP bridge translation
  callbac    k             Set PPP link callback option
  chap                   Set CHAP authentication parameters
  compression            Enable PPP Compression control negotiation
  ipcp                 Set IPCP negotiation options
  lcp                  PPP LCP configuration
  max-bad-auth           Allow multiple authentication failures
  multilink              Make interface multilink capable
  pap                    Set PAP authentication parameters
  quality                Set minimum Link Quality before link is down
  reliable-link          Use LAPB with PPP to provide a reliable link
  timeout                Set PPP timeout parameters
  use-tacacs             Use TACACS to verify PPP authentications
```

For example, if you want to use authentication to verify the validity of an incoming ISDN call, you must use PPP encapsulation. PPP also can be used to configure dialer callback and multilink, among others. Because of the feature available using PPP, and because nearly all real-world ISDN configurations use PPP-encapsulated interfaces, you will be using PPP encapsulated BRI interfaces in all of the labs.

The most commonly configured optional parameter involves the use of authentication, which means using either PAP or CHAP, as discussed in the sections that follow.

Example: Authentication Using the Password Authentication Protocol (PAP)

PAP is a simple method for a remote router to verify the validity of a remote node. The primary drawback is that it is not a secure method, meaning that the username and password are sent across the ISDN network in plain text and can be seen easily using a protocol analyzer. Because the PAP process is sent across the link without encryption, anyone with a protocol analyzer easily can obtain this information. PAP also offers no protection against playback and trial-and-error (dictionary or brute force) attacks. Because of this, CHAP is the preferred method of authentication. Still, it supplies a rudimentary authentication method supported by Cisco.

To configure PAP, you need to configure four things:

Step 1 Configure the remote router's username and password in global configuration mode, using the **username** *name* **password** *password* command. The username must match the host name that is configured on the remote router exactly, and it is case-sensitive.

Step 2 Under interface configuration mode, you need to set up PPP encapsulation on the ISDN interface using the **encapsulation ppp** command.

Step 3 Specify that you are using PAP authentication using the **ppp authentication pap** command.

Step 4 Specify the local username and password combination that you want to send to the remote ISDN router with the **ppp pap sent-username** *username* **password** *password* command. This must match what the remote router has specified in Step 1 for your router.

Example 7-7 shows the PAP authentication configuration for the calling router, and Example 7-8 shows the PAP authentication configuration for the called router.

Example 7-7 *Example PAP Authentication Configuration: Router 1 (Calling Router)*

```
ISDN-1#show running-config
Building configuration...

Current configuration:
!
version 12.0
service timestamps debug uptime
service timestamps log uptime
no service password-encryption
!
```

Example 7-7   *Example PAP Authentication Configuration: Router 1 (Calling Router) (Continued)*

```
hostname ISDN-1
!
!
username ISDN-2 password 0 CISCO
ip subnet-zero
isdn switch-type basic-dms100
!
!
!
interface Loopback0
 ip address 175.10.101.1 255.255.255.255
 no ip directed-broadcast
!
interface Ethernet0
 ip address 175.10.2.1 255.255.255.0
 no ip directed-broadcast
 no keepalive
!
interface Serial0
 no ip address
 no ip directed-broadcast
 encapsulation frame-relay
 logging event subif-link-status
 logging event dlci-status-change
 no fair-queue
 clockrate 125000
!
interface Serial1
 description PRIMARY LINK TO HQ
 bandwidth 64
 ip address 175.10.200.1 255.255.255.252
 no ip directed-broadcast
!
interface BRI0
 ip address 175.10.23.1 255.255.255.252
 no ip directed-broadcast
 encapsulation ppp
 dialer map ip 175.10.23.2 name ISDN-2 broadcast 6129319833
 dialer-group 1
 isdn switch-type basic-dms100
 isdn spid1 61293199371111
 isdn spid2 61293199381111
 ppp authentication pap
 ppp pap sent-username ISDN-1 password 7 0802657D2A36
!
router eigrp 1
 passive-interface BRI0
 network 175.10.0.0
 no auto-summary
!
```

continues

Example 7-7 *Example PAP Authentication Configuration: Router 1 (Calling Router) (Continued)*

```
no ip classless
!
dialer-list 1 protocol ip permit
!
!
line con 0
 privilege level 15
 logging synchronous
 transport input none
line aux 0
line vty 0 4
 login
!
end
```

Example 7-8 *Example PAP Authentication Configuration: Router 2 (Called Router)*

```
ISDN-2#show running-config
Building configuration...

Current configuration:
!
version 12.0
service timestamps debug uptime
service timestamps log uptime
no service password-encryption
!
hostname ISDN-2
!
logging buffered 9096 debugging
!
username ISDN-1 password 0 CISCO
ip subnet-zero
isdn switch-type basic-dms100
!
!
!
interface Loopback0
 ip address 175.10.102.1 255.255.255.255
 no ip directed-broadcast
!
interface Ethernet0
 ip address 175.10.1.1 255.255.255.0
 no ip directed-broadcast
 no keepalive
!
interface Serial0
 no ip address
 no ip directed-broadcast
 encapsulation frame-relay
```

Example 7-8   *Example PAP Authentication Configuration: Router 2 (Called Router) (Continued)*

```
 logging event subif-link-status
 logging event dlci-status-change
!
interface Serial1
 description PRIMARY LINK TO REMOTE SITE
 bandwidth 64
 ip address 175.10.200.2 255.255.255.252
 no ip directed-broadcast
 clockrate 125000
!
interface BRI0
 ip address 175.10.23.2 255.255.255.252
 no ip directed-broadcast
 encapsulation ppp
 dialer-group 1
 isdn switch-type basic-dms100
 isdn spid1 61293198331111
 isdn spid2 61293198461111
 ppp authentication pap
 ppp pap sent-username ISDN-2 password 7 01302F377024
!
no ip classless
!
dialer-list 1 protocol ip permit
!
!
line con 0
 privilege level 15
 logging synchronous
 transport input none
line aux 0
line vty 0 4
 login
!
end
```

In the configuration, the password is encrypted under the BRI0 interface. This is done by Cisco IOS Software so that anyone passing by your desk cannot obtain the password simply by looking at the configuration. This password is encrypted only in the configuration file, and the actual password (CISCO) is sent in plain text across the link.

Example: Authentication Using the Challenge Handshake Authentication Protocol (CHAP)

CHAP is used in nearly every real-world PPP authentication scheme because it offers better security than PAP. CHAP periodically verifies the identity of the remote node and uses the MD5 hash algorithm to encrypt the CHAP process. Therefore, Joe Hacker who has put a sniffer on the line will be unable to decipher what the password is. CHAP uses a three-way handshake occurring in the following sequence:

1 The central rite router issues a challenge to the remote router.

2 The remote router responds to the challenge.

3 The central site router accepts or rejects the connection.

Only three configuration steps are required to configure PPP CHAP authentication:

Step 1 Set the encapsulation type to PPP by on the ISDN interface.

Step 2 Configure CHAP on the interface using the **ppp authentication chap** command in interface configuration mode.

Step 3 Configure the username and password of the remote ISDN router(s), using the **username** *name* **password** *secret* in global configuration mode, where *name* is the host name of the remote router and *secret* is the secret password. The name is case-sensitive and must match the remote router's host name exactly (and it is case-sensitive). The secret password also must be the same on both routers. If you find that CHAP is failing, one of the first things that you should verify is that the username is specified correctly and that both routers are using the exact same password.

Example 7-9 shows the PPP CHAP configuration for Router 1, and Example 7-10 shows the PPP CHAP configuration for Router 2.

Example 7-9 *Example PPP CHAP Configuration: Router 1*

```
ISDN-1#show running-config
!
version 12.0
service timestamps debug uptime
service timestamps log uptime
no service password-encryption
!
hostname ISDN-1
!
!
username ISDN-2 password cisco
ip subnet-zero
isdn switch-type basic-dms100
!
!
!
interface Ethernet0
 ip address 175.10.2.1 255.255.255.0
 no ip directed-broadcast
!
interface Serial0
```

Example 7-9 *Example PPP CHAP Configuration: Router 1 (Continued)*

```
 no ip address
 no ip directed-broadcast
 shutdown
 no fair-queue
!
interface Serial1
 no ip address
 no ip directed-broadcast
 shutdown
!
interface BRI0
 ip address 175.10.23.1 255.255.255.248
 no ip directed-broadcast
 encapsulation ppp
 dialer map ip 175.10.23.2 name ISDN-2 broadcast 6129319833
 dialer-group 1
 isdn switch-type basic-dms100
 isdn spid1 61293199371111
 isdn spid2 61293199381111
 ppp authentication chap
!
no ip classless
!
dialer-list 1 protocol ip permit
!
!
line con 0
 privilege level 15
 logging synchronous
 transport input none
line aux 0
line vty 0 4
 login
!
end
```

Example 7-10 *Example PPP CHAP Configuration: Router 2*

```
ISDN-2#show running-config
!
version 12.0
service timestamps debug uptime
service timestamps log uptime
no service password-encryption
!
hostname ISDN-2
!
!
username ISDN-1 password cisco
```

continues

Example 7-10 *Example PPP CHAP Configuration: Router 2 (Continued)*

```
ip subnet-zero
isdn switch-type basic-dms100
!
!
!
interface Ethernet0
 ip address 172.16.1.1 255.255.255.0
 no ip directed-broadcast
!
interface Serial0
 no ip address
 no ip directed-broadcast
 shutdown
!
interface Serial1
 no ip address
 no ip directed-broadcast
 shutdown
!
interface BRI0
 ip address 175.10.23.2 255.255.255.248
 no ip directed-broadcast
 encapsulation ppp
 dialer map ip 175.10.23.1 name ISDN-1 broadcast 6129319937
 dialer-group 1
 isdn switch-type basic-dms100
 isdn spid1 61293198331111
 isdn spid2 61293198461111
 ppp authentication chap
!
no ip classless
!
dialer-list 1 protocol ip permit
!
!
line con 0
 privilege level 15
 logging synchronous
 transport input none
line aux 0
line vty 0 4
 login
!
end
```

The important configuration commands for CHAP authentication have been highlighted.

Example: Authentication Using an Alternative Host Name

Cisco IOS Software allows you to configure CHAP using a different host name than what the calling router's actual host name is.

When a remote Cisco router connects to either a Cisco or a non-Cisco central router of a different administrative control, an Internet service provider (ISP), or a rotary of central routers, it is necessary to configure an authentication username that is different from the host name. In this situation, the host name of the router is not provided or is different at different times (rotary). Also, the username and password that are allocated by the ISP might not be the remote router's host name. In such a situation, the **ppp chap hostname** command is used to specify an alternate username that will be used for authentication.

For example, consider a situation in which multiple remote devices are dialing into a central site. Using normal CHAP authentication, the username (which would be the host name) of each remote device and a shared secret must be configured on the central router. In this scenario, the configuration of the central router can get lengthy and cumbersome to manage; however, if the remote devices use a username that is different from their host name, this can be avoided. The central site can be configured with a single username and shared secret that can be used to authenticate multiple dial-in clients.

This is done using the **ppp chap hostname "alternate-host-name"** command:

```
ISDN-1(config-if)#ppp chap  hostname ?
  WORD  Alternate CHAP hostname
```

On the called router, you need to configure the username/password combination using the alternate host name of the calling router, not the actual host name. Example 7-11 shows the configuration for the calling router, and Example 7-12 shows the configuration for the called router.

Example 7-11 *CHAP Alternate Host Name Configuration: Calling Router*

```
ISDN-1#show running-config
Building configuration...

Current configuration:
!
version 12.0
service timestamps debug uptime
service timestamps log uptime
no service password-encryption
!
hostname ISDN-1
!
username ISDN-2 password cisco
ip subnet-zero
isdn switch-type basic-dms100
!
interface Ethernet0
```

continues

Example 7-11 *CHAP Alternate Host Name Configuration: Calling Router (Continued)*

```
 ip address 172.16.1.1 255.255.255.0
 no ip directed-broadcast
!
interface Serial0
 no ip address
 no ip directed-broadcast
 shutdown
 no fair-queue
!
interface Serial1
 no ip address
 no ip directed-broadcast
 shutdown
!
interface BRI0
 ip address 175.10.23.1 255.255.255.248
 no ip directed-broadcast
 encapsulation ppp
 dialer map ip 175.10.23.2 name ISDN-2 broadcast 6129319833
 dialer-group 1
 isdn switch-type basic-dms100
 isdn spid1 61293199371111
 isdn spid2 61293199381111
 ppp authentication chap
 ppp chap hostname FAKE_NAME
!
no ip classless
!
dialer-list 1 protocol ip permit
!
!
line con 0
 privilege level 15
 logging synchronous
 transport input none
line aux 0
line vty 0 4
 login
!
end
```

Example 7-12 *CHAP Alternate Host Name Configuration: Called Router*

```
ISDN-2#show running-config
Building configuration...

Current configuration:
!
version 12.0
service timestamps debug uptime
```

Example 7-12 *CHAP Alternate Host Name Configuration: Called Router (Continued)*

```
service timestamps log uptime
no service password-encryption
!
hostname ISDN-2
!
!
username FAKE_NAME password cisco
ip subnet-zero
isdn switch-type basic-dms100
!
!
!
interface Ethernet0
 ip address 172.16.1.1 255.255.255.0
 no ip directed-broadcast
!
interface Serial0
 no ip address
 no ip directed-broadcast
 shutdown
!
interface Serial1
 no ip address
 no ip directed-broadcast
 shutdown
!
interface BRI0
 ip address 175.10.23.2 255.255.255.248
 no ip directed-broadcast
 encapsulation ppp
 dialer map ip 175.10.23.1 name ISDN-1 broadcast 6129319937
 dialer-group 1
 isdn switch-type basic-dms100
 isdn spid1 61293198331111
 isdn spid2 61293198461111
 ppp authentication chap
!
no ip classless
!
dialer-list 1 protocol ip permit
!
!
line con 0
 privilege level 15
 logging synchronous
 transport input none
line aux 0
line vty 0 4
 login
!
end
```

In this example, the calling router has been authenticated by the called router with a host name of FAKENAME, even though the router's actual host name is ISDN-1. You can see this process with the **debug ppp authentication** command in Example 7-13.

Example 7-13 *Calling Router Authentication Verification*

```
ISDN-1#debug  ppp authentication
PPP authentication debugging is on
ISDN-1#ping 175.10.23.2

Type escape sequence to abort.
Sending 5, 100-byte ICMP Echos to 175.10.23.2, timeout is 2 seconds:
.!!!!
Success rate is 80 percent (4/5), round-trip min/avg/max = 40/41/44 ms
ISDN-1#
08:38:29: %LINK-3-UPDOWN: Interface BRI0:1, changed state to up
08:38:29: %ISDN-6-CONNECT: Interface BRI0:1 is now connected to 6129319833
08:38:29: BR0:1 PPP: Treating connection as a callout
08:38:30: BR0:1 PPP: Phase is AUTHENTICATING, by both
08:38:30: BR0:1 CHAP: Using alternate hostname FAKE_NAME
08:38:30: BR0:1 CHAP: O CHALLENGE id 8 len 30 from "FAKE_NAME"
08:38:30: BR0:1 CHAP: I CHALLENGE id 8 len 27 from "ISDN-2"
08:38:30: BR0:1 CHAP: Using alternate hostname FAKE_NAME
08:38:30: BR0:1 CHAP: O RESPONSE id 8 len 30 from "FAKE_NAME"
08:38:30: BR0:1 CHAP: I SUCCESS id 8 len 4
08:38:30: BR0:1 CHAP: I RESPONSE id 8 len 27 from "ISDN-2"
08:38:30: BR0:1 CHAP: O SUCCESS id 8 len 4
08:38:31: %LINEPROTO-5-UPDOWN: Line protocol on Interface BRI0:1, changed state
to up
ISDN-1#
```

Note the timeout of the first ICMP ping packet. This was because of the time it took for the ISDN call negotiation and connection process.

Example: Using PPP to Authenticate on Incoming Calls Only—Configuring Unidirectional CHAP Authentication

When two devices normally use CHAP authentication, each side sends out a challenge, to which the other side responds and is authenticated by the challenger. Each side authenticates one another independently. If you want to operate with non-Cisco routers that do not support authentication by the calling router or device, you must use the **ppp authentication chap callin** command. When using the **ppp authentication** command with the **callin** keyword, the access server authenticates the remote device only if the remote device initiated the call (for example, if the remote device "called in"). In this case, authentication is specified on incoming (received) calls only.

As depicted in Table 7-2, if Router 1 initiates a call to Router 2, Router 2 would challenge Router 1, but Router 1 would not challenge Router 2. This occurs because the **ppp**

authentication chap callin command is configured on Router 1. This is an example of a unidirectional authentication.

Table 7-2   *Unidirectional Authentication*

Router 1	Router 2
Router 1 calls Router 2 --->	
<--- Router 2 challenges Router 1	

Router 1 does not challenge Router 2 because it is configured for one-way authentication.

Example: Using PPP Link Quality

PPP link quality was covered in Chapter 4. It is important to note that this feature also applies to ISDN interfaces, as long as they are configured with PPP encapsulation.

Additional Optional Parameters: Link Quality Monitoring (LQM)

Link Quality Monitoring (LQM) is available on all serial interfaces running PPP. LQM monitors the link quality. If the quality drops below a configured percentage, the router shuts down the link. The percentages are calculated for both the incoming and the outgoing directions. The outgoing quality is calculated by comparing the total number of packets and bytes sent with the total number of packets and bytes received by the destination node. The incoming quality is calculated by comparing the total number of packets and bytes received with the total number of packets and bytes sent by the destination peer.

When LQM is enabled, *Link Quality Reports (LQRs)* are sent in place of keepalives every keepalive period. All incoming keepalives are responded to properly. If LQM is not configured, keepalives are sent every keepalive period and all incoming LQRs are responded to with an LQR. LQR is specified in RFC 1989, "PPP Link Quality Monitoring," by William A. Simpson of Computer Systems Consulting Services. To enable LQM on the interface, use the ppp quality percentage command in interface configuration mode.

The *percentage* argument specifies the link quality threshold. That percentage must be maintained, or the link is deemed to be of poor quality and is taken down. The percentages are calculated for both incoming and outgoing directions. The outgoing quality is calculated by comparing the total number of packets and bytes sent to the total number of packets and bytes received by the peer. The incoming quality is calculated by comparing the total number of packets and bytes received to the total number of packets and bytes sent by the peer.

If the link quality percentage is not maintained, the link is deemed to be of poor quality and is taken down. The policy implements a time lag so that the link does not bounce up and down.

Additional Optional Parameters: ISDN Call Screening

Besides CHAP and PAP authentication, there are alternate ways to authenticate incoming ISDN calls. Authentication based on caller ID provides even greater security than the methods described before by authenticating remote clients based not only on user ID and password, but also on dialing location. Caller ID allows the initial incoming call from the client to the server to be accepted or rejected based on the caller ID message contained in the ISDN setup message. Caller ID is not available everywhere, so be sure to check with the ISDN provider if you want to implement this feature in your network.

Only one command is needed to configure ISDN call screening. For Legacy DDR,

> **isdn caller** *remote-number* [**callback**]

For dialer profiles,

> **dialer-caller** *remote-number* [**callback**]

The **callback** option tells the router to terminate the incoming call and call back the router that originally placed the call. Callback is covered in the next section.

Example 7-14 shows how to configure caller screening.

Example 7-14 *Call Screening*

```
interface BRI 0
isdn caller 6129319937
```

This command can be repeated for each number that will be allowed to dial in. The Cisco IOS software also allows you to configure "don't care" digits in the remote number, using the letter *x*. For example, to allow all incoming calls from the 952 area code, you would use the **isdn caller 952xxxxxxx** command. You must use one *x* for each digit that you don't care about. The command **isdn caller 952x** is not the same **as isdn caller 952xxxxxxx**. The first command allows only four-digit numbers starting with 952, whereas the second command allows all seven-digit numbers starting with 952.

Use the **debug** ISDN event to troubleshoot ISDN call screening.

Additional Optional Parameters: ISDN Callback

Callback is a useful feature for networks that want to maintain a central location for all outgoing ISDN calls for billing or other business purposes. The callback feature (introduced in Cisco IOS Software Release 11.0) allows a remote router to place a call to the central site router requesting that the central site router call back the remote router. Then, the central site router disconnects the call and places a return call to the remote location. With callback configured, the ISDN bill is reduced at the remote sites because actual data transfers occur when the central office router calls back. Example 7-15 and 7-16 show the configuration for ISDN callback for the Remote Site and Headquarter routers, respectively.

| **NOTE** | Callback relies on PPP authentication, so PAP or CHAP authentication must be configured for callback to work. |

Example 7-15 *ISDN Callback Configuration: Remote Site Router*

```
Remote_Site#show running-config
Building configuration...

Current configuration:
!
version 12.0
service timestamps debug uptime
service timestamps log uptime
no service password-encryption
!
hostname Remote_Site
!
!
username Headquarters password 0 cisco
ip subnet-zero
isdn switch-type basic-dms100
!
!
!
interface Ethernet0
 ip address 172.16.1.1 255.255.255.0
 no ip directed-broadcast
!
interface Serial0
 ip address 175.10.50.1 255.255.255.252
 no ip directed-broadcast
 no fair-queue
 clockrate 125000
!
interface Serial1
 ip address 175.10.1.1 255.255.255.252
 no ip directed-broadcast
!
interface BRI0
 ip address 175.10.23.1 255.255.255.248
```

continues

Example 7-15 *ISDN Callback Configuration: Remote Site Router (Continued)*

```
 no ip directed-broadcast
 encapsulation ppp
 dialer wait-for-carrier-time 10
 dialer map ip 175.10.23.2 name Headquarters broadcast 6129319833
 dialer hold-queue 100 timeout 10
 dialer-group 1
 isdn switch-type basic-dms100
 isdn spid1 61293199371111
 isdn spid2 61293199381111
 ppp callback request
 ppp authentication chap
!
no ip classless
!
dialer-list 1 protocol ip permit
!
!
line con 0
 privilege level 15
 logging synchronous
 transport input none
line aux 0
line vty 0 4
 login
!
end
```

Example 7-16 *ISDN Callback Configuration: Headquarters Router*

```
Headquarters#show running-config
Building configuration...

Current configuration:
!
version 12.0
service timestamps debug uptime
service timestamps log uptime
no service password-encryption
!
hostname Headquarters
!
!
username Remote_Site password 0 cisco
ip subnet-zero
isdn switch-type basic-dms100
!
!
!
interface Ethernet0
```

Example 7-16 *ISDN Callback Configuration: Headquarters Router (Continued)*

```
 ip address 172.16.1.1 255.255.255.0
 no ip directed-broadcast
!
interface Serial0
 ip address 175.10.50.2 255.255.255.252
 no ip directed-broadcast
!
interface Serial1
 ip address 175.10.1.2 255.255.255.252
 no ip directed-broadcast
 clockrate 125000
!
interface BRI0
 ip address 175.10.23.2 255.255.255.248
 no ip directed-broadcast
 encapsulation ppp
 dialer callback-secure
 dialer enable-timeout 5
 dialer map ip 175.10.23.1 name Remote_Site class callback 6129319937
 dialer hold-queue 100
 dialer-group 1
 isdn switch-type basic-dms100
 isdn spid1 61293198331111
 isdn spid2 61293198461111
 ppp callback accept
 ppp authentication chap
!
no ip classless
!
!
map-class dialer callback
 dialer callback-server username
dialer-list 1 protocol ip permit
!
!
line con 0
 privilege level 15
 logging synchronous
 transport input none
line aux 0
line vty 0 4
 login
!
end
```

When an incoming call arrives and the callback router finds a best match configured for callback, the router uses the value configured by the **dialer enable-timeout** command to determine the length of time to wait before making the callback.

The minimum value of the timer is 1 second; the default value of the timer is 15 seconds. The interval set for this feature on this router must be much less than that set for DDR fast call rerouting for ISDN (that interval is set by the **dialer wait-for-carrier** command) on the calling (remote) side. Cisco recommends setting the dialer wait-for-carrier timer on the calling side to twice the length of the dialer enable-timeout timer on the callback side. In the example, we have set the dialer enable-timeout to 5 seconds on the Headquarters router, and the dialer wait-for-carrier timer to 10 seconds on the Remote_Site router.

The **dialer callback-server map class** configuration command allows the interface to return calls when callback successfully is negotiated. The **username** keyword specifies that the interface is to locate the dial string for making the return call by looking up the authenticated host name in a **dialer map** command.

The **dialer map** interface configuration command has been modified to include the **class** keyword and the name of the class, as specified in the **map-class** command. The **name** keyword is required so that when the Remote_Site router dials in, the interface can locate this **dialer map** statement and obtain the dial string for calling back the Remote_Site's router. Example 7-17 illustrates how to utilize dialer debugging to verify the callback configuration.

Example 7-17 *Verifying the Callback Configuration*

```
Remote_Site#debug dialer
Dial on demand events debugging is on
Remote_Site#ping 175.10.23.2

Type escape sequence to abort.
Sending 5, 100-byte ICMP Echos to 175.10.23.2, timeout is 2 seconds:
.....
Success rate is 0 percent (0/5)
Remote_Site#
00:30:08: BR0 DDR: Dialing cause ip (s=175.10.23.1, d=175.10.23.2)
00:30:08: BR0 DDR: Attempting to dial 6129319833
00:30:08: %LINK-3-UPDOWN: Interface BRI0:1, changed state to up
00:30:08: %ISDN-6-CONNECT: Interface BRI0:1 is now connected to 6129319833
00:30:08: BR0:1 DDR: Callback negotiated - waiting for server disconnect
00:30:09: %LINK-3-UPDOWN: Interface BRI0:1, changed state to down
00:30:09: DDR: Callback client for Headquarters 9529319833 created
00:30:09: BR0:1 DDR: disconnecting call
00:30:09: BR0:1 DDR: disconnecting call
00:30:14: %LINK-3-UPDOWN: Interface BRI0:1, changed state to up
00:30:14: %ISDN-6-CONNECT: Interface BRI0:1 is now connected to 6129319833
00:30:16: BR0:1 DDR: No callback negotiated
00:30:16: BR0:1 DDR: dialer protocol up
00:30:16:  BR0:1 DDR: Callback received from Headquarters 6129319833
00:30:16: DDR: Freeing callback to Headquarters 6129319833
00:30:16: BR0:1 DDR: Call connected, 4 packets unqueued, 4 transmitted, 0 discar
ded
00:30:17: %LINEPROTO-5-UPDOWN: Line protocol on Interface BRI0:1, changed state
to up
```

Example 7-17 *Verifying the Callback Configuration (Continued)*

```
00:30:20: %ISDN-6-CONNECT: Interface BRI0:1 is now connected to 6129319833
Headquarters
Remote_Site#ping 175.10.23.2

Type escape sequence to abort.
Sending 5, 100-byte ICMP Echos to 175.10.23.2, timeout is 2 seconds:
!!!!!
Success rate is 100 percent (5/5), round-trip min/avg/max = 44/44/44 ms
```

```
Headquarters#show dialer

BRI0 - dialer type = ISDN

Dial String      Successes   Failures    Last called   Last status
6129319937               4          0     00:00:10       successful
0 incoming call(s) have been screened.
0 incoming call(s) rejected for callback.


BRI0:1 - dialer type = ISDN
Idle timer (120 secs), Fast idle timer (20 secs)
Wait for carrier (30 secs), Re-enable (5 occs)
Dialer state is data link layer up
Dial reason: Callback return call
Time until disconnect 111 secs
Connected to 6129319937 (Remote_Site)
```

Here, you can see that the first five **ping**s were unsuccessful. This is because of the amount
of time that it took for the Headquarters router to disconnect the incoming call and then call
back the Remote_Site router. After this process was completed, the **ping**s were successful.
The callback process can be seen when issuing the **debug dialer** command. The **show
dialer** command on the Headquarters router clearly shows that the reason for its call was
"Callback return call." The **debug dialer** and **show dialer** commands are useful methods
of verifying that the routers are properly configured for ISDN callback.

Additional Optional Parameters: Using PPP Multilink

Multilink PPP is a feature that allows traffic to be load balanced over multiple WAN links.
When enabled, the multiple physical links are bonded together and are seen as one logical
link. In the case of ISDN, you can configure multiple B channels to come up to act as one
large traffic pipe. The multiple links come up in response to a user-defined threshold using
the **dialer load-threshold** command. This threshold can be defined based on inbound or
outbound traffic, or either. It is a value from 1 to 255, where 1 means that the second BRI
channel should come up almost immediately when the ISDN link is up, and 255 means that
the second BRI channel should come up only when the first channel is completely saturated.
For example, if you want to have the second B channel bond to the first when the load is 50
percent utilized, you would use the command **dialer load-threshold 127** ($255 \times .50 = 127$,

after rounding up). Configuring multilink PPP requires the following commands used under interface mode:

```
encapsulation ppp
dialer load-threshold load
ppp multilink
```

Example 7-18 shows an example configuration using PPP multilink.

Example 7-18 *PPP Multilink Configuration:*

```
Remote_Site#show running-config
Building configuration...

Current configuration:
!
version 12.0
service timestamps debug uptime
service timestamps log uptime
no service password-encryption
!
hostname Remote_Site
!
!
username Headquarters password 0 cisco
ip subnet-zero
isdn switch-type basic-dms100
!
!
!
interface Loopback0
 ip address 175.10.101.1 255.255.255.255
 no ip directed-broadcast
!
interface Ethernet0
 ip address 175.10.2.1 255.255.255.0
 no ip directed-broadcast
 no keepalive
!
interface Serial0
 no ip address
 no ip directed-broadcast
 shutdown
 no fair-queue
 clockrate 125000
!
interface Serial1
 description PRIMARY LINK TO HQ
 ip address 175.10.200.1 255.255.255.252
 no ip directed-broadcast
!
interface BRI0
 ip address 175.10.23.1 255.255.255.248
 no ip directed-broadcast
```

Example 7-18 *PPP Multilink Configuration: (Continued)*

```
 encapsulation ppp
 dialer map ip 175.10.23.2 name Headquarters broadcast 6129319833
 dialer load-threshold 25 either
 dialer-group 1
 isdn switch-type basic-dms100
 isdn spid1 61293199371111
 isdn spid2 61293199381111
 ppp multilink
!
router eigrp 1
 network 175.10.0.0
 no auto-summary
!
no ip classless
!
access-list 101 deny   eigrp any any
access-list 101 permit ip any any
dialer-list 1 protocol ip list 101
!
!
line con 0
 privilege level 15
 logging synchronous
 transport input none
line aux 0
line vty 0 4
 login
!
end
```

Here, it is specified that both B channels should be used after the first B channel has exceeded a threshold of approximately 10 percent in either outbound or inbound traffic (255 [ts\x .10 is close to 25), not 25 percent.

You can verify the multilink PPP configuration by issuing the **show dialer** command. In Example 7-19, the router is made to initiate an ISDN connection by simply **ping**ing the other side of the link.

Example 7-19 *Verifying the Multilink PPP Configuration*

```
Remote_Site#ping 175.10.23.2

Type escape sequence to abort.
Sending 5, 100-byte ICMP Echos to 175.10.23.2, timeout is 2 seconds:
.!!!!
Success rate is 80 percent (4/5), round-trip min/avg/max = 44/45/48 ms

Remote_Site#show dialer
```

continues

Example 7-19 *Verifying the Multilink PPP Configuration (Continued)*

```
BRI0 - dialer type = ISDN

Dial String      Successes    Failures    Last called    Last status
6129319833             29          62      00:00:06       successful
0 incoming call(s) have been screened.
0 incoming call(s) rejected for callback.

BRI0:1 - dialer type = ISDN
Idle timer (120 secs), Fast idle timer (20 secs)
Wait for carrier (30 secs), Re-enable (15 secs)
Dialer state is multilink member
Dial reason: ip (s=175.10.23.1, d=175.10.23.2)
Connected to 6129319833 (Headquarters)

BRI0:2 - dialer type = ISDN
Idle timer (120 secs), Fast idle timer (20 secs)
Wait for carrier (30 secs), Re-enable (15 secs)
Dialer state is idle
```

You can see that the ISDN connection was made successfully and that the first B channel is indeed a multilink member. However, the second B channel still shows that it is idle and was not bonded to the first B channel. The reason for this is that the simple **ping**s that traversed the link were not sufficient to exceed the 10 percent load that is required in this case.

To see what the load is for the first B channel, issue the **show interface bri0 1** command, as demonstrated in Example 7-20.

Example 7-20 *Displaying the Load for the First B Channel*

```
Remote_Site#show interface bri 0 1
BRI0:1 is up, line protocol is up
  Hardware is BRI
  MTU 1500 bytes, BW 64 Kbit, DLY 20000 usec, rely 255/255, load 3/255
  Encapsulation PPP, loopback not set, keepalive set (10 sec)
  LCP Open, multilink Open
  Last input 00:00:05, output 00:00:05, output hang never
  Last clearing of "show interface" counters never
  Queueing strategy: fifo
  Output queue 0/40, 0 drops; input queue 0/75, 0 drops
  5 minute input rate 1000 bits/sec, 1 packets/sec
  5 minute output rate 1000 bits/sec, 1 packets/sec
     4183 packets input, 2365973 bytes, 0 no buffer
     Received 0 broadcasts, 0 runts, 0 giants, 0 throttles
     0 input errors, 0 CRC, 0 frame, 0 overrun, 0 ignored, 0 abort
     4342 packets output, 2396289 bytes, 0 underruns
     0 output errors, 0 collisions, 33 interface resets
     0 output buffer failures, 0 output buffers swapped out
     210 carrier transitions
```

You can plainly see that the load on this B channel is only at 3/255. In this configuration, the second B channel will come up only after the first B channel has exceeded a load of 25/255, or approximately 10 percent.

You will need to create some more traffic to actually bring up both B channels in this configuration. You can do this by using the extended **ping** command, as demonstrated in Example 7-21.

Example 7-21 *Creating Additional Traffic to Bring Up Both B Channels*

```
Remote_Site#ping
Protocol [ip]:
Target IP address: 175.10.23.2
Repeat count [5]: 100
Datagram size [100]: 1500
Timeout in seconds [2]:
Extended commands [n]:
Sweep range of sizes [n]:
Type escape sequence to abort.
Sending 100, 1500-byte ICMP Echos to 175.10.23.2, timeout is 2 seconds:
!!!!!!!!!!!!!!!!!!!!!!!!!!!!!!!!!!!!!!!!!!!!!!!!!!!'!!!!!!!!!!!!!!!!!!!!!!!!!!!!!!!!!!!!!!!!!!!!
!!!!!!!!!!!!'!!!!!!
Success rate is 100 percent (100/100), round-trip min/avg/max = 212/359/428 ms
```

Now, issue the same **show int bri0 1** command to check the load on the interface, as done in Example 7-22.

Example 7-22 *Displaying the Load for Both B Channels*

```
Remote_Site#show int bri0 1
BRI0:1 is up, line protocol is up
  Hardware is BRI
  MTU 1500 bytes, BW 64 Kbit, DLY 20000 usec, rely 255/255, load 27/255
  Encapsulation PPP, loopback not set, keepalive set (10 sec)
  LCP Open, multilink Open
  Last input 00:00:04, output 00:00:04, output hang never
  Last clearing of "show interface" counters never
  Queueing strategy: fifo
  Output queue 0/40, 0 drops; input queue 0/75, 0 drops
  5 minute input rate 8000 bits/sec, 5 packets/sec
  5 minute output rate 7000 bits/sec, 4 packets/sec
     4452 packets input, 2579061 bytes, 0 no buffer
     Received 0 broadcasts, 0 runts, 0 giants, 0 throttles
     0 input errors, 0 CRC, 0 frame, 0 overrun, 0 ignored, 0 abort
     4611 packets output, 2611177 bytes, 0 underruns
     0 output errors, 0 collisions, 33 interface resets
     0 output buffer failures, 0 output buffers swapped out
     212 carrier transitions
```

You can see that the load has reached 27/255, so the second B channel should have been brought up to bond with the first B channel. There are a couple of ways to verify that this has indeed happened: using the **show dialer** and the **show ppp multilink** commands, as demonstrated in Example 7-23.

Example 7-23 *Verifying a Second B Channel with the* **show dialer** *command*

```
Remote_Site#show dialer

BRI0 - dialer type = ISDN

Dial String      Successes   Failures   Last called   Last status
6129319833              32         62    00:00:55        successful
0 incoming call(s) have been screened.
0 incoming call(s) rejected for callback.


BRI0:1 - dialer type = ISDN
Idle timer (120 secs), Fast idle timer (20 secs)
Wait for carrier (30 secs), Re-enable (15 secs)
Dialer state is multilink member
Dial reason: ip (s=175.10.23.1, d=175.10.23.2)
Connected to 6129319833 (Headquarters)

BRI0:2 - dialer type = ISDN
Idle timer (120 secs), Fast idle timer (20 secs)
Wait for carrier (30 secs), Re-enable (15 secs)
Dialer state is multilink member
Dial reason: Multilink bundle overloaded
Connected to 6129319833 (Headquarters)
```

Both channels are indeed in use, and the second B channel shows that the dial reason was because of a PPP multilink overload.

Example 7-24 shows how to verify the PPP multilink configuration.

Example 7-24 *Verifying a Second B Channel with the* **show ppp multilink** *Command*

```
ISDN-1#show ppp multilink

Bundle ISDN-2, 2 members, Master link is Virtual-Access1
Dialer Interface is BRI0
  0 lost fragments, 0 reordered, 0 unassigned, sequence 0xF8/0xF8 rcvd/sent
  0 discarded, 0 lost received, 1/255 load

Member Links: 2 (max not set, min not set)
BRI0:1
BRI0:2
```

Here, both B channels are listed as PPP multilink members.

In this case, we sent 100 1500-byte ICMP packets across the link. This was enough to bring up the secondary B channel. Both B channels were bonded to form one large virtual circuit.

Step 5: Routing Traffic over ISDN

As stated previously, there are a number of ways to ensure that traffic is routed over the ISDN interface. You want to be able to route traffic over the ISDN link when it is up, but you normally do not want this routing traffic to cause it to stay up indefinitely. One important configuration option that you should be aware of is the **passive-interface** routing command. Passive interfaces listen to incoming routing updates but will not advertise any routing information out that interface. This is particularly effective for dial-on-demand interfaces because you can suppress the routing information from causing unnecessary connections. This command is done under the routing process and is valid for nearly every routing protocol. Example 7-25 shows an example using EIGRP.

Example 7-25 *Defining a Passive Interface*

```
router eigrp 1
 passive-interface BRI0
 network 175.10.0.0
 no auto-summary
```

If the passive-interface BRI0 command is not used, the ISDN link continuously would connect as routing updates are passed. This assumes that the **broadcast** keyword is on the **dialer map** statement. The **broadcast** keyword also will pass any multicast traffic that is often used by routing protocols.

The majority of real-world applications use floating static routes for routing over ISDN so that when the primary link fails, the ISDN interface comes up. However, numerous other equally successful methods enable you to control routing information over an ISDN network, including the following:

- Floating static routes
- OSPF demand circuit
- Dialer watch
- Backup interface
- Backup load
- Snapshot routing

Example: Floating Static Routes

A floating static route is simply a static route with a higher administrative distance than that of the routing protocols, which is tagged at the end of the **ip route** command. Each routing protocol has a different administrative distance associated with it. An administrative distance is simply the degree of reliability, or cost, of the route. The lower the distance is, the more reliable the routing information is for the specified routes. If a router knows about a route from more than one means, the route with the lowest administrative distance wins out. Table 7-3 shows the default administrative distances for connected interfaces, static routes, and routing protocols.

Table 7-3   *Default Administrative Distances*

Protocol	Default Administrative Distance
Connected interface	0
Static route	1
Enhanced Interior Gateway Routing Protocol (EIGRP) summary route	5
External Border Gateway Protocol (BGP)	20
Internal EIGRP	90
IGRP	100
OSPF	110
Intermediate System-to-Intermediate System (IS-IS)	115
Routing Information Protocol (RIP)	120
Exterior Gateway Protocol (EGP)	140
External EIGRP	170
Internal BGP	200
Unknown	255

A static route becomes floating when it is assigned a higher AD than that of the routing protocols. It is called "floating" because when a route known through some other means goes away, the floating static route "floats" to the top and is used by the router. For example, if you use the command **ip route 10.1.1.0 255.255.255.0 BRI 0 200**, you have manually assigned an AD of 200 to this route. The router routes packets to 10.1.1.0/24 through the BRI 0 interface only if it knows of no other way to reach this subnet. This is useful when you want to use the ISDN network to route traffic only if the primary link has failed. This is the most common real-world method used to configure ISDN to back up a primary link failure. Figure 7-6 shows a simple network between the two routers Cheech and Chong. In this case, Frame Relay is used as the primary communication link between the two routers, with the ISDN link being used as a backup method only.

Figure 7-6   *Floating Static Route Example*

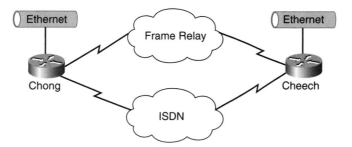

In this scenario, you want to maintain connectivity between users on the Ethernet segments between the two locations. Example 7-26 shows the configuration for the proper use of floating static routes in this scenario.

Example 7-26 *Floating Static Route Configuration*

```
Cheech#show running-config
Building configuration...

Current configuration:
!
version 11.2
no service password-encryption
no service udp-small-servers
no service tcp-small-servers
!
hostname Cheech
!
enable password cisco
!
username Chong password 0 cisco
isdn switch-type basic-dms100
!
interface Loopback0
 ip address 175.10.2.2 255.255.255.0
!
interface Ethernet0
 ip address 175.10.22.1 255.255.255.0
 no keepalive
 no mop enabled
!
interface Serial0
 ip address 175.10.123.1 255.255.255.0
 encapsulation frame-relay
 frame-relay map ip 175.10.123.2 300 broadcast
!
interface Serial1
```

continues

```
 no ip address
```

Example 7-26 *Floating Static Route Configuration (Continued)*

```
 shutdown
!
interface BRI0
 ip address 175.10.23.1 255.255.255.0
 encapsulation ppp
 isdn spid1 61293199371111
 isdn spid2 61293199381111
 dialer map ip 175.10.23.2 broadcast 6129319833
 dialer-group 1
 no fair-queue
 ppp authentication chap
!
router eigrp 1
 passive-interface BRI0
 network 175.10.0.0
 no auto-summary
!
ip classless
ip route 175.10.35.0 255.255.255.0 175.10.23.2 200
!
dialer-list 1 protocol ip permit
!
line con 0
 exec-timeout 0 0
 privilege level 15
 logging synchronous
line aux 0
line vty 0 4
 password cisco
 login
!
end
```

```
Chong#show running-config
Building configuration...

Current configuration:
!
version 11.2
no service password-encryption
no service udp-small-servers
no service tcp-small-servers
!
hostname Chong
!
enable password cisco
!
username Cheech password 0 cisco
isdn switch-type basic-dms100
!
interface Loopback0
 ip address 175.10.3.3 255.255.255.0
```

Example 7-26 *Floating Static Route Configuration (Continued)*

```
!
interface Ethernet0
 ip address 175.10.35.3 255.255.255.0
!
interface Serial0
 no ip address
 encapsulation frame-relay
 no fair-queue
!
interface Serial0.1 point-to-point
 ip address 175.10.123.2 255.255.255.0
 frame-relay interface-dlci 200
!
interface Serial0.2 point-to-point
 ip address 175.10.134.2 255.255.255.252
 shutdown
 frame-relay interface-dlci 400
!
interface Serial1
 no ip address
 shutdown
!
interface BRI0
 ip address 175.10.23.2 255.255.255.0
 encapsulation ppp
 isdn spid1 61293198331111
 isdn spid2 61293198461111
dialer map ip 175.10.23.1 broadcast 6129319937
dialer-group 1
 no fair-queue
 ppp authentication chap
!
router eigrp 1
 passive-interface BRI0
 network 175.10.0.0
 no auto-summary
!
no ip classless
ip route 175.10.22.0 255.255.255.224 175.10.23.1 200
!
dialer-list 1 protocol ip permit
!
line con 0
 exec-timeout 0 0
 privilege level 15
 logging synchronous
line aux 0
line vty 0 4
 password cisco
```

continues

Example 7-26 *Floating Static Route Configuration (Continued)*

```
 login
 !
 end
```

You have made the BRI0 interfaces passive under the EIGRP processes. This was needed
to keep the routing updates from initiating calls and keeping up the link indefinitely.
Because the dialer list specifies all IP packets as interesting, EIGRP multicast updates
would have brought the ISDN link up. An alternative to using the **passive-interface**
command is to use a more restrictive dialer list that denies EIGRP packets.

Example: OSPF Demand Circuit

As the name implies, an OSPF demand circuit enables the ISDN link to work through the
OSPF protocol. This topic was introduced in Chapter 4 and is covered in more detail in
Chapter 12, "Link-State Protocols: Open Shortest Path First (OSPF)." As stated in Chapter
12, demand circuits suppress the OSPF hello packets from traversing the ISDN link, and
ISDN calls initiate only after a logical topology change. Without this feature, these hello
packets can keep the link up indefinitely. This feature is enabled through the following
single interface command:

```
ISDN_Router#config term
ISDN_Router(config)#int bri0
ISDN_Router(config-if)#ip ospf demand-circuit
```

This seems simple enough, right? In most situations, it is. However, keep in mind that when
a change in the OSPF link-state database occurs, an ISDN call is made. Therefore, in certain
situations, such as when you are redistributing other protocols into OSPF, you must be
careful in how you implement the redistribution, to avoid routing loops that will cause these
link-state changes to occur constantly. You will see an example of this soon in the advanced
practice labs when you need to do more than simply add the **ip ospf demand-circuit**
command to make this work properly. Figure 7-7 shows the reference network that we will
use to illustrate the proper configuration for setting up the OSPF demand circuit.

Figure 7-7 *Example OSPF Demand Circuit Configuration*

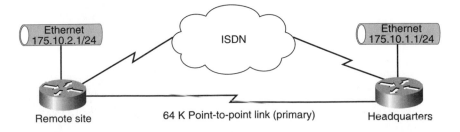

Example 7-27 shows the configuration for both the Headquarters and Remote Site routers.

Example 7-27 *OSPF Demand Circuit Configuration*

```
Remote_Site#show running-config
Building configuration...

Current configuration:
!
version 12.0
service timestamps debug uptime
service timestamps log uptime
no service password-encryption
!
hostname Remote_Site
!
!
username Headquarters password 0 cisco
ip subnet-zero
isdn switch-type basic-dms100
!
!
!
interface Loopback0
 ip address 175.10.101.1 255.255.255.255
 no ip directed-broadcast
!
interface Ethernet0
 ip address 175.10.2.1 255.255.255.0
 no ip directed-broadcast
 no keepalive
!
interface Serial0
 no ip address
 no ip directed-broadcast
 shutdown
 no fair-queue

!
interface Serial1
 description PRIMARY LINK TO HQ
 ip address 175.10.200.1 255.255.255.252
 no ip directed-broadcast
 bandwidth 64
!
interface BRI0
 ip address 175.10.23.1 255.255.255.248
 no ip directed-broadcast
 encapsulation ppp
 ip ospf demand-circuit
 ip ospf cost 9999
 dialer map ip 175.10.23.2 name Headquarters broadcast 6129319833
```

continues

Example 7-27 *OSPF Demand Circuit Configuration (Continued)*

```
 dialer-group 1
 isdn switch-type basic-dms100
 isdn spid1 61293199371111
 isdn spid2 61293199381111
!
router ospf 1
 network 175.10.0.0 0.0.255.255 area 0
!
no ip classless
!
dialer-list 1 protocol ip permit
!
!
line con 0
 privilege level 15
 logging synchronous
 transport input none
line aux 0
line vty 0 4
 login
!
end
```

```
Headquarters#show running-config
Building configuration...

Current configuration:
!
version 12.0
service timestamps debug uptime
service timestamps log uptime
no service password-encryption
!
hostname Headquarters
!
logging buffered 9096 debugging
!
username Remote_Site password 0 cisco
ip subnet-zero
isdn switch-type basic-dms100
!
!
!
interface Loopback0
 ip address 175.10.102.1 255.255.255.255
 no ip directed-broadcast
!
interface Ethernet0
 ip address 175.10.1.1 255.255.255.0
 no ip directed-broadcast
 no keepalive
!
```

Example 7-27 *OSPF Demand Circuit Configuration (Continued)*

```
interface Serial0
 no ip address
 no ip directed-broadcast
 shutdown
!
interface Serial1
 description PRIMARY LINK TO REMOTE SITE
 ip address 175.10.200.2 255.255.255.252
 no ip directed-broadcast
 clockrate 64000
 bandwidth 64
!
interface BRI0
 ip address 175.10.23.2 255.255.255.248
 no ip directed-broadcast
 encapsulation ppp
 dialer-group 1
 isdn switch-type basic-dms100
 isdn spid1 61293198331111
 isdn spid2 61293198461111
!
router ospf 1
 network 175.10.0.0 0.0.255.255 area 0
!
no ip classless
!
dialer-list 1 protocol ip permit
!
!
line con 0
 privilege level 15
 logging synchronous
 transport input none
line aux 0
line vty 0 4
 login
!
end
```

The **ip ospf demand circuit** configuration command in interface mode tells the router to not send hello packets out that interface. Without it, the OSPF hellos will keep the link up. Example 7-28 shows the output from the **show ip ospf interface bri0** command.

Example 7-28 *Using the* **show ip ospf interface** *Command*

```
Remote_Site#show ip ospf interface bri0
BRI0 is up, line protocol is up (spoofing)
  Internet Address 175.10.23.1/29, Area 0
  Process ID 1, Router ID 175.10.101.1, Network Type POINT_TO_POINT, Cost: 9999
```

continues

Example 7-28 *Using the* **show ip ospf interface** *Command (Continued)*

```
Configured as demand circuit.
Run as demand circuit.
DoNotAge LSA allowed.
Transmit Delay is 1 sec, State POINT_TO_POINT,
Timer intervals configured, Hello 10, Dead 40, Wait 40, Retransmit 5
  Hello due in 00:00:01
Neighbor Count is 1, Adjacent neighbor count is 1
  Adjacent with neighbor 175.10.102.1  (Hello suppressed)
Suppress hello for 1 neighbor(s)
```

You can see that OSPF has formed a neighbor adjacency with the Headquarters router and is suppressing the hello packets for the BRI 0 interface.

In this network, the primary link is a 64-kbps point-to-point circuit. As you will learn in the OSPF section of this book, it is generally a good idea to explicitly state the actual bandwidth of each interface that OSPF has been enabled on, which is why you used the **bandwidth 64** command on the Serial 1 interface of each router. This is because the metric used in OSPF is cost, which is calculated as 100,000,000/bandwidth.

Unless you actually state what the bandwidth is for the serial interface, OSPF assumes that it is a full T1 and incorrectly gives the interface an OSPF cost of 64. For ISDN interfaces, OSPF assumes that the link is 64 kbps and assigns it a cost of 1562. This can be seen with the **show ip ospf interface bri0** command, as demonstrated in Example 7-29.

Example 7-29 *Assigning a Cost to an ISDN Interface in an OSPF Environment*

```
Remote_Site#show ip ospf int bri0
BRI0 is up, line protocol is up (spoofing)
  Internet Address 175.10.23.1/29, Area 0
  Process ID 1, Router ID 175.10.101.1, Network Type POINT_TO_POINT, Cost: 1562
  Configured as demand circuit.
  Run as demand circuit.
  DoNotAge LSA allowed.
  Transmit Delay is 1 sec, State POINT_TO_POINT,
  Timer intervals configured, Hello 10, Dead 40, Wait 40, Retransmit 5
    Hello due in 00:00:03
  Neighbor Count is 1, Adjacent neighbor count is 1
    Adjacent with neighbor 175.10.102.1  (Hello suppressed)
  Suppress hello for 1 neighbor(s)
```

Notice that the OSPF hello packets are being suppressed and will not be sent over the ISDN network.

The problem here is that now OSPF has assigned a cost of 1562 to both the Serial 1 and BRI interfaces. It now sees these links as equal-cost path, and traffic is load balanced across both links. This causes the ISDN link to stay up indefinitely. To remedy this, it is usually a good idea to assign an artificially high OSPF cost to the BRI interfaces, ensuring that traffic is routed over this link only after the alternate paths are down.

In this example, a cost of 9999 has been assigned to the ISDN link by issuing the **ip ospf cost 9999** command. This actual cost that you implement doesn't really matter, but it needs to be high enough that OSPF will not prefer the backup ISDN link.

Under normal circumstances, the routing table should look like Example 7-30.

Example 7-30 *Testing the OSPF Demand Circuit Configuration*

```
Remote_Site#show ip route
Codes: C - connected, S - static, I - IGRP, R - RIP, M - mobile, B - BGP
       D - EIGRP, EX - EIGRP external, O - OSPF, IA - OSPF inter area
       N1 - OSPF NSSA external type 1, N2 - OSPF NSSA external type 2
       E1 - OSPF external type 1, E2 - OSPF external type 2, E - EGP
       i - IS-IS, L1 - IS-IS level-1, L2 - IS-IS level-2, * - candidate default
       U - per-user static route, o - ODR

Gateway of last resort is not set

     175.10.0.0/16 is variably subnetted, 6 subnets, 4 masks
C       175.10.200.0/00 is directly connected, Serial1
O       175.10.1.0/24 [110/1572] via 175.10.200.2, 00:00:39, Serial1
C       175.10.2.0/24 is directly connected, Ethernet0
C       175.10.23.0/29 is directly connected, BRI0
C       175.10.101.1/32 is directly connected, Loopback0
O       175.10.102.1/32 [110/1563] via 175.10.200.2, 00:00:39, Serial1
Remote_Site#ping 175.10.1.1

Type escape sequence to abort.
Sending 5, 100-byte ICMP Echos to 175.10.1.1, timeout is 2 seconds:
!!!!!
Success rate is 100 percent (5/5), round-trip min/avg/max = 16/18/20 ms
```

Now, you will administratively shut down the Serial 1 interface and verify that you still have connectivity to the Headquarters router, as demonstrated in Example 7-31.

Example 7-31 *Testing the ISDN Backup with the Primary Link Shut Down*

```
Remote_Site#conf t
Enter configuration commands, one per line.  End with CNTL/Z.
Remote_Site(config)#int s1
Remote_Site(config-if)#shut
Remote_Site(config-if)#
3d03h: %LINK-3-UPDOWN: Interface BRI0:1, changed state to up
Remote_Site(config-if)#end
Remote_Site#
3d03h: %ISDN-6-CONNECT: Interface BRI0:1 is now connected to 6129319833
```

continues

Example 7-31 *Testing the ISDN Backup with the Primary Link Shut Down (Continued)*

```
3d03h: %LINK-5-CHANGED: Interface Serial1, changed state to administratively down
n
3d03h: %SYS-5-CONFIG_I: Configured from console by console
3d03h: %LINEPROTO-5-UPDOWN: Line protocol on Interface BRI0:1, changed state to
up
3d03h: %LINEPROTO-5-UPDOWN: Line protocol on Interface Serial1, changed state to
 down
Remote_Site#
3d03h: %ISDN-6-CONNECT: Interface BRI0:1 is now connected to 6129319833 Headquarters
Remote_Site#sho ip route
Codes: C - connected, S - static, I - IGRP, R - RIP, M - mobile, B - BGP
       D - EIGRP, EX - EIGRP external, O - OSPF, IA - OSPF inter area
       N1 - OSPF NSSA external type 1, N2 - OSPF NSSA external type 2
       E1 - OSPF external type 1, E2 - OSPF external type 2, E - EGP
       i - IS-IS, L1 - IS-IS level-1, L2 - IS-IS level-2, * - candidate default
       U - per-user static route, o - ODR

Gateway of last resort is not set

     175.10.0.0/16 is variably subnetted, 6 subnets, 3 masks
O       175.10.1.0/24 [110/10009] via 175.10.23.2, 00:00:06, BRI0
C       175.10.2.0/24 is directly connected, Ethernet0
C       175.10.23.2/32 is directly connected, BRI0
C       175.10.23.0/29 is directly connected, BRI0
C       175.10.101.1/32 is directly connected, Loopback0
O       175.10.102.1/32 [110/10000] via 175.10.23.2, 00:00:06, BRI0
Remote_Site#ping 175.10.1.1

Type escape sequence to abort.
Sending 5, 100-byte ICMP Echos to 175.10.1.1, timeout is 2 seconds:
!!!!!
Success rate is 100 percent (5/5), round-trip min/avg/max = 40/43/44 ms
```

Because OSPF detected a topology change in the network, it initiated a connection. If you issue the **show dialer** command as demonstrated in Example 7-32, you can see that the reason for the ISDN call was IP traffic to the destination of 224.0.0.5. This is the multicast address used in OSPF.

Example 7-32 **show dialer** *Command Reveals the Reason for an ISDN Call*

```
Remote_Site#show dialer

BRI0 - dialer type = ISDN

Dial String      Successes   Failures    Last called   Last status
6129319833              44         62    00:01:55        successful
0 incoming call(s) have been screened.
0 incoming call(s) rejected for callback.

BRI0:1 - dialer type = ISDN
```

Example 7-32 show dialer *Command Reveals the Reason for an ISDN Call (Continued)*

```
Idle timer (120 secs), Fast idle timer (20 secs)
Wait for carrier (30 secs), Re-enable (15 secs)
Dialer state is data link layer up
Dial reason: ip (s=175.10.23.1, d=224.0.0.5)
Time until disconnect 49 secs
Connected to 6129319833 (Headquarters)

BRI0:2 - dialer type = ISDN
Idle timer (120 secs), Fast idle timer (20 secs)
Wait for carrier (30 secs), Re-enable (15 secs)
Dialer state is idle
```

When the primary link is restored, the ISDN connection tears down after the dialer idle timeout period has occurred. It can be easy to create routing loops in your network, especially when multiple routes are being redistributed. It is important to use filtering to ensure that these loops do not cause unnecessary ISDN connections.

Example: Dialer Watch

Dialer watch became a feature with Cisco IOS Software Release 11.3(2)T. It works by having the IOS "watch" the routing table to keep track of a number of user-defined routes. When one or more of the routes in the dialer watch list are removed from the routing table, an ISDN connection is initiated. The speed and effectiveness of implementing dialer watch depends on the convergence times and characteristics of the routing protocol used. EIGRP works best and normally is implemented with dialer watch, although dialer watch also is supported using OSPF and IGRP.

Dialer watch uses the ISDN network as a backup means to provide reliable connectivity between remote locations. Dialer watch monitors the routing table and initiates calls when the primary link fails and one of the routes defined in the dialer watch list is removed from the routing table. It does this in the following sequence:

1 When a watched route is deleted, dialer watch checks for at least one valid route for any of the watched IP addresses defined.

2 If there is no valid route, the primary line is considered down and unusable.

3 If there is a valid route for at least one of the defined watched IP addresses and the route is pointing to an interface other than the backup interface configured for dialer watch, the primary link is considered up. For example, if a site remote site has two Frame Relay PVCs to its headquarters, and one of the PVC's goes down, traffic still can be routed over the secondary PVC rather than over the ISDN link.

4 If the primary link goes down, the routing protocol immediately notifies the dialer watch process, and the secondary link (in this case, the ISDN line) is brought up.

5 After the secondary link is up, the primary link is checked again at the expiration of each idle timeout.

6 If the primary link remains down, the idle timer is reset.

If the primary link comes back up, the secondary link is disconnected. A disable timer can be set to delay the disconnection of the secondary link.

For the network in Figure 7-8, you will back up the connection to network 175.10.1.0/24 and to the Headquarters loopback address, ensuring connectivity despite a Frame Relay outage.

Figure 7-8 *Network Topology for Dialer Watch Configuration Example*

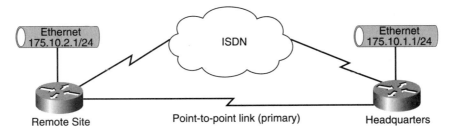

Example 7-33 shows the configuration for using dialer watch.

Example 7-33 *Dialer Watch Configuration*

```
Remote_Site#show running-config
Building configuration...

Current configuration:
!
version 12.0
service timestamps debug uptime
service timestamps log uptime
no service password-encryption
!
hostname Remote_Site
!
!
username Headquarters password 0 cisco
ip subnet-zero
isdn switch-type basic-dms100
!
!
!
interface Loopback0
 ip address 175.10.101.1 255.255.255.255
 no ip directed-broadcast
!
```

Example 7-33 *Dialer Watch Configuration (Continued)*

```
interface Ethernet0
 ip address 175.10.2.1 255.255.255.0
 no ip directed-broadcast
 no keepalive
!
interface Serial0
 no ip address
 no ip directed-broadcast
 shutdown
 no fair-queue
 clockrate 125000
!
interface Serial1
 description PRIMARY LINK TO HQ
 ip address 175.10.200.1 255.255.255.252
 no ip directed-broadcast
!
interface BRI0
 ip address 175.10.23.1 255.255.255.248
 no ip directed-broadcast
 encapsulation ppp
 dialer map ip 175.10.23.2 name Headquarters broadcast 6129319833
 dialer map ip 175.10.102.1 name Headquarters broadcast 6129319833
 dialer map ip 175.10.1.0 name Headquarters broadcast 6129319833
 dialer watch-group 1
 dialer-group 1
 isdn switch-type basic-dms100
 isdn spid1 61293199371111
 isdn spid2 61293199381111
!
router eigrp 1
 network 175.10.0.0
 no auto-summary
!
no ip classless
!
access-list 101 deny    eigrp any any
access-list 101 permit ip any any
dialer watch-list 1 ip 175.10.102.1 255.255.255.255
dialer watch-list 1 ip 175.10.1.0 255.255.255.0
dialer-list 1 protocol ip list 101
!
!
line con 0
 privilege level 15
 logging synchronous
 transport input none
line aux 0
line vty 0 4
```

continues

Example 7-33 *Dialer Watch Configuration (Continued)*

```
 login
 !
 end
```

```
Headquarters#show running-config
Building configuration...

Current configuration:
!
version 12.0
service timestamps debug uptime
service timestamps log uptime
no service password-encryption
!
hostname Headquarters
!
!
username Remote_Site password 0 cisco
ip subnet-zero
isdn switch-type basic-dms100
!
!
!
interface Loopback0
 ip address 175.10.102.1 255.255.255.255
 no ip directed-broadcast
!
interface Ethernet0
 ip address 175.10.1.1 255.255.255.0
 no ip directed-broadcast
 no keepalive
!
interface Serial0
 no ip address
 no ip directed-broadcast
 shutdown
!
interface Serial1
 description PRIMARY LINK TO REMOTE SITE
 ip address 175.10.200.2 255.255.255.252
 no ip directed-broadcast
 clockrate 125000
!
interface BRI0
 ip address 175.10.23.2 255.255.255.248
 no ip directed-broadcast
 encapsulation ppp
 dialer-group 1
 isdn switch-type basic-dms100
 isdn spid1 61293198331111
 isdn spid2 61293198461111
 !
```

Example 7-33 *Dialer Watch Configuration (Continued)*

```
router eigrp 1
 network 175.10.0.0
 no auto-summary
!
no ip classless
!
dialer-list 1 protocol ip permit
!
!
line con 0
 privilege level 15
 logging synchronous
 transport input none
line aux 0
line vty 0 4
 login
!
end
```

If any of the routes defined in the dialer-watch list still exists in the routing table, the primary interface is considered to be up, and the ISDN call will not initiate. In this example, both the routes to the Headquarters Ethernet segment and the loopback address must disappear from the routing table before dialer watch will cause the router to make a call. Using a loopback address is an effective way to use dialer watch because this interface is always up. If you specified only the Ethernet network in the dialer watch list, ISDN calls would be made whenever the Ethernet interface went down. This is not a desired result because the primary link might still be up; if the Ethernet is down, it will be just as unreachable through the backup link as it would be through the primary connection. In this example, you could have just as easily chosen only the Headquarters loopback network in the dialer watch list. Instead, both the Ethernet and loopback networks were used in the dialer watch list to illustrate that all routes being watched must no longer be in the routing table for dialing to occur.

CAUTION   The networks defined in the dialer watch list must match the network and subnet masks in the routing table exactly. For example, if the routing table shows 175.10.0.0/16 and your configuration lists **dialer watch-list 1 ip 175.10.0.0 255.255.255.0**, the dialer watch process will be incapable of detecting that 175.10.0.0/16 is no longer in the routing table.

Example: Backup Interface

Using the **backup interface** command is another effective way of using ISDN to back up a primary link failure. This command works by keeping track of the link status of the primary interface and initiating an ISDN connection only when the interface status of the primary interface changes from up to down.

NOTE   Some documentation states that the backup interface will come up when only the line protocol of the primary interface goes from up to down. This is not the case. The actual interface must be down, and the line protocol must be down also. You will see an example of where it will not work when the interface is administratively down and the line protocol is down.

Using the backup interface method is not as common as using floating static routes because the only way to test that the ISDN link is working is by actually taking down the primary link physically.

Configuring the backup interface requires only one command:

```
Router(config-if)#backup interface bri 0
```

This is performed under the primary link's interface, *not* under the ISDN interface. An optional parameter that you should be aware of is the **backup delay** command. This configuration command allows you to determine the time that the ISDN link should wait after detecting a primary link outage before initiating a call, as well as the amount of time that the backup link should wait before tearing down this call after the primary link has been restored. This is useful when the primary link experiences frequent, short outages, and you do not want the ISDN router to initiate a call every time this happens. This is done with the command sequence in Example 7-34, again done under the primary link's interface configuration mode.

Example 7-34 *Example Backup Configuration*

```
interface Serial0
 backup delay 5 60
 backup interface BRI0
 ip address 175.10.123.1 255.255.255.0
 encapsulation frame-relay
 frame-relay map ip 175.10.123.2 300 broadcast
```

Here, the primary link is the Frame Relay connection on Serial 0, and the backup link is the ISDN link on BRI 0. The ISDN link will wait 5 seconds after before calling, after the Serial 0 interface goes from up to down, and it will wait 60 seconds before ending the call after the Serial 0 interface goes from down to up. The backup delay is configured in seconds and can be a value from 0 to 4,294,967,294 seconds for both delay times. Configuring the delays is an optional parameter; if omitted, the ISDN link will come up instantly upon the primary links failure, and the call will terminate instantly upon restoration of the primary link.

Set the delays to ensure that fast bouncing circuits do not start the ISDN call. Bouncing circuits will create havoc with link-state routing protocols, especially OSPF.

When configuring the ISDN link as backup interface, the BRI 0 interface status changes from up, line protocol up (spoofing), to standby mode, line protocol down, as demonstrated in Example 7-35.

Example 7-35 *ISDN Interface Status When Using the Backup Interface Configuration*

```
Cheech#show int bri0
BRI0 is standby mode, line protocol is down
  Hardware is BRI
  Internet address is 175.10.23.1/24
  MTU 1500 bytes, BW 64 Kbit, DLY 20000 usec, rely 255/255, load 1/255
  Encapsulation PPP, loopback not set
  Last input 00:19:42, output 00:19:42, output hang never
  Last clearing of "show interface" counters 1d04h
  Queueing strategy: fifo
  Output queue 0/40, 0 drops; input queue 0/75, 0 drops
  5 minute input rate 0 bits/sec, 0 packets/sec
  5 minute output rate 0 bits/sec, 0 packets/sec
      21175 packets input, 08385 bytes, 0 no buffer
      Received 4 broadcasts, 0 runts, 0 giants, 0 throttles
      0 input errors, 0 CRC, 0 frame, 0 overrun, 0 ignored, 0 abort
      21175 packets output, 89187 bytes, 0 underruns
      0 output errors, 0 collisions, 2 interface resets
      0 output buffer failures, 0 output buffers swapped out
      3 carrier transitions
```

This interface remains in standby mode and will be unusable until the primary link fails.

Figure 7-9 shows the example network to reference for your backup interface configuration.

Figure 7-9   *Network Topology for Backup Interface Configuration Example*

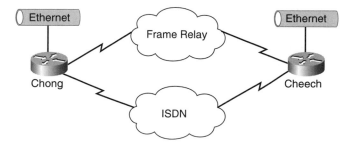

Example 7-36 shows an example backup interface configuration.

Example 7-36 *Backup Interface Configuration*

```
Cheech#show running-config
Building configuration...

Current configuration:
!
version 11.2
no service password-encryption
no service udp-small-servers
no service tcp-small-servers
!
hostname Cheech
!
enable password cisco
!
username Chong password 0 cisco
isdn switch-type basic-dms100
!
interface Loopback0
 ip address 175.10.2.2 255.255.255.0
!
interface Ethernet0
 ip address 175.10.22.1 255.255.255.0
 no keepalive
 no mop enabled
!
interface Serial0
 backup delay 5 60
 backup interface BRI0
 ip address 175.10.123.1 255.255.255.0
 encapsulation frame-relay
 frame-relay map ip 175.10.123.2 300 broadcast
!
interface Serial1
 no ip address
 shutdown
!
interface BRI0
 ip address 175.10.23.1 255.255.255.0
 encapsulation ppp
 isdn spid1 61293199371111
 isdn spid2 61293199381111
 dialer map ip 175.10.23.2 broadcast 6129319833
 dialer-group 1
 no fair-queue
 ppp authentication chap
!
router eigrp 1
 network 175.10.0.0
 no auto-summary
```

Example 7-36 *Backup Interface Configuration (Continued)*

```
!
ip classless
!
dialer-list 1 protocol ip permit
!
line con 0
 exec-timeout 0 0
 privilege level 15
 logging synchronous
line aux 0
line vty 0 4
 password cisco
 login
!
end
```

```
Chong#show running-config
Building configuration...

Current configuration:
!
version 11.2
no service password-encryption
no service udp-small-servers
no service tcp-small-servers
!
hostname Chong
!
enable password cisco
!
username Cheech password 0 cisco
isdn switch-type basic-dms100
!
interface Loopback0
 ip address 175.10.3.3 255.255.255.0
!
interface Ethernet0
 ip address 175.10.35.3 255.255.255.0
!
interface Serial0
 no ip address
 encapsulation frame-relay
 no fair-queue
!
interface Serial0.1 point-to-point
 ip address 175.10.123.2 255.255.255.0
 frame-relay interface-dlci 200
!
interface Serial1
 no ip address
```

continues

Example 7-36 *Backup Interface Configuration (Continued)*

```
 shutdown
 !
interface BRI0
 ip address 175.10.23.2 255.255.255.0
 encapsulation ppp
 isdn spid1 61293198331111
 isdn spid2 61293198461111
 dialer idle-timeout 9999
 dialer-group 1
 no fair-queue
 ppp authentication chap
 !
router eigrp 1
 network 175.10.0.0
 no auto-summary
 !
no ip classless
 !
dialer-list 1 protocol ip permit
 !
line con 0
 exec-timeout 0 0
 privilege level 15
 logging synchronous
line aux 0
line vty 0 4
 password cisco
 login
 !
end
```

No special configuration command was needed in the Chong router, and the BRI0 interface was not made passive under the EIGRP routing process. Normally, when you fail to do this, the EIGRP process keeps the ISDN link up indefinitely, but because it is configured as a backup interface, it will not call unless the Serial 0 interface goes down.

When testing the backup interface scenario, it is important to realize that it will *not* work simply by administratively shutting down the serial interface on the Cheech router. A backup interface connection will be made only when the primary link's interface is down, not administratively down. However, if you had implemented logical subinterfaces in the Cheech router, using Serial 0.1 for the Frame Relay connection to Chong, you could have configured the backup interface commands on the Serial 0.1 interface. In this case, you could have shut down the physical Serial 0 interface, and the ISDN backup connection would have worked because the Serial 0.1 interface would have gone from up to down (not administratively down). But because you configured the physical serial interface with the backup command in the previous case, you need to actually unplug the Frame Relay connection from the router (or power down the Frame Relay switch in the lab) to initiate the ISDN call.

Example 7-37 shows Cheech's routing table before the Frame Relay outage. Example 7-38 shows the same routing table after the Frame Relay outage.

Example 7-37 *Cheech's Routing Table Before Frame Relay Outage*

```
Cheech#show ip route
Codes: C - connected, S - static, I - IGRP, R - RIP, M - mobile, B - BGP
       D - EIGRP, EX - EIGRP external, O - OSPF, IA - OSPF inter area
       N1 - OSPF NSSA external type 1, N2 - OSPF NSSA external type 2
       E1 - OSPF external type 1, E2 - OSPF external type 2, E - EGP
       i - IS-IS, L1 - IS-IS level-1, L2 - IS-IS level-2, * - candidate default
       U - per-user static route, o - ODR

Gateway of last resort is not set

     175.10.0.0/24 is subnetted, 7 subnets
D       175.10.35.0 [90/2195456] via 175.10.123.2, 00:05:07, Serial0
D       175.10.5.0 [90/2323456] via 175.10.123.2, 00:05:07, Serial0
D       175.10.3.0 [90/2297856] via 175.10.123.2, 00:05:07, Serial0
C       175.10.2.0 is directly connected, Loopback0
D       175.10.23.0 [90/41024000] via 175.10.123.2, 00:04:41, Serial0
C       175.10.22.0 is directly connected, Ethernet0
C       175.10.123.0 is directly connected, Serial0
Cheech# ping 175.10.35.3

Type escape sequence to abort.
Sending 5, 100-byte ICMP Echos to 175.10.35.3, timeout is 2 seconds:
!!!!!
Success rate is 100 percent (5/5), round-trip min/avg/max = 8/8/8 ms
```

Example 7-38 *Cheech's Routing Table After Frame Relay Outage*

```
Cheech#show ip route
Codes: C - connected, S - static, I - IGRP, R - RIP, M - mobile, B - BGP
       D - EIGRP, EX - EIGRP external, O - OSPF, IA - OSPF inter area
       N1 - OSPF NSSA external type 1, N2 - OSPF NSSA external type 2
       E1 - OSPF external type 1, E2 - OSPF external type 2, E - EGP
       i - IS-IS, L1 - IS-IS level-1, L2 - IS-IS level-2, * - candidate default
       U - per-user static route, o - ODR

Gateway of last resort is not set

     175.10.0.0/16 is variably subnetted, 7 subnets, 2 masks
D       175.10.35.0/24 [90/40537600] via 175.10.23.2, 00:00:12, BRI0
D       175.10.5.0/24 [90/40665600] via 175.10.23.2, 00:00:12, BRI0
D       175.10.3.0/24 [90/40640000] via 175.10.23.2, 00:00:12, BRI0
C       175.10.2.0/24 is directly connected, Loopback0
```

continues

Example 7-38 *Cheech's Routing Table After Frame Relay Outage (Continued)*

```
C       175.10.23.2/32 is directly connected, BRI0
C       175.10.23.0/24 is directly connected, BRI0
C       175.10.22.0/24 is directly connected, Ethernet0
Cheech#ping 175.10.35.3

Type escape sequence to abort.
Sending 5, 100-byte ICMP Echos to 175.10.35.3, timeout is 2 seconds:
!!!!!
Success rate is 100 percent (5/5), round-trip min/avg/max = 40/41/44 ms
Cheech#
```

After the Frame Relay connection was unplugged from the Cheech router, it dialed into Chong after waiting 5 seconds. After restoring the connection, the ISDN call ended after 60 seconds. Again, these timers are user-configurable.

Example: Using the **backup load** Command

Using the backup interface command is also helpful in that, when the primary link becomes overly utilized, an ISDN call can be initiated to provide more bandwidth using the **backup load** command on the primary link's interface. It also provides a way to configure the routers to make an ISDN connection to back up a failed primary link. A major advantage to using this method to initiate ISDN calls is that it works over any routed or routing protocol. This is bandwidth on demand, not backup. But **backup load** does work in conjunction with **backup interface**, as follows:

A Cisco IOS interface is placed into backup mode by applying the **backup interface** command:

- The **backup interface** interface configuration command specifies the interface that is to act as the backup.

- The **backup load** command specifies the traffic threshold at which the backup interface is to be activated and deactivated.

- The **backup delay** command specifies the amount of time that is to elapse before the backup interface is activated or deactivated after a transition on the primary interface.

Backup interfaces traditionally lock the backup interface into backup state so that it is unavailable for other use. Dialer profiles eliminates this lock and allows the physical interface to be used for multiple purposes. Floating static route DDR design also eliminates this lock on the dialer interface.

Using the configuration in Example 7-39, BRI 0 is activated only when serial interface 1/0 (the primary line) goes down. The **backup delay** command configures the backup connection to activate 30 seconds after serial interface 0 goes down and to remain activated for 60 seconds after the serial interface 1/0 comes up.

Example 7-39 *Configuration Options Using Backup Delay*

```
interface serial 1/0
    ip address 172.20.1.4 255.255.255.0
    backup interface bri 2/0
    backup delay 30 60
```

Using the configuration in Example 7-40, BRI 2/0 is activated only when the load on Serial 0 (the primary line) exceeds 75 percent of its bandwidth. The backup line is deactivated when the aggregate load between the primary and backup lines is within 5 percent of the primary line's bandwidth.

Example 7-40 *Configuration Options Using Backup Load*

```
interface serial 1/0
    ip address 172.20.1.4 255.255.255.0
    backup interface bri 2/0
    backup load 75 5
```

Using the configuration in Example 7-41, BRI 2/0 is activated only when serial interface 1/00 goes down or when traffic exceeds 25 percent. If serial interface 1/0 goes down, 10 seconds will elapse before BRI 0 becomes active. When serial interface 1/0 comes up, BRI 2/0 remains active for 60 seconds. If BRI 2/0 is activated by the load threshold on serial interface 1/0, BRI 2/0 is deactivated when the aggregate load of serial interface 1/0 and BRI 2/0 returns to within 5 percent of the bandwidth of serial interface 1/0.

Example 7-41 *Using the Backup Load Configuration*

```
interface serial 1/0
    ip address 172.20.1.4 255.255.255.0
    backup interface bri 2/0
    backup load 25 5
    backup delay 10 60
```

Note the difference between PPP multilink and backup load. In PPP multilink, the dialer-load threshold value was specified as a value from 1 to 255. In backup load, the number specified to bring up the backup connection is given as a true percentage (0 to 100).

Example: Snapshot Routing

Snapshot routing works on the client/server principle in which one router (usually the headquarters router) is designated as the snapshot server, and one or more routers (remote sites) are the snapshot clients. The clients connect to the server at specific times, called the active period, to obtain their routing information from the server. The term *snapshot* gets its name from the fact that when the clients' active time expires, the ISDN call disconnects but the clients retain a "snapshot" of the routing entries. During the time that the ISDN line is idle, termed the quiet period, these routing entries remain frozen into the clients' routing tables. When the quiet period ends, the clients dial into the snapshot server to obtain the latest routing information. The quiet and active periods are configurable (5 to 1000 minutes for the active time, and 8 to 100,000 minutes for the quiet period).

Because link-state protocols rely on the use of periodic hellos to retain neighbor adjacency, snapshot routing can be used only with link-state protocols, such as IGRP and RIP for IP, RIP for IPX, and RTMP for AppleTalk.

Snapshot Client Configuration

Configuring snapshot routing is relatively simple. For the client router, only two commands are needed in interface config mode. The first one is as follows:

```
router(config-if)#snapshot client active-time quiet-time [suppress-statechange-updates]
   [dialer]
```

This command sets the active and quiet periods, in minutes. The **suppress-statechange-updates** command option disables the exchange of routing updates each time that the link comes up because of any additional traffic. The default is that routing information is exchanged whenever the ISDN link is up for any reason. The dialer option is used to tell the client router to go ahead and dial into the snapshot server in the absence of regular traffic, and to point to the appropriate dialer map specified in Step 2.

The second required command is as follows:

```
router(config-if)# dialer map snapshot sequence-number name name dial-string
```

This command defines the dialer map that includes the snapshot server router to call for routing updates.

A common point of confusion occurs when using the **help** (the **?**) the feature in this command, when a protocol address is asked for when the sequence number is really needed. Consider the configuration in Example 7-42.

Example 7-42 **dialer map snapshot** *Confusion Illustration*

```
Cheech#conf t
Cheech(config)#int bri0
Cheech(config-if)#dialer map snapshot ?
  N  Protocol specific address
```

It appears here that IOS is looking for a specific protocol address, when, in fact, only a sequence number is required. Sequence numbers are used to identify a dialer map and prioritize the sequence (a number from 1 to 254) in which the client calls the server routers, if there are multiple server routers. If only one server router exists, any sequence number will do. The point here is to remember to input only a number from 1 to 254, not to try to put in any kind of Layer 3 address.

Snapshot Server Configuration

This one is easy because only one command is needed:

```
Router(config-if)#snapshot server active-timer [dialer]
```

The *active-timer* specified in this command must match the same value that was placed on the client router.

Example Snapshot Configuration

In the simple network in Figure 7-10, Frame Relay is used as the primary communication link between the two sites, and snapshot routing is used to exchange routing information between the two locations so that connectivity will remain through the ISDN link in the case of a Frame Relay outage. We made the BRI interfaces passive to eliminate the routing updates from triggering a call.

Figure 7-10   *Snapshot Network Reference*

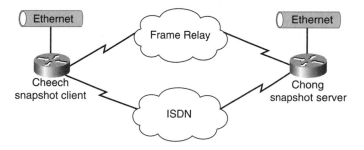

Example 7-43 illustrates the proper snapshot configuration.

Table 7-4   *Snapshot Client Router Configuration*

```
Cheech#show running-configuration
no service password-encryption
no service udp-small-servers
no service tcp-small-servers
!
hostname Cheech
!
```

continues

Table 7-4   *Snapshot Client Router Configuration (Continued)*

```
enable password cisco
!
username Chong password 0 cisco
isdn switch-type basic-dms100
!
interface Loopback0
 ip address 175.10.2.2 255.255.255.0
!
interface Ethernet0
 ip address 175.10.22.1 255.255.255.0
 no keepalive
 no mop enabled
!
interface Serial0
 ip address 175.10.123.1 255.255.255.0
 encapsulation frame-relay
 frame-relay map ip 175.10.123.2 300 broadcast
!
interface Serial1
 no ip address
 shutdown
!
interface BRI0
 ip address 175.10.23.1 255.255.255.0
 encapsulation ppp
 isdn spid1 61293199371111
 isdn spid2 61293199381111
 dialer map snapshot 1 name Chong 6129319833
 dialer map ip 175.10.23.2 broadcast 6129319833
 dialer-group 1
 snapshot client 10 20 dialer
 no fair-queue
 ppp authentication chap
!
router igrp 1
 network 175.10.0.0
!
ip classless
!
dialer-list 1 protocol ip permit
!
line con 0
 exec-timeout 0 0
 privilege level 15
 logging synchronous
line aux 0
line vty 0 4
 password cisco
 login
!
end
```

Table 7-4   *Snapshot Client Router Configuration (Continued)*

```
Chong#show running-configuration
no service password-encryption
no service udp-small-servers
no service tcp-small-servers
!
hostname Chong
!
enable password cisco
!
username Cheech password 0 cisco
isdn switch-type basic-dms100
!
interface Loopback0
 ip address 175.10.3.3 255.255.255.0
!
interface Ethernet0
 ip address 175.10.35.3 255.255.255.0
!
interface Serial0
 no ip address
 encapsulation frame-relay
 no fair-queue
!
interface Serial0.1 point-to-point
 ip address 175.10.123.2 255.255.255.0
 frame-relay interface-dlci 200
!
interface Serial1
 no ip address
 shutdown
!
interface BRI0
 ip address 175.10.23.2 255.255.255.0
 encapsulation ppp
 isdn spid1 61293198331111
 isdn spid2 61293198461111
 dialer-group 1
 snapshot server 10
 no fair-queue
 ppp authentication chap
!
router igrp 1
 network 175.10.0.0
!
no ip classless
!
dialer-list 1 protocol ip permit
!
line con 0
 exec-timeout 0 0
```

continues

Table 7-4 *Snapshot Client Router Configuration (Continued)*

```
 privilege level 15
 logging synchronous
line aux 0
line vty 0 4
 password cisco
 login
 !
end
```

An important note here is that we have not made the BRI0 interfaces passive under the
IGRP process. This is needed so that routing traffic will pass over the ISDN link and
the snapshot routing process will keep this line from coming up needlessly. To verify that the
routers do connect during the active period and that routing traffic is being passed, you can
issue the **show dialer** and **show snapshot** commands, as demonstrated in Example 7-44.

Example 7-43 *Verifying Router Connections During Active Periods and Passing of Routing Traffic*

```
Cheech#show dialer

BRI0 - dialer type = ISDN

Dial String      Successes   Failures    Last called   Last status
6129319833               85          0    00:10:22      successful
0 incoming call(s) have been screened.

BRI0:1 - dialer type = ISDN
Idle timer (120 secs), Fast idle timer (20 secs)
Wait for carrier (30 secs), Re-enable (15 secs)
Dialer state is data link layer up
Dial reason: snapshot
Time until disconnect 6 secs
Connected to 6129319833 (Chong)

BRI0:2 - dialer type = ISDN
Idle timer (120 secs), Fast idle timer (20 secs)
Wait for carrier (30 secs), Re-enable (15 secs)
Dialer state is idle
Cheech#show dialer

BRI0 - dialer type = ISDN

Dial String      Successes   Failures    Last called   Last status
6129319833               85          0    00:10:26      successful
0 incoming call(s) have been screened.

BRI0:1 - dialer type = ISDN
Idle timer (120 secs), Fast idle timer (20 secs)
Wait for carrier (30 secs), Re-enable (15 secs)
```

Example 7-43 *Verifying Router Connections During Active Periods and Passing of Routing Traffic (Continued)*

```
Dialer state is data link layer up
Dial reason: snapshot
Time until disconnect
```

The reason for this ISDN connection was to exchange snapshot routing information. Based on the previous example, these exchanges should take place every 20 minutes, for a length of 10 minutes each. In real-world applications, you might want to increase the quiet time period because causing the link to come up every 20 minutes might seem a bit excessive and costly.

The **show snapshot** command can be used to verify that the snapshot processes are working properly and to show which snapshot options are being applied, as demonstrated in Example 7-45.

Example 7-44 *Verifying Snapshot Processes and Applied Options*

```
Cheech#show snapshot
BRI0 is up, line protocol is up Snapshot client
  Options: dialer support
  Length of active period:       10 minutes
  Length of quiet period:        20 minutes
  Length of retry period:        13 minutes
   For dialer address 1
    Current state: active, remaining/exchange time: 8/2 minutes
    Connected dialer interface:
       BRI0:1
    Updates received this cycle: ip
```

Only IP routes are being passed, and you can verify that this router has been configured as a client using dialer information, with the configured active and quiet periods, along with the retry period. The retry period defaults to the configured active period plus 3 minutes.

To test that routing over the ISDN link works in the event of a Frame Relay outage, unplug the Frame Relay connection from the Cheech router. Example 7-46 and 7-47 show the routing table before and after the Frame Relay connection was unplugged.

Example 7-45 *Routing Table Before Frame Relay Outage*

```
Cheech#show ip route
Codes: C - connected, S - static, I - IGRP, R - RIP, M - mobile, B - BGP
       D - EIGRP, EX - EIGRP external, O - OSPF, IA - OSPF inter area
       N1 - OSPF NSSA external type 1, N2 - OSPF NSSA external type 2
       E1 - OSPF external type 1, E2 - OSPF external type 2, E - EGP
```

continues

Example 7-45 *Routing Table Before Frame Relay Outage (Continued)*

```
               i - IS-IS, L1 - IS-IS level-1, L2 - IS-IS level-2, * - candidate default
               U - per-user static route, o - ODR

Gateway of last resort is not set

     175.10.0.0/24 is subnetted, 6 subnets
I        175.10.35.0 [100/8576] via 175.10.123.2, 00:00:04, Serial0
I        175.10.3.0 [100/8976] via 175.10.123.2, 00:00:04, Serial0
C        175.10.2.0 is directly connected, Loopback0
C        175.10.23.0 is directly connected, BRI0
C        175.10.22.0 is directly connected, Ethernet0
C        175.10.123.0 is directly connected, Serial0
Cheech# ping 175.10.35.3

Type escape sequence to abort.
Sending 5, 100-byte ICMP Echos to 175.10.35.3, timeout is 2 seconds:
!!!!!
Success rate is 100 percent (5/5), round-trip min/avg/max = 4/7/8 ms
```

Example 7-46 *Routing Table After a Frame Relay Outage*

```
Cheech#show ip route
Codes: C - connected, S - static, I - IGRP, R - RIP, M - mobile, B - BGP
       D - EIGRP, EX - EIGRP external, O - OSPF, IA - OSPF inter area
       N1 - OSPF NSSA external type 1, N2 - OSPF NSSA external type 2
       E1 - OSPF external type 1, E2 - OSPF external type 2, E - EGP
       i - IS-IS, L1 - IS-IS level-1, L2 - IS-IS level-2, * - candidate default
       U - per-user static route, o - ODR

Gateway of last resort is not set

     175.10.0.0/16 is variably subnetted, 6 subnets, 2 masks
I        175.10.35.0/24 [100/158350] via 175.10.23.2, 00:00:00, BRI0
I        175.10.3.0/24 [100/158750] via 175.10.23.2, 00:00:00, BRI0
C        175.10.2.0/24 is directly connected, Loopback0
C        175.10.23.2/32 is directly connected, BRI0
C        175.10.23.0/24 is directly connected, BRI0
C        175.10.22.0/24 is directly connected, Ethernet0
Cheech#ping 175.10.35.3

Type escape sequence to abort.
Sending 5, 100-byte ICMP Echos to 175.10.35.3, timeout is 2 seconds:
!!!!!
Success rate is 100 percent (5/5), round-trip min/avg/max = 40/43/44 ms
```

It took only a couple seconds for the routing to converge to the ISDN link. When the Frame Relay link was restored, traffic again was routed over this link quickly.

The "Big show" and "Big D" for Troubleshooting ISDN

We will now cover some of the ISDN troubleshooting techniques that will aid in discovering and isolating common ISDN issues, as well as some tips to help you properly configure ISDN.

The "Big show" for ISDN

The following list includes some of the most useful commands when trying to isolate ISDN-related problems, and this should be among the first things done to verify whether the ISDN link is working properly.

show isdn status Command

This command tells you whether your router is properly talking to the carrier's ISDN switch. It tells you the ISDN switch type that has been configured for each interface, as well as information about the SPID status and active layer calls. Example 7-48 shows an example where the router's BRI interface is properly configured and connected to the ISDN switch.

Example 7 47 **show isdn status** *Command Output*

```
Cheech#show isdn status
The current ISDN Switchtype = basic-dms100
ISDN BRI0 interface
    Layer 1 Status:             →Shows that the interface is up and the ISDN
        ACTIVE                  →circuit has been plugged into the router
    Layer 2 Status:
        TEI = 104, State = MULTIPLE_FRAME_ESTABLISHED
        TEI = 113, State = MULTIPLE_FRAME_ESTABLISHED
    Spid Status:
        TEI 104, ces = 1, state = 5(init)
            spid1 configured, no LDN, spid1 sent, spid1 valid
            Endpoint ID Info: epsf = 0, usid = 0, tid = B
        TEI 113, ces = 2, state = 5(init)
            spid2 configured, no LDN, spid2 sent, spid2 valid
            Endpoint ID Info: epsf = 0, usid = 1, tid = B
    Layer 3 Status:
        1 Active Layer 3 Call(s)   →Shows that a connection has been made to another
router.
    Activated dsl 0 CCBs = 2
        CCB: callid=0x0, sapi=0, ces=1, B-chan=0
        CCB: callid=0x802A, sapi=0, ces=1, B-chan=1
    Total Allocated ISDN CCBs = 2
```

Depending on the router model and IOS version, it might be necessary to reset the BRI interface for the router's interface to properly connect to the ISDN switch. To illustrate this, watch what happens when we entered the bswitch type and SPID information into a Cisco 2503 running IOS version 11.2(20) in Example 7-49.

Example 7-48 *Verifying ISDN Layer 2 Status*

```
ISDN_Router#show isdn status
The current ISDN Switchtype = basic-dms100
ISDN BRI0 interface
    Layer 1 Status:
        ACTIVE
    Layer 2 Status:
        TEI = 88, State = MULTIPLE_FRAME_ESTABLISHED
    Spid Status:
        TEI 88, ces = 1, state = 5(init)
            spid1 configured, no LDN, spid1 sent, spid1 valid
            Endpoint ID Info: epsf = 0, usid = 0, tid = B
        TEI Not Assigned, ces = 2, state = 1(terminal down)
            spid2 configured, no LDN, spid2 NOT sent, spid2 NOT valid
    Layer 3 Status:
        0 Active Layer 3 Call(s)
    Activated dsl 0 CCBs = 0
    Total Allocated ISDN CCBs = 0
```

Here, you can see that SPID 1 was accepted, but SPID 2 was not. After verifying that the SPID information is indeed correct, we reset the BRI interface by issuing the **shutdown/no shutdown** commands. Example 7-50 shows the results.

Example 7-49 *Resetting the BRI Interface*

```
ISDN_Router(config)#int bri0
ISDN_Router(config-if)#shut
ISDN_Router(config-if)#no shut
ISDN_Router(config-if)#
%LINK-5-CHANGED: Interface BRI0, changed state to administratively down
%LINK-3-UPDOWN: Interface BRI0:1, changed state to down
%LINK-3-UPDOWN: Interface BRI0:2, changed state to down
%LINK-3-UPDOWN: Interface BRI0, changed state to up
ISDN Router(config-if)#end
%ISDN-6-LAYER2UP: Layer 2 for Interface BR0, TEI 88 changed to up
%ISDN-6-LAYER2UP: Layer 2 for Interface BR0, TEI 97 changed to up
%SYS-5-CONFIG_I: Configured from console by console
Blue-R8#show isdn status
The current ISDN Switchtype = basic-dms100
ISDN BRI0 interface
    Layer 1 Status:
        ACTIVE
    Layer 2 Status:
        TEI = 88, State = MULTIPLE_FRAME_ESTABLISHED
        TEI = 97, State = MULTIPLE_FRAME_ESTABLISHED
    Spid Status:
        TEI 88, ces = 1, state = 5(init)
```

Example 7-49 *Resetting the BRI Interface (Continued)*

```
            spid1 configured, no LDN, spid1 sent, spid1 valid
            Endpoint ID Info: epsf = 0, usid = 0, tid = B
    TEI 97, ces = 2, state = 5(init)
            spid2 configured, no LDN, spid2 sent, spid2 valid
            Endpoint ID Info: epsf = 0, usid = 1, tid = B
  Layer 3 Status:
      0 Active Layer 3 Call(s)
  Activated dsl 0 CCBs = 1
      CCB: callid=0x0, sapi=0, ces=1, B-chan=0
  Total Allocated ISDN CCBs = 1
```

After the interface was reset, both SPIDS were properly talking to the ISDN switch and were shown as valid. One of the first things that should be done to verify connectivity to the ISDN provider's switch is to issue the **show isdn status** command. If the SPIDs will not come active following an interface reset, power-reset the router. This has proven to get the correct signaling from the switch when all else fails.

show interface bri 0 Command

This command is useful in showing the general status of the ISDN interface. In general, after the ISDN circuit is connected to the interface and it is administratively enabled, it will be spoofing. *Spoofing* is the state in which the IOS makes the interface pretend to be up so that the routing table can point to this interface to pass traffic. Example 7-51 demonstrates the output from this command.

Example 7-50 *Checking the Status of the ISDN Interface*

```
Cheech#show int bri0
BRI0 is up, line protocol is up (spoofing)
  Hardware is BRI
  Internet address is 175.10.23.1/30
  MTU 1500 bytes, BW 64 Kbit, DLY 20000 usec, rely 255/255, load 1/255
  Encapsulation PPP, loopback not set
  Last input 00:00:01, output 00:00:01, output hang never
  Last clearing of "show interface" counters 00:00:02
  Queueing strategy: fifo
  Output queue 0/40, 0 drops; input queue 0/75, 0 drops
  5 minute input rate 0 bits/sec, 0 packets/sec
  5 minute output rate 0 bits/sec, 0 packets/sec
    1 packets input, 4 bytes, 0 no buffer
    Received 0 broadcasts, 0 runts, 0 giants, 0 throttles
    0 input errors, 0 CRC, 0 frame, 0 overrun, 0 ignored, 0 abort
    1 packets output, 4 bytes, 0 underruns
    0 output errors, 0 collisions, 0 interface resets
    0 output buffer failures, 0 output buffers swapped out
    0 carrier transitions
```

If you want to see the status of each individual B channel, you can issue the **show interface bri0 1 2** command, as demonstrated in Example 7-52.

Example 7-51 *Checking the Status of the Individual B Channels on the ISDN Interface*

```
Cheech#show interface bri0 1 2
BRI0:1 is down, line protocol is down
  Hardware is BRI
  MTU 1500 bytes, BW 64 Kbit, DLY 20000 usec, rely 255/255, load 1/255
  Encapsulation PPP, loopback not set, keepalive set (10 sec)
  LCP Closed, multilink Closed
  Closed: IPCP, CDPCP
  Last input 00:00:07, output 00:00:05, output hang never
  Last clearing of "show interface" counters 00:00:49
  Queueing strategy: fifo
  Output queue 0/40, 0 drops; input queue 0/75, 0 drops
  5 minute input rate 0 bits/sec, 0 packets/sec
  5 minute output rate 0 bits/sec, 0 packets/sec
     9 packets input, 144 bytes, 0 no buffer
     Received 9 broadcasts, 0 runts, 0 giants, 0 throttles
     0 input errors, 0 CRC, 0 frame, 0 overrun, 0 ignored, 0 abort
     10 packets output, 152 bytes, 0 underruns
     0 output errors, 0 collisions, 0 interface resets
     0 output buffer failures, 0 output buffers swapped out
     1 carrier transitions
BRI0:2 is down, line protocol is down
  Hardware is BRI
  MTU 1500 bytes, BW 64 Kbit, DLY 20000 usec, rely 255/255, load 1/255
  Encapsulation PPP, loopback not set, keepalive set (10 sec)
  LCP Closed, multilink Closed
  Closed: IPCP, CDPCP
  Last input 00:10:44, output 00:10:44, output hang never
  Last clearing of "show interface" counters 00:00:53
  Queueing strategy: fifo
  Output queue 0/40, 0 drops; input queue 0/75, 0 drops
  5 minute input rate 0 bits/sec, 0 packets/sec
  5 minute output rate 0 bits/sec, 0 packets/sec
     0 packets input, 0 bytes, 0 no buffer
     Received 0 broadcasts, 0 runts, 0 giants, 0 throttles
     0 input errors, 0 CRC, 0 frame, 0 overrun, 0 ignored, 0 abort
     0 packets output, 0 bytes, 0 underruns
     0 output errors, 0 collisions, 0 interface resets
     0 output buffer failures, 0 output buffers swapped out
     0 carrier transitions
```

In this example, both B channels are down (the ISDN line is idle).

show dialer Command

This command enables you to determine which B channels are connected, as well as determine the destination number and the time until the call will tear down. It is also useful in that it shows the reason that each call was made (in the calling router only). Example 7-53 demonstrates the output generated from this command.

Example 7-52 show dialer *Command Output*

```
Cheech#show dialer

BRI0 - dialer type = ISDN

Dial String      Successes   Failures   Last called   Last status
6129319833              31          0   00:00:15      successful
0 incoming call(s) have been screened.

BRI0:1 - dialer type = ISDN
Idle timer (120 secs), Fast idle timer (20 secs)
Wait for carrier (30 secs), Re-enable (15 secs)
Dialer state is physical layer up
Dial reason: ip (s=175.10.20.1, d=175.10.23.2)
Time until disconnect 104 secs
Connected to 6129319833 (Chong)
BRI0:2 - dialer type = ISDN
Idle timer (120 secs), Fast idle timer (20 secs)
Wait for carrier (30 secs), Re-enable (15 secs)
Dialer state is physical layer up
Dial reason: Multilink bundle overloaded
Time until disconnect 104 secs
Connected to 6129319833 (Chong)
```

In this example, both B channels are in use and are connected to a router named Chong. The first call was made as a result of an IP packet from 175.10.23.1 destined for 175.10.23.2 (which was allowed in the dialer-list). The second B channel was connected as a result of multilink bonding. (PPP multilink was configured on this particular BRI0 interface.)

show isdn active Command

As demonstrated in Example 7-54, this command is useful in showing the number of calls that are currently active, as well the number dialed and the idle time before disconnect.

Example 7-53 show isdn active *Command Output*

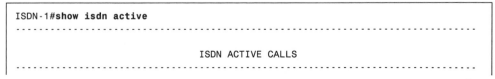

```
ISDN-1#show isdn active
----------------------------------------------------------------------
                              ISDN ACTIVE CALLS
----------------------------------------------------------------------
```

continues

Example 7-53 show isdn active *Command Output (Continued)*

```
History table has a maximum of 100 entries.
History table data is retained for a maximum of 15 Minutes.
-----------------------------------------------------------------------

Call    Calling     Called      Remote  Seconds Seconds Seconds Charges
Type    Number      Number      Name    Used    Left    Idle    Units/Currency

-----------------------------------------------------------------------

Out                 6129319833  ISDN-2    6                0       0

-----------------------------------------------------------------------
```

The "Big D" for ISDN

Included here are some of the most useful debugging commands to use when trying to determine the cause of any ISDN anomalies. Among the most common problems are calls not connecting, calls that never hang up, and dialer interfaces that continuously connect, hang up, and then connect again.

debug isdn q.921 Command

Personally, we have never found this **debug** command to be particularly useful, except when troubleshooting SPID problems. The **debug isdn q.921** command shows what is happening at Layer 2. The output in Example 7-55 shows what happens when the SPID's are improperly configured.

Example 7-54 debug q.921 *Command Output*

```
debug isdn q921
19:27:31: TX ->  IDREQ  ri = 19354  ai = 127 dsl = 0
19:27:33: TX ->  IDREQ  ri = 1339  ai = 127 dsl = 0
19:27:35: TX ->  IDREQ  ri = 22764  ai = 127 dsl = 0
19:27:37: TX ->  IDREQ  ri = 59309  ai = 127 dsl = 0
19:27:39: TX ->  IDREQ  ri = 25214  ai = 127 dsl = 0
19:27:41: TX ->  IDREQ  ri = 35423  ai = 127 dsl = 0
19:27:43: TX ->  IDREQ  ri = 12368  ai = 127 dsl = 0
19:27:45: TX ->  IDREQ  ri = 13649  ai = 127 dsl = 0
19:27:47: TX ->  IDREQ  ri = 35426  ai = 127 dsl = 0
19:27:49: TX ->  IDREQ  ri = 12419  ai = 127 dsl = 0
19:27:51: TX ->  IDREQ  ri = 14516  ai = 127 dsl = 0
19:28:04: TX ->  IDREQ  ri = 50165  ai = 127 dsl = 0
19:28:06: TX ->  IDREQ  ri = 838  ai = 127 dsl = 0
19:28:08: TX ->  IDREQ  ri = 14247  ai = 127 dsl = 0
19:28:34: TX ->  IDREQ  ri = 45592  ai = 127 dsl = 0
19:28:36: TX ->  IDREQ  ri = 54169  ai = 127 dsl = 0
```

Example 7-54 **debug q.921** *Command Output (Continued)*

```
19:28:38: TX -> IDREQ  ri = 3370   ai = 127 dsl = 0
19:29:09: TX -> IDREQ  ri = 57291  ai = 127 dsl = 0
19:29:11: TX -> IDREQ  ri = 56444  ai = 127 dsl = 0
19:29:13: TX -> IDREQ  ri = 42045  ai = 127 dsl = 0
19:29:44: TX -> IDREQ  ri = 59406  ai = 127 dsl = 0
19:29:46: TX -> IDREQ  ri = 26863  ai = 127 dsl = 0
19:29:48: TX -> IDREQ  ri = 63456  ai = 127 dsl = 0
19:30:19: TX -> IDREQ  ri = 30177  ai = 127 dsl = 0
19:30:21: TX -> IDREQ  ri = 54258  ai = 127 dsl = 0
19:30:23: TX -> IDREQ  ri = 4883   ai = 127 dsl = 0
19:30:54: TX -> IDREQ  ri = 17476  ai = 127 dsl = 0
19:30:56: TX -> IDREQ  ri = 34949  ai = 127 dsl = 0
19:30:58: TX -> IDREQ  ri = 4310   ai = 127 dsl = 0
19:31:24: TX -> IDREQ  ri = 7735   ai = 127 dsl = 0
19:31:26: TX -> IDREQ  ri = 424    ai = 127 dsl = 0
```

The router is sending identification requests (IDREQ) to the ISDN switch but is not receiving a response from the switch. If a SPID is incorrectly configured in the router, this **debug** command also shows that it was rejected.

debug isdn events Command

Debugging Q.931 can be useful when you want to check the status of incoming and outgoing ISDN calls. This **debug** command displays the call setup and teardown process, and it can give some insight on what any problems with these processes might be. Example 7-56 demonstrates sample output from this command.

Example 7-55 **debug isdn events** *Command Output*

```
BRI0: Dialing cause: BRI0: ip PERMIT
BRI0: Attempting to dial 6968900 TX -> SETUP dsl = 0 pd = 8 callref = 0x01 Bearer
Capability i = 0x8890218F Channel ID i = 0x83
Called Party Number i = 0x80, '6968900' RX RELEASE dsl = 0 pd = 8 callref = 0x01 RX
Router#
```

You can see that interesting traffic tried to initiate an ISDN connection, but the remote router did not answer the call (this is seen by the RX RELEASE) output. Normally, this problem is caused by a misconfigured dialing number or SPID. In this case, the dialing number was misconfigured.

debug dialer Command

This is probably the single most important **debug** command available. It can give insight to a number of things, such as the reason calls are initiated, whether the remote router is responding, and, in many cases, why calls fail. Example 7-57 demonstrates the output that appears when the router configuration is missing a **dialer map** or **dialer string** command.

Example 7-56 *debug dialer Command Output*

```
ISDN-1#debug dialer
1w1d: BR0 DDR: Dialing cause ip (s=175.10.23.1, d=175.10.23.2)
1w1d: BR0 DDR: No dialer string, dialing cannot occur
1w1d: BR0 DDR: Dialing cause ip (s=175.10.23.1, d=175.10.23.2)
1w1d: BR0 DDR: No dialer string, dialing cannot occur
1w1d: BR0 DDR: Dialing cause ip (s=175.10.23.1, d=175.10.23.2)
1w1d: BR0 DDR: No dialer string, dialing cannot occur
1w1d: BR0 DDR: Dialing cause ip (s=175.10.23.1, d=175.10.23.2)
1w1d: BR0 DDR: No dialer string, dialing cannot occur
1w1d: BR0 DDR: Dialing cause ip (s=175.10.23.1, d=175.10.23.2)
1w1d: BR0 DDR: No dialer string, dialing cannot occur
```

Unlike many other **debug** outputs, the debug dialer gives some intuitive information about the reason calls fail.

Perhaps the most useful information that we can obtain is the reason that calls initiate, showing which packets actually pass through the dialer list to make outgoing calls. For example, say that you are seeing the ISDN line connecting constantly, even though you have a restrictive dialer list in place. Example 7-58 shows the resulting output from the **debug dialer** command with this set of circumstances.

Example 7-57 *debug dialer Command Output*

```
ISDN-1#debug dialer
1w1d: BR0 DDR: Dialing cause ip (s=175.10.23.1, d=224.0.0.10)
1w1d: BR0 DDR: Attempting to dial 6129319833
1w1d: %LINK-3-UPDOWN: Interface BRI0:1, changed state to up
1w1d: %ISDN-6-CONNECT: Interface BRI0:1 is now connected to 6129319833
1w1d: %LINK-3-UPDOWN: Interface Virtual-Access1, changed state to up
1w1d: Vi1 DDR: dialer protocol up

1w1d: %SYS-5-CONFIG_I: Configured from console by console
1w1d: %LINEPROTO-5-UPDOWN: Line protocol on Interface BRI0:1, changed state to up
1w1d: %LINEPROTO-5-UPDOWN: Line protocol on Interface Virtual-Access1, changed
  state to up
```

The highlighted output type shows that the reason for the ISDN call is an IP packet with a source of 175.10.23.1 to a destination of 224.0.0.10. If you did your homework, you know that the 224.0.0.10 is a multicast address that EIGRP uses to announce routes. Therefore, EIGRP updates are triggering the call. To remedy this, make sure that the BRI interface is listed as passive under the EIGRP process, or deny all EIGRP packets in your dialer list.

Some extensions to the **debug dialer** command are the **debug dialer packets** and **events** commands. **debug dialer packets** will give you some in depth insight on packets that are interesting and those that are not. **debug dialer events** will show you some additional information about the call setup and teardown process.

debug ppp authentication Command

Example 7-59 reflects a situation in which the BRI interface constantly goes up and down and no traffic will traverse the link.

Example 7-58 *Authentication Failure Symptoms*

```
Cheech#ping 175.10.23.2

Type escape sequence to abort.
Sending 5, 100-byte ICMP Echos to 175.10.23.2, timeout is 2 seconds:
.....
Success rate is 0 percent (0/5)
Cheech#
%LINK-3-UPDOWN: Interface BRI0:1, changed state to up
%LINK-3-UPDOWN: Interface BRI0:1, changed state to down
%LINK-3-UPDOWN: Interface BRI0:1, changed state to up
%LINK-3-UPDOWN: Interface BRI0:1, changed state to down
%LINK-3-UPDOWN: Interface BRI0:1, changed state to up
%LINK-3-UPDOWN: Interface BRI0:1, changed state to down
%LINK-3-UPDOWN: Interface BRI0:1, changed state to up
%LINK-3-UPDOWN: Interface BRI0:1, changed state to down
%LINK-3-UPDOWN: Interface BRI0:1, changed state to up
%LINK-3-UPDOWN: Interface BRI0:1, changed state to down
Cheech#
```

A prime suspect for this type of behavior is PPP authentication failure. Example 7-60 shows the output from the **debug ppp authentication** command to indicate the symptoms of this problem.

Example 7-59 *PPP Authentication Debugging*

```
Cheech#debug ppp authentication
%LINK-3-UPDOWN: Interface BRI0:1, changed state to up
BR0:1 PPP: Treating connection as a callout
BR0:1 PPP: Phase is AUTHENTICATING, by both
BR0:1 CHAP: O CHALLENGE id 17 len 27 from "Cheech"
BR0:1 CHAP: I CHALLENGE id 17 len 26 from "Chong"
BR0:1 CHAP: O RESPONSE id 17 len 27 from "Cheech"
BR0:1 CHAP: I FAILURE id 17 len 21 msg is "MD compare failed"
%LINK-3-UPDOWN: Interface BRI0:1, changed state to down
```

As you can see, the MD compare failed, indicating that the username and password combination was incorrectly configured on one of the routers. As it turns out, Cheech had the following command in its configuration:

```
username Chong password cisco
```

Meanwhile, Chong had the following:

```
username Chong password Cisco
```

As you can see, the passwords must match exactly, and they are case-sensitive.

Useful Tips and Tricks

This section contains additional notes on some useful methods to properly configure your ISDN network. Although these notes do not apply to all ISDN networks, they address many common configuration mistakes.

- If you want to have only one router to initiate ISDN calls, omit any dialer maps or dial strings on the router that you want to be designated as the called router. The called router will obtain the next-hop and dialer information dynamically.

- For the called router, increase the dialer idle-timeout to a high value. We normally set the dialer idle-timeout value to something such as 9999 so that only the calling router can terminate the call. For example, if you want an ISDN connection to remain up for a minimum of 5 minutes after the call is placed, you must set the dialer idle-timeout value to 300 seconds on the calling router. However, if you do not also adjust the called router's idle timer value, you will see each call terminate after 120 seconds (the default), assuming that no interesting traffic has passed after the connection is made. The called router terminating the connection causes this; so to avoid this, you might want to set the idle timeout value on the called router to an artificially high number.

- Don't forget the **broadcast** keyword on your **dialer map** statements. If you are having difficulties getting routes to traverse the ISDN link, odds are good that the broadcast keyword is missing in your **dialer map** statement.

- If your link appears to stay up indefinitely, or if you see the link constantly connecting right after disconnecting, make your dialer-group list more restrictive. Also, be sure that the ISDN interfaces are listed as passive under your routing processes,

- Be sure to avoid routing loops that might cause the router to consistently dial out. This is especially true when using the OSPF demand circuit feature. This can be accomplished through distribute lists or route maps under the routing processes.

- Keep an open mind. Often, there are multiple ways to accomplish the same goal, and there are a number of ways that any ISDN network can be configured.

- For PPP authentication, be sure that the usernames are configured correctly (remember, they are case-sensitive), and be sure that the passwords match on each router.

- For OSPF demand circuit configuration, be sure to increase the OSPF cost value of the ISDN link so that the preferred path is always over the primary link. Also be sure that there are no routing loops in your network, to avoid calls that are made unnecessarily.

- Configure the optional parameters, such as authentication and caller ID last. Make sure that the ISDN link is working properly first before configuring these advanced options. After each of the steps for configuring ISDN have been completed, use the appropriate **show** and **debug** commands to verify that it is working. You should configure the routers incrementally and avoid blindly configuring all the aspects and then trying to figure out where you went wrong.

With practice, you will find the method that works best for you, and this will become your default method; however, be prepared to use various methods and understand the "knobs" so that you can address various situations.

ISDN Labs

We will now put everything that you have learned into a series of labs similar to those of the infamous CCIE Routing and Switching Lab Exam. Here, a set of requirements will be given, and it will be up to you to determine how to configure the routers based on those requirements. Solutions to these labs also are provided. You might want to continue to read the rest of this book before attempting these labs, to gain a better understanding of the routing and routed protocols that will be required in these lab configurations.

Lab 16: Configuring PPP Authentication, Callback, and Multilink over ISDN

The ABC network consists of the network topology in Figure 7-11. The primary communications link is the Frame Relay circuit, with the ISDN line used only as specified in the requirements. The CEO of this network is set in his ways. He has asked you to design a network for him that meets some specific requirements:

1 Configure the network using OSPF as the routing protocol, as shown in Figure 7-11.

2 Maintain site-to-site connectivity even after a Frame Relay outage. The ISDN link should be utilized only when there is a physical break in the frame network or when the primary frame link exceeds 50 percent utilization. The ISDN call should wait 10 seconds after the Frame Relay link goes down in case of a brief outage. The call also should get disconnected after 2 minutes upon restoration of the Frame Relay link, or after the load on this link goes back down to 25 percent. Only one PVC is expected to be used on the Frame Relay interfaces.

3 Both ISDN B channels are to be utilized immediately whenever a connection is made.

4 Use authentication, but ensure that the passwords are not encrypted over the ISDN link.

5 Both routers must be capable of initiating ISDN calls.

6 No static routes are to be used.

Figure 7-11 shows the network topology for this lab.

Figure 7-11 *Network Topology for This Lab*

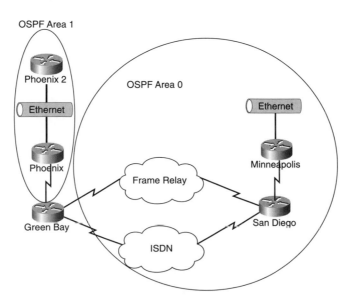

Lab 16 Solution

Example 7-61 shows the complete solution to this lab, followed by a discussion pertaining to it.

Example 7-60 *Configurations for Phoenix2, Phoenix, Green Bay, San Diego, and Minneapolis Routers*

```
Phoenix2#show running-config
Building configuration...

Current configuration:
!
version 11.2
no service password-encryption
no service udp-small-servers
no service tcp-small-servers
!
hostname Phoenix2
!
enable password cisco
!
!
interface Ethernet0
 ip address 170.10.35.2 255.255.255.0
!
interface Ethernet1
 no ip address
 shutdown
!
interface Serial0
 no ip address
 shutdown
 no fair-queue
!
interface Serial1
 no ip address
 shutdown
!
router ospf 1
 network 170.10.0.0 0.0.255.255 area 1
!
no ip classless
!
!
line con 0
 exec-timeout 0 0
 privilege level 15
 logging synchronous
line aux 0
line vty 0 4
```

continues

Example 7-60 *Configurations for Phoenix2, Phoenix, Green Bay, San Diego, and Minneapolis Routers (Continued)*

```
 password cisco
 login
 !
 end
```

```
Phoenix#show running-config
Building configuration...

Current configuration:
!
version 12.0
service timestamps debug uptime
service timestamps log uptime
no service password-encryption
!
hostname Phoenix
!
logging buffered 9096 debugging
!
ip subnet-zero
isdn switch-type basic-dms100
!
!
!
interface Ethernet0
 ip address 170.10.35.1 255.255.255.0
 no ip directed-broadcast
!
interface Serial0
 no ip address
 no ip directed-broadcast
 shutdown
!
interface Serial1
 description POINT TO POINT LINK TO GREEN BAY
 bandwidth 64
 ip address 170.10.23.2 255.255.255.252
 no ip directed-broadcast
 clockrate 125000
!
router ospf 1
 network 170.10.0.0 0.0.255.255 area 1
!
no ip classless
!
!
!
line con 0
 privilege level 15
 logging synchronous
 transport input none
line aux 0
```

Example 7-60 *Configurations for Phoenix2, Phoenix, Green Bay, San Diego, and Minneapolis Routers (Continued)*

```
line vty 0 4
 login
!
end
```

```
Green_Bay#show running-config
Building configuration...

Current configuration:
!
version 12.0
service timestamps debug uptime
service timestamps log uptime
no service password-encryption
!
hostname Green_Bay
!
!
username San_Diego password 0 isdnlab
ip subnet-zero
isdn switch-type basic-dms100
!
!
!
interface Ethernet0
 ip address 170.10.22.1 255.255.255.0
 no ip directed-broadcast
 no keepalive
!
interface Serial0
 backup delay 10 120
 backup interface BRI0
 backup load 50 25
 no ip address
 no ip directed-broadcast
 encapsulation frame-relay
 logging event subif-link-status
 logging event dlci-status-change
 no fair-queue
 clockrate 125000
!
interface Serial0.1 point-to-point
 ip address 170.10.29.1 255.255.255.252
 no ip directed-broadcast
 frame-relay interface-dlci 300
!
interface Serial1
 description POINT TO POINT LINK TO PHOENIX
 bandwidth 64
 ip address 170.10.23.1 255.255.255.252
```

continues

Example 7-60 *Configurations for Phoenix2, Phoenix, Green Bay, San Diego, and Minneapolis Routers (Continued)*

```
 no ip directed-broadcast
!
interface BRI0
 ip address 170.10.129.1 255.255.255.252
 no ip directed-broadcast
 encapsulation ppp
 dialer map ip 170.10.129.2 name San_Diego broadcast 6129319360
 dialer load-threshold 1 either
 dialer-group 1
 isdn switch-type basic-dms100
 isdn spid1 61293199371111
 isdn spid2 61293199381111
 ppp authentication pap
 ppp pap sent-username Green_Bay password 7 141E010F02082B29
 ppp multilink
!
router ospf 1
 network 170.10.22.1 0.0.0.0 area 1
 network 170.10.23.1 0.0.0.0 area 1
 network 170.10.29.1 0.0.0.0 area 0
 network 170.10.129.1 0.0.0.0 area 0
!
no ip classless
!
dialer-list 1 protocol ip permit
!
!
line con 0
 privilege level 15
 logging synchronous
 transport input none
line aux 0
line vty 0 4
 login
!
end
```

```
San_Diego#show running-config
Building configuration...

Current configuration:
!
version 11.2
no service password-encryption
no service udp-small-servers
no service tcp-small-servers
!
hostname San_Diego
!
enable password cisco
!
username Green_Bay password 0 isdnlab
```

Example 7-60 *Configurations for Phoenix2, Phoenix, Green Bay, San Diego, and Minneapolis Routers (Continued)*

```
ip subnet-zero
no ip domain-lookup
isdn switch-type basic-dms100
!
interface Ethernet0
 no ip address
 no keepalive
 media-type 10BaseT
!
interface Serial0
 backup delay 10 120
 backup interface BRI0
 backup load 50 25
 no ip address
 encapsulation frame-relay
!
interface Serial0.1 point-to-point
 ip address 170.10.29.2 255.255.255.252
 frame-relay interface-dlci 200
!
interface Serial1
 ip address 170.10.49.2 255.255.255.252
 clockrate 125000
!
!
interface BRI0
 ip address 170.10.129.2 255.255.255.252
 encapsulation ppp
 isdn spid1  61293193601111
 isdn spid2  61293197761111
 dialer map ip 170.10.129.1 name Green_Bay broadcast 6129319937
dialer load-threshold 1 either
 dialer-group 1
 no fair-queue
 ppp authentication pap
 ppp pap sent-username San_Diego password 7 09455D0D17091610
 ppp multilink
!
interface BRI1
 no ip address
 shutdown
!
interface BRI2
 no ip address
 shutdown
!
interface BRI3
 no ip address
 shutdown
!
```

continues

Example 7-60 *Configurations for Phoenix2, Phoenix, Green Bay, San Diego, and Minneapolis Routers (Continued)*

```
router ospf 1
 network 170.10.0.0 0.0.255.255 area 0
!
ip classless
!
dialer-list 1 protocol ip permit
!
line con 0
 exec-timeout 0 0
 privilege level 15
 logging synchronous
line aux 0
line vty 0 4
 exec-timeout 0 0
 privilege level 15
 logging synchronous
 no login
!
end
```

```
Minneapolis#show running-config
Building configuration...

Current configuration:
!
version 11.2
no service password-encryption
no service udp-small-servers
no service tcp-small-servers
!
hostname Minneapolis
!
enable password cisco
!
!
interface Ethernet0
 ip address 170.10.44.1 255.255.255.0
 no keepalive
!
interface Serial0
 no ip address
 shutdown
 no fair-queue
!
interface Serial1
 ip address 170.10.49.1 255.255.255.252
!
router ospf 1
 network 170.10.0.0 0.0.255.255 area 0
!
no ip classless
!
```

Example 7-60 *Configurations for Phoenix2, Phoenix, Green Bay, San Diego, and Minneapolis Routers (Continued)*

```
 !
line con 0
 privilege level 15
 logging synchronous
line aux 0
line vty 0 4
 privilege level 15
 password cisco
 no login
 !
end
```

Lab 16 Solution Discussion

We will keep our discussion here to the Green Bay and San Diego routers because the configuration for the other three routers is fairly straightforward.

Because this lab asked that the ISDN link be utilized after a physical break in the ISDN connection, using the **backup interface** command was the most appropriate solution. In addition, the lab asked you to utilize the ISDN connection if the frame link became congested, so the **backup load** command also was used. Using PPP multilink and setting the dialer load-threshold to 1 either way satisfied requirement 3. Using PAP authentication completed requirement 4. Finally, both routers used dialer maps in their configurations, satisfying requirement 5. This lab did not specifically ask you to use dialer maps, so you could have just as easily used dialer strings or dialer profiles.

Lab 17: Configuring OSPF Demand Circuits over ISDN

This lab assumes an in-depth knowledge of the various routing protocols. It might be a good idea to read Chapter 11, "Hybrid: Enhanced Interior Gateway Routing Protocol," and Chapter 12 before attempting this lab. Try to complete this lab on your own by doing some research and looking up the necessary commands first before peeking at the solution provided.

Refer to the network diagram in Figure 7-12 for reference; call this network the ABC company.

Figure 7-12 *Network Topology for This Lab*

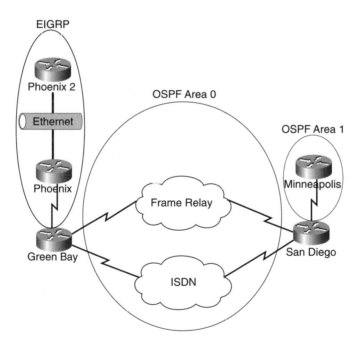

Configure the ABC network so that it satisfies the following requirements:

1 Configure OSPF and EIGRP as shown previously, and be sure to redistribute between them to ensure full IP connectivity.

2 The 56-kbps Frame Relay link is the primary means of communication between Green Bay and San Diego. You do not want OSPF traffic to be capable of initiating ISDN calls, but you do want to maintain total connectivity in the case of a Frame Relay outage. ISDN calls should be initiated upon a loss of routes.

3 Both routers must be capable of initiating calls. Toll charges from Green Bay are cheaper, so be sure that the vast majority of ISDN calls is initiated from Green Bay.

4 You want to authenticate each ISDN connection, ensuring that the passwords are hidden using MD5 encryption.

5 The Green Bay router must be configured so that it will accept incoming calls only from the San Diego router.

6 The ISDN call must disconnect 5 minutes after the routes through the Frame Relay link are restored.

7 The Frame Relay link is only 56 k. Be sure that your configurations reflect this.

8 No static routes are to be used in this lab.

Lab 17 Solution

Example 7-62 shows the final configuration solution that meets the aforementioned requirements for this lab.

Example 7-61 *Phoenix 2, Phoenix, Green Bay, San Diego, and Minneapolis Router Configurations*

```
Phoenix2#show running-config
Building configuration...

Current configuration:
!
version 11.2
no service password-encryption
no service udp-small-servers
no service tcp-small-servers
!
hostname Phoenix2
!
enable password cisco
!
!
interface Ethernet0
 ip address 170.10.35.2 255.255.255.0
!
interface Ethernet1
 no ip address
 shutdown
!
interface Serial0
 no ip address
 shutdown
 no fair-queue
!
```

continues

Example 7-61 *Phoenix 2, Phoenix, Green Bay, San Diego, and Minneapolis Router Configurations (Continued)*

```
interface Serial1
 no ip address
 shutdown
!
router eigrp 1
 network 170.10.0.0
 no auto-summary
!
no ip classless
!
!
line con 0
 exec-timeout 0 0
 privilege level 15
 logging synchronous
line aux 0
line vty 0 4
 password cisco
 login
!
end
```

```
Phoenix#show running-config
Building configuration...

Current configuration:
!
version 12.0
service timestamps debug uptime
service timestamps log uptime
no service password-encryption
!
hostname Phoenix
!
logging buffered 9096 debugging
!
ip subnet-zero
isdn switch-type basic-dms100
!
!
!
interface Ethernet0
 ip address 170.10.35.1 255.255.255.0
 no ip directed-broadcast
!
interface Serial0
 no ip address
 no ip directed-broadcast
 shutdown
!
interface Serial1
 description POINT TO POINT LINK TO GREEN BAY
```

Example 7-61 *Phoenix 2, Phoenix, Green Bay, San Diego, and Minneapolis Router Configurations (Continued)*

```
 bandwidth 64
 ip address 170.10.23.2 255.255.255.252
 no ip directed-broadcast
 clockrate 125000
!
router eigrp 1
 network 170.10.0.0
 no auto-summary
!
no ip classless
!
!
!
line con 0
 privilege level 15
 logging synchronous
 transport input none
line aux 0
line vty 0 4
 login
!
end
```
```
Green_Bay#show running-config
Building configuration...

Current configuration:
!
version 12.0
service timestamps debug uptime
service timestamps log uptime
no service password-encryption
!
hostname Green_Bay
!
!
username San_Diego password 0 isdnlab
ip subnet-zero
isdn switch-type basic-dms100
!
!
!
interface Ethernet0
 ip address 170.10.22.1 255.255.255.0
 no ip directed-broadcast
 no keepalive
!
interface Serial0
 no ip address
 no ip directed-broadcast
 encapsulation frame-relay
```

continues

Example 7-61 *Phoenix 2, Phoenix, Green Bay, San Diego, and Minneapolis Router Configurations (Continued)*

```
 logging event subif-link-status
 logging event dlci-status-change
 no fair-queue
 clockrate 125000
!
interface Serial0.1 point-to-point
 description 56K FRAME RELAY CONNECTION
 bandwidth 56
 ip address 170.10.29.1 255.255.255.252
 no ip directed-broadcast
 frame-relay interface-dlci 300
!
interface Serial1
 description POINT TO POINT LINK TO PHOENIX
 bandwidth 64
 ip address 170.10.23.1 255.255.255.252
 no ip directed-broadcast
!
interface BRI0
 ip address 170.10.129.1 255.255.255.252
 no ip directed-broadcast
 encapsulation ppp
 ip ospf cost 9999
 ip ospf demand-circuit
 dialer callback-secure
 dialer idle-timeout 300
 dialer enable-timeout 5
 dialer map ip 170.10.129.2 name San_Diego class isdnlab broadcast 6129319360
 dialer-group 1
 isdn switch-type basic-dms100
 isdn spid1 61293199371111
 isdn spid2 61293199381111
 isdn caller 6129319360 callback
 ppp callback accept
 ppp authentication chap
!
router eigrp 1
 redistribute ospf 1 metric 64 100 200 10 1500
 passive-interface BRI0
passive-interface Serial0.1
network 170.10.0.0
 no auto-summary
!
router ospf 1
 redistribute eigrp 1 metric 100 subnets route-map DENY_BRI_ROUTE
 network 170.10.29.1 0.0.0.0 area 0
 network 170.10.129.1 0.0.0.0 area 0
passive interface Serial1
!
no ip classless
!
```

Example 7-61 *Phoenix 2, Phoenix, Green Bay, San Diego, and Minneapolis Router Configurations (Continued)*

```
!
map-class dialer isdnlab
 dialer callback-server username
access-list 1 permit 170.10.129.0 0.0.0.3
dialer-list 1 protocol ip permit
route-map DENY_BRI_ROUTE deny 10
 match ip address 1
!
route-map DENY_BRI_ROUTE permit 20
!
!
!
line con 0
 privilege level 15
 logging synchronous
 transport input none
line aux 0
line vty 0 4
 login
!
end
```

```
San_Diego#show running-config
Building configuration...

Current configuration:
!
version 11.2
no service password-encryption
no service udp-small-servers
no service tcp-small-servers
!
hostname San_Diego
!
enable password cisco
!
username Green_Bay password 0 isdnlab
ip subnet-zero
no ip domain-lookup
isdn switch-type basic-dms100
!
interface Ethernet0
 no ip address
 no keepalive
 media-type 10BaseT
!
interface Ethernet1
 no ip address
 media-type 10BaseT
!
```

continues

Example 7-61 *Phoenix 2, Phoenix, Green Bay, San Diego, and Minneapolis Router Configurations (Continued)*

```
interface Ethernet2
 no ip address
 shutdown
 media-type 10BaseT
!
interface Ethernet3
 no ip address
 shutdown
 media-type 10BaseT
!
interface Ethernet4
 no ip address
 shutdown
 media-type 10BaseT
!
interface Ethernet5
 no ip address
 shutdown
 media-type 10BaseT
!
interface Serial0
 no ip address
 encapsulation frame-relay
!
interface Serial0.1 point-to-point
 description 56K FRAME RELAY CONNECTION
 ip address 170.10.29.2 255.255.255.252
 bandwidth 56
 frame-relay interface-dlci 200
!
interface Serial1
 ip address 170.10.49.2 255.255.255.252
 clockrate 125000
!
interface Serial2
 no ip address
 shutdown
!
interface Serial3
 no ip address
 shutdown
!
interface BRI0
 ip address 170.10.129.2 255.255.255.252
 encapsulation ppp
 ip ospf cost 9999
 ip ospf demand-circuit
 isdn spid1  61293193601111
 isdn spid2  61293197761111
dialer idle-timeout 300
 dialer wait-for-carrier-time 10
 dialer map ip 170.10.129.1 name Green_Bay broadcast 6129319937
```

Example 7-61 *Phoenix 2, Phoenix, Green Bay, San Diego, and Minneapolis Router Configurations (Continued)*

```
 dialer-group 1
 no fair-queue
 ppp callback request
 ppp authentication chap
!
interface BRI1
 no ip address
 shutdown
!
interface BRI2
 no ip address
 shutdown
!
interface BRI3
 no ip address
 shutdown
!
router ospf 1
 network 170.10.29.2 0.0.0.0 area 0
 network 170.10.129.2 0.0.0.0 area 0
 network 170.10.40.2 0.0 0.0 area 1
!
ip classless
!
dialer-list 1 protocol ip permit
!
line con 0
 exec-timeout 0 0
 privilege level 15
 logging synchronous
line aux 0
line vty 0 4
 exec-timeout 0 0
 privilege level 15
 logging synchronous
 no login
!
end
```

```
Minneapolis#show running-config
Building configuration...

Current configuration:
!
version 11.2
no service password-encryption
no service udp-small-servers
no service tcp-small-servers
!
hostname Minneapolis
!
```

continues

Example 7-61 *Phoenix 2, Phoenix, Green Bay, San Diego, and Minneapolis Router Configurations (Continued)*

```
enable password cisco
!
!
interface Ethernet0
 ip address 170.10.44.1 255.255.255.0
 no keepalive
!
interface Serial0
 no ip address
 shutdown
 no fair-queue
!
interface Serial1
 ip address 170.10.49.1 255.255.255.252
!
router ospf 1
 network 170.10.0.0 0.0.255.255 area 1
!
no ip classless
!
!
line con 0
 privilege level 15
 logging synchronous
line aux 0
line vty 0 4
 privilege level 15
 password cisco
 no login
!
end
```

Lab 17 Solution Discussion

Again, nothing special is going on with the Phoenix, Phoenix 2, and Minneapolis configurations. They are being used here only to generate routes. The bulk of the configuration commands needed for this lab are done with the Green Bay router.

This lab hinted at the use of OSPF demand circuit, in that it asked the ISDN link to be brought up in the case of a loss of routes over the Frame Relay connection. If the lab had asked you to have the ISDN line come up in case of physical loss of connectivity on the Frame Relay link, using the **backup interface** option would have been more appropriate.

To satisfy requirement 3, Green Bay was set up as a callback router. Requirement 4 asked for authentication using MD5 encryption, so CHAP had to be configured. We also set it up with ISDN caller ID to satisfy requirement 5. Both Green Bay and San Diego have **dialer map** statements, so both have the capability to issue ISDN calls. Requirement 6 was satisfied with setting the dialer idle-timeout to 300 seconds on both ends of the ISDN connection.

The biggest issue with this particular lab is getting the ISDN line to remain quiet when the network is stable. If you were able to do this without first looking at the solution, you should be proud of your accomplishment.

The important thing to notice about the Green Bay router configuration is the use of the **route map** statement when redistributing EIGRP into OSPF. Recall from the OSPF demand circuit section that sometimes you need to do more than simply issue the **ip ospf demand-circuit** command. This lab network is a classic example of this. When redistributing EIGRP into OSPF on the Green Bay router, you have effectively created a routing loop because the BRI interface (170.10.129.1) also is included with the EIGRP network. Because of this, this interface constantly is being redistributed into OSPF from EIGRP, and vice versa. To fix this, you needed to use a route map to deny the 170.10.129.0/30 network from being redistributed into OSPF. An alternative to using a route map would have been to use a distribute list, denying this network from being redistributed.

One other important thing to note is the use of the **ip ospf cost 9999** command under the BRI interface of the Green Bay and San Diego routers. Remember that requirement 7 of the lab basically requires you to use the **bandwidth 56** command under interface s0.1 of both routers. Because of this, OSPF actually preferred the BRI link because it had a lower cost. This was fixed by increasing the OSPF cost to an artificially high number on the BRI interface. This number didn't have to be this high, but we chose to use 9999 for emphasis. You also could have used the **ip ospf cost** command on the Serial 0.1 of these routers to decrease the cost.

Summary

The topic of ISDN is vast and comprehensive, and it is a core topic of the CCIE Routing and Switching Lab Exam. If you don't have a firm grasp of the topics described in this chapter, you have a slim chance of getting your CCIE number. The best way to prepare for the ISDN portion of this rigorous exam is to practice these topics. You cannot possibly retain the knowledge contained in this chapter if you do not have the equipment necessary to practice these topics repeatedly. We cannot stress this enough. If you don't have access to ISDN equipment, you will need to purchase an ISDN simulator and some routers with BRI interfaces. Reading about any topic is one thing. The practical knowledge obtained from actually doing it is something else entirely.

Try to add as many complexities to the ISDN topics as you can. Use different routing protocols, and note how they change the configurations. Add IPX and other routed protocols to the configurations to see how they affect the outcome. After that, try configuring BGP, DLSw, and NAT over the ISDN link. It is relatively easy to configure any single topic on a Cisco router. However, when multiple things are configured and integrated, unexpected issues can arise. The only way to learn about these issues is to practice as many different topics as you can and then integrate them.

WAN Protocols and Technologies: Asynchronous Transfer Mode (ATM)

Authoring contribution by Galina Diker Pildush

Asynchronous Transfer Mode (ATM) has been looked upon as the technology that can do it all—carry voice, data, and video information, implying that both voice and data payloads, batch and real-time, can be transferred from one part of the world to another. This is implemented with guarantees in quality, such as integrity of the information and its throughput, toward different classes of services. In my book *Cisco ATM Solutions*, I elaborate on the whys and whats with respect to ATM. It is the technology that instilled in me a sense of the simplicity and beauty within it.

The concept behind ATM is quite simple: Push into the ATM cloud equal-size payloads (an ATM cell consists of a 48-byte payload and a 5-byte header) that consist of any type of applications above it. Perform *no* error checking of these payloads; do not waste any overhead on useless things such as sequence numbers (because ATM is connection-oriented anyway), just to perform error checking of the ATM header (which is done at the silicon layer); and zoom through those payloads as fast as you can at a low layer of the OSI reference model. ATM operates on 1.25 layers of the OSI reference model—exactly, 1.25 layers! Figure 8-1 provides the information about the ingredients of an ATM cell.

Figure 8-1 *ATM Cell Format*

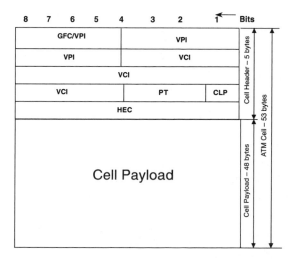

Table 8-1 lists the meaning of the cell header fields.

Table 8-1   *ATM Cell Header Fields*

Field	Size	Meaning
GFC	4 bits	Generic Flow Control: Used at the UNI level.
VPI	8 or 12 bits	Virtual Path Identifier: Part of ATM locally significant address. It is 8 bits at the UNI and 12 bits at the NNI.
VCI	16 bits	Virtual Channel Identifier: Part of the ATM locally significant address.
PT	3 bits	Payload Type. The 3 bits are used as follows: The most significant bit is used to identify the data versus the OAM cell, the next bit is used to identify congestion on the network (it is called Explicit Forward Congestion Indication [EFCI]), and the last bit is used to identify the last cell of a higher-level packet/frame. This bit, called End of Message, is important in the congestion control algorithm within the ATM cloud.
CLP	1 bit	Cell Loss Priority: Used to indicate if a cell can be discarded by the network, in case there is congestion.
HEC	8 bits	Header Error Check. The ATM cloud does not perform payload error checking, only the header error checking.

The powerful concepts of ATM's *Private Network-to-Network Interface (PNNI)* helped in the development of such protocols as MPLS with traffic engineering, which introduces a connection-oriented flavor to connectionless IP. PNNI is a routing protocol deployed by the ATM signaling protocol to establish SVCs.

Recognizing ATM's impact on the customer's enterprise networks, Cisco introduced interconnections of various protocols over ATM into its Routing and Switching CCIE certification. This chapter discusses two methods of protocol interconnectivity over ATM that address implementation from the edge device perspective:

- RFC 2684, "Multiprotocol Encapsulation over ATM Adaptation Layer 5"
- RFC 2225, "Classical IP and ARP over ATM"

The implementations of the actual ATM cloud are not currently in the CCIE practical exam. See the *Cisco ATM Solutions* book for the implementations of the cloud itself.

The whole objective of ATM internetworking is to send upper-layer information over ATM. Four implementation methods exist for achieving that goal:

- Manual method for multiple upper-layer protocols by using RFC 2684. I call it a method without any magic "upstairs" in the upper layers of the OSI reference model.
- Dynamic method for IP implementation by using RFC 2225 (Classical IP). I call it a method with the magic of transporting IP over ATM.

- Dynamic method for Layer 2 protocols by using Local-Area Network Emulation (LANE).
- Dynamic method for all Layer 2 and Layer 3 protocols by using Multiprotocol over ATM (MPOA).

This chapter focuses on the first two methods—RFC 2684 and RFC 2225.

The two labs presented in the chapter provide you with additional practical exercises. If you require information on other interconnection methods (for example LANE, MPOA, and so on) or more examples/labs, refer to the *Cisco ATM Solutions* book.

Special Components Needed for ATM Lab Studies

I recommend the following equipment for your ATM exercises:

- One LightSteam 1010 (LS1010) ATM switch
- Two or three routers with ATM interfaces

If you have problems accessing LS1010, you can attend Cisco's "Campus ATM Solutions" class before going to a lab. The class has several LS1010s with routers, providing you with the necessary gear. Also, the *Cisco ATM Solutions* book provides many configuration examples/labs to enhance your comfort level with ATM.

This chapter focuses on the routers' configurations. Typically, the LS1010 does not require any special configuration unless you have a network of LS1010s. *Cisco ATM Solutions* provides elaborate examples and explanations on LS1010 configuration, if you ever have a need to configure one.

The routers can include a 4*XXX*, 7*XXX*, or 36*XX* series model. Cisco has a rich assortment of product lines that include routers and switches with ATM interfaces. Table 8-2 illustrates this variety. It is important to note the assortment of ATM adaptation layers (AALs), User-Network Interface (UNI) types, and ATM service categories that are supported.

Table 8-2   *Cisco ATM Edge Devices Summary Table[1]*

Edge Device Model	Switch Type	Supported Traffic Type	Supported ATM Interface Speeds	Supported AAL	Supported UNI	Supported ATM Service Categories
26*XX*	Layer 3	Voice and data	1x25 Mbps 4xDS-1/E1 with (IMA) 8xDS-1/E1 with IMA DS-3/E3	AAL1, AAL2, AAL5	UNI3.0, UNI3.1, UNI4.0	UBR, ABR, CBR, nrt-VBR, rt-VBR

continues

Table 8-2   *Cisco ATM Edge Devices Summary Table[1] (Continued)*

Edge Device Model	Switch Type	Supported Traffic Type	Supported ATM Interface Speeds	Supported AAL	Supported UNI	Supported ATM Service Categories
36*XX*	Layer 3	Voice and data	1x25 Mbps; 1x (OC-3)/ (STM-1) 4xDS-1/E1 with IMA 8xDS-1/E1 with IMA DS-3/E3	AAL1, AAL2, AAL5	UNI3.0, UNI3.1, UNI4.0	UBR, ABR, nrt-VBR
3810	Layer 3	Voice and data	1xDS-1/E1	AAL1, AAL2, AAL5	UNI3.0, UNI3.1, UNI4.0	UBR, ABR, nrt-VBR
4500	Layer 3	Data	1xOC-3/ STM-1	AAL5, AAL3/4	UNI3.0, UNI3.1, UNI4.0	CBR, UBR, nrt-VBR, ABR
4700	Layer 3	Data	1xOC-3/ STM-1	AAL5, AAL3/4	UNI3.0, UNI3.1, UNI4.0	UBR, nrt-VBR, ABR
6400	Layer 3	Voice and data	1xOC-3/ STM-1 1xOC-12/ STM-4	AAL5, AAL1	UNI3.0, UNI3.1, UNI4.0	CBR,UBR, ABR, nrt-VBR
7100	Layer 3	Data	T3/E3 2xOC-3/ STM-1	AAL5	UNI3.0, UNI3.1, UNI4.0	UBR, ABR, GFR, nrt-VBR
72*XX*	Layer 3	Voice and data	8xDS-1/E1 with IMA 1xOC-3/ STM-1 1xOC-12/ STM-4 1xDS-3/E3	AAL5, AAL1	UNI3.0, UNI3.1, UNI4.0	UBR, nrt-VBR, ABR

Table 8-2   *Cisco ATM Edge Devices Summary Table[1] (Continued)*

Edge Device Model	Switch Type	Supported Traffic Type	Supported ATM Interface Speeds	Supported AAL	Supported UNI	Supported ATM Service Categories
7400	Layer 3	Data	8xDS-1/E1 with IMA 1xDS-3/E3 1xOC-3/ STM-1	AAL5, AAL1	UNI3.0, UNI3.1, UNI4.0	UBR, CBR, nrt-VBR, ABR
75XX	Layer 3	Data	1xOC-3/ STM-1 1xOC-12/ STM-4 1xDS-3/E3 8xDS-1/E1 with IMA	AAL5, AAL3/4	UNI3.0, UNI3.1, UNI4.0	UBR, nrt-VBR, ABR
76XX	Layer 3	Data	2xOC-12/ SMT-4	AAL5	UNI3.0, UNI3.1, UNI4.0	UBR, nrt-VBR, ABR
12000	Layer 3	Data	1xOC-12/ STM-4 4xOC-3/ STM-1	AAL5	UNI3.0, UNI3.1, UNI4.0	UBR, nrt-VBR, ABR,
Catalyst 2820	Layer 2	Data	1xOC-3/ STM-1	AAL5	UNI3.0, UNI3.1, UNI4.0	UBR, nrt-VBR, ABR
Catalyst 2900	Layer 2	Data	1xOC-3/ STM-1	AAL5	UNI3.0, UNI3.1, UNI4.0	CBR,UBR, nrt-VBR, ABR
Catalyst 3900	Layer 2	Data	1xOC-3/ STM-1	AAL5	UNI3.0, UNI3.1, UNI4.0	UBR, nrt-VBR, ABR

continues

Table 8-2   *Cisco ATM Edge Devices Summary Table[1] (Continued)*

Edge Device Model	Switch Type	Supported Traffic Type	Supported ATM Interface Speeds	Supported AAL	Supported UNI	Supported ATM Service Categories
Catalyst 5XXX	Layer 2	Voice and data	25 Mbps DS-1/E1 DS-3/E3 1xOC-3/STM-1 1xOC-12/STM4	AAL5	UNI3.0, UNI3.1, UNI4.0	UBR, ABR, rt-VBR, nrt-VBR, CBR, GFR
Catalyst 6000	Layer 2	Data	1xOC-12/STM-4	AAL5	UNI3.0, UNI3.1, UNI4.0	
Catalyst 85XX	Layer 2, Layer 3, Layer 1.25[2]	Voice and data	Up to 64xDS-1/E1 Up to 64xDS3/E3 96x25 Mbps 128xOC-3/STM-1 32xOC-12/STM-4 8xOC-48/STM-16	AAL1, AAL2, AAL5	UNI3.0, UNI3.1, UNI4.0	

Table 8-2 is taken from *Cisco ATM Solutions*, Galina Diker Pildush, Cisco Press.

[1] Table 8-2 information is based on Cisco's product catalog as of August 2001.

[2] A member of the Catalyst 8500 family, the Catalyst 8540MSR, can also be an ATM switch. It can accept not only new modules, but also existing LightStream 1010 modules.

Cisco has various ATM router interfaces supported on multiple platforms, as illustrated in Table 8-3.

Table 8-3   *NPM, AIP, ATM PA-A1, and ATM PA-A3 Comparison*

Physical Interfaces/ Features	NPM	AIP	ATM PA-A1	ATM PA-A3
Platform	4500, 4700	7000, 7500	7200, VIP2-based 7500	7200, VIP2-based 7500
OC-3 MMF Support	Yes	Yes	Yes	Yes
OC-3 SMF Support	Yes	Yes	Yes	Yes
DS-3/E3 Support	Yes	Yes	No	Yes
TAXI Support	No	Yes	No	No
UNI Supported	3.0/3.1/4.0	3.0/3.1	3.0/3.1	3.0/3.1/4.0
LANE Support	Yes	Yes	Yes	Yes
RFC 2684, 2225 Support	Yes	Yes	Yes	Yes
Types of VCs Supported	PVCs, SVCs	PVCs, SVCs	PVCs, SVCs	PVCs (as per 11.1 (22)C) SVCs (IOS 12.0)
Maximum pps (64 byte, bidirectional)	—	110,000 pps	150,000 pps	170,000 pps
Simultaneous SARs (# of packets)	192	256 (can be up to 512)	512	1024
Maximum number of VCs	1023	2048	2048	4096
AAL Support	AAL5	AAL3/4, AAL5	AAL5	AAL5
ATM Service Category Support	UBR, ABR	UBR	UBR	nrt-VBR, UBR, ABR

continues

Table 8-3   *NPM, AIP, ATM PA-A1, and ATM PA-A3 Comparison (Continued)*

Physical Interfaces/ Features	NPM	AIP	ATM PA-A1	ATM PA-A3
Traffic Shaping Support	Yes	Yes	None	Yes
OAM Support[1]	F4, F5	F4, F5 (as of 11.3(2)T Cisco IOS Software)	F4, F5 (as of 11.3(2)T Cisco IOS Software and 11.1(22)CC)	F4, F5 (special release 11.1(22)CC and 12.0)

Table 8-3 is taken from *Cisco ATM Solutions*, Galina Diker Pildush, Cisco Press.

Configuring RFC 2684

The complete theory behind RFC 2684 is covered in *Cisco ATM Solutions*. Here, I want to remind you that RFC 2684 (formerly RFC 1483) is an encapsulation method of all routed or bridged protocols over ATM. My formula for RFC 2684 is as follows:

> RFC 2684 is the multiprotocol encapsulation method. The encapsulation method of multiple protocols (Layer 3 or bridged) over a single VC is accomplished using LLC/SNAP; the encapsulation method of a single protocol over a single VC is done using mux. Both PVCs and SVCs are supported, provided that the ATM cloud can support PVCs or SVCs.

A *permanent virtual circuit (PVC)* is a statically defined route, whereas a *switched virtual circuit (SVC)* is a dynamically defined route through signaling. In this section, you learn the principles behind the implementation of both PVCs and SVCs.

RFC 2684 is a basic encapsulation method, without any "magic" behind it. Your protocol addresses must be manually mapped to the ATM addresses by using either the VPI/VCI pair in the PVC implementation or the NSAP/E.164 address in the SVC implementation.

Let's examine the details of PVC and SVC methods of implementations.

PVC Implementation

The PVC implementation is a static and tedious process from within the ATM network itself. If you implement the PVC-based ATM networks, please be careful to make sure that the information on the VPI/VCI numbers is precise. One mistake on a VPI/VCI number(s) can lead to devastating unpredictable results, like ending up in Moscow instead of New York for your connection. Recall that VPI/VCI numbers are locally significant addresses used in ATM's PVC implementations.

For the purpose of this chapter discussion, assume that the ATM network has been configured correctly.

You can implement PVC networks by using one of two methods:

- Static VPI/VCI assignment, where you have to enter VPI/VCI numbers manually based on the providers information
- Dynamic VPI/VCI assignment, where your edge routers obtain VPI/VCI numbers dynamically from the edge ATM switch

In either method, VPI/VCI numbers are locally significant.

NOTE   VPI/VCI numbers are similar to DLCIs in Frame Relay networks, where the DLCI is locally significant. The local significance applies all the way to the interface level. That is, if various router ATM physical interfaces have identical VPI/VCI numbers, they are treated as independent connections to the ATM network.

The static configuration involves full manual intervention. If VPI/VCI assignments change within the ATM cloud, you need to adjust the configurations within the routers manually. The dynamic discovery of VPI/VCI numbers is much more appealing because the attached routers learn the information from their respective adjacent switches dynamically. The discovered PVCs and their traffic parameters are configured on the ATM main interface or subinterface that you specify. Your router receives the PVC parameter information by using Interim Local Management Interface (ILMI).

Let's examine the syntax and configuration examples for both methods of PVC-based network implementation. Figure 8-2 illustrates our implementation example.

The three routers (A, B, and C) connected to the ATM cloud handle two protocols—IP and IPX. From the OSI model Level 3 perspective (network layer), all the routers are interconnected through one single IP and IPX networks—131.108.168.0/24 and network 100. Each of the routers has another IP and IPX network attached.

Static PVC Implementation

Example 8-1 presents the configurations for Routers A, B, and C. Notice that the subinterfaces are used to interconnect routers over the ATM cloud. You can use major interfaces instead. Use of the subinterfaces, however, positions you with a more scalable configuration.

Also, the example illustrates the use of LLC/SNAP encapsulation (as opposed to mux). LLC/SNAP encapsulation positions your VCs to carry multiple protocols, whereas mux encapsulation carries only one protocol.

Figure 8-2 *PVC-Based Configuration Example*

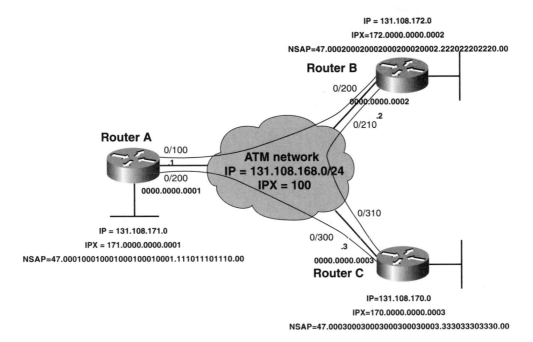

I can think of only one instance when you would need a single protocol to be carried over a single VC: when you require to do traffic shaping of individual protocols. Assume that you have IP and IPX to carry over ATM network. If you need to define different traffic-shaping parameters to IP and IPX, you would deploy mux encapsulation.

Example 8-1 *FC 2684 Static PVC Configuration for Multiprotocol Encapsulation*

```
Router A (config)# interface atm 0.1 multipoint
ip address 131.108.168.1 255.255.255.0
ipx network 100
atm pvc 10 0 100 aal5snap
atm pvc 11 0 200 aal5snap
map-group pvc-static-routerA-ip
map-group pvc-static-routerA-ipx

map-list pvc-static-routerA-ip
ip 131.108.168.2 atm-vc 10 broadcast
ip 131.108.168.3 atm-vc 11 broadcast
map-list pvc-static-routerA-ipx
ipx 100.0000.0000.0002 atm-vc 10 broadcast
```

Example 8-1   *FC 2684 Static PVC Configuration for Multiprotocol Encapsulation (Continued)*

```
ipx 100.0000.0000.0003 atm-vc 11 broadcast

Router B (config)# interface atm 0.1 multipoint
ip address 131.108.168.2 255.255.255.0
ipx network 100
atm pvc 10 0 200 aal5snap
atm pvc 11 0 210 aal5snap
map-group pvc-static-routerB-ip
map-group pvc-static-routerB-ipx

map-list pvc-static-routerB-ip
ip 131.108.168.1 atm-vc 10 broadcast
ip 131.108.168.3 atm-vc 11 broadcast
map-list pvc-static-routerB-ipx
ipx 100.0000.0000.0001 atm-vc 10 broadcast
ipx 100.0000.0000.0003 atm-vc 11 broadcast

Router C (config)# interface atm 0.1 multipoint
ipx network 100
ip address 131.108.168.3 255.255.255.0
atm pvc 10 0 300 aal5snap
atm pvc 11 0 310 aal5snap
map-group pvc-static-routerC-ip

map-list pvc-static-routerC-ip
ip 131.108.168.1 atm-vc 10 broadcast
ip 131.108.168.2 atm-vc 11 broadcast
map-list pvc-static-routerC-ipx
ipx 100.0000.0000.0001 atm-vc 10 broadcast
ipx 100.0000.0000.0002 atm-vc 11 broadcast
```

The configurations are quite simple, with no magic involved: You need to manually assign the PVCs with an encapsulation method—in this case, by using aal5snap encapsulation—and then you need to manually map the corresponding next-hop IP and IPX addresses to the corresponding PVC's VPI/VCI that takes you to the destination address of the corresponding protocol. VPI/VCI numbers must be obtained from an entity managing the ATM cloud. Cisco IOS mapping is done using *map-lists* that are defined in the global configuration mode and then referenced using *map-groups*. Please note that the example illustrates the use of two map-lists, each one dedicated for a specific protocol (in this case, IP and IPX). Although you can have one map-list referring to both protocols, I strongly recommend deploying a separate a map-list per protocol, for modularity reasons.

Figure 8-3 illustrates the complete syntax of the command, with explanations provided in Table 8-4. For more in-depth information and further examples of the static PVC implementations by using RFC 2684 encapsulation, refer to *Cisco ATM Solutions*.

Figure 8-3 *Static PVC Command Syntax*

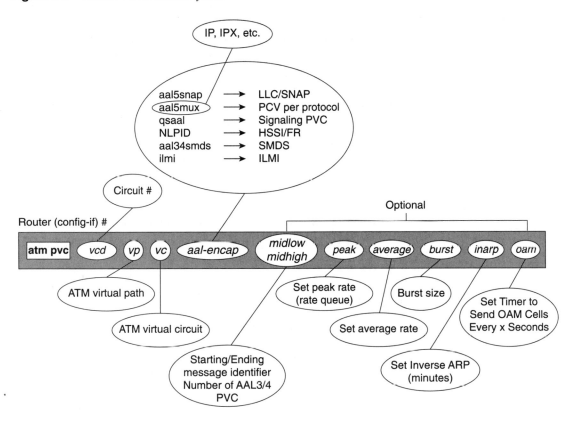

Table 8-4 *Descriptions of* **atm pvc** *Command Arguments*

Field	Description
vcd	Virtual circuit descriptor. It uniquely identifies the PVC in the router. It must be unique in the entire router because there is a reference to that number from the global configuration level. The vcd numbers stay in the routers.
vpi	Virtual path identifier. This is a part of the ATM VC address. It must match the carrier-provided VPI for a specific destination and must be unique within a physical interface of the router[1].
vci	Virtual channel identifier. This is a part of the ATM VC address. It must match the carrier-provided VCI for a specific destination and must be unique within a physical interface of the router[1].

continues

Table 8-4   *Descriptions of* **atm pvc** *Command Arguments (Continued)*

Field	Description
aal-encap	This is a mandatory parameter that identifies the ATM adaptation layer (AAL) and encapsulation type. Figure 8-2 identifies the various encapsulation types.
midlow	This is optional parameter. It is set for the aal34smds encapsulation only. It is the starting message identifier (MID) number for this PVC. The default is 0. If you set the peak and average (burst is optional) values for aal34smds encapsulation, you also must set the midlow and midhigh values. This option is not available for the ATM port adapter.
midhigh	This is optional parameter. It is set for the aal34smds encapsulation only. It is the ending MID number for this PVC. The default is 0. If you set the peak and average (burst is optional) values for aal34smds encapsulation, you also must set the midlow and midhigh values.
peak	This is an optional parameter that signifies the maximum rate at which this virtual circuit can transmit, in kilobits per second. By default, peak = 155,000 kbps.[2]
average	This is an optional parameter that signifies the average rate at which this virtual circuit transmits, in kilobits per second. By default, average = 155,000 kbps.[2]
burst	This is an optional parameter. It is the value that relates to the maximum number of ATM cells that the VC can transmit to the network at the peak rate of the PVC. The default value varies, based on the model of the router. For example, the 7XXX series default burst value = 94[2,3].
inarp x	This is an optional parameter to enable Inverse ARP on the PVC (works only for IP, which is RFC 2225, "Classical IP"). The Inverse ARP datagrams are sent every *x* minutes on this PVC. The default value is 15 minutes.
oam x	This is an optional parameter that configures the transmission of OAM F5 loopback cells every *x* seconds. The OAM F5 cells verify connectivity on the virtual circuit. The remote end must respond by echoing back such cells.

[1]   The reference to the physical interface should not be confused with the subinterface notation. Cisco routers treat the subinterfaces as real physical interfaces, each of which is a separate broadcast domain that can have unique traffic control and policy being definitions, using access lists, for example. The VPI/VCI must be unique within an actual physical interface range, simply because an ingress ATM switch has no idea how to "spell" the word *subinterface*.

[2]   The *peak*, *average*, and the *burst* numbers are the PCR, SCR, and BT values that are used by the router to perform traffic shaping using the leaky bucket algorithm, which is discussed in Chapter 4, "ATM Traffic and Network Management," of the *Cisco ATM Solutions* book.

[3]   The default *burst* value of 94 for the 7*XXX* series signifies that the default burst tolerance is 94 tokens. Each token in the 7*XXX* series handles 32 cells. In the 4*XXX* series, each token handles only one cell. Therefore, in the Cisco literature, you sometimes see a reference to "cells" in the 4*XXX* commands and to "tokens" in the 7*XXX* commands.

Information excerpted from *Cisco ATM Solutions*, Galina Diker Pildush, Cisco Press.

Dynamic PVC Implementation

The dynamic PVC setup is not as manually intensive as the static method. Still, you use PVCs, which are set up permanently through the ATM cloud. The dynamics here involve automatic discovery of the VPI/VCI numbers by using the *Integrated Local Management Interface (ILMI)*. To use ILMI, you need to define the ILMI PVC, by using VCI = 16, per ATM Forum specifications. When you enter the command **atm ilmi-pvc-discovery subinterface**, the ILMI PVC carries the PVC identifier. Example 8-2 presents more detail on dynamic PVC implementation.

Example 8-2, based on Figure 8-2, illustrates dynamic PVC implementation.

Example 8-2 *Dynamic PVC Configuration for Multiprotocol Encapsulation*

```
Router A (config)# interface atm 0
atm pvc 1 0 16 ilmi
atm ilmi-pvc-discovery subinterface
interface atm 0.1 multipoint
ip address 131.108.168.1 255.255.255.0
ipx network 100

Router B (config)# interface atm 0
atm pvc 1 0 16 ilmi
atm ilmi-pvc-discovery subinterface
interface atm 0.1 multipoint
ip address 131.108.168.2 255.255.255.0
ipx network 100

Router C (config)# interface atm 0
atm pvc 1 0 16 ilmi
atm ilmi-pvc-discovery subinterface
interface atm 0.1 multipoint
ip address 131.108.168.3 255.255.255.0
ipx network 100
```

Please note the specification of the **subinterface** keyword in the **atm ilmi-pvc-discovery** command. This enables the discovered PVCs to reside on an ATM subinterface that is specified below. The discovered PVCs are assigned to the subinterface number that matches the VPI number of the discovered PVC. In the example, the discovered PVCs must have a VPI value of 1 to be assigned to the subinterface 0.1.

Notice that static mapping is not defined. When PVC discovery is enabled on an active PVC and the router terminates that PVC, the PVC generates an ATM Inverse ARP request. This allows the PVC to resolve its own network addresses without configuring a static map.

Address mappings learned through Inverse ARP are aged out. However, mappings are refreshed periodically. This period is configurable using the **inarp** command, which has a default of 15 minutes. It is interesting to note that Inverse ARP initially was available only for IP, following RFC 2225 (Classical IP). Currently, Cisco IOS Software extends the availability of Inverse ARP to the IPX protocol as well. The "Configuring RFC 2225 (Classical IP)" section of the chapter elaborates more on this subject.

NOTE   The fact that dynamically discovered PVCs use ATM Inverse ARP requests is somewhat similar to the Classical IP behavior. Although Classical IP architecture truly does focus on IP protocol only, Cisco extended this capability to the IPX protocol as well.

SVC Implementation

The SVC implementation is much more dynamic and resilient than the PVC implementation. Why? Simply because SVCs are set up on demand, without manual intervention. If traffic needs to get from point A to point Z, signaling sets up the VC dynamically, using either a static or a dynamic ATM routing protocol, through the ATM cloud. After the VC is set up, the traffic can flow through, utilizing the preset path. After the VC is set, all the traffic from source to destination takes the same path. The beauty of an SVC is that you do not have to worry about ATM network availability (provided, of course, that the entire ATM cloud is alive). If a problem exists with one of the links that is used for a preset VC, a new VC is set up for your traffic dynamically, using Q.2931 signaling. Several methods exist for SVC setup, using static routes or dynamic routing protocols; that discussion is outside the scope of this book, however, and can be found in *Cisco ATM Solutions*.

Because SVCs are set up dynamically, the addressing scheme is different from that of PVCs. The PVC's address, which is a VPI/VCI combination, is locally significant. The local significance makes total sense—no protocol at the ingress of the ATM network carries the ATM address of the destination dynamically through the cloud. The SVC address, on the other hand, is globally significant, which also makes total sense. The ATM edge device that needs to pass on the information received through the ATM cloud is responsible for setting up the VC. It does this by using the signaling protocol, Q.2931, which carries the information about the ATM destination and QoS parameters. Path selection within the ATM cloud and number of hops (ATM switches) for this VC setup is immaterial for the IP layer.

The SVC ATM address format consists of 160 bits or 40 hexadecimal numbers, as illustrated in Figure 8-4. If you use a private ATM network, you would use an NSAP-based ATM address. If you use a public ATM network, you would use an E.164-based ATM address. *Cisco ATM Solutions* discusses the various ATM address formats in depth.

Figure 8-4   *SVC ATM Address Format*

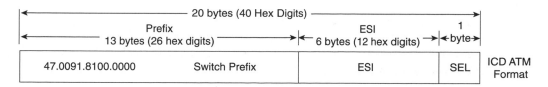

Although the address seems quite long and tedious to input (it is expressed in hexadecimal notation), do not fear. The ATM Forum foresaw that this would be a problem and allowed the addresses to be learned dynamically using ILMI. All you have to assign is the *end station identifier (ESI)*, consisting of 12 hexadecimal numbers and 2 hexadecimal selector numbers. The prefix is obtained automatically from the immediately attached ATM switch by using ILMI. Various options are available for the ESI assignment—you can use the MAC address of one of the LAN interfaces of a router, or you can assign an arbitrary address coinciding with the interface's IP address. For example, if the IP address of the ATM interfaces (or subinterface) is 177.10.168.1, you can assign the ESI to be 0177.1016.8100.

Use of ILMI requires you to set up an ILMI PVC by using VCI=16, as identified by the ATM Forum.

Table 8-5 addresses the similarities and differences of SVC implementation and PVC implementation.

Table 8-5 *SVC Versus PVC Implementation*

Similarities	Differences
Assigning an ATM address to an interface or subinterface	Different form of the ATM addresses: global addresses
Statically mapping Layer 3 next-hop a ddresses to the corresponding ATM addresses (using global ATM addresses)	Need to create PVCs for signaling and, optionally, ILMI

RFC 2684 implementation includes either manual assignment of full ATM address to the ATM edge devices or manual assignment of only the ESI portion of the NSAP address and deployment of the ILMI. Example 8-3, based on Figure 8-1, illustrates the RFC 2684 SVC implementation for the edge device routers A, B, and C. The configurations presented include RFC 2684 handling of IP and IPX protocols. Full NSAP addresses are assigned to routers A, B, and C.

Example 8-3 *RFC 2684 SVC Configuration for Multiprotocol Encapsulation*

```
Router A (config)# interface atm 0
atm pvc 5 0 5 qsaal

interface atm 0.1
ip address 138.108.168.1 255.255.255.0
atm nsap-address 47.0001000100010001000100010001.111011101110.00
map-group ip-routerA
map-group ipx-routerA

map-list ip-routerA
ip 131.108.168.2 atm-nsap 47.0002000200020002000200020002.222022202220.00 broadcast
ip 131.108.168.3 atm-nsap 47.0003000300030003000300030003.333033303330.00 broadcast

map-list ipx-routerA
```

Example 8-3 *RFC 2684 SVC Configuration for Multiprotocol Encapsulation (Continued)*

```
ipx 100.0000.0000.0002 atm-nsap 47.0002000200020002000020002.222022202220.00
broadcast
ipx 100.0000.0000.0003 atm-nsap 47.0003000300030003000030003.333033303330.00
broadcast

Router B (config)# interface atm 0
atm pvc 5 0 5 qsaal

interface atm 0.1
ip address 138.108.168.2 255.255.255.0
atm nsap-address 47.0002000200020002000020002.222022202220.00
map-group ip-routerB
map-group ipx-routerB

map-list ip-routerB
ip 131.108.168.1 atm-nsap 47.0001000100010001000010001.111011101110.00 broadcast
ip 131.108.168.3 atm-nsap 47.0003000300030003000030003.333033303330.00 broadcast

map-list ipx-routerB
ipx 100.0000.0000.0001 atm-nsap 47.0001000100010001000010001.111011101110.00
broadcast
ipx 100.0000.0000.0003 atm-nsap 47.0003000300030003000030003.333033303330.00
broadcast

Router C (config)# interface atm 0
atm pvc 5 0 5 qsaal

interface atm 0.1
ip address 138.108.168.3 255.255.255.0
atm nsap-address 47.0003000300030003000030003.333033303330.00
map-group ip-routerC
map-group ipx-routerC

map-list ip-routerC
ip 131.108.168.1 atm-nsap 47.0001000100010001000010001.111011101110.00 broadcast
ip 131.108.168.2 atm-nsap 47.0002000200020002000020002.222022202220.00 broadcast

map-list ipx-routerC
ipx 100.0000.0000.0001 atm-nsap 47.0001000100010001000010001.111011101110.00
broadcast
ipx 100.0000.0000.0002 atm-nsap 47.0002000200020002000020002.222022202220.00
broadcast
```

Example 8-4, based on Figure 8-1, illustrates another RFC 2684 SVC implementation for the same edge devices. This example illustrates the ESI portion of the ATM address assigned to the routers' interfaces. ILMI is used to obtain the NSAP prefix portion from the immediately attached ATM switch. Notice that Example 8-3 had only signaling PVCs, whereas Example 8-4 illustrates the use of two PVCs—signaling and ILMI. The signaling and ILMI PVCs must be assigned to the major interface.

Example 8-4 *RFC 2684 SVC Configuration for Multiprotocol Encapsulation*

```
Router A (config)# interface atm 0
atm pvc 5 0 5 qsaal
atm pvc 2 0 16 ilmi

interface atm 0.1
ip address 138.108.168.1 255.255.255.0
atm esi-address 111011101110.00
map-group ip-routerA
map-group ipx-routerA

map-list ip-routerA
ip 131.108.168.2 atm-nsap 47.000200020002000200020002.222022202220.00 broadcast
ip 131.108.168.3 atm-nsap 47.000300030003000300030003.333033303330.00 broadcast

map-list ipx-routerA
ipx 100.0000.0000.0002 atm-nsap 47.000200020002000200020002.222022202220.00
broadcast
ipx 100.0000.0000.0003 atm-nsap 47.000300030003000300030003.333033303330.00
broadcast
```

```
Router B (config)# interface atm 0
atm pvc 5 0 5 qsaal
atm pvc 2 0 16 ilmi

interface atm 0.1
ip address 138.108.168.2 255.255.255.0
atm esi-address 222022202220.00
map-group ip-routerB
map-group ipx-routerB

map-list ip-routerB
ip 131.108.168.1 atm-nsap 47.000100010001000100010001.111011101110.00 broadcast
ip 131.108.168.3 atm-nsap 47.000300030003000300030003.333033303330.00 broadcast

map-list ipx-routerB
ipx 100.0000.0000.0001 atm-nsap 47.000100010001000100010001.111011101110.00
broadcast
ipx 100.0000.0000.0003 atm-nsap 47.000300030003000300030003.333033303330.00
broadcast
```

```
Router C (config)# interface atm 0
atm pvc 5 0 5 qsaal
atm pvc 2 0 16 ilmi

interface atm 0.1
ip address 138.108.168.3 255.255.255.0
atm esi-address 333033303330.00
map-group ip-routerC
map-group ipx-routerC

map-list ip-routerC
```

Example 8-4   *RFC 2684 SVC Configuration for Multiprotocol Encapsulation*

```
ip 131.108.168.1 atm-nsap 47.000100010001000100010001.111011101110.00 broadcast
ip 131.108.168.2 atm-nsap 47.000200020002000200020002.222022202220.00 broadcast

map-list ipx-routerC
ipx 100.0000.0000.0001 atm-nsap 47.000100010001000100010001.111011101110.00
broadcast
ipx 100.0000.0000.0002 atm-nsap 47.000200020002000200020002.222022202220.00
broadcast
```

Summarizing, the syntax of the SVC commands for RFC 2684 is as follows:

```
Router (config-if)# atm nsap-address nsap-address
  or

Router (config-if)# atm esi-address esi
Router (config-if)# map-group name
Router (config)# map-list name
Router (config-map-list)# protocol protocol-address atm-nsap atm-nsap-address
[class class-name][broadcast]
```

Table 8-6 summarizes all the parameters that are used for configuring router interconnectivity through the SVC-based ATM networks.

Table 8-6   *Argument Description of the SVC-Associated Commands*

Argument	Description
nsap-address	Source address, specified as 40 hexadecimal digits.
esi	End-station system identifier (esi), specified as 12 hexadecimal digits. To form a full NSAP address, the 26 hexadecimal-digit prefix is learned dynamically from the ingress ATM switch with help of ILMI.
name	The name of the map list that is created at the global configuration mode. The map list name must be referenced from the interface/subinterface mode by using map-group to activate the map list.
protocol	One of the following keywords: **ip**, **ipx**, **appletalk**, **decnet**, **vines**, **apollo**, and so on, depending on the Layer 3 protocol in use.
protocol-address	Destination address that is being mapped to this SVC.
atm-nsap-address	Destination ATM NSAP address.
class-name	A reference to the traffic parameters map class lists. This is optionally available to change the traffic parameter values from their default values. With the help of **map-class** statements, you can customize the traffic-shaping parameters for various types of traffic.
broadcast	Keyword that is necessary if protocol broadcast traffic, like routing updates, needs to use the ATM interface.

Table 8-5 is excerpted from *Cisco ATM Solutions*, Galina Diker Pildush, Cisco Press.

Cisco IOS Software extends traffic-shaping capabilities to SVCs with the help of **map-class** commands:

```
Router(config-map-class)# atm forward-peak-cell-rate-clp0 rate
atm backward-peak-cell-rate-clp0 rate
atm forward-peak-cell-rate-clp1 rate
atm backward-peak-cell-rate-clp1 rate
atm forward-sustainable-cell-rate-clp0 rate
atm backward-sustainable-cell-rate-clp0 rate
atm forward-sustainable-cell-rate-clp1 rate
atm backward-sustainable-cell-rate-clp1 rate
atm forward-max-burst-size-clp0 cell-count
atm backward-max-burst-size-clp0 cell-count
atm forward-max-burst-size-clp1 cell-count
atm backward-max-burst-size-clp1 cell-count
```

The map class is referred to from the map list level by using the **class** command within the map list, as illustrated in Example 8-5.

Example 8-5 *Example of Traffic Engineering Deployment in SVC*

```
Router(config)# map-class atm contract-svcs
Router(config-map-class)# atm forward-peak-cell-rate-clp0 56000
Router(config)# map-list test ip 200.0.0.1 atm-nsap
  44.444400000000000000000000.000000000000.00 class contract-svcs
```

Configuring RFC 2225 (Classical IP)

Classical IP, specified in RFC 2225, is a dynamic method of IP interconnectivity through the ATM network. Classical IP uses RFC 2684 encapsulation. It provides a dynamic method for IP interconnectivity through the ATM network, freeing you from the necessity of configuring manually intensive mapping statements. Here is my definition of Classical IP:

> It internetworks IP only. It allows native "behavior" of IP through the ATM cloud. This implies that the IP ARP function of mapping IP addresses to the ATM PVCs or SVCs happens dynamically. The dynamics occur with the help of ARP server for the SVC scenario; in the case of PVCs, InATMARP must be configured for every PVC defined. The SVC scenario does not provide for redundancy, per the specification. Cisco has a proprietary solution to provide for redundancy. RFCs 1577 and 2225 specify the IP interoperability within a single network/subnetwork (or you can refer to it as a broadcast domain).

Classical IP utilizes a client/server architecture, which helps the ATM cloud pretend that it is a broadcast domain. Recall that IP ARP is a local broadcast. Because ATM is a nonbroadcast domain, deployment of the client/server architecture solves the problem. All the clients connect to the server, and the server performs the ARP function.

Notice that only SVC-based ATM networks deploy a client/server architecture. The PVC-based ATM networks do not require it. This is because PVC-based ATM networks have VCs pre-established and deploy locally significant ATM addressing. PVC-based ATM deploy

InATMARP to resolve VCs identifiers to the corresponding IP addresses, without involvement of an ARP server. This is exactly how InARP Frame Relay operates as well.

Please note that the original Classical IP specification, RFC 1577, does not specify ARP server redundancy. Cisco has had a proprietary solution to provide server redundancy prior to release of RFC 2225, which provisions for ARP server redundancy.

For more information on the theoretical part of Classical IP, refer to the *Cisco ATM Solutions* book.

Now let's look at the configuration examples for PVC- and SVC-based ATM networks.

PVC Implementation

Classical IP implementation through the use of PVCs uses InATMARP, which dynamically announces to the edge devices the IP addresses that are associated with the predefined PVCs. As a result, the edge devices build a dynamic ARP table between their IP addresses and the corresponding PVCs' VCD numbers.

Each router, A, B, C, and D, dynamically builds a table by using InATMARP. The table associates the IP addresses with the locally significant VCD numbers, as listed in Table 8-7.

Table 8-7   *Dynamic IP and VCD Number Assignment*

Router	IP Address	VCD Number
A	138.108.168.2	12
	138.108.168.3	13
	138.108.168.4	14
B	138.108.168.1	21
	138.108.168.3	23
	138.108.168.4	24
C	138.108.168.1	31
	138.108.168.2	32
	138.108.168.4	34
D	138.108.168.1	41
	138.108.168.2	42
	138.108.168.3	43

The syntax of PVC commands for Classical IP is identical to that of the regular PVC commands. You need to create PVCs as you would when implementing RFC 2684. Only two differences exist. You need to specify **inarp** at the end of the **atm pvc** command, and you have to omit the **map-group** statement that is referencing the corresponding map list. Table 8-4 provides all the details of the PVC command components.

Let's examine the network illustrated in Figure 8-5. You have four routers interconnected across the ATM network. The identified VCD values enable a fully meshed topology, which results in a direct VC availability from any to any router.

Figure 8-5 *Classical IP over PVC-Based ATM Network*

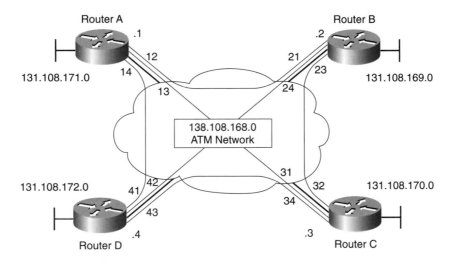

Example 8-6 presents the configuration for all routers.

Example 8-6 *Classical IP Implementation Using PVC-Based ATM Network*

```
Router A (config)# interface atm 0
no shutdown
interface atm 0.1
ip address 138.108.168.1 255.255.255.0
atm pvc 12 0 77 aal5snap inarp 5
atm pvc 13 0 78 aal5snap inarp 5
atm pvc 14 0 79 aal5snap inarp 5

Router B (config)# interface atm 0
no shutdown
interface atm 0.1
ip address 138.108.168.2 255.255.255.0
atm pvc 21 0 87 aal5snap inarp 5
atm pvc 23 0 88 aal5snap inarp 5
atm pvc 24 0 89 aal5snap inarp 5
```

Example 8-6 *Classical IP Implementation Using PVC-Based ATM Network (Continued)*

```
Router C (config)# interface atm 0
no shutdown
int atm 0.1
ip address 138.108.168.3 255.255.255.0
atm pvc 31 0 97 aal5snap inarp 5
atm pvc 32 0 98 aal5snap inarp 5
atm pvc 34 0 99 aal5snap inarp 5

Router D (config)# interface atm 0
no shutdown
int atm 0.1
ip address 138.108.168.4 255.255.255.0
atm pvc 41 0 107 aal5snap inarp 5
atm pvc 42 0 108 aal5snap inarp 5
atm pvc 43 0 109 aal5snap inarp 5
```

All the routers are configured to send Inverse ARP datagrams every 5 minutes.

SVC Implementation

Implementing Classical IP over SVC-based ATM networks is based on a client/server architecture. This implies that there must be a server providing services to many clients. Classical IP provisions one ARP server, called ATMARP server, for many clients within a single broadcast domain. No longer do you have to configure static mapping between the globally significant ATM addresses and IP addresses—the ATMARP server takes care of it dynamically.

The simplicity of the architecture provides for little configuration in both ATMARP server and clients. All you have to do is assign either your full ATM address or the ESI prefix only (in this case, each router learns the prefix dynamically from an ingress ATM switch) in both clients and servers. Then, clients have to specify the full ATM address of the ATMARP server. All clients and a server must have the signaling and the ILMI PVCs. Then, the magic begins. Clients, knowing the ATMARP server address, automatically announce themselves to the server. In turn, when the client/server VC is set, the server builds the dynamic ARP table, containing the cross-reference between the clients' IP and ATM addresses.

Figure 8-6 illustrates a sample Classical IP setup, where all four routers share one IP network, 138.108.168.0, across the ATM cloud. Router B is the ATMARP server, and routers A, C, and D are the clients.

After you define the clients, each one sets up a VC to the ATMARP server, Router B. Then, each client sends ATMARP request packets to the ATMARP server. The server, Router B, examines each ATMARP request packet and uses the information to build its ATMARP cache. This information is a dynamic cross-reference between the clients' ATM and IP addresses, as defined in Table 8-8. Using the ARP table entries, clients can communicate with each other without the need for static map list entries.

Figure 8-6 *Classical IP over SVC-Based ATM Network*

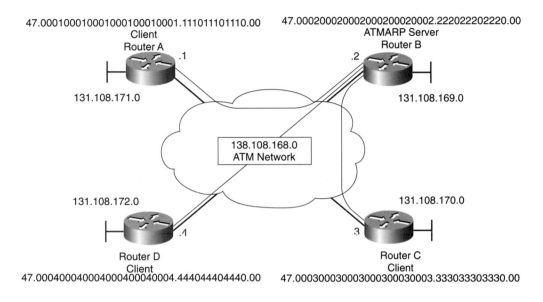

Table 8-8 *Dynamically Generated ATMARP Server Cache Entries*

IP Address	ATM (NSAP) Address
138.108.168.1	47.000100010001000100010001.111011101110.00
138.108.168.2	47.000200020002000200020002.222022202220.00
138.108.168.3	47.000300030003000300030003.333033303330.00
138.108.168.4	47.000400040004000400040004.444044404440.00

Example 8-7 depicts the configurations that are required in all four routers (routers A, C, and D are clients; Router B is the ATMARP server). Notice that static mapping no longer is required.

Example 8-7 *Classical IP Implementation Using ATM SVC-Based Network*

```
Router A (config)# interface atm 0
atm pvc 1 0 5 qsaal
no shutdown
interface atm 0.1
ip address 138.10.168.1 255.255.255.0
atm nsap-address 47.000100010001000100010001.111011101110.00
atm arp-server nsap 47.000200020002000200020002.222022202220.00

Router B (config)# interface atm 0
atm pvc 1 0 5 qsaal
```

Example 8-7 *Classical IP Implementation Using ATM SVC-Based Network (Continued)*

```
no shutdown
interface atm 0.1
ip address 138.108.168.2 255.255.255.0
atm nsap-address 47.00020002000200020002.222022202220.00
atm arp-server self

Router C (config)# interface atm 0
atm pvc 1 0 5 qsaal
no shutdown
interface atm 0.1
ip address 138.108.168.3 255.255.255.0
atm nsap-address 47.00030003000300030003.333033303330.00
atm arp-server nsap 47.00020002000200020002.222022202220.00

Router D (config)# interface atm 0
atm pvc 1 0 5 qsaal
no shutdown
interface atm 0.1
ip address 138.108.168.4 255.255.255.0
atm nsap-address 47.00040004000400040004.444044404440.00
atm arp-server nsap 47.00020002000200020002.222022202220.00
```

Example 8-7 uses a single ATMARP server within a broadcast domain. If you need ATMARP server redundancy, you need to define more than one ATMARP server in every client, as illustrated in Example 8-8, using Figure 8-7. The second ATMARP server is Router D.

Figure 8-7 *Redundant ATMARP Server Classical IP over SVC-Based ATM Network*

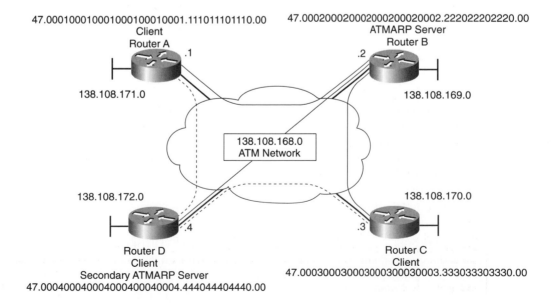

Example 8-8 *Redundant ATMARP Server Classical IP Implementation Using ATM SVC-Based Network*

```
Router A (config)# interface atm 0
atm pvc 1 0 5 qsaal
no shutdown
interface atm 0.1
ip address 138.108.168.1 255.255.255.0
atm classic-ip-extensions bfi
atm nsap-address 47.000100010001000100010001.111011101110.00
atm arp-server nsap 47.000200020002000200020002.222022202220.00
atm arp-server nsap 47.000400040004000400040004.444044404440.00

Router B (config)# interface atm 0
atm pvc 1 0 5 qsaal
no shutdown
interface atm 0.1
ip address 138.108.168.2 255.255.255.0
atm classic-ip-extensions bfi
atm nsap-address 47.000200020002000200020002.222022202220.00
atm arp-server nsap 47.000400040004000400040004.444044404440.00
atm arp-server self
Router C - Client

Router C (config)# interface atm 0
atm pvc 1 0 5 qsaal
no shutdown
interface atm 0.1
ip address 138.108.168.3 255.255.255.0
atm classic-ip-extensions bfi
atm nsap-address 47.000300030003000300030003.333033303330.00
atm arp-server nsap 47.000200020002000200020002.222022202220.00
atm arp-server nsap 47.000400040004000400040004.444044404440.00

Router D (config)# interface atm 0
atm pvc 1 0 5 qsaal
no shutdown
interface atm 0.1
ip address 138.108.168.4 255.255.255.0
atm classic-ip-extensions bfi
atm nsap-address 47.000400040004000400040004.444044404440.00
atm arp-server nsap 47.000200020002000200020002.222022202220.00
atm arp-server self
```

Notice the use of the new **atm classic-ip-extensions bfi** command, which allows the ATMARP server redundancy. Initially, clients Router A and Router C use Router B as their ARMARP server. If Router B becomes unavailable, the clients use Router D as their backup ATMARP server.

Classical IP implementation enables you to define only the ESI portions of the ATM addresses at the clients and the server, which then uses ILMI to obtain the prefix portion of their NSAP addresses from the corresponding ingress ATM switches.

Summarizing, the syntax for the clients' Classical IP implementation over SVC-based ATM networks is as follows:

```
Router(config)# int atm int#
Router(config-if)# atm pvc vcd# vpi# 5 qsaal
```

And, if the ESI portion of the address is used:

```
Router(config-if)# atm pvc vcd# vpi# 16 ilmi
Router(config)# int atm subint#
Router(config-if)# atm nsap nsap-address
```

or:

```
Router(config-if)# atm esi esi-portion-address
Router(config-if)# atm arp-server nsap nsap-address
```

The syntax for the ATMARP server implementation is as follows:

```
Router(config)# int atm int#
Router(config-if)# atm pvc vcd# vpi# 5 qsaal
```

And, if the ESI portion of the address is used:

```
Router(config-if)# atm pvc vod# vpi# 16 ilmi
Router(config)# int atm subint#
Router(config-if)# atm nsap nsap-address
```

or:

```
Router(config-if)# atm esi esi-portion-address
Router(config-if)# atm arp-server self [time-out minutes]
```

The **atm arp-server self** command declares to the router that it is the ATMARP server. The **time-out**, specified in minutes, is optional. It identifies the number of minutes that a destination entry listed in the ARP cache is kept before the server takes any action to verify the address. The default value of the ATMARP cache timeout is 20 minutes, per RFC 2225.

Lab 18: Configuring PVCs on Cisco 7XXX Routers, RFC 2684—Part I

Practical Scenario

Unfortunately for ATM, most of ATM's implementations are PVC-based. The reason I say "unfortunately" is because SVC-based networks are simpler to set up. Also, dynamic ATM QoS is available with SVC-based networks only. Knowing the steps involved in PVC-based ATM networks setup is one of the prerequisites for the CCIE examination lab.

Lab Exercise

You are running an IP-based network, which extends through the ATM cloud. You must interconnect various sites. The ATM network is PVC-based. Your service provider promised to give you all the necessary addressing to interconnect your five sites. You are running the EIGRP routing protocol. You need to maintain the following guidelines in your implementation:

- Use EIGRP as the routing protocol with autonomous system 100.

- Assign proper VPI/VCI numbers to all the PVCs.

- Maintain a fully meshed topology.

Lab Objectives

At the end of this lab, you will complete the following:

- Configure the Cisco router for operation.

- Configure a full mesh PVC environment.

- Configure RFC 2684.

Equipment Needed

The lab uses five routers and one ATM switch. For CCIE preparation, it is sufficient to obtain two routers interfacing through the ATM network. To summarize, you need the following equipment:

- At least five routers with ATM interfaces

- One LS1010 ATM switch

Physical Layout and Prestaging

- Connect the routers to the ATM switch, as shown in Figure 8-8.
- Note that, although Figure 8-8 shows five routers, you can perform a similar exercise by using only two routers interconnected through the ATM network.

Figure 8-8 *PVCs for IP*

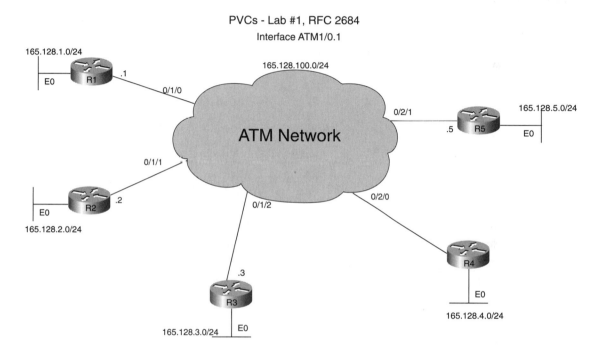

Lab 18: Configuring PVCs on Cisco 7*XXX* Routers, RFC 2684—Part II

Lab Walkthrough

You need to configure the IP routing protocol and IP addressing, which are used in both labs. After the initial configuration is complete, you need to set up eight PVCs to the other routers, creating a fully meshed topology. Your IP connectivity must extend through the ATM network.

Table 8-9 lists the commands that you need to complete this lab.

Table 8-9   *Lab Command Summary*

Command	Description
router eigrp	Turns on the EIGRP routing protocol on the router
atm pvc	Sets up bidirectional permanent virtual circuits
map-list	Maps a Layer 3 network address to a PVC
show atm vc	Displays the configured virtual circuits on the router
show atm interface atm	Displays more detail about the specified interface
show atm map	Displays the map-lists that were created by the user
Debug atm events	Displays the creation of PVCs between the router and the ATM switch
show ip route	Displays the IP routing table
ping	Tests connectivity at Layer 3

Refer to Figure 8-8 to complete the following exercises for this lab.

Step 1. Configure the Router Parameters

Configure your router with the following parameters:

- Host name: R*n* (where *n* is the router number)
- Enable password: atmlab
- Virtual terminal/console password: cisco
- IP routing: EIGRP
- EIGRP autonomous system number: 100
- IP as your *only* routed protocol

Example 8-9 shows the configuration for R1.

Example 8-9 *Router R1 Configuration Parameters*

```
R1(config)# hostname R1
!
enable password atmlab
!
router eigrp 100
 network 165.128.0.0
!
line con 0
 exec-timeout 0 0
line aux 0
line vty 0 4
 exec-timeout 0 0
 password cisco
 login
!
```

Step 2. Configure the IP Addresses for the Ethernet 0 and ATM 1/0.1 Interfaces

Configure the IP addresses for the Ethernet 0 and ATM 1/0.1 interfaces with the IP addresses, as identified in Table 8-10.

Table 8-10 *IP Address Assignment*

Router	E0	ATM1/0.1
R1	165.128.1.1/24	165.128.100.1/24
R2	165.128.2.2/24	165.128.100.2/24
R3	165.128.3.3/24	165.128.100.3/24
R4	165.128.4.4/24	165.128.100.4/24
R5	165.128.5.5/24	165.128.100.5/24

Example 8-10 shows the configuration for R1.

Example 8-10 *IP Address Configuration for Router R1*

```
R1(config)# interface e0
 ip address 165.128.1.1 255.255.255.0
interface atm1/0.1 multipoint
 ip address 165.128.100.1 255.255.255.0
```

Step 3: Configure a PVC to Every Other Router

To create a fully meshed ATM PVC network, you need to configure a PVC to every other router. Use AAL5SNAP. Use Table 8-11 for the VPI/VCI number assignment.

Table 8-11   *VPI/VCI Assignment*

From	To	VCD	VPI	VCI
R1	R2		0	112
	R3		0	113
	R4		0	114
	R5		0	115
R2	R1		0	121
	R3		0	123
	R4		0	124
	R5		0	125
R3	R1		0	131
	R2		0	132
	R4		0	134
	R5		0	135
R4	R1		0	141
	R2		0	142
	R3		0	143
	R5		0	145
R5	R1		0	151
	R2		0	152
	R3		0	153
	R4		0	154

Example 8-11 shows the configuration for R1.

Example 8-11 *PVC Configuration for Router R1*

```
R1(config)# interface atm1/0.1 multipoint
 ip address 165.128.100.1 255.255.255.0
 atm pvc 112 0 112 aal5snap
 atm pvc 113 0 113 aal5snap
 atm pvc 114 0 114 aal5snap
 atm pvc 115 0 115 aal5snap
```

Step 4: Configure LS1010 to Handle PVCs

In the CCIE lab, the ATM switch is preconfigured. For your CCIE preparation, however, you are required to configure your own switch, as demonstrated in Example 8-12. The configuration is as follows.

Example 8-12 *Configuring an ATM Switch to Be PVC-Aware*

```
ATM-Switch# version 11.3
no service pad
no service udp-small-servers
no service tcp-small-servers
!
hostname ATM-Switch
!
enable password atmlab
!
no ip domain-lookup
!
atm address 47.0091.8100.0000.0010.0739.a101.0010.0739.a101.00
atm router pnni
 node 1 level 56 lowest
  redistribute atm-static
!
interface ATM0/1/0
 no ip address
 no atm auto-configuration
 atm uni version 3.1
 atm maxvpi-bits 3
 atm maxvci-bits 10
 atm pvc 0 112  interface  ATM0/1/1 0 121
 atm pvc 0 113  interface  ATM0/1/2 0 131
 atm pvc 0 114 interface   ATM0/2/0 0 141
 atm pvc 0 115 interface   ATM0/2/1 0 151
!
interface ATM0/1/1
 no ip address
 no atm auto-configuration
atm uni version 3.1
 atm maxvpi-bits 3
 atm maxvci-bits 10
 atm pvc 0 121  interface  ATM0/1/0 0 112
 atm pvc 0 123  interface  ATM0/1/2 0 132
 atm pvc 0 124  interface  ATM0/2/0 0 142
 atm pvc 0 125  interface  ATM0/2/1 0 152
!
interface ATM0/1/2
 no ip address
 no atm auto-configuration
 atm uni version 3.1
 atm maxvpi-bits 3
 atm maxvci-bits 10
```

continues

Example 8-12 *Configuring an ATM Switch to Be PVC-Aware (Continued)*

```
  atm pvc 0 131  interface  ATM0/1/0 0 113
  atm pvc 0 132  interface  ATM0/1/1 0 123
  atm pvc 0 134  interface  ATM0/2/0 0 143
  atm pvc 0 135  interface  ATM0/2/1 0 153
!
interface ATM0/2/0
 no ip address
 no atm auto-configuration
 atm uni version 3.1
 atm maxvpi-bits 3
 atm maxvci-bits 10
 atm pvc 0 141  interface  ATM0/1/0 0 114
 atm pvc 0 142  interface  ATM0/1/1 0 124
 atm pvc 0 143  interface  ATM0/1/2 0 134
 atm pvc 0 145  interface  ATM0/2/1 0 154
!
interface ATM0/2/1
 no ip address
 no atm auto-configuration
 atm uni version 3.1
 atm maxvpi-bits 3
 atm maxvci-bits 10
 atm pvc 0 151  interface  ATM0/1/0 0 115
 atm pvc 0 152  interface  ATM0/1/1 0 125
 atm pvc 0 153  interface  ATM0/1/2 0 135
 atm pvc 0 154  interface  ATM0/2/0 0 145
!
interface Ethernet2/0/0
 ip address 10.0.0.12 255.0.0.0
!
ip classless
!
line con 0
 exec-timeout 0 0
 password cisco
 login
line aux 0
line vty 0 4
 exec-timeout 0 0
 password cisco
 login
!
end
```

Step 5: Map Your Neighbor's IP Network Number to the Appropriate PVC

Example 8-13 uses R1 to demonstrate this step of the lab.

Example 8-13 *Mapping IP Network Numbers to the Proper PVC*

```
R1(config)# interface atm1/0.1 multipoint
 ip address 165.128.100.1 255.255.255.0
 atm pvc 112 0 112 aal5snap
 atm pvc 113 0 113 aal5snap
 atm pvc 114 0 114 aal5snap
 atm pvc 115 0 115 aal5snap
 map-group ip-Pvc
 !
map-list ip-Pvc
 ip 165.128.100.2 atm-vc 112 broadcast
 ip 165.128.100.3 atm-vc 113 broadcast
 ip 165.128.100.4 atm-vc 114 broadcast
 ip 165.128.100.5 atm-vc 115 broadcast
```

Step 6: Test Your Configuration

Lab 19: Configuring Classical IP Using SVCs on Cisco 7XXX Routers, RFC 2225—Part I

Practical Scenario

Classical IP reduces many configuration steps, such as the necessity to perform manual mapping between Layer 3 addressing and ATM. This lab demonstrates the use of SVCs as well.

Lab Exercise

You are running an IP-based network that extends through the ATM cloud. You must interconnect various sites. The ATM network is SVC-based. Your service provider is not giving the details of SVC addressing. Therefore, you decided to learn the address prefixes from the provider's ingress ATM switch by using ILMI. Furthermore, you want to use Classical IP. You are running the EIGRP routing protocol. You need to maintain the following guidelines in your implementation:

- Use EIGRP as the routing protocol with autonomous system 100.
- Assign ESI portions of the NSAP address.
- Establish signaling and ILMI PVCs.
- Assign the ATM ARP server function to R2. Other routers are clients.
- Maintain a fully meshed topology.

Lab Objectives

At the end of the lab, you will complete the following:

- Enable Classical IP of the SVC network (RFC 2225).
- Configure the ARP server and client (RFC 2225).
- Implement a single logical IP subnet (LIS).

Equipment Needed

The lab uses five routers and one ATM switch. For CCIE preparation, it is sufficient to obtain two routers interfacing through the ATM network. To summarize, you need the following equipment:

- At least five routers with ATM interfaces
- One LS1010 ATM switch

Physical Layout and Prestaging

- Connect the routers to the ATM switch, as shown in Figure 8-9.
- Note that although Figure 8-9 shows five routers, you can perform a similar exercise by using only two routers interconnected through the ATM network.

Figure 8-9 illustrates the network diagram and addressing scheme used in this lab.

Figure 8-9   *Classical IP*

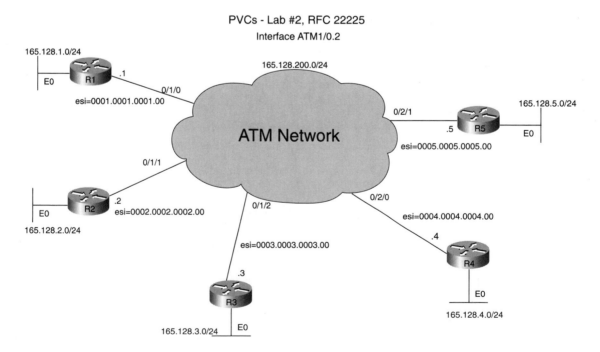

Lab 19: Configuring Classical IP Using SVCs on Cisco 7XXX Routers, RFC 2225—Part II

Lab Walkthrough

You use the same IP addressing and IP routing protocol as you used in the previous lab. The steps necessary to perform these tasks are presented here for your reference. The ATM network is SVC-based. Your IP connectivity must extend through the ATM network, creating a fully meshed environment.

This lab illustrates the extension of IP connectivity using Classical IP. In addition to Classical IP implementation, you use ILMI for a dynamic ATM address prefix assignment.

Table 8-12 lists and describes the commands that are necessary to complete this lab.

Table 8-12   *Lab Command Summary*

Command	Description
atm pvc	Used for signaling and ILMI PVCs creation
atm arp-server self	Configures the ARP server for one LIS
atm arp-server nsap	Configures the ARP server client
atm esi-address	Configures the ATM ESI portion of the NSAP (AESA) address
debug atm events	Shows the creation of PVCs between router and switch
debug atm arp	Shows ATM ARP events
show ip route	Shows the IP routing table
ping	Tests connectivity at Layer 3

Refer to Figure 8-9 to complete the steps described in the sections that follow.

Step 1. Configure the Router Parameters

Configure your router with the following parameters:

- Host name: R*n* (where *n* is the router number)
- Enable password: atmlab
- Virtual terminal/console password: cisco
- IP routing: EIGRP
- EIGRP autonomous system number: 100
- IP as your *only* routed protocol

Example 8-14 shows the results of your configuration, demonstrated for R1.

Example 8-14 *Configuring the Router Parameters*

```
R1(config)# hostname R1
!
enable password atmlab
!
router eigrp 100
 network 165.128.0.0
!
line con 0
 exec-timeout 0 0
line aux 0
line vty 0 4
 exec-timeout 0 0
 password cisco
 login
!
```

Step 2. Configure the IP Addresses for the ATM 1/0.2 Interfaces

Configure the IP addresses for the ATM 1/0.2 interfaces with the IP addresses identified in Table 8-13.

Table 8-13   *IP Address Assignment*

Router	ATM1/0.1
R1	165.128.200.1/24
R2	165.128.200.2/24
R3	165.128.200.3/24
R4	165.128.200.4/24
R5	165.128.200.5/24

Example 8-15 shows the configuration for R1.

Example 8-15 *IP Address Configuration for Router R1*

```
R1(config)# interface atm1/0.2 multipoint
 ip address 165.128.200.1 255.255.255.0
```

Step 3: Configure Two PVCs—Signaling and ILMI on the Major Interfaces on Every Router

Example 8-16 shows how to perform the configuration for this step on Router 1.

Example 8-16 *Configuring the Signaling and ILMI on PVCs*

```
R1(config)# interface atm1
 atm pvc 1 0 5 qsaal
 atm pvc 2 0 16 ilmi
interface atm 1/0.2 multipoint
 ip address 165.128.200.1 255.255.255.0
```

Step 4: Configure LS1010 to Handle PVCs

In the CCIE lab, the ATM switch is preconfigured; However, for your CCIE preparation, you are required to configure your own switch as demonstrated in Example 8-17. The configuration is as follows.

Example 8-17 *Configuring an ATM Switch to Be PVC-Aware*

```
ATM-Switch# version 11.3
no service pad
no service udp-small-servers
no service tcp-small-servers
!
hostname ATM-Switch
!
enable password atmlab
!
no ip domain-lookup
!
atm address 47.0091.8100.0000.0010.0739.a101.0010.0739.a101.00
atm router pnni
 node 1 level 56 lowest
   redistribute atm-static
!
interface ATM0/1/0
 no ip address
 no atm auto-configuration
 atm uni version 3.1
 !
interface ATM0/1/1
 no ip address
 no atm auto-configuration
 atm uni version 3.1
 !
interface ATM0/1/2
 no ip address
 no atm auto-configuration
 atm uni version 3.1
```

Example 8-17 *Configuring an ATM Switch to Be PVC-Aware (Continued)*

```
!
interface ATM0/2/0
 no ip address
 no atm auto-configuration
 atm uni version 3.1
!
interface ATM0/2/1
 no ip address
 no atm auto-configuration
 atm uni version 3.1
```

Step 5: Assign the ESI Portion of the NSAP Address to Router Interfaces

This step involves assigning the ESI portion of the NSAP address to the interface atm1/0.2 of all the routers, using Table 8-14.

Table 8-14   *IP Address Assignment*

Router	ESI Portion of the Address
R1	0001.0001.0001.00
R2	0002.0002.0002.00
R3	0003.0003.0003.00
R4	0004.0004.0004.00
R5	0005.0005.0005.00

Example 8-18 shows the configuration for this step by using R1.

Example 8-18 *Mapping the ESI Portion of the NSAP Address to the atm1/0.2 Interface*

```
R1(config)# interface atm1
 atm pvc 1 0 5 qsaal
 atm pvc 2 0 16 ilmi
interface atm 1/0.2 multipoint
 ip address 165.128.200.1 255.255.255.0
 atm esi-address 0001.0001.0001.00
```

Step 6: Define the Address of the ATM ARP Server

This step involves defining the address of the ATM ARP server in R1, R3, R4, and R5, and defining R2 to be the ATM ARP server.

R2 is the ATM ARP server that is consulted by R1, R3, R4, and R5 to resolve between IP and ATM addresses. Example 8-19 shows how to configure R2 as the ATM ARP server.

Example 8-19 *Configuring R2 as the ATM ARP Server*

```
R2(config)# interface atm1
 atm pvc 1 0 5 qsaal
 atm pvc 2 0 16 ilmi
interface atm 1/0.2 multipoint
 ip address 165.128.200.2 255.255.255.0
 atm esi-address 0002.0002.0002.00
 atm arp-server self
```

R1, R3, R4, and R5 are the clients. The configuration of a client must have the ATM ARP server NSAP address. Example 8-20 shows the configuration of a client by using R1 as the example.

Example 8-20 *Configuring the ATM ARP Server Clients*

```
R1(config)# interface atm1
 atm pvc 1 0 5 qsaal
 atm pvc 2 0 16 ilmi
interface atm 1/0.2 multipoint
 ip address 165.128.200.1 255.255.255.0
 atm esi-address 0001.0001.0001.00
 atm arp-server nsap 47.0091.8100.0000.0010.0739.a101.0002.0002.0002.00
```

Notice that the NSAP address of R2 was created using the prefix from the LS1010 and the ESI portion that was assigned to R2.

Step 7: Test Your Configuration

Summary

Cisco supports various router interconnections over ATM networks on its multiple product lines, a summary of which is provided in this chapter. Also, this chapter presents Cisco's implementation of multiprotocol encapsulation (RFC 2684) and Classical IP (RFC 2225) over PVC- and SVC-based ATM networks. The chapter provides the syntax of the relevant Cisco IOS commands, supported by the examples.

Multiprotocol encapsulation provides interconnectivity of Layer 3 and Layer 2 across the ATM networks. The examples in this chapter focus on Layer 3 support. Layer 2 support, LANE, is outside the scope of this chapter and is no longer part of the CCIE lab.

Classical IP (RFC 2225) focuses on IP only and allows dynamic address mapping between IP and ATM.

Routing Protocols

Routing protocols are the glue of the internetwork. They are the foundation of routers and are what has allowed the Internet to grow to its gargantuan size. Your mastery of routing protocols is a critical skill in designing and implementing IP networks. The upcoming sections define what routing protocols are, give the different types and metrics of each, and compare two major classes of routing protocols—distance vector protocols and link-state protocols.

Part IV includes the following chapters:

What Are Routing Protocols?

A protocol is a routed protocol if it contains an explicit network address and enough information is in its network layer address to allow for a router to make an intelligent forwarding decision. *Routing* is the process by which a packet gets from one network to another. A *routing* protocol supports a *routed* protocol by providing a means for propagating routing information. This information includes elements such as the available routes, a cost to the routes, and the next-hop address. The routing protocol uses messages between routers that allow for communication with other routers to update and maintain routing tables. It is important to note that routing protocols do not carry end-user traffic from network to network. Routing protocols only build the paths that end-user data uses to travel.

The Route Table

Many routing protocols are in use today. As different as they are from each other, they all serve the same purpose of performing routing operations and maintaining a route table.

The route table contains the following information:

- Lists of networks/routes or host routes.
- The means by which the route was learned, either dynamically from a routing protocol or statically from manual configuration.
- Administrative distances of the routes.
- The metric or cost of the route.
- The address of the next-hop router to the route.
- The current status of the route. This can include the amount of time since the last update, whether the route is in holddown, and so forth.
- The interface associated with reaching the route. This is the interface from which the packet will be forwarded to the next-hop router.

Example IV-1 depicts a complex routing table, illustrating OSPF, EIGRP, and default routing.

Example IV-1 *Routing Table*

```
r2#show ip route
Codes: C - connected, S - static, I - IGRP, R - RIP, M - mobile, B - BGP
       D - EIGRP, EX - EIGRP external, O - OSPF, IA - OSPF inter area
       N1 - OSPF NSSA external type 1, N2 - OSPF NSSA external type 2
       E1 - OSPF external type 1, E2 - OSPF external type 2, E - EGP
       i - IS-IS, L1 - IS-IS level-1, L2 - IS-IS level-2, * - candidate default
       U - per-user static route, o - ODR

Gateway of last resort is 172.16.128.1 to network 0.0.0.0

     10.0.0.0/24 is subnetted, 1 subnets
O       10.10.10.0 is a summary, 03:05:49, Null0
     129.201.0.0/24 is subnetted, 1 subnets
O E1    129.201.1.0 [110/90] via 172.16.2.66, 03:05:45, TokenRing1
     128.200.0.0/24 is subnetted, 1 subnets
D EX    128.200.1.0 [170/679936] via 172.16.192.3, 05:42:57, Serial1
     129.200.0.0/24 is subnetted, 1 subnets
O E1    129.200.1.0 [110/90] via 172.16.2.66, 03:05:45, TokenRing1
     128.201.0.0/24 is subnetted, 1 subnets
D EX    128.201.1.0 [170/679936] via 172.16.192.3, 05:42:57, Serial1
C    201.201.101.0/24 is directly connected, Loopback0
O E2 132.31.0.0/16 [110/2] via 172.16.2.66, 00:58:04, TokenRing1
O E2 131.31.0.0/16 [110/2] via 172.16.2.66, 00:58:04, TokenRing1
     172.16.0.0/16 is variably subnetted, 27 subnets, 4 masks
O IA    172.16.152.0/24 [110/71] via 172.16.2.66, 03:05:45, TokenRing1
O IA    172.16.150.0/24 [110/80] via 172.16.2.66, 03:05:45, TokenRing1
O IA    172.16.151.0/24 [110/71] via 172.16.2.66, 03:05:45, TokenRing1
C       172.16.144.0/21 is directly connected, Loopback20
C       172.16.136.0/21 is directly connected, Ethernet1
C       172.16.128.0/21 is directly connected, Ethernet0
C       172.16.192.0/24 is directly connected, Serial1
C       172.16.192.3/32 is directly connected, Serial1
```

Example IV-1 *Routing Table (Continued)*

```
O IA    172.16.42.2/32 [110/70] via 172.16.2.66, 03:05:46, TokenRing1
O IA    172.16.42.3/32 [110/70] via 172.16.2.66, 03:05:46, TokenRing1
O E2    172.16.42.0/24 [110/2] via 172.16.2.66, 03:05:46, TokenRing1
O IA    172.16.42.1/32 [110/6] via 172.16.2.66, 03:05:46, TokenRing1
O IA    172.16.21.0/24 [110/76] via 172.16.2.66, 03:05:46, TokenRing1
O IA    172.16.22.0/24 [110/71] via 172.16.2.66, 03:05:46, TokenRing1
O E2    172.16.1.0/24 [110/2] via 172.16.2.66, 03:05:46, TokenRing1
O E2    172.16.2.0/24 [110/2] via 172.16.2.66, 03:05:46, TokenRing1
D       172.16.102.0/24 [90/679936] via 172.16.192.3, 05:42:59, Serial1
D       172.16.103.0/24 [90/409600] via 172.16.128.1, 05:42:59, Ethernet0
O E2    172.16.84.0/24 [110/2] via 172.16.2.66, 03:05:47, TokenRing1
O E2    172.16.85.0/24 [110/2] via 172.16.2.66, 03:05:47, TokenRing1
O E2    172.16.81.0/24 [110/2] via 172.16.2.66, 03:05:47, TokenRing1
O E2    172.16.82.0/24 [110/2] via 172.16.2.66, 03:05:47, TokenRing1
O E2    172.16.83.0/24 [110/2] via 172.16.2.66, 03:05:47, TokenRing1
O E2    172.16.64.0/24 [110/2] via 172.16.2.66, 03:05:47, TokenRing1
C       172.16.1.64/26 is directly connected, TokenRing0
C       172.16.2.64/26 is directly connected, TokenRing1
D*EX 0.0.0.0/0 [170/20028160] via 172.16.128.1, 05:43:00, Ethernet0
```

You can see many of the routing table components mentioned previously by examining the highlighted line. The route 172.16.102.0/24 is being reported by EIGRP. The administrative distance of the route is 90, and the EIGRP metric is 67,9936. The route was reported more than 5 hours and 42 minutes ago. The next-hop router is over interface Serial1, and its IP address is 172.16.192.3.

The Routing Protocol Algorithm

All dynamic routing protocols are built around a general algorithm. The routing algorithm addresses the following areas:

- A procedure for distributing reachability information about networks to and from other routers

- A procedure for determining and recording optimal routes, based on the reachability information received from other routers

- A procedure to advertise and compensate for topology changes

When Does the Router *Route*?

By default, all Cisco routers will route all *routable* protocols, such as IP or IPX, first. If routing for the *routable* protocol is not enabled and bridging for that protocol is enabled, the router will bridge it. How a router handles a protocol depends not only on the protocol being a *routable* protocol, but also on how *routing* is enabled for that protocol. For example, if the router receives an IPX packet and has IPX routing enabled, it tries to route or forward the packet to the next-hop address. This is the normal operation of IPX. However, if the router receives an IPX packet and does not have IPX routing enabled, the router forwards that packet out any bridged interfaces, including DLSw ports. This is because the router no longer recognizes IPX as a *routable* protocol.

To successfully route a packet, a router must know the following:

- The protocol must be *routable*, and routing for that protocol suite must be enabled.
- The router must know the destination network or have a default route installed.
- A valid next-hop address must exist, or an interface pointing at the destination network must exist.

When the decision to route the packet is made, the router checks the packet to see if the final destination is a locally connected network. If the destination is local, the router forwards it out the appropriate port. If the network is not local, the router must consult the *route table*. The route table consists of known networks, the costs associated with those networks, and the path to the next-hop router. The router compares the packet to entries in its route tables by performing a longest match lookup. The entry that has the *longest match* to the destination address is the entry used to determine the forwarding path. The longest match route can also be referred to as the most explicit route. The longest match is only 100 percent true if **ip classless** is enabled, and it applies mostly to classless routing protocols.

NOTE   The longest match lookup occurs when a router must determine which entry in the route table to use in forwarding a packet. For example, imagine that the router receives a packet that has a destination network of 172.16.1.0/24. It has two routes, 172.0.0.0/8 out S1 and 172.16.0.0/16 out S2. Which interface should the router forward the packet out? This is when the router performs a longest match lookup. To accomplish this, the router compares the bits of the destination network, from left to right, with the bits in route in the routing table. The router compares each bit in sequence and stops the comparison process at the bit before the first bit that doesn't match in the route table entry being compared. The router chooses the path/route where the greatest number of consecutive bit matches has occurred. In this case, the router uses the 172.16.1.0 route over the 172.16.0.0 route because the 172.16.1.0 route is the longest match—or, in other words, more explicit.

Routing Metrics

Another important aspect of routing protocols is to provide a loop-free topology of the network while locating the best path to every destination network. Routers advertise the path to a network in terms of a metric. The metric value or metric type depends on the routing protocol. For example, RIP uses hop count as its metric, whereas OSPF uses cost. The router uses the metric value when evaluating multiple paths to the same network. The metrics for all routing protocols can be adjusted, thereby influencing which path the router will select in forwarding traffic. The following list is a brief description of the most common routing metrics:

- **Hop count**—A metric that counts router hops. The more hops, the less desirable the path.

- **Bandwidth**—A metric that measures bandwidth. The higher the bandwidth, the more preferable the path.

- **Load**—A metric that reflects the amount of traffic on a links to a path. The lower the load, the more preferable the path.

- **Delay**—A metric that measures the time that a packet takes to traverse a route. The lower the delay, the more preferable the route.

- **Reliability**—A metric that measures the probability that a link will fail. The higher the reliability, the more preferred the path.

- **Cost**—A configured metric. The lower the cost, the more preferred the route.

Because each routing protocol has a unique application of metrics, we will discuss routing protocol specific metrics in the upcoming chapters.

Administrative Distance

At any given time, more than one routing protocol can be active on a router. The router needs a way to classify the routes received from one routing protocol against the routes received from another. Cisco uses the concept of *administrative distance* to measure the trustworthiness of the source of IP routing information. The lower the value of the administrative distance is, the more preferred the route is. The distance can be changed for each routing protocol with the **distance** command. Table IV-1 lists the default administrative distances of route sources.

Table IV-1   *Default Administrative Distances on Cisco Routers*

Route Source/Type	Default Administrative Distance
Connected interface	0
Static route pointing to an interface	0
Static route to a next-hop interface	1
EIGRP summary route	5
External BGP	20
EIGRP	90
IGRP	100
OSPF	110

continues

Table IV-1   *Default Administrative Distances on Cisco Routers (Continued)*

Route Source/Type	Default Administrative Distance
IS-IS	115
RIP-1 and RIP-2	120
EGP	140
External EIGRP	170
Internal BGP	200
Unknown route	255
Unreachable	

Distance Vector and Link-State Protocols

Most routing protocols can be divided into two major classes:

- Distance vector protocols
- Link-state protocols

Cisco's EIGRP is the exception and is often referred to as a *hybrid* protocol because it combines aspects of link-state and distance vector protocols. EIGRP is closer to a distance vector protocol than a link-state protocol because it uses metrics for distance and does not use the link states for routing advertisements.

Distance Vector Protocols

Distance vector-based algorithms, also known as Bellman-Ford algorithms, pass periodic copies of a route table from router to router. Regular updates between routers happen during topology changes. Distance vector protocols advertise routes in terms of *vectors*. Each vector has a distance and direction associated with it. For example, in RIP, the subnet 172.10.0.0 is the vector, its distance is five hops away, and the direction is the next-hop router.

Here is a simplistic way of how distance vector protocols operate:

1   At a specific timed interval, the router broadcasts its entire route table out each interface. It does not include routes suppressed by filters, split horizons, or routes that exist on a different major bit boundary than the interface sending the broadcast. The broadcast contains the network or route and a metric associated with that route.

2   Each adjacent router receives the update and compares the routes in the update to the routes in the route table. The routes with the best metric, the ones with the lower metric, are stored in the forwarding table.

3 Each adjacent router now propagates its new routing table route to all its neighbors.

4 The routers continue to broadcast their route tables to their neighbors at a periodic interval. RIP, for example, uses a periodic interval of 30 seconds.

All distance vector protocols have the following common characteristics:

- **Periodic full routing updates**—At the end of a certain time limit, usually 10 to 90 seconds, a full routing table is broadcast to every neighbor.

- **Neighbors**—Neighbors can be defined as routers sharing a common data link. Distance vector routers send updates to all neighbors and depend on them to pass along that information to their neighbors.

- **Broadcast updates**—The router uses a broadcast address to locate its neighbors and to advertise its route table.

- **Route invalidation timers**—These timers provide a means for the router to start to degrade the cost of the route and eventually remove it from the route table. The timers are reset when a new update is received.

- **Split horizon**—A route pointing back to the router where it was received is called a *reverse route*. Split horizon prevents reverse routes between routers. The rule of simple split horizons states that when sending an update out an interface or subinterface, do not include networks learned from that interface. Split horizon is enabled or enforced by default on all serial interfaces and subinterfaces. We discuss split horizons more throughout the book, especially how this relates to Frame Relay point-to-point and multipoint interfaces.

- **Maximum hop count or count to infinity**—Distance vector networks have a ceiling on how many hops a route can be away before the route is declared unreachable. RIP has a maximum hop count of 16.

- **Poison reverse**—The rule for poison reverse is to advertise a route out the interface on which it was received with an unreachable metric. Different routing protocols employ this rule at different times to control routing loops.

The following is a list of distance vector routing protocols:

- IP Routing Information Protocol (RIP)
- Xerox Networking System's XNS RIP
- IPX RIP
- Cisco's Internet Gateway Routing Protocol (IGRP)
- DEC's DNA Phase IV
- AppleTalk's Routing Table Maintenance Protocol (RTMP)
- Gateway-to-Gateway Protocol (GGP)
- Exterior Gateway Protocol (EGP)

Link-State Protocols

The other class of routing protocols is called link-state protocols. As distance vector protocols are based on algorithms by R.E. Bellman, L.R. Ford, and D.R. Fulkerson, link-state protocols are based on an algorithm by E.W. Dijkstra.

Link-state protocols operate in a significantly different manner than that of distance vector protocols. Some of the major differences include the following:

- **Support for variable-length subnet masking (VLSM)**—All link-state protocols support VLSM. One reason for this is because the routing update includes a subnet mask.

- **Neighbors**—All link-state environments establish neighbors through the use of a Hello protocol.

- **Nonstub routers**—Nonstub routers retain a complete map of all paths in the network.

- **Event-triggered routing announcements**—Routing updates are propagated by a means of flooding link states from one area to the next. The SPF/Dijkstra algorithm directs the flooding of LSAs.

- **Link-state database**—The link-state database stores link-state advertisements (LSAs) as a series of records. The information in the database includes a record of router IDs, connected networks, and adjacent routers, and the cost associated with them.

- **Hierarchical topology required**—External areas require connections to backbone areas. Link-state networks must be designed around these requirements. OSPF virtual links will allow this rule to be broken, but they should be avoided.

Here is a simplistic way of how link-state protocols operate:

1 The router establishes an adjacency with each of its neighbors.

2 Each router sends link-state advertisements (LSAs) or link-state packets (LSPs) to its neighbors. One LSA is generated for each route in the table. The LSA identifies the route, the state of the route, the cost or metric of the interface associated with the route, and any neighbors connected to the route. Each neighbor that receives an advertisement forwards it to its neighbors.

3 Each router stores a copy of all the LSAs that it has received in a database.

4 The database is called a link-state database. It contains a map or tree of the entire network. The router uses the Dijkstra algorithm and calculates a shortest path to each network; it enters this information into the routing table.

The most common link-state protocols are as follows:

- Open Shortest Path First (OSPF) for IP

- Intermediate System-to-Intermediate System, for ISO IS-IS

- DEC's DNA Phase V
- Novell's NetWare Link Services Protocol (NLSP)

Distance Vector Versus Link-State Routing Protocols

Table IV-2 highlights the major differences between distance vector and link-state routing protocols.

Table IV-2 *IP Routing Protocol Comparison*

	RIP-1	RIP-2	IGRP	EIGRP	OSPF	IS-IS
Split horizon–sensitive	X	X	X			
Periodic updates	X	X	X			
Triggered updates	X	X	X	X	X	X
VLSM support		X		X	X	X
Equal-path load balancing	X	X	X	X	X	X
Unequal-path load balancing			X	X		
Automatic classful route summarization	X*	X	X	X		
Manual classless route summarization				X	X	X
Routing metric	Hop count	Hop count	Delay, MTU load, BW, reliability	Delay, MTU load, BW, reliability	Cost	Default, delay, expense, error
Authentication type **Type 1—clear text** **Type 2—MD5**	None	Type 1 Type 2	None	Type 2	Type 1 Type 2	Type 1
Hop-count limit	15	15	255	255	Unlimited	1024

continues

Table IV-2   *IP Routing Protocol Comparison (Continued)*

	RIP-1	RIP-2	IGRP	EIGRP	OSPF	IS-IS
Hierarchical design required					X	X
Scalability	Small	Small	Medium	Large	Large	Very large
Routing algorithm	Bellman-Ford	Bellman-Ford	Bellman-Ford	DUAL	Dijkstra	IS-IS
Cisco administrative distance	120	120	100	90/5**	110	115

*   Route summarization cannot be disabled.

**   5 is the distance for an EIGRP summary route.

The upcoming chapters are intended to be a technical overview of the configuration of RIP, IGRP, EIGRP, and OSPF. For a thorough and, in my opinion, one of the best explanations of routing protocols, study Jeff Doyle's book, *Routing TCP/IP,* Volumes I and II.

CHAPTER 9

Distance Vector Protocols: Routing Information Protocol Versions 1 and 2 (RIP-1 and RIP-2)

As IP-based networks enter the 21st century, one of the earliest routing protocols is still present in many modern networks. For good reason, RIP has managed to survive from the creation of IP to the present. This proves one thing about RIP—despite its limitations, it performs its job well. RIP has evolved over the years from a classful routing protocol, RIP Version 1 (RIP-1), to a classless routing protocol, RIP Version 2 (RIP-2). This chapter covers the operation, configuration, and tuning of RIP-1 and RIP-2, in addition to information on route redistribution.

Technical Overview of RIP

RFC 1058 outlines RIP-1, and RFCs 1721, 1722, and 1723 are supplemental RFCs that allow for RIP-2 extensions.

NOTE   You can find all RFCs online at http://www.isi.edu/in-notes/rfc*xxxx*.txt, where *xxxx* is the number of the RFC.

RIP operates on UDP port 520—that is, all RIP packets have a source and destination port equal to 520. RIP operates in the following manner:

1 **Initialization**—When the RIP process initializes, it sends a *request packet* out each participating interface. This request packet asks for a full routing table update from all RIP routers. This request is accomplished by broadcasts on LANs and is sent to the next-hop address on point-to-point links. The request packet is a special request, querying the neighboring devices for a full routing table update.

2   **Request received**—RIP has two message types, a *response* and a *receive* message. Each route entry in the request packet is processed and a metric is formed for the route along with the path to the route. RIP uses the hop-count metric. A hop count of 1 means a directly connected network, whereas a hop count of 16 denotes an unreachable network. The entire routing table is sent back as a response received message.

3   **Response received**—The router receives and processes the response. It can update its routing table with the addition, deletion, or modification of entries.

4   **Regular routing updates and timers**—Every 30 seconds, the router sends out the entire routing table in the form of a response message to every neighboring router. The router sets an *expiration timer* or *invalid timer* of 180 seconds when a new route is received or an update about an existing route is received. If no new update for a route is received within 180 seconds, the hop count for the route is set to 16 (unreachable). The router advertises the route with a metric of 16 until the flush timer removes the route from the routing table. The *flush timer* is set to 240 seconds, or 60 seconds longer then the expiration timer. Cisco's implementation of RIP, which is not defined in RFC 1058, uses a third timer called a *hold-down timer*. The hold-down period occurs for 180 seconds after a route is received with a higher metric. During this time, the router does not update its routing table with the new information that it received, to provide additional time for convergence.

5   **Triggered routing updates**—Whenever a metric for a route changes, the router sends only the routes that are affected by the metric change. A full routing table is not sent.

All the timers can be changed with the **timers basic** *update invalid holddown flush* command.

CAUTION   When adjusting the timers for RIP, all the timers in the routing domain must also be adjusted. Failure to do so can cause many unpredictable results.

Classful Routing (RIP-1 Only)

RIP-1 is a classful routing protocol, so it does not advertise a subnet mask along with advertised routes. For RIP to determine what the subnet mask is of the destination network, RIP uses the subnet mask of the interface in which the route was received. This is true only if the route received is a member of a directly connected major network. If the route received is not of the same major network, the router tries to match only the major bit boundary of the route—either Class A, B, or C. For this reason, it is critical to preserve a consistent bit mask in each major network throughout the entire RIP routing domain.

Figure 9-1 illustrates classful routing on a RIP-1 network. Let's examine how the wolverine and rogue routers handle the RIP process.

Figure 9-1 *Classful Routing Example*

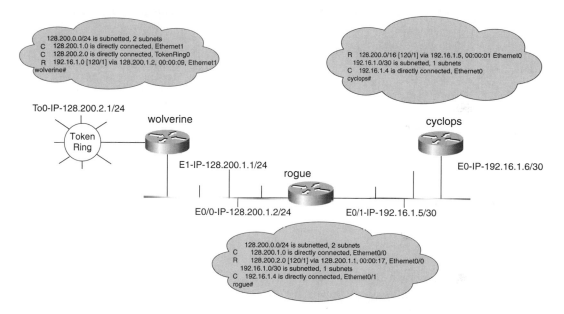

The wolverine router has two interfaces in the 128.200.0.0 major network. The 24-bit mask is consistent on every interface on the router. Therefore, the router receives updates only for the major network 128.200.0.0 on the 24-bit boundary. When the router receives the update out of this major network—for example, 192.16.1.4/30—it enters only a summary route in its routing table pointing to the major bit or class boundary of the address, summarizing the address to 192.16.1.0/24. Example 9-1 shows the output of **debug ip rip** demonstrating this concept.

Example 9-1 **debug ip rip** *Command Output on wolverine*

```
01:24:39: RIP: sending v1 update to 255.255.255.255 via Ethernet1 (128.200.1.1)
01:24:39:       subnet  128.200.2.0, metric 1
01:24:39: RIP: Update contains 1 routes
01:24:39: RIP: Update queued
01:24:39: RIP: Update sent via Ethernet1
01:24:39: RIP: sending v1 update to 255.255.255.255 via TokenRing0 (128.200.2.1)
01:24:39:       subnet  128.200.1.0, metric 1
01:24:39:       network 192.16.1.0, metric 2
01:24:39: RIP: Update contains 2 routes
01:24:39: RIP: Update queued
01:24:39: RIP: Update sent via TokenRing0
```

The rogue router has two interfaces. One is in the 128.200.0.0/16 major network, and the other is in the 192.16.1.0/24 network. When the rogue router receives the 128.200.2.0/24 and 128.200.1.0/24 subnets from its E0/0 interface, it tries to send them out its E0/1 interface. Because this interface has a different mask (30-bit), only the summary route 128.200.0.0/16 is sent to the cyclops router. Example 9-2 demonstrates this happening, through the aid of **debug ip rip**.

Example 9-2   **debug ip rip** *Command Output on rogue*

```
RIP: received v1 update from 128.200.1.1 on Ethernet0/0
     128.200.2.0 in 1 hops
RIP: sending v1 update to 255.255.255.255 via Ethernet0/0 (128.200.1.2)
     network 192.16.1.0, metric 1
RIP: sending v1 update to 255.255.255.255 via Ethernet0/1 (192.16.1.5)
     network 128.200.0.0, metric 1
```

Classless Routing (RIP-2 Only)

RIP-2 is not a new routing protocol, but it is an extension of RIP-1 provided by RFCs 1721, 1722, and 1723. The extensions provide the following enhancements to RIP:

- VLSM support. The router carries the subnet mask in the update, which allows the router to handle VLSM addressing.

- A next-hop address carried with each route entry.

- Support for external route tags.

- Multicast route updates.

- Support for MD5 authentication.

The most significant of all the enhancements is the support for VLSM, making RIP-2 a classless routing protocol. It is no longer critical to have one bit mask throughout the entire routing domain.

Most of RIP-2 operational procedures and timers are identical to those of RIP-1. RIP-2 uses the multicast address of 224.0.0.9 to send updates versus the general all-hosts broadcast used by RIP-1.

RIP-2 is fully backward compatible with RIP-1. This is accomplished by the means of a *compatibility switch* and a *receive control switch*, as defined in RFC 1723. Essentially, these switches allow you to control what type of RIP updates the router sends and receives. The router can be configured to receive only Version 1 updates, only Version 2 updates, both, or none. The router can send only Version 1 updates, send Version 2 updates as a broadcast message, send Version 2 updates as a multicast, or send no updates. The switches can be manually set with the following interface command:

```
ip rip [send | receive] version [1 | 2 | 1 2]
```

Configuring RIP-1 and RIP-2

The configuration of RIP-1 and RIP-2 is a straightforward task:

Step 1   Enable RIP and the version of RIP on the router. To enable RIP, use the **router rip** global command. At this time, also configure the version of RIP. If you want RIP-1, no additional configuration is necessary. For RIP-2, use the **version 2** command from the **config-router#** prompt.

Step 2   Add the networks on which you want to want to run RIP. This is accomplished with the command **network a.b.c.d** from the **config-router#** prompt.

Configuring RIP-1

Example 9-3 illustrates the configuration of RIP-1 on the network previously illustrated in Figure 9-1.

Example 9-3   *RIP-1 Configuration*

```
hostname wolverine
!
router rip
 network 128.200.0.0
!

hostname rogue
!
router rip
 network 128.200.0.0
 network 192.16.1.0
!

hostname cyclops
!
router rip
 network 192.16.1.0
!
```

Configuring RIP-2

Let's update the network from Figure 9-1 to a RIP-2 network. You will configure the Token Ring network on wolverine to send and receive both RIP-1 and RIP-2 updates. The Ethernet segment off wolverine, however, will send and receive only Version 2 updates. The rogue and cyclops routers will be configured to send and receive only RIP-2 updates. Example 9-4 shows the necessary router configurations to match this criteria.

Example 9-4 *RIP-2 Configuration*

```
hostname wolverine
!
interface Ethernet1
 ip address 128.200.1.1 255.255.255.0
 ip rip send version 2
 ip rip receive version 2
 media-type 10BaseT
!
interface TokenRing0
 ip address 128.200.2.1 255.255.255.0
 ip rip send version 1 2
 ip rip receive version 1 2
 ring-speed 16
!
router rip
 version 2
 network 128.200.0.0
 no auto-summary
```

```
hostname rogue
!
interface Ethernet0/0
 ip address 128.200.1.2 255.255.255.0
 ip rip send version 2
 ip rip receive version 2
!
interface Ethernet0/1
 ip address 192.16.1.5 255.255.255.252
 ip rip send version 2
 ip rip receive version 2
!
router rip
 version 2
 network 128.200.0.0
 network 192.16.1.0
 no auto-summary
```

```
hostname cyclops
!
interface Ethernet0
 ip address 192.16.1.6 255.255.255.252
 ip rip send version 2
 ip rip receive version 2
!
router rip
 version 2
 network 192.16.1.0
 no auto-summary
```

Figure 9-2 illustrates the changes in the routing tables after migrating the network to RIP-2. Notice how the individual subnets appear on wolverine and cyclops routers. Even though you are now sending RIP-2 updates, you must also use the **no auto-summary** command to prevent automatic summarization at the major class boundary.

Figure 9-2   *Classless Routing Example*

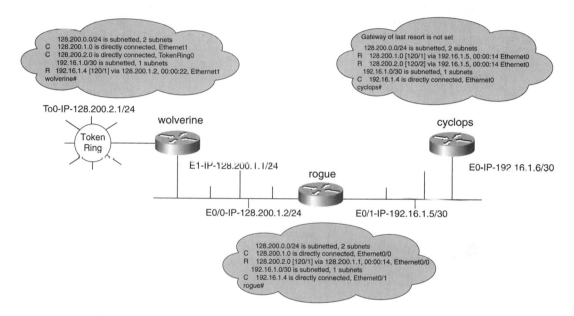

The "Big show" and "Big D" for RIP

Troubleshooting RIP can be an easy process. Most of the RIP configuration errors involve a bad **network** statement, discontinuous subnets, or split horizons. Because most of these errors are design-related, the **debug** and **show** commands for RIP are limited. Again, the list that follows is not a complete list; instead, it's a condensed list of what I find to the most useful **show** and **debug** commands. The "Big **show**" and the "Big D" commands for RIP are as follows:

- **show ip protocols** {**summary**}
- **show ip route**
- **debug ip rip** {**events**}

show ip protocols {summary} Command

This command displays all routing protocols, detailed timer and metric information, and routing update information. Example 9-5 lists the output of the **show ip protocols** command.

Example 9-5 **show ip protocols** *Command Output*

```
rogue#show ip protocols
Routing Protocol is "rip"  ←Routing Protocol Type
  Sending updates every 30 seconds, next due in 29 seconds
  Invalid after 180 seconds, hold down 180, flushed after 240   ←Timer information
  Outgoing update filter list for all interfaces is        ←Distribut list (if any)
  Incoming update filter list for all interfaces is
  Default redistribution metric is 2             ←Default metric
  Redistributing: rip, eigrp 2001              ←Redistrution is on
  Default version control: send version 1, receive any version
    Interface        Send  Recv   Key-chain
    Ethernet0/0        1    1 2   ←RIP Versions running
  Routing for Networks:        ←Networks participating in RIP
    128.200.0.0
  Passive Interface(s):
    Ethernet0/1            ←Network listening to RIP
  Routing Information Sources:
    Gateway          Distance     Last Update
    128.200.1.1         120       00:00:07 ←RIP Neighbors
  Distance: (default is 120)        ←Administrative Distance
```

show ip route Command

This command lists the router's current routing table and the one on which it makes forwarding decisions. It is possible for a route to exist or be known to the router but then have only the routes with the shortest administrative distances listed. The output from this command lists what routing protocol the route is from—in the case of Example 9-6, R for RIP. The number behind the route is the administrative distance of the route followed by the hop count. The Via field explains who the route is from, how long ago an update was received, and by what interface. Example 9-6 lists the output of the **show ip route** command used on the rogue router.

Example 9-6 **show ip route** *Command Output*

```
rogue#show ip route
Gateway of last resort is not set

     128.200.0.0/16 is variably subnetted, 4 subnets, 2 masks
R       128.200.10.0/24 [120/1] via 128.200.1.1, 00:00:17, Ethernet0/0
C       128.200.1.0/24 is directly connected, Ethernet0/0
R       128.200.2.0/24 [120/1] via 128.200.1.1, 00:00:17, Ethernet0/0
C       128.200.3.16/29 is directly connected, Ethernet0/1
rogue#
```

In this example, the route 128.200.10.0/24 has a metric of 120 and is one hop away. The RIP neighbor informing about the route is 128.200.1.1, and it sent the last update 17 seconds ago; rogue received it through its Ethernet 0/0 port.

debug ip rip {events} Command

This command shows all the RIP activity occurring in the router and also displays exactly which interfaces are advertising and receiving routes. The RIP version of the update is also displayed, along with the metric of each route in the update. Example 9-7 lists the output of the **debug ip rip** command. Notice that RIP is sending and receiving routes.

Example 9-7   debug ip rip *Command Output*

```
wolverine#debug ip rip
1d02h: RIP: received v1 update from 128.200.10.2 on TokenRing1
1d02h:      128.200.10.0 in 1 hops
1d02h: RIP: sending v1 update to 255.255.255.255 via Ethernet1 (128.200.1.1)
1d02h:      subnet  128.200.10.0, metric 1
1d02h:      subnet  128.200.2.0, metric 1
1d02h: RIP: sending v1 update to 255.255.255.255 via TokenRing0 (128.200.2.1)
1d02h:      subnet  128.200.10.0, metric 1
1d02h:      subnet  128.200.1.0, metric 1
1d02h: RIP: sending v1 update to 128.200.10.2 via TokenRing1 (128.200.10.1)
1d02h:      subnet  128.200.10.0, metric 1
1d02h:      subnet  128.200.1.0, metric 1
1d02h:      subnet  128.200.2.0, metric 1
```

Tuning, Redistribution, and Control of RIP Updates

RIP offers several parameters for tuning timers, controlling broadcasts, and controlling routes. The following is a list of some of the common parameters adjustable within RIP:

- Router(config-router)**timers basic** *update invalid holddown flush*—This allows the user to set the update, invalid, hold-down, and flush timers for RIP.

- Router(config-router)**passive-interface** *interface_name*—This command prevents the sending of routing updates on a interface; however, the router still listens to updates received from that interface.

- Router(config-router)**neighbor** *ip-address*—This command defines a RIP neighbor to exchange unicast updates with. This command should be used in conjunction with the **passive-interface** command.

- Router(config-router)**offset-list** [*access_list_0-99* {**in**|**out**} **offset** [**metric_ offset_1-16**]—Use this command to increase the value of the routing metrics. The metric offset cannot exceed 16.

The following commands are not exclusive to RIP and can be used with other routing protocols:

- Router(config-router)**distribute-list** [**1-199**] [**in** | **out**] [**interface**]—Use this command to call a standard or extended access list to filter inbound or outbound routing updates.

- Router(config-router)**distance** [**1-255**] **adjacent_neighbors_ip_address wildcard_mask** [*access_list_0-99*]—Use this command to change the administrative distance of routes received from a neighbor. If the IP address and wildcard mask are omitted, all routes for that protocol will be set to the distance value.

- Router(config-router)**redistribute** [**connected, static, bgp, igrp, eigrp, ospf, isis**] {*metric*} {*route-map*}—Use this command to redistribute other routing protocols into RIP. A route map may be added for additional route control. This sets the metric to be used for the redistribution of this specific protocol and the specified autonomous system, if the protocol uses one. The other option for setting the redistribute metrics is to use the **default-metric** command discussed in the item that follows. Whenever redistributing routes, remember that IP needs a route *to and from* a destination. Many times, mutual redistribution might be required to give IP a path to and from its destination.

- Router(config-router)**default-metric** [**1-16**]—Use this command to set the default metric of all routes redistributed into RIP. You must supply a default metric whenever redistributing.

To see how some of these concepts work, apply some to the existing lab. Figure 9-3 changes the subnet between rogue and cyclops to 128.200.3.16/29. Instead of RIP on this segment, run EIGRP as the routing protocol. Redistribute between EIGRP and RIP on the rogue router. As Figure 9-3 shows, another router, storm, has been integrated into the network. Instead of running broadcast updates on the Token Ring segment between the storm and wolverine routers, run unicast updates.

To configure RIP unicast between storm and wolverine, you must first use the **passive-interface** command to prevent RIP broadcasts from entering the Token Ring network. Next, add a **neighbor** statement to point to the router in which RIP updates are to be sent. Example 9-8 lists the RIP configuration of wolverine and storm.

Example 9-8 *RIP Unicast Configuration*

```
hostname wolverine
!
router rip
 passive-interface TokenRing1
 network 128.200.0.0
 neighbor 128.200.10.2
```

Example 9-8   *RIP Unicast Configuration (Continued)*

```
hostname storm
!
router rip
 passive-interface TokenRing0
 network 128.200.0.0
 neighbor 128.200.10.1
```

Figure 9-3   *Route Redistribution and Unicast Example*

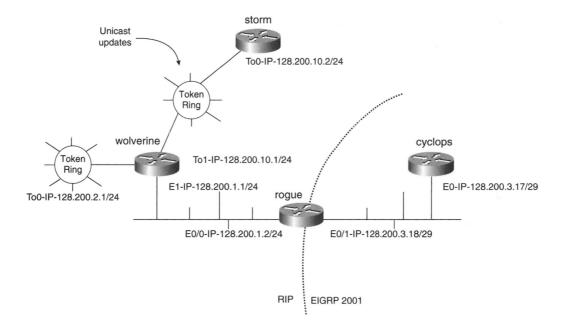

The next step is to perform mutual redistribution between EIGRP and RIP on the rogue router. Because there is only one redistribution point in the network, there is no need to perform any route filtering when using mutual redistribution. To redistribute between EIGRP and RIP, use the **redistribution** command, along with adding a default metric. The default metric chosen for RIP is 3, whereas 10000 1000 254 1 1500 is the default metric for EIGRP. Because the routing domains overlap (which means that RIP broadcasts will be heard on cyclops), use the **passive-interface** command to prevent excessive broadcasts from occurring. Example 9-9 lists the configuration of EIGRP and RIP on the rogue router.

Example 9-9 *EIGRP and RIP Configuration on rogue*

```
router eigrp 2001
 redistribute rip
 passive-interface Ethernet0/0
 network 128.200.0.0
 default-metric 10000 1000 254 1 1500
 no auto-summary
!
router rip
 redistribute eigrp 2001
 passive-interface Ethernet0/1
 network 128.200.0.0
 default-metric 2
```

At this point, the network is close to being complete. However, if you observe the routing table on storm, you see that it does not have a route to 128.200.3.16/29, as illustrated in Figure 9-4.

Figure 9-4 *Route Table Discrepancies: RIP/EIGRP Network Before Summarization*

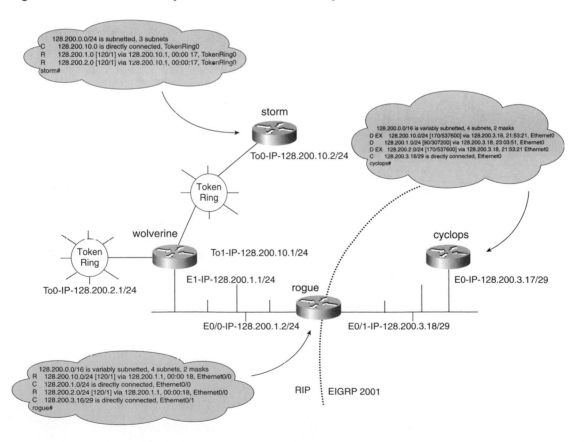

Because the Ethernet segment between rogue and cyclops is on a 29-bit boundary, and because the segment between rogue and wolverine is on a 24-bit boundary, the rogue router will not forward any 29-bit network updates out its E0/0 port. Performing a **debug ip rip** command on the rogue router as done in Example 9-10 substantiates this.

Example 9-10 **debug ip rip** *Command Output from rogue*

```
rogue#debug ip rip
RIP protocol debugging is on
RIP: sending v1 update to 255.255.255.255 via Ethernet0/0 (128.200.1.2) -
   suppressing null update    ←-no 128.200.3.x route
RIP: received v1 update from 128.200.1.1 on Ethernet0/0
     128.200.10.0 in 1 hops
     128.200.2.0 in 1 hops
RIP: sending v1 update to 255.255.255.255 via Ethernet0/0 (128.200.1.2) -
   suppressing null update
RIP: received v1 update from 128.200.1.1 on Ethernet0/0
     128.200.10.0 in 1 hops
     128.200.2.0 in 1 hops
rogue#
```

To allow full IP reachability between cyclops and storm, the route between them must be summarized on a 24-bit boundary. To accomplish this, use the following command on the cyclops router:

```
cyclops(config-if)#ip summary-address eigrp 2001 128.200.3.0 255.255.255.0
```

Observing the routing table on rogue, as in Figure 9-5, an EIGRP route 128.200.3.0/24 now exists. Because the route has a 24-bit mask, rogue can forward it out its E0/0 port, where storm will eventually receive the route.

CAUTION   Caution should be used whenever redistributing one routing protocol into another. Potential routing loops can occur if there are two or more redistribution points within the network. If there is only one redistribution point, inherent loop prevention within the routing protocol will be sufficient enough to prevent loops. When multiple redistribution points are in the network, distance vector protocols are vulnerable to loops. Use the route maps with a well-thought-out IP addressing scheme to control loops.

Figure 9-5 *Route Table Discrepancies Resolved: RIP/EIGRP Network After Summarization*

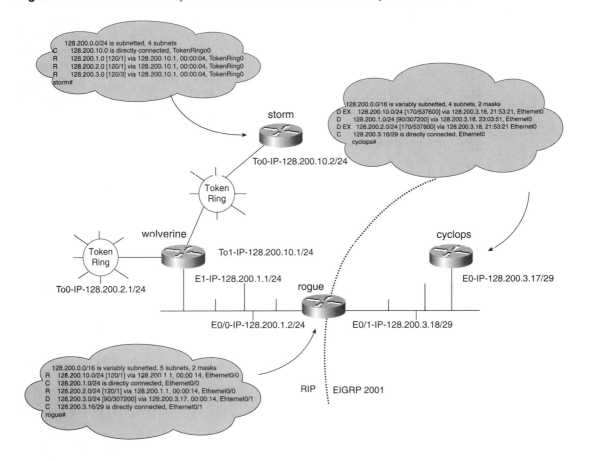

128.200.0.0/24 is subnetted, 4 subnets
C   128.200.10.0 is directly connected, TokenRing0
R   128.200.1.0 [120/1] via 128.200.10.1, 00:00:04, TokenRing0
R   128.200.2.0 [120/1] via 128.200.10.1, 00:00:04, TokenRing0
R   128.200.3.0 [120/3] via 128.200.10.1, 00:00:04, TokenRing0
storm#

128.200.0.0/16 is variably subnetted, 4 subnets, 2 masks
D EX 128.200.10.0/24 [170/537600] via 128.200.3.18, 21:53:21, Ethernet0
D   128.200.1.0/24 [90/307200] via 128.200.3.18, 23:03:51, Ethernet0
D EX 128.200.2.0/24 [170/537600] via 128.200.3.18, 21:53:21 Ethernet0
C   128.200.3.16/29 is directly connected, Ethernet0
cyclops#

storm

To0-IP-128.200.10.2/24

Token Ring

wolverine

Token Ring

To1-IP-128.200.10.1/24

cyclops

E0-IP-128.200.3.17/29

E1-IP-128.200.1.1/24

rogue

To0-IP-128.200.2.1/24

E0/0-IP-128.200.1.2/24   E0/1-IP-128.200.3.18/29

128.200.0.0/16 is variably subnetted, 5 subnets, 2 masks
R 128.200.10.0/24 [120/1] via 128.200.1.1, 00:00:14, Ethernet0/0
C 128.200.1.0/24 is directly connected, Ethernet0/0
R 128.200.2.0/24 [120/1] via 128.200.1.1, 00:00:14, Ethernet0/0
D 128.200.3.0/24 [90/307200] via 128.200.3.17, 00:00:14, Ethernet0/1
C 128.200.3.16/29 is directly connected, Ethernet0/1
rogue#

RIP : EIGRP 2001

TIP

Whenever you are working with routing protocols that don't carry a subnet mask within the routing update, such as RIP-1 and IGRP, be extremely careful to preserve a consistent bit mask throughout the entire internetwork. For example, a RIP domain might be operating on 24-bit boundary, whereas an OSPF domain might have some LAN networks at the 24-bit boundary, but its entire WAN is using a 30-bit boundary. The RIP domain will have no problem reaching the LANs because of the bit boundary match; however, it will not be capable of reaching the WAN interfaces. To allow full reachability between the two domains, the OSPF WAN networks that reside on a 30-bit boundary must be summarized to a 24-bit boundary before redistribution into RIP.

RIP Default Routing

A default route is necessary whenever connecting the Internet. Without it, the router would need a path to every single network in its routing table. A default route is configured to point to a gateway of last resort. When a router cannot find a specific match in its route table for a packet, it forwards that packet to the gateway of last resort. Cisco routers always perform classful route lookups, which means that they will not forward packets to a gateway of last resort unless the global **ip classless** command is set. The **ip classless** command is enabled by default in Cisco IOS Software Release 11.3 and later.

The concept of default routing varies by each routing protocol. Each routing protocol uses a specific method when defining and advertising a default route.

There are two steps to perform when configuring default routing with RIP:

Step 1 Define or *flag* a default network. There are two ways to accomplish this. First, RIP will recognize the address of 0.0.0.0 as a default route. Default routes like this are created by adding a static route of all 0s, as in **ip route 0.0.0.0 0.0.0.0 a.b.c.d**, to the router. When this static route is created, it is not necessary to redistribute it into RIP. It will be propagated automatically by RIP. The second way to *flag* a route as a default is through the **ip default-network a.b.c.d** command.

Step 2 Ensure that **ip classless** is enabled on the router. Without **ip classless**, routers will not forward traffic to the gateway of last resort.

In Figure 9-6, the dr_xavier router was added to the network from the previous examples. This router has a default route to the Internet, through Internet_router/Firewall. This example uses a default static route to mark the route as the default. Adding the **ip route 0.0.0.0 0.0.0.0 206.191.240.2** command to the dr_xavier router propagates a default route to rogue and cyclops. The route table for the dr_xavier router marks this route with an *, meaning that the route is the candidate default. When the route is propagated to a downstream router, it becomes a gateway of last resort, as shown in Figure 9-6.

Example 9-11 lists the configuration of the dr_xavier router.

Example 9-11 *Relevant Portions of the dr_xavier Configuration*

```
!
router rip
 network 128.200.0.0
 network 206.191.240.0
!
ip classless
ip route 0.0.0.0 0.0.0.0 206.191.240.2
!
```

Figure 9-6 *RIP Default Routing*

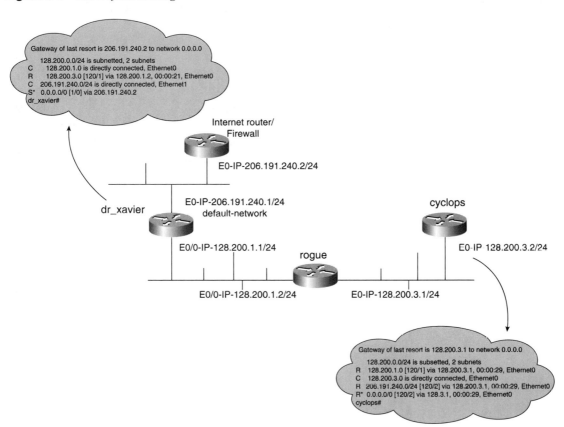

Gateway of last resort is 206.191.240.2 to network 0.0.0.0

128.200.0.0/24 is subnetted, 2 subnets
C   128.200.1.0 is directly connected, Ethernet0
R   128.200.3.0 [120/1] via 128.200.1.2, 00:00:21, Ethernet0
C   206.191.240.0/24 is directly connected, Ethernet1
S*   0.0.0.0/0 [1/0] via 206.191.240.2
dr_xavier#

Internet router/
Firewall

E0-IP-206.191.240.2/24

cyclops

dr_xavier   E0-IP-206.191.240.1/24
default-network

E0-IP 128.200.3.2/24

E0/0-IP-128.200.1.1/24   rogue

E0/0-IP-128.200.1.2/24   E0-IP-128.200.3.1/24

Gateway of last resort is 128.200.3.1 to network 0.0.0.0

128.200.0.0/24 is subsetted, 2 subnets
R   128.200.1.0 [120/1] via 128.200.3.1, 00:00:29, Ethernet0
C   128.200.3.0 is directly connected, Ethernet0
R   206.191.240.0/24 [120/2] via 128.200.3.1, 00:00:29, Ethernet0
R*   0.0.0.0/0 [120/2] via 128.3.1, 00:00:29, Ethernet0
cyclops#

Lab 20: Integrating RIP Networks: Redistribution, Route Filtering, and Control—Part I

Practical Scenario

RIP is still one of the most common routing protocols in use today. Although it might not be the dominant protocol on most major internetworks, RIP domains remain sprinkled throughout the internetwork. Integrating these domains and compensating for RIP's lack of support for VLSM can be challenging. This lab gives you practice in integrating RIP and controlling routing updates.

Lab Exercise

Habano Net runs distribution and export information for some of the finest cigar manufactures in the world. Information in Habano Net flows from cigar makers, such as montecristo and romeo_y_julieta to habanos. From here, habanos has connections to worldwide importers, such as churchill_imports. The task will be to integrate the RIP network of the cigar makers to the EIGRP networks of the exporters. Use the following parameters as your design guidelines:

- Use the IP subnet 150.100.100.0/24 for the Frame Relay network between the habanos, montecristo, and romeo_y_julieta routers. Use RIP as the routing protocol. Ensure that montecristo has IP connectivity to romeo_y_julieta.

- Use the IP subnet of 150.100.200.0/30 for the Frame Relay link between the habanos and churchill_imports router. Use EIGRP with 2001 as the autonomous system for the routing protocol.

- Mutually redistribute RIP into EIGRP on the habanos router. Ensure full IP reachability across the entire network.

- Prevent the subnet 150.100.10.0/24 on the habanos router from reaching montecristo and romeo_y_julieta.

- (Optional) Configure the habanos router so that all routes from romeo_y_julieta have an administrative distance of 5.

Lab Objectives

- Configure Habano Net as depicted in Figure 9-7, and configure IP as denoted as well. The LAN topology type is not important in this lab.

- Use Frame Relay as the data-link protocol on the WAN.

- Configure RIP and EIGRP as shown in Figure 9-7. Redistribute between RIP and EIGRP to provide full IP connectivity across the network. Prevent excess routing protocol broadcasts from entering segments that are not running that protocol.

- Prevent the subnet 150.100.10.0/24 on the habanos router from reaching montecristo and romeo_y_julieta.

- (Optional) Adjust the administrative distance of routes originating from romeo_y_julieta.

Equipment Needed

- Five Cisco routers, connected through V.35 back-to-back cable or in a similar fashion. One router will serve as a frame switch and require four serial ports.

- Four LAN segments, provided through hubs or switches.

Physical Layout and Prestaging

- Configure a Frame Relay switch to provide the PVCs as listed in Figure 9-7. See Chapter 1, "The Key Components for Modeling an Internetwork," if you need assistance in configuring a Frame Relay switch. Example 9-12 provides a sample Frame Relay switch configuration.

- Connect the hubs and serial cables to the routers as shown in Figure 9-7.

Example 9-12 *Frame Relay Switch Configuration*

```
hostname frame_switch
!
frame-relay switching
!
interface Serial0
 no ip address
 encapsulation frame-relay
 no fair-queue
 clockrate 148000
 frame-relay intf-type dce
 frame-relay route 121 interface Serial1 120
!
interface Serial1
 no ip address
 encapsulation frame-relay
 clockrate 148000
 frame-relay intf-type dce
 frame-relay route 110 interface Serial5 111
 frame-relay route 120 interface Serial0 121
 frame-relay route 130 interface Serial3 131
```

continues

Example 9-12 *Frame Relay Switch Configuration (Continued)*

```
!
interface Serial3
 no ip address
 encapsulation frame-relay
 clockrate 64000
 frame-relay intf-type dce
 frame-relay route 131 interface Serial1 130
!
interface Serial5
 no ip address
 encapsulation frame-relay
 clockrate 64000
 frame-relay intf-type dce
 frame-relay route 111 interface Serial1 110
!
```

Figure 9-7   *Habano Net*

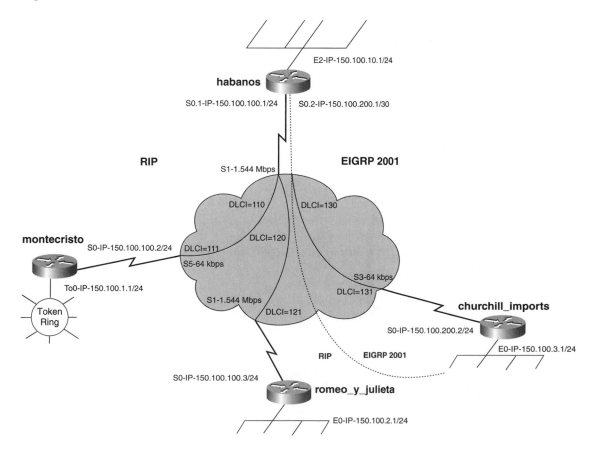

Lab 20: Integrating RIP Networks: Redistribution, Route Filtering, and Control—Part II

Lab Walkthrough

Attach the four routers in a back-to-back manner to the Frame Relay switch. Use V.35 cables or CSU/DSUs with crossover cables to connect the routers to the Frame Relay switch. Create the four LANs by the use of switches or hubs/MAUs.

When the physical connections are complete, assign IP addresses to all LAN interfaces, as depicted in Figure 9-7. Be sure that you can **ping** the router's local LAN interface before moving on.

First, we will focus on configuring the routers in the RIP domain. Start by configuring a multipoint subinterface on the habanos router. The network between habanos, montecristo, and romeo_y_julieta is a multipoint network, so you need to use **frame-relay map** statements. Example 9-13 shows this portion of the Frame Relay configuration.

Example 9-13 *Frame Relay Configuration Part 1—RIP*

```
! hostname habanos
!
interface Serial0.1 multipoint
 ip address 150.100.100.1 255.255.255.0
 no arp frame-relay
 frame-relay map ip 150.100.100.2 110 broadcast
 frame-relay map ip 150.100.100.3 120 broadcast
 no frame-relay inverse-arp
```
```
hostname montecristo
!
 interface Serial0
 ip address 150.100.100.2 255.255.255.0
 no ip directed-broadcast
 encapsulation frame-relay
 no ip mroute-cache
 frame-relay map ip 150.100.100.1 111 broadcast
 frame-relay map ip 150.100.100.3 111 broadcast
 frame-relay lmi-type cisco
```
```
hostname romeo_y_julieta
!
interface Serial0
 ip address 150.100.100.3 255.255.255.0
 no ip directed-broadcast
 encapsulation frame-relay
 no ip mroute-cache
```

Example 9-13 *Frame Relay Configuration Part 1—RIP (Continued)*

```
frame-relay map ip 150.100.100.1 121 broadcast
frame-relay map ip 150.100.100.2 121 broadcast
frame-relay lmi-type cisco
```

At this point, you should be able to **ping** the WAN interfaces that you configured.

To configure RIP, use the **router rip** and the **network 150.100.0.0** commands on each router in the RIP domain. Because the Frame Relay network is a multipoint network, you need to disable split horizons on the habanos router. Without disabling split horizons, the montecristo Token Ring network will not propagate to the romeo_y_julieta router. The opposite also is true. To disable split –horizons, use the **no ip split-horizon** command on the Serial0.1 interface on the habanos router.

Now that the RIP domain is complete, let's begin to configure the EIGRP domain. The first step is to configure a Frame Relay point-to-point network between the habanos and churchill_imports router. Example 9-14 shows the configuration, which uses Frame Relay inverse ARP.

Example 9-14 *Frame Relay Configuration Part 2—EIGRP*

```
! hostname habanos
!
interface Serial0.2 point-to-point
 ip address 150.100.200.1 255.255.255.252
 frame-relay interface-dlci 130
!
─────────────────────────────────────────────
!
hostname churchill_imports
!
interface Serial0
 ip address 150.100.200.2 255.255.255.252
 encapsulation frame-relay
 no fair-queue
 frame-relay interface-dlci 131
!
```

The EIGRP configuration is almost identical to the RIP configuration. Use the **router eigrp 2001** command along with the **network 150.100.0.0** statement on the habanos and churchill_imports routers. If you need more assistance in configuring EIGRP, see Chapter 11, "Hybrid: Enhanced Interior Gateway Routing Protocol (EIGRP)."

To have full IP connectivity, you need to mutually redistribute between RIP and EIGRP on the habanos router. To accomplish this, use the **redistribute** command along with a default metric. The default metric for RIP is 2, and the default metric for EIGRP is 10000 1000 254 1 1500. Use the **passive-interface** command to avoid sending both RIP and EIGRP route updates out the same interface. Example 9-15 shows the updated configuration on habanos.

Example 9-15 *Routing Protocol Configuration on habanos*

```
! hostname habanos
!
router eigrp 2001
  redistribute rip              ←Redistributing RIP
  passive-interface Ethernet2        ←Prevents EIGRP broadcasts
  passive-interface Serial0.1
  network 150.100.0.0
  default-metric 10000 1000 254 1 1500
!
router rip
  redistribute eigrp 2001        ←Redistributing EIGRP
  passive-interface Serial0.2       ←Prevents RIP broadcasts
  network 150.100.0.0
  default-metric 2
!
```

You now should have a full routing table on the churhcill_imports router. You can see two EIGRP routes, 150.100.100.0/24 and 150.100.10.0/24 because the EIGRP distance is lower then that of RIP. You can also see two external EIGRP routes, 150.100.2.0/24 and 150.100.1.0/24, which come from RIP being redistributed into EIGRP. Example 9-16 shows the updated routing table for the churchill_imports router.

Example 9-16 *Routing Table of churchill_imports*

```
churchill_imports#show ip route
<<<text omitted>>>
     150.100.0.0/16 is variably subnetted, 6 subnets, 2 masks
C       150.100.200.0/30 is directly connected, Serial0
D       150.100.100.0/24 [90/2681856] via 150.100.200.1, 00:29:52, Serial0
D EX    150.100.2.0/24 [170/2425856] via 150.100.200.1, 00:18:01, Serial0
C       150.100.3.0/24 is directly connected, Ethernet0
D EX    150.100.1.0/24 [170/2425856] via 150.100.200.1, 00:18:01, Serial0
D       150.100.10.0/24 [90/2195456] via 150.100.200.1, 00:29:52, Serial0
churchill_imports#
```

The configuration is almost complete; however, if you observe the routing table on montecristo in Example 9-17, you see that the 150.100.200.0/30 route is missing from the table.

Example 9-17 *Routing Table of montecristo*

```
montecristo#show ip route
<<<text omitted>>>
     150.100.0.0/24 is subnetted, 5 subnets
C       150.100.100.0 is directly connected, Serial0
R       150.100.2.0 [120/2] via 150.100.100.1, 00:00:05, Serial0
R       150.100.3.0 [120/2] via 150.100.100.1, 00:00:05, Serial0
C       150.100.1.0 is directly connected, TokenRing0
R       150.100.10.0 [120/1] via 150.100.100.1, 00:00:05, Serial0
montecristo#
```

The 150.100.200.0/30 route is missing from the table because the bit mask is on a 30-bit boundary, and RIP does not forward the update out the Serial0.1 port of the habanos router. To remedy this, you need to summarize EIGRP on a 24-bit boundary on the Frame Relay link between habanos and the churchill_imports routers. To summarize the route, use the **ip summary-address eigrp 2001 150.100.200.0 255.255.255.0** command on the Serial 0 interface of the churchill_imports router. You now can observe the routing table on montecristo and see that it has a summary route to 150.100.200.0/24, as demonstrated in Example 9-18.

Example 9-18 *Complete Routing Table on montecristo*

```
montecristo#show ip route
<<<text omitted>>>
     150.100.0.0/24 is subnetted, 6 subnets
R       150.100.200.0 [120/2] via 150.100.100.1, 00:00:02, Serial0
C       150.100.100.0 is directly connected, Serial0
R       150.100.2.0 [120/2] via 150.100.100.1, 00:00:02, Serial0
R       150.100.3.0 [120/2] via 150.100.100.1, 00:00:02, Serial0
C       150.100.1.0 is directly connected, TokenRing0
R       150.100.10.0 [120/1] via 150.100.100.1, 00:00:02, Serial0
montecristo#
```

TIP   When you are modeling complex networks, it might take a while for network convergence and routes to propagate. You can force a route update to speed this process along by using the **clear ip route *** command. This flushes all routes and force routing updates to happen.

When you have full IP connectivity, you can start to filter routes. In this model, you want prevent the route 150.100.10.0/24 from being propagated to the montecristo and romeo_y_julieta routers. To accomplish this, use a **distribute-list out** under the RIP portion of the habanos router. You also need to define an access list filtering out the network 150.100.10.0. Example 9-19 shows the final configurations.

Example 9-19 *Complete Routing Listings*

```
hostname habanos
!
interface Ethernet2
 ip address 150.100.10.1 255.255.255.0
 media-type 10BaseT
interface Serial0
 no ip address
 encapsulation frame-relay
 no ip mroute-cache
!
interface Serial0.1 multipoint
 ip address 150.100.100.1 255.255.255.0
 no ip split-horizon
 no arp frame-relay
 frame-relay map ip 150.100.100.2 110 broadcast
 frame-relay map ip 150.100.100.3 120 broadcast
 no frame-relay inverse-arp
!
interface Serial0.2 point-to-point
 ip address 150.100.200.1 255.255.255.252
 frame-relay interface-dlci 130
!
router eigrp 2001
 redistribute rip
 passive-interface Ethernet2
 passive-interface Serial0.1
 network 150.100.0.0
 default-metric 10000 1000 254 1 1500
!
router rip
 redistribute eigrp 2001
 passive-interface Serial0.2
 network 150.100.0.0
 default-metric 2
 distribute-list 10 out Serial0.1
!
ip classless
!
access-list 10 deny    150.100.10.0 0.0.0.255
access-list 10 permit any
```
```
hostname montecristo
!
ip subnet-zero
 !
 interface Serial0
 ip address 150.100.100.2 255.255.255.0
 no ip directed-broadcast
 encapsulation frame-relay
 no ip mroute-cache
 frame-relay map ip 150.100.100.1 111 broadcast
```

Example 9-19 *Complete Routing Listings (Continued)*

```
 frame-relay map ip 150.100.100.3 111 broadcast
 frame-relay lmi-type cisco
!
interface TokenRing0
 ip address 150.100.1.1 255.255.255.0
 no ip directed-broadcast
 ring-speed 16
!
router rip
 network 150.100.0.0
!
ip classless

hostname romeo_y_julieta
!
ip subnet-zero
!
 interface Ethernet0
 ip address 150.100.2.1 255.255.255.0
 no ip directed-broadcast
!
interface Serial0
 ip address 150.100.100.3 255.255.255.0
 no ip directed-broadcast
 encapsulation frame-relay
 no ip mroute-cache
 frame-relay map ip 150.100.100.1 121 broadcast
 frame-relay map ip 150.100.100.2 121 broadcast
 frame-relay lmi-type cisco
!
router rip
 network 150.100.0.0

hostname churchill_imports
!
interface Ethernet0
 ip address 150.100.3.1 255.255.255.0
!
interface Serial0
 ip address 150.100.200.2 255.255.255.252
 ip summary-address eigrp 2001 150.100.200.0 255.255.255.0
 encapsulation frame-relay
 no fair-queue
 frame-relay interface-dlci 131
!
router eigrp 2001
 network 150.100.0.0
!
```

Finally, the optional portion of the lab specifies that you need to configure the administrative distance of all routes from romeo_y_julieta to be set to 5. To produce this result, use the **distance** command under RIP. In this model, you don't want to set the entire distance of RIP to 5, but you want to set just the distance of routes from one neighbor. Therefore, you need to call an access list on the **distance** command as well, as demonstrated in Example 9-20.

Example 9-20 *Setting the Distance for Specific Routes*

```
hostname habanos
!
router rip
 redistribute eigrp 2001
 passive-interface Serial0.2
 network 150.100.0.0
 default-metric 2
 distribute-list 10 out Serial0.1
 distance 5 150.100.100.3 0.0.0.0 11      ←Set distance for routes in list 11 only
!
ip classless
!
access-list 10 deny   150.100.10.0 0.0.0.255
access-list 10 permit any
access-list 11 permit 150.100.2.0 0.0.0.255    ←Allow only 150.200.2.0 through
!
```

Finally, viewing the route table on the habanos router in Example 9-21 shows that the route 150.100.2.0 has an administrative distance of 5, versus the default distance of 120.

Example 9-21 *Setting the Distance for Specific Routes*

```
habanos#show ip route
Codes: C - connected, S - static, I - IGRP, R - RIP, M - mobile, B - BGP
       D - EIGRP, EX - EIGRP external, O - OSPF, IA - OSPF inter area
       N1 - OSPF NSSA external type 1, N2 - OSPF NSSA external type 2
       E1 - OSPF external type 1, E2 - OSPF external type 2, E - EGP
       i - IS-IS, L1 - IS-IS level-1, L2 - IS-IS level-2, * - candidate default
       U - per-user static route, o - ODR

Gateway of last resort is not set

     150.100.0.0/16 is variably subnetted, 7 subnets, 2 masks
D       150.100.200.0/24 [90/2681856] via 150.100.200.2, 00:04:42, Serial0.2
C       150.100.200.0/30 is directly connected, Serial0.2
C       150.100.100.0/24 is directly connected, Serial0.1
R       150.100.2.0/24 [5/1] via 150.100.100.3, 00:00:20, Serial0.1
D       150.100.3.0/24 [90/2195456] via 150.100.200.2, 00:04:42, Serial0.2
R       150.100.1.0/24 [120/1] via 150.100.100.2, 00:00:07, Serial0.1
C       150.100.10.0/24 is directly connected, Ethernet2
habanos#
```

CHAPTER 10

Distance Vector Protocols: Interior Gateway Routing Protocol (IGRP)

When Cisco Systems developed the Interior Gateway Routing Protocol (IGRP) around 1986, network administrators didn't have many options to deal with some of RIP's limitations. RIP's hop-count limit of 15 and its simplistic metrics weren't allowing networks to scale and distribute traffic across paths of unequal cost. OSPF would not come out for another two years, and another routing protocol was needed. As the pioneer of internetworking, Cisco developed IGRP to specifically address some of RIP's shortcomings.

IGRP has features that differentiate it from other distance vectors protocols:

- **Scalability**—A hop count limit of 255 provides a broader network diameter versus RIP's hop-count limit of 15. The default hop for IGRP is 100.

- **Faster convergence**—IGRP uses *Flash updates*, which are updates that are sent to neighboring routers when topology changes occur.

- **Sophisticated metric**—IGRP uses a composite metric based on five individual metrics—bandwidth, delay, reliability, load, and MTU—to influence routing decisions.

- **Unequal-cost load balancing**—IGRP composite routing metrics allow for load balancing across multiple unequal-cost paths.

These features provided significant enhancements over the routing protocols of the mid-1980s. But eventually, like RIP, IGRP networks will give way to their stronger brethren, Enhanced IGRP. This chapter covers the features and operation of IGRP, along with configuration and redistribution of IGRP.

Technical Overview of IGRP

IGRP is cast as a classful distance vector protocol that interfaces directly with the IP layer as protocol Type 9. It uses the concept of autonomous systems, where it periodically broadcasts its entire routing table to all of its neighbors. IGRP deploys several timers and metrics to control route validity. IGRP uses these mechanisms in the following manner:

- **Routing updates**—Upon initialization, and every 90 seconds after that, IGRP broadcasts a routing update out all IGRP interfaces. This update includes all routes, as well as the route type and metric. This update includes every route in the route table, except routes suppressed by split horizon and filters. IGRP also uses Flash updates. Whenever network topology changes, IGRP sends out a Flash update to all its neighbors. The Flash update contains the entire route table.

- **Timers**—A 90-second timer called the *update timer* triggers the sending of another routing update when the 90 seconds expires. When a route is learned from a neighbor, an *invalid timer* for the route is set to three times the update timer, or 270 seconds. A *flush timer* is also set at this time; the default value of the flush timer is seven times the update timer, or 630 seconds. All the timers are defined as follows:

  - **Update timer**—This timer dictates how long a router waits between sending route advertisements. All route advertisements are offset by a random jitter to prevent synchronization problems.

  - **Invalid timer**—This timer dictates how long a router continues to advertise a route until it receives another update. When the invalid timer expires before an update, the route is marked as unreachable.

  - **Flush timer**—This timer dictates how long a router holds and advertises the route as unreachable before removing it from the routing table.

  - **Hold-down timer**—When a route becomes unreachable, or if the next-hop router increases the metric of the route, it is placed in holddown. The hold-down timer is three times the update timer plus 10 seconds; the default value is 280 seconds. Hold-down timers also prevent the router from receiving new information during convergence periods.

The default timers can be changed with the **timers basic** *update invalid holddown flush [sleeptime]* command. The *sleeptime* parameter instructs the router to wait a specified period of time before sending a routing update after receiving a triggered update.

IGRP deploys the concepts of split horizon and poison reverse to prevent routing loops. These concepts are described as follows:

- **Split horizon**—IGRP uses split horizon to prevent routing loops. Recall from earlier chapters that split horizon is the rule that information about a route is not be sent out the same interface or subinterface from which the route was received. By default, split horizon is enabled on all interfaces. This can be disabled with the **no ip split-horizon interface** command.

- **Poison reverse**—The router sends a poison reverse update to remove a route and place it in holddown. This is done to avoid a routing loop. A split horizon update is sent when a router detects a metric increase of 1.1 or greater. IGRP does this by setting the composite metric to 4,294,967,295 and advertising the route back to the source.

IGRP Route Types

As you can see, the operation of the IGRP timers is similar to that of RIP's timers. One way in which the two routing protocols differ is in the way they advertise routes. The three major categories of IGRP routes follow:

- **Exterior route**—An exterior route is a route flagged by the **ip default-network** *a.b.c.d* command. If the router has the **ip classless** command and IGRP has a default network configured, the router forwards any packets to the default network that it does not have a specific route to.

- **Interior or subnet route**—A route is advertised as an interior route if the route is part of the major subnet class of the interface sending the route.

- **System or network route**—A route is advertised as a system route if the route is not part of the major subnet class of the interface sending the route. System routes always are advertised as a summary route on the major class boundary.

Figure 10-1 illustrates the router advertising all three types of routes. In this example, the router highlighted has the **ip default-network 206.191.241.0** command set in its configuration**.** This command flags the 206.191.241.0 route as an exterior route when advertising it.

In this example, igrp_rtr has four interfaces in the same autonomous system. The Ethernet 5 (E5) interface is in subnet 172.16.1.0/24. Therefore, IGRP advertises the 172.16.2.0 route as a *subnet route* out the E5 interface. This is because the interface sending the route is in the same major class boundary as the route itself. IGRP advertises the 172.18.1.0/24 route as a *summary route* of 172.18.0.0 out the E5 interface. This is because the sending interface is in a different major class boundary. Finally, IGRP advertises the 206.191.241.40/29 route as the *exterior route* 206.191.241.0. The receiving IGRP router treats this route as its default route, or *gateway of last resort*.

Figure 10-1 *IGRP Routing Updates*

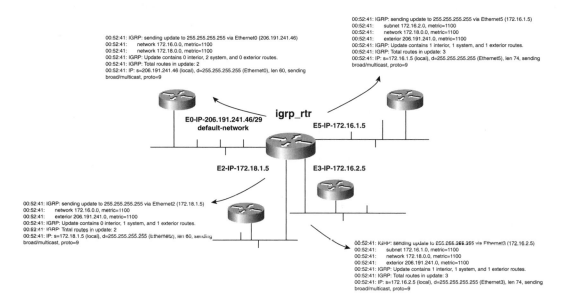

IGRP Metric Types

Another significant enhancement that IGRP provides over RIP is the use of complex composite metrics. Bandwidth, delay, load, reliability, and MTU are the submetrics. By default, IGRP chooses a route based primarily on bandwidth and delay. For a complete explanation on how the composite metric is derived and influenced by setting k values, see Chapter 11, "Hybrid: Enhanced Interior Gateway Routing Protocol (EIGRP)." The following list provides a more detailed description of the five IGRP metrics:

- **Bandwidth**—Bandwidth is expressed in units of kilobits. It must be statically configured to accurately represent the interfaces that IGRP is running on. For example, the default bandwidth of a 56-kbps interface and a T1 interface is 1544. To accurately adjust the bandwidth, use the **bandwidth** *kbps* interface subcommand. Table 10-1 highlights some common bandwidth settings.

- **Delay**—Delay is expressed in microseconds. It, too, must be statically configured to accurately represent the interface that IGRP is running on. The delay on an interface can be adjusted with the **delay** *time_in_microseconds* interface subcommand.

- **Reliability**—Reliability is a dynamic number expressed as a value from 1 to 255. Here, 255 represents a 100 percent reliable link, whereas 1 represents an unreliable link.

- **Load**—Load is a number in the range of 1 to 255 that shows the output load of an interface. This value is dynamic and can be viewed by the **show interfaces** command. Here, 1 represents a minimally loaded link, whereas 255 represents a 100 percent loaded link.
- **MTU**—This is the smallest maximum transmission unit (MTU) value in the path.

NOTE   Whenever you are influencing routing decisions in IGRP or EIGRP, use the metric of delay over bandwidth. Changing bandwidth can affect other routing protocols, such as OSPF. Changing delay affects only IGRP and EIGRP.

Table 10-1 highlights the common metrics used.

Table 10-1   *Common IGRP and EIGRP Metrics*

Medium	Bandwidth	Delay
100M ATM	100,000 kbps	100 microseconds
Fast Ethernet	100,000 kbps	100 microseconds
FDDI	100,000 kbps	100 microseconds
HSSI	45,045 kbps	20,000 microseconds
16M Token Ring	16,000 kbps	630 microseconds
10M Ethernet	10,000 kbps	1000 microseconds
T1	1544 kbps	20,000 microseconds
DS-0	64 kbps	20,000 microseconds
56K	56 kbps	20,000 microseconds

*   These metrics are not the actual metrics that get communicated in the IGRP updates. These metrics are used to derive the composite metric that actually is sent in the update.

Configuring IGRP

Configuring basic IGRP is a two-step process. Configuring IGRP calls for the definition of an autonomous system (AS). By definition, an autonomous system is a set of routers under a single administrative technical authority. IGRP, EIGRP, and BGP all use the concept of autonomous systems, but BGP is the only routing protocol that actually utilizes the AS in routing decisions. It is not required to have a registered AS when configuring IGRP or EIGRP.

This following two-step process can be followed by an optional third step to fine-tune IGRP to specific environments:

Step 1 Enable IGRP and define an autonomous system on the router. This is accomplished with the **router igrp** *autonomous_system_id* global command.

Step 2 Add the networks that you want to run IGRP on. This is accomplished with the **network** *a.b.c.d* command from the **config-router#** mode. When you enter the **network** statements, it is necessary to enter only the major class boundary.

Step 3 *Optional:* Fine-tune IGRP metrics with **bandwidth** statements, or configure IGRP timers and options.

Example 10-1 illustrates the IGRP configuration from Figure 10-1.

Example 10-1 *IGRP Configuration*

```
! hostname igrp_rtr
!
router igrp 2001          ←IGRP routing process
 network 172.16.0.0           ←Networks running IGRP
 network 172.18.0.0
 network 206.191.241.0
!
ip classless
ip default-network 206.191.241.0 ←Default Network
!
```

Before moving on to configuring other IGRP options, let's take a look at the "Big D" and the "Big show" commands for IGRP.

The "Big show" and "Big D" for IGRP

Troubleshooting IGRP is similar to troubleshooting RIP. Most of the configuration errors around IGRP involve a bad **network** statement, discontinuous subnets, or inconsistent bit masks across the IGRP domain. The following is list of what I find to be the most useful **show** and **debug** commands for IGRP.

- **show ip protocols [summary]**
- **Router#show ip route**
- **Router(config-router)#debug ip igrp [transactions | events]**

The sections that follow explain these commands in greater detail.

show ip protocols [summary] Command

This command displays all routing protocols, detailed timer and metric information, as well as routing update information. Example 10-2 lists the output of the **show ip protocols** command.

Example 10-2 *Output of the* **show ip protocols** *Command*

```
igrp_rtr#show ip protocols
Routing Protocol is "igrp 2001"     ←AS number
  Sending updates every 90 seconds, next due in 19 seconds     ←Update Timer
  Invalid after 270 seconds, hold down 280, flushed after 630 ←Other 3 timers
  Outgoing update filter list for all interfaces is
  Incoming update filter list for all interfaces is
  Default networks flagged in outgoing updates
  Default networks accepted from incoming updates
  IGRP metric weight K1=1, K2=0, K3=1, K4=0, K5=0     ←Metrics
  IGRP maximum hopcount 100
  IGRP maximum metric variance 1
  Redistributing: igrp 2001
  Routing for Networks:          ←Networks IGRP is routing for
    172.16.0.0
    172.18.0.0
    206.191.241.0
  Routing Information Sources:          ←Networks reporting routes
    Gateway         Distance      Last Update
    172.18.1.55          100      00:00:29
    206.191.241.42       100      00:00:06
    172.18.1.7           100      00:01:06
    172.16.2.4           100      00:38:38
    172.16.1.1           100      00:50:01
  Distance: (default is 100)          ←Administrative Distance

igrp_rtr#
```

show ip route Command

This command lists the router's current routing table and the one that it uses to make forwarding decisions. The output lists what routing protocol the route is from—in this case, **I** for IGRP. The number behind the route is the administrative distance of the route followed by the composite metric of IGRP. The **via** field explains who the route is from, how long ago an update was received, and by what interface it was received. Example 10-3 lists the output of the **show ip route** command. In this example, the route 206.191.241.0/24 is the default route, marked by the *. It has an administrative distance of 100 and a composite metric of 1200. The IGRP neighbor informing the router about the route is 172.18.1.5. The last update about the route occurred 52 seconds ago, through the Ethernet 0 port.

Example 10-3 show ip route *Command Output*

```
r7#show ip route
Codes: C - connected, S - static, I - IGRP, R - RIP, M - mobile, B - BGP
       D - EIGRP, EX - EIGRP external, O - OSPF, IA - OSPF inter area
       N1 - OSPF NSSA external type 1, N2 - OSPF NSSA external type 2
       E1 - OSPF external type 1, E2 - OSPF external type 2, E - EGP
       i - IS-IS, L1 - IS-IS level-1, L2 - IS-IS level-2, * - candidate default
       U - per-user static route, o - ODR

Gateway of last resort is 172.18.1.5 to network 206.191.241.0

I*   206.191.241.0/24 [100/1200] via 172.18.1.5, 00:00:52, Ethernet0
I    172.16.0.0/16 [100/1200] via 172.18.1.5, 00:00:53, Ethernet0
     172.18.0.0/24 is subnetted, 3 subnets
I       172.18.18.0 [100/1600] via 172.18.1.55, 00:00:29, Ethernet0
C       172.18.19.0 is directly connected, Loopback20
C       172.18.1.0 is directly connected, Ethernet0
r7#
```

Router(config-router)#debug ip igrp [transactions | events] Command

The **debug ip igrp transactions** command shows detailed information about the routing updates being sent and received by the various interfaces. The **debug ip igrp transactions** command provides comprehensive routing detail, listing the networks and composite metric of each network. Both the commands show which interfaces are sending and receiving routes. The **debug ip igrp events** command provides only what type of routes are being advertised and received. Example 10-4 lists the output of the **debug ip igrp transactions** command, whereas Example 10-5 lists the output of **debug ip igrp events**. Use Figure 10-1 as reference for this output, which was performed on the igrp_router.

Example 10-4 debug ip igrp transactions *Command Output*

```
01:40:07: IGRP: received update from 206.191.241.42 on Ethernet0
01:40:07:        network 172.16.0.0, metric 1121211 (neighbor 1121111)
01:40:27: IGRP: sending update to 255.255.255.255 via Ethernet0 (206.191.241.46)
01:40:27:        network 172.16.0.0, metric-1100
01:40:27:        network 172.18.0.0, metric=1100
01:40:27: IGRP: sending update to 255.255.255.255 via Ethernet1 (172.18.1.5)
01:40:27:        network 172.16.0.0, metric=1100
01:40:27:        exterior 206.191.241.0, metric=1100
01:40:27: IGRP: sending update to 255.255.255.255 via Ethernet3 (172.16.2.5)
01:40:27:        subnet 172.16.1.0, metric=1100
01:40:27:        network 172.18.0.0, metric=1100
01:40:27:        exterior 206.191.241.0, metric=1100
01:40:27: IGRP: sending update to 255.255.255.255 via Ethernet5 (172.16.1.5)
01:40:27:        subnet 172.16.2.0, metric=1100
01:40:27:        network 172.18.0.0, metric=1100
01:40:27:        exterior 206.191.241.0, metric=1100
igrp_rtr#
```

Example 10-5 debug ip igrp events *Command Output*

```
02:52:53: IGRP: sending update to 255.255.255.255 via Ethernet0 (206.191.241.46)
02:52:53: IGRP: Update contains 0 interior, 2 system, and 0 exterior routes.
02:52:53: IGRP: Total routes in update: 2
02:52:53: IGRP: sending update to 255.255.255.255 via Ethernet1 (172.18.1.5)
02:52:53: IGRP: Update contains 0 interior, 1 system, and 1 exterior routes.
02:52:53: IGRP: Total routes in update: 2
02:52:53: IGRP: sending update to 255.255.255.255 via Ethernet3 (172.16.2.5)
02:52:53: IGRP: Update contains 1 interior, 1 system, and 1 exterior routes.
02:52:53: IGRP: Total routes in update: 3
02:52:53: IGRP: sending update to 255.255.255.255 via Ethernet5 (172.16.1.5)
02:52:53: IGRP: Update contains 1 interior, 1 system, and 1 exterior routes.
02:52:53: IGRP: Total routes in update: 3
02:52:55: IGRP: received update from 172.18.1.7 on Ethernet1
02:52:55: IGRP: Update contains 1 interior, 0 system, and 0 exterior routes.
02:52:55: IGRP: Total routes in update: 1
```

Tuning, Redistribution, and Controlling IGRP Updates

Like RIP, IGRP has several parameters for tuning timers, controlling broadcasts, load-sharing, and controlling routes. The following is a list of parameters adjustable within IGRP:

- **Router(config-router)#timers basic** *update invalid holddown flush* [*sleeptime*]— This allows the user to set the update, invalid, hold-down, flush, and optional sleep timers for IGRP.

  To allow IGRP unicast updates, define a next-hop neighbor with the **neighbor** command. The command functions identically to the RIP version. For more information on configuring unicast routing updates, see Chapter 9, "Distance Vector Protocols: Routing Information Protocol Versions 1 and 2 (RIP-1 and RIP-2)."

- **Router(config-router)#passive-interface** *interface_name*—This command prevents routing updates from being sent on an interface. The router, however, still listens to broadcast or unicast updates as they are received on that interface.

- **Router(config-router)#neighbor** *a.b.c.d*—This command defines an IGRP neighbor to exchange unicast updates with. This command should be used in conjunction with the **passive-interface** command.

- **Router(config-router)#offset-list** [*access_list_0-99* [**in** | **out**] *offset* {*metric_offset_ 1-214748364*} [*interface*]—Use this command to increase the value of the routing metrics. The metric offset cannot exceed 214,748,364.

  To filter routing updates in IGRP, use a distribute list. A distribute list, as you recall, calls a standard or extended access list and filters routing updates accordingly. When redistributing one protocol into another, use the **redistribute** command along with the default metric. A route map should be used in place of a distribute list when controlling specific routes during the redistribution process. In the section on IGRP integration, you can see an example of **redistribute** and **default-metric** commands.

- **Router(config-router)#distribute-list** {*1-199*} [**in** | **out**] [*interface*]—Use this command to call a standard or extended access list to filter inbound or outbound routing updates.

- **Router(config-router)#redistribute** {**connected** | **static** | **bgp** | **rip** | **eigrp** | **ospf** | **isis**} [**metric** *metric-value*] [**route-map** *map-tag*]—Use this command to redistribute other routing protocols into IGRP. A route map can be added for additional route control. An optional metric also can be supplied for routes originating from the routing protocol being redistributed that are different from the default metric. Whenever redistributing routes, remember that IP needs a route *to and from* a destination. Many times mutual redistribution might be required to give IP a path to and from its destination.

- **Router(config-router)#default-metric** *bandwidth_kbps 1-4214748364 delay_microseconds 1-4214748364 reliability 1-255 load 1-244 mtu 1-4214748364*—Use this command to set the default metric of all routes redistributed into IGRP. Keep in mind that if the metrics are defined on the **redistribute** command shown previously, those metrics override any metrics set here. You must supply a default metric when redistributing between protocols either by using the **default-metric** command or by specifying the metrics on the **redistribute** command. A common metric to use is **default-metric 10000 1000 254 1 1500**. This metric tells the router to derive the composite metric from the values of bandwidth of 10000, a delay of 1000, a load of 1 (or no load), and an MTU of 1500. The link is 254 reliable here, where 255 is 100 percent reliable.

The following subsets of commands are used to influence routing decisions. Individual metrics can be modified, as can the administrative distance of the IGRP. Whenever influencing a specific links metric, use the **delay** command over the **bandwidth** command. Both can be used, but OSPF also is affected by **bandwidth,** whereas **delay** affects only IGRP and EIGRP.

- **Router(config-router)#metric weights 0** *k1 k2 k3 k4* k5—This command enables you to set the weight of the IGRP metric in terms of bandwidth, load, delay, and reliability.

- **Router(config-router)#distance** *weight_1-255* [*adjacent_neighbors_ip_address wildcard_mask* [*access_list_0-99*]]—Use this command to change the administrative distance of routes received from a neighbor. If the IP address and wildcard mask are omitted, all routes for that protocol are set to the distance value. For a specific example and more practice with the **distance** command, see Chapter 9 and the lab therein.

- **Router(config-if)#delay** microseconds_1-*4214748364*—This command specifies the delay of an interface in tens of microseconds. This command is used only by routing protocols and does not affect traffic on the link.

- **Router(config-if)#bandwidth** *bandwidth_kbps_1-4214748364*—This command specifies the bandwidth of an interface in kilobits per second. This command is used only by routing protocols and does not affect traffic on the link.

Unequal-Cost Load Balancing

IGRP has the capability to use unequal-cost load balancing. The router uses variance as a multiplier in choosing the upper boundary of path with the greatest metric.

Configuring unequal-cost load balancing is a three-step process:

Step 1   Configure the bandwidth on both sides of all the interfaces involved in the load-sharing group. Use the **bandwidth** *kbps* command to accomplish this.

Step 2   Define the lowest-cost metric and the highest-cost metric. From these values, compute the variance multiplier and add it to the IGRP routing process.

Step 3   *Optional:* Set the *maximum-paths* or the *traffic-share* variables.

The following example walks through the calculation of a fictional variance. IGRP has a route, and the metric of that route is 100. The router also has two more routes to that same destination, and the metrics for those routes are 200 and 300. To allow IGRP to use all three paths in sharing data, you would set the variance to 3. $(3 \times 100) = 300$, or (Best_metric) $\times$ (variance) = Largest metric of path to load share over. To properly set the variance, use the following formula:

Variance = 1 + ([(Metric of highest-cost route) / (Metric of the lowest cost route)] Rounded up to the nearest 1s decimal place)

The metric of the lowest-cost route can be discovered with the **debug ip igrp transactions** command. Be sure to change the variance and other variables on both ends of the link. The bandwidth also should be set on all serial links. The following syntax is used in configuring load balancing:

- **Router(config-router)#variance** *metric_multiplier 1-128*—Defines the metric multiplier of which routes to use in unequal-cost load balancing. The default variance is 1, which is equal-cost load balancing.

- **Router(config-router)#maximum-paths** *1-6*—By default, the router uses four equal-cost paths for load sharing, but up to six paths can be set using this command. This command also can be used to limit this number. The multiple paths that make up a single-hop transport to a common destination are called a *load-sharing group*.

- **Router(config-router)#traffic-share** {**balanced** | **min**}—If multiple minimum-cost paths exist and **traffic-share min** is configured, IGRP uses equal-cost load balancing. By default, the command is set to **balanced**, where traffic is distributed proportionally to the ratio of the metrics. For example, if the variance is set to 3 and **traffic-share** is set to **balanced**, the best route transports traffic four times that of the worst route.

- **Router(config-router)#bandwidth** *xx-kbps*—This command configures bandwidth that IGRP uses in route decisions.

For a route to be included in unequal-cost load sharing, three other conditions must be met:

- The maximum paths limit must not be exceeded as a result of adding this route to the load-sharing group.

- The downstream router must be metrically closer to the destination.

- The metric of the lowest-cost route, multiplied by the variance, must be greater than the metric of the route to be added to the load-sharing group.

Configuring IGRP Unequal-Cost Load Sharing

In the network model in Figure 10-2, there are two routers: klipsch and carver. The routers are connected by two serial links: One link is running at 56 kbps, and the other is running at T1 speeds. The routers are both running IGRP in the private autonomous system of 65,001. In this model, you want to enable unequal-cost load balancing across the serial links.

Figure 10-2 *IGRP with Unequal Metric Calculation*

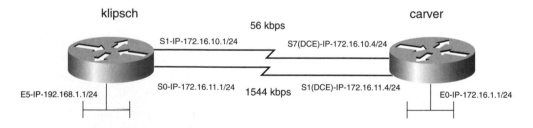

The first step, after configuring basic IGRP, is to set the bandwidth on the serial interfaces. If IGRP is enabled without tuning the bandwidth, the routers get an inconsistent view of the metrics of the network. In Example 10-6, the klipsch router has calculated a composite metric of 180,671 for the subnet 172.16.1.0 from the Serial 1 interface. On the other hand, the router has calculated a metric of 8576 for the same route from the Serial 0 interface.

How IGRP calculates the metrics for each route can be displayed by the **debug ip igrp transactions** command, as shown in Example 10-6.

Example 10-6 *Metric of the 172.16.1.0 Route on klipsch*

```
klipsch# debug ip igrp transactions
IGRP protocol debugging is on
klipsch#
00:50:05: IGRP: received update from 172.16.11.4 on Serial0
00:50:05:        subnet 172.16.10.0, metric 182571 (neighbor 180571)
00:50:05:        subnet 172.16.1.0, metric 8576 (neighbor 1100)
00:50:05: IGRP: received update from 172.16.10.4 on Serial1
00:50:05:        subnet 172.16.11.0, metric 182571 (neighbor 8476)
00:50:05:        subnet 172.16.1.0, metric 180671 (neighbor 1100)
00:50:05:        subnet 172.16.100.0, metric 182671 (neighbor 8576)
klipsch#
```

Example 10-7 illustrates how, without setting the bandwidth on both sides of the serial links, the routers might have different perspectives on the link.

Example 10-7 *Metric of 192.168.1.0 Route of carver*

```
carver#debug ip igrp transactions
IGRP protocol debugging is on
03:12:26: IGRP: received update from 172.16.11.1 on Serial1
03:12:26:        subnet 172.16.10.0, metric 10476 (neighbor 8476)
03:12:26:        network 192.168.1.0, metric 8576 (neighbor 1100)
03:12:26: IGRP: received update from 172.16.10.1 on Serial7
03:12:26:        subnet 172.16.11.0, metric 90956 (neighbor 8476)
03:12:26:        network 192.168.1.0, metric 89056 (neighbor 1100)
carver#
```

To assist in synchronizing the metrics, assign the **bandwidth** statement to the two serial interfaces. Once again, this is done with the **bandwidth** *kbps* interface command. After applying the **bandwidth** command, the metrics are consistent throughout the network, as shown in Example 10-8.

Example 10-8 **debug ip igrp transactions** *Command Output on the klipsch and carver Routers*

```
klipsch#
03:54:18: IGRP: received update from 172.16.11.4 on Serial0
03:54:18:        subnet 172.16.10.0, metric 182571 (neighbor 180571)
03:54:18:        subnet 172.16.1.0, metric 8576 (neighbor 1100)
03:54:19: IGRP: received update from 172.16.10.4 on Serial1
03:54:19:        subnet 172.16.11.0, metric 182571 (neighbor 8476)
03:54:19:        subnet 172.16.1.0, metric 180671 (neighbor 1100)
03:54:19:        network 192.168.1.0, metric 182671 (neighbor 8576)
```

continues

Example 10-8 debug ip igrp transactions *Command Output on the klipsch and carver Routers (Continued)*

```
carver#
03:49:31: IGRP: received update from 172.16.11.1 on Serial1
03:49:31:        subnet 172.16.10.0, metric 182571 (neighbor 180571)
03:49:31:        network 192.168.1.0, metric 8576 (neighbor 1100)
03:49:31: IGRP: received update from 172.16.10.1 on Serial7
03:49:31:        subnet 172.16.11.0, metric 182571 (neighbor 8476)
03:49:31:        subnet 172.16.1.0, metric 182671 (neighbor 8576)
03:49:31:        network 192.168.1.0, metric 180671 (neighbor 1100)
carver#
carver#
```

The routing table is now consistent and all traffic flows through the lowest-cost path. Notice in Figure 10-3 that the routing table for the klipsch router now reports only the lowest-cost path to the network 172.16.1.0.

Figure 10-3 *IGRP with Equal Metric Calculation*

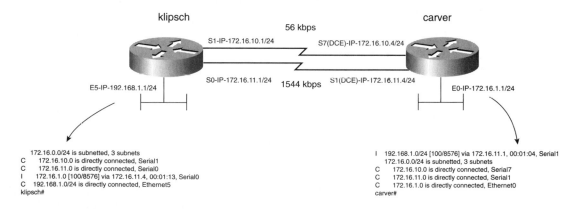

The final step is to set the variance. Recall that the formula to calculate variance is as follows:

1+ ([highest_cost_path/lowest_cost_path] Rounded up)

Therefore, in this example, you have $1 + (180671/8576) = 22$. After the variance is set, the router reports two paths to the destination network and load-share over them. The load sharing is in an inverse proportion to the variance setting. In this model, every 22nd packet crosses the lowest-cost path.

Finally, Example 10-9 lists the route table on the carver and klipsch routers when unequal-cost load balancing is in effect. Notice that all possible paths to the destination networks are listed.

Example 10-9 show ip route *Command Output Lists All Possible Paths to Remote Networks*

```
I     192.168.1.0/24 [100/8576] via 172.16.11.1, 00:01:09, Serial1
                      [100/180671] via 172.16.10.1, 00:01:10, Serial7
      172.16.0.0/24 is subnetted, 3 subnets
C        172.16.10.0 is directly connected, Serial7
C        172.16.11.0 is directly connected, Serial1
C        172.16.1.0 is directly connected, Ethernet0
carver#
```

```
      172.16.0.0/24 is subnetted, 3 subnets
C        172.16.10.0 is directly connected, Serial1
C        172.16.11.0 is directly connected, Serial0
I        172.16.1.0 [100/8576] via 172.16.11.4, 00:00:20, Serial0
                    [100/180671] via 172.16.10.4, 00:00:20, Serial1
C     192.168.1.0/24 is directly connected, Ethernet5
klipsch#
```

Example 10-10 lists the configuration of the carver and klipsch routers.

Example 10-10 *Relevant Portions of the carver and klipsch Router Configurations*

```
hostname carver
!
interface Ethernet0
 ip address 172.16.1.1 255.255.255.0
!
interface Serial1
 ip address 172.16.11.4 255.255.255.0
 bandwidth 1544
 clockrate 2000000
!
interface Serial7
 ip address 172.16.10.4 255.255.255.0
 bandwidth 56
 clockrate 56000
!
router igrp 65001
 variance 22
 network 172.16.0.0
!
ip classless
```

```
hostname klipsch
!
interface Ethernet5
 ip address 192.168.1.1 255.255.255.0
 media-type 10BaseT
!
interface Serial0
 ip address 172.16.11.1 255.255.255.0
```

continues

Example 10-10 *Relevant Portions of the carver and klipsch Router Configurations (Continued)*

```
 no ip mroute-cache
 bandwidth 1544
!
interface Serial1
 ip address 172.16.10.1 255.255.255.0
 bandwidth 56
!
router igrp 65001
 variance 22
 network 172.16.0.0
 network 192.168.1.0
!
ip classless
```

IGRP and EIGRP Integration and Migration

Migration from IGRP to EIGRP was designed to be an effortless migration. For the most part, this is true. If IGRP and EIGRP use the same Autonomous System IDs, redistribution occurs automatically. This facilitates a rather painless migration from IGRP to EIGRP. If the routing processes are in different autonomous systems, manual redistribution must be configured.

IGRP is also a classful routing protocol, which means that routing updates in the same major class or bit boundary as the interface receiving the update must have a subnet mask that matches the mask of the interface receiving the update. If the update is in a different class, it automatically is summarized at that class's major bit boundary, 8-bit, 16-bit, or 24-bit. Therefore, care must be taken to use summarization so that all the networks are at the same bit boundary throughout the portion of the network that supports only classful routing.

Expanding upon the model from the previous example, a new router has been added to the internetwork and some other subnet changes have been made, as illustrated in Figure 10-4. There now exists an EIGRP domain in the model. A router called dts is connected by a T1 serial link to the carver router.

To integrate the dts router to the network, manual redistribution is necessary. This is because the network resides in different autonomous systems. Example 10-11 highlights the IGRP and EIGRP redistribution on the carver router. The **passive-interface** commands are not necessary but are configured to prevent unnecessary EIGRP hellos and IGRP broadcast from entering networks that they shouldn't.

Figure 10-4 *IGRP and EIGRP Integration*

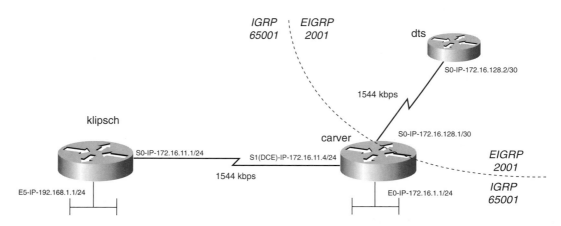

Example 10-11 *IGRP and EIGRP Redistribution on the carver Router*

```
!
router eigrp 2001
 redistribute igrp 65001      ←Redistribute IGRP into EIGRP
 passive-interface Ethernet0     ←do not send EIGRP hellos on these interfaces
passive-interface Serial1
 network 172.16.0.0
 default-metric 1544 100 254 1 1500 ←Use this metric for redistributed routes
 no auto-summary
!
router igrp 65001
 redistribute eigrp 2001      ←Redistribute EIGRP into IGRP
 passive-interface Serial0
 network 172.16.0.0
 default-metric 1544 100 254 1 1500     ←Default metric for redistributed routes
!
```

The link between the carver and dts routers is on a 30-bit boundary. IGRP is not capable of advertising this network after it is redistributed because the subnet mask does not match the subnet mask on the advertising interface. To remedy this, summarize the 172.16.128.0/30 network to 172.16.128.0/24 by using the **ip summary-address eigrp 2001 172.16.128.0 255.255.255.0** command under the Serial 0 interface of the carver router.

Downstream routers, such as klipsch, now have IP reachability to the subnet 172.16.128.0/24. Example 10-12 lists the route table of the klipsch router.

Example 10-12 *Route Table of the klipsch Router*

```
klipsch#show ip route
<<<text omitted>>>
Gateway of last resort is not set

     172.16.0.0/24 is subnetted, 3 subnets
I       172.16.128.0 [100/10476] via 172.16.11.4, 00:00:31, Serial0
C       172.16.11.0 is directly connected, Serial0
I       172.16.1.0 [100/8576] via 172.16.11.4, 00:00:31, Serial0
klipsch#
```

IGRP and Default Routing

A default route is necessary whenever connecting to the Internet because, without it, the router would need a path to every single network in its routing table. Fundamentally, a default route points to a gateway of last resort. When a router cannot find a specific match in its route table for a packet, it forwards that packet to the gateway of last resort. Cisco routers always perform a classful route lookup, which means that they do not forward packets to a gateway of last resort unless the global **ip classless** command is set. **ip classless** is enabled by default in Cisco IOS Software Release 11.3 and later.

The concept of default routing varies by each routing protocol. Each routing protocol uses a specific method when defining and advertising a default route.

The two steps to perform when configuring default routing with IGRP follow:

Step 1   Define a default network. IGRP does not recognize the address of 0.0.0.0 as a default route. Recall that the IGRP actually advertises a route as an external network. To "flag" or define a network as external, two things must happen. First, the route must be flagged by the **ip default-network** *a.b.c.d* command. Second, for the route to be advertised as external, the interface advertising the route must not be in the same major class boundary as the default network.

Step 2   Ensure that **IP classless** is enabled on the router.

In Figure 10-5, igrp_rtr has a default network of 206.191.241.40/29. The **ip default-network 206.191.241.0** command has been added to the configuration. This causes the route to be flagged as a default and as an external network. The route table for the igrp_rtr router marks this route with an *, meaning that the route is the candidate default. When the route is propagated to a downstream router, it becomes a gateway of last resort, as shown in Figure 10-5.

Figure 10-5 *GRP Default Network*

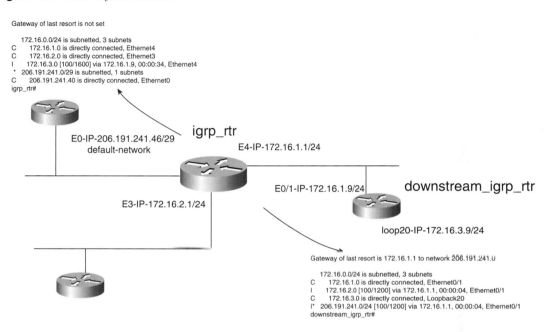

Gateway of last resort is not set

```
   172.16.0.0/24 is subnetted, 3 subnets
C    172.16.1.0 is directly connected, Ethernet4
C    172.16.2.0 is directly connected, Ethernet3
I    172.16.3.0 [100/1600] via 172.16.1.9, 00:00:34, Ethernet4
*  206.191.241.0/29 is subnetted, 1 subnets
C    206.191.241.40 is directly connected, Ethernet0
igrp_rtr#
```

igrp_rtr

E0-IP-206.191.241.46/29
default-network

E4-IP-172.16.1.1/24

E0/1-IP-172.16.1.9/24

downstream_igrp_rtr

E3-IP-172.16.2.1/24

loop20-IP-172.16.3.9/24

Gateway of last resort is 172.16.1.1 to network 206.191.241.0

```
   172.16.0.0/24 is subnetted, 3 subnets
C    172.16.1.0 is directly connected, Ethernet0/1
I    172.16.2.0 [100/1200] via 172.16.1.1, 00:00:04, Ethernet0/1
C    172.16.3.0 is directly connected, Loopback20
I*  206.191.241.0/24 [100/1200] via 172.16.1.1, 00:00:04, Ethernet0/1
downstream_igrp_rtr#
```

Example 10-13 lists the configuration of the igrp_rtr router.

Example 10-13 *Relevant Portions of the igrp_rtr Configuration*

```
router igrp 2001
 network 172.16.0.0
 network 206.191.241.0
!
ip classless
ip default-network 206.191.241.0
!
```

Lab 21: Default Routing, Filtering, and Unequal-Cost Load Sharing in IGRP Networks—Part I

Practical Scenario

Most IGRP networks have evolved into EIGRP networks, but some still remain. When working with IGRP networks, it is key to be able to control routing updates and propagate default information.

The following lab gives you practice in controlling routing updates, filtering, and default routing.

Lab Exercise

The Sea Shepherd Conservation Society (SSCS), or Sea Shepherd International, is a powerful group of environmentalists committed to defending a segment of the world's population that has no voice. The SSCS has an organized navy that goes by the code name Neptune. The navy has several ships that operate out of various ports across the globe and patrol ecological hot spots enforcing United Nations sanctions. The Neptune Navel Intelligence Network links the various departments of the navy to allow the SSCS quick access to important data. Your task is to configure an IGRP network by using the following parameters as design guidelines:

- Configure an IP network, as depicted in Figure 10-6, using IGRP as the routing protocol and 65,001 as the Autonomous System ID.

- Configure a default network to 204.30.121.0/24 from the sea_shepherd router, and propagate it throughout the IGRP domain.

- The ocean_warrior router has a private subnet of 172.16.128.0/24. Prevent only the mirage router from seeing this subnet.

- Configure the ocean_warrior router to use all possible paths to the default network.

- *Optional:* Configure IGRP so that broadcasts are less intensive on the LAN segment between the ocean_warrior, sirenian, and mirage routers.

Lab Objectives

- Configure the Neptune Naval Intelligence Network as depicted in Figure 10-6. Configure IP as denoted in the diagram. The LAN topology type is not important in this lab.

- Use HDLC as the data-link protocol on the WAN.

- Configure a default network and propagate it throughout the IGRP domain.

- Configure unequal-cost load balancing to the default network from the ocean_warrior router.

- Filter subnet 172.16.128.0/24 of the ocean_warrior router from reaching the mirage router. You might need to configure multiple access lists to accomplish this.

- *Optional:* Configure IGRP unicast updates on the LAN segment between the ocean_warrior, sirenian, and mirage routers.

Equipment Needed

- Four Cisco routers. Three will be connected through V.35 back-to-back cables or in a similar manner.

- Three LAN segments, provided through hubs or switches.

- You might want to test the configuration by adding a workstation with the IP address of 204.30.121.31 on the subnet of the sea_shepherd router.

Physical Layout and Prestaging

- Connect the hubs and serial cables to the routers, as shown in Figure 10-6.

- *Optional:* Configure an IP workstation with the address of 204.30.121.3 to test the network.

Figure 10-6 *Neptune Naval Intelligence Network*

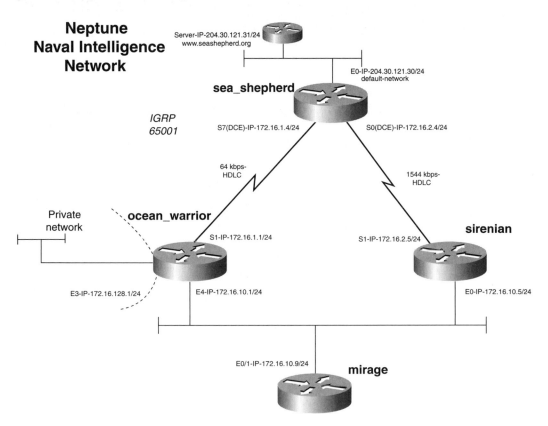

Lab 21: Default Routing, Filtering, and Unequal-Cost Load Sharing in IGRP Networks—Part II

Lab Walkthrough

Attach the two routers in a back-to-back manner to the sea_shepherd router. Use V.35 cables or CSU/DSUs with crossover cables to connect the routers. Create the three LANs by the use of switches or hubs/MAUs. The LAN segment 172.16.128.0/24 on ocean_warrior can be simulated with a loopback interface.

When the physical connections are complete, assign IP addresses to all LAN and WAN interfaces, as depicted in Figure 10-6. Be sure that you can **ping** the router's local LAN and WAN interface before moving on. Do not forget to use the **clock rate** command for the DCE side on the serial interfaces of the sea_shepherd router.

The basic IGRP configuration is similar on all the routers. Following the three-step process for IGRP configuration provided earlier in the chapter, begin by enabling IGRP on all the routers by using the **router IGRP 65001** command. The second step is to define the networks to run IGRP on. The sea_shepherd router runs IGRP on major networks 204.30.121.0 and 172.16.0.0. The ocean_warrior router runs IGRP on networks 110.0.0.0 and 172.16.0.0. The mirage and sirenian routers need to run IGRP on only the 172.16.0.0 network. Example 10-14 shows the initial IGRP configuration on the routers.

Example 10-14 *Initial IGRP Configuration for Neptune Naval Intelligence Network Routers*

```
hostname sea_shepherd
!
router igrp 65001        ←Define the IGRP process
 network 172.16.0.0         ←Networks participating in routing
 network 204.30.121.0

hostname ocean_warrior
!
router igrp 65001
 network 110.0.0.0
 network 172.16.0.0

hostname sirenian
!
router igrp 65001
 network 172.16.0.0
!

hostname mirage
!
```

continues

Example 10-14 *Initial IGRP Configuration for Neptune Naval Intelligence Network Routers (Continued)*

```
router igrp 65001
 network 172.16.0.0
!
```

At this point, full routing should exist between all the routers. Verify this with the **show ip route** command and by **ping**ing the various interfaces. The route table on the sea_shepherd router resembles Example 10-15.

Example 10-15 *Route Table of the sea_shepherd Router*

```
sea_shepherd#show ip route
<<<text omitted>>>
Gateway of last resort is not set

C    204.30.121.0/24 is directly connected, Ethernet0
     172.16.0.0/24 is subnetted, 4 subnets
I       172.16.128.0 [l00/8076] via 172.16.2.5, 00:00:32, Serial0
I       172.16.10.0 [100/8576] via 172.16.2.5, 00:00:56, Serial0
C       172.16.1.0 is directly connected, Serial7
C       172.16.2.0 is directly connected, Serial0
sea_shepherd#
```

If you observe the routing table on the mirage router, as in Example 10-16, you can see that two routes exist to the network 204.30.121.0/24. One route travels through ocean_warrior, 172.16.10.1, and one route travels through sirenian. Two routes exist because the default bandwidth has not been changed on the serial interfaces, so IGRP has inconsistent views of the metrics for the routes. To enforce consistent metrics, the **bandwidth** statement needs to be added to the serial interface on the WAN links. Without **bandwidth** statements, the sirenian and ocean_warrior routers view both of their links as the T1s. The sea_shepherd router in this example is a Cisco 2522, so the low-speed sync port measures yet a different default metric of 115 for the bandwidth. This reaffirms why you should check and configure the **bandwidth** statements for proper routing.

Example 10-16 *mirage Router Routing Table*

```
mirage#show ip route
<<<text omitted>>>
Gateway of last resort is not set

     172.16.0.0/24 is subnetted, 4 subnets
I       172.16.128.0 [100/1200] via 172.16.10.1, 00:01:10, Ethernet0/1
C       172.16.10.0 is directly connected, Ethernet0/1
I       172.16.1.0 [100/8576] via 172.16.10.1, 00:00:41, Ethernet0/1
I       172.16.2.0 [100/8576] via 172.16.10.5, 00:00:44, Ethernet0/1
I    204.30.121.0/24 [100/8676] via 172.16.10.5, 00:00:44, Ethernet0/1
                     [100/8676] via 172.16.10.1, 00:00:41, Ethernet0/1
mirage#
```

After adding **bandwidth** statements to the serial interfaces, the mirage router shows a preferred route to the 204.30.121.0/24 network through the sirenian router or 172.16.10.5. Example 10-17 lists the output of the **show ip route** command after the statements **bandwidth 64** and **bandwidth 1544** to the serial interfaces of the ocean_warrior and sirenian routers, respectively. The statements is also added to the sea_shepherd router.

Example 10-17 *mirage Routing Table After the* **bandwidth** *Statements Are Added*

```
mirage#show ip route
<<<text omitted>>>
Gateway of last resort is not set

     172.16.0.0/24 is subnetted, 4 subnets
I       172.16.128.0 [100/1200] via 172.16.10.1, 00:01:10, Ethernet0/1
C       172.16.10.0 is directly connected, Ethernet0/1
I       172.16.1.0 [100/158350] via 172.16.10.1, 00:01:10, Ethernet0/1
I       172.16.2.0 [100/8576] via 172.16.10.5, 00:00:19, Ethernet0/1
I     204.30.121.0/24 [100/8676] via 172.16.10.5, 00:00:19, Ethernet0/1
mirage#
```

The next step in the lab is to configure a default network on the sea_shepherd router. To achieve this, add the global command **ip default-network 204.30.121.0** on the sea_shepherd router. Remember, for a router to use a default route, **ip classless** also must be enabled. Viewing the route table on the mirage router, the default network is now set with the *, and a gateway of last resort is also set to network 204.30.121.0. Example 10-18 lists the routing table of mirage after the default network is set on the sea_shepherd router.

Example 10-18 *mirage Routing Table After the Default Network Is Set on sea_shepherd*

```
mirage#show ip route
<<<text omitted>>>
Codes: C - connected, S - static, I - IGRP, R - RIP, M - mobile, B - BGP
       D - EIGRP, EX - EIGRP external, O - OSPF, IA - OSPF inter area
       N1 - OSPF NSSA external type 1, N2 - OSPF NSSA external type 2
       E1 - OSPF external type 1, E2 - OSPF external type 2, E - EGP
       i - IS-IS, L1 - IS-IS level-1, L2 - IS-IS level-2, * - candidate default
       U - per-user static route, o - ODR

Gateway of last resort is 172.16.10.5 to network 204.30.121.0

     172.16.0.0/24 is subnetted, 4 subnets
I       172.16.128.0 [100/1200] via 172.16.10.1, 00:03:06, Ethernet0/1
C       172.16.10.0 is directly connected, Ethernet0/1
I       172.16.1.0 [100/158350] via 172.16.10.1, 00:01:18, Ethernet0/1
I       172.16.2.0 [100/8576] via 172.16.10.5, 00:00:27, Ethernet0/1
I     110.0.0.0/8 [100/1200] via 172.16.10.1, 00:01:18, Ethernet0/1
I*    204.30.121.0/24 [100/8676] via 172.16.10.5, 00:00:27, Ethernet0/1
mirage#
```

Another task of this lab is to configure unequal-cost load balancing to the default network from the mirage router. Recalling the process from an earlier section, you need to set the bandwidth and then derive and configure the variance. You have already accomplished the first step by taking the extra time to tune the IGRP configuration with the **bandwidth** statements earlier in the lab. For the second step, you need to derive the variance. The variance formula is as follows:

1 + ([highest_cost_path/lowest_cost_path] Rounded up)

Use **debug ip igrp transactions** to find the lowest-cost metric to 204.30.121.0/24. Example 10-19 shows the output of the command on the ocean_warrior router.

Example 10-19 debug ip igrp transactions *Command Output on the ocean_warrior Router*

```
ocean_warrior#debug ip igrp transactions
IGRP protocol debugging is on
ocean_warrior#
04:35:06: IGRP: received update from 172.16.1.4 on Serial1
04:35:06:        subnet 172.16.10.0, metric 160350 (neighbor 8576)
04:35:06:        subnet 172.16.2.0, metric 160250 (neighbor 8476)
04:35:06:        exterior network 204.30.121.0, metric 158350 (neighbor 1100) ←High
                    metric
04:35:06: IGRP: received update from 172.16.10.9 on Ethernet4
04:35:06:        subnet 172.16.10.0, metric 1200 (neighbor 1100)
04:35:06:        subnet 172.16.2.0, metric 8676 (neighbor 8576)
04:35:06:        exterior network 204.30.121.0, metric 8776 (neighbor 8676) ←low
                    metric
```

In this model, you have 1 + (158350/8776) = 20. After the variance is set, the router reports two paths to the destination network and load-shares over them. Example 10-20 shows the route table of the ocean_warrior router after the **variance 20** command was added under the IGRP process.

Example 10-20 show ip route *Command Output on the ocean_warrior Router*

```
ocean_warrior#show ip route
<<<text omitted>>>
Gateway of last resort is 172.16.1.4 to network 204.30.121.0

     172.16.0.0/24 is subnetted, 4 subnets
C       172.16.128.0 is directly connected, Ethernet3
C       172.16.10.0 is directly connected, Ethernet4
C       172.16.1.0 is directly connected, Serial1
I       172.16.2.0 [100/160250] via 172.16.1.4, 00:00:11, Serial1
                   [100/8576] via 172.16.10.5, 00:00:34, Ethernet4
I*   204.30.121.0/24 [100/158350] via 172.16.1.4, 00:00:11, Serial1
                     [100/8676] via 172.16.10.5, 00:00:34, Ethernet4
                            Two paths to the default network!
ocean_warrior#
```

Next, you need to filter the ocean_warrior subnet of 110.16.20.0/24 from the mirage router. You need to configure distribute lists on the ocean_warrior router and the sirenian router. Example 10-21 shows the configuration of the ocean_warrior distribute list. The distribute list on the sirenian router is identical except for the Ethernet port.

Example 10-21 *Configuration of the Distribution List on ocean_warrior*

```
ocean_warrior(config)#router igrp 65001
ocean_warrior(config-router)#distribute-list 10 out e4
ocean_warrior(config-router)#exit
ocean_warrior(config)#access-list 10 deny 172.16.128.0 0.0.0.255
ocean_warrior(config)#access-list 10 permit any
```

When the 172.16.128.0/24 route is filtered out the Ethernet port on the ocean_warrior router, sirenian tries to route to this route through the sea_shepherd router. A static route can be added to sirenian to prevent this. Example 10-22 now lists the route table of the mirage router without the 172.16.128.0/24 subnet.

Example 10-22 *Route Table of the mirage Router, After the Filter*

```
mirage#show ip route
<<<text omitted>>>
Gateway of last resort is 172.16.10.5 to network 204.30.121.0

     172.16.0.0/24 is subnetted, 3 subnets
C        172.16.10.0 is directly connected, Ethernet0/1
I        172.16.1.0 [100/158350] via 172.16.10.1, 00:00:08, Ethernet0/1
I        172.16.2.0 [100/8576] via 172.16.10.5, 00:00:27, Ethernet0/1
I*    204.30.121.0/24 [100/8676] via 172.16.10.5, 00:00:27, Ethernet0/1
mirage#
```

Finally, the optional portion of the lab involves limiting broadcasts on the Ethernet segment between the routers. Broadcast can be limited by enabling unicast routing updates. The **neighbor** *a.b.c.d* statement, along with the **passive interface** command, causes only unicast routing updates to occur. The last example lists the final router configs, which includes the unicast configuration.

Example 10-23 *Final Router Configurations for Neptune Naval Intelligence Network Routers*

```
hostname sea_shepherd
!
interface Ethernet0
 ip address 204.30.121.30 255.255.255.0
!
interface Serial0
 ip address 172.16.2.4 255.255.255.0
 bandwidth 1544
```

continues

Example 10-23 *Final Router Configurations for Neptune Naval Intelligence Network Routers (Continued)*

```
 no fair-queue
 clockrate 2000000
!
interface Serial7
 ip address 172.16.1.4 255.255.255.0
 bandwidth 64
 clockrate 64000
!
router igrp 65001
 network 172.16.0.0
 network 204.30.121.0
!
ip classless
ip default-network 204.30.121.0
!
```

```
hostname ocean_warrior
!
interface Ethernet3
 ip address 172.16.128.1 255.255.255.0
 media-type 10BaseT
!
interface Serial1
 ip address 172.16.1.1 255.255.255.0
 bandwidth 64
!
router igrp 65001
 variance 20
 passive-interface Ethernet4
 network 110.0.0.0
 network 172.16.0.0
 neighbor 172.16.10.5
 neighbor 172.16.10.9
 distribute-list 10 out Ethernet4
!
ip classless
!
access-list 10 deny    172.16.128.0 0.0.0.255
access-list 10 permit any
```

```
hostname sirenian
!
 interface Ethernet0
 ip address 172.16.10.5 255.255.255.0
 no ip directed-broadcast
!
interface Serial0
 ip address 172.16.2.5 255.255.255.0
 bandwidth 1544
 no ip directed-broadcast
 no ip mroute-cache
 no fair-queue
```

Example 10-23 *Final Router Configurations for Neptune Naval Intelligence Network Routers (Continued)*

```
!
router igrp 65001
 passive-interface Ethernet0
 network 172.16.0.0
 neighbor 172.16.10.1
 neighbor 172.16.10.9
 distribute-list 10 out Ethernet0
!
ip classless
ip route 172.16.128.0 255.255.255.0 172.16.10.1

hostname mirage
!
interface Ethernet0/1
 ip address 172.16.10.9 255.255.255.0
!
router igrp 65001
 passive-interface Ethernet0/1
 network 172.16.0.0
 neighbor 172.16.10.5
 neighbor 172.16.10.1
!
ip classless
```

To verify unicast updates, perform a **debug ip igrp transactions** command on the sirenian or ocean_warrior routers. By performing this command on the sirenian router in Example 10-24, notice how the updates out the Ethernet 0 port are no longer sent to a broadcast address or 255.255.255.255, but instead are sent to a specific address as specified in the **neighbor** statement.

Example 10-24 *Verifying Unicast Updates*

```
sirenian#debug ip igrp transactions
IGRP protocol debugging is on
sirenian#
01:01:40: IGRP: sending update to 255.255.255.255 via Serial0 (172.16.2.5)
01:01:40:        subnet 172.16.10.0, metric=1100
01:01:40:        subnet 172.16.1.0, metric=158350
01:01:41: IGRP: sending update to 172.16.10.9 via Ethernet0 (172.16.10.5)
01:01:41:        subnet 172.16.10.0, metric=1100
01:01:41:        subnet 172.16.1.0, metric=158350
01:01:41:        subnet 172.16.2.0, metric=8476
01:01:41:        exterior 204.30.121.0, metric=8576
01:01:41: IGRP: sending update to 172.16.10.1 via Ethernet0 (172.16.10.5)
01:01:41:        subnet 172.16.10.0, metric=1100
01:01:41:        subnet 172.16.2.0, metric=8476
01:01:41:        exterior 204.30.121.0, metric=8576
```

CHAPTER 11

Hybrid: Enhanced Interior Gateway Routing Protocol (EIGRP)

As internetworks grew in scale and diversity in the early 1990s, new routing protocols were needed. Cisco developed *Enhanced Interior Gateway Routing Protocol (IGRP)* primarily to address many of the limitations of IGRP and RIP. As WANs were growing, so was the need for a routing protocol that would use efficient address space on WAN links, as well as the LAN networks. OSPF was available, but the CPU-intensive tasks that it had to perform often overloaded the small processors of many edge or remote routers of that time. The configuration was also more complex than that of RIP or IGRP. A routing protocol was needed that could support VLSM and that could scale with large internetworks, yet that was less CPU-intensive than OSPF. In 1994, Cisco answered the call by releasing Enhanced IGRP in Cisco IOS Software Release 9.21. Today, EIGRP is used as the routing protocol on many large government and commercial internetworks. It has proven to be very stable, flexible, and fast. In addition to these characteristics, the ease of EIGRP configuration makes it one of the most popular routing protocols among network engineers.

EIGRP can be referred to as a hybrid protocol. It combines most of the characteristics of traditional distance vector protocols with some characteristics of link-state protocols. Specifically, EIGRP is "enhanced" by using four routing technologies:

- Neighbor discovery/recovery
- Reliable Transport Protocol (RTP)
- DUAL finite-state machine
- Protocol-dependent modules

This chapter covers these technologies, as well as the operation and configuration of EIGRP.

Technical Overview of EIGRP

EIGRP offers many advantages over other routing protocols, including the following:

- **Support for VLSM**—EIGRP is a classless routing protocol and carries the subnet mask of the route in its update.

- **Rapid convergence**—By using the concept of feasible successors, defined by DUAL, EIGRP is capable of preselecting the next best path to a destination. This allows for very fast convergence upon a link failure.

- **Low CPU utilization**—Under normal operation, only hellos and partial updates are sent across a link. Routing updates are not flooded and are processed only periodically.

- **Incremental updates**—EIGRP does not send a full routing update; it sends only information about the changed route.

- **Scalable**—Through the use of VLSM and a complex composite metric, EIGRP networks can be vast in size.

- **Easy configuration**—EIGRP supports hierarchical network design, but it does not require the strict configuration guidelines, such as the ones needed for OSPF.

- **Automatic route summarization**—EIGRP will perform automatic summarization on major bit boundaries.

- **MD5 route authentication**—As of Cisco IOS Software Release 11.3, EIGRP can be configured to perform MD5 password authentication on route updates.

Looking at this list, it becomes evident why EIGRP has become a popular routing protocol. It provides many of the enhancements of OSPF, without the strict configuration guidelines. It could be argued that EIGRP's weakest point is that it is a Cisco-proprietary protocol, but with the aid of redistribution, this point becomes moot.

EIGRP is a classless routing protocol. It directly interfaces to IP as protocol 88. EIGRP uses the multicast address of 224.0.0.10 for hellos and routing updates instead of an all-hosts broadcast like RIP uses. EIGRP also employs a system of hello and hold timers to maintain neighbors. Aside from the initial routing update, partial routing updates are sent only when network topology changes occur. The updates are also bounded, which means that updates are sent only to pertinent routers. Like IGRP, EIGRP uses a composite metric to calculate the best path to a destination. The sections that follow take a closer look at how EIGRP makes use of metrics, neighbors, reliable transport, and DUAL in its operation.

NOTE	Early releases of EIGRP had stability issues over low-speed serial links and problems maintaining many neighbors. Cisco significantly enhanced EIGRP with Cisco IOS Software Releases 10.3(11), 11.0(8), and 11.1(3)— early releases of EIGRP are sometimes referred to as EIGRP version 1. Cisco currently ships routers with IOS 12.0 and above.

EIGRP Metrics

EIGRP uses metrics in the same way as IGRP. Each route in the route table has an associated metric. EIGRP uses a composite metric much like IGRP, except that it is modified by a multiplier of 256. Recall from Chapter 10, "Distance Vector Protocols: Interior Gateway Routing Protocol (EIGRP)," that bandwidth, delay, load, reliability, and MTU are the submetrics. Like IGRP, EIGRP chooses a route based primarily on bandwidth and delay, or the composite metric with the lowest numerical value. When EIGRP calculates this metric for a route, it calls it the *feasible distance* to the route. EIGRP calculates a feasible distance to all routes in the network. The following list is a detailed description of the five EIGRP submetrics:

- **Bandwidth**—Bandwidth is expressed in units of kilobits. It must be statically configured to accurately represent the interfaces that EIGRP is running on. For example, the default bandwidth of a 56-kbps interface and a T1 interface is 1544 kbps. To accurately adjust the bandwidth, use the **bandwidth** *kbps* interface subcommand. Table 11-1 highlights some common bandwidth values.

- **Delay**—Delay is expressed in microseconds. It, too, must be statically configured to accurately represent the interface that EIGRP is running on. The delay on an interface can be adjusted with the **delay** *time_in_microseconds* interface subcommand. Common delay values are represented in Table 11-1.

- **Reliability**—Reliability is a dynamic number in the range of 1 to 255, where 255 is a 100 percent reliable link and 1 is an unreliable link.

- **Load**—Load is the number in the range of 1 to 255 that shows the output load of an interface. This value is dynamic and can be viewed using the **show interfaces** command. A value of 1 indicates a minimally loaded link, whereas 255 indicates a 100 percent loaded link.

- **MTU**—The maximum transmission unit (MTU) is the recorded smallest MTU value in the path, usually 1500.

NOTE   Whenever you are influencing routing decisions in IGRP or EIGRP, use the metric of delay over bandwidth. Changing bandwidth can affect other routing protocols, such as OSPF. Changing delay affects only IGRP and EIGRP.

Table 11-1 highlights the common metrics used.

Table 11-1 *Common IGRP and EIGRP Metrics*

Medium	Bandwidth	Delay
100-Mbps ATM	100,000 kbps	100 µs
Gigabit Ethernet	100,000 kbps	100 µs
Fast Ethernet	100,000 kbps	100 µs
FDDI	100,000 kbps	100 µs
HSSI	45,045 kbps	20,000 µs
16-Mbps Token Ring	16,000 kbps	630 µs
10-Mbps Ethernet	10,000 kbps	1000 µs
T1	1544 kbps	20,000 µs
DS-0	64 kbps	20,000 µs
56-kbps media	56 kbps	20,000 µs

EIGRP uses a composite metric (CM) that is derived from the five submetrics. When EIGRP computes the composite metric, it uses a formula that involves five constants or "k" values. The constant values have default value such as the following:

k1 = k3 = 1 and k2 = k4 = k5 = 0

By setting k2, k4, and k5 to 0, it essentially nullifies the submetrics of load, reliability, and MTU. This is precisely why you should first use delay and then bandwidth when trying to influence which routes EIGRP prefers. The formula EIGRP uses to calculate the composite metric is as follows:

$$CM = 256 \times ([k1 \times BW_{mim} + (k2 \times BW_{mim}) / (256\text{-}LOAD) + k3 \times DELAY_{sum}] \times X)$$

where the following is true:

$BW_{mim} = 10^7$ / bandwidth_of_slowest_link
$DELAY_{sum} = \Sigma$ (delays_along_the_path)
$X = k5$ / (reliability + k4) if and only if $k1 <> 1$, if k1 = 1 then X = 1

With the k values set at the default value you have

k1 = k3 = 1
k2 = k4 = k5 = 0
$CM = 256 \times (BW_{mim} + DELAY_{sum})$

NOTE   The router calculation of the composite metric will always differ slightly from the result when it is performed by longhand. This is because of the way the router handles floating-point mathematics; there will be slight rounding discrepancies.

Using the default values of constants, $k1 = k3 = 1$ and $k2 = k4 = k5 = 0$, the formula quickly breaks down to this:

$$(256 \times [\text{BW}_{\text{mim}} \text{ and } \text{DELAY}_{\text{sum}}])$$

Substituting the constants, you have the following:

$$\text{CM} = 256 \times ([1 \times \text{BW}_{\text{mim}} + (0 * \text{BW}_{\text{mim}}) / (256\text{-LOAD}) + 1 \times \text{DELAY}_{\text{sum}}] \times 1)$$
$$\text{CM} = 256 \times ([\text{BW}_{\text{mim}} + (0) / (256\text{-LOAD}) + \text{DELAY}_{\text{sum}}] \times 1)$$
$$\text{CM} = 256 \times (\text{BW}_{\text{mim}} + \text{DELAY}_{\text{sum}})$$

NOTE

For reference, the metric is computed the same way for IGRP, except the result of bandwidth and delay is not multiplied by 256, and the **DELAY$_{\text{sum}}$** variable is divided by 10.

$$\text{CM} = (k1 \times \text{BW}_{\text{min}} + [k2 \times \text{BW}_{\text{min}}] / [256\text{-LOAD}] + [k3 \times \text{DELAY}_{\text{sum}}] \times X)$$

where the following is true:

$\text{BW}_{\text{min}} = 10^7 /$ bandwidth of slowest link

$\text{DELAY}_{\text{sum}} = S(\text{delays\_along\_the\_path}) / 10$

$X = k5 / (\text{reliability} + k4)$ if and only if $k1 <> 1$, if $k1 = 1$ then $X = 1$

$k1 = k3 = 1$

$k2 = k4 = k5 = 0$

With k values set at the default value, you have:

$$\text{CM} = \text{BW}_{\text{min}} + \text{DELAY}_{\text{sum}}$$

To demonstrate composite metric calculation, refer to Figure 11-1. In this example, EIGRP calculates a composite metric on the alpha router to 172.16.1.0/24, which resides on the charlie router.

Assuming that the **bandwidth** statements been set by an astute engineer, the lowest bandwidth on the path between alpha and charlie routers would be 56. Therefore, you have

$$\text{BW}_{\text{mim}} = 10^7 / 56 = 178571$$

The delay is the summation of the delays on the outbound interfaces only. The summation ends with the delay on the interface in which the final subnet resides. From alpha to bravo, the delay is 20000; from bravo to charlie, it is 1000; this includes the final interface on charlie, which has a delay of 1000. Therefore, you have

$$\text{DELAY}_{\text{sum}} = 20000 + 1000 + 1000 = 22000$$

The composite metric now yields the following:

$$\text{CM} = 256 \times (178571) + 256 \times (22000) = 46277485$$

Figure 11-1 *EIGRP Routing Updates*

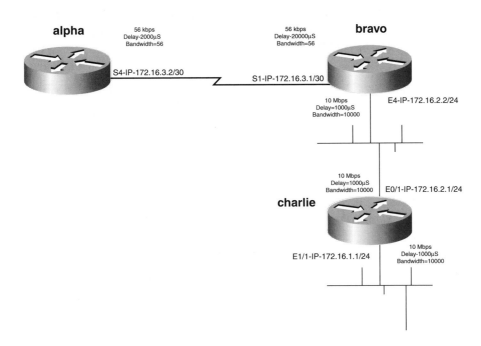

The submetrics and the composite metric can be confirmed by performing the **show ip route 172.16.1.0** command on the alpha router, as in Example 11-1. Remember, because of rounding errors, the metric does not match exactly.

Example 11-1 show ip route *Command Output Highlighting the EIGRP Metrics*

```
alpha#show ip route 172.16.1.0
Routing entry for 172.16.1.0/24
  Known via "eigrp 65001", distance 90, metric 46277376, type internal
  Redistributing via eigrp 65001
  Last update from 172.16.3.1 on Serial7, 00:50:53 ago
  Routing Descriptor Blocks:
  * 172.16.3.1, from 172.16.3.1, 00:50:53 ago, via Serial7
      Route metric is 46277376, traffic share count is 1
      Total delay is 22000 microseconds, minimum bandwidth is 56 Kbit
      Reliability 255/255, minimum MTU 1500 bytes
      Loading 1/255, Hops 2

alpha#
```

When using metrics to influence routing decisions, use the **delay** *xx* interface command. Be sure to include a delay at each side of the interface if you want symmetrical routing—that is, packets will take the same route back to the source. By default, EIGRP will perform equal-cost load balancing over routes. For example, if you perform a **show ip route** command and see two routes to a destination reported, EIGRP will load-balance over those routes.

To demonstrate the use of the delay metric, we have added another Ethernet segment between the bravo and charlie routers and a loopback interface, 172.16.128.1/24, on the charlie router, as illustrated in Figure 11-2.

Figure 11-2 *EIGRP Load Sharing*

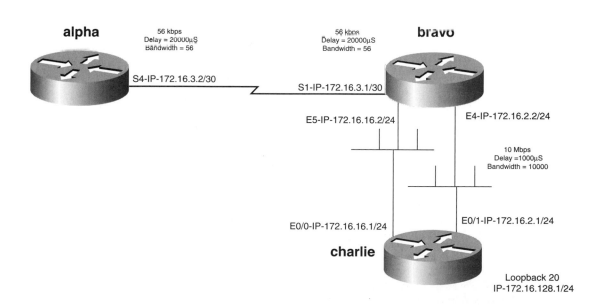

If you perform a **show ip route** command on the bravo router, as shown in Example 11-2, you see two routes to the 172.16.128.0/24 network. The **show ip eigrp topology** command also lists the routes and the composite metric to them.

Example 11-2 *Two Routes Reported to 172.16.128.0/24*

```
bravo#show ip route
Codes: C - connected, S - static, I - IGRP, R - RIP, M - mobile, B - BGP
       D - EIGRP, EX - EIGRP external, O - OSPF, IA - OSPF inter area
       N1 - OSPF NSSA external type 1, N2 - OSPF NSSA external type 2
       E1 - OSPF external type 1, E2 - OSPF external type 2, E - EGP
       i - IS-IS, L1 - IS-IS level-1, L2 - IS-IS level-2, * - candidate default
       U - per-user static route, o - ODR

Gateway of last resort is not set

     172.16.0.0/16 is variably subnetted, 4 subnets, 2 masks
D       172.16.128.0/24 [90/409600] via 172.16.2.1, 00:23:50, Ethernet4
                        [90/409600] via 172.16.16.1, 00:23:50, Ethernet5
C       172.16.16.0/24 is directly connected, Ethernet5
C       172.16.2.0/24 is directly connected, Ethernet4
C       172.16.3.0/30 is directly connected, Serial1
bravo#
```

If you want EIGRP to prefer one path to the other, add the **delay** command on each side of the interface. It is important to note that changing the delay of a link will affect only the routing protocol, not the actual throughput of the link.

Continuing with the example, set the delay of the link so that the primary link to 172.16.128.0 will be through 172.16.16.1. This can be accomplished by adding a delay of 1000 to the e4 interface of the bravo router and under the e0/1 interface of the charlie router. Example 11-3 demonstrates the configuration of delay on the bravo router.

Example 11-3 *Addition of the* **delay** *Command*

```
bravo#conf t
Enter configuration commands, one per line.  End with CNTL/Z.
bravo(config)#int e4
bravo(config-if)#delay 1000
bravo(config-if)#^Z
```

Example 11-4 shows the route table of the bravo router after the delay was added to the bravo and charlie routers.

Example 11-4 *One Route to the 172.16.128.0/24 Route*

```
bravo#show ip route
     172.16.0.0/16 is variably subnetted, 4 subnets, 2 masks
D       172.16.128.0/24 [90/409600] via 172.16.16.1, 00:00:11, Ethernet5
C       172.16.16.0/24 is directly connected, Ethernet5
C       172.16.2.0/24 is directly connected, Ethernet4
C       172.16.3.0/30 is directly connected, Serial1
bravo#
```

Keep in mind that although the second route is removed from the routing table, EIGRP still knows of the route and will keep it as a feasible successor.

The *k* values also can be manipulated to influence routing decisions. This can be accomplished with the **metric weights** tos *k1 k2 k3 k4 k5* command. Manipulating these values directly impacts how EIGRP derives the composite metric for all routes. Change the metric weights only when working with Cisco to solve specific problems.

EIGRP Neighbors

EIGRP does not periodically advertise it routes. Because of this, it needs some way to locate and then exchange routing information with adjacent devices. EIGRP accomplishes this through the use of neighbors. When EIGRP initializes, it sends out a multicast hello on address 224.0.0.10, on broadcast media. On NBMA media, X.25, Frame Relay, and ATM, the hellos are unicast every 60 seconds. EIGRP continues to send out hellos every few seconds, based on the media type. Specifically, EIGRP sends hellos every 5 seconds on the following interfaces:

- LAN broadcast media, such as Ethernet, Token Ring, and FDDI
- High-speed serial link greater than T1 speeds, such as Frame Relay HSSI links
- Point-to-point serial links, such as PPP or HDLC
- ATM and Frame Relay point-to-point subinterfaces

EIGRP sends hellos every 60 seconds on the following interfaces:

- Low-speed serial links less than T1 speeds, including Frame Relay and multipoint X.25
- ATM and Frame Relay multipoint interfaces, and ATM SVCs
- ISDN BRIs

Routers that reside on the same network receive the multicast hello and respond to form what is called an *adjacency.* Figure 11-3 and the list that follows describe the initial router exchange when forming an adjacency:

1 Hellos are sent out each interface participating in EIGRP, except interfaces quieted by the passive interfaces. All EIGRP hellos and routing updates use the multicast address of 224.0.0.10.

2 Routers on the same IP subnet receive the multicast and respond with a full routing update. This is accomplished by setting the INITialization bit in the EIGRP header; the updates include all networks that EIGRP is aware of and the metric for those routes, except for those suppressed by split horizon. This update packet establishes a neighbor relationship (adjacency). The hello packet also includes a *hold timer*, which tells the router how long it should wait before receiving a hello and declaring the route unreachable and reporting it to the DUAL process. The hold timer is set to three times the value assigned for the hello timer. This usually is 15 or 180 seconds, depending on the media.

3 The bravo router responds to the initialization packet by sending a hello with the ACK bit set. EIGRP sets the ACK bit to acknowledge all messages that it receives that have data. This is one way that EIGRP has reliable transports (discussed further in upcoming sections).

4 The bravo router now inserts the new update into its route table. Because it has a new update, it sends an update to all its neighbors.

5 The neighbors that received the update from the bravo message respond with an acknowledgment packet.

6 The router holds the adjacency by the continuous exchange of hellos. If a hello is not received by the time the hold timer expires, the router marks the route as unreachable.

Figure 11-3 *EIGRP Neighbor Establishment*

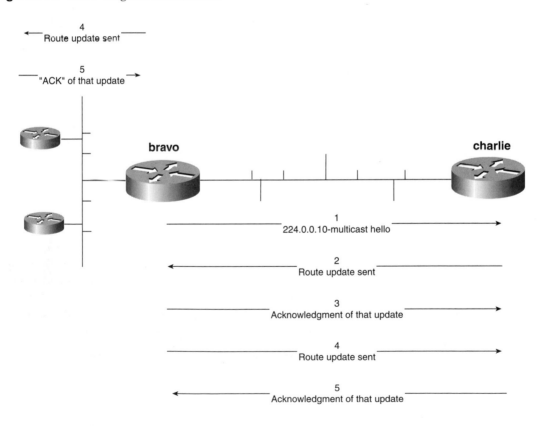

When the router forms an adjacency, it treats this as a virtual link to transport routing information.

The router begins to form a neighbor table with the following information:

- The IP address of the router that it received the hello from
- The hold timer
- The SRTT or round-trip time
- The uptime of the neighbor

The status of neighbors can be displayed with the **show ip eigrp neighbors** command, as in Example 11-5. The uptime of the neighbor should be for as long as the adjacency has been established.

Example 11-5 show ip eigrp neighbors *Command Output on the bravo Router*

```
bravo#show ip eigrp neighbors
IP-EIGRP neighbors for process 65001
H   Address               Interface   Hold Uptime    SRTT   RTO  Q   Seq
                                      (sec)          (ms)        Cnt Num
1   172.16.2.1            Et4           12 01:10:36     8   200  0   29
2   172.16.16.1           Et5           13 02:14:15     3   200  0   28
0   172.16.3.2            3e1           11 07:07:44    23  2604  0   23
bravo#
```

Stable EIGRP neighbors are the single most important element in any EIGRP network. Without stable neighbors, an EIGRP network will have difficulty operating properly. Checking the status of EIGRP neighbors should be the first step in verifying the operational status of any EIGRP network.

EIGRP Reliable Transport Protocol (RTP)

RTP ensures that EIGRP packets are received, delivered, ordered, and acknowledged. To guarantee delivery, EIGRP employs the use of a Cisco proprietary reliable multicast message. When each neighbor receives a reliable multicast packet, it is required to respond with a unicast acknowledgment. Updates also have sequence numbers; this is how the router ensures that updates are in the proper order. To facilitate RTP and the other functions of EIGRP, Cisco uses four primary types of packets, even though there are actually five. As previously mentioned, all EIGRP packets directly interface with the IP layer as protocol 88, and the multicast updates use the IP address of 224.0.0.10. The five packet types are as follows:

- **Hello**—Used to discover and maintain neighbors. This packet type uses unreliable delivery.
- **Acknowledgments (ACKs)**—Used to acknowledge updates. They are essentially hellos with no data in them. ACKs also use unreliable delivery.

- **Updates**—Contain routing information. Updates can be either unicast or multicast, depending on how they are generated. Updates use reliable delivery.

- **Queries**—Used by the DUAL process to find feasible successor for routes. The query can be unicast or multicast. Queries always use reliable delivery.

- **Replies**—Used by the DUAL process to aid in finding feasible successor for routes. Replies are always unicast and use reliable delivery.

NOTE   Some documentation refers to queries and replies as the four and fifth types of packets. The actual fifth type of packet is a request. The request never was implemented in EIGRP and was intended for route servers. IPX SAPs also use another Opcode in the EIGRP header, making them another packet type.

Diffusing Update Algorithm

The DUAL algorithm is the "brains" of EIGRP, responsible for tracking all routes by all neighbors and ensuring a loop-free topology. It is based on an algorithm first developed by E.W. Dijkstra and C.S. Scholten, and later enhanced by J.J. Garcia-Luna-Aceves.

With the help of DUAL, EIGRP and the processes previously covered, EIGRP keeps the following tables:

- **Neighbor table**—EIGRP tracks every formed adjacency in the neighbor table. A neighbor will be held until an ACK is not received after 16 unicast retransmissions to that neighbor. At this time, the neighbor is dropped. Neighbors can be displayed with the **show ip eigrp neighbors** command.

- **Topology table**—All learned routes reported by neighbors are kept in the topology table. The topology table also tracks the metrics and feasible distances associated with those routes. The topology table can be displayed with the **show ip eigrp topology** *as_number* command.

- **Route table/forwarding table**—Only the routes with the lowest composite metric are entered into the final route or forwarding table. This is the route that the router will forward to.

The process that DUAL uses to perform a loop-free topology is a detailed process. EIGRP has what is called a *feasible successor* and a *successor* to every route in its route table. The *successor* is the primary path for the route, or the path that the router will forward packets to. The *feasible successor* becomes the next-hop address only if the primary route to the destination becomes unreachable. The *feasible successor* is always downstream and, thereby, must have a distance or *feasible distance* that is less than that of the current preferred route. This prevents routing loops because the downstream router must always have a feasible cost lower than that of the current cost of the route to be considered as a feasible successor.

The DUAL process is in control of determining feasible distances, feasible successors, and the successor of the routes in the EIGRP topology table. By having a backup path already defined in the topology table, the router can quickly converge to the new path in case the primary path fails.

Protocol-Dependent Modules

EIGRP is one of the few routing protocols that can work with multiple routed protocols. Cisco implements what it calls *protocol-dependent modules* in the code that handle protocol-specific tasks. For example, IPX EIGRP needs to send and receive SAP updates. IP and IPX form neighbors using different message formats.

EIGRP operates the same way for all routed protocols—that is, it uses DUAL to find the shortest path to forward data toward. Another task of protocol-dependent modules is to pass data into the DUAL process so that a proper topology table, and eventually a route table, can be formed.

Like IGRP, EIGRP deploys the concepts of split horizon and poison reverse to prevent routing loops.

Split Horizon

Recall from earlier that *split horizon* is a routing technique in which information about routes is prevented from exiting the router interface or subinterface through which that information was received. Split horizon is most prevalent in multipoint networks. Here, routing updates flow into one subinterface but also must be sent out that very same subinterface to reach the other routers on the multipoint network. Split horizon is enabled by default and prevents specific route updates for EIGRP, IGRP, and RIP from being propagated properly in a multipoint configuration. Disable this with the **no ip split-horizon eigrp** *autonomous system* command. This command has similar forms for IPX and AppleTalk.

In Figure 11-4, the grinch router receives updates from the whos and whoville routers, but because of split horizon, the grinch does not advertise 172.16.5.0 and 172.16.6.0 out its serial 0.1 multipoint interface. Because the grinch didn't learn about the 172.16.2.0 network from its 0.1 interface, it advertises that network to the whos and whoville routers.

Figure 11-4 *EIGRP Split Horizons Route Suppression*

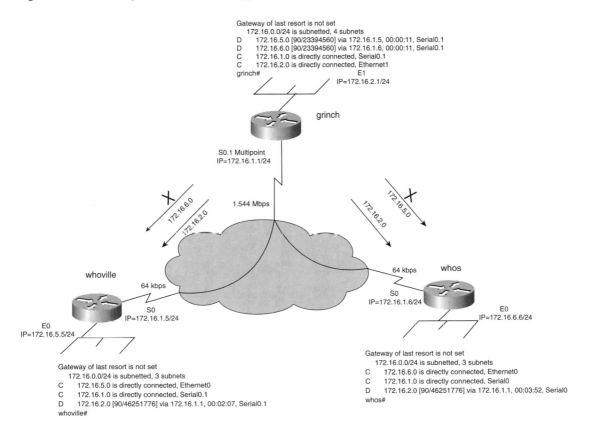

To make the whos and whoville happy again, we need to disable split horizon on the grinch by using the **no ip split-horizon eigrp** command, as demonstrated in Example 11-6.

Example 11-6 *Disabling Split Horizon on the grinch Router*

```
grinch(config)#int s0.1
grinch(config-subif)#no ip split-horizon eigrp 2001
```

Figure 11-5 illustrates how the routing tables will look after disabling split horizon on the grinch router. Notice that all routes are being propagated.

Figure 11-5 *Fully Functional EIGRP Network*

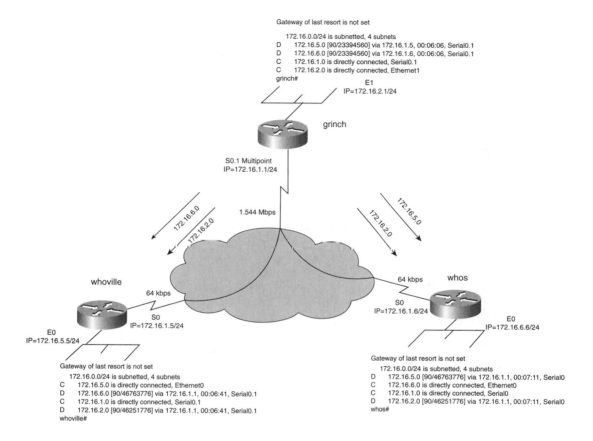

Configuring EIGRP

Configuring basic EIGRP is, for the most part, identical to configuring IGRP. Configuring EIGRP calls for the definition of an *autonomous system (AS)*. By definition, an AS is a set of routers under a single administrative technical authority. Like IGRP, EIGRP uses the concept of ASs to separate routing processes. Having a registered AS when configuring EIGRP is not required.

This following three-step process can be used to configure EIGRP. The third step is optional to specific environments.

Step 1 Enable EIGRP and define an AS on the router. This is accomplished with the **router eigrp** *autonomous_system_id* global command.

Step 2   Add the networks that you want to run EIGRP on. This is accomplished with the **network a.b.c.d** from the config-router# mode. When you enter the network statements, it is necessary to enter only the major class boundary. In Cisco IOS Software Release 12.0 and later, the **network** command adds an additional wildcard mask, much like OSPF. This is an inverse bit mask—for example, to enable EIGRP on network 172.16.1.0 only, the syntax would be **network 172.16.1.0 0.0.0.255**; however, note that *EIGRP is smart enough to convert a subnet mask to a wildcard mask if you make a mistake*. Now that's user-friendly!

Step 3   (Optional) Fine-tune EIGRP metrics with **bandwidth** statements, or configure IGRP summarization and options. By taking the time to configure bandwidth, EIGRP will have a more accurate picture of the network and also will aid in preventing EIGRP from saturating the link with broadcasts. The bandwidth always should be set on Frame Relay networks. The bandwidth can be changed with the **bandwidth kilobits** interface command. Later sections in the chapter cover bandwidth and summarizing EIGRP in greater detail.

Example 11-7 illustrates the EIGRP configuration from Figure 11-5 on the grinch router.

Example 11-7 *EIGRP Configuration*

```
! hostname grinch
!
interface Ethernet1
 ip address 172.16.2.1 255.255.255.0
 media-type 10BaseT
!
interface Serial0
 no ip address
 encapsulation frame-relay
 no ip mroute-cache
!
interface Serial0.1 multipoint
 ip address 172.16.1.1 255.255.255.0
 no ip split-horizon eigrp 2001      ←Split Horizons disabled
 bandwidth 112                        ←Bandwidth set to the sum of the remote PVCs
 frame-relay map ip 172.16.1.5 110 broadcast
 frame-relay map ip 172.16.1.6 130 broadcast
!
router eigrp 2001                     ←EIGRP routing process
 network 172.16.0.0                   ←Networks running EIGRP
 !
```

Before further discussing these and other EIGRP options in greater detail, lets take a closer look at the **show** commands for EIGRP.

The "Big show" and "Big D" for EIGRP

Cisco offers some useful tools for determining how EIGRP is working. Perhaps one of the best and most overlooked commands is **show ip eigrp neighbors**. EIGRP neighbors remind me of an old Robert Frost poem that said, "Good fences make good neighbors." Well, in EIGRP, "Good networks make good neighbors." The neighbor state is absolutely critical to EIGRP operations. Besides providing the capability to assess neighbor states, Cisco offers tools to look at the EIGRP topology table, as well as providing detailed logging of EIGRP events.

The following is a list of what we find to be the most useful **show**, logging, and **debug** commands for EIGRP:

```
show ip eigrp neighbors [as_number | interface_name]
show ip eigrp topology [as_number | active | pending | summary] [as_number subnet
subnet_mask]
show ip protocols [summary]
show ip route
debug eigrp packets
eigrp log-neighbor-changes
```

show ip eigrp neighbors Command

This can be one of the most useful commands when verifying the operational status of EIGRP. The **show ip eigrp neighbors** command shows the status of all EIGRP neighbors. The neighbor should be "up" for as long as EIGRP has been running on the link. EIGRP forms a neighbor relationship with all routers on the same subnet and in the same AS. EIGRP does not form a neighbor relationship with mismatched k values; however, a neighbor can be formed with mismatched hellos and dead timers. A neighbor with a short uptime is a clear indication of a problem. Another important field is the queue count. This field indicates the number of packets waiting to be transmitted to that neighbor. This value should be 0 or a number under 20. Consistent Q values in the range of 60 or greater are considered high. A high SRTT number can mean that the packet is experiencing some type of delay on the link. Example 11-8 provides some sample output from the **show ip eigrp neighbor** command, which provides the basis for an explanation of the other fields, which follows.

Example 11-8 **show ip eigrp neighbor** *Command Performed on the grinch Router*

```
grinch#show ip eigrp neighbors
IP-EIGRP neighbors for process 2001
H   Address               Interface     Hold Uptime    SRTT   RTO  Q   Seq
                                        (sec)          (ms)        Cnt Num
1   172.16.1.5            Se0.1          136 05:48:23    36   1302  0   15
0   172.16.1.6            Se0.1          131 05:48:24    40   1302  0   17
grinch#
```

- **Handle (H)**—A Cisco IOS internal number used to identify a neighbor. Do not confuse this with hop count.

- **Neighbor Address**—The adjacent neighbor's IP address. A neighbor should be formed between every router on that subnet running EIGRP in a common AS.

- **Interface**—The interface that is reporting the neighbor.

- **HoldTime**—The amount of time, which counts down, that EIGRP waits for a hello before tearing down the neighbor.

- **Uptime**—Statement of how long the neighbor has been up. This number should be up for as long as the link has been up.

- **Smooth Round Trip Timer (SRRT)**—The number of milliseconds that it takes for an EIGRP packet to be sent to this neighbor and for the local router to receive an acknowledgment—hence, a round-trip timer. If this number equals 0, a packet has never made a successful round trip.

- **Retransmission TimeOut (RTO)**—The amount of time, in milliseconds, that the EIGRP waits before retransmitting a packet from the retransmission queue to a neighbor.

- **Queue count (Q)**—The number of packets waiting in the queue to be sent out to this neighbor. This value should be 0 or a very low number. A high queue count indicates that data is having trouble getting through.

- **Sequence Number (Seq-Num)**—Sequence number of the last update, query, or reply that was received from this neighbor. If this number equals 0, it indicates that no reliable packets have ever been received from the neighbor, another clear indication of a problem.

NOTE   Just because a network appears in the route table does not necessarily mean that "routing" is working properly. In some instances, such as timer mismatches, networks can "phase" in and out of the route table. It is important to look at other things, such as neighbors and databases, to get a clearer view of whether "routing" is actually working properly.

show ip eigrp topology Command

This command lists the EIGRP topology table discussed earlier. The table lists all routes that EIGRP is aware of and shows whether EIGRP is actively processing information on that route. Under most normal conditions, the routes should all be in a passive state and no EIGRP process are running for that route. If the routes are active, this could indicate the dreaded *stuck in active*, or SIA, state, which is discussed in more detail in an upcoming section. The **show ip eigrp topology** command also can be extended to show information about an individual route or subnet. This information includes all relevant information about the route, including all its metrics and successors, as well as how the route was learned. Example 11-9 illustrates the use of **show ip eigrp topology**, followed by the extended version of the command.

Example 11-9 *EIGRP Topology Table of the grinch Router*

```
grinch#show ip eigrp topology
IP-EIGRP Topology Table for process 2001

Codes: P - Passive, A - Active, U - Update, Q - Query, R - Reply,
       r - Reply status

P 172.16.5.0/24, 1 successors, FD is 23394560
        via 172.16.1.5 (23394560/281600), Serial0.1
P 172.16.6.0/24, 1 successors, FD is 23394560
        via 172.16.1.6 (23394560/281600), Serial0.1
P 172.16.1.0/24, 1 successors, FD is 23368960
        via Connected, Serial0.1
P 172.16.2.0/24, 1 successors, FD is 281600
        via Connected, Ethernet1
grinch#

grinch#show ip eigrp topology 2001 172.16.5.0 255.255.255.0
IP-EIGRP topology entry for 172.16.5.0/24
  State is Passive, Query origin flag is 1, 1 Successor(s), FD is 23394560
  Routing Descriptor Blocks:
  172.16.1.5 (Serial0.1), from 172.16.1.5, Send flag is 0x0
      Composite metric is (23394560/281600), Route is Internal
      Vector metric:
        Minimum bandwidth is 112 Kbit
        Total delay is 21000 microseconds
        Reliability is 254/255
        Load is 1/255
        Minimum MTU is 1500
        Hop count is 1
grinch#
```

The fields to note in this output are as follows:

- **P**—Passive; no EIGRP computation is being performed. This is the ideal state.
- **A**—Active; EIGRP computations are "actively" being performed for this destination. Routes constantly appearing in an active state indicate a neighbor or query problem. Both are symptoms of the SIA problem.
- **U**—Update; an update packet was sent to this destination.
- **Q**—Query; a query packet was sent to this destination.
- **R**—Reply; a reply packet was sent to this destination.

- **Route information**—IP address of the route or network, its subnet mask, and the successor, or next hop to that network, or the feasible successor.

- **FD**—Feasible distance to the destination network.

- Send Flag—The type of packets that need to be sent for the entry.

  — 0x1 The router has received a query for this network and needs to send a unicast reply.

  — 0x2 The route is active, and a multicast query should be sent.

  — 0x3 The route has changed, and a multicast update should be sent.

show ip protocols Command

This command displays all routing protocols, detailed timer and metric information, as well as routing update information. Example 11-10 lists the output of the **show ip protocols** command.

Example 11-10 **show ip protocols** *Command Output*

```
grinch#show ip protocols
Routing Protocol is "eigrp 2001"          ←AS system ID
  Outgoing update filter list for all interfaces is
  Incoming update filter list for all interfaces is
  Default networks flagged in outgoing updates
  Default networks accepted from incoming updates
  EIGRP metric weight K1=1, K2=0, K3=1, K4=0, K5=0 ←'K' values
  EIGRP maximum hopcount 100
  EIGRP maximum metric variance 1
  Redistributing: eigrp 2001
  Automatic network summarization is in effect      ←Auto-summary in effect
  Routing for Networks:
    172.16.0.0                          ←Networks running EIGRP
  Routing Information Sources:
    Gateway         Distance      Last Update
    172.16.1.5          90        00:08:48       ←Routes reported, and administrative
    172.16.1.6          90        00:08:52           distance of the route.
  Distance: internal 90 external 170              ←Default admin distance

grinch#
```

show ip route Command

This command lists the router's current route or forwarding table. The output lists what routing protocol the route is from—in this case, D for EIGRP internal routes and D EX for routes redistributed into EIGRP. The number behind the route is the administrative distance of the route, followed by the composite metric of the route. The via field explains where the route is from, how long ago an update was received, and by what interface it was received. Example 11-11 lists the output of this command.

Example 11-11 show ip route *Command Output*

```
grinch#show ip route
Codes: C - connected, S - static, I - IGRP, R - RIP, M - mobile, B - BGP
       D - EIGRP, EX - EIGRP external, O - OSPF, IA - OSPF inter area
       N1 - OSPF NSSA external type 1, N2 - OSPF NSSA external type 2
       E1 - OSPF external type 1, E2 - OSPF external type 2, E - EGP
       i - IS-IS, L1 - IS-IS level-1, L2 - IS-IS level-2, * - candidate default
       U - per-user static route, o - ODR

Gateway of last resort is not set

     172.16.0.0/24 is subnetted, 4 subnets
D       172.16.5.0 [90/23394560] via 172.16.1.5, 00:17:51, Serial0.1
D       172.16.6.0 [90/23394560] via 172.16.1.6, 00:29:06, Serial0.1
C       172.16.1.0 is directly connected, Serial0.1
C       172.16.2.0 is directly connected, Ethernet1
grinch#
```

debug eigrp packets Command

The "Big D" command for EIGRP, is just that: big. As discussed earlier, debugs always should be used in conjunction with logging. However, some EIGRP debugs can be so big that additional debugs are needed to control the output of the original **debug** command. One such case is the **debug eigrp packets** command.

Use the **debug eigrp packets** command to verify that EIGRP hellos are being exchanged and that adjacencies are being established. Each EIGRP packet sent and received is listed in this output. The output of this command can be controlled with further debugs, such as **debug ip eigrp [neighbor as_number IP_address_of_neighbor]**. Use the **debug ip eigrp** command. Use this command with caution and only to look further into a problem. Do not start troubleshooting EIGRP with this command. Example 11-12 lists the output of the **debug eigrp packets** command.

Example 11-12 debug eigrp *packets Command Output*

```
grinch#debug eigrp packets
06:22:29: EIGRP: Received HELLO on Serial0.1 nbr 172.16.1.5
06:22:29:   AS 2001, Flags 0x0, Seq 0/0 idbQ 0/0
06:22:29: EIGRP: Enqueueing UPDATE on Serial0.1 nbr 172.16.1.5 iidbQ un/rely 0/1
 peerQ un/rely 0/0 serno 2-10
06:22:29: EIGRP:  Requeued unicast on Serial0.1
06:22:29: EIGRP: Sending UPDATE on Serial0.1 nbr 172.16.1.5
06:22:29:   AS 2001, Flags 0x1, Seq 7/0 idbQ 0/0 iidbQ un/rely 0/0 peerQ un/rely
 0/1 serno 2-10
```

eigrp log-neighbor-changes Command

EIGRP also offers a unique logging command that can be useful when trying to isolate problems on your network. Use the router command **eigrp log-neighbor-changes** to verify any loss of EIGRP neighbors. Example 11-13 lists the log after an EIGRP hold time has expired.

Example 11-13 *EIGRP Log After a Neighbor Change*

```
grinch(config-router)#eigrp log-neighbor-changes
06:42:12: %DUAL-5-NBRCHANGE: IP-EIGRP 2001: Neighbor 172.16.1.6 (Serial0.1) is d
own: holding time expired
```

Tuning EIGRP Updates

Like IGRP, EIGRP has several parameters for tuning timers, controlling broadcasts, load sharing, and controlling routes. The following is a list of parameters adjustable for EIGRP:

* Router(config-if)**ip hello-interval eigrp** *as_number interval_in_seconds*—Use this interface command to change the hello timer for EIGRP. The default value of this command is interface-dependant. By default, hello packets are sent every 5 seconds. The exception to this is low-speed, *nonbroadcast multiaccess media (NBMA)*, where it is 60 seconds. Low-speed is defined as rates of T1 (1.544 Mbps) or slower. All neighbors residing on a network should have equal hello timers.

* Router(config-if)**ip hold-time eigrp** *as_number holdown_timer_in_seconds*—Use this command to change the EIGRP hold timer for routes received by this interface. The timer has a default vault of 180 seconds for low-speed NBMA networks and 15 seconds for all other networks. All neighbors residing on a network should have an equal hold timer.

EIGRP Redistribution and Route Control

To filter routing updates in EIGRP, use a distribute list. A distribute list calls a standard or extended access list and filters routing updates accordingly. When redistributing one protocol into another, use the **redistribute** command along with a default metric. A route map should be used in place of a distribute list when controlling specific routes during the redistribution process. Redistribution happens automatically between IGRP and EIGRP when they are in the same autonomous systems.

* Router(config-router)**distribute-list** [**1-199**] [**in** | **out**] [*interface*]—Use this command to call a standard or extended access list to filter inbound or outbound routing updates. The **in** and **out** options always are applied from the view of the interface—in other words, to prevent a routing update from being advertised out an interface, use the **out** option. To prohibit route updates from entering an interface, use the **in** option.

- Router(config-router)**redistribute** [**connected** | **static** | **bgp** | **rip** | **igrp** | **ospf** | **isis**] *{metric} {route-map}*—Use this command to redistribute other routing protocols into EIGRP. A route map may be added for additional route control. An optional metric also can be supplied for routes originating from the routing protocol being redistributed that are different from the default metric. Whenever redistributing routes, remember that IP needs a route to and from a destination. Many times, mutual redistribution might be required to give IP a path to *and* from a destination.

   Router(config-router)**default-metric** [*bandwidth_kbps 1-4214748364*] [*delay_ ms 1-4214748364*] [**reliability** *1-255*] [**load** *1-244*] [**mtu** *1-4214748364*]—Use this command to set the default metric of all routes redistributed into EIGRP. You must supply a default metric whenever redistributing. A common metric to use is **default-metric 1544 100 254 1 1500**. This metric tells the router to derive the composite metric from the values of bandwidth of 1544 and delay of 100; with a link that is 254 reliable, where 255 is 100 percent reliable; with a load of 1, or no load; and, finally, an MTU of 1500. Perhaps more important than the actual value of the default metric is the practice of using the same metric throughout the EIGRP domain so that all redistributed routes have the same weight.

NOTE   Whenever you are redistributing one routing protocol into another, you must use a default metric or supply a metric on the redistribution command.

The following subsets of commands are used to influence routing decisions made by EIGRP. Individual metrics can be modified in addition to the administrative distance of the EIGRP. Whenever you are influencing a specific link's metric, use the **delay** command over the **bandwidth** command. Both may be used; however, recall that OSPF also is affected by **bandwidth**, whereas **delay** affects only IGRP and EIGRP.

- Router(config-router)**metric weights 0** *k1 k2 k3 k4 k5*—This command allows you to set the weight of the EIGRP metric in terms of bandwidth, load, delay, and reliability. Change these values with extreme caution; EIGRP will not form neighbors with mismatched K values.

- Router(config-router)**distance** [*1-255*] *adjacent_neighbors_ip_address wildcard_ mask [access_list_0-99]*—Use this command to change the administrative distance of routes received from a neighbor. If the IP address and wildcard mask are omitted, all routes for that protocol will be set to the distance value. For a specific example and more practice with the **distance** command, see Chapter 10, "Distance Vector Protocols: Interior Gateway Routing Protocol (IGRP)."

- **Router(config-if)delay** [*1-4214748364*]—Specifies the delay of an interface in tens of microseconds. This command is used only by routing protocols and does not affect traffic on the link.

- Router(config-if)**bandwidth** [*bandwidth_kbps 1-4214748364*]—Specifies the bandwidth of an interface in kilobits per second. This command is used only by routing protocols and does not affect traffic on the link.

- Router(config-router)**passive-interface** *interface_name*—Prevents the sending of EIGRP hellos on the link. This command operates differently on EIGRP than on IGRP. Because hellos are suppressed, no neighbors are formed; therefore, no routing updates are sent or received.

- Router(config-router)**offset-list** [**access_list_0-99** {**in** | **out**} **offset** [*metric_offset_ 1-214748364*] [interface]—Used to increase the value of the routing metrics. The metric offset cannot exceed 214748364. The offset list is applied in the same way as it is in RIP, using the EIGRP metric. For an example of the application of the offset list, see Chapter 9, "Distance Vector Protocols: Routing Information Protocol Versions 1 and 2 (RIP-1 and RIP-2).

Practical Example: Applying EIGRP Redistribution

Let's apply some of these concepts to a practical model in route redistribution and control. The model in Figure 11-6 shows three routing domains. The canada routers and the Frame Relay network reside in the EIGRP domain. Across the Frame Relay network reside two other routing domains; the mexico routers are in an IGRP domain, while the usa routers reside in an OSPF domain.

You must verify two things within the routing domains to allow IP end-to-end connectivity:

- Notice that the IGRP domain is on a 24-bit boundary. This means that when the IGRP domain receives a route, it must exist on a major bit boundary or a 24-bit boundary for the interface to accept that route.

- Mutual redistribution must occur between EIGRP and IGRP, and EIGRP and OSPF.

Beginning with the configuration for the canada_1 router, you can follow the three-step process for configuring EIGRP as listed earlier in this chapter. First, all EIGRP routers are in the autonomous system 2001; therefore, you will use this as the Autonomous System ID. Second, the networks that you are running EIGRP on reside in the major network of 172.16.0.0, which you will use in the **network** command. The third step is optional; in this case, however, you are configuring EIGRP over Frame Relay, so it's a good idea to add the **bandwidth** commands under the serial subinterfaces. In this model, you will set the bandwidth equal to the port speed of the remote routers Frame Relay interface. Example 11-14 lists the configuration of the canada_1 router.

Figure 11-6 *EIGRP Network For EIGRP Redistribution and Route Control Examples*

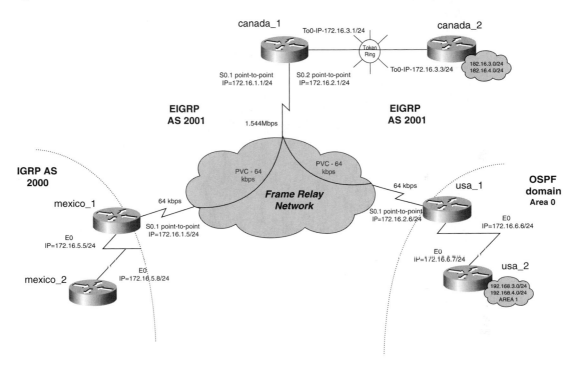

Example 11-14 *Configuration of the canada_1 Router*

```
hostname canada_1
!
interface Serial0
 no ip address
 encapsulation frame-relay
 no ip mroute-cache
!
interface Serial0.1 point-to-point
 ip address 172.16.1.1 255.255.255.0
 bandwidth 64                          ←EIGRP bandwidth set
 frame-relay interface-dlci 110
!
interface Serial0.2 point-to-point
 ip address 172.16.2.1 255.255.255.0
 bandwidth 64                          ←EIGRP bandwidth set
 frame-relay interface-dlci 130
!
interface TokenRing0
 ip address 172.16.3.1 255.255.255.0
```

continues

Example 11-14 *Configuration of the canada_1 Router (Continued)*

```
  ring-speed 16
!
router eigrp 2001                      ←EIGRP routing enabled
  network 172.16.0.0                    ←Networks running EIGRP
```

You can follow the same process to configure EIGRP for the mexico_1 and usa_1 routers, with a couple of minor differences. In both instances, you do not want to risk having any EIGRP neighbors automatically created on the Ethernet segments of these routers. To accomplish this, add the **passive-interface ethernet 0** command under EIGRP for the mexico_1 and usa_1 routers. Example 11-15 lists the configuration thus far for the mexico_1 and usa_1 routers. For more information on the IGRP and OSPF configuration portions of the configuration, see Chapter 10 and Chapter 12, "Link-State Protocols: Open Shortest Path First (OSPF)."

Example 11-15 *EIGRP Configuration of mexico_1 and usa_1 Routers*

```
hostname mexico_1
!
interface Ethernet0
 ip address 172.16.5.5 255.255.255.0
 no ip directed-broadcast
!
interface Serial0
 no ip address
 no ip directed-broadcast
 encapsulation frame-relay
 no ip mroute-cache
!
interface Serial0.1 point-to-point
 ip address 172.16.1.5 255.255.255.0
 no ip directed-broadcast
 frame-relay interface-dlci 111
!
<<<Text omitted>>>
!
router eigrp 2001
 passive-interface Ethernet0
 network 172.16.0.0
!
router igrp 2000
 passive-interface Serial0.1
 network 172.16.0.0
<<<Text omitted>>>

hostname usa_1
!
interface Ethernet0
 ip address 172.16.6.6 255.255.255.0
!
```

Example 11-15 *EIGRP Configuration of mexico_1 and usa_1 Routers (Continued)*

```
interface Serial0
 no ip address
 encapsulation frame-relay
!
interface Serial0.1 point-to-point
 ip address 172.16.2.6 255.255.255.0
 frame-relay interface-dlci 131
!
<<<Text omitted>>>
!
router eigrp 2001
 passive-interface Ethernet0
 network 172.16.0.0
!
router ospf 69
 network 172.16.6.6 0.0.0.0 area 0
<<<Text omitted>>>
```

At this point, you should have full IP connectivity within the EIGRP routing domain. To verify this, perform a **show ip route** combined with the **show ip eigrp neighbors** command on the canada_1 router, as demonstrated in Example 11-16.

Example 11-16 *Verifying EIGRP Routing*

```
canada_1#show ip route
Codes: C - connected, S - static, I - IGRP, R - RIP, M - mobile, B - BGP
       D - EIGRP, EX - EIGRP external, O - OSPF, IA - OSPF inter area
       N1 - OSPF NSSA external type 1, N2 - OSPF NSSA external type 2
       E1 - OSPF external type 1, E2 - OSPF external type 2, E - EGP
       i - IS-IS, L1 - IS-IS level-1, L2 - IS-IS level-2, * - candidate default
       U - per-user static route, o - ODR

Gateway of last resort is not set

     172.16.0.0/24 is subnetted, 5 subnets
D       172.16.5.0 [90/40537600] via 172.16.1.5, 00:45:58, Serial0.1
D       172.16.6.0 [90/40537600] via 172.16.2.6, 00:45:58, Serial0.2
C       172.16.1.0 is directly connected, Serial0.1
C       172.16.2.0 is directly connected, Serial0.2
C       172.16.3.0 is directly connected, TokenRing0
D    182.16.0.0/16 [90/304128] via 172.16.3.3, 00:43:27, TokenRing0
canada_1#
canada_1#show ip eigrp neighbors
IP-EIGRP neighbors for process 2001
H   Address                Interface    Hold Uptime    SRTT   RTO  Q  Seq
                                        (sec)          (ms)        Cnt Num
2   172.16.3.3             To0          11   00:43:36  685   4110  0  3
1   172.16.2.6             Se0.2        14   1d06h      48   2280  0  28
0   172.16.1.5             Se0.1        12   1d06h      29   2280  0  23
canada_1#
```

The important elements of the output that you are looking for are that route 172.16.5.0/24 is reported through 172.16.1.5, route 172.16.6.0/24 is reported through 172.16.2.6, and 182.16.3.0/24 and 182.16.4.0/24 are reported through 172.16.3.3. Because of EIGRP auto-summarization, 182.16.3.0/24 and 182.16.4.0 will be summarized at its natural 16 bit-boundary when these routes are advertised out the canada_2 Token Ring interface. The **show ip eigrp neighbors** command verifies that EIGRP adjacencies have been formed between canada_1 and the other two routers.

To allow EIGRP connectivity to the OSPF routing domain, you must mutually redistribute between EIGRP and OSPF on the usa_1 router. There is only one redistribution point for EIGRP and OSPF, so you do not have to take into account "route feedback" or redistribution loops. Example 11-17 shows the configuration of the usa_1 router.

Example 11-17 *Redistribution Configuration Portion of usa_1*

```
 !
router eigrp 2001
 redistribute ospf 69
 passive-interface Ethernet0
 network 172.16.0.0
 default-metric 1544 100 254 1 1500
 !
router ospf 69
 redistribute eigrp 2001 subnets
 network 172.16.6.6 0.0.0.0 area 0
 default-metric 100
 !
```

The OSPF routes 192.168.3.0/24 and 192.168.4.0/24 now appear as external EIGRP routes on the canada_1 router. Likewise, all EIGRP routes appear as OSPF external Type 2 routes on the usa_2 router.

Mutual redistribution also must be performed between the EIGRP and IGRP routing domains on the mexico_1 router. If the IGRP routing domain was in the same autonomous system as EIGRP, redistribution would not be necessary because it would occur automatically. Example 11-18 shows the configuration of the mexico_1 router.

Example 11-18 *Redistribution Configuration portion of mexico_1*

```
 !
router eigrp 2001
 redistribute igrp 2000
 passive-interface Ethernet0
 network 172.16.0.0
 default-metric 1544 100 254 1 1500
 !
router igrp 2000
 redistribute eigrp 2001
```

Example 11-18 *Redistribution Configuration portion of mexico_1 (Continued)*

```
passive-interface Serial0.1
network 172.16.0.0
default-metric 1544 100 254 1 1500
!
```

The route table for the mexico_2 router now shows all the appropriate routes for every network in the model. Example 11-19 shows the route table of mexico_2.

Example 11-19 *Route Table of the mexico_2 Router After Redistribution*

```
mexico_2#show ip route
Codes: C - connected, S - static, I - IGRP, R - RIP, M - mobile, B - BGP
       D - EIGRP, EX - EIGRP external, O - OSPF, IA - OSPF inter area
       N1 - OSPF NSSA external type 1, N2 - OSPF NSSA external type 2
       E1 - OSPF external type 1, E2 - OSPF external type 2, E - EGP
       i - IS-IS, L1 - IS-IS level-1, L2 - IS-IS level-2, * - candidate default
       U - per-user static route, o - ODR

Gateway of last report is not set

     172.16.0.0/24 is subnetted, 5 subnets
C       172.16.5.0 is directly connected, Ethernet0/0
I       172.16.6.0 [100/10676] via 172.16.5.5, 00:00:16, Ethernet0/0
I       172.16.1.0 [100/8576] via 172.16.5.5, 00:00:16, Ethernet0/0
I       172.16.2.0 [100/10576] via 172.16.5.5, 00:00:16, Ethernet0/0
I       172.16.3.0 [100/8639] via 172.16.5.5, 00:00:16, Ethernet0/0
I     192.168.4.0/24 [100/10676] via 172.16.5.5, 00:00:16, Ethernet0/0
I     182.16.0.0/16 [100/9139] via 172.16.5.5, 00:00:16, Ethernet0/0
I     192.168.3.0/24 [100/10676] via 172.16.5.5, 00:00:16, Ethernet0/0
mexico_2#
```

The redistribution in this model was relatively straightforward because all the networks in the model either are on a 24-bit boundary or are automatically summarized on a 24-bit boundary. EIGRP automatically summarizes at a major bit boundary when advertising or redistributing. During redistribution into IGRP, EIGRP automatically summarized the network 192.168.4.0/24 because it is on a 24-bit boundary along with 192.168.3.0/24. The network 182.16.0.0 was summarized when it was advertised out the s0.1 and s0.2 interfaces.

It is important to note that if the IP address of the advertising interface is in the same major class boundary as the route being advertised, automatic summarization will not occur. For example, if the router were advertising 172.16.100.0/30 out an interface with an IP address of 172.16.10.1/24, EIGRP would not summarize the route at its natural bit boundary. If the same network, 172.16.100.0/24, was advertised out an interface with the IP address of 172.17.10.1/24, EIGRP would advertise only the summary route 172.16.0.0/16, as seen in the previous model.

As you will see in the upcoming section on EIGRP summarization, we will make some subtle changes to the IP address structure, which will force the use of manual summarization before redistribution will work correctly.

Practical Example: Applying EIGRP Route Control

Now that you have a working IP network, let's examine route control through the application of route maps and distribution lists using the network in Figure 11-6 as the model again. On the usa_1 router, you will apply a distribution list preventing the route 192.168.3.0/24 from being advertised by EIGRP to the entire EIGRP domain. To carry out this task, use the **distribute-list** router command; apply an access list denying 192.168.3.0/24, while allowing other routes to be advertised. Example 11-20 highlights the configuration of the usa_1 router, allowing EIGRP to advertise only the 192.168.3.0/24 route.

Example 11-20 *Application of Distribution List*

```
router eigrp 2001
 redistribute ospf 69
 passive-interface Ethernet0
 network 172.16.0.0
 default-metric 1544 100 254 1 1500
 distribute-list 10 out Serial0.1     ←Apply access list 10 to interface s0.1
!
router ospf 69
 redistribute eigrp 2001 subnets
 network 172.16.6.6 0.0.0.0 area 0
 default-metric 100
!
ip classless
access-list 10 deny    192.168.3.0 0.0.0.255    ←deny route 192.168.3.0/24
access-list 10 permit any            ←allow all other routes to pass
!
```

Whenever you are controlling routing updates from one routing protocol to another, use a route map. In this model, a route map is used to prohibit the OSPF route of 172.16.6.0/24 from being redistributed from EIGRP into IGRP. The route map is called from the **redistribution** command in IGRP; the route map then calls and permits routes that match access list 11. Example 11-21 lists the configuration of the mexico_1 router using a route map to filter the route 172.16.6.0/24.

Example 11-21 *Calling a Route Map During Redistribution on mexico_1*

```
router eigrp 2001
 redistribute igrp 2000
 passive-interface Ethernet0
 network 172.16.0.0
 default-metric 1544 100 254 1 1500
```

Example 11-21 *Calling a Route Map During Redistribution on mexico_1 (Continued)*

```
!
router igrp 2000
 redistribute eigrp 2001 route-map noospf      ←call route map named noospf
 passive-interface Serial0.1
 network 172.16.0.0
 default-metric 1544 100 254 1 1500
 !
ip classless
!
access-list 11 deny   172.16.6.0 0.0.0.255     ←deny 172.16.6.0/24
access-list 11 permit any
route-map noospf permit 10
 match ip address 11                  ←allow routes that pass access list 11
 !
```

The route table on the mexico_2 router now shows only one route from the OSPF domain 192.168.4.0. Compare the output in Example 11-22 with that of Example 11-19 to see the application of the route map and distribution list.

Example 11-22 *The Route Table of mexico_2 After Route Filtering*

```
mexico_2#show ip route
Codes: C - connected, S - static, I - IGRP, R - RIP, M - mobile, B - BGP
       D - EIGRP, EX - EIGRP external, O - OSPF, IA - OSPF inter area
       N1 - OSPF NSSA external type 1, N2 - OSPF NSSA external type 2
       E1 - OSPF external type 1, E2 - OSPF external type 2, E - EGP
       i - IS-IS, L1 - IS-IS level-1, L2 - IS-IS level-2, * - candidate default
       U - per-user static route, o - ODR

Gateway of last resort is not set

     172.16.0.0/24 is subnetted, 4 subnets
C       172.16.5.0 is directly connected, Ethernet0/0
I       172.16.1.0 [100/8576] via 172.16.5.5, 00:00:51, Ethernet0/0
I       172.16.2.0 [100/10576] via 172.16.5.5, 00:00:51, Ethernet0/0
I       172.16.3.0 [100/8639] via 172.16.5.5, 00:00:51, Ethernet0/0
I     192.168.4.0/24 [100/10676] via 172.16.5.5, 00:00:51, Ethernet0/0
I     182.16.0.0/16 [100/9139] via 172.16.5.5, 00:00:51, Ethernet0/0
mexico_2#
```

NOTE   A route map also may be used to set an EIGRP tag, using the syntax **set tag** xx under the **route-map** command. Setting tags can be useful for looking at how routes entered a route table. The tag can be viewed in EIGRP by the **show ip eigrp topology** command, and in OSPF by **show ip ospf database**. The OSPF tag also can be entered directly on the **redistribution** command.

EIGRP Summarization

Understanding EIGRP summarization and knowing how to effectively use it are absolutely vital to the design of large EIGRP networks. EIGRP scales very well, but when the number of routes starts to climb into the hundreds, extra care should be taken to control route propagation and the query range. As much as EIGRP is plug-and-play on small networks, it is not on large networks. The larger the network is, the more care should be taken to control how routes propagation.

Summarization provides two powerful enhancements to EIGRP. First, by lowering the number of routes in the route table, it lessens the number and size of the EIGRP advertisements. Second, and more importantly, it can limit the EIGRP query range.

Controlling the Query Range Through Summarization, Addressing Stuck in Active (SIA) Route Issues

Arguably one of the most common and complex problems facing large EIGRP networks is *stuck in active (SIA)* routes. A route becomes SIA when EIGRP is "actively" running computations for the route, and it doesn't stop. EIGRP will log multiple messages similar to the following:

```
%DUAL-3-SIA: Route 192.168.1.16 Stuck-in-Active
```

Most of the time, the route shows active because it is waiting for query to return from neighbor. There can be many reasons for this:

- **The router is overutilized**—Edge routes can get flooded with query request and often don't have the CPU power to keep up with the request. Queries receive irregular replies, if any, and the route stays active.

- **The router is having memory issues**—This can be compounded from a slow processor and the router having many items in its queues.

- **Overutilized circuit**—EIGRP hellos might not be getting through, causing the neighbor to drop.

Two types of configurations can manifest the SIA situation:

- Most EIGRP networks have autosummary disabled. This is primarily because the IP addressing scheme has discontinuous subnets, so the query range is not bounded.

- Large Frame Relay networks have many remote sites coming into the same router, therefore, there are many EIGRP neighbors.

For example, in a Frame Relay network, if a single PVC goes inactive or a route starts flapping, it can cause a small *EIGRP query storm*. Figures 11-7 and 11-8 illustrate a common Frame Relay network and the query process.

Figure 11-7 *EIGRP Network*

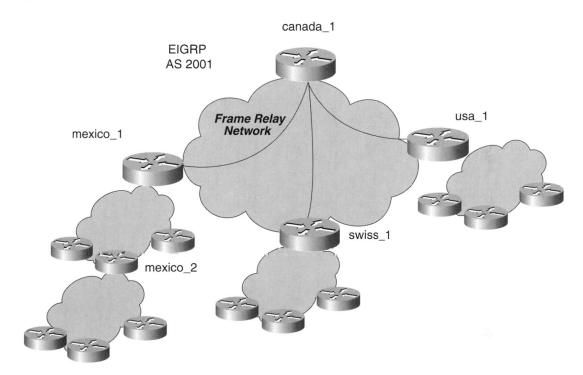

If the PVC is lost from canada_1 to mexico_1, the canada_1 router sends an EIGRP query message to all of its neighbors regarding the routes that it lost from the mexico_1 router. It is looking for a new feasible successor to the routes. In this case, the message goes to the swiss_1 and usa_1 routers. The mexico_1 router also sends a query message to all of its neighbors looking for a new feasible successor for the routes that it lost from canada_1. All routers in the EIGRP domain continue to issue queries to neighbors. The routes stay in an "active" state until EIGRP receives "replys" to the queries that it sent. If you scale this network to a router with an HSSI or T3 interface, it would be possible to have hundreds of PVCs on a single interface, and the loss of just a single PVC could generate hundreds or thousands of queries. Fortunately, summarization bounds the query process and is one of the most effective ways to control EIGRP query storms. A large EIGRP network without summarization is an SIA problem looking for an owner.

Figure 11-8 *EIGRP Query Storm*

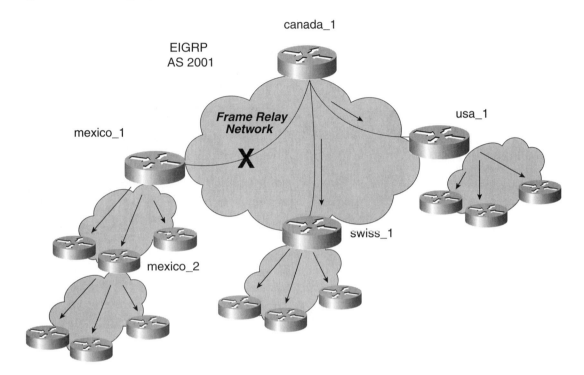

EIGRP Autosummarization

By default, EIGRP performs autosummarization in two situations:

- Autosummarization will occur at the major class boundary during redistribution from EIGRP into a classful routing protocol, such as IGRP or RIP. This type of summarization cannot be disabled.

- Autosummarization will occur at the major class boundary when the route is advertised out an interface that is on a different major class boundary. This summarization can be disabled with the command **no auto-summary** from the router(config-router) prompt.

EIGRP will not automatically summarize EIGRP external routes.

EIGRP routes that are summarized have an administrative distance of 90. In Figure 11-9, the internetwork has been modified from the previous example, adding two additional networks to the canada_2 router.

Figure 11-9 *EIGRP Autosummarization*

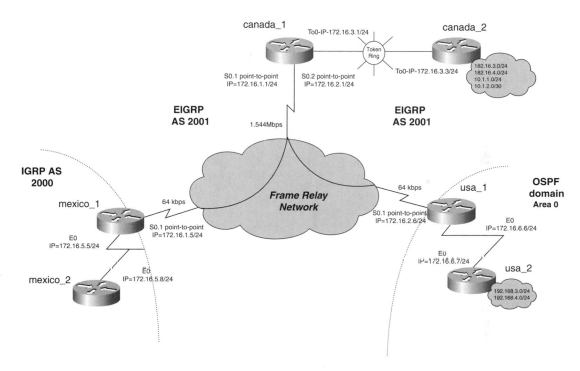

With autosummarization enabled, EIGRP on the canada_2 router advertises two summary routes to canada_1. The routes 182.16.3.0/24 and 182.16.4.0/24 are advertised as 182.16.0.0/16. The routes 10.1.1.0/24 and 10.1.2.0/30 are advertised at their natural class boundary with a route of 10.0.0.0/8. It is important to note that EIGRP summarizes the route only when advertising out an interface that is in a different class. For example, if the network between canada_1 and canada_2 is 10.1.3.0/24, the 10's network would not be summarized; only the 182.16.x.x networks would. Example 11-23 lists the route table of canada_1, highlighting the summarized routes.

Example 11-23 *Route Table of canada_1 with Summarized Routes*

```
canada_1#show ip route
Codes: C - connected, S - static, I - IGRP, R - RIP, M - mobile, B - BGP
       D - EIGRP, EX - EIGRP external, O - OSPF, IA - OSPF inter area
       N1 - OSPF NSSA external type 1, N2 - OSPF NSSA external type 2
       E1 - OSPF external type 1, E2 - OSPF external type 2, E - EGP
       i - IS-IS, L1 - IS-IS level-1, L2 - IS-IS level-2, * - candidate default
       U - per-user static route, o - ODR
```

continues

Example 11-23 *Route Table of canada_1 with Summarized Routes (Continued)*

```
Gateway of last resort is not set

     172.16.0.0/24 is subnetted, 5 subnets
D       172.16.5.0 [90/2195456] via 172.16.1.5, 01:06:41, Serial0.1
D       172.16.6.0 [90/2195456] via 172.16.2.6, 01:08:01, Serial0.2
C       172.16.1.0 is directly connected, Serial0.1
C       172.16.2.0 is directly connected, Serial0.2
C       172.16.3.0 is directly connected, TokenRing0
     192.168.4.0/32 is subnetted, 1 subnets
D EX    192.168.4.1 [170/2195456] via 172.16.2.6, 01:07:46, Serial0.2
D    10.0.0.0/8 [90/304128] via 172.16.3.3, 00:51:27, TokenRing0
D    182.16.0.0/16 [90/304128] via 172.16.3.3, 00:51:27, TokenRing0
     192.168.3.0/32 is subnetted, 1 subnets
D EX    192.168.3.1 [170/2195456] via 172.16.2.6, 01:07:46, Serial0.2
canada_1#
```

As helpful as EIGRP summarization might appear on the surface, it has serious drawbacks on most modern networks. It essentially makes a classless routing protocol enforce the discontinuous subnets rule at the major bit boundaries. When EIGRP forms a summary route to advertise, it also forms a route to null for all the networks in that summary. For example, the canada_2 router will form three routes to null for each major class network that the router has an interface in. The route to null will discard any packets that this router has an explicit route to. Example 11-24 demonstrates autosummary null routes displayed by the **show ip route** command.

Example 11-24 *EIGRP Autosummary Null Routes*

```
canada_2#show ip route
Codes: C - connected, S - static, I - IGRP, R - RIP, M - mobile, B - BGP
       D - EIGRP, EX - EIGRP external, O - OSPF, IA - OSPF inter area
       N1 - OSPF NSSA external type 1, N2 - OSPF NSSA external type 2
       E1 - OSPF external type 1, E2 - OSPF external type 2, E - EGP
       i - IS-IS, L1 - IS-IS level-1, L2 - IS-IS level-2, * - candidate default
       U - per-user static route, o - ODR

Gateway of last resort is not set

     172.16.0.0/16 is variably subnetted, 6 subnets, 2 masks
D       172.16.5.0/24 [90/2211584] via 172.16.3.1, 00:12:02, TokenRing0
D       172.16.6.0/24 [90/2211584] via 172.16.3.1, 00:12:02, TokenRing0
D       172.16.0.0/16 is a summary, 00:12:06, Null0
D       172.16.1.0/24 [90/2185984] via 172.16.3.1, 00:12:02, TokenRing0
D       172.16.2.0/24 [90/2185984] via 172.16.3.1, 00:12:02, TokenRing0
C       172.16.3.0/24 is directly connected, TokenRing0
     192.168.4.0/32 is subnetted, 1 subnets
D EX    192.168.4.1 [170/2211584] via 172.16.3.1, 00:12:02, TokenRing0
     10.0.0.0/8 is variably subnetted, 3 subnets, 3 masks
C       10.1.2.0/30 is directly connected, Loopback32
D       10.0.0.0/8 is a summary, 00:12:06, Null0
```

Example 11-24 *EIGRP Autosummary Null Routes (Continued)*

```
C       10.1.1.0/24 is directly connected, Loopback31
        182.16.0.0/16 is variably subnetted, 3 subnets, 2 masks
C       182.16.4.0/24 is directly connected, Loopback21
C       182.16.3.0/24 is directly connected, Loopback20
D       182.16.0.0/16 is a summary, 00:12:07, Null0
        192.168.3.0/32 is subnetted, 1 subnets
D EX    192.168.3.1 [170/2211584] via 172.16.3.1, 00:12:03, TokenRing0
canada_2#
```

- For autosummarization to work properly, discontinuous subnets at the major bit boundaries must be avoided at all costs. Unfortunately, on modern networks, something causes subnets to be deployed in places they shouldn't be, and EIGRP has forwarding problems. By disabling autosummarization with the **no auto-summary** command, the routes to null are not created and automatic summary routes are not forwarded. In place of autosummary, use manual summarization. Most engineers that we have worked with disable autosummarization when using EIGRP to prevent routes to the null interface.

EIGRP Manual Summarization or Route Aggregation

EIGRP manual summarization is critical to large EIGRP networks. It limits the EIGRP query and can significantly reduce the size of the routing table. There are essentially two ways to deploy manual summarization:

- Advertise an summary address or aggregate address with the following interface command:

```
ip summary-address eigrp as_number summary_address address_mask
```

- Advertise a default route with the following interface command:

```
ip summary-address eigrp as_number 0.0.0.0 0.0.0.0.
```

This command causes only the default route to be advertised; all other routing updates are suppressed.

One of the powerful functions of EIGRP is the capability to advertised multiple summary routes and default routes on different interfaces. The EIGRP network in Figure 11-10 is under the same autonomous system, and autosummary has been disabled on all the routers. In this model, EIGRP is configured to advertise a default route out the s0.2 port on the canada_1 router to the usa_1 router. The canada_1 router also advertises two summary routes, 182.0.0.0/8 and 10.0.0.0/8, out the s0.1 interface to the mexico_1 router.

Figure 11-10 *EIGRP Manual Summarization*

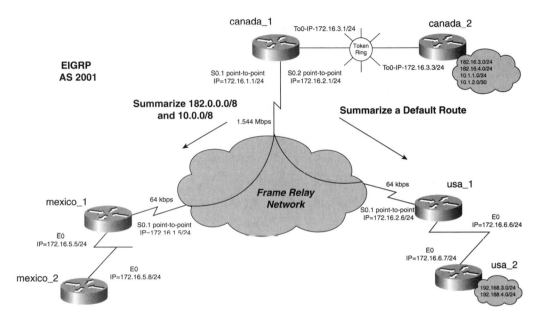

Example 11-25 lists the configuration of canada_1 router performing manual summarization.

Example 11-25 *Manual Summarization on canada_1 Serial Interfaces*

```
interface Serial0
 no ip address
 encapsulation frame-relay
 no ip mroute-cache
!
interface Serial0.1 point-to-point
 ip address 172.16.1.1 255.255.255.0
 ip summary-address eigrp 2001 182.0.0.0 255.0.0.0      ←Manual summarization
 ip summary-address eigrp 2001 10.0.0.0 255.0.0.0
 frame-relay interface-dlci 110
!
interface Serial0.2 point-to-point
 ip address 172.16.2.1 255.255.255.0
 ip summary-address eigrp 2001 0.0.0.0 0.0.0.0          ←Advertise a default route only
 frame-relay interface-dlci 130
!
interface TokenRing0
 ip address 172.16.3.1 255.255.255.0
 ring-speed 16
!
```

Example 11-25 *Manual Summarization on canada_1 Serial Interfaces (Continued)*

```
router eigrp 2001
 network 172.16.0.0
 no auto-summary
!
```

Example 11-26 lists the route table of the mexico_1 router and the usa_1 router. Notice how the routes are summarized. The usa_1 router receives only a default route 0.0.0.0, and the gateway of last resort is set.

Example 11-26 *Route Tables of mexico_1 and usa_1 with Summarization Applied*

```
mexico_1#show ip route
Codes: C - connected, S - static, I - IGRP, R - RIP, M - mobile, B - BGP
       D - EIGRP, EX - EIGRP external, O - OSPF, IA - OSPF inter area
       N1 - OSPF NSSA external type 1, N2 - OSPF NSSA external type 2
       E1 - OSPF external type 1, E2 - OSPF external type 2, E - EGP
       i - IS-IS, L1 - IS-IS level-1, L2 - IS-IS level-2, * - candidate default
       U - per-user static route, o - ODR
       T - traffic engineered route

Gateway of last resort is not set

     172.16.0.0/24 is subnetted, 5 subnets
C       172.16.5.0 is directly connected, Ethernet0
D       172.16.6.0 [90/2707456] via 172.16.1.1, 00:34:11, Serial0.1
C       172.16.1.0 is directly connected, Serial0.1
D       172.16.2.0 [90/2681856] via 172.16.1.1, 00:34:11, Serial0.1
D       172.16.3.0 [90/2185984] via 172.16.1.1, 00:34:11, Serial0.1
D     192.168.4.0/24 [90/2835456] via 172.16.1.1, 00:34:11, Serial0.1
D     10.0.0.0/8 [90/2313984] via 172.16.1.1, 00:34:11, Serial0.1    ←Summary Route
D     192.168.3.0/24 [90/2835456] via 172.16.1.1, 00:34:11, Serial0.1
D     182.0.0.0/8 [90/2313984] via 172.16.1.1, 00:34:11, Serial0.1   ←Summary Route

mexico_1#
```
```
usa_1#show ip route
Codes: C - connected, S - static, I - IGRP, R - RIP, M - mobile, B - BGP
       D - EIGRP, EX - EIGRP external, O - OSPF, IA - OSPF inter area
       N1 - OSPF NSSA external type 1, N2 - OSPF NSSA external type 2
       E1 - OSPF external type 1, E2 - OSPF external type 2, E - EGP
       i - IS-IS, L1 - IS-IS level-1, L2 - IS-IS level-2, * - candidate default
       U - per-user static route, o - ODR

Gateway of last resort is 172.16.2.1 to network 0.0.0.0

D     192.168.3.0/24 [90/409600] via 172.16.6.7, 00:45:52, Ethernet0
D     192.168.4.0/24 [90/409600] via 172.16.6.7, 00:45:52, Ethernet0
     172.16.0.0/24 is subnetted, 2 subnets
```

continues

Example 11-26 *Route Tables of mexico_1 and usa_1 with Summarization Applied (Continued)*

```
C       172.16.6.0 is directly connected, Ethernet0
C       172.16.2.0 is directly connected, Serial0.1
D*  0.0.0.0/0 [90/2185984] via 172.16.2.1, 00:44:54, Serial0.1
usa_1#
```

NOTE   In Cisco IOS Software 12.0(4)T, an administrative distance can be added to the summary address to alter the default admin distance of 90.

Default Routing with EIGRP

A default route can be injected into EIGRP in two primary ways:

- Redistribute a default static route into EIGRP so that EIGRP recognizes the route of 0.0.0.0 to be the default route. A default static route is created with the global router entry **ip route 0.0.0.0 0.0.0.0** *next_hop_IP_address*. This route then must be redistributed into EIGRP with the **redistribute static** command. If the network 0.0.0.0 is not used, you can still mark the route as a default route by using the **ip default-network** *a.b.c.d* command.

- Summarize a default route of 0.0.0.0 with the interface command **ip summary-address eigrp** *as_number* **0.0.0.0 0.0.0.0**. The example in the previous section demonstrated how to propagate a default route with this command.

With both ways, the router needs the **ip classless** global command enabled. With IP classless, the router forwards any packets toward the default route that it does not have a more specific route toward. **ip classless** is enabled by default in Cisco IOS Software Release 12.0 and later.

In Figure 11-11, the canada_1 router advertises a default route to usa_1 and mexico_1. canada_1 does this by creating a static route pointing at a next-hop address of 172.16.3.3 or the canada_2 router.

Example 11-27 lists the configuration of the canada_1 router advertising a default static route.

Example 11-27 *Advertising a Default Static Route with EIGRP on canada_1*

```
router eigrp 2001
 redistribute static          ←redistribute the static routes
 network 172.16.0.0
 default-metric 16000 630 254 1 1500     ←Don't forget the default-metric
 no auto-summary
!
ip classless                 ←IP classless must be enabled for default routing
ip route 0.0.0.0 0.0.0.0 172.16.3.3    ←The default route points at Canada_1 router
!
```

Figure 11-11 *EIGRP Default Routing*

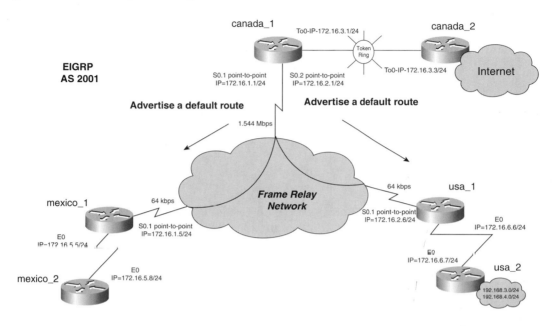

Example 11-28 lists the route table of the mexico_1 router demonstrating how the default route is received. Notice that when the route is advertised, it is an external router because it is redistributed, and it has the * denoting it is the default route. The gateway of last resort also is set.

Example 11-28 *Route Table of the mexico_1 Router*

```
mexico_1#show ip route
Codes: C - connected, S - static, I - IGRP, R - RIP, M - mobile, B - BGP
       D - EIGRP, EX - EIGRP external, O - OSPF, IA - OSPF inter area
       N1 - OSPF NSSA external type 1, N2 - OSPF NSSA external type 2
       E1 - OSPF external type 1, E2 - OSPF external type 2, E - EGP
       i - IS-IS, L1 - IS-IS level-1, L2 - IS-IS level-2, * - candidate default
       U - per-user static route, o - ODR
       T - traffic engineered route

Gateway of last resort is 172.16.1.1 to network 0.0.0.0

     172.16.0.0/24 is subnetted, 5 subnets
C       172.16.5.0 is directly connected, Ethernet0
D       172.16.6.0 [90/2707456] via 172.16.1.1, 00:04:15, Serial0.1
C       172.16.1.0 is directly connected, Serial0.1
D       172.16.2.0 [90/2681856] via 172.16.1.1, 00:04:51, Serial0.1
D       172.16.3.0 [90/2185984] via 172.16.1.1, 00:04:51, Serial0.1
```

continues

Example 11-28 *Route Table of the mexico_1 Router (Continued)*

```
D     192.168.4.0/24 [90/2835456] via 172.16.1.1, 00:04:15, Serial0.1
      10.0.0.0/8 is variably subnetted, 2 subnets, 2 masks
D        10.1.2.0/30 [90/2313984] via 172.16.1.1, 00:04:51, Serial0.1
D        10.1.1.0/24 [90/2313984] via 172.16.1.1, 00:04:52, Serial0.1
      182.16.0.0/24 is subnetted, 2 subnets
D        182.16.4.0 [90/2313984] via 172.16.1.1, 00:04:52, Serial0.1
D        182.16.3.0 [90/2313984] via 172.16.1.1, 00:04:52, Serial0.1
D     192.168.3.0/24 [90/2835456] via 172.16.1.1, 00:04:15, Serial0.1
D*EX 0.0.0.0/0 [170/2331136] via 172.16.1.1, 00:00:53, Serial0.1
mexico_1#
```

EIGRP Stub Routing

In Cisco IOS Software Release 12.0(7)T, Cisco introduced EIGRP stub routing to further control stability and reduce resource utilization. This feature was fully integrated into Release 12.0(15)S. EIGRP stub routing functions very much like that of an OSPF stub area. The stub router has one exit path from the routing domain and forwards all traffic to a central or distribution router. Another way to say this is that the stub network cannot be a transit router for EIGRP, and it can have only one EIGRP neighbor.

When configuring EIGRP stub routing, only the remote or the spoke router needs to be configured as a stub. This router responds to queries for summaries, connected routes, redistributed static routes, external routes, and internal routes with the message "inaccessible." This process greatly reduces the overhead associated with responding to queries by the remote routers. The stub router also sends special peer information to its neighbor informing its neighbor that it is a stub router.

To configure EIGRP stub routing, use the following router command under EIGRP:

```
Router(config-router)#eigrp stub [receive-only | connected | static | summary]
```

The options are described as follows:

- **receive-only**—This causes the router to not send any routes.
- **connected**—The router advertises all connected routes to the single neighbor. No redistribution is necessary.
- **static**—The router advertises all static routes to a single neighbor. The static routes still need to be redistributed into EIGRP to be advertised.
- **summary**—The router advertises summary routes.

A stub router can be configured to advertise connected and static routes at the same time, which is the case in most stub domains. Figure 11-12 shows two EIGRP stub networks configured. The mexico_1 router is configured as a stub router that advertises only its local Ethernet network. The usa_1 router advertises its local Ethernet network along with two static routes to the 192.168.3.0/24 and 192.168.4.0/24 networks. The usa_2 router has a default gateway pointing to 172.16.6.6 and has no routing enabled. The distribution router is canada_1. No additional EIGRP configuration is necessary on the distribution router.

Figure 11-12 *EIGRP Stub Routing*

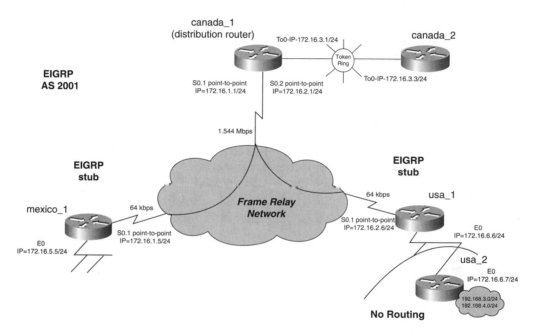

Example 11-29 lists the EIGRP configuration of the mexico_1 and the usa_1 routers.

Example 11-29 *EIGRP Stub Configuration*

```
!
hostname mexico_1
!
router eigrp 2001
 network 172.16.0.0
 default-metric 1544 100 254 1 1500
 no auto-summary
 eigrp stub connected        ←Set EIGRP stub, and advertise connected routes
!

!
hostname usa_1
!
router eigrp 2001
 redistribute static         ←Redistribute static
```

continues

Example 11-29 *EIGRP Stub Configuration (Continued)*

```
network 172.16.0.0
default-metric 1544 100 254 1 1500
no auto-summary
eigrp stub connected static      ←Set EIGRP stub, and advertise connected and static
                                    routes
!
ip classless
ip route 192.168.3.0 255.255.255.0 172.16.6.7
ip route 192.168.4.0 255.255.255.0 172.16.6.7
```

Finally, by viewing the canada_1 route table, all routes are being reported by EIGRP in the correct manner. Example 11-30 lists the route table of the canada_1 router.

Example 11-30 *Route Table of canada_1 with Two EIGRP Stub Domains*

```
canada_1#show ip route
Codes: C - connected, S - static, I - IGRP, R - RIP, M - mobile, B - BGP
       D - EIGRP, EX - EIGRP external, O - OSPF, IA - OSPF inter area
       N1 - OSPF NSSA external type 1, N2 - OSPF NSSA external type 2
       E1 - OSPF external type 1, E2 - OSPF external type 2, E - EGP
       i - IS-IS, L1 - IS-IS level-1, L2 - IS-IS level-2, * - candidate default
       U - per-user static route, o - ODR

Gateway of last resort is not set

     172.16.0.0/24 is subnetted, 5 subnets
D       172.16.5.0 [90/2195456] via 172.16.1.5, 01:03:47, Serial0.1
D       172.16.6.0 [90/2195456] via 172.16.2.6, 00:48:40, Serial0.2
C       172.16.1.0 is directly connected, Serial0.1
C       172.16.2.0 is directly connected, Serial0.2
C       172.16.3.0 is directly connected, TokenRing0
D EX 192.168.4.0/24 [170/2195456] via 172.16.2.6, 00:43:27, Serial0.2
     10.0.0.0/8 is variably subnetted, 2 subnets, 2 masks
D       10.1.2.0/30 [90/304128] via 172.16.3.3, 07:31:49, TokenRing0
D       10.1.1.0/24 [90/304128] via 172.16.3.3, 07:31:49, TokenRing0
     182.16.0.0/24 is subnetted, 2 subnets
D       182.16.4.0 [90/304128] via 172.16.3.3, 07:31:49, TokenRing0
D       182.16.3.0 [90/304128] via 172.16.3.3, 07:31:49, TokenRing0
D EX 192.168.3.0/24 [170/2195456] via 172.16.2.6, 00:43:28, Serial0.2
canada_1#
```

To verify that the router is configured as an EIGRP stub router, use the **show ip eigrp neighbor detail** command. The last line of the output will show whether stub routing is enabled and what the stub router can advertise. This output can be viewed in Example 11-41. The show **eigrp packet stub** command shows debug information about the stub status of the peer routers.

EIGRP Equal- and Unequal-Cost Load Balancing

By default, EIGRP load-shares over four equal-cost paths. For load sharing to happen, the routes to load-share over must show up in the IP forwarding table or with the **show ip route** command. Only when a route shows up in the forwarding table with multiple paths to it will load sharing occur. Use the **bandwidth** interface command on serial links to ensure that EIGRP has a consistent perspective of the metrics of the network. This also might aid in making the route show up in the IP forwarding table.

EIGRP also has the capability to use unequal-cost load balancing in the same manner as IGRP. The router uses variance as a multiplier in choosing the upper boundary of the path with the greatest metric.

Configuring EIGRP unequal-cost load balancing is a three-step process:

Step 1 Configure the bandwidth on both sides of all the interfaces involved in the load-sharing group. Use the **bandwidth** *xx_kbps* command to accomplish this.

Step 2 Define the lowest-cost metric and the highest-cost metric. From these values, compute the variance multiplier and add it to the EIGRP routing process. The composite metric that EIGRP is using can be viewed with the **show ip eigrp topology** command, as discussed in previous sections.

Step 3 (Optional) Set the *maximum-paths* or the *traffic-share* variables.

The following example walks through the calculation of a fictional variance. EIGRP has a route whose metric is 100. The router also has two more routes to that same destination whose metrics are 200 and 300. To allow EIGRP to use all three paths in sharing data, you would set the variance to 3:

$$3 \times 100 = 300$$

Another way to view it is as variance × lowest_metric = largest metric of path to load-share over—in this case, 300. To properly set the variance in a real network, use the following formula:

Variance = 1 + (*[metric of highest cost route / metric of the lowest cost route]*, rounded up to the nearest 1s decimal place)

The metric of the lowest-cost and highest-cost routes can be discovered with the **show ip eigrp topology** command. Be sure to change variance and any other variables, such as bandwidth, on both ends of the link. The bandwidth should be set on all serial links. The following is the syntax for the commands used in configuring load balancing:

```
Router(config-router)variance [metric_multiplier 1-128]
Router(config-router)maximum-paths [1-6]
Router(config-router)traffic-share {balanced | min across-interface]
Router(config-router)bandwidth xx kbps
```

The **variance** command defines the metric multiplier of which routes to use in unequal-cost load balancing. The default variance is 1, which is equal-cost load balancing.

With the **maximum-paths** command, the router uses up to six paths to share traffic across; to limit this number, use the **maximum-paths** command. The multiple paths that make up a single-hop transport to a common destination are called a *load-sharing group*. The default value is 4.

With the **traffic-share** command, if there are multiple minimum-cost paths and **traffic-share-min** is configured, EIGRP will use equal-cost load balancing. By default, the command is set to **balanced**, where traffic will be distributed proportionally to the ratio of the metrics. For example, if variance is set to 3 and traffic-share is set to balanced, the best route will transport traffic three times that of the worst route.

For a route to be included in unequal-cost load sharing, three other conditions must be met:

- The maximum-paths limit must not be exceeded as a result of adding this route to the load-sharing group.
- The downstream router must be metrically closer to the destination.
- The metric of the lowest-cost route, multiplied by the variance, must be greater than the metric of the route to be added to the load-sharing group.

Chapter 10 provides a detailed example of load sharing over IGRP, which is syntactically identical to configuring EIGRP traffic load balancing.

Lab 22: EIGRP Route Redistribution, Summarization, and Stub Routing—Part I

Practical Scenario

As EIGRP networks continue to grow in popularity, it becomes increasingly important to be able to control the query range and integrate it with other routing protocols, such as RIP and OSPF. It is also important to understand the default setting of EIGRP, such as split horizon and autosummarization.

This lab gives you practice in controlling the query range, integrating EIGRP with other routing protocols, and performing summarization.

Lab Exercise

Cisco Training Partners provide custom-tailored Cisco courses around the United States and are in the process of integrating their training facilities over a common network. Your task is to configure an EIGRP network using the following parameters as design guidelines:

- Configure an IP network, as depicted in Figure 11-13, using EIGRP as the routing protocol and 65001 as the Autonomous System ID.

- Configure the Frame Relay network as a multipoint network between the wisconsin, georgia, and ohio routers. Configure the Frame Relay network as a point-to-point network between the wisconsin and minnesota routers.

- Ensure full IP reachability with the RIP domain without using static routes or advertising a default route.

- (Optional) Configure the georgia and ohio routers as EIGRP stub routers. The routers should advertise their local LAN networks in EIGRP.

Lab Objectives

- Configure the Cisco Training Partners Network as depicted in Figure 11-13. Configure IP as denoted in the diagram. The LAN topology type is not important in this lab.

- Use Frame Relay data link protocol on the WAN.

- Configure redistribution between RIP and EIGRP.

- Ensure full IP connectivity to all IP interfaces—that is, be sure that you can **ping** all Frame Relay and LAN interfaces from the RIP domain. Also ensure that the georgia and ohio routers can **ping** each others' Frame Relay and LAN interfaces. You cannot configure any static routes or default routes on the network.

- (Optional) Configure the georgia and ohio routers as EIGRP stub routers. You will need Cisco IOS Software Release 12.0(7)T or Cisco IOS Release 12.0(15)S or 12.1 and later, the T and S trains are required.

Equipment Needed

- Six Cisco routers. Four will be connected through V.35 back-to-back cables or in a similar manner to a Frame Relay switch.

- Four LAN segments, provided through hubs or switches. The LAN topology is not significant to this lab.

Physical Layout and Prestaging

- Connect the hubs and serial cables to the routers, as shown in Figure 11-13.

- The stillwater router will run RIP only on network 172.16.0.0. Configure this router at this time. See Chapter 9 if you need assistance on this.

- A Frame Relay switch with three PVCs also is required. Example 11-31 lists the Frame Relay configuration used in this lab.

Example 11-31 *Frame Relay Switch Configuration*

```
hostname frame_switch
!
frame-relay switching
!
<<<text omitted>>>
!
interface Serial0
 no ip address
 encapsulation frame-relay
 no fair-queue
 clockrate 148000
 frame-relay intf-type dce
 frame-relay route 111 interface Serial1 110
 frame-relay route 121 interface Serial3 102
 frame-relay route 150 interface Serial5 151
!
interface Serial1
 no ip address
 encapsulation frame-relay
 clockrate 148000
 frame-relay intf-type dce
 frame-relay route 110 interface Serial0 111
!
<<<text omitted>>>
!
interface Serial3
```

Example 11-31 *Frame Relay Switch Configuration (Continued)*

```
 no ip address
 encapsulation frame-relay
 clockrate 64000
 frame-relay intf-type dce
 frame-relay route 102 interface Serial0 121
!
<<<text omitted>>>
!
interface Serial5
 no ip address
 encapsulation frame-relay
 clockrate 64000
 frame-relay intf-type dce
 frame-relay route 151 interface Serial0 150
!
```

Figure 11-13 *Cisco Training Partners Network*

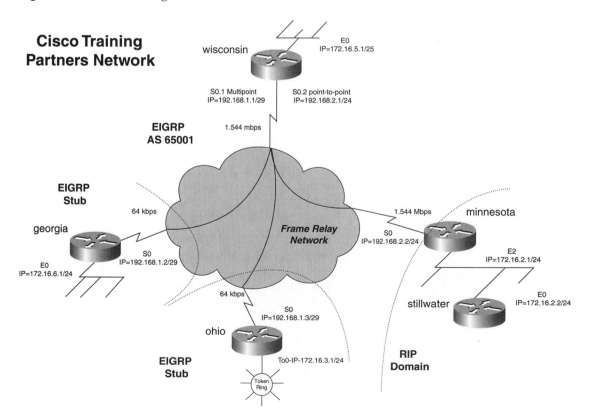

Lab 22: EIGRP Route Redistribution, Summarization, and Stub Routing—Part II

Lab Walkthrough

Configure the Frame Relay switch and attach the four routers in a back-to-back manner to the Frame Relay switch. Use V.35 cables or CSU/DSUs with crossover cables, to connect the routers. Create the four LANs by using switches or hubs/MAUs, as illustrated in Figure 11-13.

When the physical connections are complete, assign IP addresses to all LAN and WAN interfaces, as depicted in Figure 11-13. Be sure that you can **ping** each router's local LAN and WAN interface before moving on. The wisconsin router will need subinterfaces; one will be a multipoint interface and one will be a point-to-point interface. You will use **frame-relay map** statements on the multipoint interface. You will use **frame-relay interface-dlci** commands on the point-to-point interface between the wisconsin and minnesota routers. For full IP connectivity, you will need an additional **frame-relay map** statement on ohio and georgia pointing toward each other. Example 11-32 lists the Frame Relay configuration, to this point, on all routers involved.

Example 11-32 *Frame Relay Configuration on wisconsin, georgia, ohio, and minnesota Routers*

```
!
hostname wisconsin
!
<<<text omitted>>>
!
interface Serial0
 no ip address
 no ip directed-broadcast
 encapsulation frame-relay
 no ip mroute-cache
 frame-relay lmi-type cisco
!
interface Serial0.1 multipoint
 ip address 192.168.1.1 255.255.255.248
 no ip directed-broadcast
 frame-relay map ip 192.168.1.2 121 broadcast
 frame-relay map ip 192.168.1.3 150 broadcast
!
interface Serial0.2 point-to-point
 ip address 192.168.2.1 255.255.255.0
 no ip directed-broadcast
 frame-relay interface-dlci 111
```

Example 11-32 *Frame Relay Configuration on wisconsin, georgia, ohio, and minnesota Routers (Continued)*

```
!
hostname georgia
!
<<<text omitted>>>
!
interface Serial0
 ip address 192.168.1.2 255.255.255.248
 no ip directed-broadcast
 encapsulation frame-relay
 no ip mroute-cache
 frame-relay map ip 192.168.1.1 102 broadcast
 frame-relay map ip 192.168.1.3 102 broadcast
 frame-relay lmi-type cisco
!
```

```
hostname ohio
!
enable password cisco
!
<<<text omitted>>>
!
interface Serial0
 ip address 192.168.1.3 255.255.255.248
 no ip directed-broadcast
 encapsulation frame-relay
 no ip mroute-cache
 frame-relay map ip 192.168.1.1 151 broadcast
 frame-relay map ip 192.168.1.2 151 broadcast
 frame-relay lmi-type cisco
!
```

```
hostname minnesota
!
<<<text omitted>>>
!
interface Serial0
 ip address 192.168.2.2 255.255.255.0
 encapsulation frame-relay
 no ip mroute-cache
 frame-relay interface-dlci 110
```

After local WAN and LAN connectivity has been established, the network configuration will be divided into two parts. First, you will configure the EIGRP domain and then you will integrate RIP.

The basic EIGRP configuration will be similar on all the routers. Following the three-step process, begin by enabling EIGRP on all the routers using the **router eigrp 65001** command. The second step is to define the networks to run EIGRP on. The wisconsin, georgia, and ohio routers will route EIGRP on the major networks of 172.16.0.0 and 192.168.1.0.

Therefore, use these networks for your **network** statements. The wisconsin and minnesota routers will run EIGRP on 192.168.2.0 in addition to 172.16.0.0. Because this is a Frame Relay network, it's a good idea to set the bandwidth statements. Set the **bandwidth** to 128 kbps on the wisconsin interface s0.1 to accommodate the two 64-kbps PVCs. The georgia and ohio routers should have the **bandwidth** set to 64 kbps on the Frame Relay interfaces. The default bandwidth is 1.544 Mbps (T1 speed), so there is no need to modify it on the S0.2 interface on the wisconsin router. Example 11-33 lists the configuration of the wisconsin router to this point.

Example 11-33 *Configuration of the wisconsin Router*

```
hostname wisconsin
!
interface Ethernet0
 ip address 172.16.5.1 255.255.255.128
 no ip directed-broadcast
!
interface Serial0
 no ip address
 no ip directed-broadcast
 encapsulation frame-relay
 no ip mroute-cache
 frame-relay lmi-type cisco
!
interface Serial0.1 multipoint
 bandwidth 128
 ip address 192.168.1.1 255.255.255.248
 no ip directed-broadcast
 frame-relay map ip 192.168.1.2 121 broadcast
 frame-relay map ip 192.168.1.3 150 broadcast
!
interface Serial0.2 point-to-point
 ip address 192.168.2.1 255.255.255.0
 no ip directed-broadcast
 frame-relay interface-dlci 111
!
router eigrp 65001
 network 172.16.0.0
 network 192.168.1.0
 network 192.168.2.0
!
```

At first glance, it might appear that routing is working. After all, you have a route table and three EIGRP neighbors on the wisconsin router. But some EIGRP defaults must be disabled to make the network route properly. Notice in Example 11-34 that EIGRP has three neighbors in the route table. Unfortunately, the router also has injected a couple routes to null in its forwarding table.

Example 11-34 *show ip route* **and** *show ip eigrp neighbors* *Command Output on the wisconsin Router*

```
wisconsin#show ip route
Codes: C - connected, S - static, I - IGRP, R - RIP, M - mobile, B - BGP
       D - EIGRP, EX - EIGRP external, O - OSPF, IA - OSPF inter area
       N1 - OSPF NSSA external type 1, N2 - OSPF NSSA external type 2
       E1 - OSPF external type 1, E2 - OSPF external type 2, E - EGP
       i - IS-IS, L1 - IS-IS level-1, L2 - IS-IS level-2, ia - IS-IS inter area
       * - candidate default, U - per-user static route, o - ODR
       P - periodic downloaded static route

Gateway of last resort is not set

     172.16.0.0/16 is variably subnetted, 2 subnets, 2 masks
C       172.16.5.0/25 is directly connected, Ethernet0
D       172.16.0.0/16 is a summary, 00:10:58, Null0
     192.168.1.0/24 is variably subnetted, 2 subnets, 2 masks
D       192.168.1.0/24 is a summary, 00:11:33, Null0
C       192.168.1.0/29 is directly connected, Serial0.1
C     192.168.2.0/24 is directly connected, Serial0.2
wisconsin#
wisconsin#show ip eigrp neighbors
IP-EIGRP neighbors for process 65001
H   Address              Interface   Hold Uptime   SRTT   RTO  Q  Seq Type
                                     (sec)         (ms)        Cnt Num
2   192.168.1.2          Se0.1        171 00:14:00  768  4608  0  4
1   192.168.1.3          Se0.1        152 00:14:11 1544  5000  0  4
0   192.168.2.2          Se0.2        157 00:14:22    0  3000  0  11
wisconsin#
```

If you try to **ping** any routers in the 172.16.0.0 domain, it will fail. This is because the router is forwarding those packets to its null interface.

You need to correct two problems:

- The network has discontinuous subnets at the major bit boundaries. The major network 172.16.0.0/16 is divided by the networks 192.168.1.0/29 and 192.168.2.0/24. To correct this problem, disable EIGRP autosummarization on all routers in the internetwork with the **no auto-summary** EIGRP router command.

- Split horizon must be corrected, although this problem won't manifest itself until autosummarization is disabled.

Example 11-35 lists the route table of the wisconsin router now that autosummarization is disabled throughout the network. Notice that the 172.16.2.0/24, 172.16.3.0/24, and 172.16.5.0/24 routes are now in the forwarding table.

Example 11-35 **show ip route** *Command Output on the wisconsin Router*

```
wisconsin#show ip route
Codes: C - connected, S - static, I - IGRP, R - RIP, M - mobile, B - BGP
       D - EIGRP, EX - EIGRP external, O - OSPF, IA - OSPF inter area
       N1 - OSPF NSSA external type 1, N2 - OSPF NSSA external type 2
       E1 - OSPF external type 1, E2 - OSPF external type 2, E - EGP
       i - IS-IS, L1 - IS-IS level-1, L2 - IS-IS level-2, ia - IS-IS inter area
       * - candidate default, U - per-user static route, o - ODR
       P - periodic downloaded static route

Gateway of last resort is not set

     172.16.0.0/16 is variably subnetted, 4 subnets, 2 masks
C       172.16.5.0/25 is directly connected, Ethernet0
D       172.16.6.0/24 [90/20537600] via 192.168.1.2, 00:01:47, Serial0.1
D       172.16.2.0/24 [90/40537600] via 192.168.2.2, 00:54:38, Serial0.2
D       172.16.3.0/24 [90/20528128] via 192.168.1.3, 00:08:32, Serial0.1
     192.168.1.0/29 is subnetted, 1 subnets
C       192.168.1.0 is directly connected, Serial0.1
C     192.168.2.0/24 is directly connected, Serial0.2
wisconsin#
```

As mentioned previously, the other problem that you need to remedy is split horizon. If you test IP connectivity from strictly the wisconsin router, everything would appear normal. However, upon examining the forwarding table of the georgia and ohio routers, you will see that the georgia router does not have the 172.16.3.0/24 subnet. The ohio router also does not have the 172.16.6.0/24 subnet, as shown in Example 11-36.

Example 11-36 **show ip route** *Command Output on the ohio and georgia Routers*

```
ohio#show ip route
Codes: C - connected, S - static, I - IGRP, R - RIP, M - mobile, B - BGP
       D - EIGRP, EX - EIGRP external, O - OSPF, IA - OSPF inter area
       N1 - OSPF NSSA external type 1, N2 - OSPF NSSA external type 2
       E1 - OSPF external type 1, E2 - OSPF external type 2, E - EGP
       i - IS-IS, L1 - IS-IS level-1, L2 - IS-IS level-2, ia - IS-IS inter area
       * - candidate default, U - per-user static route, o - ODR
       P - periodic downloaded static route

Gateway of last resort is not set

     172.16.0.0/16 is variably subnetted, 3 subnets, 2 masks
D       172.16.5.0/25 [90/40537600] via 192.168.1.1, 00:00:52, Serial0
D       172.16.2.0/24 [90/41049600] via 192.168.1.1, 00:00:52, Serial0
C       172.16.3.0/24 is directly connected, TokenRing0
     192.168.1.0/29 is subnetted, 1 subnets
C       192.168.1.0 is directly connected, Serial0
D     192.168.2.0/24 [90/41024000] via 192.168.1.1, 00:00:53, Serial0
```

Example 11-36 show ip route *Command Output on the ohio and georgia Routers (Continued)*

```
ohio#

georgia#show ip route
Codes: C - connected, S - static, I - IGRP, R - RIP, M - mobile, B - BGP
       D - EIGRP, EX - EIGRP external, O - OSPF, IA - OSPF inter area
       N1 - OSPF NSSA external type 1, N2 - OSPF NSSA external type 2
       E1 - OSPF external type 1, E2 - OSPF external type 2, E - EGP
       i - IS-IS, L1 - IS-IS level-1, L2 - IS-IS level-2, ia - IS-IS inter area
       * - candidate default, U - per-user static route, o - ODR
       P - periodic downloaded static route

Gateway of last resort is not set

     172.16.0.0/16 is variably subnetted, 3 subnets, 2 masks
D       172.16.5.0/25 [90/40537600] via 192.168.1.1, 00:01:21, Serial0
C       172.16.6.0/24 is directly connected, Ethernet0
D       172.16.2.0/24 [90/41049600] via 192.168.1.1, 00:01:21, Serial0
     192.168.1.0/29 is subnetted, 1 subnets
C       192.168.1.0 is directly connected, Serial0
D    192.168.2.0/24 [90/41024000] via 192.168.1.1, 00:01:21, Serial0
georgia#
```

These routes are not being propagated because of EIGRP split horizon. This can be verified with the **debug ip eigrp packets** command. To allow updates to flow properly across a multipoint network, disable split horizon on that interface with the **no ip split-horizon eigrp** command on the wisconsin s0.1 interface:

```
wisconsin(config)#int s0.1
wisconsin(config-subif)#no ip split-horizon eigrp 65001
```

Example 11-37 lists the forwarding tables of the ohio and georgia routers after split horizon has been disabled on the wisconsin router.

Example 11-37 show ip route *Command Output on the ohio and georgia Routers*

```
ohio#show ip route
Codes: C - connected, S - static, I - IGRP, R - RIP, M - mobile, B - BGP
       D - EIGRP, EX - EIGRP external, O - OSPF, IA - OSPF inter area
       N1 - OSPF NSSA external type 1, N2 - OSPF NSSA external type 2
       E1 - OSPF external type 1, E2 - OSPF external type 2, E - EGP
       i - IS-IS, L1 - IS-IS level-1, L2 - IS-IS level-2, ia - IS-IS inter area
       * - candidate default, U - per-user static route, o - ODR
       P - periodic downloaded static route

Gateway of last resort is not set

     172.16.0.0/16 is variably subnetted, 4 subnets, 2 masks
D       172.16.5.0/25 [90/40537600] via 192.168.1.1, 00:00:04, Serial0
D       172.16.6.0/24 [90/41049600] via 192.168.1.1, 00:00:04, Serial0
D       172.16.2.0/24 [90/41049600] via 192.168.1.1, 00:00:04, Serial0
```

continues

Example 11-37 **show ip route** *Command Output on the ohio and georgia Routers (Continued)*

```
C        172.16.3.0/24 is directly connected, TokenRing0
         192.168.1.0/29 is subnetted, 1 subnets
C        192.168.1.0 is directly connected, Serial0
D        192.168.2.0/24 [90/41024000] via 192.168.1.1, 00:00:04, Serial0
ohio#
```

```
georgia#show ip route
Codes: C - connected, S - static, I - IGRP, R - RIP, M - mobile, B - BGP
       D - EIGRP, EX - EIGRP external, O - OSPF, IA - OSPF inter area
       N1 - OSPF NSSA external type 1, N2 - OSPF NSSA external type 2
       E1 - OSPF external type 1, E2 - OSPF external type 2, E - EGP
       i - IS-IS, L1 - IS-IS level-1, L2 - IS-IS level-2, ia - IS-IS inter area
       * - candidate default, U - per-user static route, o - ODR
       P - periodic downloaded static route

Gateway of last resort is not set

     172.16.0.0/16 is variably subnetted, 4 subnets, 2 masks
D        172.16.5.0/25 [90/40537600] via 192.168.1.1, 00:01:41, Serial0
C        172.16.6.0/24 is directly connected, Ethernet0
D        172.16.2.0/24 [90/41049600] via 192.168.1.1, 00:01:41, Serial0
D        172.16.3.0/24 [90/41040128] via 192.168.1.1, 00:00:49, Serial0
     192.168.1.0/29 is subnetted, 1 subnets
C        192.168.1.0 is directly connected, Serial0
D        192.168.2.0/24 [90/41024000] via 192.168.1.1, 00:01:41, Serial0
georgia#
```

At this point, you have full IP connectivity to all routers except the stillwater router, which resides in the RIP domain.

To fully integrate the RIP domain into EGIRP, you must ensure that the configuration has two elements:

- Mutual redistribution between RIP and EIGRP on the minnesota router
- All EIGRP routes summarized on a 24-bit boundary, the bit boundary the RIP network is on

To enable mutual redistribution on the minnesota router, use the **redistribution** and **default-metric** commands. Example 11-38 lists the configuration of the minnesota router.

Example 11-38 *EIGRP and RIP Configuration of the minnesota Router*

```
!
router eigrp 65001
 redistribute rip
 network 172.16.0.0
 network 192.168.2.0
 default-metric 1544 100 254 1 1500
```

Example 11-38 *EIGRP and RIP Configuration of the minnesota Router (Continued)*

```
 no auto-summary
!
router rip
 redistribute eigrp 65001
 network 172.16.0.0
 default-metric 4
!
```

The stillwater router now starts to receive routes from the minnesota router; however, it can receive only routes that have a 24-bit mask. The stillwater router will not have routes to the Frame Relay multipoint network, 192.168.1.0/29, or the Ethernet network, 182.16.5.0/25 on the wisconsin router. For the stillwater router to receive these routes, you must configure two summary addresses on a 24-bit boundary, on the point-to-point subnet between the wisconsin and minnesota router. Example 11-39 lists the configuration needed on the wisconsin router.

Example 11-39 *EIGRP Summarization on the wisconsin Router*

```
!
interface Serial0.2 point-to-point
 bandwidth 64
 ip address 192.168.2.1 255.255.255.0
 no ip directed-broadcast
 ip summary-address eigrp 65001 192.168.1.0 255.255.255.0 5
 ip summary-address eigrp 65001 172.16.5.0 255.255.255.0 5
 frame-relay interface-dlci 111
!
```

Example 11-40 lists the IP forwarding table of the stillwater router, followed by three **ping**s. To test complete IP connectivity, **ping**s have been issued from the stillwater router to the networks that were not originally on a 24-bit boundary.

Example 11-40 *The* **show ip route** *Command Followed by a* **ping** *on the stillwater Router*

```
stillwater#show ip route
Codes: C - connected, S - static, I - IGRP, R - RIP, M - mobile, B - BGP
       D - EIGRP, EX - EIGRP external, O - OSPF, IA - OSPF inter area
       N1 - OSPF NSSA external type 1, N2 - OSPF NSSA external type 2
       E1 - OSPF external type 1, E2 - OSPF external type 2, E - EGP
       i - IS-IS, L1 - IS-IS level-1, L2 - IS-IS level-2, * - candidate default
       U - per-user static route, o - ODR

Gateway of last resort is not set

R    192.168.1.0/24 [120/4] via 172.16.2.1, 00:00:01, Ethernet0
R    192.168.2.0/24 [120/4] via 172.16.2.1, 00:00:01, Ethernet0
     172.16.0.0/24 is subnetted, 4 subnets
```

continues

Example 11-40 *The* **show ip route** *Command Followed by a* **ping** *on the stillwater Router (Continued)*

```
R       172.16.5.0 [120/4] via 172.16.2.1, 00:00:01, Ethernet0
R       172.16.6.0 [120/4] via 172.16.2.1, 00:00:01, Ethernet0
C       172.16.2.0 is directly connected, Ethernet0
R       172.16.3.0 [120/4] via 172.16.2.1, 00:00:01, Ethernet0
stillwater#ping 192.168.1.2

Type escape sequence to abort.
Sending 5, 100-byte ICMP Echos to 192.168.1.2, timeout is 2 seconds:
!!!!!
Success rate is 100 percent (5/5), round-trip min/avg/max = 68/70/72 ms
stillwater#ping 192.168.1.3

Type escape sequence to abort.
Sending 5, 100-byte ICMP Echos to 192.168.1.3, timeout is 2 seconds:
!!!!!
Success rate is 100 percent (5/5), round-trip min/avg/max = 68/70/72 ms
stillwater#ping 172.16.5.1

Type escape sequence to abort.
Sending 5, 100-byte ICMP Echos to 172.16.5.1, timeout is 2 seconds:
!!!!!
```

The final part of this lab is optional and involves configuring the georgia and ohio routers
as EIGRP stub routers. Both routers still must advertise their connected networks; therefore,
they need to use the **connected** keyword with the **eigrp stub** command. The only routers
that need to be configured as stub routers are georgia and ohio; no configuration is necessary
on the wisconsin router. The syntax needed on both routers resembles the following:

```
georgia(config-router)#eigrp stub connected
```

To verify that a stub router is working, use the **show ip eigrp neighbors detail** command,
as in Example 11-41. The last line of the output shows whether stub routing is enabled and
what the stub router can advertise. **ping**s also should be issued from the RIP domain to the
newly configured stub areas to verify IP routing.

Example 11-41 *Verifying Stub Routing*

```
wisconsin#show ip eigrp neighbors detail 65001
IP-EIGRP neighbors for process 65001
H   Address               Interface    Hold Uptime    SRTT   RTO  Q  Seq Type
                                       (sec)          (ms)        Cnt Num
2   192.168.1.3           Se0.1         178 00:00:53    52  1140  0  25
    Version 12.0/1.1, Retrans: 1, Retries: 0
    Stub Peer Advertising ( CONNECTED ) Routes
1   192.168.1.2           Se0.1         156 00:03:11   209  1254  0  28
    Version 12.0/1.1, Retrans: 0, Retries: 0
    Stub Peer Advertising ( CONNECTED ) Routes
0   192.168.2.2           Se0.2         130 01:01:01    26  2280  0  33
    Version 11.3/1.0, Retrans: 1, Retries: 0
wisconsin#
```

The last example (11-42) lists the complete configuration of the georgia, wisconsin, and minnesota routers.

Example 11-42 *Configuration listings of georgia, wisconsin, and minnesota Routers*

```
hostname georgia
!
<<<text omitted>>>
!
interface Ethernet0
 ip address 172.16.6.1 255.255.255.0
 no ip directed-broadcast
!
interface Serial0
 bandwidth 64
 ip address 192.168.1.2 255.255.255.248
 no ip directed-broadcast
 encapsulation frame-relay
 no ip mroute-cache
 fair-queue 64 256 0
 frame-relay map ip 192.168.1.1 102 broadcast
 frame-relay map ip 192.168.1.3 102 broadcast
 frame-relay lmi-type cisco
!
router eigrp 65001
 network 172.16.0.0
 network 192.168.1.0
 no auto-summary
 eigrp stub connected
!
```

```
hostname wisconsin
!
<<<text omitted>>>
!
interface Ethernet0
 ip address 172.16.5.1 255.255.255.128
 no ip directed-broadcast
!
interface Serial0
 no ip address
 no ip directed-broadcast
 encapsulation frame-relay
 no ip mroute-cache
 frame-relay lmi-type cisco
!
interface Serial0.1 multipoint
 bandwidth 128
 ip address 192.168.1.1 255.255.255.248
 no ip directed-broadcast
 no ip split-horizon eigrp 65001
 frame-relay map ip 192.168.1.2 121 broadcast
 frame-relay map ip 192.168.1.3 150 broadcast
!
```

continues

Example 11-42 *Configuration listings of georgia, wisconsin, and minnesota Routers (Continued)*

```
interface Serial0.2 point-to-point
 ip address 192.168.2.1 255.255.255.0
 no ip directed-broadcast
 ip summary-address eigrp 65001 192.168.1.0 255.255.255.0 5
 ip summary-address eigrp 65001 172.16.5.0 255.255.255.0 5
 frame-relay interface-dlci 111
!
interface Serial1
 no ip address
 no ip directed-broadcast
 shutdown
!
interface BRI0
 no ip address
 no ip directed-broadcast
 shutdown
 isdn guard-timer 0 on-expiry accept
!
router eigrp 65001
 network 172.16.0.0
 network 192.168.1.0
 network 192.168.2.0
 no auto-summary
```

```
hostname minnesota
!
<<<text omitted>>>
!
interface Ethernet2
 ip address 172.16.2.1 255.255.255.0
 media-type 10BaseT
!
<<<text omitted>>>
!
interface Serial0
 ip address 192.168.2.2 255.255.255.0
 encapsulation frame-relay
 no ip mroute-cache
 frame-relay interface-dlci 110
!
router eigrp 65001
 redistribute rip
 network 172.16.0.0
 network 192.168.2.0
 default-metric 1544 100 254 1 1500
 no auto-summary
!
router rip
 redistribute eigrp 65001
 network 172.16.0.0
 default-metric 4
!
```

Lab 23: Default Routing, Route manipulation, and Filtering in EIGRP Networks—Part I

Practical Scenario

Most networks today are connected to the Internet in some form. Connecting to the Internet usually requires a default route to be propagated throughout the network. The following lab gives you practice in controlling routes and propagating a default route throughout EIGRP.

Lab Exercise

Small groups of Internet coffee shops and their suppliers have pooled to leverage a common connection to the Internet. Solar Bucks Inc., G & S INC of Sweden, and Barneys have decided to share common networks while providing new services to their customers. Some shops also have private networks and do not want them propagated to other coffee shops. Your task is to configure an EIGRP network using the following parameters as design guidelines:

- Configure an IP network as depicted in Figure 11-14, using EIGRP as the routing protocol and 2001 as the Autonomous System ID.

- Configure the Frame Relay network as a point-to-point network among all the routers. Do not create a multipoint network.

- Do not allow any other shops to see the subnet 172.16.3.0/24 on the barneys router.

- Inject a default route into the solar_bucks router pointing all traffic to the internet_router.

- The direct Frame link between solar_bucks and g_and_s router is very expensive. Configure EIGRP so that traffic from g_and_s will go first to barneys and then to solar_bucks. If the PVC between barneys and g_and_s drops, traffic will flow directly from g_and_s to solar_bucks.

Lab Objectives

- Configure the Internet Coffee Shop Network as depicted in Figure 11-14. Configure IP as denoted in the diagram. The LAN topology type is not important in this lab.

- Use the Frame Relay data link protocol on the WAN. Use only point-to-point networks on the Frame Relay network.

- Ensure full IP connectivity to all IP interfaces—that is, be sure that you can **ping** all Frame Relay and LAN interfaces except those that are filtered.

- Filter the network 172.16.3.0/24 from g_and_s and solar_bucks routers.

- Inject a default route into the solar_bucks router pointing all traffic to the internet_router.

- Control routes so that the traffic from the g_and_s router passes through barneys before it hits the Internet. Traffic to 172.16.50.0/0 also should go through the barneys router. Do not use policy routing.

Equipment Needed

- Five Cisco routers. Three will be connected through V.35 back-to-back cables or in a similar manner to a Frame Relay switch.

- Four LAN segments, provided through hubs or switches. The LAN topology is not significant to this lab. The Internet connection can be real or not; it does not affect the configuration of the router.

Physical Layout and Prestaging

- Connect the hubs and serial cables to the routers, as shown in Figure 11-14.

- Configure an additional router to serve as the connection to the Internet. Use EIGRP for the routing protocol.

- A Frame Relay switch with three PVCs also is required. Example 11-43 lists the Frame Relay configuration used in this lab.

Example 11-43 *Frame Relay Switch Configuration*

```
hostname frame_switch
!
frame-relay switching
!
<<<text omitted>>>
!
interface Serial0
 no ip address
 encapsulation frame-relay
 no fair-queue
 clockrate 148000
 frame-relay intf-type dce
 frame-relay route 111 interface Serial1 110
 frame-relay route 121 interface Serial3 102
!
interface Serial1
 no ip address
 encapsulation frame-relay
 clockrate 148000
 frame-relay intf-type dce
 frame-relay route 110 interface Serial0 111
 frame-relay route 130 interface Serial3 131
```

Example 11-43 *Frame Relay Switch Configuration (Continued)*

```
!
interface Serial2
 no ip address
 shutdown
!
interface Serial3
 no ip address
 encapsulation frame-relay
 clockrate 64000
 frame-relay intf-type dce
 frame-relay route 102 interface Serial0 121
 frame-relay route 131 interface Serial1 130
!
```

Figure 11-14 *Internet Coffee Shop Network*

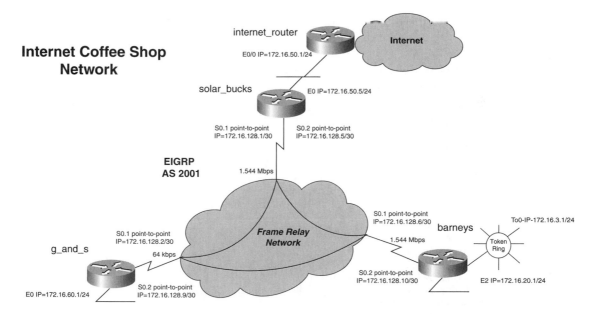

Lab 23: Default Routing, Route Manipulation, and Filtering in EIGRP Networks—Part II

Lab Walkthrough

Configure the Frame Relay switch and attach the three routers in a back-to-back manner to the Frame switch. Use V.35 cables or CSU/DSUs with crossover cables to connect the routers. Create the four LANs by the use of switches or hubs/MAUs, as illustrated in Figure 11-14.

When the physical connections are complete, assign IP addresses to all LAN and WAN interfaces, as depicted in Figure 11-14. Be sure that you can **ping** each routers' local LAN and WAN interface before moving on. You will use **frame-relay interface-dlci** commands on the point-to-point interfaces among all the routers. Example 11-44 lists the Frame Relay configuration, to this point, on all routers involved.

Example 11-44 *Frame Relay Configurations*

```
hostname solar_bucks
!
<<<text omitted>>>
!
interface Serial0
 no ip address
 no ip directed-broadcast
 encapsulation frame-relay
 no ip mroute-cache
 frame-relay lmi-type cisco
!
interface Serial0.1 point-to-point
 ip address 172.16.128.1 255.255.255.252
 no ip directed-broadcast
 frame-relay interface-dlci 121
!
interface Serial0.2 point-to-point
 ip address 172.16.128.5 255.255.255.252
 no ip directed-broadcast
 frame-relay interface-dlci 111
!
```
```
hostname g_and_s
!
<<<text omitted>>>
!
interface Serial0
 no ip address
 no ip directed-broadcast
```

Example 11-44 *Frame Relay Configurations (Continued)*

```
 encapsulation frame-relay
 no ip mroute-cache
 frame-relay lmi-type cisco
!
interface Serial0.1 point-to-point
 ip address 172.16.128.2 255.255.255.252
 no ip directed-broadcast
 frame-relay interface-dlci 102
!
interface Serial0.2 point-to-point
 ip address 172.16.128.9 255.255.255.252
 no ip directed-broadcast
 frame-relay interface-dlci 131
!
```

```
hostname barneys
!
<<<text omitted>>>
!
interface Serial0
 no ip address
 encapsulation frame-relay
 no ip mroute-cache
!
interface Serial0.1 point-to-point
 ip address 172.16.128.6 255.255.255.252
 frame-relay interface-dlci 110
!
interface Serial0.2 point-to-point
 ip address 172.16.128.10 255.255.255.252
 frame-relay interface-dlci 130
!
```

The basic EIGRP configuration for this lab is far simpler than that of the previous lab. There are no discontinuous subnets; therefore, you do not have to disable EIGRP autosummarization. The Frame Relay network is a point-to-point network, thereby making split horizon a nonissue, as well. Following the three-step process for configuring EIGRP, you simply need to enable EIGRP routing and assign the AS number of 2001. You will use the **network** statement of 172.16.0.0 on each router. This is all that you need to configure for basic EIGRP routing. Because the PVCs to the g_and_s router are only 64 kbps, set the bandwidth to 64 on all the Frame Relay links to the g_and_s router. The EIGRP portion of the solar_bucks router, which resembles all the EIGRP configurations to this point, is presented in Example 11-45.

Example 11-45 *EIGRP Configuration of All Routers to This Point*

```
!
router eigrp 2001
 network 172.16.0.0
!
```

At this time, you can verify routing by performing source **ping**s and examining the route table. When basic routing is working, you can proceed to the next portion of the lab, which requires that barneys not propagate the subnet 172.16.3.0 throughout the EIGRP domain. There are many ways to accomplish this, but for this lab, you will use a distribution list. The list will be applied to EIGRP updates leaving the s0.1 and s0.2 interfaces on the barneys router. Example 11-46 demonstrates the configuration of an access list denying the network 172.16.3.0/24 only. Access list 10 then is called by the distribution list in EIGRP. The distribution list must be applied to serial interfaces s0.1 and s0.2 to prevent the route from leaking back into the network.

Example 11-46 *Configuration of a Distribution List*

```
barneys(config)#access-list 10 deny 172.16.3.0 0.0.0.255
barneys(config)#access-list 10 permit any
barneys(config)#router eigrp 2001
barneys(config-router)#distribute-list 10 out serial 0.1
barneys(config-router)#distribute-list 10 out serial 0.2
barneys(config-router)#^z
```

By observing the forwarding table on g_and_s in Example 11-47, you can see that the route 172.16.3.0/24 is now missing. You still can **ping** the 172.16.20.0/24 subnet, so you know that the filter was a success.

Example 11-47 *Testing a Route Filter*

```
g_and_s#show ip route
Codes: C - connected, S - static, I - IGRP, R - RIP, M - mobile, B - BGP
       D - EIGRP, EX - EIGRP external, O - OSPF, IA - OSPF inter area
       N1 - OSPF NSSA external type 1, N2 - OSPF NSSA external type 2
       E1 - OSPF external type 1, E2 - OSPF external type 2, E - EGP
       i - IS-IS, L1 - IS-IS level-1, L2 - IS-IS level-2, ia - IS-IS inter area
       * - candidate default, U - per-user static route, o - ODR
       P - periodic downloaded static route

Gateway of last resort is not set

     172.16.0.0/16 is variably subnetted, 7 subnets, 3 masks
C        172.16.128.8/30 is directly connected, Serial0.2
D        172.16.128.4/30 [90/41024000] via 172.16.128.1, 00:05:14, Serial0.1
                         [90/41024000] via 172.16.128.10, 00:05:14, Serial0.2
C        172.16.128.0/30 is directly connected, Serial0.1
```

Example 11-47 *Testing a Route Filter (Continued)*

```
C       172.16.60.0/24 is directly connected, Ethernet0
D       172.16.50.0/24 [90/40537600] via 172.16.128.1, 00:05:14, Serial0.1
D       172.16.20.0/24 [90/40537600] via 172.16.128.10, 00:05:13, Serial0.2
D       172.16.0.0/16 is a summary, 01:10:38, Null0
g_and_s#ping 172.16.20.1

Type escape sequence to abort.
Sending 5, 100-byte ICMP Echos to 172.16.20.1, timeout is 2 seconds:
!!!!!
Success rate is 100 percent (5/5), round-trip min/avg/max = 40/41/44 ms
g_and_s#
```

The next portion of the lab requires solar_bucks to inject a default route into the EIGRP domain. To accomplish this task, configure a default static route pointing all traffic to the internet_routers Ethernet port, 172.16.50.1. For the routers to use the default network, ensure that IP classless is enabled. The static route is redistributed into EIGRP. Example 11-48 demonstrates the configuration of the default route on the solar_bucks router.

Example 11-48 *Configuring a Default Route for EIGRP*

```
solar_bucks(config)#ip route 0.0.0.0 0.0.0.0 172.16.50.1
solar_bucks(config)#router eigrp 2001
solar_bucks(config-router)#redistribute static
solar_bucks(config-router)#default-metric 1544 100 254 1 1500
solar_bucks(config-router)#^Z
solar_bucks#
```

By viewing the route or forwarding table on g_and_s or barneys, you can see that the default route is being propagated and is marked as an external, default candidate route, as shown in Example 11-49.

Example 11-49 *Viewing the Default Route on Barneys*

```
g_and_s#show ip route
Codes: C - connected, S - static, I - IGRP, R - RIP, M - mobile, B - BGP
       D - EIGRP, EX - EIGRP external, O - OSPF, IA - OSPF inter area
       N1 - OSPF NSSA external type 1, N2 - OSPF NSSA external type 2
       E1 - OSPF external type 1, E2 - OSPF external type 2, E - EGP
       i - IS-IS, L1 - IS-IS level-1, L2 - IS-IS level-2, * - candidate default
       U - per-user static route, o - ODR

Gateway of last resort is 172.16.128.1 to network 0.0.0.0

     172.16.0.0/16 is variably subnetted, 7 subnets, 3 masks
C       172.16.128.8/30 is directly connected, Serial0.2
```

continues

Example 11-49 *Viewing the Default Route on Barneys (Continued)*

```
D        172.16.128.4/30 [90/41024000] via 172.16.128.1, 00:20:43, Serial0.1
                         [90/41024000] via 172.16.128.10, 00:20:43, Serial0.2
C        172.16.128.0/30 is directly connected, Serial0.1
C        172.16.60.0/24 is directly connected, Ethernet0
D        172.16.50.0/24 [90/40537600] via 172.16.128.1, 00:20:43, Serial0.1
D        172.16.20.0/24 [90/40537600] via 172.16.128.10, 00:20:42, Serial0.2
D        172.16.0.0/16 is a summary, 01:26:07, Null0
D*EX 0.0.0.0/0 [170/40537600] via 172.16.128.1, 00:09:12, Serial0.1
g_and_s#
```

The final phase of the lab involves influencing EIGRP routing decisions. In the previous example, g_and_s is using solar_bucks as the preferred route to the Internet. By changing the delay on this link, you can affect the route table so that the barneys router is the preferred path to the Internet. To accomplish this, use the **delay 1000** command on each side of the PVC going between the g_and_s router and solar_bucks. Example 11-50 lists the route table of g_and_s, showing all routes now going through barneys first. A source trace can be performed to further test the configuration.

Example 11-50 *Route Table of g_and_s After the Delay Was Implemented*

```
g_and_s#show ip route
Codes: C - connected, S - static, I - IGRP, R - RIP, M - mobile, B - BGP
       D - EIGRP, EX - EIGRP external, O - OSPF, IA - OSPF inter area
       N1 - OSPF NSSA external type 1, N2 - OSPF NSSA external type 2
       E1 - OSPF external type 1, E2 - OSPF external type 2, E - EGP
       i - IS-IS, L1 - IS-IS level-1, L2 - IS-IS level-2, ia - IS-IS inter area
       * - candidate default, U - per-user static route, o - ODR
       P - periodic downloaded static route

Gateway of last resort is 172.16.128.10 to network 0.0.0.0

     172.16.0.0/16 is variably subnetted, 7 subnets, 3 masks
C        172.16.128.8/30 is directly connected, Serial0.2
D        172.16.128.4/30 [90/41024000] via 172.16.128.10, 00:00:01, Serial0.2
C        172.16.128.0/30 is directly connected, Serial0.1
C        172.16.60.0/24 is directly connected, Ethernet0
D        172.16.50.0/24 [90/41049600] via 172.16.128.10, 00:00:01, Serial0.2
D        172.16.20.0/24 [90/40537600] via 172.16.128.10, 00:00:11, Serial0.2
D        172.16.0.0/16 is a summary, 01:28:54, Null0
D*EX 0.0.0.0/0 [170/41049600] via 172.16.128.10, 00:00:02, Serial0.2
g_and_s#
```

Example 11-51 lists the final configurations.

Example 11-51 *Final Router Configurations for the Internet Coffee Shop Network*

```
hostname solar_bucks
!
<<<text omitted>>>
!
interface Ethernet0
 ip address 172.16.50.5 255.255.255.0
 no ip directed-broadcast
!
interface Serial0
 no ip address
 no ip directed-broadcast
 encapsulation frame-relay
 no ip mroute-cache
 frame-relay lmi-type cisco
!
interface Serial0.1 point-to-point
 bandwidth 64
 ip address 172.16.128.1 255.255.255.252
 no ip directed-broadcast
 delay 1000
 frame-relay interface-dlci 121
!
interface Serial0.2 point-to-point
 ip address 172.16.128.5 255.255.255.252
 no ip directed-broadcast
 frame-relay interface-dlci 111
!
<<<text omitted>>>
!
router eigrp 2001
 redistribute static
 network 172.16.50.0 0.0.0.255          ←Optional 12.0 way, listed for example only
 network 172.16.0.0
 default-metric 1544 100 254 1 1500
!
ip classless
ip route 0.0.0.0 0.0.0.0 172.16.50.1
```

```
hostname g_and_s
!
<<<text omitted>>>
!
interface Ethernet0
 ip address 172.16.60.1 255.255.255.0
 no ip directed-broadcast
!
interface Serial0
 no ip address
```

continues

Example 11-51 *Final Router Configurations for the Internet Coffee Shop Network (Continued)*

```
 no ip directed-broadcast
 encapsulation frame-relay
 no ip mroute-cache
 frame-relay lmi-type cisco
!
interface Serial0.1 point-to-point
 bandwidth 64
 ip address 172.16.128.2 255.255.255.252
 no ip directed-broadcast
 delay 1000
 frame-relay interface-dlci 102
!
interface Serial0.2 point-to-point
 bandwidth 64
 ip address 172.16.128.9 255.255.255.252
 no ip directed-broadcast
 frame-relay interface-dlci 131
!
router eigrp 2001
 network 172.16.0.0
!
ip classless
```

```
hostname barneys
!
<<<text omitted>>>
!
interface Ethernet2
 ip address 172.16.20.1 255.255.255.0
 media-type 10BaseT
!
<<<text omitted>>>
!
interface Serial0
 no ip address
 encapsulation frame-relay
 no ip mroute-cache
!
interface Serial0.1 point-to-point
 ip address 172.16.128.6 255.255.255.252
 frame-relay interface-dlci 110
!
interface Serial0.2 point-to-point
 ip address 172.16.128.10 255.255.255.252
 bandwidth 64
 frame-relay interface-dlci 130
!
<<<text omitted>>>
!
router eigrp 2001
 network 172.16.0.0
```

Example 11-51 *Final Router Configurations for the Internet Coffee Shop Network (Continued)*

```
 distribute-list 10 out Serial0.1
 distribute-list 10 out Serial0.2
!
ip classless
!
access-list 10 deny    172.16.3.0 0.0.0.255
access-list 10 permit any
```

CHAPTER 12

Link-State Protocols: Open Shortest Path First (OSPF)

Since its conception in 1987, OSPF has continued to evolve with the modern internetwork. Today, OSPF is clearly the dominant Open Systems interior routing protocol. Because of the constant RFC enhancements to OSPF, it has proven itself to be a scalable protocol with networks in the tens of thousands of nodes.

OSPF officially was documented in 1989 by the Internet Engineering Task Force (IETF) to address many of the limitations of distance vector protocols, such as RIP and IGRP. Since 1989, OSPF evolved through several RFCs, beginning with Version 1 in RFC 1131 and moving to Version 2 in RFC 1247, which was superceded by RFC 2178, to its final form, Version II in RFC 2328. In modern large networks, OSPF become the standard *open* routing protocol. The word *open* is used because the algorithm that drives OSPF, Dijkstra's Shortest Path First (SPF) algorithm, isn't proprietary to any vendor or organization. This allows for mainframes such as IBM, Unisys, and DEC, as well as other manufacturers' routers, to run OSPF.

As previously mentioned, OSPF provides many significant enhancements over current distance vector protocols:

- **Fast convergence**—OSPF uses a reliable flooding mechanism to update neighboring routers of changes in network topology. Only partial routing updates are sent upon the loss of a route. These two facts, combined with the fact that all routers in the OSPF domain have a nearly identical view of the network, allow for OSPF to converge quickly.

- **Support for VLSM, supernetting, and summarization**—OSPF can use summarization and VLSM to conserve address space and streamline routing.

- **Support for large network diameters**—By using VLSM and forcing hierarchical network design based on areas, the OSPF network diameter is virtually limitless.

- **Stub area routing**—Large networks are supported because stub-area routing reduces the routing table.

- **Efficient and reliable transport of routing updates**—Through the use of two reserved multicast addresses to transport routing updates, OSPF does not impact non-OSPF routers and devices. OSPF updates are reliable because they all are implicitly or explicitly acknowledged.

- **Efficient use of media**—Multicasts messages occur only on broadcast media. Unicast are used on NBMA and point-to-point networks.

- **Arbitrary metric based on cost**—OSPF uses a metric of cost, which can be changed, to base routing decisions on.

- **Equal-cost load balancing**—OSPF load-shares across equal-cost paths, optimizing bandwidth and multiple paths.

- **Support for Type 1 and Type II (MD5) authentication**—OSPF allows for secure route exchange by using Type 1 clear-text passwords or Type 2 MD5 authentication.

- **Support for route tagging of OSPF external routes**—Tags can be added to external routes redistributed into OSPF. Tags can be used as another control for routing policy within the autonomous system or for internal documentation.

- **Fully classless routing protocol**—OSPF supports a classless route table lookup and is not susceptible to classful routing problems, such as discontinuous subnets.

- No susceptibility to split-horizon issues.

In spite of these advantages, OSPF has been criticized as being overly complicated to configure and requiring high processor utilization. It is true that even the smallest OSPF network will require a small amount of design before implementation, and it does require more CPU cycles than other routing protocols. However, with the advent of modern CPUs, the amount of processor utilization for OSPF can be minimal. In this chapter, the technical operation of OSPF is discussed focusing more on the configuration aspects of OSPF.

Technical Overview of OSPF

OSPF is classless routing protocol that interfaces directly to IP as protocol 89. OSPF uses the concept of multicast hellos and dead timers to discover and maintain neighbors. Routing updates for OSPF are called *link-state advertisements (LSAs)*. The topology table for OSPF commonly is referred to as the *link-state database*. OSPF floods areas with LSAs until every router in the domain has a consistent image of the network, called the link-state database. When every router has the same image of the network, the SPF algorithm, or the Dijkstra algorithm, is run on the database, and a loop-free graph describing the shortest-cost path to each destination in the network is created. This is called the SPF tree. The OSPF routes in the route table or forwarding table are derived from the SPF tree. Because each router has an identical copy of the entire SPF tree, rapid convergence is possible. OSPF uses an arbitrary metric of *cost* when determining the shortest path to a destination.

Let's take a look at the major steps that OSPF goes through in building a route table, followed by a detailed examination of those steps. It is important to understand how OSPF operates over the different types of links and what type of LSAs propagates from one area to another. These details can be important when configuring OSPF over different media types.

1 When OSPF initializes, it sends hello packets out all OSPF interfaces on the multicast address of 224.0.0.5, called the AllSPFRouter address, on broadcast and point-to-point networks. The hello is unicast to specific neighbors on NBMA and multipoint networks. A router that receives the hello then verifies it against its own information about the network. The OSPF hello packet is a lot more complicated than that of EIGRP. As you will see, OSPF actually exchanges data within the hello packet.

2 When the packet has been verified, a neighbor is formed between the two routers. Neighbors, in turn, might or might not form adjacencies. An adjacency can be thought of as a virtual link between to routes used to send routing information on.

3 Each router sends its link-state information to the new neighbor.

4 Each neighbor records the new information and floods it to all its existing neighbors.

5 All routers receive the link-state information and build identical link-state databases. When the databases are complete, each router runs the SPF algorithm. The algorithm generates a loop-free path to every known route, with the local router as root. This is called the SPF tree.

6 Routes fitting the proper criteria from the SPF database then are inserted into the route table or forwarding database on the router.

Now, let's examine some of the more significant elements in greater detail.

OSPF Hello Protocol

As mentioned previously, the hello protocol in OSPF actually carries important information and forms the adjacency. By default, the hello packet is sent out every 10 seconds on all OSPF interfaces. On NBMA networks, the default hello is 30 seconds. The hello packet accomplishes these tasks:

- **Neighbor discovery**—When a router receives a hello, the packet contains the following information:
    — The router ID of the originating router
    — The area ID of the originating router interface
    — The address mask of the originating interface
    — Authentication type and authentication information for the originating interface
    — The HelloInterval of the originating interface

— The RouterDeadInterval of the originating interface

— The router priority

— The designated router (DR) and backup designated router (BDR)

— Five flags for options

— The router IDs of the originating router's neighbors

- **Adjacency criteria**—For OSPF to form an adjacency between two neighbors, the HelloInterval, RouterDeadInterval, area IDs, and authentication type and password must match.

- **Keepalive mechanism between neighbors**—The RouterDeadInterval is set to four times the hello timer. In most cases, this is 40 seconds or 120 seconds, depending on the link type. If a hello is not received by the time the RouterDeadInterval expires, the neighbor is declared down.

- **Election of DRs and BDRs on broadcast and NBMA networks**—The router ID, DR, and BDR fields, along with the router priority, help determine the state of DRs and BDRs. More information on DR and BDRs is offered in upcoming sections.

NOTE   Sometimes, the terms *neighbors* and *adjacencies* are used synonymously. In OSPF, the terms are related but mean different things. RFC 2328 defines neighboring routers as routers that have interfaces to a common network. Neighbors are maintained by and usually are dynamically discovered by OSPF's Hello Protocol. Adjacency is defined as a relationship formed between selected neighboring routers for the purpose of exchanging routing information. Not every pair of neighboring routers becomes adjacent.

OSPF Neighbors and Network Types

The old Frost poem about neighbors reads as true for OSPF as it did for EIGRP: "Good neighbors make good networks." As in EIGRP, link states can be exchanged only after the neighbors build adjacencies. Stable OSPF neighbors are important in OSPF networks. How OSPF treats the neighbor and propagates link states depends on the network type that the router and its neighbor(s) exist on. There are five types of OSPF networks:

- **Point-to-point networks**—Examples of point-to-point networks are HDLC networks, PPP, and Frame Relay networks with point-to-point subinterfaces. Link states and hellos use the multicast address of 224.0.0.5. There is no designated router or BDR election. This is a Cisco-specific network type and is not defined by an RFC.

- **Broadcast networks**—Examples include Ethernet, Token Ring, and FDDI networks. Hellos use the address 224.0.0.5 and elect a DR and a BDR. The other routers on this network send link states on the multicast address of 224.0.0.6. Only the DR and the

BDR listen to these updates on this address. They, in turn, flood the link states out address 224.0.0.5 for the other routers. The election and the role of the DR and BDR are discussed more in the next section.

- **NBMA networks**—NBMA network types include Frame Relay *natural* or multipoint interfaces and X.25 networks. On networks such as these, multicast packets are not forwarded properly to all neighbors because there exists no broadcast capability. Therefore, OSPF neighbors must be statically defined. A DR and a BDR are elected, and all OSPF packets are unicast. On NBMA networks, the DR/BDR should be the router(s) that have a PVC, SVC, or circuit to all the other routers, or what is called the *hub* router(s).

- **Point-to-multipoint**—Point-to-multipoint network types must be statically defined. The router treats a Frame Relay multipoint network like many point-to-point links. A DR and BDR are not elected, and OSPF packets are multicast.

- **Virtual links**—Virtual links are a special type of network that is used to extend Area 0. Virtual links are discussed more in the section "OSPF Virtual Links."

Designated Routers and Backup Designated Routers

On multiaccess networks, such as Ethernet, Token Ring, or FDDI, it quickly becomes inefficient for every adjacent router to advertise link states to all its neighbors. It also becomes inefficient for every router to become adjacent. Instead, OSPF elects one router and calls it the designated router. The designated router listens to link states on 224.0.0.6 and floods them on address 224.0.0.5. This is the only router besides the backup designated router that will listen for link-state updates on 224.0.0.6. The BDR will shadow the DR and take over only when the DR fails. Essentially, the DR/BDR scheme offers the following advantages:

- It streamlines routing updates through managing the flooding link states.

- DR and BDR represent the multiaccess network to the rest of the OSPF domain. By acting as a single point of control, the DR also ensures that routers on the multiaccess network have consistent link-state information.

- The concept of a BDR also speeds network synchronization. Because all routers are also adjacent to the BDR, if the DR fails, the BDR takes its place with minimum unavailability.

When the DR and the BDR are elected, new routers will establish adjacencies only with the DR and the BDR. The DR and the BDR also become adjacent with each other.

To elect the DR and BDR, the router will adhere to the following process:

1 Neighbors participating in the election must be in at least the *2-way state*. That is, each neighbor has sent and received a hello from the other neighbors participating. See the section entitled "The Basic OSPF Adjacency."

2 Priority values will be examined. Neighbors with the priority value of 0 are excluded from the process. The neighbor with the highest priority becomes the BDR. In case of a tie, the router with the highest RID wins. The default OSPF priority is 1, which can be modified with the **ip ospf priority** [*0-255*] interface command.

3 If no DRs are reported on the link, the BDR is promoted to DR, and the process begins again to select a new BDR. If there is a tie in the network, the tie is resolved by the router ID. The router with the highest router ID becomes the BDR.

4 If a router with a higher priority is added to the network, a new DR or BDR will not be selected. The DR/BDR election process happens again only if the DR or BDR fails.

5 The routers continue to exchange hellos every 10 seconds (the default on broadcast networks). If a router does not receive a hello from a neighbor within the amount of time specified by the dead timer interval, which is four times the hello interval, the neighbor is declared down.

Essentially, the election of a DR and a BDR allows OSPF to streamline routing updates through the network. In the Ethernet example in Figure 12-1, you can see how inefficient the routing process would quickly become in a large network. Without the DR/BDR, every router would need to exchange LS information with every other router on the network.

Figure 12-1 *OSPF Ethernet Network LS Propagation Without a DR and BDR (Hypothetical)*

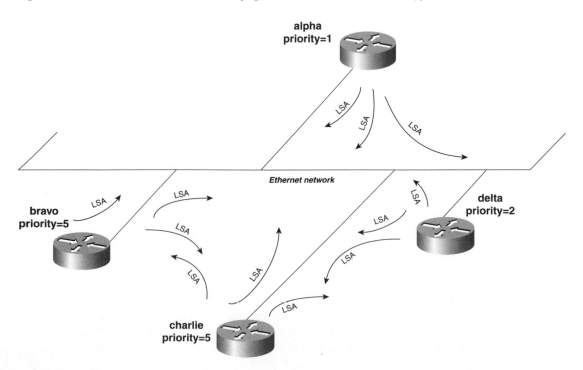

With a DR and BDR in place (see Figure 12-2), LS information, or route information, is controlled by the DR.

Figure 12-2 *LS Propagation with a DR and BDR*

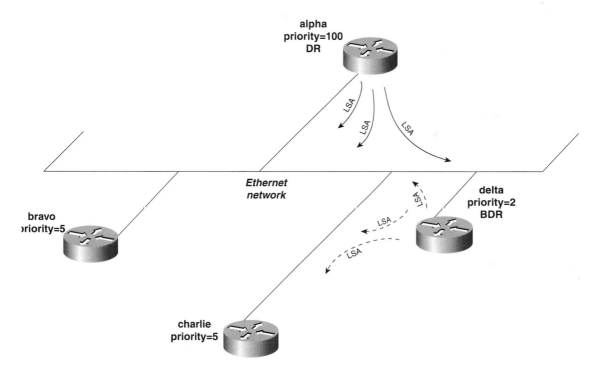

OSPF Router IDs (RIDs)

The OSPF router ID (RID) is 32-bit unique number assigned to each router running OSPF. This number uniquely identifies the router within the autonomous system. By having a unique router ID for every router within the AS, OSPF can accomplish the following:

- OSPF easily can identify duplicate LSAs.

- OSPF is used to identify the unique end points of virtual links.

- OSPF is used to determine the tie-breaker for DR and BDR negotiations, as mentioned previously.

The router ID is chosen among the interfaces configured for IP on the Cisco router. The router chooses the highest IP address from any operational IP interface. That is, the line is up and the line protocol is up for that interface. If a loopback address is configured on the router, the router chooses that address. If multiple loopback interfaces are configured, it chooses the loopback interface with the highest IP address.

To force a router ID, use a loopback interface with a high IP address, such as 192.168.200.X. It is not necessary to propagate this network in a routing protocol. The networks—or, more specifically, the IP host addresses used for router IDs—do not need to be reachable or "**ping**-able" addresses. In Cisco IOS Software Version 12.0 and above, the OSPF router ID can be hard-coded with the OSPF router command:

```
Router(config-router)#router-id ip_address
```

TIP It is highly recommended to set the router ID with **router-id** command or by using loopback interfaces. This can greatly increase OSPF network stability. For example, OSPF virtual links rely on the router ID. If the router ID is not fixed and a new network or loopback interface is added to that router, the router ID would be recalculated upon a failure of that router. This could then lead to a change in routers IDs, making the virtual link fail.

The Basic OSPF Adjacency

OSPF neighbors go through states before they can begin exchanging LSAs, as illustrated in Figure 12-3. These states are referred to as the neighbor state machine. You can examine the state of an OSPF neighbor with the **show ip ospf neighbor** command.

Figure 12-3 *A Basic OSPF Adjacency*

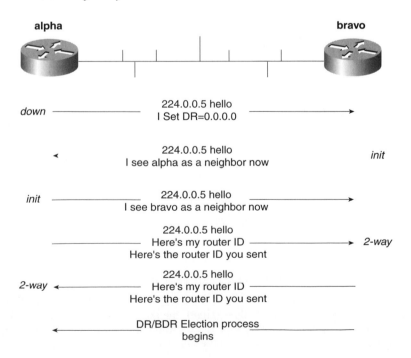

The following list briefly describes the OSPF neighbor states and how they operate:

- **Down**—This is the initial state of the neighbor, which also indicates that no hellos were heard from this neighbor within the last dead time interval.
- **Attempt**—This state applies only to neighbors on NBMA networks, where the neighbors statically are configured with the **neighbor** command. When the interface becomes active, it goes to the ATTEMPT state, or when the router is DR or BDR.
- **Init**—A hello packet has been received from the neighbor, but two-way communication hasn't taken place yet.
- **2-way**—This state indicates that a router has seen its own router ID in the Neighbor field of the Hello packet that it received from the neighbor. It also means that bidirectional conversation was established and that DR and BDR election can occur.

When an OSPF interface first becomes active, it begins to send hello packets. When two routers receive each other's hello, they place the neighbor in *init status*. When a neighbor is in init status, it places its own router ID into the hello packet. When a router receives one of the new hellos with the router ID of its neighbor, it places the neighbor in a new state of *2-way*. The *2-way* state ensures that there is two-way communication between the routers. The routers must be in this state before they can negotiate a DR/BDR and exchange LSAs.

After the routers have achieved the 2-way state, OSPF enters its final states:

- **ExStart**—The router enters a master/slave relationship and prepares for the exchange of database description packets. The neighbor with the highest interface address becomes the master.
- **Exchange**—The router sends its database description packets to neighbors in the exchange state. The database description packets describe the entire link-state database. The link-state database is synchronized after this phase. After synchronization, the router enters one of two final states:
  - **Loading**—The router also sends link-state request packets to all neighbors that are in the loading state. The loading phase requests that more recent LSAs be sent.
  - **Full**—Neighbors in this state are fully adjacent.

In summary, the OSPF adjacency is built in four phases:

1 Neighbors are discovered.
2 Bidirectional communication is established between neighbors.
3 The SPF database is synchronized.
4 Full adjacency is formed.

You can view the status of an OSPF adjacency with the **show ip ospf neighbor** command, and you can observe the actual building of the adjacency with the **debug ip ospf adj** command. These and other OSPF status commands are discussed more in upcoming sections.

In Figure 12-4, the charlie router is added to an existing OSPF network. By enabling the **debug** command, you can observe the adjacency being built, as demonstrated in Example 12-1.

Figure 12-4 *A Basic OSPF Adjacency Demonstration*

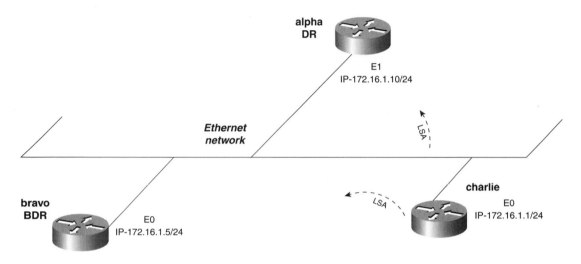

Example 12-1 **debug ip ospf adj** *Command Followed by a* **show ip ospf neighbor** *Command Demonstrating an Adjacency Forming*

```
charlie#debug ip ospf adj
OSPF adjacency events debugging is on

OSPF: Interface Ethernet0 going Up
OSPF: Build router LSA for area 0, router ID 172.16.1.1
OSPF: Build router LSA for area 0, router ID 172.16.1.1
OSPF: Build router LSA for area 0, router ID 172.16.1.1
%SYS-5-CONFIG_I: Configured from console by console
OSPF: 2 Way Communication to 172.16.1.10 on Ethernet0, state 2WAY    →Router enters
two-way state
OSPF: Build router LSA for area 0, router ID 172.16.1.1
OSPF: 2 Way Communication to 172.16.1.5 on Ethernet0, state 2WAY
OSPF: Backup seen Event before WAIT timer on Ethernet0
OSPF: DR/BDR election on Ethernet0        →DR/BDR election begins
OSPF: Elect BDR 172.16.1.5
OSPF: Elect DR 172.16.1.10
        DR: 172.16.1.10 (Id)    BDR: 172.16.1.5 (Id)
OSPF: Send DBD to 172.16.1.5 on Ethernet0 seq 0x1370 opt 0x2 flag 0x7 len 32
OSPF: Send DBD to 172.16.1.10 on Ethernet0 seq 0x218C opt 0x2 flag 0x7 len 32
OSPF: Build router LSA for area 0, router ID 172.16.1.1
OSPF: Rcv DBD from 172.16.1.10 on Ethernet0 seq 0x1137 opt 0x2 flag 0x7 len 32
```

Example 12-1 **debug ip ospf adj** *Command Followed by a* **show ip ospf neighbor** *Command Demonstrating an Adjacency Forming (Continued)*

```
   state EXSTART        →EXSTART state begins slave/master will be selected
OSPF: NBR Negotiation Done. We are the SLAVE
OSPF: Send DBD to 172.16.1.10 on Ethernet0 seq 0x1137 opt 0x2 flag 0x2 len 52
OSPF: Rcv DBD from 172.16.1.5 on Ethernet0 seq 0x16D9 opt 0x42 flag 0x7 len 32
   state EXSTART        →EXSTART state begins for the other neighbor
OSPF: NBR Negotiation Done. We are the SLAVE
OSPF: Send DBD to 172.16.1.5 on Ethernet0 seq 0x16D9 opt 0x2 flag 0x2 len 52
OSPF: Rcv DBD from 172.16.1.10 on Ethernet0 seq 0x1138 opt 0x2 flag 0x3 len 92
   state EXCHANGE       →Exchange state begins for one neighbor
OSPF: Send DBD to 172.16.1.10 on Ethernet0 seq 0x1138 opt 0x2 flag 0x0 len 32
OSPF: Database request to 172.16.1.10
OSPF: sent LS REQ packet to 172.16.1.10, length 36
OSPF: Rcv DBD from 172.16.1.5 on Ethernet0 seq 0x16DA opt 0x42 flag 0x3 len 92
state EXCHANGE          →Exchange state begins for the other neighbor
OSPF: Send DBD to 172.16.1.5 on Ethernet0 seq 0x16DA opt 0x2 flag 0x0 len 32
OSPF: Database request to 172.16.1.5
OSPF: sent LS REQ packet to 172.16.1.5, length 36
OSPF: Rcv DBD from 172.16.1.10 on Ethernet0 seq 0x1139 opt 0x2 flag 0x1 len 32 s
tate EXCHANGE
OSPF: Exchange Done with 172.16.1.10 on Ethernet0
OSPF: Send DBD to 172.16.1.10 on Ethernet0 seq 0x1139 opt 0x2 flag 0x0 len 32
OSPF: Synchronized with 172.16.1.10 on Ethernet0, state FULL     →LS database is
synced and the adjacency is in FULL status for this neighbor
OSPF: Build router LSA for area 0, router ID 172.16.1.1
OSPF: Rcv DBD from 172.16.1.5 on Ethernet0 seq 0x16DB opt 0x42 flag 0x1 len 32 s
tate EXCHANGE
OSPF: Exchange Done with 172.16.1.5 on Ethernet0
OSPF: Synchronized with 172.16.1.5 on Ethernet0, state FULL     →The same "FULL"
state is achieved with this neighbor
OSPF: Build router LSA for area 0, router ID 172.16.1.1
OSPF: Send DBD to 172.16.1.5 on Ethernet0 seq 0x16DB opt 0x2 flag 0x0 len 32
OSPF: Build router LSA for area 0, router ID 172.16.1.1
charlie#

charlie#show ip ospf neighbor

Neighbor ID     Pri   State         Dead Time   Address        Interface
172.16.1.5        1   FULL/BDR      00:00:35    172.16.1.5     Ethernet0
172.16.1.10       1   FULL/DR       00:00:30    172.16.1.10    Ethernet0
charlie#
```

In this example, 172.16.1.10, or the alpha router, became the DR because its IP address is the highest one on the link. The next highest IP address was 172.16.1.5, or the bravo router, so it was elected as the BDR.

Shortest-Path Tree (SPF) and the OSPF Metric Cost

When the LS database is synchronized within an area, the Dijkstra algorithm is run against it in two passes to form the *shortest-path (SPF)* tree. The first pass against the SPF database forms the branches, or router adjacencies within the area. The second pass adds all leaves or stub networks to the tree. When OSPF builds the tree, it determines the shortest path to each destination based on the sum *cost* to the destination. The lower the cost is, the more preferred the route is. The cost of a route is the sum of all costs of outgoing interfaces to that destination. Oddly enough, RFC 2328 offers no specific values for cost. Nortel Networks, for example, implements OSPF under RFC 2328 and uses the same formula to generate cost as Cisco Systems. In multivendor environments, take the extra time to see how cost is calculated because it will help OSPF have a consistent view of the entire internetwork.

Cisco routers calculate OSPF cost as (10^8/BW) *rounded down*, where BW is the configured or default bandwidth of the interface. Table 12-1 lists the common default OSPF cost settings.

Table 12-1 *Default OSPF Interface Cost*

Interface Type	Default Cost (10^8/BW)
FDDI, ATM, Fast Ethernet, Gigabit Ethernet (> 100 Mbps)	1
HSSI (45 Mps)	2
16-Mbps Token Ring	6
10-Mbps Ethernet	10
4-Mbps Token Ring	25
T1 (1.544 Mbps)	64
DS-0 (64 kbps)	1562
56 kbps	1785
Tunnel (9 kbps)	11111

The default cost values can be overridden with the **ip ospf cost 1-65535** interface command. The cost for a route can be viewed with the **show ip route command**. Recall that the variable behind the administrative distance is the metric cost for the router. Figure 12-5 shows a quick example of how cost is calculated. The route table of the echo router lists the cost for network 172.16.2.0 to be 70. The bandwidth of the T1 plus the 16-MB Token Ring equals 70; 64 + 6 = 70. The route to the Ethernet network has a cost of 80; 64 + 6 + 10.

Figure 12-5 *OSPF Cost Calculation*

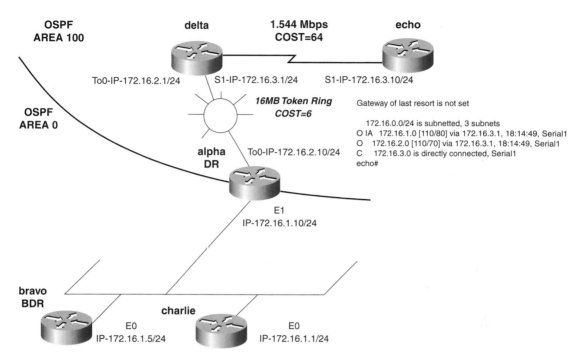

OSPF
AREA 100

delta

1.544 Mbps
COST=64

echo

To0-IP-172.16.2.1/24   S1-IP-172.16.3.1/24   S1-IP-172.16.3.10/24

OSPF
AREA 0

16MB Token Ring
COST=6

Gateway of last resort is not set

172.16.0.0/24 is subnetted, 3 subnets
O IA   172.16.1.0 [110/80] via 172.16.3.1, 18:14:49, Serial1
O   172.16.2.0 [110/70] via 172.16.3.1, 18:14:49, Serial1
C   172.16.3.0 is directly connected, Serial1
echo#

alpha
DR

To0-IP-172.16.2.10/24

E1
IP-172.16.1.10/24

bravo
BDR

charlie

E0
IP-172.16.1.5/24

E0
IP-172.16.1.1/24

OSPF Router Types, Areas, and LSAs

At the onset, we mentioned that OSPF could be considered to be CPU-intensive and difficult to configure. By now, it becomes evident that multiple SPF databases, complex algorithms, and constant CPU interrupts caused by link-state flooding can cause an increase in the router's processor utilization.

To control the flooding of link states and database synchronization, OSPF deploys the use of areas. An OSPF area can be defined as a group of routers and links that divide an OSPF domain into subdomains. Areas are identified by a 32-bit area ID, which then also can be expressed in dotted-decimal notation or as a decimal number.

There are five types of areas in OSPF:

- **Backbone area, or Area 0 (or 0.0.0.0)**—All traffic must pass through the backbone area; nonbackbone areas do not exchange packets directly. All areas also must be adjacent to Area 0. The backbone must be continuous and cannot be partitioned. Area 0 can be extended by the use of a virtual link.

- **Nonbackbone, nonstub area**—This is a normal OSPF area other than Area 0. All LSAs, except Type 7, are flooded into this area.

- **Stub area**—No external routes are advertised into a stub area, nor will they generate external LSA type 5s. A backbone area will advertise a single default route to a stub area or a network summary LSA for the destination 0.0.0.0. Some other restrictions on stub areas apply:

  — Virtual links cannot be configured across stub areas.

  — Adjacencies will not be established with any other router not configured as a stub, except for the Area Border Router.

  — No router within a stub area can be an ASBR because no external routes or LSA Type 5 can be advertised out of a stub area. In short, stub areas cannot perform redistribution.

  — LSA Types 4 and 5 are blocked into the area. Only LSA Types 1, 2, and 3 are flooded into the area.

- **Totally stubby area**—Neither external nor internal routes are advertised into this area. LSA types 3, 4, and 5 are blocked into the area, except for a single default route advertised as a LSA type 3. The router will use the default route to reach any destination outside the area.

- **Not-so-stubby area (NSSAs)**—Sometimes, it is necessary to redistribute another routing protocol, such as RIP, into a stub area. Because this violates the definition of stub area, a new area type was needed. To remedy this, RFC 1587 defines not-so-stubby areas (NSSA). An NSSA allows external routes to be advertised into the OSPF domain while retaining the other characteristics of a stub area. When external routes are redistributed into a router in an NSSA area, the router originates LSA Type 7s to advertise the new external destination(s) to routers within the NSSA area. The LSA Type 7s are converted to LSA Type 5 when flooded into Area 0 by the ABR. No LSA type 5s will exist in the NSSA area. All routers in the area must be configured NSSA.

OSPF requires a hierarchical network design through the use of areas controlled by specific router types. A router might be multiple router types; for example, ABRs are also backbone routers. The OSPF router types are as follows:

- **Internal routers**—Internal routers are routers whose interfaces all reside in the same OSPF area. All internal routers have the same SPF database.

- **Area Border Routers (ABRs)**—ABRs are routers that connect one or more areas to the backbone area. They forward all LSAs from the backbone area. The ABR always has at least one interface in Area 0 and keeps a separate SPF database for each area that it is connected to. These should be high-end routers for this reason.

- **Backbone routers**—These are routers that have at least one interface in Area 0. All interfaces might reside in Area 0, in which case the router is an internal backbone router.

- **Autonomous System Boundary Routers (ASBRs)**—Routers that redistribute another routing protocol or advertise external routes are called ASBRs.

The word LSA has been mentioned quite a bit. LSAs are what OSPF uses to build the OSPF database. OSPF floods specific LSA types to specific portions of the OSPF domain as dictated by the area and router type mentioned previously. LSA are classified by type, and each type serves a specific purpose, as described in the following list:

- **Router LSA (Type 1)**—This LSA contains information about a router and the links that it has in an area. LSA type 1s are flooded only in that area. The LSA also tells whether the router is a stub or ASBR, or whether it has one end of a virtual link. OSPF represents these routes in the forwarding table with an O.

- **Network LSA (Type 2)**—This LSA is used for transit networks within an area. It describes the set of routers attached to a network. LSA Type 2s are not flooded outside an area. OSPF represents these routes in the forwarding table with an O.

- **Summary LSAs for ABRs (Type 3)**—These LSAs advertise internal networks to routers in other areas, called OSPF interarea routes. The LSA might contain a summary network or a single network. ABRs are the only router type that generates this LSA type. OSPF represents these routes in the forwarding table with an O IA.

- **Summary LSA for ASBRs (Type 4)**—These LSAs are used to advertise the location of an ASBR. Routers searching for a path to an external network use LSA Type 4 to determine the best next hop. OSPF represents these routes in the forwarding table with an O IA. This LSA type is hard to remember, so you can think of it as the "how do I get out here LSA."

- **Autonomous system external LSAs (Type 5)**—Type 5 LSAs are used to advertise routes redistributed into OSPF. These routes are called OSPF external routes, and they are flooded throughout the entire OSPF autonomous system, except for stub, totally stubby, and NSSA areas. OSPF represents these routes in the forwarding table with an O E1 or O E2, depending on the route.

- **NSSA external LSA (Type 7)**—This type of LSA is generated for the external routes redistributed into a not-so-stubby area. They are flooded throughout the NSSA area. When they hit an ABR, the ABR advertises them as Type 5 LSAs into Area 0. Type 7 LSAs never leave the NSSA area. OSPF represents these routes in the forwarding table with an O N1 or O N2, depending on how the route was redistributed.

Table 12-2 summarizes the LSAs that are allowed in each area.

Table 12-2   *LSA Types Allowed in Each Area*

Area Type	LSA 1 and 2	LSA 3 and 4	LSA 5	LSA 7
Backbone area (Area 0)	Yes	Yes	Yes	No
Stub area	Yes	Yes	No	No
Totally stubby area	Yes	No*	No	No
Not-so-stubby area	Yes	Yes	No	Yes
Nonbackbone, nonstub area	Yes	Yes	Yes	No

*   One LSA Type 3 is used to advertise the default route

NOTE	RFC 2370 defines opaque link states. Opaque LSAs are Type 9, 10, and 11 link-state advertisements. These advertisements might be used directly by OSPF or indirectly by some application wanting to distribute information throughout the OSPF domain, such as RSVP. The function of the opaque LSA option is to provide for future extensibility of OSPF. The following section is taken directly from RFC 2370:

3.0 The Opaque LSA

Opaque LSAs are types 9, 10 and 11 link-state advertisements. Opaque LSAs consist of a standard LSA header followed by a 32-bit aligned application-specific information field. Standard link-state database flooding mechanisms are used for distribution of Opaque LSAs. The range of topological distribution (i.e., the flooding scope) of an Opaque LSA is identified by its link-state type. This section documents the flooding of Opaque LSAs.

The flooding scope associated with each Opaque link-state type is defined as follows.

Link-state type 9 denotes a link-local scope. Type-9 Opaque LSAs are not flooded beyond the local (sub)network.

Link-state type 10 denotes an area-local scope. Type-10 Opaque LSAs are not flooded beyond the borders of their associated area.

Link-state type 11 denotes that the LSA is flooded throughout the Autonomous System (AS). The flooding scope of type-11 LSAs are equivalent to the flooding scope of AS-external (type-5) LSAs. Specifically type-11 Opaque LSAs are 1) flooded throughout all transit areas, 2) not flooded into stub areas from the backbone and 3) not originated by routers into their connected stub areas. As with type-5 LSAs, if a type-11 Opaque LSA is received in a stub area from a neighboring router within the stub area the LSA is rejected.

Figure 12-6 illustrates a modern OSPF network, highlighting the different router types.

OSPF Acknowledgments

To ensure that LSAs are transmitted successfully, OSPF requires each LSA to be acknowledged. LSAs are acknowledged by one of the following acknowledgment types:

- **Implicit acknowledgment**—Occurs when the sending router receives a duplicate LSA from the neighbor. By seeing the neighbor report the LSA, the router knows "implicitly" that it received the LSA.

- **Explicit acknowldgment**—Requires the receiving router(s) to send a specific link-state acknowledgement packet in response to the LSA.

Figure 12-6 *OSPF Network Router types*

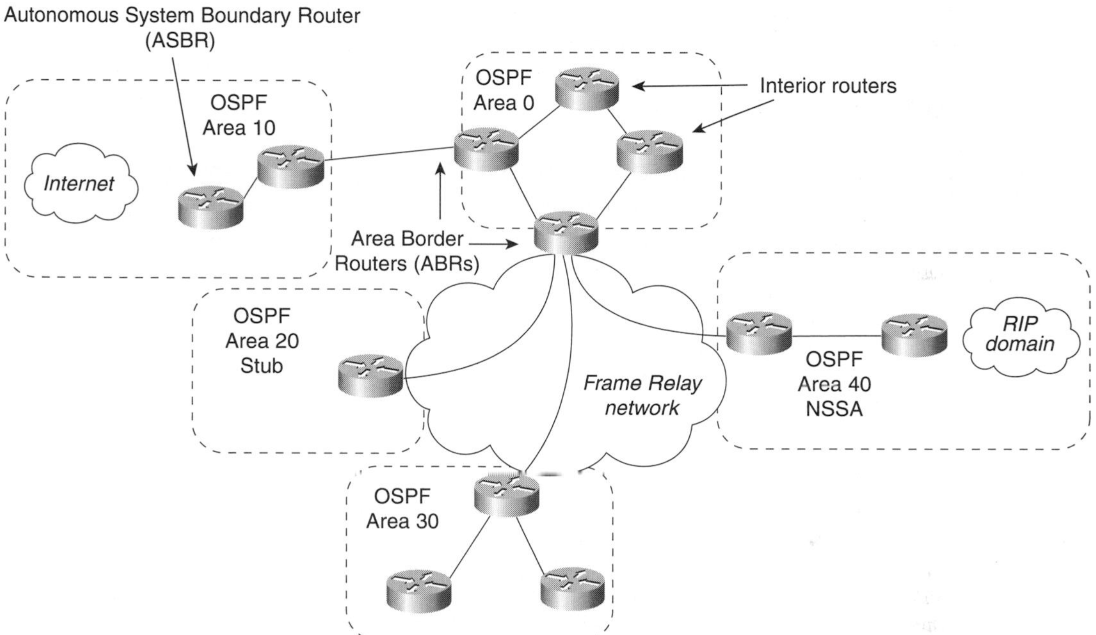

To ensure that LSAs are current and valid, each LSA has a sequence number, a checksum, and a MaxAge value. The sequence number and checksum verify that the LSA is valid, whereas the age parameter ensures that the LSA is the most current LSA. MaxAge is used to verify how old the LSA was. MaxAge is set for 3600 seconds, or 1 hour. When a router originates an LSA, it sets the MaxAge at 0. Each time the LSA is flooded by another router, its MaxAge is incremented by another timer called InfTransDelay, which has a default value of 1. When the LSA reaches the MaxAge value, the LSA is reflooded throughout the network. Routers also use the MaxAge parameter when comparing two LSAs to determine which one is more current. This type of flooding can be excessive on large stable networks. In Cisco IOS 12.1, Cisco introduced a concept called LSA flooding reduction. LSA flooding control is discussed more in upcoming sections.

OSPF Path Types

When you perform the **show ip route** command on OSPF, each route is classified in OSPF as one of six path types. The path is preceded by a tag representing the route's type. The path types and tags used are as follows:

- **(O) Intra-area paths/routes**—These are routes to networks within the same OSPF area.

- **(O IA) Interarea paths/routes**—These are routes to networks in different OSPF areas but within the same OSPF autonomous system.

- **(O E1) External Type 1 paths/routes**—When an external route is redistributed into OSPF, it must be assigned a metric or cost. Type 1 paths have a cost that is the sum of this external path/metric plus the internal cost of the path to the ASBR reporting the route.

- **(O E2) External Type 2 paths/routes**—This is the same as a Type 1 route, except for the fact that the internal cost to the ASBR is not added to the default cost of the path. By default, all routes distributed into OSPF become external Type 2 routes. This can be changed during redistribution.

- **(O N1) OSPF NSSA type 1**—When an external route is redistributed into an OSPF NSSA area, it becomes this type. Type 1 paths have a cost that is the sum of this external path/metric plus the internal cost of the path to the router reporting the route.

- **(O N2) OSPF NSSA type 2**—This is the same as a Type 1 route, except that the internal cost to the router is not added to the default cost of the path. By default, all routes distributed into OSPF NSSA area become OSPF NSSA external Type 2 routes. This can be changed during redistribution.

Example 12-2 lists a complex route table with four types of OSPF routes.

Example 12-2 *Complex OSPF Route Table*

```
skynet#show ip route
Codes: C - connected, S - static, I - IGRP, R - RIP, M - mobile, B - BGP
       D - EIGRP, EX - EIGRP external, O - OSPF, IA - OSPF inter area
       N1 - OSPF NSSA external type 1, N2 - OSPF NSSA external type 2
       E1 - OSPF external type 1, E2 - OSPF external type 2, E - EGP
       i - IS-IS, L1 - IS-IS level-1, L2 - IS-IS level-2, * - candidate default
       U - per-user static route, o - ODR

Gateway of last resort is 172.16.128.1 to network 0.0.0.0

     10.0.0.0/24 is subnetted, 1 subnets
O       10.10.10.0 is a summary, 03:05:49, Null0
     129.201.0.0/24 is subnetted, 1 subnets
O E1    129.201.1.0 [110/90] via 172.16.2.66, 03:05:45, TokenRing1
     128.200.0.0/24 is subnetted, 1 subnets
D EX    128.200.1.0 [170/679936] via 172.16.192.3, 05:42:57, Serial1
     129.200.0.0/24 is subnetted, 1 subnets
O E1    129.200.1.0 [110/90] via 172.16.2.66, 03:05:45, TokenRing1
     128.201.0.0/24 is subnetted, 1 subnets
D EX    128.201.1.0 [170/679936] via 172.16.192.3, 05:42:57, Serial1
C    201.201.101.0/24 is directly connected, Loopback0
O E2 132.31.0.0/16 [110/2] via 172.16.2.66, 00:58:04, TokenRing1
O E2 131.31.0.0/16 [110/2] via 172.16.2.66, 00:58:04, TokenRing1
     172.16.0.0/16 is variably subnetted, 27 subnets, 4 masks
O IA    172.16.152.0/24 [110/71] via 172.16.2.66, 03:05:45, TokenRing1
O IA    172.16.150.0/24 [110/80] via 172.16.2.66, 03:05:45, TokenRing1
```

Example 12-2 *Complex OSPF Route Table (Continued)*

```
O IA     172.16.151.0/24 [110/71] via 172.16.2.66, 03:05:45, TokenRing1
C        172.16.144.0/21 is directly connected, Loopback20
C        172.16.136.0/21 is directly connected, Ethernet1
C        172.16.128.0/21 is directly connected, Ethernet0
C        172.16.220.0/24 is directly connected, Loopback69
C        172.16.192.0/24 is directly connected, Serial1
C        172.16.192.3/32 is directly connected, Serial1
O IA     172.16.42.2/32 [110/70] via 172.16.2.66, 03:05:46, TokenRing1
O IA     172.16.42.3/32 [110/70] via 172.16.2.66, 03:05:46, TokenRing1
O E2     172.16.42.0/24 [110/2] via 172.16.2.66, 03:05:46, TokenRing1
O IA     172.16.42.1/32 [110/6] via 172.16.2.66, 03:05:46, TokenRing1
O IA     172.16.21.0/24 [110/76] via 172.16.2.66, 03:05:46, TokenRing1
O IA     172.16.22.0/24 [110/71] via 172.16.2.66, 03:05:46, TokenRing1
O E2     172.16.1.0/24 [110/2] via 172.16.2.66, 03:05:46, TokenRing1
O E2     172.16.2.0/24 [110/2] via 172.16.2.66, 03:05:46, TokenRing1
D        172.16.102.0/24 [90/679936] via 172.16.192.3, 05:42:59, Serial1
D        172.16.103.0/24 [90/409600] via 172.16.128.1, 05:42:59, Ethernet0
O E2     172.16.84.0/24 [110/2] via 172.16.2.66, 03:05:47, TokenRing1
O E2     172.16.85.0/24 [110/2] via 172.16.2.66, 03:05:47, TokenRing1
O E2     172.16.81.0/24 [110/2] via 172.16.2.66, 03:05:47, TokenRing1
O E2     172.16.82.0/24 [110/2] via 172.16.2.66, 03:05:47, TokenRing1
O E2     172.16.83.0/24 [110/2] via 172.16.2.66, 03:05:47, TokenRing1
O E2     172.16.64.0/24 [110/2] via 172.16.2.66, 03:05:47, TokenRing1
<<<text omitted>>>
```

This section on the technical aspects of OSPF is meant to give you a solid background on OSPF fundamentals so that the configuration commands will have a firmer meaning when used. Several books have been written on OSPF describing in further detail OSPF packet structure, as well as other OSPF intricacies. For further reading, we suggest Jeff Doyles's *Routing TCP/IP*, Volume I; Tom Thomas's *OSPF Network Design Solutions*; and John Moy's *OSPF, Anatomy of an Internet Routing Protocol*. The Cisco OSPF design guide on www.cisco.com and RFC 2328 also make good references.

Configuring OSPF

Unlike other routing protocols, OSPF requires a certain amount of predesign before implementation. Careful consideration must be applied to the OSPF network as a whole, not just a single area. The following list contains some design considerations that you should take into account when deploying OSPF:

- **Area deployment**—Area 0 must be continuous and should be located in the most stable part of the network. This usually consists of the core routers.

- **Router IDs**—Statically configure router ID (RIDs). Use the private subnet of 192.168.0.0 to accomplish this. Remember, the highest addresses become the DR and the BDR. Cisco IOS Level 12.0 and above allow for static RIDs without having to use loopback interfaces.

- **RIDs and priority used to "hard-code" DR and BDR**—Where the OSPF network type requires the use of a DR and BDR, use OSPF priority or router IDs to force the election of the DR and BDR. The DR on Frame Relay networks should be the router with a direct PVC to all the neighbors in that area. On LANs, the DR and BDR should be the higher-end routers.

- **Continuous IP addressing within an area**—When possible, all addresses in an area should be continuous. This leads toward route summarization and a natural hierarchical design.

- **Various forms of Stub areas**—Many edge routers and Frame Relay networks lead nicely toward the use of stub areas. Use the different forms of stub areas whenever possible.

- **Virtual links avoided**—Even though we will discuss virtual links, their deployment and presence is an indication of poor network design. There are a few cases in which backup links might not be directly connected to Area 0, and a virtual link will be needed. Overall, they should be avoided in production networks.

With these design considerations in mind, you will use the following seven-step task list to configure OSPF:

Step 1   **Divide the OSPF network into various areas by using the design guidelines listed previously**. Make a network diagram, and highlight Area 0, other areas, and the area types. If the network will be using a DR/BDR, mark which routers will serve that function.

Step 2   **(Optional) Assign permanent router IDs to the network**. To accomplish this, configure loopback interfaces for use as static RIDs, if on Cisco IOS Software earlier than Release 12.0. The loopback interfaces should be in a high private address space and do not need to be advertised by OSPF. We recommend using the range 192.168.*x.x.* on loopback interface 0. If the OSPF network type will elect a DR/BDR, such as in an Ethernet network, assign the routers to be the DR and BDR the higher IP addresses, such as 192.168.250.251 and 192.168.250.250. RIDs can be assigned in Cisco IOS Software 12.0 and above with the OSPF router command **router-id** **ip_address**. *Note:* OSPF must be enabled before the router ID can be assigned.

Step 3   **Enable OSPF on the router and configure RIDs**. This is accomplished with the **router ospf** *process_id* global command. Think of the process_id as an Autonomous System ID. This number should be the same on all routers within the autonomous system. At this time, also configure the RIDs that you assigned in Step 2. Use the router command **router-id** **ip_address**.

Step 4   **Configure interfaces to participate in OSPF.** The OSPF uses a network statement that is followed by a wildcard mask and an area ID.

```
network a.b.c.d wildcard_mask area X
```

A wildcard mask can be considered an inverse bit mask, where the 0 bit is a "care" bit, and a 1 bit is a "don't care" bit. For example, to run OSPF only on networks 128.10.1.0/24 to 128.10.255.0/24 in Area 0, the syntax would resemble this:

```
network 128.10.0.0 0.0.255.255 area 0
```

For another example, to run OSPF only on the network 172.16.128.4/30 in Area 100, the syntax would resemble this:

```
network 172.16.128.4 0.0.0.3 area 100
```

Use a wildcard mask of 0.0.0.0 to enable OSPF on a single interface. Use the tightest wildcard mask possible when configuring OSPF. This will prevent OSPF from advertising networks that you might be unaware of. It also prevents unnecessary OSPF hellos from entering those segments.

Step 5   **Configure OSPF neighbor support.** The OSPF network type might require additional configuration for OSPF to build an adjacency. On NBMA networks, such as Frame Relay, the OSPF configuration will be interface-dependant. Table 12-3 highlights some common network types and tells whether any additional configuration is needed.

Table 12-3   *OSPF Network Configuration Table*

Physical Interface Type	Default OSPF Network Type	Static Neighbor Needed	DR/BDR Elected	Desired Neighbor State	Priority Recommended
Broadcast media Ethernet, Token Ring, and so on	Broadcast*	No	Yes	FULL/DR FULL/BDR FULL/—	Yes
Frame Relay natural or multipoint	NMBA	Yes	Yes	FULL/ DROTHER	No
Frame Relay point-to-point	Point-to-point	No	No	FULL/—	No
Frame Relay multipoint	Point-to-multipoint**	No	No	FULL/—	No

*   If the OSPF network type on a Frame Relay network is changed to BROADCAST, it will have a DR and BDR election and priority should be set.

**   The OSPF network type of point-to-multipoint is not the default network type of any interface. OSPF point-to-multipoint networks must be statically configured.

When configuring OSPF over Frame Relay multipoint interfaces, it is necessary to configure static neighbors. Without the neighbor statements, the router's neighbor will be in a constant state of waiting and will never form an adjacency. To configure the static neighbor, use this OSPF router command:

```
Router(config-route)neighbor ip_address_of_neighbor
```

The hub router of the multipoint network, or the router that has a PVC to each site, should be statically configured as the DR. To accomplish this, set the priority of the spoke or remote routers to 0. A priority of 0 tells OSPF that this interface or neighbor will not participate in the DR/BDR election process. The DR choice can be further influenced by configuring the priority of the link on the router of the DR to the high number, such as 255. The priority can be configured with this interface command:

```
Router(config-if)ip ospf priority 0-255
```

The default OSPF priority is 1.

Another way to force an adjacency creation is simply to change the OSPF network type to something more desirable. Changing a Frame Relay multipoint network to a point-to-multipoint will make OSPF treat the multipoint network like many point-to-point networks. Changing the network type to broadcast also forces adjacency creation and DR/BDR election. To change the OSPF network type, use the following interface command:

```
Router(config-if)ip ospf network [broadcast | non-broadcast |
point-to-multipoint | point-to-point]
```

Step 6   **(Optional) Configure OSPF special area types**. To configure OSPF areas as stubs, NSSAs, and totally stubby areas, use the following OSPF router command:

```
Router(config-route)area x [nssa | stub | virtual-link ] [no-summary]
```

To configure an area as a stub or an NSSA area, simply add the **area** command followed by this parameter. For example, to configure Area 10 as a stub, the syntax would resemble this:

```
Router(config-route)area 10 stub
```

A totally stubby area is configured by configuring a normal stub area followed by the **no-summary** argument to block LS Types 3 and 4.

```
Router(config-route)area 10 stub no-summary
```

Step 7   **(Optional) Configure any optional OSPF parameters**. These include such things as hello timers, route summarization, authentication, and so on. These and other OSPF optional parameters are discussed in upcoming sections.

Practical Example: Configuring Multiple OSPF Area Types over Frame Relay

To better understand this rather lengthy process, let's apply it to an practical example. Figure 12-7 illustrates an OSPF network that is in Step 1 of the configuration process. This model of OSPF has a Frame Relay multipoint and point-to-point network. You will be configuring a totally stubby area, Area 100, for the luke router. The paul router will reside in Area 0, the backbone area, along with the Ethernet interface of the router john. The mark and mathew routers will be in OSPF Area 10. We have marked john to be the DR for the WAN and LAN networks.

Figure 12-7 *OSPF Multiple-Area Network*

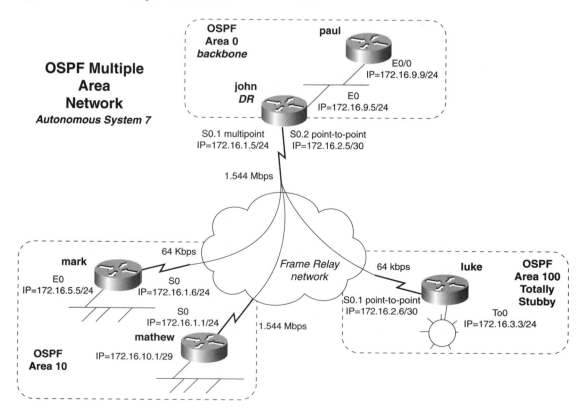

Step 2 calls for defining or configuring RIDs. In this particular network, only the mathew router is running a version of Cisco IOS Software prior to Release 12.0, so it will have to use a loopback address to configure a RID. Recall that OSPF will use the highest loopback address for a RID; this is why this step precedes enabling OSPF. On the mathew router, create a static RID with the following commands:

```
mathew(config)#int loop 0
mathew(config-if)#ip address 172.16.250.1 255.255.255.0
```

Figure 12-8 illustrates the RIDs used in this model. It should be noted that this step is optional but recommended for stability reasons.

Figure 12-8 *OSPF Static RIDs*

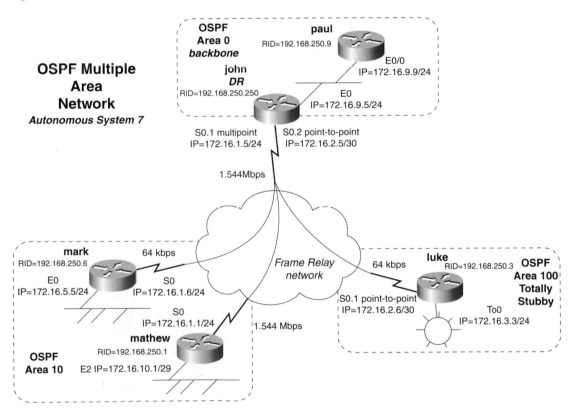

TIP   When configuring OSPF in a lab scenario, we assign our RIDs so that the last octet of the RID is the router number. For example, if you have the routers R1, R2 and R3, you would assign the RIDs to be 192.168.250.1, 192.168.250.2, and 192.168.250.3, respectively. The DR in the lab has an unusually high RID, 250, so it stands out from the rest. When viewing the OSPF database, having RIDs that somewhat "self-document" the network can be a great benefit.

Step 3 involves enabling the OSPF process and configuring RIDs. The OSPF autonomous system is 7, so you will use 7 as the OSPF process ID. During this step, you also will configure the RIDs with the router command **router-id** *ip_address*. Example 12-3 demonstrates this step on the mark and john routers.

Example 12-3 *Enabling OSPF on mark and john*

```
mark(config)#router ospf 7
mark(config-router)#router-id 192.168.250.6

john(config)#router ospf 7
john(config-router)#router-id 192.168.250.250
```

After the OSPF process is enabled on all the routers, Step 4 requires that you configure the interfaces or networks participating in OSPF. Using the router command **network** *ip_address wildcard_mask* **area** *x*, you define the networks to run OSPF and also specify the area that those networks will reside in. Example 12-4 demonstrates the configuration of **network** statements on the router john.

Example 12-4 *Configuring OSPF on the Router john*

```
john(config)#router ospf 7
john(config-router)#network 172.16.9.0 0.0.0.255 area 0
john(config-router)#network 172.16.1.0 0.0.0.255 area 10
john(config-router)#network 172.16.2.4 0.0.0.3 area 100
```

You can configure the **network** statements on the remaining routers in many ways. We personally prefer limiting the **network** statement with a specific wildcard mask to one network per statement, or to a single interface with the 0.0.0.0 as the wildcard mask. In large networks, this type of configuration might be less desirable, and you might want to use a single **network** statement to group multiple interfaces into the same OSPF area. However, if you add new interfaces and they must go into different areas, you will have to remove the **network** statement and add it again for the new **network** statement to take effect.

At this point during the configuration, OSPF builds adjacencies on the Frame Relay point-to-point network between john and luke. Another adjacency is built on the Ethernet network between john and paul. OSPF, however, will not be capable of building an adjacency on the Frame Relay multipoint network between john, mark, and mathew without additional configuration. You can verify adjacency formation by performing a **show ip ospf neighbor** command on the router john, as in Example 12-5. The **show** and **debug** commands for OSPF are discussed in the next section.

Example 12-5 show ip ospf neighbor *Performed on the Router john*

```
john#show ip ospf neighbor

Neighbor ID      Pri   State          Dead Time    Address        Interface
192.168.250.9     1    FULL/BDR       00:00:34     172.16.9.9     Ethernet0
192.168.250.3     1    FULL/  -       00:00:38     172.16.2.6     Serial0.2
john#
```

Notice how clearly the router IDs show up in the previous command. This can significantly help troubleshooting OSPF on any size network.

Step 5 calls for the configuration of additional neighbor support to remedy the adjacency situation between john, mark, and mathew. Because you took the extra time to hard-code RIDs on all the routers, the john router will be DR for the connected LAN and WAN interfaces. You will take this a step further when defining **neighbor** statements. For the router john to build an adjacency with mark and mathew, you will need to add **neighbor** statements to all the routers. By setting the OSPF priority to 0 on the interface, that router will never participate in DR/BDR election. On multipoint networks, only the routers that have PVCs to all remote locations should be eligible for DR/BDR election. The default priority of 1 will be sufficient on the **neighbor** statements of the mark and mathew routers that point toward john. Example 12-6 illustrates the relevant portions of the OSPF configuration, to this point, on john, mark, and mathew, respectively.

Example 12-6 *OSPF Configuration of john, mark, and mathew Routers*

```
hostname john
!
interface Serial0.1 multipoint
 ip address 172.16.1.5 255.255.255.0
 no ip directed-broadcast
 ip ospf priority 255          →Set this routers priority to 255, forcing the DR
 frame-relay map ip 172.16.1.6 121 broadcast
 frame-relay map ip 172.16.1.1 111 broadcast
!
interface Serial0.2 point-to-point
 ip address 172.16.2.5 255.255.255.252
 no ip directed-broadcast
 frame-relay interface-dlci 150
!
```

Example 12-6 *OSPF Configuration of john, mark, and mathew Routers (Continued)*

```
router ospf 7
 router-id 192.168.250.250
 network 172.16.1.0 0.0.0.255 area 10
 network 172.16.2.4 0.0.0.3 area 100
 network 172.16.9.0 0.0.0.255 area 0
 neighbor 172.16.1.1          →A neighbor priority of 0 will not
 neighbor 172.16.1.6          →be listed in the configuration
!
```

```
hostname mark
!
interface Serial0
 ip address 172.16.1.6 255.255.255.0
 no ip directed-broadcast
 encapsulation frame-relay
 ip ospf priority 0           →This router will not participate in DR/BDR election
 no ip mroute-cache
 frame-relay map ip 172.16.1.5 102 broadcast
 frame-relay map ip 172.16.1.1 102 broadcast
!
router ospf 7
 router-id 192.168.250.6
 network 172.16.1.0 0.0.0.255 area 10
 network 172.16.5.0 0.0.0.255 area 10
 neighbor 172.16.1.5
!
```

```
hostname mathew
!
interface Serial0
 ip address 172.16.1.1 255.255.255.0
 encapsulation frame-relay
 ip ospf priority 0           →This router will not participate in DR/BDR election
 no ip mroute-cache
 frame-relay map ip 172.16.1.5 110 broadcast
 frame-relay map ip 172.16.1.6 110 broadcast
!
router ospf 7
 network 172.16.1.0 0.0.0.255 area 10
 network 172.16.10.0 0.0.0.255 area 10
 neighbor 172.16.1.5
!
```

By adding the **neighbor** statements, OSPF now builds adjacencies over the Frame Relay multipoint network. This can be verified by performing the **show ip ospf neighbor** command on the router john. Example 12-7 demonstrates this command on john.

Example 12-7 **show ip ospf neighbor** *Command Output for Router john*

```
john#show ip ospf neighbor

Neighbor ID     Pri   State          Dead Time   Address       Interface
192.168.250.9    1    FULL/BDR       00:00:32    172.16.9.9    Ethernet0
172.16.250.1     0    FULL/DROTHER   00:01:55    172.16.1.1    Serial0.1
192.168.250.6    0    FULL/DROTHER   00:01:46    172.16.1.6    Serial0.1
192.168.250.3    1    FULL/  -       00:00:37    172.16.2.6    Serial0.2
john#
```

The mathew and mark routers will not become adjacent with each other because there is not a direct connection between them. Example 12-8 shows the active neighbor on the mathew router. The adjacency is in a FULL state, with john being the DR for the link.

Example 12-8 **show ip ospf neighbor** *Command Output for Router mathew*

```
mathew#show ip ospf neighbor

Neighbor ID     Pri   State          Dead Time   Address         Interface
192.168.250.250 255   FULL/DR        00:01:48    172.16.1.5      Serial0
mathew#
```

You could accomplish this in other ways without using **neighbor** commands. Another way is to change the OSPF network type to either broadcast or point-to-multipoint. Technically, a point-to-multipoint would be a more accurate network type to use. Configuring the same network model, you will now use the network type of point-to-multipoint to create adjacencies between mathew, mark, and john. Example 12-9 lists the relevant configuration of the john and mathew routers, using the **ip osfp network** *type* command in place of **neighbor** statements. The configuration of mark would be identical to that of mathew.

Example 12-9 *Configuration of john and mark Using Network Types*

```
hostname john
!
interface Serial0
 no ip address
 no ip directed-broadcast
 encapsulation frame-relay
 no ip mroute-cache
!
interface Serial0.1 multipoint
 ip address 172.16.1.5 255.255.255.0
 no ip directed-broadcast
 ip ospf network point-to-multipoint       →Change the default OSPF network type
to PTM
                          →Priority is not needed, no DR/BDR on PTM
 frame-relay map ip 172.16.1.6 121 broadcast
 frame-relay map ip 172.16.1.1 111 broadcast
```

Example 12-9 *Configuration of john and mark Using Network Types (Continued)*

```
!
router ospf 7
 router-id 192.168.250.250
 network 172.16.1.0 0.0.0.255 area 10
 network 172.16.2.4 0.0.0.3 area 100
 network 172.16.9.0 0.0.0.255 area 0          →No neighbors
!

hostname mathew
!
interface Serial0
 ip address 172.16.1.1 255.255.255.0
 encapsulation frame-relay
 ip ospf network point-to-multipoint
 no ip mroute-cache
 frame-relay map ip 172.16.1.5 110 broadcast
 frame-relay map ip 172.16.1.6 110 broadcast
!
router ospf 7
 network 172.16.1.0 0.0.0.255 area 10
 network 172.16.10.0 0.0.0.255 area 10
!
```

Example 12-10 lists how the neighbors look on the mathew and john routers.

Example 12-10 *OSPF Neighbors on mathew and john*

```
mathew#show ip ospf neighbor

Neighbor ID      Pri   State         Dead Time   Address      Interface
192.168.250.250  1     FULL/  -      00:01:35    172.16.1.5   Serial0
mathew#

john#show ip ospf neighbor

Neighbor ID      Pri   State         Dead Time   Address      Interface
192.168.250.9    1     FULL/BDR      00:00:36    172.16.9.9   Ethernet0
172.16.250.1     1     FULL/  -      00:01:58    172.16.1.1   Serial0.1
192.168.250.6    1     FULL/  -      00:01:58    172.16.1.6   Serial0.1
192.168.250.3    1     FULL/  -      00:00:38    172.16.2.6   Serial0.2
john#
```

Steps 6 and 7 in the OSPF configuration process are optional; they involve configuring any OSPF area types and any other OSPF enhancements. In this model, you need only to configure one more step, and that is to configure the router luke to be in a totally stubby area. To configure a totally stubby area, the area needs to first be configured as a stub area, and then the argument **no-summary** must be used. The syntax will resemble the following:

```
area 100 stub no-summary
```

These commands should be added to the john and luke routers. Example 12-11 lists the output of the **show ip ospf** and **show ip route** command on the router luke.

Example 12-11 *Verifying the Totally Stubby Area on luke*

```
luke# show ip ospf 7
 Routing Process "ospf 7" with ID 192.168.250.3
 Supports only single TOS(TOS0) routes
 Supports opaque LSA
 SPF schedule delay 5 secs, Hold time between two SPFs 10 secs
 Minimum LSA interval 5 secs. Minimum LSA arrival 1 secs
 Number of external LSA 0. Checksum Sum 0x0
 Number of opaque AS LSA 0. Checksum Sum 0x0
 Number of DCbitless external and opaque AS LSA 0
 Number of DoNotAge external and opaque AS LSA 0
 Number of areas in this router is 1. 0 normal 1 stub 0 nssa
 External flood list length 0
    Area 100
        Number of interfaces in this area is 2
        It is a stub area, no summary LSA in this area
        Area has no authentication
        SPF algorithm executed 46 times
        Area ranges are
        Number of LSA 3. Checksum Sum 0x16F14
        Number of opaque link LSA 0. Checksum Sum 0x0
        Number of DCbitless LSA 0
        Number of indication LSA 0
        Number of DoNotAge LSA 0
        Flood list length 0

luke#show ip route
Codes: C - connected, S - static, I - IGRP, R - RIP, M - mobile, B - BGP
       D - EIGRP, EX - EIGRP external, O - OSPF, IA - OSPF inter area
       N1 - OSPF NSSA external type 1, N2 - OSPF NSSA external type 2
       E1 - OSPF external type 1, E2 - OSPF external type 2, E - EGP
       i - IS-IS, L1 - IS-IS level-1, L2 - IS-IS level-2, ia - IS-IS inter area
       * - candidate default, U - per-user static route, o - ODR
       P - periodic downloaded static route

Gateway of last resort is 172.16.2.5 to network 0.0.0.0

     172.16.0.0/16 is variably subnetted, 2 subnets, 2 masks
C       172.16.2.4/30 is directly connected, Serial0.1
C       172.16.3.0/24 is directly connected, TokenRing0
O*IA 0.0.0.0/0 [110/65] via 172.16.2.5, 00:02:23, Serial0.1
luke#
```

Instead of a full routing table, the luke router will receive only a default route from john, as shown in Example 12-12.

Example 12-12 shows the relevant portions of the configurations and the route tables used in this model.

Example 12-12 *Configurations and Route Table of john, mark, mathew, luke, and paul*

```
!
hostname john
!
interface Ethernet0
 ip address 172.16.9.5 255.255.255.0
 no ip directed-broadcast
!
interface Serial0
 no ip address
 no ip directed-broadcast
 encapsulation frame-relay
 no ip mroute-cache
!
interface Serial0.1 multipoint
 ip address 172.16.1.5 255.255.255.0
 no ip directed-broadcast
 ip ospf network point-to-multipoint
 frame-relay map ip 172.16.1.6 121 broadcast
 frame-relay map ip 172.16.1.1 111 broadcast
!
interface Serial0.2 point-to-point
 ip address 172.16.2.5 255.255.255.252
 no ip directed-broadcast
 frame-relay interface-dlci 150
!
router ospf 7
 router-id 192.168.250.250
 area 100 stub no-summary
 network 172.16.1.0 0.0.0.255 area 10
 network 172.16.2.4 0.0.0.3 area 100
 network 172.16.9.0 0.0.0.255 area 0

john#
john#show ip route
Codes: C - connected, S - static, I - IGRP, R - RIP, M - mobile, B - BGP
       D - EIGRP, EX - EIGRP external, O - OSPF, IA - OSPF inter area
       N1 - OSPF NSSA external type 1, N2 - OSPF NSSA external type 2
       E1 - OSPF external type 1, E2 - OSPF external type 2, E - EGP
       i - IS-IS, L1 - IS-IS level-1, L2 - IS-IS level-2, ia - IS-IS inter area
       * - candidate default, U - per-user static route, o - ODR
       P - periodic downloaded static route

Gateway of last resort is not set

     172.16.0.0/16 is variably subnetted, 8 subnets, 4 masks
C       172.16.9.0/24 is directly connected, Ethernet0
```

continues

Example 12-12 *Configurations and Route Table of john, mark, mathew, luke, and paul (Continued)*

```
O        172.16.10.0/29 [110/74] via 172.16.1.1, 00:16:06, Serial0.1
O        172.16.5.0/24 [110/74] via 172.16.1.6, 00:16:06, Serial0.1
C        172.16.2.4/30 is directly connected, Serial0.2
O        172.16.1.6/32 [110/64] via 172.16.1.6, 00:16:06, Serial0.1
O        172.16.1.1/32 [110/64] via 172.16.1.1, 00:16:06, Serial0.1
C        172.16.1.0/24 is directly connected, Serial0.1
O        172.16.3.0/24 [110/70] via 172.16.2.6, 00:13:47, Serial0.2
john#
```

```
!
hostname mark
!
interface Ethernet0
 ip address 172.16.5.5 255.255.255.0
 no ip directed-broadcast
!
interface Serial0
 ip address 172.16.1.G 255.255.256.0
 no ip directed-broadcast
 encapsulation frame-relay
 ip ospf network point-to-multipoint
 no ip mroute-cache
 frame-relay map ip 172.16.1.5 102 broadcast
 frame-relay map ip 172.16.1.1 102 broadcast
!
router ospf 7
 router-id 192.168.250.6
 network 172.16.1.0 0.0.0.255 area 10
 network 172.16.5.0 0.0.0.255 area 10
!
mark#
mark#show ip route
Codes: C - connected, S - static, I - IGRP, R - RIP, M - mobile, B - BGP
       D - EIGRP, EX - EIGRP external, O - OSPF, IA - OSPF inter area
       N1 - OSPF NSSA external type 1, N2 - OSPF NSSA external type 2
       E1 - OSPF external type 1, E2 - OSPF external type 2, E - EGP
       i - IS-IS, L1 - IS-IS level-1, L2 - IS-IS level-2, ia - IS-IS inter area
       * - candidate default, U - per-user static route, o - ODR
       P - periodic downloaded static route

Gateway of last resort is not set

     172.16.0.0/16 is variably subnetted, 8 subnets, 4 masks
O IA    172.16.9.0/24 [110/74] via 172.16.1.5, 00:29:30, Serial0
O       172.16.10.0/29 [110/138] via 172.16.1.5, 00:29:30, Serial0
O       172.16.1.5/32 [110/64] via 172.16.1.5, 00:29:30, Serial0
C       172.16.5.0/24 is directly connected, Ethernet0
O IA    172.16.2.4/30 [110/128] via 172.16.1.5, 00:29:30, Serial0
O       172.16.1.1/32 [110/128] via 172.16.1.5, 00:29:30, Serial0
C       172.16.1.0/24 is directly connected, Serial0
O IA    172.16.3.0/24 [110/134] via 172.16.1.5, 00:15:36, Serial0
```

Example 12-12 *Configurations and Route Table of john, mark, mathew, luke, and paul (Continued)*

```
mark#
mark#

!
hostname mathew
!
interface Loopback0
 ip address 172.16.250.1 255.255.255.0
!
interface Ethernet2
 ip address 172.16.10.1 255.255.255.248
 media-type 10BaseT
!
interface Serial0
 ip address 172.16.1.1 255.255.255.0
 encapsulation frame-relay
 ip ospf network point-to-multipoint
 no ip mroute-cache
 frame-relay map ip 172.16.1.5 110 broadcast
 frame-relay map ip 172.16.1.6 110 broadcast
!
router ospf 7
 network 172.16.1.0 0.0.0.255 area 10
 network 172.16.10.0 0.0.0.255 area 10
!
mathew#
mathew#show ip route
Codes: C - connected, S - static, I - IGRP, R - RIP, M - mobile, B - BGP
       D - EIGRP, EX - EIGRP external, O - OSPF, IA - OSPF inter area
       N1 - OSPF NSSA external type 1, N2 - OSPF NSSA external type 2
       E1 - OSPF external type 1, E2 - OSPF external type 2, E - EGP
       i - IS-IS, L1 - IS-IS level-1, L2 - IS-IS level-2, * - candidate default
       U - per-user static route, o - ODR

Gateway of last resort is not set

     172.16.0.0/16 is variably subnetted, 9 subnets, 4 masks
C       172.16.250.0/24 is directly connected, Loopback0
O IA    172.16.9.0/24 [110/74] via 172.16.1.5, 00:29:44, Serial0
C       172.16.10.0/29 is directly connected, Ethernet2
O       172.16.1.5/32 [110/64] via 172.16.1.5, 00:29:44, Serial0
O       172.16.5.0/24 [110/138] via 172.16.1.5, 00:29:44, Serial0
O IA    172.16.2.4/30 [110/128] via 172.16.1.5, 00:29:44, Serial0
O       172.16.1.6/32 [110/128] via 172.16.1.5, 00:29:44, Serial0
C       172.16.1.0/24 is directly connected, Serial0
O IA    172.16.3.0/24 [110/134] via 172.16.1.5, 00:15:54, Serial0
mathew#
mathew#
```

continues

Example 12-12 *Configurations and Route Table of john, mark, mathew, luke, and paul (Continued)*

```
!
hostname luke
!
interface Serial0
 no ip address
 no ip directed-broadcast
 encapsulation frame-relay
 no ip mroute-cache
 frame-relay lmi-type cisco
!
interface Serial0.1 point-to-point
 ip address 172.16.2.6 255.255.255.252
 no ip directed-broadcast
 frame-relay interface-dlci 151
!
router ospf 7
 router-id 192.168.250.3
 area 100 stub no-summary
 network 172.16.2.4 0.0.0.3 area 100
 network 172.16.3.0 0.0.0.255 area 100
!
luke#
luke#show ip route
Codes: C - connected, S - static, I - IGRP, R - RIP, M - mobile, B - BGP
       D - EIGRP, EX - EIGRP external, O - OSPF, IA - OSPF inter area
       N1 - OSPF NSSA external type 1, N2 - OSPF NSSA external type 2
       E1 - OSPF external type 1, E2 - OSPF external type 2, E - EGP
       i - IS-IS, L1 - IS-IS level-1, L2 - IS-IS level-2, ia - IS-IS inter area
       * - candidate default, U - per-user static route, o - ODR
       P - periodic downloaded static route

Gateway of last resort is 172.16.2.5 to network 0.0.0.0

     172.16.0.0/16 is variably subnetted, 2 subnets, 2 masks
C       172.16.2.4/30 is directly connected, Serial0.1
C       172.16.3.0/24 is directly connected, TokenRing0
O*IA 0.0.0.0/0 [110/65] via 172.16.2.5, 00:14:56, Serial0.1
luke#
luke#
```

```
!
hostname paul
!
interface Ethernet0/0
 ip address 172.16.9.9 255.255.255.0
 no ip directed-broadcast
!
router ospf 7
 router-id 192.168.250.9
 network 172.16.9.0 0.0.0.255 area 0
!
paul#
```

Example 12-12 *Configurations and Route Table of john, mark, mathew, luke, and paul (Continued)*

```
paul#
paul#show ip route
Codes: C - connected, S - static, I - IGRP, R - RIP, M - mobile, B - BGP
       D - EIGRP, EX - EIGRP external, O - OSPF, IA - OSPF inter area
       N1 - OSPF NSSA external type 1, N2 - OSPF NSSA external type 2
       E1 - OSPF external type 1, E2 - OSPF external type 2, E - EGP
       i - IS-IS, L1 - IS-IS level-1, L2 - IS-IS level-2, * - candidate default
       U - per-user static route, o - ODR

Gateway of last resort is not set

     172.16.0.0/16 is variably subnetted, 8 subnets, 4 masks
C       172.16.9.0/24 is directly connected, Ethernet0/0
O IA    172.16.10.0/29 [110/84] via 172.16.9.5, 00:30:32, Ethernet0/0
O IA    172.16.1.5/32 [110/10] via 172.16.9.5, 00:31:27, Ethernet0/0
O IA    172.16.5.0/24 [110/84] via 172.16.9.5, 00:30:42, Ethernet0/0
O IA    172.16.2.4/30 [110/74] via 172.16.9.5, 00:31:27, Ethernet0/0
O IA    172.16.1.6/32 [110/74] via 172.16.9.5, 00:30:42, Ethernet0/0
O IA    172.16.1.1/32 [110/74] via 172.16.9.5, 00:30:32, Ethernet0/0
O IA    172.16.3.0/24 [110/80] via 172.16.9.5, 00:16:41, Ethernet0/0
paul#
```

Before further discussing these and other OSPF configuration options, let's take a closer look at the "Big **show**" and "Big D" commands for OSPF.

The "Big show" and "Big D" for OSPF

Like most routing protocols, Cisco provides a vast array of **show** and **debug** commands to aid in the verification of OSPF. In practical application, a majority of OSPF problems and information can be gained from three primary commands:

```
show ip ospf database
show ip ospf neighbors
debug ip ospf adj
```

Like EIGRP, one of the best and most overlooked commands is **show ip ospf neighbors**. Cisco also offers a way to examine the OSPF database, as well as providing detailed OSPF adjacency information.

The following list shows the complete syntax for what we find to the most useful **show**, **debug**, and logging commands for OSPF as detailed in upcoming sections:

```
show ip ospf neighbors [detail | interface_name]
show ip ospf [process-id area-id] database
show ip ospf interface [interface_type ]
show ip route
show ip ospf [process_id]
debug ip ospf adj
debug ip ospf events
Router(config-router)#log-adjacency-changes
clear ip ospf process
```

show ip ospf neighbors Command

This can be one of the most useful commands when verifying the operational status of OSPF. The **show ip ospf neighbor** command shows the status of all OSPF neighbors. The command also shows whether the neighboring router is a DR, a BDR, or a DROTHER. For a neighbor to form, the HelloInterval, RouterDeadInterval, area IDs, and authentication type and password must match. Neighbors should form automatically on broadcast type networks such as Ethernet, Tokin Ring, and FDDI. Additional configuration is required for OSPF NMBA networks to help neighbors form.

The **detail** argument might be appended to the **show ip ospf neighbor** statement to provide extended information on each neighbor. The detailed information includes OSPF timer and option information, state-change counters, and specific information on what routers are DR and BDR for the link. If no information is listed, when the command is performed, it means that no hellos have been received and accepted. If neighbors are not forming, the command **debug ip ospf adj** more than likely lists the reason why. Example 12-13 demonstrates the command on the router john.

Example 12-13 **show ip ospf neighbor** *Command Output for Router john*

```
john#show ip ospf neighbors

Neighbor ID     Pri   State        Dead Time   Address      Interface
192.168.250.9    1    FULL/BDR     00:00:37    172.16.9.9   Ethernet0
172.16.250.1     1    FULL/  -     00:01:57    172.16.1.1   Serial0.1
192.168.250.6    1    FULL/  -     00:01:52    172.16.1.6   Serial0.1
192.168.250.3    1    FULL/  -     00:00:35    172.16.2.6   Serial0.2
john#
```

The fields to notice in this output are as follows:

- **Neighbor ID**—The neighbor ID is the router ID of the neighbor.

- **Pri**—This is the priority of the neighbor from this router's prospective.

- **State**—This field describes the neighbor state and lists whether the neighbor is a DR or BDR, or DROTHER. The only two normal states are 2-way and FULL. A router stuck in any other state indicates a problem. The state fields are defined as follows:

  — **Down**—This is the first OSPF neighbor state. It means that no information has been received from this neighbor, but hello packets still can be sent to the neighbor in this state. If a router doesn't receive a hello packet from a neighbor within the RouterDeadInterval time (RouterDeadInterval = 4*HelloInterval by default), the neighbor state changes from full to down.

— **Attempt**—This state is valid only for neighbors in an NBMA environment that are defined by the neighbor statements. *Attempt* means that the router is sending hello packets to the neighbor but has not yet received any information.

— **Init**—This state specifies that the router has received a hello packet from its neighbor, but the receiving router's ID wasn't included in the hello packet.

— **2-Way**—This state designates that bidirectional communication has been established between two routers. *Bidirectional* means that each router has seen the other's hello packet. At this state, a router decides whether to become adjacent with this neighbor. On broadcast media, a router becomes FULL only with the DR and the BDR; it stays in the 2-way state with all other neighbors.

— **Exstart**—This is the first state in forming an adjacency. It is used to elect the master and slave routers on the link.

— **Exchange and loading**—In these states, OSPF sends link-state request packets and link-state update packets.

— **Full**—Routers are fully adjacent with each other. All the router and network LSAs are exchanged, and the routers' databases are fully synchronized.

- **Dead time**—The expected time before a router receives a hello before being declared dead.

- **[IP] address and interface**—The address is the IP address of the physical interface of the neighbor. The interface column states the interface in which the neighbor's hello was received.

show ip ospf database Command

The **show ip ospf database** command is used to show the entire OSPF database, each link state in the database, and the areas they are in. Instead of referring to the link state by type, as in Type 1, Type 2, and so on, the database uses the alphabetic character name of the link state. If OSPF is aware of a network, it is in the database. The database uses router IDs to identify the routers advertising the link state. Example 12-14 demonstrates the command on the router john.

Example 12-14 show ip ospf database *Command Output on Router john*

```
john#show ip ospf database

        OSPF Router with ID (192.168.250.250) (Process ID 7)


                Router Link States (Area 0)
```

continues

Example 12-14 show ip ospf database *Command Output on Router john (Continued)*

```
Link ID         ADV Router       Age    Seq#         Checksum Link count
192.168.250.9   192.168.250.9    450    0x80000033   0x1370   1
192.168.250.250 192.168.250.250  334    0x8000002A   0xD0DA   1

                Net Link States (Area 0)

Link ID         ADV Router       Age    Seq#         Checksum
172.16.9.5      192.168.250.250  334    0x80000024   0xC14

                Summary Net Link States (Area 0)

Link ID         ADV Router       Age    Seq#         Checksum
172.16.1.1      192.168.250.250  1592   0x8000000B   0x9242
172.16.1.5      192.168.250.250  1850   0x8000000B   0xE729
172.16.1.6      192.168.250.250  1592   0x8000000B   0x606F
172.16.2.4      192.168.250.250  1850   0x8000000B   0x577C
172.16.3.0      192.168.250.250  845    0x8000000B   0xC20B
172.16.5.0      192.168.250.250  1592   0x8000000B   0xD4F2
172.16.10.0     192.168.250.250  1594   0x8000000B   0x7356

                Router Link States (Area 10)

Link ID         ADV Router       Age    Seq#         Checksum Link count
172.16.250.1    172.16.250.1     1740   0x80000052   0x6209   3
192.168.250.6   192.168.250.6    1812   0x80000025   0xE048   3
192.168.250.250 192.168.250.250  1594   0x80000053   0x72A6   3

                Summary Net Link States (Area 10)

Link ID         ADV Router       Age    Seq#         Checksum
172.16.2.4      192.168.250.250  1595   0x80000030   0xDA1
172.16.3.0      192.168.250.250  848    0x8000000B   0xC20B
172.16.9.0      192.168.250.250  92     0x8000002F   0xDD02

                Router Link States (Area 100)

Link ID         ADV Router       Age    Seq#         Checksum Link count
192.168.250.3   192.168.250.3    694    0x80000051   0x2DA0   3
192.168.250.250 192.168.250.250  848    0x80000039   0x3291   2

                Summary Net Link States (Area 100)

Link ID         ADV Router       Age    Seq#         Checksum
0.0.0.0         192.168.250.250  848    0x8000000B   0xD202
john#
```

The fields to notice in this output are as follows:

- **ADV Router**—This is the advertising router ID.

- **Age**—This is the max age of the link state.

- **Seq# and Checksum**—These fields are used to verify link-state integrity.
- **Tag**—If an OSPF tag is added during redistribution, that will appear on a column on the right.

show ip ospf interface Command

A common problem with OSPF is incorrect network statements and wildcard masks. The best way to verify what the precise OSPF parameters are for an interface is to use the **show ip opsf interface** command. The important fields are the network type, the area, the process ID, the timers, the neighbor and the adjacency count. The DR/BDR routers and priorities also are listed. Example 12-15 demonstrates the command on the router mark.

Example 12-15 show ip ospf interface *Command Output for Router mark*

```
mark#show ip ospf interface
Ethernet0 is up, line protocol is up
  Internet Address 172.16.5.5/24, Area 10
  Process ID 7, Router ID 192.168.250.6, Network Type BROADCAST, Cost: 10
  Transmit Delay is 1 sec, State DR, Priority 1
  Designated Router (ID) 172.16.5.5, Interface address 172.16.5.5
  No backup designated router on this network
  Timer intervals configured, Hello 10, Dead 40, Wait 40, Retransmit 5
    Hello due in 00:00:06
  Index 2/2, flood queue length 0
  Next 0x0(0)/0x0(0)
  Last flood scan length is 0, maximum is 0
  Last flood scan time is 0 msec, maximum is 0 msec
  Neighbor Count is 0, Adjacent neighbor count is 0
  Suppress hello for 0 neighbor(s)
Serial0 is up, line protocol is up
  Internet Address 172.16.1.6/24, Area 10
  Process ID 7, Router ID 192.168.250.6, Network Type POINT_TO_MULTIPOINT, Cost:
64
  Transmit Delay is 1 sec, State POINT_TO_MULTIPOINT,
  Timer intervals configured, Hello 30, Dead 120, Wait 120, Retransmit 5
    Hello due in 00:00:05
  Index 1/1, flood queue length 0
  Next 0x0(0)/0x0(0)
  Last flood scan length is 1, maximum is 1
  Last flood scan time is 0 msec, maximum is 0 msec
  Neighbor Count is 1, Adjacent neighbor count is 1
    Adjacent with neighbor 192.168.250.250
  Suppress hello for 0 neighbor(s)
mark#
```

show ip route Command

This command shows the IP forwarding table or route table. Six types of OSPF routes can be listed:

- **(O)**—OSPF intra-area route, or routes from the same area
- **(O IA)**—OSPF inter-area route, or routes from another area
- **(O N1)**—OSPF NSSA Type 1
- **(O N2)**—OSPF NSSA Type 2
- **(O E1)**—OSPF external Type 1
- **(O E2)**—OSPF external Type 2

For a detailed explanation of the route types, see the previous section, "OSPF Path Types." The route in the forwarding table is followed by the administrative distance and the cost of the route. The forwarding table also lists the router reporting the network, when it was reported, and the interface that reported it.

show ip ospf Command

This command provides a comprehensive view of the OSPF areas, listing the area type, authentication, SPF counters, redistribution, as well as detailed LSA timer information. Example 12-16 demonstrates this command.

Example 12-16 show ip ospf *Command Output on Router john*

```
john#show ip ospf
 Routing Process "ospf 7" with ID 192.168.250.250
 Supports only single TOS(TOS0) routes
 Supports opaque LSA
 It is an area border router
 SPF schedule delay 5 secs, Hold time between two SPFs 10 secs
 Minimum LSA interval 5 secs. Minimum LSA arrival 1 secs
 Number of external LSA 0. Checksum Sum 0x0
 Number of opaque AS LSA 0. Checksum Sum 0x0
 Number of DCbitless external and opaque AS LSA 0
 Number of DoNotAge external and opaque AS LSA 0
 Number of areas in this router is 3. 2 normal 1 stub 0 nssa
 External flood list length 0
    Area BACKBONE(0)
        Number of interfaces in this area is 1
        Area has no authentication
        SPF algorithm executed 11 times
        Area ranges are
        Number of LSA 10. Checksum Sum 0x5A54A
        Number of opaque link LSA 0. Checksum Sum 0x0
        Number of DCbitless LSA 0
        Number of indication LSA 0
```

Example 12-16 show ip ospf *Command Output on Router john (Continued)*

```
              Number of DoNotAge LSA 0
              Flood list length 0
          Area 10
              Number of interfaces in this area is 1
              Area has no authentication
              SPF algorithm executed 35 times
              Area ranges are
              Number of LSA 6. Checksum Sum 0x40CCF
              Number of opaque link LSA 0. Checksum Sum 0x0
              Number of DCbitless LSA 0
              Number of indication LSA 0
              Number of DoNotAge LSA 0
              Flood list length 0
          Area 100
              Number of interfaces in this area is 1
              It is a stub area, no summary LSA in this area
                generates stub default route with cost 1
              Area has no authentication
              SPF algorithm executed 32 times
              Area ranges are
              Number of LSA 3. Checksum Sum 0x10A47
              Number of opaque link LSA 0. Checksum Sum 0x0
              Number of DCbitless LSA 0
              Number of indication LSA 0
              Number of DoNotAge LSA 0
              Flood list length 0

john#

Gateway of last resort is not set

     172.16.0.0/16 is variably subnetted, 8 subnets, 4 masks
O IA    172.16.9.0/24 [110/74] via 172.16.1.5, 09:11:03, Serial0
O       172.16.10.0/29 [110/138] via 172.16.1.5, 09:11:03, Serial0
O       172.16.1.5/32 [110/64] via 172.16.1.5, 09:11:03, Serial0
C       172.16.5.0/24 is directly connected, Ethernet0
O IA    172.16.2.4/30 [110/128] via 172.16.1.5, 09:11:03, Serial0
O       172.16.1.1/32 [110/128] via 172.16.1.5, 09:11:03, Serial0
C       172.16.1.0/24 is directly connected, Serial0
O IA    172.16.3.0/24 [110/134] via 172.16.1.5, 08:57:09, Serial0
mark#
```

debug ip ospf adj and debug ip ospf events Commands

Two **debug** commands provide the "Big D" for OSPF—**debug ip ospf adj** and **debug ip ospf events**. For the most part, the commands are identical. The output can be fairly heavy, so turn on logging if using this command in a production environment. This **debug** command is so comprehensive that it will alert you to a majority of common OSPF issues, such as the following:

- Mismatched subnet mask
- Mismatched hello/dead interval
- Mismatched authentication key
- Mismatched area IDs and area types

log-adjacency-changes/show log Commands

Like EIGRP, OSPF offers a special command to log adjacency changes. This command can help alert you to adjacency problems without having to wade through heavy debugs. The syntax to log adjacency changes is as follows:

```
john(config)#router ospf 7
john(config-router)#log-adjacency-changes
```

Example 12-17 lists the log after an adjacency has been dropped.

Example 12-17 **show log** *Command Output Documents a Down Neighbor*

```
john#show log
Syslog logging: enabled (0 messages dropped, 0 flushes, 0 overruns)
    Console logging: level debugging, 1228 messages logged
    Monitor logging: level debugging, 0 messages logged
    Buffer logging: level debugging, 2 messages logged
    Trap logging: level informational, 68 message lines logged

Log Buffer (10000 bytes):

1d00h: %SYS-5-CONFIG_I: Configured from console by console
1d00h: %OSPF-5-ADJCHG: Process 7, Nbr 172.16.250.1 on Serial0.1 from FULL to DOW
N, Neighbor Down
john#
```

clear ip ospf process

Available as of Cisco IOS Software Release 12.0, this command clears all OSPF neighbors, the RID, and the SPF database. This command initializes the entire OSPF process as if the router were reloaded.

Configuring OSPF Stub Areas

Three types of OSPF stub areas must be configured:

- Stub
- NSSA
- Totally stubby

To configure stub areas, use the **area** command followed by what type of stub area you want to configure. All routers on the same IP network must be in the same area, and area parameters also must match for neighbors and adjacencies to form.

To configure Area X as a stub area, enter the following:

```
Router(config-route)rea X stub
```

To configure Area X as a not-so-stubby area, enter the following:

```
Router(config-route)area X nssa {default-information originate}.
```

Use the keyword **default-information originate** on the **area** statement in the preceding example to propagate a default route to an NSSA area.

To configure Area X as a totally stubby area, enter the following:

```
Router(config-route)area X stub no-summary
```

Tuning OSPF

OSPF has several parameters for tuning timers, controlling broadcasts, and controlling routes and link-state propagation. The following list shows the syntax of the more common parameters adjustable for OSPF, explained in the text that follows.

```
Router(config-if)ip ospf hello-interval interval_in_seconds
Router(config-if)ip ospf dead-interval dead_interval_in_seconds
Router(config-if)ip ospf retransmit-interval
```

Use the **ip ospf hello-interval** interface command to change the hello timer for OSPF. The default value of this command is interface-dependent. By default, hello packets are sent every 10 seconds on broadcast and point-to-point networks, and 30 seconds on NBMA networks. All neighbors residing on a network and area should have equal hello timers. The dead-interval and wait timer automatically are changed when the hello interval is changed.

Use the **ip ospf dead-interval** command to change the dead interval received by this interface. The timer has a default vault of four times that of the hello timer, 40 seconds for broadcast and point-to-point networks, and 120 seconds for NBMA networks. Recall that the dead interval is the time that has to pass before a neighbor receives a hello before declaring it "dead."

Use the **ip ospf retransmit-interval** command to change OSPF retransmission interval. All routers in the area should have the time set to the same value.

OSPF Flooding Reduction

OSPF flooding reduction was introduced in Cisco IOS Software Release 12.1(2)T. Inherently, OSPF LSAs are refreshed every 3600 seconds. In large, fairly stable OSPF networks, this can lead to large amounts of unnecessary LSA flooding from area to area. Technically, if an LSA has not changed, why reflood it every 3600 seconds? OSPF flooding control is a new technique that changes normal LSAs into DoNotAge LSAs. Therefore, they will not get flooded every 3600 seconds across areas. For this feature to work, all routers in the area that are connected to the router performing flooding control must be running Cisco IOS Software Release 12.1(2)T or later. To enable flooding control on the interface, use the following interface command:

```
Router(config-if)#ip ospf flood-reduction
```

Additionally, you can choose to block all LSA flooding out an interface. To block OSPF flooding of LSAs on broadcast, nonbroadcast, and point-to-point interfaces, use this following interface command:

```
Router(config-if)#ospf database-filter all out
```

To block LSAs flooding to a specific neighbor, use the following router command on the **neighbor** statement:

```
Router(config-router)#neighbor ip_address database-filter all out
```

OSPF Redistribution and Route Control

To filter specific routing updates in OSPF, you must use an inbound distribution list. An OSPF router does not send routing updates in the traditional manner; therefore, only an inbound distribution list on the router receiving the update works for route control. When redistributing one protocol into another, use the **redistribute** command along with the default metric. A route map should be used in place of a distribute list when controlling specific routes during the redistribution process. A route map provides for many more options during redistribution and is a powerful routing tool.

Commands to Control Route Filtering/Redistribution

To call a standard access list to filter inbound routing updates, use the following command:

```
Router(config-router)distribute-list [1-99] [in] [interface_name]
```

The **in** option is applied from the view of the interface. In other words, to prevent a routing update from entering an interface, use the **in** option. This command filters only the route, not the LSA.

To redistribute other routing protocols into OSPF, use the following command:

```
Router(config-router)redistribute [connected | static | bgp | rip | igrp | eigrp |
    isis] [subnets] [tag tag_number] [metric cost] [metric-type {OE1 | OE2}]
    [route-map]
```

With OSPF, the keyword **subnets** always should be used when redistributing more then one network into OSPF. When redistributing routes into OSPF, only routes that are not subnetted are redistributed if the **subnets** keyword is not specified. An optional tag can be added during redistribution. This tag appears in the OSPF database and can be used to quickly identify where route redistribution occurs in the internetwork. A route map might be added for additional route control. An optional metric/cost also can be supplied for routes originating from the routing protocol being redistributed that are different from the default metric. When OSPF redistributes routes, the default route type will be an OSPF external Type 2 route (O E2). To change this to an OSPF external Type 1 route (O E1), use the **metric-type** argument on the **redistribution** command.

To set the default cost of all routes redistributed into OSPF, use the following command:

```
Router(config-router)default-metric [cost 1-4294967295]
```

You must supply a default metric whenever redistributing. A common metric to use is **default-metric 10**. Recall from the previous chapter that more important than the actual value of the default metric is the practice of using the same metric throughout the routing domain, so all redistributed routes will have the same cost.

Commands to Influence OSPF Routing Decisions

You can control routing updates within OSPF in multiple ways. Recall that OSPF calculates a cost to a destination based on a formula involving bandwidth. To influence route decisions, you can either change the bandwidth on the interface, which in turn will affect the cost of the link, or directly change the cost of the interface.

OSPF also supports the direct changing of the administrative distance with the **distance** command, much like EIGRP. OSPF also uses the passive interface command to prevent hellos from being sent on the link.

To specify the cost of an interface in OSPF, use the following command:

```
Router(config-if)cost_[cost 1-4294967295]
```

This command is used only by OSPF and does not affect the actual traffic on the link.

To specify the bandwidth of an interface in kilobits per second, use the following command:

```
Router(config-if)bandwidth [bandwidth_kbps 1-4214748364]
```

The **bandwidth** command is used only by routing protocols to derive a cost for the interface, and it also does not affect the actual traffic on the link.

To change the administrative distance of OSPF routes, use the following command:

```
Router(config-router)distance ospf {[intra-area [1-255] [inter-area [1-255]
   [external [1-255]}
```

OSPF uses three different administrative distances: intra-area, interarea, and external. Routes within an area are intra-area; routes from another area are interarea; and routes injected by redistribution are external. The default administrative distance for each type of route is 110.

To prevent the sending of OSPF hellos on the link, use the following command:

```
Router(config-router)passive-interface interface_name
```

Because hellos are suppressed, neighbors will not be formed, so no routing updates will be sent or received.

Practical Example: Route Filtering/Redistribution

Let's apply a couple of these concepts to a practical model in route filtering and redistribution to gain a better grasp of them. Figure 12-9 modifies the internetwork from the previous model in Example 12-8. The mark router is now an ASBR between the OSPF domain and a RIP domain. You also will redistribute some loopback interfaces on the router paul. On the mathew router, you will apply an inbound distribution list to filter the external networks or the loopback networks from the router paul.

Figure 12-9 *OSPF Network for Route Filtering/Redistribution*

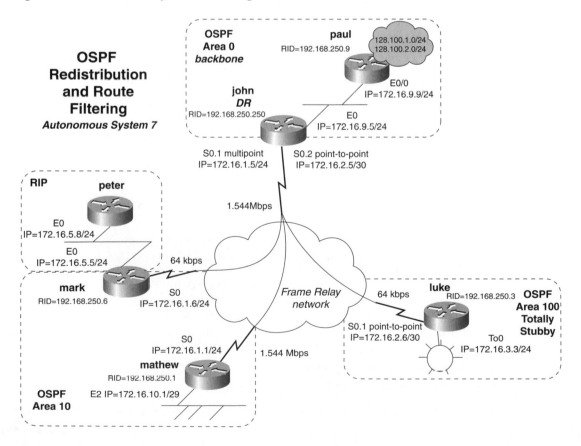

Beginning with the paul router, we have added two loopback interfaces, 128.100.1.1/24 and 128.100.2.1/24. To redistribute these networks, you will use the **redistribute connected** command with the **subnets** argument. The default metric or cost will be set to 10. In this example, a tag is set on the redistribution. Example 12-20 illustrates how the tag shows up in the OSPF database. Example 12-18 lists the relevant configuration of the router paul.

Example 12-18 *Configuration of the paul Router*

```
interface Loopback20
 ip address 128.100.1.1 255.255.255.0
 no ip directed-broadcast
!
interface Loopback21
 ip address 128.100.2.1 255.255.255.0
 no ip directed-broadcast
!
interface Ethernet0/0
 ip address 172.16.9.9 255.255.255.0
 no ip directed-broadcast
!
<<<text omitted>>>
!
router ospf 7
 router-id 192.168.250.9
 redistribute connected subnets tag 9        →redistribute the loopback interfaces
 network 172.16.9.0 0.0.0.255 area 0
 default-metric 10                           →Use a cost of 10 on redistributed networks
!
```

To verify the redistribution, perform **show ip route** on the mark router. Example 12-19 demonstrates this command.

Example 12-19 **show ip route** *on Router mark*

```
mark#show ip route
Codes: C - connected, S - static, I - IGRP, R - RIP, M - mobile, B - BGP
       D - EIGRP, EX - EIGRP external, O - OSPF, IA - OSPF inter area
       N1 - OSPF NSSA external type 1, N2 - OSPF NSSA external type 2
       E1 - OSPF external type 1, E2 - OSPF external type 2, E - EGP
       i - IS-IS, L1 - IS-IS level-1, L2 - IS-IS level-2, ia - IS-IS inter area
       * - candidate default, U - per-user static route, o - ODR
       P - periodic downloaded static route

Gateway of last resort is not set

     172.16.0.0/16 is variably subnetted, 8 subnets, 4 masks
O IA    172.16.9.0/24 [110/74] via 172.16.1.5, 08:58:07, Serial0
O       172.16.10.0/24 [110/138] via 172.16.1.5, 18:33:11, Serial0
O       172.16.1.5/32 [110/64] via 172.16.1.5, 18:33:11, Serial0
```

continues

Example 12-19 **show ip route** *on Router mark*

```
C       172.16.5.0/24 is directly connected, Ethernet0
O IA    172.16.2.4/30 [110/128] via 172.16.1.5, 08:58:08, Serial0
O       172.16.1.1/32 [110/128] via 172.16.1.5, 18:33:11, Serial0
C       172.16.1.0/24 is directly connected, Serial0
O IA    172.16.3.0/24 [110/134] via 172.16.1.5, 08:58:09, Serial0
        128.100.0.0/24 is subnetted, 2 subnets
O E2    128.100.1.0 [110/20] via 172.16.1.5, 08:58:09, Serial0    →redistributed routes
O E2    128.100.2.0 [110/20] via 172.16.1.5, 08:58:09, Serial0
```

During redistribution, we also put a tag of 9 on the routes. Example 12-20 lists the OSPF database of mark showing how the tag is propagated throughout OSPF.

Example 12-20 *OSPF Database on the Router mark*

```
mark#show ip ospf database

        OSPF Router with ID (192.168.250.6) (Process ID 7)

<<text omitted>>>

              Type-5 AS External Link States

Link ID         ADV Router      Age      Seq#        Checksum Tag
128.100.1.0     192.168.250.9   1094     0x80000024 0xDE42   9   →Tag added during
128.100.2.0     192.168.250.9   1095     0x80000024 0xD34C   9   →redistribution
172.16.9.0      192.168.250.9   844      0x80000026 0x3807   9
mark#
```

Notice that during redistribution, the 172.16.9.0 route also is redistributed. This is because the Ethernet network also is considered a local network. To prevent this from happening, add a route map to the **redistribution** command to filter any unwanted networks.

Next, you will integrate the RIP domain into OSPF on the router mark. To accomplish this, enable RIP on the mark router. When doing this, you will put the E0 interface into a passive state for OSPF and the S0 interface into a passive state for RIP. A more specific **network** command also will accomplish this, which is another good reason to limit the wildcard mask on the **network** command to a single network or interface. To enable redistribution, use the **redistribute rip subnets** command on the mark router. Likewise, you will have to redistribute OSPF into RIP. The default metric that you will use for OSPF is 10. Example 12-21 shows the OSPF portion of router mark.

Example 12-21 *Routing Protocol Configuration of mark*

```
router ospf 7
 router-id 192.168.250.6
 redistribute rip subnets      →redistribute RIP into OSPF
```

Example 12-21 *Routing Protocol Configuration of mark (Continued)*

```
 passive-interface Ethernet0    ➙No OSPF hellos are to enter E0 (optional)
 network 172.16.1.0 0.0.0.255 area 10
 default-metric 10              ➙Use 10 as the cost to the RIP domain
!
router rip
 redistribute ospf 7            ➙redistribute OSPF into RIP
 passive-interface Serial0      ➙No RIP broadcasts out S0
 network 172.16.0.0
 default-metric 3               ➙Use a hop count of 3 for OSPF routes
```

Because one redistribution point exists in the network, you do not have to worry about redistribution loops or "route feedback." Before redistribution will be complete, you have to summarize the 172.16.2.4/30 network. This is because RIP receives routes through an interface on a 24-bit boundary. In this model, you accomplished this with the **area range** command. We will discuss more about this in the next session. The best way to verify redistribution in this model is to view the route table of the router peter and verify that all the OSPF routes are reachable by **ping** tests. Example 12-22 lists the route table of peter.

Example 12-22 *Route Table of peter After Redistribution*

```
peter#show ip route
<<<text omitted>>>

Gateway of last resort is not set

     172.16.0.0/16 is variably subnetted, 8 subnets, 2 masks
R       172.16.9.0/24 [120/3] via 172.16.5.5, 00:00:01, Ethernet0
R       172.16.10.0/24 [120/3] via 172.16.5.5, 00:00:01, Ethernet0
R       172.16.1.5/32 [120/3] via 172.16.5.5, 00:00:01, Ethernet0
C       172.16.5.0/24 is directly connected, Ethernet0
R       172.16.1.1/32 [120/3] via 172.16.5.5, 00:00:02, Ethernet0
R       172.16.1.0/24 [120/1] via 172.16.5.5, 00:00:02, Ethernet0
R       172.16.2.0/24 [120/3] via 172.16.5.5, 00:00:02, Ethernet0
R       172.16.3.0/24 [120/3] via 172.16.5.5, 00:00:02, Ethernet0
R    128.100.0.0/16 [120/3] via 172.16.5.5, 00:00:02, Ethernet0
peter#
```

To demonstrate route filtering in OSPF, you will apply an inbound distribute list to the router mathew. The configuration of the mathew router resembles the following example. At the end of Example 12-23 is the new route table for mathew, without the 128.100.1.0/24 and 128.100.2.0/24 routes.

Example 12-23 *Distribute List on the mathew Router*

```
router ospf 7
 network 172.16.1.0 0.0.0.255 area 10
 network 172.16.10.0 0.0.0.255 area 10
 distribute-list 10 in Serial0          ←distribute list applied to s0
!
ip classless
!
access-list 10 deny    128.100.0.0 0.0.255.255    ←access list deny all 128.100.x.x
                                                     networks
access-list 10 permit any
!

mathew#show ip route
Codes: C - connected, S - static, I - IGRP, R - RIP, M - mobile, B - BGP
       D - EIGRP, EX - EIGRP external, O - OSPF, IA - OSPF inter area
       N1 - OSPF NSSA external type 1, N2 - OSPF NSSA external type 2
       E1 - OSPF external type 1, E2 - OSPF external type 2, E - EGP
       i - IS-IS, L1 - IS-IS level-1, L2 - IS-IS level-2, * - candidate default
       U - per-user static route, o - ODR

Gateway of last resort is not set

     172.16.0.0/16 is variably subnetted, 9 subnets, 2 masks
C        172.16.250.0/24 is directly connected, Loopback0
O IA     172.16.9.0/24 [110/74] via 172.16.1.5, 01:01:06, Serial0
C        172.16.10.0/24 is directly connected, Ethernet2
O        172.16.1.5/32 [110/64] via 172.16.1.5, 01:01:06, Serial0
O        172.16.5.0/24 [110/129] via 172.16.1.5, 01:01:06, Serial0
O        172.16.1.6/32 [110/128] via 172.16.1.5, 01:01:06, Serial0
C        172.16.1.0/24 is directly connected, Serial0
O IA     172.16.2.0/24 [110/128] via 172.16.1.5, 01:01:06, Serial0
O IA     172.16.3.0/24 [110/134] via 172.16.1.5, 01:01:06, Serial0
mathew#
```

OSPF Summarization

OSPF allows for two forms of summarization. One form of summarization is used when summarizing routes redistributed into OSPF from another routing protocol. The other form of summarization is used when summarizing an area. With both forms of summarization, summary LSAs are created and flooded toward Area 0, or the backbone area. The backbone area, in turn, floods the link states to the other areas. Use these guidelines when configuring summarization in OSPF:

- Use continuous address space in each OSPF area. This allows for easy summarization on the ABRs. Summarizing many networks into a single advertisement decreases the route table and improves the overall performance and scalability of OSPF.

- Summarize on major bit boundaries or simple octet boundaries whenever possible. If you have a classful routing protocol in your network, such as RIP or IGRP, you must summarize on bit boundaries that the classful routing protocol can receive.

- You cannot summarize Area 0 or the backbone area. All summaries are flooded into Area 0 and then are flooded out from that point. Therefore, Area 0 routes cannot be summarized.

To summarize external routes, or routes redistributed into OSPF, use the following router command on the ASBR:

```
Router(config-router)summary-address network_address network_mask [tag tag_number]
```

The **tag** parameter can be used in the same manner as it is during redistribution, to mark routes with a numeric number.

To summarize routes from one OSPF area into Area 0, use the following router command:

```
Router(config-router)area area_id range network_address network_mask
```

In Figure 12-10, we have modified the network once again. We have changed some interfaces and increased the networks in the RIP domain. OSPF Area 20 now contains the subnets 100.10.1.0/24 to 100.10.3.0/24. First, you will want to summarize these networks into a single route, 100.10.0.0/16. To accomplish this, you will use the router command **area 20 range 100.10.0.0 255.255.0.0** on the ABR, or the router john. The router john will advertise the summary route 100.10.0.0/16 to mark. This is referred to as *interarea summarization*.

This network must use another form of interarea summarization for full IP connectivity to the RIP domain. The RIP Ethernet interface has an IP address on a 24-bit boundary. Recall from Chapter 9, "Distance Vector Protocols: Routing Information Protocol Versions 1 and 2 (RIP-1 and RIP-2)," that for RIP to receive a route, it must be on a natural bit boundary 8, 16, or 24, or on the same bit boundary that the interface receiving the route is on—in this case, a 24-bit boundary. This is true for IGRP as well. All of the networks in the OSPF domain reside on a 24-bit boundary except for the Frame Relay point-to-point network between the routers john and luke. To accommodate RIP, you must summarize the Frame Relay point-to-point network at a 24-bit boundary. To summarize the 172.16.2.4/30 network into 172.16.2.0/24, use the **area 100 range 172.16.2.0 255.255.255.0** command on the router john. The router john will now advertise the summary route 172.16.2.0/24 to mark and finally to peter. Example 12-24 lists the route table on the mark router.

Figure 12-10 *Summarizing OSPF*

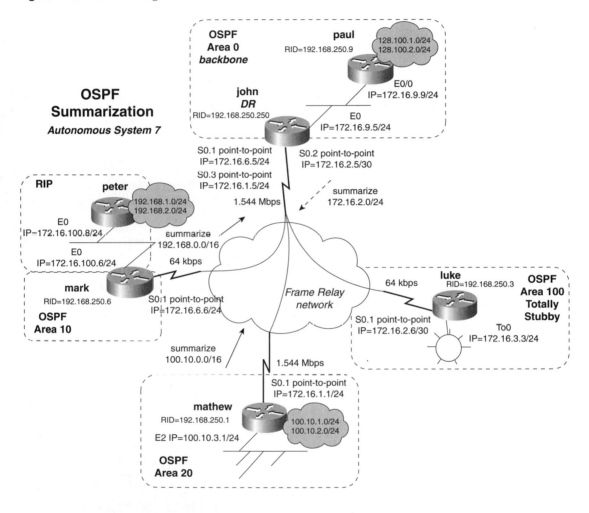

Example 12-24 *Route Table of the mark Router*

```
mark#show ip route
Codes: C - connected, S - static, I - IGRP, R - RIP, M - mobile, B - BGP
       D - EIGRP, EX - EIGRP external, O - OSPF, IA - OSPF inter area
       N1 - OSPF NSSA external type 1, N2 - OSPF NSSA external type 2
       E1 - OSPF external type 1, E2 - OSPF external type 2, E - EGP
       i - IS-IS, L1 - IS-IS level-1, L2 - IS-IS level-2, ia - IS-IS inter area
       * - candidate default, U - per-user static route, o - ODR
       P - periodic downloaded static route
```

Example 12-24 *Route Table of the mark Router (Continued)*

```
Gateway of last resort is not set

     100.0.0.0/16 is subnetted, 1 subnets
O IA    100.10.0.0 [110/129] via 172.16.6.5, 00:26:45, Serial0.1
     172.16.0.0/24 is subnetted, 6 subnets
O IA    172.16.9.0 [110/74] via 172.16.6.5, 00:26:45, Serial0.1
C       172.16.6.0 is directly connected, Serial0.1
O IA    172.16.1.0 [110/128] via 172.16.6.5, 00:26:45, Serial0.1
O IA    172.16.2.0 [110/128] via 172.16.6.5, 00:26:45, Serial0.1
O IA    172.16.3.0 [110/134] via 172.16.6.5, 00:26:45, Serial0.1
C       172.16.100.0 is directly connected, Ethernet0
     128.100.0.0/24 is subnetted, 2 subnets
O E2    128.100.1.0 [110/20] via 172.16.6.5, 00:26:45, Serial0.1
O E2    128.100.2.0 [110/20] via 172.16.6.5, 00:26:45, Serial0.1
R    192.168.1.0/24 [120/1] via 172.16.100.8, 00:00:06, Ethernet0
R    192.168.2.0/24 [120/1] via 172.16.100.8, 00:00:07, Ethernet0
mark#
```

The final summary that you want to perform is external summarization. On the mark router, you want to summarize the two RIP routes 192.168.1.0/24 and 192.168.2.0/24 into a single OSPF route 192.168.0.0/16. To perform this task, use the OSPF router command **summary-address 192.168.0.0 255.255.0.0.** Example 12-25 lists the routing protocol configurations of the john and mark routers, respectively.

Example 12-25 *john and mark Configurations*

```
hostname mark
!
router ospf 7
 router-id 192.168.250.6
 summary-address 192.168.0.0 255.255.255.0
 redistribute rip subnets
 passive-interface Ethernet0
 network 172.16.6.0 0.0.0.255 area 10
 default-metric 10
!
router rip
 redistribute ospf 7
 passive-interface Serial0
 network 172.16.0.0
 default-metric 3
!

hostname john
!
router ospf 7
 router-id 192.168.250.250
 area 7 stub
```

continues

Example 12-25 *john and mark Configurations (Continued)*

```
    area 20 range 100.10.0.0 255.255.0.0
    area 100 stub no-summary
    area 100 range 172.16.2.0 255.255.255.0
    network 172.16.1.0 0.0.0.255 area 20
    network 172.16.2.4 0.0.0.3 area 100
    network 172.16.6.0 0.0.0.255 area 10
    network 172.16.9.0 0.0.0.255 area 0
    !
```

Example 12-26 lists the route table of paul, listing all the summary routes.

Example 12-26 *Route Table of paul*

```
paul#show ip route
<<<text omitted>>>

Gateway of last resort is not set

     100.0.0.0/16 is subnetted, 1 subnets
O IA    100.10.0.0 [110/75] via 172.16.9.5, 1d22h, Ethernet0/0
     172.16.0.0/24 is subnetted, 6 subnets
C       172.16.9.0 is directly connected, Ethernet0/0
O IA    172.16.6.0 [110/74] via 172.16.9.5, 1d22h, Ethernet0/0
O IA    172.16.1.0 [110/74] via 172.16.9.5, 1d22h, Ethernet0/0
O IA    172.16.2.0 [110/74] via 172.16.9.5, 1d22h, Ethernet0/0
O IA    172.16.3.0 [110/80] via 172.16.9.5, 1d22h, Ethernet0/0
O E2    172.16.100.0 [110/10] via 172.16.9.5, 01:19:17, Ethernet0/0
     128.100.0.0/24 is subnetted, 2 subnets
C       128.100.1.0 is directly connected, Loopback20
C       128.100.2.0 is directly connected, Loopback21
O E2 192.168.0.0/16 [110/10] via 172.16.9.5, 00:01:17, Ethernet0/0
paul#
```

OSPF Default Routing

Today, most, and potentially all, networks connect to the Internet. Some routers have registered address space, while others have Internet routers, or firewalls. Being able to generate and propagate a default route is important. Recall from earlier chapters that default routing is a three-step task:

Step 1　Mark or "flag" a network as a default. A route must be "flagged" a default route before OSPF will treat it as a default route. This can be done in one of two ways with the following global commands:

`Router(config)ip default-network` *network_address*

`Router(config)ip route 0.0.0.0 0.0.0.0` *ip_address*

This particular static route does not need to be redistributed into OSPF to be propagated. OSPF will recognize the 0.0.0.0 0.0.0.0 route as a default and treat it accordingly. If you use the **default-network** statement, you need to use the keyword **always** in Step 2.

Step 2 Propagate the default network. Use the following OSPF router command:

```
default-information originate [always] [metric cost] [metric-type OE1 |
OE2] [route-map map-name]
```

Step 3 Enable IP classless. Recall from previous chapters, that for any routing protocol to forward packets to a destination that does not appear in the route table, the router needs **ip classless** enabled. By default, **ip classless** in enabled in Cisco IOS Software Release 12.0 and later.

Figure 12-11 adds another connection, 206.191.200.1, to the network that is the gateway to the Internet. To flag the network 206.191.200.0 as a default network, either of the two global configuration commands will work:

```
ip default-network 206.191.200.0
```

Or point it directly at an address:

```
ip route 0.0.0.0 0.0.0.0 206.191.200.1
```

To propagate the default network, use the **default-information originate always** command. The **always** keyword always propagates a default route if the router flags the default network with the **default-network** command.

Example 12-27 lists the configuration of paul and shows how the default route is configured.

Example 12-27 *Default Route Configuration on paul*

```
router ospf 7
 router-id 192.168.250.9
 redistribute connected subnets tag 9
 network 172.16.9.0 0.0.0.255 area 0
 default-information originate always        ←Propagate the default route
 default-metric 10
!
ip classless                      ←IP classless is always needed
ip route 0.0.0.0 0.0.0.0 206.191.200.1    ←"Flag" the route as default
!
```

Figure 12-11   *OSPF Default Routing*

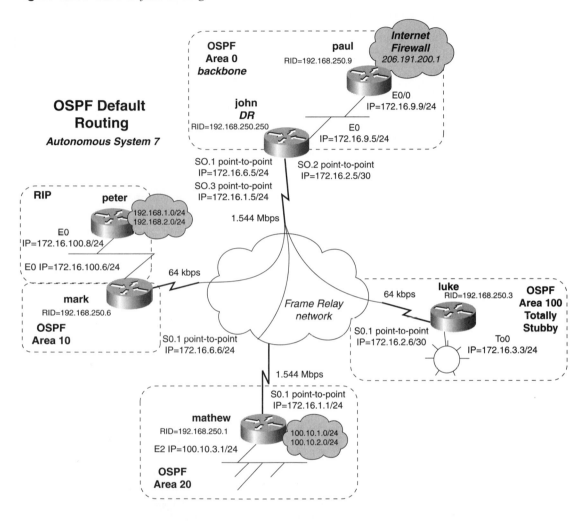

Example 12-28 lists how the route is propagated into the NSSA area on the router mathew. Notice that the gateway of last resort now is set.

Example 12-28   *Route Table of mathew*

```
mathew#show ip route
<<<text omitted>>>

Gateway of last resort is 172.16.1.5 to network 0.0.0.0

     100.0.0.0/24 is subnetted, 3 subnets
C       100.10.2.0 is directly connected, Loopback21
```

Example 12-28 *Route Table of mathew (Continued)*

```
C       100.10.3.0 is directly connected, Ethernet2
C       100.10.1.0 is directly connected, Loopback20
        172.16.0.0/24 is subnetted, 8 subnets
C       172.16.250.0 is directly connected, Loopback0
O IA    172.16.9.0 [110/74] via 172.16.1.5, 1d23h, Serial0.1
O       172.16.10.0 is a summary, 2d00h, Null0
O IA    172.16.6.0 [110/128] via 172.16.1.5, 1d23h, Serial0.1
C       172.16.1.0 is directly connected, Serial0.1
O       172.16.2.0 is a summary, 2d00h, Null0
O IA    172.16.3.0 [110/134] via 172.16.1.5, 1d23h, Serial0.1
O E2    172.16.100.0 [110/10] via 172.16.1.5, 02:54:58, Serial0.1
O E2 206.191.200.0/24 [110/20] via 172.16.1.5, 00:09:56, Serial0.1
        12.0.0.0/16 is subnetted, 1 subnets
O E2     12.16.0.0 [110/10] via 172.16.1.5, 1d23h, Serial0.1
O*E2 0.0.0.0/0 [110/1] via 172.16.1.5, 01:04:36, Serial0.1
O E2 192.168.0.0/16 [110/10] via 172.16.1.5, 01:36:57, Serial0.1
mathew#
```

OSPF Authentication

OSPF uses two forms of authentication, Type I and Type II. Both forms are fairly easy and straightforward to configure. When configuring passwords, do not enter an encryption type for the password on the interface. Instead, use the global command **service password-encryption** to enable all password protection after all the configuration is complete.

Type 1 Authentication

Type 1 authentication is clear-text authentication. If a sniffer is placed on a network, the password still can be captured, so this is less secure than Type 2. To configure Type 1 authentication, follow this two-step process:

Step 1   Enable area authentication on all routers in that area. Use this router command:

> Router(config-route)**area** *area_id* **authentication**

Step 2   Enter the clear-text password on the interface. Use this interface command:

> Router(config-if) **ip ospf authentication-key** *password.*

The passwords and authentication must match for all interfaces in that area, or adjacencies will not be formed.

Type 2 Authentication

Type 2 authentication is Message Digest 5 (MD5) cryptographic checksums. OSPF builds a hash value from the OSPF key and password. The hash is the only value sent across the link; no passwords are sent, making MD5 authentication secure. To configure Type 2 (MD5), authentication, follow this two-step process:

Step 1 Enable MD5 area authentication on all routers in that area. Use this router command:

```
Router(config-route)area area_id authentication message-digest
```

Step 2 Set a key and password on a per-interface basis. Use this interface command:

```
Router(config-if) ip ospf message-digest-key key_value md5 password
```

The *key_value* and *password* must match on all routers in that network. Different key values allow for quick changes of passwords and multiple passwords per area.

Type 1/Type 2 Authentication Example

Figure 12-12 shows a portion of a network in Area 10. Example 12-29 and Example 12-30 show Type 1 and Type 2 authentication options for OSPF in this network.

Figure 12-12 *OSPF Authentication*

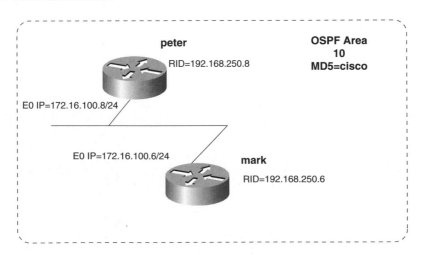

Example 12-29 *Example 12-29 OSPF Type 1 Authentication on Area 10*

```
!
hostname peter
!
interface Ethernet0
 ip address 172.16.100.8 255.255.255.0
 ip ospf authentication-key cisco    →Cisco is the password
!
router ospf 7
 network 172.16.100.8 0.0.0.0 area 10
 area 10 authentication          →Type 1 authentication enabled in area 10

hostname mark
!
interface Ethernet0
 ip address 172.16.100.6 255.255.255.0
 no ip directed-broadcast
 ip ospf authentication-key cisco
!
router ospf 7
 router-id 192.168.250.6
 area 10 authentication
 network 172.16.6.0 0.0.0.255 area 10
 network 172.16.100.6 0.0.0.0 area 10
!
```

Example 12-30 is the same configuration for Figure 12-11 using MD5 authentication.

Example 12-30 *OSPF Type 2 Authentication on Area 10*

```
!
hostname peter
!
interface Ethernet0
 ip address 172.16.100.8 255.255.255.0
 ip ospf message-digest-key 1 md5 cisco    →Cisco is the password, key=1
!
router ospf 7
 network 172.16.100.8 0.0.0.0 area 10
 area 10 authentication message-digest    →Type 2 authentication enabled in area 10

hostname mark
!
interface Ethernet0
 ip address 172.16.100.6 255.255.255.0
 no ip directed-broadcast
 ip ospf message-digest-key 1 md5 cisco
!
router ospf 7
 router-id 192.168.250.6
```

continues

Example 12-30 *OSPF Type 2 Authentication on Area 10 (Continued)*

```
area 10 authentication message-digest
network 172.16.6.0 0.0.0.255 area 10
network 172.16.100.6 0.0.0.0 area 10
!
```

OSPF Demand Circuits and Backup

Backup with OSPF can be difficult, especially with dial-on-demand backup such as ISDN. OSPF becomes difficult in the backup mode because of area connectivity. The key to how you control backup interfaces depends on what OSPF area the backup interface is in. Because of the different area properties, such as what LSA get flooded to what areas, the area selection for backup is important. Where the router is located in the network, the area type, and how it connects to Area 0 will also influence what area the backup interface goes in. Instead of going over the countless possible examples for demand circuits and OSPF backup, we instead cover configuration guidelines and issues. For specific lab examples and more information on the backup interface and OSPF demand circuits, see Chapter 5, "WAN Protocols and Technologies: Frame Relay," and Chapter 7, "WAN Protocols and Technologies: Integrated Services Digital Network (ISDN)." The sections that follow cover the configuration guidelines for OSPF demand circuits and backup.

Adhere to OSPF Design Rules

When the backup link becomes active, the network still must comply with all OSPF design guidelines. That is, Area 0 cannot be partitioned, virtual links cannot be run through stub areas, all areas must connect to Area 0, and so on. The network topology will change when in backup mode, but it still must adhere to the same OSPF guidelines.

OSPF Demand Circuits

RFC 1793 outlines the original standard for OSPF demand circuits. Essentially, OSPF demand circuits will spoof hellos, 224.0.0.5, from activating dial-on-demand circuits. It attempts to control LSA flooding by exchanging LSA information only the first time that the circuit is activated and by setting the LSA DoNotAge bit. If the dial link is in Area 0, or if the OSPF internetwork has external LSAs or LSA Type 5s or is in an NSSA area with LSA Type 7s, a demand circuit will not operate properly. Type 5 and Type 7 LSAs or NSSA LSAs force a DDR link, such as ISDN, to constantly dial. Most networks have some form of redistribution and almost always have LSA Type 5s floating around. Only a stub area used in conjunction with demand circuit will prevent the DDR link from constant dialing because of LSA Type 5s. To configure a demand circuit, use the following three-step process:

Step 1   Configure the interfaces on both sides of the network as OSPF point-to-point networks. Remember that hellos cannot be suppressed on "broadcast" networks, and virtual links cannot be run through stub areas.

Step 2   Configure the interfaces to be in the same stub area. Use the router command **Area _x_ stub**.

Step 3   Configure only one side, the "dialing" side of network, to be the demand circuit. Use the interface command **ip ospf demand-circuit**.

Area 0 Guidelines

The backup interface should go into Area 0 only if the primary interface is in Area 0. If dynamic routing is to occur, use the **backup interface** command or **dialer watch** commands. Remember, all LSAs will be flooded into Area 0. This type of constant LSA flooding to Area 0 will cause constant dialing of the interface. In cases such as this, the interface must be forced not to dial with additional configuration techniques.

OSPF Virtual Links

We discuss OSPF virtual links last because they should be used as your last option. The Cisco design guide warns that the use of virtual links is an indication of poor design, and, for the most part, this is correct. Virtual links are used to extend Area 0 across another area. They also can be thought of as tunnels for LSAs. They are deployed in cases when areas become partitioned or an area does not border Area 0. To configure a virtual link, use the following router command:

```
Router(config-route)#area transit_area_id virtual-link router_id_of_remote
```

The _area_id_ is the "transit area" that OSPF will tunnel through. The "transit area" cannot be a stub area of any kind. At the end of the tunnel will be another router terminating the virtual link; use the router ID of that router in the _router_id_ field. Virtual links use RIDs, and they are another reason why we use fixed RIDs when configuring OSPF. It is important that any timer changes or OSPF authentication applied to Area 0 also must be applied to the other side of the virtual link. Remember that a virtual link is actually an extension of Area 0. Think of the virtual link as the router's new interface into Area 0. Configure all interface options on the virtual link.

In Figure 12-13, the router peter is in Area 200. Notice that Area 200 does not directly touch Area 0. To make this network functional, you need to define a virtual link across Area 10. On the router mark, define a virtual link using Area 10 as the transit area, terminating it at the router ID of 192.168.250.250 or the router john. On the router john, configure a virtual link by using Area 10 as the transit area, and terminate the link at router ID 192.168.250.6. The precise syntax for each virtual link is highlighted in Figure 12-13.

Figure 12-13 *OSPF Virtual Links*

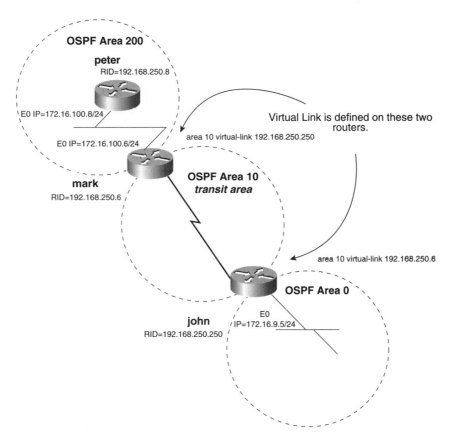

To verify the functionality of a virtual link, use the command **show ip ospf virtual-links** along with standard **show ip route** and **ping** tests. The virtual link should be up and the adjacency state should be FULL when it is operating properly. If the link does not come up, ensure that the router IDs are the ones that OSPF is using. View the OSPF database if you are unsure what the current router ID is. Example 12-31 lists the output of the **show ip ospf virtual-links** command performed on the router john.

Example 12-31 *Verifying a Virtual Link*

```
john#show ip ospf virtual-links
Virtual Link OSPF_VL0 to router 192.168.250.6 is up
  Run as demand circuit
  DoNotAge LSA allowed.
  Transit area 10, via interface Serial0.1, Cost of using 64
  Transmit Delay is 1 sec, State POINT_TO_POINT,
  Timer intervals configured, Hello 10, Dead 40, Wait 40, Retransmit 5
    Hello due in 00:00:09
    Adjacency State FULL (Hello suppressed)
    Index 2/5, retransmission queue length 0, number of retransmission 1
    First 0x0(0)/0x0(0) Next 0x0(0)/0x0(0)
    Last retransmission scan length is 1, maximum is 1
    Last retransmission scan time is 0 msec, maximum is 0 msec
john#
```

Lab 24: OSPF Multiple Area Routing, Authentication, Path Manipulation, Default Routing—Part I

Practical Scenario

Throughout this text, we have stated that most networks today are connected to the Internet in some form. Connecting to the Internet usually requires a default route to be propagated throughout the network. The following lab gives you practice in configuring multiple OSPF areas and types, authenticating an area, manipulating paths, and propagating a default route throughout OSPF.

Lab Exercise

The famous Dr. Stai has a small group of regional offices. Each office specializes in a specific area of dentistry, such as root canals or fillings. Dr. Stai wants to connect the offices over a Frame Relay network. The offices also will share a common connection to the Internet so that they can have access to the latest techniques and new pain-reduction methods. Your task is to configure an OSPF network by using the following parameters as design guidelines:

- Configure an IP network, as depicted in Figure 12-14, by using OSPF as the routing protocol and 2002 as the Autonomous System ID.

- Configure the Frame Relay network as a point-to-point network between dental_ho and the router fillings. Use a Frame Relay multipoint network between the dental_ho, crowns, and root_canals routers.

- Configure all the OSPF areas as denoted in the diagram. Area 10 is to be configured as a NSSA area.

- Inject a default route into the dental_ho router pointing all Internet traffic toward the network 128.10.1.0/24. Propagate the default route within the OSPF domain.

- Configure Type 2 authentication in Area 200.

- The root_canals router has a T1 to the dental_ho router. Configure the network so that the pain_center router will use the T1 of root_canals over the crowns router's 64-kbps link when accessing any networks across the WAN.

Lab Objectives

- Configure Dr. Stai's dental network as depicted in Figure 12-14. Configure IP as denoted in the figure, as well. The LAN topology type is not important in this lab.

- Use the Frame Relay data link protocol on the WAN. Use only multipoint networks and point-to-point networks, as indicated in the figure.

- Ensure full IP connectivity to all IP interfaces—that is, be sure that you can **ping** all Frame Relay and LAN interfaces.

- Do not change the default OSPF network type. Do not use any static routes.

- Inject a default route into the dental_ho router. Direct all IP traffic toward the subnet 128.10.1.0/24. Use a default network to accomplish this. Propagate the default route within OSPF.

- Use Type 2 authentication on Area 200. Use cisco as the password.

- Tune OSPF so that the pain_center router will have a preferred path through the router root_canals router over the crowns router. That is, all traffic from the pain_center router should travel through the router root_canals.

- (Optional) Propagate the default route only if the subnet 128.10.1.0/24 is present in the route table of the dental_ho router. If this route is not present, the default route should not get propagated because the dental_ho router cannot reach it. *Note:* You will be able to control only the default route to normal areas in this lab, so do not worry about controlling it in the NSSA area.

Equipment Needed

- Six Cisco routers. Four will be connected through V.35 back-to-back cables or in a similar manner to a Frame Relay switch.

- Three LAN segments, provided by hubs or switches. The LAN topology is not significant in this lab. The Internet connection and router can be real or not; this does not affect the configuration of the router.

Physical Layout and Prestaging

- Connect the hubs and serial cables to the routers, as shown in Figure 12-14.

- Configure an additional router to serve as the connection to the Internet. This is totally optional.

- A Frame Relay switch with three PVCs also is required. Example 12-32 lists the Frame Relay configuration used in this lab.

Example 12-32 *Frame Relay Switch Configuration*

```
hostname frame_switch
!
frame-relay switching
!
<<<text omitted>>>
!
interface Serial0
 no ip address
 encapsulation frame-relay
 no fair-queue
 clockrate 148000
 frame-relay intf-type dce
 frame-relay route 111 interface Serial1 110
 frame-relay route 121 interface Serial3 102
 frame-relay route 150 interface Serial5 151
!
interface Serial1
 no ip address
 encapsulation frame-relay
 clockrate 148000
 frame-relay intf-type dce
 frame-relay route 110 interface Serial0 111
!
interface Serial2
 no ip address
 shutdown
!
interface Serial3
 no ip address
 encapsulation frame-relay
 clockrate 64000
 frame-relay intf-type dce
 frame-relay route 102 interface Serial0 121
!
interface Serial5
 no ip address
 encapsulation frame-relay
 clockrate 64000
 frame-relay intf-type dce
 frame-relay route 151 interface Serial0 150
```

Figure 12-14 *Dr. Stai's Dental Network*

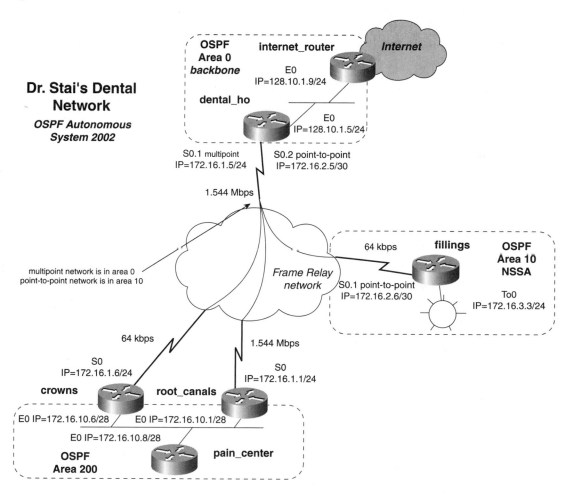

Lab 24: OSPF Multiple Area Routing, Authentication, Path Manipulation, Default Routing—Part II

Lab Walkthrough

Configure the Frame Relay switch and attach the four routers in a back-to-back manner to the Frame switch. Use V.35 cables or CSU/DSUs with crossover cables to connect the routers. Create the three LANs by the use of switches or hubs/MAUs, as illustrated in Figure 12-14.

When the physical connections are complete, assign IP addresses to all LAN and WAN interfaces, as depicted in Figure 12-14. Be sure that you can **ping** each router's local LAN and WAN interface before moving on. You will use **frame-relay interface-dlci** commands on the point-to-point interfaces and **frame-relay map** statements on the multipoint interfaces. For more information on the specifics of the Frame Relay configuration, see Chapter 5. Example 12-33 lists the Frame Relay configurations, to this point, on all routers involved.

Example 12-33 *Frame Relay Configurations*

```
hostname dental_ho
!
<<<text omitted>>>
!
interface Serial0
 no ip address
 encapsulation frame-relay
 frame-relay lmi-type cisco
!
interface Serial0.1 multipoint
 ip address 172.16.1.5 255.255.255.0
 frame-relay map ip 172.16.1.6 121 broadcast
 frame-relay map ip 172.16.1.1 111 broadcast
!
interface Serial0.2 point-to-point
 ip address 172.16.2.5 255.255.255.252
 frame-relay interface-dlci 150
!

hostname crowns
!
<<<text omitted>>>
!
interface Serial0
 ip address 172.16.1.6 255.255.255.0
 no ip directed-broadcast
```

Example 12-33 *Frame Relay Configurations (Continued)*

```
 encapsulation frame-relay
 no ip mroute-cache
 frame-relay map ip 172.16.1.5 102 broadcast
 frame-relay map ip 172.16.1.1 102 broadcast
 frame-relay lmi-type cisco
!

hostname root_canals
!
interface Serial0
 ip address 172.16.1.1 255.255.255.0
 encapsulation frame-relay
 no ip mroute-cache
 frame-relay map ip 172.16.1.5 110 broadcast
 frame-relay map ip 172.16.1.6 110 broadcast
!

hootname fillings
!
<<<text omitted>>>
!
interface Serial0
 no ip address
 encapsulation frame-relay
 frame-relay lmi-type cisco
!
interface Serial0.1 point-to-point
 ip address 172.16.2.6 255.255.255.252
 frame-relay interface-dlci 151
!
```

After the LAN and WAN interfaces are configured and basic IP connectivity is established, you can begin to configure OSPF. Recalling the detailed process to configure OSPF, you have the following:

Step 1 Perform area design and DR/BDR designation.

Step 2 Assign RIDs with the use of loopback on routers running Cisco IOS Software Release 12.0 or earlier.

Step 3 Enable OSPF, and assign RIDs on routers running Cisco IOS Software Release 12.0 or later.

Step 4 Configure OSPF interfaces.

Step 5 Configure additional neighbor support, if required.

Step 6 Configure OSPF area types.

Step 7 Configure other OSPF parameters, such as authentication.

Step 1 involves area design. In this model, we put the LAN network between crowns, root_canal and pain_center in OSPF Area 200. Area 200 also will have Type 2 authentication. The fillings router will be in an NSSA area. The multipoint Frame Relay network and the LAN network of dental_ho will reside in Area 0. The dental_ho router should be DR for the Frame Relay multipoint network because it is the only router with a PVC directly to the crowns and root_canal routers.

Step 2 involves setting RIDs on the routers that have Cisco IOS Software prior to Release 12.0. To accomplish this, use loopback interfaces on those routers. Figure 12-15 shows the diagram with the router IDs and areas that we have assigned.

Figure 12-15 *Dr. Stai's Dental Network with RIDs*

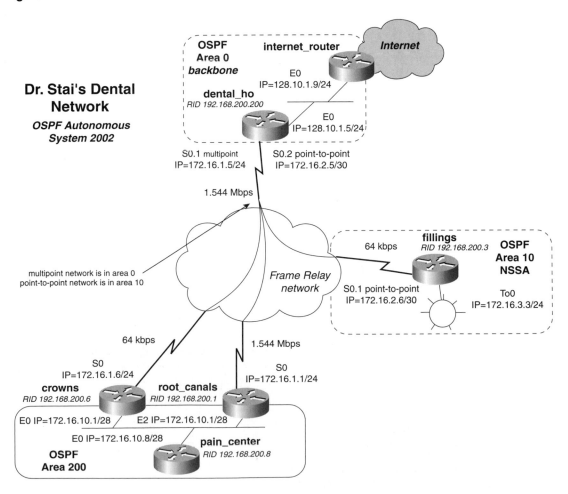

Step 3 is where the real configuration begins. On all the routers, enable OSPF in AS 2002 with the command **router ospf 2002.** On routers that have Cisco IOS Software Release 12.0, use the router command **router-id** *ip_address* to assign the static RIDs to the routers.

At Step 4, you configure which interfaces will participate in OSPF routing and what areas they will reside in. On the dental_ho router, the E0 interface will be in Area 0, along with the s0.1 multipoint interface. The s0.2 interface will be in Area 10. Example 12-34 lists the OSPF configuration, to this point, of the router dental_ho.

Example 12-34 *Preliminary OSPF Configuration of dental_ho*

```
router ospf 2002
 router-id 192.168.200.200
 network 128.10.1.5 0.0.0.0 area 0
 network 172.16.1.5 0.0.0.0 area 0
 network 172.16.2.5 0.0.0.0 area 10
 !
```

Recall from previous sections that a wildcard mask of 0.0.0.0 means match every octet of the address. In this OSPF configuration, you are telling the router to put only a single interface into an area.

The preliminary OSPF configurations on the crowns, root_canals, and pain_center routers will resemble each other. The routers that have an S0 interface will be in Area 0, while the LAN interfaces will reside in Area 200. The preliminary OSPF configuration for the crowns router is represented in Example 12-35.

Example 12-35 *Preliminary OSPF Configuration of the crowns Router*

```
router ospf 2002
 router-id 192.168.200.6
 network 172.16.1.6 0.0.0.0 area 0
 network 172.16.10.6 0.0.0.0 area 200
 !
```

The fillings router will have both interfaces in Area 10. Because this router will not need any additional neighbor support, you can skip Step 5 for this router and configure the area as an NSSA area. Example 12-36 lists the OSPF configuration of the fillings router.

Example 12-36 *Preliminary OSPF Configuration of the fillings Router*

```
router ospf 2002
 router-id 192.168.200.3
 area 10 nssa
 network 172.16.2.6 0.0.0.0 area 10
 network 172.16.3.3 0.0.0.0 area 10
 !
```

Step 5 requires you to configure the additional neighbor support needed for OSPF to form an adjacency over the Frame Relay multipoint network. For the adjacency to form properly, set the priority of the dental_ho router to be 255 and the priority of the crowns and root_ canals to 0. You also will add **neighbor** statements to the routers. Example 12-37 lists the configuration of the crowns and dental_ho routers.

Example 12-37 *OSPF Configuration of the crowns and dental_ho Router*

```
!
interface Serial0
 no ip address
 encapsulation frame-relay
 frame-relay lmi-type cisco
!
interface Serial0.1 multipoint
 ip address 172.16.1.5 255.255.255.0
 ip ospf priority 255
 frame-relay map ip 172.16.1.6 121 broadcast
 frame-relay map ip 172.16.1.1 111 broadcast
!
interface Serial0.2 point-to-point
 ip address 172.16.2.5 255.255.255.252
 frame-relay interface-dlci 150
!
interface Serial1
 no ip address
 shutdown
!
interface BRI0
 no ip address
 shutdown
!
router ospf 2002
 router-id 192.168.200.200
 area 10
 network 128.10.1.5 0.0.0.0 area 0
 network 172.16.1.5 0.0.0.0 area 0
 network 172.16.2.5 0.0.0.0 area 10
 neighbor 172.16.1.1
 neighbor 172.16.1.6
!
```

Step 6 of the configuration involves only the dental_ho and fillings router. This step requires you to configure Area 10 as an NSSA area. To configure the area as an NSSA area, simply append that **NSSA** argument into the area statements. Both routers dental_ho and fillings will need NSSA areas configured. Example 12-38 lists the OSPF configuration of the fillings router.

Example 12-38 *OSPF NSSA Configuration on fillings*

```
!
router ospf 2002
 router-id 192.168.200.3
 area 10 nssa
 network 172.16.2.6 0.0.0.0 area 10
 network 172.16.3.3 0.0.0.0 area 10
!
```

At this point, OSPF is fully operational, and you have IP connectivity to every router in the network. To verify this, we can examine the neighbors and the route table, and you can perform standard **ping** tests. To verify the NSSA area, use the **show ip ospf** command. Example 12-39 lists the output of the **show ip ospf neighbor** and **show ip ospf** commands on the dental_ho router.

Example 12-39 *Verify OSPF Operation and NSSA Configuration*

```
dental_ho#show ip ospf neighbor

Neighbor ID     Pri   State          Dead Time   Address         Interface
192.168.200.1    0    FULL/DROTHER   00:01:42    172.16.1.1      Serial0.1
192.168.200.6    0    FULL/DROTHER   00:01:44    172.16.1.6      Serial0.1
192.168.200.3    1    FULL/  -       00:00:38    172.16.2.6      Serial0.2
dental_ho#
dental_ho#show ip ospf
 Routing Process "ospf 2002" with ID 192.168.200.200
 Supports only single TOS(TOS0) routes
<<<text omitted>>>
    Area 10
        Number of interfaces in this area is 1
        It is a NSSA area
        Perform type-7/type-5 LSA translation
        generates NSSA default route with cost 1
        Area has no authentication
        SPF algorithm executed 11 times
        Area ranges are
        Number of LSA 6. Checksum Sum 0x30908
        Number of opaque link LSA 0. Checksum Sum 0x0
        Number of DCbitless LSA 0
        Number of indication LSA 0
        Number of DoNotAge LSA 0
        Flood list length 0

dental_ho#
```

The final step in the model calls for you to configure three things: a default route, authentication, and path selection. First, to configure a default route, you need to flag or mark a network as a default and then propagate it within the OSPF domain. To flag a route as a default network without using a static route, use the global command **default-network 128.10.1.0.** To propagate the network, use the OSPF command **default-information originate always**. Remember, for a router to forward packets to a default route, all routers also need the global command **ip classless** enabled. A default route will not automatically get flooded into a NSSA area. For the NSSA area to receive a default route, the argument **default-information-originate** must be appended to the **area 10 nssa** router statement. Example 12-40 lists the configuration of dental_ho, highlighting the default routing commands.

Example 12-40 *Configuration of dental_ho*

```
router ospf 2002
 router-id 192.168.200.200
 area 10 nssa default-information-originate
 network 128.10.1.5 0.0.0.0 area 0
 network 172.16.1.5 0.0.0.0 area 0
 network 172.16.2.5 0.0.0.0 area 10
 neighbor 172.16.1.1
 neighbor 172.16.1.6
 default-information originate always
 !
 ip classless
 ip default-network 128.10.0.0
```

To verify that the default route is being propagated, list the route table of any router, excluding dental_ho router. Look for a gateway of last resort to be set and a route marked by an *, indicating that it is the candidate default. Example 12-41 lists the route table of the router fillings. Notice that the route is advertised to an NSSA area as an OSPF NSSA external Type 2 route.

Example 12-41 *Route Table of fillings*

```
fillings#show ip route
Codes: C - connected, S - static, I - IGRP, R - RIP, M - mobile, B - BGP
       D - EIGRP, EX - EIGRP external, O - OSPF, IA - OSPF inter area
       N1 - OSPF NSSA external type 1, N2 - OSPF NSSA external type 2
       E1 - OSPF external type 1, E2 - OSPF external type 2, E - EGP
       i - IS-IS, L1 - IS-IS level-1, L2 - IS-IS level-2, ia - IS-IS inter area
       * - candidate default, U - per-user static route, o - ODR
       P - periodic downloaded static route

Gateway of last resort is 172.16.2.5 to network 0.0.0.0

     172.16.0.0/16 is variably subnetted, 4 subnets, 3 masks
O IA    172.16.10.0/28 [110/138] via 172.16.2.5, 00:09:18, Serial0.1
C       172.16.2.4/30 is directly connected, Serial0.1
O IA    172.16.1.0/24 [110/128] via 172.16.2.5, 00:09:18, Serial0.1
```

Example 12-41 *Route Table of fillings (Continued)*

```
C        172.16.3.0/24 is directly connected, TokenRing0
         128.10.0.0/24 is subnetted, 1 subnets
O IA     128.10.1.0 [110/74] via 172.16.2.5, 00:09:18, Serial0.1
O*N2 0.0.0.0/0 [110/1] via 172.16.2.5, 00:09:18, Serial0.1
fillings#
```

Next, you need to configure Type 2 or MD5 authentication on Area 200. You will need to enable authentication on the OSPF area statement and on the interface. Use cisco as the MD5 password. Example 12-42 lists the configuration needed for authentication on the pain_center router. The configuration must be identical on all the routers in Area 200.

Example 12-42 *MD5 Authentication on the Router pain_center*

```
interface Ethernet0
 ip address 172.16.10.8 255.255.255.240
 ip ospf message-digest-key 1 md5 cisco
!
<<<text omitted>>>
!
router ospf 2002
 network 172.16.10.8 0.0.0.0 area 200
 area 200 authentication message-digest
```

As you enable authentication throughout Area 200, routes and neighbors will start to age out and disappear. This is one obvious way to tell you that authentication is starting to work. Performing the **show ip ospf** command also lists the area as being authenticated. When all the routers have authentication enabled, neighbors and routes will start to reappear.

The final portion of the lab, excluding the optional part, involves influencing packets from the pain_center router. Traffic from this router should always take a primary path through the root_canals router. A quick view of the route table on pain_center shows two paths to the other portions of the network. One path goes through the root_canals router, and one goes through the crowns router, such as in Example 12-43.

Example 12-43 *Route Table of pain_center*

```
pain_center#show ip route
Codes: C - connected, S - static, I - IGRP, R - RIP, M - mobile, B - BGP
       D - EIGRP, EX - EIGRP external, O - OSPF, IA - OSPF inter area
       N1 - OSPF NSSA external type 1, N2 - OSPF NSSA external type 2
       E1 - OSPF external type 1, E2 - OSPF external type 2, E - EGP
       i - IS-IS, L1 - IS-IS level-1, L2 - IS-IS level-2, * - candidate default
       U - per-user static route, o - ODR
```

continues

Example 12-43 *Route Table of pain_center (Continued)*

```
Gateway of last resort is 172.16.10.1 to network 0.0.0.0

     128.10.0.0/24 is subnetted, 1 subnets
O IA    128.10.1.0 [110/84] via 172.16.10.1, 00:14:03, Ethernet0
                    [110/84] via 172.16.10.6, 00:14:03, Ethernet0
C    192.168.200.0/24 is directly connected, Loopback0
     172.16.0.0/16 is variably subnetted, 4 subnets, 3 masks
C       172.16.10.0/28 is directly connected, Ethernet0
O IA    172.16.2.4/30 [110/138] via 172.16.10.1, 00:14:03, Ethernet0
                       [110/138] via 172.16.10.6, 00:14:03, Ethernet0
O IA    172.16.1.0/24 [110/74] via 172.16.10.1, 00:14:03, Ethernet0
                       [110/74] via 172.16.10.6, 00:14:03, Ethernet0
O IA    172.16.3.0/24 [110/144] via 172.16.10.1, 00:14:04, Ethernet0
                       [110/144] via 172.16.10.6, 00:14:04, Ethernet0
O*E2 0.0.0.0/0 [110/1] via 172.16.10.1, 00:14:04, Ethernet0
               [110/1] via 172.16.10.6, 00:14:04, Ethernet0
pain_center#
```

OSPF will load-balance over these routes, but instead you want to use only one route. If the primary route becomes available, OSPF will use the backup route through the crowns router. To influence the forwarding decisions of the router, you can use the **bandwidth** command to change the cost of the link or you can directly change the cost with the interface command **ip ospf cost.** You could influence the forwarding decision in this model in many ways. The method that you will use here is to simply set the OSPF cost of the s0 interface of the root_canals router to 15. Example 12-44 shows the route table, followed by a trace performed on the pain_center after the change has been made to the root_canals router. Notice that only one primary path, through 172.16.10.1, shows up in the route table.

Example 12-44 *Route Table of pain_center Router*

```
pain_center#show ip route
Codes: C - connected, S - static, I - IGRP, R - RIP, M - mobile, B - BGP
       D - EIGRP, EX - EIGRP external, O - OSPF, IA - OSPF inter area
       N1 - OSPF NSSA external type 1, N2 - OSPF NSSA external type 2
       E1 - OSPF external type 1, E2 - OSPF external type 2, E - EGP
       i - IS-IS, L1 - IS-IS level-1, L2 - IS-IS level-2, * - candidate default
       U - per-user static route, o - ODR

Gateway of last resort is 172.16.10.1 to network 0.0.0.0

     128.10.0.0/24 is subnetted, 1 subnets
O IA    128.10.1.0 [110/35] via 172.16.10.1, 00:00:17, Ethernet0
C    192.168.200.0/24 is directly connected, Loopback0
     172.16.0.0/16 is variably subnetted, 4 subnets, 3 masks
C       172.16.10.0/28 is directly connected, Ethernet0
O IA    172.16.2.4/30 [110/89] via 172.16.10.1, 00:00:17, Ethernet0
O IA    172.16.1.0/24 [110/25] via 172.16.10.1, 00:00:17, Ethernet0
O IA    172.16.3.0/24 [110/95] via 172.16.10.1, 00:00:17, Ethernet0
```

Example 12-44 *Route Table of pain_center Router (Continued)*

```
O*E2 0.0.0.0/0 [110/1] via 172.16.10.1, 00:00:17, Ethernet0
pain_center#trace  128.10.1.5

Type escape sequence to abort.
Tracing the route to 128.10.1.5

  1 172.16.10.1 0 msec 0 msec 0 msec
  2 172.16.1.5 16 msec 24 msec *
pain_center#
```

The optional portion of the lab instructs you to propagate the default route only if the network 128.10.1.0/24 is in the route table. If the network 128.10.1.0 is not available, the router dental_ho should not propagate the default route to the rest of the OSPF domain. To accomplish this, you need to configure what is called a *conditional default route*. To configure a conditional default route (refer to Example 12-45), call a route map on the **default-information originate** command. This route map, in turn, matches a prefix list that corresponds to the network 128.10.1.0.

Example 12-45 *Conditional Default Route Configuration*

```
!
router ospf 2002
 router-id 192.168.200.200
 area 10 nssa default-information-originate
 network 128.10.1.5 0.0.0.0 area 0
 network 172.16.1.5 0.0.0.0 area 0
 network 172.16.2.5 0.0.0.0 area 10
 neighbor 172.16.1.6
 neighbor 172.16.1.1
 default-information originate always route-map condition  →calls route map
"condition"
!
ip classless
ip default-network 128.10.0.0
no ip http server
!
!
ip prefix-list cond seq 5 permit 128.10.1.0/24     →match route 128.10.1.0/24
route-map condition permit 10
 match ip address prefix-list cond                 →call prefix-list called "cond"
!
```

When the Ethernet interface is shut down, the dental_ho router no longer advertises the default route. Because the NSSA default route is controlled differently, you cannot call a route map and control default routing to the NSSA area. Future Cisco IOS Software releases might provide for this.

Example 12-46 lists the relevant portions of the routers in the lab.

Example 12-46 *Router Configurations Used in This Lab*

```
hostname dental_ho
!
interface Ethernet0
 ip address 128.10.1.5 255.255.255.0
!
interface Serial0.1 multipoint
 ip address 172.16.1.5 255.255.255.0
 ip ospf priority 255
 frame-relay map ip 172.16.1.6 121 broadcast
 frame-relay map ip 172.16.1.1 111 broadcast
!
interface Serial0.2 point-to-point
 ip address 172.16.2.5 255.255.255.252
 frame-relay interface-dlci 150
!
<<<text omitted>>>
!
router ospf 2002
 router-id 192.168.200.200
 area 10 nssa default-information-originate
 network 128.10.1.5 0.0.0.0 area 0
 network 172.16.1.5 0.0.0.0 area 0
 network 172.16.2.5 0.0.0.0 area 10
 neighbor 172.16.1.6
 neighbor 172.16.1.1
 default-information originate always route-map condition
!
ip classless
ip default-network 128.10.0.0
no ip http server
!
ip prefix-list cond seq 5 permit 128.10.1.0/24
route-map condition permit 10
 match ip address prefix-list cond
!
!
```

```
hostname crowns
!
interface Ethernet0
 ip address 172.16.10.6 255.255.255.240
 no ip directed-broadcast
 ip ospf message-digest-key 1 md5 cisco
!
interface Serial0
 ip address 172.16.1.6 255.255.255.0
 no ip directed-broadcast
 encapsulation frame-relay
 ip ospf priority 0
```

Example 12-46 *Router Configurations Used in This Lab (Continued)*

```
 no ip mroute-cache
 frame-relay map ip 172.16.1.5 102 broadcast
 frame-relay map ip 172.16.1.1 102 broadcast
 frame-relay lmi-type cisco
!
router ospf 2002
 router-id 192.168.200.6
 area 200 authentication message-digest
 network 172.16.1.6 0.0.0.0 area 0
 network 172.16.10.6 0.0.0.0 area 200
!
ip classless
!
!
```

```
hostname root_canals
!
interface Loopback0
 ip address 192.168.200.1 255.255.255.0
!
<<<text omitted>>>
!
interface Ethernet2
 ip address 172.16.10.1 255.255.255.240
 ip ospf message-digest-key 1 md5 cisco
 media-type 10BaseT
! !
interface Serial0
 ip address 172.16.1.1 255.255.255.0
 encapsulation frame-relay
 ip ospf cost 15
 ip ospf priority 0
 no ip mroute-cache
 frame-relay map ip 172.16.1.5 110 broadcast
 frame-relay map ip 172.16.1.6 110 broadcast
!
<<<text omitted>>>
!
router ospf 2002
 network 172.16.1.1 0.0.0.0 area 0
 network 172.16.10.1 0.0.0.0 area 200
 area 200 authentication message-digest
!
ip classless
!
!
```

```
hostname pain_center
```

continues

Example 12-46 *Router Configurations Used in This Lab (Continued)*

```
!
interface Loopback0
 ip address 192.168.200.8 255.255.255.0
!
interface Ethernet0
 ip address 172.16.10.8 255.255.255.240
 ip ospf message-digest-key 1 md5 cisco
!
<<<text omitted>>>
!
router ospf 2002
 network 172.16.10.8 0.0.0.0 area 200
 area 200 authentication message-digest
!
ip classless
!
!
```

```
hostname fillings
!
interface Serial0
 no ip address
 encapsulation frame-relay
 frame-relay lmi-type cisco
!
interface Serial0.1 point-to-point
 ip address 172.16.2.6 255.255.255.252
 frame-relay interface-dlci 151
!
interface TokenRing0
 ip address 172.16.3.3 255.255.255.0
 ring-speed 16
!
router ospf 2002
 router-id 192.168.200.3
 area 10 nssa
 network 172.16.2.6 0.0.0.0 area 10
 network 172.16.3.3 0.0.0.0 area 10
!
ip classless
```

Lab 25: OSPF Multiple Area Routing, Route Redistribution and Summarization—Part I

Practical Scenario

As OSPF networks continue to grow, it becomes inevitable that the network will be broken into areas. Redistribution between routing protocols is also fairly common. When integrating a classful routing protocol with a classless routing protocol, an understanding of summarization is required. The following lab gives you practice in configuring multiple OSPF areas, virtual links, redistribution, and summarization.

Lab Exercise:

The Herpetology (Herp) Information Network or HIN, is a network of herpetologists exchanging biological and ecological information on several species of reptiles and amphibians. HIN has a Frame Relay network used to disperse information across the country. The network is in a constant state of flux and suffers from this continuous change. You have been given the task of fixing the current OSPF network and integrating it with an IGRP network. You must abide by the following design guidelines:

- Configure an IP network as depicted in Figure 12-16, by using OSPF as the routing protocol and 2001 as the Autonomous System ID.

- Configure the entire Frame Relay network as three point-to-point networks, as depicted in the figure.

- Configure all the OSPF areas as denoted in the figure. The two Frame Relay point-to-point networks, between hin_hq, gecko, and tree_frog are in OSPF Area 0. The LAN interface of gecko is in OSPF Area 10, while the LAN interfaces of tree_frog and python are in OSPF Area 20. The serial interface of the python router and all the interfaces of the boa router are in OSPF Area 75.

- Configure the Frame Relay point-to-point network between hin_hq and the chameleon router to be in the IGRP routing domain. Ensure full IP connectivity from the chameleon routers LAN interface to all of the OSPF networks and interfaces.

- Configure three loopback interfaces on the chameleon router, and advertise this as a single OSPF route.

- The gecko router must not have IP visibility to the LAN network on the boa router.

Lab Objectives

- Configure the HIN as depicted in Figure 12-16. Configure IP as denoted in the diagram. The LAN topology type is not important in this lab.

- Use the Frame Relay data link protocol on the WAN. Use only point-to-point networks as indicated on the diagram.

- Ensure full IP connectivity to all IP interfaces—that is, be sure that you can **ping** all Frame Relay and LAN interfaces from all routers. You might not use any static routes.

- Do not change the default OSPF network type.

- Configure the IGRP domain on the chameleon router. Ensure that this domain has full IP reachability to the entire OSPF network.

- Configure and advertise three loopback networks on the chameleon router. These networks are 10.1.16.0/24, 10.1.17.0/24, and 10.1.18.0/24. Aggregate the networks into a single OSPF route.

- Prevent the gecko router from reaching the network 10.1.70.1/24.

- (Optional) Configure OSPF so that the tree_frog router will send OSPF hellos every 30 seconds.

Equipment Needed

- Seven Cisco routers. Four will be connected through V.35 back-to-back cables or in a similar manner to a Frame Relay switch.

- Two routers will be connected directly through V.35 back-to-back cables or in a similar manner.

- Five LANs segments, provided through hubs or switches. The LAN topology is not significant to this lab.

Physical Layout and Prestaging

- Connect the hubs and serial cables to the routers, as shown in Figure 12-16.

- A Frame Relay switch with three PVCs also is required. Example 12-47 lists the Frame Relay configuration used in this lab. Note that this is the same Frame Relay switching configuration as in the previous lab exercise.

Example 12-47 *Frame Relay Switch Configuration*

```
hostname frame_switch
!
frame-relay switching
!
<<<text omitted>>>
```

Example 12-47 *Frame Relay Switch Configuration (Continued)*

```
!
interface Serial0
 no ip address
 encapsulation frame-relay
 no fair-queue
 clockrate 148000
 frame-relay intf-type dce
 frame-relay route 111 interface Serial1 110
 frame-relay route 121 interface Serial3 102
 frame-relay route 150 interface Serial5 151
!
interface Serial1
 no ip address
 encapsulation frame-relay
 clockrate 148000
 frame-relay intf-type dce
 frame-relay route 110 interface Serial0 111
!
interface Serial2
 no ip address
 shutdown
!
interface Serial3
 no ip address
 encapsulation frame-relay
 clockrate 64000
 frame-relay intf-type dce
 frame-relay route 102 interface Serial0 121
!
interface Serial5
 no ip address
 encapsulation frame-relay
 clockrate 64000
 frame-relay intf-type dce
 frame-relay route 151 interface Serial0 150
```

Figure 12-16 *HIN*

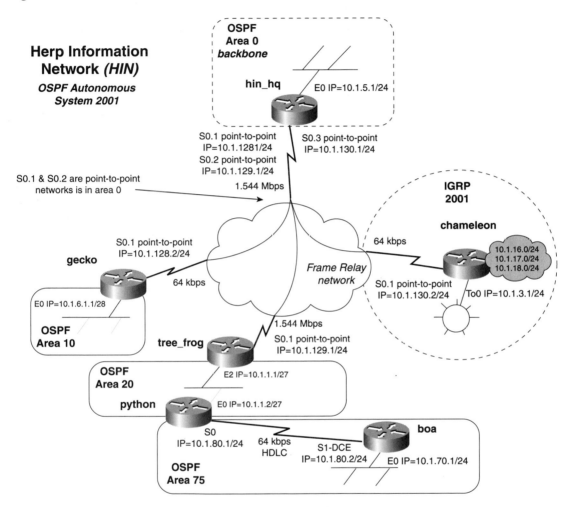

Lab 25: OSPF Multiple Area Routing, Route Redistribution and Summarization—Part II

Lab Walkthrough

Configure the Frame Relay switch and attach the four routers in a back-to-back manner to the Frame switch. Use V.35 cables or CSU/DSUs with crossover cables to connect the routers. Create the five LANs by the use of switches or hubs/MAUs, as illustrated in Figure 12-16.

When the physical connections are complete, assign IP addresses to all LAN and WAN interfaces, as depicted in Figure 12-16. Configure three loopback addresses on the chameleon router with the addresses 10.1.16.0/24, 10.1.17.0/24, and 10.1.18.0/24. Be sure that you can **ping** each router's local LAN and WAN interface before continuing. You will use **frame-relay interface-dlci** commands on all of the point-to-point interfaces. Example 12-48 lists the Frame Relay configurations, to this point, on all routers involved.

Example 12-48 *Frame Relay Configurations*

```
hostname hin_hq
!
<<<text omitted>>>
!
interface Serial0
 no ip address
 encapsulation frame-relay
!
interface Serial0.1 point-to-point
 ip address 10.1.128.1 255.255.255.0
 frame-relay interface-dlci 121
!
interface Serial0.2 point-to-point
 ip address 10.1.129.1 255.255.255.0
 frame-relay interface-dlci 111
!
interface Serial0.3 point-to-point
 ip address 10.1.130.1 255.255.255.0
 frame-relay interface-dlci 150
!

hostname gecko
!
<<<text omitted>>>
!
interface Serial0
 no ip address
 no ip directed-broadcast
 encapsulation frame-relay
```

continues

Example 12-48 *Frame Relay Configurations (Continued)*

```
 no ip mroute-cache
 frame-relay lmi-type cisco
!
interface Serial0.1 point-to-point
 ip address 10.1.128.2 255.255.255.0
 no ip directed-broadcast
 frame-relay interface-dlci 102
!

hostname tree_frog
!
interface Serial0
 no ip address
 encapsulation frame-relay
 no ip mroute-cache
!
interface Serial0.1 point-to-point
 ip address 10.1.129.2 255.255.255.0
 frame-relay interface-dlci 110
!

hostname chameleon
!
<<<text omitted>>>
!
interface Serial0
 no ip address
 encapsulation frame-relay
 frame-relay lmi-type cisco
!
interface Serial0.1 point-to-point
 ip address 10.1.130.2 255.255.255.0
 frame-relay interface-dlci 151
!
```

To configure the WAN network between python and the boa, one end will need to be configured for clocking, or DCE. Example 12-49 lists the serial configuration of the boa router, which is the DCE side of the link. This is not necessary if you are using CSU/DSUs with crossover cables.

Example 12-49 *Serial Configuration of the Router boa*

```
!
interface Serial1
 ip address 10.1.80.2 255.255.255.0
 clockrate 56000
```

After the LAN and WAN interfaces have been configured and basic IP connectivity has been established, begin to configure OSPF and IGRP. First, you will configure OSPF, and then you will integrate it with IGRP. Recalling the detailed process to configure OSPF, you have the following:

Step 1   Perform area design, DR/BDR designation.

Step 2   Assign RIDs with the use of loopback on routers prior to Cisco IOS Software 12.0.

Step 3   Enable OSPF, and assign RIDs on routers running Cisco IOS Software Release 12.0 and later.

Step 4   Configure OSPF interfaces.

Step 5   Configure additional neighbor support, if required.

Step 6   Configure OSPF area types and virtual links.

Step 7   Configure other OSPF parameters, such as summarization and redistribution.

Step 1 involves area design. In this model, the Frame Relay point-to-point networks are in OSPF Area 0. The LAN interface of the gecko router is in OSPF Area 10, while the LAN interfaces of the tree_frog and python routers are in OSPF Area 20. The serial interface of the python router and all the interfaces of the boa router are in OSPF Area 75. As you probably can tell at this point, you will need a virtual link to connect Area 75 to the rest of the OSPF network.

Step 2 involves setting RIDs on the routers that have Cisco IOS Software prior to Release 12.0. To accomplish this, you will use loopback interfaces on those routers. Figure 12-17 shows the diagram with the router IDs that you have assigned and the virtual link marked.

Again, Step 3 is where the real configuration begins. On all the routers except chameleon, you will enable OSPF in AS 2001 with the command **router ospf 2001.** On routers that have Cisco IOS Software Release 12.0, use the router command **router-id** *ip_address* to assign the static RIDs to the routers.

Step 4 involves configuring which interfaces will participate in OSPF routing and the areas in which they will reside. On the hin_hq router, the E0 interface will be in Area 0, along with the s0.1 and s0.2 point-to-point interfaces. Example 12-50 lists the OSPF configuration, to this point, of the router hin_hq.

Figure 12-17 *HIN with RIDs Assigned*

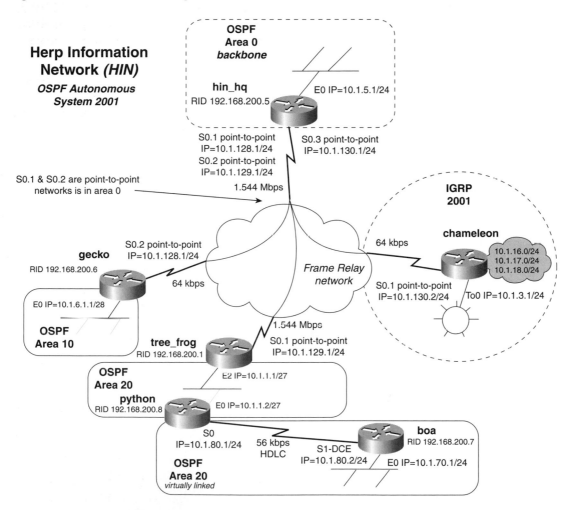

Example 12-50 *Preliminary OSPF Configuration of hin_hq*

```
router ospf 2001
 router-id 192.168.200.5
 redistribute igrp 2001 subnets tag 5
 network 10.1.5.1 0.0.0.0 area 0
 network 10.1.128.1 0.0.0.0 area 0
 network 10.1.129.1 0.0.0.0 area 0
 default-metric 64
!
```

The **network** statements in the previous example could be simplified with one command— **network 10.1.0.0 0.0.255.255 area 0**. In production networks, it pays to be specific on the mask. As changes occur in the network, new interfaces in different areas might be added. If the wildcard mask is too general, OSPF will have to be interrupted while new, more specific **network** statements are configured.

The LAN interface of the gecko router resides in OSPF Area 10, while its serial interface resides in OSPF Area 0. The tree_frog routers LAN interface resides in OSPF Area 20, while its serial interface also resides in OSPF Area 0. Example 12-51 presents the preliminary OSPF configurations for the gecko and tree_frog routers.

Example 12-51 *Preliminary OSPF Configurations of the gecko and tree_frog Routers*

```
hostname gecko
!
router ospf 2001
 router-id 192.168.200.6
 network 10.1.6.1 0.0.0.0 area 10
 network 10.1.128.2 0.0.0.0 area 0
!
```
```
hostname tree_frog
!
router ospf 2001
 network 10.1.1.1 0.0.0.0 area 20
 network 10.1.129.2 0.0.0.0 area 0
!
```

NOTE   The tree_frog router does not show a router ID because it is using a loopback interface for its RID. The tree_frog router is running a Cisco IOS Software Release prior to 12.0.

The python router will have one interface in Area 20 and one in Area 75, while the boa router will have both interfaces in Area 75. Example 12-52 lists the OSPF configuration of these routers.

Example 12-52 *Preliminary OSPF Configuration of the python and boa Routers*

```
hostname python
!
router ospf 2001
 network 10.1.80.1 0.0.0.0 area 75
 network 10.1.1.2 0.0.0.0 area 20
!
```

continues

Example 12-52 *Preliminary OSPF Configuration of the python and boa Routers (Continued)*

```
hostname boa
!
router ospf 2001
 network 10.1.0.0 0.0.255.255 area 75
!
```

Step 5 requires you to configure the additional neighbor support. In this model, adjacencies automatically form over the Frame Relay point-to-point networks. No additional neighbor configuration support is needed.

At this point, OSPF is operational, except for Area 75, and you have IP connectivity to every router in the network. To verify this, you can examine the neighbors and route table, as well as perform standard **ping**s tests. Example 12-53 lists the output of the **show ip ospf neighbor** commands on the hin_hq, gecko, tree_frog, and python routers.

Example 12-53 *Verifying OSPF Neighbors*

```
hin_hq#show ip ospf neighbor

Neighbor ID     Pri   State         Dead Time   Address       Interface
192.168.200.6    1    FULL/  -      00:00:35    10.1.128.2    Serial0.1
192.168.200.1    1    FULL/  -      00:00:32    10.1.129.2    Serial0.2
hin_hq#
```
```
tree_frog#show ip ospf neighbor

Neighbor ID     Pri   State         Dead Time   Address       Interface
192.168.200.8    1    FULL/DR       00:00:35    10.1.1.2      Ethernet2
192.168.200.5    1    FULL/  -      00:00:34    10.1.129.1    Serial0.1
tree_frog#
```
```
phython#show ip ospf neighbor

Neighbor ID     Pri   State         Dead Time   Address       Interface
192.168.200.1    1    FULL/BDR      00:00:39    10.1.1.1      Ethernet0
192.168.200.7    1    FULL/  -      00:00:35    10.1.80.2     Serial0
python#
```

Step 6 requires you to configure OSPF special areas, such as stub areas—or, in this case, virtual links. As mentioned previously, you will need a virtual link to connect Area 75 to the rest of the OSPF domain. To configure a virtual link, you need to locate the two routers that will serve as your endpoints for the virtual links. In this model, Area 20 will be your transit area; therefore, your virtual links need to be defined on the routers tree_frog and python. The syntax on the tree_frog router will be **area 20 virtual-link 192.168.200.8**, which is the RID of the python router. The python router, in turn, points to the RID of the tree_frog router. The syntax on the python router will be **area 20 virtual-link 192.168.200.1**.

Static router IDs are vital to the operation of OSPF virtual circuits. If you have trouble bringing up the virtual link and have verified that there are no configuration errors, try reloading the routers. A common problem with virtual links is RIDs, and this will reassign them in routers running Cisco IOS Software prior to Release 12.0. To view whether the virtual link is working, use the **show ip ospf virtual-link** command. The routes from the boa router also should start appearing throughout the OSPF domain. Example 12-54 lists the output of the **show ip ospf virtual-link** command on the tree_frog router.

Example 12-54 *Verifying the Virtual Link*

```
tree_frog#show ip ospf virtual-links
Virtual Link OSPF_VL0 to router 192.168.200.8 is up
  Run as demand circuit
  DoNotAge LSA allowed.
  Transit area 20, via interface Ethernet2, Cost of using 10
  Transmit Delay is 1 sec, State POINT_TO_POINT,
  Timer intervals configured, Hello 10, Dead 40, Wait 40, Retransmit 5
    Hello due in 00:00:00
    Adjacency State FULL (Hello suppressed)
tree_frog#
```

The OSPF domain is now fully functional. By viewing the route table on the boa router, you can see that you have routes to every destination in the network, as shown in Example 12-55.

Example 12-55 *Verifying the OSPF Domain*

```
boa#show ip route
Codes: C - connected, S - static, I - IGRP, R - RIP, M - mobile, B - BGP
       D - EIGRP, EX - EIGRP external, O - OSPF, IA - OSPF inter area
       N1 - OSPF NSSA external type 1, N2 - OSPF NSSA external type 2
       E1 - OSPF external type 1, E2 - OSPF external type 2, E - EGP
       i - IS-IS, L1 - IS-IS level-1, L2 - IS-IS level-2, * - candidate default
       U - per-user static route, o - ODR

Gateway of last resort is not set

     10.0.0.0/8 is variably subnetted, 8 subnets, 4 masks
O IA    10.1.1.0/27 [110/74] via 10.1.80.1, 00:28:02, Serial1
O IA    10.1.6.0/28 [110/212] via 10.1.80.1, 00:28:02, Serial1
O IA    10.1.5.0/24 [110/148] via 10.1.80.1, 00:28:02, Serial1
C       10.1.70.0/24 is directly connected, Ethernet0
C       10.1.80.0/24 is directly connected, Serial1
O IA    10.1.129.0/24 [110/138] via 10.1.80.1, 00:28:02, Serial1
O IA    10.1.128.0/30 [110/266] via 10.1.80.1, 00:28:02, Serial1
O IA    10.1.128.0/24 [110/202] via 10.1.80.1, 00:28:02, Serial1
C    192.168.200.0/24 is directly connected, Loopback0
boa#
```

To integrate the IGRP domain, configure IGRP on the chameleon and hin_hq routers.
Example 12-56 lists the IGRP configuration on the hin_hq router. Be sure to use the
passive-interface command to prevent unnecessary broadcast from the Ethernet and other
serial interfaces. The IGRP configuration on hin_hq and chameleon will be identical.

Example 12-56 *Configuring IGRP on hin_hq*

```
!
router igrp 2001
 passive-interface Ethernet0
 passive-interface Serial0.1
 passive-interface Serial0.2
 network 10.0.0.0
 !
```

Next, you need to configure redistribution between IGRP and OSPF. There is only one
redistribution point in the network, so you do not have to worry about route feedback or
redistribution loops. Example 12-57 lists the configuration of the hin_hq router, highlighting
the redistribution commands. In this example, you use an OSPF default metric of 64
because it is the cost of a T1 interface. You also use the **subnet** keyword to redistribute
multiple subnets into OSPF.

Example 12-57 *Redistribution on the hin_hq Router*

```
!
router ospf 2001
 router-id 192.168.200.5
 redistribute igrp 2001 subnets tag 5        ←Redistribute IGRP into OSPF
 network 10.1.5.1 0.0.0.0 area 0
 network 10.1.128.1 0.0.0.0 area 0
 network 10.1.129.1 0.0.0.0 area 0
 default-metric 64                    ←Default metric or cost
 !
router igrp 2001
 redistribute ospf 2001               ←Redistribute OSPF into IGRP
 passive-interface Ethernet0
 passive-interface Serial0.1
 passive-interface Serial0.2
 network 10.0.0.0
 default-metric 1544 10 254 1 1500          ←IGRP metric
 !
```

After redistribution is enabled, if you viewed the route table on the chameleon router, you
would find the results in Example 12-58.

Example 12-58 *Route Table of the chameleon Router*

```
chameleon#show ip route
Codes: C - connected, S - static, I - IGRP, R - RIP, M - mobile, B - BGP
       D - EIGRP, EX - EIGRP external, O - OSPF, IA - OSPF inter area
       N1 - OSPF NSSA external type 1, N2 - OSPF NSSA external type 2
       E1 - OSPF external type 1, E2 - OSPF external type 2, E - EGP
       i - IS-IS, L1 - IS-IS level-1, L2 - IS-IS level-2, ia - IS-IS inter area
       * - candidate default, U - per-user static route, o - ODR
       P - periodic downloaded static route

Gateway of last resort is not set

     10.0.0.0/24 is subnetted, 10 subnets
C       10.1.3.0 is directly connected, TokenRing0
I       10.1.5.0 [100/8576] via 10.1.130.1, 00:00:00, Serial0.1
C       10.1.18.0 is directly connected, Loopback22
C       10.1.17.0 is directly connected, Loopback21
C       10.1.16.0 is directly connected, Loopback20
I       10.1.70.0 [100/8486] via 10.1.130.1, 00:00:00, Serial0.1
I       10.1.80.0 [100/8486] via 10.1.130.1, 00:00:00, Serial0.1
C       10.1.130.0 is directly connected, Serial0.1
I       10.1.129.0 [100/10476] via 10.1.130.1, 00:00:00, Serial0.1
I       10.1.128.0 [100/10476] via 10.1.130.1, 00:00:00, Serial0.1
chameleon#
```

At first glance, it might appear that the route table is complete; however, upon closer examination, two routes are missing: 10.1.6.0/28 and 10.1.1.0/27. This is because IGRP can receive only routes that are on the same bit boundary as the interface receiving the routes. For the chameleon router to receive all the OSPF routes, they must be summarized on a 24-bit boundary that matches the bit boundary on its s0.1 interface. To summarize Area 20 and Area 10, use the router command **area x range** statements. The **area range** statement for the gecko router will be **area 10 range 10.1.6.0 255.255.255.0**, and the **area range** statement on the tree_frog router will be **area 20 range 10.1.1.0 255.255.255.0**. After adding the **area range** statements, the route table on the chameleon router now has all the routes to the OSPF domain, as verified by Example 12-59.

Example 12-59 *Route Table of the chameleon Router*

```
chameleon#show ip route
Codes: C - connected, S - static, I - IGRP, R - RIP, M - mobile, B - BGP
       D - EIGRP, EX - EIGRP external, O - OSPF, IA - OSPF inter area
       N1 - OSPF NSSA external type 1, N2 - OSPF NSSA external type 2
       E1 - OSPF external type 1, E2 - OSPF external type 2, E - EGP
       i - IS-IS, L1 - IS-IS level-1, L2 - IS-IS level-2, ia - IS-IS inter area
       * - candidate default, U - per-user static route, o - ODR
       P - periodic downloaded static route
```

continues

Example 12-59 *Route Table of the chameleon Router (Continued)*

```
Gateway of last resort is not set

      10.0.0.0/24 is subnetted, 12 subnets
C       10.1.3.0 is directly connected, TokenRing0
I       10.1.1.0 [100/8486] via 10.1.130.1, 00:00:28, Serial0.1
I       10.1.6.0 [100/8486] via 10.1.130.1, 00:00:28, Serial0.1
I       10.1.5.0 [100/8576] via 10.1.130.1, 00:00:28, Serial0.1
C       10.1.18.0 is directly connected, Loopback22
C       10.1.17.0 is directly connected, Loopback21
C       10.1.16.0 is directly connected, Loopback20
I       10.1.70.0 [100/8486] via 10.1.130.1, 00:00:28, Serial0.1
I       10.1.80.0 [100/8486] via 10.1.130.1, 00:00:29, Serial0.1
C       10.1.130.0 is directly connected, Serial0.1
I       10.1.129.0 [100/10476] via 10.1.130.1, 00:00:29, Serial0.1
I       10.1.128.0 [100/10476] via 10.1.130.1, 00:00:29, Serial0.1
chameleon#
```

If you have not configured the loopback interfaces on the chameleon router, do so at
this time. You want to configure the hin_hq router to advertise the routes 10.1.16.0/24,
10.1.17.0/24, and 10.1.18.0/24 as a single OSPF route. To summarize networks from
another AS, use the OSPF command **summary-address** command. The aggregate address
is 10.1.16.0 with a 255.255.252.0 mask. Example 12-60 shows the OSPF configuration of
hin_hq now.

Example 12-60 *OSPF Configuration of hin_hq*

```
router ospf 2001
 router-id 192.168.200.5
 summary-address 10.1.16.0 255.255.252.0
 redistribute igrp 2001 subnets tag 5
 network 10.1.5.1 0.0.0.0 area 0
 network 10.1.128.1 0.0.0.0 area 0
 network 10.1.129.1 0.0.0.0 area 0
 default-metric 64
!
router igrp 2001
 redistribute ospf 2001
 passive-interface Ethernet0
 passive-interface Serial0.1
 passive-interface Serial0.2
 network 10.0.0.0
 default-metric 1544 10 254 1 1500
!
```

To view the summary route, list the route table on the boa router, as in Example 12-61.

Example 12-61 *Route Table of the boa Router, Highlighting the Summary Route*

```
boa#show ip route
Codes: C - connected, S - static, I - IGRP, R - RIP, M - mobile, B - BGP
       D - EIGRP, EX - EIGRP external, O - OSPF, IA - OSPF inter area
       N1 - OSPF NSSA external type 1, N2 - OSPF NSSA external type 2
       E1 - OSPF external type 1, E2 - OSPF external type 2, E - EGP
       i - IS-IS, L1 - IS-IS level-1, L2 - IS-IS level-2, * - candidate default
       U - per-user static route, o - ODR

Gateway of last resort is not set

     10.0.0.0/8 is variably subnetted, 12 subnets, 4 masks
O E2    10.1.3.0/24 [110/64] via 10.1.80.1, 00:37:49, Serial1
O IA    10.1.1.0/27 [110/74] via 10.1.80.1, 00:27:57, Serial1
O IA    10.1.1.0/24 [110/84] via 10.1.80.1, 00:27:57, Serial1
O IA    10.1.6.0/24 [110/212] via 10.1.80.1, 00:28:57, Serial1
O IA    10.1.5.0/24 [110/148] via 10.1.80.1, 01:13:37, Serial1
O E2    10.1.16.0/22 [110/64] via 10.1.80.1, 00:17:20, Serial1
C       10.1.70.0/24 is directly connected, Ethernet0
C       10.1.80.0/24 is directly connected, Serial1
O E2    10.1.130.0/24 [110/64] via 10.1.80.1, 00:37:50, Serial1
O IA    10.1.129.0/24 [110/138] via 10.1.80.1, 01:13:37, Serial1
O IA    10.1.128.0/30 [110/266] via 10.1.80.1, 01:13:37, Serial1
O IA    10.1.128.0/24 [110/202] via 10.1.80.1, 01:13:37, Serial1
C    192.168.200.0/24 is directly connected, Loopback0
boa#
```

The final portion of the lab calls for you to prevent the LAN network of the router boa, 10.1.3.0/24, from the gecko router. To accomplish this, configure an inbound distribute list on the gecko router. Example 12-62 demonstrates configuration of the filter on the gecko router.

Example 12-62 *Configuring a Distribute List on gecko*

```
gecko(config)#router ospf 2001
gecko(config-router)#distribute-list 10 in s0.1     ←Applied to s0.1
gecko(config-router)#exit
gecko(config)#access-list 10 deny 10.1.70.0 0.0.0.255     ←deny 10.1.70.0/24
gecko(config)#access-list 10 permit any
gecko(config)#
```

To verify the access list, clear the route table on the gecko router and then relist it. Example 12-63 lists the route table of gecko after the distribute list is applied.

Example 12-63 *Route Table on gecko*

```
gecko#show ip route
Codes: C - connected, S - static, I - IGRP, R - RIP, M - mobile, B - BGP
       D - EIGRP, EX - EIGRP external, O - OSPF, IA - OSPF inter area
       N1 - OSPF NSSA external type 1, N2 - OSPF NSSA external type 2
       E1 - OSPF external type 1, E2 - OSPF external type 2, E - EGP
       i - IS-IS, L1 - IS-IS level-1, L2 - IS-IS level-2, ia - IS-IS inter area
       * - candidate default, U - per-user static route, o - ODR
       P - periodic downloaded static route

Gateway of last resort is not set

     10.0.0.0/8 is variably subnetted, 11 subnets, 5 masks
O E2    10.1.3.0/24 [110/64] via 10.1.128.1, 00:00:03, Serial0.1
O IA    10.1.1.0/27 [110/148] via 10.1.128.1, 00:00:03, Serial0.1
O IA    10.1.1.0/24 [110/138] via 10.1.128.1, 00:00:03, Serial0.1
C       10.1.6.0/28 is directly connected, Ethernet0
O       10.1.5.0/24 [110/74] via 10.1.128.1, 00:00:04, Serial0.1
O E2    10.1.16.0/22 [110/64] via 10.1.128.1, 00:00:03, Serial0.1
O IA    10.1.80.0/24 [110/202] via 10.1.128.1, 00:00:04, Serial0.1
O E2    10.1.130.0/24 [110/64] via 10.1.128.1, 00:00:04, Serial0.1
O       10.1.129.0/24 [110/128] via 10.1.128.1, 00:00:04, Serial0.1
O       10.1.128.0/24 [110/128] via 10.1.128.1, 00:00:04, Serial0.1
C       10.1.128.0/24 is directly connected, Serial0.1
gecko#
```

The optional portion of the lab involves changing the hello interval on the tree_frog router. To perform this, you need to change the **ip ospf hello-interval** on the E2 interface of the tree_frog router. If you change the timer on just one interface, the neighbor soon will drop and routing will be compromised. Whenever changing timers in OSPF, be sure to change the timers on all routers on the same IP network. In this model, you have to change the timer on the tree_frog router and also on the python router. Example 12-64 demonstrates the timer configuration on the tree_frog router.

Example 12-64 *Changing the OSPF Hello Timer on an Interface*

```
tree_frog(config)#int e2
tree_frog(config-if)#ip ospf hello-interval 30
tree_frog(config-if)#
```

To verify the timer change, check the status of the OSPF neighbors and perform the **show ip ospf interface** command on the interface. Example 12-65 lists the OSPF interface on the tree_frog router with the new timer change. The OSPF dead timer and wait timer automatically are adjusted to four times the hello timer.

Example 12-65 *Viewing the OSPF Timer Change on tree_frog*

```
tree_frog#show ip ospf interface e2
Ethernet2 is up, line protocol is up
  Internet Address 10.1.1.1/27, Area 20
  Process ID 2001, Router ID 192.168.200.1, Network Type BROADCAST, Cost: 10
  Transmit Delay is 1 sec, State BDR, Priority 1
  Designated Router (ID) 192.168.200.8, Interface address 10.1.1.2
  Backup Designated router (ID) 192.168.200.1, Interface address 10.1.1.1
  Timer intervals configured, Hello 30, Dead 120, Wait 120, Retransmit 5
    Hello due in 00:00:11
  Neighbor Count is 1, Adjacent neighbor count is 1
    Adjacent with neighbor 192.168.200.8  (Designated Router)
  Suppress hello for 0 neighbor(s)
tree_frog#
```

Examples 12-66 concludes this lab walkthrough with the complete configurations of the routers used in the model of the HIN.

Example 12-66 *Final Configurations of the HIN*

```
hostname hin_hq
!
<<<text omitted>>>
!
interface Ethernet0
 ip address 10.1.5.1 255.255.255.0
!
interface Serial0
 no ip address
 encapsulation frame-relay
!
interface Serial0.1 point-to-point
 ip address 10.1.128.1 255.255.255.0
 frame-relay interface-dlci 121
!
interface Serial0.2 point-to-point
 ip address 10.1.129.1 255.255.255.0
 frame-relay interface-dlci 111
!
interface Serial0.3 point-to-point
 ip address 10.1.130.1 255.255.255.0
 frame-relay interface-dlci 150
!
router ospf 2001
 router-id 192.168.200.5
 summary-address 10.1.16.0 255.255.252.0
 redistribute igrp 2001 subnets tag 5
 network 10.1.5.1 0.0.0.0 area 0
 network 10.1.128.1 0.0.0.0 area 0
```

continues

Example 12-66 *Final Configurations of the HIN (Continued)*

```
 network 10.1.129.1 0.0.0.0 area 0
 default-metric 64
!
router igrp 2001
 redistribute ospf 2001
 passive-interface Ethernet0
 passive-interface Serial0.1
 passive-interface Serial0.2
 network 10.0.0.0
 default-metric 1544 10 254 1 1500
!
ip classless
!
```

```
hostname gecko
!
<<<text omitted>>>
!
interface Ethernet0
 ip address 10.1.6.1 255.255.255.240
 no ip directed-broadcast
!
interface Serial0
 no ip address
 no ip directed-broadcast
 encapsulation frame-relay
 no ip mroute-cache
 frame-relay lmi-type cisco
!
interface Serial0.1 point-to-point
 ip address 10.1.128.2 255.255.255.0

 frame-relay interface-dlci 102
!
<<<text omitted>>>
!
router ospf 2001
 router-id 192.168.200.6
 area 10 range 10.1.6.0 255.255.255.0
 network 10.1.6.1 0.0.0.0 area 10
 network 10.1.128.2 0.0.0.0 area 0
 distribute-list 10 in Serial0.1
!
ip classless
!
```

```
hostname tree_frog
!
interface Loopback0
 ip address 192.168.200.1 255.255.255.0
!
```

Example 12-66 *Final Configurations of the HIN (Continued)*

```
interface Ethernet0
 no ip address
 shutdown
 media-type 10BaseT
!
interface Ethernet1
 no ip address
 shutdown
 media-type 10BaseT
!
interface Ethernet2
 ip address 10.1.1.1 255.255.255.224
 ip ospf hello-interval 30
 media-type 10BaseT
!
interface Serial0
 no ip address
 encapsulation frame-relay
 no ip mroute-cache
!
interface Serial0.1 point-to-point
 ip address 10.1.129.2 255.255.255.0
 frame-relay interface-dlci 110
!
<<<text omitted>>>
!
router ospf 2001
 network 10.1.1.1 0.0.0.0 area 20
 network 10.1.129.2 0.0.0.0 area 0
 area 20 range 10.1.1.0 255.255.255.0
 area 20 virtual-link 192.168.200.8
!
ip classless
!
```

```
hostname python
!
<<<text omitted>>>
!
interface Loopback0
 ip address 192.168.200.8 255.255.255.0
!
interface Ethernet0
 ip address 10.1.1.2 255.255.255.224
 ip ospf hello-interval 30
!interface Serial1
 ip address 10.1.80.1 255.255.255.0
!
<<<text omitted>>>
!
```

continues

Example 12-66 *Final Configurations of the HIN (Continued)*

```
router ospf 2001
 network 10.1.80.1 0.0.0.0 area 75
 network 10.1.1.2 0.0.0.0 area 20
 area 20 virtual-link 192.168.200.1
!
ip classless
!
```

```
hostname boa
!
<<<text omitted>>>
!
interface Loopback0
 ip address 192.168.200.7 255.255.255.0
!
interface Ethernet0
 ip address 10.1.70.1 255.255.255.0
!
interface Serial1
 ip address 10.1.80.2 255.255.255.0
 clockrate 56000
!
router ospf 2001
 network 10.1.0.0 0.0.255.255 area 75
!
ip classless
!
```

```
hostname chameleon
!
<<<text omitted>>>
!
interface Loopback20
 ip address 10.1.16.1 255.255.255.0
!
interface Loopback21
 ip address 10.1.17.1 255.255.255.0
!
interface Loopback22
 ip address 10.1.18.1 255.255.255.0
!
interface Serial0
 no ip address
 encapsulation frame-relay
 frame-relay lmi-type cisco
!
interface Serial0.1 point-to-point
 ip address 10.1.130.2 255.255.255.0
 frame-relay interface-dlci 151
!
```

Example 12-66 *Final Configurations of the HIN (Continued)*

```
interface TokenRing0
 ip address 10.1.3.1 255.255.255.0
 ring-speed 16
!
router igrp 2001
 network 10.0.0.0
!
ip classless
```

Transporting Non-Routable Protocols

CHAPTER 13

Configuring Bridging and Data Link Switching Plus

Most of the early protocols were designed without explicit network addresses. For that reason, the protocol does not have the same concept of *traditional Layer 3* that we have grown to love. Protocols without explicit network layer addresses, by definition, are called *nonroutable* or *bridged protocols*. Some examples of common bridged protocols are IBM Systems Network Architecture (SNA), NetBEUI, NetBIOS, and DEC LAT.

The most commonly used bridged protocols today are SNA and NetBEUI. IBM's SNA is found in many large data centers and is perhaps the most common bridged protocol that you will encounter in the field. With the advent of Windows 9*x* and Microsoft Networking, NetBEUI started to creep across many networks as well.

Along with SNA, NetBEUI, and other nonroutable protocols comes the necessary evil of transporting them across multiple LAN segments and WAN segments. We call this a necessary evil because bridged traffic is extremely broadcast-intensive. Enabling bridging across your network can severely impact the performance of your network. For this reason, when you deploy any bridging on your network, try to control it or limit the segments of the network that it has to cross.

This chapter focuses on ways to transport *nonroutable protocols* by using the following methods:

- Transparent bridging
- Integrated routing and bridging
- Source-route bridging (SRB)
- Remote source-route bridging (RSRB)
- Data link switching (DLSw)

Transparent Bridging

Transparent bridging is used to transport nonroutable protocols across Ethernet networks. Transparent bridges first were developed by DEC in the early 1980s. DEC submitted the work to the IEEE, which incorporated it into the IEEE 802.1 standard.

The basic function of a bridge is to forward data across the network. The bridge accepts frames, briefly examines them, and then makes a forwarding decision based on the information in that frame. The bridge accomplishes this by building a bridge or station table. Figure 13-1 illustrates the bridge table in a bridged network.

Figure 13-1 *A Bridged Network*

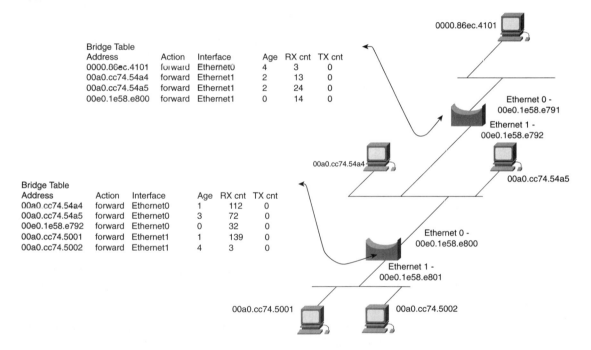

Bridges operate at the first two layers of the OSI model. Recall from Chapter 2, "LAN Protocols: Configuring Catalyst Ethernet and Token Ring Switches," that the data link layer, Layer 2, is subdivided into two layers, the MAC and LLC. Bridges primarily operate at the MAC layer, working with source and destination MAC addresses.

Transparent Bridging Operation

Basically, a bridge operates in the following manner:

1 When a transparent bridge initializes, it starts listening promiscuously to frames on the network.

2 As frames are received on an interface, the source MAC address, along with the interface/port on which it was received, are recorded in a station cache or bridge table. The bridge table keeps track of all MAC addresses that the bridge is aware of and what port they reside on.

3 As subsequent frames are received, the bridge examines the frame for destination MAC addresses. The bridge then compares the address to the addresses in the bridge table or station cache and makes one of the following decisions:

   — If the MAC address resides on the network/interface where it was received, the bridge will not forward it and, subsequently, drops the frame.

   — If the MAC address is found in the bridge table, the bridge forwards the frame only onto the interface/port specified in the table.

   — If the bridge has no record of the MAC address, it floods the frame out all ports except the port that received the frame.

4 The bridge ages each entry in the station cache and deletes it after a period of time, known as the MAX Age timer. The MAX Age timer flushes entries from the bridge table when no traffic is received with a source MAC address matching the MAC address stored in the bridge table.

Spanning Tree Review

Because bridges use the process of flooding frames from segment to segment, they need a way to control loops. Three types of loop-prevention mechanisms are available on Cisco routers:

- IEEE 802.1D Spanning-Tree Protocol (STP). This is the same protocol discussed in detail in Chapter 2.

- A digital protocol upon which this IEEE standard is based.

- An IBM form of STP used mainly for legacy transparent bridging on a Token Ring.

All forms of STP are similar, so we will focus on the primary one in use and the one used as the default for Cisco switches—802.1d.

The following information is reprinted from Chapter 2. For more details on STP, see that chapter. We also highly recommend reading Radia Perlman's book *Interconnections: Bridges and Routers*. Recall from Chapter 2 that STP transitions through the phases illustrated by Figure 13-2 and explained in the sections that follow.

Figure 13-2 *The STP Transition*

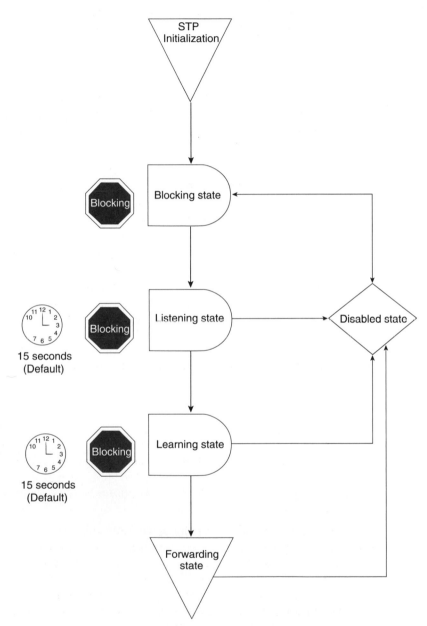

Disabled State

This state appears when a bridge having problems processes Bridged Protocol Data Units (BPDUs), when a trunk is improperly configured, or when the port is administratively down.

Listening State

When a bridge port initializes, or in the absence of BPDUs for a certain amount of time, STP transitions to the listening state. When STP is in this state, the port is actually "blocking," and no user data is sent on the link. STP follows a four-step process for convergence:

1 **Elect one root bridge**—Upon initialization, the bridge begins sending BPDUs on all bridged interfaces. A root bridge is chosen based on the bridge with the lowest bridge ID (BID). Recall that the BID is a combination of a priority and MAC address. In the event of a tie, the bridge with the lowest MAC address is chosen as root. All ports of the root bridge are put in forwarding state.

2 **Elect one root port for every nonroot bridge**—When a single root bridge has been elected, STP elects a *single* root port on each bridge/switch that is not root. The root port is the bridge's/switch's best path to the root bridge. After a root port is elected, it is put into the forwarding state. To determine what port should be a root port, STP prioritizes based on criteria in the following order:

   — Lowest root BID

   — Lowest path cost to root bridge; the cumulative cost of the all paths to root

   — Lowest sender BID

   — Lowest port ID

   When a bridge receives a BPDU, it stores it in a bridge table for that port. As new BPDUs are received on that port, they are compared to existing BPDUs. Using the four-step process listed previously, BPDUs that are more attractive or that have lower costs, are kept, and the other ones are discarded. The primary variable that influences the root port election is *the cost to the root bridge*. The cost to the root bridge is the cumulative path cost of all links to root bridge.

3 **Elect one designated port/designated bridge for every segment**—For every segment, STP elects one port that will send and receive all information from that segment to the root bridge. A root port can be thought of as the port that forwards information to the root, whereas the designated port can be thought of as the port that sends traffic away from the root. This rule applies mostly to shared-media bridges, or routers. Designated ports on switched trunk lines do not follow this rule.

4 **All remaining ports will become nondesignated ports and are put in blocking mode**.

Learning State

Ports that remain designated or root ports for a period of 15 seconds, the default forward delay, enter the learning state. In the learning state, the bridge waits another 15 seconds while it builds its bridge table.

Forwarding and Blocking States

When the bridge reaches this phase, ports that do not serve a special purpose, such a root port or a designated port, are called nondesignated ports. All designated ports are put in forwarding state, while all nondesignated ports are put in a blocking state. In the blocking state, a bridge does not send any configuration BPDUs, but it still listens to them. A blocking port also does not forward any user data.

STP Timers

STP has three basic timers that regulate and age BPDUs:

- **Hello timer**—The default hello timer is 2 seconds. This is the amount of time between configuration BPDUs sent by the root bridge.

- **Forward delay**—This timer is the default 15 seconds that the router/bridge waits while building its bridging table. The listening and learning stages each use this single 15-second timer.

- **MAX Age**—This timer indicates how long a BPDU is stored before it is flushed. If this timer expires before the interface receives a new BPDU, the interface transitions to the listening state. An expired MAX Age parameter usually is caused by a link failure. The default value is 20 seconds.

STP uses the hello timer to space BPDUs and has a keepalive mechanism. The hello timer always should prevent the MAX age value from being hit. When the MAX Age timer expires, it usually indicates a link failure. When this happens, the bridge re-enters the listening state. It takes approximately 50 seconds for STP to recover from a link failure; 20 seconds for the BPDU to age out, the MAX Age; 15 seconds for listening; and 15 seconds for the learning state.

Configuring Transparent Bridging

Configuring transparent bridging is a simple three-step process:

Step 1   Assign a bridge group number and define the Spanning-Tree Protocol. This is accomplished with this global command:

```
Router(config)# bridge-group [1-255] protocol [ieee | ibm | dec]
```

Step 2   Assign each network interface that is to be bridged to a bridge group by using the following interface command:

```
Router(config-if)# bridge-group [1-255]
```

If the interface is a Frame Relay multipoint interface, a **frame-relay map** statement will be needed to map the bridge to a DLCI. The **frame-relay map** interface command is as follows:

```
Router(config-if)# frame-relay map bridge [DLCI Number_16-1007]
broadcast
```

If the interface is a DDR interfaces, such as an ISDN interface, a dialer-map statement will be needed to transport the bridged traffic across the DDR link.

```
Router(config-if)# dialer map bridge [name {remote_host_name}]
broadcast dialer_string
```

Step 3   (Optional) Configure root for the Spanning Tree. Select which bridge or interface will serve as root. As mentioned previously, there are a couple of ways to influence root. The best and most direct way is to set the STP priority. STP priority can be set on the interface or global level, depending on how you want to influence root selection. The lower the priority, the more likely the bridge will become root. Use the following commands to influence STP root selection:

To set the bridge priority, use the following global command:

```
Router(config)# bridge-group [1-255] priority [0-65535]
```

To set the bridge port priority, use the following interface command:

```
Router(config-if)# bridge-group [1-255] priority [1-255]
```

To set the bridge path cost, use the following interface command:

```
Router(config-if)# bridge-group [1-255] path-cost [0-65535]
```

The first step in setting up transparent bridging is to define a Spanning-Tree Protocol and assign it a bridge group number. You can choose either the IEEE 802.1D Spanning-Tree Protocol or the Digital or IBM versions. The IEEE 802.1D Spanning-Tree Protocol is the preferred way of running the bridge. Use the Digital Spanning-Tree Protocol or the IBM version only for backward compatibility.

The next step is to assign each network interface to a bridge group. A bridge group is defined by Cisco as follows:

An internal organization of network interfaces on a router. Bridge groups within the same router function as distinct bridges; that is, bridged traffic and bridge protocol data units (BPDUs) cannot be exchanged between different bridge groups on a router. Furthermore, bridge groups cannot be used to multiplex or demultiplex different streams of bridged traffic on a LAN. An interface can be a member of only one bridge group.

If you are configuring bridging over a Frame Relay multipoint network or DDR network, an additional **map** statement will be needed to carry the bridged traffic over the network.

A couple of reasons exist for placing the interface into a bridge group:

- To bridge all *nonroutable* traffic among the network interfaces making up the bridge group.

- To participate in a common Spanning-Tree Algorithm by receiving and transmitting BPDUs on the LANs that are in the same bridge group. A separate spanning process runs for each configured bridge group. Each bridge group participates in a separate Spanning Tree.

In Figure 13-3, interfaces e0 and e1 are in bridge group 1. These interfaces will forward bridged traffic to another. Interface e3 is not part of the bridge group and will not receive traffic from the bridge group.

Figure 13-3 *Transparent Bridging Bridge Groups*

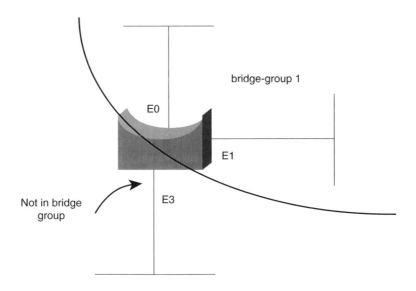

TIP   An effective way to isolate bridged traffic on switched networks is to create a VLAN just for bridged traffic. Any devices that require bridged traffic will exist on this VLAN. Data-link switching then can be used to take this VLAN traffic or bridged traffic across the LAN or WAN, without *propagating* its traffic to every segment in between.

Transparent Bridging Model

Figure 13-4 presents a practical example of transparent bridging. In this model, the workstations are MS Windows 9*x* running NetBEUI, a nonroutable protocol. For the workstations to communicate, transparent bridging must be enabled across the Frame Relay network and on the Ethernet interfaces of the routers shuttle_5 and shuttle_6.

Figure 13-4 *Transparent Bridging*

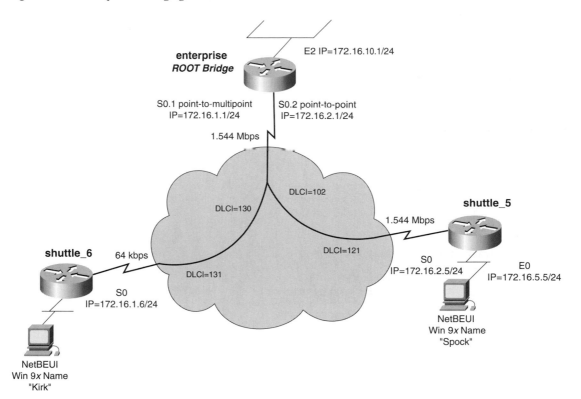

To enable transparent bridging on the enterprise router, follow the three-step process. Begin by assigning a bridge group and STP to the bridging domain. This is accomplished with the global router command **bridge group 1 protocol ieee.** In this model, you will be using 802.1d as the Spanning-Tree Protocol. The second step involves assigning interfaces to bridge groups. This is done with the interface command **bridge-group 1.** On the enterprise router, this command must be entered on the E0 interface, s0.1 and s0.2 Frame Relay interfaces. Because S0.1 is a Frame Relay multipoint, it also needs to have a **frame-relay map bridge** statement, mapping a specific DLCI to the bridge. Finally, the third step involves setting a root bridge. In this model, we have chosen the enterprise router to be the root for

STP. To force root selection, we elected to use the global router command **bridge-group 1 priority 100**, setting the bridge priority of the enterprise router/bridge to be 100. Example 13-1 lists the configuration of the enterprise router.

Example 13-1 *Transparent Bridge Configuration on the enterprise Router*

```
hostname enterprise
!
<<<text omitted>>>
!
interface Ethernet2
 ip address 172.16.10.1 255.255.255.0
 no ip directed-broadcast
 media-type 10BaseT
 bridge-group 1                        ←Assign E2 to bridge 1
!
<<<text omitted>>>
!
interface Serial0
 no ip address
 no ip directed-broadcast
 encapsulation frame-relay
 no ip mroute-cache
 logging event subif-link-status
 logging event dlci-status-change
 frame-relay lmi-type cisco
!
interface Serial0.1 multipoint
 ip address 172.16.1.1 255.255.255.0
 no ip directed-broadcast
 frame-relay map bridge 130 broadcast        ←Map statement needed for bridging
 frame-relay map ip 172.16.1.6 130 broadcast
 bridge-group 1                          ←Assign S0.1 to bridge 1
!
interface Serial0.2 point-to-point
 ip address 172.16.2.1 255.255.255.0
 no ip directed-broadcast
 frame-relay interface-dlci 102
 bridge-group 1                          ←Assign S0.2 to bridge 1
!
<<<text omitted>>>
!
bridge 1 protocol ieee             ←Define bridge 1 with 802.1d as the STP
bridge 1 priority 100              ←Set Bridge Priority to 100, forcing ROOT
!
```

The configurations of the shuttle_5 and shuttle_6 routers resemble the enterprise router's configuration. Example 13-2 lists the bridging portions of the shuttle_5 and shuttle_6 routers, respectively. Note that the Frame Relay map statements are needed only on Frame Relay multipoint networks.

Example 13-2 *Transparent Bridge Configuration on the shuttle_5 and shuttle_6 Routers*

```
hostname shuttle_5
!
interface Ethernet0
 ip address 172.16.5.5 255.255.255.0
 bridge-group 1                        ←Assign E0 to bridge 1
!
interface Serial0
 ip address 172.16.2.5 255.255.255.0
 encapsulation frame-relay
 frame-relay interface-dlci 121
 frame-relay lmi-type cisco
 bridge-group 1                        ←Assign S0 to bridge 1
!
<<<text omitted>>>
!
bridge 1 protocol ieee                 ←Define bridge 1 with 802.1d as the STP
 !
```

```
hostname shuttle_6
!!
interface Ethernet0
 ip address 172.16.6.6 255.255.255.0
 no ip directed-broadcast
 bridge-group 1                        ←Assign E0 to bridge 1
 !
interface Serial0                      ←Remember this is a multi-point!
 ip address 172.16.1.6 255.255.255.0
 no ip directed-broadcast
 encapsulation frame-relay
 no ip mroute-cache
 no fair-queue
 frame-relay map bridge 131 broadcast         ←Map bridge 1 to DLCI 131
 frame-relay map ip 172.16.1.1 131 broadcast
 bridge-group 1                        ←Assign S0 to bridge 1
!
<<<text omitted>>>
!
bridge 1 protocol ieee                 ←Define bridge 1 with 802.1d as the STP
```

Verifying Transparent Bridging, the "Big show" for Transparent Bridging and STP

Cisco offers some useful commands that aid in verifying the operation of the bridging environment. I can't recommend using any of the **debug** commands for transparent bridging. The ones available are cryptic or offer little valuable information—for example:

```
11:23:34: ST: Serial0.1 00000000000800000605CF35DA40000000000800000605CF35DA4800600
00140002000F00
```

Instead of trying to break down the bit stream that **debug spantree tree** provides, use other commands that prove to be more useful and easier to understand. The big **show** commands are as follows:

```
show bridge [bridge_number]
show spanning-tree [bridge_number]
```

show bridge Command

The **show bridge** command shows the current state of the bridge, the MAC addresses it has learned, and whether it is forwarding on specific interfaces. Age and transmit and receive counts are also listed. If the bridge number is appended to the command, it lists the known bridge ports and the STP state they are in: learning, listening, forwarding, or blocking. Example 13-3 demonstrates the versions of the **show bridge** command on the shuttle_5 router from the previous model. For a more detailed explanation of the STP states, see Chapter 2.

Example 13-3 **show bridge** *Command Output on the shuttle_5 Router*

```
shuttle_5#show bridge

Total of 300 station blocks, 296 free
Codes: P - permanent, S - self

Bridge Group 1:

    Address         Action    Interface     Age    RX count   TX count
0000.8139.6c45      forward   Ethernet0     0          248          0
0000.863c.3b41      forward   Serial0       0          126        107
00e0.b055.5789      forward   Serial0       0          506          0
00a0.cc74.54a4      forward   Ethernet0     0          449        157


shuttle_5#show bridge group

Bridge Group 1 is running the IEEE compatible Spanning Tree protocol

    Port 2 (Ethernet0) of bridge group 1 is forwarding
    Port 6 (Serial0 Frame Relay) of bridge group 1 is forwarding
```

show spanning-tree Command

The **show spanning-tree** command for bridges provides nearly identical information as the **show spanning-tree** command found on the Catalyst switches. The relevant information that this command provides is the current root of the Spanning Tree, the cost to root, its priority, as well as detailed STP timer information. For more specific information on the fields listed and their meaning, review the section, "802.1d Spanning-Tree Protocol (STP)" in Chapter 2. Example 13-4 lists the output of the **show spanning-tree** command on the enterprise router from the previous model. Note that this bridge is root and has a priority of 100, just as configured in the model.

Example 13-4 **show spanning-tree** *Command on the enterprise Router*

```
enterprise#show spanning-tree

 Bridge group 1 is executing the IEEE compatible Spanning Tree protocol
  Bridge Identifier has priority 100, address 00e0.1e58.e798
  Configured hello time 2, max age 20, forward delay 15
  We are the root of the spanning tree
  Topology change flag not set, detected flag not set
  Times:  hold 1, topology change 35, notification 2
          hello 2, max age 20, forward delay 15
  Timers: hello 0, topology change 0, notification 0
  bridge aging time 300

Port 8 (Ethernet2) of Bridge group 1 is forwarding
   Port path cost 100, Port priority 128
   Designated root has priority 100, address 00e0.1e58.e798
   Designated bridge has priority 100, address 00e0.1e58.e798
   Designated port is 8, path cost 0
   Timers: message age 0, forward delay 0, hold 0
   BPDU: sent 876, received 0

Port 13 (Serial0.1 Frame Relay) of Bridge group 1 is forwarding
   Port path cost 647, Port priority 128
   Designated root has priority 100, address 00e0.1e58.e798
   Designated bridge has priority 100, address 00e0.1e58.e798
   Designated port is 13, path cost 0
   Timers: message age 0, forward delay 0, hold 0
   BPDU: sent 632, received 2

Port 14 (Serial0.2 Frame Relay) of Bridge group 1 is forwarding
   Port path cost 647, Port priority 128
   Designated root has priority 100, address 00e0.1e58.e798
   Designated bridge has priority 100, address 00e0.1e58.e798
   Designated port is 14, path cost 0
   Timers: message age 0, forward delay 0, hold 0
   BPDU: sent 347, received 0

enterprise#
```

NOTE   Various levels of Cisco IOS Software Release 12.0 have Spanning Tree disabled by default. To enable Spanning Tree, use the command **no bridge-group** *bridge_number* **spanning-disabled.**

Verifying Transparent Bridging with Windows 9x or 2000

Windows 9x or 2000 with Microsoft networking enabled—or, more specifically, NetBEUI enabled—provides a great test application for all bridged and DLSw networks. To test any bridging type environments, use two Windows workstations with Microsoft networking and NetBEUI enabled. If you also enable Microsoft file and print sharing, you will be able to test file transfers across the bridged or DLSw network. Using the network browser or the Find Computer application in Windows, you can force broadcast data across the network. For more information on configuring Windows networking, see Chapter 1, "The Key Components for Modeling an Internetwork," or consult the Microsoft documentation.

Integrated Routing and Bridging

Integrated routing and bridging (IRB) allows you to bridge local traffic within several segments while having hosts on the bridged segments reach the hosts or routers on routed networks. It essentially can allow a routed domain to reach a bridge domain.

Using the IRB feature, you can route a given protocol between routed interfaces and bridge groups within a single router. Specifically, local or *unroutable traffic* will be bridged among the bridged interfaces in the same bridge group, while routable traffic will be routed to other routed interfaces or bridge groups.

Integrated routing and bridging uses the concept of a Bridge-Group Virtual Interface (BVI) to enable these interfaces to exchange packets for a given protocol. A BVI is a virtual interface within the router that acts like a normal *routed* interface. A BVI does not support bridging, but it actually represents the corresponding bridge group to routed interfaces within the router. The interface number is the link between the BVI and the bridge group. All Layer 3 information, such as IP address, or filters are applied to the BVI, not the actual physical interface.

IRB Considerations

Before enabling IRB, you should be aware of the following:

- The default route/bridge behavior on a router is to route all packets first and then bridge them. This is precisely why configuring transparent bridging does not impact the routed domain. However, when the IRB is enabled, the behavior changes to bridge all packets first. The bridge group must be enabled to route with command **bridge** *bridge_number* **route ip** if routing IP also is enabled.

- Packets of *nonroutable protocols,* such as local-area transport (LAT) or SNA, always are bridged. You cannot disable bridging for the nonroutable protocols.

- Bridging attributes cannot be configured on a BVI interface.

- IRB supercedes concurrent routing and bridging (CRB), which no longer should be used.

Figure 13-5 illustrates a common IRB environment. In this figure, note that there are no Layer 3 addresses on the Ethernet interfaces that are in the bridged domain. These interfaces are made part of the BVI by being members of the same bridge group. The BVI number—in this case, 10—must be the bridge number. This number is how the two domains are linked. The BVI interface is where all layer information goes for the protocol that you want to bridge and route. In this figure, you simply have an IP address. By adding an IP address to the BVI interface, it instructs the router to start to bridge IP on all interfaces that are a member of bridge group 10.

Figure 13-5 *Integrated Routing and Bridging*

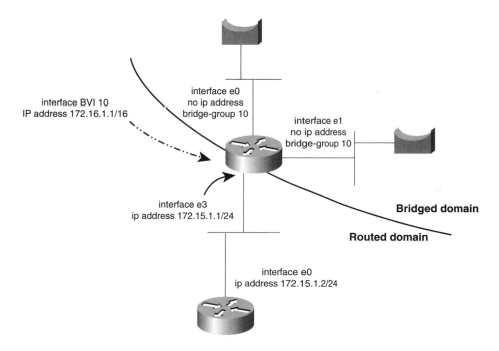

Configuring IRB

Configuring IRB is a three-step process. The steps are as follows:

Step 1 Configure transparent bridging on the interfaces that you want to bridge and route. Use the process defined earlier. Recall that this consists of creating a bridge group and assigning interfaces to that group.

Step 2   Configure IRB and the BVI. Assign the same bridge number to the BVI interface. For example if you use bridge 2, the BVI will be **interface bvi 2**. To enable IRB, use the following syntax from the router global configuration prompt:

```
Router(config)# bridge irb
Router(config)# interface bvi bridge-group_number
```

Step 3   Configure protocol-specific routing and bridging for the bridge group. This step is extremely important. As soon as you enable IRB with the **bridge irb** command, all interfaces in that bridge group, or all interfaces that have transparent bridging enabled on them, will now bridge all protocols first. This can and will have devastating effects where routing is needed for another protocol on those links. Because of this, all Layer 3 protocols must be told whether to route, bridge, or do both. To accomplish this, you must complete two steps:

(a)   Assign all Layer 3 addresses of the protocol that you want to *bridge and route* to the BVI interface. No Layer 3 addresses should reside on the physical interface for the protocol that you want to bridge and route.

(b)   Enable or disable routing and bridging on a per-protocol basis.

To enable bridging or routing per protocol, use the following syntax from the global configuration prompt:

```
Router(config)# bridge bridge_number [route | bridge] [ip | ipx |
appletalk | decnet]
```

To disable bridging or routing per protocol, use the following syntax from the global configuration prompt:

```
Router(config)# no bridge bridge_number [route | bridge] [ip | ipx |
appletalk | decnet]
```

To view whether the router is routing, bridging, or both for any given protocol, use the command **show interface irb**, as demonstrated in Example 13-5.

Example 13-5 show interface irb *Command Output*

```
irb_router#show int irb

Ethernet2

  Routed protocols on Ethernet2:
    ip          ipx

  Bridged protocols on Ethernet2:
    appletalk  clns         decnet      vines
    apollo     xns
```

Example 13-5 **show interface irb** *Command Output (Continued)*

```
Software MAC address filter on Ethernet2
  Hash Len    Address     Matches  Act     Type
  0x00:  0 ffff.ffff.ffff          0 RCV Physical broadcast
  0x2A:  0 0900.2b01.0001          0 RCV DEC spanning tree
  0x86:  0 00e0.1e58.e798          0 RCV Interface MAC address
  0xC0:  0 0100.0ccc.cccc          0 RCV CDP
  0xC2:  0 0180.c200.0000          0 RCV IEEE spanning tree
  0xC2:  1 0180.c200.0000          0 RCV IBM spanning tree
```

Practical Example: Configuring IRB

Figure 13-6 shows a network where you want to bridge and route IP on interfaces e2 and e3. To configure IRB on this router, you begin by defining a bridge group and placing the interfaces that you want to bridge and route into that bridge group. In this example, we have made bridge group 5 and placed interfaces e2 and e3 into that bridge group.

Figure 13-6 *Integrated Routing and Bridging Example*

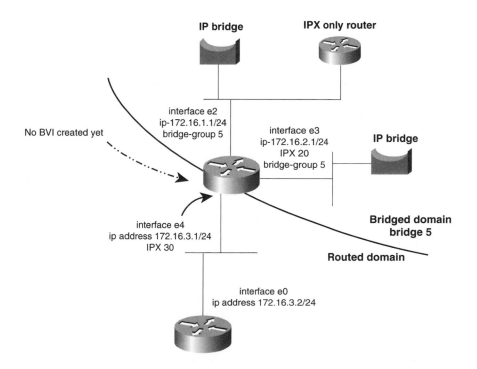

If you examine IRB, at this point, it looks much like a normal router. Example 13-6 lists the output of the **show interface irb** command on the irb_router. Notice that the router is either bridging or routing IP, but not both.

Example 13-6 show interface irb *Command Output*

```
irb_router#show int irb

Ethernet2

 Routed protocols on Ethernet2:
   ip        ipx

 Bridged protocols on Ethernet2:
   appletalk clns        decnet      vines
   apollo    xns

 Software MAC address filter on Ethernet2
   Hash Len   Address        Matches Act      Type
   0x00:  0 ffff.ffff.ffff         0 RCV Physical broadcast
   0x2A:  0 0900.2b01.0001         0 RCV DEC spanning tree
   0x86:  0 00e0.1e58.e798         0 RCV Interface MAC address
   0xC0:  0 0100.0ccc.cccc         0 RCV CDP
   0xC2:  0 0180.c200.0000         0 RCV IEEE spanning tree
   0xC2:  1 0180.c200.0000         0 RCV IBM spanning tree

Ethernet3

 Routed protocols on Ethernet3:
   ip        ipx

 Bridged protocols on Ethernet3:
   appletalk clns        decnet      vines
   apollo    xns

 Software MAC address filter on Ethernet3
   Hash Len   Address        Matches Act      Type
   0x00:  0 ffff.ffff.ffff         0 RCV Physical broadcast
   0x2A:  0 0900.2b01.0001         0 RCV DEC spanning tree
   0x85:  0 00e0.1e58.e79b         0 RCV Interface MAC address
   0xC0:  0 0100.0ccc.cccc         0 RCV CDP
   0xC2:  0 0180.c200.0000         0 RCV IEEE spanning tree
   0xC2:  1 0180.c200.0000         0 RCV IBM spanning tree

Ethernet4

 Routed protocols on Ethernet4:
   ip        ipx
irb_router#
```

The second step in the configuration involves enabling IRB and creating the BVI. Because you are using bridge 5, the BVI interface will be 5, too. When the BVI is created, the router generates the statements needed to route whatever Layer 3 protocol it discovers on a transparently bridged interface. Example 13-7 shows this happening when IRB was enabled in the model. In this model, IPX and IP are enabled on a transparently bridged interface, so both commands were generated.

Example 13-7 *Enabling IRB*

```
irb_router(config)#bridge irb
IRB: generating 'bridge 5 route ip' configuration command
IRB: generating 'bridge 5 route novell' configuration command
irb_router(config)#int bvi 5
04:17:56: %LINEPROTO-5-UPDOWN: Line protocol on Interface BVI5, changed state to
  up
irb_router(config-if)#
```

Now you want to remove the Layer 3 address of the protocol that we want to route and bridge from the physical interface. All other Layer 3 addresses, the ones that you do not want to bridge and route on, should remain on the physical interface. Assign the Layer 3 address of the protocol to bridge and route to the BVI interface. Figure 13-7 illustrates the changes that you need to make to the network.

Figure 13-7 *Addressing and Creating the BVI*

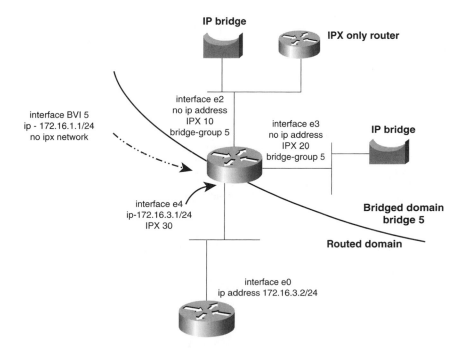

After the IP address changes have been made, the model is almost complete. At this point, IP is being bridged and routed, and this can be verified with the **show int irb** command, as in Example 13-8.

Example 13-8 show interface irb *Command Output*

```
irb_router#show int irb

BVI5

 Routed protocols on BVI5:
  ip

Ethernet2

 Routed protocols on Ethernet2:
  ip          ipx

 Bridged protocols on Ethernet2:
  appletalk  clns       decnet     ip
  vines      apollo     ipx        xns

 Software MAC address filter on Ethernet2
  Hash Len    Address        Matches  Act     Type
  0x00:  0 ffff.ffff.ffff         0 RCV Physical broadcast
  0x2A:  0 0900.2b01.0001         0 RCV DEC spanning tree
  0x86:  0 00e0.1e58.e798         0 RCV Interface MAC address
  0x86:  1 00e0.1e58.e798         0 RCV Bridge-group Virtual Interface
  0xC0:  0 0100.0ccc.cccc         0 RCV CDP
  0xC2:  0 0180.c200.0000         0 RCV IEEE spanning tree
  0xC2:  1 0180.c200.0000         0 RCV IBM spanning tree

Ethernet3

 Routed protocols on Ethernet3:
  ip          ipx

 Bridged protocols on Ethernet3:
  appletalk  clns       decnet     ip
  vines      apollo     ipx        xns

 Software MAC address filter on Ethernet3
  Hash Len    Address        Matches  Act     Type
  0x00:  0 ffff.ffff.ffff         0 RCV Physical broadcast
  0x2A:  0 0900.2b01.0001         0 RCV DEC spanning tree
  0x85:  0 00e0.1e58.e79b         0 RCV Interface MAC address
  0x86:  0 00e0.1e58.e798         0 RCV Bridge-group Virtual Interface
  0xC0:  0 0100.0ccc.cccc         0 RCV CDP
  0xC2:  0 0180.c200.0000         0 RCV IEEE spanning tree
  0xC2:  1 0180.c200.0000         0 RCV IBM spanning tree
```

Example 13-8 **show interface irb** *Command Output (Continued)*

```
Ethernet4

 Routed protocols on Ethernet4:
   ip          ipx
irb_router#
```

By observing the output of Example 13-8, you can see that the BVI appears as a normal interface, much like interface E4. Notice that only IP is running on the BVI because that is the only protocol that you want to bridge and route.

Notice in this model that you have a downstream IPX router. All IPX traffic first is bridged, and this causes problems with the downstream IPX router. To remedy this, the second part of Step 3 calls for you to disable IPX bridging with the command **no bridge 5 bridge ipx.** After keying in this command, you can view the IRB interface and note the changes. IPX no longer is bridged and routed on the interfaces E2 and E3; it is only routed. Example 13-9 lists the output of the **show irb** command, illustrating that IPX no longer is bridged and routed.

Example 13-9 **show interface irb** *Command Output*

```
irb_router#show int irb
BVI5

 Routed protocols on BVI5:
   ip

Ethernet2

 Routed protocols on Ethernet2:
   ip          ipx

 Bridged protocols on Ethernet2:
   appletalk  clns       decnet     ip
   vines      apollo     xns

 Software MAC address filter on Ethernet2
   Hash Len    Address        Matches Act      Type
   0x00:   0 ffff.ffff.ffff         0 RCV Physical broadcast
   0x2A:   0 0900.2b01.0001         0 RCV DEC spanning tree
   0x86:   0 00e0.1e58.e798         0 RCV Interface MAC address
   0x86:   1 00e0.1e58.e798         0 RCV Bridge-group Virtual Interface
   0xC0:   0 0100.0ccc.cccc         0 RCV CDP
   0xC2:   0 0180.c200.0000         0 RCV IEEE spanning tree
   0xC2:   1 0180.c200.0000         0 RCV IBM spanning tree

Ethernet3
```

continues

Example 13-9 **show interface irb** *Command Output (Continued)*

```
 Routed protocols on Ethernet3:
   ip        ipx

 Bridged protocols on Ethernet3:
   appletalk  clns      decnet    ip
   vines      apollo    xns

 Software MAC address filter on Ethernet3
   Hash Len    Address        Matches  Act      Type
   0x00:  0 ffff.ffff.ffff        0 RCV Physical broadcast
   0x2A:  0 0900.2b01.0001        0 RCV DEC spanning tree
   0x85:  0 00e0.1e58.e79b        0 RCV Interface MAC address
   0x86:  0 00e0.1e58.e798        0 RCV Bridge-group Virtual Interface
   0xC0:  0 0100.0ccc.cccc        0 RCV CDP
   0xC2:  0 0180.c200.0000        0 RCV IEEE spanning tree
   0xC2:  1 0180.c200.0000        0 RCV IBM spanning tree

Ethernet4

 Routed protocols on Ethernet4:
   ip        ipx
irb_router#
```

Example 13-10 lists the configuration that we created for this model.

Example 13-10 *IRB Configuration for This Model*

```
hostname irb_router
!
ip subnet-zero
ipx routing 00e0.1e58.e792
!
bridge irb
!
<<<text omitted>>>
!
interface Ethernet2
 no ip address
 no ip directed-broadcast
 media-type 10BaseT
 ipx network 10
 bridge-group 5
!
interface Ethernet3
 no ip address
 no ip directed-broadcast
 media-type 10BaseT
 ipx network 20
 bridge-group 5
!
```

Example 13-10 *IRB Configuration for This Model (Continued)*

```
interface Ethernet4
 ip address 172.16.3.1 255.255.255.0
 no ip directed-broadcast
 media-type 10BaseT
 ipx network 30
!
<<<text omitted>>>
!
interface BVI5
 ip address 172.16.1.1 255.255.255.0
 no ip directed-broadcast
!
router eigrp 2001
 network 172.16.0.0
!
ip classless
!
bridge 5 protocol ieee
 bridge 5 route ip
 bridge 5 route ipx
 no bridge 5 bridge ipx
!
```

Source Route Bridging (SRB)

At the same time that the IEEE 802.1 committee was considering adapting transparent bridging for the standard to connect LANs, it also was reviewing source-route bridging as an alternative. As history tells us, the IEEE 802.1 committee adopted transparent bridging. When this happened, source-route bridging was presented before the IEEE 802.5, where it found a home as the protocol to connect IBM Token Ring LANs and IEEE 802.5 LANs. Figure 13-8 represents the 802.5 Token Ring frame.

Figure 13-8 *IEEE 802.5 Token Ring Frame Format*

Token Ring 802.5	SD	AC	FC	Destination Address	Source Address	Routing Information Field	Information Field	FCS	ED	FS

Source-Route Bridging Overview

Source-route bridging uses a combination of explorer packets and a RIF field to determine the best path through the bridged network. A source-route bridge uses the routing information field (RIF) in the IEEE 802.5 MAC header of a datagram, as in Figure 13-9, to determine which rings or Token Ring network segments the packet must transit. This is where the "route" in source route comes from.

Figure 13-9 *IEEE 802.5 MAC Frame Format*

Destination Address	RII	Source Address	RIF	DATA	FCS

The RIF is inserted into the MAC header immediately following the source address field in every frame by the source station. The destination station reverses the routing field to reach the originating station. Unlike transparent Spanning Tree bridging that requires time—50 seconds to converge in the event of failures—source-route bridging allows multiple active paths through the network, which provides an extremely efficient way to use alternate paths in the event of a failure. Most importantly, source-route bridging places the burden of transmitting frames on the end stations by allowing them to determine the best routes for frames across the network. The IBM Token Ring specifies a maximum number of 8 rings and 7 bridges in the RIF, while 802.5 specifies a maximum of 14 rings and 13 bridges. Figure 13-9 represents the 802.5 MAC Frame.

The *ring* in a Token Ring network is designated in the routing information identifier (RII) by a unique 12-bit ring number ranging from 1 to 4095. Each *bridge* between two Token Rings is designated by a unique 4-bit bridge number in the RIF. The valid bridge numbers are 1 to 15. Bridge numbers must be unique only between bridges that connect the same two Token Rings. If the RII is set to 0, there will be no RIF in the frame; if the RII is set to 1, a RIF will be included in the frame.

The RIF Field

The RIF is composed of 16–bit routing control fields and routing descriptor fields. Figure 13-10 illustrates the basic RIF format.

Figure 13-10 *Basic RIF Format*

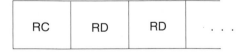

RC	RD	RD	. . .

RC = Routing Control field
RD = Routing Descriptor
Each block is 16 bits wide.

Figure 13-11 illustrates the routing control format for the RIF, followed by the descriptions of each field.

Figure 13-11 *RIF Routing Control Format*

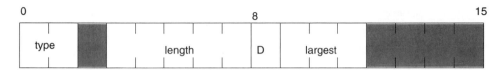

- Shaded fields are reserved.
- **type**—The explorer type is used, as follows:
  - — 00: Specific routes explorer
  - — 10: All rings, all-routes explorer
  - — 11: All rings, spanning routes (limited broadcast)
- **length**—This is the total length in bytes of the RIF.
- **D**—This is the direction, indicated as follows:
  - — **0:** Interpret route left to right (forward)
  - — **1:** Interpret route right to left (reverse)
- **largest**—This is the largest frame that can be handled by this route, as follows:
  - — **000:** 516 bytes (DDN 1822)
  - — **001:** 1500 bytes (Ethernet)
  - — **010:** 2052 bytes
  - — **011:** 4472 bytes (Token Ring and Cisco maximum)
  - — **100:** 8144 bytes (Token Bus)
  - — **101:** 11,407 bytes
  - — **110:** 17,800 bytes
  - — **111:** 65,535 (initial values)

Figure 13-12 describes the routing descriptor format of the RIF string. When you configure a static RIF or when a RIF is represented, it is represented in dotted hexadecimal.

Figure 13-12 *Routing Descriptor Format*

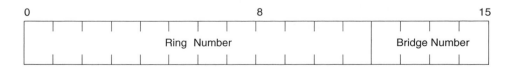

- **Ring number**—Unique decimal ring number within the bridged network.

- **Bridge number**—Unique decimal bridge number between any bridges connecting the same two rings. A bridge number of 0 indicates that the RIF is terminating.

Figure 13-13 shows an SRB network. The RIF from station Alpha to station Bravo would read as follows:

```
0830.0012.002a.00b0
```

The 0830 is the 16-bit RC field, and 0012, 002a, and 00b0 are the three 16-bit RD fields. The first four bits, from left to right, state that the explorer type is 0, or a specific routes explorer. The 8 says that the entire RIF is 8 bytes in length. The D bit is set to 0, indicating that the RIF is read from left to right, or forward. The next three bits are set to 011, which sets the frame size to be 4472, the Cisco maximum. The RD fields break down rather easily:

```
RING1-BRIDGE2 = 0012
RING2-BRIDGE10 = 002a
RING11-BRIDGE0 = 00b0
```

A bridge of 0 tells the SRB to terminate the RIF and that no more bridges follow the ring. For more information on configuring a static RIF, see the section entitled "Configuring a Static RIF."

Figure 13-13 *Source-Route Bridge—RIF*

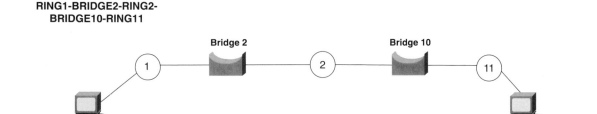

A source-route bridge can determine whether to forward an explorer into a ring by looking at the RIF field. An explorer packet will not be forwarded to a ring where a duplicate ring-bridge-ring pattern already exists in the RIF.

The information in a RIF is derived from explorer frames generated by the source node. These explorer packets traverse the entire source-route bridge network, gathering information on the possible paths the source node might use to forward traffic. SRBs use three types of explorer frames:

- **All-routes explorer or all-rings explorer**—This type of explorer is propagated from ring to ring from each SRB toward its destination. The destination station receives an all-routes explorer and forwards a directed, nonbroadcast frame back at the source that originated it.

- **Specific routes explorer or local explorer**—This type of explorer is used by the end station to locate a specific station on a local ring. NetBIOS and SNA produce these types of explorers.

- **Spanning explorer or limited routes explorer**—Spanning explorer can be propagated only if the Token Ring interface has source-bridge spanning enabled. Protocols such as NetBIOS require this type of explorer frame. When an end station receives a spanning explorer, it responds with an all-routes explorer frame sent toward the originating station.

Figures 13-14 and 13-15 illustrate how the all-routes explorers and spanning explorers operate.

Figure 13-14 *SRB All-Routes Explorer*

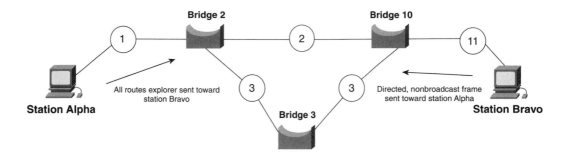

Figure 13-15 *SRB Spanning Explorer*

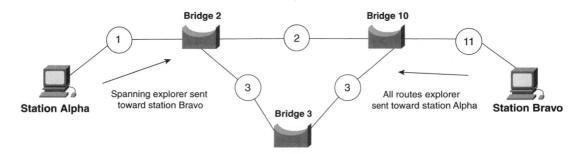

Configuring Source-Route Bridging

Source-route bridging can be configured in three primary ways:

- Basic local SRB
- Multiport local SRB
- Remote source-route bridging (RSRB)

Configuring Basic Local Source-Route Bridging

Local SRB in its simplest form exists between two rings on a router. Figure 13-16 illustrates this type of configuration.

Figure 13-16   *Basic Local SRB Configuration*

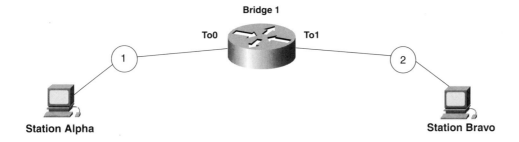

To configure this type of SRB, follow this two-step process:

Step 1   Enable the use of the RIF, if required, with the router interface command **multiring all**. The full syntax is as follows:

```
Router(config-if)#multiring {protocol-keyword | all | other}
    no multiring {protocol-keyword | all | other}
```

The Cisco IOS Software allows you to also specify a protocol. This is specified by the argument *protocol-keyword*. This keyword allows for per-protocol specification of the interface's capability to append RIFs to routed protocols. When it is enabled for a protocol, the router will source packets that include information used by source-route bridges. The protocols supported and the keywords are as follows:

— **apollo**—Apollo Domain

— **appletalk**—AppleTalk Phases 1 and 2

— **clns**—ISO CLNS

— **decnet**—DECnet Phase IV

— **ip**—IP

— **novell**—Novell IPX

— **vines**—Banyan VINES

— **xns**—XNS

Two other keywords are used with the **multiring** command. The keyword **all** enables the RIF for *all* frames, and this is the recommend use. The keyword **other** enables the RIF for *any* routed frame not included in the previous list of supported protocols. The **no multiring** subcommand with the appropriate keyword disables the use of RIF information for the protocol specified.

Step 2   Configure SRB for the Token Ring interface. This is accomplished with the following interface command:

```
Router(config-if)#source-bridge local_ring bridge_number
destination_ring
```

The configuration for SRB is shown in Example 13-11.

Example 13-11 *Local SRB Configuration*

```
interface TokenRing0
 no ip address
 no ip directed-broadcast
 ring-speed 16
 multiring all          ←RIF enabled
 source-bridge 1 1 2       ←From ring 1 thru bridge 1 to ring 2
!
interface TokenRing1
 no ip address
 no ip directed-broadcast
 ring-speed 16
 multiring all          ←RIF enabled
 source-bridge 2 1 1       ←From ring 2 thru bridge 1 to ring 1
!
```

Configuring Multiport Local Source-Route Bridging

The other type of SRB is needed when there are more than two Token Ring interfaces to bridge between. This type of configuration requires a virtual ring to be defined on the router. A virtual ring is just as the name describes, a virtual entity that connects two or more physical rings locally or remotely. A virtual ring also is referred to as a *ring group*. As you will see in the next section, "Configuring Remote Source-Route Bridging," a virtual ring can span an entire IP domain. For now, the virtual ring will be limited to the local router. Figure 13-17 contains an example of a three-port SRB. To configure SRB between rings 1,

2, and 10, you will need to configure a virtual ring. Then, you will source-bridge every *real* Token Ring to the *virtual ring*. Figure 13-18 illustrates conceptually how the network will look with the location of the *virtual ring*.

Figure 13-17 *SRB Multiport Bridging*

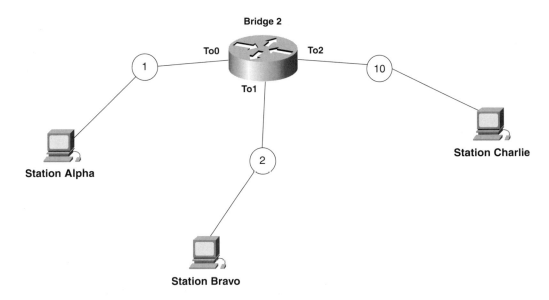

To configure this type of SRB, follow this four-step process:

Step 1 Define a virtual ring on the router. This is accomplished with this global router command:

```
Router(config)#source-bridge ring-group virtual_ring_number
```

The virtual ring number can range from 1 to 4095.

Step 2 Enable the use of the RIF, if required, with the router interface command **multiring all**. The full syntax is as follows:

```
Router(config-if)#multiring {protocol-keyword | all | other}
         no multiring {protocol-keyword | all | other}
```

Step 3 Configure SRB for the Token Ring interface. This is accomplished with the following interface command:

```
Router(config-if)#source-bridge local_ring bridge_number virtual_ring
```

Figure 13-18 *SRB Multiport Bridging Conceptual View*

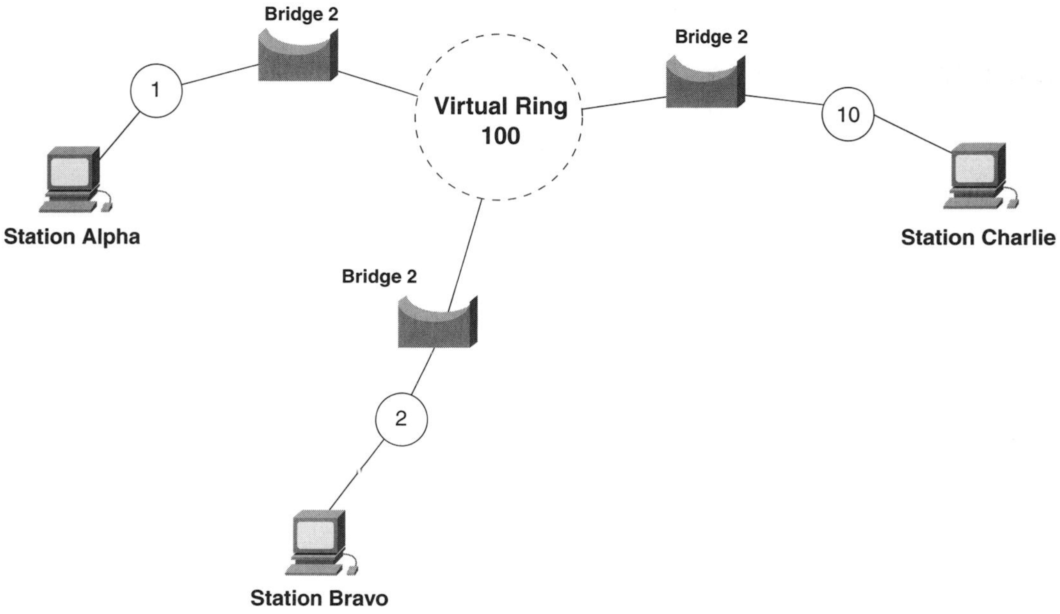

Step 4 (Optional) Enable Spanning Tree explorers. By doing so, you can reduce the number of explorers that transverse the network. NetBIOS and NetBEUI require Spanning Tree explorers to function properly. Cisco recommends enabling Spanning Tree explorers in complex multiprotocol networks. To enable them, use this interface command:

```
Router(config-if)#source-bridge spanning
```

Example 13-12 shows the configuration for local multiport SRB for the network in Figure 13-17.

Example 13-12 *Multiport SRB Configuration*

```
!
source-bridge ring-group 100      ←Configure a virtual ring of 100
!
interface TokenRing0
 no ip address
 no ip directed-broadcast
 ring-speed 16
 multiring all            ←RIF enabled
 source-bridge 1 2 100          ←From ring 1 thru bridge 2 to V-ring 100
!
interface TokenRing1
```

continues

Example 13-12 *Multiport SRB Configuration (Continued)*

```
 no ip address
 no ip directed-broadcast
 ring-speed 16
 multiring all            ←RIF enabled
 source-bridge 2 2 100        ←From ring 2 thru bridge 2 to V-ring 100
!
interface TokenRing2
 no ip address
 no ip directed-broadcast
 ring-speed 16
 multiring all            ←RIF enabled
 source-bridge 10 2 100    ←From ring 10 thru bridge 2 to V-ring 100
```

Configuring Remote Source-Route Bridging

SRB also can be configured to span a single WAN serial interface or an entire IP domain. This type of configuration is called *remote source-route bridging (RSRB)*, which involves defining a virtual ring to link the remote bridges. Figure 13-19 illustrates a Token Ring SRB network connected by a common Frame Relay network.

Figure 13-19 *RSRB Network Connected by a Frame Relay Network*

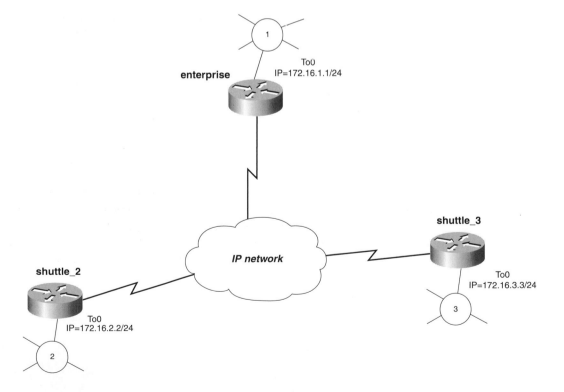

To configure RSRB, you need to define a common virtual ring to connect all the SRBs. The most logical spot for the virtual ring is the IP network, or the WAN, in this example. Figure 13-20 illustrates the RSRB with the virtual ring defined.

Figure 13-20 *RSRB Network with Virtual Ring Defined*

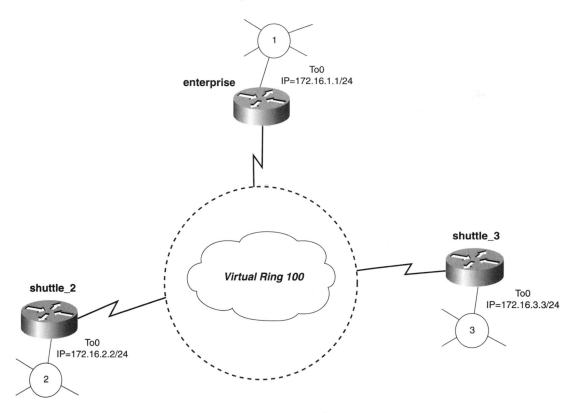

RSRB offers a variety of options to encapsulate SRB information over the IP network. The options depend primarily on the WAN interface. RSRB can be configured with four types of encapsulation: direct, FST, TCP, and Frame Relay. All four types of configurations are similar, but some require additional configuration. Table 13-1 presents an overview of the four encapsulation types, described in greater detail in the list following the table.

Table 13-1 *RSRB Encapsulation Types and Requirements*

Encapsulation Type	Link Type Required	Syntax
Direct	LAN—single hop only WAN must use HDLC only	**source-bridge remote-peer** *V_ring* **interface** *interface_name*
Frame Relay	WAN—Frame Relay only	**source-bridge remote-peer** *V_ring frame-relay* **interface** *interface_name* **frame-relay map rsrb** *dlci_number*
TCP	WAN or LAN	**source-bridge remote-peer** *V_ring* **tcp** *ip_address*
FST	WAN or LAN	**source-bridge** *fst-peername ip_address* **source-bridge remote-peer** *V_ring* **fst** *ip_address*

*   V_ring = the virtual ring

- **Direct**—Direct encapsulation is a quick way to encapsulate SRB frames over a single physical network between two routers. This command does not offer some of the advanced features of RSRB, such as local acknowledgment, but it is efficient. If direct encapsulation is used on a WAN interface, it must run HDLC as the data link protocol. Remember, direct encapsulation can be used only between two routers that are adjacent to each other.

- **Frame Relay**—Frame Relay encapsulation uses RFC 1490 to directly encapsulate RSRB in the Frame Relay frame. Frame Relay encapsulation allows you to control RSRB on a per-PVC basis. In addition to the RSRB commands, a **frame-relay map rsrb** command is needed to map the rsrb to a DLCI number on multipoint interfaces. This type of encapsulation provides less overhead than TCP, but it does not offer some of the advanced features of TCP.

- **TCP**—The TCP type of encapsulation provides the greatest benefits, but at a lower performance. Cisco recommends using this encapsulation when connecting Token Ring bridges across heterogeneous networks. TCP also provides load balancing and local acknowledgment.

- **FST**—FST stands for Fast-Sequenced Transport. Although it consumes less overhead than TCP, it still is not as fast as direct encapsulation. FST can be used to connect more than one SRB, but it does not offer local acknowledgment. An FST RSRB also needs to have an FST peer name assigned.

To configure RSRB, follow this four-step process:

Step 1   Enable the use of the RIF, if required, with the router interface command **multiring all**.

Step 2   Enable the virtual ring with the **source-bridge ring-group** *virtual_ring* command.

Step 3   Configure SRB from the physical ring to the virtual ring.

Step 4   Determine the encapsulation type to use, and configure RSRB.

— **Direct encapsulation:** Create a remote peer for each peer router and one for the local router. Use the following global router command:

— Router(config)#**source-bridge remote-peer** *virtual_ring* **interface** *interface_name*

— **Frame Relay encapsulation:** Create a remote peer for each peer router and one for the local router. Use the following global router command:

```
Router(config)#source-bridge remote-peer virtual_ring frame-relay
interface
  interface_name dlci_number [lf largest_frame_size]
```

You also must add a **frame-relay map** statement for multipoint interfaces; use the following interface command:

```
Router(config-if)#frame-relay map rsrb dlci_number
```

TCP encapsulation: Create a remote peer for each peer router and one for the local router. Use the following global router command:

```
Router(config)#source-bridge remote-peer virtual_ring tcp ip_address
  [lf largest_frame_size] [local-ack]
```

The IP address is the IP address of the remote router that you want to reach. You also must have IP connectivity to this address.

— **FST encapsulation:** First, create a source-bridge FST peer name. This peer should be a loopback address or a local Token Ring interface. Use the following global command:

```
Router(config)#source-bridge fst-peername local_ip_address
```

Next, create a remote peer for each peer router and one for the local router. Use the following global router command:

```
Router(config)#source-bridge remote-peer virtual_ring fst ip_address
  [lf largest_frame_size]
```

The IP address is the IP address of the remote router that you want to reach. You also must have IP connectivity to this address.

NOTE	We highly recommend using loopback addresses for the RSRB peers and DLSw peers. By pointing the peer to a loopback interface, you provide the peer with an interface that can be down only if the router is down or there is a problem with IP routing. A physical interface can go down, which will cause the peer to drop. This, in turn, could affect other interfaces on the remote router that might need to see the RSRB or DLSW traffic. By pointing the peer at a loopback interface, the peer will always remain up, thereby servicing all ports on the router independently of each other.

Determining Source-Route Bridge Status

You can view the status of the SRB by using the following commands:

```
show source-bridge
show source-bridge interface
```

The **show source-bridge** command displays information about all the SRBs on the router. With this command, you should verify the entries that you made to configure SRB with the output. Ensure that ring and bridge numbers match what you configured. If other bridges are active, you will see receive and transmit counts increment. This command also displays the number and type of explorers received on the network. The command also display errors and drops on the SRB. For more detailed information about this and all source-route bridging commands, read the Cisco Press title *Cisco IOS Bridging and IBM Networks Solutions*. Example 13-13 lists the output of the **show source-bridge** command.

Example 13-13 *Status of the SRB*

```
srb_router#show source-bridge

Local Interfaces:                              receive      transmit
            srn bn  trn r p s n  max hops       cnt          cnt        drops
To0           1  1  100 *   b    7  7  7        7297          2          154
To1           2  1    1     b    7  7  7          2          390          0

Global RSRB Parameters:
 TCP Queue Length maximum: 100

Ring Group 100:          ←virtual ring Number
  No TCP peername set, TCP transport disabled
   Maximum output TCP queue length, per peer: 100
  Rings:
   bn: 1  rn: 1    local  ma: 4007.781a.e789 TokenRing0              fwd: 0

Explorers: ------- input -------          ------- output -------
          spanning  all-rings    total    spanning  all-rings     total
To0           0       6856        6856        0          1           1
```

Example 13-13 *Status of the SRB (Continued)*

```
To1              0            1          1            0          390          390

  Explorer fastswitching enabled
  Local switched: 6300        flushed 0          max Bps 38400

           rings       inputs         bursts          throttles      output drops
           To0          6300              0                  0                 0
           To1             0              0                  0                 0

srb_router#
```

The **show source-bridge interface** command displays a quick overview of the SRB on the network. It displays the state, ring, and bridge number, as well as packets in and out. Use this command for a quick view on whether the bridge is operating and passing data. Example 13-14 lists the output of this command.

Example 13-14 *Status of the SRB Interfaces*

```
srb srb_router#show source-bridge interfaces

                                    v p s n r                      Packets
Interface  St  MAC-Address    srn bn  trn r x p b c IP-Address     In    Out

To0        up 0007.781a.e789   1  1   100 *   b   F               35373  7393
To1        up 0007.781a.e729   2  1    1      b   F               30158  7228
srb_router#
```

Practical Example: Configuring Remote Source-Route Bridging

Figure 13-21 models three Token Ring routers connected by a Frame Relay network. To configure RSRB on this network, you can follow the four-step process defined earlier. The first step is to enable the RIF field with the **multiring all** interface command. You will perform this on all the routers in the model. Second, you need to define a virtual ring. The logical location for the virtual ring in this model is the Frame Relay cloud. Therefore, you will make virtual ring 100 reside over the Frame Relay cloud. To configure the virtual ring 100, use the global router command **source-bring ring-group 100**.

The third step involves configuring SRB on all the routers that you want to connect through the RSRB. Example 13-15 lists the SRB configuration of the shuttle_15 and shuttle_3 routers.

Figure 13-21 *RSRB with TCP*

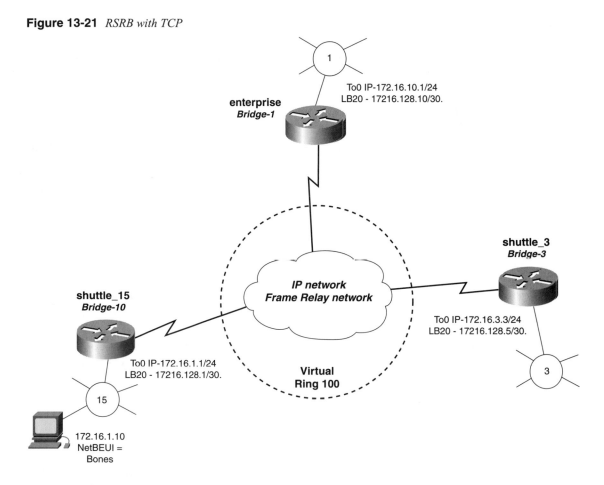

Example 13-15 *SRB Configuration of shuttle_15 and shuttle_3 Routers*

```
hostname shuttle_15
!
<<<text omitted>>>
!
interface TokenRing0
 ip address 172.16.1.1 255.255.255.0
 no ip directed-broadcast
 no ip route-cache
 no ip mroute-cache
 ring-speed 16
 multiring all                 ←RIF enabled
 source-bridge 15 10 100       ←SRB from ring 15 through bridge 10 to V-Ring 100
 source-bridge spanning        ←Enable support for NETBios and NetBEUI
```

Example 13-15 *SRB Configuration of shuttle_15 and shuttle_3 Routers (Continued)*

```
!
hostname shuttle_3
!
interface TokenRing0
 ip address 172.16.3.3 255.255.255.0
 ring-speed 16
 multiring all                ←RIF enabled
 source-bridge 3 3 100              ←SRB from ring 3 through bridge 3 to V-Ring 100
 source-bridge spanning      ←Enable support for NETBios and NetBEUI
!
```

NOTE
Using Windows 9*x* NetBEUI to Test RSRB

In this model, you can test the bridge with Windows 9*x* networking, or, specifically, NetBEUI. Without actual traffic, the RSRB will stay in a *closed* state. When the RSRB detects traffic, the bridge will transition from a *closed* state to an *open* state. In a lab environment, you can generate the traffic needed for the RSRB with Windows 9*x* configured using NetBEUI for file and print sharing. In a Windows 9*x* configuration, when the network neighborhood is browsed (or select **Start**, **Find**, **Find Computer**), this forces traffic across the RSRB. When the RSRB detects traffic, the state of the RSRB transitions from *closed* to *up*. This is an effective and easy way to test the RSRB. Use this same testing technique to test your DLSw configurations. With two workstations configured, you can print and share files over transparent, source-route, or DLSw networks. Windows 2000, Me, and NT also can be used for testing.

In this model, you will be testing the RSRB with Windows 9*x* networking. Therefore, you also will need to configure Spanning Tree explorers on the source-route bridge, as noted in Example 13-15.

The final step is to select an encapsulation to use on the RSRB and to configure it. In this model, we are using TCP and the RSRB encapsulation. Each router in the RSRB group will be configured with three **source-bridge remote-peer** statements. One peer statement is needed for each peer, and one peer statement is needed for the local router. In this model, we deployed the use of loopback interfaces to connect the RSRB. Example 13-16 shows the full RSRB configuration for the enterprise router. Example 13-17 shows the RSRB portions of the configuration of the shuttle_15 router.

Example 13-16 *RSRB Configuration of the enterprise Router*

```
hostname enterprise
!
source-bridge ring-group 100
source-bridge remote-peer 100 tcp 172.16.128.10    ←Peer for the local router
source-bridge remote-peer 100 tcp 172.16.128.5     ←Peer for the shuttle_5 router
source-bridge remote-peer 100 tcp 172.16.128.1     ←Peer for the shuttle_15 router
!
!
interface Loopback20
 ip address 172.16.128.10 255.255.255.252
 no ip directed-broadcast
!
interface Serial0
 no ip address
 no ip directed-broadcast
 encapsulation frame-relay
 no ip mroute-cache
 logging event subif-link-status
 logging event dlci-status-change
 frame-relay lmi-type cisco
!
interface Serial0.1 multipoint
 ip address 172.16.2.5 255.255.255.252
 no ip directed-broadcast
 frame-relay map ip 172.16.2.6 170 broadcast
!
interface Serial0.2 point-to-point
 ip address 172.16.2.1 255.255.255.252
 no ip directed-broadcast
 frame-relay interface-dlci 180
!
<<<text omitted>>>
!
interface TokenRing0
 ip address 172.16.10.1 255.255.255.0
 no ip directed-broadcast
 ring-speed 16
 multiring all
 source-bridge 1 1 100
 source-bridge spanning
!
router eigrp 2001
 network 172.16.0.0
 no auto-summary
```

Example 13-17 *RSRB Configuration of the shuttle_15 Router*

```
hostname shuttle_15
!
source-bridge ring-group 100
source-bridge remote-peer 100 tcp 172.16.128.1        ←Peer for the local router
source-bridge remote-peer 100 tcp 172.16.128.5        ←Peer for the shuttle_5 router
source-bridge remote-peer 100 tcp 172.16.128.10       ←Peer for the enterprise router
!
interface Loopback20
 ip address 172.16.128.1 255.255.255.252
 no ip directed-broadcast
!
interface Serial0
 ip address 172.16.2.6 255.255.255.252
 no ip directed-broadcast
 encapsulation frame-relay
 no ip route-cache
 no ip mroute-cache
 logging event subif-link-status
 logging event dlci-status-change
 frame-relay map ip 172.16.2.5 171 broadcast
!
<<<text omitted>>>
!
interface TokenRing0
 ip address 172.16.1.1 255.255.255.0
 no ip directed-broadcast
 no ip route-cache
 no ip mroute-cache
 ring-speed 16
 multiring all
 source-bridge 15 10 100
 source-bridge spanning
!
router eigrp 2001
 network 172.16.0.0
 no auto-summary
```

The RSRB configuration can be verified in the same manner as a normal source-route bridge can. Using the **show source-bridge** command, verify that the TCP peers are in a *closed* or *open* state. The bridge will not transition from closed to open without some type of data sent across it. In this model, the workstation Bones browses the network neighborhood, thereby activating the RSRB. Example 13-18 shows the output of the **show source-**bridge command performed on the enterprise router.

Example 13-18 show source-bridge *Command Output*

```
enterprise#show source-bridge

Local Interfaces:                            receive      transmit
           srn bn  trn r p s n  max hops       cnt          cnt          drops
To0          1  1  100 *   f    7  7  7        1019            0            0

Global RSRB Parameters:
 TCP Queue Length maximum: 100

Ring Group 100:
  This TCP peer: 172.16.128.10
   Maximum output TCP queue length, per peer: 100
  Peers:                  state      bg lv  pkts_rx   pkts_tx   expl_gn   drops TCP
   TCP 172.16.128.10      -              3        0         0         0       0   0
   TCP 172.16.128.5       open           3        0      1258      1019       0   0
   TCP 172.16.128.1       open           3        0       708      1019     346   0
  Rings:
  Rings:
    bn: 3  rn: 3    remote ma: 4000.30b1.270a TCP 172.16.128.5      fwd: 0
    bn: 10 rn: 15   remote ma: 4000.309a.68bb TCP 172.16.128.1      fwd: 0

Explorers: ------- input -------         ------- output -------
           spanning  all-rings   total   spanning  all-rings   total
To0           284       735      1019        0         0         0

  Explorer fastswitching enabled
  Local switched: 1019      flushed 0          max Bps 38400

           rings      inputs        bursts        throttles     output drops
           To0         1019            0              0               0

enterprise#
```

Now, modify the previous example to use Frame Relay as the encapsulation type of the
RSRB. Figure 13-22 highlights the relevant portions of the network, listing the DLCIs in use.

To configure RSRB to use Frame Relay encapsulation, follow Steps 1 to 3, which are
identical to those in the previous section. Frame Relay encapsulation requires only one
source-bridge remote-peer statement for each remote router connecting the RSRB. In this
type of RSRB, you do not configure a remote-peer statement for the local router. Instead,
you need to add a **Frame-relay** map statement for RSRB on the multipoint subinterface.
Example 13-19 lists the configuration of the enterprise and shuttle_15 routers, highlighting
the Frame Relay RSRB portions. This is the only difference between this model and the
TCP model that you just performed.

Figure 13-22 *RSRB with Frame Relay*

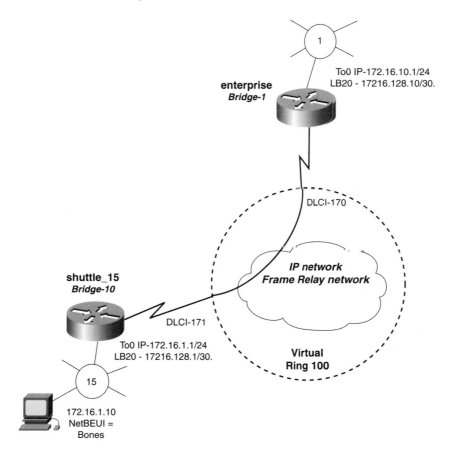

Example 13-19 *RSRB Frame Relay Encapsulation*

```
hostname enterprise
!
ip subnet-zero
!
source-bridge ring-group 100
source-bridge remote-peer 100 frame-relay interface Serial0.1 170
!
<<<text omitted>>>
!
interface Serial0
 mtu 4096
 no ip address
```

continues

Example 13-19 *RSRB Frame Relay Encapsulation (Continued)*

```
 no ip directed-broadcast
 encapsulation frame-relay
 no ip mroute-cache
 logging event subif-link-status
 logging event dlci-status-change
 frame-relay lmi-type cisco
!
interface Serial0.1 multipoint
 ip address 172.16.2.5 255.255.255.252
 no ip directed-broadcast
 frame-relay map rsrb 170 broadcast
 frame-relay map ip 172.16.2.6 170 broadcast
!
<<<text omitted>>>
!
interface TokenRing0
 ip address 172.16.10.1 255.255.255.0
 no ip directed-broadcast
 ring-speed 16
 multiring all
 source-bridge 1 1 100
 source-bridge spanning
!

hostname shuttle_15
!
ip subnet-zero
!
source-bridge ring-group 100
source-bridge remote-peer 100 frame-relay interface Serial0 171
!
interface Serial0
 mtu 4096
 ip address 172.16.2.6 255.255.255.252
 no ip directed-broadcast
 encapsulation frame-relay
 no ip route-cache
 no ip mroute-cache
 logging event subif-link-status
 logging event dlci-status-change
 frame-relay map rsrb 171 broadcast
 frame-relay map ip 172.16.2.5 171 broadcast
!
<<<text omitted>>>
!
interface TokenRing0
 ip address 172.16.1.1 255.255.255.0
 no ip directed-broadcast
 no ip route-cache
 no ip mroute-cache
```

Example 13-19 *RSRB Frame Relay Encapsulation (Continued)*

```
ring-speed 16
multiring all
source-bridge 15 10 100
source-bridge spanning
```

The status of the RSRB can be viewed with the same **show source-bridge** command used earlier. Example 13-20 lists the output of this command performed on the enterprise router.

Example 13-20 *Status of the RSRB on the enterprise Router*

```
enterprise#show source-bridge

Local Interfaces:                        receive     transmit
            srn bn  trn r p s n  max hops    cnt         cnt        drops
To0           1  1  100 *  f   7  7 7      4223          0          0

Global RSRB Parameters:
  TCP Queue Length maximum. 100

Ring Group 100:
  No TCP peername set, TCP transport disabled
   Maximum output TCP queue length, per peer: 100
   Peers:                   state    bg lv  pkts_rx  pkts_tx  expl_gn   drops TCP
    FR  Serial0.1           170 open        3        0        253       230      16
n/a
   Rings:
    bn: 1   rn: 1    local  ma: 4007.781a.e789 TokenRing0          fwd: 0
    bn: 10  rn: 15   remote ma: 4000.309a.68bb FR  Serial0.1       170  fwd: 0

Explorers: ------- input -------        ------- output -------
          spanning all-rings    total    spanning all-rings    total
To0         1886     2337       4223       0        0           0

  Explorer fastswitching enabled
  Local switched: 4223      flushed 0         max Bps 38400

          rings      inputs       bursts        throttles    output drops
          To0        4223         0             0            0

enterprise#
```

Configuring Other SRB Functions and Features

Cisco provides many useful options for controlling traffic and fine-tuning the source-route bridge environment. Some of the more common features are as follows:

- RSRB TCP and LLC2 local acknowledgment
- Setting largest frame

- Setting Spanning Tree explorers
- Static RIFs
- LSAP and MAC filters

The sections that follow discuss some of these options and how to use them.

RSRB TCP LLC2 Local Acknowledgments

SNA sessions are complete end-to-end sessions. Every frame sent by a front-end processor must be acknowledged by the station or controller receiving the frame. If the SNA session must cross vast geographical distances over low-speed links such as 64 kpbs, there is a high probability of *T1 timer* expirations. The T1 time is a predefined period of time that a host expects the receiving host to respond, either positively or negatively, to the frame sent to it. All LLC2 frames, including supervisory frames RR, RNR, and REJ, must be acknowledged in an end-to-end manner. Figure 13-23 represents a typical LLC2 session in an RSRB environment.

Figure 13-23 *LLC2 Session Without Local Acknowledgment*

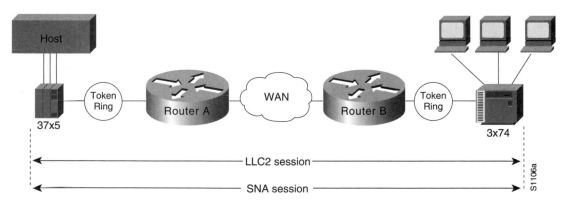

Cisco offers local acknowledgment for TCP-based RSRBs. Local acknowledgment solves the T1 timer problem without having to change the configuration of the end nodes. With local acknowledgment enabled, all LLC2 frames are acknowledged by the router. The only LLC2 frames that cross the network are *I frames*, or information frames. Figure 13-24 demonstrates LLC2 local acknowledgment.

To configure local acknowledgment between two RSRBs, use the argument **local-ack** on the **source-bridge remote-peer** statement:

```
Router(config)#source-bridge remote-peer virtual_ring tcp ip_address local-ack
```

Because the router must maintain a full LLC2 session with every host, the number of *simultaneous* sessions that it can support could be a factor. Cisco recommends using local acknowledgment only when you are experiencing T1 timer problems or LLC2 problems. Local acknowledgment will not affect NetBIOS timeouts.

Figure 13-24 *LLC2 Session with Local Acknowledgment*

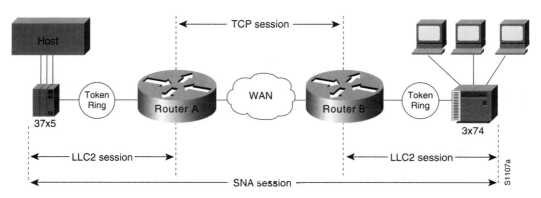

Setting the Largest Frame Size

In mixed environments, such as Token Ring and Ethernet, to prevent a lot of segmentation throughout the network, you can fix the largest frame size to 1500 or another value. By setting the frame size to 1500, less segmentation will occur as frames cross Ethernet and Token Ring segments of the network. This easily is accomplished using the **lf** argument on the Frame Relay, TCP, and FST **remote-peer** statements:

```
Router(config)#source-bridge remote-peer virtual_ring frame-relay interface
    interface_name dlci_number [lf largest_frame_size]
Router(config)#source-bridge remote-peer virtual_ring tcp ip_address
    [lf largest_frame_size] [local-ack]
Router(config)#source-bridge remote-peer virtual_ring fst ip_address
    [lf largest_frame_size]
```

Configuring Spanning Tree Explorers

By default, Cisco routers use all-routes explorer frames to generate the RIF. In large redundant networks, the number of explorers can multiply exponentially as they are duplicated and forwarded throughout the network. Recall from the previous section that Spanning Tree explorers reduce the number of explorers on the network. Spanning Tree nodes will forward Spanning Tree explorers only to nodes that are configured for Spanning Tree. To enable the **spanning tree** explorers, use the following Token Ring interface command:

```
Router(config-if)#source-bridge spanning
```

Microsoft NetBIOS also uses Spanning Tree; therefore, as a rule of thumb in the field, we always configure Spanning Tree explorers when using Microsoft Windows networking.

Configuring a Static RIF

Cisco provides a way to statically configure a RIF on a router. To configure a static RIF, you must be familiar with route control and route descriptor frames. Recall the figures from the previous section of source-route bridging.

Figure 13-25 illustrates the routing control format for the RIF, followed by the descriptions of each field.

Figure 13-25   *RIF Routing Control Format*

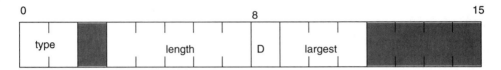

- Shaded fields are reserved.
- **type**—Explorer type is used, as follows:
    - **00:** Specific routes explorer
    - **10:** All rings, all-routes explorer
    - **11:** All rings, spanning routes (limited broadcast)
- **length**—This is the total length in bytes of the RIF.
- **D**—This is the direction, indicated as follows:
    - **0:** Interpret route left to right (forward)
    - **1:** Interpret route right to left (reverse)
- **largest**—This is the largest frame that can be handled by this route, as follows:
    - **000:** 516 bytes (DDN 1822)
    - **001:** 1500 bytes (Ethernet)
    - **010:** 2052 bytes
    - **011:** 4472 bytes (Token Ring and Cisco maximum)
    - **100:** 8144 bytes (Token bus)
    - **101:** 11407 bytes
    - **110:** 17800 bytes
    - **111:** 65535 (initial values)

Figure 13-26 describes the routing descriptor format of the RIF string. When you configure a static RIF, it is in dotted-hexadecimal format.

Figure 13-26   *Routing Descriptor Format*

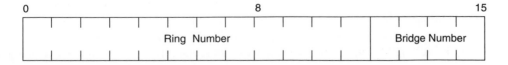

- **Ring number**—Unique decimal ring number within the bridged network.
- **Bridge number**—Unique decimal bridge number between any bridges connecting the same two rings. A bridge number of 0 indicates that the RIF is terminating.

Figure 13-27 presents an SRB network.

Figure 13-27 *Source-Route Bridge: RIF*

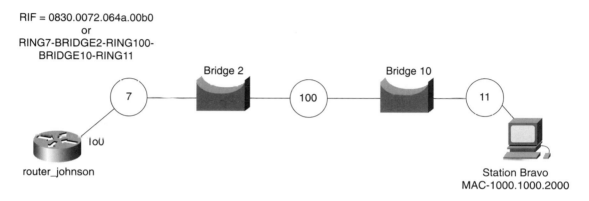

The static RIF from router_johnson to station Bravo would read as follows:

```
0830.0072.064a.00b0
```

Use the previous figures to break down the RIF into its significant components. The 0830 is the 16-bit RC field. Reading from left to right, the bit pattern is as follows:

Bit	0	1	2	3	4	5	6	7	8	9	10	11	12	13	14	15
	0	0	0	0	1	0	0	0	0	0	1	1	0	0	0	0

The first two bits, from left to right again, equal 00. This sets the explorer type to be a specific routes explorer; you want to use this explorer type because this is a static RIF. Bit 3 is set to 0 and is reserved. The next five bits set the length of the RIF in bytes. In this example, the RIF—not just the ring-bridge-ring part, but the whole RIF—is eight bytes. The next bit, the D bit, is set to 0, indicating that the RIF is read from left to right, or forward. The next three bits are set to 011, which sets the frame size to be 4472, the Cisco maximum. The last four bits are reserved.

The RD fields, the next three bytes, break down rather easily.

The next three bytes, 0072, 064a, and 00b0, are the three 16-bit RD fields. The first three bits of each byte, are the ring number in hexadecimal format. The last bit is the ring number in hexadecimal format. For the RIF in this example, you have the following:

```
RING7-BRIDGE2 = 0072
RING100-BRIDGE10 = 064a
RING11-BRIDGE0 = 00b0
```

A bridge of 0 tells the SRB to terminate the RIF and that no more bridges follow the ring.

To configure a static RIF on a router, use the following global router command:

```
Router(config)#rif mac-address rif-string {interface-name | ring-group ring}
```

Example 13-21 demonstrates the configuration of the static RIF from router_johnson to station bravo.

Example 13-21 *Static RIF Configuration*

```
router_johnson(config)#rif 1000.1000.2000 0830.0072.064a.00b0 to0
```

LSAP, MAC, and NetBIOS Filters

We will discuss LSAP and MAC filters more in the upcoming sections. For now, we simply want to show you the syntax for applying the filters to a source-route bridge environment.

To configure LSAP filters for IEEE 802 encapsulated frames, use the following syntax:

```
Router(config-if)#source-bridge input-lsap-list access_list_number
Router(config-if)#source-bridge output-lsap-list access_list_number
Router(config)#rsrb remote-peer ring-group group [tcp ip_address | fst ip_address |
  interface interface_name] lsap-output-list access_list_number
```

The LSAP access lists is in the range of 200 to 299 and filters based on LSAP type code.

To filter based on IEEE 802 source addresses, use the following syntax:

```
Router(config-if)#source-bridge input-address-list access_list_number
Router(config-if)#source-bridge output-address-list access_list_number
```

The access list number ranges from 700 to 799.

To filter based on NetBIOS name, use the following commands:

```
Router(config-if)#netbios input-access-filter host station_name
Router(config-if)#netbios output-access-filter host station_name
Router(config)#rsrb remote-peer ring-group [tcp ip_address | fst ip_address |
  interface interface_name] netbios-output-list access_list_number
```

Data Link Switching Plus (DLSw+)

Data Link Switching (DLSw), as we know it today, was pioneered in 1995 by the Advanced Peer-to-Peer Networking (APPN) Implementers' Workshop (AIW), sponsored by IBM. It was not the first RFC on DLSw. IBM wanted to create a way to transport LLC2 frames across TCP/IP networks and drafted RFC 1434 in 1993. The concept was sound, but it lacked (surprise) multivendor interoperability.

The goal of the APPN AIW goal was to evolve the original DLSw RFC, RFC 1434, with new features. The original work later was turned into the first standard for DLSw, titled RFC 1795. RFC 1795 defines what commonly is called Data Link Switching Version 1.

DLSw version II was developed in 1997 and is documented in RFC 2166, which provided enhancements that allowed DLSw networks to scale better and provide better availability than either RSRB or standard-only implementations. Cisco Systems refers to its implementation of DLSw as DLSw Plus (DLSw+). One of the most notable features about DLSw+ is the concept of *border peers and peer groups.*

NOTE	For the purpose of this text, consider DLSw to be synonymous with DLSW Version 1, Version 2, and Cisco's implementation's DLSW+. When we discuss material where the version or implementation is relevant, we will note that.

DLSw+ Features

In 1991, RSRB was the only option that many network engineers had to bridge their Token Ring or LLC2 networks over an IP-based network. In a short time, thousands of RSRB networks were springing up. Soon, however, RSRB networks were sidelined by the newer way to transport LLC2 over an IP network, DLSw. By 1995, all future work on RSRB glided to a halt because the industry clearly was embracing DLSw. Since then, it has surfaced to become the most dynamic and one of the most reliable ways to transport legacy protocols across the modern internetwork.

DLSw provides a method of running SNA and NetBIOS over IP. DLSw also provides better scalability, functionality, manageability, and control than RSRB. DLSw addresses several RSRB limitations by including key features such as local acknowledgment for devices on Ethernet and SDLC for physical unit (PU) 2.1 devices. DLSw also provides higher availability with load balancing and backup features.

Some of the advantages DLSw+ offers over RSRB are as follows:

- Multivendor interoperability
- DLC timeouts
- DLC acknowledgments over the WAN
- Circuit-level flow and congestion control
- Peer priority and port load sharing
- Local acknowledgment on Ethernet
- Backup, dynamic, and fault-tolerant peers
- Enhanced broadcast reduction
- UDP for UI frames
- RIF termination, allowing a wider network diameter
- Broadcast optimization with peer groups and border peer caching

- Enhanced support, including the following:
    - Media conversion built in (PU 2.0, 2.1, and 4)
    - Support for end systems on Token Ring LANE, Token Ring ISL, and SRB FDDI
    - Detailed capabilities exchange
    - SNA DDR

NOTE

DLSw, the Only Way to Integrate Legacy Protocols

In the field, I have found DLSw+ to be one of the most reliable and fairly straightforward protocols to configure. SNA is a time-sensitive protocol, and the ease in which DLSw transports it across the internetwork is exceptional. When I learned to configure DLSw+, it quickly became our *only* choice for transporting nonroutable protocols, such as SNA, NetBEUI, and NetBIOS. Hopefully, when you finish this section, you, too, will feel this way.

DLSw+ Technical Overview

IEEE 802.2 LLC Type 2 was designed under the assumption that network transit delay would be small and predictable. After all, Token Ring and Ethernet are LAN protocols. When remote bridging is used over vast geographical distances, the network delay can vary drastically with the load on the link. When the delay becomes too large, LLC2 timeouts occur and retransmissions start happening. Because the frame is only delayed, LLC2 can become confused when it starts to see duplicate frames, and it might start tearing down LLC2 sessions. Figure 13-28 illustrates how LLC2 has end-to-end acknowledgment in a traditional bridged environment.

Figure 13-28 *LLC2 End-to-End Acknowledgment*

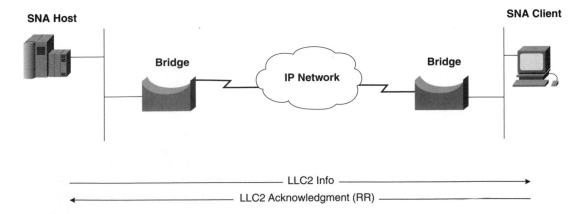

DLSw+ terminates the LLC Type 2 connection on the DLSw+ device/router. LLC Type 2 connections no longer cross the WAN and are exposed to large delays. The only delays that occur at the LLC layer are now on the LAN. This inherently reduces traffic on the WAN as well. SDLC links, polling, and poll response occur locally and no longer transverse the WAN. Broadcasting of search frames is controlled by the DLSw+ router and are no longer flooded after the router locates the target station. Figure 13-29 illustrates how acknowledgments are handled in a DLSw+ environment.

Figure 13-29 *LLC2 with Local Acknowledgment*

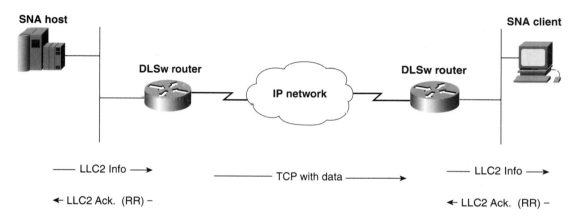

As mentioned, DLSW+ provides a method of transport for SNA, NetBIOS, and NetBEUI over TCP/IP. DLSW+ refers to routers as *peers*. When the TCP or other transport protocol makes a connection with another router, it is called a *peer connection*. When this type of peer connection is formed, a DLSw circuit is established between the two end stations. Data between the two end stations is passed on the circuit. A single peer can support multiple circuits. DLSW+ supports the following circuit types:

- SNA PU Type 2.0/2.1 and SNA PU Type 4
- SDLC PU1 Type 1 through PU Type 4
- NetBIOS
- Windows 9.*x* NetBEUI

By default, every 30 seconds, DLSw+ peers send keepalive messages to all peers. The keepalive mechanism is used to ensure that the peer is alive. If three keepalives are missed, the peer will be torn down.

The data-link switch—or Cisco router, in our case—uses a Switch-to-Switch Protocol (SSP) to establish DLSw peers. A pair of routers uses a peer connection to multiplex data links over a reliable transport using SSP protocol. Before DLSw can occur between two routers, the routers must establish a peer relationship with each other. The transport protocol for DLSw peer connections is TCP. The Cisco implementation, DLSW+, allows for four types of transport methods:

- **TCP encapsulation**—TCP is used where local acknowledgment is required, and it aids in preventing data-link control timeouts. TCP also provides backup peers and other capabilities that allow for nondistruptive rerouting around link failures.

  TCP is the most flexible and reliable of all the transports. Unfortunately, it also has the most overhead because of the 20 bytes for the TCP header, 20 bytes for the IP header, and 16 bytes for the DLSw header. In modern networks, this amount of overhead is becoming irrelevant. DLSw TCP encapsulation listens on TCP port 2067 and transmits on TCP port 2065 by default. Priority can be assigned by the TCP port number. Table 13-3 lists the ports and the corresponding priority.

  Table 13-2 *TCP Port Priority*

Priority	Port
High	2065
Medium	1981
Normal	1982
Low	1983

  TCP encapsulation also allows the most comprehensive control over the capabilities exchanges and explorer traffic, by the use of LSAP, DMAC, and NetBIOS name filters. TCP peers can exist on any type of LAN or WAN topology that supports TCP/IP.

- **Fast Sequence Transport (FST) encapsulation**—FST is a low-overhead method of transporting DLSw over IP. This method does not have reliable delivery of frames or local acknowledgment. All keepalive frames flow end to end with FST transport. FST uses IP as the transport and reroutes around link failures. FST encapsulation can be used only when the end systems reside on Token Ring. FST peers can exist over HDLC, Ethernet, Token Ring, FDDI, ATM, and Frame Relay.

- **Direct encapsulation**—Direct encapsulation provides a low-overhead option for transporting LLC across HDLC or Frame Relay links. It includes only the 16 byte DLSw header, along with the frame header that it is being transported in. The *direct* method does not have reliable delivery of frames or local acknowledgment. As with FST, keepalive frames flow end to end, and direct encapsulation can be used only when the end systems reside on Token Ring.

- **LLC2 encapsulation (DLSw Lite)**—This method of encapsulation is another low-overhead method, 16 bytes, utilizing RFC 1490, which allows for direct encapsulation of a protocol in the Frame Relay frame. Naturally, this method can be used only over Frame Relay. DLSw+ Lite supports local acknowledgment and reliable delivery of frames. Link failures are disruptive to DLSw Lite peers.

DLSw Circuit Establishment

Circuit establishment occurs between two end systems. SNA circuit establishment occurs when a SNA TEST or XID explorer frame with a specific MAC address is generated from an end station. The DLSw router sends a CANUREACH frame to each active peer. The correct peer responds with an ICANREACH frame. After a series of XIDs and other information is exchanged, a circuit is established. Each circuit has a unique ID that allows a TCP peer connection to support multiple circuits. The ID is composed of the source and destination MAC address, source and destination LSAPs, and a data-link control port ID. Only when the circuit becomes *connected* can data can be exchanged between the hosts. Each DLSw router caches the MAC addresses and NetBIOS names to prevent future explorer frames from crossing the network. Figures 13-30 and 13-31 are adopted from RFC 1795 and illustrate the complete process of DLSw circuits for SNA and NetBIOS.

NetBIOS stations establish circuits in a similar manner. Instead of issuing a CANUREACH frame, NetBIOS issues a NetBIOS NAME-QUERY frame that specifies a NetBIOS name. Figure 13-31 illustrates the complete circuit establishment process for NetBIOS.

DLSw Capabilities Exchange

A key process that occurs during DLSw circuit establishment is the *capabilities exchange*. The capabilities exchange the process that differentiates DLSw from other bridging technologies. The exchange is a special DLSw SSP control message that describes the capabilities of the sending DLSw router. The initial capabilities exchange is always the first SSP message sent when a new connection between two DLSw devices occur. It is used to identify the DLSw version and other options that the DLSw device is capable of.

SSP uses the concept of control vectors to exchange information between DLSw devices. Required control vectors must occur first and in the following order:

1 Vendor ID

2 DLSw version number

3 Initial pacing window

4 Supported SAP list

Figure 13-30 *SNA Circuit Establishment*

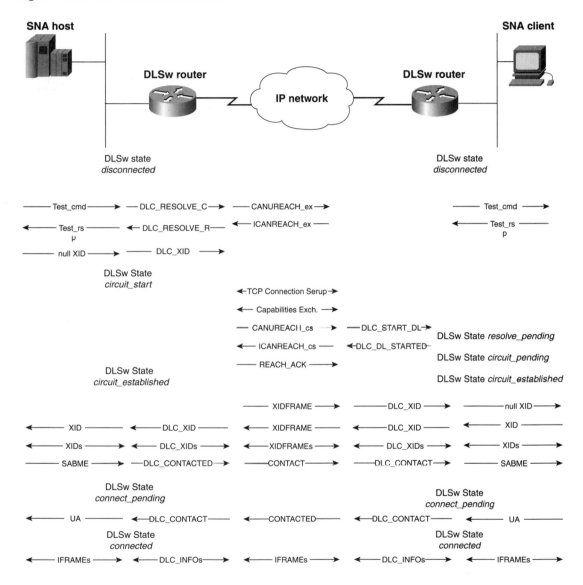

Figure 13-31 *NetBIOS Circuit Establishment*

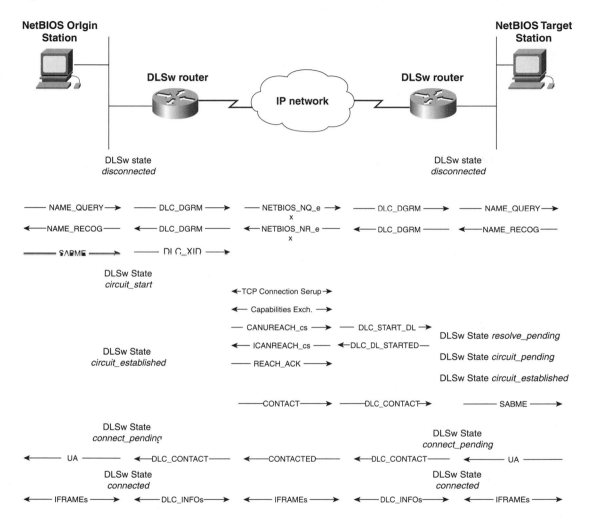

The remainder of the control vectors can occur in any order:

- Vendor ID control vector.
- DLSw version control vector. This indicates the DLSw standard in use.
- Initial pacing window control vector. This is used for flow control.
- Version string control vector.
- MAC address exclusivity control vector. This includes only MAC addresses that this switch can reach.
- Supported SAP list control vector. This is a list of all SAPs.
- TCP connections control vector. This specifies the number of TCP connections to support.
- NetBIOS name exclusivity control vector.
- MAC address list control vector.
- NetBIOS name list control vector.
- Vendor context control vector.
- Reserved for future use.
- Vendor-specific.

Cisco's implementation of the TCP connections control vector states that only one TCP connection will be used to transport data. When a DLSw+ circuit first is established, two TCP connections are active. DLSw+ states that the TCP connection with the highest IP address will be torn down, leaving only one TCP connection to transport data.

After the capabilities exchange occurs, the DLSw router can proceed to complete circuit setup. Only after a circuit is *connected* can data be exchanged on it.

DLSw Flow Control

DLSw uses a form of adaptive pacing for flow control. DLSw specifies two independent, unidirectional circuit flow-control mechanisms on a per-circuit basis. DLSw uses a dynamic window based on buffer size, TCP transmit queue, and end station flow-control mechanisms.

DLSw RIF Termination and RIF Passthrough

DLSw supports RIF termination when used with source-route bridges. All remote devices/bridges appear to be attached to the virtual ring. By default, the RIF is terminated by the DLSw router. DLSw peers also can be configured to have RIF passthrough. When configuring RIF passthrough, be sure that the virtual rings on both peers match and that both peers have RIF passthrough enabled.

Canonical and Noncanonical Address Formats

Recall from Chapter 2 that Ethernet uses canonical bit format and Token Ring uses noncanonical format. When DLSw receives a frame from Ethernet, it converts it to non-canonical format. DLSw works strictly in noncanonical format as it passes data from peer to peer. When the frame arrives at the interface it is destined for, DLSW checks to see whether the interface is Ethernet or Token Ring. If the interface is Ethernet, the frame is converted back to canonical format and is sent out the interface. If the interface is Token Ring, the frame is passed unchanged to the Token Ring interface. Care should be taken whenever using SNA attached Ethernet devices so that they operate in canonical format. Most SNA devices, such as IBM 3174s, do operate in canonical format on Ethernet.

Configuring DLSw+

For the purpose of this text, we will discuss configuring DLSw only with Token Ring and Ethernet networks. For comprehensive information on configuring DLSw for FDDI, SDLC, and QLLC, see *Cisco IOS Bridging and IBM Network Solutions*, by Cisco Press.

Configuring DLSw involves a four-step task. Essentially, you need to create a bridge for the LAN interface and define local and remote DLSw peers. Naturally, there will be a few steps in between, but basically, that is all there is to configure for DLSw. This might again explain why it has become so popular so quickly.

The four-step task lists the steps necessary to configure DLSw:

Step 1   Configure IP loopback interfaces, and add them to the routing domain on every router that you want to enable DLSw on. As in RSRB and OSPF, the use of loopback addresses provides greater stability for the DLSw peers. Using logical interfaces, the DLSw peer connections are not dependent on the operational status of a physical interface. This can be important on multi-interfaced routers. Be sure that the loopback's IP address is reachable by the remote peer router. We usually circulate loopback addresses with a routing protocol.

Step 2   Define a local peer for DLSw. The creation of a local peer activates the DLSw code in the router. The local peer's IP address should be that of the loopback interface configured in Step 1. The local peer is where you specify all local DLSw+ parameters. The basic syntax needed for a DLSw is listed, followed by the syntax of the whole command. We will talk about most of these additional arguments in upcoming sections.

```
Router(config)#dlsw local-peer [peer-id ip_address]
Router(config)#dlsw local-peer [peer-id ip_address] [group
peer_group_1-255]
   [border] [cost 1-5] [lf largest_frame_516-11407] [keepalive seconds]
   [passive] [promiscuous] [init-pacing-window size_1-2000]
   [max-pacing-window size][biu-segment]
```

Step 3 Enable transparent bridging for Ethernet interfaces, and/or enable source-route bridging for Token Ring interfaces. The source-route bridge automatically is linked to DLSW through the virtual ring. The Ethernet transparent bridge needs to have additional syntax to link it to DLSw, as noted later. You can think of the bridge as a *broadcast or LLC2 capture entity*. When the frame is captured, it can be transported to the remote peer. Traffic from a remote peer is forwarding only into the virtual ring or transparent bridge group defined by the **dlsw bridge-group** command. For more information on transparent and source-route bridging, see the previous sections on those topics.

— **Ethernet:** Enable transparent bridging on the Ethernet interface running SNA, NetBIOS, or another LLC2 protocol. This example uses bridge 10.

```
Router(config)#bridge 10 protocol ieee
Router(config)#dlsw bridge-group 10
Router(config-if)#bridge-group 10
```

The full syntax for the **dlsw bridge-group** command is as follows:

```
Router(config)# dlsw bridge-group group-number [llc2 [N2 number]
[ack-delay-time milliseconds] [ack-maxnumber]
[idle-time milliseconds] [local-window number]
[t1-time milliseconds] [tbusy-timemilliseconds]
[tpf-time milliseconds] [trej-time milliseconds]
[txq-maxnumber] [xid-neg-val-time milliseconds]
[xid-retry-time milliseconds]] [locaddr-priority
lu address priority list number] [sap-priority
priority list number]
```

— **Token Ring:** Enable source-route bridging on the Token Ring interface running SNA, NetBIOS, or another LLC2 protocol. You must define a virtual ring for SRB. This example creates a virtual ring of 100, and the ring number of the Token Ring interface is 1.

```
Router(config)#source-bridge ring-group 100
Router(config-if)#source-bridge 1 2 100
```

Step 4 Decide what encapsulation type you will use for the peers. As mentioned previously, you have four types of encapsulation to choose from. Table 13-3 lists the various encapsulation types, along with some of the capabilities supported with that encapsulation type.

Table 13-3 *DLSw Encapsulation Support Matrix*

Encapsulation Type	Reliable Delivery	Local Ack	Nondisruptive Rerouting Around Link Failures	Overhead of DLSw**	End-Station Topology Supported	Support for Backup Peers
TCP	Yes	Yes	Yes	56 bytes	All	Yes
FST	No	No	No*	36 bytes	Token Ring only	Yes
Direct	No	No	No	16 bytes	Token Ring only	No
DLSw Lite	Yes	Yes	No*	20 bytes	Token Ring, Ethernet, SDLC, QLLC	No

*   FST and DLSw can be configured in manners to provide disruptive rerouting around link failures. Note that the session will drop during disruptive rerouting.

** Overhead does not include the DLC or frame headers on the overhead associated with DLSw.

Use the following global configuration commands to configure the various encapsulation types on the remote peer. The IP address of the remote peer should be the IP address of the loopback interface of the remote router. The first command in each list shows the minimum configuration needed for the remote peer, followed by the complete syntax of the remote peer statement for that encapsulation type.

— TCP encapsulation:

```
Router(config)#dlsw remote-peer 0 tcp ip_address
Router(config)# dlsw remote-peer list-number tcp ip-address [backup-peer
  [ip-address| frame-relay interface serial number dlci-number|
  interface name]] [bytes-netbios-out bytes-list-name]
[circuit-weight weight] [cluster cluster-id]
[cost cost] [dest-mac mac-address]
[dmac-output-list access-list-number]
[host-netbios-out host-list-name] [inactivity]
[dynamic] [keepalive seconds] [lf size] [linger
minutes] [lsap-output-list list] [no-llc
minutes] [passive] [priority] [rif-passthru
virtual-ring-number] [tcp-queue-max size]
[timeout seconds]
```

— FST encapsulation:

```
Router(config)#dlsw remote-peer 0 fst ip_address
Router(config)# dlsw remote-peer list-number fst ip-address
[backup-peer [ip-address] [bytes-netbios-outbytes-list-name]
[circuit-weight weight] [cost cost] [dest-mac
mac-address] [dmac-output-list access-list-number]
[host-netbios-out host-list-name] [keepalive seconds]
[lf size][linger minutes] [lsap-output-list list]
```

— Direct encapsulation for Frame Relay:

You also must add a **frame-relay map dlsw** statement, if the interface is a multipoint interface:

```
Router(config)#dlsw remote-peer 0 frame-relay interface serial number
DLCI_number
Router(config-if)#frame-relay map dlsw DLCI_number
```

— Direct encapsulation for HDLC:

```
Router(config)#dlsw remote-peer 0 interface serial number
Router(config)# dlsw remote-peer list-number interface
serial number [bytes-netbios-out bytes-list-name]
[circuit-weight weight] [cost cost] [dest-mac mac-address]
[dmac-output-list access-list-number]
[host-netbios-out host-list-name] [keepalive seconds] [lf size]
[linger minutes] [lsap-output-list list] pass-thru
```

— **LLC2 encapsulation for Frame Relay (DLSw Lite):** You also must add a **frame-relay map llc2** statement if the interface is a multipoint interface:

```
Router(config)#dlsw remote-peer 0 frame-relay interface serial
  number DLCI_number
Router(config-if)#frame-relay map llc2 DLCI_number
dlsw remote-peer list-number frame-relay interface serial number
dlci-number [bytes-netbios-out bytes-list-name] [circuit-weight weight]
[cost cost] [dest-mac mac-address] [dmac-output-list access-list-number]
[host-netbios-out host-list-name] [keepalive seconds] [lf size]
[linger minutes] [lsap-output-list list] pass-thru
```

Practical Example: DLSw TCP and FST Peers

Figure 13-32 models a Frame Relay network connecting four routers. In this model, you will want to create two types of DLSw connections. From the router skywalker, you want to create a TCP peer to the router solo. From the vader router, you want to create an FST peer to the router chewbacca.

Figure 13-32 *DLSw TCP and FST Peers*

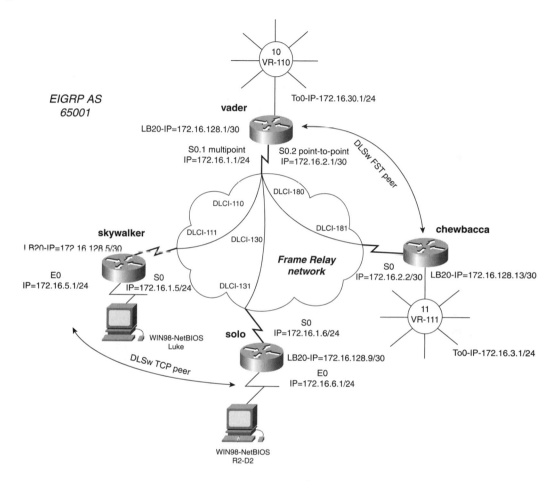

Begin by focusing the TCP peer between skywalker and solo. Following the four-step configuration process, begin by creating loopback interfaces on skywalker and solo. When the loopback interfaces are configured and IP addresses are assigned to them, make sure that they are advertised by the routing protocol. The loopback address will serve as the local and remote peers, so it is essential that IP connectivity exits between them. In this model, you are using EIGRP as the routing protocol, so EIGRP must advertise all loopback addresses. Before moving on to Step 2, be sure that you can **ping** all the relevant IP addresses in the model. You do not want to waste time troubleshooting peers if IP connectivity does not exist.

In Step 2, you configure the DLSw local peer for each router. Remember, the IP address that you will use will be the loopback addresses. To configure the local peer, use the global configuration command **dlsw local-peer peer-id** *ip_address.* For example, to configure the local peer for the skywalker router, enter **dlsw local-peer peer-id 172.16.128.5.**

After the local peers are configured, define a transparent bridge group. For Ethernet networks, you must configure transparent bridging on the Ethernet segment where the end stations reside. The transparent bridge group then is linked to DLSw with the global command **dlsw bridge-group** *bridge-group.* Example 13-22 lists the relevant portions of the configuration of the solo router, up to this point.

Example 13-22 *DLSw TCP Configuration of the solo Router*

```
hostname solo
!
<<<text omitted>>>
!
dlsw local-peer peer-id 172.16.128.9      ←IP address of Loopback 20
dlsw remote-peer 0 tcp 172.16.128.5      ←Configured in step-4, IP address of
                                          skywalker
dlsw bridge-group 1                  ←Must match the bridge group on E0
!
interface Loopback20
 ip address 172.16.128.9 255.255.255.252
 no ip directed-broadcast
!
interface Ethernet0
 ip address 172.16.6.1 255.255.255.0
 no ip directed-broadcast
 bridge-group 1                     ←Transparent Bridging enabled for E0
!
interface Serial0
 ip address 172.16.1.6 255.255.255.0
 no ip directed-broadcast
 encapsulation frame-relay
 no ip mroute-cache
 frame-relay map ip 172.16.1.5 131 broadcast
 frame-relay map ip 172.16.1.1 131 broadcast
 frame-relay lmi-type cisco
!
<<<text omitted>>>
!
router eigrp 65001
 network 172.16.0.0
 no auto-summary
!
ip classless
no ip http server
!
bridge 1 protocol ieee              ←Transparent Bridging enabled
!
```

To configure the remote peer for TCP, use the global command **dlsw remote-peer 0 tcp** *ip_address*. Unless you are using a DLSw port list, use 0, which implies that no list is in use. The previous example demonstrated the use of this command on the solo router. Example 13-23 lists the configuration of the skywalker router.

Example 13-23 *DLSw TCP Configuration of the skywalker Router*

```
hostname skywalker
!
<<<text omitted>>>
!
dlsw local-peer peer-id 172.16.128.5
dlsw remote-peer 0 tcp 172.16.128.9
dlsw bridge-group 1
!
interface Loopback20
 ip address 172.16.128.5 255.255.255.252
!
interface Ethernet0
 ip addrooo 172.16.5.1 255.255.255.0
 bridge-group 1
!
interface Serial0
 ip address 172.16.1.5 255.255.255.0
 encapsulation frame-relay
 no arp frame-relay
 frame-relay map ip 172.16.1.6 111 broadcast
 frame-relay map ip 172.16.1.1 111 broadcast
 no frame-relay inverse-arp
 frame-relay lmi-type cisco
!
<<<text omitted>>>
!
router eigrp 65001
 network 172.16.0.0
 no auto-summary
!
<<<text omitted>>>
!
bridge 1 protocol ieee
```

To verify the configuration, you can view the status of the peers with the **show dlsw peers** command. Example 13-24 displays the output of this command on the solo router. Only when the peer is in a connect state can it create a circuit transport data. It is important to note that a "connected peer" does not mean that DLSw is fully functional. DLSw circuits, denoted by the ckts column, are the only indication that an end-to-end session exists within a TCP peer. We will discuss this command more in the next section.

Example 13-24 **show dksw peers** *Command Output*

```
solo#show dlsw peers
Peers:                  state     pkts_rx    pkts_tx  type  drops ckts TCP    uptime

 TCP 172.16.128.5    CONNECT        255        444  conf      0    1   0 00:39:33

Total number of connected peers: 1
Total number of connections:     1

solo#
```

Example 13-25 demonstrates another way to view more comprehensive information about
a DLSw circuit. The command used in this example is **show dlsw circuits.**

Example 13-25 *show dlsw circuits Command Output*

```
solo#show dlsw circuits
Index            local addr(lsap)    remote addr(dsap)  state       uptime
1778384900       0000.613c.dc82(F0)  0005.332e.2a25(F0) CONNECTED   00:12:27
Total number of circuits connected: 1
```

NOTE   In this model, we use Windows 98 workstations with NetBEUI and Windows networking
enabled to create DLSw circuits. Using Windows networking provides a great application for
testing DLSw. To actually create a circuit, you must browse the network neighborhood and
log into that workstation and access a network resource, such as viewing a drive. It is
important to test your network with as many real applications as possible. This is the *only*
way to actually tell whether your configurations are successful. For example, in this model,
if you did not have workstations, you would never see a circuit be created. So, you might
be thinking, "This is okay—I can status the peers and DLSw capabilities, and get a good
idea that my configuration works." But let's just say you forgot to enable bridging on the
Ethernet interface. The peer will still become active, and, really, from a DLSw point of
view, everything *is* configured properly. However, because of this critical error, DLSw
forwards any traffic to the Ethernet segment. Figure 13-33 displays the workstation R2-D2
finding and then viewing the files on luke.

To configure the FST peer in the model, you can begin adding the loopback interfaces and
addresses to the vader and chewbacca routers.

In Step 2, you add a local peer to each router, pointing at the loopback interface just created.
The command for a local FST peer is identical to that of a TCP peer. For example, on
the vader router, the syntax would be **dlsw local-peer peer-id 172.16.128.1**, and on the
chewbacca router, it would be **dlsw local-peer peer-id 172.16.128.13.**

Figure 13-33 *Using Windows 9x to Test DLSw*

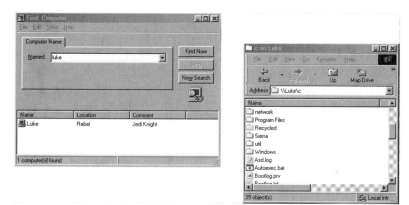

The next step is to configure source-route bridging using a virtual ring for all the interfaces that have end stations on them. The virtual ring is the link that ties DLSw to the source-route bridge. There is no need to configure a command similar to the **dlsw bridge-group** command.

Step 4 calls for configuring a DLSw remote FST peer. The syntax to accomplish this on the chewbacca router would be **dlsw remote-peer 0 fst 172.16.128.1**. Example 13-26 lists the configurations of the chewbacca and vader routers, respectively.

Example 13-26 *FST Peer Configurations of the chewbacca and vader Routers*

```
hostname chewbacca
!
<<<text omitted>>>
!
source-bridge ring-group 111                  ←virtual ring
dlsw local-peer peer-id 172.16.128.13         ←IP address of Loopback 20
dlsw remote-peer 0 fst 172.16.128.1           ←FST peer to Loopback address of vader
!
interface Loopback20
 ip address 172.16.128.13 255.255.255.252
!
interface Serial0
 ip address 172.16.2.2 255.255.255.252
 encapsulation frame-relay
 frame-relay interface-dlci 181
 frame-relay lmi-type cisco
!
<<<text omitted>>>
!
interface TokenRing0
 ip address 172.16.3.1 255.255.255.0
 ring-speed 16
 source-bridge 11 2 111                        ←SRB enabled
```

continues

Example 13-26   *FST Peer Configurations of the chewbacca and vader Routers (Continued)*

```
 source-bridge spanning
!
router eigrp 65001
 network 172.16.0.0
 no auto-summary
!
```

```
hostname vader
!
<<<text omitted>>>
!
source-bridge ring-group 110
dlsw local-peer peer-id 172.16.128.1
dlsw remote-peer 0 fst 172.16.128.13
!
!
interface Loopback20
 ip address 172.16.128.1 255.255.255.252
 no ip directed-broadcast
!
<<<text omitted>>>
!
interface Serial0
 no ip address
 no ip directed-broadcast
 encapsulation frame-relay
 no ip mroute-cache
 logging event subif-link-status
 logging event dlci-status-change
 frame-relay lmi-type cisco
!
interface Serial0.1 multipoint
 ip address 172.16.1.1 255.255.255.0
 no ip directed-broadcast
 no ip split-horizon eigrp 65001
 frame-relay map ip 172.16.1.5 110 broadcast
 frame-relay map ip 172.16.1.6 130 broadcast
!
interface Serial0.2 point-to-point
 ip address 172.16.2.1 255.255.255.252
 no ip directed-broadcast
 frame-relay interface-dlci 180
!
<<<text omitted>>>
!
interface TokenRing0
 ip address 172.16.30.1 255.255.255.0
 no ip directed-broadcast
 ring-speed 16
 source-bridge 10 1 110
 source-bridge spanning
!
```

Example 13-26 *FST Peer Configurations of the chewbacca and vader Routers (Continued)*

```
<<<text omitted>>>
!
router eigrp 65001
 network 172.16.0.0
 no auto-summary
!
```

Again, to view the status of a peer, you can use the **show dlsw peer** command, as shown in Example 13-27.

Example 13-27 *Status of the FST Peer on the chewbacca Router*

```
chewbacca#show dlsw peers
Peers:                  state     pkts_rx   pkts_tx type  drops ckts TCP   uptime

  FST 172.16.128.1    CONNECT      1635      1371  conf      0   1  - 02:23:08

        Expected: 230  Next Send: 194  Seq errors: 0
Total number of connected peers: 1
Total number of connections:     1

chewbacca#
```

The "Big show" and "Big D" for DLSw+

The **show** and **debug** commands for DLSw+ are comprehensive; there are many commands and subcommands for debugging and display DLSw+ info. Again, instead of listing every possible **show** and **debug** command relating to DLSw, we will focus on just a few, or the "Big **show**" and "Big D." For reference, the examples presented in the sections on each of these significant **show** and **debug** commands are generated from the previous model.

The "Big D" for DLSw consists of **debug dlsw peers**, **debug dlsw core**, **debug dlsw reachability**, and their subcommands. As with all **debug** commands, the output can be rather plentiful, so make sure that logging is enabled with the global configuration command **logging buffered 10000**.

The syntax for the "Big show" and the "Big D" is as follows:

```
show dlsw peer [interface interface_name | ip-address ip_address_of_peer]
show dlsw reachability [mac-address mac_address][netbios-name name]
show dlsw circuits [detail] [circuit_number] [mac-address address | sap-value value
| circuit_id]
show dlsw capabilities [interface type number | ip_address ip_address | local]
debug dlsw peers [interface type number | ip_address ip_address ]
debug dlsw reachability [error | verbose] [netbios | sna]
debug dlsw core [flow-control | messages] [state | xis]
```

show dlsw peer Command

This command displays current peer information for static peers and connected peers. The output in Example 13-28 lists the peer type, TCP, FST, or interface number for direct encapsulated peer. The *type* field describes whether the peer is configured, promiscuous, or a peer on demand (POD).

Example 13-28 show dlsw peer *Command Output*

```
skywalker#show dlsw peer
Peers:                 state     pkts_rx    pkts_tx  type  drops ckts TCP    uptime

 TCP 172.16.128.9    CONNECT       1863         847  conf      0    1   0 04:19:26

Total number of connected peers: 1
Total number of connections:     1
```

The possible *states* that a peer can be in are as follows:

- **Connect**—The DLSw peer is up and has a transport active to the peer. This is the normal state that a peer should be in.

- **DISCONNECT**—The local peer does not have a valid or active transport to the remote peer.

- **CAP_EXG**—The local peer is in the capabilities exchange mode with the remote peer. It is awaiting a capabilities response.

- **WAIT_RD**—This is the final step in peer establishment. The local peer's TCP write pipe, TCP port 2065, is waiting for the remote peer to open the read port, TCP port 2067.

- **WAN_BUSY**—The TCP outbound queue is full, and the packet cannot be transmitted.

The **show dlsw peer** also displays the number of packets transmitted and received, along with drops. The TCP column is the TCP queue for the peer. This number should remain low, less than 10 and at 0 a majority of the time. A high TCP number is an indication of congestion or throughput problems to the remote peer. The ckts column lists the number of active circuits on the peer.

show dlsw reachability Command

This command is useful when verifying what end stations DLSw has in its current cache. The reachability cache is a table that the DLSw checks when it receives a request to initiate a session. It checks the cache in an attempt to locate the resource requested. If the destination address is not in the cache, DLSw queries its peers. Example 13-29 lists the output of this command.

Example 13-29 show dlsw reachability *Command Output on the solo Router*

```
solo#show dlsw reachability
DLSw Local MAC address reachability cache list
Mac Addr         status     Loc.    port                       rif
```

Example 13-29 show dlsw reachability *Command Output on the solo Router (Continued)*

```
0000.613c.dc82   FOUND      LOCAL    TBridge-001    --no rif--
0006.3acf.7aa6   FOUND      LOCAL    TBridge-001    --no rif--

DLSw Remote MAC address reachability cache list
Mac Addr         status     Loc.     peer
0005.332e.2a25   FOUND      REMOTE   172.16.128.5(2065) max-lf(1500)

DLSw Local NetBIOS Name reachability cache list
NetBIOS Name     status     Loc.     port              rif
R2-D2            FOUND      LOCAL    TBridge-001    --no rif--

DLSw Remote NetBIOS Name reachability cache list
NetBIOS Name     status     Loc.     peer
LUKE             FOUND      REMOTE   172.16.128.5(2065) max-lf(1500)

solo#
```

The Status field describes the local peer's relationship with that entry. The Location field describes whether the end station is considered local or remote to the router. The possible values for the status field are listed here:

- **FOUND**—The router has located the end station.
- **NOT_FOUND**—The end station has not responded to queries from this router or peer.
- **SEARCHING**—The router is sending queries for the station in an attempt to locate it.
- **UNCONFIRMED**—The station is a static entry, such as with a DLSW ICANREACH entry.
- **VERIFY**—Cache is going stale, and the router is verifying it.

Other information includes the displaced peer/port or the peer the station is accessible from. The RIF and largest frame also are listed. The value —**no rif**— in the RIF fields means that the station does not support a RIF, such as an Ethernet station.

It is important to note that this information is cached, so entries will be aged and flushed. If a station currently is sending or trying to send data, it should be listed in the output of the command.

show dlsw circuits Command

Use this command to display end-to-end sessions of peers using TCP encapsulation or Frame Relay direct encapsulation with local acknowledgment. This command displays the local MAC address and remote address along with SAP that they are using. Example 13-30 lists the circuit between the workstations luke and R2-D2. The SAP value is (F0), for NetBIOS. The second half of the example shows the detailed listing of circuit.

Example 13-30 **show dlsw circuits** *Command Output on solo Router*

```
solo#show dlsw circuits
Index           local addr(lsap)    remote addr(dsap)   state         uptime
2919235595      0000.613c.dc82(F0)  0005.332e.2a25(F0)  CONNECTED     00:01:17
Total number of circuits connected: 1


solo#show dlsw circuits detail
Index           local addr(lsap)    remote addr(dsap)   state         uptime
2919235595      0000.613c.dc82(F0)  0005.332e.2a25(F0)  CONNECTED     00:01:28
        PCEP: 49AC68     UCEP: 142AFC
        Port:TB1         peer 172.16.128.5(2065)
        Flow-Control-Tx  CW:20, Permitted:39; Rx CW:20, Granted:29; Op: Repeat
        Congestion: Low(02), Flow Op: Half: 0/0 Reset 0/0
        RIF = --no rif--
        Bytes:          2702/6467      Info-frames:        41/31
        XID-frames:        0/0         UInfo-frames:        0/0
Total number of circuits connected: 1

solo#
```

Circuits can be in one of two states, CONNECTED or CKT_ESTABLISHED. When the
circuit is registering as CKT_ESTABLISHED, DLSw has set up the circuit properly, but
the end stations have not, or cannot, initiated a session across the circuit. A restart of the
end station might help clear this condition.

show dlsw capabilities Command

This command lists the control vectors that the local peer will exchange with other peers
during the *capabilities exchange*. The output of this command is useful when SAP and
NetBIOS filters are applied to DLSw peers. Example 13-31 lists the output of this
command.

Example 13-31 **show dlsw capabilities** *Command Output on solo Router*

```
solo#show dlsw capabilities
DLSw: Capabilities for peer 172.16.128.5(2065)
  vendor id (OUI)          : '00C' (cisco)
  version number           : 2
  release number           : 0
  init pacing window       : 20
  unsupported saps         : none
  num of tcp sessions      : 1
  loop prevent support     : no
  icanreach mac-exclusive  : no
  icanreach netbios-excl.  : no
  reachable mac addresses  : none
  reachable netbios names  : none
```

Example 13-31 show dlsw capabilities *Command Output on solo Router (Continued)*

```
        V2 multicast capable     : yes
        DLSw multicast address   : none
        cisco version number     : 1
        peer group number        : 0
        peer cluster support     : no
        border peer capable      : no
        peer cost                : 3
        biu-segment configured   : no
        UDP Unicast support      : yes
        Fast-switched HPR supp.   : no
        NetBIOS Namecache length : 15
        local-ack configured     : yes
        priority configured      : no
        cisco RSVP support       : no
        configured ip address    : 172.16.128.5
        peer type                : conf
        version string           :
Cisco Internetwork Operating System Software
IOS (tm) 2500 Software (C2500-JS-L), Version 12.1(2)T,  RELEASE SOFTWARE (fc1)
Copyright (c) 1986-2000 by cisco Systems, Inc.
Compiled Tue 16-May-00 15:28 by ccai
```

debug dlsw peers Command

Figures 13-30 and 13-31 from the previous section can be useful when used in conjunction with the **debug**s listed. Use the figures as a guide to help you locate where in the data flows you might be having a problem.

This command provides comprehensive information about the peer status and current actions. Use this **debug** when a peer will not connect or stay active. Example 13-32 lists the output from the **debug** DLSw peers during a NetBIOS session establishment.

Example 13-32 debug dlsw peer *Command Output During NetBIOS Session Establishment*

```
solo#debug dlsw peers
DLSw peer debugging is on
solo#
01:55:59: %SYS-5-CONFIG_I: Configured from console by console
01:55:59: %LINEPROTO-5-UPDOWN: Line protocol on Interface DLSw Port0, changed state
          to up
01:56:00: DLSw: passive open 172.16.128.5(11000) -> 2065
01:56:00: DLSw: START-TPFSM (peer 172.16.128.5(2065)): event:TCP-RD PIPE OPENED
state:DISCONN
01:56:00: DLSw: dtp_action_c() opening write pipe for peer 172.16.128.5(2065)
01:56:00: DLSw: END-TPFSM (peer 172.16.128.5(2065)): state:DISCONN->WWR_RDOP

01:56:00: DLSw: Async Open Callback 172.16.128.5(2065) -> 11010
01:56:00: DLSw: START-TPFSM (peer 172.16.128.5(2065)): event:TCP-WR PIPE OPENED
```

continues

Example 13-32 **debug dlsw peer** *Command Output During NetBIOS Session Establishment (Continued)*

```
01:56:00: DLSw: dtp_action_i() write pipe opened for peer 172.16.128.5(2065)
01:56:00: DLSw: CapExId Msg sent to peer 172.16.128.5(2065)
01:56:00: DLSw: END-TPFSM (peer 172.16.128.5(2065)): state:WWR_RDOP->WAIT_CAP

01:56:00: DLSw: START-TPFSM (peer 172.16.128.5(2065)): event:SSP-CAP MSG RCVD st
ate:WAIT_CAP
01:56:00: DLSw: dtp_action_j() cap msg rcvd from peer 172.16.128.5(2065)
01:56:00: DLSw: Recv CapExId Msg from peer 172.16.128.5(2065)
01:56:00: DLSw: received fhpr capex from peer 172.16.128.5(2065): support: false
, fst-prio: false
01:56:00: DLSw: Pos CapExResp sent to peer 172.16.128.5(2065)
01:56:00: DLSw: END-TPFSM (peer 172.16.128.5(2065)): state:WAIT_CAP->WAIT_CAP

01:56:00: DLSw: START-TPFSM (peer 172.16.128.5(2065)): event:SSP-CAP MSG RCVD st
ate:WAIT_CAP
01:56:00: DLSw: dtp_action_j() cap msg rcvd from peer 172.16.128.5(2065)
01:56:00: DLSw: Recv CapExPosRsp Msg from peer 172.16.128.5(2065)
01:56:00: DLSw: END-TPFSM (peer 172.16.128.5(2065)): state:WAIT_CAP->WAIT_CAP

01:56:00: DLSw: Processing delayed event:SSP-CAP EXCHANGED - prev state:WAIT_CAP

01:56:00: DLSw: START-TPFSM (peer 172.16.128.5(2065)): event:SSP-CAP EXCHANGED s
tate:WAIT_CAP
01:56:00: DLSw: dtp_action_k() cap xchged for peer 172.16.128.5(2065)
01:56:00: DLSw: closing read pipe tcp connection for peer 172.16.128.5(2065)
01:56:00: DLSw: END-TPFSM (peer 172.16.128.5(2065)): state:WAIT_CAP->PCONN_WT

01:56:00: DLSw: Processing delayed event:TCP-PEER CONNECTED - prev state:PCONN_W
T
01:56:00: DLSw: START-TPFSM (peer 172.16.128.5(2065)): event:TCP-PEER CONNECTED
state:PCONN_WT
01:56:00: DLSw: dtp_action_m() peer connected for peer 172.16.128.5(2065)
01:56:00: DLSw: END-TPFSM (peer 172.16.128.5(2065)): state:PCONN_WT->CONNECT
01:56:31: DLSw: START-TPFSM (peer 172.16.128.5(2065)): event:DLX-KEEPALIVE REQ s
tate:CONNECT
01:56:31: DLSw: dtp_action_q() keepalive request from peer 172.16.128.5(2065)
01:56:31: DLSw: Keepalive Response sent to peer 172.16.128.5(2065))
01:56:31: DLSw: END-TPFSM (peer 172.16.128.5(2065)): state:CONNECT->CONNECT
```

debug dlsw reachability Command

This command provides a clear picture of the end station's MAC address and the associated SSAPs and DSAPs. The **debug** also provide information on the message type that is being issued by that end station. Use this **debug** if end stations are not showing up in the DLSw reachability cache. Example 13-33 demonstrates the output from this command.

Example 13-33 debug dlsw reachability *Command Output During a NetBIOS NAME_QUERY*

```
solo#debug dlsw reachability
DLSw reachability debugging is on at event level for all protocol traffic
09:51:40: CSM: Received CLSI Msg : UDATA_STN.Ind   dlen: 79 from DLSw Port0
09:51:40: CSM:   smac 0000.613c.dc82, dmac c000.0000.0080, ssap F0, dsap F0
09:51:40: CSM: Received frame type NETBIOS NAME_QUERY from 0000.613c.dc82, DL0
09:51:40: CSM: Received CLSI Msg : CONECT_STN.Ind   dlen: 47 from DLSw Port0
09:51:40: CSM:   smac 0000.613c.dc82, dmac 0005.332e.2a25, ssap F0, dsap F0
09:51:43: CSM: Received CLSI Msg : UDATA_STN.Ind   dlen: 86 from DLSw Port0
09:51:43: CSM:   smac 0006.3acf.7aa6, dmac ffff.ffff.ffff, ssap AA, dsap AA
```

debug dlsw core Command

This command provides visibility to virtually everything that is occurring in the DLSw code. If no subcommands are added, all core debugging is enabled. Naturally, this command generates a lot of output and should be used to narrow down specific problems. Again, use this command in the field only with console logging buffered.

DLSw+ Advanced Configuration

DLSw provides many features that allow for easier peer configuration, explorer control, and backup and filtering capabilities. This section covers configuration of some of the more advanced features of DLSw+. These features include the following:

- DLSw+ promiscuous peers configurations
- DLSw+ backup configurations
- DLSw+ border peers, peer groups, and demand peers
- Controlling DLSw explorers with ring lists, bridge group lists, and port lists
- DLSw+ dynamic peers
- Configuring DLSw+ reachability with the **icanreach** command

DLSw+ Promiscuous Peer Configuration

DLSw+ allows you to configure different types of peers. The peer types that you have configured up to this point have been static peers. That is, a remote peer needs to be defined for every DLSw peer that you want to connect to. In large DLSw networks, where there are many peers, this type of configuration can be rather lengthy. When a local peer is configured in *promiscuous mode*, it automatically accepts peer connections from remote peers without having a specific remote peer configured. To configure a local peer as promiscuous, use the following syntax:

```
Router(config)#dlsw local-peer peer-id ip_address promiscuous
```

Figure 3-34 illustrates a DLSw+ network, with the vader router using its local peer as promiscuous. With the local peer as promiscuous, there is no need to configure any **remote-peer** statements for the skywalker, solo, and chewbacca routers. The remote routers, however, still need a **remote-peer** statement pointing at the promiscuous peer.

Figure 13-34 *Promiscuous Peers*

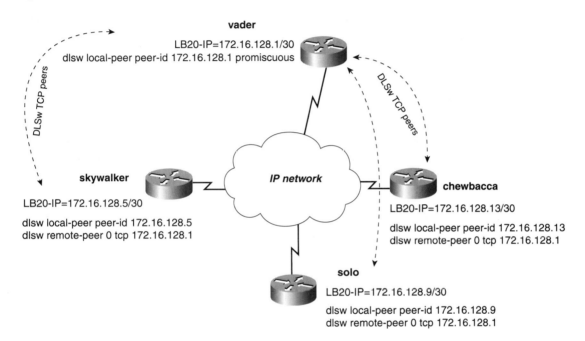

Promiscuous peers have standard default values for all remote peers that connect to them. For example, use this command if you want to change keepalive values or other such parameters for the remote peers that connect to the promiscuous peers. To change these default values or apply access lists, use the following syntax:

```
Router(config)#dlsw prom-peer-defaults [bytes-netbios-out bytes-list-name] [cost 1-5]
    [dest-mac destination_mac_address] [dmac-output-list access-list-number]
    [host-netbios-out host-list-name] [keepalive seconds] [lf largest_frame_516-11407]
    [LSAP-output-list list] [tcp-queue-max size]
```

DLSw+ Backup Configurations

DLSw offers a couple of methods to configure redundancy, depending on whether you want to keep the DLSw peer active. One method is configuring a peer as a *backup peer*. When a peer is configured as backup, it becomes active only when the router loses connectivity to the primary peer or DLSw router. The other method is used primarily to provide peer stability during a link failure. In this method, you tweak DLSw timeout and keepalives, to essentially keep the peer up during a routing protocol convergence, or during the time that it takes to activate a DDR or backup link.

DLSw+ Backup Peers

Backup peers are created by simply adding the *backup-peer* argument to the new remote peer. Before creating a backup peer, you must define the primary peer. The backup peer must point at a different DLSw router than the primary peer. The **linger** keyword tells the router not to disconnect the backup peer until the primary has been up for *X* amount of seconds. Without the **linger** keyword, the primary peer immediately becomes active when connectivity is restored.

LLC2 sessions automatically are terminated when the linger timer expires, and this can be an undesirable result of the backup peer. If the **linger** keyword is omitted, the backup peer stays active when the primary peer comes online, but no new circuits will be created over the backup link. Existing LLC2 circuits on the backup link remain active. Therefore, do not use the **linger** option if you do not want to terminate active circuits on the backup peer. If a linger value of 0 is used, the backup peer stays active until it fails, despite the status of the primary peer. The positive side of the linger option is that it will greatly stabilize the DLSw peers during situations in which a link might be flapping. The steps and syntax for configuring a backup peer are as follows:

Step 1 Configure a primary peer to the primary DLSw router.

```
dlsw remote-peer 0 tcp primary_peers_ip_address
```

Step 2 Configure a backup peer to a new DLSw router.

```
dlsw remote-peer 0 tcp backup_peers_ip_address backup-peer
    primary_peers_ip_address linger timeout_in_minutes
```

In Figure 13-35, the solo router has a primary peer to the falcon router and a backup peer to skywalker. The peers on falcon and vader are configured as promiscuous, so no remote peer statements are needed for DLSw routers to establish a peer connection with these routers. On the router solo, we have configured a backup peer to skywalker. The statement **dlsw remote-peer 0 tcp 172.16.128.5 backup-peer 172.16.128.1 linger 5** instructs the solo router to establish a new peer to the skywalker router if the peer to falcon fails.

Example 13-34 shows the output of the **show dlsw peer** command on the solo router from the previous figure. Notice that the backup peer is in a disconnect state while the primary is up.

Figure 13-35 *Backup and Promiscuous Peers*

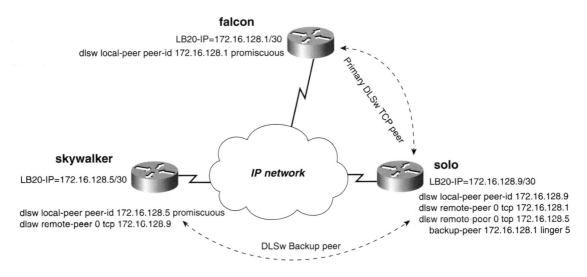

Example 13-34 **show dlsw peer** *Command Output on solo Router Reveals Backup Peer Status*

```
solo#show dlsw peer
Peers:                  state     pkts_rx   pkts_tx  type  drops ckts TCP    uptime

 TCP 172.16.128.1       CONNECT      1268        190  conf      1    0    0 00:21:56

 TCP 172.16.128.5       DISCONN         0          0  conf      0    0    -         -

Total number of connected peers: 1
Total number of connections:     1

solo#
```

When the primary peer fails, the backup peer to the skywalker router will become active,
as in Example 13-35.

Example 13-35 *show dlsw peer Command Output on solo Router Reveals Backup Peer Status*

```
solo#show dlsw peer
Peers:                  state     pkts_rx   pkts_tx  type  drops ckts TCP    uptime

 TCP 172.16.128.5       CONNECT         2          4  conf      0    0    0 00:00:29

 TCP 172.16.128.1       DISCONN         0          0  conf      0    0    -         -
```

Example 13-35 *show dlsw peer Command Output on solo Router Reveals Backup Peer Status (Continued)*

```
Total number of connected peers: 1
Total number of connections:    1

solo#
```

When the primary peer between the solo and falcon routers becomes active again, the solo router waits until after the linger timer expires—in this example, 5 minutes—until it disconnects the backup peer and reconnects the primary peer.

DLSw+ Backup over DDR

The other method of DLSw+ backup involves keeping the peer connection established during a link failure. For example, if you are using an ISDN link for backup, you might want to keep the peer active while the ISDN line dials and makes a connection. The time for link such as this to converge can exceed the DLSw+ keepalive timers and force the peer down. The DLSw+ keepalives operate on TCP port 2065, which also makes it hard to control significant traffic with ACLs because data and keepalives use the same TCP port number. The **no keepalive** argument also keeps an ISDN link from dialing because of this type of traffic. Whenever setting the keepalive to 0, DLSw+ cannot tell whether the peer is still active based on keepalives. Therefore, it *never* tears down the peer based on missed keepalives. By adding a timeout value, the peer automatically is disconnected if no data has been received from a peer for the length of the timeout value.

To configure DLSw+ to operate in environments like this, you can control the timeout values and keepalives of DLSw+. To configure this form of backup, follow this two-step process:

Step 1   Use the keywords **keepalive 0** on the local peer for both routers.

Step 2   Assign a **timeout** value to the **remote-peer** statement on both routers.

In Figure 13-36, the solo router has a DLSw+ TCP peer and an ISDN backup connection to the falcon router.

To keep the peer active while ISDN converges, set the keepalive to 0 and the timeout value to 5 minutes, or 300 seconds. Example 13-36 illustrates the peer from solo to the falcon router remaining active during convergence, while IP connectivity temporary doesn't exist.

Figure 13-36 *Backup Peers over DDR*

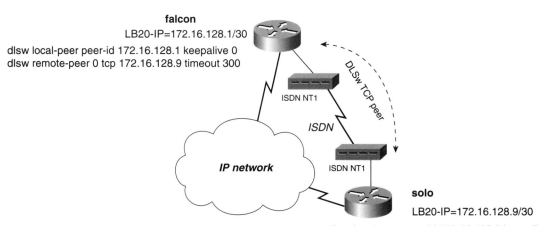

falcon
LB20-IP=172.16.128.1/30

dlsw local-peer peer-id 172.16.128.1 keepalive 0
dlsw remote-peer 0 tcp 172.16.128.9 timeout 300

ISDN NT1

ISDN

IP network

ISDN NT1

solo
LB20-IP=172.16.128.9/30

dlsw local-peer peer-id 172.16.128.9 keepalive 0
dlsw remote-peer 0 tcp 172.16.128.1 timeout 300

Example 13-36 *DLSw+ Peer Remaining Active, While No IP Connectivity Exists*

```
solo#show dlsw peer
Peers:                  state    pkts_rx  pkts_tx  type  drops ckts TCP    uptime

 TCP 172.16.128.1    CONNECT       14        2  conf     0    0   0 00:01:37

Total number of connected peers: 1
Total number of connections:     1

solo#ping 172.16.128.1

Type escape sequence to abort.
Sending 5, 100-byte ICMP Echos to 172.16.128.1, timeout is 2 seconds:
.....
Success rate is 0 percent (0/5)
solo#
```

DLSw+ Border Peers, Peer Groups, and Demand Peers

Border peers and peer groups provide an effective way to scale DLSw networks that require any-to-any reachability and to control explorers. A DLSw router that requires any-to-any reachability would need a **remote-peer** statement to every router that it has a connection to. For example, Figure 13-37 illustrates a common network.

Figure 13-37 *DLSw Full Reachability*

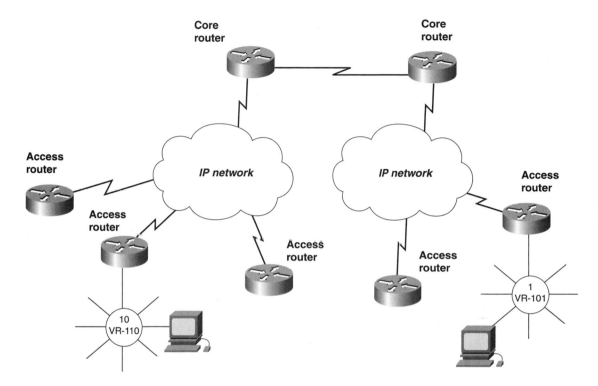

Only two workstations are illustrated in the figure, but they represent workstations that would reside on all the LAN segments of the access routers. For the workstations on the access routers to reach any workstations on any other access router, multiple remote peers statements are needed.

Figure 13-38 represents all of the **remote-peer** statements that would be needed for any-to-any reachability to take place.

In this small network, you would have to configure 42 **remote-peer** statements. You easily can see how this type of network doesn't scale well. Besides, the amount of configuration associated with this type of network is the amount of explorer traffic traveling from peer to peer, which is more harmful than some extra keystrokes.

Figure 13-38 *TCP Peers Required in a Fully Meshed Network*

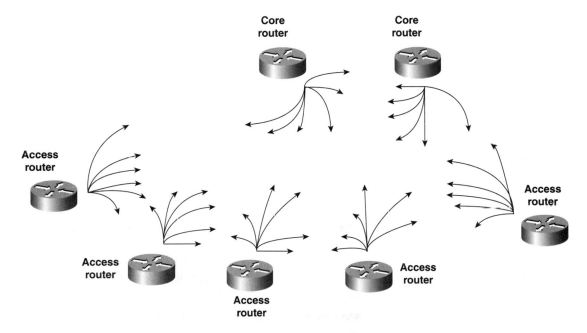

Cisco DLSw+ supports the concept of peer groups and border peers and peer-on-demand. A peer group is a group of routers with one or more members designated as a border peer. The border peer's role is to forward explorers for routers in the peer group. When the border peer receives an explorer, it checks its *local, remote, and group cache* before forwarding the explorer to other routers. When the border peer checks its cache, if it gets a hit in its *local cache*, it does not forward the explorer to other routers. The *remote cache* contains information on reachability within the peer group. If the border peer gets a hit on this type of cache, it forwards the explorer only to routers in the same group. The *group cache* contains information about the other peer groups to which the border peer does not belong. When the border peer gets a hit in this cache, it forwards the explorer only to border peers.

Figure 13-39 illustrates how the network would look if you divided it into two peer groups. Each peer group must have one border router to handle the proper forwarding of explorers for that group. The border peers also must have a peer between them.

Figure 13-39 *DLSw Border Peers and Peer Groups*

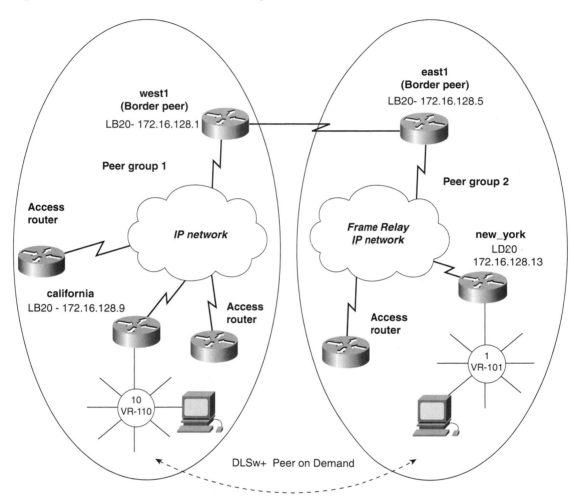

To configure border peers and peer groups, use the following process:

Step 1 Divide the network into peer groups.

Step 2 Configure the peer group so that there is a single peer from all the routers to one peer within that group. This router with all the peers will be configured as the border peer. To configure a peer group, use the keyword **group** *x* on the **local-peer** statement. To configure a peer as a border peer, use the keyword **border** on the **local-peer** statement.

Step 3 Configure a DLSw peer between border peers.

Step 4   Optional: Configure DLSw peer-on-demand. For any-to-any reachability, such as with a NetBIOS or APPN applications, you must configure DLSw peer-on-demand. The peer-on-demand will allow a demand peer to be created between end stations that do not have a static peer configured between them. A demand peer is formed when a router in a peer group requests services from another router either in the group or external to it. To configure peer-on-demand, use the following syntax:

```
dlsw peer-on-demand-defaults [tcp 25-2000]
```

The command **dlsw peer-on-demand** allows for a peer to be created "on demand," or a demand peer. Do not confuse demand peers with dynamic peers—these two are different types of peers. The default values for the demand peer can be changed with the following global configuration command:

```
Router(config)#dlsw peer-on-demand-defaults [fst] [bytes-netbios-out bytes-list-name]
[cost 1-5] [dest-mac destination_mac_address] [dmac-output-list access list-number]
[host-netbios-out host-list-name] [keepalive seconds] [lf largest_frame_516-11407]
[lsap-output-list list] [port-list port-list-number][priority] [tcp-queue-max size]
```

When configuring border peers and peer groups, keep the following rules in mind:

- In a single group, every member peer must peer to every border peer in its group.
- All border peers in a group must peer to each other.
- All border peers within a group must peer to every border peer in the other peer groups.
- Border peers forward explorers to all member peers in their group, all border peers in their group, and one border peer in every other group.

In Figure 13-39, we have assigned IP addresses to routers and divided them into two peer groups. The west router will serve as the border peer for group 1, while the east router will serve as the border peer for group 2. Example 13-37 lists the DLSw configuration of the routers in Figure 13-39.

Example 13-37 *Configuring Border Peers and Peer Groups*

```
Configuration of the west router:

dlsw local-peer peer-id 172.16.128.1 group 1 border promiscuous
dlsw remote-peer 0 tcp 172.16.128.5
!
!
Configurations of the routers in group 1, such as the california router:

dlsw local-peer peer-id 172.16.128.9 group 1 promiscuous
dlsw remote-peer 0 tcp 172.16.128.1
dlsw peer-on-demand-defaults tcp-queue-max 50
!
Configuration of the east router:

dlsw local-peer peer-id 172.16.128.5 group 2 border promiscuous
```

Example 13-37 *Configuring Border Peers and Peer Groups (Continued)*

```
dlsw remote-peer 0 tcp 172.16.128.1
!
!
Configurations of the routers in group 2, such as the new_york router:

dlsw local-peer peer-id 172.16.128.13 group 2 promiscuous
dlsw remote-peer 0 tcp 172.16.128.5
dlsw peer-on-demand-defaults tcp-queue-max 50
!
```

Controlling DLSw+ Explorers with Ring Lists, Bridge Group Lists, and Port Lists

Because you can configure only a single local peer on a router, this makes it difficult to control explorers among peers. A ring list allows you to specify which virtual rings or bridge groups will receive explorers from a specific remote peer.

For example, in Figure 13-40, the yoda router has two Ethernet interfaces. One Ethernet interface, E0, is in bridge group 1; the other interface, E1, is in bridge group 2.

Figure 13-40 *DLSw Bridge Group Lists*

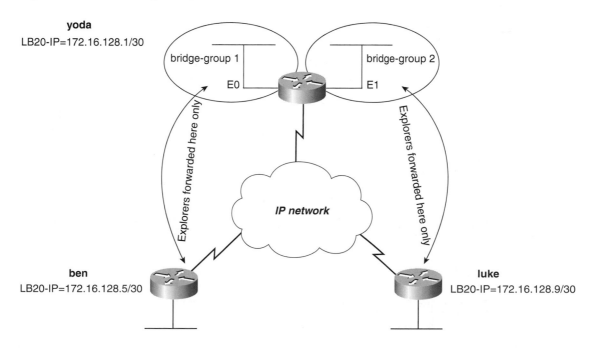

In this model, you want to control DLSw+ so that explorers from the router ben will be forwarded only to the E0 interface, or bridge group 1. Explorers from the router luke should be forwarded only to the E1 interface on the yoda router. To accomplish this type of configuration, DLSw+ supports the use of ring and port lists. To create a ring or port list, use the following procedure:

Step 1 Separate the Token Ring and Ethernet bridging domains. For Ethernet networks, separate the bridging domains by placing Ethernet segments in different bridge groups. For example, E0 will be in bridge group 1, and E1 will be in bridge group 2. In this example, you also need to add the commands **bridge 1 protocol ieee** and **bridge 2 protocol ieee**. For every bridge group, you will need to add that bridge group to DLSw+. In the previous example, you would need two commands to accomplish this— **dlsw bridge-group 1** and **dlsw bridge-group 2.**

For Token Ring networks, you would create separate virtual rings and source-route bridge each Token Ring interface to the various virtual rings. For example, Token Ring 0 would have the command **source-bridge 10 1 100** to source-route bridge the interface to virtual ring 100. The other interface would be source-route bridged to another virtual ring.

Step 2 Create a ring list. For Token Ring networks, create a ring list with the following global command:

```
Router(config)#dlsw ring-list list_number_1-255 rings virtual-ring(s)
```

For Ethernet networks, create a ring list with the following global command:

```
Router(config)#dlsw bgroup-list list_number_1-255 bgroups
bridge_group_number(s)
```

Step 3 Call the ring list on the DLSw+ **remote-peer** statement. For example, if you use the command **dlsw bgroup-list 1 bgroups 1** to create a ring list for Ethernet, you could call this list on the remote peer statement with the command **dlsw remote-peer 1 tcp** *ip_address.*

In Figure 13-41, we created two bridge groups on the router yoda. Each bridge group then is added to a DLSw bgroup list. The peer to the router ben will call bgroup list 1, and the peer to the router luke will call bgroup list 2.

Explorers from luke will be forwarded only to the E1 interface on the router yoda. Explorers from the router ben will be forwarded only to the E0 interface on the yoda router. Example 13-38 lists the configuration of the yoda router.

Figure 13-41 *DLSw+ Bridge Group Lists Example*

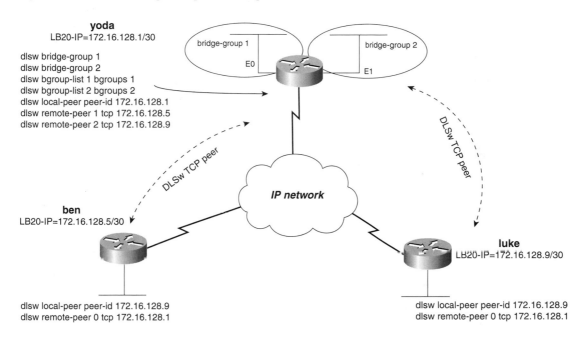

Example 13-38 *Configuration of the yoda Router*

```
hostname yoda
!
<<<text omitted>>>
!
dlsw local-peer peer-id 172.16.128.1
dlsw bgroup-list 1 bgroups 1
dlsw bgroup-list 2 bgroups 2
dlsw remote-peer 1 tcp 172.16.128.5
dlsw remote-peer 2 tcp 172.16.128.9
dlsw bridge-group 1
dlsw bridge-group 2
!
interface Loopback20
 ip address 172.16.128.1 255.255.255.252
 no ip directed-broadcast
!
interface Ethernet0
 no ip address
 no ip directed-broadcast
 media-type 10BaseT
```

continues

Example 13-38 *Configuration of the yoda Router (Continued)*

```
 bridge-group 1
!
interface Ethernet1
 no ip address
 no ip directed-broadcast
 media-type 10BaseT
 bridge-group 2
!
<<<text omitted>>>
!
bridge 1 protocol ieee
bridge 2 protocol ieee
```

A port list might be used to map traffic on a local interface, either a Token Ring or a serial interface, to a remote peer. The syntax to accomplish this is as follows:

```
Router(config)#dlsw port-list list_number_1-255 [token-ring | serial]
interface_number
```

The port list is called in the same manner as the ring list or bridge list, on the **remote-peer** statement.

DLSw+ Dynamic Peers

A *dynamic peer* is yet another type of DLSw peer. A dynamic peer is a peer that becomes active only when certain criteria are met, such as MAC address or SAP type. To configure a dynamic peer, use the keyword **dynamic** on the remote peer statement. The **inactivity** timer also should be set when creating a dynamic peer. A dynamic peer will stay active 10 minutes after the last circuit has disconnected from the peer. When you create a dynamic peer, the router automatically adds a timeout value and disables keepalives. This is for the same reasons mentioned in the previous section on configuring backup over DDR.

If you are using promiscuous peers with dynamic peers, be sure to modify the default values of the promiscuous peers to disable the keepalives. This can be done with the **dlsw prom-peer-defaults** command, as mentioned previously.

In Figure 13-42, the solo router has a dynamic peer configured to skywalker. The **remote-peer** statement instructs the peer to be *dynamic* and to become active only when the output SAP filter 201 is met. The peer will remain active for 5 minutes after the last circuit has disconnected. The router inserts the keepalive 0 and timeout 90 on the remote peer statement automatically. The SAP filter in this example is access list 201, which permits only SAP 0xF0F0, the NetBIOS SAP. We will discuss SAP filters more in the next section.

Figure 13-42 *DLSw Dynamic Peer*

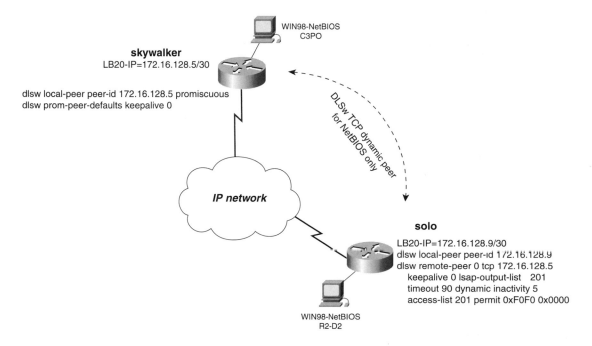

Example 13-39 lists the configuration of the solo router, with the dynamic peer configured to skywalker.

Example 13-39 *Configuration of the solo Router*

```
hostname solo
!
<<<text omitted>>>
!
dlsw local-peer peer-id 172.16.128.9
dlsw remote-peer 0 tcp 172.16.128.5 keepalive 0 lsap-output-list 201 timeout 90
   dynamic inactivity 5
dlsw bridge-group 1
!
interface Loopback20
 ip address 172.16.128.9 255.255.255.252
 no ip directed-broadcast
!
interface Ethernet0
 ip address 172.16.6.1 255.255.255.0
 no ip directed-broadcast
 bridge-group 1
!
```

continues

Example 13-39 *Configuration of the solo Router (Continued)*

```
<<<text omitted>>>
!
access-list 201 permit 0xF0F0 0x0000          ←NETBIOS SAP
bridge 1 protocol ieee
```

NOTE   Do not confuse dynamic peers with promiscuous or demand peers. This can be hard to do because all of these peer types are *dynamic* in some form.

Configuring DLSw+ Reachability with the **icanreach** Command

During the DLSw+ capabilities exchange, routers also exchange what resources they can reach in the control vectors. This is information that can be statically configured on the router. By configuring what SAP, MAC address, and NetBIOS names the router can reach, it can greatly reduce the number of explorers sent to remote peers. Along with the resources that the router can reach, you can configure the SAP values that the router cannot reach. If a router has a static entry defined by the **icannotreach** command, it also reports that to its peers. The peer keeps track of what resources it cannot reach and avoids sending explorers to those peers. To configure DLSW+ reachability, use the following commands:

```
Router(config)#dlsw icanreach [mac-address | saps | netbios-name]
Router(config)#dlsw icannotreach [saps] <0-FE> Even SAP Value (hex)
```

When using the **icanreach saps** command, be careful because it will deny all other SAPs. In other words, there is an implicit "deny all SAPs" that follow the use of this command. It is best to use the **icannotreach** command to deny explicit SAPs.

Use the **mac-exclusive** parameters and the **netbios-exclusive** arguments to advertise reachability to a single address or host. These commands must be used with another statement, **dlsw icanreach mac address** or **netbios name**:

```
Router(config)#dlsw icanreach [mac-exclusive | netbios-exclusive]
```

In Figure 13-43, we have configured DLSw reachability on the falcon router. In this example, the falcon router will advertise that it can reach only a single MAC address, 3745.1000.1010. Example 13-40 lists the configuration needed on the falcon router to accomplish this.

Example 13-40 *Configuration DLSw+ Reachability on the falcon Router*

```
!
dlsw local-peer peer-id 172.16.128.5 promiscuous
dlsw icanreach mac-exclusive
dlsw icanreach mac-address 3745.1000.1010 mask ffff.ffff.ffff
dlsw bridge-group 1
!
```

Figure 13-43 *DLSw Reachablity*

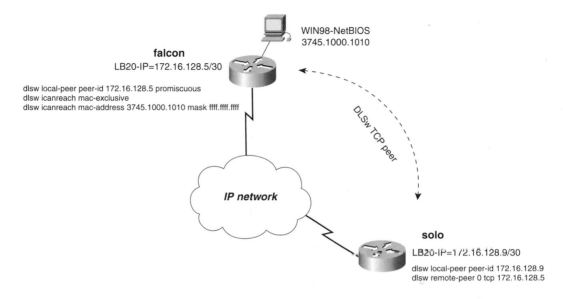

By viewing the DLSw reachability on the solo router in Example 13-41, you can see that the MAC address is the only one being advertised by the falcon router. The status is unconfirmed because it is a static entry.

Example 13-41 *The DLSw Reachability on the solo Router*

```
solo#show dlsw reach
DLSw Local MAC address reachability cache list
Mac Addr        status    Loc.    port              rif
0000.613c.dc82  FOUND     LOCAL   TBridge-001    --no rif--
0006.3acf.7aa6  FOUND     LOCAL   TBridge-001    --no rif--
0007.781a.e7a9  FOUND     LOCAL   TBridge-001    --no rif--

DLSw Remote MAC address reachability cache list
Mac Addr        status    Loc.    peer
3745.1000.1010  UNCONFIRM  REMOTE  172.16.128.5(2065)

DLSw Local NetBIOS Name reachability cache list
NetBIOS Name    status    Loc.    port              rif
R2-D2           FOUND     LOCAL   TBridge-001    --no rif--

DLSw Remote NetBIOS Name reachability cache list
NetBIOS Name    status    Loc.    peer
```

To view details about what addresses and SAP the router now can reach, use the **show dlsw capabilities** command. Example 13-42 lists the capabilities on the solo router. Notice that one MAC address is reported, and the max-exclusive column now is set to yes.

Example 13-42 *The DLSw+ Capabilities of the solo Router*

```
solo#show dlsw capabilities
DLSw: Capabilities for peer 172.16.128.5(2065)
  vendor id (OUI)          : '00C' (cisco)
  version number           : 2
  release number           : 0
  init pacing window       : 20
  unsupported saps         : none
  num of tcp sessions      : 1
  loop prevent support     : no
  icanreach mac-exclusive  : yes
  icanreach netbios-excl.  : no
  reachable mac addresses  : 3745.1000.1010 <mask ffff.ffff.ffff>
  reachable netbios names  : none
  V2 multicast capable     : yes
  DLSw multicast address   : none
  cisco version number     : 1
  peer group number        : 0
  peer cluster support     : no
  border peer capable      : no
  peer cost                : 3
  biu-segment configured   : no
  UDP Unicast support      : yes
  Fast-switched HPR supp.  : no
  NetBIOS Namecache length : 15
  local-ack configured     : yes
  priority configured      : no
  cisco RSVP support       : no
  configured ip address    : 172.16.128.5
  peer type                : prom
  version string           :
Cisco Internetwork Operating System Software
IOS (tm) 2500 Software (C2500-JS-L), Version 12.1(2)T,  RELEASE SOFTWARE (fc1)
Copyright (c) 1986-2000 by cisco Systems, Inc.
Compiled Tue 16-May-00 15:28 by ccai

solo#
```

You also can use the **dlsw reachability** command to help you test DLSw networks. By configuring a router with a **dlsw icanreach** *dummyname*, you can easily tell whether your DLSw configuration is working by examining the reachability of its peer routers.

Filtering Traffic in Bridged Environments

In this section, we discuss the various methods for filtering in a bridged environment. If you are not familiar with access lists you might want to skip ahead to Chapter 14, "Understanding IP Access Lists." Even though that chapter deals strictly with IP access lists, the concepts, rules, and tips apply to all access lists.

Filtering for bridges and data-link switches occurs at the data link layer. Cisco provides three primary types of filters for the data link layer:

* Service access point (SAP) filters
* MAC filters
* NetBIOS name filters

Filtering SAPs

For SNAP encapsulated frames, an access list filters based on the 2-byte TYPE field given after the DSAP/SAP/OUI fields of the frame. For IEEE 802.2 frames, access lists filter on the DSAP/SSAP fields. The syntax for an access list to filter based on SAPs is as follows:

```
Router(config)#access-list [200-299] [deny | permit] [0x0-0xFFFF] <0x0-0xFFFF>
```

The first value is the protocol type code, and the second value is the protocol type-code mask. The valid range for access lists that filter based on the protocol type field or SAP is 200 to 299. The access list is entered in hexadecimal format, where the hexadecimal address is followed by a wildcard mask. The wildcard mask is applied to the address, where a 1 bit means "don't care" and a 0 bit is a "care" bit. An all 0's masks means that you must match the address bit for bit, to yield a TRUE result for the access list. For more information on access-list formats and the wildcard mask, skip ahead to Chapter 14.

SNA SAPs

SNA uses multiple SAPs. Fortunately, they can be filtered with a single SAP of 0x0D0D. The primary SAPs that SNA uses are as follows:

0x04 = IBM SNA path control (individual)
0x05 = IBM SNA path control (group)
0x08 = IBM SNA 3270 terminals
0x09 = IBM SNA
0x0c = IBM SNA 3270 terminals

All five SAPs can be filtered with the single "wildcard" SAP of 0x0D0D, which will include all SAP types. The access list to allow only SNA SAPs would resemble the following:

```
Router(config)#access-list 200 permit 0x0d0d 0x0000
```

Or, simply:

```
Router(config)#access-list 200 permit 0x0d0d
```

NetBIOS SAPs

NetBIOS traffic uses the following SAP values:

0xf0 = IBM NetBIOS commands
0xf1 = IBM NetBIOS responses

The hexadecimal address and the appropriate wildcard mask for these two SAPS is **0xf0f0 0x0101.** The access list to allow only NetBIOS SAPs resembles the following:

```
Router(config)#access-list 200 permit 0xf0f0 0x0101
```

Filtering simply the NetBIOS commands is sufficient to control all NetBios traffic as well.

```
Router(config)#access-list 200 permit 0x0d0d
```

IPX SAPs

IPX using 802.2 encapsulation uses the following SAP value:

0xe0 = Novell NetWare

The access list to allow only IPX SAPs resembles the following:

```
Router(config)#access-list 200 permit 0xe0e0 0x0000
```

Or, simply:

```
Router(config)#access-list 200 permit 0xe0e0
```

Filtering and Blocking all SAPs

All access lists, the 200 series included, have an implicit **deny any** at the end of the list. The implicit **deny** does not show up in the configuration when it is displayed.

The access list to allow all SAPs resembles the following:

```
Router(config)#access-list 200 permit 0x0000 0xffff
```

Conversely, the access list to deny all SAPs would look like the following:

```
Router(config)#access-list 200 deny 0x0000 0xffff
```

CAUTION	Extreme care should be used whenever integrating IPX networks with DLSw. By default, Cisco routers will bridge IPX traffic. That means that DLSw also will pass IPX packets, unless **ipx routing** is enabled on the DLSw router. However, a router might be configured only for IP serving a primary DLSw peer for the SNA network, or an "SNA/DLSw peering router." If IPX also is running on the backbone of this network, "SNA peering routing" doesn't carry any IPX traffic; IPX routing isn't configured for this router. If the SNA/DLSw peering router has any interfaces that receive IPX traffic, it will not route IPX, but it will bridge it across all the DLSw peers. Soon IPX networks will be showing up all over, and the serial links can come to a screeching halt, all because they are bridging an entire IPX domain. Fortunately, this can be easily corrected by enabling IPX on the SNA/DLSw peering router or by filtering the IPX SAP, if the proper Cisco IOS Software isn't available.

MAC Filtering

The access list range of 700 allows filtering based on MAC address. The syntax for a 700 series list is as follows:

```
Router(config)#access-list [700-799] [deny | permit] [MAC_address]
<MAC_address_mask>
```

Most often, this access list is entered with just a single MAC address. This is primarily because MAC addresses are not inclusive, unless you define them yourself. For example, to configure an access list to allow only MAC address 0060.5cf3.5da4, you would use the following syntax:

```
access-list 701 permit 0060.5cf3.5da4
```

NetBIOS Name Filtering

To filter NetBIOS based on the name, use the following syntax:

```
Router(config)#netbios access-list host access_list_name [deny | permit] pattern
```

For example, to filter a NetBIOS name of HARLY, you would use the following syntax:

```
netbios access-list host denyharly deny HARLY
```

The following should be kept in mind when using NetBIOS access lists:

- Access-list arguments are case-sensitive. Most NetBIOS names are in uppercase.
- The station names included in the access lists are compared with the source name field for NetBIOS commands 00 and 01 (ADD_GROUP_NAME_QUERY and ADD_NAME_QUERY), as well as the destination name field for NETBIOS commands 08, 0a, and 0e (DATAGRAM, NAME_QUERY, and NAME_RECOGNIZED).

Practical Example: Filtering in a Bridged Environment

All of these access lists can be applied in a number of ways. All of the aforementioned filters mentioned can be applied to the physical interface, a DLSw peer, or a source-route bridge. The syntax needed to apply these filters to a source-route bridge or DLSw peer is listed in the previous sections.

Figure 13-44 presents a DLSw network with routers solo and chewbacca. You want to apply an LSAP filter so that only SNA SAPs will cross the DLSw link between the two routers. To accomplish this, configure an access list in the 200s range, denying SAP 0x0d0d, like the following:

```
access-list 201 permit 0x0d0d
```

Attach the filter to the **remote-peer** statement of each router, using the **lsap-output-list** argument.

Figure 13-44 *DLSw LSAP Filters*

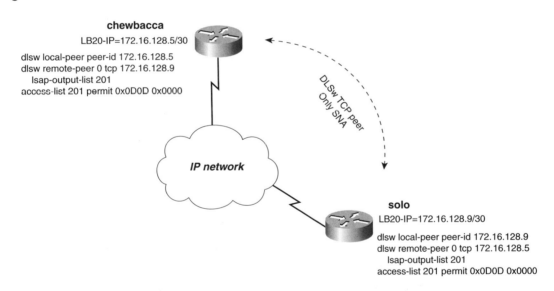

chewbacca
LB20-IP=172.16.128.5/30

dlsw local-peer peer-id 172.16.128.5
dlsw remote-peer 0 tcp 172.16.128.9
  lsap-output-list 201
access-list 201 permit 0x0D0D 0x0000

DLSw TCP peer
Only SNA

IP network

solo
LB20-IP=172.16.128.9/30

dlsw local-peer peer-id 172.16.128.9
dlsw remote-peer 0 tcp 172.16.128.5
  lsap-output-list 201
access-list 201 permit 0x0D0D 0x0000

Lab 26: Transparent Bridging, Remote Source-Route Bridging, LSAP Filtering—Part I

Practical Scenario

Nonroutable protocols such as NetBIOS and SNA are still much alive in the modern internetwork. There are many ways to transport these protocols across the network. This lab gives you practice in performing transparent bridging and RSRB, setting root, and LSAP filters.

Lab Exercise

An underground network of crime fighters exists in secret locations from the valleys of California to the hills of northern Wisconsin. The specific locations are secret, and the routers are identified only by code names, such as trashman and beerbelly. The crime fighters want to link their existing networks, to utilize the super computer H.O.O.V.E.R. Their supercomputers, H.O.O.V.E.R. and H.O.O.V.E.R.2, are SNA mainframes, so the remote sites must be bridged to the crime fighters' headquarters. Your task is to configure a bridged and routed network, using the following design guidelines:

- Configure an IP network, as depicted in Figure 13-45, using EIGRP as the routing protocol and 2001 as the Autonomous System ID.

- Configure the Frame Relay network as depicted in Figure 13-45. Do not configure DLSw in this lab.

- Configure the network so that the routers lone_rhino and trashman can transport SNA to the HQ site or the wolf router.

- Configure the router beerbelly so that it has SNA access to the mainframe H.O.O.V.E.R.2. The H.O.O.V.E.R.2 mainframe requires a RIF. Ensure that your configuration supports this.

- Do not allow NetBIOS traffic from Ring 2 on the beerbelly router to Ring 1 on the wolf router.

- Set the wolf router to be root of the transparent bridging domain.

- A "double secret" workstation is located off the Token Ring interface on the beerbelly router. Because this workstation is so secret, you need to configure a static RIF to it. Configure the RIF as follows: Secret Workstation MAC = 0101.0027.0081; RING2-BRIDGE9-RING50-BRIDGE5-RING52-BRIDGE13-RING7.

Lab Objectives

- Configure the crime fighters network as depicted in Figure 13-45. Configure IP as denoted in the figure. Use EIGRP as the routing protocol, with an Autonomous System ID of 2001.

- Use Frame Relay as the data link protocol on the WAN. Configure a Frame Relay multipoint network between the wolf, lone_rhino, and trashman routers. Configure a Frame Relay point-to-point network between the wolf and beerbelly routers.

- Configure transparent bridging on the Ethernet interfaces of the lone_rhino, trashman, and wolf routers. Bridge these routers over the Frame Relay network.

- Configure remote source-route bridging between the Token Ring interfaces of the beerbelly and wolf routers.

- Configure source-route bridging so that NetBIOS traffic will not be forwarded by the remote source-route bridge.

- Configure a static RIF on the beerbelly router with the following guidelines: MAC = 0101.0027.0081; RING2-BRIDGE9-RING50-BRIDGE5-RING52-BRIDGE13-RING7.

Equipment Needed

- Five Cisco routers. Four will be connected through V.35 back-to-back cables or in a similar manner to a Frame Relay switch.

- Five LANs segments, provided by hubs or switches. One router will need a Token Ring interface and an Ethernet interface. One other router will need to be Token Ring as well.

Physical Layout and Prestaging

- Connect the hubs and serial cables to the routers as shown in Figure 13-45.

- A Frame Relay switch with three PVCs also is required. Example 13-43 lists the Frame Relay configuration used in this lab.

Example 13-43 *Frame Relay Switch Configuration*

```
hostname frame_switch
!
interface Serial0
 no ip address
 encapsulation frame-relay
 no fair-queue
 clockrate 148000
 frame-relay intf-type dce
 frame-relay route 111 interface Serial1 110
!
interface Serial1
 no ip address
 encapsulation frame-relay
 clockrate 148000
 frame-relay intf-type dce
 frame-relay route 110 interface Serial0 111
 frame-relay route 130 interface Serial3 131
 frame-relay route 100 interface Serial5 181
!
<<<text omitted>>>
!
interface Serial3
 no ip address
 encapsulation frame-relay
 clockrate 64000
 frame-relay intf-type dce
 frame-relay route 131 interface Serial1 130
!
<<<text omitted>>>
!
interface Serial5
 no ip address
 encapsulation frame-relay
 clockrate 64000
 frame-relay intf-type dce
 frame-relay route 181 interface Serial1 180
```

Figure 13-45 *Crime Fighters Network*

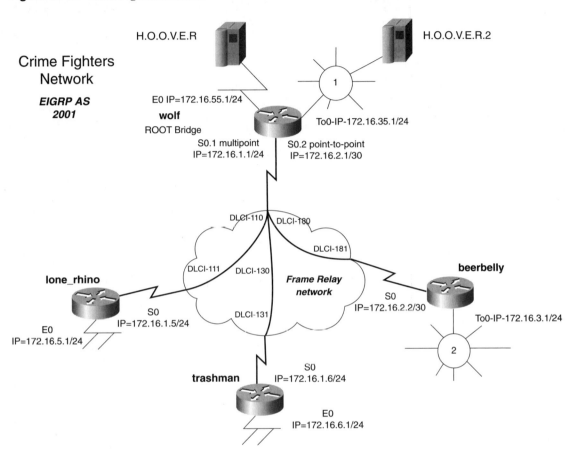

Lab 26: Transparent Bridging, Remote Source-Route Bridging, LSAP Filtering—Part II

Lab Walkthrough

Configure the Frame Relay switch and attach the four routers in a back-to-back manner to the Frame switch. Use V.35 cables or CSU/DSUs with crossover cables to connect the routers. Create the three Ethernet LANs and two Token Ring LANs by the use of switches or hubs/MAUs, as illustrated in Figure 13-45.

When the physical connections are complete, assign IP addresses to all LAN and WAN interfaces, as depicted in Figure 13-45. On the wolf router, configure a Frame Relay multipoint network to the routers lone_rhino and trashman. Configure a Frame Relay point-to-point network between the wolf router and the beerbelly router. Configure EIGRP as the routing protocol. For the trashman subnet to be advertised to the lone_rhino router, you must disable EIGRP split horizon on the wolf router. Example 13-44 provides the EIGRP and the frame configurations of the wolf, lone_rhino, trashman, and beerbelly routers. For specific information on the configuration details, see Chapter 5, "WAN Protocols and Technologies: Frame Relay," and Chapter 11, "Hybrid: Enhanced Interior Gateway Routing Protocol (EGIRP)."

Example 13-44 *Frame Relay and EIGRP Configurations of wolf, lone_rhino, and beerbelly*

```
hostname wolf
!
<<<text omitted>>>
!
interface Serial0
 no ip address
 no ip directed-broadcast
 encapsulation frame-relay
 no ip mroute-cache
 logging event subif-link-status
 logging event dlci-status-change
 frame-relay lmi-type cisco
!
interface Serial0.1 multipoint
 ip address 172.16.1.1 255.255.255.0
 no ip directed-broadcast
 no ip split-horizon eigrp 2001          ←Split horizon disabled
 frame-relay map ip 172.16.1.5 110 broadcast    ←Map statement to lone_rhino
 frame-relay map ip 172.16.1.6 130 broadcast    ←Map statement to trashman
!
interface Serial0.2 point-to-point
 ip address 172.16.2.1 255.255.255.0
 no ip directed-broadcast
 frame-relay interface-dlci 180          ←Inverse ARP
```

continues

Example 13-44 *Frame Relay and EIGRP Configurations of wolf, lone_rhino, and beerbelly (Continued)*

```
!
<<<text omitted>>>
!
router eigrp 2001                    ←Routing EIGRP
 passive-interface Ethernet0
 network 172.16.0.0
 no auto-summary
!
```

```
hostname lone_rhino
!
<<<text omitted>>>
!
interface Serial0
 ip address 172.16.1.5 255.255.255.0
 encapsulation frame-relay
 frame-relay map ip 172.16.1.6 111 broadcast    ←Map statement to trashman
 frame-relay map ip 172.16.1.1 111 broadcast    ←Map statement to wolf
!
<<<text omitted>>>
!
router eigrp 2001                    ←Routing EIGRP
 network 172.16.0.0
 no auto-summary
!
```

```
hostname trashman
!
<<<text omitted>>>
!
interface Serial0
 ip address 172.16.1.6 255.255.255.0
 no ip directed-broadcast
 encapsulation frame-relay
 no ip mroute-cache
 frame-relay map ip 172.16.1.5 131 broadcast    ←Map statement to lone_rhino
 frame-relay map ip 172.16.1.1 131 broadcast    ←Map statement to wolf
 frame-relay lmi-type cisco
!
<<<text omitted>>>
!
router eigrp 2001                    ←Routing EIGRP
 network 172.16.0.0
 no auto-summary
!
```

```
hostname beerbelly
!
<<<text omitted>>>
!
interface Serial0
 ip address 172.16.2.2 255.255.255.0
```

Example 13-44 *Frame Relay and EIGRP Configurations of wolf, lone_rhino, and beerbelly (Continued)*

```
 encapsulation frame-relay
 frame-relay interface-dlci 181
 frame-relay lmi-type cisco
!
<<<text omitted>>>
!
router eigrp 2001
 network 172.16.0.0
 no auto-summary
!
```

After the Frame Relay network is configured and you have full IP reachability, you can begin to configure the bridging environment.

Your first task is to configure transparent bridging between the Ethernet segments of the wolf, lone_rhino, and trashman routers. You also must set the root of the Spanning Tree to be the wolf router. To accomplish this, you can follow this three-step configuration task list.

Step 1   Configure a bridge number and Spanning Tree for that bridge.

Step 2   Configure the interfaces to be a part of that bridge group.

Step 3   Configure a root bridge.

Beginning with Step 1, use the router command **bridge-group 1 protocol ieee** to create the bridge group on all the routers that you want to configure transparent bridging on. Step 2 involves assigning the physical or logical interfaces to the bridge group that you created. This is done with the interface command **bridge-group 1.** On Frame Relay multipoint interfaces, such as the S0.1 interface on wolf and the s0 interfaces on lone_rhino and trashman, you need to configure a **frame-relay map bridge** statement. Example 13-45 demonstrates Steps 1 and 2 being performed on the wolf router.

Example 13-45 *Transparent Bridging Configuration on the wolf Router*

```
wolf(config)#bridge 1 protocol ieee
wolf(config)#interface ethernet 0
wolf(config-if)#bridge-group 1
wolf(config)#interface serial 0.1
wolf(config-subif)#bridge-group 1
wolf(config-subif)#frame-relay map bridge 110 broadcast
wolf(config-subif)#frame-relay map bridge 130 broadcast
wolf(config-subif)#
```

Example 13-46 demonstrates the transparent bridging configuration on the lone_rhino router.

Example 13-46 *Transparent Bridging Configuration on the lone_rhino Router*

```
lone_rhino(config)#bridge 1 protocol ieee
lone_rhino(config)#interface e0
lone_rhino(config-if)#bridge-group 1
lone_rhino(config-if)#exit
lone_rhino(config)#interface s0
lone_rhino(config-if)#bridge-group 1
lone_rhino(config-if)#frame-relay map bridge 111 broadcast
```

The configuration for transparent bridging on the trashman is nearly identical to the configuration on the lone_rhino router. The **frame-relay map** statement for the trashman router would read **frame-relay map bridge 131 broadcast**. At this point, transparent bridging is working. You can determine the status of the bridge with the **show bridge** command, as shown in Example 13-47.

Example 13-47 *Viewing the Status of the Transparent Bridge*

```
trashman#show bridge

Total of 300 station blocks, 295 free
Codes: P - permanent, S - self

Bridge Group 1:

    Address       Action    Interface    Age    RX count    TX count
0060.5cf3.5e65    forward   Ethernet0     0          44           0
0050.5475.e1ad    forward   Serial0       0          10           0
0000.8108.caae    forward   Serial0       0          20           0
0000.863c.3b41    forward   Serial0       3           2           0
00e0.b05a.66e4    forward   Serial0       3           1           0

trashman#
```

The bridge should start displaying MAC address and should be forwarding out the serial and Ethernet interfaces. If you are not seeing this, ensure that the Frame Relay and Ethernet interfaces are all in the same bridge group. Also be sure that you have **frame-relay map** statements for the bridge.

Step 3 calls for configuration of the root of Spanning Tree to be the wolf router. This model might not be the same for yours; the root of Spanning Tree is the trashman router. To check which router is the current root, use the **show spanning-tree** command. Example 13-48 demonstrates this command on the trashman router. Notice that trashman is the current root for STP.

Example 13-48 *Viewing STP on the trashman Router*

```
trashman#show spanning-tree

 Bridge group 1 is executing the IEEE compatible Spanning Tree protocol
  Bridge Identifier has priority 32768, address 0060.5cf3.5da4
  Configured hello time 2, max age 20, forward delay 15
  We are the root of the spanning tree
  Port Number size is 9
  Topology change flag not set, detected flag not set
  Times:  hold 1, topology change 35, notification 2
          hello 2, max age 20, forward delay 15
  Timers: hello 1, topology change 0, notification 0
  bridge aging time 300

 Port 2 (Ethernet0) of Bridge group 1 is forwarding
    Port path cost 100, Port priority 128
    Designated root has priority 32768, address 0060.5cf3.5da4
    Designated bridge has priority 32768, address 0060.5cf3.5da4
    Designated port is 2, path cost 0
    Timers: message age 0, forward delay 0, hold 0
    BPDU: sent 0, received 0

 Port 6 (Serial0 Frame Relay) of Bridge group 1 is forwarding
    Port path cost 647, Port priority 128
    Designated root has priority 32768, address 0060.5cf3.5da4
    Designated bridge has priority 32768, address 0060.5cf3.5da4
    Designated port is 6, path cost 0
    Timers: message age 0, forward delay 0, hold 0
    BPDU: sent 0, received 0

trashman#
```

To change the root so that it resides on the wolf router, use the following global command
on the wolf router:

```
wolf(config)#bridge 1 priority 100
```

By viewing STP on the trashman router as demonstrated in Example 13-49, you can see
that the root is now the wolf router and that the priority has been changed to 100.

Example 13-49 *Viewing STP on the trashman Router*

```
trashman#show spanning-tree
Bridge group 1 is executing the IEEE compatible Spanning Tree protocol
  Bridge Identifier has priority 32768, address 0060.5cf3.5da4
  Configured hello time 2, max age 20, forward delay 15
  Current root has priority 100, address 00e0.1e58.e792
  Root port is 6 (Serial0), cost of root path is 647
  Port Number size is 9
  Topology change flag not set, detected flag not set
```

continues

Example 13-49 *Viewing STP on the trashman Router (Continued)*

```
      Times:  hold 1, topology change 35, notification 2
              hello 2, max age 20, forward delay 15
      Timers: hello 0, topology change 0, notification 0
      bridge aging time 300

  Port 2 (Ethernet0) of Bridge group 1 is forwarding
     Port path cost 100, Port priority 128
     Designated root has priority 100, address 00e0.1e58.e792
     Designated bridge has priority 32768, address 0060.5cf3.5da4
     Designated port is 2, path cost 647
     Timers: message age 0, forward delay 0, hold 0
     BPDU: sent 0, received 0

  Port 6 (Serial0 Frame Relay) of Bridge group 1 is forwarding
     Port path cost 647, Port priority 128
     Designated root has priority 100, address 00e0.1e58.e792
     Designated bridge has priority 100, address 00e0.1e58.e792
     Designated port is 12, path cost 0
     Timers: message age 2, forward delay 0, hold 0
     BPDU: sent 0, received 57

  trashman#
```

The next portion of the lab involves configuring the beerbelly router so that its Token Ring network can have SNA access to the mainframe H.O.O.V.E.R.2 on the Token Ring network on the wolf router. The SNA application requires a RIF, so you must account for this in your configuration as well. To transport SNA across the WAN, you will use RSRB, primarily because you cannot use DLSw+ in the lab.

Recalling the four-step process for configuring RSRB, you have the following:

Step 1   Enable the use of the RIF, if required, with the router interface command **multiring all** command.

Step 2   Enable the virtual ring with the **source-bridge ring-group** *virtual_ring* command.

Step 3   Configure SRB from the physical ring to the virtual ring.

Step 4   Determine the encapsulation type to use, and configure RSRB. In this exercise, you will use TCP as the encapsulation type.

To create a remote peer for each peer router and one for the local router with TCP as the encapsulation type, use the following global router command:

```
  source-bridge remote-peer virtual_ring tcp ip_address
     [lf largest_frame_size] [local-ack]
```

Before you begin configuring RSRB, you should take the extra time to label a common virtual ring on the diagram and to configure the loopback address for the RSRB peers. Figure 13-46 is a new diagram of the network illustrating the loopback address/interfaces and the common virtual ring of 101.

Figure 13-46 *Crime Fighters Network*

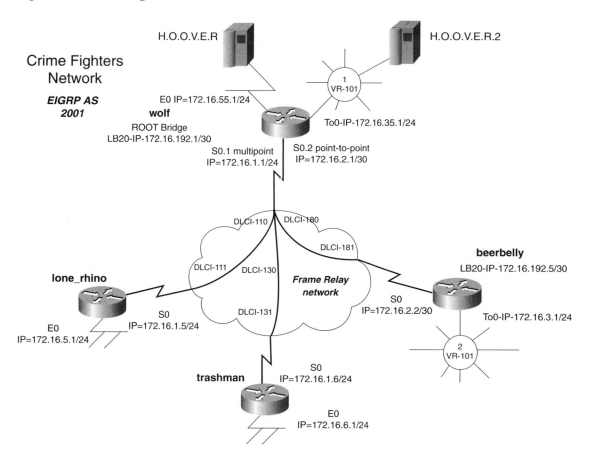

In this model, the H.O.O.V.E.R.2 mainframe requires a RIF field. Therefore, in Step 1, you must enable the RIF on all Token Ring interfaces with the interface command **multiring all**. Step 2 calls for configuring a virtual ring. In this model, we have chosen to use a virtual ring of 101. The virtual ring is configured on the wolf and the beerbelly routers with the global command **source-bridge ring-group 101.** Step 3 involves configuring SRB on the Token Ring interfaces that you want to join to the RSRB group. The configuration for SRB on the beerbelly router resembles the following:

```
beerbelly(config-if)#source-bridge 2 1 101
```

The **source-bridge** command on the wolf router resembles the following:

```
wolf(config-if)#source-bridge 1 1 101
```

Example 13-50 shows the source-route bridge configuration of beerbelly.

Example 13-50 *Configuration of beerbelly, up to This Point*

```
hostname beerbelly
!
<<<text omitted>>>
!
source-bridge ring-group 101          ←virtual ring
!
interface Loopback20                  ←Loopback for RSRB peers
 ip address 172.16.192.5 255.255.255.252
!
<<<text omitted>>>
!
interface TokenRing0
 ip address 172.16.3.1 255.255.255.0
 ring-speed 16
 multiring all                        ←RIF enabled
 source-bridge 2 1 101                ←SRB from Ring 2 to Ring 101
```

Step 4 calls for configuring RSRB peers and the transport type. In this model, you are using TCP for the RSRB transport. Therefore, you need to configure one RSRB TCP peer on each local router pointing at itself and one RSRB TCP peer pointing at the other router—or, more specifically, the other router's loopback address. Example 13-51 illustrates the configuration of RSRB needed on the beerbelly and wolf routers. The RSRB **remote-peer** statements on beerbelly will match the **remote-peer** statement on the wolf router exactly. Remember that you always need a remote peer for the local router in RSRB configuration.

Example 13-51 *Configuration of the beerbelly Router*

```
!
source-bridge ring-group 101
source-bridge remote-peer 101 tcp 172.16.192.5
source-bridge remote-peer 101 tcp 172.16.192.1
!
```

At this point, the RSRB configuration is operational. To determine the status of the RSRB, use the command **show source-bridge.** Example 13-52 displays the status of the RSRB on the wolf router. If the RSRB has detected traffic, it should be in an "open" state.

Example 13-52 *Viewing the RSRB on the wolf Router*

```
wolf#show source-bridge

Local Interfaces:                              receive      transmit
            srn bn  trn r p s n  max hops        cnt          cnt       drops
To0           1  1  101 *  b     7  7  7          40           0          0

Global RSRB Parameters:
 TCP Queue Length maximum: 100

Ring Group 101:
  This TCP peer: 172.16.192.1
   Maximum output TCP queue length, per peer: 100
  Peers:                   state     bg lv  pkts_rx  pkts_tx  expl_gn  drops TCP
    TCP 172.16.192.1        -          3       0        0        0        0  0
    TCP 172.16.192.5       open        3       0        4        2        0  0
  Rings:
    bn: 1   rn: 1    local  ma: 4007.781a.e789 TokenRing0         fwd: 0
    bn: 1   rn: 2    remote ma: 4000.30b1.270a TCP 172.16.192.5   fwd: 0

Explorers: ------- input -------      ------- output -------
          spanning  all-rings    total     spanning  all-rings    total
To0           0        40         40           0         0          0

  Explorer fastswitching enabled
  Local switched: 40       flushed 0        max Bps 38400

          rings       inputs        bursts        throttles     output drops
          To0          40            0               0               0

wolf#
```

When the RSRB is up and operational, apply the filter to it. In this model, you want to prevent the RSRB from transporting NetBIOS. To filter NetBIOS on the RSRB, you need to configure a SAP filter, denying SAP 0xf0. Because there is an implicit **deny** for all SAPs, you must add another line to override this. You then can apply the SAP filter to the RSRB with the command **rsrb remote-peer lsap-output-list.** Example 13-53 lists the relevant portions of the configuration from the wolf router.

Example 13-53 *Filtering SAP on a RSRB*

```
rsrb remote-peer 101 tcp 172.16.192.5 lsap-output-list 201 ←filter to peer
172.16.192.5
!
access-list 201 deny   0xF0F0 0x0000            ←Deny NETBIOS
access-list 201 permit 0x0000 0xFFFF            ←Permit all SAPs
!
```

The final portion of this lab involves configuring a static RIF on the beerbelly router. The RIF that you need to configure is the following:

```
MAC = 0101.0027.0081; RING2-BRIDGE9-RING50-BRIDGE5-RING52-BRIDGE13-RING7
```

Recall from the previous section that a static RIF is built from left to right. The first byte in our static RIF will be 0a30.

The first two bits, from left to right again, equal 00. This sets the explorer type to be a specific routes explorer. You want to use this explorer type because this is a static RIF. The bit 3 is set to 0, and it is reserved. The next five bits set the length of the RIF in bytes. In this example, the RIF is 10 bytes, or 0x0a. The next bit, the D or direction bit, is set to 1, indicating that the RIF is read from left to right, or forward. The next three bits are set to 011, which sets the frame size to be 4472, the Cisco maximum. The last four bits are reserved.

The RD fields, the next 4 bytes, break down rather easily: The next four bytes, 0029, 0325, 0034d, and 0070, are the four 16-bit RD fields. The first three bits of each byte are the ring number in hexadecimal format. The last bit is the ring number in hexadecimal format. For the RIF in this example, you have the following:

RING2 to BRIDGE9 = 0029
RING50 to BRIDGE5 = 0325
RING52 to BRIDGE13 = 034d
RING7 to BRIDGE0 = 0070

A bridge of 0 tells the SRB to terminate the RIF and that no more bridges follow the ring. Example 13-54 demonstrates the configuration of the static RIF on the beerbelly router, followed by the **show rif** command.

Example 13-54 *Configuring and Viewing a Static RIF*

```
beerbelly#conf t
Enter configuration commands, one per line.  End with CNTL/Z.
beerbelly(config)#rif 0101.0027.0081 0a30.0029.0325.034d.0070 to0
beerbelly(config)#exit

beerbelly#show rif
Codes: * interface, - static, + remote

Dst HW Addr    Src HW Addr    How    Idle(min) Vlan Routing Information Field
0101.0027.0081 N/A            To0        -        -  0A30.0029.0325.034D.0070
0000.30b1.270a N/A            To0        *        - -
beerbelly#
```

Example 13-55 shows the complete configurations used in this lab.

Example 13-55 *Final Configuration Listings*

```
hostname wolf
!
source-bridge ring-group 101
source-bridge remote-peer 101 tcp 172.16.192.1
source-bridge remote-peer 101 tcp 172.16.192.5
rsrb remote-peer 101 tcp 172.16.192.5 lsap-output-list 201
!
interface Loopback20
 ip address 172.16.192.1 255.255.255.252
 no ip directed-broadcast
!
interface Ethernet0
 ip address 172.16.55.1 255.255.255.0
 no ip directed-broadcast
 media-type 10BaseT
 bridge-group 1
!
<<<text omitted>>>
!
interface Serial0
 no ip address
 no ip directed-broadcast
 encapsulation frame-relay
 no ip mroute-cache
 logging event subif-link-status
 logging event dlci-status-change
 frame-relay lmi-type cisco
!
interface Serial0.1 multipoint
 ip address 172.16.1.1 255.255.255.0
 no ip directed-broadcast
 no ip split-horizon eigrp 2001
 frame-relay map bridge 130 broadcast
 frame-relay map bridge 110 broadcast
 frame-relay map ip 172.16.1.5 110 broadcast
 frame-relay map ip 172.16.1.6 130 broadcast
 bridge-group 1
!
interface Serial0.2 point-to-point
 ip address 172.16.2.1 255.255.255.0
 no ip directed-broadcast
 frame-relay interface-dlci 180
!
<<<text omitted>>>
!
interface TokenRing0
 ip address 172.16.35.1 255.255.255.0
 no ip directed-broadcast
```

continues

Example 13-55 *Final Configuration Listings (Continued)*

```
 ring-speed 16
 multiring all
 source-bridge 1 1 101
!
router eigrp 2001
 passive-interface Ethernet0
 network 172.16.0.0
 no auto-summary
!
<<<text omitted>>>
!
access-list 201 deny    0xF0F0 0x0000
access-list 201 permit 0x0000 0xFFFF
!
bridge 1 protocol ieee
bridge 1 priority 100
```

```
hostname lone_rhino
!
<<<text omitted>>>
!
interface Ethernet0
 ip address 172.16.5.1 255.255.255.0
 bridge-group 1
!
interface Serial0
 ip address 172.16.1.5 255.255.255.0
 encapsulation frame-relay
 frame-relay map bridge 111 broadcast
 frame-relay map ip 172.16.1.6 111 broadcast
 frame-relay map ip 172.16.1.1 111 broadcast
 bridge-group 1
!
<<<text omitted>>>
!
router eigrp 2001
 network 172.16.0.0
 no auto-summary
!
<<<text omitted>>>
!
bridge 1 protocol ieee
```

```
hostname trashman
!
<<<text omitted>>>
!
interface Ethernet0
 ip address 172.16.6.1 255.255.255.0
```

Example 13-55 *Final Configuration Listings (Continued)*

```
 no ip directed-broadcast
 bridge-group 1
!
interface Serial0
 ip address 172.16.1.6 255.255.255.0
 no ip directed-broadcast
 encapsulation frame-relay
 no ip mroute-cache
 frame-relay map bridge 131 broadcast
 frame-relay map ip 172.16.1.5 131 broadcast
 frame-relay map ip 172.16.1.1 131 broadcast
 frame-relay lmi-type cisco
 bridge-group 1
!
<<<text omitted>>>
!
router eigrp 2001
 network 172.16.0.0
 no auto-summary
!
<<<text omitted>>>
!
bridge 1 protocol ieee
```

```
hostname beerbelly
!
!
rif 0101.0027.0081 0A30.0029.0325.034D.0070 TokenRing0
!
<<<text omitted>>>
!
source-bridge ring-group 101
source-bridge remote-peer 101 tcp 172.16.192.5
source-bridge remote-peer 101 tcp 172.16.192.1
rsrb remote-peer 101 tcp 172.16.192.1 lsap-output-list 201
!
interface Loopback20
 ip address 172.16.192.5 255.255.255.252
!
interface Serial0
 ip address 172.16.2.2 255.255.255.0
```

continues

Example 13-55 *Final Configuration Listings (Continued)*

```
 encapsulation frame-relay
 frame-relay interface-dlci 181
 frame-relay lmi-type cisco
!
<<<text omitted>>>
!
interface TokenRing0
 ip address 172.16.3.1 255.255.255.0
 ring-speed 16
 multiring all
 source-bridge 2 1 101
!
<<<text omitted>>>
!
router eigrp 2001
 network 172.16.0.0
 no auto-summary
!
<<<text omitted>>>
!
access-list 201 deny   0xF0F0 0x0000
access-list 201 permit 0x0000 0xFFFF
```

Lab 27: DLSw+ TCP, LLC2, Promiscuous, Dynamic, and Backup Peer Configuration—Part I

Practical Scenario

DLSw+ provides an effective way, if not the best way, to transport legacy protocols over a TCP network. Advanced configuration of DLSw+ can be used to control traffic and to provide enhanced backup capabilities. This lab gives you extensive practice in configuring multiple types of DLSw+ peers. In this lab, you will practice configuring DLSw+ TCP peers, LLC2 peers, promiscuous peers, backup peers, and dynamic peers. You also will control traffic with SAP filters and port lists.

Lab Exercise

Our original crime fighters are back in this exercise. They currently transport SNA and NetBIOS across a Frame Relay network, using transparent bridging and remote source-route bridging. The crime fighters have two supercomputers, the H.O.O.V.E.R. and H.O.O.V.E.R.2. They would like to provide access to these computers by DLSw. Your task is to configure DLSw+ with the following strict guidelines set forth by the crime fighters:

- Configure an IP network, as depicted in Figure 13-47, using EIGRP as the routing protocol and 2001 as the Autonomous System ID.

- Configure the Frame Relay network as depicted in Figure 13-47.

- Configure the DLSw+ peers on the network as depicted in Figure 13-48. Abide by the following guidelines:

    — Configure DLSw+ Lite between the wolf router Ethernet 2 segment and trashman's Ethernet segment. This is the only *remote-peer* statement that you can configure on the wolf router.

    — Configure DLSw+ so that trashman only has visibility and reachability to the Ethernet segment that the H.O.O.V.E.R.2 mainframe is on. No other DLSw+ peer should see the Ethernet segment that H.O.O.V.E.R.2 resides on.

    — Configure a dynamic SNA TCP peer from lone_rhino to the wolf router. This peer should time out after seven minutes without traffic. Only SNA can bring up this dynamic peer. The peer should transport only SNA between the Ethernet segment of lone_rhino and the E0 segment of the wolf router, where the H.O.O.V.E.R mainframe resides.

— Configure a TCP peer to transport data from the Token Ring segment on the beerbelly router to the Ethernet segment that the H.O.O.V.E.R mainframe resides on, on the wolf router.

— Configure a backup peer from trashman to the lone_rhino router, backing up the peer from trashman to the wolf. The backup peer should remain up as long as a circuit is active. If the primary peer becomes active, ensure that it will not tear down the active circuit on the backup peer.

Lab Objectives

- Configure the Crime Fighters Network as depicted in Figures 13-47 and 13-48. Configure IP as denoted. Use EIGRP as the routing protocol, with an Autonomous System ID of 2001. Because this network is an evolution of the previous lab, you might use that same configuration to begin this lab.

- Use Frame Relay as the data link protocol on the WAN. Configure a Frame Relay multipoint network between the wolf, lone_rhino, and trashman routers. Configure a Frame Relay point-to-point network between the wolf and beerbelly routers.

- Configure the DLSw+ peers on the network as depicted in Figure 13-48. Abide by the following guidelines:

  — Configure DLSw+ Lite between the wolf router Ethernet 2 segment and trashman's Ethernet segment. This is the only **remote-peer** statement that you can configure on the wolf router.

  — Configure DLSw+ so that trashman only has visibility and reachability to the Ethernet segment that the H.O.O.V.E.R.2 mainframe is on. No other DLSw+ peer should see the Ethernet segment that H.O.O.V.E.R.2 resides on.

  — Configure a dynamic SNA TCP peer from lone_rhino to the wolf router. This peer should time out after seven minutes without traffic. Only SNA can bring up this dynamic peer. The peer should transport only SNA between the Ethernet segment of lone_rhino and the E0 segment of the wolf router, where the H.O.O.V.E.R mainframe resides.

  — Configure a TCP peer to transport data from the Token Ring segment on the beerbelly router to the Ethernet segment that the H.O.O.V.E.R mainframe resides on, on the wolf router.

  — Configure a backup peer from trashman to the lone_rhino router, backing up the peer from trashman to the wolf. The backup peer should remain up as long as a circuit is active. If the primary peer becomes active, ensure that it will not tear down the active circuit on the backup peer.

Equipment Needed

- Five Cisco routers. Four will be connected through V.35 back-to-back cables or in a similar manner to a Frame Relay switch.

- Five LANs segments, provided by hubs or switches. One router will need two Ethernet interfaces. One other router will need to be a Token Ring interface.

Physical Layout and Prestaging

Note: You can use the same Frame Relay configuration from the previous lab.

- Connect the hubs and serial cables to the routers, as shown in Figure 13-47.

- A Frame Relay switch with three PVCs also is required. Example 13-56 lists the Frame Relay configuration used in this lab.

Example 13-56 *Frame Relay Switch Configuration*

```
hostname frame_switch
!
interface Serial0
 no ip address
 encapsulation frame-relay
 no fair-queue
 clockrate 148000
 frame-relay intf-type dce
 frame-relay route 111 interface Serial1 110
!
interface Serial1
 no ip address
 encapsulation frame-relay
 clockrate 148000
 frame-relay intf-type dce
 frame-relay route 110 interface Serial0 111
 frame-relay route 130 interface Serial3 131
 frame-relay route 180 interface Serial5 181
!
<<<text omitted>>>
!
interface Serial3
 no ip address
 encapsulation frame-relay
 clockrate 64000
 frame-relay intf-type dce
 frame-relay route 131 interface Serial1 130
!
<<<text omitted>>>
!
```

continues

Example 13-56 *Frame Relay Switch Configuration (Continued)*

```
interface Serial5
 no ip address
 encapsulation frame-relay
 clockrate 64000
 frame-relay intf-type dce
 frame-relay route 181 interface Serial1 180
```

Figure 13-47 *Crime Fighters Network, Part II*

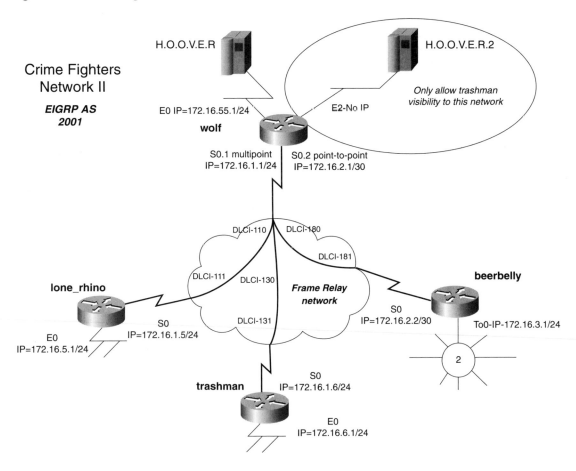

Figure 13-48 *Crime Fighters Network with DLSw Peers*

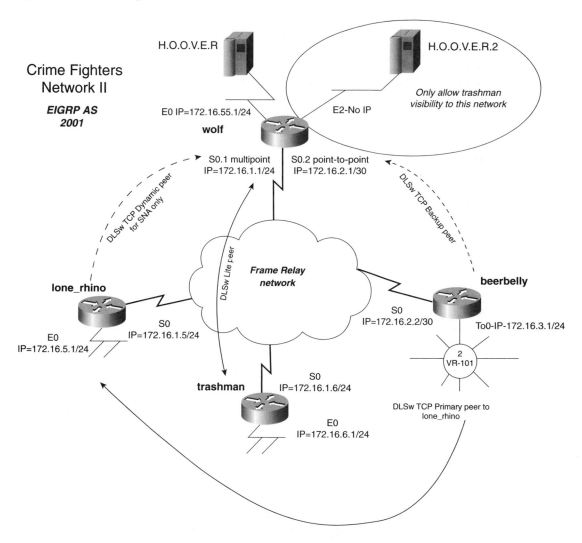

Lab 27: DLSw+ TCP, LLC2, Promiscuous, Dynamic, and Backup Peer Configuration—Part II

Lab Walkthrough

This lab continues from the previous lab; the only difference in the physical layout is that of the wolf router, which now has two Ethernet interfaces and no Token Ring interfaces. If you use the same configurations from the previous lab, be sure to disable transparent bridging on the WAN and RSRB.

Configure the Frame Relay switch and attach the four routers in a back-to-back manner to the frame switch. Use V.35 cables or CSU/DSUs with crossover cables to connect the routers. Create the four Ethernet LANs and Token Ring LANs by the using switches and hubs/MAUs, as illustrated previously in Figure 13-47.

When the physical connections are complete, assign IP addresses to all LAN and WAN interfaces, as depicted in Figure 13-47. On the wolf router, configure a Frame Relay multipoint network to the routers lone_rhino and trashman. Configure a Frame Relay point-to-point network between the wolf router and the beerbelly router. Configure EIGRP as the routing protocol. For trashman's subnet to be advertised to the lone_rhino router, you must disable EIGRP split horizon on the wolf router. Example 13-57 provides the EIGRP and the frame configurations of the wolf, lone_rhino, trashman, and beerbelly routers.

Example 13-57 *Frame Relay and EIGRP Configurations of wolf, lone_rhino, and beerbelly*

```
hostname wolf
!
<<<text omitted>>>
!
interface Serial0
 no ip address
 no ip directed-broadcast
 encapsulation frame-relay
 no ip mroute-cache
 logging event subif-link-status
 logging event dlci-status-change
 frame-relay lmi-type cisco
!
interface Serial0.1 multipoint
 ip address 172.16.1.1 255.255.255.0
 no ip directed-broadcast
 no ip split-horizon eigrp 2001          ←Split horizon disabled
 frame-relay map ip 172.16.1.5 110 broadcast    ←Map statement to lone_rhino
 frame-relay map ip 172.16.1.6 130 broadcast    ←Map statement to trashman
 !
```

Example 13-57 *Frame Relay and EIGRP Configurations of wolf, lone_rhino, and beerbelly (Continued)*

```
interface Serial0.2 point-to-point
 ip address 172.16.2.1 255.255.255.0
 no ip directed-broadcast
 frame-relay interface-dlci 180          ←Inverse ARP
!
<<<text omitted>>>
!
router eigrp 2001                        ←Routing EIGRP
 passive-interface Ethernet0
 network 172.16.0.0
 no auto-summary
!
```

```
hostname lone_rhino
!
<<<text omitted>>>
!
interface Serial0
 ip address 172.16.1.5 255.255.255.0
 encapsulation frame-relay
 frame-relay map ip 172.16.1.6 111 broadcast    ←Map statement to trashman
 frame-relay map ip 172.16.1.1 111 broadcast    ←Map statement to wolf
!
<<<text omitted>>>
!
router eigrp 2001                        ←Routing EIGRP
 network 172.16.0.0
 no auto-summary
!
```

```
hostname trashman
!
<<<text omitted>>>
!
interface Serial0
 ip address 172.16.1.6 255.255.255.0
 no ip directed-broadcast
 encapsulation frame-relay
 no ip mroute-cache
 frame-relay map ip 172.16.1.5 131 broadcast    ←Map statement to lone_rhino
 frame-relay map ip 172.16.1.1 131 broadcast    ←Map statement to wolf
 frame-relay lmi-type cisco
!
<<<text omitted>>>
!
router eigrp 2001                        ←Routing EIGRP
 network 172.16.0.0
 no auto-summary
!
```

continues

Example 13-57 *Frame Relay and EIGRP Configurations of wolf, lone_rhino, and beerbelly (Continued)*

```
hostname beerbelly
!
<<<text omitted>>>
!
interface Serial0
 ip address 172.16.2.2 255.255.255.0
 encapsulation frame-relay
 frame-relay interface-dlci 181
 frame-relay lmi-type cisco
!
<<<text omitted>>>
!
router eigrp 2001
 network 172.16.0.0
 no auto-summary
!
```

The abbreviated process to configure DLSw+ is as follows:

Step 1   Configure loopback address for peers.

Step 2   Configure local peers.

Step 3   Configure SRB or transparent bridging.

Step 4   Configure remote peers.

Figure 13-49 illustrates the network, highlighting some more specific configuration details. Figure 13-49 illustrates bridge groups, virtual rings, and the loopback address that you will use for local and remote peers.

Step 1 in configuring DLSW is to assign the loopback interfaces, as denoted in Figure 13-49. EIGRP will propagate these addresses because they are in the same major bit boundary configured previously. When you can **ping** all the loopback interfaces, move on to the next step.

Step 2 involves assigning local peers to the routers. In this model, you accomplish this by using the global router command **dlsw local-peer peer-id** *loopback_IP_address.* You are allowed to configure only a single remote-peer on the wolf router. Therefore, the wolf's local peer must be configured as promiscuous. If you want to save some time configuring remote peers, you also should configure the local peer of the lone_rhino router to be promiscuous. The syntax to configure the local peer on the wolf is as follows:

```
wolf(config)#dlsw local-peer peer-id 172.16.192.1 promiscuous
```

Figure 13-49 *Crime Fighters Network with DLSw Peers*

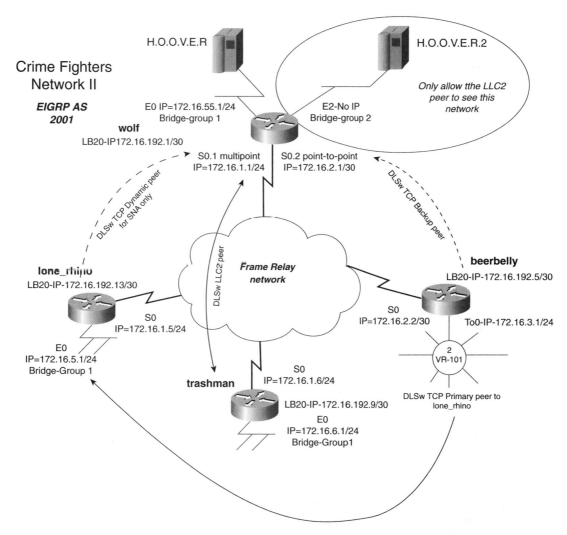

The third step involves configuring transparent or source-route bridging on the routers and interfaces that you want to add to the DLSw domain. For the routers lone_rhino, trashman, and beerbelly, this is accomplished in the exact same manner as it was in the previous lab; therefore, we will not spend a lot of time going over the details of this portion of the configuration. The wolf router, on the other hand, needs two bridge groups configured. Ethernet 0 will be in bridge group 1, and Ethernet 2 will be in bridge group 2. You need to do this to set up the DLSw bridge list when you configure the remote peers. Example 13-58 lists the transparent bridging portion and DLSw portion of the wolf router to this point.

Example 13-58 *Transparent Bridging on the wolf Router*

```
hostname wolf
!
dlsw local-peer peer-id 172.16.192.1 promiscuous    ←Local Peer, Loopback 20
dlsw bridge-group 1                    ←Link to bridge 1
dlsw bridge-group 2                    ←Linkn to bridge 2
!
interface Loopback20
 ip address 172.16.192.1 255.255.255.252
 no ip directed-broadcast
!
interface Ethernet0
 ip address 172.16.55.1 255.255.255.0
 no ip directed-broadcast
 media-type 10BaseT
 bridge-group 1                        ←In bridge 1
!
<<<text omitted>>>
!
interface Ethernet2
 no ip address
 no ip directed-broadcast
 media-type 10BaseT
 bridge-group 2                        ←In bridge 2
!
<<<text omitted>>>
!
bridge 1 protocol ieee                 ←STP for bridge 1 and bridge 2
bridge 2 protocol ieee
```

When the transparent bridge groups are configured, they need to be attached to DLSw domain with the command **dlsw bridge-group** *X* command. This command is demonstrated in the previous example for the wolf router. For source-route bridging, such as found on the beerbelly router, the virtual ring links the SRB to the DLSw domain. Example 13-59 lists the configuration of the beerbelly router to this point.

Example 13-59 *SRB Configuration on the beerbelly Router*

```
hostname beerbelly
!
<<<text omitted>>>
!
source-bridge ring-group 101              ←virtual ring
dlsw local-peer peer-id 172.16.192.5      ←Local Peer- Loopback address
!
interface Loopback20
 ip address 172.16.192.5 255.255.255.252
!
```

continues

Example 13-59 *SRB Configuration on the beerbelly Router (Continued)*

```
interface Serial0
 ip address 172.16.2.2 255.255.255.0
 encapsulation frame-relay
 frame-relay interface-dlci 181
 frame-relay lmi-type cisco
!
<<<text omitted>>>
!
interface TokenRing0
 ip address 172.16.3.1 255.255.255.0
 ring-speed 16
 multiring all
 source-bridge 2 1 101              ←SRB enabled
!
<<<text omitted>>>
!
router eigrp 2001
 network 172.16.0.0
 no auto-summary
!
<<<text omitted>>>

beerbelly#
```

Step 4 of the DLSw+ configuration process involves configuring remote peers for all the routers. All of the remote peers are different in this model, so we will focus on a router at a time, starting with the wolf router.

The wolf router is allowed only one remote peer, and that is why its local peer is configured as promiscuous. The one remote peer that you need to define is a DLSw+ Lite or LLC2 peer to the trashman router. You also must limit what Ethernet segments the router trashman has reachability to. To accomplish this, use a DLSw bridge list defining only bridge 2. The bridge list then will be attached to the remote peer statement for the trashman router. When configuring a LLC2 peer, you also need to add a **frame relay map llc2** statement to the S0.1 interface. Example 13-60 lists the DLSw configuration of the wolf router.

Example 13-60 *DLSw Configuration of the wolf Router*

```
hostname wolf
!
<<<text omitted>>>
!
dlsw local-peer peer-id 172.16.192.1 promiscuous
dlsw bgroup-list 2 bgroups 2                         ←allows only bridge 2
dlsw remote-peer 2 frame-relay interface Serial0.1 130   ←LLC2 remote peer w/bridge
list
dlsw bridge-group 1                ←DLSW link to bridge groups
dlsw bridge-group 2
```

continues

Example 13-60 *DLSw Configuration of the wolf Router (Continued)*

```
!
interface Loopback20
 ip address 172.16.192.1 255.255.255.252
 no ip directed-broadcast
!
interface Ethernet0
 ip address 172.16.55.1 255.255.255.0
 no ip directed-broadcast
 media-type 10BaseT
 bridge-group 1                         ←Bridge group 1
!
<<<text omitted>>>
!
interface Ethernet2
 no ip address
 no ip directed-broadcast
 media-type 10BaseT
 bridge-group 2                         ←Bridge group 2
!
<<<text omitted>>>
!
interface Serial0
 no ip address
 no ip directed-broadcast
 encapsulation frame-relay
 no ip mroute-cache
 logging event subif-link-status
 logging event dlci-status-change
 frame-relay lmi-type cisco
!
interface Serial0.1 multipoint
 ip address 172.16.1.1 255.255.255.0
 no ip directed-broadcast
 no ip split-horizon eigrp 2001
 frame-relay map llc2  130 broadcast           ←LLC2 MAP statement for DLSW
 frame-relay map ip 172.16.1.5 110 broadcast
 frame-relay map ip 172.16.1.6 130 broadcast
!
interface Serial0.2 point-to-point
 ip address 172.16.2.1 255.255.255.0
 no ip directed-broadcast
 frame-relay interface-dlci 180
!
<<<text omitted>>>
!
router eigrp 2001
 network 172.16.0.0
 no auto-summary
!
```

Example 13-60 *DLSw Configuration of the wolf Router (Continued)*

```
bridge 1 protocol ieee
bridge 2 protocol ieee
!
```

Example 13-61 represents the other side of the configuration, the trashman router.

Example 13-61 *DLSw Configuration of the trashman Router*

```
hostname trashman
!
<<<text omitted>>>
!
dlsw local-peer peer-id 172.16.192.9
dlsw remote-peer 0 frame-relay interface Serial0 131          ←LLC2 peer
!
interface Loopback20
 ip address 172.16.192.9 255.255.255.0
 no ip directed-broadcast
!
interface Ethernet0
 ip address 172.16.6.1 255.255.255.0
 no ip directed-broadcast
 bridge-group 1
!
interface Serial0
 ip address 172.16.1.6 255.255.255.0
 no ip directed-broadcast
 encapsulation frame-relay
 no ip mroute-cache
 frame-relay map llc2  131 broadcast              ←LLC2 map statement
 frame-relay map ip 172.16.1.5 131 broadcast
 frame-relay map ip 172.16.1.1 131 broadcast
 frame-relay lmi-type cisco
!
<<<text omitted>>>
!
router eigrp 2001
 network 172.16.0.0
 no auto-summary
!
<<<text omitted>>>
!
bridge 1 protocol ieee
```

The remote peer configuration of the beerbelly router involves configuring a primary peer to the lone_rhino router and a backup peer to the wolf router. This peer cannot tear down LLC2 session when the primary becomes active again. Therefore, you do not want to add the **linger** option. Example 13-62 shows the configuration of the beerbelly router.

Example 13-62 *DLSw Configuration of the beerbelly Router*

```
hostname beerbelly
!
<<<text omitted>>>
!
source-bridge ring-group 101
dlsw local-peer peer-id 172.16.192.5
dlsw remote-peer 0 tcp 172.16.192.13                    ←Primary Peer
dlsw remote-peer 0 tcp 172.16.192.1 backup-peer 172.16.192.13 ←Backup Peer
!
interface Loopback20
 ip address 172.16.192.5 255.255.255.252
!
interface Serial0
 ip address 172.16.2.2 255.255.255.0
 encapsulation frame-relay
 frame-relay interface-dlci 181
 frame-relay lmi-type cisco
!
<<<text omitted>>>
!
interface TokenRing0
 ip address 172.16.3.1 255.255.255.0
 ring-speed 16
 multiring all
 source-bridge 2 1 101
!
<<<text omitted>>>
!
router eigrp 2001
 network 172.16.0.0
 no auto-summary
```

The last remote peer that you need to configure is a dynamic TCP peer from lone_rhino to the wolf router. When you configure this peer, you need to include an LSAP-OUTPUT-FILTER to allow only SNA to pass. The SAP value for SNA is 0x0d0d. To make the peer dynamic, simply add the **dynamic** and **inactivity** keywords to the remote peer statement. The inactivity timer that you need to specify is seven minutes. Example 13-63 lists the configuration of the lone_rhino router. The keepalive value and a timeout value automatically are added when a dynamic peer is configured.

Example 13-63 *Configuration of the lone_rhino Router*

```
hostname lone_rhino
!
<<<text omitted>>>
!
dlsw local-peer peer-id 172.16.192.13 promiscuous
```

Example 13-63 *Configuration of the lone_rhino Router (Continued)*

```
dlsw remote-peer 0 tcp 172.16.192.1 keepalive 0 lsap-output-list 201 timeout 90
  dynamic inactivity 7                       ←dynamic peer
dlsw bridge-group 1
!
interface Loopback20
 ip address 172.16.192.13 255.255.255.252
!
interface Ethernet0
 ip address 172.16.5.1 255.255.255.0
 bridge-group 1
!
interface Serial0
 ip address 172.16.1.5 255.255.255.0
 encapsulation frame-relay
 frame-relay map ip 172.16.1.6 111 broadcast
 frame-relay map ip 172.16.1.1 111 broadcast
!
<<<text omitted>>>
!
router eigrp 2001
 network 172.16.0.0
 no auto-summary
!
ip classless
no ip http server
!
access-list 201 permit 0x0D0D 0x0000        ←Allow SNA only
!
bridge 1 protocol ieee
```

You can verify the configuration by viewing peers on the various routers. By deactivating the serial link on the lone_rhino router, the backup peer should become active on the beerbelly router. Use Windows networking to verify reachability, as we discussed earlier in this chapter. To test the dynamic peer, you might want to switch the SAP to NetBIOS and use WIN 9*x*. It might be hard to easily simulate a SAP 0x0d.

Example 13-64 displays all the possible peers on the wolf router, including the backup peer for beerbelly. Notice that one peer is an LLC2 peer, and the other two are TCP promiscuous peers.

Example 13-64 *DLSW Peers on the wolf Router*

```
wolf#show dlsw peer
Peers:                  state     pkts_rx   pkts_tx  type  drops ckts TCP   uptime

 LLC2 Se0.1    130 CONNECT        50        50 conf      0    0  - 00:23:38
```

continues

Example 13-64 *DLSW Peers on the wolf Router (Continued)*

```
  TCP 172.16.192.5    CONNECT          14       53  prom     0    0    0 00:06:19

  TCP 172.16.192.13   CONNECT          12        9  prom     0    0    0 00:01:02

Total number of connected peers: 3
Total number of connections:     3

wolf#
```

Example 13-65 displays all the possible peers on the lone_rhino router, including the dynamic peer for the wolf router. Notice that one peer is an LLC2 peer, and the other two are TCP promiscuous.

Example 13-65 *DLSW Peers on the lone_rhino Router*

```
wolf#show dlsw peer
Peers:               state    pkts_rx  pkts_tx  type  drops ckts TCP    uptime

  TCP 172.16.192.5   CONNECT       26       32  prom     0    0    0 00:12:34

  TCP 172.16.192.1   CONNECT        2        5  dynam    0    0    0 00:00:06

Total number of connected peers: 2
Total number of connections:     2

lone_rhino#
```

Example 13-66 displays all the possible peers on the beerbelly router. Notice that the backup peer is down at this time.

Example 13-66 *DLSW Peers on the beerbelly Router*

```
wolf#show dlsw peer
Peers:               state    pkts_rx  pkts_tx  type  drops ckts TCP    uptime

  TCP 172.16.192.13  CONNECT       43       32  conf     0    0    0 00:15:23

  TCP 172.16.192.1   DISCONN        0        0  conf     0    0    -       -

Total number of connected peers: 1
Total number of connections:     1

beerbelly#
```

Lab 28: DLSw+ Reachability, Border Peers, Demand Peers, and Resilient Peers—Part I

Practical Scenario

DLSw+ provides a way to control explorers and scale a DLSW network with the concept of border peers. Border peers greatly reduce the number of explorers on the link and the configuration of remote peers. This lab will give you experience configuring DLSw+ border peers, peer groups, and demand peers. This lab will also give you practice configuring DLSw resiliency.

Lab Exercise

The United States and Canada have established a tourism network. The tourism network will allow tourists to access to the latest information about popular sites in each country. Your task is to configure DLSw with the following guidelines:

- Configure an IP network as depicted in Figure 13-50 using EIGRP as the routing protocol and 2001 as the Autonomous System ID.
- Configure the WAN links to all use HDLC protocol. Configure the dual WAN links between the us_tour router and the us_border router so that one is a backup for the other. Both links should not be active at the same time.
- Configure the DLSw peers on the network as depicted in Figure 13-50. Abide by the following guidelines:
  - Configure any-to-any SNA and NetBIOS reachability from all the Ethernet segments in the network.
  - Do not configure a peer between the us_tour and the canada_tour routers.
  - Do not bridge across any WAN interfaces.
  - Configure DLSw reachability such so the us_tour router advertises reachability to the station named US_STATIONS and the Canada_tour router advertises reachability to the station named CANADA_STATIONS.
  - Configure the peer between the us_tour router and the us_border router to remain up during the loss of the primary HDLC link. This peer should not drop while the network is converging over the new link.

Lab Objectives

- Configure the network as depicted in Figure 13-50. Configure IP as denoted. Use EIGRP as the routing protocol, with an Autonomous System ID of 2001.

- Configure the WAN links to all use HDLC protocol. Configure the dual WAN links between the us_tour router and the us_border router so that one is a backup for the other. Both links cannot be active at the same time.

- Configure the DLSw peer groups and border peers as depicted in Figure 13-50. Abide by the following guidelines:

  — Configure two DLSw peer groups. Peer group 10 contains the U.S. routers, and peer group 20 contains the Canadian routers. Configure reachability between these two groups.

  — Configure DLSw so that a peer-on-demand will be created between the us_tour and the canada_tour routers. Do not configure a peer between the us_tour and canada_tour routers.

  — Configure DLSw reachability so that the us_tour router advertises reachability to the station named US_STATIONS and the Canada_tour router advertises reachability to the station named CANADA_STATIONS.

  — Configure the peer between the us_tour router and the us_border router to remain up during the loss of the primary HDLC link. This peer should not drop while the network is converging over the new link.

Equipment Needed

- Four Cisco routers, connected together through V.35 back-to-back cables or in a similar manner.

- Four LANs segments, provided by hubs or switches. The LAN topology is not significant for this lab.

Physical Layout and Prestaging

- Connect the hubs and serial cables to the routers as shown in Figure 13-50.

- You might want to use Windows 9x workstations to test the peer-on-demand configuration.

Figure 13-50 *U.S.–Canadian Tourism Network*

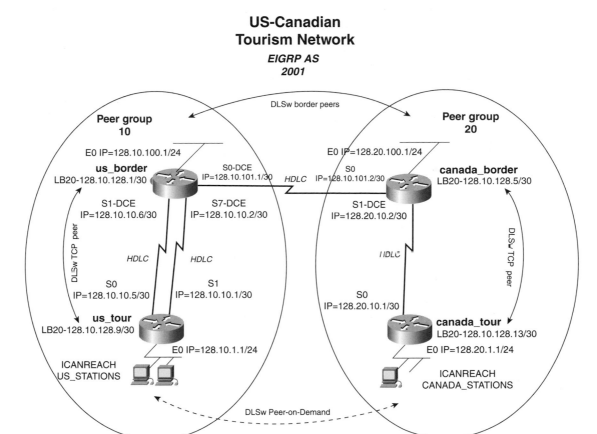

**US-Canadian
Tourism Network**

*EIGRP AS
2001*

Lab 28: DLSw+ Reachability, Border Peers, Demand Peers, and Resilient Peers—Part II

Lab Walkthrough

Begin by attaching the four routers in a back-to-back manner as illustrated in Figure 13-50. Use V.35 cables or CSU/DSUs with crossover cables to connect the routers. Create the four Ethernet LANs by the use of switches and hubs/MAUs, as illustrated in Figure 13-50.

When the physical connections are complete, assign IP addresses to all LAN and WAN interfaces, as depicted in Figure 13-50. To configure the WAN interfaces, one end of the link must be configured as DCE if you are using back-to-back cables. Use the interface command **clock rate** *speed* to set one side of the link to be DCE. The WAN protocol is HDLC, so no further configuration is necessary to make the link active. The model specifies that you can have only one serial link active at a time between the us_border and us_tour routers. To configure one link to back up the other, use the **backup interface** command. Example 13-67 lists the serial configuration of the us_border router.

Example 13-67 *Serial Configuration of the us_border Router*

```
hostname us_border
!
<<<text omitted>>>
!
interface Serial0
 ip address 128.10.101.1 255.255.255.252
 no fair-queue
 clockrate 64000
!
interface Serial1
 backup delay 0 0
 backup interface Serial7
 ip address 128.10.10.6 255.255.255.252
 clockrate 64000
!
<<<text omitted>>>
!
interface Serial7
 ip address 128.10.10.1 255.255.255.252
 clockrate 64000
!
<<<text omitted>>>
!
```

Example 13-67 *Serial Configuration of the us_border Router (Continued)*

```
router eigrp 2001
 network 128.10.0.0
 no auto-summary
```

When you can **ping** all of the routers' local interfaces, configure EIGRP as the routing protocol. This model has two major subnets; thus, the canada_border router will need two network statements, one for 128.20.0.0 and one for 128.10.0.0. Example 13-68 lists the EIGRP configuration of the canada_border router.

Example 13-68 *EIGRP Configuration of the canada_border Router*

```
!
router eigrp 2001
 network 128.10.0.0
 network 128.20.0.0
 no auto-summary
!
```

Begin the DLSw configuration by configuring the peer between the U.S. routers first. Recall the following four-step process for configuring DLSw:

Step 1 Configure loopback address for peers.

Step 2 Configure local peers.

Step 3 Configure SRB or transparent bridging.

Step 4 Configure remote peers.

Begin by configuring loopback addresses on all the routers. You will use these for the local and remote peers.

Step 2 calls for configuring local peers. The U.S. routers will be in peer group 10. To the local peer to a peer group, use the **group** keyword on the **local-peer** statement. The us_border router actually will be the border peer for peer group 10. To configure a border peer, simply include the keyword **border** on the **local-peer** statement. The Canada routers will be in peer group 20, and the canada_border router will be the border peer for that peer group.

To configure transparent bridging to satisfy Step 3, add the Ethernet interface to a bridge group with the interface command **bridge-group** *x*. STP also must be enabled with the global command **bridge 1 protocol IEEE**, where 1 is the transparent bridge number. The transparent bridging portion for all of the router configurations will be identical. Example 13-69 lists the transparent bridging configuration of the us_tour router. This example also demonstrates the command needed to attach the bridge group to a DLSw domain.

Example 13-69 *Transparent Bridging Configuration*

```
dlsw bridge-group 1              ←Attach bridge 1 to DLSW
!
<<<text omitted>>>
!
interface Ethernet0
 ip address 128.10.1.1 255.255.255.0
 no ip directed-broadcast
 media-type 10BaseT
 bridge-group 1
!
<<<text omitted>>>
!
bridge 1 protocol ieee
!
```

Step 4 involves configuring a TCP peer from the us_tour router to the us_border router. This peer needs to be configured so that it will not drop when a serial line converges. To prevent a peer from dropping during a link failure, assign a **timeout 500** value and a **keepalive 0** value to the remote peer on both sides of the link. The us_tour router will need to be configured for a peer-on-demand from the canada_tour router. To configure a peer-on-demand, use the following global command:

```
us_tour(config)#dlsw peer-on-demand-defaults tcp-queue-max 50
```

The last DLSw command that you need to configure on the us_tour router is for DLSw reachability. To advertise reachability to the station US_STATION, use the following DLSw command:

```
us_tour(config)#dlsw icanreach netbios-name US_STATIONS
```

Example 13-70 shows the complete configuration of the us_tour router.

Example 13-70 *Configuration of the us_tour Router*

```
hostname us_tour
!
<<<text omitted>>>
!
dlsw local-peer peer-id 128.10.128.9 group 10
dlsw remote-peer 0 tcp 128.10.128.1 keepalive 0 timeout 500
dlsw icanreach netbios-name US_STATIONS
dlsw peer-on-demand-defaults tcp-queue-max 50
dlsw bridge-group 1
!
!
interface Loopback20
 ip address 128.10.128.9 255.255.255.252
 no ip directed-broadcast
!
interface Ethernet0
```

Example 13-70 *Configuration of the us_tour Router (Continued)*

```
 ip address 128.10.1.1 255.255.255.0
 no ip directed-broadcast
 media-type 10BaseT
 bridge-group 1
!
<<<text omitted>>>
!
interface Serial0
 ip address 128.10.10.5 255.255.255.252
 no ip directed-broadcast
 no ip mroute-cache
!
interface Serial1
 ip address 128.10.10.1 255.255.255.252
 no ip directed-broadcast
!
<<<text omitted>>>
!
router eigrp 2001
 network 128.10.0.0
 no auto-summary
!
<<<text omitted>>>
!
bridge 1 protocol ieee
!
```

The us_border peer has one additional peer configured to the canada_border router. Example 13-71 shows the complete configuration of the us_border router.

Example 13-71 *Configuration of the us_border Router*

```
hostname us_border
!
dlsw local-peer peer-id 128.10.128.1 group 10 border
dlsw remote-peer 0 tcp 128.10.128.9 keepalive 0 timeout 500
dlsw remote-peer 0 tcp 128.10.128.5
dlsw bridge-group 1
!
interface Loopback20
 ip address 128.10.128.1 255.255.255.252
!
interface Ethernet0
 ip address 128.10.100.1 255.255.255.0
 bridge-group 1
!
interface Serial0
 ip address 128.10.101.1 255.255.255.252
 no fair-queue
```

continues

Example 13-71 *Configuration of the us_border Router (Continued)*

```
 clockrate 64000
!
interface Serial1
 backup delay 0 0
 backup interface Serial7
 ip address 128.10.10.6 255.255.255.252
 clockrate 64000
!
<<<text omitted>>>
!
interface Serial7
 ip address 128.10.10.1 255.255.255.252
 clockrate 64000
!
<<<text omitted>>>
!
router eigrp 2001
 network 128.10.0.0
 no auto-summary
!
<<<text omitted>>>
!
bridge 1 protocol ieee
```

To view the static NetBIOS reachability from the us_border peer, enter the **show dlsw reachability** command as demonstrated in Example 13-72. You should now see the NetBIOS name US_STATIONS being reported to the border router.

Example 13-72 *Viewing the Reachability on the us_border Router*

```
us_border#show dlsw reachability
DLSw Remote MAC address reachability cache list
Mac Addr        status    Loc.    port                rif

DLSw Local MAC address reachability cache list
Mac Addr        status    Loc.    peer
0000.613c.dc82  FOUND     REMOTE  128.10.128.5(2065)

DLSw Local NetBIOS Name reachability cache list
NetBIOS Name    status    Loc.    port                rif


DLSw Remote NetBIOS Name reachability cache list
NetBIOS Name    status    Loc.    peer
US_STATIONS     UNCONFIRM  REMOTE  128.10.128.9(2065)

us_border#
```

The configuration of canada_border router and canada_tour routers mirrors that of the two U.S. routers. Example 13-73 shows the complete configurations of these routers.

Example 13-73 *Configurations of the Canada Routers*

```
hostname canada_border
!
<<<text omitted>>>
!
dlsw local-peer peer-id 128.10.128.5 group 20 border
dlsw remote-peer 0 tcp 128.10.128.1
dlsw remote-peer 0 tcp 128.10.128.13
dlsw bridge-group 1
!
!
interface Loopback20
 ip address 128.10.128.5 255.255.255.252
!
interface Ethernet0
 ip address 128.20.100.1 255.255.255.0
 bridge-group 1
!
interface Serial0
 ip address 128.10.101.2 255.255.255.252
 no fair-queue
!
interface Serial1
 ip address 128.20.10.2 255.255.255.252
 clockrate 64000
!
<<<text omitted>>>
!
router eigrp 2001
 network 128.10.0.0
 network 128.20.0.0
 no auto-summary
!
<<<text omitted>>>
!
bridge 1 protocol ieee
!
```

```
hostname canada_tour
!
!
dlsw local-peer peer-id 128.10.128.13 group 20
dlsw remote-peer 0 tcp 128.10.128.5
dlsw icanreach netbios-name CANADA_STATIONS
dlsw peer-on-demand-defaults tcp-queue-max 50
dlsw bridge-group 1
!
<<<text omitted>>>
!
```

continues

Example 13-73 *Configurations of the Canada Routers (Continued)*

```
interface Loopback20
 ip address 128.10.128.13 255.255.255.252
!
interface Ethernet0
 ip address 128.20.1.1 255.255.255.0
 bridge-group 1
!
interface Serial0
 ip address 128.20.10.1 255.255.255.252
 no fair-queue
!
<<<text omitted>>>
!
router eigrp 2001
 network 128.20.0.0
 network 128.10.0.0
 no auto-summary
!
<<<text omitted>>>
!
bridge 1 protocol ieee
```

To verify the configuration, view the DLSw reachability on the border routers. You should
see the static ICANREACH from the peers within the same group as the border peer. As
mentioned previously, a Windows workstation is a great way to test DLSw. By putting
workstations on the various LAN segments, you can generate traffic, create circuits, and
force explorers. Example 13-74 shows a workstation connected to the DLSw domain,
issuing an explorer for the NetBIOS station BORDER-PATROL.

Example 13-74 *Verifying the Configuration*

```
us_border#show dlsw reachability
DLSw Remote MAC address reachability cache list
Mac Addr        status    Loc.    port                    rif

DLSw Local MAC address reachability cache list
Mac Addr        status    Loc.    peer
0000.613c.dc82  FOUND     REMOTE  128.10.128.5(2065)

DLSw Local NetBIOS Name reachability cache list
NetBIOS Name    status    Loc.    port                    rif
BORDER-PATROL   SEARCHING LOCAL

DLSw Remote NetBIOS Name reachability cache list
NetBIOS Name    status    Loc.    peer
TOURIST         FOUND     REMOTE  128.10.128.5(2065)
US_STATIONS     UNCONFIRM  REMOTE 128.10.128.9(2065)

us_border#
```

Verifying the DLSw peer connections and DLSw capabilities is another way to ensure that the DLSw network is operating. Example 13-75 illustrates the **show dlsw peer** command on the canada_border router.

Example 13-75 *Verifying the Peers on the canada_border Router*

```
canada_border#show dlsw peer
Peers:                  state    pkts_rx   pkts_tx  type  drops ckts TCP   uptime

 TCP 128.10.128.1    CONNECT       65        85  conf      0    0   0 00:32:20

 TCP 128.10.128.13   CONNECT       67       103  conf      0    0   0 00:33:00

Total number of connected peers: 2
Total number of connections:     2

canada_border#
```

PART VI

Controlling Networks and Network Access

CHAPTER 14

Understanding IP Access Lists

In many modern networks, there eventually comes a point when full IP reachability is no longer desirable. The reasons for this can range from security concerns to political concerns, such as the merging of two companies with the same IP address space assigned. And sooner, or later, the request will come "Can we just allow. . .?", and you will be forced to deal with access lists.

Controlling routing updates, traffic paths, and protocols can be one of the more challenging aspects of router configuration. Understanding binary math and how it relates to the access list is critical to access lists. Critical to traffic filters is understanding the protocol characteristics of the protocol that you are trying to filter.

This chapter covers access lists in general and explains why binary arithmetic is important. It also covers the different types of IP access lists: standard, extended, dynamic, and named.

NOTE Understanding the way a protocol works is key to writing a filter for it. When writing a filter for an IP protocol, you must know what port a client uses to initiate a connection to a server. You also must know the port number on which the server sends data to the client because the two might not be the same. As you will see later in this section, FTP is a good example of a protocol that sends data on a different port than the port on which the session is initiated. If you're having problems writing specific IP traffic filters, consult a reference such as Richard Stevens' *TCP/IP Illustrated* or Douglas Comer's *Internetworking with TCP/IP* for more details on how that specific protocol might be operating.

Understanding How Access Lists Operate

Essentially, an access list is a set of conditions that are executed sequentially from top to bottom. When a condition is matched, no further comparisons are made, and a true or false result is returned to the process that called the list. The types of access lists have grown over the years. Cisco IOS Software Release 12.0. adds some extended ranges for IP, as Example 14-1 lists.

Example 14-1 *Access List Range in Cisco IOS Software Release 12.0.*

```
router(config)#access-list ?
  <1-99>       IP standard access list
  <100-199>    IP extended access list
  <1000-1099>  IPX SAP access list
  <1100-1199>  Extended 48-bit MAC address access list
  <1200-1299>  IPX summary address access list
  <1300-1999>  IP standard access list (expanded range)
  <200-299>    Protocol type-code access list
  <2000-2699>  IP extended access list (expanded range)
  <300-399>    DECnet access list
  <400-499>    XNS standard access list
  <500-599>    XNS extended access list
  <600-699>    Appletalk access list
<700 790>      48-bit MAC address access list
  <800-899>    IPX standard access list
  <900-999>    IPX extended access list
```

Standard access lists filter based on one condition, the match of an address. When you think of access lists, think of them as conditions that are either true or false; they return this result to the process that called them. It is important to think of them in this way because you will use access lists not only to filter packets on interfaces, but also for route maps, redistribution, and other features, such as Network Address Translation (NAT). Therefore, don't limit your thinking of access lists in terms of "networks" or "packets," but consider what process is calling the access list and what is returned to that process. The access list merely returns the result of the condition in the list, either **true** or **false**. The process that called the list is then carried out or denied based on the result of the condition.

You should follow a few rules and suggestions when configuring any access list:

- There is an implicit **deny** at the end of all access lists. This will not appear in your configuration listing.

- The access list is executed from top to bottom in sequential order. When a condition is true, processing in the list comes to a halt, and no further comparisons are made.

- Access list entries should filter in the order from specific to general. Specific hosts should be denied first, and groups or general filters should come last.

- New lines are always added to the end of the access list. A **no access-list** *x* command will remove the whole list; you cannot selectively add and remove lines.

- An undefined access list will permit any or all traffic.

- When configuring an access list, always configure the list first and then apply it to the process, whether it's a standard packet filter, a route map, or a **redistribute** statement. This way, it is easy to test your list and remove it quickly.

- An IP access list will send an ICMP host unreachable message to the sender of the packet and then will discard the packet into the bit bucket.

- Apply the filter as close as possible to the source of traffic that you want to filter. Security filters usually block inbound access, whereas traffic filters usually prohibit traffic from crossing a link and use outbound filters.

- Care should be used whenever removing an access list. If the access list is applied to a production interface and the access list is removed, there will be a default **deny any** applied to the interface, and all traffic will be halted.

- Outbound filters do not affect traffic originating on the router.

Access Lists, Wildcard Masks, and Binary Math

Everything digital speaks the language of ones and zeros, and access lists are no exception. Standard and extended access lists use the concept of a *wildcard mask*, a binary number expressed in dotted-decimal notation. In an access list, the address bits, or the first address entry, are compared to a corresponding wildcard mask. If the wildcard mask has a 0 bit, it means that the corresponding bit location in the access list address must match the bit value of the compared packet. This is sometimes called a *care bit*. If the wildcard mask has a 1, it means that this bit value will not be compared to anything; sometimes it is called a *don't care bit*. The concept of the care and don't care bits becomes clear only when everything is broken down into binary form.

Figure 14-1 shows a simple access list configured on the router's Ethernet 0/0 port. The text following the figure provides a step-by-step look at how this works.

Figure 14-1 *Simple Access List Example*

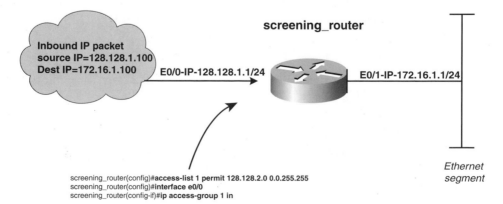

The first step in understanding the access list is to write out both of the lines of the access list in binary. Figure 1 shows the following access list:

`access-list 1 permit 128.128.2.0 0.0.255.255`

Writing out the first part of the list in binary yields the following:

128	.128	.2	.0
1000 0000	1000 0000	0000 0010	0000 0000

You will use the first part of the access list as the comparison bits. The second half of the access list tells what bits you should care about or must match from the comparison bits. Writing the second half of the access list in binary yields this result:

0	.0	.255	.255
0000 0000	0000 0000	1111 1111	1111 1111

Now, if you lay the two together, you can see directly what bits are significant. In this case, you can see that you care about every bit in the first two octets only because every value in them is set to 0.

1000 0000	1000 0000	0000 0010	0000 0000
0000 0000	0000 0000	1111 1111	1111 1111

Essentially, the first bit of whatever address you compare this access list to must be a 1, and the next 7 bits must be 0. The second octet says the same thing. In the third and fourth octet, there are all 1 bits in the wildcard mask. Therefore, you don't care whether these bits match because you're basically ignoring the last two octets; this means that these bits can be either a 1 or a 0.

This example uses a standard access list, so the router will use the source IP address of the incoming packet for its comparison. Breaking out the source address, you have the following:

128	.128	.1	.100
1000 0000	1000 0000	0000 0001	0100 0100

Examining the first bit, you can see that it is a 1. From the previous comparison, you know that you care about this bit and that it has to be a 1. The second bit is 0; again, the wildcard mask indicates that you care about this bit and that it has to be a 0. Stepping through the rest of the example, it becomes apparent that this comparison will yield a true or positive result.

The process that the router uses is called a *logical OR*, or a *Boolean OR*. Much as a router uses a logical AND between the destination packet's address and the mask on the router's interface to find out whether a particular address resides on that subnet, a logical OR is used in access lists.

A logical AND states that when comparing two binary numbers, the result will yield a 1 if, and only if, both bits are 1. For example, performing a logical AND on two addresses, 128.128.1.1 and 255.255.255.0, would yield 128.128.1.0.

1000 0000	1000 0000	0000 0001	0000 0001
1111 1111	**1111 1111**	**1111 1111**	**0000 0000**
1000 0000	1000 0000	0000 0001	0000 0000
Yields: 128.128.1.0			

A logical OR is just the opposite. It states that when comparing two binary numbers, the result will yield a 0 if and only if both bits are 0. For example, performing a logical OR on the same address pair (128.128.1.1 and 255.255.255.0) yields 255.255.255.1.

1000 0000	1000 0000	0000 0001	0000 0001
1111 1111	**1111 1111**	**1111 1111**	**0000 0000**
1111 1111	1111 1111	1111 1111	0000 0001
Yields: 255.255.255.1			

You can now apply the concept of the logical OR to access lists. All access lists, standard or extended, yield a true result if a logical OR is performed between the wildcard mask and the test address, and if this result equals the result of performing a logical OR between the address and mask pair of the access list. For example, assume the use of the following standard access list:

```
access-list 1 permit 128.128.0.0 0.0.255.255
```

You are given two packets with the source addresses of 128.128.1.1 and 128.192.1.1. Which address will pass the access list?

Performing a logical OR on the test address and the wildcard mask, 128.128.1.1 and 0.0.255.255, yields 128.128.255.255. Next, you can perform a logical OR on the address and mask pair of the access list. Performing a logical OR on 128.128.0.0 and 0.0.255.255 yields 128.128.255.255. Notice that the results are the same, so the access list yields a **true** result for the address 128.128.1.1. Using the second address, you perform a logical OR of 128.192.1.1 and 0.0.255.255, which yields 128.192.255.255. Compare this result with a logical OR of the access list address and mask pair. A logical OR of 128.128.0.0 and

0.0.255.255 yields 128.128.255.255. Notice this time that the results of 128.128.255.255 and 128.192.255.255 do not equal each other, so, in this case, this address of 128.192.1.1 would yield a **false** result.

In this example, the bit boundaries are set cleanly to highlight the example, and performing the logical OR might seem like a lot of work. But when you start performing the same exercise with access lists such as **access-list 1 permit 64.35.100.150 0.4.10.254**, breaking down the numbers in binary form and using the logical OR is the only way to understand which bits are significant and which ones are not.

Standard IP Access Lists

Until this point, this chapter has have talked about access lists in a general sense. Now, you will learn about the specific types of IP access lists and how to configure them.

A standard access list falls within the range of 1 and 99, and 1300 and 1999 in Cisco IOS Release 12.0. The **log** keyword can be added to the end of any access list. It causes an informational logging message about the packet that matches the entry to be sent to the console. The syntax for the standard IP access list is shown here:

```
access-list x {deny | permit} a.b.c.d wildcard_mask {log}
```

The *a.b.c.d* argument is the IP address that the wildcard mask is OR'd with to yield a **true** or **false** result.

The standard access list can be applied in a number of ways:

- As a packet filter
- As a route filter
- To define significant traffic for a feature such as NAT or a DDR link

Of course, there are many more, and that is why you can't limit your use of access lists to packet filters.

The example in this section uses standard access lists to filter routes, deny network access, and deny virtual terminal access. Figure 14-2 illustrates a simple network running EIGRP as its routing protocol. From this example, you can configure multiple access lists to accomplish the following:

- Prevent jefferson from having a route to 172.16.2.0/24
- Allow user 172.16.1.129 Telnet access to henry, and deny all other access
- Prevent all users from 172.16.1.0/24 access to Token Ring 128.200.1.2

Figure 14-2 *Standard IP Access List Example*

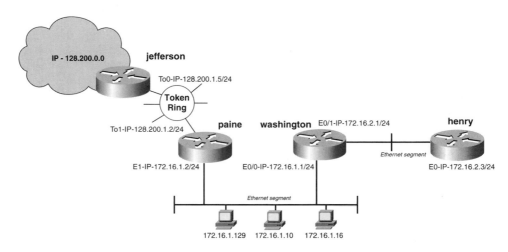

Under normal circumstances, with the **eigrp no auto-summary** command added to each router, the route table of the jefferson router would look like Example 14-2.

Example 14-2 *Route Table of the jefferson Router*

```
jefferson#show ip route
Codes: C - connected, S - static, I - IGRP, R - RIP, M - mobile, B - BGP
       D - EIGRP, EX - EIGRP external, O - OSPF, IA - OSPF inter area
       N1 - OSPF NSSA external type 1, N2 - OSPF NSSA external type 2
       E1 - OSPF external type 1, E2 - OSPF external type 2, E - EGP
       i - IS-IS, L1 - IS-IS level-1, L2 - IS-IS level-2, * - candidate default
       U - per-user static route, o - ODR
       T - traffic engineered route

Gateway of last resort is not set

     172.16.0.0/24 is subnetted, 2 subnets
D       172.16.1.0 [90/297728] via 128.200.1.2, 00:00:31, TokenRing0
D       172.16.2.0 [90/323328] via 128.200.1.2, 00:00:18, TokenRing0
     128.200.0.0/24 is subnetted, 1 subnets
C       128.200.1.0 is directly connected, TokenRing0
jefferson#
```

One way to prevent jefferson from having access to 172.16.2.0/24 is to use a standard access list called by a distribution list on the paine router. Example 14-3 demonstrates the addition of the access list to the paine router. Recall from the previous chapters on routing protocols that a distribute list is used to filter route updates.

Example 14-3 *Adding a Distribution List Calling a Standard Access List*

```
paine(config)#router eigrp 2001
paine(config-router)#distribute-list 1 out to1
paine(config-router)#exit
paine(config)#access-list 1 deny 172.16.2.0 0.0.0.255
paine(config)#access-list 1 permit any
paine(config)#exit
paine#
```

Example 14-4 lists the route table of the jefferson router after the access list has been applied.

Example 14-4 *Route Table of the jefferson Router*

```
jefferson#show ip route
Codes: C - connected, S - static, I - IGRP, R - RIP, M - mobile, B - BGP
       D - EIGRP, EX - EIGRP external, O - OSPF, IA - OSPF inter area
       N1 - OSPF NSSA external type 1, N2 - OSPF NSSA external type 2
       E1 - OSPF external type 1, E2 - OSPF external type 2, E - EGP
       i - IS-IS, L1 - IS-IS level-1, L2 - IS-IS level-2, * - candidate default
       U - per-user static route, o - ODR
       T - traffic engineered route

Gateway of last resort is not set

     172.16.0.0/24 is subnetted, 2 subnets
D       172.16.1.0 [90/297728] via 128.200.1.2, 00:00:31, TokenRing0
C       128.200.1.0 is directly connected, TokenRing0
jefferson#
```

Following the guidelines listed at the beginning of the chapter, you filter the most specific address first and then permit the general address. There is an implicit **deny** any at the end of the access list, so you need to permit routing updates that you are not filtering before the implicit **deny**. Table 14-1 lists access list shortcuts.

Table 14-1 *Access List Shortcuts*

Address	Mask	Returns a True Value	Shortcut Keyword
0.0.0.0	255.255.255.255	Any address returns a **true**	**any**
a.b.c.d	0.0.0.0	An exact match to the address *a.b.c.d*	**host**

To limit Telnet access on the henry router, you can apply a standard access list to the vty ports on the routers. Recall from Chapter 1, "The Key Components for Modeling an

Internetwork," that a **show line** command lists the vty or the Telnet access ports. Use the following command to apply an access list to a port on a router:

access-class *access-list_number* {**in** | **out**}

In this case, you want to allow the address 172.16.1.129 Telnet access to henry while denying access to all the others. To accomplish this, you need to locate the absolute line numbers of the vty sessions. This can be done with the **show line** command. Then apply an access group, calling an access list only to those line numbers. Example 14-5 lists the commands needed to limit Telnet access to one address on the router henry.

Example 14-5 *Controlling Telnet Access with Standard IP Access Lists*

```
henry#show line
 Tty Typ    Tx/Rx      A Modem  Roty AccO AccI  Uses    Noise   Overruns
 *  0 CTY               -   -     -    -    -     0       0       0/0
    1 AUX   9600/9600   -   -     -    -    -     0       0       0/0
    2 VTY               -   -     -    -    -     2       0       0/0
                                                              ←Telnet sessions
    3 VTY               -   -     -    -    -     0       0       0/0
    4 VTY               -   -     -    -    -     0       0       0/0
    5 VTY               -   -     -    -    -     0       0       0/0
    6 VTY               -   -     -    -    -     0       0       0/0

henry#conf t
Enter configuration commands, one per line.  End with CNTL/Z.
henry(config)#access-list 1 permit 172.16.1.129 0.0.0.0
henry(config)#line 2 6
henry(config-line)#access-class 1 in
henry(config-line)#^Z
```

Finally, you must stop all users on subnet 172.16.1.0/24 from accessing the Token Ring network. To accomplish this, you will use the most common application of an access list by applying it with an IP access group.

Access groups are used to apply an access list to an interface. When you configure an access group, it is applied in an *in* or *out* fashion. The **in** or **out** options represent how the access list will be applied from the perspective of the interface. **out** applies the access list to all outgoing packets, whereas **in** applies the access list to all incoming packets. The **out** option will not filter packets that originate on the router itself. As mentioned previously, if no access list is defined, when an access group is applied to an interface, the default action of the router is to filter all traffic. You can apply only one outbound and one inbound access list per interface.

Use the following command to apply an access list to an interface on a router:

ip access-group *x* {**in** | **out**}

Example 14-6 illustrates the commands needed to accomplish denying the 172.16.1.0/24 subnet access to the Token Ring.

Example 14-6 *Controlling Network Access with Standard IP Access Lists*

```
paine#conf t
Enter configuration commands, one per line.  End with CNTL/Z.
01:42:01: %SYS-5-CONFIG_I: Configured from console by console
paine(config)#access-list 5 deny 172.16.1.0 0.0.0.255
paine(config)#access-list 5 permit any
paine(config)#int to1
paine(config-if)#ip access-group 5 out
paine(config-if)#^Z
```

Extended IP Access Lists

Extended IP access lists apply the same concepts that you just learned; however, they have much more control over whether to filter off a source and destination address, along with IP protocol type filtering. The general syntax for extended IP access lists is shown here:

access-list {**100-199** | **2000-2699**} {**permit** | **deny**} *protocol_type Source_address Source_address_wildcard destination_address destination_address_wildcard* [*protocol specific options*] [**precedence** *precedence*][**tos** *tos*][**log**][**established**]

The access list range is 100 to 199 and has an extended range of 2000 to 2699 in Cisco IOS Release 12.0.0 and later. The *protocol_type* keyword is a special value that will cause the access list to look for a match in the Protocol field of the IP header. Table 14-2 lists the values as of Cisco IOS Release 12.0.

Table 14-2 *Extended IP Access List* protocol_type *Values for Cisco IOS Release 12.0*

Value	What It Means
<0-255>	An IP protocol number
ahp	Authentication Header Protocol
eigrp	Cisco's EIGRP routing protocol
esp	Encapsulation Security Payload
gre	Cisco's GRE tunneling
icmp	Internet Control Message Protocol
igmp	Internet Gateway Message Protocol
igrp	Cisco's IGRP routing protocol
ip	Any Internet protocol
ipinip	IP in IP tunneling
nos	KA9Q NOS–compatible IP over IP tunneling
ospf	OSPF routing protocol

Table 14-2   *Extended IP Access List* protocol_type *Values for Cisco IOS Release 12.0 (Continued)*

pcp	Payload Compression Protocol
pim	Protocol Independent Multicast
tcp	Transmission Control Protocol
udp	User Datagram Protocol

As you can see, the *protocol_type* field grows with every release of Cisco IOS Software. Specifying the protocol type can be a simple way to avoid complex filters. For example, specifying the protocol type when filtering routing protocols such as IGRP, EIGRP, and OSPF instead of filtering by the individual IP multicast messages that these routing protocols use can simplify your configuration when using the *protocol_type* keyword. Table 14-3 lists the currently supported TCP port numbers under Cisco IOS Release 12.0.

Table 14-3   *Extended IP Access List TCP Port Numbers Supported Under Cisco IOS Release 12.0*

Value	What It Means
<0-65535>	Port number
bgp	Border Gateway Protocol (179)
chargen	Character generator (19)
cmd	Remote commands (rcmd, 514)
daytime	Daytime (13)
discard	Discard (9)
domain	Domain Name Service (53)
echo	Echo (7)
exec	Exec (rsh, 512)
finger	Finger (79)
ftp	File Transfer Protocol (21)
ftp-data	FTP data connections (used infrequently, 20)
gopher	Gopher (70)
hostname	NIC host name server (101)
ident	Ident Protocol (113)
irc	Internet Relay Chat (194)
klogin	Kerberos login (543)
kshell	Kerberos shell (544)
login	Login (rlogin, 513)

continues

Table 14-3 *Extended IP Access List TCP Port Numbers Supported Under Cisco IOS Release 12.0 (Continued)*

Value	What It Means
lpd	Printer service (515)
nntp	Network News Transport Protocol (119)
pim-auto-rp	PIM Auto-RP (496)
pop2	Post Office Protocol v2 (109)
pop3	Post Office Protocol v3 (110)
smtp	Simple Mail Transport Protocol (25)
sunrpc	Sun Remote Procedure Call (111)
Syslog	Syslog (514)
Tacacs	TAC Access Control System (49)
Talk	Talk (517)
telnet	Telnet (23)
Time	Time (37)
Uucp	UNIX-to-UNIX Copy Program (540)
Whois	Nicname (43)
www	World Wide Web (HTTP, 80)

Table 14-4 lists the currently supported UDP port numbers under Cisco IOS Release 12.0.

Table 14-4 *Extended IP Access List UDP Port Numbers Supported Under Cisco IOS Release 12.0*

Value	What It Means
<0-65535>	Port number
biff	Biff (mail notification, comsat, 512)
bootpc	Bootstrap Protocol (BOOTP) client (68)
bootps	Bootstrap Protocol (BOOTP) server (67)
discard	Discard (9)
dnsix	DNSIX security protocol auditing (195)
domain	Domain Name Service (DNS, 53)
echo	Echo (7)
isakmp	Internet Security Association and Key Management Protocol (500)
mobile-ip	Mobile IP registration (434)
nameserver	IEN116 name service (obsolete, 42)

Table 14-4   *Extended IP Access List UDP Port Numbers Supported Under Cisco IOS Release 12.0 (Continued)*

Value	What It Means
netbios-dgm	NetBIOS datagram service (138)
netbios-ns	NetBIOS name service (137)
netbios-ss	NetBIOS session service (139)
ntp	Network Time Protocol (123)
pim-auto-rp	PIM Auto-RP (496)
rip	Routing Information Protocol (router, in.routed, 520)
snmp	Simple Network Management Protocol (161)
snmptrap	SNMP Traps (162)
sunrpc	Sun Remote Procedure Call (111)
syslog	System Logger (514)
tacacs	TAC Access Control System (49)
talk	Talk (517)
tftp	Trivial File Transfer Protocol (69)
time	Time (37)
who	Who service (rwho, 513)
xdmcp	X Display Manager Control Protocol (177)

Another enhancement in extended access lists that is not offered by standard access lists is that you can specify a match on where traffic originates and where it is destined. At the end of the access list, you can set precedence and type-of-service (TOS) values. Here, the router examines the IP packet header for these values. The precedence values range from 0 to 7, while the TOS values range from 0 to 15. The **established** keyword is used to check for the ACK or RESET flags in the TCP header. If one flag is set, a match occurs. This command is used to pass existing data streams through the access list.

Let's take a look at an extended access list that will be used on a connection to the Internet. In this example, an extended access list is configured on the inbound BRI interface to the Internet. Figure 14-3 illustrates the network topology for the next example.

Figure 14-3 *Extended Access List Example*

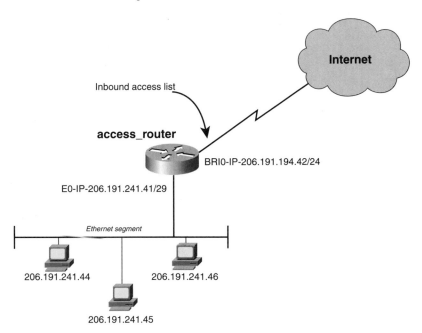

Now, let's add the syntax in Example 14-7 to the access_router.

Example 14-7 *Applying an Extended Access List to the access_router*

```
access_router(config)#access-list 199 permit tcp any any established
access_router(config)#access-list 199 deny   ip 206.191.241.40 0.0.0.7 any
access_router(config)#access-list 199 deny   ip host 206.191.194.42 host
  206.191.194.42
access_router(config)#access-list 199 permit icmp any any echo
access_router(config)#access-list 199 permit icmp any any echo-reply
access_router(config)#access-list 199 permit tcp any 206.191.241.40 0.0.0.7 eq www
access_router(config)#access-list 199 permit tcp any 206.191.241.40 0.0.0.7 eq smtp
access_router(config)#access-list 199 permit tcp any 206.191.241.40 0.0.0.7 eq
  domain
access_router(config)#access-list 199 permit udp any 206.191.241.40 0.0.0.7 eq
  domain
access_router(config)#access-list 199 deny   tcp any 206.191.241.40 0.0.0.7 lt 1024
access_router(config)#access-list 199 deny   tcp any 206.191.241.40 0.0.0.7 gt 1023
access_router(config)#access-list 199 permit udp any 206.191.241.40 0.0.0.7 gt 1023
access_router(config)#access-list 199 deny   udp any 206.191.241.40 0.0.0.7 gt 50000
access_router(config)#access-list 199 deny   udp any 206.191.241.40 0.0.0.7 lt 1024
```

Now, apply the access list to the BRI interface with the following commands:

```
access_router(config)#int bri 0
access_router(config-if)#ip access-group 199 in
```

The first line of the access list in Example 14-6 invokes the **established** keyword. This keyword looks for the ACK or the RESET bits set in the TCP header. This inherently allows existing data streams to qualify as a match. The **established** keyword should be used on any TCP traffic that is user-interactive, such as WWW.

The second line and third lines in Example 14-6 are used to prevent spoof attacks. The second line states that it will deny IP traffic from subnet 206.191.241.40/29. This is the subnet assigned to the Ethernet port, and you should not accept any packets coming from an outside network that are in the same source address range as the Ethernet segment. The third line prevents a spoof attack on the BRI port. The next two lines of the extended access list permit ICMP echo and echo-reply, consequently allowing **ping**s in and out of our network. Remember to lay out the address in binary form, if you have difficulty determining which bits are significant. The next few lines in Example 14-6 are straightforward.

In the next subset of lines, you have the following:

```
access-list 199 permit tcp any 206.191.241.40 0.0.0.7 eq www
access-list 199 permit tcp any 206.191.241.40 0.0.0.7 eq smtp
access-list 199 permit tcp any 206.191.241.40 0.0.0.7 eq domain
access-list 199 permit udp any 206.191.241.40 0.0.0.7 eq domain
```

The first entry allows TCP from any source address or network to go to just the subnet of 206.191.241.40. This would include addresses .41, .42, .43, .44, .45, and .46 only if the TCP port is 80 for HTTP or WWW traffic. The second and third lines allow for the same subnet to inbound access from Simple Mail Transport Protocol (SMTP), port 25, and POP3 mail, port 110. Finally, we have two DNS entries: One allows for DNS that might be operating on TCP port 53, and the other allows for DNS, UDP port 53 access, the more common transport for DNS services.

In the last subset of lines in Example 14-6, you see these lines:

```
access-list 199 deny    tcp any 206.191.241.40 0.0.0.7 lt 1024
access-list 199 deny    tcp any 206.191.241.40 0.0.0.7 gt 1023
access-list 199 permit udp any 206.191.241.40 0.0.0.7 gt 1023
access-list 199 deny    udp any 206.191.241.40 0.0.0.7 gt 50000
access-list 199 deny    udp any 206.191.241.40 0.0.0.7 lt 1024
```

The first line of this subset of entries denies TCP traffic on ports less than 1024 and from any source network to the specific subnet of 206.191.241.40/29. The next line does the same for ports greater than 1023. The next line allows UDP ports greater then 1023 to pass, while the last two lines deny UDP ports greater then 50000 and deny UDP ports less than 1024. Basically, this subset is filtering some of the well-known UDP TCP ports. The implicit **deny any** would have caught all of these ports and the entry may seem redundant; however, sometimes it is desirable to "see" the actual ports being denied in the configuration and being logged when someone is trying to access them. In this example, you could also filter inclusive ports with a **range** statement. For example, these two lines could be combined into single entry:

```
access-list 199 deny   tcp any 206.191.241.40 0.0.0.7 lt 1024
access-list 199 deny   tcp any 206.191.241.40 0.0.0.7 gt 1023
```

or:

```
access-list 199 deny   tcp any 206.191.241.40 0.0.0.7 range 1 65535
```

CAUTION   Enhancements to the **access-list** commands are backward compatible; migrating from earlier releases to Release 11.1 will convert your access lists automatically. Releases earlier than Release 11.1 are not upwardly compatible with these enhancements. If you save an access list with these images later then Release 11.1 and then use software earlier than Release 11.1, the resulting access list will not be interpreted correctly. This can cause severe security problems.

In other words, access lists from Cisco IOS Releases 11.1 and later are backward and forward compatible. Releases earlier than 11.1 are not backward or forward compatible. So, your lists run the chances of being destroyed if the router would come up under a different Cisco IOS Release image or was downgraded somehow.

Displaying Access Lists

By now, you might want to display or troubleshoot your access lists. To view the access lists, use the following commands from the **enable** prompt:

*   **show access-list**—Displays access lists from all protocols. This command displays the number of packets that pass each line of an access list. Use the **clear access-list counter** command to clear these counters.

*   **show ip access-list** [*access-list number*]—Displays all IP access lists defined. If you select a specific access list for display, only that list will be displayed. This command displays the number of packets that pass each line of an access list. Use the **clear access-list counter** command to clear these counters.

*   **show log**—This command is used in conjunction with the **log** keyword trailing any access list. Be sure to have a **logging buffered** command in the configuration to capture all the console messages. This message includes the access list number, information on whether the packet was permitted or denied, the protocol, and if applicable, the source and destination addresses. To prevent huge log files, the router generates this message only for the first packet that matches and then at 5-minute intervals, including the number of packets permitted or denied in the previous 5-minute interval.

Example 14-8 lists the output of the **show ip access-list** command.

Example 14-8 show ip access-list *Command Output*

```
access_router# show ip access-lists
Standard IP access list 69
    permit 206.191.241.0, wildcard bits 0.0.0.255 log
Extended IP access list 101
    deny udp host 172.16.16.2 host 204.221.151.211 eq domain
    permit tcp any any established (15992 matches)
    permit ip any 192.168.5.0 0.0.0.255 (43 matches)
    permit ip any 204.221.151.0 0.0.0.255 (169 matches)
    permit icmp any any echo (78 matches)
    permit icmp any any echo-reply (9 matches)
    permit tcp any any eq www (216 matches)
    permit udp any any
Extended IP access list 110
    permit ip any any (37779 matches)
    permit tcp any any established
Extended IP access list 199
    permit tcp any any established (175 matches)
    deny ip 206.191.241.40 0.0.0.7 any
    deny ip host 206.191.194.42 host 206.191.194.42
    permit icmp any any echo
    permit icmp any any echo-reply
    permit tcp any 206.191.241.40 0.0.0.7 eq www
    permit tcp any 206.191.241.40 0.0.0.7 eq smtp
    permit tcp any 206.191.241.40 0.0.0.7 eq domain
    permit udp any 206.191.241.40 0.0.0.7 eq domain
    deny tcp any 206.191.241.40 0.0.0.7 lt 1024
    deny tcp any 206.191.241.40 0.0.0.7 gt 1023
    permit udp any 206.191.241.40 0.0.0.7 gt 1023 (13 matches)
    deny udp any 206.191.241.40 0.0.0.7 gt 50000
    deny udp any 206.191.241.40 0.0.0.7 lt 1024
access_router#
```

Dynamic Access Lists

A dynamic access list is an access list that allows temporary access after a user has authenticated with the router. For example, in the field, you might want a Cisco engineer from the TAC to help you troubleshoot your network by logging into the routers. A dynamic access list could be created giving Cisco complete privileges for a predetermined amount of time. After a configured time limit expires, the session is closed and traffic is again denied. This form of access list is also referred to as *lock-and-key security*.

To configure a dynamic access list, you need to perform the following steps:

Step 1   Define a username and password.

Step 2   Define the username with the **autocommand** and **timeout** arguments; these must match a timeout value specified on the dynamic access list.

Step 3   Define a *one-line* dynamic access list allowing what traffic you want to pass after that user has authenticated. This line also should include the timeout value, which must match the one mentioned in the earlier bulleted item.

Step 4   Define an extended access list, in the same range as the dynamic access list, that will serve as the normal packet filter for the interface where you apply it to. This must allow Telnet access to the interface it is applied to because this is for Telnet authentication. Finally, apply this access list to an interface.

Step 5   Add the **login local** port to the vty line numbers; these are displayed by the **show line** command.

Recalling the same network from the earlier example, you now learn how to clear all the access lists and enable any-to-any routing. In Figure 14-4, every router has the 128.200.0.0 subnet in its routing table, and there is full reachability.

Figure 14-4 *Dynamic Access List Example*

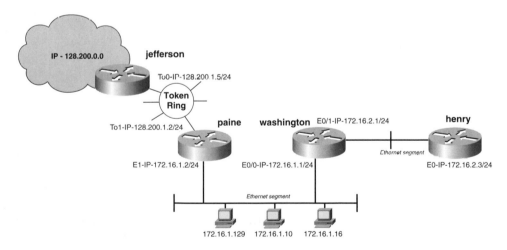

In this example, you will define a dynamic access list on the router paine Ethernet 0 port. You will allow only users on the 172.16.1.0/24 subnet to authenticate, and then you will allow them access to the full 128.200.0.0 subnet. The access list will prevent any packets from unauthenticated users from entering into the interface. After someone has authenticated, you will allow all the devices on subnet 172.16.1.0/24 access for five minutes before closing the dynamic access list.

First, add a username and password needed for authentication:

```
username franklin password ben
username franklin autocommand access-enable timeout 5
```

The second line states that a special **autocommand** will be run when user franklin logs in. **access-enable** is a special command that will not be displayed by the question mark (context-sensitive help)—yes, you will have to remember this one! The timeout value is an idle timeout—in this case, it is set for five minutes. This means that the access list will close after no traffic has been detected for five minutes.

Next, define the dynamic access list:

```
access-list 101 dynamic allowben timeout 5 permit ip 172.16.1.0 0.0.0.255 any
access-list 101 permit tcp 172.16.1.0 0.0.0.255 host 172.16.1.2 eq telnet
```

The name for the access list must be unique and can be set to anything. What is important is the timeout value, which is an absolute timeout value. If you use both timers, either they must be equal or the idle timeout must be less than the absolute timeout value. The rest of the access list will allow IP traffic the subnet 172.16.1.0/24 access to any network, after authenticated.

The following list provides some Cisco rules and recommendations for configuring dynamic access list timers:

- Either define an idle timeout now with the **timeout** keyword in the **access-enable** command in the **autocommand** command, or define an absolute timeout value later with the **access-list** command. You must define either an idle timeout or an absolution timeout; otherwise, the temporary access list entry will remain configured indefinitely on the interface (even after the user has terminated the session) until the entry is removed manually by an administrator.

- If you configure an idle timeout, the idle timeout value should be equal to the dialer-idle timeout value.

- If you configure both idle and absolute timeouts, the idle timeout value must be less than or equal to the absolute timeout value.

The next line is your normal access list that will always be in place until someone has authenticated. This access list must begin with a permit of Telnet to the interface where the filter is applied. Without allowing Telnet, the user could never authenticate. In this case, you will allow only users on the same subnet of 172.16.1.0/24 to authenticate, while denying all other traffic. You can now apply the access list to the Ethernet 0 port of the paine router. This is done with the **ip access-group 101 in** command under the Ethernet 0 interface.

Finally, you must enable Telnet access under the vty ports, along with the appropriate enable passwords. See Chapter 1 if you need additional help with absolute line numbers. Example 14-9 lists the configuration of the paine router.

Example 14-9 *paine Router Configuration*

```
hostname paine
!
enable password 7 02050D480809
!
username franklin password 7 02040155
username franklin autocommand access-enable timeout 5
!
!
interface Ethernet0
 no ip address
 shutdown
 media-type 10BaseT
!
interface Ethernet1
 ip address 172.16.1.2 255.255.255.0
 ip access-group 101 in
 media-type 10BaseT
!
<<<text omitted>>>
!
interface TokenRing1
 ip address 128.200.1.2 255.255.255.0
 ring-speed 16
!
router eigrp 2001
 network 128.200.0.0
 network 172.16.0.0
 no auto-summary
!
ip classless
!
access-list 101 dynamic allowben timeout 5 permit ip 172.16.1.0 0.0.0.255 any
access-list 101 permit tcp 172.16.1.0 0.0.0.255 host 172.16.1.2 eq telnet
!
!
line con 0
line aux 0
line vty 0 4
 login local
!
end
```

To test the configuration, either attach a workstation to the Ethernet segment of 172.16.1.0/24 or use the washington router. The router will always use the address closest to the destination for the source address of IP packets. If you want to source a Telnet session from a different port, use the following command:

```
ip telnet source-interface interface_name
```

Example 14-10 first illustrates an unsuccessful **ping** from washington to jefferson. The user then authenticates with paine, followed by successful **ping**s to jefferson. After five minutes, the router paine will close the temporary hole and deny future access inbound to its Ethernet port. Notice how the Telnet session is immediately closed after authentication—this is normal operation.

Example 14-10 *Testing the Dynamic Access List*

```
washington#
washington#ping 128.200.1.5

Type escape sequence to abort.
Sending 5, 100-byte ICMP Echos to 128.200.1.5, timeout is 2 seconds:
U.U.U
Success rate is 0 percent (0/5)
washington#
washington#
washington#telnet 172.16.1.2
Trying 172.16.1.2 ... Open


User Access Verification

Username: franklin
Password:
[Connection to 172.16.1.2 closed by foreign host]
washington#
washington#
washington#ping 128.200.1.5

Type escape sequence to abort.
Sending 5, 100-byte ICMP Echos to 128.200.1.5, timeout is 2 seconds:
!!!!!
Success rate is 100 percent (5/5), round-trip min/avg/max = 4/6/8 ms
washington#
<<<After 5 minutes expires>>>
washington#ping 128.200.1.5

Type escape sequence to abort.
Sending 5, 100-byte ICMP Echos to 128.200.1.5, timeout is 2 seconds:
U.U.U
Success rate is 0 percent (0/5)
washington#
```

Named Access Lists

With the introduction of Cisco IOS Release 11.2, Cisco introduced a way to label access lists with unique names. Named access lists allow the use of descriptive names for an access list versus the less descriptive use of numbers. This can be beneficial to network administrators using large numbers of access lists.

To configure a named access list, first define the access list as standard or extended, with the following command:

```
ip access-list {standard | extended} access_list_name
```

After this line is entered, the router prompts you for the next entries under the access list. The syntax offered for standard access lists at the access list prompt is shown here:

```
{permit | deny} a.b.c.d [wildcard_mask]
```

The syntax offered for an extended access list is as follows:

```
{permit | deny} protocol_type source_address source_address_wildcard
destination_address destination_address_wildcard [protocol specific options] {log}
```

All the same rules and syntax apply to both cases, except for the access list number preceding each line, as in a normal access list. Figure 14-5 illustrates a simple named access list applied to an Ethernet interface.

Figure 14-5 *Named Access List Example*

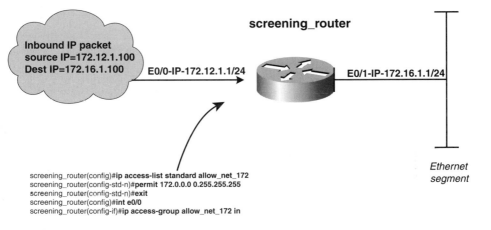

In the example in Figure 14-5, a named access list called **allow_net_172** was applied to the Ethernet 0/0 port. The command for attaching an access list to an interface is the **access-group** command, which uses the *name* of the access list instead of numbers.

Lab 29: Configuring Access Lists, Named Access Lists, and EIGRP Route Filters—Part I

Practical Scenario

This chapter has stressed the importance of understanding access lists in binary. This exercise underscores this fact. In the field, you will want to make your access lists as small and efficient as possible.

Lab Exercise

The State Patrol and the County Sheriff use a national fingerprinting system at FBI headquarters. Because of the enormous growth in access and use of the system, the FBI wants to cut down on the number of networks that it can see and reach. The bureau has implemented a policy that they will route only to the even subnets for the State Patrol locations and only to the odd subnets for the County Sheriff locations. Because the State Patrol and the County Sheriff have overlapping subnets, extreme care must be taken when implementing this policy. Use the following parameters as your design guidelines:

- EIGRP is the routing protocol for this entire network. The autonomous System ID is 2001.

- Control routing updates so that the FBI router routes receive only even subnets from the State Patrol router and odd subnets from the County Sheriff router.

- The two clouds represent IP networks that the router is attached to. These clouds will be simulated by creating a route generator.

- Use named access lists.

Lab Objectives

- Configure the network as depicted in Figure 14-6. Use EIGRP as the routing protocol.

- Allow only routing updates in which the subnet is an even number to be advertised from the state_patrol router. Allow only routing updates in which the subnet is an odd number to be advertised from the county_sheriff router.

- Construct your access list with as few lines as possible.

- Check the network by issuing a **trace** from the fbi_hq router to the addresses 150.100.2.1, which should go to the state_patrol router. Also verify proper route advertisement by observing what routers report what routes.

Equipment Needed

- Three Cisco routers. The routers should be connected through V.35 back-to-back cables or in a similar manner.

- One LAN segment, provided through hub or switch.

Physical Layout and Prestaging

- Connect the hubs and serial cables to the routers, as shown in Figure 14-6.

- Simulate a LAN segment, as shown in Figure 14-6.

- Configure route generators on the state_patrol and county_sheriff routers. Do this by configuring 10 loopback addresses on the routers; use the same range for both routers—150.100.1.0/24 through 150.100.10.0/24.

- Use EIGRP as the routing protocol.

Figure 14-6 *National Fingerprinting System—WAN Access*

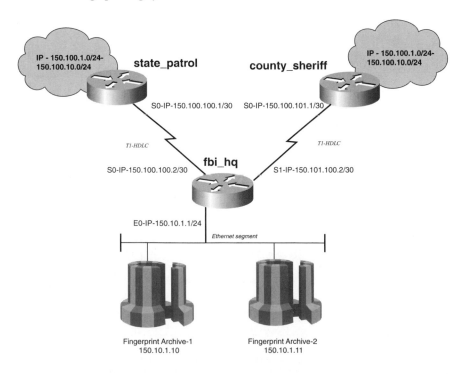

Lab 29: Configuring Access Lists, Named Access Lists, and EIGRP Route Filters—Part II

Lab Walkthrough

After completing the physical installation, you should establish IP connectivity among all the routers. At this point, don't be concerned about **ping**ing loopback addresses of the routers. There will be a routing loop until the filters are applied.

Beginning with the fbi_router router, configure the IP addresses of Ethernet and two serial interfaces. Because you are configuring the DCE side of both links, be sure to include the **clock rate** command under the serial interface. Configure the state_patrol router first. When you can **ping** the serial interface of the fbi_hq router from the state_patrol router, configure EIGRP. Seeing individual subnets will be important, so you will need to add the **no auto-summary** command under EIGRP. To configure the state_patrol router as a route generator, use MS Notepad and make a file similar to the following:

```
int loop 20
ip add 150.100.1.1 255.255.255.0
int loop 21
ip add 150.100.2.1 255.255.255.0
int loop 22
ip add 150.100.3.1 255.255.255.0
int loop 23
ip add 150.100.4.1 255.255.255.0
int loop 24
ip add 150.100.5.1 255.255.255.0
int loop 25
ip add 150.100.6.1 255.255.255.0
int loop 26
ip add 150.100.7.1 255.255.255.0
int loop 27
ip add 150.100.8.1 255.255.255.0
int loop 28
ip add 150.100.9.1 255.255.255.0
int loop 29
ip add 150.100.10.1 255.255.255.0
```

Cutting and pasting this text will be quicker than performing the manual key-ins. When you are finished and can see the routes on the fbi_hq router, proceed to configure the local_sheriff router in the same manner. When you are finished, the routing table of the fbi_hq router should appear like Example 14-11.

Example 14-11 **show ip route** *Command on fbi_hq Router*

```
fbi_hq# show ip route
Codes: C - connected, S - static, I - IGRP, R - RIP, M - mobile, B - BGP
       D - EIGRP, EX - EIGRP external, O - OSPF, IA - OSPF inter area
       N1 - OSPF NSSA external type 1, N2 - OSPF NSSA external type 2
       E1 - OSPF external type 1, E2 - OSPF external type 2, E - EGP
       i - IS-IS, L1 - IS-IS level-1, L2 - IS-IS level-2, * - candidate default
```

continues

Example 14-11 **show ip route** *Command on fbi_hq Router (Continued)*

```
          U - per-user static route, o - ODR

Gateway of last resort is not set

     150.10.0.0/24 is subnetted, 1 subnets
C       150.10.1.0 is directly connected, Ethernet0
     150.100.0.0/16 is variably subnetted, 12 subnets, 2 masks
C       150.100.100.0/30 is directly connected, Serial0
C       150.100.101.0/30 is directly connected, Serial1
D       150.100.2.0/24 [90/2297856] via 150.100.100.1, 00:00:07, Serial0
                       [90/2297856] via 150.100.101.1, 00:00:07, Serial1
D       150.100.3.0/24 [90/2297856] via 150.100.100.1, 00:00:07, Serial0
                       [90/2297856] via 150.100.101.1, 00:00:07, Serial1
D       150.100.1.0/24 [90/2297856] via 150.100.100.1, 00:00:07, Serial0
                       [90/2297856] via 150.100.101.1, 00:00:07, Serial1
D       150.100.6.0/24 [90/2297856] via 150.100.100.1, 00:00:07, Serial0
                       [90/2297856] via 150.100.101.1, 00:00:07, Serial1
D       150.100.7.0/24 [90/2297856] via 150.100.100.1, 00:00:07, Serial0
                       [90/2297856] via 150.100.101.1, 00:00:07, Serial1
D       150.100.4.0/24 [90/2297856] via 150.100.100.1, 00:00:08, Serial0
                       [90/2297856] via 150.100.101.1, 00:00:08, Serial1
D       150.100.5.0/24 [90/2297856] via 150.100.100.1, 00:00:08, Serial0
                       [90/2297856] via 150.100.101.1, 00:00:08, Serial1
D       150.100.10.0/24 [90/2297856] via 150.100.100.1, 00:00:08, Serial0
                        [90/2297856] via 150.100.101.1, 00:00:08, Serial1
D       150.100.8.0/24 [90/2297856] via 150.100.100.1, 00:00:09, Serial0
                       [90/2297856] via 150.100.101.1, 00:00:09, Serial1
D       150.100.9.0/24 [90/2297856] via 150.100.100.1, 00:00:09, Serial0
                       [90/2297856] via 150.100.101.1, 00:00:09, Serial1
```

Notice that both route generators are advertising the same routes to the fbi_hq router. If you performed only a **ping**, you might be persuaded to believe that everything was okay. But performing a source trace from the Ethernet interface of the fbi_hq router shows that you have a routing issue. Example 14-12 lists the output from a source **trace** and **ping**.

Example 14-12 **trace** *and* **ping** *Commands from fbi_hq*

```
fbi_hq# ping 150.100.1.1

Type escape sequence to abort.
Sending 5, 100-byte ICMP Echos to 150.100.1.1, timeout is 2 seconds:
!!!!!
Success rate is 100 percent (5/5), round-trip min/avg/max = 1/2/4 ms
fbi_hq# trace
Protocol [ip]:
Target IP address: 150.100.1.1
Source address: 150.10.1.1
Numeric display [n]:
Timeout in seconds [3]:
```

Example 14-12 **trace** *and* **ping** *Commands from fbi_hq (Continued)*

```
Probe count [3]:
Minimum Time to Live [1]:
Maximum Time to Live [30]:
Port Number [33434]:
Loose, Strict, Record, Timestamp, Verbose[none]:
Type escape sequence to abort.
Tracing the route to 150.100.1.1

  1 150.100.100.1 4 msec
    150.100.101.1 4 msec
    150.100.100.1 8 msec
```

Focusing on the state_patrol router, you need to write a named access list that will allow only the even subnets to be advertised to the fbi_hq router. These subnets would be 0, 2, 4, 6, 8, and 10 of the 150.100.0.0 network. If you wrote 1 through 10 in binary, you would have the following:

0000 0001 = 1
0000 0010 = 2
0000 0011 = 3
0000 0100 = 4
0000 0101 = 5
0000 0110 = 6
0000 0111 = 7
0000 1000 = 8
0000 1001 = 9
0000 1010 = 10

Notice that all the even subnets have a 0 in the first bit from the right. Therefore, tell the access list that the third octet must have a 0 in the first position. Example 14-13 shows how to configure the access list with these parameters. The wildcard mask is 0.0.254.255 because you want to match on the 0 in the first position on the third octet of the first part of the access list.

Example 14-13 *Named Access List to Allow Even Subnets*

```
state_patrol(config)#ip access-list standard alloweven
state_patrol(config-std-nacl)#permit 150.100.0.0 0.0.254.255
state_patrol(config-std-nacl)#exit
state_patrol(config)#router eigrp 2001
state_patrol(config-router)#distribute-list alloweven out s0
state_patrol(config-router)#^Z
```

Moving on to the local_sheriff router, you need to perform a similar exercise. Here, you want to allow only the odd subnets to pass to the fbi_hq router. Using the same logic as for the access list in Example 14-13, put a 1 in the first position of the third octet of the source address of the access list. You can use the same wildcard mask, stating that the first bit must be 1 in the third octet, by using the mask of 0.0.254.255. Example 14-14 demonstrates the configuration of the local_sheriff router.

Example 14-14 *Named Access List to Allow Odd Subnets*

```
county_sheriff(config)#ip access-list standard allowodd
county_sheriff(config-std-na)#permit 150.100.1.0 0.0.254.255
county_sheriff(config-std-na)#exit
county_sheriff(config)#router eigrp 2001
county_sheriff(config-router)#distribute-list allowodd out s0
county_sheriff(config-router)#^Z
county_sheriff#
```

To test the final configurations, go to the fbi_hq router and perform a **show ip route** and source **trace**. Example 14-15 lists the output from the fbi_hq router. Notice that only the even subnets are being reported from 150.100.100.1 in through interface Serial 0. The odd subnets are now coming from 150.100.101.1 in through interface Serial 1.

Example 14-15 show ip route *and* **trace** *Commands on fbi_hq Router*

```
fbi_hq# show ip route

Codes: C - connected, S - static, I - IGRP, R - RIP, M - mobile, B - BGP
       D - EIGRP, EX - EIGRP external, O - OSPF, IA - OSPF inter area
       N1 - OSPF NSSA external type 1, N2 - OSPF NSSA external type 2
       E1 - OSPF external type 1, E2 - OSPF external type 2, E - EGP
       i - IS-IS, L1 - IS-IS level-1, L2 - IS-IS level-2, * - candidate default
       U - per-user static route, o - ODR

Gateway of last resort is not set

     150.10.0.0/24 is subnetted, 1 subnets
C       150.10.1.0 is directly connected, Ethernet0
     150.100.0.0/16 is variably subnetted, 12 subnets, 2 masks
C       150.100.100.0/30 is directly connected, Serial0
C       150.100.101.0/30 is directly connected, Serial1
D       150.100.2.0/24 [90/2297856] via 150.100.100.1, 00:01:35, Serial0
D       150.100.3.0/24 [90/2297856] via 150.100.101.1, 00:01:30, Serial1
D       150.100.1.0/24 [90/2297856] via 150.100.101.1, 00:01:30, Serial1
D       150.100.6.0/24 [90/2297856] via 150.100.100.1, 00:01:35, Serial0
D       150.100.7.0/24 [90/2297856] via 150.100.101.1, 00:01:30, Serial1
D       150.100.4.0/24 [90/2297856] via 150.100.100.1, 00:01:35, Serial0
D       150.100.5.0/24 [90/2297856] via 150.100.101.1, 00:01:30, Serial1
D       150.100.10.0/24 [90/2297856] via 150.100.100.1, 00:01:35, Serial0
D       150.100.8.0/24 [90/2297856] via 150.100.100.1, 00:01:35, Serial0
D       150.100.9.0/24 [90/2297856] via 150.100.101.1, 00:01:31, Serial1
fbi_hq#
fbi_hq#trace
Protocol [ip]:
```

Example 14-15 **show ip route** *and* **trace** *Commands on fbi_hq Router (Continued)*

```
Target IP address: 150.100.1.1
Source address: 150.10.1.1
Numeric display [n]:
Timeout in seconds [3]:
Probe count [3]:
Minimum Time to Live [1]:
Maximum Time to Live [30]:
Port Number [33434]:
Loose, Strict, Record, Timestamp, Verbose[none]:
Type escape sequence to abort.
Tracing the route to 150.100.1.1

  1 150.100.101.1 0 msec 0 msec *
fbi_hq#
```

Example 14-16 shows the complete configuration for the state_patrol, county_sheriff, and fbi_hq routers.

Example 14-16 *Complete Configurations for state_patrol, county_sheriff, and fbi_hq Routers*

```
hostname state_patrol
!
ip subnet-zero
!
 interface Loopback20
 ip address 150.100.1.1 255.255.255.0
 no ip directed-broadcast
!
interface Loopback21
 ip address 150.100.2.1 255.255.255.0
 no ip directed-broadcast
!
interface Loopback22
 ip address 150.100.3.1 255.255.255.0
 no ip directed-broadcast
!
interface Loopback23
 ip address 150.100.4.1 255.255.255.0
 no ip directed-broadcast
!
interface Loopback24
 ip address 150.100.5.1 255.255.255.0
 no ip directed-broadcast
!
interface Loopback25
 ip address 150.100.6.1 255.255.255.0
 no ip directed-broadcast
```

continues

Example 14-16 *Complete Configurations for state_patrol, county_sheriff, and fbi_hq Routers (Continued)*

```
!
interface Loopback26
 ip address 150.100.7.1 255.255.255.0
 no ip directed-broadcast
!
interface Loopback27
 ip address 150.100.8.1 255.255.255.0
 no ip directed-broadcast
!
interface Loopback28
 ip address 150.100.9.1 255.255.255.0
 no ip directed-broadcast
!
interface Loopback29
 ip address 150.100.10.1 255.255.255.0
 no ip directed-broadcast
!
<<<text omitted>>>
!
interface Serial0
 ip address 150.100.100.1 255.255.255.252
 no ip directed-broadcast
!
<<<text omitted>>>
!
router eigrp 2001
 network 150.100.0.0
 distribute-list alloweven out Serial0
 no auto-summary
!
ip access-list standard alloweven
 permit 150.100.0.0 0.0.254.255
```

```
hostname county_sheriff
!
ip subnet-zero
!
 interface Loopback20
 ip address 150.100.1.1 255.255.255.0
 no ip directed-broadcast
!
interface Loopback21
 ip address 150.100.2.1 255.255.255.0
 no ip directed-broadcast
!
interface Loopback22
 ip address 150.100.3.1 255.255.255.0
 no ip directed-broadcast
!
interface Loopback23
 ip address 150.100.4.1 255.255.255.0
```

Example 14-16 *Complete Configurations for state_patrol, county_sheriff, and fbi_hq Routers (Continued)*

```
 no ip directed-broadcast
!
interface Loopback24
 ip address 150.100.5.1 255.255.255.0
 no ip directed-broadcast
!
interface Loopback25
 ip address 150.100.6.1 255.255.255.0
 no ip directed-broadcast
!
interface Loopback26
 ip address 150.100.7.1 255.255.255.0
 no ip directed-broadcast
!
interface Loopback27
 ip address 150.100.8.1 255.255.255.0
 no ip directed-broadcast
!
interface Loopback28
 ip address 150.100.9.1 255.255.255.0
 no ip directed-broadcast
!
interface Loopback29
 ip address 150.100.10.1 255.255.255.0
 no ip directed-broadcast
!
<<<text omitted>>>
!
interface Serial0
 ip address 150.100.101.1 255.255.255.252
 no ip directed-broadcast
!
<<<text omitted>>>
!
router eigrp 2001
 network 150.100.0.0
 distribute-list allowodd out Serial0
 no auto-summary
!
ip access-list standard allowodd
permit 150.100.1.0 0.0.254.255
```

```
hostname fbi_hq
!
interface Ethernet0
 ip address 150.10.1.1 255.255.255.0
!
interface Serial0
 ip address 150.100.100.2 255.255.255.252
 no fair-queue
```

continues

Example 14-16 *Complete Configurations for state_patrol, county_sheriff, and fbi_hq Routers (Continued)*

```
 clockrate 2000000
!
interface Serial1
 ip address 150.100.101.2 255.255.255.252
 clockrate 2000000
!
<<<text omitted>>>
!
router eigrp 2001
 network 150.10.0.0
 network 150.100.0.0
 no auto-summary


fbi_hq#
```

Lab 30: Configuring Dynamic Access Lists and Traffic Filters by Using Named Access Lists—Part I

Practical Scenario

As more networks grow together, either by the Internet or internally, you will be required to control access to them. The best way to control access is not to advertise the private subnet with a routing protocol. However, IP access might be required at times, so you will have to advertise your networks with a routing protocol. To control access on a packet level, you will have to use an access list.

Lab Exercise

The upstart company of Wavester.com provides secure FTP and TFTP access to its huge MP3 archive. Many universities were experiencing high and expensive Internet usage. To the delight of the students, Wavester now offers direct T1 access to its archives. In this lab, you will configure a T1 to the Wavester site. The only protocols that can travel across the link are FTP, TFTP, ping, and routing protocols. Place this filter in the most effective location using the following criteria:

- OSPF is the routing protocol. All new sites are to be configured as stub areas.
- Control traffic so that only FTP, TFTP, and ping go across the serial link. Allow FTP access only to the server 150.10.1.10 from the 132.31.5.16/27 subnet.
- Use named access lists.
- Configure an access list that denies Telnet access to graceland until a user authenticates with the wavester router. Then allow access only from the 132.31.5.16/27 subnet.

Lab Objectives

- Configure the network as depicted in Figure 14-7. Use OSPF as the routing protocol. Configure the router jo_college to be in a stub area.
- Allow only Telnet, FTP, TFTP, ping, and routing protocols to cross the serial link. Allow FTP access only to the server 150.10.1.10.
- Configure another access list on wavester that prevents Telnet to the graceland router from the 132.31.5.16 subnet. When the user theking with password elvis authenticates with wavester, Telnet access from the 132.31.5.16/27 subnet will be allowed into graceland. The authentication should expire 10 minutes from login.

Equipment Needed

- Three Cisco routers. Two of the routers should be connected through V.35 back-to-back cables or in a similar manner.

- Two LAN segments, provided through hubs or switches.

- Two workstations for testing FTP, and TFTP file transfers. Use software found at http://download.cnet.com/ for the FTP and TFTP clients and servers. FTP uses different ports to send data than it does for its initial connection. Applying your filter to a live FTP client and server environment will manifest errors that you will not see without a live connection. Remember that the router will source its packets from the closest interface to its destination, so workstations are required for proper testing of access lists.

Physical Layout and Prestaging

- Connect the hubs and serial cables to the routers, as shown in Figure 14-7.

- Simulate the LAN segments, as shown in Figure 14-7.

- Attach a workstation to the Ethernet segment of the wavester router. This workstation will serve as the FTP and TFTP server. Attach another workstation to the Ethernet segment of the jo_college router to serve as the FTP and TFTP client. You can download network utilities from http://download.cnet.com/.

- The router can also be used to test TFTP, but be aware of where it sources its packets from because this will affect where you place your filters.

- Use OSPF as the routing protocol. Place the graceland router and the wavester router into Area 0, and put the jo_college router into stub Area 100. Ensure full IP connectivity before applying any filters.

Figure 14-7 *Wavester.com Network*

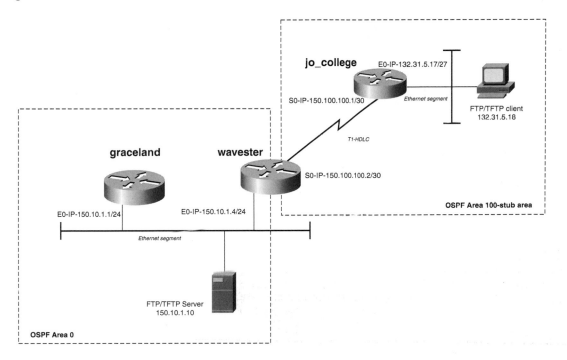

Lab 30: Configuring Dynamic Access Lists and Traffic Filters by Using Named Access Lists—Part II

Lab Walkthrough

After completing the physical installation, you should establish IP connectivity among all the routers. Configure OSPF Area 0 on the Ethernet interface of the graceland and wavester routers. Put the serial interface of the wavester into OSPF Area 100. Use the **area 100 stub** command to make jo_college a stub router. When you have full IP connectivity from the 132.31.5.18 subnet to the 150.10.1.1 subnet, begin to test file transfers.

Configure a workstation as an FTP and TFTP server on the Ethernet segment of the wavester router. Test file transfers with the FTP client software or the router. Ensure that you can transfer files back and forth before proceeding to configure filters. You can download network utilities from http://download.cnet.com/.

The first access list to configure goes on the jo_college router. This access list must allow Telnet, FTP, OSPF, TFTP, and ICMP through it. Place the access list close to the source of traffic that you want to filter, which is the FTP/TFTP client. The named access list should look like Example 14-17.

Example 14-17 *IP Named Access List*

```
ip access-list extended allow_filetrans
 permit tcp any any established
 permit tcp 132.31.5.16 0.0.0.15 any eq telnet
 permit tcp 132.31.5.16 0.0.0.15 host 150.10.1.10 eq ftp
 permit tcp 132.31.5.16 0.0.0.15 host 150.10.1.10 gt 1023
 permit ospf any any
 permit udp any any eq tftp
 permit icmp any any echo
 permit icmp any any echo-reply
```

The first line of the access list allows established connections or connections with the ACK or RST bits set in the TCP header to pass. The second line allows Telnet access from the subnet of 132.31.5.16 to anywhere. The wildcard mask in the second line is derived from laying out the .16 subnet in binary and looking at the significant bits. If you want to allow the hosts only on the .16 subnet, you need to match on the first 4 bits in the fourth octet.

0001 0000 = subnet 16
0000 1111 = wildcard mask = 15

Therefore, the wildcard mask of 0.0.0.15 will allow hosts on subnet 132.31.5.16/27 to pass.

The next three lines are used for FTP access:

```
permit tcp 132.31.5.16 0.0.0.15 host 150.10.1.10 eq ftp
permit tcp 132.31.5.16 0.0.0.15 host 150.10.1.10 gt 1023
permit tcp host 150.10.1.10 132.31.5.16 0.0.0.15 gt 1023
```

FTP initiates a session from the client to the server on TCP port 21, but it sends data on random ports above 1023. It is a common misconception that FTP uses TCP port 20 to send data. When configuring an access list for FTP, you must allow TCP ports greater than 1023.

The next line in the access list allows OSPF packets, while the following line allows UDP equal to port 69, TFTP. Another common pitfall when writing access lists is to filter the routing protocol. Of course, when this happens, all the routes in the routing table disappear, thereby making it an easy error to spot.

Finally, the last two lines allow ICMP echo and echo-reply. These lines enable you to still **ping** the remote routers. Apply the filter to the Ethernet interface with the following command:

```
ip access-group allow_filetrans in
```

After the access list is applied, try to transfer files to and from the FTP/TFTP server. A live test of the application is the only way to properly test any type of traffic filters.

The next step in the lab is to configure a dynamic access list on the wavester router. This access list must allow Telnet to this router while denying Telnet access to the graceland router. When the user theking authenticates, Telnet access is granted to graceland for 10 minutes. The access list to accomplish this looks like Example 14-18.

Example 14-18 *Dynamic Access List on wavester*

```
ip access-list extended allowtelnet
 dynamic allowking timeout 10 permit tcp 132.31.5.16 0.0.0.15 host 150.10.1.1 eq
telnet
 permit tcp 132.31.5.16 0.0.0.15 host 150.101.100.2 eq telnet
 deny   tcp any host 150.10.1.1 eq telnet
 permit ip any any
```

The first line of the access list is a **dynamic** command that permits Telnet from the 132.31.5.16/27 subnet to the specific host address of 150.10.1.1. When a user authenticates, this access list stays open for 10 minutes. The next line allows Telnet access to the serial interface of the wavester router, which is needed for authentication to take place. The next line is the line that denies Telnet access from anywhere to the graceland router's Ethernet port. Finally, the last line of the access list will permit any IP traffic. The access list is applied to the serial interface with the **ip access-group allowtelnet in** command.

The second part of configuring a dynamic access list is to configure a username, password, and **autocommand**. The **autocommand** timeout value must match what is used in the dynamic line of the access list, if you are using both timeouts. Example 14-19 shows the username combinations on the wavester router.

Example 14-19 *Username Passwords for Dynamic Access Lists*

```
username theking password elvis
username theking autocommand access-enable timeout 10
```

Before testing the configuration for Telnet access, be sure to configure the routers' vty sessions to support Telnet. To test the dynamic access list, first try to Telnet to the graceland router from the jo_college router. The session should be denied. Next, Telnet to the serial interface of the wavester router and log in as theking with the password elvis. The session should immediately close and jump you back to the jo_college router. Now, Telnet to the graceland router, and your login will be accepted.

Example 14-20 shows the complete configurations for the wavester and jo_college routers.

Example 14-20 *jo_college and wavester Router Configurations*

```
hostname jo_college
!
enable password cisco
!
username cisco password 0 cisco
ip subnet-zero
 !
 <<<text omitted>>>
!
interface Ethernet0
 ip address 132.31.5.17 255.255.255.240
 ip access-group allow_filetrans in
 no ip directed-broadcast
!
interface Serial0
 ip address 150.100.100.1 255.255.255.252
 no ip directed-broadcast
!
<<<text omitted>>>
!
router ospf 69
 network 132.31.5.17 0.0.0.0 area 100
 network 150.100.100.1 0.0.0.0 area 100
 area 100 stub
!
ip classless
!
ip access-list extended allow_filetrans
 permit tcp any any established
 permit tcp 132.31.5.16 0.0.0.15 any eq telnet
 permit tcp 132.31.5.16 0.0.0.15 host 150.10.1.10 eq ftp
 permit tcp 132.31.5.16 0.0.0.15 host 150.10.1.10 gt 1023
 permit tcp host 150.10.1.10 132.31.5.16 0.0.0.15 gt 1023
 permit ospf any any
 permit udp any any eq tftp
```

Example 14-20 *jo_college and wavester Router Configurations (Continued)*

```
 permit icmp any any echo
 permit icmp any any echo-reply
 !
line con 0
 transport input none
line aux 0
line vty 0 4
end
```
```
hostname wavester
!
username theking password 0 elvis
username theking autocommand access-enable timeout 10
clock timezone PAC -8
!
interface Ethernet0
 ip address 150.10.1.4 255.255.255.0
!
interface Serial0
 ip address 150.100.100.2 255.255.255.252
 ip access-group allowtelnet in
 no fair-queue
 clockrate 2000000
!
<<<text omitted>>>
!
router ospf 69
 network 150.10.1.4 0.0.0.0 area 0
 network 150.100.100.2 0.0.0.0 area 100
 area 100 stub
!
ip classless
!
ip access-list extended allowtelnet
 dynamic allowking timeout 10 permit tcp 132.31.5.16 0.0.0.15 host 150.10.1.1 eq
 telnet
 permit tcp 132.31.5.16 0.0.0.15 host 150.101.100.2 eq telnet
 deny   tcp any host 150.10.1.1 eq telnet
 permit ip any any
!
line con 0
line aux 0
line vty 0 4
 login local
!
end
```

PART **VII**

Enhanced Network Protocols

CHAPTER 15

Configuring Network Address Translation (NAT)

The phenomenal growth of the Internet spawned a tremendous squeeze on IP address space. Some of the stronger solutions offered to relieve this pressure are classless interdomain routing (CIDR) and IPv6. CIDR can be viewed as the short-term solution until IPv6 becomes the dominant version of IP in use. But many private networks and ISPs have yet to migrate to IPv6. Perhaps one reason for the delay to migrate to IPv6 is the huge success of an intermediate solution called Network Address Translation (NAT).

NAT allows many private companies and individuals to implement private address space for their networks, provided under RFC 1918, thereby conserving valuable public address space. NAT also provides ways for addresses in the same routing domain to "overlap" each other yet reach the common hosts. The translation of addresses by NAT inherently provides a level of security directly needed when transporting data across the Internet. This chapter discusses how NAT operates and covers NAT terminology. It also explores the three major implementations of NAT—NAT pools, static NAT, and NAT overload.

NAT Technical Overview

RFC 1631, "The Network Address Translator (NAT)," outlines NAT, which is most often installed on a router in a stub domain—that is, a network with a single exit point. Specifically, NAT handles two types of translations:

- Outside address translation entry
- Inside translation entry

To explain how these translations work, it is important to understand NAT terminology.

NAT Terminology

Some terms mentioned earlier apply to all NAT configurations. The term *inside* refers to networks that are private and that reside inside your routing domain. The inside is the address that you will be translating. The term *outside* refers to networks that are "visible" and most often routable to the outside world. The term *global* is used with *inside* and *outside* as well; think of the term to mean that this address space is assigned by NIC. Table 15-1 details how the words are used together.

Table 15-1　*NAT Terminology*

NAT Term	Definition
Inside local address(es)	The IP address(es) assigned to the host(s) on the network that is to translate. This network should be one of the networks provided by RFC 1918.
Inside global address(es)	A routable and legitimate IP address, assigned by the NIC or ISP. This range must be routable to the Internet or destination network(s).
Outside local address(es)	The IP address of an outside host(s), as it is viewed by the inside host(s). This space is reachable from an inside network and might or might not be registered IP address space. It is used primarily in static translations.
Outside global address(es)	The IP address assigned to a host(s) on the outside network; this is routable and visible to Internet. It is a registered address and is used primarily in static translations.

NAT processes a packet that originates from an inside network in the following manner:

1　When NAT receives a packet from an inside interface that passes the criteria set for translation, it searches the NAT table for an outside address-translation entry whose outside local address is equal to the destination IP address of the packet.

2　If no match is found in the lookup, the packet is dropped.

3　If an entry is found, NAT replaces the destination address in the packet with the outside global address from the table entry.

4　NAT proceeds to search the NAT table to see if an inside local address is equal to the source IP address in the packet.

5　If an entry is found, NAT replaces the source address in the packet with the inside global address.

6　If no entry is found, NAT creates a new inside address entry and inserts it in the packet.

NAT processes a packet that originates from an outside network in the following manner:

1 When NAT receives a packet that originated from an outside interface that passes the criteria set for translation, it searches its address translation table for an entry where the inside global address is equal to the destination address of the packet.

2 If no entry is found, the packet is dropped.

3 If an entry is found, NAT replaces the destination address with the inside local address from the translation table.

4 The router searches the NAT table for an outside global address that is equal to the source IP address of the packet.

5 If an entry is found, NAT replaces the source address with the outside local address from the table entry.

6 If NAT does not find an entry, it creates one and performs the same task.

7 Any time NAT modifies the header, the router also needs to recalculate and replace the IP and TCP checksums.

Figure 15-1 shows a workstation on a private network of 172.16.1.0/24 that it is running a TCP application that needs to reach a public university network of 128.100.1.0/24.

Figure 15-1 *NAT Translation Example*

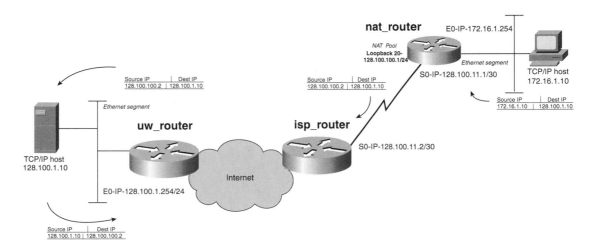

The public network of 128.100.1.0/24 or the UW has no visibility to the private network 172.16.1.0. However, 172.16.1.0 does have a route to the 128.100.1.0/24 subnet. As a packet originates from the host 172.16.1.10 to 128.100.1.10, it will have a source IP address of 172.16.1.10 and a destination IP address of 128.100.1.10. As the packet enters the NAT inside interface (E0) of the NAT router, it is routed through an NAT outside interface, S0.

When this happens, the router follows a list of user-defined criteria to determine whether address translation should take place. This is usually accomplished by checking an access list. If translation is to happen, the router translates according to how NAT is configured. This example uses a NAT pool of 254 addresses in the 128.100.100.0/24 range. These are the *inside global addresses*.

NAT now makes an association table between 172.16.1.10 and 128.100.100.2. It replaces the source IP address 172.16.1.10 of the packet with 128.100.100.2 and forwards the packet out its S0 port. This example uses a loopback interface for a NAT pool; the IP address is 128.100.100.1. NAT uses the next available address on this subnet for its association—in this example, it uses 128.100.100.2. When the UW router receives the packet, it will have appeared to come from the subnet 128.100.100.0/24. This network is reachable by this router, and it can service the request.

On the NAT router, you must have at least one globally reachable IP address; in this example, this is referred to as an *inside global address*. This address or pool of addresses is where NAT replaces the original source IP address with a new source IP address specified by NAT. When this packet reaches its destination, the host on the other side thinks that the packet comes from the global inside address, or the pool. Example 15-1 shows the results of a **ping** from 172.16.1.10 to 128.100.1.10. You can see the translations taking place by using the **debug ip nat** command along with the **show ip nat translations** command.

Example 15-1 *NAT Translation Example*

```
nat_router#deubg ip nat
00:17:30: NAT*: s=172.16.1.10->128.100.100.2, d=128.100.1.10 [4097]
00:17:30: NAT*: s=128.100.1.10, d=128.100.100.2->172.16.1.10 [4097]
00:17:31: NAT*: s=172.16.1.10->128.100.100.2, d=128.100.1.10 [4353]
00:17:31: NAT*: s=128.100.1.10, d=128.100.100.2->172.16.1.10 [4353]
00:17:32: NAT*: s=172.16.1.10->128.100.100.2, d=128.100.1.10 [4609]
00:17:32: NAT*: s=128.100.1.10, d=128.100.100.2->172.16.1.10 [4609]
00:17:33: NAT*: s=172.16.1.10->128.100.100.2, d=128.100.1.10 [4865]
00:17:33: NAT*: s=128.100.1.10, d=128.100.100.2->172.16.1.10 [4865]
nat_router#
nat_router#show ip nat translations
Pro Inside global     Inside local      Outside local     Outside global
--- 128.100.100.2     172.16.1.10       - - -             - - -
```

For reference, this type of NAT is called *dynamic translation*, and it is discussed in greater detail in a later section. Example 15-2 lists the configuration of the nat_router from Figure 15-1.

Example 15-2 *NAT Dynamic Pool Configuration for the nat_router*

```
hostname nat_router
!
ip subnet-zero
 !
 interface Loopback20
```

Example 15-2 *NAT Dynamic Pool Configuration for the nat_router (Continued)*

```
 ip address 128.100.100.1 255.255.255.0
 no ip directed-broadcast
!
interface Ethernet0
 ip address 172.16.1.254 255.255.255.0
 no ip directed-broadcast
 ip nat inside
!
interface Serial0
 ip address 128.100.11.1 255.255.255.252
 no ip directed-broadcast
 ip nat outside
!
<<<text omitted>>>
!
router eigrp 2001
 network 128.100.0.0
!
ip nat pool publicpool 128.100.100.2 128.100.100.254 netmask 255.255.255.0←Notice
   that 128.100.11.1 is not part of the pool since it is the address of the Loopback
   interface.
ip nat inside source list 69 pool publicpool
ip classless
!
access-list 69 permit 172.16.1.0 0.0.0.255
!
```

NAT and RFC 1918

Many of the benefits of NAT are derived from the goal of conserving public IP address space. As you can see from the preceding example, NAT allows you to have private addressing while accessing services outside your routing domain. RFC 1918, "Address Allocation for Private Internets," sets aside ranges of addresses that ISPs will not forward. This allows for the design of many internetworks capable of accessing Internet services without having to worry about having registered addresses. Specifically, RFC 1918 reserves the IP address ranges listing in Table 15-2.

Table 15-2   *IP Address Range for RFC 1918*

IP Address Class	IP Address Range
Class A	10.0.0.0 to 10.255.255.255
Class B	172.16.0.0 to 172.31.255.255
Class C	192.168.0.0 to 192.168.255.255

NOTE   When using private address space, use it wisely. Unfortunately, many network designs have implemented using the 10s network with 24-bit mask on point-to-point links, 16-bit masks on Ethernet segments, and so on. Just because the address space is vast, don't let this lead to sloppy IP address schemes. Remember that proper subnetting helps with route summarization and route propagation, both of which can have a significant impact on large internetworks. Many internetworks are also built around the 10s subnet. In the few years that this RFC has been out, many networks have merged and have had address overlaps on the 10s subnet, while the thousands of networks that reside on the 172.16.0.0 remain unused. My point again is to use this space wisely; treat it as you would if the address spaces were registered. Be original in your design. You will find that the little extra time you take in proper IP design will benefit you immensely as your internetwork scales and grows together with other internetworks.

Configuring NAT

NAT translation can be configured in three primary ways:

- **Dynamic translation**—NAT translates inside addresses to a pool of global addresses. After a period of time, the translation times out and global address goes back to the pool to be reused. The timeout value for all NAT translations is based on protocol. The timeout values are listed in the later section "Clearing and Changing NAT Translations."

- **Static translation**—NAT uses a one-for-one address mapping. This allows the outside network to initiate a session to the inside network based on the NAT address.

- **Overload of a single IP address**—This involves multiplexing addresses in which many local IP addresses use port address translation (PAT) to share a single global IP address.

All three methods of configuration follow a similar four-step process:

Step 1   Define NAT inside and outside networks. First, define what networks are to be translated. You might not want all inside networks to be translated. Also note where they reside from your router's perspective, and mark that interface as a NAT inside interface. Second, locate the exit point of your routing domain, where the destination networks exist; usually this is the Internet. Configure this exit interface as a NAT outside interface. You can have multiple inside and outside interfaces. These steps are accomplished using the **ip nat inside** and **ip nat outside** commands at the interface or subinterface prompts.

Step 2   Ensure that IP reachability exits between the destination network/Internet and the address/pool that you are translating to. If you are configuring a dynamic or static translation, you must ensure that the outside network can reach the subnet of your inside global network. The inside global network is the network that you are translating your addresses into. Put the subnet of the global address on a loopback interface, and ensure that the subnet is propagated via a routing protocol or a static route. This is to ensure that the subnet is reachable from the outside network.

Step 3 Configure the specific networks that are to be translated. If you are configuring dynamic NAT pools, this step is accomplished with the following command:

```
ip nat inside source [list {1-99} | route-map] pool pool_name
  overload
```

Use an access list or a route map to match the networks that will be translated. Take into account all networks that might pass through the interface, not just the local network. The **pool** argument defines what pool will be used for translation. The **overload** argument enables the router to use one global address for many local addresses.

If you are configuring static translation, use the following command:

```
ip nat inside source static local_ip_addr global_ip_addr
```

Step 4 Configure the address pool. This step is covered in Step 3 if you are using a static translation. When using dynamic translation, first "anchor" the global subnet to a loopback address. For example, if you are translating to the subnet of 150.100.100.0/24, put this subnet on a loopback address instead of using a secondary IP address on a "real" interface. This way, NAT will work on multiple interfaces if one goes down. This also prevents potential routing issues on IP secondary interfaces. To define the pool, use the following command:

```
ip nat pool pool_name starting_ip_addr ending_ip_addr {netmask
  netmask | prefix-length prefix-length}
```

Configuring NAT Dynamic Translation

Using the four-step process listed, now you will walk through the NAT configuration that you did earlier in this chapter. Figure 15-2 illustrates a private IP network of 172.16.1.0/24.

This network needs reachability to the Internet—specifically, the host 128.100.1.10 on the UW Ethernet segment. The router nat_router has a T1 connection to the Internet through the isp_router. The ISP has assigned the network 128.100.100.0/24 to nat_router for access to the Internet. The engineers who support nat_router do not want to change all the IP host addresses from a 172.16.1.x network to a 128.100.100.x network, so they use dynamic NAT.

Figure 15-2 *Dynamic NAT Example*

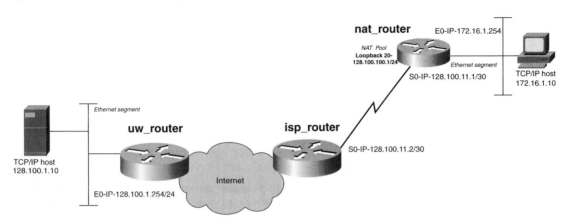

First, you must define NAT inside and outside networks. The inside network is where the networks to be translated reside, while the outside network is your destination network. In this example, your E0 port will become your NAT inside interface, while your S0 port will be your NAT outside interface. Figure 15-3 highlights the inside and outside networks.

Figure 15-3 *NAT Inside and Outside Networks*

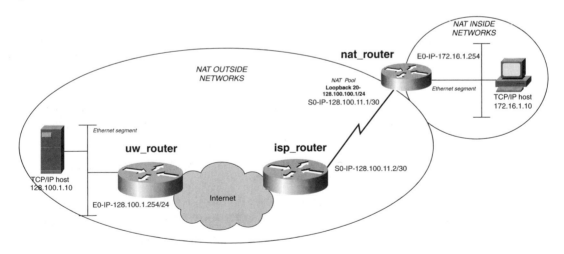

To configure the inside and outside interface, use the **ip nat [inside | outside]** command. Example 15-3 demonstrates the use of the command.

Example 15-3 *Configuring Inside and Outside Interfaces*

```
nat_router(config)#interface e0
nat_router(config-if)#ip nat inside
nat_router(config-if)#exit
nat_router(config)#interface s0
nat_router(config-if)#ip nat outside
```

The next step requires you to "anchor" the subnet that you are translating to on this router. You do this by assigning the network given to you from your ISP—in this case, 128.100.100.0/24 to a local interface. Use the first host address on the loopback interface, and use 128.100.100.2 to 128.100.100.254 as the address pool. The second part of this step requires that you have a route to the outside network and that the outside networks have a route to the subnet 128.100.100.0/24. For this example, you add a static default route on the nat_router and you use the **ip classless** command, which would appear as follows:

```
interface Loopback20
 ip address 128.100.100.1 255.255.255.0
 ip classless
 ip route 0.0.0.0 0.0.0.0 128.100.11.2
```

Relevant to this example but not shown is a static route on the isp_router to the subnet 128.100.100.0/24. This route must be propagated by the isp_router to any and all destination networks, such as the uw_router. At this point, before proceeding, ensure that all routers have IP reachability to the 128.100.100.0/24 subnet. Without IP reachability, NAT will fail.

The third step in the process is to use the **ip nat inside source** command to define the networks to be translated. In this example, you will use the following commands:

```
ip nat inside source list 69 pool publicpool
access-list 69 permit 172.16.1.0 0.0.0.255
```

This command sequence calls access list 69 and compares the source network of the packet coming in the inside interface to the list. If the source IP address is in the subnet range of 172.16.1.x, the network is translated to the IP pool called publicpool.

Finally, the last step is defining the pool publicpool using the **ip nat pool** command:

```
ip nat pool publicpool 128.100.100.2 128.100.100.254 netmask 255.255.255.0
```

This statement uses the IP address range of 128.100.100.2 to 128.100.100.254, with a subnet mask of 255.255.255.0 for translation. Because 128.100.100.1 is the address of the loopback address, you do not want to include it in the pool range. Example 15-4 lists the relevant portions the configuration of the nat_router.

Example 15-4 *NAT Dynamic Translation Configuration*

```
hostname nat_router
!
!
ip subnet-zero
!
 interface Loopback20
 ip address 128.100.100.1 255.255.255.0
 no ip directed-broadcast
!
interface Ethernet0
 ip address 172.16.1.254 255.255.255.0
 no ip directed-broadcast
 ip nat inside
!
interface Serial0
 ip address 128.100.11.1 255.255.255.252
 no ip directed-broadcast
 ip nat outside
!
<<<text omitted>>>
!
ip nat pool publicpool 128.100.100.2 128.100.100.254 netmask 255.255.255.0
ip nat inside source list 69 pool publicpool
ip classless
ip route 0.0.0.0 0.0.0.0 128.100.11.2
!
access-list 69 permit 172.16.1.0 0.0.0.255
```

Configuring NAT Static Translation

Configuring static translation is similar to configuring dynamic translation, except that you do not configure an IP pool. Instead, you configure a one-to-one address map of which specific hosts are to be translated to a specific address. A static translation can be used as an inside static translation or can have an outside static translation. Most implementations of NAT simply use an inside static translation, but when NAT is overlapping, you might want to use an outside source translation.

Building on the previous example of NAT illustrated in Figure 15-3, modify it so that only one address, 172.16.1.10, will be translated to 128.100.100.10. To configure static NAT, follow the same steps as previously defined, which include defining the inside and outside networks. Define the loopback address to "anchor" the global network and ensure routing between this subnet, 128.100.100.0/24, and the outside networks. The only part that is different from dynamic NAT configuration is defining how networks get translated. Instead of using the **ip nat inside source list** *x* command, use the **ip nat inside static** command. Specifically, this example uses the following command:

```
ip nat inside source static 172.16.1.10 128.100.100.10
```

This command causes the address 172.16.1.10 to be mapped to 128.100.100.10. No other translations will occur on the router. Example 15-5 lists how the configuration would appear with a static configuration.

Example 15-5 *NAT Static Translation Example*

```
hostname nat_router
!
ip subnet-zero
!
 interface Loopback20
 ip address 128.100.100.1 255.255.255.0
 no ip directed-broadcast
!
interface Ethernet0
 ip address 172.16.1.254 255.255.255.0
 no ip directed-broadcast
 ip nat inside
!
interface Serial0
 ip address 128.100.11.1 255.255.255.252
 no ip directed-broadcast
 ip nat outside
!
<<<text omitted>>>
!
ip nat inside source static 172.16.1.10 128.100.100.10
ip classless
ip route 0.0.0.0 0.0.0.0 128.100.11.2
```

Configuring Easy IP and Port Address Translation (PAT)

Perhaps "Easy IP" expresses the best example of overloading a single IP address for NAT. Easy IP combines NAT overload/PAT and PPP/Internet Protocol Control Protocol (IPCP). However, NAT TCP overload is not limited to PPP.

For the purposes of this text, TCP overload and PAT are synonymous. PAT provides for many-to-one IP translations. Essentially, this allows many IP addresses to share or be translated into a single IP address. PAT uses a unique source port number on the inside global IP address to distinguish between each translation.

Easy IP (Phase 1) enables a Cisco router to automatically negotiate its own registered WAN address, and it enables local hosts to access the global networks or Internet through this single IP address. Many ISPs use IPCP to dynamically assign an IP address to the remote serial interface. Because this address is unknown until it is assigned, NAT static and dynamic translations cannot be configured. Therefore, to accommodate this type of configuration, Cisco uses Easy IP. Essentially, this is what happens:

Step 1   A remote router makes a PPP connection to the ISP or a central site router. Easy IP uses PPP/IPCP to obtain an address from a DHCP server residing at the central site or ISP.

Step 2   Easy IP receives the new "dynamic" address and assigns it to WAN interface.

Step 3   Easy IP then uses port address translation (PAT) to perform a many-to-one address/port association, using multiple inside local addresses and the new global "dynamic" address.

NOTE   To configure Easy IP, you must have Cisco IOS Software Release 11.3 or later.

To configure Easy IP, you can begin by following the four-step process outlined earlier. The main difference occurs in Step 4 and the enabling of IPCP. Figure 15-4 illustrates a typical home user or small office with an ISDN connection to an ISP. The home user does not have any registered IP address space and obtains an address when dialing up the ISP. This user also has multiple workstations that must access the Internet, providing an ideal candidate for Easy IP.

Figure 15-4   *Easy IP Example*

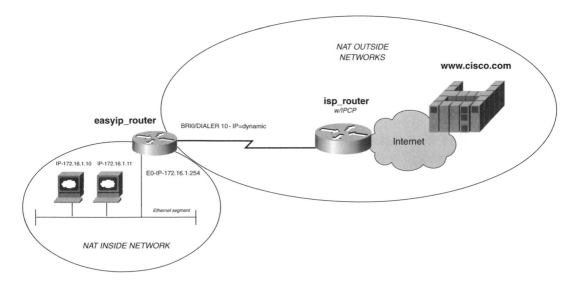

The first step is to define inside and outside networks. Here, the inside network is the Ethernet, while the BRI or Dialer 10 interface is the outside network. Use the same NAT commands, **ip nat inside** and **ip nat outside**, to define these networks on the appropriate interfaces.

The next step is to ensure that routing exists between the router and the Internet. Because only one exit point exists, use a default static route pointing to the dialer interface. Be sure to include the **ip classless** command when using a default route.

The third step involves defining what networks are to be translated and how they are translated. Here, you will point your translation to the Dialer 10 interface because the IP address is unknown. Use the **overload** command, which tells the router to use PAT. Doing so enables many connections to the Internet through one IP address. The command will look like the following:

```
ip nat inside source list 10 interface Dialer10 overload
```

Because you don't have an address pool to define static translations, Step 4 is a good place to configure IPCP. To configure IPCP, you must have PPP as your Layer 2 encapsulation, and you must have Cisco IOS Software Release 11.3 or greater. The command to enable IPCP is **ip address negotiated** under the serial or dialer interface. Example 15-6 illustrates the dialer configuration and IPCP needed on the easyip_router.

Example 15-6 *IPCP and Dialer Configuration for Easy IP*

```
interface BRI0
 no ip address
 no ip directed-broadcast
 encapsulation ppp
 dialer pool-member 10
 isdn switch-type basic-ni
 isdn spid1 71538154750101 3815475
 isdn spid2 71538154760101 3815476
 ppp multilink
!
interface Dialer10
 ip address negotiated        ←IPCP configuration
 no ip directed-broadcast
 ip nat outside
 encapsulation ppp
 no ip mroute-cache
 dialer remote-name isp_router
 dialer idle-timeout 300
 dialer string 4262200
 dialer hold-queue 80
 dialer load-threshold 10 either
 dialer pool 10
 dialer-group 10
 compress stac
```

continues

Example 15-6 *IPCP and Dialer Configuration for Easy IP (Continued)*

```
no cdp enable
ppp authentication pap
ppp pap sent-username ksolie password 7 1304474B5B5D577E
ppp multilink
!
```

Notice that most ISPs also use PAP for authentication. This also might be a requirement for your configuration to the ISP. For more information on the dialer configurations or ISDN setup, see Chapter 4, "WAN Protocols and Technologies: Point-to Point Protocol (PPP)," and Chapter 7, "WAN Protocols and Technologies: Integrated Services Digital Network (ISDN)."

Example 15-7 lists the entire configuration needed for Easy IP.

Example 15-7 *Easy IP Configuration*

```
hostname easyip_router
!
ip subnet-zero
!
isdn switch-type basic-ni
!
interface Ethernet0
 ip address 172.16.1.254 255.255.255.0
 no ip directed-broadcast
 ip nat inside
!
interface BRI0
 no ip address
 no ip directed-broadcast
 encapsulation ppp
 dialer pool-member 10
 isdn switch-type basic-ni
 isdn spid1 71538154750101 3815475
 isdn spid2 71538154760101 3815476
 ppp multilink
!
interface Dialer10
 ip address negotiated
 no ip directed-broadcast
 ip nat outside
 encapsulation ppp
 no ip mroute-cache
 dialer remote-name isp_router
 dialer idle-timeout 300
 dialer string 4262200
 dialer hold-queue 80
 dialer load-threshold 10 either
 dialer pool 10
 dialer-group 10
```

Example 15-7 *Easy IP Configuration (Continued)*

```
   no cdp enable
   ppp authentication pap
   ppp pap sent-username ksolie password 7 1304474B5B5D577E
   ppp multilink
   !
ip nat inside source list 10 interface Dialer10 overload

ip classless
ip route 0.0.0.0 0.0.0.0 Dialer10
!
access-list 10 permit 172.16.1.0 0.0.0.255
access-list 110 permit ip any any
dialer-list 10 protocol ip list 110
```

The "Big show" and "Big D" for NAT

The "big **show**" commands for NAT are **show ip nat translations** for detailed NAT table listings and **show ip nat** statistics for a broader view of the translations occurring on the router.

The **show ip nat translations** command displays all NAT translations on the router. It lists the protocol, along with the inside and outside global and local translations. Example 15-8 demonstrates the use of the command from the previous Easy IP model. This example shows two workstations, 172.16.1.10 and 172.16.1.11, accessing two hosts on the Internet, using the same inside local address, 206.191.194.42. The address 206.191.194.42 was the address assigned dynamically from the ISP when you connected.

Example 15-8 show ip nat translations *Command Output*

```
easyip_router#show ip nat translations
Pro Inside global      Inside local       Outside local      Outside global
tcp 206.191.194.42:1169 172.16.1.10:1169   198.133.219.25:80  198.133.219.25:80
tcp 206.191.194.42:1168 172.16.1.10:1168   198.133.219.25:80  198.133.219.25:80
tcp 206.191.194.42:1171 172.16.1.10:1171   198.133.219.25:80  198.133.219.25:80
tcp 206.191.194.42:1170 172.16.1.10:1170   198.133.219.25:80  198.133.219.25:80
tcp 206.191.194.42:1173 172.16.1.10:1173   198.133.219.25:80  198.133.219.25:80
tcp 206.191.194.42:1172 172.16.1.10:1172   198.133.219.25:80  198.133.219.25:80
tcp 206.191.194.42:1167 172.16.1.10:1167   198.133.219.25:80  198.133.219.25:80
udp 206.191.194.42:1050 172.16.1.11:1050   206.191.193.1:53   206.191.193.1:53
udp 206.191.194.42:1048 172.16.1.11:1048   206.191.193.1:53   206.191.193.1:53
udp 206.191.194.42:1049 172.16.1.11:1049   206.191.193.1:53   206.191.193.1:53
udp 206.191.194.42:1046 172.16.1.11:1046   206.191.193.1:53   206.191.193.1:53
udp 206.191.194.42:1044 172.16.1.11:1044   206.191.193.1:53   206.191.193.1:53
tcp 206.191.194.42:1045 172.16.1.11:1045   63.251.8.23:80     63.251.8.23:80
udp 206.191.194.42:1057 172.16.1.11:1057   206.191.193.1:53   206.191.193.1:53
easyip_router#
```

NOTE	The easiest way to test NAT in any of the three configurations is to test for IP connectivity from the inside network to a host on the outside network. This can be accomplished with a source **ping**, assuming that you're translating ICMP traffic.

The **show ip nat statistics** command summarizes NAT's operation on the router. It lists the active translations and tells whether they are static, dynamic, or extended. This command also shows the NAT inside and outside interfaces. Example 15-9 lists the output of this command on the easy_ip router.

Example 15-9 show ip nat statistics *Command*

```
easyip_router#show ip nat statistics
Total active translations: 12 (0 static, 12 dynamic; 12 extended)
Outside interfaces:
  BRI0:1, BRI0:2, Dialer10, Virtual-Access1
Inside interfaces:
  Ethernet0
Hits: 2304  Misses: 190
Expired translations: 134
Dynamic mappings:
-- Inside Source
access-list 10 interface Dialer10 refcount 12
```

In this example, the translations are all dynamic and extended. In the code, **Hits** refers to the number of times that Cisco IOS Software does a translation table lookup and finds an entry, whereas **Misses** refers to the number of times that it fails to find an existing translation and must create a new one. **Expired translations** lists a cumulative count of translations that have expired since the router was booted.

The **show ip nat translations verbose** command displays more detailed information about each translation than the **show ip nat translations** command, including the time it was created, the time it was in use, and expiration time. Any flags, such as extended port translation, are also noted. Example 15-10 lists the output of the command from the previous Easy IP example.

Example 15-10 show ip nat translation verbose *Command Output*

```
easyip_router#show ip nat translations verbose
Pro Inside global     Inside local     Outside local     Outside global
tcp 206.191.194.42:1066 172.16.1.11:1066  128.11.25.241:80   128.11.25.241:80
    create 00:00:23, use 00:00:22, left 23:59:37, flags:extended
```

Example 15-10 **show ip nat translation verbose** *Command Output (Continued)*

```
tcp 206.191.194.42:1063 172.16.1.11:1063  128.11.25.252:80    128.11.25.252:80
    create 00:00:23, use 00:00:23, left 23:59:36, flags:extended
tcp 206.191.194.42:1065 172.16.1.11:1065  128.11.25.241:80    128.11.25.241:80
    create 00:00:23, use 00:00:23, left 23:59:36, flags:extended
easyip_router#
```

A limited number of debugs are available for NAT, and they all stem from the **debug ip nat** command. The syntax is as follows:

```
debug ip nat [detailed]
```

The **debug ip nat** command displays each individual port and address pair association of all active translations. The detailed variation of this command adds additional information with an interface perspective. It also displays port negotiation messages. A heavy warning is warranted to anyone using this command on a production router: The output from a single workstation can be high. Notice in Example 15-11 how many messages are generated per millisecond on a single workstation. Use this command only to track down specific NAT problems.

Example 15-11 **debug ip nat detailed** *Output from the easy_ip Router*

```
easyip_router#debug ip nat detailed
IP NAT detailed debugging is on
00:24:07: NAT: i: udp (172.16.1.10, 137) -> (206.191.193.1, 53) [25601]
00:24:07: NAT: ipnat_allocate_port: wanted 137 got 137
00:24:07: NAT: s=172.16.1.10->206.191.194.42, d=206.191.193.1 [25601]
00:24:07: NAT: o: udp (206.191.193.1, 53) -> (206.191.194.42, 137) [44225]
00:24:07: NAT: s=206.191.193.1, d=206.191.194.42->172.16.1.10 [44225]
00:24:51: NAT: i: udp (172.16.1.10, 1046) -> (206.191.193.1, 53) [25857]
00:24:51: NAT: ipnat_allocate_port: wanted 1046 got 1046
00:24:51: NAT: s=172.16.1.10->206.191.194.42, d=206.191.193.1 [25857]
00:24:51: NAT: o: udp (206.191.193.1, 53) -> (206.191.194.42, 1046) [22909]
00:24:51: NAT: s=206.191.193.1, d=206.191.194.42->172.16.1.10 [22909]
00:24:51: NAT: i: udp (172.16.1.10, 1047) -> (206.191.193.1, 53) [26113]
00:24:51: NAT: ipnat_allocate_port: wanted 1047 got 1047
```

CAUTION   Use the **debug ip nat** commands with extreme caution. A single workstation can generate several entries per millisecond. Use the command with the **logging buffered** global configuration command.

Clearing and Changing NAT Translations

NAT TCP translations will time out after a default of 24 hours. You can change the timeout values on a per-protocol basis with the following commands:

- **ip nat translation timeout** *seconds*—Specifies the timeout value that applies to dynamic translation, except for ones with overload translations. The default is 86,400 seconds, or 24 hours.

- **ip nat translation udp-timeout** *seconds*—Specifies the timeout value of UDP translations. The default is 300 seconds, or 5 minutes.

- **ip nat translation dns-timeout** *seconds*—Specifies the timeout value for DNS. The default is 60 seconds.

- **ip nat translation tcp-timeout** *seconds*—Specifies the TCP timeout values. The default is 86,400 seconds or 24 hours.

- **ip nat translation finrst-timeout** *seconds*—Specifies the timeout for NAT TCP flows after a FIN or RST bit is set in the TCP header. The default is 60 seconds.

- **ip nat translation icmp-timeout** *seconds*—Specifies the timeout for NAT ICMP packets. The default is 60 seconds.

- **ip nat translation port-timeout [tcp | udp]** *port_number seconds*—Specifies the timeout value for specific TCP or UDP port numbers.

- **ip nat translation syn-timeout**—Specifies the timeout value for NAT TCP flows after the SYN bit is set, and gives no further data.

To clear NAT translations or statistics, use the following commands:

- **clear ip nat translations** [*\|*inside* inside_address* | **outside** outside_address* | **tcp** *port_number* | **udp** *port_number*]

- **clear ip nat statistics**

NAT Limitations and Uses

NAT provides a great alternative to readdressing your network to provide access to the Internet and other IP services. NAT also provides inherent security for the inside network by preventing outside network hosts from initiating sessions. However, NAT does have its limitations. Many protocols, such as SNMP and BOOTP, embed an IP address in the data stream. Some applications ignore the source address of the IP header and, in turn, use the embedded address in the data stream for routing back to the host in which the message was received. In these instances, NAT will fail. NAT recognizes some of these traffic types, and special sets of instructions are used to handle that type of traffic, such as FTP. Table 15-3 lists those traffic types that are supported and not supported by NAT.

Table 15-3 *Traffic Type Support for NAT*

Traffic Types/Applications Supported by NAT	Traffic Types/Applications Not Supported by NAT
Any TCP/UDP traffic that does not carry source or destination IP address in the application data stream	IP multicast.
	In Cisco IOS Software Release 12.0.(1)T, the following are now supported:
	Data packet source address translation
	PIM, Auto-RP, PIM V2, and BSR
	mstat, mrinfo, and mtrace
	SDR advertisement or app. payload
HTTP	Routing table updates.
TFTP	DNS zone transfers.
TELNET	BOOTP.
Archie	Talk, ntalk.
Finger	SNMP.
NTP	Netshow.
NFS	
Rlogin, RSH, RCP	

The following carry IP addresses in the application data stream and are supported by NAT:

ICMP.

FTP. (See the following section for nonstandard port operation.)

Net BIOS over TCP/IP (Datagram and name services only; session service support will be supported in a future IOS.)

Progressive Networks' RealAudio, RTSP is not supported.

White Pines' CuSeeMe.

Xing Technologies' SteamWorks.

DNS "A" and "PTR" queries.

H.323-IOS 12.0(1)/12.0(1)T and later.

NetMeeting 2.1, 2.11, 3.01—IOS 12.0(1)/12.0(1)T and later.

NetMeeting Directory (ILS Servers)—12.1(5)T.

VDOLive—IOS 11.3(4)/11.3(4)T and later.

Vxtreme—IOS 11.3(4)/11.3(4)T and later.

NOTE	NAT pools and translations are subject to the Subnet 0 rule. Translations will fail if the NAT pool is on IP Subnet 0. Cisco IOS Software Release 12.0 and later have the **ip subnet zero** command enabled by default. If you want to use Subnet 0 for your NAT pool on devices running Cisco IOS Software with releases earlier than 12.0, you will need to use the **ip subnet zero** command.

NAT and Nonstandard FTP Port Numbers

When using FTP, the arguments to the **ftp port** command include an IP address embedded in the data stream. To accommodate this, Cisco routers recognize port 21 and take the appropriate steps in replacing the data with the new translated address and recomputing the necessary checksums. A problem happens when FTP is using nonstandard port numbers. NAT cannot recognize the data stream as being an FTP request, so it passes the packet along without the necessary modifications. Naturally, the request will fail when it reaches the host because the address in the payload differs from the address in the IP header.

In Cisco IOS Software Release 11.3(3) and Cisco IOS Software Release 11.2.(13), Cisco introduced the capability to use nonstandard TCP port numbers for FTP. The command **ip nat service list** [*1-100*] **ftp tcp port** *xxxx* calls an access list of the networks to be translated and then looks for FTP packets operating on port *xxxx*. If the router finds a match, it makes the necessary changes to that packet for FTP to operate.

Lab 31: Configuring Dynamic NAT and Using Non-Standard FTP Port Numbers—Part I

Practical Scenario

As internetworks grow together and access to the Internet increases, so will the need to use NAT. To add security to a network, NAT can also be deployed. By not propagating a subnet with a routing protocol, you can protect an internal network from any outside session initiation.

Lab Exercise

The Durand school district decided to merge two smaller high schools to form one large district. The JP Memorial School will be getting a T1 HDLC link to the Durand High School. The dhs_router has registered CIDR blocks of 200.100.1.16/29 and 200.100.1.32/29. The jpms router is using an unregistered IP address range of 9.3.3.0/24. The jpms_router requires access to the Internet, while restricting FTP and **ping** access to the server 200.100.1.18. Use the following parameters as your design guidelines:

- Configure the network so that the workstations on the subnet 9.3.3.0/24 can access to the Internet, while restricting access to the 200.100.1.16/29 subnet.

- Control access so that NAT works to the Internet, but only NAT ICMP and FTP when traffic is destined toward the host 200.100.1.18.

- Use the CIDR block of 200.100.1.32/29 for your address pool.

- *Optional:* Configure FTP to work on port 2021 instead of port 21.

Lab Objectives

- Configure the network as depicted in Figure 15-5. Use a loopback address to simulate the Internet. For lab purposes, you will use the address of 198.133.219.25/24 on a loopback interface to simulate the Internet.

- Configure NAT so that the 9.3.3.0/24 subnet can reach the address 198.133.219.25. Restrict NAT access to only FTP, and **ping** to the host of 200.100.1.18. You should not be able to **ping** 200.100.1.17 from the 9.3.3.0/24 subnet.

- Do not make a route to the jpms_router's Ethernet from the dhs_router. Do not propagate the 9.3.3.0/24 subnet with a routing protocol.

Equipment Needed

- Two Cisco routers. The routers should be connected through V.35 back-to-back cables or in a similar manner. Cisco IOS Software Release 11.2 or later and releases 11.2(13) or 11.3(3) and later for the optional portion of the lab.

- Two LAN segments, provided through hubs or switches.

- Two IP workstations, one to serve as an FTP server and one to serve as the client workstation. You can download FTP server and client software from DOWNLOAD.CNET.COM.

Physical Layout and Prestaging

- Connect the hubs and serial cables to the routers, as shown in Figure 15-5.

- Connect the two Ethernet hubs to the routers to form two LAN segments, as shown in Figure 15-5.

- Connect and configure two IP-based workstations, as shown in Figure 15-5. Make the workstation 200.100.1.18 the FTP server, and make 9.3.3.10 the FTP client. Copy a test file into the public directory of the FTP server for testing.

- *Optional:* Configure FTP to operate on port 2021 instead of port 21. Do this by changing the server software to run on port 2021. You also need to make sure that the client is set to connect on 2021.

Figure 15-5 *DHS School District—Dynamic NAT*

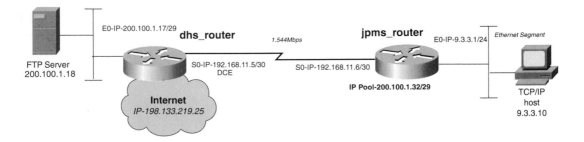

Lab 31: Configuring Dynamic NAT and Using Non-Standard FTP Port Numbers—Part II

Lab Walkthrough

After completing the physical installation of the serial link and the two Ethernet segments, establish IP connectivity between the appropriate subnets.

Beginning with the dhs_router, configure the IP addresses of Ethernet and serial interfaces. The Serial 0 port is the DCE side of the link, so this side will have the **clockrate** command. You are not allowed to "see" the 9.3.3.0/24 subnet from this router. Instead, you will have assigned the router a CIDR block 200.100.1.32/29 for NAT. This is the network that you need a route to. Therefore, you will make a static route to it on the dhs_router.

For the lab purpose, you may or may not have a connection to the Internet. If you don't have a connection to the Internet, simulate an IP host by adding a loopback interface with the address 198.133.219.25. You should be able to **ping** this address from the 9.3.3.0/24 subnet when NAT is working properly. Example 15-12 lists the configuration for the dhs_router.

Example 15-12 *dhs_router Configuration*

```
hostname dhs_router
!
<<<text omitted>>>
!
interface Loopback20
 ip address 198.133.219.25 255.255.255.0
!
interface Ethernet0
 ip address 200.100.1.17 255.255.255.248
!
interface Serial0
 ip address 192.168.11.5 255.255.255.252
 no fair-queue
 clockrate 2000000
!
<<<text omitted>>>
!
no ip classless
ip route 200.100.1.32 255.255.255.248 192.168.11.6
```

The configuration for the jpms_router will be a little more involved. Begin by assigning the appropriate IP addresses to the Ethernet and serial interfaces. You need to configure a default route pointing to 192.168.11.5. Don't forget to include the **ip classless** command when using a default route:

```
ip classless
ip route 0.0.0.0 0.0.0.0 192.168.11.5
```

At this point, you should be able to **ping** the "Internet" address of 198.133.219.25 from the router. If you issue a source **ping** from the router's Ethernet 0 interface or from the workstation 9.3.3.10, you should not be able to reach the "Internet" or the 200.100.1.16/29 subnet.

You can now begin to configure NAT on the jpms_router. First, define the inside and outside networks. Figure 15-6 illustrates the inside and outside networks from the jpms_router's perspective. After defining the inside and outside networks, configure them by using the **ip nat outside** command on the serial interface and **ip nat inside** on the Ethernet interface.

Figure 15-6 *DHS School District Inside and Outside Networks*

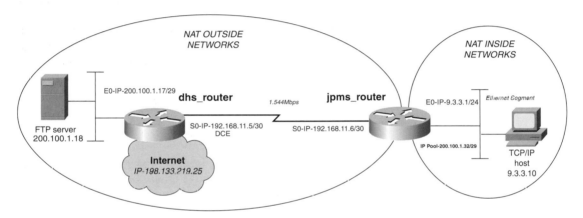

The next step in configuring NAT is to ensure that IP routing exists between the pool and the dhs_router. You have the IP subnet of 200.100.1.32/29 assigned to you from DHS. You must tell the jpms_router that this subnet exists on it. To accomplish this, use a loopback interface and assign the IP address of 200.100.1.33 to it. Note that this is the only subnet that you have a static router to on the dhs_router.

The third step in configuring NAT is to define the range of addresses and protocols that get translated. In this case, you want to translate FTP and ICMP to only one host, 200.100.1.18, when going to the 200.100.1.16/29 subnet. You also want to translate any addresses destined toward the Internet. To achieve this, use a route map on the **ip nat inside source** command. The route map can call an extended access list, where you can make decisions on specific traffic types. You also must use the **pool** keyword on this command. Example 15-13 demonstrates the command, along with the route map and access list needed on the jpms_router.

Example 15-13 *Configuring the Addresses and Protocols to Be Translated*

```
jpms_router(config)#ip nat inside source route-map trans_nat pool legalpool
jpms_router(config)#route-map trans_nat permit 10
jpms_router(config-route-map)# match ip address 101
```

Example 15-13 *Configuring the Addresses and Protocols to Be Translated (Continued)*

```
jpms_router(config-route-map)#exit
jpms_router(config)# access-list 101 permit icmp 9.3.3.0 0.0.0.255
  host 200.100.1.18 echo
jpms_router(config)# access-list 101 permit icmp 9.3.3.0 0.0.0.255
  host 200.100.1.18 echo-reply
jpms_router(config)# access-list 101 permit tcp 9.3.3.0 0.0.0.255
  host 200.100.1.18 eq ftp
jpms_router(config)# access-list 101 deny   ip 9.3.3.0 0.0.0.255
  200.100.1.16 0.0.0.7

jpms_router(config)#access-list 101 permit ip 9.3.3.0 0.0.0.255 any
```

The last step is to define and configure your NAT pool. Because you do not want to translate the host address of the loopback interface, the pool will have a starting address of 200.100.1.34 and an ending address of 200.100.1.38, ignoring the broadcast address of 200.100.1.39. Using the following command, you can configure the NAT pool, called legalpool:

```
jpms_router(config)# ip nat pool legalpool 200.100.1.34 200.100.1.38
  netmask 255.255.255.248
```

Example 15-14 provides the entire configuration for the jpms_router.

Example 15-14 *Configuration of the jpms_router*

```
hostname jpms_router
!
<<<text omitted>>>
!
 interface Loopback20
 ip address 200.100.1.33 255.255.255.248
 no ip directed-broadcast
!
interface Ethernet0
 ip address 9.3.3.1 255.255.255.0
 no ip directed-broadcast
ip nat inside
!
interface Serial0
 ip address 192.168.11.6 255.255.255.252
 no ip directed-broadcast
 ip nat outside
 no ip mroute-cache
!
<<<text omitted>>>
!
ip nat pool legalpool 200.100.1.34 200.100.1.38 netmask 255.255.255.248
ip nat inside source route-map trans_nat pool legalpool
ip classless
```

continues

Example 15-14 *Configuration of the jpms_router (Continued)*

```
ip route 0.0.0.0 0.0.0.0 192.168.11.5
!
access-list 101 permit icmp 9.3.3.0 0.0.0.255 host 200.100.1.18 echo
access-list 101 permit icmp 9.3.3.0 0.0.0.255 host 200.100.1.18 echo-reply
access-list 101 permit tcp 9.3.3.0 0.0.0.255 host 200.100.1.18 eq ftp
access-list 101 deny   ip 9.3.3.0 0.0.0.255 200.100.1.16 0.0.0.7
access-list 101 permit ip 9.3.3.0 0.0.0.255 any
route-map trans_nat permit 10
 match ip address 101


jpms_router#
```

You can now test the configuration with the workstation 9.3.3.10 on the jpms_router. To properly test this particular NAT configuration, you need two IP workstations. The one on dhs_router will be running FTP server software, and the workstation on the jpms_router will be configured as the FTP client. **ping** the FTP server from the client workstation. You should be able to **ping** the server but not the Ethernet port of the dhs_router. You should also be able to **ping** the address 198.133.219.25. Test the FTP portion of the configuration by initiating an FTP session from the client to the server.

Be sure that you can transfer a file across the network. If you are having problems, ensure that the dhs_router can reach the IP pool on the jpms_router. We are not running any routing protocols, so the routers, servers, and stations that you are using for this test need to have the appropriate default or static routing to gain reachability. Verify that your route map calls the correct access list. Use the **show access-list** command to ensure that your access list is taking hits and is properly configured. In addition, be sure that your NAT pool host addresses are on the same subnet as your loopback interface. This "anchors" the subnet to that router and eventually to the NAT pool. Example 15-15 lists the **show** commands illustrating NAT translations while testing the network.

Example 15-15 *Configuring NAT Inside and Out*

```
 jpms_router#show ip nat trans
Pro Inside global      Inside local      Outside local      Outside global
icmp 200.100.1.33:512  9.3.3.10:512      200.100.1.18:512   200.100.1.18:512
tcp 200.100.1.33:1076  9.3.3.10:1076     200.100.1.18:21    200.100.1.18:21
tcp 200.100.1.33:1077  9.3.3.10:1077     200.100.1.18:20    200.100.1.18:20
tcp 200.100.1.33:1072  9.3.3.10:1072     200.100.1.18:21    200.100.1.18:21
jpms_router#
jpms_router#show ip nat stat
Total active translations: 1 (0 static, 1 dynamic; 1 extended)
Outside interfaces:
  Serial0
Inside interfaces:
  Ethernet0
```

Example 15-15 *Configuring NAT Inside and Out (Continued)*

```
Hits: 3727  Misses: 87
Expired translations: 89
Dynamic mappings:
-- Inside Source
route-map trans_nat pool legalpool refcount 1
 pool legalpool: netmask 255.255.255.248
        start 200.100.1.33 end 200.100.1.38
        type generic, total addresses 6, allocated 1 (16%), misses 0
jpms_router#
jpms_router# show access-lists
Extended IP access list 101
    permit icmp 9.3.3.0 0.0.0.255 host 200.100.1.18 echo (1 match)
    permit icmp 9.3.3.0 0.0.0.255 host 200.100.1.18 echo-reply
    permit tcp 9.3.3.0 0.0.0.255 host 200.100.1.18 eq ftp (2 matches)
    deny ip 9.3.3.0 0.0.0.255 200.100.1.16 0.0.0.7 (4 matches)
    permit ip 9.3.3.0 0.0.0.255 any (1 match)
jpms_router#
```

The optional portion of this lab illustrates some new features of NAT that Cisco has introduced to help deal with some well-known applications that transport an IP address in the data stream. FTP is one such application. Because this application is so well known, when a Cisco router identifies port number 21 in a NAT translation, it modifies the data portion of the packet and also the IP header and checksums. This solution works great as long as FTP operates on port 21. When FTP connections occur on a port other then 21, NAT cannot properly handle the packet. Example 15-16 shows the **debug ip nat detailed** output of a packet failing to be translated properly.

Example 15-16 debug ip nat detailed *List of an FTP Port Failure*

```
jpms_router#debug ip nat detailed
IP NAT detailed debugging is on
jpms_router#
11:36:27: NAT: i: udp (9.3.3.10, 1154) -> (206.191.193.1, 53) [36138]
11:36:27: NAT: i: udp (9.3.3.10, 1154) -> (204.221.151.213, 53) [36394]
11:36:27: NAT: o: icmp (192.168.11.5, 53) -> (200.100.1.33, 1154) [524]
11:36:31: NAT: i: udp (9.3.3.10, 1154) -> (206.191.193.1, 53) [36650]
11:36:31: NAT: i: udp (9.3.3.10, 1154) -> (204.221.151.213, 53) [36906]
11:36:31: NAT: o: icmp (192.168.11.5, 53) -> (200.100.1.33, 1154) [525]
11:36:38: NAT: i: tcp (9.3.3.10, 1155) -> (200.100.1.18, 2021) [37162]
11:36:41: NAT: i: tcp (9.3.3.10, 1155) -> (200.100.1.18, 2021) [37418]
11:36:47: NAT: i: tcp (9.3.3.10, 1155) -> (200.100.1.18, 2021) [37674]
11:36:59: NAT: i: tcp (9.3.3.10, 1155) -> (200.100.1.18, 2021) [37930]
11:37:24: NAT: i: tcp (9.3.3.10, 1156) -> (200.100.1.18, 2021) [38442]
11:37:27: NAT: i: tcp (9.3.3.10, 1156) -> (200.100.1.18, 2021) [38698]
11:37:31: NAT: deleting alias for 200.100.1.33
11:37:33: NAT: i: tcp (9.3.3.10, 1156) -> (200.100.1.18, 2021) [38954]
11:37:45: NAT: i: tcp (9.3.3.10, 1156) -> (200.100.1.18, 2021) [39210]
```

continues

Example 15-16 **debug ip nat detailed** *List of an FTP Port Failure (Continued)*

```
11:38:11: NAT: i: tcp (9.3.3.10, 1157) -> (200.100.1.18, 2021) [39466]
11:38:14: NAT: i: tcp (9.3.3.10, 1157) -> (200.100.1.18, 2021) [39722]
11:38:20: NAT: i: tcp (9.3.3.10, 1157) -> (200.100.1.18, 2021) [39978]
11:38:32: NAT: i: tcp (9.3.3.10, 1157) -> (200.100.1.18, 2021) [40234]
11:40:09: NAT: i: udp (9.3.3.10, 1158) -> (206.191.193.1, 53) [40490]
11:40:09: NAT: map match trans_nat
11:40:09: NAT: installing alias for address 200.100.1.33
11:40:09: NAT: alias insert failed for 200.100.1.33
```

The inbound interface never receives a packet back from 200.100.1.18. Compare this output to Example 15-17, where you have a successful connect to a FTP sever on port 21.

Example 15-17 *A Successful FTP NAT Translation, Listed by* **debug ip nat detailed**

```
jpms_router#debug ip nat detailed
IP NAT detailed debugging is on
jpms_router#
11:33:03: NAT: created edit_context (9.3.3.10,1145) -> (200.100.1.18,21)
11:33:03: NAT: o: tcp (200.100.1.18, 21) -> (200.100.1.33, 1145) [40457]
11:33:03: NAT: i: tcp (9.3.3.10, 1145) -> (200.100.1.18, 21) [11791]
11:33:03: NAT: o: tcp (200.100.1.18, 21) -> (200.100.1.33, 1145) [40713]
11:33:03: NAT: i: tcp (9.3.3.10, 1145) -> (200.100.1.18, 21) [12047]
11:33:03: NAT: o: tcp (200.100.1.18, 21) -> (200.100.1.33, 1145) [41225]
11:33:03: NAT: i: tcp (9.3.3.10, 1145) -> (200.100.1.18, 21) [12303]
11:33:03: NAT: o: tcp (200.100.1.18, 21) -> (200.100.1.33, 1145) [41481]
11:33:03: NAT: i: tcp (9.3.3.10, 1145) -> (200.100.1.18, 21) [12559]
```

Here, you are receiving inbound and outbound requests to 200.100.1.18 on port 21, demonstrating a successful translation.

To allow FTP through NAT on a port other then 21, use the **ip nat service** command and add an access list identifying the FTP hosts. In this lab, you have to make an additional modification to your access list to include TCP port 2021. Example 15-18 shows the configuration changes.

Example 15-18 *Using Nonstandard FTP Port Numbers and NAT*

```
jpms_router(config)#ip nat service list 1 ftp tcp port 2021
jpms_router(config)# access-list 1 permit 200.100.1.18
jpms_router(config)# no access-list 101
jpms_router(config)# access-list 101 permit icmp 9.3.3.0 0.0.0.255
  host 200.100.1.18 echo
jpms_router(config)# access-list 101 permit icmp 9.3.3.0 0.0.0.255
  host 200.100.1.18 echo-reply
jpms_router(config)# access-list 101 permit tcp 9.3.3.0 0.0.0.255
  host 200.100.1.18 eq 2021
```

Example 15-18 *Using Nonstandard FTP Port Numbers and NAT (Continued)*

```
jpms_router(config)# access-list 101 deny    ip 9.3.3.0 0.0.0.255
  200.100.1.16 0.0.0.7
jpms_router(config)#access-list 101 permit ip 9.3.3.0 0.0.0.255 any
```

NAT now recognizes that port 2021 to host 200.100.1.18 is an FTP data stream, and it makes the necessary modifications to support that protocol. Example 15-19 lists the output from the **show debug ip nat detailed** command, showing the use of FTP port 2021 successfully.

Example 15-19 debug ip nat detailed *List of FTP on Port 2021*

```
11:48:17: NAT: i: tcp (9.3.3.10, 1164) -> (200.100.1.18, 2021) [52266]
11:48:17: NAT: o: tcp (200.100.1.18, 2021) -> (200.100.1.33, 1164) [4645]
11:48:17: NAT: i: tcp (9.3.3.10, 1164) -> (200.100.1.18, 2021) [52522]
11:48:17: NAT: o: tcp (200.100.1.18, 2021) -> (200.100.1.33, 1164) [5157]
11:48:17: NAT: i: tcp (9.3.3.10, 1164) -> (200.100.1.18, 2021) [52778]
11:48:17: NAT: o: tcp (200.100.1.18, 2021) -> (200.100.1.33, 1164) [5413]
```

Lab 32: Configuring Static NAT and DLSw—Part I

Practical Scenario

As automation increases through the network, many users have IP addresses of applications defined in specific user setups. When IP addresses change, it can cause a great deal of labor changing individual scripts and host files on many workstations. In cases such as this, a static mapping of NAT addresses is desirable, to avoid using a different translation address every time the service is required. Static mapping also allows outside networks to make session initiations to the inside network. Keep in mind that this works only if the application does not transport the IP addresses in the data stream.

Lab Exercise

Harms Co., a leading consulting and guide company in northern Wisconsin, is going through an IP address migration. To avoid having to change all the addresses and host tables at once, Harms Co. will use NAT to assist in the migration. The subnet 190.10.1.0/24 previously resided on the Ethernet segment of the green_bay router. Many hosts (not depicted in Figure 15-7 for this lab) have static entries to the hosts on the 190.10.1.0/24 subnet. The new subnet 210.168.1.0/24 will be placed on the Ethernet segment of the green_bay router. NAT will be required to preserve the current host tables of the workstations that reside on the Ethernet segment of the harms_co router. Based on this scenario, the configuration exercises for this lab are as follows:

- Configure the network as depicted in Figure 15-7. Configure the network with EIGRP as the routing protocol. Use an autonomous System ID of 7.
- Configure green_bay so that the router does not circulate the new subnet of 210.168.1.0/24 in EIGRP.
- Configure static translations as follows:
    — 210.168.1.254 translates to 190.10.1.1
    — 210.168.1.250 translates to 190.10.1.2
- *Optional:* Configure a DLSw peer between the harms_co router and the green_bay router. Use 198.100.1.10 as the local peer on harms_co, and use 210.168.1.254 as the local peer on the green_bay router.

Lab Objectives

- Configure the network as depicted in Figure 15-7. Use EIGRP as the routing protocol, and do not propagate the 210.168.1.0/24 subnet in EIGRP.

- Configure NAT static translations as follows:
    - 210.168.1.254 translates to 190.10.1.1
    - 210.168.1.250 translates to 190.10.1.2

Equipment Needed

- Three Cisco routers. Two routers should be connected through V.35 back-to-back cables or in a similar manner. The third router will connect to another router by an Ethernet segment. Cisco IOS Software Release 11.2 or later is also required.
- Two LAN segments, provided through hubs or switches.
- Two IP workstations will aid in the testing of the NAT configuration.

Physical Layout and Prestaging

- Connect the hubs and serial cables to the routers, as shown in Figure 15-7.
- Connect the two Ethernet hubs to the routers to form two LAN segments, as shown in Figure 15-7.
- Connect and configure two IP-based workstations, as shown in Figure 15-7. This is optional, but it will aid in testing the NAT configuration.

Figure 15-7 *The Harms Co. Network—Static NAT with DLSw*

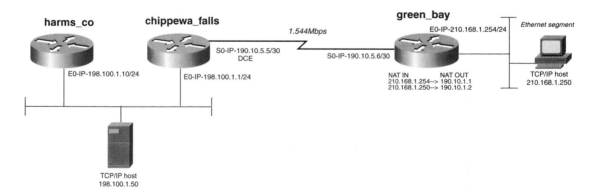

Lab 32: Configuring Static NAT and DSLw—Part II

Lab Walkthrough

After completing the physical installation of the serial link and the two Ethernet segments, establish IP connectivity between the appropriate subnets. Use EIGRP as the routing protocol on all routers. Be sure that you do not route the subnet 210.168.1.0/24 with EIGRP.

Beginning with the green_bay router, define which networks will be the inside and outside networks. In this lab, networks 198.100.1.0/24 and 190.10.5.4/30 are outside networks, while 210.168.1.0/24 and 190.10.1.0/24 are inside networks. Configure the E0 port with the **ip nat inside** command, and configure the S0 port with the **ip nat outside** command.

Next, you must ensure that IP connectivity exists between the IP subnet 190.10.1.0/24 and the rest of the network. Do this by creating a loopback interface and using an IP host address from the 190.10.1.0/24 subnet. You should be able to **ping** this address/subnet from the harms_co router when routing is established. Example 15-20 lists the commands needed to accomplish the first two steps on NAT configuration.

Example 15-20 *Configuring NAT on the green_bay Router*

```
green_bay(config)#int e0
green_bay(config-if)#ip nat inside
green_bay(config-if)#int s0
green_bay(config-if)#ip nat outside
green_bay(config-if)#exit
green_bay(config)#router eigrp 7
green_bay(config-router)#network 190.10.0.0
green_bay(config-router)#^Z
green_bay#
```

You now can define what addresses you want to translate with NAT. On the green_bay router, you want to translate address 210.168.1.250 to 190.10.1.2 and 210.168.1.254 to 190.10.1.1. This can be done with the following global NAT command:

```
ip nat inside source static 210.168.1.250 190.10.1.2
ip nat inside source static 210.168.1.254 190.10.1.1
```

At this point, the workstation 210.168.1.250 can reach the rest of the network. Hosts on the outside networks also can reach 210.168.1.250 and 210.168.1.254 through 190.10.1.2 and 190.10.1.1, respectively. Example 15-21 shows the NAT table from the green_bay router.

Example 15-21 **show ip nat translations** *on the green_bay Router*

```
green_bay#show ip nat trans
Pro Inside global      Inside local      Outside local      Outside global
tcp 190.10.1.2:1084    210.168.1.250:1084  198.100.1.50:21    198.100.1.50:21
```

Example 15-21 **show ip nat translations** *on the green_bay Router (Continued)*

```
--- 190.10.1.2        210.168.1.250      ---              ---
--- 190.10.1.1        210.168.1.254      ---              ---
green_bay#
```

Example 15-22 lists the chippewa_falls configuration and the green_bay configuration, respectively.

Example 15-22 *chippewa_falls and green_bay Router Configurations*

```
hostname chippewa_falls
!
<<<text omitted>>>
!
interface Ethernet0
 ip address 198.100.1.1 255.255.255.0
!
interface Serial0
 ip address 190.10.5.5 255.255.255.252
 no fair-queue
 clockrate 2000000
!
<<<text omitted>>>
!
router eigrp 7
 network 198.100.1.0
 network 190.10.0.0

hostname green_bay
!
<<<text omitted>>>
!
 interface Loopback20
 ip address 190.10.1.3 255.255.255.0
 no ip directed-broadcast
!
interface Ethernet0
 ip address 210.168.1.254 255.255.255.0
 no ip directed-broadcast
 ip nat inside
!
interface Serial0
 ip address 190.10.5.6 255.255.255.252
 no ip directed-broadcast
 ip nat outside
 no ip mroute-cache
 no fair-queue
!
<<<text omitted>>>
!
```

continues

Example 15-22 *chippewa_falls and green_bay Router Configurations (Continued)*

```
router eigrp 7
 network 190.10.0.0
 !
ip nat inside source static 210.168.1.250 190.10.1.2
ip nat inside source static 210.168.1.254 190.10.1.1
<<<text omitted>>>
```

The optional portion of this lab exploits a DLSw issue with NAT. First, you will walk through the configuration as specified. Configure DLSw using 210.168.1.254 as the local peer on the green_bay router, with a remote peer pointing toward 198.100.1.10. Example 15-23 shows the DLSw configuration.

Example 15-23 *DLSw Configuration Using 210.168.1.254 as the Local Peer on the green_bay Router with a Remote Peer Pointing Toward 198.100.1.10*

```
dlsw local-peer peer-id 210.168.1.254
 dlsw remote-peer 0 tcp 198.100.1.10
 dlsw bridge-group 1
 !
interface Ethernet0
 ip address 210.168.1.254 255.255.255.0
 no ip directed-broadcast
 ip nat inside
 bridge-group 1
```

Example 15-24 shows the configuration of DLSw on the harms_co router.

Example 15-24 *DLSw Configuration on the harms_co Router*

```
dlsw local-peer peer-id 198.100.1.10 promiscuous
dlsw bridge-group 1
 !
interface Ethernet1
 ip address 198.100.1.10 255.255.255.0
 media-type 10BaseT
 bridge-group 1
```

This configuration is correct; however, DLSw will encounter an error because of NAT. By watching the peers, you can observe that they never connect, despite the fact that there is IP connectivity between them. RFC 1795 specifies how TCP connections are handled with a control vector. During the capabilities exchange, a control vector is negotiated. DSLw uses two TCP sessions for data exchange. Cisco routers will use only one TCP session and will tear down the other TCP connection. When the router determines what TCP session to tear down, it looks for the highest IP address on the peer statement and drops that TCP connection.

In this lab, the harms_co router believes that its IP address is 198.100.1.10 and that the remote peer address is 190.10.1.2. Therefore, it tears down its TCP connection. On the green_bay router, it sees its IP address as 210.168.1.254 and the remote peer address as 198.100.1.10. Therefore, it tears down its TCP connection. Because both sides tear down what they believe is the highest IP address, the connection is terminated. Example 15-25 demonstrates this with the **debug dlsw peer** and **debug dlsw core** commands.

Example 15-25 debug *Showing the Teardown of TCP Sessions*

```
harms_co#
02:21:02: DLSw: passive open 190.10.1.1(11009) -> 2065
02:21:02: DLSw: START-TPFSM (peer 190.10.1.1(2065)): event:TCP-RD PIPE OPENED st
ate:DISCONN
02:21:02: DLSw: dtp_action_c() opening write pipe for peer 190.10.1.1(2065)
02:21:02: DLSw: END-TPFSM (peer 190.10.1.1(2065)): state:DISCONN->WWR_RDOP

02:21:02: DLSw: Async Open Callback 190.10.1.1(2065) -> 11006
02:21:02: DLSw: START-TPFSM (peer 190.10.1.1(2065)): event:TCP-WR PIPE OPENED st
ate:WWR_RDOP
02:21:02: DLSw: dtp_action_i() write pipe opened for peer 190.10.1.1(2065)
02:21:02: DLSw: END-TPFSM (peer 190.10.1.1(2065)): state:WWR_RDOP->WAIT_CAP

02:21:02: DLSw: START-TPFSM (peer 190.10.1.1(2065)): event:SSP-CAP MSG RCVD stat
e:WAIT_CAP
02:21:02: DLSw: dtp_action_j() cap msg rcvd from peer 190.10.1.1(2065)
02:21:02: DLSw: Recv CapExId Msg from peer 190.10.1.1(2065)
02:21:02: DLSw: Unknown CV D9 with length 3 from peer 190.10.1.1(2065)
02:21:02: DLSw: Pos CapExResp sent to peer 190.10.1.1(2065)
02:21:02: DLSw: CapExId Msg sent to peer 190.10.1.1(2065)
02:21:02: DLSw: END-TPFSM (peer 190.10.1.1(2065)): state:WAIT_CAP->WAIT_CAP

02:21:02: DLSw: START-TPFSM (peer 190.10.1.1(2065)): event:SSP-CAP MSG RCVD stat
e:WAIT_CAP
02:21:02: DLSw: dtp_action_j() cap msg rcvd from peer 190.10.1.1(2065)
02:21:02: DLSw: Recv CapExPosRsp Msg from peer 190.10.1.1(2065)
02:21:02: DLSw: END-TPFSM (peer 190.10.1.1(2065)): state:WAIT_CAP->WAIT_CAP

02:21:02: DLSw: Processing delayed event:SSP-CAP EXCHANGED - prev state:WAIT_CAP
02:21:02: DLSw: START-TPFSM (peer 190.10.1.1(2065)): event:SSP-CAP EXCHANGED sta
te:WAIT_CAP
02:21:02: DLSw: dtp_action_k() cap xchged for peer 190.10.1.1(2065)
02:21:02: DLSw: closing read pipe tcp connection for peer 190.10.1.1(2065)
02:21:02: DLSw: END-TPFSM (peer 190.10.1.1(2065)): state:WAIT_CAP->PCONN_WT

02:21:02: DLSw: Processing delayed event:TCP-PEER CONNECTED - prev state:PCONN_W
T
02:21:02: DLSw: START-TPFSM (peer 190.10.1.1(2065)): event:TCP-PEER CONNECTED st
ate:PCONN_WT
02:21:02: DLSw: dtp_action_m() peer connected for peer 190.10.1.1(2065)
02:21:02: DLSw: END-TPFSM (peer 190.10.1.1(2065)): state:PCONN_WT->CONNECT
```

continues

Example 15-25 debug *Showing the Teardown of TCP Sessions (Continued)*

```
02:21:02: DLSw: dlsw_tcpd_fini() for peer 190.10.1.1(2065)
02:21:02: DLSw: START-TPFSM (peer 190.10.1.1(2065)): event:ADMIN-CLOSE CONNECTIO
N state:CONNECT
02:21:02: DLSw: dtp_action_b() close connection for peer 190.10.1.1(2065)
02:21:02: DLSw: END-TPFSM (peer 190.10.1.1(2065)): state:CONNECT->DISCONN

02:21:03: DLSw: freeing 190.10.1.1
```

The workaround for this problem is to ensure that both sides of the DLSw connection view
the other peers in a consistent numerical order. Instead of translating to 190.10.1.0/24, you
need to translate to an IP address higher than 198.100.1.10, such as 199.100.1.0/24. This
way the local peer on the green_bay router will always be the higher of the two peers, even
through NAT translations. A quicker workaround is to add a loopback interface to the
harms_co router that is lower then 190.10.1.1, and making this the new local peer. For
example, you can add a loopback interface with the IP address of 100.100.1.1 and make this
the new local peer, as done in Example 15-26.

Example 15-26 *Configuring a Loopback Interface as the Local Peer*

```
dlsw local-peer peer-id 100.100.1.1 promiscuous
dlsw bridge-group 1
!
interface Loopback20
 ip address 100.100.1.1 255.255.255.0
```

Now, you can add a new remote peer to the green_bay router pointing at 100.100.1.1, and
the DLSw peer will connect through a NAT translation.

CHAPTER 16

Using Hot Standby Routing Protocol (HSRP)

You might think that Cisco should have named HSRP (the Hot Standby Routing Protocol) as HSDG instead, for *Hot Standby Default Gateway*. This is exactly what HSRP provides to the hosts residing on local LANs. It seems that the name HSRP can imply a lot of things about "backup" that it actually doesn't provide. Many times, it has been necessary to explain exactly what HSRP can do for a customer's network besides give it a great name.

HSRP provides a consistent and reachable network layer address for IP and, in limited forms, IPX. By providing a constant address, even upon failure, a form of redundancy can occur. The most common deployment of HSRP is in LAN environments, where two routers "share" a common host address between them. This common address, called the *hot standby address*, is used as the default gateway for all the local hosts on that LAN segment. One router acts as the primary router and actually receives traffic destined for the hot standby address. The secondary router ignores this traffic until a configured set of circumstances is reached that affects the router's *HSRP priority* or *standby priority*. When the secondary router's priority exceeds the primary, it starts servicing requests for the hot standby address becoming the primary router. From the workstation's point of view, it has a single default gateway, pointing to the hot standby address. Figure 16-1 illustrates a common HSRP deployment.

In Figure 16-1, all the TCP/IP clients have a default gateway set to 172.16.1.1. The default gateway tells the IP client to forward any traffic not found on a local subnet to a specific IP address. The 172.16.1.1 address then is used as the *HSRP virtual address*. In this example, the router caladan is configured to track the serial interface to arakas. This means that if the serial interface enters a *down* state, it decrements the router's priority by 10 or by another configured value. While the serial interface is up, caladan receives and forwards IP packets from the workstations. If the serial interface on caladan drops, giedi_prime becomes the primary HSRP router. It immediately starts to service IP packets from the workstations, preserving all active sessions. The loss of the caladan router is completely transparent to the workstations on the LAN segment.

HSRP is most effective in scenarios that involve hosts defaulting traffic to a single network address, such as in Figure 16-1.

Figure 16-1 *HSRP in a Typical Network*

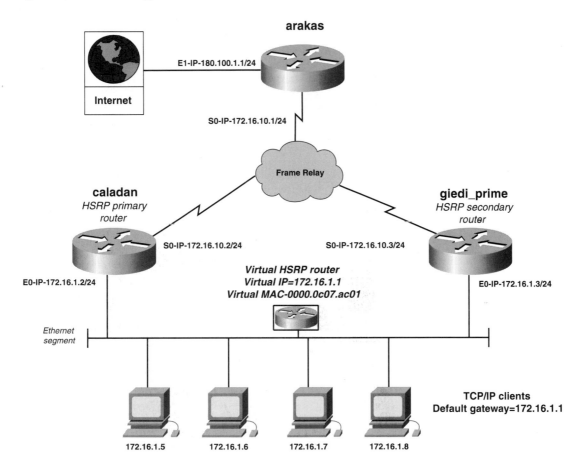

HSRP Overview and Configuration

HSRP uses the exchange of multicast messages to communicate a configured priority with other routers in the same *standby group*. The priority defines which router will be the primary and which router(s) will be secondary in the group. The default priority is 100; the router with the highest priority will be the primary for the group. If the priorities are the same, the first router up becomes the primary. Any prioritization is then based on the IP address. If a new router (at the same priority) joins, it doesn't bump the current primary router, even if its IP address is higher; however, it can bump the current standby router.

If priorities are different, a new router joining with a higher priority becomes active, even if preemption is not configured; however, if the router is already up and its priority changes (because of tracking or reconfiguration), it won't bump the primary without preemption configured.

HSRP uses three types of multicast messages to exchange standby group information:

- **Hello**—The hello message contains the sending router's priority and state information. Hellos are exchanged every three seconds. If a router fails to send a hello in a specified amount of time, the receiving router, if priority dictates, becomes the primary router for the group.

- **Coup**—When a secondary router becomes the primary router, it sends a coup message to the routers in the group.

- **Resign**—When the primary router is about to shut down, or when it has received a hello message with a higher priority than its own, it forfeits the primary position with a resign message.

To configure HSRP, use the following guidelines:

Step 1 Pick a virtual address to use for the HSRP address. This address must be in the same address space that is assigned to the LAN interface where you want to run HSRP. This is also referred to as the *standby IP address*. Each router in the standby group must define the virtual IP address using the **standby** *group_number* **ip** *a.b.c.d* command.

The standby group number is a unique number that identifies 1 to 255 standby groups on Ethernet and FDDI, and 0 to 2 different groups on Token Ring. If you do not specify a group, standby group 0 is used.

If you are configuring HSRP on VLAN trunks, each VLAN or Ethernet subinterface must be in a different standby group.

Step 2 Decide which router is to be the primary router. Configure a priority of at least 101 on this router. Also add the **preempt** command to make this router eligible for the primary router election. Step 2 can be accomplished with the **standby** *group_number* **preempt** and **standby** *group_number* **priority** *1-255* commands:

— The **preempt** command enables the router to become the primary if it has the highest priority in the group.

— The **priority** command assigns a priority to the router. The default priority is 100, and the router with the highest priority becomes the primary router, or active router.

Step 3   Configure tracking, authentication, and timers on the primary router using the following commands:

— **standby** *group_number* **track** *interface_name* [*cost*]

— When HSRP tracks an interface, it tells the HSRP process to decrement 10 from the priority if the interface goes down. This command can force the HSRP group to switch its primary and secondary routers based on whether an interface is active. The default cost is 10 and can be modified.

— **standby** *group_number* **authentication** *character_string*

This command establishes authentication messages to be included in the HSRP multicast. This ensures that only authorized routers can become part of the HSRP group. The string must match all routers in the HSRP group.

— **standby** *group_number* **timers** *hello_interval_seconds holddown_timer_seconds*

The **timers** argument sets the interval between hello messages and the hold-down timer. The hold-down timer specifies how long the router waits before it declares the active router to be down. The defaults for these timers are 3 and 10 seconds, respectively. These timers must match among all routers in the group.

— **standby** *group_number* **mac-address** *H.H.H*

This command allows for the static entry of a MAC address. This can be useful for management or in filtering the HSRP addresses from downstream devices.

Step 4   Configure the other routers in the standby group as secondary routers by using a priority of 99 or less.

Step 5   Configure preempt, tracking, authentication, and timers on the secondary routers.

NOTE   HSRP requires a routing protocol that converges rapidly, such as EIGRP or OSPF, to transport packets without interruption. HSRP is designed to reroute packets upon router or link failure without any retransmissions or drops occurring. For this to happen, the router must be capable of converging quickly during a failure.

Configuring HSRP Between Routers

Using Figure 16-1 as an example, you will configure HSRP between the routers caladan and giedi prime. In this scenario, multiple IP clients reside on the Ethernet segment of 172.16.1.0/24. All the TCP/IP clients need access to arakasarakas for access to the Internet; caladan and giedi prime have access to arakas through the Frame Relay network. To exchange routing information, all routers are running EIGRP as the routing process.

HSRP will provide the IP clients with uninterrupted access to arakas. To accomplish this, caladan is selected as the primary router, and giedi prime is the secondary router. You will use 172.16.1.1 as the virtual IP address between the two routers. Because the ultimate destination of the clients is arakas, you should track on the serial interfaces. By tracking on the serial interface, you can force giedi prime to become the primary if the link to arakas fails.

NOTE	When tracking is used, two potential situations can cause giedi prime to become the primary router. One is a loss of the connection to caladan, such as physical loss to the Ethernet port on caladan. The second situation involves the loss of physical connectivity between arakas and caladan, causing the serial interface on caladan to drop.

First, you will configure caladan. To do so, you need to add a standby group to the E0 interface. You already know that caladan is going to be the primary, so you will need a priority greater than 100; for this example, use 105. You also want to track on the serial interface. The default tracking cost is 10, so if the caladan router looses its serial link, it will have an HSRP cost of 95. Make note of this value because you need to configure the priority of giedi prime to be greater then 95 but less then 105. Example 16-1 demonstrates the configuration of caladan.

Example 16-1 *Configuring HSRP on the Primary Router*

```
caladan(config)#interface ethernet 0
caladan(config-if)#standby 1 ip 172.16.1.1
caladan(config-if)#standby 1 priority 105
caladan(config-if)#standby 1 preempt
caladan(config-if)#standby 1 track s0
```

When a member of an HSRP group goes from the *standby* state to the *active* state, the following message is generated:

```
01:10:14: %STANDBY-6-STATECHANGE: Standby: 1: Ethernet0 state Speak
  -> Standby
01:10:14: %STANDBY-6-STATECHANGE: Standby: 1: Ethernet0 state Standby
  -> Active
```

To configure giedi_prime, you must set the standby group to be the same as caladan, which is standby group 1. You also must use the same virtual IP address as caladan. The use of the **preempt** argument will allow giedi prime to become the primary router, if that router's priority exceeds caladan's. Perhaps the most important command is the **priority** command. On the primary router, you have a priority of 105 and tracking on the serial interface. The priority of the primary router, caladan, will be 95 if it loses its serial interface. Therefore, the priority of the secondary, giedi_prime, needs to be greater then 95. In this example, you will use 101. A value of 101 also provides the router with a higher priority than any new routers that might be added to the network with a default priority of 100.

Example 16-2 demonstrates the configuration of giedi prime.

Example 16-2 *Configuring HSRP on the Secondary Route*

```
giedi_prime(config)#interface ethernet 0
giedi_prime(config-if)#standby 1 ip 172.16.1.1
giedi prime(config-if)#standby 1 priority 101
giedi_prime(config-1f)#standby 1 preempt
giedi_prime(config-if)#standby 1 track s0
```

To verify the functionality of HSRP, use the **show standby** command. This command shows which router is primary, tells whether it can preempt, and gives the virtual IP and MAC addresses used in that group. Example 16-3 illustrates the **show standby** command on caladan, the primary router, and giedi prime, the secondary router.

Example 16-3 **show standby** *Command Output for the Primary and Secondary Routers*

```
caladan#show standby
Ethernet0 - Group 1
  Local state is Active, priority 105, may preempt        ←Active=Primary router
  Hellotime 3 holdtime 10
  Next hello sent in 00:00:02.496
  Hot standby IP address is 172.16.1.1 configured        ←Virtual IP address
  Active router is local
  Standby router is 172.16.1.3 expired
  Standby virtual mac address is 0000.0c07.ac01
  Tracking interface states for 1 interface, 1 up:
    Up    Serial0
caladan#


giedi_prime#show standby
Ethernet0 - Group 1
  Hellotime 3 holdtime 10
  Next hello sent in 00:00:02.540
  Hot standby IP address is 172.16.1.1 configured
```

Example 16-3 show standby *Command Output for the Primary and Secondary Routers (Continued)*

```
   Active router is 172.16.1.2 expires in 00:00:09
   Standby router is local
   Tracking interface states for 1 interface, 1 up:
     Up   Serial0
giedi_prime#
```

To add authentication, simply add the **standby 1 authentication** *password* command under the Ethernet interface. Be sure that all routers in the group are authenticating. Example 16-4 shows the configurations in their entirety.

Example 16-4 *caladan*

```
hostname caladan
!
<<<text omitted>>>
!
 interface Ethernet0
 ip address 172.16.1.2 255.255.255.0
 no ip redirects          ←this is added by the router when standby is enabled
no ip directed-broadcast
 standby 1 priority 105
 standby 1 preempt
 standby authentication cisco        ←cisco is the password and is case sensitive
 standby 1 ip 172.16.1.1
 standby 1 track Serial0
!
interface Serial0
 ip address 172.16.10.2 255.255.255.0
 no ip directed-broadcast
 encapsulation frame-relay
 no ip mroute-cache
 no fair-queue
 frame-relay map ip 172.16.10.1 21 broadcast
 frame-relay map ip 172.16.10.3 21 broadcast
!
router eigrp 2001
 network 172.16.0.0
!
```

```
hostname giedi_prime
!
<<<text omitted>>>
!
interface Ethernet0
 ip address 172.16.1.3 255.255.255.0
 no ip redirects
```

continues

Example 16-4 *caladan (Continued)*

```
 delay 1000000      ←influence EIGRP, to not load-share
 standby 1 priority 101
 standby 1 preempt
 standby authentication cisco        ←cisco is the password and is case sensitive
 standby 1 ip 172.16.1.1
 standby 1 track Serial0
!
interface Serial0
 ip address 172.16.10.3 255.255.255.0
 encapsulation frame-relay
 no fair-queue
 frame-relay map ip 172.16.10.1 31 broadcast
 frame-relay map ip 172.16.10.2 31 broadcast
!
router eigrp 2001
 network 172.16.0.0
!
```

The "Big show" and "Big D" for HSRP

Still building on the first example, this section demonstrates the use of the **show** and **debug** commands for HSRP:

```
show standby {brief | interface}
debug standby
```

The **show standby** command shows whether this interface is in standby mode or active mode. Active mode indicates that interface or router is the primary, while standby indicates that it's the secondary or backup interface or router. The **show standby** command also shows the hello timers, virtual MAC address in use, and any tracking information. Example 16-5 lists the output from the **show standby** command on the caladan router.

Example 16-5 show standby *Command Output*

```
caladan#show standby
Ethernet0 - Group 1
  Local state is Active, priority 105, may preempt
  Hellotime 3 holdtime 10
  Next hello sent in 00:00:02.496
  Hot standby IP address is 172.16.1.1 configured
  Active router is local
  Standby router is 172.16.1.3 expired
  Standby virtual mac address is 0000.0c07.ac01
  Tracking interface states for 1 interface, 1 up:
    Up   Serial0
caladan#
```

The **debug standby** command shows hello timer and hold timer settings. In addition, this command displays standby group information, such as which router is active and what the priorities are for the active and standby routers. Example 16-6 lists the output from the **debug standby** command, as seen on giedi prime.

Example 16-6 *Edebug standby Command Output for giedi prime*

```
giedi_prime#debug standby
SB1:Ethernet0 Hello in 172.16.1.2 Active pri 105 hel 3 hol 10 ip 172.16.1.1
SB1:Ethernet0 Hello out 172.16.1.3 Standby pri 95 hel 3 hol 10 ip 172.16.1.1
SB1:Ethernet0 Hello in 172.16.1.2 Active pri 105 hel 3 hol 10 ip 172.16.1.1
SB1:Ethernet0 Hello out 172.16.1.3 Standby pri 95 hel 3 hol 10 ip 172.16.1.1
SB1:Ethernet0 Hello in 172.16.1.2 Active pri 105 hel 3 hol 10 ip 172.16.1.1
SB1:Ethernet0 Hello out 172.16.1.3 Standby pri 95 hel 3 hol 10 ip 172.16.1.1
```

Lab 33: Configuring HSRP, Tracking, and Asymetrical Routing—Part I

Practical Scenario

HSRP is an effective way to provide a fault-tolerant default gateway for TCP/IP. HSRP is mostly deployed in IP environments, where there are IP hosts with static default gateways. If there is router redundancy on the network, IP clients will still forward IP packets to the default gateway address, even if that default gateway router is down. There can still be a valid path out of the network, but the clients will fail because they know only how to forward packets to the default gateway. In these cases, HSRP provides a gateway address that can be shared among many routers, thereby closing the client loophole in redundant networks.

Lab Exercise

The 4th Army Com Net runs a Frame Relay network between Headquarters Company and Charlie Company. The workstations at Charlie Company are IP-based and require uninterrupted access to the headquarters master and backup server. The data passed between the companies is critical; if one router fails, the other router should resume its function. Use the following parameters as your design guidelines:

- The workstations at Charlie Company are IP-based. They have static default gateways configured pointing to 10.25.61.3. Configure the network so that the workstations have uninterrupted access to headquarters_co, even upon failure of the charlie_1 or charlie_2 routers; charlie_1 should be the primary router.

- If the charlie_1 or charlie_2 serial interface fails, ensure that the router is not the primary router.

Lab Objectives

- Configure the network as depicted in Figure 16-2. Use RIP V2 as the routing protocol. Configure RIP to perform asymmetrical routing with the primary router in HSRP. That is, if charlie_1 is the primary router, traffic should flow from the workstations to charlie_1, to headquarters_co, and back down through charlie_1 to the workstations. Traffic should not flow from the headquarters_co router to charlie_2 router, unless charlie_2 is the active HSRP router.

- Configure HSRP between charlie_1 and charlie_2. Configure the charlie_1 router to be the primary router for HSRP.

- Configure tracking on the serial interfaces.
- *Optional:* Improve the design of the Charlie Company network so that it operates more efficiently in an HSRP environment by using EIGRP as the routing protocol.

Equipment Needed

- Four Cisco routers, three to serve as routers in the network, and one to serve as the frame switch. The frame switch will need to have three serial ports. The routers should be connected through V.35 back-to-back cables or in a similar manner.
- Two LAN segments, provided through hubs or switches.
- *Optional:* Two IP workstations, one to serve as a Charlie Company workstation and one to serve as the headquarters servers.

Physical Layout and Prestaging

- Connect the hubs and serial cables to the routers as shown in Figure 16-2. Configure a Frame Relay switch in a multipoint configuration so that it provides PVC from headquarters_co to charlie_1 and charlie_2. The diagram does not show the frame switch or the frame switch configuration.
- Connect the two Ethernet hubs to the routers to form two LAN segments, as shown in Figure 16-2, with one segment connecting charlie_1 to charlie_2 and the other segment off of headquarters_co.
- Connect and configure two IP-based workstations, as shown in Figure 16-2, with the default gateway set to 25.100.61.3.
- Configure the headquarters_co router as shown with RIP version 2 as the routing protocol.
- *Optional:* Improve the design of the Charlie Company network so that it operates more efficiently in an HSRP environment by using EIGRP as the routing protocol.

Figure 16-2 *4th Army Com Net*

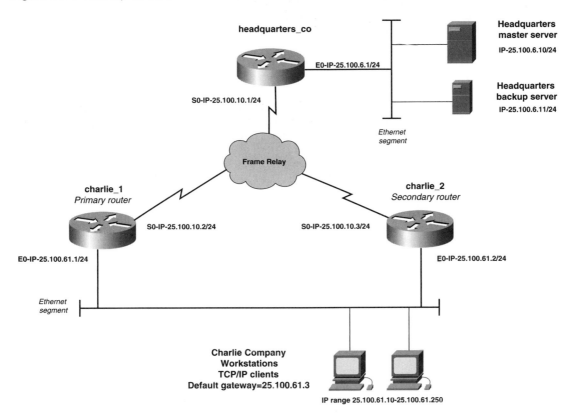

Lab 33: Configuring HSRP, Tracking, and Asymetrical Routing—Part II

Lab Walkthrough

After completing the physical installation and the Frame Relay switch configuration, you should establish IP connectivity among all the routers. Example 16-7 lists the Frame Relay configuration used in this lab.

Example 16-7 *Frame Relay Switch Configuration*

```
hostname frame_switch
!
frame-relay switching
!
<<<text omitted>>>
!
interface Serial0
 no ip address
 encapoulation frame-relay
 no fair-queue
 clockrate 148000
 frame-relay intf-type dce
 frame-relay route 131 interface Serial1 31
 frame-relay route 121 interface Serial3 21
!
interface Serial1
 no ip address
 encapsulation frame-relay
 clockrate 148000
 frame-relay intf-type dce
 frame-relay route 31 interface Serial0 131
!
interface Serial2
 no ip address
 shutdown
!
interface Serial3
 no ip address
 encapsulation frame-relay
 clockrate 64000
 frame-relay intf-type dce
 frame-relay route 21 interface Serial0 121
!
```

Beginning with the headquarters_co router, configure the IP addresses of Ethernet and serial interfaces. Because you are configuring a multipoint Frame Relay network, you should use **frame-relay map** statements. Make the **map** statements point to the IP address of charlie_1 and charlie_2, like the following:

```
frame-relay map ip 25.100.10.2 121 broadcast
frame-relay map ip 25.100.10.3 131 broadcast
```

Next, configure RIP Version 2 (RIP-2) as the routing protocol, as done in Example 16-8. RIP-2 is configured by adding the **version 2** argument under the routing protocol. In this model, you will also added the **distance** argument. The **distance** argument will point a primary route to charlie_1; charlie_2 has an administrative distance of 125, which is 5 higher than a normal RIP distance of 120. This will force all outbound traffic to first go to the charlie_1 router, and the network to have asymetrical routing.

Example 16-8 *RIP-2 Configuration*

```
router rip
 version 2
 network 25.0.0.0
 distance 125 0.0.0.3 255.255.255.0
```

The same set of commands will be needed on all routers in the 4th Army Com Net that are not running Cisco IOS Software Release 12.0. Next, configure the serial and Ethernet interfaces to send and receive RIP-2 updates by using the following commands:

```
ip rip send version 2
ip rip receive version 2
```

Again, these same statements will be used on all the routers in 4th Army Com Net.

When you are finished with the configuration for the headquarters_co router, it will look like Example 16-9.

Example 16-9 *Configuration of the headquarters_co Router*

```
hostname headquarters_co
!
interface Ethernet0
 ip address 25.100.6.1 255.255.255.0
 ip rip send version 2
 ip rip receive version 2
 media-type 10BaseT
!
interface Serial0
 ip address 25.100.10.1 255.255.255.0
 ip rip send version 2
 ip rip receive version 2
 encapsulation frame-relay
 no ip mroute-cache
 frame-relay map ip 25.100.10.2 121 broadcast
 frame-relay map ip 25.100.10.3 131 broadcast
!
<<<<text omitted>>>
```

Example 16-9 *Configuration of the headquarters_co Router (Continued)*

```
!
router rip
 version 2
 network 25.0.0.0
 distance 125 0.0.0.3 255.255.255.0
!

headquarters_co#
```

Moving on to the IP configuration of the Charlie Company routers, you should begin by adding IP addresses to the Ethernet and serial interfaces of each router. As mentioned previously, each router will also need to be configured for RIP-2. Follow the same steps as previously noted for the RIP-2 configuration. Because this is a multipoint Frame Relay network, you will also need to add **frame-relay map** statements. When you are finished with the IP configuration for each router, the configurations should resemble Example 16-10.

Example 16-10 *charlie_1 and charlie_2 IP Configurations*

```
hostname charlie_1
!
<<<text omitted…
 !
 interface Ethernet0
 ip address 25.100.61.1 255.255.255.0
 no ip directed-broadcast
 ip rip send version 2
 ip rip receive version 2
!
interface Serial0
 ip address 25.100.10.2 255.255.255.0
 no ip directed-broadcast
 ip rip send version 2
 ip rip receive version 2
 encapsulation frame-relay
 no ip mroute-cache
 frame-relay map ip 25.100.10.1 21 broadcast
 frame-relay map ip 25.100.10.3 21 broadcast
 frame-relay lmi-type cisco
 !
<<<text omitted>>>
 !
router rip
 version 2
 network 25.0.0.0
 !
<<<text omitted>>>
```

continues

Example 16-10 *charlie_1 and charlie_2 IP Configurations (Continued)*

```
charlie_1#

hostname charlie_2
!
interface Ethernet0
 ip address 25.100.61.2 255.255.255.0
 ip rip send version 2
 ip rip receive version 2
!
interface Serial0
 ip address 25.100.10.3 255.255.255.0
 ip rip send version 2
 ip rip receive version 2
 encapsulation frame-relay
 frame-relay map ip 25.100.10.1 31 broadcast
 frame-relay map ip 25.100.10.2 31 broadcast
!
<<<text omitted>>>
router rip
 version 2
 network 25.0.0.0
!
```

After establishing end-to-end IP connectivity, you can begin to configure HSRP. Following the steps for HSRP, you must first define the HSRP or virtual router IP address. All the workstations at Charlie Company point to a default gateway address of 25.100.61.3. Therefore, this will be your HSRP address. Each router will need the **preempt** and the **priority** statements as well.

Because charlie_1 will be the primary router, you should set its priority above the default of 100. Before setting the priority, take into consideration the circumstance at which you will want this router to not be the primary. In this model, you want charlie_1 to be the primary until the link fails. If you set the priority of charlie_1 to 105 and use the default tracking cost of the serial interfaces on charlie_1 and charlie_2 of 10, this will put the priority at 95 upon the loss of a serial link. Therefore, you will need to set the priority of charlie_2 to greater then 95 but less then 105. Example 16-11 demonstrates the configuration of the charlie_1 router.

Example 16-11 *Configuration of charlie_1 Router for HSRP*

```
charlie_1#conf t
Enter configuration commands, one per line.  End with CNTL/Z.
charlie_1(config)#interface ethernet 0
charlie_1(config-if)#standby 1 ip 25.100.61.3
charlie_1(config-if)#standby 1 preempt
charlie_1(config-if)#standby 1 priority 105
04:08:11: %STANDBY-6-STATECHANGE: Standby: 1: Ethernet0 state Speak      -> Stan
```

Example 16-11 *Configuration of charlie_1 Router for HSRP (Continued)*

```
dby
04:08:11: %STANDBY-6-STATECHANGE: Standby: 1: Ethernet0 state Standby    -> Active
charlie_1(config-if)#standby 1 track serial 0
```

When configuring HSRP, a state change message will be sent when HSRP becomes active. When this is complete, verify the HSRP configuration with the **show standby ethernet 0** command, as demonstrated in Example 16-12. Look for the local state to be "active," and make sure that the active router is "local." Also ensure that the host standby IP address is the one that you configured.

Example 16-12 *Status of the Primary Router*

```
charlie_1#show standby ethernet 0
Ethernet0 - Group 1
  Local state is Active, priority 105, may preempt
  Hellotime 3 holdtime 10
  Next hello sent in 00:00:00.678
  Hot standby IP address is 25.100.61.3 configured
  Active router is local
  Standby router is 25.100.61.2 expired
  Standby virtual mac address is 0000.0c07.ac01
  Tracking interface states for 1 interface, 1 up:
    Up    Serial0
charlie_1#
```

The configuration of the charlie_2 router will be identical to the configuration of the charlie_1 router, except for the priority, which can be left at the default of 100. Setting the priority at 101 is still preferred, to ensure that this router is second only to the primary. This also helps to break any possible "tie-breakers" with new routers that might be added to the HSRP group in the future. When this is complete, verify HSRP on charlie_2 with the **show standby Ethernet 0** command, as listed in Example 16-13.

Example 16-13 *Status of the Standby Router*

```
charlie_2#show standby ethernet 0
Ethernet0 - Group 1
  Local state is Standby, priority 101, may preempt
  Hellotime 3 holdtime 10
  Next hello sent in 00:00:01.336
  Hot standby IP address is 25.100.61.3 configured
  Active router is 25.100.61.1 expires in 00:00:09
  Standby router is local
  Tracking interface states for 1 interface, 1 up:
    Up    Serial0
charlie_2#
```

In this example, you want to verify that the local state is standby and that it may preempt, or take over as the active router, if priority warrants it. Example 16-14 shows the HSRP configuration for both Ethernet interfaces on charlie_1 and charlie_2.

Example 16-14 *HSRP Configurations for charlie_1 and charlie_2*

```
charlie_1#
 interface Ethernet0
 ip address 25.100.61.1 255.255.255.0
 no ip redirects
 no ip directed-broadcast
 ip rip send version 2
 ip rip receive version 2
 standby 1 priority 105
 standby 1 preempt
 standby 1 ip 25.100.61.3
 standby 1 track Serial0

charlie_2#
 interface Ethernet0
 ip address 25.100.61.2 255.255.255.0
 no ip redirects
 ip rip send version 2
 ip rip receive version 2
 standby 1 priority 101
 standby 1 preempt
 standby 1 ip 25.100.61.3
 standby 1 track Serial0
 !
```

To test the HSRP configuration for functionality, attach an IP-based workstation, as shown in Figure 16-2. Make sure that the default gateway on the workstation is pointing to 25.100.61.3. This workstation should be capable of **ping**ing the IP address of the E0 port of the headquarters_co router or the headquarters servers, if you have them configured. To test the failover process, go to the frame switch and disable the serial interface attached to the charlie_1 router. HSRP will note that the interface is down and will subtract the cost associated with the interface—in this case, the default of 10. This will put the priority of charlie_1 at 95, less than charlie_2, so charlie_2 should be active. You can verify the failover by performing traceroute functions on the workstations and by using the **show standby interface** command. Example 16-15 lists the **show standby interface** output on charlie_2 after you have downed the frame switch serial interface attached to charlie_1. Note the state change from standby to active.

Example 16-15 show standby *Command Output After Failover*

```
charlie_2#show standby ethernet 0
Ethernet0 - Group 1
  Local state is Active, priority 101, may preempt
  Hellotime 3 holdtime 10
```

Example 16-15 **show standby** *Command Output After Failover (Continued)*

```
    Next hello sent in 00:00:00.952
    Hot standby IP address is 25.100.61.3 configured
    Active router is local
    Standby router is 25.100.61.1 expires in 00:00:07
    Tracking interface states for 1 interface, 1 up:
      Up   Serial0
charlie_2#
```

Also ensure that IP routing is working by issuing test **ping**s from the workstations and by looking at the routing table of headquarters_co router. Example 16-16 lists the routing table of headquarters_co, before and after the failover. It first shows RIP updates coming from 25.100.10.2, the primary router. After failover, the routing updates start to come from 25.100.10.3, with an administrative distance of 125.

Example 16-16 *IP Route Table Before and After Failover Tests*

```
headquarters_co#show ip route
Codes: C - connected, S - static, I   IGRP, R - RIP, M - mobile, B - BGP
<<<text omitted>>>

     25.0.0.0/24 is subnetted, 3 subnets
R       25.100.61.0 [120/1] via 25.100.10.2, 00:00:01, Serial0
C       25.100.10.0 is directly connected, Serial0
C       25.100.6.0 is directly connected, Ethernet0
headquarters_co#

! AFTER WE DOWN THE FRAME INTERFACE WE HAVE THE FOLLOWING:
headquarters_co#show ip route
Codes: C - connected, S - static, I - IGRP, R - RIP, M - mobile, B - BGP
<<<text omitted>>>

Gateway of last resort is not set

     25.0.0.0/24 is subnetted, 3 subnets
R       25.100.61.0/24 is possibly down,
          routing via 25.100.10.2, Serial0
C       25.100.10.0 is directly connected, Serial0
C       25.100.6.0 is directly connected, Ethernet0
headquarters_co#

headquarters_co#show ip route
Codes: C - connected, S - static, I - IGRP, R - RIP, M - mobile, B - BGP
<<<text omitted>>>

Gateway of last resort is not set
```

continues

Example 16-16 *IP Route Table Before and After Failover Tests (Continued)*

```
         25.0.0.0/24 is subnetted, 3 subnets
R         25.100.61.0 [125/1] via 25.100.10.3, 00:00:17, Serial0
C         25.100.10.0 is directly connected, Serial0
C         25.100.6.0 is directly connected, Ethernet0
headquarters_co#
```

The time that it takes for RIP-2 to converge from the primary router to the backup router can be a few minutes. This leads to the optional part of the lab. To improve the design of the 4th Army Com Net, you could change the routing protocol from RIP-2 to EIGRP or OSPF. By switching the routing protocol, IP convergence can happen much quicker. This, in turn, better supports the functionality and purpose of HSRP.

In this model, you use EIGRP because the migration from RIP to EIGRP can be quite easy. The best way to migrate to EIGRP is simply to add the **router eigrp** command with an autonomous system and network address. Because the administrative distance of EIGRP is less than that of RIP, the routing table will automatically converge from RIP to EIGRP, as shown in Example 16-17.

Example 16-17 *IP Routing Table of headquarters_co Router on EIGRP*

```
headquarters_co#show ip route
Codes: C - connected, S - static, I - IGRP, R - RIP, M - mobile, B - BGP
       D - EIGRP, EX - EIGRP external, O - OSPF, IA - OSPF inter area
<<<text omitted>>>

Gateway of last resort is not set


     25.0.0.0/24 is subnetted, 3 subnets
D         25.100.61.0 [90/2195456] via 25.100.10.2, 00:00:02, Serial0
C         25.100.10.0 is directly connected, Serial0
C         25.100.6.0 is directly connected, Ethernet0
headquarters_co#
```

To influence the routes advertised by EIGRP, add a DELAY to the Ethernet segment of charlie_2. This way, when EIGRP reports that route to headquarters_co, it will be weighted. This then will cause EIGRP to have a preferred route to the subnet 25.100.61.0/24, through the charlie_1 router. The delay should be added to the Ethernet interface instead of the serial interface because traffic destined for the headquarters master server from charlie_2 should leave through the serial interface. If the delay is put there, EIGRP will want to route this traffic through the Ethernet port to charlie_1 first. When your EIGRP configuration is complete, remove the RIP portions of the configuration with the **no router rip** command. This command will remove all RIP-related statements.

CHAPTER 17

Configuring Network Time Protocol (NTP) and Simple Network Time Protocol (SNTP)

Bob poured feverishly over the latest trace of the chronic link problem. There was a strong chance that it was this same problem that they had experienced just one week earlier. Bob wasn't his real name; it was a name that all the guys called him because he was the "new guy." Bob knew almost every acronym in the Telco industry, and he also knew that the ATM was indeed faster then Ethernet. In the middle of his spaghetti network, he had finally found a "smoking gun." He would finally prove his worth to the whole group by cracking this chronic problem. Carefully continuing down the trace, he came to two places where the link had failed: The timestamps read 12:01:21 OCT 18, 1999 and 11:23:40 OCT 18, 1999. Quickly turning to the log of the remote site, Bob found 105 failures, all dated from 11:57:42.079 UTC Mar 1 1993 to 03:32:12.022 UTC Mar 17. Hmmmmmmm . . ..

Sadly, Bob would have to wait for another day and unfortunately, another failure, to correlate his findings. The next time, however, it will be different: Bob is going to add the Network Time Protocol (NTP) to his acronym list.

NTP Overview

NTP was designed to provide an accurate and stable clock to remote sources across an unmanaged, global Internet environment. Before NTP, other protocols such as Daytime protocol, Time protocol, and ICMP timestamp provided this service. Digital Time Service (DTS) accomplished many of the same objectives as NTP. However, NTP provides for the use of stratum information in clock selection and provides an accurate compensation for inherent clock frequency errors. DTS does not use a stratum or compensate for inherent frequency errors.

The concept of a stratum was conceived directly from the telephone industry, under BELL 86. The accuracy of each NTP server was defined with a stratum number. The most accurate server stratum starts at 1 and increments from there. The implementation of a stratum allows NTP to select from multiple clock sources and judge which one to synchronize with.

The stratum value of 1 requires the accuracy provided by atomic clocks. You will not be able to configure a Cisco router to supply or have a stratum 1 clock, for obvious reasons.

NOTE   Atomic clocks have oscillators that can maintain extremely precise frequencies that correspond to natural phenomenon. The earliest and ultimate oscillators are our celestial bodies. But because of their vastness and our lack of scientific knowledge about them, scientists base atomic clocks on the orbital states of an electron instead of the orbital states of planets and our solar system. The atom provides a stable and accurate model on which scientists can perform accurate measurements. Atomic oscillators are based on the transitions of hydrogen, cesium, and rubidium atoms.

NOTE   To test NTP, I used the shareware TARDIS2000 V1.2, available at c/net's DOWNLOAD.COM or http://download.cnet.com. Two public NTP/SNTP clocks' addresses that you can use in your models are zeus.tamu.edu or 128.194.103.14, and tmc.edu or 128.249.1.1.

After you synchronize with them, most atomic clocks provide a stratum level of 3 or greater to the client. Consider 3 to be a highly reliable stratum level when using NTP.

NTP was specifically designed to produce three products:

- **Clock offset**—Clock offset is the amount by which to adjust the local clock so that it corresponds to the reference clock.

- **Round-trip delay**—Round-trip delay makes it possible for a reference clock to launch a message to arrive back at the reference clock at a specific time.

- **Dispersion**—Dispersion is the maximum error of the local clock relative to the reference or NTP server.

These products are all produced in relation to the local clock, and they use Greenwich Mean Time, UTC, or Coordinated Universal Time as a common reference in time. If the local clock is unreliable, it will affect NTP synchronization, as well as the values provided by NTP, which also provides these values with a relatively simple data flow and little overhead to the network. NTP accomplishes this by using User Datagram Protocol (UDP) port 123. Data integrity is provided by UDP checksums; no flow control or retransmission facilities are provided or necessary.

NTP can be used in a variety of ways. Perhaps the most common use of NTP is for an NTP client to obtain a valid clock from an external source through IP. If multiple clients are synchronizing off the same source, this allows for entire network synchronization. Network clock synchronization can provide several useful functions:

- As the tragic story of Bob illustrates, NTP can be a useful protocol when trying to correlate network anomalies, such as link or neighbor failures.

- Network clock synchronization helps to correlate time accurate logs and debug information from multiple routers.

- Network-management platforms, such as CiscoWorks and HP OpenView, will be more effective and accurate in reporting network statistics.

NTP was first described in RFC 958, but since its first release, it has evolved many times. NTP version 3 is the dominant version of NTP today. RFC 1305 outlines NTP and obsoletes RFCs 1119, 1059, and 958. RFC 2030 outlines the Simple Network Time Protocol (SNTP), which is an adaptation of NTP Version 3. The only significant change in SNTP Version 4 is its adaptation to properly interpret an IPv6 header and OSI addressing.

NOTE   You can find all RFCs online at www.isi.edu/in-notes/rfc*xxxx*.*txt*, where *xxxx* is the number of the RFC.

Configuring NTP

NTP can be configured to support a number of different environments. The following are the most common implementations of NTP and are the ones that you will be configuring in this chapter:

- **NTP broadcast client mode**—The router can be configured to passively listen for NTP broadcasts, avoiding a static entry to one specific time server.

- **NTP static client mode**—The router can be configured to listen and exchange messages between statically configured NTP servers.

- **NTP master mode**—The router can be configured as an NTP server forwarding NTP broadcasts.

- **NTP peer associations**—The router can be configured to form an NTP peer association with another router. The router can either synchronize to the other system or allow the other system to synchronize to it.

- **NTP options and time-related configurations**—NTP options include perform authentication and setting the calendar. Time-related options include setting daylight saving time and the current time zone.

Configuring NTP Broadcast Client Mode

Cisco routers can be configured to receive NTP broadcasts on an interface-by-interface level. This type of configuration should be used in LAN environments and can be used to avoid the need to statically configure multiple NTP servers. To configure a router to receive NTP broadcasts, use the **ntp broadcast client** command under the interface nearest the NTP server or on the interface receiving the NTP broadcast. Figure 17-1 shows a LAN configured with an NTP server. The NTP server has a stratum of 5 and an IP address of 206.191.241.44.

Figure 17-1 *NTP Broadcast Client*

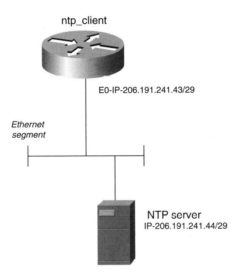

Example 17-1 provides the configuration for the router to receive NTP broadcasts on its Ethernet 0 interface.

Example 17-1 *Configuring an NTP Broadcast Client*

```
ntp_client(config)#int ethernet 0
ntp_client(config-if)#ntp broadcast client
ntp_client(config-if)#exit
ntp_
```

To verify that the clock has synchronized, use the **show ntp associations** and **show ntp status** commands. Examples 17-2 and 17-3 demonstrate the use of these commands on the ntp_client router.

Example 17-2 *The* **show ntp associations** *Command*

```
ntp_clent#show ntp associations

        address        ref clock    st  when  poll reach  delay  offset    disp
* 206.191.241.44  128.194.103.14   5    7   8192   76    4.1    0.05   910.5
  * master (synced), # master (unsynced), + selected, - candidate, ~ configured
ntp_clent#
```

Example 17-2 highlights the key values to look at. When NTP is synchronized, an asterisk (*) denotes that the router has received UDP packets from the address listed immediately after the asterisk and that the router has synchronized with that NTP server. The st field indicates that the clock source is a stratum 5 clock. The ref clock field (reference clock) indicates the clock that the NTP source synchronized to. If the number is 127.127.7.1 and the device is a Cisco router, the clock is synchronized with itself.

Example 17-3 *The* **show ntp status** *Command*

```
ntp_clent#show ntp status
Clock is synchronized, stratum 0, reference is 206.191.241.44
nominal freq is 250.0000 Hz, actual freq is 250.0093 Hz, precision is 2**19
reference time is BCF2162C.BDF0EE87 (09:33:16.741 CSTDST Wed Jun 14 2000)
clock offset is -91.9576 msec, root delay is 4.14 msec
root dispersion is 135.64 msec, peer dispersion is 43.67 msec
ntp_clent#
```

The first line in Example 17-3 provides a clear indication that the clock has synchronized from an address of 206.191.241.44. Here, the stratum has been adjusted to one greater than the original stratum of the master clock. In this example, the router has some optional time-related commands configured. We have set daylight savings time and have set an offset from UTC of six hours. These options will be covered in later sections.

Configuring NTP Static Client Mode

Another way to configure the NTP client is to statically map it to a specific time server. A static NTP server should be used when you want to receive an NTP broadcast from a specific host. An example is when you want to point to the Internet and synchronize the router with one of the atomic clocks on it.

Building on the first model, let's configure another NTP client on the same router, pointing to an atomic clock on the Internet. At TMC.EDU, or 128.249.1.1, is an atomic clock that you can use as a NTP server. Figure 17-2 illustrates the new NTP configuration performed in Example 17-4.

Figure 17-2 *NTP Static Client*

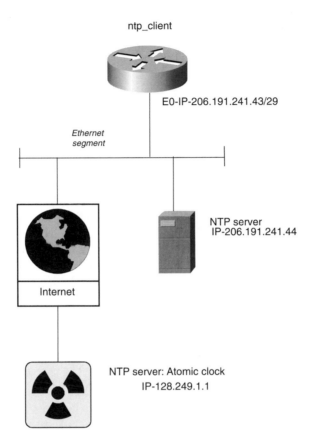

ntp_client

E0-IP-206.191.241.43/29

Ethernet segment

Internet

NTP server
IP-206.191.241.44

NTP server: Atomic clock
IP-128.249.1.1

Example 17-4 *Configuration of the ntp_client Router*

```
hostname ntp_client
!
clock timezone CST -6
 !
<<<text omitted>>>
!
interface Ethernet0
 ip address 206.191.241.43 255.255.255.248
 no ip directed-broadcast
 ntp broadcast client
!
<<<text omitted>>>
!
ntp clock-period 17179279          ←This is added by the router
```

To configure the router to receive its NTP broadcast from a specific host, use the **ntp server a.b.c.d** command. This is a global command, and the router can have multiple NTP servers configured at any one time.

You can now perform the same **show** commands, **show ntp assoc** and **show ntp status**, to verify the synchronization.

Example 17-5 shows NTP slowly converging to the new NTP server. RFC 1305 points out that clock synchronization requires long periods and multiple comparisons to maintain accurate time. The time for synchronization to occur will range, depending on multiple factors. Be prepared to wait a while for clock synchronization; however, if the clocks do not synchronize in an hour or sooner, you might want to review your NTP design. In the labs and examples presented here, NTP synchronized in less than five minutes.

Example 17-5 *The* **show ntp assoc** *and* **show ntp status** *Command*

```
ntp_client#show ntp stat
Clock is synchronized, stratum 6, reference is 206.191.241.44
nominal freq is 250.0000 Hz, actual freq is 250.0096 Hz, precision is 2**19
reference time is BCF258FA.69DAF6F5 (14:18:18.413 CSTDST Wed Jun 14 2000)
clock offset is -16.8153 msec, root delay is 4.06 msec
root dispersion is 409.61 msec, peer dispersion is 392.78 msec
ntp_client#
ntp_client#show ntp ass

        address         ref clock      st  when  poll reach  delay  offset     disp
 ~128.249.1.1        0.0.0.0           16    -    64    0    0.0    0.00   16000.←NTP
configured but no synced
 * 206.191.241.44    128.194.103.14     5   46  8192   77    4.1   -16.82    392.8
  * master (synced), # master (unsynced), + selected, - candidate, ~ configured
ntp_client#

ntp_client#show ntp ass

        address         ref clock      st  when  poll reach  delay  offset     disp
*~128.249.1.1       139.78.160.41       3   11   512  377  114.5   30.71    26.0 ←NTP Sync
  206.191.241.44    128.194.103.14      5   26  8192   77    4.1   15.23     20.0
  * master (synced), # master (unsynced), + selected, - candidate, ~ configured
ntp_client#show ntp stat
Clock is synchronized, stratum 4, reference is 128.249.1.1
nominal freq is 250.0000 Hz, actual freq is 250.0093 Hz, precision is 2**19
reference time is BCF26309.F694401F (15:01:13.963 CSTDST Wed Jun 14 2000)
clock offset is 30.7128 msec, root delay is 151.06 msec
root dispersion is 97.17 msec, peer dispersion is 26.05 msec
ntp_client#
```

Configuring NTP Master Mode

Cisco routers can also use NTP to function as authoritative NTP servers. When configuring a router as an NTP server, you should take care when setting the stratum level. This value should range somewhere between 6 and 15; the default is 8. The clocks in the mid- and upper-class routers, such as the 36xx, 47xx, and 7k series routers, are much more reliable and provide a calendar function. Use these types of routers for your NTP servers.

To configure a Cisco router as an authoritative NTP server, use the **ntp master** [*stratum_number*]command in global configuration mode. Figure 17-3 shows a Cisco 4700 router as the NTP master and a Cisco 2500 router as the NTP client. The 4700 is a good choice as the NTP server because it has a more reliable clock than the 2500 router. You will use the **ntp master** command on the server, and the client can be configured as either a static client or a broadcast client.

Figure 17-3 *NTP Configuration: Using a Router as an NTP Server*

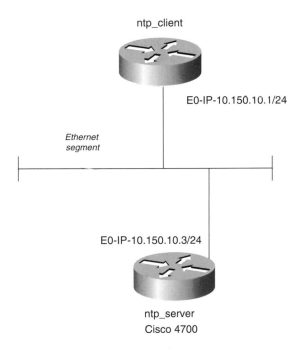

Example 17-6 illustrates the configuration of an NTP master and an NTP static client.

Example 17-6 *Configuration of an NTP Master and Client*

```
ntp_server#conf t
Enter configuration commands, one per line.  End with CNTL/Z.
ntp_server(config)#ntp master 7
ntp_server(config)#exit
ntp_server#
```

Example 17-6 *Configuration of an NTP Master and Client (Continued)*

```
ntp_client#conf t
Enter configuration commands, one per line.  End with CNTL/Z.
ntp_client(config)#ntp server 10.150.10.3
ntp_client(config)#exit
ntp_client#
```

Use the **show ntp status** to verify that the clock is synchronized, and use **show ntp associations** for detailed information on the clock/server that the router has synchronized with. Example 17-7 shows the output for these commands. Again, you are looking for the clock to be synchronized and for the reference address to be 10.150.10.3, which is the NTP master.

Example 17-7 **show ntp status** *and* **show ntp associations** *Command Output*

```
ntp_client#show ntp status
Clock is synchronized, stratum 8, reference is 10.150.10.3
nominal freq is 250.0000 Hz, actual freq is 250.0000 Hz, precision is 2**19
reference time is BD13BB90.AE4D80D0 (03:03:44.000 UTC Mon Jul 10 2000)
clock offset is 1.2767 msec, root delay is 3.78 msec
root dispersion is 1.97 msec, peer dispersion is 0.67 msec
ntp_client#
ntp_client#show ntp associations

      address         ref clock    st  when  poll reach  delay  offset   disp
*~10.150.10.3      127.127.7.1     7    60    64  377     3.8    1.28    0.7
 * master (synced), # master (unsynced), + selected, - candidate, ~ configured
ntp_client#
```

Configuring NTP Peer Associations

An NTP peer association is much like that of a static peer. An NTP association can be a peer association, meaning that it allows this system to synchronize to another system or allows the other system to synchronize to it. This type of NTP configuration can be deployed in the standard Cisco hierarchical three-layer network design practice (core, distribution, and access layers). At the core level reside NTP master servers, which can be routers or actual NTP servers. The distribution-level routers have a single peer to the core routers. The access-level routers, in turn, peer to the distribution routers. This keeps many NTP broadcasts, however slight they may be, from all going to the same host, yet it provides complete network time synchronization across the internetwork. If a peer loses synchronization, by the rules of NTP, it will not synchronize with any other external sources. Therefore, locate your central peers where a potential loss of physical connectivity makes it logical for the clock to become unsynchronized.

In Figure 17-4, the access routers have a single NTP peer pointing to the distribution router's Ethernet segment. The distribution routers have a single NTP peer pointing to the core router.

The core router could be initiating the time source or, in this case, synchronizing to a more reliable external time source. To configure NTP peers, use the **ntp peer** *ip_address* command, in which the IP address is the NTP time source that you want to synchronize to. There is no need to put an **ntp peer** statement on both sides of the connection. The access routers in Figure 17-4 will have a single **ntp peer** statement, as will the distribution and the core routers, each pointing only at the IP address where they want to get the time source. Example 17-8 lists the syntax needed to accomplish NTP peering for Figure 17-4.

Figure 17-4 *NTP Peer Associations*

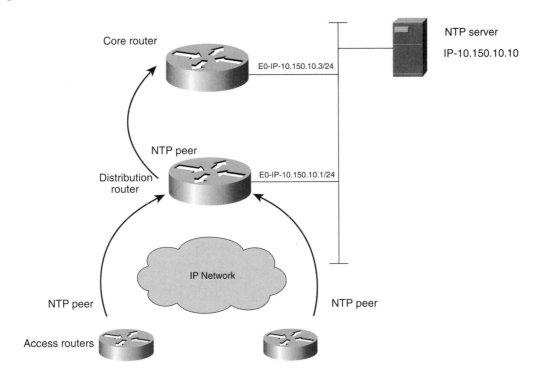

Example 17-8 *NTP Peer Configurations for Figure 17-4*

```
Access routers:
ntp peer 10.150.10.1

Distribution router:
ntp peer 10.150.10.3

Core router:
ntp server 10.150.10.10        or
ntp master 6
```

Configuring NTP Authentication and Other Clock-Related Options

NTP also provides Message Digest 5 (MD5) authentication of NTP packets for applications that require a secure time source. For applications that bill and track by the minute or the second, it is critical that a secure and reliable clock is kept across the network. Configuring MD5 authentication involves three steps:

Step 1 Enable NTP authentication. Use the **ntp authenticate** global command.

Step 2 Define authentication keys. Configure an MD5 password and an authentication key to use with it. Use the **ntp authentication-key** *key_number* **md5** *md5_password* global command.

Step 3 Define a trusted key. Using the same *key_number* as in Step 2, define a trusted key that will be used among the routers when authenticating NTP. Use the **ntp trusted-key** *key_number* command to accomplish this.

Figure 17-5 shows two routers configured for NTP authentication. The ntp_t_server router is the NTP master. The ntp_t_client router is the NTP client.

Figure 17-5 *NTP Master and Client Configuration with MD5 Authentication*

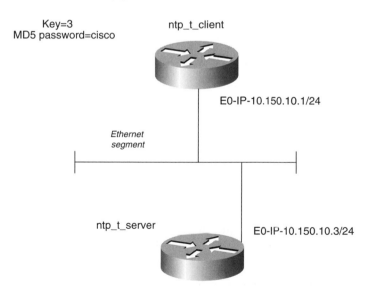

The **ntp authentication** commands for both routers will be identical. You must enable authentication to each router and then define the authentication and trusted keys. Example 17-9 demonstrates the commands needed to configure the NTP master; Example 17-10 demonstrates the commands needed for the client.

Example 17-9 *Configuring Authentication for NTP on the Master*

```
ntp_t_server(config)#ntp master 6
ntp_t_server (config)#ntp authenticate
ntp_t_server (config)#ntp authentication-key 3 md5 cisco
ntp_t_server (config)#ntp trusted-key 3
```

Example 17-10 *Configuring Authentication for NTP on the Client*

```
ntp_t_client(config)#ntp server 10.150.10.3
ntp_t_client(config)#ntp authenticate
ntp_t_client(config)#ntp authentication-key 3 md5 cisco
ntp_t_client(config)#ntp trusted-key 3
```

Using the same **show** commands mentioned previously, **show ntp status** and **show ntp associations**, you can verify that NTP is synchronized as demonstrated in Example 17-11.

Example 17-11 **show ntp stat** *and* **show ntp assoc** *Command Output*

```
ntp_t_client#show ntp stat
Clock is synchronized, stratum 7, reference is 10.150.10.3
nominal freq is 250.0000 Hz, actual freq is 249.9990 Hz, precision is 2**19
reference time is BD15D137.C52F08AF (17:00:39.770 UTC Tue Jul 11 2000)
clock offset is 1.4114 msec, root delay is 3.77 msec
root dispersion is 1.46 msec, peer dispersion is 0.03 msec

ntp_t_client#show ntp associations

      address          ref clock      st  when  poll reach  delay  offset    disp
*~10.150.10.3     127.127.7.1      6    37    64   377     3.8    1.41     0.0
 * master (synced), # master (unsynced), + selected, - candidate, ~ configured
ntp_t_client#
```

Configure Clock and Time Zones

Inherently critical to having a common clock across the network is having that clock correct and uniform. That includes setting the time zone and daylight saving time. The default time zone is UTC, or Greenwich Mean Time. NTP also can periodically update the calendar, if one is present on the router, as in the Cisco 3600, 7000, and higher-end series routers.

To configure time-zone values, use the following commands from the global configuration mode:

- **clock timezone** *timezone_name* [*hours_plus_or_minus_from_UTC*] [*minutes_offset_from_UTC*]
- **clock summertime** *summer_timezone_name* [*recurring|date*]
- **ntp update-calendar**

When you configure a time zone, you can enter the time zone name, such as PAC or CST for Pacific and Central time accordingly, or you can make up a name. You can also set the hours (+23 to –23) and minutes offset from UTC time. When you configure daylight saving time with the **clock summertime** command, you can enter a time zone name that will appear when running in daylight saving mode. You also can configure any daylight saving offset or specifics that your local government has implemented. The default rules on daylight saving time is that the router or switch will advance the clock one hour on the first Sunday in April at 2:00 a.m., and move the clock back one hour on the last Sunday in October at 2:00 a.m.

Apply these commands to routers in Figure 17-5. Set the time zone on ntp_t_server to U.S. Central time, and enable daylight saving time. CST time is a –6 hour offset from Greenwich Mean Time, so you will want to adjust the offset accordingly. Example 17-12 demonstrates how to set the master clock on Figure 17-5 to Central time.

Example 17-12 *Setting the Time Zone and Daylight Saving Time*

```
ntp_t_server (config)#clock timezone CST -6
ntp_t_server (config)#clock summer-time CDT recurring
```

Performing a **show clock** on the ntp_t_master router results in the output in Example 17-13.

Example 17-13 **show clock** *Command Output Indicates Daylight Saving Time in Effect*

```
ntp_t_serverr#show clock
13:44:49.063 CDT Tue Jul 11 2000
ntp_t_server#
```

Note that the CDT is the time zone name, which denotes that we are running on daylight saving time.

TIP

NTP does not pass time zone information in its updates. To configure the proper time zone, you must use the **clock timezone** command on all the routers in the network. I recommend setting all the clocks to UTC, the default, if the network is large or global. If the network is smaller, the routers should be set to the time zone that the core routers are in. Without a common time zone, problem and event correlation can be much more difficult.

NOTE

The **ntp clock-period** that appears in the router's configuration listing is added automatically into the router configs when NTP is enabled. It serves to jump-start the NTP frequency compensation when the router is rebooted.

Configuring the Simple Network Time Protocol (SNTP)

On smaller routers that do not support NTP, such as the Cisco 100x series, the 80x series, and other lower-end routers, you can deploy SNTP. However, SNTP lacks some of the enhanced features of NTP: It cannot be an NTP server, and it provides no authentication and statistics mechanisms. SNTP can be configured in two ways, much like NTP:

- Configure the router to passively listen for SNTP broadcasts on a wire.
- Statically map SNTP to a specific server.

If both methods are configured, the router accepts a tie from a broadcast server, but it prefers time from the static server, assuming that the stratum levels are equal.

To configure SNTP on the smaller Cisco platforms, use the following global commands:

- **sntp server** *server_IP_address*—This command statically maps an SNTP server to the router for SNTP updates. It performs just like the NTP server command.
- **sntp broadcast client**—This command passively listens for SNTP broadcast on the router interfaces.
- **show sntp**—This command shows SNTP status.

The example in this section uses a Cisco 804, called skynet_2, and an NTP server on its LAN interface, as illustrated in Figure 17-6.

Figure 17-6 *SNTP Configuration Topology*

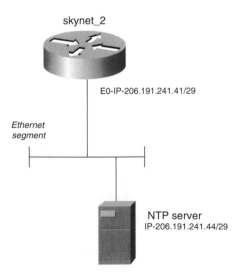

skynet_2

E0-IP-206.191.241.41/29

Ethernet
segment

NTP server
IP-206.191.241.44/29

To configure this router to receive updates from an unknown source, simply add the **sntp broadcast client** configuration command. You will also add the appropriate time zone for the U.S. Central time and set daylight saving time. Example 17-14 demonstrates this process.

Example 17-14 *Configuring SNTP on a Cisco 804 Router*

```
skynet_2(config)#sntp broadcast client
skynet_2(config)#clock timezone CST -6
skynet_2(config)#clock summer-time CDT recurring
skynet_2(config)#exit

skynet_2#show sntp
SNTP server      Stratum   Version    Last Receive
206.191.241.44     14        3           00:00:39    Synced  Bcast

Broadcast client mode is enabled.

skynet_2#show clock
14:12:45.116 CDT Tue Jul 11 2000
```

Note that the SNTP has synchronized to the server 206.191.241.44 with a stratum 14, without statically configuring it. The **show clock** command shows the clock to be in daylight saving time.

The "Big show" and "Big D" for NTP and SNTP

You have already seen and used the three primary **show** commands for NTP and SNTP. Those commands are as follows:

- **show ntp status**—This command provides detailed status of NTP synchronization, along with the three primary elements of NTP: delay, offset, and dispersion.

- **show sntp**—This command displays whether SNTP is configured if it has not found a valid clock source. If SNTP is synchronized, this command displays the IP address and the stratum of the server.

- **show ntp associations [detailed]**—This command displays any statically configured NTP peers, along with the clock selection and whether the peer is synchronized.

Example 17-15 lists the output from the **show ntp status** command. The output details that you want to look for here are that the clock in synchronized, with a valid stratum, usually less then 16. You also need information about a reference clock. The clock offset, root delay, root, and peer dispersion should be relatively small numbers, in the millisecond range, when the clocks are synchronized.

Example 17-15 **show ntp status** *Command Output*

```
ntp_t_client#show ntp status
Clock is synchronized, stratum 7, reference is 10.150.10.3
nominal freq is 250.0000 Hz, actual freq is 249.9984 Hz, precision is 2**19
reference time is BD1604F7.3618FF07 (20:41:27.211 UTC Tue Jul 11 2000)    ←Correct
    time!
clock offset is 0.3951 msec, root delay is 3.78 msec
root dispersion is 0.44 msec, peer dispersion is 0.03 msec
ntp_t_client#
```

Example 17-16 lists the output from a **show ntp status** command, where the clock hasn't synchronized. Notice that the stratum is not set and no reference clock exists.

Example 17-16 *Bad Output from the* **show ntp status** *Command*

```
timex#show ntp stat
Clock is unsynchronized, stratum 16, no reference clock
nominal freq is 250.0000 Hz, actual freq is 250.0003 Hz, precision is 2**19
reference time is BD15D99C.4AC66EE0 (17:36:28.292 UTC Tue Jul 11 2000)
clock offset is -0.1224 msec, root delay is 31.14 msec
root dispersion is 1.45 msec, peer dispersion is 0.14 msec
timex#
```

Example 17-17 lists the output from the **show sntp** command. The relevant information to look for here is the IP address of the SNTP server, a valid stratum, and confirmation that the clock is synchronized. If no valid SNTP broadcasts are found, this command displays only that the SNTP client mode is enabled.

Example 17-17 **show sntp** *Command Output*

```
skynet_2#show sntp
SNTP server      Stratum    Version    Last Receive
206.191.241.44     14         3         00:00:44      Synced  Bcast

Broadcast client mode is enabled.
```

Example 17-18 lists the output from the **show ntp associations** command. The key indicator is the *, which indicates that the master clock is synchronized and gives the IP address and stratum of that clock. The bottom of the example lists the extended version of this command, which includes information on delay, offset, and dispersion. The first line of the output provides a quick view of the primary NTP association.

Example 17-18 show ntp associations *Command Output*

```
timex#show ntp associations

        address        ref clock      st  when  poll reach  delay  offset   disp
*~10.150.10.1       10.150.10.3       7   38    64   377    6.1   -0.51    0.1
 * master (synced), # master (unsynced), + selected, - candidate, ~ configured
timex#
timex#show ntp associations detail
10.150.10.1 configured, our_master, sane, valid, stratum 7
ref ID 10.150.10.3, time BD160B37.3911241E (21:08:07.222 UTC Tue Jul 11 2000)
our mode active, peer mode passive, our poll intvl 64, peer poll intvl 64
root delay 3.78 msec, root disp 0.41, reach 377, sync dist 5.432
delay 6.07 msec, offset -0.5087 msec, dispersion 0.09
precision 2**19, version 3
org time BD160B48.A2712FA3 (21:08:24.634 UTC Tue Jul 11 2000)
rcv time BD160B48.A3598FCA (21:08:24.638 UTC Tue Jul 11 2000)
xmt time BD160B48.A19B718B (21:08:24.631 UTC Tue Jul 11 2000)
filtdelay =     6.07    6.04    6.03    6.13    6.03    6.09    6.01    6.06
filtoffset =   -0.51   -0.41   -0.40   -0.43   -0.48   -0.43   -0.41   -0.39
filterror =     0.02    0.99    1.97    2.94    3.92    4.90    5.87    6.85

timex#
```

Cisco provides many debugs for NTP, but perhaps the most useful one is **debug ntp select**. This **debug** shows the status of NTP peers, along with the packet exchange as it is occurring. Most of the other debugs indicate only when an event is triggered, such as **debug ntp events** and **debug ntp sync.** These display only information when state changes happen and give no indications of internal workings.

Example 17-19 lists the output of the **debug ntp select** command, which indicates that the output packet is going to the NTP server 10.150.10.3, your configured clock. You also see the offset measured from the survivor clock, which indicates that the clocks have been compared.

Example 17-19 debug ntp select *Command Output*

```
03:42:37: NTP: nlist 1, allow 0, found 0, low -0.001984, high 0.002411
03:42:37: NTP: candidate 10.150.10.3 cdist 96.002197 error 0.000305
03:42:37: NTP: survivor 10.150.10.3 offset 0.000226, cdist 96.00220

03:43:23: NTP: nlist 1, allow 0, found 0, low -0.001785, high 0.002151
03:43:23: NTP: candidate 10.150.10.3 cdist 96.001968 error 0.000076
03:43:23: NTP: survivor 10.150.10.3 offset 0.000185, cdist 96.00197

03:43:41: NTP: nlist 1, allow 0, found 0, low -0.002045, high 0.002411
03:43:41: NTP: candidate 10.150.10.3 cdist 96.002228 error 0.000336
03:43:41: NTP: survivor 10.150.10.3 offset 0.000185, cdist 96.00223
```

Lab 34: Configuring NTP Servers, Clients, and Authentication—Part I

Practical Scenario

NTP is a critical component to network management. Without a common clock, it is difficult to track and correlate any network anomalies. By having NTP configured, all the routers will be synchronized to the same clock, and troubleshooting the network will be much easier.

Lab Exercise

You are an engineer at management.com networks. You will be in charge of synchronizing all the routers in the network to one common clock source. Before rolling out NTP to the whole network, you will perform a proof-of-concept test with the following conditions:

- At this time, you do not have access to an NTP server, and you must find a way for the router to provide NTP service to the network.

- All routers are located in the United States–Pacific Time zone, which is an 8-hour offset from Greenwich Mean Time or UTC. Ensure that this is the time zone for the network, and use the name of PAC for a description.

- Make NTP pass secure updates.

- The remote router, client_router, should have a stratum of 6 when its clock is synchronized to the mngt_router.

- (Optional) Set up all the routers for daylight saving time. Use S-PAC for the description when in daylight saving time.

Lab Objectives

- Configure the network as depicted in Figure 17-7. Use OSPF as the routing protocol, and put the client router in a stub area.

- Configure the management router as an NTP server and the client router as an NTP client.

- Use MD5 authentication for NTP; use cns for the password with a key of 2.

- Set the appropriate stratum level.

Equipment Needed

- Two Cisco routers. The routers should be connected through V.35 back-to-back cables or in a similar manner. The routers must support NTP—a Cisco 2500 or greater series. To model this network, we used Cisco 4700 and Cisco 2500 series routers.

- Two LAN segments, provided through hubs or switches.

Physical Layout and Prestaging

- Connect the hubs and serial cables to the routers, as shown in Figure 17-7. Use HDLC as the WAN protocol.

- Connect the two Ethernet hubs to the routers to form two LAN segments, as shown in Figure 17-7.

Figure 17-7 *Management.Com Networks: NTP Proof-of-Concept*

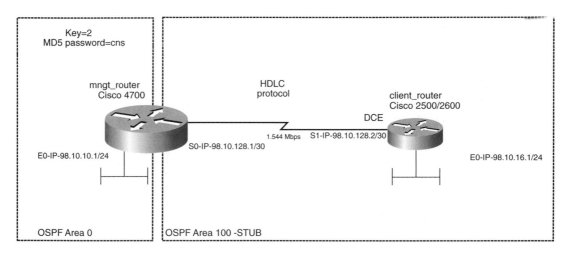

Lab 34: Configuring NTP Servers, Clients, and Authentication—Part II

Lab Walkthrough

After completing the physical installation of the LAN and WAN segments, you should establish IP connectivity among all the routers. Before trying to configure NTP, be sure to perform source **ping**s from each router's Ethernet to verify end-to-end connectivity.

Beginning with the mngt_router, configure the IP address of the Ethernet E0 port and the serial port. This is not the DCE side of the serial link, so no **clock rate** command is needed. The WAN protocol is HDLC, so you do not need to configure an encapsulation type on this link.

On the client_router, you need to configure an IP address on the E0 port and the S1 port. Because this side is the DCE end, you need to add the **clock rate** command.

Before moving on to OSPF, be sure that each router can **ping** the other router's serial port. The WAN is considered a local network, and the remote end should be reachable.

To configure OSPF on the mngt_router, you need to add two **network** statements and an **area** subcommand. Example 17-20 lists the relevant IP configuration for the mngt_router as it stands at this point.

Example 17-20 *Relevant IP Configuration for the mngt_router*

```
! hostname mngt_router
!
interface Ethernet0
 ip address 98.10.10.1 255.255.255.0
 media-type 10BaseT
!
interface Serial0
 ip address 98.10.128.1 255.255.255.252
 no ip mroute-cache
!
router ospf 100
 network 98.10.10.1 0.0.0.0 area 0
 network 98.10.128.1 0.0.0.0 area 100
 area 100 stub
```

Configuring OSPF on the client_router is similar. Because the entire router exists in a stub area, you can simplify the config by using a wildcard mask on the network statement. Again, you also need the **area stub** command for Area 100. Example 17-21 lists the relevant IP configuration for the client_router.

Example 17-21 *Relevant IP Configuration for the client_router*

```
hostname client_router
!
interface Ethernet0
 ip address 98.10.16.1 255.255.255.0
!
interface Serial0
 no ip address
 shutdown
 no fair-queue
!
interface Serial1
 ip address 98.10.128.2 255.255.255.252
 clockrate 2000000
!
router ospf 100
 network 98.10.0.0 0.0.255.255 area 100
 area 100 stub
!
```

Moving on to the NTP portion of the config, you need to configure the following:

- NTP master with a stratum level of 5 on the mngt_router
- MD5 authentication with trusted key of 2 and a password of cns
- NTP client on the client_router so that its stratum is 6 when synced
- Time zone of PAC with an offset of –8 from UTC
- Optionally, daylight saving time across the network, with the name of S-PAC

To configure the NTP on the mngt_router, you need to add the command **ntp master 5**. The 5 sets the stratum to 6 on the client side when it synchronizes with the client_router. To enable authentication, follow this three-step process:

Step 1   Enable authentication.

Step 2   Define authentication keys.

Step 3   Define trusted keys.

Example 17-22 illustrates performing these commands on the master_router. The exact same **authentication** commands will be used on the client_router.

Example 17-22 *Configure NTP and MD5 Authentication on the mngt_router*

```
mngt_router(config)#ntp master 5
mngt_router(config)#ntp authenticate
mngt_router(config)#ntp authentication-key 3 md5 cns
mngt_router(config)#ntp trusted-key 3
mngt_router(config)#exit
```

Configuring the client router is similar to configuring the master, except that you use the **ntp server 98.10.128.1** command in place of the **ntp master** command. The authentication portions of the configuration will be identical to those of the mngt_router.

Check the status of NTP synchronization by using the **show ntp status** and **show ntp assoc** commands. Performing these commands on the client_router generates the output listed in Example 17-23.

Example 17-23 **show ntp status** *and* **show ntp assoc** *Command Output*

```
client_router#show ntp status
Clock is synchronized, stratum 6, reference is 98.10.128.1
nominal freq is 250.0000 Hz, actual freq is 250.0000 Hz, precision is 2**19
reference time is BD19C766.31F0D0F5 (17:07:50.195 UTC Fri Jul 14 2000)
clock offset is -0.3234 msec, root delay is 4.46 msec
root dispersion is 0.52 msec, peer dispersion is 0.15 msec
client_router#
client_router#show ntp assoc

      address         ref clock      st  when  poll reach  delay  offset    disp
*~98.10.128.1      127.127.7.1       5    59    64   377     4.5    -0.32     0.2
 * master (synced), # master (unsynced), + selected, - candidate, ~ configured
client_router#
```

Example 17-23 verifies that the clock is synchronized and that the stratum is set to 6. Also note that the clock has the appropriate reference, which should be the one that you configured.

Finally, you need to set the time and clock in accordance with the time zone and name specified in the lab. To configure this, use the **clock timezone PAC −8** command on both the client and the host router. Now when you view the time, the UTC time should be replaced with PAC time and should be offset by 8 hours.

The optional part of the lab consists of adding daylight saving time to the network. This is accomplished by using the **clock summer-time S-PAC recurring** command on both routers. If you are in daylight saving time, your router will now have output similar to Example 17-24.

Example 17-24 **show ntp status** *While in Daylight Saving Time*

```
client_router#show ntp status
Clock is synchronized, stratum 6, reference is 98.10.128.1
nominal freq is 250.0000 Hz, actual freq is 250.0000 Hz, precision is 2**19
reference time is BD19CA66.316D2935 (10:20:38.193 S-PAC Fri Jul 14 2000)
clock offset is -0.5572 msec, root delay is 4.49 msec
root dispersion is 0.66 msec, peer dispersion is 0.06 msec
client_router#
```

Example 17-25 shows the configurations for both routers.

Example 17-25 *Configurations for the mngt_router and the client_router*

```
hostname client_router
!
enable password cisco
!
clock timezone PAC -8
clock summer-time S-PAC recurring
!
interface Ethernet0
 ip address 98.10.16.1 255.255.255.0
!
<<<text omitted>>>
!
interface Serial1
 ip address 98.10.128.2 255.255.255.252
 clockrate 2000000
!
<<<text omitted>>>
!
router ospf 100
 network 98.10.0.0 0.0.255.255 area 100
 area 100 stub
!
ip classless
!
<<<text omitted>>>
!
ntp authentication-key 2 md5 070C2F5F 7
ntp authenticate
ntp trusted-key 2
ntp clock-period 17179866
ntp server 98.10.128.1
```

```
hostname mngt_router
!
enable password cisco
!
clock timezone PAC -8
clock summer-time S-PAC recurring
!
!
interface Ethernet0
 ip address 98.10.10.1 255.255.255.0
 media-type 10BaseT
!
<<<text omitted>>>
!
interface Serial0
 ip address 98.10.128.1 255.255.255.252
```

continues

Example 17-25 *Configurations for the mngt_router and the client_router (Continued)*

```
 no ip mroute-cache
!
<<<text omitted>>>
!
router ospf 100
 network 98.10.10.1 0.0.0.0 area 0
 network 98.10.128.1 0.0.0.0 area 100
 area 100 stub
!
ip classless
!
<<<text omitted>>>
!
ntp authentication-key 2 md5 104D070A 7
ntp authenticate
ntp trusted-key 2
ntp master 5
```

Lab 35: Configuring NTP Servers, Clients, and Peer Associations—Part I

Practical Scenario

As mentioned previously, NTP is a critical component to network management and for applications that may require an accurate time source. Cisco routers can be configured to synchronize to an external time source and, in turn, have other routers synchronize to them.

Lab Exercise

Independent Ticket, Inc. runs a concert ticket sales application that requires an accurate clock to ensure that ticket sales start and stop at the correct times. This particular application is run by a small group of bands that want to coordinate their own ticket sales instead of relying on existing ticket monopolies. The bands all have 56-kbps links to a small central site that provides common venue information, as well as a secure NTP server. The bands Metallica and Pearl Jam have recently signed up for NTP services. You are tasked to configure the new metallica and pearl_jam routers with the following conditions:

- The network will have a core router, ticket_central, with two 56-kbps HDLC links to the metallica and pearl_jam routers.

- An NTP server resides on the backbone Ethernet segment of the ticket_central router. The NTP server has an IP address of 206.191.241.45. Configure the ticket_central router to synchronize to this server.

- Configure the metallica and pearl_jam routers to form a peer association with the ticket_central router.

- All routers are located in the United States–Pacific time zone, which is an 8-hour offset from Greenwich Mean time or UTC. Ensure that this is the time zone for the network, and use the name of PAC for a description.

- (Optional) Prevent any NTP broadcast from being broadcast onto the Ethernet segments of the metallica and pearl_jam routers.

Lab Objectives

- Configure the network as depicted in Figure 17-8. Use EIGRP as the routing protocol, with an autonomous System ID of 2001.

- Configure the ticket_central router as an NTP master, and source its clock from 206.191.241.45, the NTP server.

- Configure the metallica and pearl_jam routers to form a peer association with the ticket_central router.
- The stratum level should be 5 at the remote sites.

Equipment Needed

- Three Cisco routers. Two routers should be connected through V.35 back-to-back cables to the serial ports of the ticket_central router.
- Three LAN segments, provided through hubs or switches.
- An NTP server located on the Ethernet segment of the ticket_central router. Use the shareware site download.com to download an NTP server for the lab. The NTP server that we used is called TARDIS 2000 and is available at this site. Any NTP server or another router could also serve this function.

Physical Layout and Prestaging

- Connect the hubs and serial cables to the routers, as shown in Figure 17-8. Use HDLC as the WAN protocol.
- Connect the three Ethernet hubs to the routers to form three LAN segments, as shown in Figure 17-8.
- Configure EIGRP across the network, use 2001 as the Autonomous System ID.
- Add and configure the NTP server on the Ethernet segment of the ticket_central router. Enable NTP broadcast, and set the stratum level to 3 on the software. The IP address of the server is 206.191.241.45.

Figure 17-8 *NTP Peer Association Configuration*

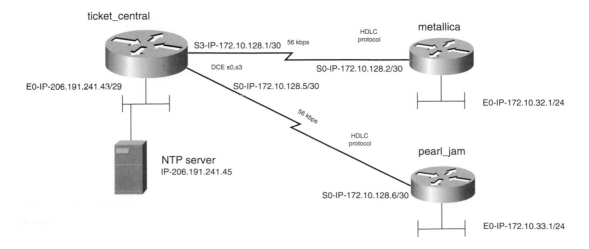

Lab 35: Configuring NTP Servers, Clients, and Peer Associations—Part II

Lab Walkthrough

After completing the physical installation of the LAN and WAN segments, you should establish IP connectivity among all the routers. Before trying to configure NTP, be sure to perform source **ping**s from each router's Ethernet to verify end-to-end connectivity.

Beginning with the ticket_central router, configure the IP address of the E0 port and the two serial ports. This end is the DCE side of the serial link, so a **clock rate** command is needed; use the **clock rate 56000** command on the S0 and S3 interfaces. The WAN protocol is HDLC, so you will not need to configure an encapsulation type on this link.

On the metallica and pearl_jam routers, you need to configure an IP address on the E0 ports and the S0 ports. When the IP addresses are configured and the links are brought up, you should be able to **ping** other routers' serial ports.

When the interfaces are up, configure EIGRP on all the routers, and use the autonomous System ID of 2001. Example 17-26 lists the relevant IP configuration for the all the routers in the lab.

Example 17-26 *Relevant IP Configuration for the Routers in This Lab*

```
hostname ticket_central
!
interface Ethernet0
 ip address 206.191.241.43 255.255.255.248
!
interface Serial0
 ip address 172.10.128.1 255.255.255.252
 no fair-queue
 clockrate 56000
!
<<<text omitted>>>
!
interface Serial3
 ip address 172.10.128.5 255.255.255.252
 clockrate 56000
!
<<<text omitted>>>
!
router eigrp 2001
 network 206.191.241.0
 network 172.10.0.0
```

continues

Example 17-26 *Relevant IP Configuration for the Routers in This Lab (Continued)*

```
hostname pearl_jam
!
interface Ethernet0
 ip address 172.10.33.1 255.255.255.0
!
interface Serial0
 ip address 172.10.128.6 255.255.255.252
 no ip directed-broadcast
 no ip mroute-cache
 no fair-queue
!
<<<text omitted>>>
!
router eigrp 2001
 network 172.10.0.0
```
```
hostname metallica
!
interface Ethernet0
 ip address 172.10.32.1 255.255.255.0
!
interface Serial0
 ip address 172.10.128.2 255.255.255.252
 no ip directed-broadcast
 no ip mroute-cache
 no fair-queue
!
<<<text omitted>>>
!
router eigrp 2001
 network 172.10.0.0
!
```

To configure NTP on the ticket_central router, you must configure it as a both a client and a master. First, use the **ntp server 206.191.241.45** command to point to the NTP server off its E0 port. At this time, you can also configure this router as an NTP master. To accomplish this, use the **ntp master** command. There is no need to add a stratum because you want to preserve the stratum number that the NTP server broadcasts. The last step is to set the time zone to Pacific time, with an 8-hour offset. This is done by using the **clock timezone PAC –8** command. Example 17-27 lists the NTP configuration of the ticket_central router.

Example 17-27 *NTP Configuration of ticket_central*

```
ticket_central(config)#clock timezone PAC -8
ticket_central(config)#ntp server 206.191.241.45
ticket_central(config)#ntp master
```

Check the status of NTP by using the **show ntp status** command. Look for the clock to be synchronized; it should have a reference clock of 206.191.241.45.

Finally, you can configure the NTP peer associations on the metallica and pearl_jam routers. Use the **ntp peer 172.10.128.1** and **ntp peer 172.10.128.5** commands, respectively, on these routers. Use the same **clock timezone PAC –8** command to set the time zone to Pacific time.

Use the **show ntp status** and **show ntp associations** commands on the remote routers to verify NTP synchronization. Example 17-28 lists the output of these commands on the metallica router.

Example 17-28 *Verifying NTP Synchronization*

```
metallica#show ntp status
Clock is synchronized, stratum 5, reference is 172.10.128.1
nominal freq is 250.0000 Hz, actual freq is 250.0010 Hz, precision is 2**19
reference time is BD1D1551.469209A4 (21:17:05.275 PAC Sun Jul 16 2000)
clock offset is -10.3164 msec, root delay is 34.47 msec
root dispersion is 70.31 msec, peer dispersion is 3.02 msec
metallica#
metallica#show ntp associations

      address         ref clock     st  when  poll reach  delay  offset    disp
*~172.10.128.1    206.191.241.45     4    39    64   377   30.3  -10.32     3.9
 * master (synced), # master (unsynced), + selected, - candidate, ~ configured
metallica#
```

Notice that the reference clock in the **show ntp associations** command is that of your original NTP server, 206.191.241.45. The stratum of 5 indicates that the stratum is being passed and incremented from the original NTP server.

The optional part of this exercise consists of preventing NTP broadcasts on the Ethernet segments of the remote routers. To disable NTP broadcasts of any interface on a router, use the **ntp disable** command under the interface that you want to disable the broadcast from entering. Example 17-29 lists the configurations of the metallica and pearl_jam routers.

Example 17-29 *Configurations of the metallica and pearl_jam Routers*

```
hostname metallica
!
clock timezone PAC -8
!
interface Ethernet0
ip address 172.10.32.1 255.255.255.0
```

continues

Example 17-29 *Configurations of the metallica and pearl_jam Routers (Continued)*

```
 ntp disable
!
interface Serial0
 ip address 172.10.128.2 255.255.255.252
 no ip directed-broadcast
 no ip mroute-cache
 no fair-queue
!
<<<text omitted>>>
!
router eigrp 2001
 network 172.10.0.0
!
<<<text omitted>>>
!
ntp clock-period 17179749
ntp peer 172.10.128.1


hostname pearl_jam
!
!
clock timezone PAC -8
!
interface Ethernet0
 ip address 172.10.33.1 255.255.255.0
 ntp disable
!
interface Serial0
 ip address 172.10.128.6 255.255.255.252
 no fair-queue
!
<<<text omitted>>>
!
router eigrp 2001
 network 172.10.0.0
!
<<<text omitted>>>
!
ntp clock-period 17179636
ntp peer 172.10.128.5
```

PART VIII

CCIE Preparation and Self-Assessment

CHAPTER 18

The CCIE Practical Exam: Preparation and CCIE Practice Labs

"There are no shortcuts to success, and don't waste time looking them."

These words come from one of my personal heroes, retired General Colin Powell. His words of advice ring true for soldiers as well as anyone striving to become a CCIE. There exists no single source of CCIE knowledge, no all-in-one book, including this text, that will get you into the ranks of the CCIEs. And as Powell's words echo, "don't waste time looking for them." At the time of this writing, September 2001, Cisco states that there are 6678 active CCIEs in the world. When you compare this number to how Cisco predominates the market, the ranks of the CCIEs still remain very slim.

The CCIE program is constantly changing to reflect current market trends. In 1997, all the tests were made standard. In 1999, Cisco offered more then the core "routing and switching" exam. You could specialize in WAN switching, or SNA and others. These specialization certifications also have changed in recent years. In 2000, voice and ATM where introduced, whereas years before that, switches were emerging in the lab. In 2001, the test moved from a two-day, 16-hour test to a one-day, 8 1/2-hour test. With all the changes the CCIE practical/lab has gone through, one thing does remain the same: Over time, it constantly gets harder. For instance, when I became a CCIE, I did not have to know voice, Token Ring switching, or ATM. This is precisely why there is no single source for CCIE information: The test is and will be ever-changing.

The best place to find the most current information about the CCIE program is on the Web at www.cisco.com/go/ccie.

The New One-Day CCIE Lab Exam

I was fortunate enough to talk to Lorne Braddock Sr., the manager of the CCIE program, about the move from a two-day test to a one-day test. Like many CCIEs, I had a knee-jerk reaction to the move. I was aware of the huge backload that Cisco was experiencing with people waiting to get into the lab; in some cases, the waiting list was approaching a year long. Many Cisco partners required people to get certified to retain or gain a preferred partner status. For many Cisco partners, the revenue difference between a gold and silver partnership is in the millions. Another problem for Cisco and its customers was the difficulty in scheduling a two-day exam that you can get sent home early on. This not only costs time and money to Cisco's customers, but it also leaves many open lab slots.

Moving to a one-day, 8 1/2-hour test resolved many of these problems, but the question remained—what do you cut? The program decided to enhance the Layer 1 or physical aspect of the written test. The physical portion of the lab exam was a rather "technically" small portion of the lab exam, but it did consume some time. Another portion of the exam that could be cut was the troubleshooting portion. The reality is that if you spent the last 8 1/2-hours successfully configuring this very difficult exam, you are not going to get stumped when someone changes the router password or an IP address. I personally know a lot of CCIEs, and of those who have failed the exam, no one has ever failed the troubleshooting portion. Therefore, the four hours of troubleshooting also was cut from the lab exam.

In a nutshell, Cisco made the written portion of the CCIE exam more difficult because it deals with more physical layer topics. The lab exam now is a one-day, 8 1/2-hour exam in which time will be critical factor.

How Do I Become a CCIE?

The first step with any serious undertaking is to take a hard, honest assessment of your current skills. Know your strengths and acknowledge your weaknesses. Cisco has specifically designed the CCIE practical exam to weed out candidates with little "hands-on" or "field" experience. When you take your personal assessment, be very honest with past experience. This will help you identify the areas that you need to focus on. For instance, many people (unless they have worked with SNA) have little field experience in DLSw. Modeling DLSw in the lab will give you the valuable experience that you need for the practical exam.

The second step is to dedicate and commit yourself to passing the exam. Plan to commit yourself to one to three years of intense training to become certified. You must be willing to read a lot of books and spend months in the lab. You must take your current understanding of topologies and protocols to the next level. You won't be "memorizing" how Spanning Tree works, but you will be "understanding" how and why it needs to work. Anything short of very serious preparation will leave you short when test day arrives.

Perhaps the most critical part of your studies will be the last two to three months. By this time, you should have all of your "formal" or "classroom" education out of the way, and you should be applying it in the lab. You should have read most of your books, and you will be focusing on the advanced elements of the technologies that you are working with. During the last two months, spend as much time in the lab configuring as many different network scenarios as you can think of. Read through all the configuration guides and browse the CD. Make yourself aware of the ways to tune each protocol or feature set. This also will help you become familiar with the configuration guides and CD; they will be your only source of information during the lab exam. You will have this information available; however, the new test is very time-intensive. If you have to look up commands and study manuals, chances are good that you will run out of time during the practical exam.

Finally, if you do come up short on test day, don't give up. Yes, people have passed the lab on the first try, but a majority of *us* had to come back on another day. Hang in there, and, remember, "Nothing worthwhile ever comes easy."

Good luck.

CCIE: Recommended Study Resources and Topics Outline

This book serves as only one of many that you will have to read during your studies. The following books are a brief list of the ones that will be of great value during your studies; another list is provided on the CCIE page, mentioned previously:

Stevens: *TCP/IP Illustrated*
Comer: *Internetworking with TCP/IP*
Perlman: *Interconnections, Second Edition: Bridges, Routers, Switches, and Internetworking Protocols*
Doyle: *Routing TCP/IP,* Volume I and II
Halabi: *Internetwork Routing Architectures*
Hamilton/Clark: *Cisco LAN Switching*
Caslow, Bruce: *Bridges, Routers, and Switches*
Cisco Press: *CCIE Network Design and Case Studies*
Diker-Pildush: *Cisco ATM Solutions*

Table 18-1 provides a rough outline (but by no means a complete list) of CCIE study topics. It offers a solid starting point for a list of topics that the CCIE candidate should become *very* familiar with.

Table 18-1 *CCIE Study Topic Outline*

Main Topic	Subtopics
Frame Relay	Frame Relay switching
	Frame Relay subinterfaces
	Point-to-point links and multipoint links
	Frame Relay map statements: bridge, LLC, DLSw and other keywords
	RFC 1490 encapsulation
	Bridging over Frame
	Voice over Frame
	PPP over Frame
	Frame Relay ARP and Inverse ARP operation
	Frame Relay traffic shaping
HDLC	Compression types
PPP	PPP authentication: PAP/CHAP
	PPP callback
	PPP multilink
	DDR techniques
	Compression types
	IPCP
ISDN	Dialer maps/DDR
	Running every protocol over ISDN: IPX, IP, and so on
	How to handle routing protocols over ISDN, such as EIGRP, OSPF, IGRP, and others
	Snapshot routing
	Dialer watch
	Demand circuits
	Complex IPX and IP ACLs to control dialing

Table 18-1   *CCIE Study Topic Outline (Continued)*

Main Topic	Subtopics
BGP	Route reflectors
	Use of loopbacks
	Synchronization rule
	IBGP versus EBGP
	Route maps and route redistribution
	AS path filters
	BGP path selection process and path manipulation: MED, local preference, weight, and so on
	BGP confederations
	BGP communities
	Advertising supernets, summarization
	BGP maps
OSPF	Redistribution to and from every routing protocol
	Summarization with summary address and area range statements
	OSPF over Frame and X.25
	OSPF demand circuits
	Route maps and route filters with OSPF
	OSPF costs and administrative distance
	Stub areas, NSS areas, and backbone areas
	Authentication: Type I and Type II
	Designated router and BDR selection: **priority** command
	Default route propagation

continues

Table 18-1 *CCIE Study Topic Outline (Continued)*

Main Topic	Subtopics
EIGRP	EIGRP for IP and IPX
	Redistribution to and from every routing protocol
	Summarization
	Route maps and route filters with EIGRP
	MD5 authentication
	EIGRP over ISDN
	Split-horizon issues with multipoint networks
	Administrative distance
IGRP	Redistribution to and from every routing protocol
	Snapshot routing/IGRP over ISDN
	Split-horizon issues with multipoint networks
	Default networks
	Administrative distance
	Issues from lack of VLSM support
RIP	Redistribution to and from every routing protocol
	Snapshot routing/RIP over ISDN
	Split-horizon issues with multipoint networks
	RIP Version 1, issues from lack of VLSM support
	RIP Version 2
IPX	IPX routing protocols: NLSP/RIP/EIGRP
	Static SAPs, SAP filtering and propagation
	Network filtering
	Redistribution between NLSP, RIP, and EIGRP
	ACLs to control IPX dialing over ISDN
	Snapshot routing/IPX over ISDN
	Tunneling IPX
	Split-horizon issues with multipoint networks
	SPX and watchdog spoof
	IPX frame types, such as type 20 frames

Table 18-1   *CCIE Study Topic Outline (Continued)*

Main Topic	Subtopics
DLSw	TCP, FST, direct, and Frame Relay peers
	Backup peers
	Promiscuous peers
	Border peers and peer groups
	Costed peers
	Explorer control and LLC control with DLSw LSAP filters
Bridging	Transparent bridging
	Spanning Tree control
	Bridging over Frame Relay
	Source-route bridging
	Remote source-route bridging
	Translational bridging
	Explorer control and flooding
	LSAP filters
	Integrated routing and bridging
	Default gateways
Controlling routing and traffic	Standard access lists
	Extended access lists
	Named access lists
	Dynamic and reflective access lists
	Route maps and policy routing
	Propagating default routes
Queuing	Weighted fair queuing
	Priority queuing
	Custom queuing
	Generic and Frame Relay traffic shaping
	RSVP, WRED basic configurations

continues

Table 18-1 *CCIE Study Topic Outline (Continued)*

Main Topic	Subtopics
General Cisco IOS Software topics	Access server configuration
	Jump register configuration
	Password recovery for Catalyst switches and routers
	Configuration through TFTP and autoinstall
	Exec control: timeouts, privilege levels, and so on
	Security
	Logging
Cisco IOS Software features	NAT: Dynamic, static, and pooled
	NTP: NTP authentication and stratum settings
	DNS
	HSRP: tracking and priority
	IRDP
	Snapshot routing
	Dialer watch
	Mobile IP
	ARP manipulation
	SNMP: read/write keys, set and get traps
	UDP flooding: IP Forward command
	GRE tunneling
Catalyst switches	Cat 55*xx* VLAN creation
	Cat 39*xx* VLAN creation
	Cat 29*xx* VLAN creation
	VTP domains
	Spanning Tree control
	Port security and IP access control
	ISL, 802.1Q trunking
	VLAN propagation and control over trunks
	Routing between VLANs
	Multicast routing

Table 18-1   *CCIE Study Topic Outline (Continued)*

Main Topic	Subtopics
Multicast routing	Joining multicast groups
	Sparse- and dense-mode operation
ATM	Classical IP, routing over ATM
	VPI, VCD, and VCI definition
	ARP control
	PVC mapping
Voice	Voice over IP
	Voice over Frame
	Voice over ATM
	FXO and FXS and E&M circuits
	H.323
VPN	Encryption types
	IPSec-protected BGR tunnels
	IPSec transport and tunnel mode
	Transform sets, crypto maps
	"Key" authentication
Removed topics (removed in 2)	ATM LANE
	AppleTalk
	LAT
	DECnet
	Apollo
	Banyan VINES
	ISO CLNS
	XNS
	X.25

The practice labs are designed to give you an accurate representation of what a CCIE Lab Exam actually looks like. Many topics on the practice labs are not covered in this volume. As mentioned previously, one book—not even one this size—can possibly cover all the topics on the CCIE exam, at least in any depth. Topics such as BGP, IPX, multicast, and IPSec will be covered in *CCIE Practical Studies,* Volume II.

The labs are divided into two parts and are timed labs. Each lab has different hardware requirements and might require some prestaging to make the labs operate properly. As with the real lab, the answers are not provided. The solutions are posted on Cisco Press Web site at www.ciscopress.com/1587200023. We are doing this to encourage you to actually practice the labs and to exhaust all possible means of designing a solution before having to look at the answers. You should allow yourself 8 1/2 hours to complete each lab.

CCIE Practice Lab: "Skynet"

Equipment List

- One Frame Relay switch: four serial ports
- One access server/backbone router: eight asynchronous interfaces, one Ethernet port
- Two lab routers: one Ethernet, two serial interfaces
- Three lab routers: one Token Ring, two serial interfaces
- One lab router: two Ethernet ports, one Token Ring port
- Three Ethernet hubs, four Token Ring hubs/MAUs
- The hubs and MAUs may be substituted for a Catalyst 5000 with the appropriate number of ports. This lab is designed to be performed without any Catalyst switches. It is the only lab that does not require a switch.

Prestaging: Frame Switch Configuration

Configure the Frame Relay switch with the PVCs as depicted in Figure 18-1; do not time yourself on this portion of the lab. Example 18-1 lists the configuration for the Frame Relay switch.

Example 18-1 *Frame Relay Switch Configuration*

```
hostname frame_switch
!
frame-relay switching
!
<<<text omitted>>>
!
interface Serial0
 no ip address
 encapsulation frame-relay
 no fair-queue
 clockrate 148000
 frame-relay lmi-type ansi
 frame-relay intf-type dce
 frame-relay route 121 interface Serial1 120
 frame-relay route 152 interface Serial5 151
!
interface Serial1
 no ip address
 encapsulation frame-relay
 clockrate 148000
 frame-relay lmi-type ansi
 frame-relay intf-type dce
```

continues

Example 18-1 *Frame Relay Switch Configuration (Continued)*

```
 frame-relay route 110 interface Serial5 111
 frame-relay route 120 interface Serial0 121
 frame-relay route 130 interface Serial3 131
!
interface Serial3
 no ip address
 encapsulation frame-relay
 clockrate 64000
 frame-relay lmi-type ansi
 frame-relay intf-type dce
 frame-relay route 131 interface Serial1 130
!
interface Serial5
 no ip address
 encapsulation frame-relay
 clockrate 64000
 frame-relay lmi-type ansi
 frame-relay intf-type dce
 frame-relay route 111 interface Serial1 110
 frame-relay route 151 interface Serial0 152
!
```

Figure 18-1 *Frame Relay Switch Configuration*

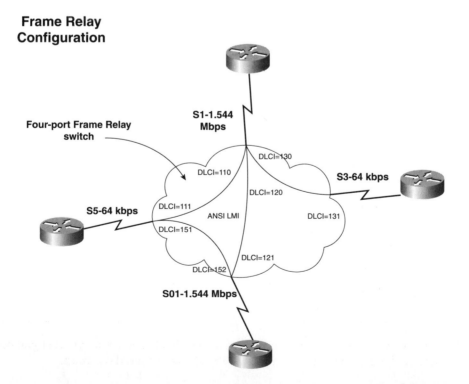

Frame Relay Configuration

Four-port Frame Relay switch

S1-1.544 Mbps

S3-64 kbps

S5-64 kbps

DLCI=110
DLCI=111
DLCI=151
DLCI=130
DLCI=120
DLCI=131
DLCI=121
DLCI=152
ANSI LMI

S01-1.544 Mbps

Prestaging: Backbone Router Configuration

Configure R7 as a backbone router. Configure R7 as an external BGP peer to R2's IP address of 192.128.128.2/24. Use 2010 as the Autonomous System ID for this router. Configure loopback interfaces on this router with the following addresses:

128.200.1.1/24
128.201.1.1/24
128.202.1.1/24

Use the **network** command to circulate the networks. Example 18-2 illustrates the configuration of the backbone router R7.

Example 18-2 *Backbone Router Configuration*

```
hostname r7_backbone_router
!
interface Loopback20
 ip address 128.200.1.1 255.255.255.0
!
interface Loopback21
ip address 128.201.1.1 255.255.255.0
!
interface Loopback22
ip address 128.202.1.1 255.255.255.0
!
interface Ethernet1
 description place in vlan 3 - backbone 1
 ip address 192.128.128.1 255.255.255.0
 media-type 10BaseT
 ip rip send version 2
 ip rip receive version 2
!
 router rip
 version 2
 no auto-summary
 network 192.128.128.0
 network 128.200.0.0
 network 128.201.0.0
 network 128.202.0.0
!
router bgp 2010
 no synchronization
 network 192.128.128.0
 network 128.200.0.0
 network 128.201.0.0
 network 128.202.0.0
 neighbor 192.128.128.2 remote-as 2001
 neighbor 192.128.128.2 ebgp-multihop 10
!
```

The following portion of the lab is timed, and it should begin after the configuration and physical installation of the Frame Relay switch and the backbone router.

Timed Portion

Lab Rules

- No static routes or floating static routes are used unless specifically stated.

- Follow the instructions exactly. Be careful to propagate routes only where and when instructed. Use the PVCs only as directed by the instructions.

- Primary configurations might need to be modified for Part II configurations to work. Proceed to Part II only when you are finished with the primary configurations.

- You can use the configuration guides and the Cisco Documentation CD-ROM for your only reference material.

- You have 8 1/2 hours to complete the lab. Do not talk to anyone during this phase.

- It is recommended that you read the entire lab before beginning.

- Make an accurate and precise network illustration.

- Use Figure 18-2 as a reference for the physical layout of the lab.

Section I: Basic IP Configuration

1 Access server: Configure the access server/router so that all the routers and the switches can be accessed through reverse Telnet. Password-protect all routers and switches with the password cisco.

2 IP address assignment: Assign an IP addresses to all physical interfaces as denoted in Figure 18-2. Use the major network of 140.100.x.x on all interfaces. Use a 24-bit mask on all interfaces except for the following:

R1: Allow for 30 host addresses on the Token Ring interface. Use a 30-bit address on the PPP and Frame link between R1 and R4.

R2: Use an IP address of 192.128.128.2/24 on the Ethernet interface. Assign a 30-bit subnet to the HDLC link between R2/R5.

R3: Configure the IPX network DEAD on a loopback interface.

R4: Use a 27-bit mask on the Token Ring interface. Configure 10 loopback interfaces; use the IP addresses of 199.199.1.1/24 to 199.199.10.1/24.

R5: Configure the Token Ring to support 14 hosts. Configure three loopback addresses, with the IP addresses of 151.100.1.1/24, 151.101.1.1/24, and 172.16.1.1/24. Assign a 30-bit subnet to the HDLC link between R2/R5.

R6: Assign the IP address of 10.10.10.1/24 to the Ethernet interface on VLAN 2.

Full IP and IPX connectivity to all Ethernet, Token Ring, and loopback interfaces will be expected unless noted.

3 Document the network thoroughly; include all OSPF areas, IP/IPX address, IPX networks, and so on.

Figure 18-2 *Network Diagram for "Skynet"*

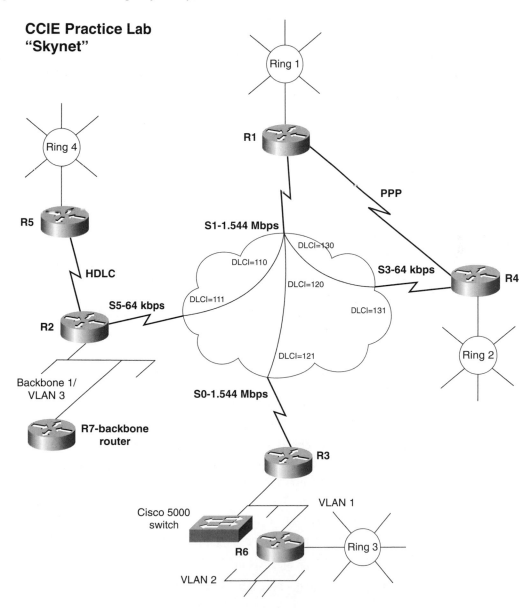

Section II: Catalyst/LAN Configuration

1 Configure the VLANs as depicted in Figure 18-2. Configure the Token Ring segments, and connect R2 to the backbone routers Ethernet segment.

Section III: OSPF and Frame Relay Configuration

1 Configure the Frame Relay network as shown in Figure 18-2. You may use subinterfaces only on R1. Use only the DLCIs shown in the diagram to route traffic. Traffic from R2 to R3 should all go through R1.

2 R1, R2, and R3 should share the same IP subnet. Configure OSPF Area 0 between the routers; do not use the **ip ospf network** command when configuring OSPF. Configure the Frame link between R1 and R4 to also be in OSPF Area 0.

3 Configure the PPP link between R1 and R4 to be in OSPF Area 10. Ring 2 is in OSPF Area 20. This link should become active only upon a loss of Frame service.

4 Change the OSPF hello time on the serial link of R3 so that hellos are broadcast every 60 seconds.

5 Advertise the 10 loopback addresses on R4, 199.199.1.1 to 199.199.10.1, through OSPF without assigning an area to them.

Section IV: Routing Protocols and Redistribution

1 Configure IGRP on VLAN 1 on R3/R6, and Ring 3 on R6 only. Do not allow IGRP broadcast onto VLAN 2.

2 Configure RIP 2 on R2 going to the backbone router. Configure R2 to send and receive only version II updates to and from the backbone router.

3 Prevent the subnet of the Token Ring network on R4 from reaching R7.

4 Configure EIGRP on the HDLC link between R2/R5. Configure EIGRP on Ring 4 of R5. Use 2020 as the Autonomous System ID.

5 Summarize the loopback networks of 151.100.1.1 and 151.101.1.1 into one advertisement. Ensure that R6 can **ping** all EIGRP networks, without adding a static route.

Section V: IPX Configuration

1 Configure IPX NLSP on R5's Ring 4 and on R2.

2 Configure IPX RIP/SAP on all LAN interfaces only.

3 Configure IPX EIGRP on the Frame Relay WAN links.

4 Apply a static SAP to R6 that is three hops away out its Token Ring interface. The SAP offers print services and should be configured as such.

5 Prevent R3 from propagating this SAP across the WAN.

6 R3 should have a loopback interface configured with the IPX network DEAD; prevent only R4 from receiving this route.

Section VI: Bridging

1 Transparently bridge SNA from VLAN 1 to VLAN 3/Backbone 1, across the Frame Relay network.

2 Force the selection of ROOT bridge to go to R1.

Section VII: MISC IOS Configuration

1 Configure CHAP authentication on the PPP link between R1 and R4. Use ccie as the password.

2 Apply an inbound filter to R5, filtering just the even subnets from the loopback range 199.199.1.1 to 199.199.10.1 on R4.

3 Apply an inbound traffic filter to R6 so that only routing protocols, **ping**s, and WWW can enter the router and have access to the WWW hosts on Ring 3 and VLAN 2.

4 The user skynet resides on R1. Allow this user access to all IP services on Ring 3 and VLAN 2. This access should be valid for only 10 minutes.

Part II

Section VIII: BGP Configuration

1 R1, R2, and R3 are in autonomous system 2001. R5 is in autonomous system 65001. Configure an EBGP peer from R2 to 192.128.128.1, which is in autonomous system 2010. Configure an EBGP peer from R5 to R2.

2 Configure IBGP from R2 to R1 and R1 to R3; do not configure a peer R2 to R3. Ensure that all BGP routers are receiving the routes 128.20x.1.0 from the backbone router.

3 Have R5 advertise the supernet of 128.200.0.0 into the rest of the lab network, R1, R2, R3, R4, R6, R7; suppress all other subnets of 128.200.0.0.

4 Have R5 advertise the 172.16.1.0/24 subnet via BGP. Advertise the routes with a metric of 75.

5 When the backbone router receives the 172.16.1.0 route, it should appear to come from AS 2011.

6 Change the BGP hello timer on R5 to be 5 minutes.

Section IX: DLSw Configuration

1 Configure a DLSw TCP peer between Ring 2 and Ring 3.

2 Configure a DLSw FST peer between Ring 1 and Ring 4.

3 Configure an additional peer between R1 and R4 so that full NetBIOS reachability will occur from Ring 3 to Ring 4, while minimizing explorer traffic.

4 Configure a TCP peer from Ring 2 to Ring 1; allow this peer to always stay up and active, even upon a loss of Frame Relay service.

5 Configure the peer of R5 to forward only frames destined toward the MAC address 3745.0001.0101.

Section X: Miscellaneous Cisco IOS Software Features

1 The 10's network on VLAN 2 of R6 should not be advertised by a routing protocol. Configure the users of this VLAN so that they can reach the entire network, without changing the IP address or advertising the subnet 10.10.10.0.

2 Configure multicast routing on R1, R3, and R6. R6 will join the multicast group of 224.10.10.10. R6 should respond to **ping**s from R3 and R1.

CCIE Practice Lab: "Darth Reid"

Equipment List

- One Frame switch: four serial ports
- One access server: eight asynchronous interfaces, one Ethernet port
- One backbone router: two Ethernet ports
- Two lab routers: one Ethernet, one ISDN, one serial interface
- Two lab routers: one Ethernet, one Token Ring, one serial interface
- Catalyst 5000 switch
- Catalyst 3900 switch

Prestaging: Frame Switch Configuration

Configure the Frame Relay switch with the PVCs as depicted in Figure 18-3; do not time yourself on this portion of the lab. Example 18-3 lists the configuration for the Frame Relay switch.

Figure 18-3 *Frame Relay Switch Configuration*

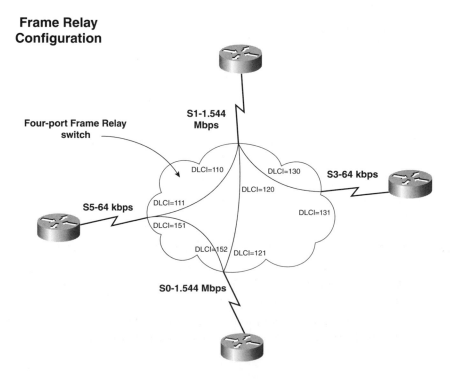

Example 18-3 *Frame Relay Switch Configuration*

```
hostname frame_switch
!
frame-relay switching
!
<<<text omitted>>>
!
interface Serial0
 no ip address
 encapsulation frame-relay
 no fair-queue
 clockrate 148000
 frame-relay lmi-type cisco
 frame-relay intf-type dce
 frame-relay route 121 interface Serial1 120
 frame-relay route 152 interface Serial5 151
!
interface Serial1
 no ip address
 encapsulation frame-relay
 clockrate 148000
 frame-relay lmi-type cisco
 frame-relay intf-type dce
 frame-relay route 110 interface Serial5 111
 frame-relay route 120 interface Serial0 121
 frame-relay route 130 interface Serial3 131
!
interface Serial3
 no ip address
 encapsulation frame-relay
 clockrate 64000
 frame-relay lmi-type ansi
 frame-relay intf-type dce
 frame-relay route 131 interface Serial1 130
!
interface Serial5
 no ip address
 encapsulation frame-relay
 clockrate 64000
 frame-relay intf-type dce
 frame-relay route 111 interface Serial1 110
 frame-relay route 151 interface Serial0 152
!
```

Prestaging: Backbone Router Configuration

Configure R6 as a backbone router. Configure R6 as an external BGP peer to R1's IP address of 160.100.2.1 and R7's IP address of 160.100.1.1. Use 2001 as the Autonomous

System ID for this router. Configure loopback interfaces on this router with the following addresses:

160.100.100.1/24
197.192.100.1/24
197.192.101.1/24
197.192.102.1/24.

Use the **network** command to circulate the networks. Example 18-4 illustrates the configuration of the backbone router R6.

Example 18-4 *Backbone Router Configuration*

```
hostname r6_backbone_router
!
interface Loopback20
 ip address 192.190.100.1 255.255.255.0
!
interface Loopback21
 ip address 192.190.101.1 255.255.255.0
!
interface Loopback22
 ip address 192.190.102.1 255.255.255.0
!
interface Loopback23
 ip address 160.100.100.1 255.255.255.0
!
interface Loopback24
 ip address 160.100.128.1 255.255.255.0
!
interface Loopback25
 ip address 160.100.129.1 255.255.255.0
!
interface Loopback26
 ip address 160.100.130.1 255.255.255.0
!
interface Ethernet1
description place on vlan 20 - Backbone 1
 ip address 160.100.2.254 255.255.255.0
 media-type 10BaseT
!
interface Ethernet2
description place on vlan 10 - Backbone 2
 ip address 160.100.1.254 255.255.255.0
 media-type 10BaseT
!
router rip
 passive-interface Ethernet1
 network 160.100.0.0
```

continues

Example 18-4 *Backbone Router Configuration*

```
 network 192.190.100.0
 network 192.190.101.0
 network 192.190.102.0
!
router bgp 2001
 no synchronization
 network 160.100.100.0 mask 255.255.255.0
 network 160.100.128.0 mask 255.255.255.0
 network 160.100.129.0 mask 255.255.255.0
 network 160.100.130.0 mask 255.255.255.0
 neighbor 160.100.1.1 remote-as 2010
 neighbor 160.100.1.1 ebgp-multihop 10
 neighbor 160.100.2.1 remote-as 2010
 neighbor 160.100.2.1 ebgp-multihop 10
!
 ip route 133.10.0.0 255.255.0.0 160.100.2.1
```

The following portion of the lab is timed and should begin after the configuration and
physical installation of the Frame Relay switch and the backbone router. Do not configure
any other routers at this time.

Timed Portion

Lab Rules

- No static routes or floating static routes are used unless specifically stated.

- Follow the instructions exactly. Be careful to propagate routes only where and when instructed. Use the PVCs only as directed by the instructions.

- Primary configurations might need to be modified for Part II configurations to work. Proceed to Part II only when you are finished with the primary configurations.

- You can use the configuration guides and the Cisco Documentation CD-ROM for your only reference material.

- You have 8 1/2 hours to complete the lab. Do not talk to anyone during this phase.

- It is recommended that you read the entire lab before beginning.

- Make an accurate and precise network illustration.

- Use Figure 18-4 as reference for the physical layout of the lab.

Section I: Basic IP Configuration

1 Access server: Configure the access server/router so that all the routers and the switches can be accessed through reverse Telnet. Password-protect all routers and switches with the password cisco.

2 IP address assignment: Assign an IP addresses to all physical interfaces, as denoted in Figure 18-6. Use the major network of 133.10.*x.x* on all interfaces. Use a 24-bit mask on all interfaces except for the following:

   R2: Use an IP address of 160.100.2.1/24 on the Ethernet interface; make this VLAN 20.

   R4: Use a 28-bit mask on the loopback interface, and use a 26-bit mask on the Ethernet interface.

   R1: Allow for 30 hosts on the loopback interface. Add an additional loopback with the address of 128.200.1.1/24.

   R3: Use a 25-bit mask on the loopback interface. Use an IP address of 160.100.1.1/24 on the Ethernet interface; make this VLAN 10.

   R5: Use a 26-bit mask on the Ethernet interface.

3 Full IP and IPX connectivity to all Ethernet, Token Ring, and loopback interfaces will be expected unless noted.

4 Document the network thoroughly; include all OSPF areas, IP/IPX address, IPX networks, and so on.

Figure 18-4 *Network Diagram for "Darth Reid"*

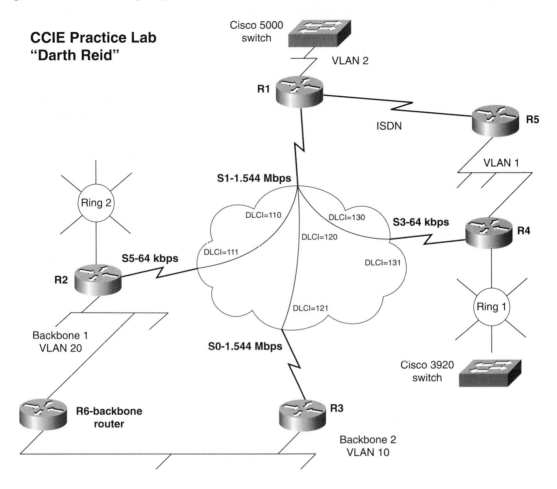

Section II: Catalyst Configuration

1 Connect the R1, R4, and R5 routers to the Catalyst 5000. Connect the two Token Ring routers to the Catalyst 3900 Token Ring switch.

2 Configure the Backbone 1 segment and Backbone 2 segment to be in separate VLANs of your choice.

3 Configure R1 Ethernet as VLAN 2 on the Catalyst 5K. Configure the R4/R5 Ethernet segment as VLAN 1 on the Catalyst 5K. Assign an IP address in VLAN 2 IP range.

4   Configure the Catalyst so that only users on VLAN 1 can access the switch through Telnet. Do not use an access list on any routers to control access to the Catalyst 5K.

5   Configure the switch so that all VLAN 2 traffic can be monitored with a sniffer/analyzer on port 2/10.

6   Configure the MAXAGE of VLAN 2 Spanning Tree 25 seconds.

7   Configure VLAN 2 so that the only device that can be used on its port is R1. If R1 is unplugged and another device is plugged into that port, the catalyst should deactivate the port.

8   Configure the Token Ring switch so that it can be managed and configured through Telnet.

Section III: OSPF and Frame Relay Configuration

1   Configure the Frame Relay network as shown in Figure 18-4. You may use subinterfaces only on R1. Use only the PVCs shown in the diagram to route traffic. Traffic from R2 to R3 should all go through R1.

2   R1, R3, and R4 should share the same IP subnet. Configure OSPF Area 0 between the routers; do not change the **ip ospf network** type when configuring OSPF.

3   Configure R4/R5 Ethernet to be in OSPF Area 30. Configure the R4's Token Ring to be in Area 30. Add a loopback interface on R5 with an IP address of 192.168.1.1/24. Put this address in OSPF Area 50. Prevent the R3 from seeing this route, but ensure that all other routers can.

4   Configure Frame Relay traffic shaping on the PVC between R1 and R2 so that it responds to BECNs. The CIR provided by the carrier is 32 K. The local port speed on R2 is 64 K, while the local port speed of R1 is 1.54 Mb.

Section IV: ISDN Configuration

1   Configure the ISDN interfaces, between R1 and R5, as a part of the OSPF backbone. Configure the router so that only R5 places a call. Be sure that you can ping the local ISDN interfaces before moving on.

2   Configure R5 to place a call only when it detects a topology change in OSPF and if traffic is destined for opposite router. Routes should be passed between R1 and R5.

Section V: Routing Protocols and Redistribution

1   Configure IGRP on the Frame Relay link between R1 and R2. R2's Token Ring and R1's Ethernet also should be in the IGRP domain. Ensure that all OSPF routes can be seen by R2. Ensure that R2 can issue a source **ping** to all configured addresses.

2   Configure EIGRP between R1, VLAN 2 and R4 Ring 1.

3   Configure RIP on R3's Ethernet port connecting to Backbone 1; use 160.100.1.1/24 for the IP address. Ensure that OSPF is not running on this interface. Redistribute RIP into OSPF. R3 should be capable of **ping**ing R2's Token Ring.

4   When RIP is configured properly, you should see routes through RIP on R3. Filter the routes so that only 192.190.102.0/24 will be redistributed into the lab. Do not allow any routes from the lab network to be advertised onto Backbone 1.

5   Add an additional loopback address to R4; use 161.100.1.1/24 as the IP address. Place the loopback into the EIGRP domain. Summarize EIGRP so that the lab network has only one route for both 160.100.1.0 and 161.100.1.0.

6   Configure the Ethernet interface of R2 on Backbone 1 with an IP address 160.100.2.1/24. Do not place the network into IGRP domain with the **network** command, but allow full connectivity to the entire network.

Section VI: BGP

1   Configure BGP on R2 and R3, using an Autonomous System ID of 2010. Configure two EBGP peers to 160.100.1.254 and 160.100.2.254 in AS 2001, yielding two exit points to your AS. Configure BGP on R1 and build an IBGP neighbor to R2 and R3. Ensure that R1 contains multiple routes from AS 2001.

2   Advertise the 128.200.1.0/24 route on R1 through BGP.

3   Configure R2 and R3 so that all incoming BGP routes have a weight of 700.

4   Configure all the routes going to AS 2001 so that AS 2001 will not advertise these routes to any other autonomous systems.

5   Configure the routes coming from AS 2001 to be summarized into 1 route, and then redistribute it into OSPF.

6   Ensure that you can **ping** all BGP routes, including 160.100.100.1, even if R2 or R3's Ethernet interface is down.

Section VII: Miscellaneous Cisco IOS Software Configuration

1   On the Ethernet segment of R1, write a traffic filter blocking data from the following sources: *(Use as few lines as possible.)*

Deny FTF, HTTP from 131.24.194.x

Deny FTF, HTTP from 131.25.194.x

Deny FTF, HTTP from 135.152.1.1

Deny FTF, HTTP from 227.24.194.x

Deny FTF, HTTP from 131.24.195.x

Deny FTF, HTTP from 131.24.196.x

2 Configure R1, R4, and R5 as members of the multicast group 224.10.10.1. Configure R1 and R4 to direct multicast traffic between the two VLANs. You can use any mode of multicast transport that you want.

3 Configure HSRP between R4 and R5. Let R4 serve as the primary default gateway. If R4 loses its frame interface, the default gateway should become R5's Ethernet interface.

Part II

Section VIII: IPX Configuration

1 Configure an IPX network on all interfaces except the loopback interfaces and the backbones. Use IPX EIGRP on the Frame Relay network, and use IPX RIP on all LAN interfaces.

2 Configure a static SAP on R5. The SAP is file services SAP, called FILESERV, and it is two hops away on network 0xBB00. You can use a static route, if needed.

3 Prevent R3 from seeing the SAP FILESERV.

4 Configure IPX over ISDN on R1 and R5. Configure IPX so that routes are passed from R5 to R1 over ISDN.

Section IX: DLSw Configuration

1 Configure a DLSw TCP peer between VLAN 2 and Ring 2. Do not configure a remote peer on R2.

2 Allow only SNA traffic to cross from VLAN 2 headed for Ring 2. Use as few lines as possible in the ACL.

3 A large amount of IP fragmentation is occurring on VLAN 2. Tune DLSw so that the IP fragmentation will not occur as often.

Section X: Bridging

1 Configure remote source-route bridging from Ring 1 to Ring 2. One IBM mainframe resides on each Token Ring. Many retransmissions are occurring on the serial links between R2 and R4. This results in duplicate frames reaching the remote host at the same time as the first frame reaches the remote host. The duplication breaks LLC2, resulting in the loss of sessions between the two IBM mainframes. Prevent this from happing. Your solution should take into account scaling issues as well.

CCIE Practice Lab: "The Lab, the Bad, the Ugly"

Equipment List

- One Frame Relay switch: four serial ports
- One access server: eight asynchronous interfaces, one Ethernet port
- Two lab routers: one Ethernet, two serial interfaces, one ISDN BRI
- Two lab routers: one Token Ring, two serial interfaces
- One lab router: one Ethernet port, two serial interfaces
- Two Token Ring hubs/MAUs
- One Catalyst 5000
- If you have another Catalyst available, it will help simulate the trunk; however, it is not required.

Prestaging: Frame Switch Configuration

Configure the Frame Relay switch with the PVCs as depicted in Figure 18-5; do not time yourself on this portion of the lab. Example 18-5 lists the configuration for the Frame Relay switch.

Example 18-5 *Frame Relay Switch Configuration*

```
hostname frame_switch
!
frame-relay switching
!
<<<text omitted>>>
!
interface Serial0
 no ip address
 encapsulation frame-relay
 no fair-queue
 clockrate 148000
 frame-relay lmi-type ansi
 frame-relay intf-type dce
 frame-relay route 121 interface Serial1 120
 frame-relay route 152 interface Serial5 151
!
interface Serial1
 no ip address
 encapsulation frame-relay
 clockrate 148000
```

continues

Example 18-5 *Frame Relay Switch Configuration (Continued)*

```
 frame-relay lmi-type ansi
 frame-relay intf-type dce
 frame-relay route 110 interface Serial5 111
 frame-relay route 120 interface Serial0 121
 frame-relay route 130 interface Serial3 131
 frame-relay route 140 interface Serial3 141
 !
interface Serial3
 no ip address
 encapsulation frame-relay
 clockrate 64000
 frame-relay lmi-type ansi
 frame-relay intf-type dce
 frame-relay route 131 interface Serial1 130
 frame-relay route 141 interface Serial1 140
 !
interface Serial5
 no ip address
 encapsulation frame-relay
 clockrate 64000
 frame-relay lmi-type ansi
 frame-relay intf-type dce
 frame-relay route 111 interface Serial1 110

 frame-relay route 151 interface Serial0 152
 !
```

The following portion of the lab is timed, and it should begin after the configuration and physical installation of the Frame switch and the backbone router. Do not configure any other routers at this time.

Figure 18-5 *Frame Relay Switch Configuration*

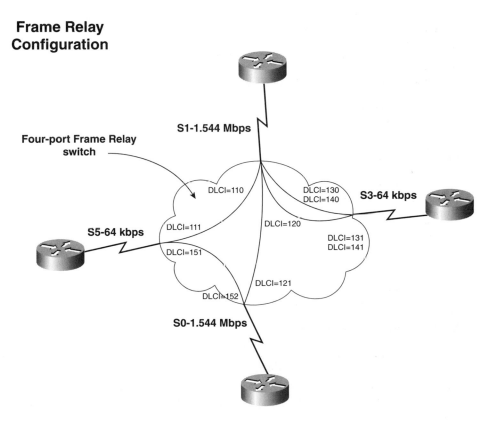

Timed Portion

Lab Rules

- No static routes or floating static routes are used unless specifically stated.

- Follow the instructions exactly. Be careful to propagate routes only where and when instructed. Use the PVCs only as directed by the instructions.

- Primary configurations might need to be modified for Part II configurations to work. Proceed to Part II only when you are finished with the primary configurations.

- You can use the configuration guides and the Cisco Documentation CD-ROM for your only reference material.

- You have 8 1/2 hours to complete the lab. Do not talk to anyone during this phase.

- It is recommended that you read the entire lab before beginning.

- Make an accurate and precise network illustration.

- Use Figure 18-6 as reference for the physical layout of the lab.

Section I: Basic IP Configuration

1 Access server: Configure the access server/router so that all the routers and the switches can be accessed through reverse Telnet. Password-protect all routers and switches with the password cisco.

2 IP address assignment: Assign an IP addresses to all physical interfaces, as denoted in Figure 18-6. Use the major network of 165.10.*x.x* on all interfaces. Use a 24-bit mask on all interfaces except for the following:

R1: Use a 30-bit address on the HDLC link between R1 and R2.

R2: Assign an IP address of 172.16.1.1/24 to a loopback interface.

R4: Assign the IP address of 165.10.10.1 to the Ethernet interface. Assign an IP address of 200.128.1.1/24 to a loopback interface.

R8: Assign the IP address of 10.10.10.1/24 to the Token Ring interface.

3 Full IP and IPX connectivity to all Ethernet, Token Ring, and loopback interfaces will be expected unless noted.

4 Document the network thoroughly; include all OSPF areas, IP/IPX address, IPX networks, and so forth.

Figure 18-6 *Network Diagram for "The Lab, the Bad, the Ugly"*

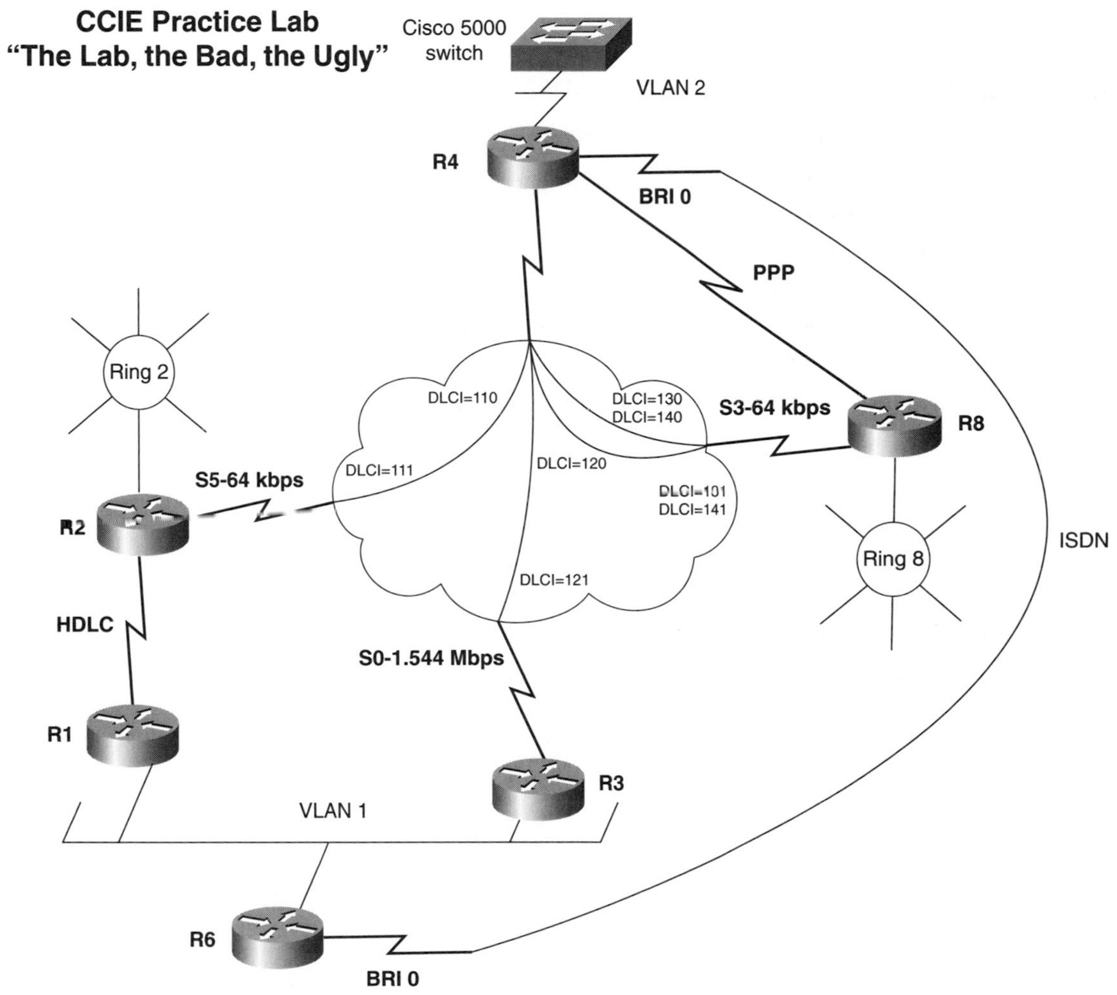

Section II: Catalyst/LAN Configuration

1 Configure the VLANs as depicted in Figure 18-6. R1, R3, and R6 reside on VLAN 1, while VLAN 2 resides on R4. Configure the Token Ring segments at this time.

2 Configure a full-duplex, ISL trunk on port 1/1. Set Spanning Tree so that the root for VLAN 2 is always your switch. You might or might not have another switch to connect to in this lab. This will not impact your configuration.

3 Configure VTP, such that ETP updates will be listened to and forwarded, but not used to update the VLAN database.

Section III: OSPF and Frame Relay Configuration

1 Configure the Frame Relay network as shown on Figure 18-6.

2 R1, R3, and R4 should share the same IP subnet; configure OSPF Area 10 between the routers.

3 Configure VLAN 1 to be in OSPF Area 0. Configure R2's Ring 2 in Area 100. Configure the HDLC link between R1/R2 to be in Area 30.

4 Configure Type II Authentication between R1 and R2. Use lbu as the password.

5 Log any OSPF adjacency changes on the backbone area.

Section IV: Routing Protocols and Redistribution

1 Configure IGRP on VLAN 2 and on the Frame Relay circuit between R4/R8; use 2010 as the Autonomous System ID. Ensure full IP reachability to the OSPF network.

2 Configure the PPP backup link on R4/R8 to become active only upon loss of Frame Relay service. The PPP link should pass all routes; you may not use a static route for this.

3 Prevent the route of the Token Ring network on R8 from reaching R4.

Section V: ISDN Configuration

1 Configure the ISDN interfaces on R4 and R6. Be sure that you can **ping** the R4/R6's ISDN interfaces before moving on.

2 Configure CHAP authentication on the ISDN link. Use ccie as the password.

3 Configure the ISDN interfaces as part of the OSPF domain. Put the interfaces in OSPF Area 20.

Section VI: IPX Configuration

1 Configure IPX on VLAN 1, VLAN 2, Ring 2, and Ring 8.

2 Configure IPX EIGRP on R1, R2, R3, and R6. Create a tunnel from R3 to R4 across the Frame Relay network. Ensure that all the IPX networks are visible on all routers.

3   Configure IPX RIP/SAP between R4 and R8 across the Frame Relay network. Make IPX traffic from R4 to R8 use a separate PVC from IP traffic.

4   Configure IPX SAP on Ring 2, which supports print services. This SAP is called fakeprint and has socket 451. Ensure that R4 can see this SAP.

5   Apply a static SAP to R6 that is three hops away out its Ethernet interface. The SAP offers print services and should be configured as such.

Section VII: Bridging

1   Transparently bridge SNA from VLAN 1 to VLAN 2 across the Frame Relay network. Make R4 the root of the Spanning Tree.

2   Bridge and route IPX on VLAN 2 of R4.

Section VIII: Miscellaneous Cisco IOS Software Configuration

1   Configure custom queuing on R4 with the following guidelines: EIGRP, OSPF, and IPX traffic have a byte size of 500 and need 25 percent of the link. WWW traffic has a byte count of 1412 and will get 10 percent of the link. The byte size for the default queue is 700 and will get 65 percent of the link.

2   The subnet 10.10.10.0/24 on R8 should not be circulated by any routing protocol. There are two hosts on this network, 10.10.10.5 and 10.10.10.10. These hosts need full reachability to the lab network. Allow these two hosts to have the same IP address each time they are translated.

3   A mainframe resides on VLAN 2. It has three IP addresses; 165.10.10.100, 165.10.10.101, and 165.10.10.102. These IP addresses correspond to a single MAC address of 2200.0001.0001. Configure the router, R4, to support forwarding traffic to the single MAC address for all three IP addresses.

4   Apply an outbound traffic filter to R6 Ethernet interface so that only routing protocols, **ping**, and WWW can leave the router.

Part II

Section IX: BGP configuration

1 R1, R3, and R6 are in autonomous system 2001. R2 is in autonomous system 5, and R4 is in autonomous system 2010. Configure an EBGP peer from R2 to R1. Also configure an EBGP from R1 to R4 and from R3 to R4 so that there are two exit points from AS 2001.

2 On R4, assign and advertise the loopback network 200.128.1.0/24 through BGP. On R2, advertise the loopback network of 172.16.1.0/24 through BGP.

3 Configure IBGP from R1 to R3 and from R1 to R6; do not configure a peer from R3 to R6. Ensure that all BGP routers are receiving these routes.

4 Manipulate the AS path throughout the BGP network so that the most desirable route to AS 2010 from AS 5 goes from R2 to R1 to R3 to R4. Make sure that the most desirable path to AS 5 from AS 2010 goes from R4 to R3 to R1 to R2.

Section X: DLSw Configuration

1 Configure a DLSw FST peer between R2, Ring 2, and R8, Ring 8. Filter all NetBIOS names starting with the letters "lab" between Ring 2 and Ring 8.

2 Configure a DLSw TCP peer between R2, Ring 2, and R6, VLAN 1.

3 If R2 loses its peer to R6, have another peer become active, pointing at R1. R2 should not have a "connected" peer and connectivity to R1 unless the peer from R2 to R6 is lost. The peer from R2 to R1 should terminate LLC2 sessions five minutes after TCP connectivity is restored from R2 to R6.

Section XI: Miscellaneous Cisco IOS Software Features

1 Configure static RIF of R8 so that it looks like the following:

Ring8-Bridge7-Ring9-Bridge11-Ring10-host—2200.600E.900E MAC address

2 Configure R2 as an NTP server. Synchronize the clock of R6 to R2. Authenticate NTP with MD5 encryption. Use cisco as the password.

3 Configuring priority queuing on the frame interface of R3. Assign Telnet, EIGRP, and IPX to the high-priority queue, and assign WWW to the low-priority queue. Everything else should be assigned the default.

CCIE Practice Lab: "The Enchilada"

Equipment List

- One Frame Relay switch: five serial ports
- One Access Server: 10 asynchronous interfaces, 1 Ethernet port
- Two Cisco 3810s or 3600s: one Ethernet, one serial interface, one FXS port with telephone headset
- One lab router: one Token Ring, one serial interface, one ISDN BRI
- One lab router: one Ethernet port, one Token Ring, one serial interface, one ISDN BRI
- Two lab routers: one Ethernet port, one ATM interface
- One lab router: one 100-MB Ethernet port, one serial port
- One Catalyst 3900
- One Catalyst 5000
- One ATM switch

Prestaging: Frame Switch Configuration

Configure the Frame Relay switch with the PVCs as depicted in Figure 18-7; do not time yourself on this portion of the lab. Example 18-6 lists the configuration for the Frame switch.

Example 18-6 *Frame Relay Switch Configuration*

```
hostname frame_switch
!
frame-relay switching
!
<<<text omitted>>>
!
interface Serial0
 no ip address
 encapsulation frame-relay
 no fair-queue
 clockrate 148000
 frame-relay lmi-type ansi
 frame-relay intf-type dce
 frame-relay route 121 interface Serial1 120
```

continues

Example 18-6 *Frame Relay Switch Configuration (Continued)*

```
!
interface Serial1
 no ip address
 encapsulation frame-relay
 clockrate 148000
 frame-relay intf-type dce
 frame-relay route 110 interface Serial5 111
 frame-relay route 120 interface Serial0 121
 frame-relay route 130 interface Serial3 131
 frame-relay route 140 interface Serial2 141
!
interface Serial2
 no ip address
 encapsulation frame-relay
 clockrate 64000
 frame-relay intf-type dce
 frame-relay route 141 interface Serial1 140
!
interface Serial3
 no ip address
 encapsulation frame-relay
 clockrate 64000
 frame-relay intf-type dce
 frame-relay route 131 interface Serial1 130
!
interface Serial5
 no ip address
 encapsulation frame-relay
 clockrate 64000
 frame-relay intf-type dce
 frame-relay route 111 interface Serial1 110
!
```

Figure 18-7 *Frame Relay Switch Configuration*

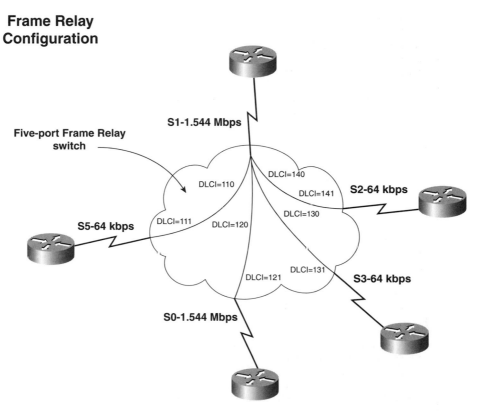

Frame Relay Configuration

Five-port Frame Relay switch

S1-1.544 Mbps

DLCI=140

DLCI=110

DLCI=141   **S2-64 kbps**

DLCI=130

S5-64 kbps   DLCI=111   DLCI=120

DLCI=131

DLCI=121   **S3-64 kbps**

S0-1.544 Mbps

The following portions of the lab are timed, and the lab should begin after the configuration and physical installation of the Frame switch and the backbone router. Do not configure any other routers at this time.

Timed Portion

Lab Rules

- No static routes or floating static routes are used unless specifically stated.

- Follow the instructions exactly. Be careful to propagate routes only where and when instructed. Use the PVCs only as directed by the instructions.

- Primary configurations might need to be modified for Part II configurations to work. Proceed to Part II only when you have finished the primary configurations.

- You can use the configuration guides and the Cisco Documentation CD-ROM for your only reference material.

- You have 8 1/2 hours to complete the lab. Do not talk to anyone during this phase.

- It is recommended that you read the entire lab before beginning.

- Make an accurate and precise network illustration.

- Use Figure 18-8 as a reference for the physical layout of the lab.

Section I: Basic IP Configuration

1 Access server: Configure the access server/router so that all the routers and the switches can be accessed through reverse Telnet. Password-protect all routers and switches with the password cisco.

2 IP address assignment: Assign an IP addresses to all physical interfaces, as denoted in Figure 18-8. Use the major network of 155.100.*x.x* on all interfaces. Use a 24-bit mask on all interfaces except for the following:

   R1: Use a 25-bit address on VLAN 1 between R1 and R5.

   R2: Use a 27-bit address on VLAN 20.

   R3: Use a 28-bit address on VLAN 30.

   R4: Assign Ring 2 an IP address of 10.11.10.0/24.

3 Full IP and IPX connectivity to all Ethernet, Token Ring, and loopback interfaces will be expected unless noted.

4 Document the network thoroughly; include all OSPF areas, IP/IPX address, IPX networks, and so on.

Figure 18-8 *Network Diagram for "The Enchilada"*

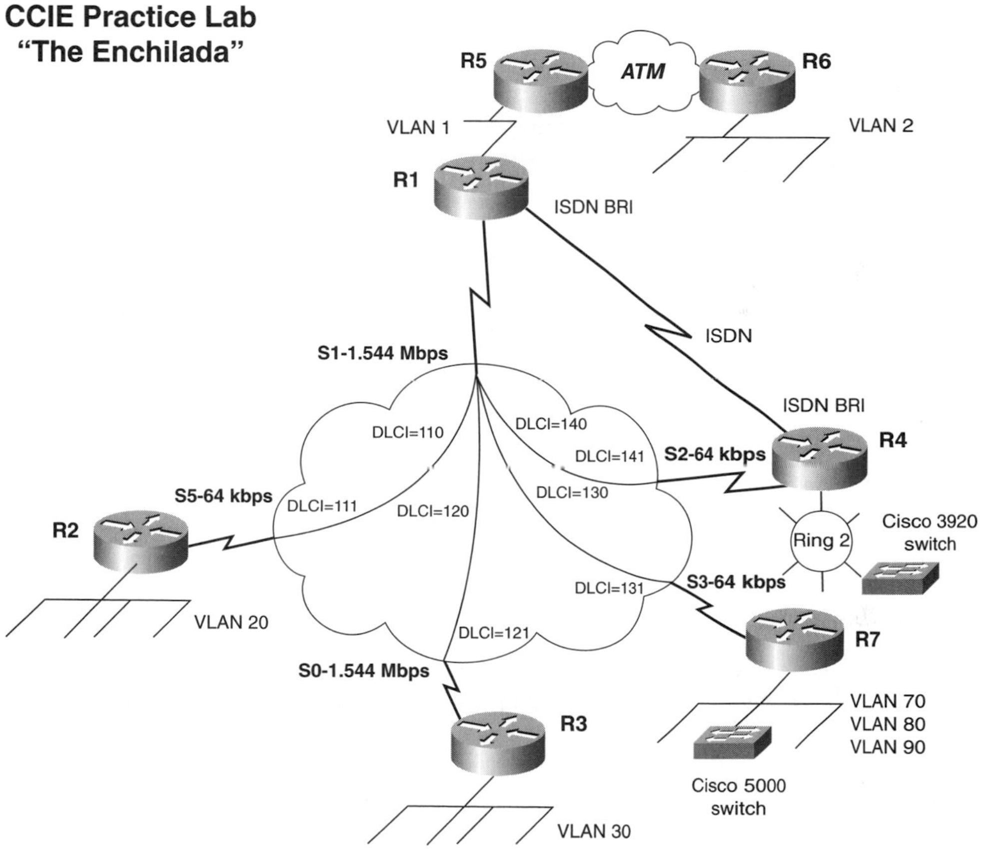

CCIE Practice Lab "The Enchilada"

Section II: Catalyst/LAN Configuration

1   Configure the VLANs as depicted in Figure 18-8. VLAN 70, VLAN 80, and VLAN 90 reside off the 100-MB port on R7. Configure the router to route between the VLANs.

2   Configure the Catalyst Ethernet and Token Ring switches so that they can be managed through Telnet from any router in the lab.

3   Configure the Token Ring segments at this time. Do not use the default Token Ring VLAN.

4   Configure a full-duplex 802.1Q trunk on port 1/1 of the Catalyst switch. Prevent STP for VLANs 70, 80, and 90 from being propagated down this trunk. *It is not important whether this link is attached; the configuration of the switch will be the same.*

Section III: OSPF and Frame Relay Configuration

1   Configure the Frame Relay network as shown in Figure 18-8.

2   R1, R2, and R3 should share the same IP subnet; use subinterfaces only on R1. Configure this subnet to be in Area 0. Do not use the OSPF **network** command. Configure the Frame Circuit between R1 and R7 to be in OSPF Area 10.

3   Configure VLAN 20 to be in OSPF Area 20. Configure VLAN 30 to be in OSPF Area 30. Configure VLANs 70, 80, 90 to be in OSPF Area 70.

4   Configure Area 30 to send link-state type 7's, to any new OSPF routers that might be on VLAN30.

5   Authenticate Area 0 with Type II authentication. Use cisco as the password.

Section IV: Routing Protocols and Redistribution

1   Configure IGRP on Ring 2 and on the Frame Relay circuit between R1/R4. Ensure full IP reachability to the OSPF network.

2   Prevent the subnet of the Token Ring network on R4 from reaching R7.

Section V: ATM and EIGRP

1   R5 and R6 both connect to the ATM switch. Configure classical IP over ATM between the routers so that the routers can **ping** each other.

2   Configure EIGRP on VLAN 1 of R5 and over the ATM cloud to R6. Redistribute EIGRP into OSPF. Make sure that the entire EIGRP network is reachable from the IGRP and OSPF domains.

Section VI: ISDN Configuration

1   Configure the ISDN interfaces on R1 and R4. Make only R4 place the call to R1. Be sure that you can **ping** the R1/R4's ISDN interfaces before moving on.

2   Configure the ISDN interfaces as part of the IGRP backbone. Ensure that the link becomes active only upon loss of IGRP routes from R1.

Section VII: Voice over IP

1 Configure Voice over IP between R2 and R3. Use the FXS ports to create a ringdown circuit between the two routers.

Section VIII: IPX Configuration

1 Configure IPX on VLAN 1, VLAN 20, and VLAN 30.

2 Configure IPX EIGRP on R1, R2, R3, and R5. Configure IPX on Ring 2 of R4; use IPX RIP/SAP on the frame link between R4 and R1. Ensure that all routers see all IPX networks.

3 Configure IPX SAP on R5, which supports file services. This SAP is called fakefserver and has socket 452. Ensure that all routers can see this SAP.

4 On R2, apply a SAP filter blocking all SAPs that start with the letters "fake."

5 Configure VLAN 30 so that SAPs are advertised only when a new server comes online.

Section IX: Miscellaneous Cisco IOS Software Configuration

1 Workstations on VLAN 20 need to gain their IP addresses through the DHCP server on VLAN1. Configure R2 to support this.

2 Configure R3 so that workstations VLAN 30 can dynamically locate their default gateway. They are not using DHCP.

3 Configure multicast routing on R1, R2, and R5. Configure R1 as a member of the multicast group 224.0.7.7. R1 should respond to **ping**s from R2 and R5.

4 Configure R1, R2, and R5 to dynamically configure the Cat5k for multicast.

Part II

Section X: BGP Configuration

1   R2, and R7 are in autonomous system 2001. R5 is in autonomous system 5, and R4 is in autonomous system 4. Configure an IBGP peer from R2 to R7. Also configure an EBGP from R2 to R5 and from R7 to R4.

2   On R4, assign and advertise the loopback network 220.128.1.0/24 through BGP. On R5, assign and advertise the loopback network 24.128.1.0/24, 24.128.2.0/24 through BGP.

3   Have R5 advertise a default route to the ATM network if—and only if—it has the route 220.128.1.0/24.

4   Configure R4 so that all routes from AS 2001 have a weight of 350.

Section XI: DLSw Configuration

1   Configure a DLSw TCP peer from R1, VLAN 1 to R2, VLAN 20. On VLAN 20, there is an SNA host with the MAC address of 2200.900e.0001. Allow only explorer frames destined toward this address to cross the DLSw peer.

2   Configure a DLSw TCP peer between R4, Ring 2, and R1, VLAN 1.

3   Allow the peer on R4 to stay "connected," even upon a loss of the Frame Service. It might take up to three minutes for the network to converge over the ISDN link. The peer should not become disconnected during this time.

Section XII: Miscellaneous Cisco IOS Software Features

1   Transparently bridge from VLAN 30 to VLAN 1, across the Frame Relay cloud.

2   Configure R1 as an NTP server. Configure a peer association so that R4 synchronizes to R1. When R4 is synchronized, allow R2 and R3 to synchronize off R4. If R4 is not synchronized with R1, R2 and R3 should not synchronize.

3   Bridge and route IPX on VLAN 30.

CCIE Practice Lab: "The Unnamed Lab"

Equipment List

- One Frame Relay switch: three serial ports
- One access server: eight asynchronous interfaces, one Ethernet port
- Two lab routers: one Ethernet, two serial interfaces, one ISDN BRI
- Two lab routers: one Token Ring, one Ethernet, one serial interface
- Two lab routers: one Ethernet port, one serial interface
- Two lab routers: one Ethernet port, one ATM interface
- One Catalyst 3900
- One Catalyst 5000

Prestaging: Frame Switch Configuration

Configure the Frame Relay switch with the PVCs as depicted in Figure 18-9; do not time yourself on this portion of the lab. Example 18-7 lists the configuration for the Frame Relay switch.

Example 18-7 *Frame Relay Switch Configuration*

```
hostname frame_switch
!
frame-relay switching
!
<<<text omitted>>>
!
interface Serial0
 no ip address
 encapsulation frame-relay
 no fair-queue
 clockrate 148000
 frame-relay lmi-type ansi
 frame-relay intf-type dce
 frame-relay route 121 interface Serial1 120
 frame-relay route 141 interface Serial3 140
!
interface Serial1
 no ip address
 encapsulation frame-relay
 clockrate 148000
```

continues

Example 18-7 *Frame Relay Switch Configuration (Continued)*

```
    frame-relay intf-type dce
    frame-relay route 120 interface Serial0 121
    frame-relay route 130 interface Serial3 131
 !
interface Serial3
 no ip address
 encapsulation frame-relay
 clockrate 64000
 frame-relay intf-type dce
 frame-relay route 131 interface Serial1 130
 frame-relay route 140 interface Serial0 141
 !
```

Figure 18-9 *Frame Relay Switch Configuration*

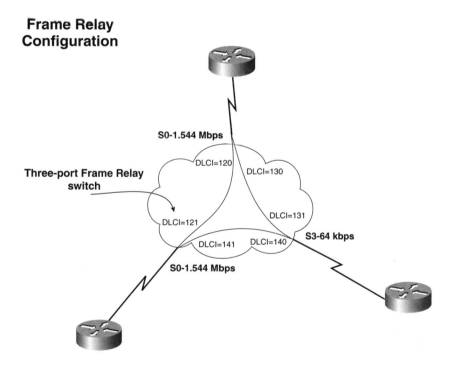

**Frame Relay
Configuration**

S0-1.544 Mbps

**Three-port Frame Relay
switch**

DLCI=120

DLCI=130

DLCI=121

DLCI=131

DLCI=141   DLCI=140   **S3-64 kbps**

S0-1.544 Mbps

The following portion of the lab is timed, and it should begin after the configuration and physical installation of the Frame switch and the backbone router. Do not configure any other routers at this time.

Prestaging: Backbone Router Configuration

Configure a backbone router and attach it to Backbone 1. Example 18-8 illustrates the configuration of the backbone router.

Example 18-8 *Backbone Router Configuration*

```
hostname r6_backbone_router
!
interface Loopback20
 ip address 192.190.100.1 255.255.255.0
!
interface Loopback21
 ip address 192.190.101.1 255.255.255.0
!
interface Loopback22
 ip address 192.190.102.1 255.255.255.0
!
interface Loopback23
 ip address 160.100.100.1 255.255.255.0
!
interface Loopback24
 ip address 160.100.128.1 255.255.255.0
!
interface Loopback25
 ip address 160.100.129.1 255.255.255.0
!
interface Loopback26
 ip address 160.100.130.1 255.255.255.0
!
interface Ethernet0
 description place on vlan 2 - Backbone 2
 ip address 133.7.77.254 255.255.255.0
 media-type 10BaseT
!
interface Ethernet1
description place on vlan 10 - backbone 1
 ip address 160.100.2.254 255.255.255.0
 media-type 10BaseT
!
router rip
 no auto-summary
 network 160.100.0.0
 network 192.190.100.0
 network 192.190.101.0
 network 192.190.102.0
!
```

continues

Example 18-8 *Backbone Router Configuration (Continued)*

```
router bgp 2001
 no synchronization
 network 160.100.100.0 mask 255.255.255.0
 network 160.100.128.0 mask 255.255.255.0
 network 160.100.129.0 mask 255.255.255.0
 network 160.100.130.0 mask 255.255.255.0
 neighbor 160.100.2.1 remote-as 2010
 neighbor 160.100.2.1 ebgp-multihop 10
!
```

The following portion of the lab is timed, and it should begin after the configuration and physical installation of the Frame Relay switch and the backbone router. Do not configure any other routers at this time.

Timed Portion

Lab Rules

- No static routes or floating static routes are used unless specifically stated.

- Follow the instructions exactly. Be careful to propagate routes only where and when instructed. Use the PVCs only as directed by the instructions.

- Primary configurations might need to be modified for Part II configurations to work. Proceed to Part II only when you finish the primary configurations.

- You can use the configuration guides and the Cisco Documentation CD-ROM for your only reference material.

- You have 8 1/2 hours to complete this portion of the lab. Do not talk to anyone during this phase.

- It is recommended that you read the entire lab before beginning.

- Make an accurate and precise network illustration.

- Use Figure 18-10 as a reference for the physical layout of the lab.

Section I: Basic IP Configuration

1 Access server: Configure the access server/router so that all the routers and the switches can be accessed through reverse Telnet. Password-protect all routers and switches with the password cisco.

2 IP address assignment: Assign an IP addresses to all physical interfaces, as denoted in Figure 18-10. Use the major network of 133.7.*x.x* on all interfaces. Configure a loopback address on each router; use 133.7.*x.x*, where *x.x* is the router number. For example, R5's loopback would be 133.7.5.5. Use a 24-bit mask on all interfaces except for the following:

R1: Use the IP address of 160.100.2.1/24 on the Ethernet segment; use VLAN 10 for this segment.

R2, R3, R6: Use a 22-bit address on VLAN 30 between all the routers.

R3: Use a 26-bit address on Ring 1.

R4: Use the IP address of 10.10.10.1 on Ring 2. Allow the subnet on the ring to have 14 hosts on it. Use the IP address of 133.7.77.1/24 on VLAN 2.

R5: Use a 26-bit address on VLAN 55.

3 Full IP and IPX connectivity to all Ethernet, Token Ring, and loopback interfaces will be expected unless noted.

4 Document the network thoroughly; include all OSPF areas, IP/IPX address, IPX networks, and so on.

Figure 18-10 *Network Diagram for "The Unnamed lab"*

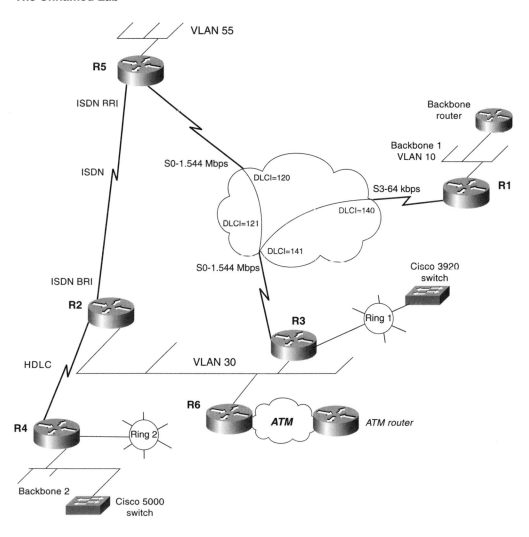

CCIE Practice Lab
"The Unnamed Lab"

Section II: Catalyst/LAN Configuration

1 Configure the VLANs as depicted in Figure 18-10. Assign an IP address of 133.7.10.254 to the Catalyst. Configure the Catalyst switch that so it can be managed/telnetted from any router in the lab.

2 Configure the Catalyst ports in VLAN 30 so that they will work only with R2, R3, and R6. If any other device is plugged into these ports, have the Catalyst deactivate the port.

3 Configure the Catalysts so that if the backplane of the switch gets overloaded, the ports in VLAN 30 get serviced before the ports on VLAN 55.

4 Password-protect VTP. Use the password of Cisco_CCIE.

Section III: OSPF and Frame Relay Configuration

1 Configure the Frame Relay network as shown on Figure 18-10. Use only the PVCs as defined in Figure 18-10. Do not allow any dynamic PVC mapping from R1 to R5.

2 R1, R3, and R5 should share the same IP subnet. Configure this subnet to be in Area 10.

3 Configure VLAN 30 to be in OSPF Area 0. Configure VLAN 55 to be in OSPF Area 55.

4 Configure Ring 1 of R3 to be in Area 20. Configure the ISDN network between R5 and R2 to be in Area 100.

Section IV: Routing Protocols and Redistribution

1 Configure IGRP on HDLC circuit between R2/R4 and on Backbone 2. Redistribute IGRP into OSPF. Do not put Ring 2 into any routing protocol.

2 Advertise a default route to R4's Backbone 2 without configuring summarization or using a static route. Ensure that every interface on R4 except Ring 2 has complete IP connectivity to the lab network.

3 Configure RIP on R1's Ethernet segment or Backbone 1. Some routes will come from the backbone network. They are 192.190.100.0/24, 192.190.101.0/24, and 192.190.102.0/24. Advertise these as one network into the rest of lab network.

4 Prevent all lab routes from being broadcast unto the Backbone 1 segment.

5 Ensure full IP reachability between OSPF, IGRP, and RIP domains, except for the network on Ring 2.

Section V: ATM and EIGRP

1 Configure the ATM interface on R6 to be part of the EIGRP autonomous system 2010.

2 Configure R6 so that it can **ping** the ATM lab router without using Inverse ARP.

3 Configure MD5 authentication for EIGRP AS 2010.

Section VI: ISDN Configuration

1 Configure the ISDN interfaces on R2 and R5. Configure the ISDN calling so that only R5 can place a call. Use CHAP authentication; use cisco11 as the password. Ensure that you can **ping** the local ISDN interfaces before moving on.

2 Configure the ISDN interfaces as part of the OSPF domain. Ensure that the link becomes active only upon changes in the routing table, unless otherwise stated. Only TCP traffic should bring up the link; routing updates should not.

Section VII: IPX Configuration

1 Configure IPX networks on all interfaces except the loopbacks, ISDN network, Backbone 2, and the ATM network.

2 Configure IPX NLSP on the HDLC network on R2/R4 and on Ring 2. Use IPX RIP on VLAN 30. Use IPX EIGRP on Frame, VLAN 55, and on Backbone 1 of R1. Ensure that all routers have IPX reachability to all IPX networks.

3 Configure IPX SAP on R5, which supports print services. This SAP is called fakepserver and has socket 451. Ensure that all routers can see this SAP.

4 Configure R2 so that the IPX network assigned to VLAN 55 will not be propagated to R4.

Section VIII: Miscellaneous Cisco IOS Software Configuration

1 The IP network assigned to Ring 2 should not be advertised by any routing protocol. Allow the users of this ring to have full IP reachability to the lab network without using redistribution, static routes, or default routes.

2 Deny R1 from **ping**ing R2, but allow R2 to **ping** R1.

Part II

Section IX: BGP Configuration

1 R1, R2, and R6 are in autonomous system 2010. R4 is in autonomous system 2020. The Backbone 1 router is in autonomous 2001. Configure an IBGP peer from R1 to R2 and from R2 to R6.

2 Configure an EBGP peer from R2 to R4. Configure an EBGP peer from R1 to the Backbone 1 router, 160.100.2.254, in autonomous system 2001.

3 Synchronize BGP with OSPF.

4 On R4 assign and advertise the 10's network through BGP.

5 Three subnets are being advertised from the backbone router: 192.190.100.0 to 192.190.102.0. Summarize the subnets into the supernet of 192.0.0.0/8. Advertise only this subnet and suppress all other routes.

Section X: DLSw Configuration

1 Configure a DLSw TCP peer between R3, Ring 1, and R5, VLAN 55. Configure another TCP peer from R3 to R1's Backbone 1.

2 Allow only NetBIOS reachability from Ring 1 to Backbone 1.

3 Configure R5 to advertise local reachability to a server called unnamed.

Section XI: Miscellaneous Cisco IOS Software Features

1 Configure R5 so that IP **ping** traffic from VLAN 55 destined toward VLAN 30 will take the ISDN link. All other IP traffic will take the frame circuit.

2 Configure R4 so that only SNA traffic to MAC address 3745.0001.0001 is allowed on Ring 2.

3 Configure R1 so that when the user unnamed logs into the router, that user immediately is put in enable mode.

4 Configure the access server so that the reverse Telnet sessions to the routers in the lab will never time out.

Appendixes

ISDN Switch Types, Codes, and Values

This appendix contains a list of the supported switch types. It also contains the ISDN cause codes, cause values, bearer capability values, and progress description field values that are valid within the **debug** commands for ISDN.

NOTE   The ITU-T carries out the functions of the former Consultative Committee for International Telegraph and Telephone (CCITT).

Switch Types

Table A-1 lists the ISDN switch types supported by the ISDN interface.

Table A-1   *Supported ISDN Switch Types*

Identifier	Description
basic-1tr6	German 1TR6 ISDN switches
basic-5ess	AT&T basic rate switches
basic-dms100	NT DMS-100 basic rate switches
basic-net3	NET3 ISDN and Euro-ISDN switches (UK and others), also called E-DSS1 or DSS1
basic-ni1	National ISDN-1 switches
basic-nwnet3	Norway Net3 switches
basic-nznet3	New Zealand Net3 switches
basic-ts013	Australian TS013 switches
None	No switch defined
ntt	Japanese NTT ISDN switches (ISDN BRI only)
primary-4ess	AT&T 4ESS switch type for the United States (ISDN PRI only)
primary-5ess	AT&T 5ESS switch type for the United States (ISDN PRI only)

continues

Table A-1   *Supported ISDN Switch Types (Continued)*

Identifier	Description
primary-dms100	NT DMS-100 switch type for the United States (ISDN PRI only)
primary-net5	NET5 ISDN PRI switches (Europe)
primary-ntt	INS-Net 1500 for Japan (ISDN PRI only)
primary-ts014	Australian TS014 switches (ISDN PRI only)
vn2	French VN2 ISDN switches (ISDN BRI only)
vn3	French VN3 ISDN switches (ISDN BRI only)
vn4	French VN4 ISDN switches (ISDN BRI only)

Cause Code Fields

Table A-2 lists the ISDN cause code fields that display in the following format within the **debug** commands:

i=0x y1 y2 z1 z2 [a1 a2]

Table A-2   *ISDN Cause Code Fields*

Field	Value—Description
0x	The values that follow are in hexadecimal.
y1	**8**—ITU-T standard coding.
y2	**0**—User
	1—Private network serving local user
	2—Public network serving local user
	3—Transit network
	4—Public network serving remote user
	5—Private network serving remote user
	7—International network
	A—Network beyond internetworking point
z1	Class (the more significant hexadecimal number) of cause value. Refer to Table A-3 for detailed information about possible values.
z2	Value (the less significant hexadecimal number) of cause value. Refer to Table A-3 for detailed information about possible values.
a1	(Optional) Diagnostic field that is always 8.

Table A-2   *ISDN Cause Code Fields (Continued)*

Field	Value—Description
a2	(Optional) Diagnostic field that is one of the following values:
	0—Unknown
	1—Permanent
	2—Transient

The following is sample output of this form from the **debug isdn q931** command:

Cause i = 0x8790

Cause Values

Table A-3 lists descriptions of the cause value field of the cause information element. The notes referred to in the Diagnostics column follow the table. For the **debug isdn q931** command output, drop the highest bit of the cause value before using this table. For example, a cause value of 0x90 becomes 0x10.

Table A-3   *ISDN Cause Values*

Decimal Value	Hex Value	Cause	Diagnostics	Explanation
1	01	Unallocated (unassigned) number	Note 10	The ISDN number was sent to the switch in the correct format; however, the number is not assigned to any destination equipment.
2	02	No route to specified transit network	Transit network identity (Note 9)	The ISDN exchange is asked to route the call through an unrecognized intermediate network.
3	03	No route to destination	Note 10	The call was routed through an intermediate network that does not serve the destination address.

continues

Table A-3   *ISDN Cause Values (Continued)*

Decimal Value	Hex Value	Cause	Diagnostics	Explanation
6	06	Channel unacceptable		The service quality of the specified channel is insufficient to accept the connection.
7	07	Call awarded and being delivered in an established channel		The user is assigned an incoming call that is being connected to an already-established call channel.
16	10	Normal call clearing	Note 10	Normal call clearing has occurred.
17	11	User busy		The called system acknowledges the connection request but is incapable of accepting the call because all B channels are in use.
18	12	No user responding		The connection cannot be completed because the destination does not respond to the call.
19	13	No answer from user (user alerted)		The destination responds to the connection request but fails to complete the connection within the prescribed time. The problem is at the remote end of the connection.
21	15	Call rejected	Note 10; user supplied diagnostic (Note 4)	The destination is capable of accepting the call, but it rejected the call for an unknown reason.
22	16	Number changed		The ISDN number used to set up the call is not assigned to any system.

Table A-3   *ISDN Cause Values (Continued)*

Decimal Value	Hex Value	Cause	Diagnostics	Explanation
26	1A	Nonselected user clearing		The destination is capable of accepting the call, but it rejected the call because it was not assigned to the user.
27	1B	Designation out of order		The destination cannot be reached because the interface is not functioning correctly and a signaling message cannot be delivered. This might be a temporary condition, but it could last for an extended period of time. For example, the remote equipment might be turned off.
28	1C	Invalid number format		The connection could not be established because the destination address was presented in an unrecognizable format or because the destination address was incomplete.
29	1D	Facility rejected	Facility identification (Note 1)	The facility requested by the user cannot be provided by the network.
30	1E	Response to STATUS ENQUIRY		The status message was generated in direct response to the previous receipt of a status inquiry message.

continues

Table A-3 *ISDN Cause Values (Continued)*

Decimal Value	Hex Value	Cause	Diagnostics	Explanation
31	1F	Normal, unspecified		Reports the occurrence of a normal event when no standard cause applies. No action is required.
34	22	No circuit/channel available		The connection cannot be established because no appropriate channel is available to take the call.
38	26	Network out of order		The destination cannot be reached because the network is not functioning correctly, and the condition might last for an extended period of time. An immediate reconnect attempt will probably be unsuccessful.
41	29	Temporary failure		An error occurred because the network is not functioning correctly. The problem will be resolved shortly.
42	2A	Switching equipment congestion		The destination cannot be reached because the network-switching equipment is temporarily overloaded.
43	2B	Access information discarded	Discarded information element identifier(s) (Note 5)	The network cannot provide the requested access information.

Table A-3   *ISDN Cause Values (Continued)*

Decimal Value	Hex Value	Cause	Diagnostics	Explanation
44	2C	Requested circuit/channel not available		The remote equipment cannot provide the requested channel for an unknown reason. This might be a temporary problem.
47	2F	Resources unavailable, unspecified		The requested channel or service is unavailable for an unknown reason. This might be a temporary problem.
49	31	Quality of service unavailable	Table A-2	The requested quality of service cannot be provided by the network. This might be a subscription problem.
50	32	Requested facility not subscribed	Facility identification (Note 1)	The remote equipment supports the requested supplementary service by subscription only.
57	39	Bearer capability not authorized	Note 3	The user requested a bearer capability that the network provides, but the user is not authorized to use it. This might be a subscription problem.
58	3A	Bearer capability not presently available	Note 3	The network normally provides the requested bearer capability, but it is unavailable at the present time. This might be the result of a temporary network problem or to a subscription problem.

continues

Table A-3 *ISDN Cause Values (Continued)*

Decimal Value	Hex Value	Cause	Diagnostics	Explanation
63	3F	Service or option not available, unspecified		The network or remote equipment was incapable of providing the requested service option for an unspecified reason. This might be a subscription problem.
65	41	Bearer capability not implemented	Note 3	The network cannot provide the bearer capability requested by the user.
66	42	Channel type not implemented	Channel Type (Note 6)	The network or the destination equipment does not support the requested channel type.
69	45	Requested facility not implemented	Facility Identification (Note 1)	The remote equipment does not support the requested supplementary service.
70	46	Only restricted digital information bearer capability is available		The network is incapable of providing unrestricted digital information bearer capability.
79	4F	Service or option not implemented, unspecified		The network or remote equipment is incapable of providing the requested service option for an unspecified reason. This might be a subscription problem.
81	51	Invalid call reference value		The remote equipment received a call with a call reference that is not currently in use on the user-network interface.

Table A-3   *ISDN Cause Values (Continued)*

Decimal Value	Hex Value	Cause	Diagnostics	Explanation
82	52	Identified channel does not exist	Channel identity	The receiving equipment is requested to use a channel that is not activated on the interface for calls.
83	53	A suspended call exists, but this call identity does not		The network received a call resume request. The call resume request contained a call identify information element that indicates that the call identity is being used for a suspended call.
84	54	Call identity in use		The network received a call resume request. The call resume request contained a Call Identify information element that indicates that it is in use for a suspended call.
85	55	No call suspended		The network received a call resume request when there was not a suspended call pending. This might be a transient error that will be resolved by successive call retries.

continues

Table A-3   *ISDN Cause Values (Continued)*

Decimal Value	Hex Value	Cause	Diagnostics	Explanation
86	56	Call having the requested call identity has been cleared	Clearing cause	The network received a call resume request. The call resume request contained a call identity information element, which once indicated a suspended call. However, the suspended call was cleared either by timeout or by the remote user.
88	58	Incompatible destination	Incompatible parameter (Note 2)	This indicates that an attempt was made to connect to non-ISDN equipment—for example, to an analog line.
91	5B	Invalid transit network selection		The ISDN exchange was asked to route the call through an unrecognized intermediate network.
95	5F	Invalid message, unspecified		An invalid message was received, and no standard cause applies. This is usually the result of a D-channel error. If this error occurs systematically, report it to your ISDN service provider.

Table A-3   *ISDN Cause Values (Continued)*

Decimal Value	Hex Value	Cause	Diagnostics	Explanation
96	60	Mandatory information element is missing	Information element identifier(s) (Note 5)	The receiving equipment received a message that did not include one of the mandatory information elements. This is usually the result of a D-channel error. If this error occurs systematically, report it to your ISDN service provider.
97	61	Message type nonexistent or not implemented	Message type	The receiving equipment received an unrecognized message, either because the message type was invalid or because the message type was valid but not supported. The cause is either a problem with the remote configuration or a problem with the local D channel.
98	62	Message not compatible with call state or message type nonexistent or not implemented	Message type	The remote equipment received an invalid message, and no standard cause applies. This cause is a D-channel error. If this error occurs systematically, report it to your ISDN service provider.

continues

Table A-3 *ISDN Cause Values (Continued)*

Decimal Value	Hex Value	Cause	Diagnostics	Explanation
99	63	Information element nonexistent or not implemented	Information element identifier(s) (Notes 5 and 7)	The remote equipment received a message that includes information elements that were not recognized. This is usually the result of a D-channel error. If this error occurs systematically, report it to your ISDN service provider.
100	64	Invalid information element contents	Information element identifier(s) (Note 5)	The remote equipment received a message that includes invalid information in the information element. This is usually the result of a D-channel error.
101	65	Message not compatible with call state	Message type	The remote equipment received an unexpected message that does not correspond to the current state of the connection. This is usually the result of a D-channel error.
102	66	Recovery on timer expires	Timer number (Note 8)	An error-handling (recovery) procedure was initiated by a timer expiry. This is usually a temporary problem.
111	6F	Protocol error, unspecified		This is the result of an unspecified D-channel error when no other standard cause applies.

Table A-3   *ISDN Cause Values (Continued)*

Decimal Value	Hex Value	Cause	Diagnostics	Explanation
127	7F	Internetworking, unspecified		An event occurred, but the network does not provide causes for the action that it takes. The precise problem is unknown.

Note 1—The coding of facility identification is network-dependent.

Note 2—An incompatible parameter is composed of an incompatible information element identifier.

Note 3—The format of the diagnostic field for causes 39, 3A, and 41 is shown in the ITU-T Q.850 specification, Table 3b/Q.850.

Note 4—The user-supplied diagnostic field is encoded according to the user specification, subject to the maximum length of the cause information element. The coding of user-supplied diagnostics should be made in such a way that it does not conflict with the coding described in Table A-2.

Note 5—Locking and nonlocking shift procedures described in the ITU-T Q.931 specification apply. In principle, information element identifiers are in the same order as the information elements in the received message.

Note 6—The following coding is used:
• Bit 8—Extension bit

• Bits 7 through 5—Spare

• Bits 4 through 1—According to Table 4-15/Q.931 octet 3.2, channel type in ITU-T Q.931 specification

Note 7—When only locking shift information element is included and no variable-length information element identifier follows, it means that the codeset in the locking shift itself is not implemented.

Note 8—The timer number is coded in IA5 characters. The following coding is used in each octet:
• Bit 8—Spare "0"

• Bits 7 through 1—IA5 character

Note 9—The diagnostic field contains the entire transit network selection or network-specific facilities information element, as applicable.

Note 10—See Table A-2 for the coding that is used.

Bearer Capability Values

Table A-4 lists the ISDN bearer capability values that display in the following format within the **debug** commands:

0x8890 for 64 kbps or 0x8890218F for 56 kbps

Table A-4   *ISDN Bearer Capability Values*

Field Value	Description
0x	Indication that the values that follow are in hexadecimal
88	ITU-T coding standard; unrestricted digital information
90	Circuit mode, 64 kbps
21	Layer 1, V.110/X.30
8F	Synchronous, no in-band negotiation, 56 kbps

Progress Field Values

Table A-5 lists the values of the Progress description field contained in the ISDN Progress indicator information element.

Table A-5   *ISDN Progress Description Field Values*

Bits	Decimal Number	Description
0000001	1	The call is not end-to-end ISDN; further call progress information may be available in-band.
0000010	2	The destination address is non-ISDN.
0000011	3	The origination address is non-ISDN.
0000100	4	The call has returned to the ISDN.
0001000	8	In-band information or an appropriate pattern is now available.
0001010	10	A delay in response has occurred at the destination interface.

All other values for the Progress description field are reserved.

The 'Abridged' OSI Reference Model

Almost every book on networking has some reference to the OSI reference model; this one will be no exception. However, instead of repeating the same text that you've probably already read 50 times, I would like to offer a new twist on the model in Table B-1. This information is presented here in less then 10 words per level, as an "abridged" OSI reference model. To read "unabridged" versions, refer to *Interconnections, Second Edition: Bridges, Routers, Switches, and Internetworking Protocols* by Radia Perlman or *Networking Standards a Guide to OSI ISDN, LAN, and MAN* Standards by William Stallings.

Table B-1   *OSI Reference Model Quick Reference*

OSI Layer	"10-Word Description"
Application layer	Governs end-user applications and services; FTP, WWW browsers, Telnet, SMTP
Presentation layer	Handles data formats, encoding, and transfer; GIF, JPEG, ASCII, EBCDIC, HTML
Session layer	Handles application dialogue control, data grouping, and recovery; NFS, SQL, NetBIOS
Transport layer	Manages network connections; reliable (TCP and SPX) and unreliable(UDP) transport
Network layer	Addresses and routes packets, packet fragmentation; IP, IPX, AppleTalk
Data link layer	Controls physical layer data flow; Frame Relay, ATM, PPP, IEEE 802.x
Physical layer	Defines electrical and physical specifications; EIA/TIA-232, V.35, 10Basex, B8ZS, NRZI

RFC List

Table C-1 provides a list of some of the more common RFCs found throughout the text. The complete text version of these RFCs can be found at www.isi.edu.

Table C-1 *List of RFCs*

RFC Number	Notes	RFC Title
RFC 2125		The PPP Bandwidth Allocation Protocol (BAP)\
		The PPP Bandwidth Allocation Control Protocol (BACP)
RFC 2037		Entity MIB using SMTv2
RFC 2030		Simple Network Time Protocol (SNTP) Version 4 for IPv4, IPv6 and OSI
RFC 2018		TCP Selective Acknowledgment Options
RFC 1997		BGP Communities Attribute
RFC 1994	Supersedes RFC 1334	PPP Challenge Handshake Authentication Protocol (CHAP)
RFC 1990	Supersedes RFC 1717	The PPP Multilink Protocol (MP)
RFC 1989	Supersedes RFC 1333	PPP Link Quality Monitoring
RFC 1918		Address Allocation for Private Internets
RFC 1907		Management Information Base for version 2 of the Simple Network Management Protocol (SNMPv2)
RFC 1906		Transport Mappings for Version 2 of the Simple Network Management Protocol (SNMPv2)
RFC 1905		Protocol Operations for Version 2 of the Simple Network Management Protocol (SNMPv2)

continues

Table C-1 *List of RFCs (Continued)*

RFC Number	Notes	RFC Title
RFC 1904		Conformance Statements for Version 2 of the Simple Network Management Protocol (SNMPv2)
RFC 1903		Textual Conventions for Version 2 of the Simple Network Management Protocol (SNMPv2)
RFC 1902		Structure of Management Information for Version 2 of the Simple Network Management Protocol (SNMPv2)
RFC 1901	Supersedes RFCs 1441–1450	Introduction to Community-based SNMPv2
RFC 1889		RTP: A Transport Protocol for Real-Time Applications
RFC 1850		OSPF Version 2 Management Information Base
RFC 1812		Requirements for IP Version 4 Routers
RFC 1795		DLSw: Switch-to-Switch Protocol
RFC 1793		Extending OSPF to Support Demand Circuits
RFC 1771		A Border Gateway Protocol 4
RFC 1745		BGP4/IDRP for IP—OSPF Interaction
RFC 1724		RIP Version 2 MIB Extension
RFC 1723		RIP Version 2 Carrying Additional Information
RFC 1722		RIP Version 2 Protocol Applicability Statement
RFC 1717	Replaced by RFC 1990	The PPP Multilink Protocol (MP)
RFC 1695		Definitions of Managed Objects for ATM Management Version 8.0 Using SMIv2
RFC 1661	Supersedes RFC 1548	The PPP (Point-to-Point Protocol)
RFC 1647		TN3270 Enhancements
RFC 1646		Cisco Supports Luname Selection Method Only
RFC 1638		PPP Bridging Control Protocol (BCP)
RFC 1634	Supersedes 1362 and 1551	Novell IPX over Various WAN Media (IPXWAN)

Table C-1 *List of RFCs (Continued)*

RFC Number	Notes	RFC Title
RFC 1633		Integrated Services in the Internet Architecture: an Overview
RFC 1631		The IP Network Address Translator (NAT)
RFC 1618		PPP over ISDN
RFC 1604		Definitions of Managed Objects for Frame Relay Services
RFC 1587		The OSPF Not-So-Stubby Area (NSSA) Option
RFC 1583	Supersedes RFC 1247	OSPF Version 2
RFC 1577		Classical IP and ARP over ATM
RFC 1576		TN3270 Current Practices
RFC 1559		DECnet Phase IV MIB Extensions
RFC 1552		The PPP Internetwork Packet Exchange Control Protocol (IPXCP)
RFC 1549		PPP in HDLC Framing
RFC 1548	Replaced by RFC 1661	The Point-to-Point Protocol (PPP)
RFC 1541	Supersedes RFC 1531	Dynamic Host Configuration Protocol
RFC 1531	Replaced by RFC 1541	Dynamic Host Configuration Protocol
RFC 1519		Classless Inter-Domain Routing (CIDR): an Address Assignment and Aggregation Strategy
RFC 1510		The Kerberos Network Authentication Service (V5)
RFC 1492		An Access Control Protocol, Sometimes Called TACACS
RFC 1490		Multiprotocol Interconnect over Frame Relay
RFC 1483		Multiprotocol Encapsulation over ATM Adaptation Layer 5
RFC 1469		IP Multicast over Token-Ring Local Area Networks
RFC 1450	Replaced By RFC 1907	MIB for SNMP Version 2
RFC 1403		BGP OSPF Interaction

continues

Table C-1 *List of RFCs (Continued)*

RFC Number	Notes	RFC Title
RFC 1397		Default Route Advertisement in BGP2 and BGP3 Versions Of The Border Gateway Protocol
RFC 1395		BootP Vendor Information Extensions
RFC 1393		Traceroute Using an IP Option
RFC 1390		Transmission of IP and ARP over FDDI Networks
RFC 1382		SNMP MIB Extension for X.25 Packet Layer
RFC 1381		SNMP MIB Extension for x.25 LAPB
RFC 1378		The PPP AppleTalk Control Protocol (ATCP)
RFC 1377		The PPP OSI Network Layer Control Protocol (OSINLCP)
RFC 1376		The PPP DECnet Phase IV Control Protocol (DNCP)
RFC 1370		Applicability Statement for OSPF
RFC 1362		Novell IPX Over Various WAN Media (IXPWAN)
RFC 1356		Multiprotocol Interconnect on x.25 and ISDN in the Packet Mode
RFC 1350		THE TFTP PROTOCOL (REVISION 2)
RFC 1349		Type of Service in the Internet Protocol Suite
RFC 1348		DNS NSAP RRs
RFC 1334	Replaced by RFC 1994	PPP Authentication Protocols
RFC 1333	Replaced by RFC 1989	PPP Link Quality Monitoring
RFC 1332		The PPP Internet Protocol Control Protocol (IPCP)
RFC 1331	Replaced by FRC 1548	The Point-to-Point Protocol (PPP) for the Transmission of Multi-protocol Datagrams over Point-to-Point Links
RFC 1323		TCP Extensions for High Performance
RFC 1315		Management Information Base for Frame Relay DTEs
RFC 1305		Network Time Protocol (Version 3) Specification, Implementation and Analysis

Table C-1   *List of RFCs (Continued)*

RFC Number	Notes	RFC Title
RFC 1294	Replaced by RFC 1940	Multiprotocol Interconnect over Frame Relay
RFC 1293		Inverse Address Resolution Protocol
RFC 1286		Definitions of Managed Objects for Bridges
RFC 1285		FDDI Management Information Base
RFC 1269		Definitions of Managed Objects for the Border Gateway Protocol (Version 3)
RFC 1268		Application of BGP in the Internet
RFC 1267		A Border Gateway Protocol (BGP-3)
RFC 1256		ICMP Router Discovery Messages
RFC 1253		OSPF Version 2 Management Information Base
RFC 1247	Replaced by RFC 1583	OSPF Version 2
RFC 1236		IP to x.121 Address Mapping for DDN
RFC 1234		Tunneling IPX Traffic through IP Networks
RFC 1231		IEEE 802.5 Token Ring MIB
RFC 1220		Point-to-Point Protocol Extensions for Bridging
RFC 1219		On the Assignment of Subnet Numbers
RFC 1215		A Convention for Defining Traps for use with SNMP
RFC 1213		Management Information Base for Network Management of TCP/IP-Based internets: MIB II
RFC 1212		Concise MIB Definitions
RFC 1209		The Transmission of IP Datagrams over SMDS Service
RFC 1196		The Finger User Information Protocol
RFC 1195		Use of OSI IS-IS for Routing in TCP/IP and Dual Environments
RFC 1191		Path MTU Discovery
RFC 1188	Replaced by RFC 1390	A Proposed Standard for the Transmission of IP Datagrams over FDDI Networks

continues

Table C-1   *List of RFCs (Continued)*

RFC Number	Notes	RFC Title
RFC 1172		The Point-to-Point (PPP) Initial Configuration Options
RFC 1171	Replaced By RFC 1331	PPP for the Transmission of Multi-Protocol Datagrams Over Point-to-Point Links
RFC 1166		INTERNET NUMBERS
RFC 1164		Application of the BGP in the Internet
RFC 1163		A Border Gateway Protocol (BGP)
RFC 1157		A Simple Network Management Protocol (SNMP)
RFC 1156	Replaced by RFC 1213	MIB for TCP/IP
RFC 1155	Replaced by FRC 1212	Structure and Identification of Management Information for TCP/IP-based Internets
RFC 1144		Compressing TCP/IP Headers for Low-Speed Serial Links
RFC 1141		Incremental Updating of the Internet Checksum
RFC 1139		An Echo Function for ISO 8473 (ping)
RFC 1136		Administrative Domains and Routing Domains: A model for routing in the Internet
RFC 1122		Requirements for Internet Hosts— Communication Layers
RFC 1119	Obsoletes RFC 119, 1059, 958	Network Time Protocol (NTP) Version 3
RFC 1112		Host Extensions for IP Multicasting
RFC 1108	DCA draft	IP Security Option (IPSO)
RFC 1101		DNS Encoding of Network Names and Other Types
RFC 1091		Telnet Terminal-Type Option
RFC 1084		BootP Extensions
RFC 1080		Telnet Remote Flow Control Option
RFC 1079		Telnet Terminal Speed Option
RFC 1069		Guidelines for the use of Internet-IP addresses in the ISO Connectionless-Mode Network Protocol
RFC 1060		Assigned Numbers

Table C-1 *List of RFCs (Continued)*

RFC Number	Notes	RFC Title
RFC 1058		Routing Information Protocol (RIP)
RFC 1055		Standard for the Transmission of IP Datagrams over Serial Lines (SLIP)
RFC 1042		Standard for the Transmission of IP Datagrams over IEEE 802 Networks
RFC 1035		Domain Names—Implementation and Specification
RFC 1034		Domain Names—Concepts and Facilities
RFC 1027		Using ARP to Implement Transparent Subnet Gateway (Proxy ARP)
RFC 1009		Requirements for Internet Gateways
RFC 995	Replaced by ISO 9542	End System to Intermediate System Routing Exchange Protocol for use in conjunction with ISO 8473
RFC 994	Replaced by ISO 8473	Protocol for Providing the Connectionless-Mode Network Service
RFC 982		Guidelines for the Specification of the Top of the Structure of the Domain Specific Part (DSP) of the ISO Standard NSAP Address
RFC 951		Bootstrap Protocol (BootP)
RFC 950		Internet Standard Subnetting Procedure
RFC 925		Multi-LAN Address Resolution (PROXY ARP)
RFC 922		Broadcasting Internet Datagrams in the Presence of Subnets (IP-BROAD)
RFC 919		BROADCASTING INTERNET DATAGRAMS
RFC 906		Bootstrap Loading Using TFTP
RFC 904		Exterior Gateway Protocol (EGP) Formal Specification
RFC 903		Reverse Address Resolution Protocol
RFC 896		Congestion Control in TCP/IP Internetworks

continues

Table C-1 *List of RFCs (Continued)*

RFC Number	Notes	RFC Title
RFC 895		Standard for the Transmission of IP Datagrams over Experimental Ethernet Networks
RFC 894		A Standard for the Transmission of IP Datagrams over Ethernet
RFC 891		Hello Protocol
RFC 879		The TCP Maximum Segment Size and Related Topics
RFC 877		Standard for the Transmission of IP Datagrams over Public Data Networks
RFC 874		Telnet Protocol Specification
RFC 863		Discard Protocol
RFC 862		Echo Protocol
RFC 860		TELNET TIMING MARK OPTION
RFC 858		TELNET SUPPRESS GO AHEAD OPTION
RFC 857		TELNET ECHO OPTION
RFC 856		TELNET BINARY TRANSMISSION
RFC 855		TELNET OPTION SPECIFICATION
RFC 854	MIL STD 1782	TELNET PROTOCOL SPECIFICATION
RFC 827		EXTERIOR GATEWAY PROTOCOL (EGP)
RFC 826		An Ethernet Address Resolution Protocol (ARP)
RFC 815		IP DATAGRAM REASSEMBLY ALGORITHMS
RFC 813		WINDOW AND ACKNOWLEDGMENT STRATEGY IN TCP
RFC 793	MIL STD 1778	Transmission Control Protocol (TCP)
RFC 792		Internet Control Message Protocol (ICMP)
RFC 791	MIL STD 1777	Internetwork Protocol (IP)
RFC 783		Trivial File Transfer Protocol (TFTP Version 2)
RFC 779		Telnet Send-Location Option
RFC 768		User Datagram Protocol (UDP)

Common Cable Types and Pinouts

This appendix provides the following pinout information:

- Console Port Pinouts (RJ-45)
- Auxiliary Port Pinouts (RJ-45)
- EIA-530 DTE Cable Pinout (DB-60 to DB-25)
- EIA/TIA-232 DTE Cable Pinout (DB-60 to DB-25)
- EIA/TIA-232 DCE Cable Pinout (DB-60 to DB-25)
- EIA/TIA-449 DTE Cable Pinout (DB-60 to DB-37)
- EIA/TIA-449 DCE Cable Pinout (DB-60 to DB-37)
- V.35 DTE Cable Pinout (DB-60 to 34-Pin)
- V.35 DCE Cable Pinout (DB-60 to 34-Pin)
- X.21 DTE Cable Pinout (DB-60 to DB-15)
- X.21 DCE Cable Pinout (DB-60 to DB-15)
- Ethernet (AUI) Cable Pinout (DB-15)
- Token Ring Port Pinout (DB-9)
- Asynchronous Breakout Cable Pinout (8-Pin RJ-45)
- Asynchronous-Line Cable Pinout (68-Pin SCSI
- Pinouts for the RJ-45-to-DB-25 Adapters
- Asynchronous Device Cabling Options

Console and Auxiliary Port Signals and Pinouts

The console port is configured as data communications equipment (DCE), and the auxiliary port is configured as data terminal equipment (DTE). The console and auxiliary ports both use RJ-45 connectors. RJ-45-to-DB-25 adapters are available for connection to modems and other external communications equipment. Both ports are configured as asynchronous serial ports.

Table D-1 shows the pinouts for the console port and Table D-2 shows the pinouts for the auxiliary port.

NOTE   Table D-16 and Table D-17 show the pinouts for the adapters.

Table D-1   *Console Port Pinouts (RJ-45)*

Console Port (DTE)		
Pin[1]	Signal	Input/Output
1	–	–
2	DTR	Output
3	TxD	Output
4	GND	–
5	GND	–
6	RxD	Input
7	DSR	Input
8	–	–

[1]   Any pin not referenced is not connected.

Table D-2   *Auxiliary Port Pinouts (RJ-45)*

Auxiliary Port (DTE)		
Pin[1]	Signal	Input/Output
1	RTS	Output
2	DTR	Output
3	TXD	Output
4	GND	–
5	GND	–
6	RXD	Input
7	DSR	Input
8	CTS	Input

[1]   Any pin not referenced is not connected.

Serial Cable Assemblies and Pinouts

The following illustrations and tables provide assembly drawings and pinouts for the EIA-530 DCE, and EIA/TIA-232, EIA/TIA-449, V.35, and X.21 DTE and DCE cables.

EIA-530

Figure D-1 shows the EIA-530 serial cable assembly, and Table D-3 lists the pinouts.

Figure D-1   *EIA-530 Serial Cable Assembly*

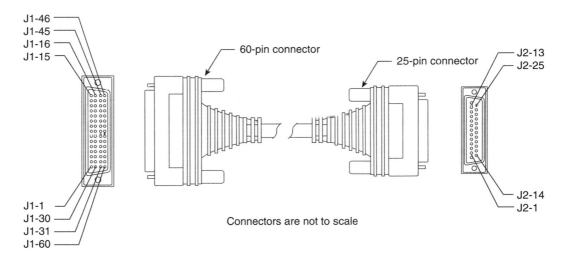

Connectors are not to scale

Arrows indicate signal direction: → indicates DTE to DCE, and ← indicates DCE to DTE.

Table D-3   *EIA-530 DTE Cable Pinout (DB-60 to DB-25)*

60 Pin[1]	Signal	25 Pin	Signal	Direction DTE DCE[2]
J1-11	TxD/RxD+	J2-2	BA(A), TxD+	→
J1-12	TxD/RxD–	J2-14	BA(B), TxD-	→
J1-28	RxD/TxD+	J2-3	BB(A), RxD+	←
J1-27	RxD/TxD–	J2-16	BB(B), RxD-	←
J1-9	RTS/CTS+	J2-4	CA(A), RTS+	→
J1-10	RTS/CTS-	J2-19	CA(B), RTS-	→
J1-1	CTS/RTS+	J2-5	CB(A), CTS+	←

continues

Table D-3   *EIA-530 DTE Cable Pinout (DB-60 to DB-25) (Continued)*

60 Pin[1]	Signal	25 Pin	Signal	Direction DTE DCE[2]
J1-2	CTS/RTS-	J2-13	CB(B), CTS-	←
J1-3	DSR/DTR+	J2-6	CC(A), DSR+	←
J1-4	DSR/DTR-	J2-22	CC(B), DSR-	←
J1-46	Shield_GND	J2-1	Shield	Shorted
J1-47	MODE_2	-	-	
J1-48	GND	-	-	Shorted
J1-49	MODE_1	-	-	
J1-5	DCD/DCD+	J2-8	CF(A), DCD+	←
J1-6	DCD/DCD-	J2-10	CF(B), DCD-	←
J1-24	TxC/RxC+	J2-15	DB(A), TxC+	←
J1-23	TxC/RxC-	J2-12	DB(B), TxC-	←
J1-26	RxC/TxCE+	J2-17	DD(A), RxC+	←
J1-25	RxC/TxCE-	J2-9	DD(B), RxC-	←
J1-44	LL/DCD	J2-18	LL	→
J1-45	Circuit_GND	J2-7	Circuit_ GND	-
J1-7	DTR/DSR+	J2-20	CD(A), DTR+	→
J1-8	DTR/DSR-	J2-23	CD(B), DTR-	→
J1-13	TxCE/TxC+	J2-24	DA(A), TxCE+	→
J1-14	TxCE/TxC–	J2-11	DA(B), TxCE–	→

[1] Any pin not referenced is not connected.

[2] The EIA-530 interface cannot be operated in DCE mode. A DCE cable is not available for the EIA-530 interface.

EIA/TIA-232

Figure D-2 shows the EIA/TIA-232 cable assembly; Table D-4 lists the DTE pinout; and Table D-5 lists the DCE pinout. Arrows indicate signal direction: → indicates DTE to DCE, and ← indicates DCE to DTE.

Figure D-2 *EIA/TIA-232 Cable Assembly*

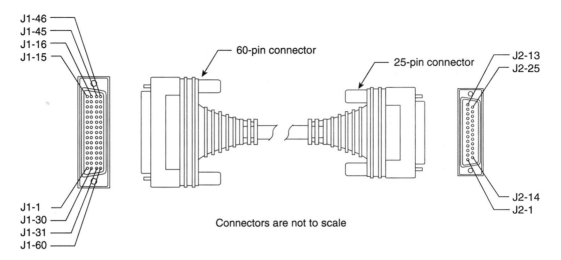

Table D-4 *EIA/TIA-232 DTE Cable Pinout (DB-60 to DB-25)*

60 Pin[1]	Signal	Description	Direction	25 Pin	Signal
J1-50	MODE_0	Shorting group	-	-	-
J1-51	GND	Shorting group	-	-	-
J1-52	MODE_DCE	Shorting group	-	-	-
J1-46	Shield GND	Single	-	J2-1	Shield GND
J1-41	TxD/RxD	Twisted pair no. 5	→	J2-2	TxD
Shield	-			Shield	-
J1-36	RxD/TxD	Twisted pair no. 9	←	J2-3	RxD
Shield	-		-	Shield	-
J1-42	RTS/CTS	Twisted pair no. 4	→	J2-4	RTS
Shield	-		-	Shield	-
J1-35	CTS/RTS	Twisted pair no. 10	←	J2-5	CTS
Shield	-		-	Shield	-
J1-34	DSR/DTR	Twisted pair no. 11	←	J2-6	DSR
Shield	-		-	Shield	-
J1-45	Circuit GND	Twisted pair no. 1	-	J2-7	Circuit GND
Shield	-		-	Shield	-

continues

Table D-4   *EIA/TIA-232 DTE Cable Pinout (DB-60 to DB-25) (Continued)*

60 Pin[1]	Signal	Description	Direction	25 Pin	Signal
J1-33	DCD/LL	Twisted pair no. 12	←	J2-8	DCD
Shield	-		-	Shield	-
J1-37	TxC/NIL	Twisted pair no. 8	←	J2-15	TxC
Shield	-		-	Shield	-
J1-38	RxC/TxCE	Twisted pair no. 7	←	J2-17	RxC
Shield	-		-	Shield	-
J1-44	LL/DCD	Twisted pair no. 2	→	J2-18	LTST
Shield	-		-	Shield	-
J1-43	DTR/DSR	Twisted pair no. 3	→	J2-20	DTR
Shield	-		-	Shield	-
J1-39	TxCE/TxC	Twisted pair no. 6	→	J2-24	TxCE
Shield	-		-	Shield	-

[1] Any pin not referenced is not connected.

Table D-5   *EIA/TIA-232 DCE Cable Pinout (DB-60 to DB-25)*

60 Pin[1]	Signal	Description	Direction	25 Pin	Signal
J1-50	MODE_0	Shorting group	-	-	-
J1-51	GND	Shorting group	-	-	-
J1-46	Shield GND	Single	-	J2-1	Shield GND
J1-36	RxD/TxD	Twisted pair no. 9	←	J2-2	TxD
Shield	-		-	Shield	-
J1-41	TxD/RxD	Twisted pair no. 5	→	J2-3	RxD
Shield	-		-	Shield	-
J1-35	CTS/RTS	Twisted pair no. 10	←	J2-4	RTS
Shield	-		-	Shield	-
J1-42	RTS/CTS	Twisted pair no. 4	→	J2-5	CTS
Shield	-		-	Shield	-
J1-43	DTR/DSR	Twisted pair no. 3	→	J2-6	DSR
Shield	-		-	Shield	-
J1-45	Circuit GND	Twisted pair no. 1	-	J2-7	Circuit GND
Shield	-		-	Shield	

Table D-5   *EIA/TIA-232 DCE Cable Pinout (DB-60 to DB-25) (Continued)*

60 Pin[1]	Signal	Description	Direction	25 Pin	Signal
J1-44	LL/DCD	Twisted pair no. 2	→	J2-8	DCD
Shield	-		-	Shield	-
J1-39	TxCE/TxC	Twisted pair no. 7	-→	J2-15	TxC
Shield	-		-	Shield	-
J1-40	NIL/RxC	Twisted pair no. 6	→	J2-17	RxC
Shield	-		-	Shield	-
J1-33	DCD/LL	Twisted pair no. 12	←	J2-18	LTST
Shield	-		-	Shield	-
J1-34	DSR/DTR	Twisted pair no. 11	←	J2-20	DTR
Shield	-		-	Shield	-
J1-38	RxC/TxCE	Twisted pair no. 8	←	J2-24	TxCE
Shield	-		-	Shield	-

[1] Any pin not referenced is not connected.

EIA/TIA-449

Figure D-3 shows the EIA/TIA-449 cable assembly; Table D-6 lists the DTE pinout; Table D-7 lists the DCE pinout. Arrows indicate signal direction: → indicates DTE to DCE, and ← indicates DCE to DTE.

Figure D-3   *EIA/TIA-449 Cable Assembly*

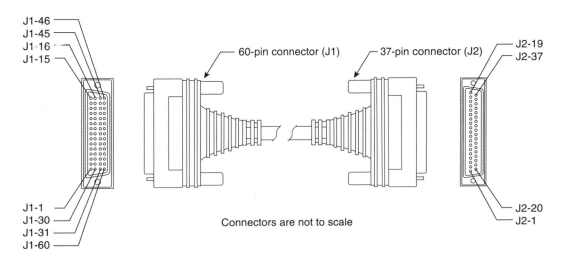

Table D-6   *EIA/TIA-449 DTE Cable Pinout (DB-60 to DB-37)*

60 Pin[1]	Signal	Description	Direction	37 Pin	Signal
J1-49	MODE_1	Shorting group	-	-	-
J1-48	GND	Shorting group	-	-	-
J1-51	GND	Shorting group	-	-	-
J1-52	MODE_DCE	Shorting group	-	-	-
J1-46	Shield_GND	Single		J2-1	Shield GND
J1-11	TxD/RxD+	Twisted pair no. 6	→	J2-4	SD+
J1-12	TxD/RxD-		→	J2-22	SD-
J1-24	TxC/RxC+	Twisted pair no. 9	←	J2-5	ST+
J1-23	TxC/RxC-		←	J2-23	ST-
J1-28	RxD/TxD+	Twisted pair no. 11	←	J2-6	RD+
J1-27	RxD/TxD-		←	J2-24	RD-
J1-9	RTS/CTS+	Twisted pair no. 5	→	J2-7	RS+
J1-10	RTS/CTS-		→	J2-25	RS-
J1-26	RxC/TxCE+	Twisted pair no. 10	←	J2-8	RT+
J1-25	RxC/TxCE-		←	J2-26	RT-
J1-1	CTS/RTS+	Twisted pair no. 1	←	J2-9	CS+
J1-2	CTS/RTS-		←	J2-27	CS-
J1-44	LL/DCD	Twisted pair no. 12	→	J2-10	LL
J1-45	Circuit_GND		-	J2-37	SC
J1-3	DSR/DTR+	Twisted pair no. 2	←	J2-11	DM+
J1-4	DSR/DTR-		←	J2-29	DM-
J1-7	DTR/DSR+	Twisted pair no. 4	→	J2-12	TR+
J1-8	DTR/DSR-		→	J2-30	TR-
J1-5	DCD/DCD+	Twisted pair no. 3	←	J2-13	RR+
J1-6			←	J2-31	RR-
J1-13	TxCE/TxC+		→	J2-17	TT+
J1-14	TxCE/TxC-	Twisted pair no. 7	→	J2-35	TT-
J1-15	Circuit_GND	Twisted pair no. 9	-	J2-19	SG
J1-16	Circuit_GND		-	J2-20	RC

[1] Any pin not referenced is not connected.

Table D-7   *EIA/TIA-449 DCE Cable Pinout (DB-60 to DB-37)*

60 Pin[1]	Signal	Description	Direction	37 Pin	Signal
J1-49	MODE_1	Shorting group	-	-	---
J1-48	GND	Shorting group	-	-	-
J1-46	Shield_GND	Single	-	J2-1	Shield GND
J1-28	RxD/TxD+	Twisted pair no. 11	←	J2-4	SD+
J1-27	RxD/TxD-		←	J2-22	SD-
J1-13	TxCE/TxC+	Twisted pair no. 7	→	J2-5	ST+
J1-14	TxCE/TxC-		→	J2-23	ST-
J1-11	TxD/RxD+	Twisted pair no. 6	→	J2-6	RD+
J1-12	TxD/RxD-		→	J2-24	RD-
J1-1	CTS/RTS+	Twisted pair no. 1	←	J2-7	RS+
J1-2	CTS/RTS-		←	J2-25	RS-
J1-24	TxC/RxC+	Twisted pair no. 9	→	J2-8	RT+
J1-23	TxC/RxC-		→	J2-26	RT-
J1-9	RTS/CTS+	Twisted pair no. 5	→	J2-9	CS+
J1-10	RTS/CTS-		→	J2-27	CS-
J1-29	NIL/LL	Twisted pair no. 12	→	J2-10	LL
J1-30	Circuit_GND		-	J2-37	SC
J1-7	DTR/DSR+	Twisted pair no. 4	→	J2-11	DM+
J1-8	DTR/DSR-		→	J2-29	DM-
J1-3	DSR/DTR+	Twisted pair no. 2	←	J2-12	TR+
J1-4	DSR/DTR-		←	J2-30	TR-
J1-5	DCD/DCD+	Twisted pair no. 3	→	J2-13	RR+
J1-6	DCD/DCD-		→	J2-31	RR-
J1-26	RxC/TxCE+	Twisted pair no. 10	←—	J2-17	TT+
J1-25	RxC/TxCE–		←—	J2-35	TT–
J1-15	Circuit_GND	Twisted pair no. 8	_	J2-19	SG
J1-16	Circuit_GND		_	J2-20	RC

[1] Any pin not referenced is not connected.

V.35

Figure D-4 shows the V.35 cable assembly; Table D-8 lists the DTE pinout; Table D-9 lists the DCE pinout. Arrows indicate signal direction: $\rightarrow$ indicates DTE to DCE, and $\leftarrow$ indicates DCE to DTE.

Figure D-4   *V.35 Cable Assembly*

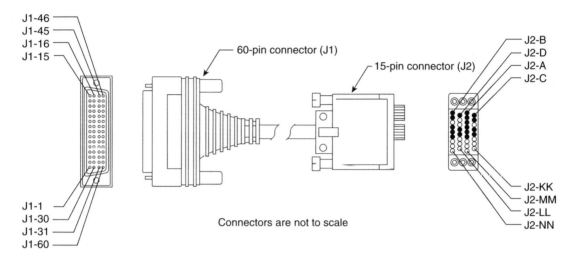

Table D-8   *V.35 DTE Cable Pinout (DB-60 to 34-Pin)*

60 Pin[1]	Signal	Description	Direction	34 Pin	Signal
J1-49	MODE_1	Shorting group	-	-	-
J1-48	GND	Shorting group	-	-	-
J1-50	MODE_0	Shorting group	-	-	-
J1-51	GND	Shorting group	-	-	-
J1-52	MODE_DCE	Shorting group	-	-	-
J1-53	TxC/NIL	Shorting group	-	-	-
J1-54	RxC_TxCE	Shorting group	-	-	-
J1-55	RxD/TxD	Shorting group	-	-	-
J1-56	GND	Shorting group	-	-	-
J1-46	Shield_GND	Single	-	J2-A	Frame GND
J1-45	Circuit_GND	Twisted pair no. 12	-	J2-B	Circuit GND
Shield	-		-	Shield	-

Table D-8 *V.35 DTE Cable Pinout (DB-60 to 34-Pin) (Continued)*

60 Pin[1]	Signal	Description	Direction	34 Pin	Signal
J1-42	RTS/CTS	Twisted pair no. 9	→	J2-C	RTS
Shield	-		-	Shield	-
J1-35	CTS/RTS	Twisted pair no. 8	←	J2-D	CTS
Shield	-		-	Shield	-
J1-34	DSR/DTR	Twisted pair no. 7	←	J2-E	DSR
Shield	-		-	Shield	-
J1-33	DCD/LL	Twisted pair no. 6	←	J2-F	RLSD
Shield	-		-	Shield	-
J1-43	DTR/DSR	Twisted pair no. 10	→	J2-H	DTR
Shield	-		-	Shield	-
J1-44	LL/DCD	Twisted pair no. 11	→	J2-K	LT
Shield	-		-	Shield	-
J18	TxD/RxD+	Twisted pair no. 1	→	J2-P	SD+
J17	TxD/RxD-		→	J2-S	SD-
J1-28	RxD/TxD+	Twisted pair no. 5	←	J2-R	RD+
J1-27	RxD/TxD-		←	J2-T	RD-
J1-20	TxCE/TxC+	Twisted pair no. 2	→	J2-U	SCTE+
J1-19	TxCE/TxC-		→	J2-W	SCTE-
J1-26	RxC/TxCE+	Twisted pair no. 4	←	J2-V	SCR+
J1-25	RxC/TxCE-		←	J2-X	SCR-
J1-24	TxC/RxC+	Twisted pair no. 3	←	J2-Y	SCT+
J1-23	TxC/RxC-		←	J2-AA	SCT-

[1] Any pin not referenced is not connected.

Table D-9 *V.35 DCE Cable Pinout (DB-60 to 34-Pin)*

60 Pin[1]	Signal	Description	Direction	34 Pin	Signal
J1-49	MODE_1	Shorting group	-	-	-
J1-48	GND	Shorting group	-	-	-
J1-50	MODE_0	Shorting group	-	-	-
J1-51	GND	Shorting group	-	-	-

continues

Table D-9 *V.35 DCE Cable Pinout (DB-60 to 34-Pin) (Continued)*

60 Pin[1]	Signal	Description	Direction	34 Pin	Signal
J1-53	TxC/NIL	Shorting group	-	-	-
J1-54	RxC_TxCE	Shorting group	-	-	-
J1-55	RxD/TxD	Shorting group	-	-	-
J1-56	GND	Shorting group	-	-	-
J1-46	Shield_GND	Single	-	J2-A	Frame GND
J1-45	Circuit_GND	Twisted pair no. 12	-	J2-B	Circuit GND
Shield	-		-	Shield	-
J1-35	CTS/RTS	Twisted pair no. 8	←	J2-C	RTS
Shield	-		-	Shield	-
J1-42	RTS/CTS	Twisted pair no. 9	→	J2-D	CTS
Shield	-		-	Shield	-
J1-43	DTR/DSR	Twisted pair no. 10	-→	J2-E	DSR
Shield	-		-	Shield	-
J1-44	LL/DCD	Twisted pair no. 11	→	J2-F	RLSD
Shield	-		-	Shield	-
J1-34	DSR/DTR	Twisted pair no. 7	←	J2-H	DTR
Shield	-		-	Shield	-
J1-33	DCD/LL	Twisted pair no. 6	←	J2-K	LT
Shield	-		-	Shield	-
J1-28	RxD/TxD+	Twisted pair no. 5	←	J2-P	SD+
J1-27	RxD/TxD-		←	J2-S	SD-
J1-18	TxD/RxD+	Twisted pair no. 1	→	J2-R	RD+
J1-17	TxD/RxD-		→	J2-T	RD-
J1-26	RxC/TxCE+	Twisted pair no. 4	←	J2-U	SCTE+
J1-25	RxC/TxCE-		←	J2-W	SCTE-
J1-22	NIL/RxC+	Twisted pair no. 3	→	J2-V	SCR+
J1-21	NIL/RxC-		→	J2-X	SCR-
J1-20	TxCE/TxC+	Twisted pair no. 2	→	J2-Y	SCT+
J1-19	TxCE/TxC-		→	J2-AA	SCT-

[1] Any pin not referenced is not connected.

X.21

Figure D-5 shows the X.21 cable assembly; Table D-10 lists the DTE pinout; Table D-11 lists the DCE pinout. Arrows indicate signal direction: → indicates DTE to DCE, and ← indicates DCE to DTE.

Figure D-5 *X.21 Cable Assembly*

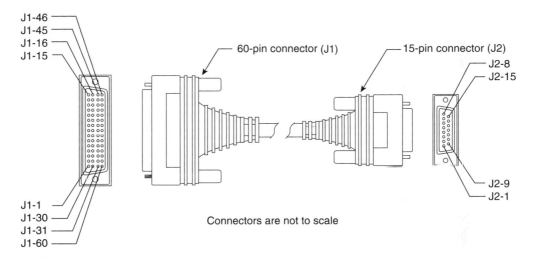

Table D-10 *X.21 DTE Cable Pinout (DB-60 to DB-15)*

60 Pin[1]	Signal	Description	Direction	15 Pin	Signal
J1-48	GND	Shorting group	-	-	-
J1-47	MODE_2	Shorting group	-	-	-
J1-51	GND	Shorting group	-	-	-
J1-52	MODE_DCE	Shorting group	-	-	-
J1-46	Shield_GND	Single	-	J2-1	Shield GND
J1-11	TxD/RxD+	Twisted pair no. 3	→	J2-2	Transmit+
J1-12	TxD/RxD-		→	J2-9	Transmit-
J1-9	RTS/CTS+	Twisted pair no. 2	→	J2-3	Control+
J1-10	RTS/CTS-		→	J2-10	Control-
J1-28	RxD/TxD+	Twisted pair no. 6	←	J2-4	Receive+
J1-27	RxD/TxD-		←	J2-11	Receive-

continues

Table D-10 *X.21 DTE Cable Pinout (DB-60 to DB-15) (Continued)*

60 Pin[1]	Signal	Description	Direction	15 Pin	Signal
J1-1	CTS/RTS+	Twisted pair no. 1	←	J2-5	Indication+
J1-2	CTS/RTS-		←	J2-12	Indication-
J1-26	RxC/TxCE+	Twisted pair no. 5	←	J2-6	Timing+
J1-25	RxC/TxCE-		←	J2-13	Timing-
J1-15	Control_GND	Twisted pair no. 4	-	J2-8	Control GND
Shield	-		-	Shqield	-

[1] Any pin not referenced is not connected.

Table D-11 *X.21 DCE Cable Pinout (DB-60 to DB-15)*

60 Pin[1]	Signal	Description	Direction	15 Pin	Signal
J1-48	GND	Shorting group	-	-	-
J1-47	MODE_2	Shorting group	-	-	-
J1-46	Shield_GND	Single	-	J2-1	Shield GND
J1-28	RxD/TxD+	Twisted pair no. 6	←	J2-2	Transmit+
J1-27	RxD/TxD-		←	J2-9	Transmit-
J1-1	CTS/RTS+	Twisted pair no. 1	←	J2-3	Control+
J1-2	CTS/RTS-		←	J2-10	Control-
J1-11	TxD/RxD+	Twisted pair no. 3	→	J2-4	Receive+
J1-12	TxD/RxD–		→	J2-11	Receive-
J1-9	RTS/CTS+	Twisted pair no. 2	→	J2-5	Indication+
J1-10	RTS/CTS-		→	J2-12	Indication-
J1-24	TxC/RxC+	Twisted pair no. 4	→	J2-6	Timing+
J1-23	TxC/RxC-		→	J2-13	Timing-
J1-15	Control_GND	Twisted pair no. 5	-	J2-8	Control GND
Shield	-		-	Shield	-

[1] Any pin not referenced is not connected.

Ethernet Cable Assembly and Pinout

Figure D-6 shows an Ethernet (AUI) cable assembly, and Table D-12 lists an AUI cable pinout.

Figure D-6   *Ethernet (AUI) Cable Assembly*

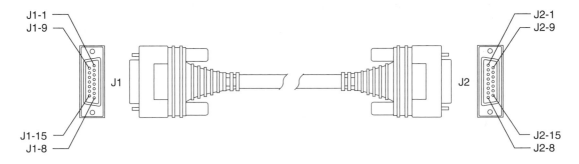

Table D-12   *Ethernet (AUI) Cable Pinout (DB-15)*

Pin[1]	Ethernet Circuit	Signal
3	DO-A	Data Out Circuit A
10	DO-B	Data Out Circuit B
11	DO-S	Data Out Circuit Shield
5	DI-A	Data In Circuit A
12	DI-B	Data In Circuit B
4	DI-S	Data In Circuit Shield
2	CI-A	Control In Circuit A
9	CI-B	Control In Circuit B
1	CI-S	Control In Circuit Shield
6	VC	Voltage Common
13	VP	Voltage Plus
14	VS	Voltage Shield (L25 and M25)
Shell	PG	Protective Ground

[1] Any pin not referenced is not connected.

Token Ring Pinout

Table D-13 lists the pinout for the Token Ring interface port.

Table D-13   *Token Ring Port Pinout (DB-9)*

9 Pin[1]	Signal
1	Receive
3	+5V[2]
5	Transmit
6	Receive
9	Transmit

[1] Pins 2, 4, 7, and 8 are ground

[2] 600 mA maximum

Asynchronous Serial Ports

Figure D-7 shows the RJ-45 breakout cable with pinouts for the 68-pin SCSI port and the RJ-45 serial port. Table D-14 contains the pinout for the RJ-45 end, and Table D-15 contains the pinout for the 68-pin SCSI type connector.

Figure D-7   *Asynchronous Serial Interface Breakout Cable Assembly*

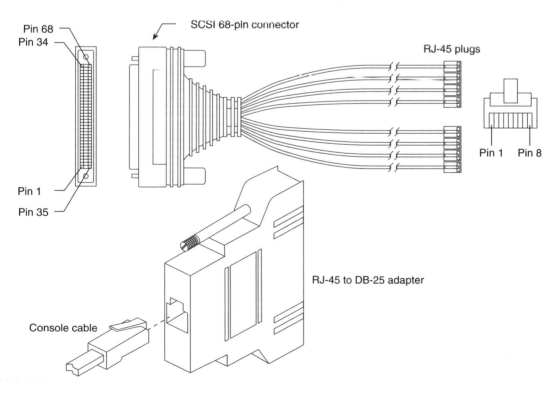

Table D-14 *Asynchronous Breakout Cable Pinout (8-Pin RJ-45)*

8 Pin RJ-45	Signal	Direction
1	CTS	←
2	DSR/DCD	←
3	RXD	←
4	RXD/GND	-
5	TXD/GND	-
6	TXD	→
7	DTR	→
8	RTS	→

NOTE   The Asynchronous breakout cable is equivalent to a console or auxiliary port with a roll-over RJ-45 cable attached. See Table D-17 for asynchronous device connection options.

Table D-15 *Asynchronous-Line Cable Pinout (68-Pin SCSI)*

RJ-45 Plug	Pin	Signal	68-Pin SCSI (J1)
1	1	CTS	39
	2	DSR	5
	3	RXD	38
	4	RXD GND	4
	5	TXD GND	37
	6	TXD	3
	7	DTR	36
	8	RTS	2
2	1	CTS	43
	2	DSR	9
	3	RXD	42
	4	RXD GND	8
	5	TXD GND	41
	6	TXD	7
	7	DTR	40
	8	RTS	6

continues

Table D-15 *Asynchronous-Line Cable Pinout (68-Pin SCSI) (Continued)*

RJ-45 Plug	Pin	Signal	68-Pin SCSI (J1)
3	1	CTS	47
	2	DSR	13
	3	RXD	46
	4	RXD GND	12
	5	TXD GND	45
	6	TXD	11
	7	DTR	44
	8	RTS	10
4	1	CTS	51
	2	DSR	17
	3	RXD	50
	4	RXD GND	16
	5	TXD GND	49
	6	TXD	15
	7	DTR	48
	8	RTS	14
5	1	CTS	55
	2	DSR	21
	3	RXD	54
	4	RXD GND	20
	5	TXD GND	53
	6	TXD	19
	7	DTR	52
	8	RTS	18
6	1	CTS	59
	2	DSR	25
	3	RXD	58
	4	RXD GND	24
	5	TXD GND	57
	6	TXD	23

Table D-15 *Asynchronous-Line Cable Pinout (68-Pin SCSI) (Continued)*

RJ-45 Plug	Pin	Signal	68-Pin SCSI (J1)
	7	DTR	56
	8	RTS	22
7	1	CTS	63
	2	DSR	29
	3	RXD	62
	4	RXD GND	28
	5	TXD GND	61
	6	TXD	27
	7	DTR	60
	8	RTS	26
8	1	CTS	67
	2	DSR	33
	3	RXD	66
	4	RXD GND	32
	5	TXD GND	65
	6	TXD	31
	7	DTR	64
	8	RTS	30

RJ-45 Adapter Pinouts

Refer to Table D-16 for a list of the pins used on the RJ-45-to-DB-25 adapters, used with an RJ-45 cable, to connect terminals and modems to the Cisco 2500 series access server. The cable you use may be a roll-over cable or a straight cable.

A roll-over cable can be detected by comparing the two modular ends of the cable. Holding the cables in your hand, side-by-side, with the tab at the back, the wire connected to the pin on the outside of the left plug should be the same color as the pin on the outside of the right plug. If your cable was purchased from Cisco, pin 1 will be white on one connector, and pin 8 will be white on the other (a roll-over cable reverses pins 1 and 8, 2 and 7, 3 and 6, and 4 and 5). (See Figure D-8.)

Figure D-8   *Identifying a Roll-Over Cable*

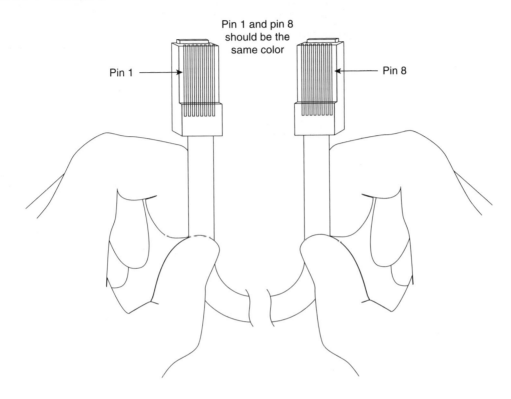

The Cisco 2500 series access server ships with a rolled cable. Connection to a terminal or a modem will require an RJ-45-to-DB-25 adapter, and possibly a DB-25-to-DB9 adapter. Refer to Table D-17 for the cable and adapter configurations that can be used to connect terminals and modems to the Cisco 2500 series access server.

Table D-16   *Pinouts for the RJ-45-to-DB-25 Adapters*

Adapter	DTE M/F Pins[1]	DCE M/F Pins	MMOD Pins[2]
RJ-45 Pins	DB-25 Pins		
1	4	5	5
2	20	6	8
3	2	3	3
4	7	7	7
5	7	7	7
6	3	2	2

Table D-16 *Pinouts for the RJ-45-to-DB-25 Adapters (Continued)*

Adapter	DTE M/F Pins[1]	DCE M/F Pins	MMOD Pins[2]
RJ-45 Pins	DB-25 Pins		
7	6	20	20
8	5	4	4

[1] The female data terminal equipment (FDTE) adapter that is available from Cisco is labeled "Terminal."

[2] The MMOD adapter that is available from Cisco is labeled "Modem."

Table D-17 *Asynchronous Device Cabling Options*

Access Server Port	RJ-45 Cable Type	DB-25 Adapter	End Device
Console or auxiliary	Rolled	FDTE[1]	Terminal
Console or auxiliary	Straight	FDCE	Terminal
Auxiliary or console	Rolled	MMOD[2]	Modem[3]

[1] The FDTE RJ-45-to-DB-25 adapter is labeled "Terminal."

[2] The MMOD RJ-45-to-DB-25 adapter is labeled "Modem."

[3] The asynchronous breakout cable (see Table D-14 and Table D-15) is functionally equivalent to a roll-over cable.

Bibliography

This appendix provides a list of resources used to create this book. Without the hard work, insight, and creativity of the authors, engineers, and professionals behind this documentation, this book would not have been possible.

Resource	Title/ Resource Type	Web Page	Chapter	Author
	Configuring IP Routing Protocol- Independent Features		Pages P1C- 189 to 215	
Access Services Configuration Guide, Release 11.1				Cisco
Advanced IP Network Design				Alvaro Retanna, Don Slice, Russ White
Bridging and IBM Networking Command Reference; Cisco IOS Software Release 12.0				Cisco
Bridging and IBM Networking Configuration Guide	*Configuring Source-Route Bridging*			

continues

Resource	Title/ Resource Type	Web Page	Chapter	Author
Bridging and IBM Networking Configuration Guide, Cisco IOS Software Release 12.0				
Bridging and IBM Networking Configuration Guide, Release 11.1				Cisco
Catalyst 2900 Series XL and Catalyst 350 Series XL Software Configuration Guide	*Configuring VLANs*		Chapter 8	
Catalyst 3920 Token Ring Switch User Guide, Release 1.0				
Catalyst 5000 Series Software Configuration Guide, Release 4.2				
Catalyst 6000 Family Software Configuration Guide			Chapters 5, 6, and 11	
Catalyst Token Ring Switching Implementation Guide	*Port Operation Modes*		Chapter 1	
Cisco: Understanding Service Access Point Access Control Lists	*Understanding Service Access Point Access Control Lists*			

Resource	Title/ Resource Type	Web Page	Chapter	Author
Cisco Document 78-2414-02 Rev A0	*Update for Catalyst 5000 Series Configuration Guide and Command Reference*			
Cisco IOS Desktop Switching Software Configuration Guide	*Creating and Maintaining VLANs*		Chapter 5	
Cisco IOS Quality of Service Solutions Configuration Guide	*Configuring Frame Relay and Frame Relay Traffic Shaping*			
Cisco IOS Switching Services Configuration Guide, Cisco IOS Release 12.0				Cisco
Cisco IOS Wide-Area Networking Configuration Guide	*Configuring Frame Relay*			
Debug Command Reference, Cisco IOS Software Release 12.0				Cisco
Dial Solutions Command Reference, Cisco IOS Software Release 11.03				Cisco
DLSW+ Design and Implementation Guide			Chapters 1, 2, 3, 4, 5, 7, and 9	

continues

Resource	Title/ Resource Type	Web Page	Chapter	Author
Enabling Enterprise Multihoming with Cisco IOS Network Address Translation (NAT)	Whitepaper, 1997			Akkiraju, Delgadillo, Rekhter
Installation and Maintenance of Cisco Router, Volume 1, version 11.3a	Student Guide			
Installation and Maintenance of Cisco Router, Volume 2, version 11.3a	Student Guide			
Installation and Maintenance of Cisco Router, Volume 3, version 11.3a	Student Guide			
Internetwork Design Guide				Cisco
Internetworking Case Studies				Cisco
Internetworking Technology Overview, June 1999	*Enhanced IGRP*		Chapter 36	
Internetworking Technology Overview, June 1999	*Mixed-Media Bridging*		Chapter 24	
Internetworking Technology Overview, June 1999	*Token Ring/ IEEE 802.5*		Chapter 9	

Resource	Title/ Resource Type	Web Page	Chapter	Author
Introduction to Cisco Router Configuration: Student Guide, Release 11.0				Cisco
IP Routing Primer				Robert Wright
Network Time Protocol (Version 3) Specification, Implementation. and Analysis				D. Mills
Quality of Service Solutions Configuration Guide	*Configuring Frame Relay and Frame Relay Traffic Shaping*			
Router Products Configuration and Reference			Chapters 1 and 19	
Router Products Configuration and Reference	*Configuring Source-Route Bridging*		Chapter 1	
Router Products Configuration and Reference	*Configuring Transparent Bridging*		Chapter 1	
Router Products Configuration Guide	*Configuring DLSw+*		Chapter 30	
Simple Network Time Protocol (SNTP), version 4 for IPv4, IPv6 and OSI				D. Mills

continues

Resource	Title/ Resource Type	Web Page	Chapter	Author
Software Configuration Guide, Release 5.4	*Configuring Faster EtherChannel and Gigabit EtherChannel*		Chapter 7	
Software Configuration Guide, Release 6.1			Chapters 9 and 12	
Software Configuration Guide, Release 5.2	*Configuring Spanning Tree*		Chapter 8	
Statement of Direction	*10 Gigabit Ethernet Position Statement*			
Web Site	"APPN Implementer's Workshop Closed Pages Document"	Info.internet.isi.edu/ in-notes/rfc/files/ rfc2166.txt		
Web Site	"Avoiding Routing Loops When Using Dynamic NAT"	Cisco.com/warp/ public/556/4.html		
Web Site	"Cisco IOS Network Address Translation (NAT)"	Cisco.com/warp/ public/701/60.html		
Web Site	"Configuration Notes for the Enhanced Implementation of EIGRP"	www.cisco.com/ warp/public/103/ 12.html		
Web Site	"Configuring IP Enhanced IGRP"	www.cisco.com/ univercd/cc/td/doc/ product/software/ ios120/12cgcr/ np1_c/1cprt1/ 1ceigrp.htm		
Web Site	"Data Link Switching"	www.cisco.com/ warp/public/100/ 49.html		

Resource	Title/ Resource Type	Web Page	Chapter	Author
Web Site	"Data Link Switching: Switch-to-Switch Protocol AIW DLSw RIG: DLSw Closed Pages, DLSw Standard Version 1.0"	Info.internet.isi.edu/ in-notes/rfc/files/ frc1795.txt		
Web Site	"DLSw and Network Address Translation (NAT)"	Cisco.com/warp/ public/697/6.html		
Web Site	"DLSw+ SAP/ MAC Filtering Techniques"	Cisco.com/warp/ public/697/ dlswfilter.shtml		
Web Site	"Enhanced IGRP Stub Routing"	www.cisco.com/ univercd/cc/td/doc/p roduct/software/ ios120/120newft/ 120limit/120s/ 120s15/eigrpstb.htm		
Web Site	"Enhanced Interior Gateway Routing Protocol"	www.cisco.com/ warp/customer/103/ eigrp1.html		
Web Site	"Enhanced Interior Gateway Routing Protocol"	www.cisco.com/ warp/customer/103/ eigrp5.html		
Web Site	"Enhanced Interior Gateway Routing Protocol"	www.cisco.com/ warp/public/ customer/103/ eigrp6.html		
Web Site	"Frame Relay Traffic Shaping"	www.cisco.com/ warp/public/125/ 21.html		
Web Site	"Introduction to Enhanced IGRP (EIGRP)"	www.cisco.com/ warp/public/459/ 7.html		

continues

Resource	Title/ Resource Type	Web Page	Chapter	Author
Web Site	"ISDN Switch Types, Codes, and Values"	www.cisco.com/ univercd/dd/td/ doc/product/ software/ios112/ dbook/disdn.html		
Web Site	"NAT Pools and Subnet Zero"	www.cisco.com/ warp/public/556/ 7.html		
Web Site	"NAT: Local and Global Definitions"	www.cisco.com/ warp/public/556/ 8.html		
Web Site	"Password Recovery Techniques"	www.cisco.com/ warp/public/701/ 22.html		
Web Site	"RIF Passthrough in DLSw+ Training Supplement"	www.cisco.com/ warp/public/779/ largeent/sna/trng/ rif_pt/rif_pt.html		
Web Site	"Troubleshooting Token Ring"	www.cisco.com/ univercd/cc/td/doc/ cisintwk/itg_v1/ tr1906.html		
Web Site	"Understanding and Configuring FastEtherChannel on Cisco Switching and Routing Devices"	www.cisco.com/ warp/ublic/473/ 4.html		
Web Site	"Understanding and Configuring Spanning Tree Protocol (STP) on Catalyst Switches"	www.cisco.com/ warp/public/473/ 5.html		
Web Site	"Using Nonstandard FTP Port Numbers with NAT"	www.cisco.com/ warp/public/556/ 6.html		

Resource	Title/ Resource Type	Web Page	Chapter	Author
Web Site	"Using the Border Gateway Protocol for Interdomain Routing"	www.cisco.com/ univ-src/3.6/data/ doc/cintrnet/ics/ icsbgp4.html		
Web Site	"Configuring a Gateway of Last Resort Using IP Command"	www.cisco.com/ warp/public/105/ default.html		
Cisco IOS IP and IP Routing Configuration Guide			PC1-C149 to 180	
Cisco IOS Software Release 12.1(2)T	*OSPF Flooding Reduction*			
Web Site	RFC 2328, "OSPF Version 2"	Faqs.org/rfcs/rfcs/ rfc2328.html		
Advanced Cisco Router Configuration: Student Guide, Release 11.0				Cisco
Introduction to Cisco Router Configuration: Student Guide, Revision 11.3				Cisco
Advanced Cisco Router Configuration: Student Guide, Release 11.2				Cisco
Cisco 1000BaseT GBIC	Data Sheet			Cisco
Router Products Configuration and Reference	*Configuring Transparent Bridging*		Chapter 1	

continues

Resource	Title/ Resource Type	Web Page	Chapter	Author
Web Site	"Connectors and Cables"	Cisco.com/univercd/ cc/td/doc/product/ lan/c2900x1/ gbic/ig_gbic/ mamopins.html		
Layer 3 Switching Software Feature and Configuration Guide	*Configuring Bridging*			

INDEX

Symbols & Numerics

μ-law, 413

2-way neighbor state (OSPF), 749
16-bit boot register, 26. *See also* CONFREG utility
    accessing, 34
    boot field, 30
    configuring
        on Catalyst switches, 36–38
        on Cisco routers, 38–39
    CONFREG utility, corresponding bit positions,
        44–45
    default settings, 27–30
802.1q trunking protocol, 143
802.3 subcommittee, 118
1000Base-CX Gigabit Ethernet, 127
1000Base-LX Gigabit Ethernet, 127
1000Base-SX Gigabit Ethernet, 126
1000Base-T Gigabit Ethernet, 127

A

A B C D signaling, 417
Abort at message, break signal output, 42
ABRs (area border routers), 754
AbS (analysis by synthesis), 414
absolute line number
    clearing, 56
    listing, 54–55
    modifying, 56
access groups, 997
access lists
    access groups, 997
    applying
        in bridged environments, 940
        to interfaces, 997
        to serial interfaces, 1025
    configuration guidelines, 990
    displaying, 1004–1005
    dynamic, configuring, 1005–1009
    extended IP
        configuring, 998–1004
        precedence values, 1001
        Protocol field values, 998–999

supported TCP port numbers, 999–1000
        supported UDP port numbers, 1000–1001
        syntax, 998
    filtering
        MAC addresses, 939
        NetBIOS names addresses, 939
        SAPs, 937–938
    logical AND, 993
    logical OR, 993
    named
        configuring, 1009–1010
        example, 1024
        filtering even subnets, 1015
    naming conventions, 1007
    operation of, 989–990
    standard, 994–995
        applying to ports, 996
        implicit deny, 996
    testing, 1025
    traffic filtering over serial links, configuring,
        1021–1027
    wildcard masks, 991
access servers, 7, 10
    cabling options, 9
    Cisco 2511, 7
    configuring, 98–100
    reverse Telnet sessions, configuring, 53–55
    show line command output, 70–71
    testing configuration, 100–101
access-enable command, 1007
accessing 16-bit boot register, 34
ACKs (acknowledgments)
    EIGRP, 679–680
    OSPF, 756
active mode (HSRP), 1076
ACTIVE status (PVCs), 348, 358
adapters, RJ-45-to-DB-25 pinouts, 9–10
adaptive cut-through switching, 136
adding modems to routers, 68–75
address formats
    DLSw+, 903
    SVC-based ATM, 569–570
address mappings
    ATM, 568–569
    Frame Relay
        configuring, 349–350
        displaying, 361

C

E

F

H

I

K

L

O

P

S

T

W

Skyline Computer Corporation

Skyline Computer—Integrated Solutions and Learning

Skyline Computer is a leading provider of integrated solutions for Cisco® internetworking technologies delivering Cisco Certified training, hardware, and professional services. Our dedication to customer service will keep you coming back—as evidenced by Skyline Computer being selected as Cisco Training Partner of the Year in 2001.

As a Certified Cisco Training Partner, Skyline offers the full range of educational curriculum for the Cisco Certification tracks CCNA®, CCDA®, CCNP®, CCDP®, CQS, CCIP™, and CCIE®. Skyline also specializes in customized education for all Cisco-based technologies and disciplines, such as SNA, CIP, WAN, AVVID, and Security.

Skyline Computer expands to include remote network lab access

With *CCIE Practical Studies*, Volume I, you are learning how to build and use networking labs. Skyline Computer will enhance your learning experience with a series of remote network labs available now. These labs are actual networking hardware arranged in a variety of designs, including some identical to scenarios in this book. You work on actual equipment without having to invest in additional hardware. With a basic Internet connection you can work through scenarios and labs from this book, as well as test and experiment with other network designs assembled by the experts at Skyline Computer.

Learn more about how Skyline Computer can increase your knowledge and training results through practical learning on remote network labs. Go to **www.skylinecomputer.com/rl_skylabs.com** and discover what innovative learning solutions can do for your growth as a networking professional.

Cisco Press

Go to ciscopress.com in February and March 2002 for news about a special promotion from Skyline Computer and Cisco Press.

Hey, you've got enough worries.

Don't let IT training be one of them.

Get on the fast track to IT training at InformIT,
your total Information Technology training network.

 | **www.informit.com** |

■ Hundreds of timely articles on dozens of topics ■ Discounts on IT books from all our publishing partners, including Cisco Press ■ Free, unabridged books from the InformIT Free Library ■ "Expert Q&A"—our live, online chat with IT experts ■ Faster, easier certification and training from our Web- or classroom-based training programs ■ Current IT news ■ Software downloads ■ Career-enhancing resources

Train with authorized Cisco Learning Partners.

Discover all that's possible on the Internet.

One of the biggest challenges facing networking professionals is how to stay current with today's ever-changing technologies in the global Internet economy. Nobody understands this better than Cisco Learning Partners, the only companies that deliver training developed by Cisco Systems.

Just go to **www.cisco.com/go/training_ad**. You'll find more than 120 Cisco Learning Partners in over 90 countries worldwide.* Only Cisco Learning Partners have instructors that are certified by Cisco to provide recommended training on Cisco networks and to prepare you for certifications.

To get ahead in this world, you first have to be able to keep up. Insist on training that is developed and authorized by Cisco, as indicated by the Cisco Learning Partner or Cisco Learning Solutions Partner logo.

Visit **www.cisco.com/go/training_ad** today.

CISCO SYSTEMS

EMPOWERING THE
INTERNET GENERATION™

CCIE Professional Development

Cisco BGP-4 Command and Configuration Handbook

William R. Parkhurst, Ph. D., CCIE

1-58705-017-X • **AVAILABLE NOW**

Cisco BGP-4 Command and Configuration Handbook is a clear, concise, and complete source of documentation for all Cisco IOS Software BGP-4 commands. If you are preparing for the CCIE exam, this book can be used as a laboratory guide to learn the purpose and proper use of every BGP command. If you are a network designer, this book can be used as a ready reference for any BGP command.

Cisco LAN Switching

Kennedy Clark, CCIE; Kevin Hamilton, CCIE

1-57870-094-9 • **AVAILABLE NOW**

This volume provides an in-depth analysis of Cisco LAN switching technologies, architectures, and deployments, including unique coverage of Catalyst network design essentials. Network designs and configuration examples are incorporated throughout to demonstrate the principles and enable easy translation of the material into practice in production networks.

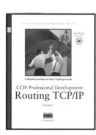

Routing TCP/IP, Volume I

Jeff Doyle, CCIE

1-57870-041-8 • **AVAILABLE NOW**

This book takes the reader from a basic understanding of routers and routing protocols through a detailed examination of each of the IP interior routing protocols. Learn techniques for designing networks that maximize the efficiency of the protocol being used. Exercises and review questions provide core study for the CCIE Routing and Switching exam.

Routing TCP/IP, Volume II

Jeff Doyle, CCIE, Jennifer DeHaven Carroll, CCIE

1-57870-089-2 • **AVAILABLE NOW**

Routing TCP/IP, Volume II, provides you with the expertise necessary to understand and implement BGP-4, multicast routing, NAT, IPv6, and effective router management techniques. Designed not only to help you walk away from the CCIE lab exam with the coveted certification, this book also helps you to develop the knowledge and skills essential to a CCIE.

Cisco Press   **www.ciscopress.com**

Cisco Press Solutions

Enhanced IP Services for Cisco Networks
Donald C. Lee, CCIE

1-57870-106-6 • AVAILABLE NOW

This is a guide to improving your network's capabilities by understanding the new enabling and advanced Cisco IOS services that build more scalable, intelligent, and secure networks. Learn the technical details necessary to deploy Quality of Service, VPN technologies, IPsec, the IOS firewall and IOS Intrusion Detection. These services will allow you to extend the network to new frontiers securely, protect your network from attacks, and increase the sophistication of network services.

Developing IP Multicast Networks, Volume I
Beau Williamson, CCIE

1-57870-077-9 • AVAILABLE NOW

This book provides a solid foundation of IP multicast concepts and explains how to design and deploy the networks that will support appplications such as audio and video conferencing, distance-learning, and data replication. Includes an in-depth discussion of the PIM protocol used in Cisco routers and detailed coverage of the rules that control the creation and maintenance of Cisco mroute state entries.

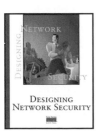

Designing Network Security
Merike Kaeo

1-57870-043-4 • AVAILABLE NOW

Designing Network Security is a practical guide designed to help you understand the fundamentals of securing your corporate infrastructure. This book takes a comprehensive look at underlying security technologies, the process of creating a security policy, and the practical requirements necessary to implement a corporate security policy.

Cisco Press   **www.ciscopress.com**

Cisco Press Solutions

EIGRP Network Design Solutions
Ivan Pepelnjak, CCIE
1-57870-165-1 • **AVAILABLE NOW**

EIGRP Network Design Solutions uses case studies and real-world configuration examples to help you gain an in-depth understanding of the issues involved in designing, deploying, and managing EIGRP-based networks. This book details proper designs that can be used to build large and scalable EIGRP-based networks and documents possible ways each EIGRP feature can be used in network design, implmentation, troubleshooting, and monitoring.

Top-Down Network Design
Priscilla Oppenheimer
1-57870-069-8 • **AVAILABLE NOW**

Building reliable, secure, and manageable networks is every network professional's goal. This practical guide teaches you a systematic method for network design that can be applied to campus LANs, remote-access networks, WAN links, and large-scale internetworks. Learn how to analyze business and technical requirements, examine traffic flow and Quality of Service requirements, and select protocols and technologies based on performance goals.

Cisco IOS Releases: The Complete Reference
Mack M. Coulibaly
1-57870-179-1 • **AVAILABLE NOW**

Cisco IOS Releases: The Complete Reference is the first comprehensive guide to the more than three dozen types of Cisco IOS releases being used today on enterprise and service provider networks. It details the release process and its numbering and naming conventions, as well as when, where, and how to use the various releases. A complete map of Cisco IOS software releases and their relationships to one another, in addition to insights into decoding information contained within the software, make this book an indispensable resource for any network professional.

Cisco Press　　　　　　　　　　　　　　　　**www.ciscopress.com**

Cisco Press Solutions

Residential Broadband, Second Edition
George Abe

1-57870-177-5 • AVAILABLE NOW

This book will answer basic questions of residential broadband networks
such as: Why do we need high speed networks at home? How will high speed
residential services be delivered to the home? How do regulatory or commercial
factors affect this technology? Explore such networking topics as xDSL, cable,
and wireless.

Internetworking Technologies Handbook, Third Edition
Cisco Systems, et al.

1-58705-001-3 • AVAILABLE NOW

This comprehensive reference provides a foundation for understanding and
implementing contemporary internetworking technologies, providing you with
the necessary information needed to make rational networking decisions.
Master terms, concepts, technologies, and devices that are used in the
internetworking industry today. You also learn how to incorporate networking
technologies into a LAN/WAN environment, as well as how to apply the OSI
reference model to categorize protocols, technologies, and devices.

OpenCable Architecture
Michael Adams

1-57870-135-X • AVAILABLE NOW

Whether you're a television, data communications, or telecommunications professional, or simply an interested business person, this book will help you understand the technical and business issues surrounding interactive television services.
It will also provide you with an inside look at the combined efforts of the cable,
data, and consumer electronics industries' efforts to develop those new services.

Performance and Fault Management
Paul Della Maggiora, Christopher Elliott, Robert Pavone, Kent Phelps, James
Thompson

1-57870-180-5 • AVAILABLE NOW

This book is a comprehensive guide to designing and implementing effective
strategies for monitoring performance levels and correctng problems in Cisco
networks. It provides an overview of router and LAN switch operations to help
you understand how to manage such devices, as well as guidance on the essential MIBs, traps, syslog messages, and show commands for managing Cisco
routers and switches.

Cisco Press Fundamentals

Internet Routing Architectures, Second Edition

Sam Halabi with Danny McPherson

1-57870-233-x • AVAILABLE NOW

This book explores the ins and outs of interdomain routing network design with emphasis on BGP-4 (Border Gateway Protocol Version 4)--the de facto interdomain routing protocol. You will have all the information you need to make knowledgeable routing decisions for Internet connectivity in your environment.

Voice over IP Fundamentals

Jonathan Davidson and James Peters

1-57870-168-6 • AVAILABLE NOW

Voice over IP (VoIP), which integrates voice and data transmission, is quickly becoming an important factor in network communications. It promises lower operational costs, greater flexibility, and a variety of enhanced applications. This book provides a thorough introduction to this new technology to help experts in both the data and telephone industries plan for the new networks.

For the latest on Cisco Press resources and Certification and

Training guides, or for information on publishing opportunities, visit

www.ciscopress.com

Cisco Press

Cisco Press books are available at your local bookstore, computer store, and online booksellers.

Cisco Press

Committed to being your long-term learning resource while you grow as a Cisco Networking Professional

Help Cisco Press **stay connected** to the issues and challenges you face on a daily basis by registering your product and filling out our brief survey. Complete and mail this form, or better yet ...

Register online and enter to win a FREE book!

Jump to **www.ciscopress.com/register** and register your product online. Each complete entry will be eligible for our monthly drawing to win a FREE book of the winner's choice from the Cisco Press library.

May we contact you via e-mail with information about **new releases, special promotions**, and **customer benefits**?

❒ Yes   ❒ No

E-mail address _____

Name _____

Address _____

City _____ State/Province _____

Country_____ Zip/Post code _____

Where did you buy this product?

❒ Bookstore   ❒ Computer store/Electronics store   ❒ Direct from Cisco Systems
❒ Online retailer   ❒ Direct from Cisco Press   ❒ Office supply store
❒ Mail order   ❒ Class/Seminar   ❒ Discount store
❒ Other

When did you buy this product? _____ **Month** _____ **Year**

What price did you pay for this product?

❒ Full retail price   ❒ Discounted price   ❒ Gift

Was this purchase reimbursed as a company expense?

❒ Yes   ❒ No

How did you learn about this product?

❒ Friend   ❒ Store personnel   ❒ In-store ad   ❒ cisco.com
❒ Cisco Press catalog ❒ Postcard in the mail   ❒ Saw it on the shelf ❒ ciscopress.com
❒ Other catalog   ❒ Magazine ad   ❒ Article or review
❒ School   ❒ Professional organization ❒ Used other products
❒ Other_____

What will this product be used for?

❒ Business use   ❒ School/Education
❒ Certification training ❒ Professional development/Career growth
❒ Other_____

How many years have you been employed in a computer-related industry?

❒ less than 2 years   ❒ 2–5 years   ❒ more than 5 years

Have you purchased a Cisco Press product before?

❒ Yes   ❒ No

Cisco Press

c i s c o p r e s s . c o m

How many computer technology books do you own?
❏ 1 ❏ 2–7 ❏ more than 7

Which best describes your job function? (check all that apply)
❏ Corporate Management ❏ Systems Engineering ❏ IS Management ❏ Cisco Networking
❏ Network Design ❏ Network Support ❏ Webmaster Academy Program
❏ Marketing/Sales ❏ Consultant ❏ Student Instuctor
❏ Professor/Teacher ❏ Other _____

Do you hold any computer certifications? (check all that apply)
❏ MCSE ❏ CCNA ❏ CCDA
❏ CCNP ❏ CCDP ❏ CCIE ❏ Other _____

Are you currently pursuing a certification? (check all that apply)
❏ MCSE ❏ CCNA ❏ CCDA
❏ CCNP ❏ CCDP ❏ CCIE ❏ Other _____

On what topics would you like to see more coverage?

_____

_____

Do you have any additional comments or suggestions?

_____

_____

Thank you for completing this survey and registration. Please fold here, seal, and mail to Cisco Press.

CCIE Practical Studies, Volume I (1-58720-002-3)

Place
Stamp
Here

ciscopress.com
Indianapolis, IN 46290
201 West 103rd Street
Cisco Press

□ **YES!** I'm requesting a **free** subscription to *Packet*™ magazine.

□ No. I'm not interested at this time.

□ Mr.
□ Ms.

First Name (Please Print)   Last Name

Title/Position (Required)

Company (Required)

Address

City   State/Province

Zip/Postal Code   Country

Telephone (Include country and area codes)   Fax

E-mail

Signature (Required)   Date

□ I would like to receive additional information on Cisco's services and products by e-mail.

1. Do you or your company:
- A □ Use Cisco products   C □ Both
- B □ Resell Cisco products   D □ Neither

2. Your organization's relationship to Cisco Systems:
- A □ Customer/End User   E □ Integrator   J □ Consultant
- B □ Prospective Customer   F □ Non-Authorized Reseller   K □ Other (specify):
- C □ Cisco Reseller   G □ Cisco Training Partner
- D □ Cisco Distributor   I □ Cisco OEM

3. How many people does your entire company employ?
- A □ More than 10,000   D □ 500 to 999   G □ Fewer than 100
- B □ 5,000 to 9,999   E □ 250 to 499
- C □ 1,000 to 4,999   F □ 100 to 249

4. Is your company a Service Provider?
- A □ Yes   B □ No

5. Your involvement in network equipment purchases:
- A □ Recommend   B □ Approve   C □ Neither

6. Your personal involvement in networking:
- A □ Entire enterprise at all sites   F □ Public network
- B □ Departments or network segments at more than one site   D □ No involvement
- C □ Single department or network segment   E □ Other (specify):

7. Your Industry:
- A □ Aerospace   G □ Education (K–12)   K □ Health Care
- B □ Agriculture/Mining/Construction   U □ Education (College/Univ.)   L □ Telecommunications
- C □ Banking/Finance   H □ Government—Federal   M □ Utilities/Transportation
- D □ Chemical/Pharmaceutical   I □ Government—State   N □ Other (specify):
- E □ Consultant   J □ Government—Local
- F □ Computer/Systems/Electronics

CPRESS

PACKET™

Packet magazine serves as the premier publication linking customers to Cisco Systems, Inc. Delivering complete coverage of cutting-edge networking trends and innovations, *Packet* is a magazine for technical, hands-on users. It delivers industry-specific information for enterprise, service provider, and small and midsized business market segments. A toolchest for planners and decision makers, *Packet* contains a vast array of practical information, boasting sample configurations, real-life customer examples, and tips on getting the most from your Cisco Systems' investments. Simply put, *Packet* magazine is straight talk straight from the worldwide leader in networking for the Internet, Cisco Systems, Inc.

We hope you'll take advantage of this useful resource. I look forward to hearing from you!

Cecelia Glover
Packet Circulation Manager
packet@external.cisco.com
www.cisco.com/go/packet